Social
Research
Methods

Alan Bryman

Fifth edition

OXFORD

UNIVERSITY PRESS

OXFORD
UNIVERSITY PRESS

Great Clarendon Street, Oxford, OX2 6DP,
United Kingdom

Oxford University Press is a department of the University of Oxford.
It furthers the University's objective of excellence in research, scholarship,
and education by publishing worldwide. Oxford is a registered trade mark of
Oxford University Press in the UK and in certain other countries

Second edition 2004
Third edition 2008
Fourth edition 2012

Impression: 1

Published in the United States of America by Oxford University Press
198 Madison Avenue, New York, NY 10016, United States of America

British Library Cataloguing in Publication Data
Data available

Library of Congress Control Number: 2015940141

ISBN 978–0–19–968945–3

Printed in Italy by L.E.G.O. S.p.A.

For Sophie and Daniel

Acknowledgements

Many people have helped me with this book, many of them unwittingly. Generations of research methods students at Loughborough University and the University of Leicester have plied me with ideas through their questioning of what I have said to them. I wish to thank several people at or connected with OUP: Tim Barton for suggesting to me in the first place that I might like to think about writing a book like this; Angela Griffin for her editorial help during the passage of the first edition of this book; Patrick Brindle and Katie Allan for their help and suggestions during the preparation of the second edition; Angela Adams for her constant support and encouragement with the revised and third edition; Kirsty Reade for copious support and suggestions in the course of preparing the fourth edition; Hilary Walford for her attention to detail when copy-editing the typescript for earlier editions of this book; Philippa Hendry for steering the production of the book; and Sarah Brett and Lucy Hyde for help with earlier editions. For this fifth edition, I would like to thank my editor, Sarah Iles, for her support, and my copy editor, Lucy Metzger, and my proof reader, Jonathon Price, for greatly improving the text. I also wish to thank Alan Beardsworth for his helpful and always constructive comments on drafts of the first edition of the book and Michael Billig for valuable comments on part of the first edition. I would like to say a big thank you to Emma Bell who co-authored the first, revised, third, and fourth editions of the business school adaptation of this book, *Business Research Methods*. I also wish to thank Alan Radley, Darrin Hodgetts, and Andrea Cullen for their permission to include two photographs from their study of images of homelessness and Carol Wolkowitz for supplying me with and her permission to use the photographs of the body work landscape of South Florida. These photographs are all in Chapter 19. I also wish to thank the *Nottingham Evening Post* for their kind permission to reproduce two newspaper articles in Chapter 13. The photograph in Plate 19.5 is Copyright DaimlerChrysler Corporation and is used with permission. I wish to thank the students who completed the questionnaires that were used for preparing the 'Student experience' features of this and the previous edition. I also wish to thank the reviewers who prepared helpful comments on the previous editions for Oxford University Press. Finally, I would like to thank Sue for all the hard work she has put into proofreading this and earlier editions of the book. I rely very much on her attention to detail.

As usual, Sue, Sarah, and Darren have supported me in many ways and put up with my anxieties and with my sudden disappearances to my study. When Sarah became a university student herself, she gave me many insights into a consumer's perspective on a book like this, for which I am grateful. Everyone except me is, of course, absolved of any responsibility for any of the book's substantive deficiencies.

Brief contents

Detailed contents

About the author

Alan Bryman was appointed Professor of Organizational and Social Research in the School of Management at the University of Leicester in August 2005. He was head of the School during 2008 and 2009. Prior to his move to Leicester, he was Professor of Social Research at Loughborough University, where he had worked for thirty-one years. He is now an Emeritus Professor of the University of Leicester.

His main research interests are in leadership, especially in higher education, research methods (particularly mixed methods research), and the 'Disneyization' and 'McDonaldization' of modern society. In 2003–4 he completed a project on mixed methods research as part of the Economic and Social Research Council's Research Methods Programme. This research has been used to inform Chapter 27.

He has published widely in the field of Social Research, including: *Quantitative Data Analysis with IBM SPSS 17, 18 and 19: A Guide for Social Scientists* (Routledge, 2011) with Duncan Cramer; *Business Research Methods* (Oxford University Press, 4th edition 2015) with Emma Bell; *The SAGE Encyclopedia of Social Science Research Methods* (Sage, 2004) with Michael Lewis-Beck and Tim Futing Liao; *The Disneyization of Society* (Sage, 2004); *Handbook of Data Analysis* (Sage, 2004) with Melissa Hardy; *The SAGE Handbook of Organizational Research Methods* (Sage, 2009) with David Buchanan; and *The SAGE Handbook of Leadership* (Sage, 2011) with David Collinson, Keith Grint, Brad Jackson, and Mary Uhl-Bien.

He has contributed articles to a range of academic journals including *Journal of Management Studies*; *Human Relations*; *International Journal of Social Research Methodology*; *Leadership Quarterly*; *Leadership*; *Studies in Higher Education*; and *American Behavioral Scientist*. He is also on the editorial board of *Leadership* and *Qualitative Research in Organizations and Management: An International Journal*.

Introducing the students

For many readers of this book one of the main reasons for using it will be to enable you to undertake a research project of your own, perhaps for the first time. With this in mind, I have included boxed features entitled 'Student experience', which are based on the experiences of undergraduate and postgraduate social science students who have done a research project, usually as part of their final year dissertation. The aim of these boxes is to provide insight and advice based on the experiences of real students in their own words, or in other words, to 'tell it like it is', as Nichols and Beynon (1977) have put it. This feature is based on a set of questionnaires completed by undergraduate and postgraduate students from different UK university social science departments.

I am extremely grateful to the students for being willing to share their experiences of doing a research project and hope that sharing what they have learned from this process with the readers of this book will enable others to benefit from their experience. A number of these students assisted on the previous edition of this book.

For more information on the students and to download the original questionnaires in the form of podcasts, visit the Online Resource Centre at:

www.oxfordtextbooks.co.uk/orc/brymansrm5e/

Guide to the book

Focus of the book

This book has been written with two groups of readers in mind. In the first are undergraduates in subjects such as sociology, social policy, human geography, and education who at some point in their degree take a course, and often more than one course, in the area of research methods. The book covers a wide range of research methods, approaches to research, and ways of carrying out data analysis, so it is likely to meet the needs of the vast majority of students in this position.

The second group, which in most cases overlaps with the first, comprises undergraduates and postgraduates who do a research project as part of the requirement for their degree programmes. This can take many forms, but one of the most common is that a small-scale research project is carried out and a dissertation based on the investigation is presented. In addition, students are often expected to carry out mini-projects in relation to certain modules. Chapter 4 has been written specifically for students doing research projects. This chapter thus builds on earlier discussion of research questions in Chapter 1, reinforcing a topic that is central to the whole process of doing research. The accent in the chapters in Parts Two and Three is on the practice of social research and as such these chapters will be extremely useful in helping students make informed decisions about doing their research. In addition, when each research method is examined, its uses and limitations are explored in order to help students to make these decisions. In Part Four, Chapter 28 provides advice on writing up research.

In addition to providing students with practical advice on doing research, the book also explores the nature of social research. This means that it attends to issues relating to fundamental concerns about what doing social research entails. For example:

- Is a natural science model of the research process applicable to the study of society?
- If not, why not?
- Why do some people feel it is inappropriate to employ such a model?
- If we do use a natural science model, does that mean that we are making certain assumptions about the nature of social reality?

- Equally, do those writers and researchers who reject such a model have an alternative set of assumptions about the nature of social reality?
- What kind or kinds of research findings are regarded as legitimate and acceptable?
- To what extent do values have an impact on the research process?
- Should we worry about the feelings of people outside the research community concerning what we do to people during our investigations?

These and many other issues impinge on research in a variety of ways and will be confronted at different stages throughout the book. While knowing how to do research—how best to design a questionnaire, how to observe, how to analyse documents, and so on—is crucial to an education in research methods, so too is a broad appreciation of the wider issues that impinge on the practice of social research. Thus, so far as I am concerned, the role of an education in research methods is not just to provide the skills that will allow you to do your own research, but also to provide you with the tools for a critical appreciation of how research is done and with what assumptions. One of the most important abilities that an understanding of research methods and methodology provides is an awareness of the need not to take evidence that you come across (in books, journals, and so on) for granted.

Why use this book?

There are likely to be two main circumstances in which this book is in your hands at the moment. One is that you have to study one or more modules in research methods for a degree in one of the social sciences or there are methodological components to one of your substantive modules (for example, a module in organizational behaviour). The other is that you have to conduct an investigation in a social scientific field, perhaps for a dissertation or project report, and you need some guidelines about how to approach your study. It may be that you are wondering why you need to study research methods as a field and why people such as the author of this book do social research at all.

Why is it important to study research methods?

To some students, there does not seem a great deal of point to studying research methods. They might take the view that, if they have to conduct an investigation, why not adopt a 'need to know' approach? In other words, why not just look into how to do your research when you are on the verge of carrying out your investigation? Quite aside from the fact that this is an extremely risky strategy, it neglects the opportunities that a training in research methods offers. In particular, you need to bear in mind the following:

- A training in research methods sensitizes you to the *choices* that are available to social researchers. In other words, it makes you aware of the range of research methods that can be employed to collect data and the variety of approaches to the analysis of data. Such an awareness will help you to make the most appropriate choices for your project, since you need to be aware of when it is appropriate or inappropriate to employ particular techniques of data collection and analysis.

- A training in research methods provides you with an awareness of the 'dos' and 'don'ts' when employing a particular approach to collecting or analysing data. Thus, once you have made your choice of research method (for example, a questionnaire), you need to be aware of the practices you should follow in order to implement that method properly. You also need to be aware of the many pitfalls to be avoided.

- A training in research methods provides you with insights into the overall research process. It provides a general vantage point for understanding how research is done. As such, it illuminates the various stages of research, so that you can plan your research and think about such issues as how your research methods will connect with your research questions.

- A training in research methods provides you with an awareness of what constitutes good and poor research. It therefore provides a platform for developing a critical awareness of the limits and limitations of research that you read. This can be helpful in providing a critical reading of research that you encounter for substantive modules in fields such as the sociology of work or the sociology of consumption.

- The skills that a training in research methods imparts are transferable ones. Knowing about how to sample, how to design a questionnaire, how to conduct semi-structured interviewing or focus groups and so on are skills that are relevant to research in other spheres (such as firms and public sector organizations).

- Studying research methods by using this book exposes you to a multitude of examples from real-life research. I have always learned a lot by reading research and finding out how others have carried out research and what lessons they seem to have learned. In view of this, the book is full of examples. I have tried to illustrate most of the major points with an example and often more than one. Most of my examples derive from published research, and it is clearly the case that you will find it difficult to generate research of an equivalent level because of your limited resources, time, and experience. On the other hand, you can get close, and it is important to learn about the benchmarks that good practice in published work provide. In your own research, it may be that, to use a well-known term devised by Herbert Simon (1960), you will need to *satisfice*. (Simon devised this term to forge a contrast with the model of rational decision-making that was pervasive in economics. He argued that, when working in organizations, people satisfice when they make decisions rather than find the most appropriate means to achieve given ends. Satisficing means that the search for an appropriate course of action is governed by the principle of looking for what is satisfactory, rather than for what is optimal.) The important issue is to know in what ways you are needing to satisfice and what the implications are of doing so.

Thus, I feel that a training in research methods has much to offer and that readers of this book will recognize the opportunities and advantages that it provides.

Erin Sanders, one of the students who have contributed to this book, herself expresses the usefulness of a knowledge of research methods for a student embarking on a research project:

I think students often read a good deal around their subject and have a working knowledge of the literature about their topic—but rarely read about methods and methodologies. Knowing about research methods is incredibly helpful when conducting research, and too often it is left out of the research process.

Structure of the book

Social research has many different traditions, one of the most fundamental of which is the distinction between quantitative and qualitative research. This distinction lies behind the structure of the book and the way in which issues and methods are approached.

The book is divided into four parts.

Part One comprises six scene-setting chapters. It deals with basic ideas about the nature of social research.

- Chapter 1 outlines some of the main stages that arise in the course of doing most kinds of social research. It also aims to explore some of the ways in which social research is located in a wider context in which a variety of factors influence why social research is done in particular ways. Most of the topics and areas covered in this chapter are addressed in much greater detail in later chapters. The goal of the chapter is to provide insights into some of the groundwork associated with thinking about social research methods and their practice.

- Chapter 2 examines such issues as the nature of the relationship between theory and research and the degree to which a natural science approach is an appropriate framework for the study of society. It is here that the distinction between quantitative and qualitative research is first encountered. They are presented as different *research strategies* with different ways of conceptualizing how people and society should be studied. It is also shown that there is more to the distinction between them than whether an investigation includes the collection of quantitative data.

- In Chapter 3, the idea of a *research design* is introduced. This chapter allows an introduction to the basic frameworks within which social research is carried out, such as social survey research, case study research, and experimental research. These first three chapters provide the basic building blocks for the rest of the book.

- Chapter 4 takes you through the mains steps that are involved in planning and designing a research project and offers advice on how to manage this process. It also includes a discussion of *research questions*—what they are, why they are important, and how they come to be formulated.

- Chapter 5 is designed to help you to get started on your research project by introducing the main steps in conducting a critical review of the literature.

- Chapter 6 considers the ways in which ethical issues impinge on researchers and the kinds of principles that are involved.

Part Two contains ten chapters concerned with quantitative research.

- Chapter 7 explores the nature of quantitative research and as such provides a context for the later chapters. The next four chapters are largely concerned with aspects of social survey research.

- Chapter 8 deals with sampling issues—how to select a sample and the considerations that are involved in assessing what can be inferred from different kinds of sample. It also begins with an introduction to survey research that acts as a backdrop to the discussion of sampling and to the subject matter of the following three chapters.

- Chapter 9 is concerned with the kind of interviewing that takes place in survey research—that is, structured interviewing.

- Chapter 10 covers the design of questionnaires. This involves a discussion of how to devise self-administered questionnaires, such as postal questionnaires.

- Chapter 11 examines the issue of how to ask questions for questionnaires and structured interviews.

- Chapter 12 covers structured observation, which is a method that has been developed for the systematic observation of behaviour.

- Chapter 13 presents content analysis, a method that provides a rigorous framework for the analysis of a wide range of documents.

- Chapter 14 deals with the analysis of data collected by other researchers and by official bodies. The emphasis then switches to the ways in which we can analyse quantitative data.

- Chapter 15 presents a range of basic tools for the analysis of quantitative data. The approach taken is non-technical. The emphasis is upon how to choose a method of analysis and how to interpret the findings. No formulae are presented.

- Chapter 16 shows you how to use computer software—in the form of SPSS, the most widely used software for analysing quantitative data—in order to implement the techniques you learned in Chapter 15.

Part Three contains nine chapters on aspects of qualitative research.

- Chapter 17 has the same role in relation to Part Three as Chapter 7 has in relation to Part Two. It provides an overview of the nature of qualitative research and as such provides the context for the other chapters in this part.

- Chapter 18 examines the main sampling strategies employed in qualitative research. Just like quantitative researchers, qualitative researchers typically have to sample research participants, documents, or whatever the unit of analysis is. As will be seen, the sampling principles involved are clearly different from those usually employed by quantitative researchers.

- Chapter 19 is concerned with ethnography and participant observation, which are the source of some of the most well-known studies in social research. The two terms are often used interchangeably and refer to the immersion of the researcher in a social setting.

- Chapter 20 deals with the kinds of interview that qualitative researchers conduct, which is typically semi-structured interviewing or unstructured interviewing.

- Chapter 21 explores the focus group method, whereby groups of individuals are interviewed on a specific topic.
- Chapter 22 examines two ways in which qualitative researchers analyse language: conversation analysis and discourse analysis.
- Chapter 23 deals with the examination of documents in qualitative research. The emphasis then shifts to the analysis of qualitative data.
- Chapter 24 explores some approaches to the analysis of qualitative data.
- Chapter 25 shows you how to use computer software—a relatively new development in qualitative research—to assist with your analysis.

It is striking that certain issues recur across Parts Two and Three: sampling, interviewing, observation, documents, and data analysis. However, as you will see, quantitative and qualitative research constitute contrasting approaches to such activities.

Part Four contains chapters that go beyond the quantitative/qualitative research contrast.

- Chapter 26 deals with some of the ways in which the distinction between quantitative and qualitative research is less fixed than is sometimes supposed.
- Chapter 27 presents some ways in which quantitative and qualitative research can be combined to produce what is referred to as mixed methods research.
- Chapter 28 has been included to help with writing up research, an often neglected area of the research process.

The fifth edition

This fifth edition contains both many differences from the fourth edition. The main revisions are:

- A new 'Research in the news' feature in several chapters. I hope that this will bring across some of the ways in which social research seeps into the mass media and how the research that is reported sometimes raises interesting methodological issues.
- The three previous editions of this book had a chapter on 'E-research'. I decided that this separation of Internet-based research methods no longer made sense as these methods have become mainstream and stand alongside traditional, established methods. To take two examples: Web surveys are increasingly a feature of typical surveys; mixed mode surveys, in which

respondents can answer questionnaires through one of several modes, have become mainstream. Increasingly, respondents have the choice of answering a questionnaire online or by returning it in the mail. To separate out Web surveys has come to make less and less sense. To take another example, traditional ethnography increasingly incorporates elements of online ethnography, for example, by examining relevant websites and online community postings. Again, it makes less and less sense to treat the two forms of ethnography as separate.

- There are new sections on a variety of topics, including Big Data, computer-assisted content analysis, mixed mode surveys, Skype interviewing, using mobile phones as a platform for surveys, experience and event sampling, mobile interviewing, and thematic synthesis for systematic reviews.
- Many sections have been substantially expanded and updated to include important developments.
- New examples have been introduced and some from the previous editions have been replaced.

How to use the book

The book can be used in a number of different ways. However, I would encourage all readers at least to look at the chapter guide at the beginning of each chapter so that they can decide whether they need the material covered there and also to gain a sense of the range of issues the book does in fact address.

- **Wider philosophical and methodological issues**. If you do not need to gain an appreciation of the wider philosophical context of enquiry in social research, Chapter 2 can largely be ignored. If an emphasis on such issues *is* something you are interested in, Chapter 2 along with Chapter 26 should be a particular focus of attention.
- **Survey research**. Chapters 8 through 11 deal with the kinds of topics that need to be addressed in survey research. In addition, Chapter 15 examines ways of analysing the kinds of data that are generated by survey researchers.
- **Practical issues concerned with doing quantitative research**. This is the province of the whole of Part Two. In addition, you would be advised to read Chapter 3, which maps out the main research designs employed, such as experimental and cross-sectional designs, which are frequently used by quantitative researchers.
- **Practical issues concerned with doing qualitative research**. This is the province of the whole of Part Three. In addition, you would be advised to read

Chapter 3, which maps out the main research designs employed, such as the case study, which is frequently employed in qualitative research.

- **Analysing data**. Chapters 15 and 24 explore the analysis of quantitative and qualitative research data respectively, while Chapters 16 and 25 introduce readers to the use of computer software in this connection. It may be that your module on research methods does not get into issues to do with analysis, in which case these chapters would be omitted.

- **Formulating research questions**. As I have already said in this Guide, I see the asking of research questions as fundamental to the research process. Advice on what research questions are, how they are formulated, where they come from, and so on is provided in Chapters 1 and 4.

- **Doing your own research project**. I hope that the whole of this book will be relevant to students doing their own research projects or mini-projects, but Chapter 4 is the one where specific advice relating to this issue is located. In addition, I would alert you to the practical tips that have been devised and the checklists of points to remember.

- **Writing**. This issue is very much connected with the previous point. It is easy to forget that your research has to be *written up*. This is as much a part of the research process as the collection of data. Chapter 28 discusses a variety of issues to do with writing up research.

- **Wider responsibilities of researchers**. It is important to bear in mind that as researchers we bear responsibilities to the people and organizations that are the recipients of our research activities. Ethical issues are raised at a number of points in this book and Chapter 6 is devoted to a discussion of them. The fact that an entire chapter has been given over to a discussion of ethics is a measure of their importance in terms of the need to ensure that all researchers should be ethically sensitive.

- **The quantitative/qualitative research contrast**. The distinction between quantitative and qualitative research is used in two ways: as a means of organizing the research methods and methods of analysis available to you; and as a way of introducing some wider philosophical issues about social research. Chapter 2 outlines the chief areas of difference between quantitative and qualitative research. These are followed up in Chapter 17. I also draw attention to some of the limitations of adhering to an excessively strict demarcation between the two research strategies in Chapter 26, while Chapter 27 explores ways of integrating them. If you do not find it a helpful distinction, these chapters can be avoided or skimmed.

- **The Internet**. The Internet plays an increasingly important role in the research process. At various junctures I provide important websites where key information can be gleaned. I also discuss in Chapter 5 the use of the Internet as a route for finding references for your *literature review*, itself another important phase of the research process. You will find that most of the references that you discover when you do an online search will then themselves be accessible to you in electronic form. Finally, many of the chapters explore the Internet as a platform for doing research in the form of such research methods as Web surveys, electronic focus groups, and email surveys.

Guided tour of textbook features

Chapter guide

This chapter and the three that follow it are concerned with principles and practices associated with social survey research. Sampling principles are not exclusively concerned with survey research; for example, they are relevant to the selection of documents for content analysis (see Chapter 13). However, in this chapter the emphasis will be on sampling in connection with the selection of people who would be asked questions by interview or questionnaire. The chapter explores:

Research in the news 13.1
Psycho versus *Finding Nemo*

An article in *The Times* on 17 December 2014 appeared with the intriguing title 'Cartoons more brutal than Psycho'. The opening paragraph reads:

Forget about *Psycho*'s shower scene; if you want grisly suspense just watch the first five minutes of *Finding Nemo*. And do you think Tarantino is violent? Then pity Snow White's stepmother who, scientists note, 'was struck by lightning, forced off a cliff and crushed by a boulder while being chased by seven vengeful dwarves'.

The author, Tom Whipple, who is *The Times*' science correspondent, then goes on to explain that a 'study in the *British Medical Journal* has found that major characters are far more likely to die—and often die badly—in cartoons meant for children than they are in films made for adults'.

Research in focus 17.2
Reliability for qualitative researchers

Gladney et al. (2003) report the findings of an exercise in which two multidisciplinary teams of researchers were asked to analyse qualitative interviews with eighty Texas school students. The interviews were concerned with reflections on violence on television; reasons for violence among some young people; and reasons for some young people *not* being violent. One group of raters read interview transcripts of the interviews; the other group listened to the audio-taped recordings. Thus, the dice were slightly loaded in favour of different themes being identified by the two groups. In spite of this there was remarkable consistency between the two groups in the themes identified. For example, in response to the question 'Why are some young people violent?', Group One identified the following themes: family/parental influence; peer influence; social influence; media influence; and coping. Group Two's themes were: the way they were raised; media influence; appearance; anger, revenge, protection; and environmental or peer influence. Such findings are quite reassuring and are interesting because of their clear concern with reliability in a qualitative research context. Exercises such as this can be viewed as a

Key concept 1.1
What are research questions?

A research question is a question that provides an explicit statement of what it is the researcher wants to find out about. A research purpose can be presented as a statement (for example, 'I want to find out whether (or why) . . .'), but a question forces the researcher to be more explicit about what is to be investigated. A research question must have a question mark at the end of it or else it is not a question. Research in focus 1.1 provides an example of a study with several research questions. A hypothesis is in a sense a form of research question, but it is not stated as a question and provides an anticipation of what will be found out.

A helpful list of types of research question has been provided by Denscombe (2010), who in an earlier book proposed the following six types:

1. Predicting an outcome (does *y* happen under circumstances *a* and *b*?).
2. Explaining causes and consequences of a phenomenon (is *y* affected by *x* or is *y* a consequence of *x*?).
3. Evaluating a phenomenon (does *y* exhibit the benefits that it is claimed to have?).

Thinking deeply 5.2
What do examiners look for in a literature review?

Holbrook et al. (2007) conducted an analysis of examiners' reports on PhD theses. They analysed 1,310 reports relating to 501 theses in 'Australia (a PhD thesis is examined by at least two examiners). These reports are naturally-occurring documents, in that examiners have to provide these reports as part of the process of examining a PhD candidate. In the course of writing a report, examiners frequently if not invariably comment on the literature review. While these findings are obviously specific to PhD theses, the features that examiners look for are also applicable in general terms to other kinds of writing, such as an undergraduate or a postgraduate dissertation.

Holbrook et al. analysed the reports using computer-assisted qualitative data analysis software, which will be covered in Chapter 25. The analysis of these reports suggests that comments concerning the literature review were of three basic kinds:

Tips and skills
The Harvard and note approaches to referencing

The examples below show some fictitious examples of referencing in published work. Note that in published articles there is usually a list of references at the end; books using the Harvard system usually have a list of references, whereas a bibliography is used with the short-title system of notes. The punctuation and style of references—such as where to place a comma, or whether to capitalize a title in full or just the first word—varies considerably from source to source. For example, with Harvard referencing, in some books and journals the surname of the author is separated from the date in the text with a comma—for example (Name, 1999)—but in others, such as this this book, there is no comma. However, the main thing is to be consistent. Select a format

Chapter guide

Each chapter opens with a guide that highlights the upcoming themes and issues to be discussed and provides you with an idea of the scope and coverage the chapter offers.

Research in the news

How is research disseminated by the media and what issues arise when it gets shared through secondary channels? Research in the news offers examples of how research has been portrayed in the media. Each example is discussed, outlining the potential role research has on influencing public opinion, encouraging debate and informing readers. It also considers the responsibility and choice presented to media outlets regarding how they utilize research and whether the choices made always retain its integrity.

Research in focus boxes

Research in focus boxes provide a sense of place for the theories and concepts discussed in the chapter text. Each box examines a key piece of published research, breaking it down so that you can develop an understanding of how research is structured, carried out, assessed and evaluated.

Key concept boxes

This feature explains key terms by asking '*What is . . . ?*' or by listing a series of important points about a particular issue or topic. These boxes highlight key terminology that you can then use in your own work. Complex ideas are also explained in more detail. Key concepts are indicated in purple type for quick reference and are defined in the Glossary.

Thinking deeply boxes

Thinking deeply boxes encourage you to consider an area in greater depth; either analysing a topic or issue further, or explaining the ins and outs of a current debate or significant discussion that has occurred between researchers. This feature introduces you to some of the complexities involved in using social research methods.

Tips and skills boxes

As you acquire the skills needed to become a competant researcher, these boxes will provide guidance and advice on key aspects of the research process and help you avoid common mistakes.

Student experience
Using supervisors

Several students wrote about the role that their supervisors played in their research projects. Isabella Robbins mentions that her supervisor played an important role in relation to her analysis of her qualitative data.

The emerging themes were strong and in that sense the analysis was not problematic, but I guess the problems came in mapping the analysis onto the theory. My way of dealing with this was to talk about the analysis at supervisions and to incorporate the ideas that came of these discussions.

Cornelius Grebe provided the following advice about relationships with supervisors:

I have learned to be very clear about my expectations of my supervisors: what kind of professional and personal relationship I thrive in and what form of support exactly I need from them.

 To read more, go to the Online Resource Centre: www.oxfordtextbooks.co.uk/orc/brymansrm5e/

Supervisor tips
How to annoy your dissertation supervisor and cause yourself problems: five easy steps

Supervisors were asked about some of the chief frustrations associated with supervising dissertation students. There were some recurring themes in their responses. Here are some easy ways to annoy your supervisor and create problems for yourself:

1. *Don't turn up to pre-arranged supervision meetings.* Quite aside from the rudeness of doing this, a failure to turn up begins to ring alarm bells about whether the student is veering off course.

2. *Leave the bulk of the work until the last minute.* Supervisors know full well that research must be paced because it requires a great deal of forethought and because things can go wrong. The longer students leave their dissertation work, the more difficult it becomes to do thorough research and to rectify problems.

3. *Ignore what your supervisor advises you to do.* Supervisors are extremely experienced researchers, so that ignoring their advice is irritating and certainly not in a student's interest.

✔ *Checklist*
Planning a research project

○ Do you know what the requirements for your dissertation are, as set out by your university or department?

○ Have you made contact with your supervisor?

○ Have you allowed enough time for planning, collecting and analysing data, and writing up your research project?

○ Do you have a clear timetable for your research project with clearly identifiable milestones for the achievement of specific tasks?

⏩ *Key points*

- Social research and social research methods are embedded in wider contextual factors. They are not practised in a vacuum.
- Social research practice comprises elements that are common to all or at least most forms of social research. These include: a literature review; concepts and theories; research questions; sampling of cases; data collection; data analysis; and a writing-up of the research finding.
- Attention to these steps is what distinguishes academic social research from other kinds of social research.

❓ *Questions for review*

Reviewing the existing literature

- What are the main reasons for writing a literature review?
- How can you ensure that you get the most from your reading?
- What are the main advantages and disadvantages associated with systematic review?
- What type of research questions is systematic review most suited to addressing?
- What are the main reasons for conducting a narrative literature review?

Glossary

Terms with an entry elsewhere in the Glossary are in colour.

Abductive, abduction A form of reasoning with strong ties to *induction* that grounds social scientific accounts of social worlds in the perspectives and meanings of participants in those social worlds.

Biographical method See *life history method.*

Bivariate analysis The examination of the relationship between two variables, as in *contingency tables* or *correlation.*

Student experience boxes

In these boxes, research students from a variety of UK universities share their first-hand experience of research in practice and any difficulties that have arisen along the way. These boxes will help you to anticipate and resolve research problems as you move through your dissertation or project.

Supervisor tips boxes

Supervisor tips boxes draw on interviews with dissertation and thesis supervisors from a variety of universities around the UK and, like the Student experience boxes, provide valuable insights into the research practices and problems encountered by previous students. These boxes will help you to foresee and resolve any issues you may encounter whilst undertaking your own dissertation or project.

Checklists

Most chapters include a helpful checklist of issues to consider when engaging in certain aspects of research (such as doing a literature review, devising a structured interview schedule, or conducting a focus group). They list key points from the text and provide an easy point of reference to call on as you conduct your own research.

Key points

Each chapter concludes with a list that summarises the most important topics, issues and terminology referenced within the chapter. These lists concisely review key points and act as a brief reminder of the chapter's coverage.

Questions for review

At the end of each chapter there is also a series of questions to help you test your understanding of key concepts and ideas.

Glossary

At the end of the book is a glossary that provides definitions of key research terms. For ease of reference the glossary includes many of the definitions listed in the Key concept boxes. Glossary terms are also highlighted in purple text in the chapters.

Guided tour of the ORC: lecturer resources

www.oxfordtextbooks.co.uk/orc/brymansrm5e/

This textbook is accompanied by a full suite of online resources, which are freely available to adopting lecturers. Our comprehensive supplements will save you time in preparing lectures, planning seminars, and creating assessments for your students. To register for a password, simply follow the steps on the Social Research Methods homepage.

PowerPoint slides

A suite of customizable PowerPoint slides has been included for use in lecture presentations. Arranged by chapter theme and tied specifically to the lecturer's guide, the slides may also be used as handouts in class.

Seminar outlines

A series of seminar outlines accompany the textbook in a chapter-by-chapter format so that students are able to easily prepare for, follow, and consolidate their seminar learning. Each seminar proposal includes appropriate learning objectives, advice on any seminar preparation required, a list of necessary equipment, and a series of suggested activities that will actively engage your students with each topic.

Exam- or coursework-based questions

To run alongside the suggested seminar outlines a selection of exam- or coursework-based questions have been included for each chapter. Each question is accompanied by an indicative answer.

Figures and tables from the text

All figures and tables from the text are provided in high resolution format for downloading into presentation software or for use in assignments and exam material.

Test bank

This customizable resource contains ten questions per chapter with answers and feedback, allowing you to create your own personalized testing sessions. These can be used to monitor students' understanding and progress during the term, or in formal assessment at the end of the course.

Data collection

Structured methods of data collection include questionnaires and interviews used in survey studies: the researcher designs research tools relative to what needs to be known;

Less structured methods include participation observation and semi-structured interviewing: the researcher can keep an open mind about what needs to be known.

OXFORD

Chapter 13: Content Analysis

The use of documents is often under-utilised in student-led research, but can be a valuable point of gaining experience of working with 'real' data. Not only do documents such as newspapers often circumvent the need for lengthy ethical review, they also provide a lot of data with relatively little expense. Methods of analysing documents, such as content analysis, can, therefore, be utilised to demonstrate the complex realities of working with data. This seminar is designed to introduce students to the process of conducting content analysis and makes use of the example that is described on pages 298-303 and in Figures 13.1 & 13.2. The example concerning the representation of crime in local newspapers will provide them with an empirical framework by which they can gain experience of working with 'real' data and demonstrate the importance of coding schemes and coding manuals and their use in facilitating data analysis

Learning objectives

1. To consolidate students' understanding of key terms in the process of content analysis
2. To develop students' knowledge and experience conducting content analysis
3. To embed students' critical understanding of the advantages and disadvantages of content analysis in an empirical example

---

Bryman: Social Research Methods, 5th edition

Coursework based questions

These suggested course based questions can be used alongside the suggested seminar outlines to use in your teaching.

- What are some of the main criticisms that are frequently levelled at qualitative research?
- Can online personal interviews really be personal interviews?
- What is mixed methods research?

Figure 2.3
Influences on social research

Theory   Practical considerations   Epistemology

Social research

Values   Ontology

Which of the following can be regarded as a core ingredient of a dissertation apply.

- ☐ a. A literature review
- ☐ b. A justification of research methods
- ☐ c. A discussion of the findings in relation to the research questions
- ☐ d. An abstract

General Feedback

Bryman shows the core ingredients of most dissertations etc. to include a litera methods, and a discussion of the findings in relation to the research questions, concluding sections. An abstract is usually required in addition by academic in summary of the dissertation or article, rather than as constituting an integral pa
Page reference: 15

Guided tour of the ORC: student resources

www.oxfordtextbooks.co.uk/orc/brymansrm5e/

Multiple-choice questions

Consolidate your understanding of research methods by checking how much you have learnt with these self-marking multiple-choice questions. Questions are categorised by chapter and instant feedback is provided, including handy page references that refer you back to the textbook.

Annotated web links

A series of annotated web links to the best social research websites, organized by chapter, enables you to extend your understanding by reading the latest perspectives on social research issues.

Flashcard glossary

Online flashcards have been designed to help you understand and memorize the key terms used in the book. The flashcards can also be downloaded onto mobile devices.

Student researcher's toolkit

This toolkit is divided into two main parts:

1. An interactive research project guide, which takes you step by step through each of the key research phases, ensuring that you do not overlook any research step, and providing guidance and advice on every aspect of social research, from dealing with your supervisor to ways of organizing and writing your dissertation.

2. Dos and don'ts of social research: a quick practical checklist drawn from experience of common pitfalls.

Student experience podcasts

Learn from previous UK social research students who have completed their own research projects. Download podcasts where they recount their research experiences, outlining the processes they went through and the problems they resolved as they moved through each research phase. The questionnaires they answered are also available on the ORC as Word documents.

Guide to using Excel in data analysis

Using Excel to an advanced level can be one of the trickiest aspects of a research project. This interactive guide takes you step by step from the very first stages of using Excel to more advanced topics such as descriptive statistics, contingency tables, charting and regression, and statistical significance.

Abbreviations

ASA	American Sociological Association
BCS	British Crime Survey
BHPS	British Household Panel Survey
BPS	British Psychological Society
BSA	British Social Attitudes [survey]
BSA	British Sociological Association
BSE	bovine spongiform encephalopathy
CA	conversation analysis
CACA	computer-assisted content analysis
CAPI	computer-assisted personal interviewing
CAQDAS	computer-assisted/aided qualitative data analysis software
CATI	computer-assisted telephone interviewing
CCSE	Cultural Capital and Social Exclusion [project]
CCTV	closed-circuit television
CDA	critical discourse analysis
CF	cystic fibrosis
CJD	Creutzfeldt Jakob disease
CV	curriculum vitae
DA	discourse analysis
DOI	digital object identifier
ECA	ethnographic content analysis
EPPI	Evidence for Policy and Practice Information and Coordinating Centre
ESDS	Economic and Social Data Service
ESRC	Economic and Social Research Council
FES	Family Expenditure Survey
FIAC	Flanders Interaction Analysis Categories
FMD	foot and mouth disease
FRE	*Framework for Research Ethics*
GESIS	Gesellschaft Sozialwissenschaftlicher Infrastruktureinrichtungen eV (German Social Science Infrastructure Services)
GHS	General Household Survey
GLF	General Lifestyle Survey
HETUS	Harmonized European Time Use Studies
HISS	hospital information support system
HRT	hormone replacement therapy
ICI	Imperial Chemical Industries
IRB	Institutional Review Board
ISP	Internet service provider
ISSP	International Social Survey Programme
IT	information technology
KWIC	key word in context
LFS	Labour Force Survey
NCDS	National Child Development Study
NFS	National Food Survey
NGO	non-governmental organizations
NHS	National Health Service

NSPCC	National Society for the Prevention of Cruelty to Children
NS-SEC	National Statistics Socio-Economic Classification
NUD*IST	Non-numerical Unstructured Data Indexing Searching and Theorizing
NVIVO	QSR NUD*IST Vivo
ONS	Office for National Statistics
ORACLE	Observational Research and Classroom Learning Evaluation
QLL	qualitative longitudinal research
RCT	randomized controlled trial
RDD	random digit dialing
REC	Research Ethics Committee
REF	*Research Ethics Framework*
RGF	*Research Governance Framework for Health and Social Care*
SCPR	Social and Community Planning Research
SE	standard error [of the mean]
SPSS	Statistical Package for the Social Sciences
SRA	Social Research Association
SSCI	Social Sciences Citation Index
TB	tuberculosis
UKDA	UK Data Archive
WERS	Workplace Employment Relations Survey
WI	Women's Institute
WoK	Web of Knowledge

Part One
The Research Process

Part One of this book provides the groundwork for the more specialized chapters in Parts Two, Three, and Four. In Chapter 1, basic ideas in thinking about social research methods are outlined. Chapters 2 and 3 are concerned with two ideas that will recur during the course of this book—the idea of **research strategy** and the idea of **research design**. Chapter 2 outlines a variety of considerations that impinge on the practice of social research and relates these to the issue of research strategy. Two research strategies are identified: **quantitative** and **qualitative research**. Chapter 3 identifies the different research designs that are employed in social research. Chapters 4 and 5 are concerned with providing advice to students on some of the issues that they need to consider if they have to prepare a dissertation based upon a relatively small-scale research project. Chapter 4 deals with planning and formulating **research questions**, including the principles and considerations that need to be taken into account in designing a small-scale research project, while Chapter 5 is about how to get started by reviewing the literature. Chapter 6 deals with ethics in social research.

1

The nature and process of social research

 ## *Chapter outline*

 ## *Chapter guide*

This chapter introduces some fundamental considerations in conducting social research. It begins by outlining what we mean by social research and the reasons why we conduct it. The bulk of the chapter then moves on to consider three areas:

- *The context of social research methods*. This entails considering issues such as the role of theory in relation to social research, the role of values and of ethical considerations in the research process, the significance of assumptions about the nature of the social world and about how knowledge about it should be produced, and the ways in which political considerations may emerge in social research.

- *The elements of the research process*. The whole book is dedicated to the elements of social research, but here the essential stages are given a preliminary treatment. The elements identified are: a literature review; formulating concepts and theories; devising research questions; sampling; data collection; data analysis; and writing up findings.

- *The messiness of social research*. This section acknowledges that social research often does not conform to a neat, linear process and that researchers may find themselves facing unexpected contingencies and difficulties. At the same time, it is suggested that a familiarity with the research process and its principles is crucial to navigating through the unexpected.

All of the issues presented in these three sections will be treated in much greater detail in later chapters, but they are introduced here to provide an early encounter with them.

Introduction

This book is concerned with the ways that social researchers go about their craft. This means that it is concerned with the approaches that are employed by social researchers when conducting research in all its phases—formulating research objectives, choosing research methods, securing research participants, collecting, analysing and interpreting data, and disseminating findings to others. An understanding of social research methods is important for several reasons, but two stand out. First, it is hoped that it will help readers to avoid some of the pitfalls that arise when relatively inexperienced people try to do social research, such as failing to match research questions to research methods, asking ambiguous questions

in **questionnaires**, and engaging in practices that are ethically dubious. If you are expected to conduct a research project, an education in research methods is important, not just for ensuring that the correct procedures are followed but also for gaining an appreciation of the choices available to you. Second, an understanding of social research methods is important from the point of view of being a consumer of published research. When people take degrees in the social sciences, they read a lot of published research in the substantive areas they study. A grounding in the research process and a familiarity with potential pitfalls provides an invaluable critical edge when reading the research of others.

What is meant by 'social research'?

The term 'social research' as used in this book denotes *academic* research on topics relating to questions relevant to the social scientific fields, such as sociology, human geography, social policy, politics, and criminology. Thus, social research involves research that draws on the social sciences for conceptual and theoretical inspiration. Such research may be motivated by developments and changes in society, such as the rise in worries about security or binge-drinking,

but it employs social scientific ideas to shed light on those changes. It draws upon the social sciences for ideas about how to formulate research topics and issues and how to interpret and draw implications from research findings. What distinguishes social research of the kind discussed in this book is that it is rooted in and draws on the ideas and intellectual traditions of the social sciences. This book is about the methods that are used to create that kind of research.

Why do social research?

The rationale for doing social research has been outlined in the previous section to a certain extent. Academics conduct such research because, in the course of reading the literature on a topic or when reflecting on what is going on in modern social life, questions occur to them. They may notice a gap in the literature or an inconsistency between a number of studies or an unresolved issue in the literature. These circumstances commonly act as springboards for social research. Another is when there is a development in society that provides an interesting point of departure for

a research question. For example, noting the widespread use of social media on portable devices, a researcher might become interested in studying how far it has affected the nature and quality of interaction in social life. In exploring this issue, the researcher may draw upon the literature on technology and on social interaction to provide insights into how to approach the issue. There is no single reason why people do social research of the kind emphasized in this book, but, at its core, it is done because there is an aspect of our understanding of what goes on in society that is unresolved.

The context of social research methods

Social research and its associated methods do not take place in a vacuum. In this book, a number of factors that form the context of social research will be mentioned. The following factors form part of the context within which social research and its methods operate:

- The *theories* that social scientists use to understand the social world have an influence on what is researched and how research findings are interpreted. In other words, the topics that are investigated are profoundly influenced by the available theoretical ideas. Thus, if a researcher was interested in the impact of the use of online social media on sociability, it is quite likely that he or she would take into account prevailing theories about how technology is used and its impacts. In this way, social research is informed and influenced by theory. It also contributes to theory because the findings of a study will feed into the stock of knowledge to which the theory relates.

- The existing knowledge about an area in which a researcher is interested forms an important part of the background within which social research takes place. This means that someone planning to conduct research must be familiar with the *literature* on the topic of interest. You must be acquainted with what is already known about the research area in which you are interested so that you can build on it and avoid covering the same ground as others.

 Reviewing the literature is the main focus of Chapter 5 and is also an ingredient of other chapters, such as Chapter 28.

- The researcher's views about the nature of the *relationship between theory and research* also have implications for research. For some researchers, theory is addressed at the beginning of a research project. The researcher might engage in some theoretical reflections out of which a **hypothesis** is formulated and subsequently tested. An alternative position is to view theory as an outcome of the research process—that is, as something that is arrived at after research has been carried out. This difference has implications for research: the first approach implies that a set of theoretical ideas drive the collection and analysis of data, whereas the second suggests a more open-ended strategy in which theoretical ideas emerge out of the data. Of course, the choice is rarely as stark as this account of the relationship between theory and research implies, but it does suggest that there are contrasting views about the role of theory in relation to research.

 The relationship between theory and research is a major focus of Chapter 2.

- The assumptions and views about how research should be conducted influence the research process. It is often assumed that a 'scientific' approach should be followed, in which a hypothesis is formulated and then tested using precise measurement techniques. Such research definitely exists, but the view that this is how research should be done is not universally shared. Considerations of this kind are referred to as **epistemological** ones. They raise questions about the issue of how the social world should be studied and

whether a scientific approach is the right stance to adopt. Some researchers favour an approach that avoids a scientific model, arguing that people and social institutions are very different from the subject matter of the scientist and that an approach is needed that is more sensitive to the special qualities of people and their social institutions.

 Epistemological issues are a major focus in Chapter 2.

- The assumptions about the nature of social phenomena influence the research process too. According to some writers, the social world should be viewed as being external to social actors and something over which they have no control. It is simply there, acting upon and influencing their behaviour, beliefs, and values. We might view the culture of an organization as a set of values and behavioural expectations that exert a powerful influence over those who work in the organization and into which new recruits have to be socialized. But we could also view it as something that is in a constant process of reformulation and reassessment, as members of the organization continually modify it through their practices and through small innovations in how things are done. Considerations of this kind are referred to as **ontological** ones. They invite us to consider the nature of social phenomena—are they relatively inert and beyond our influence or are they very much a product of social interaction? As for epistemological issues discussed in the previous point, the stance that the researcher takes on them has implications for the way in which social research is conducted.

 Ontological issues are a major focus of Chapter 2.

- The *values* of the research community have significant implications for research. This can take a number of forms. *Ethical issues* have been a point of discussion, and indeed often of considerable dissension, over the years, but in recent times they have soared in prominence. It is now almost impossible to do certain kinds of research without risking the condemnation of the research community and possible censure from the organizations in which researchers are employed. Nowadays, there is an elaborate framework of bodies that scrutinize research proposals for their ethical integrity, so that transgression of ethical principles becomes ever less likely. Certain kinds of research require special provision with regard to ethics, such as research involving children or vulnerable adults. Thus, ethical values and the institutional arrangements that have arisen in response to the clamour for ethical caution have implications for what and who can be researched and for how research can be conducted—to the point where certain research methods and practices are no longer employed. Another way in which the values of the research community can impinge on the researcher is that in certain fields, such as in social policy, there is a strong view that those being researched should be involved in the research process. For example, when social researchers conduct research on service users, it is often suggested that the users of those services should be involved in the formulation of research questions and of instruments such as questionnaires. While such views are not universally held (Becker et al. 2010), they form a consideration that researchers in some fields feel compelled to consider when contemplating certain kinds of investigation.

 Ethical issues are addressed in Chapter 6 and touched on in several other chapters.

- Related to the previous issue is the question of what research is for. So far, I have tended to stress the academic nature and role of social research—namely, that it is to add to the stock of knowledge about the social world. However, many social scientists feel that research should have a practical purpose and that it should make a difference to the world around us. Such an emphasis means that, for some researchers, the social sciences should emphasize *implications for practice*. For researchers in social science disciplines such as social policy, an emphasis on investigations having demonstrable implications for practice is more widely held than in other disciplines. Also, there are research approaches that are largely designed to examine issues that will have implications for people's everyday lives, such as **evaluation research** and **action research**, which will be touched upon in Chapters 3 and 17 respectively. However, even in such fields as social policy, a commitment to an emphasis on practice is not universally held. In a survey of UK social policy researchers in 2005, Becker, Bryman, and Sempik (2006) found that 53 per cent of all those questioned felt that it was *equally* important for research to have potential value for policy and practice and to lead to the accumulation of knowledge, a further 34 per cent felt it was more important for research to have potential value for policy and practice, and 13 per cent felt it was more important for social policy research to lead to the accumulation of knowledge.
- Social research operates within a wider *political context*. For example, much social research is funded by

government bodies, and these tend to reflect the orientation of the government of the day. This will mean that certain research issues are somewhat more likely to receive financial support than others. Further, for research supported by the Economic and Social Research Council (ESRC), the major funding body for UK social science research, prospective applicants are supposed to demonstrate how potential users of the research will be involved or engaged if the research receives financial support. The notion of a 'user' is capable of being interpreted in a number of different ways, but it is likely to be more straightforward for an applicant to demonstrate the involvement of users when research has a more applied focus. In other words, the stipulation that users must be involved could be taken to give a slight advantage to research with a focus on practice.

 The political context of research is examined in Chapter 6.

- The *training and personal values* of the researcher form a component of the context of social research methods in that they may influence the research area, the research questions, and the methods employed to investigate these. Our experiences and our interests frequently have some influence on the issues we research. As academic social researchers, the issues that interest us have to connect to the wider disciplines of the social sciences. An example referred to in Chapter 2 is O'Reilly's (2000) study of British expatriates living on Spain's Costa Del Sol. The issue was of interest to her because she and her partner were planning to live there. This clearly constitutes a personal interest, but it is not exclusively so, because she used the topic as a lens for raising issues about transnational migration, an issue that has been of great interest to social scientists in recent years. I also mention in Chapter 2 my own interest in the ways in which social science research is reported in the mass media. This grew out of a hurtful experience reported in Haslam and Bryman (1994), which led me to develop an interest in the issue, to read a great deal of the literature on the reporting of both science and social science in the media, and to develop it into a research project. Also, social researchers, as a result of their training and sometimes from personal preferences, frequently develop attachments to, or at least preferences for, certain research methods and approaches. One of the reasons why I try to cover a wide range of research methods is that I am convinced that it is important for researchers to be familiar with a diversity of methods and how to implement them. The development of methodological preferences carries the risk of researchers becoming blinkered about what they know, but such preferences often do emerge and have implications for the conduct of research.

It is impossible to arrive at an exhaustive list of factors that are relevant to this section, but the discussion has been designed to provide a flavour of the ways in which social research and the choice of research methods are not hermetically sealed off from wider influences.

Elements of the process of social research

In this section and the rest of this chapter, I will introduce the main elements of most research projects. It is common for writers of textbooks on social research methods to compile flow charts of the research process, and I am not immune to this temptation, as you will see from, for example, Figures 2.1, 8.1, and 17.1! At this point, I am not going to try to sequence the various stages of the research process, as the sequencing varies somewhat according to different research strategies and approaches. All I want to do here is to introduce some of the main elements—in other words, elements that are common to all or most varieties of social research. Some of them have already been touched on in the previous section and all will be addressed in more detail in later chapters.

Literature review

The existing literature is an important element in all research. When we have alighted upon a topic or issue that interests us, we must read further to determine a number of things. We need to know:

- what is already known about the topic;
- what concepts and theories have been applied to the topic;
- what research methods have been applied to the topic;
- what controversies exist about the topic and how it is studied;
- what clashes of evidence (if any) exist;
- who the key contributors to research on the topic are.

Many topics have a rich tradition of research, so it is unlikely that many people, such as students doing an undergraduate or postgraduate Master's dissertation, will be able to conduct an exhaustive review of the literature in such areas. What is crucial is that you read the key books and articles and the main figures who have written in the field. As I suggest in Chapter 5, it is crucial that you are aware of what is already known, so that you cannot be accused of not doing your homework and therefore of naively going over old ground. Also, being able to link your own research questions, findings, and discussion to the existing literature is an important way of demonstrating the credibility and contribution of your research. However, a literature review

is not simply a summary of the literature. The written literature review is expected to be critical. This does not necessarily mean that you are expected to be highly negative about the authors you read, but it does mean that you are supposed to assess the significance of their work and how each item fits into the narrative about the literature that you construct when writing a literature review.

 Reviewing the literature is the main focus of Chapter 5 and is also an ingredient of other chapters, such as Chapter 28.

Concepts and theories

Concepts are the way that we make sense of the social world. They are labels that we give to aspects of the social world that seem to have common features that strike us as significant. The social sciences have a strong tradition of concepts, many of which have become part of the language of everyday life. Concepts such as bureaucracy, power, social control, status, charisma, labour process, cultural capital (see Research in focus 1.1 for an example using this concept), McDonaldization, alienation, and so on are very much part of the theoretical edifice that generations of social scientists have constructed. Concepts are a key ingredient of theories. Indeed, it is almost impossible to imagine a theory that did not have at least one concept embedded in it.

 The role of concepts is discussed further in Chapter 7.

Concepts serve several purposes in social research. They are important to how we organize and signal to intended audiences our research interests. They help us to think about and be more disciplined about what we want to investigate and at the same time help with the organization of our research findings. In the section on 'The context of social research methods' it was noted briefly that the relationship between theory and research is often portrayed as involving a choice between theories driving the research process in all its phases and theories as a product of the research process. This is invariably depicted as the contrast between respectively **deductive** and **inductive** approaches to the relationship between theory and research.

The contrast between inductive and deductive approaches to theory and research will be expanded upon in Chapter 2.

This contrast has implications for concepts. Concepts may be viewed as something we start out with and that represent key areas around which data are collected. In other words, we might collect data in order to shed light on a concept or more likely several concepts and how they are connected. This is the approach taken in the investigation reported in Research in focus 1.1. The alternative view is that concepts are outcomes of research. According to this second view, concepts help us to reflect upon and organize the data that we collect. Of course, these are not mutually exclusive positions. In research, we often start out with some key concepts that help us to orient to our subject matter but, as a result of collecting and interpreting data, we possibly revise those concepts, or new ones emerge through our reflections.

One of the reasons why familiarity with the existing literature is so important is that it alerts us to some of the main concepts that past researchers have employed and how useful or limited those concepts have been in helping to unravel the main issues. Research in focus 1.1 provides an example of this tendency in that the concept of cultural capital is employed for its possible insights into the process of students being accepted or rejected when applying for entry to Oxford University. Even when we are reading the literature solely as consumers of research—for example, when writing an essay—knowing what the key concepts are, who is responsible for them, and what controversies there are (if any) surrounding them can be crucial.

Research questions

Research questions have been mentioned in passing on a couple of occasions, and they are implicit in the discussion thus far. Research questions are important in research,

Key concept 1.1
What are research questions?

A research question is a question that provides an explicit statement of what it is the researcher wants to find out about. A research purpose can be presented as a statement (for example, 'I want to find out whether (or why) . . . '), but a question forces the researcher to be more explicit about what is to be investigated. A research question must have a question mark at the end of it or else it is not a question. Research in focus 1.1 provides an example of a study with several research questions. A hypothesis is in a sense a form of research question, but it is not stated as a question and provides an anticipation of what will be found out.

A helpful list of types of research question has been provided by Denscombe (2010), who in an earlier book proposed the following six types:

1. Predicting an outcome (does y happen under circumstances a and b?).
2. Explaining causes and consequences of a phenomenon (is y affected by x or is y a consequence of x?).
3. Evaluating a phenomenon (does y exhibit the benefits that it is claimed to have?).
4. Describing a phenomenon (what is y like or what forms does y assume?).
5. Developing good practice (how can we improve y?).
6. Empowerment (how can we enhance the lives of those we research?).

White (2009) was uneasy about Denscombe's last category, arguing that an emphasis on political motives of this kind can impede the conduct of high-quality research. This difference of opinion can be attributed to differences in viewpoint about the purposes of research highlighted in the section on 'The context of social research methods'. Rather than the sixth type of research question above, White proposes an alternative:

7. Comparison (do a and b differ in respect of x?).

There are many ways that research questions can be categorized, and it is also difficult to arrive at an exhaustive list, but these seven types provide a rough indication of the possibilities as well as drawing attention to a controversy about the wider goals of research.

Research in focus 1.1
Research questions in a study of cultural capital

The focus of the article by Zimdars, Sullivan, and Heath (2009) is the recruitment of students to Oxford University. Recruitment to UK universities and to the elite universities of Oxford and Cambridge has been the focus of political controversy in recent years, because the failure to recruit sufficient numbers of state-school students is seen as elitist and as restricting social mobility. Admissions officers in Oxford and Cambridge universities in particular are often portrayed as displaying class prejudices that constrain the life chances of young people from less privileged backgrounds. The researchers' aim was 'to assess whether cultural capital is linked to success in gaining admission for those who apply' (Zimdars et al. 2009: 653). They then go on to outline their research questions:

Specifically, we address the following questions:

1. How do Oxford applicants vary in their cultural participation and cultural knowledge, according to parents' education, social class, gender and ethnicity?
2. Does cultural capital predict acceptance to Oxford?
3. If so, does its effect remain once we control for examination performance?
4. Is cultural capital more important for admission to the arts and humanities faculties than to the sciences?
5. To what extent does cultural capital mediate the effect of social class, parents' education, private schooling, ethnicity and gender?

(Zimdars et al. 2009: 653)

At one level, this research seeks to address issues of relevance to social and educational policy. As noted in the section on 'The context of social research methods', social research sometimes explores issues that are mainly to do with policy and practice. But the researchers are also keen to draw on theory and one key concept in particular—Bourdieu's concept of cultural capital—to help understand the processes underlying the low level of acceptance of state-school applicants at Oxford. Cultural capital refers to an individual's ability to distinguish him- or herself through cultural experiences and competencies. It is argued that such cultural expertise allows the middle class to reproduce itself both culturally and socially and serves to reduce the social and economic opportunities of working-class children.

Zimdars et al. draw primarily on a questionnaire survey of Oxford applicants who applied for entry in 2002. Of particular interest is that the researchers found cultural knowledge to be a more important factor in success at gaining entry than mere cultural participation through visiting museums, galleries, etc. As the authors put it: 'What matters is a relationship of familiarity with culture, rather than just participation in culture' (Zimdars et al. 2009: 661). As such, these findings are only partially supportive of Bourdieu's ideas at least so far as they relate to the issue of gaining admission to Oxford.

because they force you to consider that most basic of issues—what is it about your area of interest that you want to know? Most people beginning research start with a general idea of what it is they are interested in. Research questions force you to consider the issue of what it is you want to find out about much more precisely and rigorously. Developing research questions is a matter of narrowing down and focusing more directly on what it is that you want to know about.

Research questions are, therefore, important. Having no research questions or poorly formulated research questions will lead to poor research. If you do not specify clear research questions, there is a great risk that your research

will be unfocused and that you will be unsure about what your research is about and what you are collecting data for. It does not matter how well you design a questionnaire or how skilled an interviewer you are; you must be clear about your research questions. Equally, it does not matter whether your research is for a project with a research grant of £300,000, a doctoral thesis, or a small mini-project. Research questions are crucial because they will:

- guide your literature search;
- guide your decisions about the kind of research design to employ;

- guide your decisions about what data to collect and from whom;
- guide your analysis of your data;
- guide your writing-up of your data;
- stop you from going off in unnecessary directions; and
- provide your readers with a clearer sense of what your research is about.

It has been suggested that research questions will help to guide your literature search for your literature review. However, it is also possible, if not likely, that reading the literature may prompt you to revise your research questions and may even suggest some new ones. Therefore, at an early stage of a research study, research questions and the literature relating to them are likely to be intertwined. A plausible sequence at the beginning of a research project is that initial contact with the literature relating to an area of interest suggests one or two research questions and that further reading guided by the initial research questions gives rise to a revision of them or possibly some new ones.

 In Chapter 4, there will be more discussion of research questions and how they can be developed.

Student experience
Generating and changing research questions

Hannah Creane elaborated on her answers regarding her research questions in an email. She writes:

> the three initial research questions I had formulated when I began the study were: what makes a child a child?; what makes an adult an adult?; and to what extent can the child be seen as a 'mini' adult? However, while writing this up I realized that those questions were no longer really the guiding questions for my research. The study has evolved and become more of an empirical reflection of the generational changes within childhood rather than looking specifically at what childhood actually is. It seems to me that the two appropriate questions in relation to the study as a whole now are: What makes a child a child as opposed to an adult?; and to what extent has this changed across the generations?

 To read more, go to the Online Resource Centre: www.oxfordtextbooks.co.uk/orc/brymansrm5e/

Sampling cases

Social research is not always carried out on people. For example, we may want to examine mass-media content and employ a technique such as **content analysis**.

 Content analysis is covered in Chapter 13.

With something like media content, the data come from newspaper articles or television programmes rather than from people. Because of this, it is common for writers on social research methods to use the term 'case' to cover the wide variety of objects on which or from which data will be collected. Much if not most of the time, 'cases' will be people. In social research we are rarely in a position in which we can interview, observe, or send questionnaires to all individuals who are appropriate to our research and equally we are unlikely to be able to analyse the content of all articles in all newspapers relating to an area of media content that interests us. Time and cost issues always constrain the number of cases we can include in our research, so we almost always have to sample.

As we will see in later chapters, there are a number of different principles behind sampling. Many people associate sampling with surveys and the quest for **representative samples**. This approach to sampling invariably lies behind sampling for opinion polls of the kind that we often encounter in newspapers. Such sampling is usually based on principles to do with searching for a sample that can represent (and therefore act as a microcosm of) a wider **population**. If newspapers could not make claims about the representativeness of the samples used for the opinion polls they commission, the findings they report about the prospects for political parties would be less significant.

 In Chapter 8, the principles that lie behind the quest for the representative sample will be explained.

These principles do not apply solely to questionnaire **survey research** of the kind described in Research in focus 1.1 but may also apply to other kinds of investigation—for example, when sampling newspaper articles for a content analysis of media content. By no means all forms of social science research prioritize representative samples. In

Part Three we will encounter sampling principles that are based not on the idea of representativeness but on the notion that samples should be selected on the basis of their appropriateness to the purposes of the investigation. Also, in **case study** research, there may be just one or two units of analysis. With such research, the goal is to understand the selected case or cases in depth. Sampling issues are relevant to such research as well. Quite aside from the fact that the case or cases have to be selected according to criteria relevant to the research, those individuals who are members of the case study context have to be sampled according to criteria too. However, the chief point to register is that sampling is an inevitable feature of most social research and therefore is an important stage of any investigation.

Data collection

To many people, data collection represents the key point of any research project, and it is not surprising therefore that this book probably gives more words and pages to this stage in the research process than any other. Some of the methods of data collection covered, such as interviewing and questionnaires, are probably more familiar to many readers than some of the others. Some methods entail a rather structured approach to data collection—that is, the researcher establishes in advance the broad shape of what he or she needs to find out about and designs research instruments to implement what needs to be known. The questionnaire is an example of such an instrument; the researcher establishes what he or she needs to know to answer the research questions that drive the project and designs questions in the questionnaire that will allow data to be collected to answer those research questions. Similarly, something like a **structured interview**—the kind of interview used in survey investigations—includes a host of questions designed for the same purpose. It is unfortunate that we use the same word—question—for both research questions and the kinds of questions that are posed in questionnaires and interviews. They are very different: a research question is a question designed to indicate what the purpose of an investigation is; a questionnaire question is one of many questions that are posed in a questionnaire that will help to shed light on and answer one or more research questions.

It is also possible to discern in this book methods of data collection that are unstructured. In Part Three, research methods will be encountered that emphasize a more open-ended view of the research process, so that there is less restriction on the kinds of things that can be found out about. Research methods such as **participant observation** and **semi-structured interviewing** are used so that the researcher can keep an open mind about the shape of what he or she needs to know about, so that concepts and

theories can emerge out of the data. This is the inductive approach to theorizing and conceptualization referred to above. Such research is usually still geared to answering research questions, but these are often expressed in a less explicit form than the research questions encountered in more structured research of the kind encountered in Research in focus 1.1. This can be seen by comparing the specificity of these research questions with those of a study of retired senior managers by Jones, Leontowitsch, and Higgs (2010):

> Our aim was to explore the experiences of retirement, changes in lifestyle and social roles and the meanings associated with retirement amongst early retirees from higher management. Research questions included: to what extent do our respondents construct a new balance of activities? Do respondents construct new discourses of everyday life? Does the move by respondents into leisure retirement create new tensions in other parts of their lives?
>
> (Jones et al. 2010: 105)

These research questions derived in part from the concept of the 'quasi-subject' in modern societies, whereby people 'become authors of their own biographies—authors who have to continually construct identities and biographical narratives in order to give meaning to lives that are lived out in the face of uncertainty' (Jones et al. 2010: 104). In order to explore the research questions, semi-structured interviews with twenty relevant retirees were undertaken. The interviews were designed 'to encourage a conversation and to allow participants to give their own account of retirement' (Jones et al. 2010: 108). This is a noticeably less structured approach to data collection, reflecting the open-ended nature of the research questions.

The collection of data, then, can entail different sorts of approach in terms of how structured or open-ended the implementation of the methods is. An issue that arises in all research is that of *quality*. How do you do good research and how do you recognise it when you read it? The assessment of research quality relates to all phases of the research process, but the quality of data-collection procedures is bound to be a key concern. The assessment of quality has become a prominent issue among social researchers and also for policy-makers with an interest in academic research. It has become a much more significant topic since the publication of the first edition of this book in 2001. There are several reasons for the greater prominence of research quality assessment, some of which will be mentioned in later chapters. However, the key point to appreciate for now is that, with the increased importance of research quality assessment, debates have arisen about issues such as whether there can be quality criteria that apply to all forms of research. As we will see, especially in Chapter 17, there has been a clear position among some methodologists that a 'horses for courses' approach is required whereby the application of quality criteria needs to take into account the kind of investigation to which they are being applied.

Data analysis

Data analysis is a stage that incorporates several elements. At the most obvious level, it might be taken to mean the application of statistical techniques to data that have been collected.

 Quantitative data analysis and the software for implementing it are discussed in Chapters 15 and 16.

However, quite aside from the fact that by no means all data are amenable to statistical analysis and that, even when some data might be appropriate to such analysis, alternative approaches are sometimes taken, there are other things going on when data are being analysed. For a start, the raw data have to be *managed*. This means that the researcher has to check the data to establish whether there are any obvious flaws. For example, if we take the kind of research conducted by Jones et al. (2010) on early retirees, the interviews are usually audio-recorded and then subsequently transcribed. The researcher needs to be alert to possible hearing mistakes that might affect the meaning of people's replies. The preparation of the data for **transcription** enables the researcher to introduce the transcripts into a computer software program.

 The use of qualitative data analysis software is discussed in Chapter 25.

In the case of the research by Jones et al., once the transcripts had been incorporated within the software, the authors say they conducted a **thematic analysis**. This means that they examined the data to extract core themes that could be distinguished both between and within transcripts. One of the main elements of the identification of themes was through **coding** each transcript. With the analysis of qualitative data, coding is a process whereby the data are broken down into their component parts and those parts are then given labels. The analyst then searches for recurrences of these sequences of coded **text** within and across cases and also for links between different **codes**. Thus, there is a lot going on in this process: the data are being managed, in that the transcripts are being made more accessible than if the researcher just kept listening and relistening to the recordings; the researcher is making sense of the data through coding the transcripts; and the data are being interpreted—that is, the researcher is seeking to link the process of making sense

of the data with the research questions that provided the starting point, as well as with the literature relating to retirement and also with the theoretical ideas the authors use to illuminate the issue.

Data analysis is fundamentally about *data reduction*—that is, it is concerned with reducing the large body of information that the researcher has gathered so that he or she can make sense of it. Unless the amount of data collected is reduced—for example, in the case of quantitative data by producing tables or averages and in the case of qualitative data by grouping textual material into categories like themes—it is more or less impossible to interpret the material.

A further issue to bear in mind with data analysis is that it can refer to the analysis of either primary or secondary data. With primary data analysis, the researchers who were responsible for collecting the data conduct the analysis, as was the case with both the Zimdars et al. (2009) and Jones et al. (2010) studies. Secondary data analysis occurs when someone else analyses such data. Nowadays, researchers who work in universities are encouraged to deposit their data in archives, which then allow others to analyse the data that are deposited. Given the time and cost of most social research, this is a sensible thing to do, as it increases the likely payoff of an investigation, and it may be that a researcher conducting secondary analysis can explore the research questions in which he or she is interested without having to go through the time-consuming and lengthy process of having to collect primary data.

 Secondary analysis is discussed in Chapters 14 and 24.

Writing up

The finest piece of research would be useless if it were not disseminated to others. We do research so that it can be written up, thereby allowing others to read what we have done and concluded. It might be argued that writing up should not be part of the subject matter for a book on social research methods. However, since dissemination is so important to researchers, it is appropriate for it to be included.

 Chapter 28 is devoted to writing up.

There are slightly different ways in which social research gets written up, and these vary according to the different styles of doing research. For example, more structured kinds of research like that presented in Research in focus 1.1 are sometimes written up differently from more open-ended research of the sort represented by the Jones et al.

Table 1.1
Stages in the research process in relation to two studies

Stage	Description of stage	Example (Zimdars et al. 2009)*	Example (Jones et al. 2010)
Literature review	A critical examination of existing research relating to the phenomena of interest and of relevant theoretical ideas.	Literature concerning social stratification as it relates to educational access and concerning the notion of cultural capital.	Literature concerning retirement and the notion of the 'quasi-subject' in second modernity.
Concepts and theories	The ideas that drive the research process and that shed light on the interpretation of the resulting findings. These findings contribute to the ideas.	Academic attainment; cultural capital; social background.	Early retirement; quasi-subject; discourse; lifestyle.
Research question(s)	A question or questions providing an explicit statement of what it is the researcher wants to know about.	'1. How do Oxford applicants vary in their cultural participation and cultural knowledge, according to parents' education, social class, gender and ethnicity? 2. Does cultural capital predict acceptance to Oxford? 3. If so, does its effect remain once we control for examination performance? 4. Is cultural capital more important for admission to the arts and humanities faculties than to the sciences? 5. To what extent does cultural capital mediate the effect of social class, parents' education, private schooling, ethnicity and gender?' (Zimdars et al. 2009: 653).	'To what extent do our respondents construct a new balance of activities? Do respondents construct new discourses of everyday life? Does the move by respondents into leisure retirement create new tensions in other parts of their lives?' (Jones et al. 2010: 105).
Sampling cases	The selection of cases (in these studies, people) that are relevant to the research questions.	'A representative sample of 1,700 applicants with British qualifications who applied to Oxford during the 2002 admissions cycle' (Zimdars et al. 2009: 653).	Sample of twenty early retirees obtained initially through databases of organizations working with retired people.
Data collection	Gathering data from the sample so that the research questions can be answered.	Questionnaire survey. Data obtained on degree attainment of each applicant. Also, interviews with admissions tutors and observation of admissions meetings.	Semi-structured interviews.
Data analysis	The management, analysis, and interpretation of the data.	Statistical analysis of the questionnaire data. Thematic analysis of interview transcripts.	Thematic analysis of interview transcripts.
Writing up	Dissemination of the research and its findings.	Research written up as a doctoral thesis and as articles, including Zimdars et al. (2009). Main sections in Zimdars et al. (2009): • Introduction • Operationalization • Research questions • Data and methods • Discussion • Appendix	Research written up as an article in Jones et al. (2010). Main sections: • Introduction • Background • Methods • Findings • Discussion • Conclusion

* Zimdars (2007) consulted for further information.

(2010) study. However, there are some core ingredients that most dissertations, theses, and research articles will include. These are:

- *Introduction*. Here the research area and its significance are outlined. The research questions may also be introduced here.

- *Literature review*. What is already known about the research area is sketched out and examined critically.

- *Research methods*. Here the research methods employed (sampling, methods of data collection, methods of data analysis) are presented and justified.

- *Results*. The findings are presented.

Figure 1.1

The seven elements of the research process and where to find them in this book

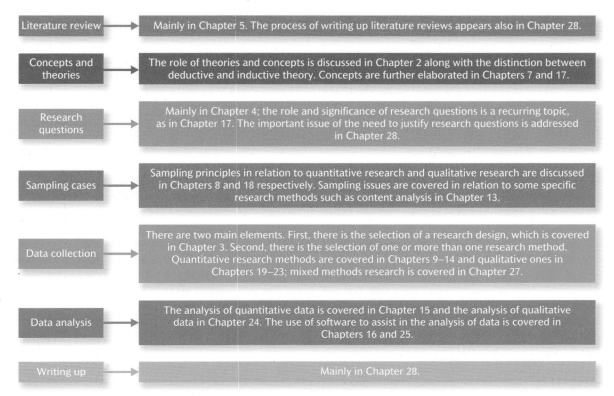

Literature review	→ Mainly in Chapter 5. The process of writing up literature reviews appears also in Chapter 28.
Concepts and theories	→ The role of theories and concepts is discussed in Chapter 2 along with the distinction between deductive and inductive theory. Concepts are further elaborated in Chapters 7 and 17.
Research questions	→ Mainly in Chapter 4; the role and significance of research questions is a recurring topic, as in Chapter 17. The important issue of the need to justify research questions is addressed in Chapter 28.
Sampling cases	→ Sampling principles in relation to quantitative research and qualitative research are discussed in Chapters 8 and 18 respectively. Sampling issues are covered in relation to some specific research methods such as content analysis in Chapter 13.
Data collection	→ There are two main elements. First, there is the selection of a research design, which is covered in Chapter 3. Second, there is the selection of one or more than one research method. Quantitative research methods are covered in Chapters 9–14 and qualitative ones in Chapters 19–23; mixed methods research is covered in Chapter 27.
Data analysis	→ The analysis of quantitative data is covered in Chapter 15 and the analysis of qualitative data in Chapter 24. The use of software to assist in the analysis of data is covered in Chapters 16 and 25.
Writing up	→ Mainly in Chapter 28.

- *Discussion*. The findings are discussed in relation to their implications for the literature and for the research questions previously introduced.

- *Conclusion*. The significance of the research is reinforced for the reader.

These elements are not an exhaustive list, because writing conventions differ in various ways, but they are recurring elements of the final written outputs. Table 1.1 summarizes the seven elements of the research process examined in this section and Figure 1.1 shows where in this book to look for information about each stage. The latter will be especially useful for readers conducting investigations of their own, as it provides a guide to the book from the point of view of the principal steps in conducting research.

 # The messiness of social research

Social research is often a lot less smooth than the accounts of the research process you read in books like this. The purpose of this book is to provide an overview of the research process as well as advice on how it should be done. In fact, research is full of false starts, blind alleys, mistakes, and enforced changes to research plans. However, in a book like this it is impossible to cover all such contingencies, largely because many of them are one-off events and almost impossible to anticipate. We know that research can get messy from the confessional accounts of the research process that have been written (e.g. the contributors to P. Hammond

1964; Bell and Newby 1977; Bryman 1988b; Townsend and Burgess 2009a; Streiner and Sidani 2010). If social research is messy, why do we invariably not get a sense of that when we read reports of research in books and academic journal articles? Of course, research often does go relatively smoothly and, in spite of minor hiccoughs, proceeds roughly according to plan. However, it is also the case that reports of research often present rather sanitized accounts of how the research was produced, without a sense of the sometimes difficult problems the researcher(s) had to overcome. This is not to say that social researchers deceive us, but rather that the accounts of the findings and how they were arrived at tend to follow an implicit template that emphasizes some aspects of the research process but not others. They tend to emphasize how the specific findings presented in the report were arrived at and to use standard methodological terminology of the kind presented in this book to express the underlying process. Research reports typically display the various elements discussed in the previous section—the relevant literature is reviewed, the key concepts and theories are discussed, the research questions are presented, the sampling procedures and methods of data collection are explained and justified, the findings are presented and discussed, and some conclusions are drawn. The ups and downs of research tend not to feature within this template. This tendency is not unique to *social* research: in Chapter 22 a study of how scientists present and discuss their work will be examined, and this shows that here too certain core aspects of the production of 'findings' tend to be omitted from the written account (Gilbert and Mulkay 1984).

It is also the case that, regardless of the various ways in which research can be knocked off its path, this book can deal only with generalities. It cannot cover every eventuality, so that it is quite possible that when conducting an investigation you will find that these generalities do not fit perfectly with the circumstances in which you find yourself. It is important to be aware of that possibility and not to interpret any slight departures you have to make from the advice provided in this book as a problem with your skills and understanding. It could be argued that, in light

of the different ways in which social researchers can be stymied in their research plans, a book on research methods, outlining how research is and should be conducted, is of little value. Needless to say, I would not subscribe to such a view. Many years ago, I was involved in several studies of construction projects. One of the recurring themes in the findings was the different ways that such projects could be knocked off their course: unpredictable weather, sudden shortages of key supplies, illness, accidents, previously reliable subcontractors letting the project manager down, clients changing their minds or being unavailable at key points, sudden changes in health and safety regulation, poor-quality supplies, poor-quality work, early excavation revealing unanticipated problems—any of these could produce significant interruptions to even the best-planned construction project. But never was it suggested that the principles of construction and of construction management should be abandoned. Without such principles, project managers would be at an even greater loss to know how to proceed. Much the same is true of research projects. There are plenty of things that can go wrong. As Townsend and Burgess (2009b) write in the introduction to their collection of 'research stories you won't read in textbooks', two of the recurring themes from the accounts they collected are the need for flexibility and the need for perseverance. However, at the same time it is crucial to have an appreciation of the methodological principles and the many debates and controversies that surround them, and these are outlined in the next twenty-seven chapters. These principles provide a road map for the journey ahead.

 ## Key points

- Social research and social research methods are embedded in wider contextual factors. They are not practised in a vacuum.

- Social research practice comprises elements that are common to all or at least most forms of social research. These include: a literature review; concepts and theories; research questions; sampling of cases; data collection; data analysis; and a writing-up of the research finding.

- Attention to these steps is what distinguishes academic social research from other kinds of social research.

- Although we can attempt to formulate general principles for conducting social research, we have to recognize that things do not always go entirely to plan.

 ## Questions for review

What is meant by 'social research'?

- What is distinctive about academic social research?

Why do social research?

- If you were about to embark on a research project now or in the near future, what would be the focus of it and why?

The context of social research methods

- What are the main factors that impinge on social research and the implementation of social research methods identified in the chapter? Can you think of any that have not been touched on?

Elements of the process of social research

- Why is a literature review important when conducting research?
- What role do concepts and theories play in the process of doing social research?
- Why are researchers encouraged to specify their research questions? What kinds of research questions are there?
- Why do researchers need to sample? Why is it important for them to outline the principles that underpin their sampling choices?
- Outline one or two factors that might affect a researcher's choice of data-collection instrument.
- What are the main differences between the kinds of data analysed by Zimdars et al. (2009) and Jones et al. (2010)?
- How might you structure the report of the findings of a project that you conducted?

The messiness of social research

- If research does not always go according to plan, why should we bother with methodological principles at all?

Online Resource Centre

www.oxfordtextbooks.co.uk/orc/brymansrm5e/

Visit the Online Resource Centre to enrich your understanding of social research strategies. Follow up links to other resources, test yourself using multiple choice questions, and gain further guidance and inspiration from the Student Researcher's Toolkit.

2

Social research strategies: quantitative research and qualitative research

Chapter outline

Chapter guide

The chief aim of this chapter is to show that a variety of considerations enter into the social research process. The distinction that is commonly drawn among writers on and practitioners of social research between *quantitative research* and *qualitative research* is explored in relation to these considerations. This chapter explores:

- the relationship between theory and research, in particular whether theory guides research (known as a *deductive* approach) or whether theory is an outcome of research (known as an *inductive* approach);

- *epistemological* issues—that is, ones to do with what is regarded as appropriate knowledge about the social world; one of the most crucial aspects is the question of whether a natural science model of the research process is appropriate for the study of the social world;

- *ontological* issues—that is, ones to do with whether the social world is regarded as something external to social actors or as something that people are in the process of creating;

- the ways in which these issues relate to the widely used distinction in the social sciences between two types of *research strategy*: quantitative and qualitative research; there is also a preliminary discussion, which will be followed up in Chapter 27, that suggests that, while quantitative and qualitative research represent different approaches to social research, we should be wary of driving a wedge between them;

- the ways in which *values* and *practical issues* also impinge on the social research process.

Introduction

This book is about social research. It attempts to equip people who have some knowledge of the social sciences with an appreciation of how social research should be conducted and what it entails. But the practice of social research does not exist in a bubble, sealed off from the social sciences and the various intellectual positions of their practitioners. Two points are of particular relevance here.

First, methods of social research are closely tied to different visions of how social reality should be studied. Methods are not simply neutral tools: they are linked with the ways in which social scientists perceive the connection between different viewpoints about the nature of social reality and how it should be examined. However, it is possible to overstate this point. While methods are not neutral, they are not entirely saturated with intellectual inclinations either. Secondly, there is the question of how research methods and practice connect with the wider social scientific enterprise. Research data are invariably collected in relation to something. The 'something' may be a burning social problem or, more usually, a theory.

This is not to suggest that research is entirely dictated by theoretical concerns. Sometimes simple 'fact-finding' exercises are published. Fenton et al. (1998) conducted a quantitative content analysis of social research reported in the British mass media. They examined national and regional newspapers, television and radio, and also magazines. They admit that one of the main reasons for conducting the research was to establish the amount and types of research that are represented. Sometimes, research exercises are motivated by a concern about a pressing social problem. McKeganey and Barnard (1996) conducted qualitative research involving observation and

interviews with prostitutes and their clients in Glasgow. One factor that seems to have prompted this research was the concern about the role of prostitutes in spreading HIV infection (McKeganey and Barnard 1996: 3). Another scenario occurs when research is done on a topic when a specific opportunity arises. Rubin et al. (2005) carried out a survey of Londoners just under two weeks after the bombings of 7 July 2005 in order to gauge people's behavioural and emotional reactions. The authors conducted social **survey research** using a structured telephone interview approach on a **sample** of Londoners. Of course, the authors were influenced by theories about and previous research on stress following traumatic events, but the specific impetus for the research was not planned (see Research in focus 8.5 for more on this study). Yet another stimulus for research can arise out of personal experiences. Lofland and Lofland (1995) note that many research publications emerge out of the researcher's personal biography. For example, Atkinson's (2006) motivation for conducting a study of Welsh National Opera was partly to do with a long-standing enthusiasm since he first began going to the opera as a child. Another example is O'Reilly's (2000) investigation of British expatriates living on the Costa del Sol in Spain; this stemmed from her dream of moving to the area, which she eventually did. My interest in the representation of social science research in the mass media (Fenton et al. 1998) can be attributed to a difficult encounter with the press reported in Haslam and Bryman (1994).

By and large, however, research data achieve significance in sociology when viewed in relation to theoretical concerns. This raises the issue of the nature of the relationship between theory and research.

Student experience
Personal experience as a basis for research interests

For her research, Isabella Robbins was interested in the ways in which mothers frame decisions regarding vaccinations for their children. This topic had a particular significance for her. She writes:

As the mother of three children I have encountered some tough decisions regarding responsibility towards my children. Reading sociology, as a mature student, gave me the tools to help understand my world and to contextualize some of the dilemmas I had faced. In particular, I had experienced a difficult decision regarding the vaccination status of my children.

To read more, go to the Online Resource Centre: www.oxfordtextbooks.co.uk/orc/brymansrm5e/

Theory and research

Characterizing the link between theory and research is by no means straightforward. There are several issues at stake here, but two stand out in particular. First, there is the question of what form of theory one is talking about. Secondly, there is the matter of whether data are collected to test or to build theories. Theory is important because it provides a backcloth and justification for the research that is being conducted. It also provides a framework within which social phenomena can be understood and the research findings can be interpreted.

What type of theory?

The term 'theory' is used in many different ways, but its most common meaning is as an explanation of observed regularities—for example, why sufferers of schizophrenia are more likely to come from working-class than middle-class backgrounds, or why work alienation varies by technology. But such theories tend not to be the

focus of modules in social theory, which typically focus much more on theories with a higher level of abstraction. Examples of such theories include structural-functionalism, **symbolic interactionism**, critical theory, poststructuralism, structuration theory, and so on. What we see here is a distinction between theories of the former type, which are often called *theories of the middle range* (Merton 1967), and *grand theories*, which operate at a more abstract level. According to Merton, grand theories offer few indications to researchers as to how they might guide or influence the collection of empirical evidence. So, if someone wanted to test an aspect of a grand theory or to draw an inference from it that could be tested, the level of abstractness is likely to be so great that the researcher would find it difficult to make the necessary links with the real world. There is a paradox here, of course. Even highly abstract ideas, such as Parsons's notions of 'pattern variables' and 'functional requisites', must have some connection with an external reality, in that they are

Research in focus 2.1
Grand theory and social research

Butler and Robson (2001) used Bourdieu's concept of social capital as a means of understanding the gentrification of areas of London. While the term 'social capital' has acquired an everyday usage, Butler and Robson follow Bourdieu's theoretical use of it, which draws attention to the social connectedness and the interpersonal resources that those with social capital can draw on to pursue their goals. While the term has attracted the interest of social policy researchers and others concerned with social exclusion, its use in relation to the middle class has been less prominent, according to Butler and Robson. Bourdieu's treatment implies that those with social capital cultivate significant social connections and then draw upon those connections as resources for their goals. Butler and Robson conducted semi-structured interviews with 'gentrifiers' in each of three inner London areas. Responding to a tendency to view gentrification in rather unitary terms, the authors selected the three areas to examine what they refer to as the 'variability' of the process. To that end, the areas were selected to reflect variation in two factors: the length of time over which gentrification had been occurring and the middle-class groupings to which each of the areas appealed. The selection of areas in terms of these criteria was aided by **census** data. Of the three areas, Telegraph Hill was the strongest in terms of social capital. According to the authors, this is revealed in 'its higher levels of voluntary co-operation and sense of geographically focused unity' (Butler and Robson 2001: 2159). It is the recourse to these networks of sociality that accounts for the successful gentrification of Telegraph Hill. Battersea, one of the other two areas, entails a contrasting impetus for gentrification in Bourdieu's terms. Here, economic capital was more significant for gentrification than the social capital that was important in Telegraph Hill. The role of economic capital in Battersea can be seen in the 'competitive access to an increasingly desirable and expensive stock of housing and an exclusive circuit of schooling centred on private provision' (Butler and Robson 2001: 2159). In the former, it is sociality that provides the motor for gentrification, whereas in Battersea gentrification is driven by market forces and is only partially influenced by patterns of social connectedness. This study is an interesting example of the way in which a relatively high-level theoretical notion—social capital and its kindred concept of economic capital—associated with a social theorist can be employed to illuminate research questions concerning the dynamics of modern urban living.

likely to have been generated out of Parsons's reading of research or his reflections upon that reality or others' writings on it. However, the level of abstractness of the theorizing is so great as to make it difficult for these notions to be deployed in research. For research purposes, then, Merton argues that grand theories are of limited use in connection with social research, although, as the example in Research in focus 2.1 suggests, an abstract concept such as social capital (Bourdieu 1984) can have some pay-off in research terms. Instead, middle-range theories are 'intermediate to general theories of social systems which are too remote from particular classes of social behavior, organization and change to account for what is observed and to those detailed orderly descriptions of particulars that are not generalized at all' (Merton 1967: 39).

Typically, it is not grand theory that guides social research. Middle-range theories are much more likely to be the focus of empirical enquiry. In fact, Merton formulated the idea as a means of bridging what he saw as a growing gulf between grand theory and empirical findings. This is not to say that there were no middle-range theories before he wrote: there definitely were, but Merton sought to clarify what is meant by 'theory' when social scientists write about the relationship between theory and research.

Middle-range theories, unlike grand ones, operate in a limited domain, whether it is juvenile delinquency, voting behaviour, educational attainment, or ethnic relations (see Research in focus 2.2). They vary in their range of application. For example, labelling theory represents a middle-range theory in the sociology of deviance. Its exponents sought to understand deviance in terms of the causes and effects of the societal reaction to deviation. It was held to be applicable to a variety of different forms of deviance, including crime and mental illness. By contrast, Cloward and Ohlin's (1960) differential association

theory was formulated specifically in connection with juvenile delinquency, and in subsequent years this tended to be its focus. Middle-range theories represent attempts to understand and explain a limited aspect of social life.

Even the grand/middle-range distinction does not entirely clarify the issues involved in asking the deceptively simple question of 'what is theory?' This is because the term 'theory' is frequently used in a manner that means the background literature in an area of social enquiry. The analysis of the representation of social research in the media by Fenton et al. (1998) was undertaken against a background of similar analyses in the USA and of studies of the representation of natural science research in the media in several different countries. In many cases, the relevant background literature relating to a topic fuels the focus of an article or book and acts as the equivalent of a theory, as with the research referred to in Research in focus 2.3. The literature in a certain domain acts as an impetus in several ways: the researcher may seek to resolve an inconsistency between different findings or between different interpretations of findings; the researcher may have spotted a neglected aspect of a topic; certain ideas may not previously have been tested a great deal; the researcher may feel that existing approaches being used for research on a topic are deficient, and so provides an alternative approach; and so on.

Social scientists are sometimes prone to being dismissive of research that has no obvious connections with theory—in either the grand or the middle-range senses of the term. Such research is often dismissed as naive **empiricism** (see Key concept 2.1). It would be harsh, not to say inaccurate, to brand as naive empiricism the numerous studies in which the publications-as-theory strategy is employed, simply because their authors have not been preoccupied with theory. Such research is conditioned by and directed towards research questions that arise out of

Research in focus 2.2
Conflict and contact theory: two middle-range theories

In the study of ethnic relations, there are two theories of relationships between ethnic groups that have very different implications for inter-ethnic harmony. One theory—the conflict theory—proposes that when ethnic groups mix in neighbourhoods and other contexts, there is a greater likelihood of a sense of threat and apprehension, resulting in such responses as greater discrimination on ethnic grounds and a greater tendency to stereotype. By contrast, the contact theory suggests that mixing between ethnic groups creates a greater sense of familiarity which reduces the sense of threat and apprehension which in turn creates a superior climate for inter-ethnic relations in which discrimination and stereotyping are reduced. Each theory is about the effects of ethnic diversity on the quality of inter-group relations. They have both been the focus of considerable research as students of ethnic relations try to establish the strengths and limitations of each theory (e.g. Hughes et al. 2011; Laurence 2014; Sturgis et al. 2011; Sturgis et al. 2014a).

Research in focus 2.3
Background literature as theory: emotional labour and hairstylists

One component of R. S. Cohen's (2010) mixed methods study of hairstylists' relationships with their clients was a **postal questionnaire** survey of all salons and barbers' shops in a northern city in England. Of the 328 enterprises contacted, 40 per cent replied to the questionnaire. The goal of the research was to examine how far the giving of emotional favours was affected by the nature of the relationship with the client in terms of whether the worker was an owner or a paid employee. Cohen's survey data show that owners are more likely to stay late for clients and to try to find a space for them between clients who have been booked in. Hochschild's (1983) book, in which the term 'emotional labour' was first coined, and the studies that have used the concept form the starting point of Cohen's research. The significance of this work is evident from Cohen's two opening sentences:

> Since Hochschild (1983) first suggested that interactive service workers carry out emotional labour in the course of their work, this proposition has become widely accepted. However the relationship of emotional labour, and client–worker social interactions more generally, to the structural relations of employment has received surprisingly little attention . . .

> (R. S. Cohen 2010: 197)

Thus, the literature on emotional labour forms the background to the study and the main impetus for the interpretation of the findings, some of which are gleaned from qualitative data deriving from semi-structured interviews with some owners and employees. For the latter, interactions with clients are much more likely to take the form of what Hochschild (1983) called 'surface acting', a superficial form of emotional labour and emotional engagement with the client.

Key concept 2.1
What is empiricism?

The term 'empiricism' is used in a number of different ways, but two stand out. First, it is used to denote a general approach to the study of reality that suggests that only knowledge gained through experience and the senses is acceptable. In other words, this position means that ideas must be subjected to the rigours of testing before they can be considered knowledge. The second meaning of the term is related to this and refers to a belief that the accumulation of 'facts' is a legitimate goal in its own right. It is this second meaning that is sometimes referred to as 'naive empiricism'.

an examination of the literature. The data collection and analysis are subsequently geared to the illumination of the research issue or problem that has been identified at the outset. The literature acts as a proxy for theory. In many instances, theory is latent or implicit in the literature.

Research that appears to have the characteristics of a fact-finding exercise should not be dismissed as naive empiricism either. McKeganey and Barnard's (1996) research on prostitutes and their clients is a case in point. Superficially, even if the concern with HIV infection is stripped away, the research could be read as naive empiricism but this would be a harsh and inaccurate judgement.

For example, the authors relate their research findings to the literature reporting other investigations of prostitutes in a number of different countries. They also illuminate their findings by drawing on ideas that are very much part of the sociologist's conceptual toolkit. One example is Goffman's (1963) notion of 'stigma' and the way in which the stigmatized individual seeks to manage a spoiled identity; another is Hochschild's (1983) concept of 'emotional labour', a term she coined to denote the way service workers often contrive a demeanour of friendliness when dealing with clients, even when they are extremely difficult (see also Research in focus 2.3).

It is not possible to tell from McKeganey and Barnard's (1996) report whether the concepts of stigma and emotional labour influenced their data collection. However, raising this question invites consideration of another question: in so far as any piece of research is linked to theory, what was the role of that theory? Up to this point, I have written as though theory guides and influences the collection and analysis of data. In other words, research is done in order to answer questions posed by theoretical considerations. But an alternative position is to view theory as something that emerges after the collection and analysis of some or all of the data associated with a project. We begin to see here the significance of a second factor in considering the relationship between theory and research—whether we are referring to deductive or inductive theory.

Deductive and inductive theory

Deductive theory represents the commonest view of the nature of the relationship between theory and social research, whereby the researcher draws on what is known about in a particular domain and on relevant theoretical ideas in order to deduce a hypothesis (or hypotheses) that must then be subjected to empirical scrutiny. Embedded within the hypothesis will be concepts that will need to be translated into researchable entities. The researcher must both skilfully deduce a hypothesis and then translate it into operational terms. This means that the researcher needs to specify how data can be collected in relation to the concepts that make up the hypothesis.

This view of the role of theory in relation to research is very much the one that Merton had in mind in connection with middle-range theory, which, he argued, 'is principally used in sociology to guide empirical inquiry' (Merton 1967: 39). Theory and the hypothesis deduced from it come first and drive the process of gathering data (see Research in focus 2.4 for an example of a deductive approach to the relationship between theory and data). The sequence can be depicted as following the steps outlined in Figure 2.1.

The last step, revision of theory, involves a movement that is in the opposite direction from **deduction**—it involves **induction**, as the researcher infers the implications of his or her findings for the theory that prompted the whole exercise. The findings are fed back into the stock of theory and the research findings associated with a certain domain of enquiry. This can be seen in the case of the final reflections of Butler and Robson's (2001) study of gentrification in three areas of London (see Research in focus 2.1) when they write:

> Each of the three groups has played on its strengths, where it has them. Gentrification, given this, cannot in any sense be considered to be a unitary phenomenon,

Figure 2.1
The process of deduction

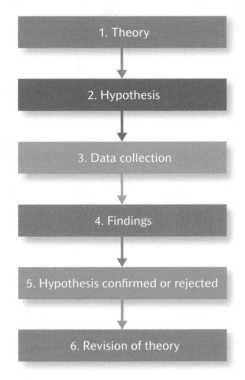

but needs to be examined in each case according to its own logic and outcomes. The concept of social capital, when used as an integrated part of an extended conceptual framework for the apprehension of all forms of middle-class capital relations, can thus play an important part in discriminating between differing types of social phenomena.

(Butler and Robson 2001: 2160)

In these final reflections they show how their findings and the interpretations of those findings can be fed back into both the stock of knowledge concerning gentrification in cities and, in the third of the three sentences, the concept of social capital and its uses.

However, while the element of induction undoubtedly exists in the process outlined in Figure 2.1, this approach is typically depicted as predominantly deductive. Moreover, it is important to bear in mind that, when this deductive approach, which is usually associated with quantitative research, is put into operation, it often does not follow the sequence outlined in its pure form. As previously noted, 'theory' may refer to the literature on a certain topic in the form of the accumulated knowledge gleaned from books and articles. Also, even when theory or theories can be

Research in focus 2.4
A deductive study

Röder and Mühlau (2014) note that egalitarian attitudes with respect to gender vary a great deal between nations. They focus especially on what happens when migrants move from a country in which egalitarian attitudes are weak to one where they are strong and often actively promoted, a scenario that they propose is common. They also note that there is relatively little research on gender-egalitarian values among migrants, but they review the studies that do exist. Their review of the literature leads them to propose five hypotheses, such as:

(H2) (a) Second-generation migrants have a more egalitarian-gender ideology than the first generation; and (b) the gender relations of the origin country exert less influence on the gender attitudes for second-generation immigrants than for first-generation immigrants.

(Röder and Mühlau 2014: 903)

This hypothesis comprises three central concepts: second-generation immigrants; gender-egalitarian attitudes; and gender relations of the origin country (i.e. the country from which an immigrant has emigrated).

In order to test the hypotheses, the authors used data from the European Social Survey, which is conducted by structured interview every two years and collects data from samples in all European Union countries and several other European countries (**www.europeansocialsurvey.org/**, accessed 13 August 2014). The authors had to be clear about what they meant by a second-generation immigrant, who is defined as having been born in the country in which they now live but who has one or both parents who were born abroad. The measurement of gender-egalitarian attitudes was based on two questions asked on the questionnaire. Both questions take the form of statements with which respondents are asked to give their level of agreement on a five-point scale, with 'strongly agree' at one end and 'strongly disagree' at the other. The two statements are: 'When jobs are scarce, men should have more right to a job than women' and 'A woman should be prepared to cut down on her paid work for the sake of her family'. This style of questioning is known as a Likert scale (see Key concept 7.2). For the measurement of gender relations of the origin country, the researchers compiled an index that was based on information for each country about female representation on parliaments; female representation in managerial and professional posts; and the earnings difference between men and women.

The hypotheses were broadly confirmed and the authors conclude that the 'gender ideology is affected by an intergenerational acculturation process' (Röder and Mühlau 2014: 915). This study demonstrates the process whereby hypotheses are deduced from existing theory and then tested.

discerned, explicit hypotheses are not always deduced from them in the way that Röder and Mühlau (2014) did in Research in focus 2.4. A further point to bear in mind is that the deductive process appears very linear—one step follows the other in a clear, logical sequence. However, there are many instances where this is not the case: a researcher's view of the theory or literature may have changed as a result of the analysis of the collected data; new theoretical ideas or findings may be published by others before the researcher has generated his or her findings; or the relevance of a set of data for a theory may become apparent *after* the data have been collected.

This may all seem rather surprising and confusing. There is a certain logic to the idea of developing theories and then testing them. In everyday contexts, we commonly think of theories as things that are quite revealing but that need to be tested before they can be considered valid or useful. However, while the process of deduction outlined in Figure 2.1 does undoubtedly occur, it is better considered as a general orientation to the link between theory and research. As a general orientation, its broad shape may often be discernible in social research, but it is also the case that we often find departures from it. In some research *no* attempt is made to follow the sequence outlined in Figure 2.1. Some researchers prefer an *inductive* approach to the relationship between theory and research. With an inductive stance, theory is the *outcome* of research which involves drawing generalizable inferences out of observations. Figure 2.2 attempts to capture the essence of the difference between inductivism and deductivism.

However, just as deduction entails an element of induction, the inductive process is likely to entail a degree of

Figure 2.2

Deductive and inductive approaches to the relationship between theory and research

Deductive approach

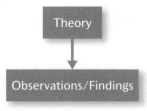

Inductive approach

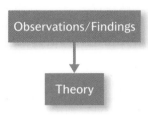

deduction. Once the phase of theoretical reflection on a set of data has been carried out, the researcher may want to collect further data in order to establish the conditions in which a theory will and will not hold. Such a general strategy is often called *iterative*: it involves a weaving back and forth between data and theory. It is particularly evident in **grounded theory**, which will be examined in Chapter 24, but in the meantime the basic point is to note that induction represents an alternative strategy for linking theory and research, although it contains a deductive element too.

The research by O'Reilly et al. (2012) is a striking illustration of an inductive approach for two main reasons. First, it uses a grounded theory approach to the analysis of data and the generation of theory. This approach, which was first outlined by Glaser and Strauss (1967), is regarded as especially strong in terms of generating theories out of data. This contrasts with the nature of some supposedly inductive studies, which generate interesting and illuminating findings but whose theoretical significance is not entirely clear. They provide insightful empirical generalizations, but little theory. Secondly, in

Research in focus 2.5
An inductive study

O'Reilly et al. (2012) discuss how one of the authors (Kelley O'Reilly) went about conducting an analysis of her qualitative data on interactions between customers and front-line employees (abbreviated as FLEs). Her initial data were collected at a site in the USA which sold through a variety of channels, including store, telephone and Internet. Around 50 per cent of her interviews (and a large amount of observation) derived from this site. She refers to her research as the 'Silo Study' because the notion of FLEs working in *service silos* (i.e. separate areas from which could not easily break out) became a linchpin of her analysis of her findings. The notion of people working in silos (for example, because they are unwilling to share information with each other) is a common sense notion but for O'Reilly, the theoretical construct of the silo was imbued with a somewhat different meaning because the silos had been strategically created by senior managers. Service silos were meant to act as mechanisms of control in the sense that FLEs were deliberately constrained in the range of what they could do. The need for this response arose from management's recognition that its existing arrangements could no longer cope with the volume of activity. The service silo approach, however, had implications for the quality of relations with customers. In O'Reilly's dissertation (2010), on which the article is based, the service silo and its impact on relations with customers is exemplified when she asks one of her participants how he would return a product. His reply is deeply sarcastic:

> Well I can't really return that defective product for you Mrs. Customer. . . I know it is only 69 cents, but I can't walk to the shelf and get you one that works. I am going to give you a sticker and you've got to go to a separate line, because the company doesn't trust me to make 69 cent decisions.
>
> (quoted in O'Reilly 2010: 116)

As O'Reilly (2010) notes, the participant's reply draws attention to his lack of empowerment to deal with the issue himself, even though the monetary amount involved is trivial.

In this study, the inductive nature of the relationship between theory and research can be seen in the way that O'Reilly's theoretical idea (the notion of the 'service silo' as a purposely designed managerial control strategy) derives from her data rather than being formed before she had collected her data.

much the same way that the deductive strategy is associated with quantitative research, an inductive strategy of linking data and theory is typically associated with qualitative research. It is not a coincidence that the research referred to in Research in focus 2.5 is based on in-depth, semi-structured interviews and observations that produced qualitative data in the form of the researcher's field notes and the respondents' detailed answers to her questions. However, as will be shown below, this characterization of the inductive strategy as associated with qualitative research is not entirely straightforward: not only does some qualitative research *not* generate theory, but also theory is often used as a background to qualitative investigations.

It is useful to think of the relationship between theory and research in terms of deductive and inductive strategies, but as the previous discussion has implied, the issues are not as clear-cut as they are sometimes presented. Deductive and inductive strategies are possibly better thought of as tendencies rather than as separated by a hard-and-fast distinction. But these are not the only issues that impinge on the conduct of social research.

Epistemological considerations

An epistemological issue concerns the question of what is (or should be) regarded as acceptable knowledge in a discipline. In the social sciences, a central issue is the question of whether the social world can and should be studied according to the same principles, procedures, and ethos as the natural sciences. The position that affirms the importance of imitating the natural sciences is invariably associated with an epistemological position known as positivism (see Key concept 2.2).

A natural science epistemology: positivism

The doctrine of **positivism** is difficult to pin down and outline in a precise manner, because authors use it in different ways. For some writers, it is a descriptive category—one that describes a philosophical position that can be discerned in research—though there are still disagreements about what it comprises; for others, it is a negative term used to describe crude and often superficial practices of data collection.

It is possible to see in the five principles in Key concept 2.2 a link with some of the points that have been raised about the relationship between theory and research. For example, positivism entails elements of both a deductive approach (principle 2) and an inductive strategy (principle 3). Also, a fairly sharp distinction is drawn between theory and research. The role of research is to test theories and to provide material for the development of laws. But either of these connections between

Key concept 2.2
What is positivism?

Positivism is an epistemological position that advocates the application of the methods of the natural sciences to the study of social reality and beyond. The term stretches beyond this principle, though the constituent elements vary between authors. However, positivism may be taken to entail the following principles:

1. Only phenomena and hence knowledge confirmed by the senses can genuinely be warranted as knowledge (the principle of *phenomenalism*).

2. The purpose of theory is to generate hypotheses that can be tested and that will thereby allow explanations of laws to be assessed (the principle of *deductivism*).

3. Knowledge is arrived at through the gathering of facts that provide the basis for laws (the principle of *inductivism*).

4. Science must (and presumably can) be conducted in a way that is value free (that is, *objective*).

5. There is a clear distinction between scientific statements and normative statements and a belief that the former are the true domain of the scientist. This last principle is implied by the first because the truth or otherwise of normative statements cannot be confirmed by the senses.

theory and research carries with it the implication that it is possible to collect observations in a manner that is not influenced by pre-existing theories. Moreover, theoretical terms that are not directly amenable to observation are not considered genuinely scientific; they must be susceptible to the rigours of observation. This implies greater epistemological status being given to observation than to theory.

It should be noted that it is a mistake to treat positivism as synonymous with science and the scientific. In

Key concept 2.3
What is realism?

Realism shares two features with positivism: a belief that the natural and the social sciences can and should apply the same kinds of approach to the collection of data and to explanation, and a commitment to the view that there is an external reality to which scientists direct their attention (in other words, there is a reality that is separate from our descriptions of it). There are two major forms of realism:

- *Empirical realism* simply asserts that, through the use of appropriate methods, reality can be understood. This version of realism is sometimes referred to as *naive realism* to reflect the fact that it is often assumed by realists that there is a perfect (or at least very close) correspondence between reality and the term used to describe it. As such, it 'fails to recognise that there are enduring structures and generative mechanisms underlying and producing observable phenomena and events' and is therefore 'superficial' (Bhaskar 1989: 2). This is perhaps the most common meaning of the term. When writers in the social sciences employ the term 'realism' in a general way, it is invariably this meaning to which they are referring.

- *Critical realism* is a specific form of realism whose manifesto is to recognize the reality of the natural order and the events and discourses of the social world and holds that 'we will only be able to understand—and so change—the social world if we identify the structures at work that generate those events and discourses. . . . These structures are not spontaneously apparent in the observable pattern of events; they can only be identified through the practical and theoretical work of the social sciences' (Bhaskar 1989: 2).

Critical realism implies two things. First, it implies that, whereas positivists take the view that the scientist's conceptualization of reality actually directly reflects that reality, realists argue that the scientist's conceptualization is simply a way of knowing that reality. As Bhaskar (1975: 250) has put it: 'Science, then, is the systematic attempt to express in thought the structures and ways of acting of things that exist and act independently of thought.' Critical realists acknowledge and accept that the categories they use to understand reality are likely to be provisional. Thus, unlike naive realists, critical realists recognize that there is a distinction between the objects that are the focus of their enquiries and the terms they use to describe, account for, and understand them. Secondly, by implication, critical realists unlike positivists are content to include in their explanations theoretical terms that are not directly amenable to observation. As a result, hypothetical entities that account for regularities in the natural or social orders (the 'generative mechanisms' to which Bhaskar refers) are acceptable for realists, but not for positivists. Generative mechanisms are the entities and processes that are constitutive of the phenomenon of interest. For critical realists, it is acceptable that generative mechanisms are not directly observable, since they can be admitted into theoretical accounts on the grounds that their effects are observable. Also crucial to a critical realist understanding is the identification of the context that interacts with the generative mechanism to produce an observed regularity in the social world. An appreciation of context is crucial to critical realist explanations because it serves to shed light on the conditions that promote or impede the operation of the causal mechanism. What makes critical realism *critical* is that the identification of generative mechanisms offers the prospect of introducing changes that can transform the status quo. A further point to note about critical realism is that the form of reasoning involved in the identification of generative causal mechanisms is neither inductive nor deductive. It is referred to by Blaikie (2004b) as **retroductive** reasoning, which entails making an inference about the causal mechanism that lies behind and is responsible for regularities that are observed in the social world. Research in focus 26.2 provides an example of research using a critical realist approach. This example can be read profitably at this stage even though it is in a much later chapter.

fact, philosophers of science and of the social sciences differ quite sharply over how best to characterize scientific practice, and since the early 1960s there has been a drift away from viewing it in positivist terms. Thus, when writers complain about the limitations of positivism, it is not entirely clear whether they mean the philosophical term or a scientific approach more generally. **Realism** (in particular, **critical realism**), for example, is another philosophical position that provides an account of the nature of scientific practice (see Key concept 2.3).

The crux of the epistemological considerations that form the central thrust of this section is the rejection, by some writers and traditions, of the application of principles of the natural sciences to the study of social reality. A difficulty here is that it is not easy to disentangle the natural science model from positivism as the butt of their criticisms. In other words, it is not always clear whether they are denouncing the application of a general natural scientific approach or of positivism in particular. There is a long-standing debate about the appropriateness of the natural science model for the study of society, but, since the account that is offered of that model tends to have largely positivist overtones, it would seem that it is positivism that is the focus of attention rather than other accounts of scientific practice (such as critical realism—see Key concept 2.3).

Interpretivism

Interpretivism is a term given to an epistemology that contrasts with positivism (see Key concept 2.4). The term subsumes the views of writers who have been critical of the application of the scientific model to the study of the social world and who have been influenced by different intellectual traditions. They share a view that the subject matter of the social sciences—people and their institutions—is fundamentally different from that of the natural sciences. The study of the social world therefore requires a different logic of research procedure, one that reflects the distinctiveness of humans as

against the natural order. Von Wright (1971) has depicted the epistemological clash as being between positivism and **hermeneutics** (a term that is drawn from theology and that, when imported into the social sciences, is concerned with the theory and method of the interpretation of human action). This clash reflects a division between an emphasis on the *explanation* of human behaviour, which is the chief ingredient of the positivist approach, and the *understanding* of human behaviour. The latter is concerned with the empathic understanding of human action rather than with the forces that are deemed to act on it. This contrast reflects long-standing debates that precede the emergence of the modern social sciences but that find their expression in such notions as the advocacy by Max Weber (1864–1920) of an approach referred to in his native German as *Verstehen* (which means understanding). Weber (1947: 88) described sociology as a 'science which attempts the interpretive understanding of social action in order to arrive at a causal explanation of its course and effects'. Weber's definition seems to embrace both explanation *and* understanding here, but the crucial point is that the task of 'causal explanation' is undertaken with reference to the 'interpretive understanding of social action' rather than to external forces that have no meaning for those involved in that social action.

One of the main intellectual traditions that has been responsible for the anti-positivist position has been **phenomenology**, a philosophy that is concerned with the question of how individuals make sense of the world around them and how in particular the philosopher should bracket out preconceptions in his or her grasp of that world. The initial application of phenomenological ideas to the social sciences is attributed to the work of Alfred Schutz (1899–1959), whose work did not come to the notice of most English-speaking social scientists until the translation from German of his major writings in the 1960s, some twenty or more years after they had been written. His work was profoundly influenced by Weber's concept of *Verstehen*, as well as by phenomenological philosophers such as Husserl. Schutz's position is well

Key concept 2.4
What is interpretivism?

Interpretivism is a term that usually denotes an alternative to the positivist orthodoxy that has dominated the social sciences for decades. It is founded upon the view that a strategy is required that respects the differences between people and the objects of the natural sciences and therefore requires the social scientist to grasp the subjective meaning of social action. Its intellectual heritage includes Weber's notion of *Verstehen*; the hermeneutic–phenomenological tradition; and symbolic interactionism.

captured in the following passage, which has been quoted on numerous occasions:

> The world of nature as explored by the natural scientist does not 'mean' anything to molecules, atoms and electrons. But the observational field of the social scientist—social reality—has a specific meaning and relevance structure for the beings living, acting, and thinking within it. By a series of common-sense constructs they have pre-selected and pre-interpreted this world which they experience as the reality of their daily lives. It is these thought objects of theirs which determine their behaviour by motivating it. The thought objects constructed by the social scientist, in order to grasp this social reality, have to be founded upon the thought objects constructed by the common-sense thinking of men [and women!], living their daily life within the social world.
>
> (Schutz 1962: 59)

Two points are particularly noteworthy in this quotation. First, it asserts that there is a fundamental difference between the subject matter of the natural sciences and the social sciences and that an epistemology is required that reflects and capitalizes upon that difference. The fundamental difference resides in the fact that social reality has a meaning for human beings and therefore human action is meaningful—that is, it has a meaning for them and they act on the basis of the meanings that they attribute to their acts and to the acts of others. This leads to the second point—namely, that it is the job of the social scientist to gain access to people's 'common-sense thinking' and hence to interpret their actions and their social world from their point of view. It is this particular feature that social scientists claiming allegiance to phenomenology have typically emphasized. In the words of the authors of a research methods text whose approach is described as phenomenological: 'The phenomenologist views human behavior . . . as a product of how people interpret the world. . . . In order to grasp the meanings of a person's behavior, *the phenomenologist attempts to see things from that person's point of view*' (Bogdan and Taylor 1975: 13–14; emphasis in original).

In this exposition of *Verstehen* and phenomenology, I have skated over some complex issues. In particular, Weber's examination of *Verstehen* is far more complex than the above commentary suggests, because the empathetic understanding that seems to be implied above was not the way in which he applied it (Bauman 1978), while the question of what is and is not a genuinely phenomenological approach to the social sciences is a matter of some dispute (Heap and Roth 1973). However, the similarity in the writings of the hermeneutic–phenomenological tradition and of the *Verstehen* approach, with their emphasis upon social action as being meaningful to actors and therefore needing to be interpreted from their point

of view, coupled with the rejection of positivism, contributed to a stream of thought often referred to as interpretivism (e.g. J. A. Hughes 1990).

Verstehen and the hermeneutic–phenomenological tradition do not exhaust the intellectual influences on interpretivism. The theoretical tradition in sociology known as *symbolic interactionism* has also been regarded by many writers as a further influence. Again, the case is not clear-cut. There has been hot debate over the implications for empirical research of the ideas of the founders of symbolic interactionism, in particular George Herbert Mead (1863–1931), who discusses the way in which our notion of self emerges through an appreciation of how others see us. However, the general tendency has been to view symbolic interactionism as occupying similar intellectual space to the hermeneutic–phenomenological tradition and so as broadly interpretative in approach. This tendency is largely the product of the writings of Herbert Blumer, a student of Mead's who acted as his mentor's spokesman and interpreter, and his followers (Hammersley 1989; R. Collins 1994). Not only did Blumer coin the term 'symbolic interaction'; he also provided a gloss on Mead's writings that has clear interpretative overtones. Symbolic interactionists argue that interaction takes place in such a way that the individual is continually interpreting the symbolic meaning of his or her environment (which includes the actions of others) and acts on the basis of this imputed meaning. In research terms, according to Blumer (1962: 188), 'the position of symbolic interaction requires the student to catch the process of interpretation through which [actors] construct their actions', a statement that brings out clearly his views of the research implications of symbolic interactionism and of Mead's thought.

The affinity between symbolic interactionism and the hermeneutic–phenomenological tradition should not be exaggerated. The two are united in their antipathy for positivism and have in common an interpretative stance. However, symbolic interactionism is a type of social theory that has distinctive epistemological implications; the hermeneutic–phenomenological tradition, by contrast, is best thought of as an epistemological approach in its own right. Blumer may have been influenced by the hermeneutic–phenomenological tradition, but there is no concrete evidence of this. There are other intellectual currents that have affinities with the interpretative stance, such as the working-through of the ramifications of the works of the philosopher Ludwig Wittgenstein (Winch 1958), but the hermeneutic–phenomenological, *Verstehen*, and symbolic interactionist traditions can be considered major influences.

Taking an interpretative stance can mean that the researcher may come up with surprising findings, or at least findings that appear surprising from a position outside the particular social context being studied. Research in focus 2.6 provides an example of this possibility.

Research in focus 2.6
Interpretivism in practice

Foster (1995) conducted an **ethnography** comprising participant observation and semi-structured interviews in a housing estate in East London, referred to as Riverside. The estate had a high level of crime, as indicated by **official statistics** on crime. However, Foster found that residents did not perceive the estate to be a high-crime area. This perception could be attributed to a number of factors, but a particularly important reason was the existence of 'informal social control'. People expected a certain level of crime, but they felt fairly secure because informal social control allowed levels of crime to be contained. Informal social control comprised a number of different aspects. One aspect was that neighbours often looked out for each other. In the words of one of Foster's interviewees: 'If I hear a bang or shouting I go out. If there's aggravation I come in and ring the police. I don't stand for it.' Another aspect of informal social control was that people often felt secure because they knew each other. Another respondent said: 'I don't feel nervous . . . because people do generally know each other. We keep an eye on each other's properties . . . I feel quite safe because you know your neighbours and you know they're there . . . they look out for you' (Foster 1995: 575).

As the example in Research in focus 2.6 suggests, when the social scientist adopts an interpretative stance, he or she does not simply reveal how members of a social group interpret the world around them. The social scientist will aim to place the interpretations that have been elicited into a social scientific frame. There is a double interpretation going on: the researcher provides an interpretation of others' interpretations. Indeed, there is a third level of interpretation going on, because the researcher's interpretations have to be further interpreted in terms of the concepts, theories, and literature of a discipline. Thus, taking the example in Research in focus 2.6, Foster's (1995) suggestion that Riverside is not perceived as a high-crime area by residents is her interpretation of her subjects' interpretations. She then had the additional job of placing her interesting findings into a social scientific frame, which she accomplished by relating them to concepts and discussions in criminology of such things as informal social control, neighbourhood watch schemes, and the role of housing as a possible cause of criminal activity.

The aim of this section has been to outline how epistemological considerations—especially those relating to the question of whether a natural science approach, and in particular a positivist one, can supply legitimate knowledge of the social world—are related to research practice. There is a link with the earlier section in that a deductive approach to the relationship between theory and research is typically associated with a positivist position. Key concept 2.2 suggests that inductivism is also a feature of positivism (third principle), but, in the working-through of its implementation in social research, it is the deductive element (second principle) that tends to be emphasized. Similarly, the third level of interpretation that a researcher engaged in interpretative research must bring into operation is a component of the inductive strategy described in the previous section. However, while such interconnections between epistemological issues and research practice exist, it is important not to overstate them, since they represent tendencies rather than definitive points of correspondence. Thus particular epistemological principles and research practices do not necessarily go hand-in-hand in a neat unambiguous manner. This point will be made again on several occasions and will be a special focus of Chapter 26.

Ontological considerations

Questions of social **ontology** are concerned with the nature of social entities. The central point of orientation here is the question of whether social entities can and should be considered objective entities that have a reality external to social actors, or whether they can and should be considered social constructions built up from the perceptions and actions of social actors. These two positions are referred to respectively as **objectivism** and **constructionism**. Their differences can be illustrated by reference to two of the most common and central terms in social science—'organization' and 'culture'.

Key concept 2.5
What is objectivism?

Objectivism is an ontological position that asserts that social phenomena and their meanings have an existence that is independent of social actors. It implies that social phenomena and the categories that we use in everyday discourse have an existence that is independent or separate from actors.

Objectivism

Objectivism is an ontological position that implies that social phenomena confront us as external facts that are beyond our reach or influence (see Key concept 2.5).

We can discuss organization or *an* organization as a tangible object. It has rules and regulations. It adopts standardized procedures for getting things done. People are appointed to different jobs within a division of labour. There is a hierarchy. It has a mission statement. And so on. The degree to which these features exist from organization to organization is variable, but in thinking in these terms we are tending to the view that an organization has a reality that is external to the individuals who inhabit it. Moreover, the organization represents a social order in that it exerts pressure on individuals to conform to the requirements of the organization. People learn and apply the rules and regulations. They follow the standardized procedures. They do the jobs to which they are appointed. They are told what to do and tell others what to do. They learn and apply the values in the mission statement. If they do not do these things, they may be reprimanded or even fired. The organization is therefore a constraining force that acts on and inhibits its members.

The same can be said of culture. Cultures and subcultures can be viewed as repositories of widely shared values and customs into which people are socialized so that they can function as good citizens or as full participants. Cultures and subcultures constrain us because we internalize their beliefs and values. In the case of both organization and culture, the social entity in question comes across as something external to the actor and as having an almost tangible reality of its own. It has the characteristics of an object and of having an objective reality. These are the 'classic' ways of conceptualizing organization and culture.

Constructionism

However, we can consider an alternative ontological position—*constructionism* (Key concept 2.6). This position

Key concept 2.6
What is constructionism?

Constructionism is an ontological position (often also referred to as constructivism) that asserts that social phenomena and their meanings are continually being accomplished by social actors. It implies that social phenomena are not only produced through social interaction but are in a constant state of revision. In recent years, the term has also come to include the notion that researchers' own accounts of the social world are constructions. In other words, the researcher always presents a specific version of social reality, rather than one that can be regarded as definitive. Knowledge is viewed as indeterminate. This sense of constructionism is usually allied to the ontological version of the term. In other words, these are linked meanings. Both meanings are antithetical to *objectivism* (see Key concept 2.5), but the second meaning is also antithetical to *realism* (see Key concept 2.3). The first meaning might be thought of usefully as constructionism in relation to the social world; the second as constructionism in relation to the nature of knowledge of the social world (and indeed the natural world).

Increasingly, the notion of constructionism in relation to the nature of knowledge of the social world is being incorporated into notions of constructionism, but in this book I will be using the term in relation to the first meaning, whereby constructionism is presented as an ontological position in relating to social objects and categories—that is, one that views them as socially constructed.

challenges the suggestion that categories such as organization and culture are pre-given and therefore confront social actors as external realities that they have no role in influencing.

Let us take organization first. Strauss et al. (1973), drawing on insights from symbolic interactionism, carried out research in a psychiatric hospital and proposed that it was best conceptualized as a 'negotiated order'. Instead of taking the view that order in organizations is a pre-existing characteristic, they argue that it is worked at. Rules were far less extensive and less rigorously imposed than might be supposed from the classic account of organization. Indeed, Strauss et al. (1973: 308) refer to them as 'much less like commands, and much more like general understandings'. Precisely because relatively little of the spheres of action of doctors, nurses, and other personnel was prescribed, the social order of the hospital was an outcome of agreed-upon patterns of action that were themselves the products of negotiations between the different parties involved. The social order was in a constant state of change because the hospital was 'a place where numerous agreements are continually being terminated or forgotten, but also as continually being established, renewed, reviewed, revoked, revised. . . . In any pragmatic sense, this is the hospital at the moment: this is its social order' (Strauss et al. 1973: 316–17). The authors argue that a preoccupation with the formal properties of organizations (rules, organizational charts, regulations, roles) tends to neglect the degree to which order in organizations has to be accomplished in everyday interaction, though this is not to say that the formal properties have *no* element of constraint on individual action.

Much the same kind of point can be made about the idea of culture. Instead of seeing culture as an external reality that acts on and constrains people, it can be taken to be an emergent reality in a continuous state of construction and reconstruction. Becker (1982: 521), for example, has suggested that 'people create culture continuously. . . . No set of cultural understandings . . . provides a perfectly applicable solution to any problem people have to solve in the course of their day, and they therefore must remake those solutions, adapt their understandings to the new situation in the light of what is different about it.' Like Strauss et al., Becker recognizes that the constructionist position cannot be pushed to the extreme: it is necessary to appreciate that culture has a reality that 'persists and antedates the participation of particular people' and shapes their perspectives, but it is not an inert objective reality that possesses only a sense of constraint: it acts as a point of reference but is always in the process of being formed.

Neither the work of Strauss et al. nor that of Becker pushes the constructionist argument to the extreme.

Each admits to the pre-existence of their objects of interest (organization and culture respectively). However, in each case we see an intellectual preference for stressing the active role of individuals in the construction of social reality. Constructionism essentially invites the researcher to consider the ways in which social reality is an ongoing accomplishment of social actors rather than something external to them and that totally constrains them.

Constructionism also suggests that the categories that people employ in helping them to understand the world around them are in fact social products. The categories do not have built-in essences; instead, their meaning is constructed in and through interaction. Thus, a category such as 'masculinity' might be treated as a social construction. This notion implies that, rather than being treated as a distinct entity, masculinity is construed as something whose meaning is built up during interaction. That meaning is likely to be a highly fleeting one, in that it will vary by both time and place. This kind of stance frequently displays a concern with the language that is employed to present categories in particular ways. It suggests that the social world and its categories are not external to us, but are built up and constituted in and through interaction. This tendency can be seen particularly in **discourse analysis**, which is examined in Chapter 22. As Potter (1996: 98) observes: 'The world . . . is *constituted* in one way or another as people talk it, write it and argue it.' This sense of constructionism is antithetical to realism (see Key concept 2.3). Constructionism frequently results in an interest in the representation of social phenomena. Research in focus 2.7 provides an illustration of this idea in relation to the representation of the breast cancer epidemic in the USA.

The term 'constructionism' is also frequently used to reflect the indeterminacy of our knowledge of the social world (see Key concept 2.6 and the idea of constructionism in relation to the nature of knowledge of the social world). However, in this book, I will be using the term in connection with the notion that social phenomena and categories are social constructions.

Relationship to social research

Questions of social ontology cannot be divorced from issues concerning the conduct of social research. Ontological assumptions and commitments will feed into the ways in which research questions are formulated and research is carried out. If a research question is formulated in such a way as to suggest that organizations and cultures are objective social entities that act on individuals, the researcher is likely to emphasize the formal properties of organizations or the beliefs and values of members of the culture. Alternatively, if the researcher

Research in focus 2.7
Constructionism in action

Lantz and Booth (1998) have shown that the notion of a breast cancer epidemic can be treated as a social construction. They note that US data show a rise in the incidence of the disease since the early 1980s, which has led to the depiction of the trend as an epidemic. The authors examined a variety of popular magazines using **qualitative content analysis** (see Key concept 13.1 for a brief description of this method). They note that many of the articles draw attention to the lifestyles of modern women, including such phenomena as delaying first births, diet, alcohol consumption, and having careers. The authors argue that these articles

> ascribe blame to individual behaviors by listing a wide array of individual risk factors (many of which are not behaviors of 'traditional' women), and then offering prudent prescriptions for prevention. Women are portrayed as victims of an insidious disease, but also as victims of their own behaviors, many of which are related to the control of their own fertility. . . . These articles suggest that nontraditional women experience pathological repercussions within their bodies and, in turn, may be responsible for our current epidemic of breast cancer.

> (Lantz and Booth 1998: 915–16)

This article suggests that, as a social category, the breast cancer epidemic is being represented in popular magazines in a particular way—one that blames the victims and the lifestyles of modern women in particular. This is in spite of the fact that fewer than 20 per cent of cases of breast cancer are in women under the age of 50. Lantz and Booth's study is fairly representative of a constructionist ontology in suggesting that the epidemic is not simply being construed as a social fact but is being ascribed a particular meaning (one that blames the victims of the disease). In this way, the representation of the disease in popular magazines forms an important element in its social construction.

formulates a research question so that the tenuousness of organization and culture as objective categories is stressed, it is likely that an emphasis will be placed on the active involvement of people in reality construction. In either case, it might be supposed that different approaches to the design of research and the collection of data will be required. Later in the book, Research in focus 20.8 provides an illustration of a study with a strong commitment to a constructionist ontology and its implications for the research process.

Research strategy: quantitative and qualitative research

Many writers on methodological issues find it helpful to distinguish between **quantitative research** and **qualitative research**. The status of the distinction is ambiguous, because it is regarded by some writers as fundamental and by others as no longer useful or even simply as 'false' (Layder 1993: 110). However, there is little evidence of a decline in the use of the distinction. The quantitative/qualitative distinction will be employed a great deal in this book, because it represents a useful means of classifying different methods of social research and because it is a helpful umbrella for a range of issues concerned with the practice of social research.

On the face of it, there would seem to be little to the quantitative/qualitative distinction other than the fact that quantitative researchers employ measurement and qualitative researchers do not. It is certainly the case that there is a predisposition among researchers along these lines, but many writers have suggested that the differences are deeper than the superficial issue of the presence or absence of quantification. For many writers, quantitative and qualitative research differ with respect to their epistemological foundations and in other respects too. Indeed, if we examine the areas that have been the focus of the previous three sections—the connection between

Table 2.1
Fundamental differences between quantitative and qualitative research strategies

	Quantitative	Qualitative
Principal orientation to the role of theory in relation to research	Deductive; testing of theory	Inductive; generation of theory
Epistemological orientation	Natural science model, in particular positivism	Interpretivism
Ontological orientation	Objectivism	Constructionism

theory and research, epistemological considerations, and ontological considerations—quantitative and qualitative research can be taken to form two distinctive clusters of research strategy. By a **research strategy**, I simply mean a general orientation to the conduct of social research. Table 2.1 outlines the differences between quantitative and qualitative research in terms of the three areas.

Thus, quantitative research can be represented as a research strategy that emphasizes quantification in the collection and analysis of data and that

- entails a deductive approach to the relationship between theory and research, in which the accent is placed on the testing of theories;
- has incorporated the practices and norms of the natural scientific model and of positivism in particular; and
- embodies a view of social reality as an external, objective reality.

By contrast, qualitative research can be construed as a research strategy that usually emphasizes words rather

Research in focus 2.8
Mixed methods research—an example

In 2001, Britain was profoundly affected by an outbreak of foot and mouth disease (FMD) affecting sheep, cattle, and swine. Efforts to contain the disease had a big impact on people's movements. Poortinga et al. (2004) were interested in how far the public trusted the information the government was supplying and how it perceived the risks associated with the disease. Such issues were of interest in part because the researchers felt that the ways in which the public responds to a crisis was an important topic, but also because the issues connect with the influence in recent years of the notion of the 'risk society' (Beck 1992), which has attracted a good deal of sociological attention. At the height of the disease during 2–5 April 2001, the researchers conducted a survey using a **self-administered questionnaire** (see Chapter 10) to samples in two contrasting areas: Bude in Cornwall and Norwich in Norfolk. These two areas were chosen because they were very differently affected by FMD. The questionnaire covered the following areas: level of agreement with statements about the outbreak of the disease (for example, 'My main concerns about FMD are to do with the possible impacts on human health'); perceptions of who was to blame; level of agreement with statements about the government's handling of FMD; degrees of trust in various sources of information about the disease; and personal information, such as any connection with the farming or tourist industries. In addition, a qualitative research method—**focus groups** (see Chapter 21)—was employed. In May and June 2001, these groups were convened and members of the groups were asked about the same kinds of issues covered in the questionnaire. Focus group participants were chosen from among those who had indicated in their questionnaire replies that they were willing to be involved in a focus group discussion. Three focus groups took place. While the questionnaire data were able to demonstrate the variation in such things as trust in various information sources, the focus groups revealed 'valuable additional information, especially on the reasons, rationalizations and arguments behind people's understanding of the FMD issue' (Poortinga et al. 2004: 86). As a result, the researchers were able to arrive at a more complete account of the FMD crisis than could have been obtained by either a quantitative or a qualitative research approach alone. This and other possible advantages of mixed methods research will be explored further in Chapter 27.

than quantification in the collection and analysis of data and that

- emphasizes an inductive approach to the relationship between theory and research, in which an emphasis is placed on the generation of theories;

- has rejected the practices and norms of the natural scientific model, and of positivism in particular, in preference for an emphasis on how individuals interpret their social world; and

- embodies a view of social reality as a constantly shifting emergent property of individuals' creation.

There is, in fact, considerably more to the quantitative/qualitative distinction than this contrast. In Chapters 7 and 17 the nature of quantitative and then qualitative research respectively will be outlined in much greater detail, while in Chapters 26 and 27 the contrasting features will be further explored. In particular, a number of distinguishing features flow from the commitment of the

Research in focus 2.9
Mixed methods research—an example

This second example of mixed methods research is probably one of the biggest studies in the UK using the approach—the Cultural Capital and Social Exclusion (CCSE) project. Like the research referred to in Research in Focus 2.1, the CCSE project was profoundly influenced by Bourdieu and in particular by his influential research on cultural capital and its role in the reproduction of social divisions (Bourdieu 1984). While the CCSE project was inspired by Bourdieu's research, at the same time the CCSE researchers had some reservations about Bourdieu's methodological and theoretical approaches and about the relevance of his research beyond the period in which it was conducted and its milieu (France). The CCSE research was designed around three research questions:

- What is the nature of cultural capital in Britain? What kinds of social exclusion are generated by the differential distribution of cultural capital across class positions?

- What are the relationships between economic capital, social capital and cultural capital, in particular how is cultural capital related to other forms of capital?

- What role does cultural capital play in relation to existing patterns of social exclusion? How can a closer knowledge of this assist in developing cultural policies designed to offset the effects of social exclusion?

(www.esrc.ac.uk/my-esrc/grants/R000239801/outputs/Download/ ad321d38-a2b2-4ce8-9273-35520a9bda63, accessed 1 August 2014)

Each of these three research questions was broken down into several sub-questions. In order to address these research questions, the authors employed three main research methods:

1. Twenty-five focus groups, with each group being made up of a distinctive group of members, for example, Pakistani middle class, supervisors, self-employed.

2. A structured interview survey of a large representative sample of 1,781 respondents within the UK.

3. Semi-structured interviews with forty-four individuals from thirty households. The interviewees were sampled from the survey on the basis of socio-demographic and cultural capital characteristics. The interviewers also took notes about the households. In addition, eleven interviews were conducted with 'elite' individuals, because it was felt that these were not sufficiently present in the sample.

Thus, the CCSE project comprised two qualitative research methods (focus groups and semi-structured interviewing) and one quantitative method (a structured interview survey). The mixed methods aspect of this research fulfilled several roles for the researchers. For example, although the focus groups yielded findings that could be linked to the survey ones, they were also used to inform the design of the survey questions. There will be further reference to the utility of the mixed methods approach in Chapter 27, while the components of the CCSE project will be referred to in the interim chapters.

Sources: Silva and Wright (2008); Bennett et al. (2009); Silva et al. (2009); www.esrc.ac.uk/my-esrc/grants/R000239801/ outputs/Download/ad321d38-a2b2-4ce8-9273-35520a9bda63 (accessed 1 August 2014).

quantitative research strategy to a positivist epistemology and from the rejection of that epistemology by practitioners of the qualitative research strategy. In other words, the three contrasts in Table 2.1 are basic, though fundamental, ones.

However, the interconnections between the different features of quantitative and qualitative research are not as straightforward as Table 2.1 and the previous paragraph imply. While it is useful to contrast the two research strategies, it is necessary to be careful about hammering a wedge between them. Qualitative research can, for instance, be used in order to test theories or at least shed light on them; it is not a research strategy that is solely concerned with the generation of theory. For example, Hughes et al. (2011) were concerned to shed light on the contact theory of inter-group relations (see Research in focus 2.2) by conducting an investigation of three communities in Northern Ireland with roughly equal proportions of Protestants and Catholics. While not about *ethnic* relations, the study was designed to explore inter-group relations from the vantage point of contact theory.

The point that is being made in this section is that quantitative and qualitative research represent different research strategies and that each carries with it striking differences in terms of the role of theory, epistemological issues, and ontological concerns. However, the distinction is not a hard-and-fast one: studies that have the broad characteristics of one research strategy may have a characteristic of the other. I will say more about the common features in quantitative and qualitative research in Chapter 26. Moreover, many writers argue that the two can be combined within an overall research project, and Chapter 27 examines precisely this possibility. In Chapter 27, I will examine what is increasingly referred to as **mixed methods research**. This term is widely used nowadays to refer to research that combines methods associated with both quantitative and qualitative research.

In Research in focus 2.8 and 2.9, I present examples of mixed methods studies partly to provide some early insights into the possibility of doing mixed methods research, but also to show how a wedge should not be driven between quantitative and qualitative research. When contrasting the two approaches, it is easy to see them as incompatible, but as the examples in Research in focus 2.8 and 2.9 show, they can be fruitfully combined. This point will be amplified throughout Chapter 27.

Influences on the conduct of social research

It is clear that social research is influenced by a variety of factors. Figure 2.3 summarizes the influences that have been examined so far, but has added two more—the impact of *values* and of *practical considerations*.

Values

Values reflect either the personal beliefs or the feelings of a researcher. We might expect that social scientists should be value free and objective in their research. After all, it might be argued that research that simply reflected the personal biases of its practitioners could not

be considered valid and scientific because it was bound up with their subjectivities. Such a view is held with less and less frequency among social scientists nowadays. Émile Durkheim (1858–1917) wrote that one of the corollaries of his injunction to treat social facts as things was that all 'preconceptions must be eradicated' (Durkheim 1938: 31). Since values are a form of preconception, his advice was at least implicitly to do with suppressing them when conducting research. His position is unlikely to be regarded as credible nowadays, because there is a growing recognition that it is not feasible to keep researchers' values totally in check. These can intrude at any or all of a number of points in the process of social research:

- choice of research area;
- formulation of research questions;
- choice of method;
- formulation of research design and data-collection techniques;
- implementation of data collection;
- analysis of data;
- interpretation of data;
- conclusions.

Figure 2.3

Influences on social research

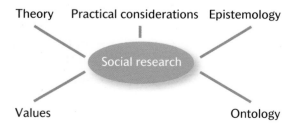

There are, therefore, numerous points at which bias and the intrusion of values can occur. Values can materialize at any point during the course of research. The researcher may develop an affection or sympathy for the people being studied. It is quite common, for example, for researchers working within a qualitative research strategy, and in particular when they use participant observation or very intensive interviewing, to develop a close affinity with the people whom they study to the extent that they find it difficult to disentangle their stance as social scientists from their subjects' perspective. This possibility may be exacerbated by the tendency that Becker (1967) identified for sociologists in particular to be very sympathetic to underdog groups. Equally, social scientists may be repelled by the people they study. The social anthropologist Colin Turnbull (1973) reports the results of his research into an African tribe known as the Ik. Turnbull was appalled by what he witnessed: a loveless (and for him unlovable) tribe that left its young and very old to die. While Turnbull was able to point to the conditions that had led to this state of affairs, he was very honest in his disgust for what he witnessed, particularly during the period of his initial stay among the tribe. However, that very disgust is a product of Western values about the family, and it is likely, as he acknowledged, that these will have influenced his perception of what he witnessed.

Another position in relation to the whole question of values and bias is to recognize and acknowledge that research cannot be value free but to ensure that the incursion of values in research is restrained and to be self-reflective and so exhibit **reflexivity** (see Key concept 17.6) about the part played by such factors. As Turnbull (1973: 13) put it at the beginning of his book on the Ik: 'the reader is entitled to know something of the aims, expectations, hopes and attitudes that the writer brought to the field with him, for these will surely influence not only how he sees things but even what he sees.' Researchers are increasingly prepared to forewarn readers of their biases and assumptions and how these may have influenced their findings. There has been a growth since the mid-1970s of collections of inside reports of what doing a piece of research was really like, as against the generalities presented in social research methods textbooks (like this one!). These collections frequently function as 'confessions', an element of which is often the writers' willingness to be open about their personal biases.

Still another approach is to argue for consciously value-laden research. This is a position taken by some feminist writers who have argued that only research on women that is intended *for* women will be consistent with the wider political needs of women. Mies (1993: 68) has argued that in feminist research the 'postulate of *value free research*, of neutrality and indifference towards the research objects, has to be replaced by *conscious partiality*, which is achieved through partial identification with the research objects' (emphases in original).

Student experience
The influence of feminism on research questions

Sarah Hanson is very clear about the influence of feminism on her research and on her research questions in particular.

My research project focused on the representation of women through the front covers of five women's magazines, combining the application of feminist theory with the decoding practices of content analysis. Throughout the project I wanted to understand the nature of women's magazines, the influences they have on women's sense of self and identity and the role the magazines play. I asked: do women's magazines support or destroy women's identity and do they encourage self-respect or self-scrutiny? I wanted to combine theory with fact, focusing on the meanings behind the presentation of images and text.

Similarly, for her research on non-governmental organizations (NGOs) and sex workers in Thailand, Erin Sanders wrote that she 'employed a feminist methodology—and as such attempted to engage with my research participants, particularly the sex workers, as a "friend" rather than as a "researcher"'. She also writes:

I chose to use a feminist methodology because I wanted to eliminate the power imbalance in the research relationship. As there are a number of power issues with a 'White', 'Western' woman interviewing 'Non-White', 'Non-Western' sex workers, I had hoped a feminist methodology . . . would help redress some of the power issues.

 To read more, go to the Online Resource Centre: www.oxfordtextbooks.co.uk/orc/brymansrm5e/

The significance of feminism in relation to values goes further than this, however. In particular, several feminist social researchers around the early 1980s proposed that the principles and practices associated with quantitative research were incompatible with feminist research on women. For such writers as Oakley (1981), quantitative research was bound up with male values of control that can be seen in the general orientation of the research strategy—control of the research subject/respondent and control of the research context and situation. Moreover, the research process was seen as one-way traffic, whereby researchers extract information from the people being studied and give little, or more usually nothing, in return. For many feminists, such a strategy bordered on exploitation and was incompatible with feminism's values of sisterhood and non-hierarchical relationships between women. The opposition towards quantitative research resulted in a preference for qualitative research among feminists. Not only was qualitative research seen as more consistent with the values of feminism; it was seen as more adaptable to those values. Feminist qualitative research came to be associated with an approach in which the investigator rejected a value-neutral approach and engaged with their research participants as people and not simply as respondents to research instruments. The stance of feminism in relation to both quantitative and qualitative approaches demonstrates the ways in which values have implications for the process of social investigation. In more recent years, there has been a softening of the attitudes of feminists towards quantitative research. Several writers have acknowledged a viable and acceptable role for quantitative research, particularly when it is employed in conjunction with qualitative research (Jayaratne and Stewart 1991; Oakley 1998). This issue will be picked up in Chapters 17, 26, and 27.

There are, then, different positions that can be taken up in relation to values and value freedom. Far fewer writers than in the past overtly subscribe to the position that the principle of objectivity can be put into practice. Quantitative researchers sometimes seem to be writing in a way that suggests an aura of objectivity (Mies 1993), but we simply do not know how far they subscribe to such a position. There is a greater awareness today of the limits to objectivity, so that some of the highly confident, sometimes naive, assertions on the subject, such as Durkheim's, have fallen into disfavour. A further way in which values are relevant to the conduct of social research is through adherence to ethical principles or standards. This issue will be followed up in Chapter 6.

Practical considerations

Nor should we neglect the importance and significance of *practical issues* in decisions about how social research should be carried out. There are a number of different dimensions to this issue.

- Choices of research strategy, design, or method have to be tailored to the research question being investigated. If we are interested in teasing out the relative importance of different causes of a social phenomenon, it is quite likely that a quantitative strategy will fit our needs, because, as will be shown in Chapter 7, the assessment of cause is one of its keynotes. Alternatively, if we are interested in the worldviews of members of a certain social group, a qualitative research strategy that is sensitive to how participants interpret their social world may be preferable.

- If a researcher is interested in a topic on which little or no research has been done in the past, quantitative research may be difficult to employ, because there is little prior literature from which to draw leads. A more exploratory stance may be preferable, and therefore qualitative research may serve the researcher's needs better, since it is typically associated with the generation rather than the testing of theory (see Table 2.1) and with a relatively unstructured approach to the research process (see Chapter 17).

- The nature of the topic and/or of the people being investigated may be another factor. For example, if the researcher needs to engage with individuals or groups involved in illicit activities, such as football hooliganism (Pearson 2009; Poulton 2012), drug dealing (P. A. Adler 1985), or the murky underworld of organs-trading (Scheper-Hughes 2004), it is unlikely that survey research would gain the confidence of participants involved or achieve the necessary rapport. In fact, the idea of conducting survey research in such contexts or on such respondents looks rather ridiculous. It is not surprising, therefore, that researchers in these areas have tended to use qualitative research where there is an opportunity to gain the confidence of the subjects of the investigation or even in some cases not reveal their identity as researchers, albeit with ethical dilemmas of the kind discussed in Chapter 6. By contrast, it seems unlikely that the hypothesis described in Research in focus 2.4 could have been tested with a qualitative method such as participant observation.

While practical considerations may seem rather mundane and uninteresting compared with the lofty realm inhabited by the philosophical debates surrounding discussions about epistemology and ontology, they are important ones. All social research is a coming-together of the ideal and the feasible, so that there will be many circumstances in which the nature of the topic or of the participants in an investigation and the constraints on a researcher loom large in decisions about how best to proceed.

Student experience
A practical consideration in the choice of research method

One of the factors that influenced Rebecca Barnes's choice of the semi-structured interview for her study of violence in women's same-sex intimate relationships was that she felt that the topic is a highly sensitive area and that she therefore needed to be able to observe her interviewees' emotional responses.

> I felt that, given the sensitivity of the research topic, semi-structured, in-depth interviews would be most appropriate. This gave me the opportunity to elicit women's accounts of abuse in a setting where I was able to observe their emotional responses to the interview and endeavour to minimize any distress or other negative feelings that might result from participating in the research.

 To read more, go to the Online Resource Centre: www.oxfordtextbooks.co.uk/orc/brymansrm5e/

 ## Key points

- Quantitative and qualitative research constitute different approaches to social investigation and carry with them important epistemological and ontological considerations.
- Theory can be depicted as something that precedes research (as in quantitative research) or as something that emerges out of it (as in qualitative research).
- Epistemological considerations loom large in considerations of research strategy. To a large extent, these revolve around the desirability of employing a natural science model (and in particular positivism) versus interpretivism.
- Ontological considerations, concerning objectivism versus constructionism, also constitute important dimensions of the quantitative/qualitative contrast.
- Values may impinge on the research process at different times.
- Practical considerations in decisions about research methods are also important factors.
- Feminist researchers have tended to prefer a qualitative approach, though there is some evidence of a change of viewpoint in this regard.

 ## Questions for review

Theory and research

- If you had to conduct some social research now, what would the topic be and what factors would have influenced your choice? How important was addressing theory in your consideration?
- Outline, using examples of your own, the difference between grand and middle-range theory.
- What are the differences between inductive and deductive theory and why is the distinction important?

Epistemological considerations

- What is meant by each of the following terms: positivism; realism; and interpretivism? Why is it important to understand each of them?

- What are the implications of epistemological considerations for research practice?

Ontological considerations

- What are the main differences between epistemological and ontological considerations?

- What is meant by objectivism and constructionism?

- Which theoretical ideas have been particularly instrumental in the growth of interest in qualitative research?

Research strategy: quantitative and qualitative research

- Outline the main differences between quantitative and qualitative research in terms of: the relationship between theory and data; epistemological considerations; and ontological considerations.

- To what extent is quantitative research solely concerned with testing theories and qualitative research with generating theories?

Influences on the conduct of social research

- What are some of the main influences on social research?

....

Online Resource Centre

www.oxfordtextbooks.co.uk/orc/brymansrm5e/

Visit the Online Resource Centre to enrich your understanding of social research strategies. Follow up links to other resources, test yourself using multiple choice questions, and gain further guidance and inspiration from the Student Researcher's Toolkit.

....

3

Research designs

Chapter guide

In focusing on the different kinds of research design, we are paying attention to the different frameworks for the collection and analysis of data. Research design is, therefore, a framework for the generation of evidence that is chosen to answer the research question(s) in which the investigator is interested. A research design also relates to the criteria that are employed when evaluating social research. This chapter is structured as follows.

- Reliability, replication, and validity are presented as criteria for assessing the quality of social research. The latter entails an assessment in terms of several criteria covered in the chapter: measurement validity; internal validity; external validity; and ecological validity.

- The suggestion that such quality criteria are mainly relevant to quantitative research is examined, along with the proposition that an alternative set of criteria should be employed in relation to qualitative research. This alternative set of criteria, which is concerned with the issue of trustworthiness, is outlined briefly.

- Five prominent research designs are then outlined:
  - experimental and related designs (such as the quasi-experiment);
  - cross-sectional design, the most common form of which is survey research;
  - longitudinal design and its various forms, such as the panel study and the cohort study;
  - case study design;
  - comparative design.

- Each research design is considered in terms of the criteria for evaluating research findings.

Introduction

In the previous chapter, the idea of *research strategy* was introduced as a broad orientation to social research. The context for its introduction was the distinction between quantitative and qualitative research as contrasting research strategies. However, the decision to adopt one or the other strategy will not get you far along the road of doing a piece of research. Two other key decisions will have to be made (along with many tactical decisions about how the research will be carried out and the data analysed). These decisions concern choices about *research design* and *research method*. On the face of it, these two terms would seem to mean the same thing, but it is crucial to draw a distinction between them (see Key concepts 3.1 and 3.2).

Research methods can be and are associated with different kinds of research design. The latter represents a structure that guides the execution of a research method and the analysis of the subsequent data. The two terms are often confused. For example, one of the research designs to be covered in this chapter—the case study—is very often referred to as a *method*. A case study entails the detailed exploration of a specific case, which could be a community, organization, or person. But, once a case has been selected, a research method or research methods are needed to collect data. Simply selecting an organization and deciding to study it intensively are not going to provide data. Do you observe? Do you conduct interviews? Do you examine documents? Do you administer questionnaires? You may in fact use any or all of these research methods, but the crucial point is that choosing a case study approach will not in its own right provide you with data.

In this chapter, five different research designs will be examined: experimental design and its variants, including **quasi-experiments**; cross-sectional or survey design; longitudinal design; case study design; and **comparative design**. However, before embarking on the nature of and differences between these designs, it is useful to consider some recurring issues in social research that cut across some or all of these designs.

Key concept 3.1
What is a research design?

A **research design** provides a framework for the collection and analysis of data. A choice of research design reflects decisions about the priority being given to a range of dimensions of the research process. These include the importance attached to:

* expressing causal connections between **variables**;
* generalizing to larger groups of individuals than those actually forming part of the investigation;
* understanding behaviour and the meaning of that behaviour in its specific social context;
* having a temporal (that is, over time) appreciation of social phenomena and their interconnections.

Key concept 3.2
What is a research method?

A research method is simply a technique for collecting data. It can involve a specific instrument, such as a self-administered questionnaire or a structured **interview schedule**, or participant observation whereby the researcher listens to and watches others.

Quality criteria in social research

Three of the most prominent criteria for the evaluation of social research are **reliability**, **replication**, and **validity**. Each of these terms will be treated in much greater detail in later chapters, but in the meantime a fairly basic treatment of them can be helpful.

Reliability

Reliability is concerned with the question of whether the results of a study are repeatable. The term is commonly used in relation to the question of whether the measures that are devised for concepts in the social sciences (such as poverty, racial prejudice, relationship quality, religious orthodoxy) are consistent. In Chapter 7 we will be looking at the idea of reliability in greater detail, particularly the different ways it can be conceptualized. Reliability is especially at issue in connection with quantitative research. The quantitative researcher is likely to be concerned with the question of whether a measure is stable or not. After all, if we found that IQ tests, which were designed as measures of intelligence, were found to fluctuate, so that people's IQ scores were wildly different when administered on two or more occasions, we would be concerned about it as a measure. We would consider it an unreliable measure—we could not have faith in its consistency.

Replication

The idea of reliability is very close to another criterion of research—replication and more especially **replicability**. Sometimes researchers choose to replicate the findings of others. There are various reasons for doing so, such as a feeling that the original results do not match other existing evidence. In order for replication to take place, a study must be capable of replication—it must be repli*cable*. This is a very obvious point: if researchers do not spell out their procedures in detail, replication is impossible. Ironically, replication in social research is quite rare. When Burawoy (1979) found that by accident he was conducting case study research in a US factory that had been studied three decades earlier by another researcher (Donald Roy), he thought about treating his own investigation as a replication. However, the low status of replication in academic life persuaded him to resist this option. He writes: 'I knew that to replicate Roy's study would not earn me a dissertation let alone a job. . . . [In] academia the real reward comes not from replication but from originality!' (Burawoy 2003: 650). Nonetheless, an investigation's capacity to be replicated—replicability—is highly valued by many social researchers working within a quantitative research tradition. See Research in focus 7.7 for an example of a replication study.

Validity

A further and in many ways the most important quality criterion is *validity*. Validity is concerned with the integrity of the conclusions that are generated from a piece of research. The idea of validity will be examined in greater detail in later chapters, but in the meantime it is important to be aware of the main facets of validity that are typically distinguished:

- *Measurement validity*. **Measurement validity** relates primarily to quantitative research and to the search for measures of social scientific concepts. It is to do with the question of whether a measure that is devised for a concept really does reflect the concept that it is supposed to be denoting. Does the IQ test really measure variations in intelligence? If we take the study reported in Research in focus 2.4, there are three concepts that needed to be measured in order to test the hypotheses: second-generation immigrants; gender-egalitarian attitudes; and gender relations of the origin country (i.e. the country from which an immigrant has emigrated). The question then is: do the measures really represent the concepts they are supposed to be tapping? If they do not, the study's findings will be questionable. Measurement validity is related to reliability: if a measure of a concept is unstable in that it fluctuates and hence is unreliable, it simply cannot be providing a valid measure of the concept in question. In other words, the assessment of a measure's validity presupposes that it is reliable. If a measure is unreliable because it does not give a stable reading of the underlying concept, it cannot be valid, because a valid measure reflects the concept it is supposed to be measuring.

- *Internal validity*. **Internal validity** relates mainly to the issue of **causality**, which will be dealt with in greater detail in Chapter 7. Internal validity is concerned with the question of whether a conclusion that incorporates a causal relationship between two or more variables holds water. If we suggest that x causes y, can we be sure that it is x that is responsible for variation in y and not something else that is producing an apparent causal relationship? In the study examined in Research in focus 2.4, the authors were quoted as concluding that 'gender ideology is affected by an intergenerational acculturation process' (Röder and Mühlau 2014: 915). Internal validity raises the question: can we be sure that the intergenerational acculturation process really does cause variation in gender ideology and that this apparent causal relationship is genuine and not produced by something else (i.e. another variable)? In discussing issues of causality, it is common to refer to the factor that has a causal impact as the **independent variable** and the effect as the **dependent variable** (see Key concept 3.3). In the case of Röder and Mühlau's research, the 'intergenerational acculturation process' was an independent variable and 'gender ideology' was the dependent variable. Internal validity raises the question: how confident can we be that the independent variable really is at least in part responsible for the variation that has been identified in the dependent variable?

- *External validity.* **External validity** is concerned with the question of whether the results of a study can be generalized beyond the specific research context. In the research by Poortinga et al. (2004) on foot and mouth disease (see Research in focus 2.8), data were collected from 229 respondents in Bude and 244 respondents in Norwich. Can their findings about the attitudes to the handling of the outbreak be generalized beyond these respondents? In other words, if the research was not externally valid, it would apply to the 473 respondents alone. If it was externally valid, we would expect it to apply more generally to the populations of these two towns at the time of the outbreak of the disease. It is in this context that the issue of how people are selected to participate in research becomes crucial. This is one of the main reasons why quantitative researchers are so keen to generate representative samples (see Chapter 8).

- *Ecological validity.* **Ecological validity** is concerned with the question of whether social scientific findings are applicable to people's everyday, natural social settings. As Cicourel (1982: 15) has put it: 'Do our instruments capture the daily life conditions, opinions, values, attitudes, and knowledge base of those we

study as expressed in their natural habitat?' This criterion is concerned with the question of whether social research sometimes produces findings that may be technically valid but have little to do with what happens in people's everyday lives. If research findings are not ecologically valid, they are in a sense *artefacts* of the social scientist's arsenal of data collection and analytic tools. The more the social scientist intervenes in natural settings or creates unnatural ones, such as a laboratory or even a special room to carry out interviews, the more likely it is that findings will not be ecologically valid. The findings deriving from a study using questionnaires may have measurement validity and a reasonable level of internal validity, and they may be externally valid, in the sense that the findings can be generalized to other samples, but the unnaturalness of having to answer a questionnaire may mean that the findings have limited ecological validity.

- *Inferential validity.* An issue that is sometimes neglected is whether the authors of a report of research produce inferences and draw conclusions that are warranted by their research and the findings generated from it. This consideration is often bound up with the question of the connection between the research design used and the interpretation of the findings deriving from it. For example, if a researcher infers cause and effect, a consideration is whether a research design has been used that is capable of allowing such an inference to be made. As will be shown below, inferring causality from research based on a cross-sectional design is risky and often simply wrong so that an important quality issue is whether the inferences generated by researchers are warranted by the research design and the procedures they adopted.

Key concept 3.3
What is a variable?

A variable is simply an attribute on which cases vary. 'Cases' can obviously be people, but they can also include things such as households, cities, organizations, schools, and nations. If an attribute does not vary, it is a **constant**. If all couples exhibited the same approach to money matters, in which financial decisions were always a product of the same amount of discussion, this attribute of such couples would be a constant and not a variable. Constants are rarely of interest to social researchers. Writers distinguish between different types of variable. The most basic distinction is between *independent variables* and *dependent variables*. The former are considered to have a causal influence on the latter. In addition, it is important to distinguish between variables—whether independent or dependent—in terms of their measurement properties. This is an important issue in the context of quantitative data analysis. See Chapter 15 for an explanation of the distinction between the following types of variable: **interval/ratio variables**; **ordinal variables**; **nominal variables**; and **dichotomous variables**; see Table 15.1 for brief descriptions of them.

Relationship with research strategy

So far the discussion has been geared mainly to quantitative rather than to qualitative research. Both reliability and measurement validity are essentially concerned with the adequacy of measures, which are most obviously a concern in quantitative research. Internal validity is concerned with the soundness of findings that specify a causal connection, an issue that is most commonly of concern to quantitative researchers. External validity *may* be relevant to qualitative research (see Chapter 18), but the question of the representativeness of research participants has a more obvious application to quantitative research, with its preoccupation with sampling procedures that maximize the opportunity for generating a representative sample. Ecological validity relates to the naturalness of the research approach and has considerable relevance to both qualitative and quantitative research.

Some writers have sought to apply the concepts of reliability and validity to qualitative research (e.g. LeCompte and Goetz 1982; Kirk and Miller 1986; Peräkylä 1997), but others argue that the grounding of these ideas in quantitative research renders them inappropriate for qualitative research. Such writers as Kirk and Miller (1986) have applied concepts of validity and reliability to qualitative research but have very slightly changed the sense in which the terms are used. Qualitative researchers sometimes propose that the studies they produce should be judged or evaluated according to different criteria from those

Key concept 3.4
What is naturalism?

Naturalism is an interesting and mercifully rare instance of a term that not only has different meanings, but also has meanings that can actually be contradictory! It is possible to identify three different meanings.

- *Naturalism means viewing all objects of study—whether natural or social ones—as belonging to the same realm and a consequent commitment to the principles of natural scientific method.* This meaning, which has clear affinities with positivism, implies that all entities belong to the same order of things, so that there is no essential difference between the objects of the natural sciences and those of the social sciences (M. Williams 2000). For many naturalists, this principle implies that there should be no difference between the natural and the social sciences in the ways in which they study phenomena. This version of naturalism essentially proposes that there is a unity between the objects of the natural and the social sciences and that, because of this, there is no reason for social scientists not to employ the approaches of the natural scientist.

- *Naturalism means being true to the nature of the phenomenon being investigated.* According to Matza, naturalism is 'the philosophical view that strives to remain true to the nature of the phenomenon under study' (1969: 5) and 'claims fidelity to the natural world' (1969: 8). This meaning of the term represents a fusion of elements of an interpretivist epistemology and a constructionist ontology, which were examined in Chapter 2. Naturalism is taken to recognize that people attribute meaning to behaviour and are authors of their social world rather than passive objects.

- *Naturalism is a style of research that seeks to minimize the intrusion of artificial methods of data collection.* This meaning implies that the social world should be as undisturbed as possible when it is being studied (Hammersley and Atkinson 1995: 6).

The second and third meanings overlap considerably, in that it could easily be imagined that, in order to conduct a naturalistic enquiry in the second sense, a research approach that adopted naturalistic principles in the third sense would be required. Both the second and third meanings are incompatible with, and indeed opposed to, the first meaning. Naturalism in the first sense is invariably viewed by writers drawing on an interpretivist epistemology as not 'true' to the social world, precisely because it posits that there are no differences between humans and the objects of the natural sciences; it therefore ignores the capacity of humans to interpret the social world and to be active agents; and, in its preference for the application of natural science methods, it employs artificial methods of data collection. When writers are described as *anti-naturalists*, it is invariably the first of the three meanings that they are criticizing.

used in relation to quantitative research. Lincoln and Guba (1985) propose that alternative terms and ways of assessing qualitative research are required. For example, they propose **trustworthiness** as a criterion of how good a qualitative study is. Each aspect of trustworthiness has a parallel with the quantitative research criteria.

- *Credibility*, which parallels internal validity—that is, how believable are the findings?
- *Transferability*, which parallels external validity—that is, do the findings apply to other contexts?
- *Dependability*, which parallels reliability—that is, are the findings likely to apply at other times?
- *Confirmability*, which parallels objectivity—that is, has the investigator allowed his or her values to intrude to a high degree?

The issue of the application of quality criteria to qualitative research will be returned to in Chapter 17.

In addition, one of the criteria previously cited—ecological validity—may have been formulated largely in the context of quantitative research, but it is in fact a feature in relation to which qualitative research fares rather well. Qualitative research often involves a *naturalistic* stance (see Key concept 3.4). This means that the researcher seeks to collect data in naturally-occurring situations and environments, as opposed to fabricated, artificial ones. This characteristic probably applies particularly well to ethnographic research, in which participant observation is a prominent element of data collection, but it is sometimes suggested that it applies also to the sort of interview approach typically used by qualitative researchers, which is less directive than the kind used in quantitative research (see e.g. Research in focus 2.5). We might expect that much qualitative research is stronger than quantitative investigations in terms of ecological validity.

By and large, these issues in social research have been presented because some of them will emerge in the context of the discussion of research designs in the next section, but in a number of ways they also represent background considerations for many issues to be examined later in the book.

Research designs

In this discussion of research designs, five different types will be examined: experimental design; cross-sectional or survey design; longitudinal design; case study design; and comparative design. Variations on these designs will be examined in their relevant subsections.

Experimental design

True **experiments** are quite unusual in sociology, but they are employed in related areas of enquiry, such as social psychology and organization studies, while researchers in social policy sometimes use them in order to assess the impact of new reforms or policies. Why, then, bother to introduce experimental designs at all if they are rarely used? The chief reason, quite aside from the fact that they are sometimes employed, is that a true experiment is often used as a yardstick against which non-experimental research is assessed. Experimental research is frequently held up as a benchmark because it engenders considerable confidence in the robustness and trustworthiness of causal findings. In other words, true experiments tend to be very strong in terms of internal validity.

Manipulation

If experiments are so strong in this respect, why then do social researchers not make far greater use of them? The reason is simple: in order to conduct a true experiment,

it is necessary to *manipulate* the independent variable in order to determine whether it does have an influence on the dependent variable. Experimental participants are likely to be allocated to one of two or more experimental groups, each of which represents different types or levels of the independent variable. It is then possible to establish how far differences between the groups are responsible for variations in the level of the dependent variable. Manipulation, then, entails intervening in a situation and establishing the impact of the manipulation on participants. However, the vast majority of independent variables with which social researchers are concerned cannot be manipulated. If we are interested in the effects of gender on work experiences, we cannot *manipulate* gender so that some people are made male and others female. If we are interested in the effects of variations in social class on social and political attitudes or on health, we cannot assign people to different social class groupings. As with the huge majority of such variables, the levels of social engineering that would be required are beyond serious contemplation.

Before moving on to a more complete discussion of experimental design, it is important to introduce a basic distinction between the *laboratory experiment* and the *field experiment*. As its name implies, the laboratory experiment takes place in a laboratory or in a contrived setting, whereas field experiments occur in real-life settings, such as in classrooms and organizations, or as a result of the implementation of reforms or new policies. It is experiments of the latter type that are most likely to touch on areas of interest to social researchers. In order to illustrate the nature of manipulation and the idea of a field experiment, Research in focus 3.1 describes a well-known piece of experimental research.

Classical experimental design

Research in focus 3.1 includes most of the essential features of what is known as the classical experimental design, which is also often referred to as the *randomized experiment* or **randomized controlled trial** (RCT). Two groups are established, and it is this that forms the experimental manipulation and therefore the independent variable—in this case, teacher expectations. The spurters form what is known as the *experimental group* or *treatment group* and the other students form a control group. The experimental group receives the *experimental treatment*—teacher expectancies—but the control group does not receive an experimental treatment. The dependent variable—student performance—is measured before and after the experimental manipulation, so that a before-and-after analysis can be conducted (see Figure 3.1). Moreover, the spurters and the non-spurters were assigned randomly

to their respective groups. Because of this use of **random assignment** to the experimental and control groups, the researchers were able to feel confident that the only difference between the two groups was the fact that teachers expected the spurters to fare better at school than the others. They would have been confident that, if they did establish a difference in performance between the two groups, it was due to the experimental manipulation alone.

In order to capture the essence of this design, the following simple notation will be employed:

Obs An **obs**ervation made in relation to the dependent variable; there may well be two or more observations, such as IQ test scores and reading grades before (*pre-test*) and after (*post-test*) the experimental manipulation.

Exp The **exp**erimental treatment (the independent variable), such as the creation of teacher expectancies. **No Exp** refers to the absence of an experimental treatment and represents the experience of the control group.

T The **t**iming of the observations made in relation to the dependent variable, such as the timing of the administration of an IQ test.

Research in focus 3.1
A field experiment

As part of a programme of research into the impact of self-fulfilling prophecies (for example, where someone's beliefs or expectations about someone else influence how the latter behaves), Rosenthal and Jacobson (1968) conducted research into the question of whether teachers' expectations of their students' abilities in fact influence the school performance of the latter. The research was conducted in a lower-class locality in the USA with a high level of children from minority group backgrounds. In the spring of 1964, all the students completed a test that was portrayed as a means of identifying 'spurters'—that is, students who were likely to excel academically. At the beginning of the following academic year, all the teachers were notified of the names of the students who had been identified as spurters. In fact, 20 per cent of the schoolchildren had been identified as spurters. However, the students had actually been administered a conventional IQ test and the so-called spurters had been selected randomly. The test was readministered eight months after the original one. The authors were then able to compare the differences between the spurters and the other students in terms of changes in various measures of academic performance, such as IQ scores, reading ability, and intellectual curiosity. Since there was no evidence for there being any difference in ability between the spurters and the rest, any indications that the spurters did in fact differ from their peers could be attributed to the fact that the teachers had been led to expect the former would perform better. The findings show that such differences did in fact exist, but that the differences between the spurters and their peers tended to be concentrated in the first two or three years of schooling. In other words, the evidence for a teacher expectancy effect was patchy. Nonetheless, this is an influential experiment that is widely believed to provide firm evidence of a teacher expectancy effect. For a useful brief review of some of the subsequent studies and reflections on Rosenthal and Jacobson's study, see Hammersley (2011: 106–9).

Figure 3.1

Classical experimental design (*with illustration of the effect of teacher expectancies on IQ*)

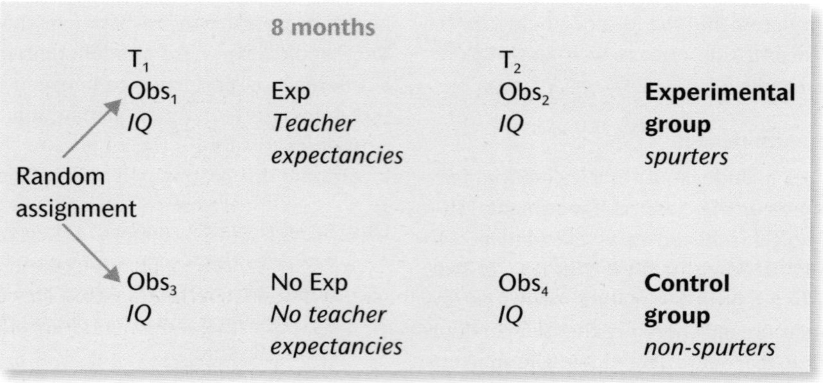

Classical experimental design and validity

What is the purpose of the control group? Surely it is what happens to the spurters (the experimental group) that really concerns us? In order for a study to be a true experiment, it must control (in other words, eliminate) the possible effects of rival explanations of a causal finding, so that we can be confident that teacher expectancies really do have an impact on student performance. We might then be in a position to take the view that such a study is internally valid. The presence of a control group *and* the random assignment of subjects to the experimental and control groups enable us to eliminate rival explanations. To see this, consider some of the rival explanations that might occur if there were *no* control group. There would then have been a number of potential threats to internal validity (see Research in focus 3.2). This list of threats is based on Campbell (1957) and Cook and Campbell (1979), but not all the threats to internal validity they refer to are included.

In the case of each of these threats to internal validity, each of which raises the prospect of a rival interpretation of a causal finding, the presence of a control group coupled with random assignment allows us to eliminate these threats so that our confidence in the causal finding, that teacher expectancies influence student performance, is greatly enhanced.

However, simply because research is considered internally valid does not mean that questions cannot be raised about it. When quantitative research has been used, further criteria can be applied to evaluate a study. First, there is the question of measurement validity. In the case of the Rosenthal and Jacobson study, there are potentially two aspects to this. One is the question of whether academic performance has been adequately measured. Measures such as reading scores seem to possess face validity, in the sense that they appear to exhibit a correspondence with what they are measuring. However, given the controversy surrounding IQ tests and what they measure (Kamin 1974), we might feel somewhat uneasy about how far gains in IQ test scores can be regarded as indicative of academic performance. Similarly, to take another of the authors' measures—intellectual curiosity—how confident can we be that this too is a valid measure of academic performance? Does it really measure what it is supposed to measure? The second question relating to measurement validity is whether the experimental manipulation really worked. In other words, did the random identification of some schoolchildren as spurters adequately create the conditions for the self-fulfilling prophecy to be examined? The procedure very much relies on the teachers being taken in by the procedure, but it is possible that they were not all equally duped. If so, this would contaminate the manipulation.

Secondly, is the research externally valid? This issue is considered in Research in focus 3.3.

Thirdly, are the findings ecologically valid? The fact that the research is a field experiment rather than a laboratory experiment seems to enhance this aspect of the Rosenthal and Jacobson research. Also, the fact that the students and the teachers seem to have had little if any appreciation of the fact that they were participating in an experiment may also have enhanced ecological validity, though this aspect of the research raises enormous *ethical* concerns, since deception seems to have been a

Research in focus 3.2
Threats to internal validity (and their application to the Rosenthal and Jacobson 1968 study)

The following is a list of possible threats to the internal validity of an investigation and shows how each is mitigated in the Rosenthal and Jacobson (1968) study by virtue of its being a true experiment.

- *History.* This refers to events other than the manipulation of teacher expectancies that may occur in the environment and that could have caused the spurters' scores to rise. The actions of the school head to raise standards in the school may be one such type of event. If there were no control group, we could not be sure whether it was the teachers' expectancies or the head's actions that were producing the increase in spurters' grades. If there is a control group, we are able to say that history would have an effect on the control-group participants too, and therefore differences between the experimental and control groups could be attributed to the impact of teacher expectancies alone.

- *Testing.* This threat refers to the possibility that subjects may become more experienced at taking a test or may become sensitized to the aims of the experiment as a result of the pre-test. The presence of a control group, which presumably would also experience the same effect, allows us to discount this possibility if there is a difference in levels of the dependent variable between the experimental and control groups.

- *Instrumentation.* This threat refers to the possibility that changes in the way a test is administered could account for an increase (or decrease) in scores between the pre-test and post-test—for example, if slight changes to the test had been introduced. Again, if there is a control group, we can assume that a change in testing would have affected the control group as well.

- *Mortality.* This relates to the problem of attrition in many studies that span a long period of time, in that participants may leave. School students may leave the area or move to a different school. Since this problem is likely to afflict the control group too, it is possible to establish its significance as a threat relative to the impact of teacher expectancies.

- *Maturation.* Quite simply, people change, and the ways in which they change may have implications for the dependent variable. The students identified as spurters might have improved anyway, regardless of the effect of teacher expectancies. Maturation should affect the control group subjects as well. If we did not have a control group, it could be argued that any change in the students' school performance was attributable to the possibility that they would have improved anyway. The control group allows us to discount this possibility.

- *Selection.* If there are differences between the two groups, which would arise if they had been selected by a non-random process, variations between the experimental and control groups could be attributed to pre-existing differences in their membership. However, since a random process of assignment to the experimental and control groups was employed, this possibility can be discounted.

- *Ambiguity about the direction of causal influence.* The very notion of an independent variable and dependent variable presupposes a direction of causality. However, there may be occasions when the temporal sequence in a study is unclear, so that it is not possible to establish which variable affects the other. Since the creation of teacher expectancies preceded the improvements in academic achievement in the earlier years of school, in the Rosenthal and Jacobson study the direction of causal influence is clear.

significant and probably necessary feature of the investigation. The question of ethical issues is in many ways another dimension of the validity of a study and will be the focus of Chapter 6. The fact that Rosenthal and Jacobson made intensive use of various instruments to measure academic performance might be considered a source of concerns about ecological validity, though this is an area which is relevant to most quantitative research.

Research in focus 3.3
Threats to external validity (and their application to the Rosenthal and Jacobson 1968 study)

Campbell (1957) and Cook and Campbell (1979) identify five major threats to the external validity and hence **generalizability** of an investigation.

- *Interaction of selection and treatment.* This threat raises the question: to what social and psychological groups can a finding be generalized? Can it be generalized to a wide variety of individuals who might be differentiated by ethnicity, social class, region, gender, and type of personality? In the case of the Rosenthal and Jacobson study, the students were largely from lower social class groups and a large proportion were from ethnic minorities. This might be considered a limitation to the generalizability of the findings.

- *Interaction of setting and treatment.* This threat relates to the issue of how confident we can be that the results of a study can be applied to other settings. In particular, how confident can we be that Rosenthal and Jacobson's findings are generalizable to other schools? There is also the wider issue of how confident we can be that the operation of self-fulfilling prophecies can be discerned in non-educational settings. In fact, Rosenthal and others have been able to demonstrate the role and significance of the self-fulfilling prophecy in a wide variety of different contexts (Rosnow and Rosenthal 1997), though this does not answer the question of whether the specific findings can be generalized. One reason for being uneasy about Rosenthal and Jacobson's findings is that they were allowed a great deal of freedom for conducting their investigation. The high level of cooperation from the school authorities was very unusual and may suggest that the school was not typical, though whether there is such a thing as a 'typical school' is questionable.

- *Interaction of history and treatment.* This threat raises the question of whether the findings can be generalized to the past and to the future. The Rosenthal and Jacobson research was conducted over forty years ago. How confident can we be that the findings would apply today? Also, their investigation was conducted at a particular point in the school academic year. Would the results have been the same if the research had been conducted at another point in the year?

- *Interaction effects of pre-testing.* As a result of being pre-tested, participants in an experiment may become sensitized to the experimental treatment. Consequently, the findings may not be generalizable to groups that have *not* been pre-tested, because in the real world people are rarely pre-tested in this way. The findings may therefore be partly determined by the experimental treatment and partly by how far pre-test sensitization influenced the way in which participants responded to the treatment. In the Rosenthal and Jacobson research all students were pre-tested at the end of the previous academic year.

- *Reactive effects of experimental arrangements.* People are frequently aware of the fact that they are participating in an experiment. Their awareness may influence how they respond to the experimental treatment and therefore affect the generalizability of the findings. Since Rosenthal and Jacobson's subjects do not appear to have been aware of the fact that they were participating in an experiment, this problem is unlikely to have arisen. The issue of **reactivity** and its potentially damaging effects is a recurring theme in relation to many methods of social research.

A fourth issue that might be raised is the question of replicability. The authors lay out very clearly the procedures and measures that they employed. If anyone were to carry out a replication, he or she would be able to obtain further information from the authors if necessary. Consequently, the research is replicable, although there has not been an exact replication. Clairborn (1969) conducted one of the earliest replications and followed a procedure that was very similar to Rosenthal and Jacobson's. The study was carried out in three middle-class, suburban schools, and the timing of the creation of teacher expectancies was different from that in the original Rosenthal and Jacobson study. Clairborn failed to replicate Rosenthal and Jacobson's findings. This failure to replicate casts doubt on the external validity of the original research and suggests that the first three threats referred to in Research in focus 3.3 may have played a part in the differences between the two sets of results.

The classical experimental design is the foundation of the randomized controlled trial (RCT), which has increasingly become the gold-standard research design in health-related fields. With an RCT, the aim is to test 'alternative ways of handling a situation' (Oakley 2000: 18). This may entail comparing the impact of an intervention with what would have happened if there had been no intervention or comparing the impacts of different kinds of intervention (such as different forms of treatment of an illness). The randomization of experimental participants is crucial, as it means that the members of the different groups in the experiment are to all intents and purposes alike.

The laboratory experiment

Many experiments in fields such as social psychology are laboratory rather than field experiments. One of the main advantages of the former over the latter is that the researcher has greater influence over the experimental arrangements. For example, it is easier to assign subjects randomly to different experimental conditions in the laboratory than in an ongoing, real-life organization. The researcher therefore has a higher level of control, which is likely to enhance the internal validity of the study. It is also likely that laboratory experiments will be more straightforward to replicate, because they are less bound up with a certain milieu that is difficult to reproduce.

However, laboratory experiments such as the one described in Research in focus 3.4 suffer from a number of limitations. First, the external validity is likely to be difficult to establish. There is the interaction of setting and treatment, since the setting of the laboratory is likely to be unrelated to real-world experiences and contexts. Also, there is likely to be an interaction of selection and treatment. In the case of the study described in Research in focus 3.4, there are a number of difficulties: the subjects were students, who are not representative of the general population, so that their responses to the experimental treatment may be distinctive; they were recruited in a non-random way; and they were given incentives to participate, which may further demarcate them from others, since not everyone is equally likely to accept inducements. There will have been no problem of interaction effects of pre-testing, because, as in many experiments, there was no pre-testing. However, it is quite feasible that **reactive effects** may have been set in motion by the experimental arrangements. Secondly, the ecological validity of the study may be poor, because we do not know how well the findings are applicable to everyday life. However, while

Research in focus 3.4
A laboratory experiment on ethnic discrimination

Blommaert et al. (2014) were interested in the part played by ethnic discrimination in job recruitment and recruited 272 students in Utrecht in the Netherlands to act as participants. The participants were asked to act as if they were employers or personnel managers. They were given two fictitious job descriptions and two sets of twenty-four CVs. One job was as a customer advisor in a bank, requiring an intermediate or higher vocational qualification; the other was as a recruiter in a human resource management firm, requiring a higher vocational qualification or a degree. For each job, participants had to rate each candidate's CV in terms of suitability and to select three applicants whom they would invite for a job interview. The authors write that within each set of CVs, 'there were sixteen [CVs] in which ethnicity, gender, level of education and work experience were varied systematically' (Blommaert et al. 2014: 737). Within these sixteen CVs, there were eight native Dutch applicants and a corresponding set of eight non-native Dutch applicants with exactly the same mixes of education, gender and work experience. Around half of the participants were told that the non-native Dutch applicants were Moroccan-Dutch and the rest were told the applicants were Turkish-Dutch.

The researchers found that ethnic discrimination was a factor in ratings of suitability. Native Dutch applicants were typically viewed as more suitable than the Moroccan-Dutch or the Turkish-Dutch applicants, although ethnicity was not regarded as the most important factor in judging suitability, since gender, education, and work experience emerged as more important in this connection. The same findings emerged when invitation for a job interview was the dependent variable, suggesting again that ethnic discrimination had an impact but that it was less important than the applicants' gender, educational level, and work experience. Thus, by varying several variables in the artificial CVs, namely ethnicity, gender, educational level, and work experience, the authors were able to establish the relative causal impact of these variables on the two dependent variables (suitability and invitation for interview).

the study may lack what is often called *mundane realism*, it may nonetheless enjoy *experimental realism* (Aronson and Carlsmith 1968). The latter means that the subjects are very involved in the experiment and take it very seriously.

Quasi-experiments

Several writers have drawn attention to the possibilities offered by *quasi-experiments*—that is, studies that have certain characteristics of experimental designs but that do not fulfil all the internal validity requirements. A large number of different types of quasi-experiments have been identified (Shadish et al. 2002), and it is not proposed to cover all of them here. One of the principal types of quasi-experiment arises when, although there is an experimental and a control group, participants to the two groups are not randomly assigned (see Research in focus 3.7 for an example). The absence of random assignment often arises because there are practical difficulties associated with implementing it. Another form of quasi-experiment occurs in the case of 'natural experiments'. These are 'experiments' in the sense there is manipulation of a social setting, but this occurs as part of a naturally-occurring attempt to alter social arrangements. In such circumstances, it is invariably not possible to assign subjects randomly to experimental and control groups. An example is provided in Research in focus 3.5. The absence of random assignment in the research casts some doubt on internal validity, since the groups may not have been equivalent.

However, the results of such studies are still compelling, because they are not artificial interventions in social life and because their ecological validity appears strong. Most writers on quasi-experimentation discount natural experiments in which there is no control group or basis for comparison (Cook and Campbell 1979), but occasionally one comes across a single-group natural experiment that is particularly striking (see Research in focus 3.6). Experimental designs and more especially quasi-experimental designs have been particularly prominent in evaluation research studies (see Key concept 3.5 and Research in focus 3.7).

Possibly because of the various difficulties noted in this section, Grant and Wall (2009) have observed that quasi-experiments are relatively rarely used in organizational research. However, they also note that there may be ways of addressing some of the concerns regarding internal validity that beset quasi-experiments. For example, they suggest that it may be possible to strengthen causal inferences when it is not possible to assign experimental and control group participants randomly and the researcher has limited or no control over the experimental manipulation. This might be done by seeking out further information that will help to discount some of the rival interpretations of a causal link that arise from the absence of a true experimental design. However, it is unlikely that such a view will find favour among writers who adopt a purist view about the need for experimental designs in order to generate robust causal inferences.

Research in focus 3.5
A quasi-experiment

Since the mid-1980s, a group of researchers has been collecting medical and psychiatric data on a cohort of over 10,000 British civil servants. The first wave of data collection took place between late 1985 and early 1988 and comprised clinical measurement (for example, blood pressure, ECG, cholesterol) and a self-administered questionnaire that generated data on health, stress, and minor psychiatric symptoms. Further measurements of the same group took place in 1989/90 and 1992/3. In the mid-1980s, the UK government decided to transfer many of the executive functions of government to executive agencies operating on a more commercial basis than previously; this afforded the opportunity to examine the health effects of a major organizational change. Ferrie et al. (1998) report the results of their Phase 1 and Phase 3 data. They distinguished between three groups: those experiencing a change; those anticipating they would be affected by the change; and a 'control group' of those unaffected by the change. The authors found significant adverse health effects among those experiencing and anticipating change compared to the control group, although the extent of the effects of the major organizational change (or its anticipation) varied markedly between men and women. This study uses a quasi-experimental design, in which a control group is compared to two treatment groups. It bears the hallmarks of a classical experimental design, but there is no random assignment. Subjects were not randomly assigned to the three groups. Whether they were affected (or anticipated being affected) by the changes depended on decisions deriving from government and civil service policy.

Research in focus 3.6
A natural experiment

The effects of television and video violence on children is one of the most contested areas of social research and one that frequently causes the media to become especially shrill. St Helena in the South Atlantic provided a fascinating laboratory for the examination of the various claims when television was introduced to the island for the first time in the mid-1990s. The television viewing habits of a large sample of schoolchildren and their behaviour are being monitored and will continue to be monitored for many years to come. The project leader, Tony Charlton, was quoted in *The Times* as saying: 'The argument that watching violent television turns youngsters to violence is not borne out . . . The children have been watching the same amounts of violence, and in many cases the same programmes, as British children. But they have not gone out and copied what they have seen on TV' (Midgley 1998: 5). A report of the findings in *The Times* in April 1998 found that 'the shared experience of watching television made them less likely to tease each other and to fight, and more likely to enjoy books' (Frean 1998: 7). The findings derive from 900 minutes of video footage of children at play during school breaks, diaries kept by around 300 of the children, and ratings by teachers. The reports of the research in academic journals confirm that there was no evidence to suggest that the introduction of television had led to an increase in anti-social behaviour (e.g. Charlton et al. 1998, 1999).

Key concept 3.5
What is evaluation research?

Evaluation research, as its name implies, is concerned with the evaluation of such occurrences as social and organizational programmes or interventions. The essential question that is typically asked by such studies is: has the intervention (for example, a new policy initiative or an organizational change) achieved its anticipated goals? A typical design may have one group that is exposed to the treatment (that is, the new initiative), and a control group that is not. Since it is often neither feasible nor ethical to assign research participants randomly to the two groups, such studies are usually quasi-experimental. The use of the principles of experimental design is fairly entrenched in evaluation research, but other approaches have emerged in recent years, including approaches to evaluation based on qualitative research. While there are differences of opinion about how qualitative evaluation should be carried out, the different views typically coalesce around a recognition of the importance of an in-depth understanding of the context in which an intervention occurs, the diverse viewpoints of the stakeholders, and the examination of the range of outcomes of the intervention (Greene 1994, 2000).

Pawson and Tilley (1997) advocate an approach that draws on the principles of *critical realism* (see Key concept 2.3) and that sees the outcome of an intervention as the result of generative mechanisms and the contexts of those mechanisms. A focus of the former element entails examining the causal factors that inhibit or promote change when an intervention occurs. Pawson and Tilley's approach is supportive of the use of both quantitative and qualitative research methods. Tilley (2000) outlines an early example of the approach in the context of an evaluation of closed-circuit television (CCTV) in car parks. He observes that there are several mechanisms by which CCTV might deter car crime, such as deterrence of offenders; greater usage of car parks, which in itself produces surveillance; more effective use of security staff; and greater sensitivity among drivers to car security. Examples of contexts are: patterns of usage (such as if the car park is one that fills up and empties during rush-hour periods or one that is in more constant use); blind spots in car parks; and the availability of other sources of car crime for potential offenders. In other words, whether the mechanisms have certain effects is influenced by the contexts within which CCTV is installed. The kind of evaluation research advocated by Pawson and Tilley maps these different combinations of mechanism and context in relation to different outcomes.

Research in focus 3.7
A quasi-experimental evaluation

Koeber (2005) reports the findings of a quasi-experiment in which he evaluated the use of multimedia presentations (PowerPoint) and a course website (Blackboard) for teaching introductory sociology at a US university. One group of students acted as the experimental group, in that it was taught using these two ways of presenting learning materials simultaneously; the other group acted as a control group and did not experience the multimedia and website methods. There was no random assignment, but in several respects the two groups were comparable. Therefore, this is not a true experiment, but it has the features of a typical quasi-experiment, in that the researcher tried to make the two treatments as comparable as possible. It is an evaluation study, because the researcher is seeking to evaluate the utility of the two teaching methods. The findings are interesting, in that there was no significant evidence of a difference in the performance of students (measured by their final grades for the course) between those who experienced the newer methods and those who experienced the more traditional ones. However, those students who were taught with the newer methods tended to perceive the course in more favourable terms, in that they were more likely to perceive various aspects of the course (for example, course design, rapport with students, and the value of the course) in a positive way. Also, the experimental groups were less likely to perceive the course demands as difficult and to view the course workload as high.

Significance of experimental design

As was stated at the outset, the chief reason for introducing the experiment as a research design is because it is frequently considered to be a yardstick against which quantitative research is judged. This occurs largely because of the fact that a true experiment will allow doubts about internal validity to be allayed and reflects the considerable emphasis placed on the determination of causality in quantitative research. As we will see in the next section, **cross-sectional designs** of the kind associated with survey research are frequently regarded as limited, because of the problems of unambiguously inferring causality when using such designs.

Logic of comparison

However, before exploring such issues, it is important to draw attention to an important general lesson that experiments teach us. A central feature of any experiment is the fact that it entails a *comparison*: at the very least it entails a comparison of results obtained by an experimental group with those produced by a control group. In the case of the Blommaert et al. (2014) experiment in Research in focus 3.4, there is no control group: the research entails a comparison of the effects of two different types of ethnicity (native Dutch versus non-native Dutch) in relation to job recruitment. The advantage of carrying out any kind of comparison such as this is that we understand the phenomenon that we are interested in better when we compare it with something else that is similar to it. The case for arguing that non-native ethnic

groups are discriminated against when they are seeking jobs is much more persuasive when we view their experiences in relation to the experiences of native applicants. While experimental design is typically associated with quantitative research, the potential for comparison provides a more general lesson that transcends matters of both research strategy and research design. While the experimental design is associated with quantitative research, the logic of comparison provides lessons of broad applicability and relevance. This issue is given more specific attention below in relation to the comparative design.

Cross-sectional design

The cross-sectional design is often called a survey design, but the idea of the survey is so closely connected in most people's minds with questionnaires and structured interviewing that the more generic term *cross-sectional design* is preferable. While the research methods associated with surveys are certainly frequently employed within the context of cross-sectional research, so too are many other research methods, including **structured observation**, content analysis, official statistics, and diaries. All these research methods will be covered in later chapters, but in the meantime the basic structure of the cross-sectional design will be outlined.

The cross-sectional design is defined in Key concept 3.6. A number of elements of this definition have been emphasized.

Key concept 3.6
What is a cross-sectional research design?

A cross-sectional design entails the collection of data on *a sample of cases* and at *a single point in time* in order to collect a body of *quantitative* or *quantifiable data* in connection with two or more variables (usually many more than two), which are then examined to detect *patterns of association*.

- *A sample of cases*. Researchers employing a cross-sectional design are interested in variation. That variation can be in respect of people, families, organizations, nation states, or whatever. Variation can be established only when more than one case is being examined. Usually, researchers employing this design will select quite a large number of cases for a variety of reasons: they are more likely to encounter variation in all the variables in which they are interested; they can make finer distinctions between cases; and the requirements of sampling procedure are likely to necessitate larger numbers (see Chapter 8).

- *At a single point in time*. With a cross-sectional design, data on the variables of interest are collected more or less simultaneously. When an individual completes a questionnaire, which may contain fifty or more variables, the answers are supplied at essentially the same time. This contrasts with an experimental design. In the classic experimental design, a participant in the experimental group is pre-tested, then exposed to the experimental treatment, and then post-tested. Days, weeks, months, or even years may separate the different phases. In the case of the Rosenthal and Jacobson (1968) study, eight months separated the pre- and post-testing of the schoolchildren in the study.

- *Quantitative or quantifiable data*. In order to establish variation between cases (and then to examine associations between variables—see the next point), it is necessary to have a systematic and standardized method for gauging variation. One of the most important advantages of quantification is that it provides the researcher with a consistent benchmark. The advantages of quantification and of measurement will be addressed in greater detail in Chapter 7.

- *Patterns of association*. With a cross-sectional design it is only possible to examine relationships between variables. There is no time ordering to the variables, because the data are collected more or less simultaneously, and the researcher does not (invariably because he or she cannot) manipulate any of the variables. This creates

the problem referred to in Research in focus 3.2 as 'ambiguity about the direction of causal influence'. If the researcher discovers a relationship between two variables, he or she cannot be certain whether this implies a causal relationship, because the features of an experimental design are not present. All that can be said is that the variables are related. This is not to say that it is not possible to draw causal inferences from research based on a cross-sectional design. As will be shown in Chapter 15, there are a number of ways in which the researcher is able to draw certain causal inferences, but these inferences rarely have the standing of causal findings deriving from an experimental design. As a result, cross-sectional research invariably lacks the internal validity that is found in most experimental research (see the example in Research in focus 3.8).

In this book, the term 'survey' will be reserved for research that employs a cross-sectional research design and in which data are collected by questionnaire or by structured interview (see Key concept 3.7). This will allow me to retain the conventional understanding of what a survey is while recognizing that the cross-sectional research design has a wider relevance—that is, one that is not necessarily associated with the collection of data by questionnaire or by structured interview.

Reliability, replicability, and validity

How does cross-sectional research measure up in terms of the previously outlined criteria for evaluating quantitative research: reliability, replicability, and validity?

- The issues of reliability and measurement validity are primarily matters relating to the quality of the measures that are employed to tap the concepts in which the researcher is interested, rather than matters to do with a research design. In order to address questions of the quality of measures, some of the issues outlined in Chapter 7 would have to be considered.

- Replicability is likely to be present in most cross-sectional research to the degree that the researcher spells out procedures for selecting respondents; designing

Research in focus 3.8
Cross-sectional design and the direction of cause and effect

Bengtsson, Berglund, and Oskarson (2013) report some of the findings of a cross-sectional survey in which data on class position and ideological orientation were collected by postal questionnaire. Data were collected from a representative sample of the Swedish population. Although data were collected on 2,374 individuals, the authors were especially interested in the significance of work-related variables for ideological orientations and therefore included only the 1,289 members of their sample who were employed at the time. The authors note:

> As survey data are cross-sectional, the directions of the relationships have been assumed on theoretical grounds. . . . We therefore cannot exclude reverse causality, i.e. that ideological orientations affect occupational choices, and thus, class position. However, most research assumes the same direction of the relationships as we do, although there are exceptions.

(Bengtsson et al. 2013: 704)

There is, therefore, some ambiguity about the direction of causal influence in a study such as this, though the authors seek to justify their assumptions about the direction of cause and effect on theoretical grounds.

---

measures of concepts; administering research instruments (such as structured interview or self-administered questionnaire); and analysing data. Most quantitative research based on cross-sectional research designs specifies such procedures to a large degree.

- Internal validity is typically weak. As suggested above, it is difficult to establish causal direction from the resulting data. Cross-sectional research designs produce associations rather than findings from which causal inferences can be unambiguously made. However, procedures for making causal inferences from cross-sectional data will be referred to in Chapter 15, though most researchers feel that the resulting causal findings rarely have the internal validity of those deriving from experimental designs.

- External validity is strong when, as in the study described in Research in focus 3.8, the sample from which data are collected has been randomly selected.

When non-random methods of sampling are employed, external validity is questionable. Sampling issues in survey research will be addressed in Chapter 8.

- Since much cross-sectional research makes considerable use of research instruments, such as self-administered questionnaires and structured **observation schedules**, ecological validity may be jeopardized because the very instruments disrupt the 'natural habitat', as Cicourel (1982) calls it.

Non-manipulable variables

As was noted at the beginning of the section on experimental design, in most social research it is not possible to manipulate the variables in which we are interested: they are **non-manipulable variables**. This is why quantitative researchers tend to employ a cross-sectional research design rather than an experimental one. Researchers need to be cautious and refer to relationships rather than

---

Key concept 3.7
What is survey research?

Survey research comprises a cross-sectional design in relation to which data are collected predominantly by questionnaire or by structured interview on *a sample of cases drawn from a wider population* and at *a single point in time* in order to collect a body of *quantitative* or *quantifiable data* in connection with a number of variables (usually many more than two), which are then examined to detect *patterns of association*.

Research in focus 3.9
Qualitative research within a cross-sectional design

Bisdee, Daly, and Price (2013) carried out a study of the connection between gender and the management of household money among older couples. They write that they were especially interested in the extent to which ageing influences the roles of men and women in relation to the management of money and the different responses of women to their situation. The authors carried out semi-structured interviews with forty-five heterosexual couples who were interviewed initially together and then simultaneously separately. Couples were identified through a **maximum variation sampling** approach (see Key concept 18.2 for an explanation of this term) 'so as to include a range in terms of age, health. . ., ethnicity, social grade, income level and marital history' (Bisdee et al. 2013: 164). The interviews were recorded and transcribed, yielding a large corpus of qualitative data.

causality, as Eschleman et al. did in Research in the news 3.1, or argue on theoretical grounds that a variable is more likely to be an independent than a dependent variable (see Research in focus 3.8 for an example).

Thus some of the variables in which social scientists are interested, and which are often viewed as potentially significant independent variables, simply cannot be manipulated other than by extreme measures. However, some variables, such as our ethnicity, age, gender, and social backgrounds, are not only 'givens' that are not amenable to the kind of manipulation that is necessary for a true experimental design but also extremely unlikely to be dependent variables. They will almost inevitably be independent variables, so that we are on pretty safe ground when inferring causal direction when these variables are involved in research showing relationships between them and other variables. However, there are also many variables that *could* be manipulated but which cannot be due to ethical and practical constraints and which therefore generate doubt about the direction of causal inference (see Research in the news 3.1).

The very fact that we can regard certain variables as givens provides us with a clue as to how we can make causal inferences in cross-sectional research. Many of the variables in which we are interested can be *assumed* to be temporally prior to other variables. For example, we can assume that, if we find a relationship between ethnic status and alcohol consumption, the former is more likely to be the independent variable because it is temporally prior to alcohol consumption. In other words, while we cannot manipulate ethnic status, we can draw causal inferences from cross-sectional data.

Structure of the cross-sectional design

The cross-sectional research design is not easy to depict in terms of the notation previously introduced, but Figure 3.2 captures its main features, except that in this case Obs simply represents an observation made in relation to a variable.

Research in the news 3.1
The ethical and practical difficulties of manipulation

On 8 October 2014, *The Times* had a short article entitled 'Bullying bosses make staff lazy and inefficient'—**www.thetimes.co.uk/tto/science/article4230054.ece**. There is a clear causal inference here (bullying bosses *make* staff lazy), even though the authors of the paper referred to in the article warned against drawing such an inference (Eschleman et al. 2014). Instead, they wrote of the *relationship* between abusive supervision and what they refer to as 'counterproductive work behaviours', which leaves open the possibility that this kind of work behaviour is the cause rather than the effect of abusive supervision. An experiment to uncover whether abusive supervision really is the independent variable is the obvious solution, but as the authors note: 'an experimental design is impractical because ethical and logistical constraints prevent the manipulation of abusive supervision' (Eschleman et al. 2014: 11).

Figure 3.2
A cross-sectional design

$$
\begin{array}{c}
T_1 \\
Obs_1 \\
Obs_2 \\
Obs_3 \\
Obs_4 \\
Obs_5 \\
\ldots \\
Obs_n
\end{array}
$$

Figure 3.3
The data rectangle in cross-sectional research

	Obs_1	Obs_2	Obs_3	Obs_4	$\ldots$	Obs_n
$Case_1$						
$Case_2$						
$Case_3$						
$Case_4$						
$Case_5$						
$\ldots$						
$Case_n$						

Figure 3.2 implies that a cross-sectional design comprises the collection of data on a series of variables (Obs_1 Obs_2 Obs_3 Obs_4 Obs_5 ... Obs_n) at a single point in time, T_1. The effect is to create what Marsh (1982) referred to as a 'rectangle' of data that comprises variables Obs_1 to Obs_n and cases $Case_1$ to $Case_n$, as in Figure 3.3. For each case (which may be a person, household, city, nation, etc.) data are available for each of the variables, Obs_1 to Obs_n, all of which will have been collected at T_1. Each cell in the matrix will have data in it.

Cross-sectional design and research strategy

This discussion of the cross-sectional design has placed it firmly in the context of quantitative research. Also, the evaluation of the design has drawn on criteria associated with the quantitative research strategy. It should also be noted, however, that qualitative research often entails a form of cross-sectional design. A fairly typical form of such research is when the researcher employs semi-structured interviewing with a number of people. Research in focus 3.9 provides an illustration of such a study.

While clearly within the qualitative research tradition, the study described in Research in focus 3.9 bears many research design similarities with cross-sectional studies within a quantitative research tradition, like the research described in Research in focus 3.8. Moreover, it is a very popular mode of qualitative research. The research was not preoccupied with such criteria of quantitative research as internal and external validity, replicability, measurement validity, and so on. In fact, it could be argued that the conversational interview style made the study more ecologically valid than research using more formal instruments of data collection. It is also striking that the study was concerned with the factors that influence couples' management of household finances (such as the development of health problems). The very notion of

an 'influence' carries a connotation of causality, suggesting that qualitative researchers are interested in the investigation of causes and effects, albeit not in the context of the language of variables that pervades quantitative research. Also, the emphasis was much more on elucidating the *experience* of something like the management of household finances than is usually the case with quantitative research. However, the chief point in providing the illustration is that it bears many similarities to the cross-sectional design in quantitative research. It entailed the interviewing of quite a large number of people and at a single point in time. Just as with many quantitative studies using a cross-sectional design, the examination of early influences on people's past and current behaviour is based on their retrospective accounts of factors that influenced them in the past.

Longitudinal design(s)

The longitudinal design represents a distinct form of research design. Because of the time and cost involved, it is a relatively little-used design in social research, so it is not allocated a great deal of space here. In the form in which it is typically found in social science subjects such as sociology, social policy, and human geography, it is usually an extension of survey research based on a self-administered questionnaire or structured interview research within a cross-sectional design. Consequently, in terms of reliability, replication, and validity, the longitudinal design is little different from cross-sectional research. However, a longitudinal design can allow some insight into the time order of variables and therefore may be more able to allow causal inferences to be made.

Research in focus 3.10
Understanding Society (formerly the British Household Panel Survey)

Understanding Society, the UK Household Longitudinal Study, began life in 1991 as the British Household Panel Survey (BHPS), when a national representative sample of 10,264 individuals in 5,538 households were interviewed for the first time in connection with six main areas of interest:

- household organization;
- labour market behaviour;
- income and wealth;
- housing;
- health; and
- socio-economic values.

BHPS participants were interviewed annually. As a result of the continuous interviewing, it is possible to highlight areas of social change. For example, Laurie and Gershuny (2000) show that there have been changes in the ways in which couples manage their money. Over a relatively short five-year period (1991–5), there was a small decline in the proportion of men having a final say in financial decisions and a corresponding small increase in those reporting equal say, although interestingly these trends refer to aggregated replies of partners—around a quarter of partners give different answers about who has the final say!

The BHPS was replaced in 2009 by the Understanding Society survey, which is based on a panel of about 40,000 UK households. Similar procedures to the BHPS are adopted and eligible adults are interviewed annually face-to-face or by telephone using computer-assisted interviewing. See **www.understandingsociety.ac.uk/about#part2** (accessed 18 September 2014).

With a longitudinal design a sample is surveyed and is surveyed again on at least one further occasion. It is common to distinguish two types of longitudinal design: the *panel study* and the *cohort study*. With the former type, a sample, often a randomly selected national one, is the focus of data collection on at least two (and often more) occasions. Data may be collected from different types of case within a panel study framework: people, households, organizations, schools, and so on. An illustration of this kind of study is the Understanding Society survey (see Research in focus 3.10).

In a cohort study, either an entire cohort of people or a random sample of them is selected as the focus of data collection. The cohort is made up of people who share a certain characteristic, such as all being born in the same week, or who all have a certain experience, such as being unemployed or getting married on a certain day or in the same week. The National Child Development Study (NCDS) is an example of a cohort study (see Research in focus 3.11). A new cohort study—the Economic and Social Research Council (ESRC) Millennium Cohort Study—began at the turn of the present millennium.

Panel and cohort studies share similar features. They have a similar design structure: Figure 3.4 portrays this structure and implies that data are collected in at least two waves on the same variables on the same people. Both panel and cohort studies are concerned with illuminating social change and with improving the understanding of causal influences over time. The latter means that longitudinal designs are somewhat better able to deal with the problem of 'ambiguity about the direction of causal influence' that plagues cross-sectional designs. Because certain potentially independent variables can be identified at T_1, the researcher is in a better position to infer that purported effects that are identified at T_2 or later have occurred *after* the independent variables. This does not deal with the entire problem about the ambiguity of causal influence, but it at least addresses the problem of knowing which variable came first. In all other respects, the points made previously about cross-sectional designs are the same as those for longitudinal designs.

Research in focus 3.11
The National Child Development Study

The National Child Development Study (NCDS) is based on all 17,000 children born in Great Britain in the week of 3–9 March 1958. The study was initially motivated by a concern over levels of perinatal mortality, but the data collected reflect a much wider range of issues than this focus implies. Data were collected on the children and their families at age 7. In fact, the study was not originally planned as a longitudinal study. The children and their families have been followed up in 1965, 1969, 1974, 1981, 1991, 1999/2000, 2004/5, 2008/9, and 2013. Data are collected in relation to a number of areas, including physical and mental health; family; parenting; occupation and income; and housing and environment. For further information, see Fox and Fogelman (1990); Hodges (1998); and **www.cls.ioe.ac.uk/MicrositeHome.aspx?sitesectionid=50&sitesectiontitle=National%20 Child%20Development%20Study** (accessed 18 September 2014).

A new cohort study—the Millennium Cohort Study—began in 2000–1 based on a sample of all children born in England and Wales over a twelve-month period from 1 September 2000 and all children born in Scotland and Northern Ireland from 1 December 2000. The sample has been followed up on four occasions since the original wave of data collection. For further information, see **www.cls.ioe.ac.uk/page.aspx?sitesectionid=851&sitese ctiontitle=Welcome+to+the+Millenium+Cohort+Study** (accessed 18 September 2014).

Panel and cohort designs differ in important respects too. A panel study, such as the BHPS, that takes place over many years can distinguish between age effects (the impact of the ageing process on individuals) and cohort effects (effects due to being born at a similar time), because its members will have been born at different times. A cohort study, however, can distinguish only ageing effects, since all members of the sample will have been born at more or less the same time. Also, a panel study, especially one that operates at the household level, needs rules to inform how to handle new entrants to households (for example, as a result of marriage or elderly relatives moving in) and exits from households (for example, as a result of marriage break-up or children leaving home).

Figure 3.4
The longitudinal design

T_1	$\cdots$	T_n
Obs_1		Obs_1
Obs_2		Obs_2
Obs_3		Obs_3
Obs_4		Obs_4
Obs_5		Obs_5
$\cdots$		$\cdots$
Obs_n		Obs_n

Panel and cohort studies share similar problems. First, there is the problem of sample attrition through death, moving, and so on, and through subjects choosing to withdraw at later stages of the research. Menard (1991) cites the case of a study of adolescent drug use in the USA in which 55 per cent of subjects were lost over an eight-year period. However, attrition rates are by no means always as high as this. In 1981 the National Child Development Study managed to secure data from 12,537 members of the original 17,414 cohort, which is quite an achievement bearing in mind that twenty-three years would have elapsed since the birth of the children. In 1991 data were elicited from 11,407. The problem with attrition is largely that those who leave the study may differ in some important respects from those who remain, so that the latter do not form a representative group. There is some evidence from panel studies that the problem of attrition declines with time (Berthoud 2000a); in other words, those who do not drop out after the first wave or two of data collection tend to stay on the panel. Secondly, there are few guidelines as to when is the best juncture to conduct further waves of data collection. Thirdly, it is sometimes suggested that many longitudinal studies are poorly thought out and that they result in the collection of large amounts of data with little apparent planning. Fourthly, there is evidence that a *panel conditioning* effect can occur whereby continued participation in a longitudinal study affects how respondents behave. Menard (1991) refers to a study of family caregiving in which 52 per cent of respondents indicated that they responded differently to providing care for relatives as a result of their participation in the research.

Surveys, such as the General Household Survey, the British Social Attitudes survey, and the Crime Survey for England and Wales (see Table 14.1), that are carried out on a regular basis on samples of the population are not truly longitudinal designs because they do not involve the same people being interviewed on each occasion. They are perhaps better thought of as involving a repeated cross-sectional design or trend design in which samples are selected on each of several occasions. They are able to chart change, but they cannot address the issue of the direction of cause and effect because the samples are always different.

It is easy to associate longitudinal designs more or less exclusively with quantitative research. However, qualitative research sometimes incorporates elements of a longitudinal design. This is especially noticeable in ethnographic research, when the **ethnographer** is in a location for a lengthy period of time or when interviews are carried out on more than one occasion to address change. See Research in focus 3.12 for an example of the latter.

Most longitudinal studies will be planned from the outset in such a way that sample members can be followed up at a later date. However, it can happen that the idea of conducting a longitudinal study occurs to the researchers only after some time has elapsed. Provided there are good records, it may be possible to follow up sample members for a second wave of data collection or even for further waves. See Research in focus 8.5 for an example. Research in focus 3.13 provides a further and extremely unusual but fascinating example of a longitudinal design from the USA with both planned and unplanned elements. This is also an interesting mixed methods study, in that it combines quantitative and qualitative research.

Research in focus 3.12
Qualitative longitudinal research: the Timescapes project

Qualitative longitudinal research (often abbreviated to QLL) that involves repeat qualitative interviews with research participants has become more common since the turn of the century. This is particularly apparent with the 'Timescapes' project, which is a major project that began life in February 2007. The aim is to interview and re-interview people on several occasions to capture social changes and shifts in people's life courses and in their thoughts and feelings. It comprises seven relatively independent projects. Through these projects the researchers aim to track the lives of around 400 people. One of the projects is entitled 'Masculinities, Identities and Risk: Transition in the Lives of Men as Fathers' and aims to get a sense of how masculine identities change in the wake of first-time fatherhood. This particular study builds on research that originally began in Norfolk in 1999, well before the Timescapes project began. Thirty fathers were interviewed in 2000–1 both before and after the birth of their first child. Each man was interviewed three times (two interviews were scheduled after the child's birth). This group of men was then followed up in 2008. A further set of interviews was conducted with eighteen men from south Wales in 2008–9 with the same pattern of one interview before and two interviews after birth. In the course of the interviews, use was made of photographs of families and men with their children to stimulate reflection on fatherhood. The use of photographs in interviews is explored in Chapters 19 and 20. The materials will eventually be made available for secondary analysis (see the section on 'Secondary analysis of qualitative data' in Chapter 24).

Sources:

Guardian, 20 Oct. 2009:
www.guardian.co.uk/education/2009/oct/20/timescapes-leeds-research-memories?INTCMP=SRCH.

Project website:
www.timescapes.leeds.ac.uk.

For information on the masculinities project, see
www.timescapes.leeds.ac.uk/research/masculinities-fatherhood-risk/index.html.

For some methodological reflections on the Timescapes project, see
www.timescapes.leeds.ac.uk/resources/publications.html.

All the above websites were accessed 18 September 2014.

Research in focus 3.13
A planned and unplanned longitudinal design

In the 1940s Sheldon and Eleanor Glueck of the Harvard Law School conducted a study concerned with how criminal careers begin and are maintained. The study entailed a comparison of 500 delinquents and 500 non-delinquents in Massachusetts. The two samples were matched in terms of several characteristics, such as age, ethnicity, and the socio-economic status of the neighbourhoods from which they were drawn. The sample was aged around 14 at the time and was followed up at ages 25 and 33. The data were collected by various means: interviews with the 1,000 participants, their families, and various key figures in their lives (for example, social workers and school teachers); observations of the home; and records of various agencies that had any connection with the participants and their families. Data concerning criminal activity were collected for each individual by examining records relating to court appearances and parole. While all these sources of data produced quantitative information, qualitative data were also collected through answers to **open-ended questions** in the interviews. Around the mid-1990s, Laub and Sampson (2003, 2004) began to follow up the 500 men who had been in the delinquent sample. By this time, they would have been aged 70. Records of death and criminal activity were searched for all 500 men, so that patterns of ongoing criminal activity could be gleaned. Further, they managed to find and then interview fifty-two of the original delinquent sample. These cases were selected on the basis of their patterns of offending over the years, as indicated by the criminal records. The interviews were **life history interviews** to uncover key turning points in their lives and to find out about their experiences. This is an extremely unusual example of a longitudinal study that contains planned elements (the original wave of data collection, followed by the ones eleven and eighteen years later) and an unplanned element conducted by Laub and Sampson many years later.

Case study design

The basic case study entails the detailed and intensive analysis of a single case. As Stake (1995) observes, case study research is concerned with the complexity and particular nature of the case in question. Some of the best-known studies in sociology are based on this kind of design. They include research on:

- a single community, such as Whyte's (1955) study of Cornerville in Boston, Gans's (1962) study of the East End of Boston, M. Stacey's (1960) research on Banbury, O'Reilly's (2000) and Benson's (2011) research on communities of expatriate Britons living on the Costa del Sol in Spain and rural France respectively, or Banks's (2012, 2014) online covert ethnography of an online gambling community;

- a single school, such as studies by Ball (1981) and by Burgess (1983) on Beachside Comprehensive and Bishop McGregor respectively and by Khan (2011, 2014) of an elite school in the USA;

- a single family, such as O. Lewis's (1961) study of the Sánchez family or Brannen and Nilsen's (2006) investigation of a family of low-skilled British men, which contained four generations, in order to uncover changes in 'fathering' over time;

- a single organization, such as studies of a factory by Burawoy (1979) and Cavendish (1982), or of pilferage in a single location (Ditton 1977), or of a single police service (Holdaway 1982, 1983), or of a restaurant (Demetry 2013), or of a single call centre (Callaghan and Thompson 2002; Nyberg 2009), or of a single opera company (Atkinson 2006);

- a person, like the famous study of Stanley, the 'jackroller' (Shaw 1930); such studies are often characterized as using the life history or biographical approach (see the section on 'Life history and oral history interviewing' in Chapter 20); and

- a single event, such as the Cuban Missile Crisis (Allison 1971), the events surrounding the media reporting of a specific issue area (Deacon, Fenton, and Bryman 1999), a Balinese cockfight (Geertz 1973b), or a study of a disaster incident (Vaughan 1996, 2004).

What is a case?

The most common use of the term 'case' associates the case study with a location, such as a community or organization. The emphasis tends to be upon an intensive examination of the setting. There is a tendency to associate case studies with qualitative research, but this is not appropriate. Case studies do tend to use qualitative methods,

Research in focus 3.14
A case study

Atkinson (2006) describes how he conducted an **ethnography** of the Welsh National Opera company. He followed several productions from the initial stages of rehearsal 'through to the first night and beyond' (Atkinson 2006: 25). For each production he engaged in daily participant observation for around six weeks during the rehearsal periods. His focus was particularly upon how the everyday work of the opera company was accomplished.

such as participant observation and unstructured interviewing, because these methods are viewed as conductive to the generation of an intensive, detailed examination of a case. However, case studies are frequently sites for the employment of *both* quantitative and qualitative research (see Chapter 27). In some instances, when an investigation is based exclusively upon quantitative research, it can be difficult to determine whether it is a case study or a cross-sectional research design. The same point can often be made about case studies based upon qualitative research. The crucial issue is to be clear about what the unit of analysis is. Let us say that the research is carried out in a single location, which could be an organization or community. Sometimes, research is carried out in a single location but the location itself is not part of the object of analysis—it simply acts as a backcloth to the collection of data. When this occurs, the sample from which the data were collected is the object of interest and the location is largely incidental and of little significance. Research in focus 3.15 provides an example in which the location is not the primary object of interest, though its significance does creep in at one point. On other occasions, the location is either primarily or at least to a significant extent

the object of interest. For example, we can be in no doubt that in Research in focus 3.14, the Welsh National Opera was Atkinson's object of analysis. This opera company is the primary focus of his attention and understanding its workings is crucial to his goal of revealing 'in considerable detail, the everyday, practical work of making an opera' (Atkinson 2006: 190).

With a case study, the case is an object of interest in its own right, and the researcher aims to provide an in-depth examination of it. Unless a distinction of this or some other kind is drawn, it is impossible to distinguish the case study as a special research design, because almost any kind of research can be construed as a case study: research based on a national, random sample of the population of Great Britain would have to be considered a case study of Great Britain! What distinguishes a case study is that the researcher is usually concerned to reveal the unique features of the case. This is known as an *idiographic* approach. Research designs such as the cross-sectional design are known as *nomothetic*, in that they are concerned with generating statements that apply regardless of time and place. However, an investigation may have elements of both (see Research in focus 3.15).

Research in focus 3.15
A cross-sectional design with case study elements

Sometimes, an investigation may have both cross-sectional and case study elements. For example, Leonard (2004) was interested in the utility of the notion of social capital for research into neighbourhood formation. She conducted her study in a Catholic housing estate in West Belfast, where she carried out semi-structured interviews with 246 individuals living in 150 households. Her findings relate to the relevance of the concept of social capital, so that the research design looks like a cross-sectional one. However, on certain occasions she draws attention to the uniqueness of Belfast with its history in recent times of conflict and the search for political solutions to the problems there. At one point she writes: 'In West Belfast, as the peace process develops, political leaders are charged with connecting informal community networks to more formal institutional networks' (Leonard 2004: 939). As this comment implies, it is more or less impossible in a study like this to generate findings concerning community formation without reference to the special characteristics of Belfast and its troubled history.

With experimental and cross-sectional designs, the typical orientation to the relationship between theory and research is a deductive one. The research design and the collection of data are guided by specific research questions that derive from theoretical concerns. However, when a qualitative research strategy is employed within a cross-sectional design, as in Research in focus 3.9, the approach tends to be inductive. In other words, whether a cross-sectional design is inductive or deductive tends to be affected by whether a quantitative or a qualitative research strategy is employed. The same point can be made of case study research. When the predominant research strategy is qualitative, a case study tends to take an inductive approach to the relationship between theory and research; if a predominantly quantitative strategy is taken, it tends to be deductive.

Reliability, replicability, and validity

The question of how well the case study fares in the context of the research design criteria cited early on in this chapter—measurement validity, internal validity, external validity, ecological validity, reliability, and replicability—depends in large part on how far the researcher feels that these are appropriate for the evaluation of case study research. Some writers on case study research, such as Yin (2009), consider that they are appropriate criteria and suggest ways in which case study research can be developed to enhance its ability to meet the criteria; for others, like Stake (1995), they are barely mentioned, if at all. Writers on case study research whose point of orientation lies primarily with a qualitative research strategy tend to play down or ignore the salience of these factors, whereas those writers who have been strongly influenced by the quantitative research strategy tend to depict them as more significant.

However, one question on which a great deal of discussion has centred concerns the *external validity* or *generalizability* of case study research. How can a single case possibly be representative so that it might yield findings that can be applied more generally to other cases? For example, how could the findings from Atkinson's (2006) research, referred to in Research in focus 3.14, be generalizable to all opera companies? The answer, of course, is that they cannot. It is important to appreciate that case study researchers do not delude themselves that it is possible to identify typical cases that can be used to represent a certain class of objects, whether it is factories, mass-media reporting, police services, or communities. In other words, they do *not* think that a case study is a sample of one.

Types of case

Following on from the issue of external validity, it is useful to consider a distinction between different types of case that is sometimes made by writers. Yin (2009) distinguishes five types.

- The *critical case*. Here the researcher has a well-developed theory, and a case is chosen on the grounds that it will allow a better understanding of the circumstances in which the hypothesis will and will not hold. The study by Festinger et al. (1956) of a religious cult whose members believed that the end of the world was about to happen is an example. The fact that the event did not happen by the appointed day allowed the researchers to test the authors' propositions about how people respond to thwarted expectations.

- The *extreme* or *unique case*. The unique or extreme case is, as Yin observes, a common focus in clinical studies. Margaret Mead's (1928) well-known study of growing up in Samoa was motivated by her belief that the country represented a unique case. She argued that, unlike most other societies, Samoan youth do not suffer a period of anxiety and stress in adolescence. The factors associated with this relatively trouble-free period in their lives were of interest to her, since they might contain lessons for Western youth. Fielding (1982) conducted research on the extreme right-wing organization the National Front. While the National Front was not unique on the British political scene, it was extremely prominent at the time of his research and was beginning to become an electoral force. As such, it held an intrinsic interest that made it essentially unique. Another example of an extreme case is that of Roseto, discussed in Research in the news 3.2.

- The *representative* or *typical case*. I prefer to call this an *exemplifying* case, because notions of representativeness and typicality can sometimes lead to confusion. With this kind of case, 'the objective is to capture the circumstances and conditions of an everyday or commonplace situation' (Yin 2009: 48). Thus a case may be chosen because it exemplifies a broader category of which it is a member. The notion of exemplification implies that cases are often chosen not because they are extreme or unusual in some way but because either they epitomize a broader category of cases or they will provide a suitable context for certain research questions to be answered. An illustration of the first kind of situation is Lynd and Lynd's (1929, 1937) classic community study of Muncie, Indiana, in the USA, which they dubbed 'Middletown' precisely because it seemed to typify American life at the time. The second rationale for selecting exemplifying cases is that they allow the researcher to examine key social processes. For example, a researcher may seek access to an organization because it is known to have implemented a new technology and he or she wants to know what the

Research in the news 3.2
An extreme case: the Roseto effect

On 28 March 2008, the *Huffington Post* posted an online story with the title 'The Mystery of the Rosetan People'. The article appeared in the same year as the publication of a popular non-fiction book by Malcolm Gladwell (2008) entitled *Outliers: The Story of Success*, whose introductory chapter, which introduces the concept of an outlier, is called 'The Roseto Story'. The case of Roseto, Pennsylvania, is (or more precisely was) an interesting instance of an extreme case. The so-called 'Roseto effect' was first noticed in the early 1960s when it was observed by a medical researcher that among the inhabitants of this little town there was a much lower incidence of heart disease than elsewhere in the USA. As Gladwell points out, the researchers were intrigued by the fact that people were dying of old age rather than the diseases that were increasingly killing off Americans. The researchers searched for the reasons behind this difference. It turned out not to be to do with smoking less or better diet or less alcohol consumption but with the close family ties and close-knit community relationships that had been imported by these mainly Italian American families from their native Italy. A high level of happiness and low levels of stress pervaded Roseto. However, as the author of the post points out, the researchers predicted that as the population of Roseto became more Americanized, its health patterns would follow those of the wider society, and that indeed is what happened. The mortality data that were examined in the 1990s revealed that the Roseto effect had disappeared. However, for a while Roseto was a fascinating extreme case and it was precisely this lack of typicality that prompted the medical researchers to ask questions about what lay behind the apparent health advantage of living in Roseto. That is where Gladwell's book comes in: it is about what lies behind the success of highly successful people. He argues that the medical researchers involved in the Roseto story had to think differently about the causes of illness and heart disease and to convince the medical establishment of their views.

Source: **www.huffingtonpost.com/dr-rock-positano/the-mystery-of-the-roseta_b_73260.html** (accessed 19 December 2014).

impact of that new technology has been. The researcher may have been influenced by various theories about the relationship between technology and work and by the considerable research literature on the topic, and as a result seeks to examine the implications of some of these theoretical and empirical deliberations in a particular research site. The case merely provides an apt context for the working-through of these research questions. To take a concrete example, Russell and Tyler's (2002) study of one store in the 'Girl Heaven' UK chain of retail stores for 3–13-year-old girls does not appear to have been motivated by the store being critical or unique, or by it providing a context that had never before been studied, but was to do with the capacity of the research site to illuminate the links between gender and consumption and the commodification of childhood in modern society.

- The *revelatory case*. The basis for the revelatory case exists 'when an investigator has an opportunity to observe and analyse a phenomenon previously inaccessible to scientific investigation' (Yin 2009: 48). As examples, Yin cites Whyte's (1955) study of Cornerville, and Liebow's (1967) research on unemployed black men.

- The *longitudinal case*. Yin suggests that a case may be chosen because it affords the opportunity for investigation at two or more junctures. However, many case studies comprise a longitudinal element, so that it is more likely that a case will be chosen both because it is appropriate to the research questions on one of the other four grounds and also because it can be studied over time.

Any case study can involve a combination of these elements, which can best be viewed as rationales for choosing particular cases. For example, Margaret Mead's (1928) study of growing up in Samoa has been depicted above as an extreme case, but it also has elements of a critical case because she felt that it had the potential to demonstrate that young people's responses to entering their teenage years are not determined by nature alone. She used growing up in Samoa as a critical case to demonstrate that culture has an important role in the development of humans, thus enabling her to cast doubt on biological determinism.

It may be that it is only at a very late stage that the singularity and significance of the case becomes apparent

(Radley and Chamberlain 2001). Flyvbjerg (2003) provides an example of this. He shows how he undertook a study of urban politics and planning in Aalborg in Denmark, thinking it was a critical case. After conducting his fieldwork for a while, he found that it was in fact an extreme case. He writes as follows:

> Initially, I conceived of Aalborg as a 'most likely' critical case in the following manner: if rationality and urban planning were weak in the face of power in Aalborg, then, most likely, they would be weak anywhere, at least in Denmark, because in Aalborg the rational paradigm of planning stood stronger than anywhere else. Eventually, I realized that this logic was flawed, because my research [on] local relations of power showed that one of the most influential 'faces of power' in Aalborg, the Chamber of Industry and Commerce, was substantially stronger than their equivalents elsewhere. Therefore, instead of a critical case, unwittingly I ended up with an extreme case in the sense that both rationality and power were unusually strong in Aalborg, and my case study became a study of what happens when strong rationality meets strong power in the area of urban politics and planning. But this selection of Aalborg as an extreme case happened to me, I did not deliberately choose it.
>
> (Flyvbjerg 2003: 426)

Thus, we may not always appreciate the nature and significance of a 'case' until we have subjected it to detailed scrutiny.

One of the standard criticisms of the case study is that findings deriving from it cannot be generalized. Advocates of case study research counter suggestions that the evidence they present is limited because it has restricted external validity by arguing that it is not the purpose of this research design to generalize to other cases or to populations beyond the case. This position is very different from that taken by practitioners of survey research. Survey researchers are invariably concerned to be able to generalize their findings to larger populations and frequently use **random sampling** to enhance the representativeness of their samples and therefore the external validity of their findings. Case study researchers argue strenuously that this is not the purpose of their craft.

Case study as intensive analysis

Instead, case study researchers tend to argue that they aim to generate an intensive examination of a single case, in relation to which they then engage in a theoretical analysis. The central issue of concern is the quality of the theoretical reasoning in which the case study researcher engages. How well do the data support the theoretical arguments that are generated? Is the theoretical analysis incisive? For example, does it demonstrate connections between different conceptual ideas that are developed out of the data? The crucial question is not whether the findings can be generalized to a wider universe but how well the researcher generates theory out of the findings. This view of generalization is called 'analytic generalization' by Yin (2009) and 'theoretical generalization' by J. C. Mitchell (1983). It places case study research firmly in the inductive tradition of the relationship between theory and research. However, a case study design is not necessarily associated with an inductive approach (see Research in focus 26.1). Thus, case studies can be associated with both theory generation and theory testing. Further, as M. Williams (2000) has argued, case study researchers are often in a position to generalize by drawing on findings from comparable cases investigated by others. This issue will be returned to in Chapter 18.

Longitudinal research and the case study

Case study research frequently includes a longitudinal element. The researcher is often a participant of an organization or member of a community for many months or years. Alternatively, he or she may conduct interviews with individuals over a lengthy period. Moreover, the researcher may be able to inject an additional longitudinal element by analysing archival information and by retrospective interviewing. Research in focus 3.16 provides an illustration of such research.

Another way in which a longitudinal element occurs is when a case that has been studied is returned to at a later stage. A particularly interesting instance of this is the Middletown study that was mentioned previously. The town was originally studied by Lynd and Lynd in 1924–5 (Lynd and Lynd 1929) and was restudied to discern trends and changes in 1935 (Lynd and Lynd 1937). In 1977 the community was restudied yet again (Bahr et al. 1983), using the same research instruments but with minor changes. Burgess (1987) was similarly concerned with continuity and change at the comprehensive school he had studied in the early 1970s (Burgess 1983) when he returned to study it ten years later. However, as he observes, it is difficult for the researcher to establish how far change is the result of real differences over the two time periods or of other factors, such as different people at the school, different educational issues between the two time periods, and the possible influence of the initial study itself.

Comparative design

It is worth distinguishing one further kind of design: comparative design. Put simply, this design entails studying two contrasting cases using more or less identical methods. It embodies the logic of comparison, in that it implies

Research in focus 3.16
A case study of ICI

Pettigrew (1985) conducted research into the use of organizational development expertise at Imperial Chemical Industries (ICI). The fieldwork was conducted between 1975 and 1983. He carried out 'long semistructured interviews' in 1975–7 and again in 1980–3. During the period of the fieldwork he also had fairly regular contact with members of the organization. He writes: 'The continuous real-time data collection was enriched by retrospective interviewing and archival analysis . . . ' (Pettigrew 1985: 40).

that we can understand social phenomena better when they are compared in relation to two or more meaningfully contrasting cases or situations. The comparative design may be realized in the context of either quantitative or qualitative research. Within the former, the data-collection strategy will take the form outlined in Figure 3.5. This figure implies that there are at least two cases (which may be organizations, nations, communities, police forces, etc.) and that data are collected from each, usually within a cross-sectional design format.

One of the more obvious forms of such research is in cross-cultural or cross-national research. In a useful definition, Hantrais (1996) has suggested that such research occurs

> when individuals or teams set out to examine particular issues or phenomena in two or more countries with the

Figure 3.5
A comparative design

	T_1
	Obs_1
	Obs_2
	Obs_3
Case 1	Obs_4
	Obs_5
	$\ldots$
	Obs_n
	Obs_1
	Obs_2
	Obs_3
	Obs_4
Case n	Obs_5
	$\ldots$
	Obs_n

express intention of comparing their manifestations in different socio-cultural settings (institutions, customs, traditions, value systems, life styles, language, thought patterns), using the same research instruments either to carry out secondary analysis of national data or to conduct new empirical work. The aim may be to seek explanations for similarities and differences or to gain a greater awareness and a deeper understanding of social reality in different national contexts.

The research by Röder and Mühlau (2014) referred to in Research in focus 2.4 is an illustration of cross-cultural research that entails a secondary analysis of survey evidence collected in twenty-seven nations. A further example is Gallie's (1978) survey research on the impact of advanced automation on comparable samples of industrial workers in both England and France. Gallie was able to show that national traditions of industrial relations were more important than technology in explaining worker attitudes and management–worker relations, a finding that was important in terms of the technological determinism thesis that was still current at the time.

Cross-cultural research is not without problems, such as managing and gaining the funding for such research (see Thinking deeply 3.1); ensuring, when existing data, such as official statistics or survey evidence, are submitted to a secondary analysis, that the data are comparable in terms of categories and data-collection methods; ensuring, when new data are being collected, that the need to translate data-collection instruments (for example, questions in interview schedules) does not undermine genuine comparability; and ensuring that samples of respondents or organizations are equivalent. This last problem raises the further difficulty that, even when translation is carried out competently, there is still the potential problem of insensitivity to specific national and cultural contexts. On the other hand, cross-cultural research helps to reduce the risk of failing to appreciate that social science findings are often, if not invariably, culturally specific. For example, Crompton and Birkelund (2000) conducted

Thinking deeply 3.1
Forms of cross-cultural research

As its name implies, cross-cultural research entails the collection and/or analysis of data from two or more nations. Some possible models for the conduct of cross-cultural research are as follows.

1. A researcher, perhaps in conjunction with a research team, collects comparable data in two or more countries. Gallie's (1978) research on the impact of advanced automation on industrial workers is an illustration of this model, in that he took comparable samples of industrial workers from two oil refineries in England and two in France.

2. A central organization coordinates the work of national organizations. The European Social Survey, which has been carried out every two years since 2001, is an example in that the administration of the surveys in each participating country is overseen by a central body (see http://www.europeansocialsurvey.org/about/, accessed on 14 July 2015). See also Research in focus 2.4.

3. A secondary analysis is carried out of data that are comparable, but where the coordination of their collection is limited or non-existent. This kind of cross-cultural analysis might occur if researchers seek to ask survey questions in their own country that have been asked in another country. The ensuing data may then be analysed cross-culturally. A further form of this model is through the secondary analysis of officially collected data, such as unemployment statistics. Wall's (1989) analysis of the living arrangements of the elderly in eighteen European countries is an example of such research. The research uncovered considerable diversity in terms of such factors as whether the elderly lived alone and whether they were in institutional care. This approach suffers from problems arising from the deficiencies of many forms of official statistics (see Chapter 14) and problems of cross-national variations in official definitions and collection procedures.

4. Teams of researchers in participating nations are recruited by a person or body that coordinates the programme, or alternatively researchers in different countries with common interests make contact and coordinate their investigations. Each researcher or group of researchers has the responsibility of conducting the investigation in his/her/their own country. The work is coordinated in order to ensure comparability of research questions, of survey questions, and of procedures for administering the research instruments. This model differs from the second model above in that it usually entails a specific focus on certain research questions. Research by Benson, Bridge, and Wilson (2015) on the school choice strategies of middle-class families in London and Paris is an example, in that teams of researchers in both cities interviewed comparable samples of parents using 'a pre-agreed interview guide' in order to explore parents' strategies. A further example can be found in Research in focus 27.8.

5. Although not genuinely cross-cultural research in the sense of a coordinated project across nations, another form can occur when a researcher compares what is known in one country with new research in another country. For example, Richard Wright, a criminologist who has carried out a considerable amount of research into street robberies in the USA, was interested in how far findings relating to this crime would be similar in the UK. In particular, US research highlighted the role of street culture in the motivation to engage in such robbery. He was involved in a project that entailed semi-structured interviews with imprisoned street robbers in south-west England (Wright et al. 2006). In fact, the researchers found that street culture played an important role in the UK in a similar way to the USA.

research using semi-structured interviewing with comparable samples of male and female bank managers in Norway and Britain. They found that, in spite of more family-friendly policies in Norway, bank managers in both countries struggle to manage career and domestic life. It might have been assumed that countries with greater attachment to such policies would ease these pressures, but cross-cultural research of this kind shows how easy it is to make such an erroneous inference.

Comparative research should not be treated as solely concerned with comparisons between nations. The logic of comparison can be applied to a variety of situations.

The Social Change and Economic Life Initiative entailed identical studies (mainly involving survey research) in six contrasting labour markets, which were chosen to reflect different patterns of economic change in the early to mid-1980s and in the then recent past. By choosing meaningful contrasts, the significance of the different patterns for a variety of experiences of both employers and employees could be portrayed (Penn, Rose, and Rubery 1994). Such designs are not without problems: the differences that are observed between the contrasting cases may not be due exclusively to the distinguishing features of the cases. Thus, some caution is necessary when explaining contrasts between cases in terms of differences between them.

In terms of issues of reliability, validity, replicability, and generalizability, the comparative study is no different from the cross-sectional design. The comparative design is essentially two or more cross-sectional studies carried out at more or less the same point in time.

The comparative design can also be applied in relation to a qualitative research strategy. When this occurs, it takes the form of a **multiple-case study** (see Research in focus 3.17). In recent years, a number of writers have argued for a greater use of case study research that includes more than one case. Essentially, a multiple-case (or multi-case) study occurs whenever the number of cases examined exceeds one. The main argument in favour of the multiple-case study is that it improves theory building. By comparing two or more cases, the researcher is in a better position to establish the circumstances in which a theory will or will not hold (Eisenhardt 1989; Yin 2009). Moreover, the comparison may itself suggest concepts that are relevant to an emerging theory.

Related to this point is the fact that there is a growing awareness that the case study and the multiple-case study in particular may play a crucial role in relation to the understanding of causality. However, this awareness reflects a different notion of causality from that

Research in focus 3.17
Multiple-case study research based on difference between cases: research on two London neighbourhoods and four Scottish neighbourhoods

In their study of the factors that contribute to the sense of 'place' and of belonging among middle-class residents in two London neighbourhoods, Benson and Jackson (2013) adopted a multiple-case study approach. One neighbourhood is described by the authors as an inner urban neighbourhood and the other as a commuter belt village. The two neighbourhoods differed particularly in terms of both how far white British residents predominated and levels of owner occupation and, by implication, rented accommodation. Semi-structured interviews were conducted with samples of middle-class residents and the authors' conclusions derive from a comparison of the two environments. For example, they write: 'The comparison of the discursive practices of place-making in two very different neighbourhoods has demonstrated that middle-class place-attachments need to be understood within the context of circulating representations of place' (Benson and Jackson 2013: 806). This kind of conclusion demonstrates the value of being able to forge a comparison through a multiple-case study approach. The comparison allows the distinctive and common features of cases to be drawn out.

Atkinson and Kintrea (2001) were interested in the implications of what are known as *area effects*. Area effects are to do with the implications of living or working in an area for life chances and attitudes. The authors were concerned with the implications of area effects for the experience of poverty. More specifically, is the experience of poverty worse if one lives in a poor area than if one lives in an economically mixed area? Are those who are economically disadvantaged more likely to experience social exclusion in one type of area rather than another (that is, economically deprived or mixed)? The researchers selected an economically disadvantaged area and an economically and socially mixed area in Glasgow for comparison. They selected a similar pair of areas in Edinburgh, thus allowing a further element of comparison because of the greater buoyancy of this city compared to Glasgow. Thus, four areas were selected altogether and samples in each were questioned using a survey instrument. The quantitative comparisons of the data led the researchers to conclude that, by and large, it is 'worse to be poor in a poor area than one which is socially mixed' (Atkinson and Kintrea 2001: 2295).

outlined earlier in this chapter. In the discussion of independent and dependent variables, the underlying perception of cause and effect is indicative of what is often referred to as a 'successionist' understanding of causation. As the term 'successionist' implies, this notion of causality entails an effect following on from an independent variable that precedes it. Critical realism (see Key concept 2.3) operates with a different understanding of causation, which is to seek out generative mechanisms that are responsible for observed regularities in the social world and how they operate in particular contexts. Case studies are perceived by critical realist writers as having an important role for research within this tradition, because the intensive nature of most case studies enhances the researcher's sensitivity to the factors that lie behind the operation of observed patterns within a specific context (Ackroyd 2009). The multiple-case study offers an even greater opportunity, because the researcher will be in a position to examine the operation of generative causal mechanisms in contrasting or similar contexts. Thus, Delbridge's (2004) ethnographic study of two 'high-performance' companies in south Wales was able to identify in both firms patterns of resistance and independence that persisted in spite of management efforts to intensify work and to minimize slack in the production process. However, the extent to which informal organization and subversion were found to operate differed considerably between the two firms, and important to this variation was the quality of the relationships between the workers themselves. This represents the causal mechanism producing the variation in resistance between the two factories. The crucial contextual factor was the operation of a blame culture in one of the firms (a Japanese-owned company), whereby any mistake had to be attributed to an individual, which had implications for the quality of relationships among the operatives because of the disputes and disagreements that ensued. Consequently, through the use of a multiple-case study, Delbridge was able to show how variation in informal organization and resistance (an observed regularity) could be understood through its generative causal mechanism (the quality of worker relationships) and through the significance of context (the presence or otherwise of a blame culture).

Research in focus 3.17 provides examples of one approach to selecting cases for a multiple-case study, namely using contrasting features as a means of both selecting cases and forging comparisons that allow the implications for the data of the contrasting features to be demonstrated. In the second example in Research in focus 3.17, cases were selected on the basis of quantitative **indicators** of economic deprivation. For example, both the economically deprived areas in Edinburgh and Glasgow were in the top 5 per cent of deprived areas in Scotland. With case selection approaches such as these, the findings that are common to the cases can be just as interesting and important as those that differentiate them. The study by Benson and Jackson (2013) entailed a qualitative research strategy, whereas the Atkinson and Kintrea's research entailed a predominantly quantitative one.

An alternative strategy is to select cases on the basis of *similarity* rather than difference. Research in focus 3.18 provides two examples of this strategy. The advantage of this strategy is that the researcher is able to say that any differences that are found between the cases in terms of the main focus of the research are likely to be due to the factors that the researcher reveals as important rather than to differences between the cases at the outset. This is in a sense a more open-ended approach to selecting cases than selecting them in terms of pre-existing characteristics (as in the studies in Research in focus 3.17). Selecting in terms of pre-existing difference means that the researcher is suggesting that he or she expects one or more factors to be significant for the focus of the research (e.g. place-making or feelings of deprivation). Selecting cases in terms of difference requires a rationale for the criteria employed. The examples in Research in focus 3.18 entail largely matched cases and the aim is to uncover the factors that may be responsible for differences that are observed (e.g. the quality of inter-ethnic relations or whether an organizational reform is successfully embedded).

Not all writers are convinced about the merits of multiple-case study research. Dyer and Wilkins (1991), for example, argue that it tends to mean that the researcher pays less attention to the specific context and more to the ways in which the cases can be contrasted. Moreover, the need to forge comparisons tends to mean that the researcher needs to develop an explicit focus at the outset, whereas critics of the multiple-case study argue that it may often be preferable to adopt a more open-ended approach. These concerns about retaining contextual insight and a rather more unstructured research approach are very much associated with the goals of qualitative research (see Chapter 17).

The key to the comparative design is its ability to allow the distinguishing characteristics of two or more cases to act as a springboard for theoretical reflections about contrasting findings. It is something of a hybrid, in that in quantitative research it is frequently an extension of a cross-sectional design and in qualitative research it is frequently an extension of a case study design. It even exhibits certain features that are similar to experiments and quasi-experiments, which also rely on forging a comparison.

Research in focus 3.18
Multiple-case study research based on similarity between cases: research on three Northern Ireland neighbourhoods and on three US hospitals

The research by Hughes et al. (2011) of three Northern Ireland neighbourhoods was briefly referred to in Chapter 2. For this research on the 'contact hypothesis' (Research in focus 2.2), the researchers examined three neighbourhoods with broadly similar proportions of Protestant and Catholic residents, although the areas differed in terms of terms of a measure of 'multiple deprivation' with one community being considerably less deprived than the other two. However, it is the fact that the three areas were 'among the most ethnically mixed in Northern Ireland' (Hughes et al. 2011: 971) that was central to the research. Hughes et al. conducted semi-structured interviews with residents in the areas. In this study the focus was on similarity rather than difference across the neighbourhoods in terms of the key variable (proportion of Protestant and Catholic residents).

Kellogg (2009, 2011) reports findings on the introduction of a new patient safety programme (a reduction in the number of hours worked by surgical residents—surgeons who are still in training—in US hospitals). Initially, two hospitals were studied (Kellogg 2009), but further fieldwork was carried out in a third as well (Kellogg 2011). The hospitals (referred to as Advent, Bayshore, and Calhoun) were selected in large part because of their similarity, and Kellogg presents a table showing the dimensions on which they were similar (Kellogg 2011: 39–40). She found that the outcomes of the change differed between the three hospitals, which allowed her to examine the kinds of factors responsible for the differences in outcome in spite of the similarities between the hospitals. For example, Kellogg shows that the change 'ultimately failed' at Bayshore and Calhoun but that at Advent, 'reformers were victorious' (Kellogg 2011: 169). Because the three hospitals were similar at the outset, the differences in outcome could not be attributed to pre-existing characteristics. Kellogg draws attention to the ways in which forces for reform and forces for retaining as much of the status quo as possible produced different outcomes at the three hospitals.

Bringing research strategy and research design together

Finally, we can bring together the two research strategies covered in Chapter 2 with the research designs outlined in this chapter. Table 3.1 shows the typical form associated with each combination of research strategy and research design and a number of examples that either have been encountered so far or will be covered in later chapters. Table 3.1 refers also to research methods that will be encountered in later chapters but that have not been referred to so far. The Glossary will give you a quick reference to terms used that are not yet familiar to you. Strictly speaking, Table 3.1 should comprise a third column for mixed methods research, as an approach that combines both quantitative and qualitative research. This has not been done because the resulting table would be

too complicated, since mixed methods research can entail the combined use of different research *designs* (for example, a cross-sectional design and a multiple-case study) as well as methods. However, the quantitative and qualitative components of some of the mixed methods studies referred to in this book *are* included in the table.

The distinctions are not always perfect. In particular, in some qualitative research it is not obvious whether a study is an example of a longitudinal design or a case study design. Life history studies, research that concentrates on a specific issue over time (e.g. Deacon, Fenton, and Bryman 1999), and ethnography in which the researcher charts change in a single case are examples of studies that cross the two types. Such studies are perhaps

Table 3.1
Research strategy and research design

Research design	Research strategy	
	Quantitative	Qualitative
Experimental	*Typical form*. Most researchers using an experimental design employ quantitative comparisons between experimental and control groups with regard to the dependent variable.	No typical form. However, Bryman (1988a: 151–2) notes a study in which qualitative data on schoolchildren were collected within a quasi-experimental research design (Hall and Guthrie 1981).
	Examples. Research in focus 3.2, 3.4; Research in the news 6.1.	
Cross-sectional	*Typical form*. Survey research or structured observation on a sample at a single point in time. Content analysis on a sample of documents.	*Typical form*. Qualitative interviews or focus groups at a single point in time. Qualitative content analysis of a set of documents relating to a single period.
	Examples. Research in focus 1.1, 2.8, 2.9, 3.8, 7.7, 8.1, 8.5, 13.2.	*Examples*. Research in focus 2.8, 2.9, 3.9, 20.1, 20.4 (see also Table 1.1), 20.5.
Longitudinal	*Typical form*. Survey research on a sample on more than one occasion, as in panel and cohort studies. Content analysis of documents relating to different time periods.	*Typical form*. Ethnographic research over a very long period, qualitative interviewing on more than one occasion, or qualitative content analysis of documents relating to different time periods. Such research warrants being dubbed longitudinal when there is a concern to map change.
	Examples. Research in focus 3.10, 3.11, 3.13.	*Examples*. Research in focus 3.12, 19.2.
Case study	*Typical form*. Survey research on a single case with a view to revealing important features about its nature.	*Typical form*. The intensive study by ethnography or qualitative interviewing of a single case, which may be an organization, life, family, or community.
	Examples. The choice by Goldthorpe et al. (1968) of Luton as a site for testing the thesis of *embourgeoisement*.	*Examples*. Research in focus 2.5, 2.6, 3.14, 17.4, 19.1, 23.1.
Comparative	*Typical form*. Survey research in which there is a direct comparison between two or more cases, as in cross-cultural research.	*Typical form*. Ethnographic or qualitative interview research on two or more cases.
	Examples. Research in focus 2.4, 7.1; Gallie (1978).	*Examples*. Research in focus 2.1, 3.17, 3.18, 17.3; Gambetta and Hammill (2005); Prichard et al. (2014).

better conceptualized as longitudinal case studies than as belonging to one category of research design. A further point to note is that there is no typical form in the qualitative research strategy/experimental research design cell.

Qualitative research in the context of true experiments is very unusual. However, as noted in the table, Bryman (1988a) refers to a qualitative study by Hall and Guthrie (1981), which employed a quasi-experimental design.

›› *Key points*

- There is an important distinction between a research method and a research design.
- It is necessary to become thoroughly familiar with the meaning of the technical terms used as criteria for evaluating research: reliability; validity; and replicability; and the types of validity: measurement; internal; external; and ecological.

- It is also necessary to be familiar with the differences between the five major research designs covered: experimental; cross-sectional; longitudinal; case study; and comparative. In this context, it is important to realize that the term 'experiment', which is often used somewhat loosely in everyday speech, has a specific technical meaning.

- There are various potential threats to internal validity in non-experimental research.

- Although the case study is often thought to be a single type of research design, it in fact has several forms. It is also important to be aware of the key issues concerned with the nature of case study evidence in relation to such issues as external validity (generalizability).

Questions for review

- In terms of the definitions used in this book, what are the chief differences between each of the following: a research method; a research strategy; and a research design?

Criteria in social research

- What are the differences between reliability and validity and why are these important criteria for the evaluation of social research?

- Outline the meaning of each of the following: measurement validity; internal validity; external validity; and ecological validity.

- Why have some qualitative researchers sought to devise alternative criteria to reliability and validity when assessing the quality of investigations?

- Why have some qualitative researchers not sought to devise alternative criteria to reliability and validity when assessing the quality of investigations?

Research designs

- What are the main research designs that have been outlined in this chapter?

- A researcher reasons that people who read broadsheet newspapers are likely to be more knowledgeable about personal finance than readers of tabloid newspapers. He interviews 100 people about the newspapers they read and their level of financial knowledge. Sixty-five people read tabloids and thirty-five read broadsheets. He finds that the broadsheet readers are on average considerably more knowledgeable about personal finance than tabloid readers. He concludes that reading broadsheets enhances levels of knowledge of personal finance. Assess his reasoning.

Experimental design

- How far do you agree with the view that the main importance of the experimental design for the social researcher is that it represents a model of how to infer causal connections between variables?

- Following on from the previous question, if experimental design is so useful and important, why is it not used more?

- What is a quasi-experiment?

Cross-sectional design

- In what ways does the survey exemplify the cross-sectional research design?

- Assess the degree to which the survey researcher can achieve internally valid findings.

- To what extent is the survey design exclusive to quantitative research?

Longitudinal design(s)

● Why might a longitudinal research design be superior to a cross-sectional one?

● What are the main differences between panel and cohort designs in longitudinal research?

Case study design

● What is a case study?

● Is case study research exclusive to qualitative research?

● What are some of the principles by which cases might be selected?

Comparative design

● What are the chief strengths of a comparative research design?

● Why might comparative research yield important insights?

Online Resource Centre

www.oxfordtextbooks.co.uk/orc/brymansrm5e/

Visit the Online Resource Centre to enrich your understanding of research designs. Follow up links to other resources, test yourself using multiple choice questions, and gain further guidance and inspiration from the Student Researcher's Toolkit.

4

Planning a research project and formulating research questions

Chapter outline

Chapter guide

The goal of this chapter is to provide advice to students on some of the issues that they need to consider if they have to prepare a dissertation based upon a relatively small-scale project. Increasingly, social science students are required to produce such a dissertation as part of the requirements for their degrees. In addition to providing help with the conduct of research, which will be the aim of the chapters that come later in this book, more specific advice on tactics in carrying out and writing up social research for a dissertation can be useful. It is against this background that this chapter has been written. The chapter explores a wide variety of issues, such as:

- advice on timing;
- advice on generating research questions;
- advice on conducting a project;
- advice on writing a research proposal.

Introduction

This chapter provides advice for readers about carrying out their own research project. The chapters in Parts Two, Three, and Four provide more detailed information about the choices available to you and how to implement them. But beyond this, how might you go about conducting a small project of your own? I have in mind here the kind of situation that is increasingly common among undergraduate and postgraduate degree programmes in the social sciences—the requirement to write a dissertation often of around 10,000 to 15,000 words. Also, the advice is especially directed at students conducting projects with a component of empirical research in which they collect new data or conduct a secondary analysis of existing data.

 ## Getting to know what is expected of you by your institution

Your institution or department will have specific requirements concerning features that your dissertation should comprise and a range of other matters relating to it. These include such things as the form of binding; how it is to be presented; whether an abstract is required; how big the page margins should be; the format for referencing; number of words; the structure of the dissertation; how much advice you can get from your supervisor; whether or not a proposal is required; plagiarism; deadlines; how much (if any) financial assistance you can expect; and so on.

The advice here is simple: *follow the requirements, instructions, and information you are given*. If anything in this book conflicts with your institution's guidelines and requirements, ignore this book! I very much hope this is not something that will occur very much, but if it does, follow your institution's guidelines.

 ## Thinking about your research area

It is likely that you will be asked to start thinking about what you want to research before you are due to start work on your dissertation. It is worth giving yourself a good deal of time. As you are doing your various modules, begin to think about whether there are any topics that might interest you and that might provide you with a researchable area.

 ## Using your supervisor

Most institutions allocate students to dissertation supervisors. Institutions vary in what can be expected of supervisors; in other words, they vary in terms of what kinds of and how much assistance supervisors will give to students allocated to them. Equally, students vary a great deal in how frequently they see their supervisors and in their use of them. My advice here is simple: use your supervisor to the fullest extent that you are allowed and follow the pointers you are given. Your supervisor will be someone who is well versed in the research process and who will be able to provide you with help and feedback at all stages of your research, subject to your institution's regulations in this regard. If your supervisor is critical of your research questions, your interview schedule, drafts of your dissertation, or whatever, try to respond positively. Follow the suggestions that he or she provides, since the feedback will invariably be accompanied by reasons for the criticisms and suggestions for revision. It is not a personal attack. Supervisors regularly have to go through the same process themselves when they submit an article to a peer-refereed journal or apply for a research grant or give a conference paper. So respond to criticisms and suggestions positively and be glad that you are being given the opportunity to address deficiencies in your work before it is formally examined.

A further point is that students who get stuck at the start of their dissertations or who get behind with their work sometimes respond to the situation by avoiding their supervisors. They then get caught up in a vicious circle that results in their work being neglected and perhaps rushed at the end. Try to avoid this situation by confronting the fact that you are experiencing difficulties in beginning your work or are getting behind, and seek out your supervisor for advice.

Student experience
Using supervisors

Several students wrote about the role that their supervisors played in their research projects. Isabella Robbins mentions that her supervisor played an important role in relation to her analysis of her qualitative data.

> The emerging themes were strong and in that sense the analysis was not problematic, but I guess the problems came in mapping the analysis onto the theory. My way of dealing with this was to talk about the analysis at supervisions and to incorporate the ideas that came of these discussions.

Cornelius Grebe provided the following advice about relationships with supervisors:

> I have learned to be very clear about my expectations of my supervisors: what kind of professional and personal relationship I thrive in and what form of support exactly I need from them.

 To read more, go to the Online Resource Centre: www.oxfordtextbooks.co.uk/orc/brymansrm5e/

Supervisor tips
How to annoy your dissertation supervisor and cause yourself problems: five easy steps

Supervisors were asked about some of the chief frustrations associated with supervising dissertation students. There were some recurring themes in their responses. Here are some easy ways to annoy your supervisor and create problems for yourself:

1. *Don't turn up to pre-arranged supervision meetings.* Quite aside from the rudeness of doing this, a failure to turn up begins to ring alarm bells about whether the student is veering off course.

2. *Leave the bulk of the work until the last minute.* Supervisors know full well that research must be paced because it requires a great deal of forethought and because things can go wrong. The longer students leave their dissertation work, the more difficult it becomes to do thorough research and to rectify problems.

3. *Ignore what your supervisor advises you to do.* Supervisors are extremely experienced researchers, so that ignoring their advice is irritating and certainly not in a student's interest.

4. *Hand in shoddy drafts as late as possible.* It is not your supervisor's role to write the dissertation for you, so you should hand in work that allows him or her to offer advice and suggestions, not a rewrite of your work. Also, supervisors have several dissertation students as well as other often urgent commitments, so they need to be given a reasonable amount of time to consider your work.

5. *Forget what you were taught in your research methods module or your research training module.* Instruction that you will have received on how to do research was meant to help you with your future research needs; it was not a hurdle for you to jump over and then move on.

 # Managing time and resources

All research is constrained by time and resources. There is no point in working on research questions and plans that cannot be carried through because of time pressure or because of the costs involved. Two points are relevant here.

1. Work out a timetable—preferably in conjunction with your supervisor—detailing the different stages of your research (including the literature review and writing up). The timetable should specify the different stages and the calendar points at which you should start and finish them. Some

stages are likely to be ongoing—for example, searching the literature for new references (a process that will be covered in Chapter 5)—but that should not prove an obstacle to developing a timetable. Securing access to an organization is sometimes required for student projects, but students typically underestimate the time it can take to do this. For his research on commercial cleaning, Ryan (2009) spent nearly two years trying to secure access to a suitable firm.

2. Find out what, if any, resources will be available for carrying out your research. For example, will you receive help from your institution with such things as travel costs, photocopying, secretarial assistance, postage, stationery, costs of an online survey platform, and so on? Will the institution be able to loan you hardware such as recording equipment and transcription machines if you need to record and transcribe your interviews? Has your institution got the software you need, such as **SPSS** or a qualitative data analysis package such as **NVivo**? This kind of information will help you to establish how far your research design and methods are financially feasible and practical. The imaginary 'gym study' used in Chapter 15 is an example of an investigation that would be feasible within the kind of time frame usually allocated to undergraduate and postgraduate dissertations. However, it would require such facilities as formatting the questionnaire; photocopying covering letters and questionnaires; postage for sending the questionnaires out and for any follow-up letters to non-respondents; return postage for the questionnaires; and the availability of a quantitative data analysis package such as SPSS.

Student experience
Managing time

One of the most difficult aspects of doing a research project for many students is managing their time. Sarah Hanson was explicit on this point:

> Never underestimate how long it will take you to complete a large project like a dissertation. Choose a topic you have passion about. The more you enjoy your research the more interesting it will be to read. Be organized: post-it notes, folders, wall planners, anything that keeps you on track from day to day will help you not to be distracted from the purpose of your study.

Both Hannah Creane and Lily Taylor felt that, unless your time is managed well, the analysis phase tends to be squeezed—often with undesirable consequences. Indeed, it is my experience too from supervising students' dissertations that they allow far too little time for data analysis and writing up. Here is what Hannah and Lily respectively wrote in response to a question asking what one single bit of advice they would give to others.

> Get your research done as soon as possible. The process of analysis is pretty much an ongoing one and can take a very long time, so the sooner you have all your data compiled the better. It also means that you have more time to make more extensive analysis rather than just noticing the surface emergent trends.

> Make sure you give yourself enough time to carry out the project, don't underestimate the amount of time data analysis can take!

Amy Knight felt she managed her time quite well when preparing an undergraduate dissertation on gender and recycling:

> Effective time management is needed when completing a large research project such as a dissertation. I spent a lot of my summer between my second and third year collecting relevant literature and putting together draft chapters. I would also recommend setting personal targets—for example, aiming to complete the literature review chapter within a month of starting your third year. Setting targets worked well for me as it spread my workload; it also meant that I could get effective feedback from my dissertation supervisor with plenty of time to make adjustments.

Similarly, Rebecca Barnes wrote that, if she were doing her research again:

> I would also allocate more time for data analysis and writing, as largely because of the long period of time which it took to recruit participants, these phases of my research were subject to considerable time pressures.

 To read more, go to the Online Resource Centre: www.oxfordtextbooks.co.uk/orc/brymansrm5e/

Supervisor tips
Allow time to gain access and for ethical scrutiny

One area where students often fail to build in sufficient time when conducting research projects is to do with the tendency to underestimate how much time it can take to gain access to organizations and other settings and to get clearance for their research through an ethics committee. Access issues are mainly covered in Chapter 19 and ethical issues in Chapter 6. Some institutions adopt a relatively light-touch approach over ethics, provided no obvious ethical issues are suggested by a student's proposal. Others submit all proposals to more detailed scrutiny. Supervisor A wrote:

> Criminological subject matter does not lend itself easily to empirical study by dissertation: one often wishes to study illegal and upsetting subjects that raise a range of ethical concerns (**informed consent**; researcher safety; data confidentiality; disclosure), that, combined with access difficulties, mean resolution timescales are often well beyond the time available to students.

It is also clear that many supervisors act as initial ethical advisers and steer students away from ethically questionable topics or approaches. Supervisor C wrote that he intervened in students' choice of topic and/or research methods 'when there is a clear possibility of ethical problems or the proposed timetable is unrealistic or if the methods are incongruent with the research aims'.

Supervisor F wrote: 'Topics are chosen by students—where these raise ethical or practical issues students are encouraged to reflect on their choices and the issues raised.' Supervisor I took a similar view: 'I help to steer them away from topics where there might be problems accessing data, ensuring safety in undertaking data collection (especially qualitative fieldwork) or dealing with ethical issues.' The very fact that your initial ideas about your research may have to be reconsidered because of ethical concerns is likely to slow down your research slightly, so it is worth giving ethical and access issues consideration very early on.

There is a clear message in the material covered in this section: allow sufficient time for the various stages of the research process. Securing access, analysing data, and writing up findings have been particularly highlighted as areas where students often miscalculate the amount of time required. Another time-related issue is that it can take a long time to secure clearance from research ethics committees to conduct your investigation. The issue of ethics is given more detailed consideration in Chapter 6. However, one final point needs to be registered: even with a really well-planned project, unexpected problems can throw out your timetable. For example, McDonald, Townsend, and Waterhouse (2009) report that they successfully negotiated access to the Australian

Student experience
Devising a timetable for writing up

Lily Taylor found it helpful to have a timetable of deadlines for the different sections of the report she had to write.

> I produced a first draft of my report and made sure that I got it done in plenty of time before the deadline. I was then able to go over my work and make the necessary changes. I made sure that I had a checklist with mini deadlines for each section. This made sure that I kept on top of my work and progressed at a steady rate.

Isabella Robbins writes that she 'devised a writing up timetable with a plan of the thesis'. Cornelius Grebe adopted a similar approach to his writing up. He writes: 'I agreed submission dates for individual draft chapters with my supervisors.'

To read more, go to the Online Resource Centre: www.oxfordtextbooks.co.uk/orc/brymansrm5e/

Student experience *and* supervisor tips
Leave enough time for analysis and writing

I have long held the view that a recurring error in students' preparations for their dissertations is that many do not allow sufficient time for the analysis and writing-up stages. This tendency results in both of these stages being rushed, when they actually require a great deal of time for reflection and redrafting. Several of the supervisors reported similar experiences with their students.

Supervisor C wrote that one of the most common problems encountered by dissertation students was not allowing 'sufficient time for re-drafting' and for Supervisor G it was 'leaving the writing until the last minute'. Several of them also commented that they encourage their students to consider issues about analysis *before* the collection of the data. Supervisor D writes that a common refrain is: 'I've collected all this data and I don't know what to do with it!' This supervisor went on to write that he or she encourages students

> to think about their analysis during or shortly after the construction of their research questions. By the time they are thinking about research design they should have a rough idea about what their analysis will look like (i.e. they must do as it will link their research design to their research questions).

Several of the students made similar observations about their own experiences. For example, Alice Palmer notes of her own experience with writing:

> As long as you have something written, you are on your way to improving it. I aimed to write a couple of hundred words a day, no matter how inspired I was feeling. I wrote more if I felt it was going well, but at least I could steadily move towards a target, which is less stressful than having no idea where you will be in a week's time.

Mark Girvan writes of a group project in which he was involved:

> DO NOT leave things late! Our research project suffered through a lack of urgency, meaning that we did not have as much time as we would have liked to write up our report. Too much was left to the last minute, which meant that what we produced was not of the high quality of which we believe we were capable.

organizations that were involved in a number of research projects in which the researchers were engaged. However, changes to personnel meant that those who had agreed to give them access (often called 'gatekeepers' in the research methods literature) left or moved on, so that the researchers had to forge new relationships and effectively had to renegotiate the terms of their investigations, which considerably slowed down the progress of their research. Such disruptions to research are impossible to predict. It is important not only to realize that they can occur but also to introduce a little flexibility into your research timetable so that you can absorb their impact.

Formulating suitable research questions

Many students want to conduct research into areas that are of personal interest to them. This is not a bad thing at all and, as I noted in Chapter 2, many social researchers start from this point as well (see also Lofland and Lofland 1995: 11–14). However, you must move on to develop research questions. This recommendation applies to qualitative research as well as quantitative research. As is explained in Chapter 17, qualitative research tends to be more open-ended than quantitative research, and in Chapter 19 I refer to some notable studies that appear not to have been driven by specific research questions. However, very open-ended research is risky and can lead to the collection of too much data and, when it comes to writing up, to confusion about your focus. So, unless your supervisor advises you to the contrary, I would definitely formulate some research questions, even if they turn out to be somewhat less specific than the kinds we often find in quantitative research. In other words, what is it about your area of interest that you want to know?

Marx (1997) has suggested a wide range of possible sources of research questions (see Thinking deeply 4.1). As this list makes clear, research questions can spring from a wide variety of sources. Figure 4.1 outlines the main steps in developing research questions. Research questions in quantitative research are sometimes more specific than in qualitative research. Indeed, some qualitative researchers advocate a very open approach with no research questions. This is a very risky approach, because it can result in collecting data without a clear sense of what to observe or what to ask your interviewees. There is a growing tendency for qualitative researchers to advocate a more focused approach (e.g. Hammersley and Atkinson 1995: 24–9).

As Figure 4.1 implies, we usually start out with a general research area that interests us. It may derive from any of several sources:

- *Personal interest/experience*. My interest in theme parks can be traced back to a visit to Disney World in Orlando in 1991, and my interest in the representation of social science research in the mass media goes back

to a difficult encounter with the press (referred to in Chapters 1 and 2).

- *Theory*. Someone might be interested in testing or exploring aspects of labour process theory, or in the theory of the risk society, or in the implications of Actor Network Theory for the use of technologies in everyday life.

- *The research literature*. Studies relating to a research area such as modern consumerism might stimulate an interest in the nature of the shopping experience in contemporary society. Writing about the field of organization studies, Sandberg and Alvesson (2011) note that spotting gaps in the literature is the chief way of identifying research questions. The main strategies for doing this are spotting overlooked or under-researched areas and identifying areas of research that have not been previously examined using a particular theory or perspective. Alvesson and Sandberg (2011) recommend greater development of research questions through what they call 'problematization', which entails challenging the assumptions that are

Thinking deeply 4.1
Marx's sources of research questions

Marx (1997) suggests the following as possible sources of research questions.

- Intellectual puzzles and contradictions.

- The existing literature.

- Replication.

- Structures and functions. For example, if you point to a structure such as a type of organization, you can ask questions about the reasons why there are different types and the implications of the differences.

- Opposition. Marx identifies the sensation of feeling that a certain theoretical perspective or notable piece of work is misguided and of exploring the reasons for your opposition.

- A social problem. But remember that this is just the source of a research question; you still have to identify social scientific (for example, sociological) issues in relation to a social problem.

- 'Gaps between official versions of reality and the facts on the ground' (Marx 1997: 113). An example here is something like Delbridge's (1998) ethnographic account of company rhetoric about Japanized work practices and how they operate in practice.

- The counter-intuitive: for example, when common sense seems to fly in the face of social scientific truths.

- 'Empirical examples that trigger amazement' (Marx 1997: 114). Marx gives, as examples, deviant cases and atypical events.

- New methods and theories. How might they be applied in new settings?

- 'New social and technical developments and social trends' (Marx 1997: 114).

- Personal experience.

- Sponsors and teachers. But do not expect your teachers to provide you with detailed research questions.

Figure 4.1
Steps in selecting research questions

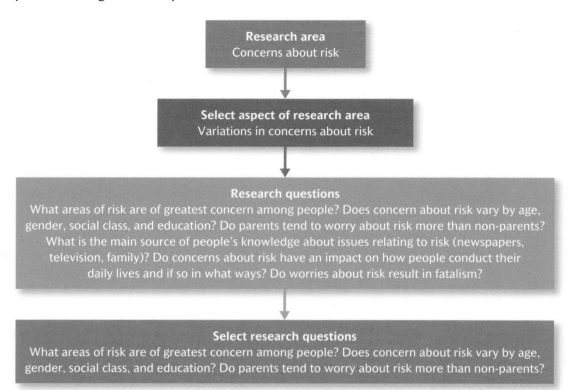

| **Research area** |
| Concerns about risk |

| **Select aspect of research area** |
| Variations in concerns about risk |

Research questions
What areas of risk are of greatest concern among people? Does concern about risk vary by age, gender, social class, and education? Do parents tend to worry about risk more than non-parents? What is the main source of people's knowledge about issues relating to risk (newspapers, television, family)? Do concerns about risk have an impact on how people conduct their daily lives and if so in what ways? Do worries about risk result in fatalism?

Select research questions
What areas of risk are of greatest concern among people? Does concern about risk vary by age, gender, social class, and education? Do parents tend to worry about risk more than non-parents?

embedded in the literature. Such assumptions might be located within a root metaphor (Morgan 1997) or paradigm (Burrell and Morgan 1979). Challenging them can result in the formulation of alternative assumptions that can be used as a springboard for generating innovative research questions. As Alvesson and Sandberg recognize, 'gap spotting' is itself a creative process because gaps in the literature are frequently identified by arranging or positioning them in certain ways. However, because such a process rarely involves challenges to assumptions, research questions are rarely innovative and rarely likely to engender significant theoretical departures.

- *Puzzles*. An interesting example of this can be found in a research article by Hodson (2004) in which he employs data from the Workplace Ethnography Project (see Research in focus 13.5). In this article he notes that writings on modern work imply two rather inconsistent views concerning the extent to which workplaces today are a source of social fulfilment. Some writers construe modern workplaces as intrinsically attractive environments to which people are drawn; other writers view people's commitment to social life at the workplace as

stemming from job and career insecurities. Hodson set up these two different points of view explicitly as essentially rival hypotheses. Similarly, Wright et al. (2006) collected semi-structured interview data on street robbers in the UK to shed light on two different views of the motivation for engaging in this crime. One view, which draws on rational choice theory, depicts street robbery as motivated by a trade-off between the desire for financial gain against the necessity to reduce the likelihood of detection. The other view of street robbery portrays it as a cultural activity from which perpetrators derived an emotional thrill and which helped to sustain a particular lifestyle.

- *New developments in society*. Examples might include the rise of the Internet and the diffusion of new models of organization—for example, call centres.
- *Social problem*. An example might be the impact of asylum-seekers being viewed as a social problem by some sectors of society. This seems to have been one of the main factors behind the work of Lynn and Lea (2003), who examined the discourses surrounding the notion of the asylum-seeker in the UK (see Research in focus 22.8).

Student experience
Theory as an influence on research questions

Rebecca Barnes's interest in feminist theories relating to patriarchy influenced her selection of woman-to-woman partner abuse as a focus for her enquiries.

> I became interested in the topic of woman-to-woman partner abuse as an undergraduate. My first encounter with this subject area took the form of a theoretical engagement with feminist explanations for domestic violence—primarily emphasizing patriarchy—and the ways in which emerging knowledge about violence and abuse in female same-sex relationships challenges this understanding. It was as a result of this first encounter that I became aware of the scarcity of research in this area, particularly in the UK, where this subject was virtually uncharted territory. I was at this point interested in pursuing postgraduate study, and thus decided to conduct my own UK-based study of woman-to-woman partner abuse for my PhD.

Theoretical ideas stimulated Gareth Matthews's interest in migrant labour. In his case, it was labour process theory that was the focus of his theoretical enquiry.

> Primarily, my interest stems from a more general interest in Marxist labour process theory, which I believe to be highly relevant to an understanding of the content of modern work-forms as well as the claims that are made by academics about these. Since Braverman published *Labour and Monopoly Capital* in 1974, the labour process debate has taken many twists and turns, and the 'core' elements of the theory are now somewhat different from those expounded by Braverman. I do not seek simply to reiterate the importance of Braverman's formulation, but instead have attempted to explore the space between this and more modern theoretical propositions—in the light of real and perceived changes in the world of work and workers. . . . Essentially, my approach stems from the belief that the employment relation cannot simply be 'read off' from analyses of the content of jobs, and that it must instead be examined through an analysis of forces that operate at various levels (i.e. the workplace, the labour market, the state, etc.), and from the interaction between these forces and employers' necessarily contradictory aims and pressures.

 To read more, go to the Online Resource Centre: www.oxfordtextbooks.co.uk/orc/brymansrm5e/

Student experience
New developments in society as a spur to research questions

Lily Taylor was interested in the role of debt on the student experience. What, in other words, is the impact of top-up fees on students' experiences of higher education?

> Increasingly today more students are put off university because of the amount of debt most students will leave with. Particularly with the topical debate at the time over the tuition fee system and top-up fees, I believed it was an interesting area to look at. Students are supposed to be concerned and worried about essay deadlines and attending lectures and seminars, yet finance today seems to be the main anxiety for most university students.

 To read more, go to the Online Resource Centre: www.oxfordtextbooks.co.uk/orc/brymansrm5e/

These sources of interest are not mutually exclusive. For example, the investigation reported in Research in focus 2.1 was motivated by at least two of the above sources: an interest in exploring the concept of social capital (theory) and understanding the process of gentrification (a new development in society).

As these types of source suggest, in research we often start out with a general research area that interests us.

This research area has to be narrowed down so that we can develop a tighter focus, out of which research questions can be developed. We can depict the process of generating research questions as a series of steps that are suggested in Figure 4.1. The series of stages is meant to indicate that, when developing research questions, the researcher is involved in a process of progressive focusing down so that he or she moves from a general research

Student experience
The nature of research questions

Some of the students worked with quite explicit and narrowly formulated research questions. For example, Rebecca Barnes writes:

> My research questions were: What forms and dynamics of abuse do women experience in same-sex relationships? What opportunities and challenges do women experience with respect to seeking support for woman-to-woman partner abuse? What impacts does being abused by a female partner have upon women's identities and biographies? How are women's accounts of woman-to-woman partner abuse similar to and different from heterosexual women's accounts of partner abuse?

Isabella Robbins was similarly explicit about her research questions:

- How do mothers frame their decisions regarding childhood vaccination? In particular, do they present this as a matter of moral obligation (to their child/to the community)?
- Do mothers consider they have a choice regarding childhood vaccination? If so, in what sense do they see this as a choice and what, if any, constraints do they identify as they seek to exercise that choice?
- How do women place themselves and their decisions about childhood vaccination, in terms of the discourse of risk, responsibility, autonomy, and expertise?
- What role do women accord to partners, mothers, siblings, and professionals in their decision-making about childhood vaccination?

Others opted for research questions that were somewhat more general and wider in focus. Erin Sanders writes of her research questions for her study:

> What are the policy goals of women's NGOs in Thailand? How do these goals relate to the needs of women in the sex industry?

In a similar vein, Gareth Matthews writes:

> My research questions were quite general. (i) What is the role of migrant workers in the UK's hospitality sector? (ii) What can this tell us about the relevance and usefulness of Marxist labour process theory?

Gareth went on to write:

> These questions stem from my theoretical concerns, and a desire for the thesis to be guided by the findings and theoretical developments in relation to these findings during the course of the research. I did not want to begin with a specific hypothesis, and then to proceed by attempting to 'prove' or 'disprove' this, but sought instead to start with a general theoretical belief about work, and then to remain open-minded so as to allow the direction of research to be guided by the qualitative findings as they unfolded.

To read more, go to the Online Resource Centre: www.oxfordtextbooks.co.uk/orc/brymansrm5e/

area down to specific research questions. In making this movement, we have to recognize that:

- We cannot answer all the research questions that occur to us. This is not just to do with issues of time and the cost of doing research. It is very much to do with the fact that we must keep a clear focus, so that our research questions relate to each other and form a coherent set of issues.

- We therefore have to select from the possible research questions that we arrive at.

- In making our selection, we should be guided by the principle that the research questions we choose should be related to one another. If they are not, our research will probably lack focus and we may not make as clear a contribution to understanding as would be the case if research questions were connected. Thus, in the example in Figure 4.1, the research questions relating to risk are closely connected.

In the section on 'Criteria for evaluating research questions' below, some suggestions are presented about the kinds of considerations that should be taken into account when developing your own research questions.

Criteria for evaluating research questions

Research questions for a dissertation or project should exhibit the following characteristics.

- They should be *clear*, in the sense of being intelligible.

- They should be *researchable*—that is, they should allow you to do research in relation to them. This means that they should not be formulated in terms that are so abstract that they cannot be converted into researchable points.

- They should have some *connection(s) with established theory and research*. This means that there should be a literature on which you can draw to help illuminate how your research questions should be approached. Even if you find a topic that has been scarcely addressed by social scientists, it is unlikely that there will be no relevant literature (for example, on related or parallel topics).

- Your research questions should be *linked* to each other. Unrelated research questions are unlikely to be acceptable, since you should be developing an argument in your dissertation. You could not very readily construct a single argument in relation to unrelated research questions.

- They should at the very least hold out the prospect of being able to make an *original contribution*—however small—to the topic.

- The research questions should be *neither too broad* (so that you would need a massive grant to study them) *nor too narrow* (so that you cannot make a reasonably significant contribution to your area of study).

If you are stuck about how to formulate research questions (or other phases of your research), it is always a good idea to look at journal articles to see how other researchers have formulated them. Also, look at past dissertations for ideas. What should become clear is that it is crucial for research questions to be *justified*. You need to show how your research questions came about and why they are important. Marx's list of sources of research questions in Thinking Deeply 4.1 is helpful, but you have to demonstrate the link between your research questions and a body of literature. As noted in the third point in the list of bullet points that precedes this paragraph, research questions 'should have some connection(s) with established theory and research', but in addition to the questions *having* a connection, that connection has to be *demonstrated*.

As an example we can examine the study from Research in focus 1.1 (see also Table 1.1). The researchers begin by noting the results of research showing that the British power elite is dominated by Oxford and Cambridge undergraduates, which leads Zimdars et al. (2009) to propose that admissions tutors at these universities act as gatekeepers to entry into the elite. They also note the potential significance for understanding this process of social reproduction of Bourdieu's theory of cultural reproduction, which 'seeks to explain the link between social class of origin and social class of destination in terms of the impact of cultural capital on educational attainment' (Zimdars et al. 2009: 650). In a section with the heading 'Research Questions', the authors go on to write that they 'aim to assess whether cultural capital is linked to success in gaining admission to Oxford University for those who apply' (Zimdars et al. 2009: 653). Following a set of reflections on the issue, they outline their five research questions, which can be found in Research in focus 1.1. Thus, the authors justify and demonstrate the significance of their research questions through identifying a social problem and the literature relating to it and then proposing the use of an established theoretical perspective (Bourdieu's theory of cultural capital) as a plausible account of the process of social and cultural reproduction. Thus, the authors take the reader through the rationale and justification for their research questions by forging several links with a social problem, the research literature relating to it, and a theoretical tradition.

Supervisor tips
The problem of research questions

Several of the supervisors were contacted for their views on the experiences of students doing small projects, dissertations, and theses. They were asked whether they felt it is important for students to formulate research questions; all nine felt it is crucial. Some of them identified problems with the identification and formulation of research questions as a difficult area for many students. When asked the three most common problems encountered by dissertation students, Supervisor A replied 'vague research questions', while Supervisor D presented the issue as a drama:

Me	'What are your research questions?'
Student	'I want to do something on [topic x].'
Me	'But what do you want to find out?'
Student	'[silence]'

Supervisors also came up with some helpful advice to students. Supervisor A said: 'Draft your research questions and tentative methods: make it [the research] realistic and doable in three months.' Supervisor I said: 'Keep your research questions focused and don't be over ambitious in terms of the scope of your study'. Supervisor H says he encourages students 'to return to the research questions and their proposal to see if it is still appropriate. Ask them to think about what they are actually trying to find out.'

Supervisor D also wrote about the problem of students choosing research methods before formulating research questions. Similarly, Supervisor I wrote: 'Although we teach them that they should choose methods and methodologies on the basis of the nature of the research question, I feel some students choose the method and then decide on the research question.' In other words, students decide what method they intend to use and then think about possible research questions. To some extent, this is not surprising, because, although teachers of research methods and writers of textbooks such as the present one observe that the choice of method should be shaped by the research question(s) being asked, researchers do not always follow this practice (Bryman 2007a).

Supervisor tips
Research questions provide guidance

Research questions can provide students with important guidance when they may have difficulty 'seeing the wood for the trees'. Students sometimes feel overwhelmed by the data they have collected. Returning to the original research questions can be instructive, as Supervisor I helpfully advises:

> Students can sometimes be overwhelmed by the amount of data they have collected and experience difficulty organizing the final dissertation. Everything seems to be relevant to them. I encourage them to answer the research questions they set themselves at the beginning of the exercise and nothing but the research questions. I tell them to write the key research questions (usually no more than three) on a postcard or post-it and place it at eye level just above the computer screen.

Supervisor D advises students to consider analysis issues early and in relation to the research questions they are asking:

> I try to encourage them to think about their analysis during or shortly after the construction of their research questions. By the time they are thinking about research design, they should have a rough idea about what their analysis will look like (i.e. they must do, as it will link their research design to their research questions).

Writing your research proposal

In preparation for your dissertation, you may be required to write a short proposal outlining what your research will be about and how you intend to go about it. This is a useful way of preparing for your research and it will encourage you to consider many of the issues covered in the next section. In addition to outlining your topic area, your research questions, and your proposed research design and methods, the proposal will ask you to demonstrate some knowledge of the relevant literature—for example, by identifying several key authors or significant research studies. This information may be used as the basis for allocating a supervisor who is knowledgeable in your research area or who has experience with your proposed research approach. The proposal is also a useful basis for discussion of your research project with your supervisor, and, if it includes a timetable, this can provide a template for planning regular meetings with your supervisor to review your progress. Developing a timetable can be very important in making you think about aspects of the overall research process, such as the different stages of your research and their timing, and in giving you a series of ongoing goals to aim for. Even if you are not required to produce a research proposal, it is worth constructing a timetable and asking your supervisor to look at it, so that you can assess how (un)realistic your goals are and whether you are allowing enough time for each component of the research process.

When writing a research proposal, there are a number of issues that you will probably need to cover.

- What is your research topic or, alternatively, what are your research objectives?

- Why is your research topic (or why are those research objectives) important?

- What is your research question or what are your research questions?

- What does the literature have to say about your research topic/objectives and research question(s)?

- How are you going to go about collecting data relevant to your research question(s)? In other words, what research methods are you intending to use?

- Why are the research methods/sources you have selected the appropriate ones for your research question(s)?

- Who will your research participants be and how will they be selected (or if the research will employ documents, what kinds of documents will be the focus of your attention and how will they be selected)?

- If your research requires you to secure access to organizations, have you done so? If you have not, what obstacles do you anticipate?

- What resources will you need to conduct your research (for example, postage, travel costs, recording and transcription equipment, photocopying, software) and how will those resources be funded?

- What is your timetable for the different stages of the project?

- What problems do you anticipate in doing the research (for example, access to organizations)?

- What are the possible ethical problems associated with your research?

- How will you analyse your data?

Writing a proposal is therefore useful in getting you started and encouraging you to set realistic objectives for your research project. In some higher education institutions, the research proposal may form part (albeit a small one) of the overall assessment of the dissertation or report that is produced out of the research. While the research proposal is a working document and the ideas that you set out in it can be refined and developed as your research progresses, it is important to bear in mind that, if you keep changing your mind about your area of research and your research design, you will use up valuable time needed to complete the dissertation within the deadline.

Preparing for your research

Do not begin your data collection until you have identified your research questions reasonably clearly. Develop your data-collection instruments with these research questions at the forefront of your thinking. If you do not do this, there is the risk that your results will not allow you to illuminate the research questions. If at all possible, conduct a small pilot study to determine how well your research instruments work.

You will also need to think about access and sampling issues. If your research requires you to gain access to or the cooperation of one or more closed settings such as an organization, you need to confirm at the earliest opportunity that you have the necessary permission to conduct your work. You also need to consider how you will go about gaining access to people. These issues lead you into sampling considerations, such as the following.

- Who do you need to study in order to investigate your research questions?

- How easily can you gain access to a **sampling frame**?

- What kind of sampling strategy will you employ (for example, **probability sampling**, **quota sampling**, **theoretical sampling**, **convenience sampling**)?

- Can you justify your choice of sampling method?

Also, while preparing for your data collection, you should consider whether there are any ethical problems associated with your research methods or your approach to contacting people (see Chapter 6).

 # Doing your research and analysing your results

Since doing your research and analysing your results are what the bulk of this book will be about, it is not necessary at this stage to go into detail, but here are some useful hints about practicalities.

- Keep good records of what you do. A research **diary** can be helpful here, but there are several other things to bear in mind. For example, if you are doing a survey by postal questionnaire, keep good records of who has replied, so that you know who should be sent reminders. If participant observation is a component of your research, remember to keep good field notes and not to rely on your memory.

- Make sure that you are thoroughly familiar with any hardware you are using in collecting your data, such as audio-recorders for interviewing, and make sure it is in good working order (for example, batteries that are not flat or close to being flat).

- Do not wait until all your data have been collected to begin coding. This recommendation applies to both quantitative and qualitative research. If you are

conducting a questionnaire survey, begin coding your data and entering them into SPSS or whatever package you are using after you have put together a reasonably sized batch of completed questionnaires. In the case of qualitative data, such as interview transcripts, the same point applies, and, indeed, it is a specific recommendation of the proponents of grounded theory that data collection and analysis should be intertwined.

- Remember that the transcription of recorded interviews takes a long time. Allow at least six hours' transcription for every one hour of recorded interview talk, at least in the early stages of transcription.

- Become familiar with any data analysis packages as soon as possible. This familiarity will help you to establish whether you definitely need them and will ensure that you do not need to learn everything about them at the very time you need to use them for your analysis.

- Do not at any time take risks with your personal safety (see Tips and skills 'Safety in research').

 ## Tips and skills
Safety in research

In the middle of December 2002, a 19-year-old female student who had just started a degree course in sociology and community studies at Manchester Metropolitan University went missing. It was believed that, in order to complete a coursework assignment, she had gone to conduct a life history interview with a person aged over 50. Since she was interested in the homeless, it was thought that she had gone to interview a homeless person. Because of concerns about her safety, her tutor had advised her to take a friend and to conduct the interview in a public place. In fact, she had not gone to conduct the interview and to everyone's relief turned up in Dublin. There is an important lesson in this incident. You must bear in mind that social research may on occasions place you in potentially dangerous situations. You should avoid taking personal risks at all costs and you should resist any attempts to place yourself in situations where personal harm is a real possibility. Just as you should ensure that no harm comes to research participants (as prescribed in the discussion of ethical principles in Chapter 6), individuals involved in directing others' research should not place students and researchers in situations in which they might come to harm. Equally, lone researchers should avoid such situations. Sometimes, as with the interviews with the homeless, there is some possibility of being in a hazardous situation, in which case, if the researcher feels confident about doing the interview, he or she needs to take precautions before going ahead with the interview. The advice given by the student's tutor—to take someone with her and to conduct the interview in a public place—was very sensible for a potentially dangerous interview. If you have a mobile telephone, keep it with you and keep it switched on. Personal attack alarms may also be useful. You should also make sure that, if your interviews or your periods of observation are part of a programme of work, you establish a routine whereby you keep in regular contact with others. However, there may be situations in which there is no obvious reason to think that the situation may be dangerous, but where the researcher is faced with a sudden outburst of abuse or threatening behaviour. This can arise when people react relatively unpredictably to an interview question or to being observed. If there are signs that such behaviour is imminent (for example, through body language), begin a withdrawal from the research situation. Further guidelines on these issues can be found in Craig et al. (2000).

Lee (2004) draws an important distinction between two kinds of danger in fieldwork: ambient and situational. The former refers to situations that are avoidable and in which danger is an ingredient of the context. Fieldwork in conflict situations of the kind encountered by the researcher who took on the role of a bouncer (Hobbs et al. 2003) would be an example of this kind of danger. Situational danger occurs 'when the researcher's presence or activities evoke aggression, hostility or violence from those within the setting' (Lee 2004: 1285). While problems surrounding safety may be easier to anticipate in the case of ambient danger, they are less easy to foresee in connection with situational danger. However, that is not to say that ambient danger is entirely predictable. It was only some time after she had begun her research in a hospital laboratory that Lankshear (2000) realized that there was a possibility of her being exposed to dangerous pathogens.

Sources: P. Barkham and R. Jenkins, 'Fears for Fresher who Vanished on Mission to talk to the Homeless', *The Times*, 13 December 2002; S. McIntyre, 'How did Vicky Vanish?', *Daily Mail*, 13 December 2002; R. Jenkins, 'Wasteland Search for Missing Student', *The Times*, 14 December 2002.

Checklist
Planning a research project

....

○ Do you know what the requirements for your dissertation are, as set out by your university or department?

○ Have you made contact with your supervisor?

○ Have you allowed enough time for planning, collecting and analysing data, and writing up your research project?

○ Do you have a clear timetable for your research project with clearly identifiable milestones for the achievement of specific tasks?

○ Have you got sufficient financial and practical resources (for example, money to enable travel to research site, recording device) to enable you to carry out your research project?

○ Have you formulated some research questions and discussed these with your supervisor?

○ Are the research questions you have identified capable of being answered through your research project?

○ Do you have the access that you require in order to carry out your research?

○ Do you know which research participants or what materials (e.g. documents) are needed to answer your research questions and how to locate and sample them?

○ Have you established which research method(s) you are planning to use and why?

○ Are you familiar with the data analysis software that you will be using to analyse your data?

○ Have you allowed others to comment on your work so far and responded to their feedback?

○ Have you checked out whether there are likely to be any ethical issues that might be raised in connection with your research?

○ Have you allowed enough time for getting clearance through an ethics committee, if that is required for your research?

》 *Key points*

- Follow the dissertation guidelines provided by your institution.
- Thinking about your research subject can be time-consuming, so allow plenty of time for this aspect of the dissertation process.
- Use your supervisor to the fullest extent allowed and follow the advice offered by him or her.
- Plan your time carefully and be realistic about what you can achieve in the time available.
- Formulate some research questions to express what it is about your area of interest that you want to know.
- Writing a research proposal is a good way of getting started on your research project and encouraging you to set realistic objectives.
- Consider access and sampling issues at an early stage and consider testing your research methods by conducting a pilot study.
- Keep good records of what you do in your research as you go along and don't wait until all your data have been collected before you start coding.

❓ *Questions for review*

Managing time and resources

- Why is it important to devise a timetable for your research project?

Formulating suitable research questions

- Why are research questions necessary?
- What are the main sources of research questions?
- What are the main steps involved in developing research questions?
- What criteria can be used to evaluate research questions?

Writing your research proposal

- What is the purpose of the research proposal and how can it be useful?

Online Resource Centre

www.oxfordtextbooks.co.uk/orc/brymansrm5e/

Visit the Online Resource Centre to enrich your understanding of planning a research project and formulating research questions. Follow up links to other resources, test yourself using multiple choice questions, and gain further guidance and inspiration from the Student Researcher's Toolkit.

5
Getting started: reviewing the literature

Chapter outline

Chapter guide

The chapter provides guidance for students on how to get started on their research project. Once you have identified your research questions (see Chapter 4), the next step in any research project is to search the existing literature and write a literature review. The principal task at this early stage involves reviewing the main ideas and research relating to your chosen area of interest. This provides the basis for writing a literature review, which forms an important part of the dissertation. This chapter will advise students on how to go about searching the literature and engaging critically with the ideas of other writers. It will also help you to understand some of the expectations of the literature review and provide some ideas about how to assess the quality of existing research.

Reviewing the existing literature

Reviewing the existing literature relating to your topic of interest is a crucial stage in conducting research. The aim of the literature review is to establish what is already known about the topic and to frame the review in such a way that it can act as a background and justification for your investigation. Increasingly, a distinction is drawn between two kinds of literature review: *narrative reviews* and *systematic reviews*. Narrative reviews are the traditional kind of literature review in which the researcher provides an account of what is already known about the area of interest as a prelude to conducting his or her own research. Narrative reviews can be stand-alone reviews; in other words, the aim may be to provide an account of the literature as an end in itself. For example, the researcher may want to review the research on British migrants abroad and to link the findings to theories of identity. In such a case, the narrative review is not a prelude to doing research. Systematic reviews tend to be stand-alone reviews; in other words, they are not typically carried out as a prelude to doing research, although the results of doing a systematic review may act as a springboard for subsequent research. Systematic reviewers use very explicit procedures to arrive at a synthesis of a body of literature. The typical context for the application of systematic review procedures is a research question of the 'what works?' kind. For example, Yager et al. (2013) conducted a systematic review to assess the effectiveness of classroom-based programmes designed to improve the body image of secondary school students.

When people refer to 'doing your literature review', it is nearly always the traditional narrative review to which they are referring. Students may conduct a systematic review, but this will typically be an exercise in its own right rather than a precursor to doing their own research. The bulk of the advice in this chapter relates to doing a narrative review, as this is the typical type of literature review that will be expected of you in the context of doing a project or dissertation. I also make the point below that some systematic review procedures are creeping into the conduct of narrative reviews. This is not to say that the distinction is breaking down but that there is a recognition that there are aspects of systematic reviews that are both desirable (such as the explicitness of searching the literature) and readily incorporated into narrative reviews.

 # Narrative review

Most literature reviews take the form of **narrative reviews**. This means that they seek to arrive at an overview of a field of study through a reasonably comprehensive assessment and critical interpretation of the literature, usually as a prelude to conducting one's own research in the area. An example of a narrative review is given in Research in focus 5.1.

Literature reviews are typically of the narrative kind, regardless of whether they are meant to be springboards for the reviewer's own investigation (for example, when the literature is reviewed as a means of specifying what is already known in connection with a research topic, so that research questions can be identified that the reviewer will then examine) or are ends in their own right (as a means of summarizing what is known in an area). When I examine examples of writing up research in Chapter 28, I will show that the literature relating to the researcher's area of interest is always reviewed as a means of establishing

why the researcher conducted the research and what its contribution is likely to be. Such reviews are still mainly narrative reviews. Compared to systematic reviews, narrative reviews can appear rather haphazard (thus making them difficult to reproduce), of questionable comprehensiveness, and lacking in discrimination in terms of the kind of evidence used, though such a view is by no means always held (see Thinking deeply 5.3). It may be that this accounts for the growing incorporation of procedures associated with systematic reviews into narrative reviews (see Thinking deeply 5.4).

A narrative review is an examination of theory and research relating to your field of interest that outlines what is already known and that frames and justifies your research question(s). It therefore both acts as a background to what you want to research and provides a platform for establishing what the contribution of your research will be.

 ## Research in focus 5.1
A narrative review

The research referred to in Research in focus 2.4 will be used as an example of the construction of a narrative review as background for an empirical study. Röder and Mühlau (2014) begin by making several assertions that are backed up by the literature. For example, they note that egalitarian gender roles are increasingly promoted at the policy level in many countries but that there are considerable differences between countries in terms of attitudes towards the role of women. Two articles are cited to support the first point and one to support the second. In this way, the literature is being used to locate the relevance of the issues addressed in the article. In the second paragraph, the authors write that 'comparatively little research systematically explores the gender-role attitudes of migrant men and women in this context' (2014: 899). They then go on to examine the literature that relates to this issue. For example, they explain that the literature 'has shown the more socially conservative values of immigrants and their children' (2014: 900) and three articles are cited to support this point. They then point to some of the limitations of this literature. The third paragraph raises a further but related issue, namely 'whether acculturation occurs largely within the first generation, or mainly between generations' (2014: 900), and they refer to some studies that relate to this issue but which do not actually answer the question. In the fourth paragraph we are told that the article also 'explores gender differences in acculturation patterns' (2014: 900) and some relevant research evidence is examined. In the next section of the article, the authors examine the research literature relating to gender egalitarianism in post-industrial societies. They note that the literature shows that migrants to Europe often come from countries where gender relations are less equal; they propose that this raises the question of whether these attitudes continue on arrival in Europe both within and across generations, which is the focus of the next section of the article. In this next section, they examine research relating to the issue of the significance of 'origin-country context' for immigrants' gender attitudes. This leads them to propose the first of five hypotheses, which is immediately followed by a consideration of the evidence that exists for this hypothesis. The following section deals with the issue of inter-generational acculturation, and at one point the authors write:

> Unlike members of mainstream society, immigrant children partake of two different cultural spheres. They grow up in immigrant families and communities that consider unequal gender roles part of their ethnic identity and aim to transmit their cultural values to their children. In many cases, this includes active strategies to shelter their children from the exposure to mainstream society by locating their families in ethnically segregated neighborhoods, selecting educational institutions, limiting the contact of their children with peers from mainstream society, and arranging intra-ethnic marriages (Portes and Rumbaut 2001). Some empirical studies suggest that these strategies are only partially successful. For example, foreign-born Arab women usually have less egalitarian values than Arab women born in the United States (Read 2003). Similarly, second-generation Turks in Germany have attitudes that lie between those of natives and first-generation Turks (Diehl, Koenig, and Ruckdeschel 2009). Based on these theoretical arguments and empirical findings, we expect that inter- generational acculturation has as a consequence that the gap in gender egalitarianism between mainstream society and immigrants is reduced for the second generation, and that intergenerational acculturation also reduces the differences among second-generation immigrant groups; i.e., that the origin-country context loses its influence on outcomes.

> (Röder and Mühlau 2014: 903)

This statement immediately precedes the second hypothesis, which is presented in Research in focus 2.4. The chief points to note about this literature review are:

- A story, or more precisely a series of stories, is built up about the literature. There is a story about the growing prevalence of egalitarian gender role attitudes in many countries and its significance for migrants who come from countries where these attitudes are not prevalent, and there is a story about the possible significance of acculturation across generations, that is, the possibility that across generations, the non-egalitarian attitudes become eroded.

- The literature is *used* to position the significance of the article. The authors show that there is existing research relating to these issues but that it is sparse and sometimes indirect.

- The literature is employed as a means of justifying the authors' hypotheses.

- The review is structured through the use of sub-headings around a number of themes.

What Röder and Mühlau do *not* do is just provide a series of points about the literature. Instead, they use the stories they devise about the literature to guide the reader towards what they take to be significant and important about it. The reader is told about what the existing research says, why it is relevant but deficient, what its significance is for the research that the authors carried out, and how it justifies their hypotheses.

Why do you need to review the existing literature? The most obvious reason is that you want to know what is already known about your area of interest so that you do not simply 'reinvent the wheel'. Your literature review demonstrates that you are able to engage in scholarly review based on your reading and understanding of the work of others. Beyond this, using the existing literature on a topic is a means of developing an argument about the significance of your research and where it leads. The simile of a *story* is also sometimes used in this context (see Thinking deeply 5.1).

Thinking deeply 5.1
The presentation of literature in articles based on qualitative research on organizations

Further useful advice on relating your own work to the literature can be gleaned from an examination of the ways in which articles based on qualitative research on organizations are composed. In their examination of such articles, Golden-Biddle and Locke (1993, 1997) argue that good articles in this area develop a story—that is, a clear and compelling framework around which the writing is structured. This idea is very much in tune with Wolcott's (1990a: 18) recommendation to 'determine the basic story you are going to tell'. Golden-Biddle and Locke's research suggests that the way the author's position in relation to the literature is presented is an important component of storytelling. They distinguish two processes in the ways that the literature is conveyed.

1. Constructing intertextual coherence. This refers to the way in which existing knowledge is represented and organized; the author shows how contributions to the literature relate to each other and the research reported. The techniques used are:
   - *Synthesized coherence* puts together work that is generally considered unrelated; theory and research previously regarded as unconnected are pieced together. There are two prominent forms:
     i. very incompatible references (bits and pieces) are organized and brought together;
     ii. connections are forged between established theories or research programmes.
   - *Progressive coherence* portrays the building up of an area of knowledge around which there is considerable consensus.
   - *Non-coherence* recognizes that there have been many contributions to a certain research programme, but that there is considerable disagreement among practitioners.

Each of these strategies is designed to leave room for a contribution to be made.

2. Problematizing the situation. The literature is then subverted by locating a problem. The following techniques were identified:
   - *Incomplete*. The existing literature is not fully complete; there is a gap (see also Sandberg and Alvesson 2011).
   - *Inadequate*. The existing literature on the phenomenon of interest has neglected ways of looking at it that can greatly improve our understanding of it; alternative perspectives or frameworks can then be introduced.
   - *Incommensurate*. This argues for an alternative perspective that is superior to the literature as it stands. It differs from 'inadequate problematization' because it portrays the existing literature as 'wrong, misguided, or incorrect' (Golden-Biddle and Locke 1997: 43).

The key point about Golden-Biddle and Locke's account of the way the literature is construed in this field is that it is used by writers to achieve a number of things.

- They demonstrate their competence by referring to prominent writings in the field (Gilbert 1977).
- They develop their version of the literature in such a way as to show and to lead up to the contribution they will be making in the article.
- The gap or problem in the literature that is identified corresponds to the research questions.

The idea of writing up one's research as storytelling acts as a useful reminder that reviewing the literature, which is part of the story, should link seamlessly with the rest of the article and not be considered as a separate element.

A competent review of the literature is at least in part a means of affirming your credibility as someone who is knowledgeable in your chosen area. This is not simply a matter of reproducing the theories and opinions of other scholars, but also involves being able to interpret what they have written, possibly by using their ideas to support a particular viewpoint or argument. Denney and Tewkesbury (2013) report that 77 per cent of reviewers of manuscripts submitted for publication in journals in the field of criminal justice and criminology say that the quality of the literature review is a significant influence on their judgements. This finding is unlikely to be specific to this field and will almost certainly apply to the literature review that forms part of a student's project or dissertation.

The purpose of examining the existing literature should be to identify the following issues:

- What is already known about this area?
- What concepts and theories are relevant to this area?
- What research methods and research designs have been employed in studying this area?
- Are there any significant controversies?
- Are there any inconsistencies in findings relating to this area?
- Are there any unanswered research questions in this area?
- How does the literature relate to your research questions?

This last issue points to the possibility that you will be able to revise and refine your research questions in the process of reviewing the literature. Answering these seven questions will provide the material you need for establishing the contribution of your own research because you can demonstrate how it links with what is already known in the area.

Tips and skills
Ways of conceptualizing a literature review

Bruce's (1994) study of research students' early experiences of the dissertation literature review identified six qualitatively different ways in which the review process was experienced or understood by postgraduates. The six conceptions included:

1. *List*. The literature review is understood as a list comprising pertinent items representing the literature of the subject.

2. *Search*. The review is a process of identifying relevant information and the focus is on finding or looking, which may involve going through sources (for example, article, database) to identify information.

3. *Survey*. Students also see the literature review as an investigation of past and present writing or research on a subject; this investigation may be active (critical/analytical) or passive (descriptive).

4. *Vehicle*. The review is also seen as having an impact on the researcher, because it is seen as a vehicle for learning that leads to an increase in his or her knowledge and understanding. Within this conception the review acts as a sounding board through which the student can check ideas or test personal perceptions.

5. *Facilitator*. The literature review can be understood as directly related to the research that is about to be or is being undertaken, the process helping the researcher to identify a topic, support a methodology, provide a context, or change research direction. The review thus helps to shape the course of the student's research.

6. *Report*. The review is understood as a written discussion of the literature, drawing on previously conducted investigations. The focus is on 'framing a written discourse about the literature which may be established as a component part of a thesis or other research report' (Bruce 1994: 223).

These six conceptions reflect the varying relationship between the student and the literature, the earlier ones being more indirect—the student works with items that represent the primary literature, such as bibliographic citations—and the latter conceptions being more direct—the student works with source material, rather than, for example, a representative abstract. The conceptions can also be seen as cumulative, since a student who adopts the facilitator conception may also continue to hold the conception of the literature review as a survey. Bruce therefore recommends that students be encouraged to adopt the higher-level conceptions (3–6), because through these the other ways of experiencing the literature review (1–3) become more meaningful.

Tips and skills
Reasons for writing a literature review

The following is a list of reasons for writing a literature review.

- You need to know what is already known in connection with your research area, because you do not want to be accused of reinventing the wheel.
- The person reading and assessing your work may not be familiar with the specific details of the area you are researching and so needs to be given some background information about it.
- You can learn from other researchers' mistakes and avoid making the same ones.
- You can learn about different theoretical and methodological approaches to your research area.
- It may help you to develop an analytic framework.
- It may lead you to consider the inclusion of variables in your research that you might not otherwise have thought about.
- It may suggest further research questions for you.
- It will help with the interpretation of your findings.
- It gives you some pegs on which to hang your findings.
- It provides a platform for you to establish the significance of your research.
- It is expected!

Getting the most from your reading

Since a great deal of time during the early stages of your research project will be taken up with reading the existing literature in order to write your review, it is important to make sure you prepare yourself for this stage. Getting the most out of your reading involves developing your skills in being able to read actively and critically. When you are reading the existing literature try to do the following.

- Take good notes, including the publication details of the material you read. It is infuriating to find that you forgot to record the volume number of an article that you read and that needs to be included in your bibliography. This may necessitate a trip to the library on occasions when you are already hard pressed for time.

- Develop critical reading skills. In reviewing the literature you should do more than simply summarize what you have read. You should, whenever appropriate, be critical in your approach. It is worth developing these skills and recording relevant critical points in the course of taking notes. Developing a critical approach does not necessarily mean simply criticizing the work of others. It entails moving beyond mere description and asking questions about the significance of the work. It entails attending to such issues as: How does the item relate to others you have read? Are there any apparent strengths and deficiencies—perhaps in terms of methodology or in terms of the credibility of the conclusions drawn? What

theoretical ideas have influenced the item you are reading? What are the implications of the author's ideas and/or findings? What was the author's objective in conducting the research? What are the main conclusions and are they warranted on the basis of the data provided in the item? What are the author's assumptions?

- Your search for literature should be guided by your research questions, but as well you should use your review of the literature as a means of showing why your research questions are important. For example, if one of your arguments in arriving at your research questions is that, although a lot of research has been done on X (a general topic or area, such as the secularization process, female entrepreneurship, or inter-ethnic relations), little or no research has been done on X_1 (an aspect of X), the literature review is the point where you can justify this assertion. Alternatively, it might be that there are two competing positions with regard to X_1 and you are going to investigate which one provides a better understanding. In the literature review, you should outline the nature of the differences between the competing positions. The literature review, then, allows you to locate your own research within a tradition of research in an area. Indeed, reading the literature is itself often an important source of research questions, so that there is an interplay between research questions and the literature.

- Bear in mind that you will want to return to much of the literature that you examine in the discussion of your findings and in your conclusion. Doing this allows you to demonstrate the significance of your research.

- Do not try to get everything you read into a literature review. Trying to force everything you have read into your review (because of all the hard work involved in uncovering and reading the material) is not going to help you. The literature review must assist you in developing an argument, and bringing in irrelevant material may undermine your ability to get your argument across.

- Reading the literature is not something that you should stop doing once you begin designing your research. You should continue your search for and reading of relevant literature throughout your research. This means that, if you have written a literature review before beginning your data collection, you will need to regard it as provisional. Indeed, you may want to make quite

substantial revisions of your review towards the end of writing up your work.

- Do not just summarize the literature you have read. Quite aside from the fact that it is boring to read such a summary, it does not tell the reader what you have made of the literature or how it fits into your research project or relates to your research questions. Try to use the literature to tell a story about it. Some useful suggestions about how to develop the literature in this way can be found in Thinking deeply 5.1. The different ways of construing the literature that are presented in this box are derived from a review of qualitative studies of organizations, but the approaches identified have a much broader applicability, including to quantitative research.

- The study by Holbrook et al. (2007) referred to in Thinking deeply 5.2 contains some useful implications

Thinking deeply 5.2
What do examiners look for in a literature review?

Holbrook et al. (2007) conducted an analysis of examiners' reports on PhD theses. They analysed 1,310 reports relating to 501 theses in Australia (a PhD thesis is examined by at least two examiners). These reports are naturally-occurring documents, in that examiners have to provide these reports as part of the process of examining a PhD candidate. In the course of writing a report, examiners frequently if not invariably comment on the literature review. While these findings are obviously specific to PhD theses, the features that examiners look for are also applicable in general terms to other kinds of writing, such as an undergraduate or a postgraduate dissertation.

Holbrook et al. analysed the reports using computer-assisted qualitative data analysis software, which will be covered in Chapter 25. The analysis of these reports suggests that comments concerning the literature review were of three basic kinds:

1. *Comments about coverage of the literature.* This was by far the most common type of comment and signals whether the candidate has covered and made sense of a broad swathe of the literature.

2. *Identification of errors.* This type of comment relates to such things as references being omitted from the bibliography, misreporting of references, and inconsistent presentation of referencing and quotations.

3. *Comments about 'use and application' of the literature.* Although this was the least common of the types of comment made by examiners, it attracts the bulk of the attention of Holbrook et al. It is made up of a number of subcategories of comment:
   - whether the literature is used to develop and sustain an argument;
   - whether the author shows clear familiarity with the literature;
   - whether the review develops a critical assessment of the literature (the ability to 'weigh up the literature and subject it to critical appraisal, ideally to lead to a new or interesting perspective'; Holbrook et al. 2007: 348);
   - whether the review connects the literature to findings;
   - whether the author demonstrates an appreciation of the disciplinary context of the literature.

One of the main themes running through these latter remarks is that the student should not just summarize the literature, simply because he or she knows that a literature review has to be undertaken. Examiners look for evidence that the candidate *uses* the literature—to develop an argument, to connect with his or her findings, or to develop a distinctive stance on the subject. However, undoubtedly, the thing that disconcerts examiners most is evidence of poor coverage of the literature, as it signals a lack of engagement with and a limited appreciation of the subject.

Student experience
Importance of doing a literature review

Lily Taylor does not appear to need convincing about the necessity of doing a literature review. As she notes:

> Looking at significant work that related to mine was good in the sense that it enabled me to look at the use of methodology and access key concepts and characteristics of the work.

For several of the students, the literature in their chosen area had an influence on their research questions. For example, Alice Palmer writes about her dissertation research on the changing role of the modern stay-at-home mother:

> Lots of reading to identify gaps in previous research was the most important way of formulating research questions. However, it is also important to follow 'gut feelings' about what needs investigating, even if it has been done before, because things could have changed over time.

Amy Knight wrote in connection with her project on recycling and gender differences:

> I completed extensive reading focusing on the topics of recycling and gender differences. In previous studies gender differences regarding levels of environmental concern tended to be similar (that females demonstrated higher levels of environmental concern than men). However, previous published research was inconclusive regarding recycling habits and gender differences. I was interested to see whether levels of environmental concern could also link to recycling habits hence the two research questions.

 To read more, go to the Online Resource Centre: www.oxfordtextbooks.co.uk/orc/brymansrm5e/

from a study of PhD examiners' reports for conducting a literature review. One of the most central implications of it is to emphasize the importance of having a comprehensive coverage of the literature. While comprehensive coverage might be an expectation for PhD candidates, this may be more difficult to achieve for undergraduate and postgraduate dissertations. At the very least, it implies that it is essential to make sure that key references are included in the review.

I do not agree with the tendency among some social scientists (who are often supporters of systematic reviews) to demonize the traditional narrative review (see Thinking deeply 5.3). What are often being criticized are poorly-conducted literature reviews, and these do not inevitably represent all reviews that are not systematic reviews. Also, systematic reviews are invariably guided by a research question, and this is not necessarily an appropriate stance for reviews which act as background to an empirical study. Here the goal is usually to show what is already known about theory and research relating to the area with which the author's research is concerned.

Here are a few tips when conducting a narrative literature review:

- Be reasonably comprehensive in your coverage of the literature. This will mean becoming familiar with

online and other ways of searching the literature, which is the focus of the rest of this chapter. At the very least, ensure you cover the principal publications relating to your area of interest.

- Do not just describe the content of each item in your literature review. Try to comment on each item and show how it relates to other items of literature.

- Try to be balanced in your presentation of the literature. Do not favour some authors or research with greater attention unless you want to make a particular point about their work: for example, that you are going to try to reproduce their methods in a different context.

- Bring together (i.e. synthesize) the material that you include. Forge an argument about the various items of literature. A common flaw in students' literature reviews is a tendency to present the literature review as a series or list of points so that it looks more like a set of notes (A says this, B notes that, C says something else, D says yet something else, etc., etc.). Show how the items of literature that you cover in your literature review relate to each other. Synthesize them and build up an argument about them.

- Building up an argument means creating a 'story' about the literature. This means asking yourself: what key

Tips and skills
Useful expressions in writing a literature review and coming to a conclusion

Bloggs et al. (2006) **drew on** Weber's (1947) concept of charismatic leadership for their research on why some departments in a large multinational firm were more effective than others. In particular, they **utilized** Weber's suggestion that having a compelling vision is a core competence of a charismatic leader. However, **according to** Cynic (2008) their research failed to take into account followers' views of leaders' visions and instead relied too much on what the leaders said about themselves. In addition, Sceptic et al. (2009) **suggest that** it is impossible to say with certainty that charismatic leadership was the cause of differences in effectiveness in the research by Bloggs et al. **Therefore, research in this field requires a greater emphasis on followers' views of leaders and the use of a research design that allows the effect of charismatic leadership to be properly inferred.**

Useful expressions for reporting the research and writings of others

An attempt to come to your own conclusions

point or points do you want to get across about the literature as a whole?

- Consider dividing the review up into themes or sub-themes that will help to structure the literature review. Do not quote too much. Try to use your own words. This is part of putting your own imprint on the literature and so part of building up a story about it.
- Include your own criticisms where appropriate. This is part of producing a critical stance on the literature, but it is not the only way. A component of coming up with a critical stance is showing how the work of the authors you review has made a distinctive contribution to the field.
- Examine some literature reviews. I do this in Chapter 28, where articles using quantitative, qualitative, and

mixed methods research are examined. Become familiar with some of the expressions social scientists use in writing their literature reviews (for examples, see the Tips and skills feature in this chapter on 'Useful expressions in writing a literature review and coming to a conclusion').

- Try to come up with a conclusion about the literature. OK, you have reviewed all these articles and books, but now tell your readers what you think your review demonstrates. Be clear about what you want to show through your literature review. If you want to show that there is a gap in the literature or that there is an inconsistency or that existing research has been dominated by a particular approach, make sure you hammer that point home. Do not leave it implicit.

Systematic review

In recent years, considerable attention has been lavished on the notion of **systematic review** (see Key concept 5.1). This is an approach to reviewing the literature that adopts explicit procedures. It has emerged as a focus of interest for two main reasons. One is that it is sometimes suggested (see e.g. Tranfield et al. 2003) that many reviews of the literature tend to 'lack thoroughness' and reflect the biases of the researcher. Proponents of systematic review suggest that adopting explicit procedures makes such biases less likely to surface. Second, in fields such as medicine, there has been a growing movement towards

evidence-based solutions to illnesses and treatments. Systematic reviews of the literature are often seen as an accompaniment to evidence-based approaches, as their goal is to provide advice for clinicians and practitioners based on all available evidence. Such reviews are deemed to be valuable for decision-makers, particularly in areas where there is conflicting evidence concerning treatments (as often occurs in the case of medicine).

The systematic review approach is beginning to diffuse into other areas, such as social policy, so that policy-makers and others can draw on reviews that summarize

Key concept 5.1
What is a systematic review?

Systematic review has been defined as 'a replicable, scientific and transparent process … that aims to minimize bias through exhaustive literature searches of published and unpublished studies and by providing an audit trail of the reviewer's decisions, procedures and conclusions' (Tranfield et al. 2003: 209). Such a review is often contrasted with the traditional narrative review. The proponents of systematic review suggest that it is more likely to generate unbiased and comprehensive accounts of the literature, especially in fields in which the aim is to understand whether a particular intervention has particular benefits, than those using the traditional review, which is often depicted by these proponents as haphazard. A systematic review that includes only quantitative studies and which seeks to summarize those studies quantitatively is a **meta-analysis** (see Chapter 14). In recent times, the development of systematic review procedures for qualitative studies has attracted a great deal of attention, especially in the social sciences. **Meta-ethnography** (see Chapter 24) is one such approach to the synthesis of qualitative findings, but currently there are several different methods, none of which is in widespread use (Mays et al. 2005).

the balance of the evidence in certain areas of practice. Tranfield and colleagues contrast systematic reviews with what they describe as 'traditional narrative reviews'. An example of systematic review is given in Research in focus 5.2. However, advocates of systematic review acknowledge that, unlike medical science, where systematic reviews are commonplace and often highly regarded, social scientific fields are often characterized by low consensus concerning key research questions because of the different theoretical approaches. Moreover, medical science is often concerned with research questions to do with answers to the question 'What works?'. Such questions are fairly well suited to systematic review in such fields as social policy, but they are less often encountered in other social science fields such as sociology.

Nonetheless, systematic review has attracted a great deal of attention in recent years, so it is worth exploring its main steps. Accounts of the systematic review process vary slightly, but they tend to comprise the following steps in roughly the following order.

1. *Define the purpose and scope of the review.* The review needs an explicit statement of the purpose of the review (invariably in the form of or leading to a research question) so that decisions about key issues, such as what kinds of research need to be searched for and what kinds of samples the research should relate to, can be made in a consistent way. It is often argued that, for a systematic review, the researcher and his or her team should assemble a panel to advise them on the precise formulation of the research question(s) to be examined and also to assist with suggestions for keywords for Step 2 (below).

2. *Seek out studies relevant to the scope and purpose of the review.* The reviewer should seek out studies relevant to the research question(s). The search will be based on keywords and terms relevant to the purpose defined in Step 1. The search strategy must be described in terms that allow it to be replicated. The reviewer has to consider which kinds of publication outlets should be incorporated. It is tempting to search for research published only in articles in peer-reviewed journals, because they are relatively easy to find using databases such as the Social Sciences Citation Index (SSCI, about which more will be said below) using keywords. However, to rely solely on peer-reviewed journal articles would imply omitting other sources of evidence, most notably studies reported in books, in articles in non-peer-reviewed journals, and in what is often referred to as 'grey literature' (for example, conference papers and reports by various bodies).

3. *Assess the relevance of each study for the research question(s).* The searches at Step 2 will produce a vast number of possible candidates for inclusion in the review based on the keywords and hand-searching through various possible publication outlets. These studies will be gradually whittled down for their degree of fit with the research question(s). This stage usually entails examining abstracts of articles and often articles themselves in order to establish their appropriateness and rejecting those that do not fit. This stage invariably results in a huge decrease in the number of studies to be reviewed. Thus, in the research referred to in Research in focus 5.2, Step 2 resulted in the identification of 7,048 reports; this number was reduced to 135 reports with the application of Step 3,

Research in focus 5.2
Healthy eating among young people

Shepherd et al. (2006) have published an account of the procedures they used to examine the barriers to healthy eating among young people aged 11–16 years and the factors that facilitate healthy eating. Table 5.1 sets out the chief steps in doing a systematic review, as outlined in the main text of this chapter, and the corresponding procedures and practices in the review by Shepherd et al. These authors used methods for systematic review that have been developed by the Evidence for Policy and Practice Information and Coordinating (EPPI) Centre at the Institute of Education, University of London. The EPPI Centre has a very comprehensive website that details its approach and its main methods and provides full reports of many of the systematic reviews its members have conducted (http://eppi.ioe.ac.uk/cms/Default. aspx?tabid=53&language=en-US, accessed 19 September 2014).

One of the features that is especially noteworthy concerning the summary in Table 5.1 is that intervention studies (for example, training parents in nutrition and evaluating the outcomes of such an intervention) and non-intervention studies (for example, a cohort or an interview study) were separated out for the purposes of presenting a summary account of the findings and appraising the quality of the studies, although a final matrix was formed that synthesized the key elements across both types of study. Assessing the quality of studies is an important component of a systematic review, so that only reliable evidence forms the basis for such things as policy changes. Different quality criteria were employed for the two types of study. In the case of the non-intervention studies, the following seven criteria were used:

(i)   an explicit theoretical framework and/or literature review;

(ii)   a clear statement of the aims and objectives of the research;

(iii)   a clear account of the context within which the research was conducted;

(iv)   a clear account of the nature of the sample and how it was formed;

(v)   a clear description of methods of data collection and analysis;

(vi)   'analysis of the data by more than one researcher' (Shepherd et al. 2006: 242); and

(vii)   whether sufficient information was provided to allow the reader to see how the conclusions were derived from the data.

The application of the corresponding criteria for the intervention studies resulted in just seven of the studies being viewed as methodologically sound. None of the eight non-intervention studies were methodologically sound in terms of all seven of the above appraisal criteria, although four met six of the seven criteria and a further two met five of the seven criteria. Of the eight non-intervention studies, five used a self-administered questionnaire to generate data, two used focus groups, and one used interviews. Thus, the category 'non-intervention study' includes research methods associated with both quantitative and qualitative research. It is quite common for systematic reviews to end up being based on quite small numbers of studies, because the explicit criteria for inclusion coupled with the quality criteria represent standards that very few investigations can meet. When presenting their synthesis of their review findings, the authors separated the findings of the seven methodologically sound intervention studies from those pertaining to the fifteen other intervention studies. Regarding the findings of the non-intervention studies, the authors report that several barriers to and facilitators of healthy eating were identified. For example, they write: 'Facilitating factors included information about nutritional content of foods/better labeling, parents and family members being supportive; healthy eating to improve or maintain one's personal appearance, will-power and better availability/lower pricing of healthy snacks' (Shepherd et al. 2006: 255). The authors linked such findings with intervention studies, arguing that 'juxtaposing barriers and facilitators alongside effectiveness studies allowed us to examine the extent to which the needs of young people had been adequately addressed by evaluated interventions' (Shepherd et al. 2006: 255).

Table 5.1

Steps in systematic review in connection with a systematic review of barriers to, and facilitators of, healthy eating among young people (Shepherd et al. 2006)

Steps in systematic review	Corresponding practices in Shepherd et al. (2006)
1. Define the purpose and scope of the review	A. Review question: 'What is known about the barriers to, and facilitators of, healthy eating among young people?' (Shepherd et al. 2006: 243).
2. Seek out studies relevant to the scope and purpose of the review	B. The authors employed a combination of terms to do with healthy eating (e.g. 'nutrition'), terms to do with health promotion or with the causes of health or ill-health (e.g. 'at-risk populations'), and terms indicative of young people (e.g. 'teenager'). In order for a study to be included in the review, in addition to being about 'the barriers to, and facilitators of, healthy eating among young people', the study had to be either an outcome evaluation (usually to evaluate the outcome of an intervention) or a non-intervention study (e.g. an interview study) in the UK, in English. Further, guidelines were formulated separately for these two types of study. For a non-intervention study to be included, it had to be about attitudes, views, experiences, etc. of healthy eating; to provide insights into respondents' own definitions of healthy eating and factors affecting it; and to 'privilege young people's views' (Shepherd et al. 2006: 241). Several online bibliographical databases were searched (including SSCI and PsycINFO). Lists of references and other sources were also searched.
3. Assess the relevance of each study for the research question(s)	C. An initial 7,048 references were gradually trimmed to 135 reports (relating to 116 studies). Of the 116 studies, seventy-five were intervention studies, thirty-two were non-intervention studies, and nine were prior systematic reviews. Application of the full set of inclusion criteria resulted in just twenty-two outcome evaluations and eight non-intervention studies meeting the criteria for what the authors refer to as 'in-depth systematic review' (Shepherd et al. 2006: 242).
4. Appraise the studies from Step 3	D. 'Data for each study were entered independently by two researchers into a specialized computer database' (Shepherd et al. 2006: 241). In doing so, the reviewers sought to summarize the findings from each study and appraise its methodological quality. Separate quality criteria were employed for intervention and non-intervention studies. The application of eight criteria for the intervention studies resulted in just seven being regarded as 'methodologically sound' and the results of just these seven studies are the focus of the authors' summary.
5. Analyse each study and synthesize the results	E. Separate syntheses of findings were conducted for the two types of study and a third synthesis for the intervention and non-intervention studies jointly. The authors write of this third synthesis: 'a matrix was constructed which laid out the barriers and facilitators identified by young people [in the non-intervention studies] alongside descriptions of the interventions included in the in-depth systematic review of outcome evaluations. The matrix was stratified by four analytical themes to characterize the levels at which the barriers and facilitators appeared to be operating: the school, family and friends, the self and practical and material resources' (Shepherd et al. 2006: 241). In forming the matrix, one column summarized barriers and facilitators identified in the non-intervention studies and there were further separate columns for the seven 'soundly evaluated interventions' and the fifteen 'other evaluated interventions'. For example, at one point in the matrix, the synthesis shows that in the non-intervention studies, one facilitator associated with 'Healthy eating and the self' is that 'Concerns over appearance (e.g. being overweight, acne) may prompt young people to moderate their intake of fast foods/unhealthy foods' (2006: 253). This facilitator is shown in the matrix to have been derived from two of the eight non-intervention studies.

whereby the initial sample of reports was examined and assessed for relevance to the review questions.

4. *Appraise the quality of studies from Step 3.* The systematic review process includes an appraisal of the quality of studies that are deemed to be relevant to the research questions. This stage necessitates a specification of quality criteria, such as whether an appropriate research design and research methods were used and whether the chosen research design and research methods were implemented according to the standards of good research practice for

those research designs and research methods. Checklists for assessing quality are available, but it is necessary to use those that are appropriate for the kinds of research being examined. The issue of quality criteria in relation to quantitative and qualitative research is covered in Chapters 7 and 17 respectively. Sometimes, systematic reviewers will exclude studies that fail to meet minimum criteria, although that may mean that the review is then conducted on an extremely small sample of remaining studies. Alternatively, reviewers will categorize studies in terms of the extent to which they meet the quality criteria that are specified and may take this categorization into account when synthesizing the research.

5. *Extract the results of each study and synthesize the results.* A formal protocol should be used to record features such as: date when the research was conducted; location; sample size; data-collection methods; and the main findings. A synthesis of the results then has to be produced. If the findings of a group of studies are quantitative in character, a meta-analysis (see Chapter 14) may be conducted. This phase will involve producing summary statistics from the quantitative data supplied with each study. In the case of other kinds of systematic review, such as those based on qualitative research or where there is a combination of both quantitative and qualitative studies, systematic reviewers seek to arrive at a 'narrative synthesis' of the research. This uses a narrative to bring together the key findings relating to the research question, often accompanied by simple statistical summaries such as the percentage of studies that examined a certain issue or that adopted a particular perspective. One advantage of a narrative synthesis is that it can be used as a platform for reviewing and summarizing both quantitative and qualitative studies. By contrast, synthesis techniques such as meta-analysis and meta-ethnography can mainly be used for summarizing quantitative and qualitative studies respectively (see Chapters 14 and 24).

Tips and skills
Using systematic review in a student research project

The systematic review approach does contain some elements that cannot easily be applied in a student research project because of limitations of time and resources. For example, you are unlikely to be able to assemble a panel of experts in methodology and theory to meet you regularly and discuss the boundaries of the review. However, there are some aspects of the approach that can be applied to students' research. For example, it will be extremely useful to meet your supervisor regularly during the planning stage of your literature review in order to define the boundaries of the subject and to come up with likely search terms. Your supervisor's knowledge of the subject can be invaluable at this stage. Also, a systematic review approach to the literature requires a transparent way of searching for and examining the literature as well as keeping records of what you have done. These practices are feasible for a student research project. However, the experience of one student who was intending to conduct a systematic review for a PhD in the field of political science suggests that students can become engulfed by the sheer volume of literature that has to be screened and analysed (Daigneault et al. 2014). The student in question was intending for the systematic review to be the core of his thesis and not a literature review that would act as a precursor to data collection. He had to give up due to the sheer volume of material he was having to consider as well as for other reasons. Clearly, the decision to include a systematic review should not be taken lightly and may be difficult for students doing undergraduate or postgraduate dissertations to implement. In Daigneault's case, he underestimated the amount of time required to screen articles for relevance and often the difficulty of doing so in the face of large numbers of article titles and abstracts that were not as informative as he would have liked.

On the other hand, there has been growing interest in **rapid reviews**, which conform to many of the principles of systematic reviews but are deliberately limited in scope in one or more respects so that the review can be completed in a much shorter time frame than would normally apply with a full systematic review, for example by restricting the scope of the review to a particular year or years, or by economizing on effort in areas such as the number of databases used. Gannan et al. (2010) examined a substantial number of such reviews in medicine and uncovered some that took as little as a month, but as they note, the shorter the time frame the greater the risk that the principles and strengths of systematic reviews will be compromised. Harker and Kleijnen (2012) uncovered forty-six rapid reviews in the field of health technology assessment and found that there was a wide variety of departures from the typical systematic review. For example, 47 per cent of studies were found to have no research question(s), which in itself is a big departure from a fully-fledged systematic review. The mean length of time taken from start to finish was 9.7 months when one 'outlier' that took an inordinately long time is excluded. While the prospect of doing a rapid review may appear attractive to many students lacking the time to conduct a full systematic review, the lack of agreement about what a rapid review is and the uncertainty about the value of the approach (Harker and Kleijnen 2012) suggest that it should only be considered with a great deal of caution.

Thinking deeply 5.3
Debates about the role of systematic review in education research

Debates about the role of systematic review in education research are of potential relevance to social policy researchers because of the similarities shared between these two applied fields of study. Both education and social policy research draw on a range of social science disciplines, involve the study of practitioners, and are sometimes criticized for not focusing sufficiently on the concerns of practitioners and policy-makers. Evans and Benefield (2001) have argued that the medical model of systematic review can be adapted for application in education research. This would enable researchers to 'say something more precise and targeted' about the effectiveness of specific interventions, or in other words to provide evidence about 'what works' (Evans and Benefield 2001: 538). Systematic reviews would thus help to make research evidence more usable.

However, Hammersley (2001) criticizes the assumption in systematic review about the superiority of the positivist model of research, which is expressed through the methodological criteria applied in evaluating the validity of studies (experiments being more highly valued), and through the explicit procedures used to produce reviews that are intended to be 'objective'. This 'takes little or no account of the considerable amount of criticism that has been made of that model since at least the middle of the twentieth century' (Hammersley 2001: 545). Moreover, Hammersley suggests that the dichotomy portrayed between rational-rule-following systematic review and irrational-judgement narrative review is overstated, because even the simplest rule-following involves an element of interpretation. He concludes:

> What all this means, I suggest, is that producing a review of the literature is a distinctive task in its own right. It is not a matter of 'synthesising data'; or, at least, there is no reason why we should assume that reviewing *must* take this form. Rather, it can involve judging the validity of the findings and conclusions of particular studies, and thinking about how these relate to one another, and how their interrelations can be used to illuminate the field under investigation. This will require the reviewer to draw on his or her tacit knowledge, derived from experience, and to *think* about the substantive and methodological issues, not just to apply replicable procedures.
>
> (Hammersley 2001: 549)

Pearson and Coomber (2009) provide some evidence that supports Hammersley's contention that systematic review necessarily entails an element of interpretation. They report the results of a participant observation study of a systematic review process. The domain with which the reviewers were concerned was the development of guidance in connection with substance misuse. Pearson and Coomber found that the reviewers prioritized internal validity over external validity considerations in selecting studies for inclusion. Also, the reviewers elected to play down the significance of one kind of intervention—life skills training—because a report was made available to them that provided a strong critique of it. However, Pearson and Coomber note that an examination of the summaries of research on life skills training generated by the reviewers suggests there was a good case for including it in the guidance on treatment. Thus, the fact of a report not being selected through the systematic review process seems to have been instrumental in the lack of attention given to life skills training, implying a degree of subjectivity in the review process.

MacLure (2005: 409) suggests that the prioritization of systematic review in education research is worrying because 'it is hostile to anything that cannot be seen, and therefore controlled, counted and quality assured'; it thus degrades the status of reading, writing, thinking, and interpreting as activities that are crucial to the development of analysis and argument. Although systematic review has so far not been as widely adopted in social research, the concerns expressed by education researchers are of potential relevance, particularly to qualitative researchers. However, one of the most interesting aspects of Hammersley's (2001) critique is that he implies that systematic review is inconsistent with its own principles, in that there appears to be no or very little evidence that systematic reviews lead to better evidence (and therefore presumably to better evidence-based practice)!

Denyer and Tranfield (2009) propose that the review document should be structured much like a research report in which the purpose of the review, its methods, its findings, the discussion of the findings, and a conclusion are clearly specified.

Tranfield et al. (2003) suggest that the systematic review process provides a more reliable foundation on which to design research, because it is based on a comprehensive understanding of what we know about a subject. It is therefore likely to be relevant to researchers as a way of summarizing findings, so that it is not just practitioners who benefit from systematic reviews. Supporters of systematic review also recommend the approach for its transparency, because the grounds on which studies were selected and how they were analysed are clearly articulated and replicable. It has sometimes been suggested that not all areas of literature lend themselves to a systematic review approach, because they are not always concerned with research questions to do with exploring whether a certain independent variable has certain kinds of effects. Meta-analysis of quantitative studies requires this kind of research question, but qualitative studies and indeed some sorts of quantitative investigation are not necessarily in this format. This impression may have been created because many early systematic reviews were of the 'what works?' or 'does X work?' kind, where the literature relating to various kinds of intervention would be appraised and reviewed. In more recent years, a wider range of research questions have been subjected to systematic review, as it has begun to include both qualitative studies and quantitative non-intervention studies.

However, one of the limitations of systematic review stems from situations where research questions are not capable of being defined in terms of the effect of a particular variable, or where the subject boundaries are more fluid and open or more subject to change. This is often the

Thinking deeply 5.4
Incorporating systematic review practices into narrative reviews

It is always risky to speculate, but I have a hunch that some narrative reviews will incorporate some of the practices associated with systematic review. Even though some writers such as those mentioned in Thinking deeply 5.3 object to systematic review for its tendency towards a mechanical approach to reviewing the literature, it could be that some reviewers will be attracted to its emphasis on such features as transparency about how searches were conducted and/or comprehensiveness in the literature search. This is especially likely to be the case when reviewers work on their own, as systematic review requires more than one person to assist in such steps as the formulation of research questions, the selection of keywords, and the assessment of quality.

I tried to incorporate some systematic review practices into a narrative literature review I carried out on leadership effectiveness at departmental level in higher education (Bryman 2007c). The systematic review practices were apparent in:

- use of an explicit research question to guide the review. The question was: 'What styles of or approaches to leadership are associated with effective leadership in higher education?' (Bryman 2007c: 693).

- the specification of the literature search procedures so that they were reproducible, the combination of key terms for searching for the literature in more than one online database (SSCI, Educational Resources Information Center, Google Scholar, and others) and hand-searching through the bibliographies of numerous key articles. The terms used were: leader* or manage* or administrat* plus higher education* or university* or academic plus effective* (the asterisks are 'wild cards' so that 'leader*' will pick up 'leader', 'leaders', 'leading', and 'leadership').

- the use of quality appraisal criteria to decide which articles should be within the review's scope. The quality appraisal criteria were: 'the aims of the research were clearly stated; they made clear the ways in which data were collected (sampling, research instruments used, how data were analysed), did so in a systematic way, and indicated how the methods were related to the aims; provided sufficient data to support interpretations; and outlined the method of analysis' (Bryman 2007c: 695). From many hundreds of 'hits', only twenty articles both related to the research question and met the appraisal criteria.

case in social research. This is not a convincing criticism because systematic reviews can be conducted in areas of research which are not to do with the effects of a particular variable. Rees et al. (2013) conducted a systematic review of the evidence about the perceptions of young people aged 12–18 years concerning obesity, body size and shape, and weight. None of the research questions was expressed in terms of causes and effects and instead they were about perceptions, such as 'What are young people's views about influences on body size?' (Rees et al. 2013: 16).

Another criticism is that the systematic review approach can lead to a bureaucratization of the process of reviewing the literature, because it is more concerned with the technical aspects of how the review is done than with the analytical interpretations generated by it. Thus, in systematic reviews, there are copious descriptions of search terms used, how potential candidates for inclusion in the review were sieved, databases used, etc. A further potential limitation of the approach relates to its applicability to qualitative research studies and in particular to the methodological judgements that inform decisions about quality and so determine the inclusion or exclusion of an article from a literature review. The systematic review approach assumes that an objective judgement about the quality of an article can be made. Particularly in relation to qualitative research, there is a lack of consensus on how the appraisal of the quality of studies should be carried out (see Chapter 17). There is also some unease among some writers concerning the claimed superiority of replicable procedures over interpretation that is implicit in some writings (see Thinking deeply 5.3). Nonetheless, some systematic review procedures seem to be creeping into narrative reviews (see Thinking deeply 5.4).

 # Searching the existing literature

Students often have in mind a few initial references when they begin a project. These may come from recommended reading in course modules, or from textbooks. The bibliographies provided at the end of textbook chapters or articles will usually provide you with a raft of further relevant references that can also be followed up. A literature search relies on careful reading of books, journals, and reports in the first instance. After identifying a few keywords that help to define the boundaries of your chosen area of research (see the section below on 'Keywords and defining search parameters'), you can search electronic databases of published literature for previously published work in the field.

Electronic databases

Online bibliographical databases accessible on the Internet are an invaluable source of journal references. An increasing number of these will also provide access to the full text of an article in electronic format—these are usually referred to as e-journals. You will need to find out whether your institution can give you a user name and password to gain access to these databases, so look on your library's home page, or ask a member of library staff.

Probably the single most useful source for the social sciences is the Social Sciences Citation Index (SSCI), which fully indexes over 3,000 major social science journals covering all social science disciplines dating back to 1970. To gain access to this website, most UK users will need an Athens username and password. It can be accessed from the ISI Web of Knowledge (WoK) home page at **http://wok.mimas.ac.uk/** (accessed 19 September 2014). The Citation Indexes collectively are also known as the Web of Science.

The SSCI database provides references and abstracts, and some libraries add full-text links for articles from some of the most important social science journals published worldwide. This database is therefore very useful as an initial source in your literature search, because, if you search the database effectively, you can be relatively confident that you have covered the majority of recent academic journals that may have published articles on your topic of interest. Here are some introductory guidelines for searching SSCI.

1. Navigate your way from your library's website to the SSCI.

2. You can then search by Topic or by Author by entering the appropriate keywords or names into the appropriate boxes below **Basic Search**.

3. Click on **Search**. Note that the default is to search 1970 to the current date; you can change this by using the pull down menus below **TIMESPAN**.

4. You will then get a list of items that meet your criteria, ordered from most recent downwards. If you click on any item, you will get full bibliographical details, along with an abstract, keywords supplied by the author, and contact information about the author(s).

A feature of SSCI is its complete coverage of journal contents, so, in addition to research and scholarly articles, it also contains book reviews and editorial material, which invariably can be identified through keyword searches. You will need to experiment with the use of keywords, because this is usually the way in which databases like these are searched, though author searches are also possible. Finally, when you click on any item in the list of references that SSCI supplies, a feature that is often useful is the 'Times cited' link. If you find an article that is relevant to your dissertation, then you can click to see which other articles have cited it. This does two things. First it allows you to see how an article has been used in more recent research, and in particular whether it has been challenged. Second, it gives an impression of whether the article and the ideas in it have been developed with new data. For example, at the time of writing this chapter (19 September 2014), my article on the Disneyization of society published in 1999 in *Sociological Review* has been cited in fifty-six other papers about related subjects, such as emotional labour and retailing. However, it is important to realize that articles in other journals may have cited the article. The reason that these would not turn up in an SSCI search is that those responsible for it operate a screening process, which means that by no means all journals achieve entry into the database. The screening process takes into account the reputation and impact of the journal concerned.

Student experience
Strategies for finding references

The students who supplied information concerning their strategies for doing their literature reviews used a variety of approaches. As well as searching the journals, Erin Saunders got help from her supervisor and others.

> I was recommended a number of relevant texts by my supervisor—and from there I located other sources by using the bibliographies of these texts. As well, I did an extensive journal search for articles that were related to my topic. I also contacted a number of academics in the field to ask for specific suggestions. Then I read as much of the literature as I could, identifying key themes and ideas.

Hannah Creane's approach was to focus on key names in the sociological literature on childhood.

> Initially I read a few core textbooks that cover the general aspects of sociology, and picked out from them the main names of sociologists who have written about childhood and, in particular, childhood as a social construction. From there I read the books of some of the key names within the field of childhood study, and just simply kept looking up the names of sociologists whom they had referenced. I kept going like this until I felt I had enough literature to back up my findings and theories that I made in the light of my own research.

Rebecca Barnes proceeded by identifying key texts and then using bibliographies.

> Once I started to locate the core texts, this process gathered more momentum, since I was able to draw on bibliographies in those sources to identify other relevant references.

To read more, go to the Online Resource Centre: www.oxfordtextbooks.co.uk/orc/brymansrm5e/

You can also use the Cited Reference Search to search for articles that cite an article that you know about already. This can help you find other related research and also see what other authors thought of your original article. This is particularly useful if your article is a few years old.

Also very useful is Scopus, which is available at **www.elsevier.com/online-tools/scopus** (accessed 19 September 2014). Scopus describes itself as 'the largest abstract and citation database of peer-reviewed literature'. You will need an Athens or other username and password to get into the database. The 'Document search' may meet your initial needs. This allows you to search in terms of keywords. You need to select the 'Author search' tab to do an author search. You need to specify the date range of articles you wish to search for (it goes back to 1960) and to untick the subject areas not relevant to your search. Scopus tends to include a wider range of journals than SSCI. Like SSCI, when you select an item, Scopus will bring up the abstract, as well as the full reference, when a particular item is selected for further examination. It also brings up the number of times the article has been cited, and you can produce a full list of references that have cited the selected article. It also supplies what Scopus refers to as 'Related documents'.

Also useful for searching for references is Google Scholar—see Tips and skills 'Using information on the Web' for details of how to use this search tool.

Most academic publishers have begun to offer full-text versions of articles in their journals through their own websites, and these allow you to search by author name or by keywords. You are usually directed to these websites when you search for and select a journal through your library's website. Nowadays, you will often have access to articles in journals ahead of print. This means that once an article has been accepted for publication and copy-edited, it will be available to read on the journal's website even though it has not been published in print. Also, online articles are often supplemented by additional material which is only available online. This supplementary material usually comprises such things as additional graphs or tables or questionnaires. These items are valuable if you want to evaluate an article on methodological grounds. Again, you will need to check with your librarian to find out which of these resources you can use and how to access them. The Ingentaconnect website (**www.ingentaconnect.com/**, accessed 19 September 2014) offers full-text versions from various publishers, and you will be able to access full-text versions of articles in journals to which your library subscribes.

In addition to scholarly books and journals, newspaper archives can provide a valuable supplementary resource through which to review the emergence of new topics in areas of social concern. Most newspapers require you to have a subscription in order to be able to search their online databases (for example, *Financial Times*, *Daily* and *Sunday Telegraph*, *The Times*). However, most academic libraries will have a subscription to some individual newspapers or to a service such as Proquest or LexisNexis, which allows you to search several newspapers at once; you may need a password to access them. Newspapers and periodicals can be a rich source of information about certain topics that make good stories for journalists, such as social problems, policy initiatives, or trade union disputes. The level of analysis can also be high. For an academic dissertation, such publications should always be seen as secondary to published literature in books and journals, but it takes some time for academic articles to be published, so for recent events newspapers may be the only source of information.

A word of warning about using Google and other search engines for research: Internet search engines are very useful for researching all sorts of things. However, they merely find sites; they do not evaluate them. So be prepared to look critically at what you have found. Remember that anyone can put information on the Web, so, when looking at websites, you need to evaluate whether the information you have found is useful. The following points are worth considering.

- Who is the author of the site and what is his or her motive for publishing?
- Where is the site located? The URL can help you here. Is it an academic site (.ac) or a government site (.gov), a non-commercial organization (.org) or a commercial one (.com or .co)?
- How recently was the site updated? Many sites will give you a 'last updated' date, but you can get clues as to whether a page is being well maintained by whether the links are up to date and by its general appearance.

Try to confine your literature search to reliable websites, such as those mentioned in this chapter. For more on this issue, see Tips and skills 'Using information on the Web'.

Tips and skills
Using email alerts

One way of expanding your literature search is through email alerts. These supply you with an email when an issue of a journal that you are interested in is published. You can also be sent email alerts when articles with certain keywords or written by particular authors are published. One of the main ways of setting up email alerts is through Zetoc, through the British Library. You will need to sign in with a username and password. An Athens username and password will usually achieve this. To find Zetoc, go to **http://zetoc.mimas.ac.uk/** (accessed 19 September 2014).

Alternatively, you can use Scopus for sending alerts when articles on nominated topics or by nominated authors are published. Go to **www.scopus.com/alert/form/MyAlerts.url** (accessed 19 September 2014).

There is also a Scopus app for the iPhone, iPod Touch, and iPad that can be downloaded from **http://itunes. apple.com/app/scopus-alerts-lite-take-your/id365300810?mt=8** (accessed 19 September 2014).

Tips and skills
Using information on the Web

The Internet provides an enormous and richly varied source of freely available information about social research that can be quickly and easily accessed without the need for university agreements to gain access to them. However, there is a difficulty in relying on this: the strength of the Internet in providing access to huge amounts of information is also its weakness, in that it can be very difficult to differentiate what is useful and reliable from that which is too simplistic, too commercially oriented, too highly opinionated, or just not sufficiently academic. The worst thing that can happen is that you end up quoting from sources from the Web that are quite simply misleading and incorrect. Therefore, it is important to be selective in your use of information on the Internet and to build up a list of favourite websites that you can check regularly for information.

However, such sources have to be evaluated critically. For example, while writing this chapter for the third edition of this book, I encountered the following definition of qualitative research in Wikipedia, which is very popular among students.

> Qualitative research is one of the two major approaches to *research methodology* in *social sciences*. Qualitative research involves an indepth understanding of *human behaviour* and the *reasons* that govern human behaviour. Unlike *quantitative research*, qualitative research relies on reasons behind various aspects of *behaviour*. Simply put, it investigates the why and how of *decision-making*, as compared to what, where, and when of quantitative research. Hence, the need is for smaller but focused *samples* rather than large *random samples*, which qualitative research categorizes into patterns as the primary basis for organizing and reporting results.

(**http://en.wikipedia.org/wiki/Qualitative_research**, accessed 12 February 2007)

This is a very misleading characterization of both quantitative and qualitative research. It implies that quantitative researchers are not concerned with examining the 'reasons behind various aspects of behaviour'. This is a quite extraordinary notion. The whole point of the preoccupation with causality and the very notions of independent and dependent variables that are part of the basic vocabulary of quantitative research (see Chapter 7) would suggest the opposite: quantitative researchers are deeply concerned about exploring the reasons behind behaviour. Also, qualitative researchers are concerned to explore 'what, where, and when', in that they frequently engage in descriptions of what is happening at certain events or on particular occasions and where they take place, and often draw inferences about their timing. Further, quantitative researchers 'categorize ... data into patterns', but the nature and character of those patterns assume a different form. This is a very poor definition and characterization of qualitative research and demonstrates the risk of using Web sources in an unquestioning way. Wikipedia contains some very good entries, but it has to be treated with caution, as do Web sources generally. Interestingly, the above quotation can no longer be found at **http://en.wikipedia.org/wiki/Qualitative_research**.

Searching tool
Google has a really useful product called 'Google Scholar', which can be accessed from the Google home page. This product provides a simple way to search broadly for academic literature. Searches are focused on peer-reviewed papers, theses, books, abstracts, and articles, from academic publishers, professional societies, preprint repositories, universities, and other scholarly organizations. Google Scholar also enables you to see how often an item has been cited by other people. This can be very useful in assessing the importance of an idea or a particular scholarly writer. See **http://scholar.google.com**.

Current affairs
For case study analyses and keeping up to date on current social issues, the BBC News website is reasonably well balanced and quite analytical: **www.bbc.co.uk**.

Statistics on social trends
The Office for National Statistics makes a huge amount of data about social trends available on its website: **www.statistics.gov.uk**.

European statistics relating to specific countries, industries, and sectors can be found on Europa, the portal to the European Union website: http://europa.eu/index_en.htm.

Other useful websites that are relevant to research methods
Teaching Resources and Materials for Social Scientists: www.data-archive.ac.uk/media/185474/tramsswebsite_archive.pdf.

Exploring online research methods: www.restore.ac.uk/orm/self-study.htm.

Qualitative data analysis: http://onlineqda.hud.ac.uk/.

Research ethics: www.ethicsguidebook.ac.uk.

Access to various data that can be used for secondary analysis: http://ukdataservice.ac.uk/.

(All websites mentioned in this box were accessed 19 September 2014 unless stated otherwise.)

Student experience
Literature review as ongoing

The literature review is often viewed as a distinct phase in the research process, but in fact it is invariably an ongoing component of a research project. While email alerts such as those provided by Zetoc (see Tips and skills 'Using email alerts') may be a useful way of keeping on top of the literature, they also mean that the literature review may not draw to a close at an early stage. Rebecca Barnes found that searching the literature was an ongoing process.

> Although at the beginning of my PhD, I dedicated a more prolonged period of time to searching for and reviewing literature, this process has been an ongoing part of the research process. I used electronic databases such as Cambridge Sociological Abstracts to identify sources which could be useful, and I was also fortunate in stumbling across a bibliography of sources for same-sex domestic violence on the Internet. ... I also subscribe to Zetoc alerts, which means that rather than having to spend time regularly updating the literature which I have, I am informed of many new articles as soon as they are published.

Rebecca's experience is not unusual. Isabella Robbins, who was doing a PhD at the time, describes the literature review as feeling like 'a process that has been ongoing for about six years', while Sarah Hanson suggests that it can be difficult to bring the review to a close.

> The only difficulty I encountered was that I couldn't stop reading; I had finished my literature review and had started writing my dissertation, but I kept stumbling upon book after book, which then had to be encompassed into the literature review. I ended up writing and rewriting my literature review.

In a similar vein Jonathan Smetherham wrote of the literature review for an undergraduate dissertation that he began with some material with which he was familiar and then:

> I developed research questions and then used these as the basis for doing a more probing lit review. By this stage, I had seen a few of the 'big names' cropping up repeatedly, so I began searching out their scholarly work for greater insight. ... However, after the actual research project had been conducted in the field, I did essentially rewrite the literature review, as the scope of my study changed so considerably during the data-collection process. However, this was a much more focused and efficient exercise—in part due to the impending deadline, and in part because the review was no longer an exploratory exercise but something which was sharp, crisp and focused.

To read more, go to the Online Resource Centre: www.oxfordtextbooks.co.uk/orc/brymansrm5e/

The catalogue of your own institution's library is an obvious route to finding books, but so too are the catalogues of other university libraries. COPAC contains the holdings of over seventy of the largest university research libraries plus the British Library. It can be found at **http://copac.ac.uk** (accessed 19 September 2014).

A well-known website such as Amazon can also be extremely helpful for searching for books.

Keywords and defining search parameters

For all these online databases, you will need to work out some suitable keywords that can be entered into the search engines and that will allow you to identify suitable references. Journal articles often include lists of keywords. When you find two or three articles that are relevant to your research and that have lists of keywords, it may be useful to use some of these keywords that are relevant to your research for searching for other articles. You will also need to think of synonyms or alternative terms and try to match your language to that of the source you are searching. For example, in the example in Thinking deeply 5.4, I used 'manage*' and 'administrat*' as well as 'leader*' (see Thinking deeply 5.4 for the use of asterisks as wild cards). This is not because I think that management and administration are the same as leadership but because I realized quite early on that some authors use these terms either as synonyms for leadership or in very similar ways. Be prepared to experiment and to amend your keywords as your research progresses; you may find as you search the literature that there are other ways of describing your subject.

In most databases, typing in the title of your project, or a sentence or long phrase, as your search term is not advisable, as, unless someone has written something with the same title, you are unlikely to find very much. You need to think in terms of keywords (see Tips and skills 'Keywords').

Tips and skills
Keywords

For all kinds of review—narrative or systematic—using keywords for searching online databases of articles is crucial. However, it is not as easy as it seems. For example, though the authors of the article in Research in focus 24.9 searched the literature thoroughly using keywords, they note that, after they had completed the meta-ethnography on lay experiences of diabetes, they 'were made aware of a meta-ethnography based on 43 qualitative reports concerned with the "lived experience of diabetes"' (Campbell et al. 2003: 683). Not only were they unable to uncover this article, which had been published in 1998, through their search, but also the authors of the other meta-ethnography had included only three of the seven articles Campbell et al. had used. Searching for keywords requires some experimentation and should not be regarded as a one-off exercise.

Use the 'Help' function provided in the databases themselves to find out how to use your keywords to best effect. The advice on using 'operators' such as AND, OR, and NOT can be especially helpful.

In some areas of research, there are very many references. Try to identify the major ones and work outwards from there. Move on to the next stage of your research at the point that you identified in your timetable, so that you can dig yourself out of the library. This is not to say that your search for the literature will cease, but that you need to force yourself to move on. Seek out your supervisor's advice on whether you need to search the literature much more. Figure 5.1 outlines one way of searching the literature. The most important thing to remember, as the note at the end of the figure suggests, is to keep a good record of the process so that you can keep track of what you have done. Also, when you give your supervisor drafts of your literature review, make sure you include all the references and their details so that he or she can adequately assess the coverage and quality of your review.

Figure 5.1

One way of searching the literature

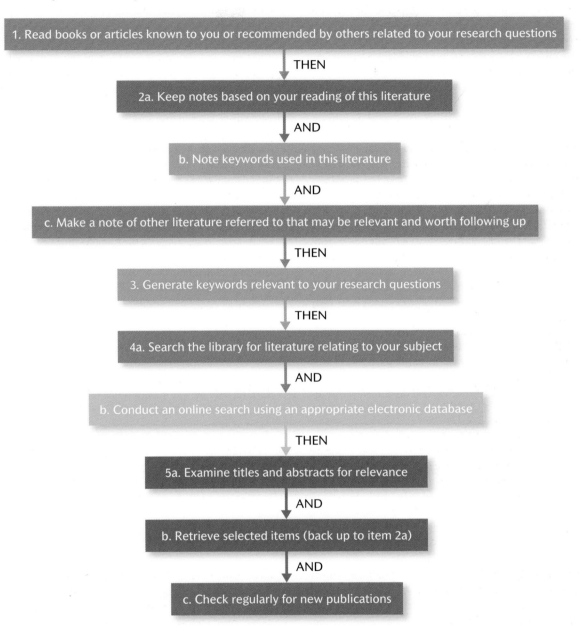

1. Read books or articles known to you or recommended by others related to your research questions

THEN

2a. Keep notes based on your reading of this literature

AND

b. Note keywords used in this literature

AND

c. Make a note of other literature referred to that may be relevant and worth following up

THEN

3. Generate keywords relevant to your research questions

THEN

4a. Search the library for literature relating to your subject

AND

b. Conduct an online search using an appropriate electronic database

THEN

5a. Examine titles and abstracts for relevance

AND

b. Retrieve selected items (back up to item 2a)

AND

c. Check regularly for new publications

Note: At each stage, keep a record of what you have done and your reasons for certain decisions. This will be useful to you for remembering how you proceeded and for writing up a description and justification of your literature search strategy, which can form part of your methods section. When making notes on literature that you read, make notes on content and method, as well as relevance, and keep thinking about how each item will contribute to your critical review of the literature.

Referencing your work

Referencing the work of others is an important academic convention because it emphasizes that you are aware of the historical development of your subject, particularly if you use the Harvard (or author–date) method, and shows that you recognize that your own research builds on the work of others. Referencing in your literature review is thus a way of emphasizing your understanding and knowledge of the subject. In other parts of your dissertation referencing will serve somewhat different purposes—for example, it will show your understanding of methodological considerations or help to reinforce your argument. A reference is also sometimes described as a 'citation' and the act of referencing as 'citing'.

A key skill in writing your literature review is keeping a record of what you have read, including all the bibliographic details about each article or book that will go into your bibliography or list of references. For larger research projects it can be useful to use note cards or software packages that are designed specifically for this purpose such as EndNote or Reference Manager, but for a student research project it will probably be sufficient to keep an electronic record of all the items that you have read in a Word document, although you should bear in mind that you may not include all of these in your final bibliography. However, the main thing is to ensure that you keep your bibliographic records up to date and do not leave this updating until the very end of the writing-up process, when you will probably be under significant time pressure.

Your institution will probably have its own guidelines as to which style of referencing you should use in your dissertation, and if it does you should definitely follow them. However, the two main methods used are:

- *Harvard* or author–date. The essence of this system is that, whenever you paraphrase the argument or ideas of an author or authors in your writing, you add in parentheses immediately afterwards the surname of the author(s) and the year of publication. If you are quoting the author(s), you put quotation marks around the quotation, and after the year of publication you include the page number where the quotation is from. All books, articles, and other sources that you have cited in the text are then given in a list of references at the end of the dissertation in alphabetical order by author surname. This is by far the most common referencing system in social research and the one that followed in this book. It is, therefore, the style that I would encourage you to use if your university does not require you to follow its own guidelines.

- *Footnote or numeric.* This approach involves the use of superscript numbers in the text that refer to a note at the foot of the page or the end of the text, where the reference is given in full together with the page number if it is a direct quotation. If a source is cited more than once, an abbreviated version of the reference is given in any subsequent citation, which is why this is often called the short-title system. As well as being used to refer to sources, footnotes and endnotes are often used to provide additional detail, including comments from the writer about the source being cited. This is a particular feature of historical writing. One of the advantages of the footnote or numeric method is that it can be less distracting to the reader in terms of the flow of the text than the Harvard method, where sometimes particularly long strings of references can make a sentence or a paragraph difficult to follow. Software packages such as Word make the insertion of notes relatively simple, and many students find that this is a convenient way of referencing their work. However, when students use this method, they often use it incorrectly, as it is quite difficult to use it well, and they are sometimes unsure whether or not also to include a separate bibliography. The footnote approach to referencing does not necessarily include a bibliography, but a bibliography can be an important factor in the assessment of students' work (see Thinking deeply 5.2). As not having a bibliography is a potential disadvantage to this style of referencing, your institution may recommend that you do not use it.

The role of the bibliography

What makes a good bibliography or list of references? You might initially think that length is a good measure, since a longer bibliography containing more references might imply that the author has been comprehensive in his or her search of the literature. This is true only up to a point, since it is also important for the bibliography to be selectively focused—it should not include everything that has ever been written about a subject but instead should reflect the author's informed judgement of the importance and suitability of sources. This incorporates some of the judgements about quality that were discussed earlier on in this chapter. One common proxy for quality is the reputation of the journal in which an article is published. However, although this is a useful indicator, it is not one that you should rely on exclusively, since there might be articles in lesser-status journals that are relevant. But it is important to be aware of these judgements of quality and to seek the advice of your supervisor in making them. Another important feature of a good bibliography relates to secondary referencing. This is when you refer to an article

Tips and skills
The Harvard and note approaches to referencing

The examples below show some fictitious examples of referencing in published work. Note that in published articles there is usually a list of references at the end; books using the Harvard system usually have a list of references, whereas a bibliography is used with the short-title system of notes. The punctuation and style of references—such as where to place a comma, or whether to capitalize a title in full or just the first word—varies considerably from source to source. For example, with Harvard referencing, in some books and journals the surname of the author is separated from the date in the text with a comma—for example (Name, 1999)—but in others, such as this this book, there is no comma. However, the main thing is to be consistent. Select a format for punctuating your references, such as the one adopted by a leading journal in your subject area, and then stick to it.

An example of a Harvard reference to a book
In the text:

As Name and Other (2011) argue, the line between migration and tourism is becoming increasingly blurred.

… and in the bibliography or list of references:

Name, A., and Other, S. (2011). *Title of Book in Italics*. Place of Publication: Publisher.

An example of a Harvard reference with a direct quotation from a book
In the text:

However, research on tourism was found to be very relevant to an understanding of migrants' experiences 'because the motivations of tourists and migrants are increasingly similar' (Name and Other 2011: 123).

… and in the bibliography or list of references:

Name, A., and Other, S. (2011). *Title of Book in Italics*. Place of Publication: Publisher.

An example of a Harvard reference to a journal article
In the text:

Research by Name (2012) has drawn attention to the importance of the notion of authenticity for both migrants and tourists.

… and in the bibliography or list of references:

Name, A. (2003). 'Title of Journal Article', *Journal Title*, 28(4): 109–38.

> Refers to volume (issue) numbers
> ↓

Issue numbers are often not included, as in the case of the References in this book.

An example of a Harvard reference to a chapter in an edited book
In the text:

As Name (2009) suggests, tourists are often motivated by a quest for authentic experiences …

… and in the bibliography or list of references:

Name, A. (2009). 'Title of Book Chapter', in S. Other (ed.), *Title of Book in Italics*. Place of Publication: Publisher, pp. 124–56.

> ↑
> Abbreviation for 'Editor'

An example of a secondary reference using the Harvard method
In the text:

This is because the line between migration and tourism is becoming increasingly blurred. (Name and Other 2011, cited in Other 2014).

… and in the bibliography or list of references:

Name, A. and Other, S. (2011). *Title of Book in Italics*. Place of Publication: Publisher, cited in G. Other (2004), *Title of Book in Italics*. Place of Publication: Publisher.

An example of a Harvard reference to an Internet site
In the text:

Scopus describes itself as 'the largest abstract and citation database of peer-reviewed literature' (Scopus 2014).

… and in the bibliography or list of references:

Scopus (2014). **www.elsevier.com/online-tools/scopus** (accessed 19 September 2014).

Note: it is very important to give the date of access, as some websites change frequently (or even disappear! See Tips and skills 'Using information on the Web' for an example).

An example of a note reference to a book
In the text:

On the other hand, research by Name[3] has drawn attention to the influence of intrinsic factors on employee motivation …

… and in the notes:

[3] A. Name and S. Other, *Title of Book in Italics*. Place of Publication, Publisher, 2011, pp. 170–7.

An example of a note reference to an Internet site
In the text:

Scopus describes itself as 'the largest abstract and citation database of peer-reviewed literature'.[39]

… and in the notes:

[39] Scopus (2014). **www.elsevier.com/online-tools/scopus** (accessed 19 September 2014).

Bear in mind that it is essential when preparing your own referencing in the text and the bibliography or list of references that *you follow the conventions and style that are recommended by your institution for preparing an essay, dissertation, or thesis.*

Tips and skills
Using bibliographic software

EndNote and Reference Manager are two of the leading Windows-based software tools used for publishing and managing bibliographies. Your university may have a site licence for one of these packages. They are used by academic researchers, information specialists, and students to create bibliographic records equivalent to the manual form of index cards. This allows you to compile your own personal reference database. These records can then be automatically formatted to suit different requirements—for example, to comply with the referencing requirements of a particular scholarly journal. A further advantage to the software is that it can enable you to export references directly from databases such as the Social Sciences Citation Index (SSCI). The software also has search options that help you to locate a particular reference, although the extent of these features varies from one package to another.

In the long run, this can save you time and effort and reduce the possibility of errors. However, for a student research project it may not be worthwhile for you to take the time to learn how to use this software if it is only to be used for the dissertation. On the other hand, if knowledge of the software may be useful to you in the longer term—for example, if you are thinking of going on to pursue an academic career by doing a PhD, or if you are intending to work in a field where research skills are valued—then it may be worth learning how to use the software. More details about these products can be found on their websites (both accessed 22 September 2014):

http://thomsonreuters.com/endnote/

www.refman.com

Thinking deeply 5.5
The problem of using secondary literature sources

Be careful when using second-hand accounts of theories or findings. It is well known that these are sometimes misleadingly represented in publications—though hopefully not in this book! An interesting case is the *Affluent Worker* research that is described later in this book in Research in focus 24.8. This research entailed a survey in the 1960s of predominantly affluent workers in three firms in Luton. It is regarded as a classic of British sociology. One of the authors of the books that were published from this research conducted a search for books and articles that discussed the findings of this research. Platt (1984) shows that several authors misinterpreted the findings. Examples of such misinterpretation follow.

- *The study was based on just car workers*. It was not—only one of the three companies was a car firm.
- *The study was based on just semi-skilled or mass production workers*. It was not—there were a variety of skill levels and technological forms among the manual sample.
- *The research 'found' instrumentalism*—that is, an instrumental orientation to work. This is misleading—instrumentalism was an inference about the data, not a finding as such.

The point of this discussion is the need to be vigilant about possibly recycling incorrect interpretations of theoretical ideas or research findings.

or book that has been cited in another source such as a textbook and you do not, or cannot, access the original article or book from which it was taken. Relying heavily on secondary references can be problematic, because you are dependent upon the interpretation of the original text that is offered by the authors of the secondary text. This may be adequate for some parts of your literature review, but there is always the potential for different interpretations of the original text, and this potential increases the further removed you are from the original source. So it is a good idea to be cautious in the use of secondary references and to go back to the original source if you can, particularly if it is an important one for your subject. Thinking

deeply 5.5 gives an example of how an author's work can be referenced in ways that involve reinterpretation and misinterpretation long after the date of publication. A further feature of a good bibliography stems from the relationship between the list of references at the end and the way in which they are used in the main body of the text. It is not helpful to include references in a list of references that are not even mentioned in the text. If references are integrated into the text in a way that shows you have read them in detail and understood their implications, this is much more impressive than if a reference is inserted in a way that does not closely relate to what is being said in the text.

Avoiding plagiarism

An issue to bear in mind when writing up your literature review is the need to avoid plagiarizing the work that you are reading. Plagiarism is a notoriously slippery notion. To plagiarize is defined in *The Concise Oxford Dictionary* as to 'take and use another person's (thoughts, writings, inventions …) as one's own'. Similarly, the online Encarta UK English Dictionary defines it as 'the process of copying another person's idea or written work and claiming it as original'. Plagiarism does not just relate to the literature you read in the course of preparing an essay or

report. Taking material in a wholesale and unattributed way from sources such as essays written by others or from websites is also a context within which plagiarism can occur. Further, it is possible to self-plagiarize, as when a person lifts material that he or she has previously written and passes it off as new work. Plagiarism is commonly regarded as a form of academic cheating; as such it differs little, if at all, in the minds of many academics from other academic misdemeanours such as fabricating research findings.

There is a widespread view that the incidence of plagiarism among students is increasing, though whether this is in fact the case is difficult to establish unambiguously. Indeed, it is difficult to establish how widespread plagiarism is, and there are quite substantial variations in estimates of its prevalence. In a study of two assignments for a business course at a New Zealand university, Walker (2010) found that just over one-quarter of the two assignments together exhibited some level of plagiarism. He also found that the level of plagiarism declined between the two assignments, suggesting that students were less inclined to plagiarize for the second assignment when they had been notified of the marker's comments on the first assignment. It is widely viewed that the Internet is one of the main—if not *the* main—motor behind the perceived increase in the prevalence of plagiarism. The ease with which text can be copied from websites, e-journal articles, e-books, online essays sold commercially, and numerous other sources and then pasted into essays is often viewed as one of the main factors behind the alleged rise in plagiarism cases among university students.

There are several difficulties with plagiarism as an issue in higher education. One is that universities vary in their definitions of what plagiarism is (Stefani and Carroll 2001). Further, they vary in their response to it when it is uncovered. They also vary in both the type and the severity of punishment. Further, within any university, academic and other staff differ in their views of the sinfulness of plagiarism and how it should be handled (Flint et al. 2006). There is also evidence that students are less convinced than academic staff that plagiarism is wrong and that it should be punished. Research at an Australian university implies that staff are more likely than students to believe that plagiarism is common among students (J. Wilkinson 2009). Major reasons for plagiarism on which staff and students largely agreed were: a failure to understand referencing rules; laziness or bad time management; and the ready availability of material on the Internet. Interestingly, students were less likely than staff to agree with the statement 'Students receive adequate guidance from staff about what is an [*sic*] isn't acceptable in terms of referencing in assignments', implying that many students feel they do not receive sufficient advice. These findings point, at the very least, to the need to be fully acquainted with your institution's regulations on plagiarism and its advice on proper referencing.

In view of all these uncertainties of both the definition of and the response to plagiarism, students may wonder whether they should take the issue of plagiarism seriously. My answer is that they most definitely should take it seriously. Academic practice places a high value on the originality of the work that is presented in any kind of output. To pass someone else's ideas and/or writings off as your own is widely regarded as morally dubious at best. Thus, while there are several grey areas with regard to plagiarism, as outlined in the previous paragraph, it is important not to overstate their significance. There *is* widespread condemnation of plagiarism in academic circles and it *is* nearly always punished when found in the work of students (and indeed that of others). You should therefore avoid plagiarizing the work of others at all costs. So concerned are universities about the growth in the number of plagiarism cases that come before examination boards and the likely role of the Internet in facilitating it that they are making more and more use of plagiarism detection software, which trawls the Internet for such things as strings of words (for example, Turnitin UK; see **http://turnitin. com/static/index.html**, accessed 22 September 2014, for more information). Thus, as several writers (e.g. McKeever 2006) have observed, the very technological development that is widely perceived as promoting the incidence of plagiarism—the Internet—is increasingly the springboard for its detection. Even well-known and ubiquitous search engines such as Google are sometimes employed to detect student plagiarism through the search for unique strings of words.

The most important issue from the student's point of view is that he or she should avoid plagiarism at all costs, as the penalties may be severe, regardless of the student's own views on the matter. First, do not 'lift' large sections of text without making it clear that they are in fact quotations. This makes it clear that the text in question is not your own work but that you are making a point by quoting someone. It is easy to get this wrong. In June 2006 it was reported that a plagiarism expert at the London School of Economics had been accused of plagiarism in a paper he published on plagiarism! A paragraph was found that copied verbatim a published source by someone else and that had not been acknowledged properly as from another source. The accused person defended himself by saying that this was due to a formatting error. It is common practice in academic publications to indent a large section of material that is being quoted, thus:

> The most important issue from the student's point of view is that they should avoid plagiarism at all costs, as the penalties may be severe, regardless of the student's own views on the matter. First, do not 'lift' large sections of text without making it clear that they are in fact quotations. This makes it clear that the text in question is not your own work but that you are making a point by quoting someone. It is easy to get this wrong. In June 2006 it was reported that a plagiarism expert

at the London School of Economics had been accused of plagiarism in a paper he published on plagiarism! A paragraph was found that copied verbatim a published source by someone else and that had not been acknowledged properly as from another source. The accused person defended himself by saying that this was due to a formatting error. It is common practice in academic publications to indent a large section of material that is being quoted.

(Bryman 2015)

The lack of indentation meant that the paragraph in question looked as though it was his own work. While it may be that this is a case of 'unintentional plagiarism' (Park 2003), distinguishing the intentional from the unintentional is by no means easy. Either way, the credibility and possibly the integrity of the author may be undermined. It is also important to realize that, for many if not most institutions, simply copying large portions of text and changing a few words will also be regarded as plagiarism.

Second, do not pass other people's ideas off as your own. This means that you should acknowledge the source of any ideas that you present that are not your own. It was this aspect of plagiarism that led to the author of *The Da Vinci Code*, Dan Brown, being accused of plagiarism. His accusers did not suggest that he had taken large chunks of text from their work and presented it as his own. Instead, they accused him of lifting their ideas from a non-fiction book they had written (*The Holy Blood and the Holy Grail*). However, Dan Brown *did* acknowledge his use of their historical work on the grail myth, though only in a general way in a list of acknowledgements, as novelists mercifully do not continuously reference ideas that they use in their work. Brown's accusers lost their case, but there have been other high-profile cases of plagiarism that *have* been proved. For example, in 2003, the UK Prime Minister's Director of Communications and Strategy issued a briefing to journalists on the concealment of weapons in Iraq. This was found to have been copied from several sources and became known as the 'dodgy dossier'. The fact that so much of it had been taken from the work of others undermined its credibility.

One of the most important messages of this section will hopefully be that you should guard against plagiarism at all costs. But it should also be clear that you should find out what your university and possibly departmental guidelines on the matter are. Research in an Australian university revealed that only half of the students in the study had read the university's misconduct policy and that those who had read it had a better understanding of plagiarism (Gullifer and Tyson 2014).

Quite aside from the rights and wrongs of plagiarism, it is not likely to impress your tutor if it is clear from reading the text that large chunks of your essay or report have been lifted from another source with just your own words interspersing the plagiarized text. In fact, that is often in my experience a giveaway—the contrast in styles is frequently very apparent and prompts the tutor to explore the possibility that some or much of the assignment you submit has in fact been plagiarized. Nor is it likely to impress most tutors if much of the text has been lifted but a few words changed here and there, along with a sprinkled few written by you. However, equally it has to be said that frequent quoting with linking sentences by you is not likely to impress either. When I have been presented with essays of that kind, I have frequently said to the student concerned that it is difficult to establish just what his or her own thoughts on the issue are.

Try therefore to express your ideas in your own words and acknowledge properly those ideas that are not your own. Plagiarism is something you may get away with once or twice, but it is so imprinted on the consciousness of many of us working in universities nowadays that you are unlikely to get away with it regularly. It is also extremely irritating to find that your own work has been plagiarized. I was asked to act as an external examiner of a doctoral thesis and found that large sections of one of my books had been taken and presented as the student's own work. I found this extremely annoying. A colleague to whom I mentioned the incident remarked that the only thing worse than plagiarism is incompetent plagiarism—incompetent because the student had plagiarized the work of someone he or she knew would be the external examiner. However, on reflection, the colleague was mistaken. Plagiarism is wrong—regardless of whether it is competently implemented or not. It is precisely for this reason that, in May 2007, Google banned advertisements from companies that write customized essays for students (**http://news.bbc.co.uk/1/hi/education/6680457.stm**, accessed 22 September 2014). Advice on plagiarism can usually be found in handbooks provided by students' institutions, as well as from **www.plagiarism.org/** (accessed 22 September 2014).

One final point to note is that plagiarism is like a moving target. What it is, how it should be defined, how it can be detected, how it should be penalized: all these issues and others are in a state of flux. It is very much a shifting situation, precisely because of the perception that it is increasing in frequency. The penalties can be severe, and, as I have witnessed when students have been presented with evidence of their plagiarism, it can be profoundly embarrassing and distressing for them. The message is simple: do not do it and make sure that you know exactly what it is and how it is defined at your institution, so that you do not inadvertently commit the sin of plagiarism.

Checklist

Questions to ask yourself when conducting and writing a literature review

○ Have you reflected on what your audience is expecting from the literature review?

○ Is your list of references up to date in your current areas of interest? Are there new areas of interest that you need to search on? Is it reasonably comprehensive?

○ What literature searching have you done recently?

○ What have you read recently? Have you found time to read?

○ What have you learned from the literature? Has this changed in any way your understanding of the subject in which you are working?

○ Is your search for the literature and the review you are writing being guided by your research questions? Has your reading of the literature made you think about revising your research questions?

○ Is what you have read going to influence or has it influenced your research design in any way? Has it given you ideas about what you need to consider and incorporate?

○ Have you addressed any key controversies in the literature and any different ways of conceptualizing your subject matter?

○ Have you been writing notes on what you have read? Do you need to reconsider how what you have read fits into your research?

○ Have you adopted a critical approach to presenting your literature review?

○ What story are you going to tell about the literature? In other words, have you worked out what is going to be the message about the literature that you want to tell your readers?

○ Has someone read a draft of your review to check on your writing style and the strength of your arguments about the literature?

》 *Key points*

● Writing a literature review is a means of reviewing the main ideas and research relating to your chosen area of interest.

● A competent literature review confirms you as someone who is competent in the subject area.

● A great deal of the work of writing a literature review is based upon reading the work of other researchers in your subject area; key skills can be acquired to help you get the most from your reading.

● Systematic review is a method that is gaining in popularity in social research as a way of enhancing the reliability of literature searching and review.

● Narrative review is a more traditional approach that has advantages of flexibility, which can make it more appropriate for inductive research and qualitative research designs.

Questions for review

Reviewing the existing literature

- What are the main reasons for writing a literature review?
- How can you ensure that you get the most from your reading?
- What are the main advantages and disadvantages associated with systematic review?
- What type of research questions is systematic review most suited to addressing?
- What are the main reasons for conducting a narrative literature review?
- In what type of research is narrative review most appropriate?

Searching the existing literature

- What are the main ways of finding existing literature on your subject?
- What is a keyword and how is it useful in searching the literature?

Referencing your work

- Why is it important to reference your work?
- What are the main referencing styles used in academic work and which of these is preferred by your institution?
- What is the role of the bibliography and what makes a good one?

Avoiding plagiarism

- What is plagiarism?
- Why is it taken so seriously by researchers?

 ### Online Resource Centre
www.oxfordtextbooks.co.uk/orc/brymansrm5e/

Visit the Online Resource Centre to enrich your understanding of how to review the literature. Follow up links to other resources, test yourself using multiple choice questions, and gain further guidance and inspiration from the Student Researcher's Toolkit.

6

Ethics and politics in social research

 ## Chapter outline

 ## Chapter guide

Ethical issues arise at a variety of stages in social research. This chapter deals with the concerns about ethics that might arise in the course of conducting research. The professional bodies concerned with the social sciences have been keen to spell out the ethical issues that can arise, and some of their statements will be reviewed in this chapter. Ethical issues cannot be ignored, as they relate directly to the integrity of a piece of research and of the disciplines that are involved. While ethical issues constitute the main emphasis of this chapter, related issues to do with the politics of research are also discussed. This chapter explores:

- some famous, even infamous, cases in which transgressions of ethical principles have occurred, though it is important not to take the view that ethical concerns arise only in relation to these extreme cases;

- different stances that can be and have been taken on ethics in social research;

- the significance and operation of four areas in which ethical concerns particularly arise: whether harm comes to participants; informed consent; invasion of privacy; and deception;

- some of the difficulties associated with ethical decision-making;

- some of the main political dimensions of research, from gaining access to research situations to the publication of findings.

Introduction

Discussions about the ethics of social research bring us into a realm in which the role of values in the research process becomes a topic of concern. Ethical considerations revolve around such issues as:

- How should we treat the people on whom we conduct research?

- Are there activities in which we should or should not engage in our relations with them?

Questions about ethics in social research also bring in the role of professional associations, such as the British Sociological Association (BSA) and the Social Research Association (SRA), which have formulated codes of ethics. The BSA's and SRA's codes will be referred to on several occasions in this chapter.

Statements of professional principles are frequently accessible from the Internet. Some of the most useful codes of ethics can be found at the following sites.

- British Sociological Association (BSA), *Statement of Ethical Practice*: **www.britsoc.co.uk/media/27107/StatementofEthicalPractice.pdf**.

- Social Research Association (SRA), *Ethical Guidelines*: **http://the-sra.org.uk/research-ethics/ethics-guidelines/**(accessed 14 July 2015).

- British Psychological Society (BPS), *Code of Conduct, Ethical Principles, and Guidelines*: **http://www.bps.org.uk/what-we-do/ethics-standards/ethics-standards**.

- American Sociological Association (ASA), *Code of Ethics*: **http://www.asanet.org/about/ethics.cfm**.

- The Economic and Social Research Council (ESRC), *Framework for Research Ethics* (see Tips and skills 'The ESRC's *Framework for Research Ethics*' below): **http://www.esrc.ac.uk/about-esrc/information/framework-for-research-ethics/**(accessed 14 July 2015).

All these statements were accessed on 23 May 2015.

Writings about ethics in social research are frequently frustrating for four reasons.

1. Writers often differ quite widely from each other over ethical issues and questions. In other words, they differ over what is and is not ethically acceptable.

2. The main elements in the debates do not seem to move forward a great deal. The same kinds of points that were made in the 1960s were being rehashed in the late 1990s and at the start of the present century. One thing that *has* changed is that ethical issues are nowadays more central to discussions about research than ever before. This may be due to a greater sensitivity to ethical issues, but it is also to do with a greater concern among representatives of universities, research funding bodies, and professional associations to exhibit good ethical credentials. One social scientist has turned sociological thinking onto the current research environment by suggesting that concerns about ethical issues today have the characteristics of a 'moral panic' (Van den Hoonaard 2001).

3. Debates about ethics have often accompanied well-known, not to say notorious, cases of alleged ethical transgression. They include: the study of a religious cult by a group of disguised researchers (Festinger et al. 1956); the use of pseudo-patients in the study of mental hospitals (Rosenhan 1973); and Rosenthal and Jacobson's (1968) field experiment to study teacher expectations in the classroom (Research in focus 3.1). The problem with this emphasis on notoriety is that it can be taken to imply that ethical concerns reside only in such extreme cases, when in fact the potential for ethical transgression is much more general than this. See Research in focus 6.1 and 6.2 for two cases that have acquired a celebrated status for their notoriety. It is striking that the research referred to in Research in focus 6.1 and 6.2 relates to investigations that occurred some decades ago. One of the reasons that authors (like me!) keep returning to these two cases is partly to do with the starkness of their ethical transgressions, but it is also to do with the fact that it would be difficult and most probably impossible to find such clear-cut cases of bad ethical practices in more recent years. That is a product of the greater ethical awareness among social researchers as well as the greater significance of ethical guidelines and research ethics committees nowadays. That it is not to say that research like that in Research in focus 6.1 and in Research in focus 6.2 is inconceivable today, but that it is a lot less likely to occur. However, Research in focus 6.2 includes a partial replication of the Milgram experiment. Also, Research in the news 6.1 contains an account of much more recent research which engendered considerable outrage.

4. Related to this last point is the fact that these extreme and notorious cases of ethical violation tend to be associated with particular research methods—notably disguised observation and the use of deception in experiments. Again, the problem with this association of ethics with certain studies (and methods) is that it implies that ethical concerns are associated with some methods but not others. As a result, the impression could be gleaned that other methods, such as questionnaires or overt observation, are immune from ethical problems. That is not the case. For example, conducting questionnaire or overt observation research with children will raise a lot of ethical issues that may not arise when the research is on adults.

Research in focus 6.1
The infamous case of the sociologist as voyeur

An investigation that has achieved particular notoriety because of its ethics (or lack of them, some might argue) is Humphreys's (1970) infamous study of homosexual encounters in public toilets ('tearoom trade'). Humphreys's research interest was in impersonal sex, and, in order to shed light on this area, he took on the role of 'watchqueen'—that is, someone who watches out for possible intruders while men meet and engage in homosexual sex in public toilets. As a result of his involvement in these social scenes, Humphreys was able to collect the details of active participants' car licence numbers. He was then able to track down their names and addresses and ended up with a sample of 100 active tearoom-trade participants. He then conducted an interview survey of a sample of those who had been identified and of a further sample that acted as a point of comparison. The interview schedule was concerned with health issues and included some questions about marital sex. In order to reduce the risk of being remembered, Humphreys waited a year before contacting his respondents and also changed his hair style.

Research in focus 6.2
The infamous case of the psychologist as Nazi concentration camp commandant

Milgram (1963) was concerned with the circumstances associated with the use of brutality in the Nazi concentration camps of the Second World War. In particular, he was interested in the processes whereby a person can be induced to cause extreme harm to another by virtue of being ordered to do so. To investigate this issue further, Milgram devised a laboratory experiment. Volunteers were recruited to act out the role of teachers who punished learners (who were accomplices of the experimenter) by submitting them to electric shocks when they gave incorrect answers to questions. The shocks were not, of course, real, but the teachers/volunteers were not aware of this. The level of electric shock was gradually increased with successive incorrect answers, until the teacher/volunteer refused to administer more shocks. Learners had been trained to respond to the rising level of electric shock with simulated but appropriate howls of pain. In the room was a further accomplice of Milgram's who cajoled the teacher/volunteer to continue to administer shocks, suggesting that it was part of the study's requirements to continue and that they were not causing permanent harm, in spite of the increasingly shrill cries of pain. Milgram's study shows that people can be induced to cause very considerable pain to others, and as such he saw it as shedding light on the circumstances leading to the horrors of the concentration camp.

The obedience study raises complex ethical issues, particularly in relation to the potential harm incurred by participants as a result of the experiments. It is worth noting that it was conducted over forty years ago and it is extremely unlikely that it would be considered acceptable to a university ethics committee or to researchers today. However, in 2006 Burger (2009) conducted a 'partial replication' of the Milgram experiment. Burger hypothesized that there would be little or no difference between Milgram's findings and his own some forty-five years later. The replication is 'partial' for several reasons such as: participants did not proceed beyond the lowest simulated voltage level that Milgram used (150 volts; 79 per cent of Milgram's teachers went beyond this point); participants were intensively screened for emotional and psychological problems and excluded if there was evidence of such problems; people who had studied some psychology were excluded (because the Milgram studies are so well known); and participants of all adult ages were included rather than up to the age of 50, as in the original studies. Burger also reckons that his sample was more ethnically diverse than Milgram's would have been. The replication had to be partial, because, as Burger puts it, 'current standards for the ethical treatment of participants clearly place Milgram's studies out of bounds' (Burger 2009: 2). Burger found that the propensity for obedience was only slightly lower than forty-five years previously, though, as A. G. Miller (2009) observes, the adjustments Burger had to make probably render comparisons with Milgram's findings questionable.

Researchers' ethical qualms do not extend to television, however. In March 2010, newspapers reported a French documentary based on a supposed game show called 'Game of Death' and broadcast on prime-time television. Eighty contestants signed contracts agreeing to inflict electric shocks on other participants. Shocks were administered when the other contestant failed to answer a question correctly. The shocks continued up to the highest voltage, with the contestants being egged on by an audience and a presenter. Only sixteen contestants stopped before administering the highest shock level, which would have been fatal. As in the Milgram experiment, the participants receiving the shocks were actors who simulated howls of agony and the shocks themselves were of course also fake. An account of this programme, which refers to Milgram, can be found at **www.independent.co.uk/news/media/tv-radio/the-evil-that-reality-television-contestants-do-1923218. html**.

Also, the following is a CNN news item that refers to Burger's research as well as Milgram's and includes a slideshow that contains a commentary from Burger: **http://edition.cnn.com/2008/HEALTH/12/19/ milgram.experiment.obedience/**.

Footage from the original Milgram experiments can be found on YouTube and makes fascinating viewing. However, some of these clips are spoof versions of the experiment!

All these websites were accessed on 22 September 2014.

In this chapter, I will introduce the main ethical issues and debates about ethics. I am not going to try to resolve them, because they are not readily capable of resolution. This is why the ethical debate has scarcely moved on since the 1960s. What *is* crucial is to be aware of the ethical principles involved and of the nature of the concerns about ethics in social research. It is only if researchers are aware of the issues involved that they can make informed decisions about the implications of certain choices. If nothing else, you should be aware of the possible disapproval and possible censure that will be coming your way if you make certain kinds of choice. My chief concern lies with the ethical issues that arise in relations between researchers and research participants in the course of an investigation. This focus by no means exhausts the range of ethical issues and dilemmas that might arise, such as in relation to the funding of social research or how findings are used by non-researchers. However, the ethical issues that arise in the course of doing research are the ones that are most likely to impinge on students. Writers on research ethics adopt different stances concerning the ethical issues that arise in connection with relationships between researchers and research participants. Key concept 6.1 outlines some of these stances.

Key concept 6.1
Stances on ethics

Authors on social research ethics can be characterized in terms of the stances they take on the issue. The following stances can be distinguished.

- *Universalism.* A universalist stance takes the view that ethical precepts should never be broken. Infractions of ethical principles are wrong in a moral sense and are damaging to social research. This kind of stance can be seen in the writings of Erikson (1967), Dingwall (1980), and Bulmer (1982). Bulmer does, however, point to some forms of what appears to be disguised observation that may be acceptable. One is retrospective covert observation, which occurs when a researcher writes up his or her experiences in social settings in which he or she participated but not as a researcher. An example would be Van Maanen (1991b), who wrote up his experiences as a ride operator in Disneyland many years after he had been employed there in vacation jobs. Even a universalist such as Erikson (1967: 372) recognizes that it 'would be absurd . . . to insist as a point of ethics that sociologists should always introduce themselves as investigators everywhere they go and should inform every person who figures in their thinking exactly what their research is all about'.

- *Situation ethics*. E. Goode (1996) has argued for deception to be considered on a case-by-case basis. In other words, he argues for what Fletcher (1966: 31) has called a 'situation ethics', or more specifically 'principled relativism', which can be contrasted with the universalist ethics of some writers. This argument has two ways of being represented.

  1. *The end justifies the means*. Some writers argue that, unless there is some breaking of ethical rules, we would never know about certain social phenomena. Fielding (1982) essentially argues for this position in relation to his research on the National Front, an extreme right-wing organization that was politically influential in the 1970s. Without some kind of disguised observation, this important movement and its appeal would not have been studied. Similarly, for their covert participant observation study of websites supportive of individuals with eating disorders (known as 'pro-ana' websites—see Research in focus 19.9), Brotsky and Giles (2007: 96) argue that deception was justified, 'given the charges laid against the pro-ana community (that they are effectively sanctioning self-starvation), and the potential benefit of our findings to the eating disorders clinical field'. This kind of argument is usually linked to the second form of a situationist argument in relation to social research ethics.

  2. *No choice*. It is often suggested that we have no choice but to dissemble on occasions if we want to investigate the issues in which we are interested. This view can be discerned in the writings of Holdaway (1982) and Homan and Bulmer (1982). For example, Brotsky and Giles (2007: 96) write: 'it was felt highly unlikely that access would be granted to a researcher openly disclosing the purpose of her study'.

- *Ethical transgression is pervasive*. It is often observed that virtually all research involves elements that are at least ethically questionable. This occurs whenever participants are not given absolutely all the details on a piece of research, or when there is variation in the amount of knowledge about research. Punch (1994: 91), for example, observes that 'some dissimulation is intrinsic to social life and, therefore, to fieldwork'. He quotes Gans (1962: 44) in support of this point: 'If the researcher is completely honest with people about his activities, they will try to hide actions and attitudes they consider undesirable, and so will be dishonest. Consequently, the researcher must be dishonest to get honest data.'

- *Anything goes (more or less)*. The writers associated with arguments relating to situation ethics and a recognition of the pervasiveness of ethical transgressions are arguing not for an 'anything-goes' mentality, but for a certain amount of flexibility in ethical decision-making. However, Douglas (1976) has argued that the kinds of deception in which social researchers engage are trivial compared to those perpetrated by powerful institutions in modern society (such as the mass media, the police, and industry). His book is an inventory of tactics for deceiving people so that their trust is gained and they reveal themselves to the researcher. Very few researchers subscribe to this stance. Denzin (1968) comes close to an anything-goes stance when he suggests that social researchers are entitled to study anyone in any setting provided the work has a 'scientific' purpose, does not harm participants, and does not deliberately damage the discipline.

- *Deontological versus consequentialist ethics*. Another distinction that has attracted interest in recent years is between deontological and consequentialist ethics. Deontological ethics considers certain acts as wrong (or good) in and of themselves. Consequentialist ethics looks at the consequences of an act for guidance as to whether it is right or wrong. In relation to the consideration of ethical issues in social research, deontological arguments tend to prevail—in terms of the issues covered below, deceiving research participants or *not* providing them with the opportunity for informed consent is regarded as ethically wrong. Consequentialist arguments do sometimes surface, however. For example, you sometimes see the argument that an activity such as covert observation is wrong because it can harm the reputation of the profession of social research or of an organization. As such, other social researchers would be adversely affected by the ethically dubious decision to engage in covert observation.

Tips and skills
Ethics committees

In addition to needing to be familiar with the codes of practice produced by professional associations such as the British Sociological Association, the American Sociological Association, and the Social Research Association, you should be familiar with the ethical guidelines of your university or college. Most higher education organizations have ethics committees that issue guidelines about ethical practice. These guidelines are often based on or influenced by the codes developed by professional associations. Universities' and colleges' guidelines provide indications of what are considered ethically unacceptable practices. Sometimes you will need to submit your proposed research to an ethics committee of your university or college. This is likely to occur if there is some uncertainty about whether your proposed research is likely to be in breach of the guidelines, or if you want to go ahead with research that you know raises ethical issues but you wish to obtain permission to do it anyway.

The ethical guidelines and the ethics committee are there to protect research participants, but they are also involved in protecting institutions, so that researchers will be deterred from behaving in ethically unacceptable ways that might rebound on institutions. Ethically inappropriate behaviour could cause problems for institutions if it gave rise to legal action against them or to adverse publicity. However, ethics committees and their guidelines exist to help and protect researchers too, so that they are less likely to conduct research that could damage their reputations.

One of the main approaches used by ethics committees is to ask researchers to indicate whether their research entails certain procedures or activities which are often derived from professional guidelines such as the BSA's *Statement of Ethical Practice* or the Economic and Social Research Council (ESRC)'s *Framework for Research Ethics* (*FRE*) (see Tips and skills 'The ESRC's *Framework for Research Ethics*' below). These include covert observation, so that effectively the researcher self-declares whether he or she is likely to engage in ethically dubious practices. This process usually entails completing a form to show that you have considered potential ethical issues that might arise. This form is likely to ask questions such as 'Will there be any potential harm, discomfort, physical or psychological risks for research participants?' and the researcher needs to answer 'Yes' or 'No'. If there is a possibility that you may engage in such a practice, the proposed research is then 'flagged' for full scrutiny by the ethics committee. In such an instance, the researcher is required to provide a full account of the research and the rationale for using the ethically dubious practice(s). This can slow down research progress considerably and can result in the committee refusing to allow it to proceed.

In recent years, research ethics committees (often called Institutional Review Boards in the USA) have become quite controversial. Some writers see them as too influenced by a natural science model of the research process and as therefore hostile to social research and to qualitative research in particular (Lincoln and Tierney 2004). Further, they are sometimes seen as having gone too far in terms of their role of protecting institutions from litigious disgruntled research participants (Van den Hoonard 2001). It has also been suggested that they divert attention from the need to be constantly vigilant for ethical problems that might arise in the course of doing research (Guillemin and Gillam 2004). In other words, there is a concern that, once the researcher has jumped over the bureaucratic hurdle of the ethics committee, he or she may feel that the ethical issues have been covered. This is clearly not the case, as ethical issues can and invariably do arise at all stages of the research process.

Ethical principles

Discussions about ethical principles in social research, and perhaps more specifically about transgressions of them, tend to revolve around certain issues that recur in different guises, but they have been usefully broken down by Diener and Crandall (1978) into four main areas:

1. whether there is *harm to participants*;
2. whether there is a *lack of informed consent*;
3. whether there is an *invasion of privacy*;
4. whether *deception* is involved.

I will look at each of these in turn, but it should be appreciated that these four principles overlap somewhat. For example, it is difficult to imagine how the principle of informed consent could be built into an investigation in which research participants were deceived. However, there is no doubt that these four areas form a useful classification of ethical principles in and for social research.

Harm to participants

Research that is likely to harm participants is regarded by most people as unacceptable. But what is harm? Harm can entail a number of facets: physical harm; harm to participants' development; loss of self-esteem; stress; and 'inducing subjects to perform reprehensible acts', as Diener and Crandall (1978: 19) put it. In several studies that we have encountered in this book, there has been real or potential harm to participants.

- In the Rosenthal and Jacobson (1968) study (Research in focus 3.2), it is at least possible that the pupils who had not been identified as 'spurters' who would excel in their studies were adversely affected in their intellectual development by the greater attention received by the spurters.

- In the Festinger et al. (1956) study of a religious cult (mentioned in Chapter 3 and discussed more fully in Chapter 26 in the section entitled 'The natural science model and qualitative research'), it is quite likely that the fact that the researchers joined the group at a crucial time—close to the projected end of the world—fuelled the delusions of group members.

- Many of the participants in the Milgram (1963) experiment on obedience to authority (Research in focus 6.2) experienced high levels of stress and anxiety as a consequence of being incited to administer electric shocks. It could also be argued that Milgram's observers were 'inducing subjects to perform reprehensible acts'.

- Many of the participants in Humphreys's (1970) research (see Research in focus 6.1) were married men who are likely to have been fearful of detection as practising homosexuals. It is conceivable that his methods could have resulted in some of them becoming identified.

- In manipulating people's emotions, it could be argued that the Facebook experiment referred to in Research in the news 6.1 could have harmed some of the unwitting participants, especially those who were exposed to a reduction in positive emotion.

Research in the news 6.1

An experiment on Facebook users performed by Kramer, Guillory, and Hancock (2014) suggests that incidents such as those described in Research in focus 6.1 and 6.2 should not be regarded as symptomatic of problems rooted in the past. A massive sample of 689,003 Facebook users was randomly selected in order to investigate whether exposure to positive or negative emotional expressions caused a change in users' own affective expressions as expressed in their own posts. Two experiments were created: one in which an experimental group was exposed for a one-week period to a reduction in positive emotions in friends' news feeds compared to a control group; in the other experiment, the experimental group was exposed to a reduction in negative emotions and compared to the control group. However, participants were not offered the opportunity to give explicit informed consent. Instead, the researchers claim that their investigation 'was consistent with Facebook's Data Use Policy, to which all users agree prior to creating an account on Facebook, constituting informed consent for this research' (Kramer et al. 2014: 8789). In other words, the researchers were relying on an implicit informed consent. The research engendered a storm of protest in the mass media in both the UK, for example:

www.theguardian.com/technology/2014/jun/29/facebook-users-emotions-news-feeds

www.bbc.co.uk/news/technology-28051930 (both accessed 2 July 2014)

—and in the USA, for example:

www.nytimes.com/2014/06/30/technology/facebook-tinkers-with-users-emotions-in-news-feed-experiment-stirring-outcry.html?_r = 0 (accessed 2 July 2014).

It is the lack of explicit informed consent that lies at the heart of this outcry, and Facebook has since admitted that it should have done things differently—see www.bbc.co.uk/news/technology-29475019 (accessed 8 October 2014).

The BSA *Statement of Ethical Practice* enjoins researchers to 'anticipate, and to guard against, consequences for research participants which can be predicted to be harmful' and 'to consider carefully the possibility that the research experience may be a disturbing one'. Similar sentiments are expressed by the SRA's *Ethical Guidelines*, for example, when it is advocated that the 'social researcher should try to minimize disturbance both to subjects themselves and to the subjects' relationships with their environment'.

The issue of harm to participants is further addressed in ethical codes by advocating care over maintaining the confidentiality of records. This means that the identities and records of individuals should be maintained as confidential. This injunction also means that care needs to be taken when findings are being presented to ensure that individuals are not identified or identifiable. The case of a study of an American town, Springdale (a pseudonym), by Vidich and Bensman (1968) is instructive in this regard. The research was based on Vidich's participant observation within the town for over two years. The published book on the research was uncomplimentary about the town and many of its leaders and was written in what many people felt was a rather patronizing tone. To make matters worse, it was possible to identify individuals through the published account. The town's inhabitants responded with a Fourth of July Parade in which many of them wore badges with their pseudonyms, and an effigy of Vidich was set up so that it was peering into manure. The townspeople also responded by announcing their refusal to cooperate in any more social research. They were clearly upset by the publication and to that extent were harmed by it. This example also touches on the issue of privacy, which will be addressed below.

As this last case suggests, the issue of confidentiality raises particular difficulties for many forms of qualitative research. In quantitative research, it is relatively easy to make records anonymous and to report findings in a way that does not allow individuals to be identified. However, this is often less easy with qualitative research, where particular care has to be taken with regard to the possible identification of persons and places. The use of pseudonyms is a common recourse, but may not eliminate entirely the possibility of identification. This issue raises particular problems with regard to the secondary analysis of qualitative data (see Chapter 24), since it is very difficult, though by no means impossible, to present **field notes** and interview transcripts in a way that will prevent people and places from being identified. As Alderson (1998) has suggested, the difficulty is one of being able to ensure that the same safeguards concerning confidentiality can be guaranteed when secondary analysts examine such records as those provided by the original primary researcher.

A further area of ethical consideration relates to the possibility of harm to the researcher, an issue that was introduced in Tips and skills 'Safety in research' (see Chapter 4). In other words, the person seeking clearance for their research from an ethics committee may be encouraged to consider the possibility of physical or emotional harm through exposure to a fieldwork setting. Even if such a consideration is not stipulated in an ethics form, it is something that you should consider very seriously.

The need for confidentiality can present dilemmas for researchers. Westmarland (2001) has discussed the dilemmas she faced when observing violence by the police towards people being held in custody. She argues that, while a certain level of violence might be deemed acceptable, in part to protect the officers themselves and the public, there is an issue of at what point it is no longer acceptable and the researcher needs to inform on those involved. Moreover, such a level of violence may be consistent with the police's occupational culture. The problem for the ethnographer is compounded by the fact that blowing the whistle on violence may result in a loss of the researcher's credibility among officers, premature termination of the investigation, or inability to gain access in the future. In the process, career issues are brought to the fore for the researcher, which connects with the discussion of political issues towards the end of this chapter. Similarly, in a feminist study of girls' experiences of violence, Burman et al. (2001: 455) encountered some distressing revelations that prompted them to ask 'exactly what, and how much, should be disclosed, to whom, and how should this be done'. Thus, the important injunction to protect confidentiality may create dilemmas for the researcher that are by no means easy to resolve.

The issue of confidentiality is clearly a very important one. Israel and Hay (2004) treat it as a separate principle of ethics in its own right. As they observe, if researchers do not observe the confidentiality of what is said to them, 'who would talk to them in the future?' (Israel and Hay 2004: 94). Thus, quite aside from the intrinsic wrongness of not keeping confidences, there is the consequentialist argument that it could harm generations of future researchers.

One of the problems with the harm-to-participants principle is that it is not possible to identify in all circumstances whether harm is likely, though that fact should not be taken to mean that there is no point in seeking to protect participants from harm. Kimmel (1988) notes in this connection the example of the Cambridge–Summerville Youth Study. In 1939 an experiment was conducted on boys aged 5–13 who either were identified as likely to become delinquent or were average in this regard. The 506 boys were equally divided in terms of this characteristic. They were randomly assigned either to an experimental

Tips and skills
Data protection

One aspect of confidentiality and the management of it is that, in the UK, the Data Protection Act (1998) confers obligations on people and organizations who hold personal data on others and it confers rights on those about whom such information is held. The Information Commissioner's website points out the Act comprises eight principles whose main purpose 'is to protect the interests of the individuals whose personal data is being processed' and which state that data must be:

- Fairly and lawfully processed
- Processed for limited purposes
- Adequate, relevant and not excessive
- Accurate and up to date
- Not kept for longer than is necessary
- Processed in line with your rights
- Secure
- Not transferred to other countries without adequate protection

The second area covered by the Act provides individuals with important rights, including the right to find out what personal information is held on computer and most paper records (http://ico.org.uk/for_organisations/data_protection/the_guide, accessed 22 September 2014).

These principles are important to bear in mind, as it is clear that it is easy to fall foul of them when conducting social research. However, Section 33 of the Act effectively exempts personal information collected for research purposes from some of these principles. According to this section, the researcher must ensure that 'personal data held for [research] purposes may be kept indefinitely as long as it is not used in connection with decisions affecting particular individuals, or in a way that is likely to cause damage or distress' (http://ico.org.uk/for_organisations/data_protection/the_guide, accessed 22 September 2014).

Holmes (2012: 88–90) provides some important and useful suggestions about how to protect confidentiality and participants' data. Her tips include:

- not storing participants' names and addresses or letter correspondence on hard drives;
- using identifier codes on data files and storing the list of participants and their identifier codes separately in a locked cabinet;
- ensuring that transcribers sign a letter saying they will conform to the Data Protection Act;
- ensuring transcripts do not include participants' names;
- keeping copies of transcripts in a locked cabinet.

The central aim of this Tips and skills feature is to reinforce the point that there is an environment that takes confidentiality and data protection issues very seriously and that it is important for students and researchers generally to be attuned to their obligations and what is required of them.

group in which they received preventative counselling or to a no-treatment control group. In the mid-1970s the records were re-examined and were quite shocking: 'Treated subjects were more likely than controls to evidence signs of alcoholism and serious mental illness, died at a younger age, suffered from more stress-related diseases, tended to be employed in lower-prestige occupations, and were more likely to commit second crimes' (Kimmel 1988: 19).

In other words, the treatment brought about a train of negative consequences for the group. This is an extreme example and relates to experimental research, which is not a research design that is commonly employed in social research (see Chapter 3), but it does illustrate the difficulty of anticipating harm to respondents. The ASA *Code of Ethics* suggests that if there is more than 'minimal risk for participants', then informed consent, the focus of the next section, is essential.

Lack of informed consent

The issue of informed consent is in many respects the area within social research ethics that is most hotly debated. The bulk of the discussion tends to focus on what is variously called disguised or covert observation. Such observation can involve covert participant observation (Key concept 19.2), or simple or contrived observation (Key concept 14.3), in which the researcher's true identity is unknown. The principle means that prospective research participants should be given as much information as might be needed to make an informed decision about whether or not they wish to participate in a study. Covert observation transgresses that principle, because participants are not given the opportunity to refuse to cooperate. They are involved, whether they like it or not.

Lack of informed consent is a feature of the research described in Research in focus 6.1 and 6.2 and Research in the news 6.1. In Humphreys's research, informed consent is absent, because the men for whom he acted as a watchqueen were not given the opportunity to refuse participation in his investigation. Similar points can be made about several other studies encountered in this book, such as Festinger et al. (1956), Winlow et al. (2001), Brotsky and Giles (2007), Pearson (2009), Sallaz (2009), and Lloyd (2012). The principle of informed consent also entails the implication that, even when people know they are being asked to participate in research, they should be fully informed about the research process. As the SRA *Ethical Guidelines* suggest:

> Inquiries involving human subjects should be based as far as practicable on the freely given informed consent of subjects. Even if participation is required by law, it should still be as informed as possible. In voluntary inquiries, subjects should not be under the impression that they are required to participate. They should be aware of their entitlement to refuse at any stage for whatever reason and to withdraw data just supplied. Information that would be likely to affect a subject's willingness to participate should not be deliberately withheld, since this would remove from subjects an important means of protecting their own interests.

Similarly, the BSA *Statement* says:

> As far as possible participation in sociological research should be based on the freely given informed consent of those studied. This implies a responsibility on the sociologist to explain as fully as possible, and in terms meaningful to participants, what the research is about, who is undertaking and financing it, why it is being undertaken, and how it is to be disseminated and used.

Thus, while Milgram's experimental subjects were volunteers and therefore knew they were going to participate in research, there is a lack of informed consent because they were not given full information about the nature of the research and its possible implications for them.

However, as Homan (1991: 73) has observed, implementing the principle of informed consent 'is easier said than done'. At least two major points stand out here.

- It is extremely difficult to present prospective participants with absolutely all the information that might be required for them to make an informed decision about their involvement. In fact, relatively minor transgressions probably pervade most social research, such as deliberately underestimating the amount of time that an interview is likely to take so that people are not put off being interviewed and not giving absolutely all the details about one's research for fear of contaminating people's answers to questions.

- In ethnographic research, the researcher is likely to come into contact with a wide spectrum of people, and ensuring that absolutely everyone has the opportunity for informed consent is not practicable because it would be extremely disruptive in everyday contexts. For example, in his research on football fans, Pearson (2012) was initially a covert participant observer but in a later phase he adopted an overt role. He notes that during this later phase, he sought consent for his research from Manchester United supporters through an online discussion forum. He outlined his research plans and the reasons for his research and notified members of the forum that if they objected he would ensure that he would not record their behaviour or conversations, regardless of whether they took place in person or online. Pearson says that the response was 'overwhelmingly positive' though one person asked to be excluded. However, Pearson notes: 'As the group was a fluid one with new or casual members appearing all the time (some of whom did not post on the forum), it was impossible to ensure that all members knew exactly what I was doing, why, and how it could affect them' (Pearson 2012: 23). Therefore, some supporters are likely to have been informed but some were not. This is a common problem for ethnographers, who are likely to encounter people in the course of their research who form part of the social setting but whose involvement is fleeting and who therefore are not given the opportunity for informed consent.

In spite of the widespread condemnation of violations of informed consent and the view that covert observation is especially vulnerable to accusations of unethical practice in this regard, studies using the method still appear periodically (e.g. Brotsky and Giles 2007; Pearson 2009). The defence is usually of the 'end-justifies-the-means' kind, which is further discussed below. What is interesting in this present context is that the BSA *Statement* essentially leaves the door ajar for covert observation. The phrase 'as far as possible' regarding informed consent in the last quotation from the *Statement* does this, but the BSA then goes even further in relation to **covert research**:

> There are serious ethical and legal issues in the use of covert research but the use of covert methods may be justified in certain circumstances. For example, difficulties arise when research participants change their behaviour because they know they are being studied. Researchers may also face problems when access to spheres of social life is closed to social scientists by powerful or secretive interests. . . . However, covert methods violate the principles of informed consent and may invade the privacy of those being studied. . . . Participant or non-participant observation in non-public spaces or experimental manipulation of research participants without their knowledge should be resorted to only where it is impossible to use other methods to obtain essential data. . . . In such studies it is important to safeguard the anonymity of research participants. Ideally, where informed consent has not been obtained prior to the research it should be obtained post-hoc.

While this statement does not condone the absence of informed consent associated with covert research, it is not unequivocally censorious either. It recognizes that covert research 'may avoid certain problems' and refers, without using the term, to the possibility of reactivity associated with overt observational methods. It also recognizes that covert methods can help to get over the difficulty of gaining access to certain kinds of setting. The passage entails an acknowledgement that covert methods jeopardize the principle of informed consent along with the privacy principle (see the section on 'Invasion of privacy' below), but it implies that covert research can be used 'where it is impossible to use other methods to obtain essential data'. The difficulty here clearly is how a researcher is to decide whether it is in fact impossible to obtain data other than by covert work. Similarly, in the ESRC's *Framework for Research Ethics* (see Tips and skills 'The ESRC's *Framework for Research Ethics*'), it is proposed: 'Deception (i.e. research without consent) should only be used as a last resort when no other approach is possible.'

I suspect that, by and large, covert observers typically make their judgements in this connection on the basis of the *anticipated* difficulty of gaining access to a setting or of encountering reactivity problems, rather than as a response to difficulties they have actually experienced. For example, Holdaway (1982: 63) has written that, as a police officer, his only alternatives to covert participant observation were either equally unethical (but less desirable) or 'unrealistic'. Similarly, Homan justified his use of covert participant observation of a religious sect on the grounds that sociologists were viewed very negatively by group members and therefore 'it seemed probable that the prevalence of such a perception would prejudice the effectiveness of a fieldworker declaring an identity as sociologist' (Homan and Bulmer 1982: 107). Pearson (2009) writes that he employed covert participant observation for a study of football hooliganism because his early attempts to conduct the research by interview proved unreliable: hardcore violent hooligans played down their involvement, whereas non-violent ones exaggerated theirs. The issue of the circumstances in which violations of ethical principles, such as informed consent, are deemed acceptable will reappear in the discussion below. It also has to be recognized that covert participant observation can cause difficulties for researchers because of their need to be consistent in the persona they project. Pearson (2009) felt that he had to engage in criminal acts in order to sustain his research and his identity among the hooligans with whom he consorted. He writes:

> On one occasion, for example, when I believed it necessary to prove my reliability to the subjects, I individually confronted a small group of rival supporters in a public house. The attempt was purely 'for show' as I predicted the group would intervene and prevent any serious physical confrontation. Nonetheless, the action was both criminal (threatening behaviour) and in the short term seriously distorted the field. My justification for this action at the time was that it enhanced my position in the field and I was accepted for the remainder of the season as one of the 'hardcore' despite my continual 'opting out' of more serious offences.
>
> (Pearson 2009: 248–9)

The principle of informed consent is also bound up to some extent with the issue of harm to participants. Erikson (1967) has suggested that, if the principle is not followed and if participants are harmed as a result of the research, the investigator is more culpable than if they did not know. For example, he writes: 'If we happen to harm people who have agreed to act as subjects, we can at least argue that they knew something of the risks involved' (Erikson 1967: 369). While this might seem like a recipe for seeking a salve for the social researcher's conscience, it does point to an important issue—namely, that the researcher is more likely to be vilified if participants were adversely affected when they were unsuspecting accomplices than when they were informed participants.

However, it is debatable whether that means that the researcher is any less culpable for that harm. Erikson implies they are less culpable, but this is a potential area for disagreement.

Informed consent forms

Increasingly, researchers prefer to obtain the informed consent of research participants by getting them to sign informed consent forms. The advantage of such forms is that they give respondents the opportunity to be fully informed of the nature of the research and the implications of their participation at the outset. Further, the researcher has a signed record of consent if any concerns are subsequently raised by participants or others. The chief possible problem is that the requirement to sign the form may prompt rather than alleviate concerns on the part of prospective participants, so that they end up declining to be involved. Also, the direction of qualitative studies can be less predictable than that of quantitative ones, so it is difficult to be specific within forms about some issues. Tips and skills 'A sample interview consent form' and 'A sample study information sheet' provide an indication of the kinds of features that might be taken into account in seeking participants' informed consent. There is very useful advice on consent forms and other aspects of ethical practice in relation to research at: **www. ethicsguidebook.ac.uk/** (accessed 23 September 2014);

www.data-archive.ac.uk/create-manage/consent- ethics/consent (accessed 23 September 2014).

Invasion of privacy

This third area of ethical concern relates to the issue of the degree to which invasions of privacy can be condoned. The right to privacy is a tenet that many of us hold dear, and transgressions of that right in the name of research are not regarded as acceptable. It is very much linked to the notion of informed consent, because, to the degree that informed consent is given on the basis of a detailed understanding of what the research participant's involvement is likely to entail, he or she in a sense acknowledges that the right to privacy has been surrendered for that limited domain. The BSA *Statement* makes a direct link in the passage quoted in the previous section ('Lack of informed consent') when it suggests: 'covert methods violate the principles of informed consent and may invade the privacy of those being studied.' Of course, the research participant does not abrogate the right to privacy entirely by providing informed consent. For example, when people agree to be interviewed, they will frequently refuse to answer certain questions on whatever grounds they feel are justified. Often, these refusals will be based on a feeling that certain questions delve into private realms, which respondents do not wish to make public, regardless of the fact that the interview is in private. Examples might

---

Tips and skills
A sample interview consent form

- I, the undersigned, have read and understood the Study Information Sheet provided . . . .
- I have been given the opportunity to ask questions about the Study.
- I understand that taking part in the Study will include being interviewed and audio-recorded.
- I have been given adequate time to consider my decision and I agree to take part in the Study.
- I understand that my personal details such as name and employer address will not be revealed to people outside the project.
- I understand that my words may be quoted in publications, reports, Web pages and other research outputs but my name will not be used.
- I agree to assign the copyright I hold in any material related to this project to [name of researcher].
- I understand that I can withdraw from the Study at any time and I will not be asked any questions about why I no longer want to take part.

Name of Participant: _____ Date:

Researcher Signature: _____ Date:

[Based on examples from UK Data Archive (2009) and several UK universities]

Tips and skills
A sample study information sheet

Thank you very much for agreeing to participate in this study. This Information Sheet explains what the study is about and how we would like you to take part in it.

The purpose of the study is to [give a short explanation of the study].

In order to elicit your views, we would like you to be interviewed by one of the researchers involved in the Study at the University of [University name]. If you agree to this, the interview will be audio-recorded and will last approximately one hour. You will also be asked to keep a workplace diary for four weeks. For you to take part in this aspect of the Study the consent of your line manager will be required. Details of how to go about this will be given when you attend for interview.

The information provided by you in the interview and workplace diary will be used for research purposes. It will not be used in a manner which would allow identification of your individual responses.

At the end of the Study, anonymized research data will be archived at the UK Data Archive in order to make it available to other researchers in line with current data-sharing practices.

The study has been considered by an Institutional Ethics Committee at the University of [University name] and has been given a favourable review.

All reasonable travel and subsistence expenses that you incur through taking part in the Study will be reimbursed, but please keep all receipts.

Once again, we would like to thank you for agreeing to take part in this Study. If you have any questions about the research at any stage, please do not hesitate to contact us.

[Researcher contact addresses, telephone, email addresses]

be questions about income, religious beliefs, or sexual activities.

Covert methods are usually deemed to be violations of the privacy principle on the grounds that participants are not being given the opportunity to refuse invasions of their privacy. Such methods also mean that they might reveal confidences or information that they would not have revealed if they had known about the status of the confidant as researcher. The issue of privacy is invariably linked to issues of anonymity and confidentiality in the research process, an area that has already been touched on in the context of the question of whether harm comes

Student experience
Informed consent forms

For Rebecca Barnes, 'ethical issues were a paramount concern, especially given the extremely sensitive and emotive nature of the topic'. She designed a participant information sheet and a consent form 'in order to make participants aware of their rights, and to advise them of the possible negative consequences of participating in the research'. Erin Sanders writes that she did not develop a consent form:

> because the women I interviewed didn't read English and I can't write in Thai, I didn't have a signed consent form. I was able to get verbal consent—but now I feel it might have been better to have a document translated into Thai—so that they understood the research—but also understood their rights and the steps that would be taken to safeguard their identities.

 To read more, go to the Online Resource Centre: www.oxfordtextbooks.co.uk/orc/brymansrm5e/

Student experience
Anonymity and confidentiality

Rebecca Barnes writes that, in the participant information sheet she prepared, she stopped short of *guaranteeing* anonymity and confidentiality.

> I assured participants that I would do my utmost to uphold confidentiality and anonymity, but I was cautious about guaranteeing confidentiality and anonymity. Factors outside a researcher's control such as theft of confidential documents make such guarantees misleading. Nonetheless, I did do everything that I could to ensure confidentiality and anonymity, such as using pseudonyms in transcripts and beyond; storing interview tapes, transcripts, and participants' contact details separately. Also, when I transcribed the interviews, I altered specific details that could make a participant identifiable, such as the area in which they live, their occupation, and other details such as pubs or nightclubs that participants referred to. I ensured that the details that I changed did not change the meaning of participants' words in any way.

 To read more, go to the Online Resource Centre: www.oxfordtextbooks.co.uk/orc/brymansrm5e/

to participants. The BSA *Statement* forges this kind of connection: 'The anonymity and privacy of those who participate in the research process should be respected. Personal information concerning research participants should be kept confidential. In some cases it may be necessary to decide whether it is proper or appropriate to record certain kinds of sensitive information.'

Issues about ensuring anonymity and confidentiality in relation to the recording of information and the maintenance of records relates to all methods of social research. In other words, while covert research may pose certain kinds of problem regarding the invasion of privacy, other methods of social research are implicated in possible difficulties in connection with anonymity and confidentiality. This was clearly the case with the Springfield research (Vidich and Bensman 1968), which was based on open participant observation. The issue here was that the absence of safeguards concerning the protection of the identity of some members of the community meant that certain matters about them came into the public domain that should have remained private.

Deception

Deception occurs when researchers represent their work as something other than what it is. The experiment by Milgram referred to in Research in focus 6.2 involved deception. Participants were led to believe they were administering real electric shocks. Deception in various degrees is probably quite widespread in experimental research, because researchers often want to limit participants' understanding of what the research is about so that they respond more naturally to the experimental treatment.

However, deception is by no means the exclusive preserve of social psychology experiments. E. Goode (1996), for example, placed four fake and slightly different dating advertisements in periodicals. He received nearly 1,000 replies and was able to conduct a content analysis of them. Several of the studies referred to in this book entail deception: Rosenthal and Jacobson (1968) deceived teachers into believing that particular children in their charge were likely to excel at school, when they had in fact been randomly selected; Festinger et al. (1956) deceived cult members that they were in fact real converts; Rosenhan's (1973) associates deceived admissions staff at mental hospitals that they were mentally ill; Holdaway (1982) deceived his superiors and peers that he was functioning solely as a police officer; and Brotsky (Brotsky and Giles 2007) posed as an anorexic and posted messages onto a 'pro-ana' website on that basis.

The ethical objection to deception seems to turn on two points. First, it is not a nice thing to do. While the SRA *Guidelines* recognize that deception is widespread in social interaction, it is hardly desirable. Second, there is the question of professional self-interest. If social researchers became known as snoopers who deceived people as a matter of professional course, the image of our work would be adversely affected and we might experience difficulty in gaining financial support and the cooperation of future prospective research participants. As the SRA *Guidelines* put it: 'It remains the duty of social researchers and their collaborators, however, not to pursue methods of inquiry that are likely to infringe human values and sensibilities. To do so, whatever the methodological advantages, would be to endanger the reputation of social research and the mutual trust between social researchers and society which is a prerequisite for much research.' Similarly, Erikson (1967: 369) has argued that disguised observation 'is liable to damage the reputation of sociology in the larger society and close off promising areas of research for future investigators'.

One of the chief problems with the discussion of this aspect of ethics is that deception is, as some writers observe, widespread in social research (see the stance 'Ethical transgression is pervasive' in Key concept 6.1). It is rarely feasible or desirable to provide participants with a totally complete account of what your research is about. As Punch (1979) found in the incident that is referred to in Chapter 19 (in the section on 'Active or passive' participation), he could hardly announce to the suspect that he was not in fact a police officer and then launch into a lengthy account of his research. Bulmer (1982), whose stance is predominantly that of a universalist in ethics terms (see Key concept 6.1), nonetheless recognizes that there are bound to be instances such as this and deems them justifiable. However, it is very difficult to know where the line should be drawn here.

Ethics and the issue of quality

Possibly one of the most interesting developments in connection with ethical issues is that a criterion of the ethical integrity of an investigation is its *quality*. For example, the ESRC's *FRE* states as the first of six principles that 'Research should be designed, reviewed and undertaken to ensure integrity, quality and transparency' (*FRE*:3). See Tips and skills 'The ESRC's *Framework for Research Ethics*' below for more on this set of guidelines. Similarly, a list of criteria for assessing the quality of qualitative research studies includes the criterion 'Evidence of consideration of ethical issues' (Spencer et al. 2003). This list of criteria was devised in connection with a report produced for the UK government's Cabinet Office. Also, the *Research Governance Framework for Health and Social Care* states that 'research which is not of sufficient quality to contribute something useful to existing knowledge is unethical' (Department of Health 2005: para. 2.3.1). Whether this link that is increasingly being forged between ethical integrity and research quality is a distinctively UK orientation, as hinted at by Israel and Hay (2004: 52), is an interesting question.

In the UK, the Health Research Agency oversees a framework for the ethical approval of health-related research (**www.hra.nhs.uk/research-community**, accessed 26 May 2015). The researcher must submit an application using the Integrated Research Application System (IRAS) which is then reviewed by a Research Ethics Committee (**www.hra.nhs.uk/research-community/applying-for-approvals/**, accessed 26 May 2015). A helpful overview of the process can be found in a flowchart prepared by the Agency: **www.hra.nhs.uk/resources/applying-to-recs/nhs-rec-application-process-flowchart/** (accessed 26 May 2015). Three points should be noted about the system by anyone thinking of conducting research that will require clearance by an REC. First, it is a slow process, so plenty of time needs to be allowed. Second, under an earlier though fundamentally similar version of the system, only around 15 per cent of applications gained clearance without further consideration. Most applications (around 64 per cent) resulted in issues being raised to which the applicant had to respond. Around 6 per cent were declined first time around. The rest were either considered by the REC not to be part of their remit or were withdrawn (Dixon-Woods et al. 2007). Third, RECs frequently raise issues about the quality of the research (see Thinking deeply 6.1).

A further issue is that gaining clearance for one's research may have implications for the research process, which in turn may have an impact on research quality. Graffigna et al. (2010) report their experiences in gaining ethical clearance for a qualitative cross-national study of young people's attitudes to HIV/AIDS in Italy and Canada. The two Italian researchers were located in a department of psychology in their university and the Canadian researcher in a nursing department. Data were collected from university students using both face-to-face and online focus groups in both countries (see Chapter 21 for a discussion of face-to-face and online focus groups). The research was concerned with the perceived gap between health knowledge and safe practices. The Italian researchers were required to go through an ethical clearance process for the social sciences, whereas the Canadian researcher, because she was located in a nursing department, was required to go through an ethical clearance process for the health sciences. The former was relatively loosely structured and relied considerably on the researchers' conscience, although consent forms were required for participants. For the Canadian researcher, having to go through a health sciences track for ethical clearance, the process was much more structured and prescriptive, with a technique for recruiting research participants that was allowed in Italy being proscribed for the Canadian study. Graffigna et al. call this technique 'random walking', whereby the Italian researchers walked throughout the campus garnering interest in participation. The process of clearance also took longer in Canada,

Thinking deeply 6.1
Ethics and quality in a study of REC letters

Angell et al. (2008) conducted a content analysis (see Key concept 13.1 for a brief description of this technique) of 141 letters written on behalf of RECs. These were letters written to applicants seeking ethical clearance to proceed with research involving the NHS. The letters analysed were either of two types: either they signalled an unfavourable decision (that is, the research could not go ahead because of concerns about ethical issues) or they gave a provisional decision (that is, clarification of certain issues was required or the applicant needed to indicate that he or she would change certain procedures in line with the REC's recommendations). Angell et al. found that issues relating to the quality of the proposed research, which the authors refer to as 'scientific issues', were raised in the context of 74 per cent of the letters analysed. The three most common concerns were: concerns about the sample; issues relating to the choice of methods; and concerns about the research question. For example, in the case of issues relating to the choice of methods, the most common complaint from RECs was that the rationale for the choice of method was unclear. However, they frequently also made judgements about the appropriateness of a method or how it was to be implemented. The point of this research is that it demonstrates that, at least as far as RECs are concerned, the distinction between ethics and scientific quality is not a stable one and that they frequently shade into each other. Thus, what is and is not an ethical issue is by no means a clear-cut matter.

in part because of concerns about the confidentiality of the data collected through online focus groups.

The authors conducted a discourse analysis (see Chapter 22) of the data and found some differences between the Canadian and Italian students. For example, the Italian students had less awareness of the disease but were more prone to irrational fears about it; the Canadian students had a greater sense of being able to control the disease. The authors argue that, while these differences may reflect cross-cultural differences, 'some of this variation might also have been due to the differences in recruitment, sampling and consent procedures specified by the IRB panels in Canada and Italy' (Graffigna et al. 2010: 348; IRB is an abbreviation of Institutional Review Board and is a term used in North America to refer to a research ethics committee). The authors feel that the random walking recruitment technique engendered a more heterogeneous sample than the Canadian sample, which

Student *and* supervisor experience
Not doing research involving the NHS

The ethical approval process can be very offputting for students. This was certainly the case for Isabella Robbins, who decided not to go through the NHS to conduct her investigation of childhood vaccinations because of the problems of getting ethical clearance.

> I avoided using state organizations—e.g. the NHS—because of the lengthy and problematic system of gaining ethical approval. I was advised to approach self-help and informal groups. I sent a letter of introduction to leaders and chairpersons of organizing committees running these groups, outlining the aims and objectives of my project. I prepared a leaflet outlining my research and I asked group leaders to post leaflets and posters in the halls where these groups are held.

Similarly, Supervisor C, when asked for the three most important pieces of advice he gives students when beginning a research project, wrote as one of the three: 'Do not conduct research with NHS patients or staff unless you have submitted an application for NHS ethical approval several months previously.' This point very much relates to the issue of building in sufficient time for submitting your research proposal to ethical scrutiny, as noted in Chapter 4.

To read more, go to the Online Resource Centre: www.oxfordtextbooks.co.uk/orc/brymansrm5e/

was recruited through posters and leaflets. The Canadian IRB rejected the technique, because people might feel coerced to participate. They also insisted on a much more detailed consent form than the one required in Italy. The authors argue that their recruitment technique resulted in the Canadian participants having a greater investment in and being more committed to the research, because they had actively needed to respond to the literature about the project. Thus, the different ethical requirements experienced in Italy and Canada had implications for the comparability of the research design and of its findings.

The point of this brief section is only partly to draw attention to the way in which ethical issues are becoming entangled with matters of research quality, because there is a significant implication of this development. This implication is that it is increasingly likely that committees charged with the task of considering applications for ethical clearance will be commenting on the quality of researchers' proposed procedures. If quality is deemed to be a component of the ethical domain, it is at the very

least distinctly possible that applicants for ethical clearance will find themselves having to defend decisions to do with their sampling, their **interview guide**, or their questionnaire on technical grounds, in addition to the areas, such as those previously covered, that are part of the traditional domain of ethical considerations (for example, informed consent or harm to participants). At the very least, as the case described by Graffigna et al. (2010) implies, the decisions made by ethics committees will have implications for the direction of research. It is not surprising, therefore, that, although social researchers are generally supportive of good ethical practice in research, there is a sense of growing frustration among many of them about the amount of time it can take to proceed with their research because of the lengthy process of clearance, especially when it involves the NHS, and growing evidence of ethics committee decisions affecting the design and quality of investigations (see e.g. Hammersley (2009) and A. G. Miller (2009) from a UK and North American perspective respectively).

Tips and skills
The ESRC's *Framework for Research Ethics*

In the UK context, the publication by the Economic and Social Research Council (ESRC) in 2005 of a document (the *Research Ethics Framework*, *REF*) outlining its position on ethical issues and providing guidance on ethical matters was very significant. It was revised in 2010 and renamed the *Framework for Research Ethics* (*FRE*). A new edition was published in September 2012. The ESRC is the major agency in the UK for funding social scientific research. It provides funding both for research projects, usually carried out by academics who apply for support for significant investigations, and for postgraduate research in the form of studentships. The *FRE* outlines the Council's requirements in terms of ethical practice(s) for the research it supports. There is a broader perspective, too, in that the ESRC intends through the *FRE* to influence the ethical practices of social science research generally; in other words, it intends the influence of the *FRE* to extend beyond research it supports. The *FRE* lays down six principles of ethical research on page 3.

1. As noted above, ethical research is of a high quality. Thus, if a study is poorly designed, quite aside from the fact that it almost certainly would not receive financial support from the ESRC, it is unethical.

2. 'Research staff and participants must normally be informed fully about the purpose, methods and intended possible uses of the research, what their participation in the research entails and what risks, if any, are involved.'

3. Confidentiality of information must be maintained and anonymity of participants respected.

4. The involvement of research participants must be entirely voluntary.

5. Harm to participants must be avoided.

6. 'The independence of research must be clear, and any conflicts of interest or partiality must be explicit.' This draws attention to the possible role of affiliation bias to which some writers on ethics in research draw attention (Bell and Bryman 2007).

It is striking that the inclusion of the issue of quality in principle 1, of research staff in principle 2 (thus including researcher safety within the purview of research ethics), and of possible conflicts of interest in principle 6 extends the reach of ethical issues when compared to those explored by Diener and Crandall (1978), which were reviewed above.

Also of considerable significance are the ESRC's proposals for the ways in which ethical issues should be given due consideration. The following are the main points concerning the Council's expectations regarding the process of handling ethical issues.

- ESRC does not expect ethical approval to have been obtained before submitting a proposal for funding. However, applicants need to specify what ethical approval is needed and how it will be achieved.
- When a proposal is peer-reviewed, reviewers and assessors are asked to comment on the self-assessment. This may lead to rejection if reviewers or assessors feel the self-assessment is wholly inadequate.
- If the application is successful, the ESRC will not release funds until there is a written confirmation from the institution where the research is to be conducted that the ethical approval outlined in the self-assessment has been completed.
- In some cases, only an 'expedited review' will be required. This will be when the risk of harm to participants or others is small. It will normally involve a member (or possibly more) of a research ethics committee conducting the review.
- When full ethical review is deemed to be needed, a research ethics committee will conduct such a review. The ESRC has laid down guidelines concerning who should be members of such committees.
- Institutions must ensure that there are mechanisms in place to monitor ongoing research projects so that any changes to the ethical issues involved in an investigation can be addressed. This provision is meant to ensure that ethical approval is an ongoing activity.

It is interesting to note the ESRC's views on what kinds of research would *not* be viewed as appropriate for expedited review—that is, projects that involve more than what is referred to as 'minimal risk' of harm to participants or others connected to the research. Examples it provides are:

- research involving vulnerable groups;
- research involving people who lack capacity;
- research involving sensitive topics;
- research involving deceased persons, body parts or other human elements;
- research using administrative data or secure data, especially when the data need to be linked and/or where participants may be identified;
- research involving groups that necessitate permission from a gatekeeper (for example, children, elderly);
- research involving deception or lack of full informed consent;
- research involving access to records or personal/confidential information;
- 'research which would or might induce psychological stress, anxiety or humiliation, or cause more than minimal pain' (*FRE*: 9, emphasis removed);
- research involving intrusive interventions or research methods;
- research involving threats to the safety of researchers;
- research involving members of the public engaged in a research role;
- research involving investigations outside the UK where issues to do with local customs and practices may arise;
- research involving online data collection, especially when visual images and/or sensitive topics are concerned;
- other research methods in which visual and vocal elements figure strongly, due to possible problems of identifying people;
- '*research which may involve data sharing of confidential information beyond the initial consent given*' (*FRE*: 9, emphasis in original).

One of the most striking features about this list is that it is much longer than the one provided in the *REF*, published in 2005. There are many other observations that could be made about the *FRE*, but these are particularly salient ones. I have spent some time on it, because it is likely to influence many universities' and colleges' practices with regard to ethical review. As such, it is likely to implicate many students conducting research projects of various kinds and levels. The *FRE* can be found at http://www.esrc.ac.uk/about-esrc/information/framework-for-research-ethics/index.aspx (accessed 23 May 2015).

Student experience
Ethical approval takes time

In Chapter 4, the point was made on several occasions about the need to manage your time when preparing a dissertation. Many of the stages take longer than you might imagine. In the case of Emma Taylor's group project looking into the impact of drinking laws in Scotland on behaviour and attitudes towards drinking, the length of time required to gain ethical clearance for the administration of the students' questionnaire was considerable:

> our group had faced many ethical barriers in terms of what we could ask people and where we could ask it. Initially, we had had a completely different research question to what we used in the end—this was due to it being rejected by ethics, meaning we had to completely change our research project, which cost us time and effort.

Similarly, Alice Palmer wrote somewhat poignantly that one thing she would have done differently was that she 'would have taken more care with the ethics paperwork earlier on as that was the only really stressful part and my failure to use the official university ethics forms came back to haunt me later'.

 To read more, go to the Online Resource Centre: www.oxfordtextbooks.co.uk/orc/brymansrm5e/

The difficulties of ethical decision-making

The difficulty of drawing the line between ethical and unethical practices can be revealed in several ways. The issue of some members of social settings being aware of the researcher's status and the nature of his or her investigation has been mentioned on several occasions. Manuals about interviewing are full of advice about how to entice interviewees to open up about themselves. Interviewers frequently err on the low side when asked how long an interview will take. Women may use their identity as women to influence female interviewees in in-depth interviews to probe into their lives and reveal inner thoughts and feelings, albeit with a commitment to feminist research (Oakley 1981; Finch 1984). Qualitative research is frequently very open-ended, and, as a result, research questions are either loose or not specified, so that it is doubtful whether ethnographers in particular are able to inform others accurately about the nature of their research. Perhaps, too, some interviewees find the questions we ask unsettling or find the cut and thrust of a focus group discussion stressful, especially if they inadvertently reveal more than they might have intended.

There are, in other words, many ways in which there is the potential for deception and, relatedly, lack of informed consent in social research. These instances are, of course, a very far cry from the deceptions perpetrated in the research summarized in Research in focus 6.1 and

6.2, but they point to the difficulty of arriving at ethically informed decisions. Ethical codes give advice on patently inappropriate practices, though sometimes leaving some room for manœuvre, as we have seen, but less guidance on marginal areas of ethical decision-making. Indeed, guidelines may even be used by research participants *against* the researcher when they seek to limit the boundaries of a fieldworker's investigation (Punch 1994).

It also has to be recognized that there is sometimes a clash between the ethically desirable and the practical. For example, it was previously noted that some researchers like to secure the informed consent of research participants by asking them to sign a consent form. However, it has been shown that the requirement to sign such a form reduces prospective participants' willingness to be involved in survey research. For example, one study from the USA showed that 13 per cent of respondents were willing to participate in a study but not if they were required to sign a consent form (Singer 2003). The problem then is that, if signed consent is insisted upon, it seems likely that the resulting sample will be biased (see Chapter 8 for a discussion of sampling bias). This has led Groves et al. (2009) to recommend that, for survey research, it is the interviewer who should sign the form, indicating that the respondent has given his or her verbal informed consent.

New media and ethical considerations

In this section, I will look at ethical issues in relation to both using the Internet as a platform for doing social research and the use of visual images. Both of these media have experienced growth in use in the last two decades.

Ethics and the Internet

Conducting research by using the Internet as a method of data collection raises specific ethical issues that are only now starting to be widely discussed and debated. Some issues relate to the many venues or environments in which these new forms of communication and possibilities for research occur, including blogs, listservs or discussion groups, email, chatrooms, social media, instant messaging, and newsgroups. The behaviour of Internet users is governed by 'netiquette', the conventions of politeness or definitions of acceptable behaviour that are recognized by online communities, as well as by service providers' acceptable use policies and by data protection legislation, and those contemplating using the Internet as a method of data collection should familiarize themselves with these. This section is concerned with the specific ethical issues raised by Internet research. One of the problems faced by social researchers wanting to use the Internet for data collection is that we are clearly in the middle of a huge growth in the amount of research being conducted in this way (M. Williams 2007). Not only is this trend creating the problem of over-researched populations who suffer from respondent fatigue; some of those involved in doing research with this new technology are not adhering to ethical principles. As a result, fatigue and suspicion are beginning to set in among prospective research participants, creating a less than ideal environment for future Internet researchers. In addition, the continual emergence of new platforms for doing research via the Internet throws up new problems as researchers struggle to absorb the ethical and other implications of using them.

The Association of Internet Researchers recommends that researchers start by considering the ethical expectations established by the venue (**http://aoir.org/reports/ethics2.pdf**, accessed 21 March 2014). For instance, is there a posted site polity that notifies users that the site is public and specifies the limits to privacy? Or are there mechanisms that users can employ to indicate that their exchanges are private? The more the venue is acknowledged to be public, the less obligation there is on the researcher to protect the confidentiality and anonymity of individuals using the venue, or to seek their informed consent. A further issue is that there are often very large numbers of people involved in the submission of postings, and many of these will no longer be active participants, thus making it difficult if not impossible to seek informed consent.

However, the distinction between public and private space on the Internet is blurred and contested. Online newsgroups and discussion groups are a particular focus of concern for researchers. They offer the opportunity to analyse naturally-occurring data but there are ethical concerns about the extent to which the communications that are posted are public. Hewson et al. (2003) suggest that data that have been deliberately and voluntarily made available in the public Internet domain, such as newsgroups, can be used by researchers without the need for informed consent, provided anonymity of individuals is protected. In the course of her research on websites for female sex workers and their male clients, Sanders (2005) acted as a 'lurker', whereby she observed the activity on message boards without revealing her identity as a researcher. She did not reveal her identity because she did not want to influence participants' behaviour and did not want to trigger hostility that might have adversely affected her research.

Whether electronic communications are public or private is clearly a matter of considerable debate. Pace and Livingston (2005: 39) argue that such electronic communications should be used for research only if:

- the information is publically archived and readily available;
- no password is required to access the information;
- the material is not sensitive in nature;
- no stated site policy prohibits the use of the material.

These authors suggest that, if these conditions do not pertain, informed consent needs to be obtained and should be obtained without disrupting ongoing online activity. They also argue that identities and confidentiality must be protected. These guidelines are not without problems. For example, who decides whether material is 'sensitive in nature'? What is or is not sensitive is likely to be highly debatable, so treating it as a principle is not in the least straightforward. Issues such as this bring out the difficulties associated with ethical decision-making. Kozinets (2010) takes a quite lenient approach, arguing that when members of an 'online community' post communications on the Internet, the analysis of such materials is not 'human subjects research' because the communications are publicly available documents provided that '*the researcher does not record the identity of the communicators and if the researcher can legally and easily gain access to these communications or archives*' (p. 142, emphasis in original). Under such circumstances, no consent is required. Thus,

Student experience
The ethics of Internet research

Isabella Robbins used Internet message boards to gain additional data on mothers whose children had not been vaccinated. She was concerned about the ethics of using these media, and this is how she dealt with the issues.

In terms of the ethics of using data from the Internet, I would argue that the Internet is in the realm of the public sphere. I decided that I did not want to contact the women on the message board, because I considered this forum did provide these women with a useful forum in which to debate difficult issues. I considered it unethical to break into that forum. I don't consider that what I was doing was covert. The message board had very visual reminders that the message board is a public space, warning women not to use names, addresses, and phone numbers (although some did). I did contact the press office of the message board, and they referred me to their terms and conditions of using the message board. This acknowledged that it is a public space, and that people using it take responsibility for that. They did not object to me using this data. I told them what I intended to do with it, and that the message board and data would be anonymized.

To read more, go to the Online Resource Centre: www.oxfordtextbooks.co.uk/orc/brymansrm5e/

we find that when posts on online discussion boards or Facebook postings or tweets are being quoted, the name of the originator is often omitted. For example, a study that is referred to in Chapter 23 in the section on 'Social media'—an analysis of tweets relating to acute NHS hospitals in England—anonymized the sources quoted thus: '[@named hospital] Your a&e department is absolutely filthy it makes the hospital visit even more unpleasant. #unsatisfactory' (quoted in Greaves et al. in press). The originator and the hospitals are anonymized.

The issue raised by Kozinets relates to the principle of protecting research participants from harm and the related issues of individual anonymity and confidentiality. Stewart and Williams (2005) suggest that complete protection through anonymity is almost impossible in Internet research, since, in computer-mediated communication, information about the origin of a computer-generated message, revealed for instance in the header, is very difficult to remove. It is also more difficult to guarantee confidentiality, because the data are often accessible to other participants. In a similar vein, DeLorme et al. (2001) suggest that the Internet raises particular ethical concerns for qualitative researchers that arise from the difficulty of knowing who has access to information. For example, a message posted on an Internet discussion group can be accessed by anyone who has a computer and an Internet connection. In addition, some Internet environments provide access to 'lurkers', making it difficult for researchers to protect the confidentiality of data that they collect, since others can discover identities even if the researcher conceals them.

However, the debates about the ethics of Internet research and the development of guidelines for researchers

are ongoing, and, even though traditional ethical guidelines may need to be revised to reflect the ethical issues raised by Internet research, researchers should continue to be guided by the ethical principles discussed in this chapter. For a helpful overview of ethical issues in online research, see **www.bps.org.uk/news/guidelines-internet-mediated-research** (accessed 2 October 2014).

Ethics and visual images

Research methods using visual media such as photographs have become increasingly popular as embellishments of traditional techniques, and these too raise ethical issues. An example is the rise of visual ethnography, which is discussed in Chapter 19. It is clearly desirable to obtain the informed consent of those who appear in photographs, but it may not be possible to do this for absolutely everyone who appears. Some people may be in the background and may have moved off before they can be asked to provide their informed consent. Further, the significance of a photograph may become apparent only when the visual and non-visual data are being analysed, and by then it may not be possible to establish informed consent with those affected. In my book on Disneyization (Bryman 2004), I would very much have liked to use a photograph I took while in the Asia region of Disney's Animal Kingdom in Orlando, Florida. I had taken a photograph of one of the 'cast members' who was dressed in thematically appropriate attire because he had been holding an insect that had intrigued both of us. It occurred to me later that it would have been an excellent illustration of the use of the body in theming, but I felt it was inappropriate to use it because of the lack of informed consent. One solution is to 'pixelate' people's faces so that they cannot be identified, a technique that is shown in Plate 19.4.

A further area raised by visual media is in relation to a category of visual research known as **photo-elicitation**, which sometimes takes the form of getting research participants to take their own photographs and then encouraging them to discuss the images. As Clark (2013) notes, the problem here is that it is in a sense the research participant who needs to secure informed consent when people appear in photographs. In the case of one of his

research projects he notes how one of the areas of ethical anxiety for his research participants was the uses that Clark and his co-researchers intended for the images that were taken. Some research participants were very cautious and either declined to take any photographs or took photographs but limited the access of Clark and his co-researchers to them. Further, as Clark observes, since consent was negotiated by participants, there is a lingering uncertainty about what exactly the implications of the negotiations for research use were and therefore what such photographs can be used for.

Politics in social research

Ethics are by no means the only context within which issues to do with wider principles are relevant to and intrude into social research. Ethical issues are part of a wider consideration of the role that values play in the research process, but the ways in which values are relevant is not just to do with the ethical dimensions of research. In Chapter 2, in the section on 'Influences on the conduct of social research', it was noted that values intrude in all phases of the research process—from the choice of a research area to the formulation of conclusions. This means that the social researcher never conducts an investigation in a moral vacuum: he or she is influenced by a variety of presuppositions that in turn have implications for the conduct of social research. This view is widely accepted among social researchers, and claims that social research can be conducted in a wholly objective, value-neutral way are now heard far less frequently. While quantitative research is sometimes depicted as being committed to objectivity (e.g. Lincoln and Guba 1985), it is not at all clear that nowadays this principle is as widely endorsed among quantitative researchers as a desirable and feasible feature as qualitative researchers would have us believe.

For some writers on social research, a 'conscious partiality', as Mies (1993: 68) calls it, is celebrated. Particularly among feminist researchers, to do research on women in an objective, value-neutral way would be undesirable (as well as being difficult to achieve), because it would be incompatible with the values of feminism. Instead, many feminist researchers advocate a stance that extols the virtues of a commitment to women and exposing the conditions of their disadvantage in a male-dominated society. Much of such research has been concerned to change the situation of women, as well as to heighten our understanding of the disadvantages from which they suffer.

Considerations of this kind begin to draw attention to the way in which *politics* (in the non-party-political sense of the working-through of power and contests over

its exercise) plays an important role in social research. Politics becomes important in different contexts and ways.

- Social researchers are sometimes put in the position where they *take sides*. This is precisely what many feminist researchers do when they focus on women's disadvantages in the family, the workplace, and elsewhere, and on the possibilities for improving their position. However, some writers have argued that this process of taking sides is pervasive in much sociology (see Thinking deeply 6.2).

- Related to this point is the issue of *funding* research. Much social research is funded by organizations such as firms and government departments. Such organizations frequently have a vested interest in the outcomes of the research. The very fact that some research is funded, while other research is not, suggests that political issues may be involved, in that we might anticipate that such organizations will seek to invest in studies that will be useful to them and that will be supportive of their operations and worldviews. Frequently, they are proactive, in that they may contact researchers to carry out an investigation or they will launch a call for researchers to tender bids for an investigation in a certain area. When social researchers participate in such exercises, they are participating in a political arena because they are having to tailor their research concerns and even research questions to a body that defines or at least influences those research concerns and research questions. Bodies such as government departments (e.g. the Home Office) are going to be influenced by notions of relevance to their work and by their understanding of ministers' concerns. As a result, as G. Hughes (2000) observes in relation to research in the field of crime, an investigation of gun crimes among Britain's 'underclass' is more likely to be looked upon favourably for funding than one concerned with state-related misdemeanours. R. Morgan (2000) points out that research funded by the Home Office typically is empirical; adopts quantitative research; is concerned with the costs and benefits of a policy or innovation; is short-termist (in the sense that the cost–benefit analysis is usually concerned with immediate impacts rather than longer-term ones); and is uncritical (in the sense that the research does not probe government policy but is concerned with the effectiveness of ways of implementing policy). In addition, many agencies restrict what researchers are able to write about their findings by insisting on seeing drafts of all proposed publications. Even such bodies as the UK's major funder of social research, the ESRC, increasingly mould their research programmes to what are perceived to be areas of concern in society and seek to involve non-academics as evaluators and audiences for research. Such features are related to the fact that the ESRC is itself involved in a political process of seeking to secure a continuous stream of funding from government, and being able to demonstrate relevance is one way of indicating standing in this regard. This predisposition on the part of the ESRC was enhanced in 2009 when it committed itself to what is often referred to as an 'impact agenda'. Applicants for research funding are required 'to consider the potential scientific, societal and economic impact of their research' (**www.esrc. ac.uk/funding-and-guidance/impact-toolkit/what- how-and-why/esrc-expects.aspx**, accessed 6 October 2014). This requirement means applicants must specify not just the anticipated academic impacts of the proposed research but also non-academic ones. Specifying non-academic impacts requires a consideration of who might benefit from the research and how they might benefit. The impact agenda was met with disquiet among many researchers, who felt that it meant that applicants needed to have a good idea of what their findings would be as early as the application stage (see, for example, the article 'Petition Decries "Impact" Agenda in Research' at **http://www.timeshighereducation.co.uk/406931.article**, accessed 6 October 2014). However, the main point to register is that the impact agenda represents in many researchers' eyes a ratcheting-up of a perceived preference for research that can be shown to be relevant so that future flows of government support will not be jeopardized. The ESRC has now developed an 'Impact toolkit' which is meant to help researchers to maximize the impact of their research (**www.esrc.ac.uk/funding-and-guidance/ impact-toolkit/**—accessed 6 October 2014).

- Gaining *access*, for example to an organization, is also a political process. Access is usually mediated by gatekeepers, who are concerned about the researcher's motives: what the organization can gain from the investigation, what it will lose by participating in the research in terms of staff time and other costs, and potential risks to its image. Often, gatekeepers will seek to influence how the investigation takes place: what kinds of questions can be asked, who can and who cannot be the focus of study, the amount of time to be spent with each research participant, the interpretation of findings, and the form of any report to the organization itself. Reiner (2000b) suggests that the police, for example, are usually concerned about how they are going to be represented in publications in case they are portrayed unfavourably to agencies to which they are accountable. Firms are also invariably concerned about issues of how they are going to be represented. Consequently, gaining access is almost always a matter of negotiation, and as such inevitably turns into a political process. The results of this negotiation are often referred to as 'the research bargain'.

- Once in the organization, researchers often find that *getting on* in organizations entails a constant process of negotiation and renegotiation of what is and is not permissible. In other words, there may be several layers of gatekeepers in any research project, so that issues of access become an ongoing feature of research. For example, for their research on cargo vessels, Sampson and Thomas (2003: 171) sought initial access through ship-owning or managing companies, but found that 'the *key* gatekeeper is invariably the captain'. Captains varied in the degree of willingness to accommodate the researchers' investigative and other needs, and their chief officers, who represented a further layer of access, were frequently delegated responsibility for dealing with the fieldworkers. These officers also varied a great deal, with the researchers quoting one case in which the chief officer wanted to call a meeting about how the interviews should be conducted and another giving a much freer rein. Moreover, researchers are often treated with suspicion and reticence because of uncertainty about their motives, such as whether they are really working for management. It is unwise to assume that, simply because gatekeepers have given the researcher access, the researcher will have a smooth passage in their subsequent dealings with the people they study. Some research participants, perhaps because they are suspicious or because they doubt the utility of social research, will obstruct the research process. Researchers may also find themselves becoming embroiled in the internal politics of organizations as factional disputes rear their heads, and they may even become pawns in such clashes if groups attempt to enlist them in getting over a particular viewpoint.

- When research is conducted in *teams*, politics may loom large, since the different career and other

Thinking deeply 6.2
Taking sides in social research: the Becker–Gouldner dispute

In the late 1960s there was an interesting dispute between two sociologists who were leaders in the field in the USA and beyond: Howard S. Becker (1928–) and Alvin Gouldner (1920–80). Their debate raised many issues concerning the role of values and politics in research, but the issue of taking sides in research is a particularly interesting aspect of their dispute. Becker (1967) argued that it is not possible to do research that is unaffected by our personal sympathies. When we conduct research, we are often doing so in the context of hierarchical relationships (police–criminal, managers–workers, warders–prisoners, doctors–patients, teachers–students). Becker felt that it is difficult in the context of such relationships not to take sides; instead, the bigger dilemma is deciding which side we are on. Becker recognized that within the field in which he conducted his research at the time—the sociology of deviance—the sympathies of many practitioners lay with the underdogs in these hierarchical relationships. At the very least, the sociologist of deviance may seek to express or represent the point of view of criminals, prisoners, mental patients, or others, even if he or she does not go as far as to identify with them. However, when sociologists of deviance take the perspective of such groups, Becker argued that they are more likely to be accused of bias, because they are ascribing credibility to those whom society shuns and in many cases abhors. Why is a study stressing the underdog's perspective more likely to be regarded as biased? Becker proffered two reasons: because members of the higher group are widely seen as having an exclusive right to define the way things are in their sphere and because they are regarded as having a more complete picture. In other words, credibility is differentially distributed in society.

Gouldner (1968) argued that Becker exaggerated the issues he described in that by no means all research entails the need to take sides. He also argued that it was a mistake to think that, simply because the researcher takes the point of view of a section of society seriously, he or she necessarily sympathizes with that group. Liebling (2001) has argued that it is possible to see the merits of more than one side. Taking the case of prison research in the UK, she shows that not only is it possible to recognize the virtues of different perspectives, but it is also possible to do so without incurring too much wrath on either side—in her case, prison officials and prisoners. However, taking sides is a common occurrence, especially when the researcher believes that injustices are being heaped on a downtrodden group. Goffman (2014) notes that although she used information from a variety of sources (such as parole officers) for her ethnography of black men who were on the run from the law in Philadelphia, she admits to taking the perspective of the men and their families. At times, this stance turns into a tangible anger when she describes what come across as the underhand actions of the police and the pressures they often pile on the women in the men's lives in order to find and prosecute them. She experiences the physical aspects of this treatment while at the house of one of her main informants:

> The door busting open brought me fully awake. . . . Two officers came through the door, both of them white, in SWAT gear, with guns strapped to the sides of their legs. The first officer pointed a gun at me. . . The second officer in pulled me out of the cushions and, gripping my wrists, brought me up off the couch and onto the floor, so that my shoulders and spine hit first and my legs came down after. . . . I wondered if he'd broken my nose or cheek. . . . His boot pressed into my back, right at the spot where it had hit the floor, and I cried for him to stop. He put my wrists in plastic cuffs behind my back. . . My shoulder throbbed, and the handcuffs pinched.

> (Goffman 2014: 61)

It is no wonder that she writes that she 'took the perspective of 6th street residents' (2014: xiv).

objectives of team members and their different (and sometimes divergent) perceptions of their contributions may form a quite separate political arena. However, this is unlikely to be a set of circumstances that will affect most undergraduate or postgraduate students, although the growing use of team-based assignments at both levels suggests that it could become more relevant to many students. On the other hand, supervisors of postgraduate research and undergraduate dissertations may themselves be evaluated in terms of the number of postgraduate students seen through to completion or in terms of the quality of undergraduate dissertations for which they were responsible. Therefore, wider political processes of this kind may be relevant to many of this book's readers.

- There may be pressure to restrict the *publication* of findings. Hughes (2000) cites the case of a study of plea-bargaining in the British criminal justice system as a case in point. The researchers had uncovered what were deemed at the time to be disconcerting levels of informal bargaining, which were taken to imply that the formal judicial process was being weakened. The English legal establishment sought to thwart the dissemination of the findings and was persuaded to allow publication to go ahead only when a panel of academics confirmed the validity of the findings.

- The *use* made by others of findings can be the focus of further political machinations. In the 1960s a study that showed the persistence of streaming and social-class differentials in a comprehensive school (at a time when comprehensive schooling was a political issue, having just been introduced by the Labour government) was used by right-wing writers on education at the time as a critique of the case for comprehensive schooling.

- One further aspect that warrants mention in this section relates to what Savage (2010) refers to as the politics of *method*. He argues that the social sciences and sociology in particular emerged as credible disciplines in the UK because their practitioners asserted expertise in the practice of certain research methods that they used in a neutral and broadly 'scientific' manner. Thus, early researchers' use of sampling techniques, questionnaires, and interviewing was associated with a claim to be taken seriously as an academic discipline, allowing them to carve out a niche that differentiated them in terms of expertise from the discipline of economics. It is not that the early UK sociologists were claiming that they were the only professionals to use these research methods; after all, market researchers were well-known practitioners. Rather, they claimed an expertise in the use of these research methods for uncovering and exploring 'the social' as a domain that either had not previously been addressed by other academics or that had been addressed in a loose and largely unsystematic manner. This was a political battle for what Savage refers to as 'jurisdiction', out of which sociology largely emerged as a winner. However, Savage also argues (see also Savage and Burrows 2007) that this jurisdiction is under threat owing to others using the very research methods over which sociologists used to claim special expertise and the emergence of new kinds of data about social issues in which sociologists play little or no role. As a result, the field of research methods can be viewed as an arena in which there are competing claims to methodological proficiency with regard to revealing the nature of the social.

These are just a small number of ways in which we can talk about a politics of the research process.

 ## *Checklist*
Issues to consider in connection with ethical issues

○ Have you read and incorporated into your research the principles associated with at least one of the major professional associations mentioned in this chapter?

○ Have you read and incorporated the requirements for doing ethical research in your institution?

○ Have you found out whether all proposed research needs to be submitted to the body in your institution that is responsible for the oversight of ethical issues?

○ If only certain types of research need to be submitted, have you checked to see whether your proposed research is likely to require clearance?

○ Have you checked to ensure that there is no prospect of any harm coming to participants?

○ Does your research conform to the principle of informed consent, so that research participants understand:

　○ what the research is about?

　○ the purposes of the research?

  ○ who is sponsoring it?

  ○ the nature of their involvement in the research?

  ○ how long their participation is going to take?

  ○ that their participation is voluntary?

  ○ that they can withdraw from participation in the research at any time?

  ○ what is going to happen to the data (e.g. how they are going to be kept)?

○ Are you confident that the privacy of the people involved in your research will not be violated?

○ Do you appreciate that you should not divulge information or views to your research participants that other research participants have given you?

○ Have you taken steps to ensure that your research participants will not be deceived about the research and its purposes?

○ Have you taken steps to ensure that the confidentiality of data relating to your research participants will be maintained?

○ Once the data have been collected, have you taken steps to ensure that the names of your research participants and the location of your research (such as the name of the organization(s) in which it took place) are not identifiable?

○ Does your strategy for keeping your data in electronic form comply with data protection legislation?

○ Once your research has been completed, have you met obligations that were a requirement of doing the research (for example, submitting a report to an organization that allowed you access)?

》 *Key points*

- This chapter has been concerned with a limited range of issues concerning ethics in social research, in that it has concentrated on ethical concerns that might arise in the context of collecting and analysing data. My concern has mainly been with relations between researchers and research participants. Other ethical issues can arise in the course of social research.

- While the codes and guidelines of professional associations provide some guidance, their potency is ambiguous and they often leave the door open for some autonomy with regard to ethical issues.

- The main areas of ethical concern relate to: harm to participants; lack of informed consent; invasion of privacy; and deception.

- Covert observation and certain notorious studies have been particular focuses of concern.

- The boundaries between ethical and unethical practices are not clear-cut.

- Writers on social research ethics have adopted several different stances in relation to the issue.

- While the rights of research participants are the chief focus of ethical principles, issues of professional self-interest are also of concern.

- Ethical issues sometimes become difficult to distinguish from ones to do with the quality of research.

- The Internet and other new media have opened up new arenas for ethical decision-making.

- There are political dimensions to the research process that have points of affinity with the influence of values.

- The political dimensions of research are concerned with issues to do with the role and exercise of power at the different stages of an investigation.

Questions for review

- Why are ethical issues important in relation to the conduct of social research?
- Outline the different stances on ethics in social research.

Ethical principles

- Does 'harm to participants' refer to physical harm alone?
- What are some of the difficulties that arise in following this ethical principle?
- Why is the issue of informed consent so hotly debated?
- What are the main difficulties of following this ethical principle?
- Why is the privacy principle important?
- Why does deception matter?
- How helpful are notorious studies such as Milgram's electric shock experiments and Humphreys's study in terms of understanding the operation of ethical principles in social research?

Ethics and the issue of quality

- Why do issues to do with ethics sometimes become difficult to distinguish from issues to do with the quality of research?
- Is it possible to maintain a distinction between ethics and research quality?

The difficulties of ethical decision-making

- To what extent do new media throw up new areas of ethical concern?
- How easy is it to conduct ethical research?
- Read one of the ethical guidelines referred to in this chapter. How effective is it in guarding against ethical transgressions?

Politics in social research

- What is meant by suggesting that politics plays a role in social research?
- In what ways does politics manifest itself in social research?

 Online Resource Centre

www.oxfordtextbooks.co.uk/orc/brymansrm5e/

Visit the Online Resource to enrich your understanding of ethics and politics in social research. Follow up links to other resources, test yourself using multiple choice questions, and gain further guidance and inspiration from the Student Researcher's Toolkit.

Part Two

Quantitative Research

Part Two of this book is concerned with quantitative research. Chapter 7 sets the scene by exploring the main features of this research strategy. Chapter 8 discusses the ways in which we sample people to carry out survey research. Chapter 9 focuses on the structured interview, which is one of the main methods of data collection in quantitative research and in survey research in particular. Chapter 10 is concerned with another prominent method of gathering data through survey research—questionnaires that people complete themselves. Chapter 11 provides guidelines on how to ask questions for structured interviews and questionnaires. Chapter 12 discusses structured observation, a method that provides a systematic approach to the observation of people. Chapter 13 addresses content analysis, which is a distinctive and systematic approach to the analysis of a wide variety of documents. Chapter 14 discusses the possibility of using, in your own research, data collected by other researchers or official statistics. Chapter 15 presents some of the main tools you will need to conduct quantitative data analysis. Chapter 16 shows you how to use computer software in the form of SPSS—a very widely used package of programs—to implement the techniques learned in Chapter 15.

These chapters will provide you with the essential tools for doing quantitative research. They will take you from the very general issues to do with the generic features of quantitative research to the very practical issues of conducting surveys and analysing your own data.

7

The nature of quantitative research

 ## Chapter outline

 ## Chapter guide

This chapter is concerned with the characteristics of quantitative research, an approach that has been the dominant strategy for conducting social research. Its influence has waned slightly since the mid-1970s, when qualitative research became increasingly influential. However, it continues to exert a powerful influence. The emphasis in this chapter is very much on what quantitative research typically entails, though a later part of the chapter outlines the ways in which there are frequently departures from this ideal type. This chapter explores:

- the main steps of quantitative research, which are presented as a linear succession of stages;

- the importance of concepts in quantitative research and the ways in which measures may be devised for concepts; this discussion includes an examination of the idea of an *indicator*, which is devised as a way of measuring a concept for which there is no direct measure;

- the procedures for checking the reliability and validity of the measurement process;

- the main preoccupations of quantitative research, which are described in terms of four features: measurement; causality; generalization; and replication;
- some criticisms that are frequently levelled at quantitative research.

Introduction

In Chapter 2, quantitative research was outlined as a distinctive research strategy. In very broad terms, it was described as entailing the collection of numerical data, a deductive view of the relationship between theory and research, a preference for a natural science approach (and for positivism in particular), and an objectivist conception of social reality. A number of other features of quantitative research were outlined, but in this chapter we will be examining it in greater detail.

It should be clear by now that the description 'quantitative research' does not mean that quantification of aspects of social life is all that distinguishes it from a qualitative research strategy. The very fact that it has a distinctive epistemological and ontological position suggests that there is a good deal more to it than the mere presence of numbers. In this chapter, the main steps in quantitative research will be outlined. I will also examine some of the principal preoccupations of the strategy and how certain issues of concern among practitioners are addressed, such as questions about measurement validity.

The main steps in quantitative research

Figure 7.1 outlines the main steps in quantitative research. This is very much an ideal-typical account of the process: it is rarely found in this pure form, but it represents a useful starting point for getting to grips with the main ingredients and the links between them. Research is rarely as linear or as straightforward as the figure implies, but its aim is to do no more than capture the main steps and provide a rough indication of their interconnections.

Some of the chief steps have been covered in Chapters 1, 2, and 3. The fact that we start off with theory signifies that a broadly deductive approach to the relationship between theory and research is taken. It is common for outlines of the main steps of quantitative research to suggest that a hypothesis is deduced from the theory and is tested. This notion has been incorporated into Figure 7.1. However, a great deal of quantitative research does not entail the specification of a hypothesis, and instead theory acts loosely as a set of concerns in relation to which the social researcher collects data. The specification of hypotheses to be tested is particularly likely to be found in experimental research but is often found as well in survey research, which is usually based on a cross-sectional design (see Research in focus 3.8).

The next step entails the selection of a research design, a topic that was explored in Chapter 3. As we have seen, the selection of a research design has implications for a variety of issues, such as the external validity of findings and researchers' ability to impute causality to their findings. Step 4 entails devising measures of the concepts in which the researcher is interested. This process is often referred to as *operationalization*, a term originally used in physics to refer to the operations by which a concept (such as temperature or velocity) is measured (Bridgman 1927). Aspects of this issue will be explored below in this chapter.

The next two steps entail the selection of a research site or sites and then the selection of participants. Thus, in social survey research an investigator must first be concerned to establish an appropriate setting for his or her research. A number of decisions may be involved. The well-known *Affluent Worker* research undertaken by Goldthorpe et al. (1968: 2–5) involved two decisions about a research site or setting. First, the researchers needed a community that would be appropriate for the testing of the 'embourgeoisement' thesis (the idea that affluent workers were becoming more middle-class in their attitudes and lifestyles). As a result of this consideration, Luton was selected. Second, in order to come up with a sample of 'affluent workers' (Step 6), it was decided that people working for three of Luton's leading employers should be interviewed. Moreover, the researchers wanted the firms selected to cover a range of production technologies, because of evidence at that time that technologies had implications for workers' attitudes and behaviour. As a result of these considerations, the three firms were selected. Industrial

Figure 7.1
The process of quantitative research

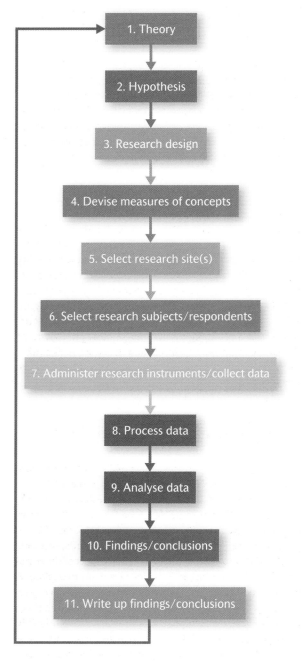

1. Theory

2. Hypothesis

3. Research design

4. Devise measures of concepts

5. Select research site(s)

6. Select research subjects/respondents

7. Administer research instruments/collect data

8. Process data

9. Analyse data

10. Findings/conclusions

11. Write up findings/conclusions

two steps are likely to include the assignment of subjects into control and treatment groups.

Step 7 involves the administration of the research instruments. In experimental research, this is likely to entail pre-testing subjects, manipulating the independent variable for the experimental group, and post-testing respondents. In cross-sectional research using survey research instruments, it will involve interviewing the sample members by structured interview schedule or distributing a self-administered questionnaire. In research using structured observation, this step will mean one or more observers watching the setting and the behaviour of people and then assigning categories to each element of behaviour.

Step 8 simply refers to the fact that, once information has been collected, it must be transformed into 'data'. In the context of quantitative research, this is likely to mean that it must be prepared so that it can be quantified. With some information this can be done in a relatively straight-forward way—for example, information relating to such things as people's ages, incomes, number of years spent at school, and so on. For other variables, quantification will entail *coding* the information—that is, transforming it into numbers to facilitate the quantitative analysis of the data, particularly if the analysis is going to be carried out by computer. Codes act as tags that are placed on data about people to allow the information to be processed by the computer. This consideration leads into Step 9—the analysis of the data. In this step, the researcher is concerned to use a number of techniques of quantitative data analysis to reduce the amount of data that needs to be processed, to test for relationships between variables, to develop ways of presenting the results of the analysis to others, and so on.

On the basis of the analysis of the data, the researcher must interpret the results of the analysis. It is at this stage that the 'findings' will emerge. The researcher will consider the connections between the findings that emerge out of Step 9 and the various preoccupations that acted as the impetus of the research. If there is a hypothesis, is it supported? What are the implications of the findings for the theoretical ideas that formed the background to the research?

Then the research must be written up. It cannot take on significance beyond satisfying the researcher's personal curiosity until it enters the public domain by being written up as a paper to be read at a conference or as a report to the agency that funded the research or as a book or academic journal article. In writing up the findings and conclusions, the researcher is doing more than simply relaying what has been found to others: readers must be convinced that the research conclusions are important and that the findings are robust. Thus, a significant part of the research process entails convincing others of the significance and validity of one's findings.

workers were then sampled, again in terms of selected criteria that were to do with the researchers' interests in embourgeoisement and in the implications of technology for work attitudes and behaviour. Research in focus 7.1 provides a more recent example of research that involved similar deliberations about selecting research sites and sampling respondents. In experimental research, these

Research in focus 7.1
Selecting research sites and sampling respondents: the study of Scottish neighbourhoods

In the case of the research by Atkinson and Kintrea (2001), four Scottish neighbourhoods were selected to reflect variations in both social mix and deprivation. This research was described in Research in focus 3.17, where the criteria for selecting the four neighbourhoods were outlined. Within each of the four areas, a survey was conducted of householders and/or their partners at 200 randomly sampled postcode addresses. Questions were asked in relation to five areas: patterns of daily life; barriers to choice of neighbourhood; social networks; stigma and reputation; and unemployment, education, and illness (Atkinson and Kintrea 2001: 2285). Thus, there are two levels of sampling: initially of neighbourhoods and then of individuals within households.

Once the findings have been published, they become part of the stock of knowledge (or 'theory' in the loose sense of the word) in their domain. Thus, there is a feedback loop from Step 11 back up to Step 1. The presence of an element of both deductivism (Step 2) and inductivism (the feedback loop) is indicative of the positivist foundations of quantitative research. Similarly, the emphasis on the translation of concepts into measures (Step 4) is symptomatic of the principle of phenomenalism (see Key concept 2.2) that is also a feature of positivism. It is to this important phase of translating concepts into measures that

we now turn. As we will see, certain considerations follow on from the emphasis on measurement in quantitative research. These considerations are to do with the validity and reliability of the measures devised by social scientists and will figure prominently in the following discussion.

As noted at the outset of presenting the model in Figure 7.1, this sequence of stages is a kind of ideal-typical account that is probably rarely found in this pure form. At the end of this chapter, the section 'Is it always like this?' deals with three ways in which the model may not be found in practice.

Concepts and their measurement

What is a concept?

Concepts are the building blocks of theory and are the points around which social research is conducted. Just think of the numerous concepts that have already been mentioned in relation to research examples cited so far in this book:

> Cultural capital, social capital, gentrification, ethnic discrimination, gender values, ideological orientation, abusive supervision, school choice strategy, poverty, social class, job search method, deskilling, emotional labour, emotional contagion, informal social control, negotiated order, culture, academic achievement, teacher expectations.

Each represents a label that we give to elements of the social world that seem to have common features and that strike us as significant. As Bulmer (1984: 43) succinctly puts it, concepts 'are categories for the organisation of ideas and observations'. For example, with the concept of social mobility, we notice that some people improve their socio-economic position relative to their parents, others stay roughly the

same, and others are downwardly mobile. Out of such considerations, the concept of social mobility is reached.

If a concept is to be employed in quantitative research, a measure will have to be developed for it so that it can be quantified. Concepts can then take the form of independent or dependent variables. In other words, concepts may provide an explanation of a certain aspect of the social world, or they may stand for things we want to explain. A concept such as social mobility may be used in either capacity: as a possible explanation of certain attitudes (are there differences between the downwardly mobile and others in terms of their political dispositions or social attitudes?) or as something to be explained (what are the causes of variation in social mobility?). Equally, we might be interested in evidence of changes in amounts of social mobility over time or in variations between comparable nations in levels of social mobility. As we start to investigate such issues, we are likely to formulate theories to help us understand why, for example, rates of social mobility vary between countries or over time. This will in turn generate new concepts, as we try to tackle the explanation of variation in rates.

Why measure?

There are three main reasons for the preoccupation with measurement in quantitative research.

1. Measurement allows us to delineate *fine differences* between people in terms of the characteristic in question. This is very useful, since, although we can often distinguish between people in terms of extreme categories, finer distinctions are much more difficult to recognize. We can detect clear variations in levels of job satisfaction—people who love their jobs and people who hate their jobs—but small differences are much more difficult to identify.

2. Measurement gives us a *consistent device* or yardstick for making such distinctions. A measurement device provides a consistent instrument for gauging differences. This consistency relates to two things: our ability to be consistent over time and our ability to be consistent with other researchers. In other words, a measure should be something that is influenced neither by the timing of its administration nor by the person who administers it. Obviously, saying that the measure is not influenced by timing is not meant to indicate that measurement readings do not change: they are bound to be influenced by social change. What it means is that the measure should generate consistent results, other than those that occur as a result of natural changes. Whether a measure actually possesses this quality has to do with the issue of *reliability*, which was introduced in Chapter 3 and which will be examined again below.

3. Measurement provides the basis for *more precise estimates of the degree of relationship between concepts* (for example, through **correlation** analysis, which will be examined in Chapter 15). Thus, if we measure both job satisfaction and the things with which it might be related, such as stress-related illness, we will be able to produce more precise estimates of how closely they are related than if we had not proceeded in this way.

Indicators

In order to provide a measure of a concept (often referred to as an **operational definition**, a term deriving from the idea of operationalization), it is necessary to have an indicator or indicators that will stand for the concept (see Key concept 7.1). There are a number of ways in which indicators can be devised:

Key concept 7.1
What is an indicator?

It is worth making two distinctions here. First, there is a distinction between an *indicator* and a *measure*. The latter can be taken to refer to things that can be relatively unambiguously counted, such as personal income, household income, age, number of children, or number of years spent at school. Measures, in other words, are quantities. If we are interested in some of the causes of variation in personal income, the latter can be quantified in a reasonably direct way. We use indicators to tap concepts that are less directly quantifiable. If we are interested in the causes of variation in job satisfaction, we will need indicators that will stand for the concept of job satisfaction. These indicators will allow job satisfaction to be measured, and we can treat the resulting quantitative information as if it were a measure. An indicator, then, is something that is devised or already exists and that is employed *as though it were a measure of a concept*. It is viewed as an indirect measure of a concept, such as job satisfaction. We see here a second distinction between *direct* and *indirect* indicators of concepts. Indicators may be direct or indirect in their relationship to the concepts for which they stand. Thus, an indicator of marital status has a much more direct relationship to its concept than an indicator (or set of indicators) relating to job satisfaction. Sets of attitudes always need to be measured by batteries of indirect indicators. So too do many forms of behaviour. When indicators are used that are not true quantities, they will need to be coded to be turned into quantities. Directness and indirectness are not qualities inherent to an indicator: data from a survey question on amount earned per month may be a direct measure of personal income. However, if we treat personal income as an indicator of social class, it becomes an indirect measure. The issue of indirectness raises the question of where an indirect measure comes from—that is, how does a researcher devise an indicator of something such as job satisfaction? Usually, it is based on common-sense understandings of the forms the concept takes or on anecdotal or qualitative evidence relating to that concept.

- through a question (or series of questions) that is part of a structured interview schedule or self-administered questionnaire; the question(s) could be concerned with the respondents' report of an attitude (for example, job satisfaction) or their social situation (for example, poverty) or a report of their behaviour (for example, leisure pursuits);

- through the recording of individuals' behaviour using a structured observation schedule (for example, pupil behaviour in a classroom);

- through official statistics, such as the use of Home Office crime statistics to measure criminal behaviour;

- through an examination of blog content using content analysis—for example, to examine bullying stories following the suicide of a teenager who had been tormented online (Davis et al. 2015).

Indicators, then, can be derived from a wide variety of different sources and methods. Very often the researcher has to consider whether one indicator of a concept will be sufficient. This consideration is frequently a focus for survey researchers. Rather than just a single indicator of a concept, the researcher may feel that it is preferable to ask a number of questions in the course of a structured interview or a self-administered questionnaire that tap into a certain concept (see Research in focus 7.2 and 7.3 for examples).

Research in focus 7.2
A multiple-indicator measure of a concept

Research on the conflict and contact theories of ethnic group relations was referred to in Research in focus 2.2. One of the studies referred to is Sturgis et al. (2014a), which examined whether ethnic diversity in London neighbourhoods had an impact on their social cohesion. Social cohesion was measured by giving respondents three statements and asking them to indicate their level of agreement or disagreement with each statement on a five-point scale running from 'Yes, I strongly agree' to 'No, I strongly disagree'. There was a middle point on the scale that allowed for a neutral response. This approach to investigating a cluster of attitudes is known as a **Likert scale**, though in many cases researchers use a seven-point rather than a five-point scale for responses. See Key concept 7.2 for a description of what a Likert scale entails. The three statements were as follows.

1. People in this area can be trusted.

2. People act with courtesy to each other in public space in this area.

3. You can see from the public space here in the area that people take pride in their environment.

Using multiple-indicator measures

What are the advantages of using a multiple-indicator measure of a concept? The main reason for their use is a recognition that there are potential problems with a reliance on just a single indicator:

- It is possible that a single indicator will incorrectly classify many individuals. This may be due to the wording of the question or to misunderstanding. But if there are a number of indicators, then if some people are misclassified through a particular question, it will be possible to offset its effects.

- A single question may need to be of an excessively high level of generality and so may not reflect the true state of affairs for the people replying to it. Alternatively, a question may cover only one aspect of the concept in question. For example, if you were interested in job satisfaction, would it be sufficient to ask people how satisfied they were with their pay? Almost certainly not, because most people would argue that there is more to job satisfaction than just satisfaction with pay. This single indicator would be missing out on such things as satisfaction with conditions, with the work itself, and with other aspects of

Key concept 7.2
What is a Likert scale?

The investigation of attitudes is a prominent area in much survey research. One of the most common techniques for investigating attitudes is the Likert scale, named after Rensis Likert, who developed the method. The Likert scale is essentially a **multiple-indicator** or **multiple-item measure** of a set of attitudes relating to a particular area. The goal of the Likert scale is to measure intensity of feelings about the area in question. In its most common format, it comprises a series of statements (known as **items**) that focus on a certain issue or theme. Each respondent is then asked to indicate his or her level of agreement with the statement. Usually, the format for indicating level of agreement is a five-point scale going from 'strongly agree' to 'strongly disagree', but seven-point scales and other formats are used too. There is usually a middle position of 'neither agree nor disagree' or 'undecided' indicating neutrality on the issue. Each respondent's reply on each item is scored, and then the scores for each item are aggregated to form an overall score. Normally, since the scale measures intensity, the scoring is carried out so that a high level of intensity of feelings in connection with each indicator receives a high score (for example, on a five-point scale, a score of 5 for very strong positive feelings about an issue and a score of 1 for very negative feelings). The social cohesion referred to in Research in focus 7.2 is an example of a Likert scale. Variations on the typical format of indicating degrees of agreement are scales referring to frequency (for example, 'never' through to 'always' or 'very often') and evaluation (for example, 'very poor' through to 'very good'). An example of the former can be found in the study by Eschleman et al. (2014) which was referred to in Research in the news 3.1. In this study, 'abusive supervision' was measured through five items asking whether the respondent's supervisor 'ridicules me' or 'puts me down in front of others' using a five-point scale from 'never' to 'very often'. An example of a Likert scale using evaluation of items is a study by Krahn and Galambos (2014: 100) in which 'intrinsic work values' was measured through three items ('feeling of accomplishment, make most of decisions yourself, interesting work') using a five-point scale from 'not important at all' to 'very important'.

There are several points to bear in mind about the construction of a Likert scale. The following are particularly important.

- The items must be statements and not questions.
- The items must all relate to the same object (job, organization, ethnic groups, unemployment, sentencing of offenders, etc.).
- The items that make up the scale should be interrelated (see the discussion of **internal reliability** in this chapter and Key concept 7.3).

It is useful to vary the phrasing so that some items imply a positive view of the phenomenon of interest and others a negative one. This variation is advised in order to identify respondents who exhibit **response sets** (see the sections on 'Response sets' in Chapters 9 and 10).

the work environment. By asking a number of questions, the researcher can get access to a wider range of aspects of the concept.

- You can make much finer distinctions. An example is the Eschleman et al. (2014) measure of counterproductive work behaviour directed at the supervisor (see Research in focus 7.4). If we took just one of the indicators as a measure, we would be able to array people only on a scale of 1 to 5, assuming that answers indicating 'rarely' were assigned 1 and answers of 'very often' were assigned 5, the three other points being scored 2, 3, and 4. However, with a multiple-indicator measure of nine indicators the range is 9 (9×1) to 45 (9×5). Key concept 7.2 provides some information about the kind of scale (a Likert scale) that was used in this study.

Research in focus 7.3
A multiple-indicator measure of religious beliefs

In Kelley and De Graaf's (1997) research on religious beliefs, two of the main concepts in which they were interested—national religiosity and family religious orientation—were each measured by a single indicator. However, religious orthodoxy was measured by four survey questions, answers to which were aggregated for each respondent to form a 'score' for that person. Answers to each of the four questions were given a score and then aggregated to form a religious belief score. The four questions were as follows.

1. Please indicate which statement below comes closest to expressing what you believe about God:
   - I don't believe in God.
   - I don't know whether there is a God and I don't believe there is any way to find out.
   - I don't believe in a personal God, but I do believe in a higher power of some kind.
   - I find myself believing in God some of the time, but not at others.
   - While I have doubts, I feel that I do believe in God.
   - I know God really exists and I have no doubts about it.

2. Which best describes your beliefs about God?
   - I don't believe in God and I never have.
   - I don't believe in God, but I used to.
   - I believe in God now, but I didn't used to.
   - I believe in God now and I always have.

3. How close do you feel to God most of the time?
   - Don't believe in God.
   - Not close at all.
   - Not very close.
   - Somewhat close.
   - Extremely close.

4. There is a God who concerns Himself with every human being, personally.
   - Strongly agree.
   - Agree.
   - Neither agree nor disagree.
   - Disagree.
   - Strongly disagree.

Dimensions of concepts

One elaboration of the general approach to measurement is to consider the possibility that the concept in which you are interested comprises different **dimensions**. This view is particularly associated with Lazarsfeld (1958). The idea behind this approach is that, when the researcher is seeking to develop a measure of a concept, the different aspects or components of that concept should be considered. This specification of the dimensions of a concept would be undertaken with reference to theory and research associated with that concept. Examples of this kind of approach can be discerned in Seeman's (1959) delineation of five dimensions of alienation (powerlessness, meaninglessness, normlessness, isolation, and self-estrangement). The idea is that people scoring high on one dimension may not necessarily score high on other dimensions, so that for each respondent you end up with a multidimensional 'profile'. Research in focus 7.4 demonstrates the use of dimensions in connection with the concept of counterproductive work behaviour.

However, in much if not most quantitative research, there is a tendency to rely on a single indicator of concepts.

For many purposes this is adequate. It would be a mistake to believe that investigations that use a single indicator of core concepts are somehow deficient. In any case, some studies, like that by Kelley and De Graaf (1997, see Research in focus 7.3), employ both single- and multiple-indicator measures of concepts. What *is* crucial is whether measures are reliable and whether they are valid representations of the concepts they are supposed to be tapping. It is to this issue that we now turn.

Research in focus 7.4
Specifying dimensions of a concept: the case of counterproductive work behaviour

This example is taken from the study by Eschleman et al. (2014) referred to in Research in the news 3.1, which was concerned with the relationship between abusive supervision and counterproductive work behaviour (CWB). This latter variable was conceptualized as being made up of two dimensions: forms of CWB directed at the supervisor and forms of CWB directed at the organization. Nine Likert scale items were used to measure the former and ten to measure organization-directed forms of CWB. Each item was presented as a statement to which the respondent indicated the frequency with which he or she engaged in that behaviour on a five-point scale going from 'rarely' to 'very often'. Representative items of the two dimensions are: 'Made fun of your supervisor at work' and 'Put little effort into your work'. Internal reliability for the two dimensions was high at .96 and .94 respectively.

Reliability and validity

Although the terms 'reliability' and 'validity' seem to be almost synonymous, they have quite different meanings in relation to the evaluation of measures of concepts, as was seen in Chapter 3.

Reliability

As Key concept 7.3 suggests, reliability is fundamentally concerned with issues of consistency of measures. There are at least three different meanings of the term. These are outlined in Key concept 7.3 and elaborated upon below.

Stability

The most obvious way of testing for the stability of a measure is the *test–retest* method. This involves administering a test or measure on one occasion and then readministering it to the same sample on another occasion—that is:

$$T_1 \qquad T_2$$
$$\text{Obs}_1 \quad \text{Obs}_2$$

We should expect to find a high correlation between Obs_1 and Obs_2. Correlation is a measure of the strength of the relationship between two variables. This topic will be covered in Chapter 15 in the context of a discussion about quantitative data analysis. Let us imagine that we develop a multiple-indicator measure that is supposed to tap 'preoccupation with social media' (the extent to which social media infiltrate participants' social worlds and thinking). We would administer the measure to a sample of respondents and readminister it some time later. If the correlation is low, the measure would appear to be unstable, implying that respondents' answers cannot be relied upon.

However, there are a number of problems with this approach to evaluating reliability. Respondents' answers at

Key concept 7.3
What is reliability?

Reliability refers to the consistency of a measure of a concept. The following are three prominent factors involved when considering whether a measure is reliable:

- *Stability*. This consideration, often referred to as *test–retest reliability*, entails asking whether a measure is stable over time, so that we can be confident that the results relating to that measure for a sample of respondents do not fluctuate. This means that, if we administer a measure to a group and then readminister it, there will be little variation over time in the results obtained.

- *Internal reliability*. The key issue is whether the indicators that make up the **scale** or index are consistent—in other words, whether respondents' scores on any one indicator tend to be related to their scores on the other indicators.

- *Inter-rater reliability*. When a great deal of subjective judgement is involved in such activities as the recording of observations or the translation of data into categories and where more than one 'rater' is involved in such activities, there is the possibility that there is a lack of consistency in their decisions. This can arise in a number of contexts, for example: in content analysis where decisions have to be made about how to categorize media items; when answers to open-ended questions have to be categorized; or in structured observation when observers have to decide how to classify participants' behaviour.

T_1 may influence how they reply at T_2, resulting in greater consistency between Obs_1 and Obs_2 than is in fact the case. Second, events may intervene between T_1 and T_2 that influence the degree of consistency. For example, if a long span of time is involved, technological changes and other development could influence preoccupation with social media. Berthoud (2000b) notes that an index of ill-health devised from the British Household Panel Survey (BHPS) achieved a high test–retest reliability. He notes that this is very encouraging, because 'some of the variation between tests (a year apart) will have been caused by genuine changes in people's health' (Berthoud 2000b: 170). There is no easy way of disentangling the effects of a lack of stability in the measure from 'real' changes in people's health over the year in question.

There are no clear solutions to these problems, other than by introducing a complex research design that turns the examination of reliability into a major project in its own right. Perhaps for these reasons, many if not most reports of research findings do not appear to carry out tests of stability. Indeed, longitudinal research is often undertaken precisely in order to identify social change and its correlates.

Internal reliability

This meaning of reliability applies to multiple-indicator measures such as those examined in Research in focus 7.2 and 7.3. When you have a multiple-item measure in which each respondent's answers to each question are aggregated to form an overall score, the possibility is raised that the indicators do not relate to the same thing; in other words, they lack coherence. We need to be sure that all our 'preoccupation with social media' indicators are related to each other. If they are not, some of the items may actually be unrelated to preoccupation with social media and therefore indicative of something else.

One way of testing internal reliability is the *split-half* method. We can take the counterproductive work behaviour directed at the organization measure developed by Eschleman et al. (2014) as an example (see Research in focus 7.4). The ten indicators would be divided into two halves with five in each group. The indicators would be allocated on a random or an odd–even basis. The degree of correlation between scores on the two halves would then be calculated. In other words, the aim would be to establish whether respondents scoring high on one of the two groups also scored high on the other group of indicators. The calculation of the correlation will yield a figure, known as a coefficient, that varies between 0 (no correlation and therefore no internal consistency) to 1 (perfect correlation and therefore complete internal consistency). It is usually expected that a result of 0.80 and above implies an acceptable level of internal reliability, although for many purposes 0.7 and above is accepted. Do not worry if these figures appear somewhat opaque. The meaning of correlation will be explored in much greater detail later on. The chief point to carry away with you at this stage is that the correlation establishes how closely respondents' scores on the two groups of indicators are related.

Nowadays, most researchers use a test of internal reliability known as 'Cronbach's alpha' (see Key concept 7.4). Its use has grown as a result of its incorporation into computer software for quantitative data analysis. In the study discussed in Research in focus 7.2, the Cronbach's alpha value for the dimension of counterproductive work behaviour was .94, which is very high.

Inter-rater reliability

The idea of inter-rater reliability is briefly outlined in Key concept 7.3. The issues involved are rather too advanced to be dealt with at this stage and will be touched on briefly in later chapters. Cramer (1998: Chapter 14) provides a very detailed treatment of the issues and appropriate techniques.

Key concept 7.4
What is Cronbach's alpha?

To a very large extent we are leaping ahead too much here, but it is important to appreciate the basic features of what this widely used test means. Cronbach's alpha is a commonly used test of internal reliability. Essentially it calculates the average of all possible split-half reliability coefficients. A computed alpha coefficient will vary between 1 (denoting perfect internal reliability) and 0 (denoting no internal reliability). The figure 0.80 is typically employed as a rule of thumb to denote an acceptable level of internal reliability, though many writers work with a slightly lower figure. In the case of Kelley and De Graaf's (1997) measure of religious orthodoxy (see Research in focus 7.3), which comprised four indicators, alpha was 0.93. The alpha levels varied between 0.79 and 0.95 for each of the fifteen national samples that make up the data. Berthoud (2000b: 169) writes that a minimum level of 0.60 is 'good' and cites the case of an index of ill-health used in the BHPS that achieved a level of 0.77.

Validity

Measurement validity has to do with whether a measure of a concept really measures that concept (see Key concept 7.5). When people argue about whether a person's IQ score really measures or reflects that person's level of intelligence, they are raising questions about the measurement validity of the IQ test in relation to the concept of intelligence. Whenever students or lecturers debate whether formal examinations provide an accurate measure of academic ability, they too are raising questions about measurement validity.

Writers distinguish between a number of ways of testing measurement validity, which really reflect different ways of gauging the validity of a measure of a concept. These different ways of testing measurement validity will now be outlined.

Key concept 7.5
What is validity?

Validity refers to the issue of whether an indicator (or set of indicators) that is devised to gauge a concept really measures that concept. Several ways of establishing validity are explored in the text: face validity; concurrent validity; predictive validity; construct validity; and convergent validity. Here the term is being used as a shorthand for what was referred to as *measurement validity* in Chapter 3. Validity should therefore be distinguished from the other terms introduced in Chapter 3: internal validity; external validity; and ecological validity.

Face validity

At the very minimum, a researcher who develops a new measure should establish that it has **face validity**—that is, that the measure apparently reflects the content of the concept in question. Face validity might be established by asking other people whether the measure seems to be getting at the concept that is the focus of attention. In other words, people, possibly those with experience or expertise in a field, might be asked to act as judges to determine whether on the face of it the measure seems to reflect the concept concerned. Face validity is, therefore, an essentially intuitive process.

Concurrent validity

The researcher might seek also to gauge the **concurrent validity** of the measure. Here the researcher employs a *criterion* on which cases (for example, people) are known to differ and that is relevant to the concept in question. A new measure of job satisfaction can serve as an example. A criterion might be absenteeism, because some people are more often absent from work (other than through illness) than others. In order to establish the concurrent validity of a measure of job satisfaction, we might see how far people who are satisfied with their jobs are less likely than those who are not satisfied to be *absent* from work. If a lack of correspondence were found, such as there being no difference in levels of job satisfaction among frequent absentees, doubt might be cast on whether our measure is really addressing job satisfaction. Wood and Williams (2007) discuss the problem of asking people in questionnaires how much they spend on gambling, because self-reported gambling expenditure tends to be inconsistent with actual revenue that accrues from gambling. The authors asked a large random sample of residents in Ontario, Canada, how much they had spent in the last month in twelve different ways. They note that even slight variations in the wording of questions could result in very different estimates of expenditure on the part of respondents, a concern that relates to issues that are discussed in Chapter 11. However, some questions did produce answers that were more consistent with an estimate of gambling expenditure per person in Ontario, which acted as the concurrent validity criterion. The authors recommend the following question on the basis of its performance in the validity test and its face validity:

> Roughly how much money do you spend on [specific gambling activity] in a typical month? What we mean here is how much you are ahead or behind, or your net win or loss in a typical month.
>
> (Wood and Williams 2007: 68)

The question required aggregating respondents' estimates of their gambling expenditure on each of several gambling activities. Research in focus 7.5 and 10.1 provide further examples of testing for concurrent validity.

Predictive validity

Another possible test for the validity of a new measure is **predictive validity**, whereby the researcher uses a *future* criterion measure, rather than a contemporary one, as in the case of concurrent validity. With predictive validity, the researcher would take future levels of absenteeism as the criterion against which the validity of a new measure of job satisfaction would be examined. The difference from concurrent validity is that a future rather than a simultaneous criterion measure is employed. Research in focus 7.5 provides an example of testing for predictive validity.

Construct validity

Some writers advocate that the researcher should also estimate the **construct validity** of a measure. Here, the researcher is encouraged to deduce hypotheses from a theory that is relevant to the concept. For example, drawing upon ideas about the impact of technology on the experience of work, the researcher might anticipate that people who are satisfied with their jobs are less likely to work on routine jobs; those who are not satisfied are more likely to work on routine jobs. We could investigate this theoretical deduction by examining the relationship between job satisfaction and job routine. However, some caution is required in interpreting the absence of a relationship between job satisfaction and job routine in this example. First, either the theory or the deduction that is made from it might be misguided. Second, the measure of job routine could be an invalid measure of that concept.

Convergent validity

In the view of some methodologists, the validity of a measure ought to be gauged by comparing it to measures of the same concept developed through other methods. For example, in addition to using a test of concurrent validity for their research on gambling expenditure, Wood and Williams (2007) used a diary to estimate gambling expenditure for a subsample of their respondents that could then be compared to questionnaire estimates. Respondents began the diary shortly after they had answered the survey question and continued completing it for a thirty-day period. This validity test allowed the researchers to compare what was actually spent in the month after the question was asked (assuming the diary estimates were correct) with what respondents *thought* they spent on gambling.

An interesting instance of convergent *in*validity is described in Research in the news 7.1. The British Crime Survey (BCS) was consciously devised to provide an alternative measure of levels of crime that would act as a check on the official statistics. The two sets of data are collected in quite different ways: the official crime statistics are collected as part of the bureaucratic processing of offenders in the course of the activities of members of

Research in focus 7.5
Assessing the internal reliability and the concurrent and predictive validity of a measure of organizational climate

Patterson et al. (2005) describe how they validated a measure they developed of organizational climate. This is a rather loose concept that was first developed in the 1960s and 1970s to refer to the perceptions of an organization by its members. Four main dimensions of climate were developed based around the following notions:

1. *human relations model:* feelings of belonging and trust in the organization and the degree to which there is training, good communication, and supervisory support;

2. *internal process model:* the degree of emphasis on formal rules and on traditional ways of doing things;

3. *open systems model:* the extent to which flexibility and innovativeness are valued;

4. *rational goal model:* the degree to which clearly defined objectives and the norms and values associated with efficiency, quality, and high performance are emphasized.

An Organizational Climate Measure, comprising 95 items in a four-point Likert format (definitely false, mostly false, mostly true, definitely true) was developed and administered to employees in 55 UK organizations, with 6,869 completing a questionnaire—a response rate of 57 per cent. A **factor analysis** (see Key concept 7.6) was conducted to explore the extent to which there were distinct groupings of items that tended to go together. This procedure yielded seventeen scales, such as autonomy, involvement, innovation and flexibility, and clarity of organizational goals.

The *internal reliability* of the scales was assessed using Cronbach's alpha, showing that all scales were at a level of 0.73 or above. This suggests that the measure's constituent scales were internally reliable.

Concurrent *validity* was assessed following semi-structured interviews, with each company's managers in connection with their organization's practices. The interview data were coded to provide criteria against which the validity of the scales could be gauged. In most cases, the scales were found to be concurrently valid. For example, the researcher examined the correlation between a scale designed to measure the emphasis on tradition and the degree to which practices associated with the 'new manufacturing paradigm' (Patterson et al. 2005: 397) were adopted, as revealed by the interview data. The correlation was –0.42, implying that those firms that were perceived as rooted in tradition tended to be less likely to adopt new manufacturing practices. Here the adoption of new manufacturing practices was treated as a criterion to assess the extent to which the scale measuring perceptions of tradition really was addressing tradition. If the correlation had been small or had been positive, the concurrent validity of the scale would have been in doubt.

To assess *predictive validity*, the researchers asked a senior **key informant** at each company to complete a questionnaire one year after the main survey had been conducted. The questionnaire was meant to address two of the measure's constituent scales, one of which was the innovation and flexibility scale. It asked the informants to assess their company in terms of its innovativeness in a number of areas. For example, the correlation between the innovation and flexibility scale and informants' assessments of their companies in terms of innovativeness with respect to products achieved a correlation of 0.53. This implies that there was indeed a correlation between perceptions of innovativeness and flexibility and a subsequent indicator of innovativeness.

the British criminal justice system, whereas the BCS entails the collection of data by interview from a national sample of possible victims of crime. In the case reported in Research in the news 7.1 a lack of **convergent validity** was found. However, the problem with the convergent approach to testing validity is that it is not possible to establish which of the two measures represents the more accurate picture. The BCS is not entirely flawless in its approach to the measurement of crime levels, and, in any case, the 'true' picture with regard to the volume of crime

Research in the news 7.1
Home Office crime statistics, convergent validity, and reliability

Few official statistics receive as much critical attention as the Home Office's crime statistics.

An article in the *Sunday Times* (Burrell and Leppard 1994) proclaimed the government's claims about the fall in crime a sham. The opening paragraph put the point as follows:

> The government's much heralded fall in crime is a myth. Hundreds of thousands of serious crimes have been quietly dropped from police records as senior officers massage their statistics to meet new Home Office targets. . . . Crime experts say at least 220,000 crimes, including burglary, assault, theft and car crimes, vanished from official statistics last year as a result of police manipulation of the figures.

What gave the 'crime experts' and the reporters the confidence to assert that the much-trumpeted fall in crime was a myth because the figures on which the claim was made had been massaged? The answer is that data from the British Crime Survey (BCS) had 'recently reported that actual crime rose faster over the past two years than during the 1980s' (see Research in focus 8.2 for details of the BCS). With each wave of data collection, a large, randomly selected sample of individuals is questioned by structured interview. The survey is not based on a panel design, since the same people are not interviewed with each wave of data collection. The BCS, which is now called the Crime Survey for England and Wales (**www.crimesurvey.co.uk/index.html**), is an example of what is known as a 'victimization survey', whereby a sample of a population is questioned about its experiences as victims of crime. The idea is that unreported crime and other crime that does not show up in the official statistics will be revealed. The authors of the *Sunday Times* article were suggesting that when the Home Office statistics are examined in relation to the BCS, the former are shown to be invalid. This is essentially an exercise in testing for convergent validity.

Because of the newsworthiness of crime, the statistics and the BCS (and its successor) have frequently been in the news since this item. On 20 November 2013, the crime figures made front page news in *The Times* with the headline 'We Regularly Fiddle Crime Numbers, Admit Police' (**www.thetimes.co.uk/tto/news/politics/article3926668.ece**). Such revelations clearly cast doubt on the crime statistics as a valid measure of the volume of underlying crime. However, the revelations also cast doubt on the test–retest reliability of the figures since we cannot be sure how far the patterns of 'fiddling' have been constant over time. An insight into this is provided by another *Times* article with the title 'Police Figures Show a Fall in Reporting . . . But Thousands of Crimes go Unreported' (**www.thetimes.co.uk/tto/news/uk/crime/article3984544.ece**). This article, which was published on 24 January 2014, revealed that crime figures published the previous day showed 'another' decline in offences but that in Kent there was an 8 per cent increase following an audit of its crime reporting procedures. This information casts doubt on the validity and stability of the crime statistics. However, as a *Times* article published on 21 November 2013 observes, the Crime Survey is not without problems as it does not include murders, offending against businesses, or cyber offending (**www.thetimes.co.uk/tto/news/uk/article3927463.ece**).

(All websites accessed 9 October 2014.)

---

at any one time is almost a metaphysical notion (Reiner 2000b). While the authors of the news item were able to draw on anecdotal evidence to support their thesis that the figures were being massaged and this together with the BCS evidence casts doubt on the official statistics, it would be a mistake to hold that the survey evidence necessarily represents a definitive and therefore unambiguously valid measure.

Research in focus 7.6 provides a brief account of the development of a scale using the Likert procedure and some of the ways in which reliability and validity were assessed.

Research in focus 7.6
Developing a Likert scale:
the case of attitudes to vegetarians

Chin et al. (2002) describe how they went about developing a scale designed to measure pro- or anti-vegetarian attitudes. They note that non-vegetarians sometimes see vegetarianism as deviant and that, as a result, vegetarians are sometimes regarded with suspicion if not hostility. The authors developed a scale comprising thirty-three items. Each item is a statement to which the respondent is asked to indicate strength of agreement or disagreement on a seven-point scale. The items were arrived at following interviews with both vegetarians and non-vegetarians; a review of the literature on vegetarianism; field observations (though it is not clear of what or whom); brainstorming within the team; and an examination of attitude scales addressing other forms of prejudice for possible wording and presentation. The items were meant to tap four areas:

- forms of behaviour in which vegetarians engage that are viewed as irritating—for example, 'Vegetarians preach too much about their beliefs and eating habits' (possibly a double-barrelled item—see Chapter 11);
- disagreement with vegetarians' beliefs—for example, 'Vegetarians are overly concerned with animal rights';
- health-related aspects of being a vegetarian—for example, 'Vegetarians are overly concerned about gaining weight';
- appropriate treatment of vegetarians—for example, 'It's OK to tease someone for being a vegetarian'.

The scale was tested out on a sample of university undergraduates in the USA. Some items from the scale were dropped because they exhibited poor internal consistency with the other items. Cronbach's alpha was conducted for the remaining twenty-one items and found to be high at 0.87 (see Key concept 7.4). The construct validity (see the subsection above on the meaning of this term) of the scale was also tested by asking the students to complete other scales that the researchers predicted would be associated with pro- or anti-vegetarian attitudes. One method was that the authors hypothesized that people with authoritarian attitudes would be more likely to be anti-vegetarians. This was confirmed, although the relationship between these two variables was very small. However, contrary to their hypothesis, the scale for attitudes towards vegetarianism was *not* found to be related to political conservatism. The scale emerges as internally reliable (see Key concept 7.3 on the meaning of this term) but as having questionable construct validity.

Reflections on reliability and validity

There are, then, a number of different ways of investigating the merit of measures that are devised to represent social scientific concepts. However, the discussion of reliability and validity is potentially misleading, because it would be wrong to think that all new measures of concepts are submitted to the rigours described above. In fact, most measurement is undertaken using what Cicourel (1964) called 'measurement by fiat'. By the term 'fiat', Cicourel was referring not to a well-known Italian car manufacturer but to the notion of 'decree'. He meant that most measures are simply asserted. Fairly straightforward but minimal steps may be taken to ensure that a measure is reliable and/or valid, such as testing for internal reliability when a multiple-indicator measure has been devised and examining face validity. But in many if not the majority of cases in which a concept is measured, no further testing takes place. This point will be further elaborated below.

It should also be borne in mind that, although reliability and validity are analytically distinguishable, they are related because validity presumes reliability. This means that, if your measure is not reliable, it cannot be valid. This point can be made with respect to each of the three criteria of reliability that have been discussed. If the measure is not stable over time, it simply cannot be providing a valid measure. The measure could not be tapping the concept it is supposed to be related to if the measure fluctuated. If the measure fluctuates, it may be measuring different things on different occasions. If a measure lacks internal reliability, it means that a multiple-indicator measure is actually measuring two or more different things. Therefore, the measure cannot be valid. Finally, if there is a lack of inter-rater consistency, it means that observers cannot agree on the meaning of what they are observing, which in turn means that a measure cannot be valid.

The main preoccupations of quantitative researchers

Both quantitative and qualitative research can be viewed as exhibiting a set of distinctive but contrasting preoccupations. These preoccupations reflect epistemologically grounded beliefs about what constitutes acceptable knowledge. In this section, four distinctive preoccupations that can be discerned in quantitative research will be outlined and examined: measurement, causality, generalization, and replication.

Measurement

The most obvious preoccupation is with measurement, a feature that is scarcely surprising in the light of much of the discussion in the present chapter so far. From the position of quantitative research, measurement carries a number of advantages that were previously outlined. It is not surprising, therefore, that issues of reliability and validity are a concern for quantitative researchers, though this is not always manifested in research practice.

Causality

In most quantitative research there is a very strong concern with explanation. Quantitative researchers are rarely concerned merely to describe how things are, but are keen to say why things are the way they are. This emphasis is also often taken to be a feature of the natural sciences. Thus, researchers are often not only interested in a phenomenon such as racial prejudice as something to be described, for example, in terms of how much prejudice exists in a certain group of individuals, or what proportion of people in a sample are highly prejudiced and what proportion are largely lacking in prejudice. Rather, they are likely to want to explain it, which means examining the causes of variation in racial prejudice. The researcher may seek to explain racial prejudice in terms of personal characteristics (such as levels of authoritarianism) or in terms of social characteristics (such as education, or social mobility experiences). In reports of research you will often come across the idea of 'independent' and 'dependent' variables, which reflect the tendency to think in terms of causes and effects. Racial prejudice might be regarded as the dependent variable, which is to be explained, and authoritarianism as an independent variable, which therefore has a causal influence upon prejudice.

When an experimental design is being employed, the independent variable is the variable that is manipulated. There is little ambiguity about the direction of causal influence. However, with cross-sectional designs which are used in most survey research, there is ambiguity about the direction of causal influence in that data concerning variables are simultaneously collected. Therefore, we cannot say that an independent variable precedes the dependent one. To refer to independent and dependent variables in the context of cross-sectional designs, we must *infer* that one causes the other, as in the example concerning authoritarianism and racial prejudice in the previous paragraph. We must draw on common sense or theoretical ideas to infer the likely temporal precedence of variables. However, there is always the risk that the inference will be wrong (see Research in focus 27.7 for an example).

The concern about causality is reflected in the preoccupation with internal validity that was referred to in Chapter 3. There it was noted that a criterion of good quantitative research is frequently the extent to which there is confidence in the researcher's causal inferences. Research that exhibits the characteristics of an experimental design is often more highly valued than cross-sectional research, because of the greater confidence in the causal findings associated with the former. For their part, quantitative researchers who employ cross-sectional designs are invariably concerned to develop techniques that will allow causal inferences to be made. Moreover, the rise of longitudinal research such as Understanding Society (as described in Research in focus 3.10) almost certainly reflects a quest to improve the ability to generate findings that permit a causal interpretation.

Generalization

In quantitative research, researchers are usually concerned to be able to say that their findings can be generalized beyond the confines of the particular context in which the research was conducted. Thus, if a study of racial prejudice is carried out by a questionnaire with a number of people who answer the questions, we might want to say that the results can apply to individuals other than those who participated in the study. This concern reveals itself in survey research in the attention that is often given to the question of how one can create a representative sample. Given that it is rarely feasible to send questionnaires to or interview whole populations (such as all members of a town, or the whole population of a country, or all members of an organization), we have to sample. However, we will want the sample to be as representative as possible in order to be able to say that the results are not unique to the particular group upon whom the research was conducted; in other words, we want to be able to generalize the findings beyond the cases (for example, the people) that make up the sample. The preoccupation with generalization can be viewed as an attempt to emulate the law-like findings of the natural sciences.

Probability sampling, which will be explored in Chapter 8, is the main way in which researchers seek to generate a representative sample. This procedure largely eliminates bias from the selection of a sample by using a process of random selection. The use of random selection does not guarantee a representative sample, because, as will be seen in Chapter 8, there are factors that operate over and above the sampling approach used that can jeopardize the representativeness of a sample. A related consideration here is this: even if we did have a representative sample, what would it be representative *of*? The simple answer is that it will be representative of the population from which it was selected. This is certainly the answer that sampling theory gives us. Strictly speaking, we cannot generalize beyond that population. This means that, if the members

of the population from which a sample is taken are all inhabitants of a town, city, or region, or are all members of an organization, we can generalize only to the inhabitants or members of the town, city, region, or organization. But it is very tempting to see the findings as having a more pervasive applicability, so that, if the sample were selected from a large city such as Birmingham, the findings would be relevant to similar cities. We should not make inferences beyond the population from which the sample was selected, but researchers frequently do so. The desire to be able to generalize is often so deeply ingrained that the limits to the generalizability of findings are frequently forgotten or sidestepped.

The concern with generalizability or external validity is particularly strong among quantitative researchers using cross-sectional and longitudinal designs. There is a concern about generalizability among experimental research, as the discussion of external validity in Chapter 3 suggested, but users of this research design usually give greater attention to internal validity issues.

Student experience
Generalizability in a student project

For his team-based survey research on students at his university, Joe Thomson felt that issues to do with reliability and validity were important. In particular, it appears from the following comment that the generalizability of the findings was seen as especially significant.

Again, the main considerations were reliability and validity of the research. Thus the methods used reflected this; the questionnaire went through a modification period where we as a group not only tested it on our sample but also received information from staff who worked within the area our research project was aimed at. We knew that the sample had to be representative of the whole university, so the number of members from the group interviewing students from different halls was in ratio to the number of students who lived within those residences.

To read more, go to the Online Resource Centre: www.oxfordtextbooks.co.uk/orc/brymansrm5e/

Replication

The natural sciences are often depicted as wishing to reduce to a bare minimum the contaminating influence of the scientist's biases and values. The results of a piece of research should be unaffected by the researcher's special characteristics or expectations or whatever. If biases and lack of objectivity were pervasive, the claims of the natural sciences to provide a definitive picture of the world would be seriously undermined. As a check upon the influence of these potentially damaging problems, scientists may seek to replicate—that is, to reproduce—each other's

experiments. If there was a failure to replicate, so that a scientist's findings repeatedly could not be reproduced, serious questions would be raised about the validity of his or her findings. Consequently, scientists are often very explicit about their procedures so that an experiment is capable of replication. Likewise, quantitative researchers in the social sciences often regard replication, or more precisely the ability to replicate, as an important ingredient of their activity. It is easy to see why: the possibility of a lack of objectivity and of the intrusion of the researcher's values would appear to be much greater when examining the social world than when the natural scientist investigates the natural order. Consequently, it is often regarded as important that researchers spell out clearly their procedures so that they can be replicated by others, even if the research does not end up being replicated.

Whether research is in practice replicated is another matter. Replication is not a high-status activity in the natural and social sciences, because it is often regarded as a pedestrian and uninspiring pursuit. It is striking that, in the example referred to in Research in focus 7.7, the exercise is referred to as a replication *and extension* of several previous studies, conveying the impression that it is not *just* a replication.

Research in focus 7.7
Replicating a study of tipping

Brewster and Lynn (2014) conducted what they refer to as a 'replication, extension, and exploration of consumer racial discrimination in tipping' (2014). They note that some previous research has shown that black service workers fare less well than their white counterparts when it comes to tipping. One of the principal studies that the authors sought to replicate was one in which Lynn had been involved and which demonstrated that black restaurant servers received lower tips than white servers. Brewster and Lynn argue that their replication is important because of some limitations in one of the measures used in the earlier study (a measure of service quality). However, they also position their research as an extension of the earlier investigation by using a more robust measure of service skills which is used as a **mediating variable**. This kind of variable is deemed to be a potential explanation of the ethnicity-tipping relationship because if it is found that (as with previous research) black servers receive lower tips, it could be that this is because their service skills tend to be poorer and therefore they are given less financial recognition for their work by diners.

As they were exiting a restaurant, diners were asked to complete a questionnaire about their experience. They were asked about the race of the server and how much they left as a tip. Server skill was measured through two kinds of questions. First, diners were asked how much they liked various features of their servers, such as friendliness, attentiveness, and appearance. Second, they were asked, using a Likert scale, whether they agreed or disagreed with statements such as whether the server smiled when greeting them and maintained eye contact. Brewster and Lynn confirmed earlier research showing that white servers receive superior tips to black servers. However, service quality was found not to act as a mediating variable; in other words, the racial difference in tipping could not be explained by differences in the perceived service quality that diners experienced. Further, the race of the diner was found not to be relevant to the tipping behaviour.

This replication was conducted in a northern city in the USA whereas the study that was being replicated had been conducted in a southern city. If the findings had been different, this could have been attributed to differences in the location of the research or to differences in the way the data were collected. However, the findings of the earlier study were successfully replicated so that Brewster and Lynn were able to draw attention to the apparent robustness of the relationship between race and tipping.

Moreover, standard replications do not form the basis for attractive articles, so far as many academic journal editors are concerned. Consequently, replications of research appear in print far less frequently than might be supposed. A further reason for the low incidence of published replications is that it is difficult to ensure in social science research that the conditions in a replication are precisely the same as those that pertained in an original study. So long as there is some ambiguity about the degree to which the conditions relating to a replication are the same as those in the initial study, any differences in findings may be attributable to the design of the replication rather than to some deficiency in the original study. To some extent, this is the case with the research referred to in Research in focus 7.7, as the initial study and the replication were carried out in different parts of the United States. Nonetheless, it is often regarded as crucial that the methods taken in generating a set of findings are made explicit, so that it is *possible* to replicate a piece of research. Thus, it is replic*ability* that is often regarded as an important quality of quantitative research.

e critique of quantitative research

, quantitative research along with its epis- nd ontological foundations has been the focus of a great deal of criticism, particularly from exponents and spokespersons of qualitative research. To a very large extent, it is difficult to distinguish between different kinds of criticism when reflecting on the different critical points that have been proffered. These include criticisms of quantitative research in general as a research strategy; criticisms of the epistemological and ontological foundations of quantitative research; and criticisms of specific methods and research designs with which quantitative research is associated.

Criticisms of quantitative research

To give a flavour of the critique of quantitative research, four criticisms will be covered briefly.

1. *Quantitative researchers fail to distinguish people and social institutions from 'the world of nature'.* The phrase 'the world of nature' is from the writings of Schutz (1962) and the specific quotation from which it has been taken can be found in Chapter 2 in the section on 'Interpretivism'. Schutz and other phenomenologists accuse social scientists who employ a natural science model of treating the social world as if it were no different from the natural order. In so doing, they draw attention to one of positivism's central tenets—namely, that the principles of the scientific method can and should be applied to all phenomena that are the focus of investigation. As Schutz argues, this tactic essentially means turning a blind eye to the differences between the social and the natural world. More particularly, as was observed in Chapter 2, it therefore means ignoring and riding roughshod over the fact that people interpret the world around them, whereas this capacity for self-reflection cannot be found among the objects of the natural sciences ('molecules, atoms, and electrons', as Schutz put it).

2. *The measurement process possesses an artificial and spurious sense of precision and accuracy.* There are a number of aspects to this criticism. For one thing, it has been argued that the connection between the measures developed by social scientists and the concepts they are supposed to be revealing is assumed rather than real; hence, Cicourel's (1964) notion of 'measurement by fiat'. Testing for validity in the manner described in the previous section cannot really address this problem, because the very tests themselves entail measurement by fiat. A further way in which writers such as Cicourel regard the measurement process as flawed is that it presumes that when, for example, members of a sample respond to a question on a questionnaire (which is itself taken to be an indicator of a concept), they interpret the key terms in the question similarly. In the view of many writers, respondents simply do not interpret such terms similarly. A common response to this problem is to use questions with fixed-choice answers, but this approach merely provides 'a solution to the problem of meaning by simply ignoring it' (Cicourel 1964: 108).

3. *The reliance on instruments and procedures hinders the connection between research and everyday life.* This issue relates to the question of ecological validity that was raised in Chapter 3. Many methods of quantitative research rely heavily on administering research instruments to participants (such as structured interviews and self-administered questionnaires) or on controlling situations to determine their effects (as in experiments). However, as Cicourel (1982) asks, how do we know if survey respondents have the requisite knowledge to answer a question or whether they are similar in their sense of the topic being important to them in their everyday lives? Thus, if respondents answer a set of questions designed to measure racial prejudice, can we be sure that they are equally aware of what it is and what its manifestations are and can we be sure that it is of equal concern to them in the ways in which it connects with everyday life? One can go even further and ask how well their answers relate to their everyday lives. People may answer a question designed to measure racial prejudice, but respondents' actual behaviour may be at variance with their answers (as discussed in Thinking deeply 12.2).

4. *The analysis of relationships between variables creates a static view of social life that is independent of people's lives.* Blumer (1956: 685) argued that studies that aim to bring out the relationships between variables omit 'the process of interpretation or definition that goes on in human groups'. This means that, for example, we do not know how an apparent relationship between two or more variables has been produced by the people on whom the research was conducted. This criticism incorporates the first and third criticisms that have been referred to—that the meaning of events to individuals is ignored and that we do not know how such findings connect to everyday contexts—but adds a further element—namely, that it creates a sense of a static social world that is separate from the individuals who make it up. In other words, quantitative research is seen as carrying an objectivist ontology that reifies the social world.

We can see in these criticisms the application of a set of concerns associated with a qualitative research strategy that reveals the combination of an interpretivist epistemological orientation (an emphasis on meaning from the individual's point of view) and a constructionist ontology (an emphasis on viewing the social world as the product of individuals rather than as something beyond them). The criticisms may appear very damning, but, as we will see in Chapter 17, quantitative researchers have a powerful battery of criticisms of qualitative research in their arsenal as well!

 # Is it always like this?

One of the problems with characterizing any research strategy, research design, or research method is that to a certain extent one is always outlining an ideal-typical approach. In other words, one tends to create something that represents that strategy, design, or method, but that may not reflect it in its entirety in research practice. This gap between the ideal type and actual practice can arise as a result of at least two major considerations. First, it arises because those of us who write about and teach research methods cannot cover every eventuality that can arise in the process of social research, so that we tend to provide accounts of the research process that draw upon common features. Thus, a model of the process of quantitative research, such as that provided in Figure 7.1, should be thought of as a general *tendency* rather than as a definitive description of all quantitative research. A second reason why the gap can arise is that, when writing about and teaching research methods, we are essentially providing an account of *good practice*. However, these practices are often not followed in the published research that students are likely to encounter in the substantive courses that they will be taking. This failure to follow the procedures associated with good practice is not necessarily due to incompetence on the part of social researchers (though in some cases it can be!), but is much more likely to be associated with matters of time, cost, and feasibility—in other words, the pragmatic concerns that cannot be avoided when one does social research.

Reverse operationism

As an example of the first source of the gap between the ideal type and actual research practice we can take the case of something that I call 'reverse operationism' (Bryman 1988a: 28). The model of the process of quantitative research in Figure 7.1 implies that concepts are specified and that measures and indicators are then devised for them. This is the basis of the idea of **operationism** or **operationalism**, a term that derives from physics (Bridgman 1927), and that implies a deductive view of how research should proceed. However, this view of research neglects the fact that measurement can entail more of an inductive element than Figure 7.1 implies. Sometimes, measures are developed that in turn lead

to conceptualization. One way in which this can occur is when a statistical technique known as *factor analysis* is employed (see Key concept 7.6). In order to measure the concept of 'charismatic leadership', a term that owes a great deal to Weber's (1947) notion of charismatic authority, Conger and Kanungo (1998) generated twenty-five items to provide a multiple-item measure of the concept. These items derived from their reading of existing theory and research on the subject, particularly in connection with charismatic leadership in organizations. When the items were administered to a sample of respondents and the results were factor analysed, it was found that the items bunched around six factors, each of which, to all intents and purposes, represents a dimension of the concept of charismatic leadership:

1. strategic vision and articulation behaviour;
2. sensitivity to the environment;
3. unconventional behaviour;
4. personal risk;
5. sensitivity to organizational members' needs;
6. action orientation away from the maintenance of the status quo.

The point to note is that these six dimensions were not specified at the outset: the link between conceptualization and measurement was an inductive one. Nor is this an unusual situation so far as research is concerned (Bryman 1988a: 26–8).

Reliability and validity testing

The second reason why the gap between the ideal type and actual research practice can arise is because researchers do not follow some of the recommended practices. A classic case of this tendency is that, while, as in the present chapter, much time and effort are expended on the articulation of the ways in which the reliability and validity of measures should be determined, often these procedures are not followed. There is evidence from analyses of published quantitative research in organization studies (Podsakoff and Dalton 1987), a field that draws extensively on ideas and methods used in the social sciences, that writers rarely

Key concept 7.6
What is factor analysis?

Factor analysis is employed in relation to multiple-indicator measures to determine whether groups of indicators tend to bunch together to form distinct clusters, referred to as factors. Its main goal is to reduce the number of variables with which the researcher needs to deal. It is used in relation to multiple-item measures, such as Likert scales, to see how far there is an inherent structure to the large number of items that often make up such measures. Researchers sometimes use factor analysis to establish whether the dimensions of a measure that they expect to exist can be confirmed. The clusters of items that are revealed by a factor analysis need to be given names (for example, innovation and flexibility or autonomy in the study discussed in Research in focus 7.5). It is a complex technique that is beyond the level at which this book is pitched (see Bryman and Cramer 2011: Chapter 13), but it has considerable significance for the development of measures in many social scientific fields.

report tests of the stability of their measures and even more rarely report evidence of validity (only 3 per cent of articles provided information about measurement validity). A large proportion of articles used Cronbach's alpha, but, since this device is relevant only to multiple-item measures, because it gauges internal consistency, the stability and validity of many measures that are employed in the field of organization studies are unknown. This is not to say that the measures are necessarily *un*stable and *in*valid, but that we simply do not know. The reasons why the procedures for determining stability and validity are rarely used are almost certainly the cost and time that are likely to be involved. Researchers tend to be concerned with substantive issues and are less than enthusiastic about engaging in the kind of development work that would be required for a thoroughgoing determination of measurement quality. However, what this means is that Cicourel's (1964) previously cited remark about much measurement in sociology being 'measurement by fiat' has considerable weight.

The remarks on the lack of assessment of the quality of measurement should not be taken as a justification for readers to neglect this phase in their work. My aim is merely to draw attention to some of the ways in which practices described in this book are not always followed and to suggest some reasons why they are not followed.

Sampling

A similar point can be made in relation to sampling, which will be covered in the next chapter. As we will see, good practice is strongly associated with *random* or *probability sampling*. However, quite a lot of research is based on **non-probability samples**—that is, samples that have not been selected in terms of the principles of probability sampling, to be discussed in Chapter 8. Sometimes the use of non-probability samples will be due to the impossibility or extreme difficulty of obtaining **probability samples**. Another reason is that the time and cost involved in securing a probability sample are too great relative to the level of resources available. And yet a third reason is that sometimes the opportunity to study a certain group presents itself and represents too good an opportunity to miss. Again, such considerations should not be viewed as a justification and hence as a set of reasons for ignoring the principles of sampling to be examined in the next chapter, not least because not following the principles of probability sampling carries implications for the kind of statistical analysis that can be employed (see Chapter 15). Instead, my purpose as before is to draw attention to the ways in which gaps between recommendations about good practice and actual research practice can arise.

≫ *Key points*

....

- Quantitative research can be characterized as a linear series of steps moving from theory to conclusions, but the process described in Figure 7.1 is an ideal type from which there are many departures.

- The measurement process in quantitative research entails the search for indicators.

- Establishing the reliability and validity of measures is important for assessing their quality.

- Quantitative research can be characterized as exhibiting certain preoccupations, the most central of which are: measurement; causality; generalization; and replication.

- Quantitative research has been subjected to many criticisms by qualitative researchers. These criticisms tend to revolve around the view that a natural science model is inappropriate for studying the social world.

Questions for review

The main steps in quantitative research

- What are the main steps in quantitative research?

- To what extent do the main steps follow a strict sequence?

- Do the steps suggest a deductive or inductive approach to the relationship between theory and research?

Concepts and their measurement

- Why is measurement important for the quantitative researcher?

- What is the difference between a measure and an indicator?

- Why might multiple-indicator approaches to the measurement of concepts be preferable to those that rely on a single indicator?

Reliability and validity

- What are the main ways of thinking about the reliability of the measurement process? Is one form of reliability the most important?

- 'Whereas validity presupposes reliability, reliability does not presuppose validity.' Discuss.

- What are the main criteria for evaluating measurement validity?

The main preoccupations of quantitative researchers

- Outline the main preoccupations of quantitative researchers. What reasons can you give for their prominence?

- Why might replication be an important preoccupation among quantitative researchers, in spite of the tendency for replications in social research to be fairly rare?

The critique of quantitative research

- 'The crucial problem with quantitative research is the failure of its practitioners to address adequately the issue of meaning.' Discuss.

- How central is the adoption by quantitative researchers of a natural science model of conducting research to the critique by qualitative researchers of quantitative research?

Is it always like this?

- Why do social researchers sometimes not test the validity and/or reliability of measures that they employ?

Online Resource Centre
www.oxfordtextbooks.co.uk/orc/brymansrm5e/

Visit the Online Resource to enrich your understanding of the nature of quantitative research. Follow up links to other resources, test yourself using multiple choice questions, and gain further guidance and inspiration from the Student Researcher's Toolkit.

8

Sampling in quantitative research

 ## *Chapter outline*

 ## *Chapter guide*

This chapter and the three that follow it are concerned with principles and practices associated with social survey research. Sampling principles are not exclusively concerned with survey research; for example, they are relevant to the selection of documents for content analysis (see Chapter 13). However, in this chapter the emphasis will be on sampling in connection with the selection of people who would be asked questions by interview or questionnaire. The chapter explores:

- the role of sampling in relation to the overall process of doing survey research;
- the related ideas of generalization (also known as external validity) and of a representative sample; the latter allows the researcher to generalize findings from a sample to a population;
- the idea of a *probability sample*—that is, one in which a random selection process has been employed;
- the main types of probability sample: the simple random sample; the systematic sample; the stratified random sample; and the multi-stage cluster sample;
- the main issues involved in deciding on sample size;

- different types of non-probability sample, including quota sampling, which is widely used in market research and opinion polls;
- some of the issues raised by sampling for online surveys;
- potential sources of error in survey research.

Introduction to survey research

This chapter is concerned with some important aspects of conducting a survey, but it presents only a partial picture, because there are many other steps. In this chapter I am concerned with the selection of individuals for survey research, although the principles involved apply equally to other approaches to quantitative research, such as content analysis. Chapters 9, 10, and 11 deal with the data-collection aspects of conducting a survey, while Chapters 15 and 16 deal with issues to do with the analysis of data.

Figure 8.1 aims to outline the main steps involved in doing survey research. Initially, the survey will begin with general research issues that need to be investigated. These are gradually narrowed down so that they become research questions, which may take the form of hypotheses. The movement from research issues to research questions is likely to be the result of reading the literature relating to the issues, such as relevant theories and evidence (see Chapters 1 and 4).

Once the research questions have been formulated, the planning of the fieldwork can begin. In practice, decisions relating to sampling and the data collection instrument will overlap, but they are presented in Figure 8.1 as part of a sequence. The figure is meant to illustrate the main phases of a survey, and these different steps (other than those to do with sampling, which will be covered in this chapter) will be followed through in Chapters 9–11 and 15–16.

The survey researcher needs to decide what kind of population is suited to the investigation of the topic and also needs to formulate a research instrument and consider how it should be administered. By 'research instrument' is meant simply something like a **structured interview** schedule or a **self-administered questionnaire**. Moreover, there are several different ways of administering such instruments. Figure 8.2 outlines the main types. Types 1 through 5 are covered in Chapter 9. Types 6 through 10 are covered in Chapter 10.

Introduction to sampling

Many of the readers of this book will be university or college students. At some point in your stay at your university (I will use this term from now on to include colleges) you may have wondered about the attitudes of your fellow students to various matters, or about their behaviour in certain areas, or something about their backgrounds. If you decided to examine any of these three areas, you might consider conducting structured interviews or sending out questionnaires in order to find out about their behaviour, attitudes, or backgrounds. You will, of course, have to consider how best to design your interviews or questionnaires, and the issues that are involved in designing these research instruments and administering them will be the focus of Chapters 9–11. However, before getting to that point you are likely to be confronted with a problem. Let us say that your university is quite large and has around 9,000 students. It is extremely unlikely that you will have the time and resources to conduct a survey of all these students. It is unlikely that you would be able to send questionnaires to all 9,000 and even more unlikely that you would be able to interview all of them, since conducting survey research by interview is considerably more

expensive and time-consuming, all things being equal, than by postal questionnaire (see Chapter 10). It is almost certain that you will need to **sample** students from the total population of students in your university.

The need to sample is commonly encountered in quantitative research. In this chapter I will be almost entirely concerned with matters relating to sampling in relation to survey research involving data collection by structured interview or questionnaire. Other methods of quantitative research also involve sampling considerations, as will be seen in Chapters 12 and 13, where we will examine structured observation and content analysis respectively. The principles of sampling involved are more or less identical to those used in connection with these other methods, but frequently other factors need to be considered as well.

But will any old sample suffice? Would it be sufficient to locate yourself in a central position on your campus and then interview those students who come past you and whom you are in a position to interview? Alternatively, would it be sufficient to go around your student union asking people to be interviewed? Or again to send questionnaires to everyone on your course?

Figure 8.1
Steps in conducting a social survey

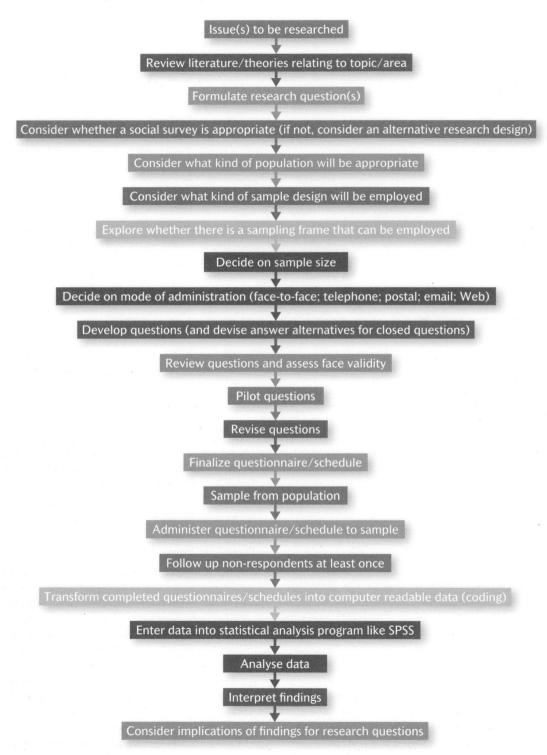

Figure 8.2
Main modes of administration of a survey

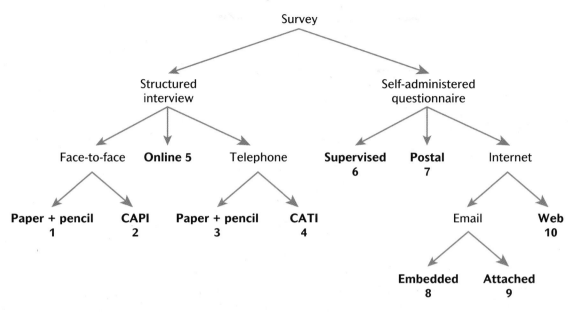

Notes: CAPI is computer-assisted personal interviewing; CATI is computer-assisted telephone interviewing.

The answer depends on whether you want to *generalize* your findings to the entire student body in your university. If you do, it is unlikely that any of the three sampling strategies proposed in the previous paragraph would provide you with a *representative sample* of all students in your university. In order to be able to generalize your findings from your sample to the population from which it was selected, the sample must be representative. See Key concept 8.1 for an explanation of key terms concerning sampling.

Why might the strategies for sampling students previously outlined be unlikely to produce a representative sample? There are various reasons, of which the following stand out.

- The first two approaches depend heavily upon the availability of students during the time that you search them out. Not all students are likely to be equally available at that time, so the sample will not reflect unavailable students who may differ in some way from available students.

- The first two approaches also depend on the students going to the locations. Not all students will necessarily pass the point where you locate yourself or go to the student union, or they may vary greatly in the frequency with which they do so. Their movements are likely to reflect such things as where their halls of residence or accommodation are situated, or where their departments are located, or their social habits. Again, to rely on these locations would mean missing out on students who do not frequent them.

- It is possible that your decisions about which people to approach will be influenced by your judgements about how friendly or cooperative the people concerned are likely to be or by how comfortable you feel about interviewing students of the same (or opposite) gender to yourself, as well as by many other factors.

- The problem with the third strategy is that students on your course by definition take the same subject as each other and therefore will not be representative of all students in the university.

In other words, with the three sampling approaches, your decisions about whom to sample are influenced too much by personal judgements, by prospective respondents' availability, or by your implicit criteria for inclusion. Such limitations mean that, in the language of survey sampling, your sample will be *biased*. A biased sample is one that does not represent the population from which the sample was selected. Sampling bias will occur if some members of the population have little or no chance of being selected for inclusion in the sample. As far as possible, bias should be removed from the selection of your sample. In fact, it is incredibly difficult to remove bias altogether and to derive a truly representative sample. What needs to be done is to ensure that steps are taken to minimize bias.

Key concept 8.1
Basic terms and concepts in sampling

- *Population*: basically, the universe of units from which the sample is to be selected. The term 'units' is employed because it is not necessarily people who are being sampled—the researcher may want to sample from a universe of nations, cities, regions, firms, etc. Finch and Hayes (1994), for example, based part of their research upon a random sample of wills. Their population, therefore, was a population of wills. Thus, 'population' has a much broader meaning than the everyday use of the term, whereby it tends to be associated with a city or nation's entire population and to refer to people only.

- *Sample*: the segment of the population that is selected for investigation. It is a subset of the population. The method of selection may be based on a probability or a non-probability approach (see below).

- *Sampling frame*: the listing of all units in the population from which the sample will be selected.

- *Representative sample*: a sample that reflects the population accurately so that it is a microcosm of the population.

- *Sampling bias*: a distortion in the representativeness of the sample that arises when some members of the population (or more precisely the sampling frame) stand little or no chance of being selected for inclusion in the sample.

- *Probability sample*: a sample that has been selected using random selection so that each unit in the population has a known chance of being selected. It is generally assumed that a *representative sample* is more likely to be the outcome when this method of selection from the population is employed. The aim of probability sampling is to keep *sampling error* (see below) to a minimum.

- *Non-probability sample*: a sample that has not been selected using a random selection method. Essentially, this implies that some units in the population are more likely to be selected than others.

- *Sampling error*: error in the research findings due to the difference between a sample and the population from which it is selected. This may occur even if probability sampling has been employed.

- *Non-sampling error*: error in the research findings due to the differences between the population and the sample that arise either from deficiencies in the sampling approach, such as an inadequate sampling frame or **non-response** (see below), or from such problems as poor question wording, poor interviewing, or flawed processing of data.

- *Non-response*: a source of non-sampling error that is particularly likely to happen when individuals are being sampled. It occurs whenever some members of the sample refuse to cooperate, cannot be contacted, or for some reason cannot supply the required data (for example, because of mental incapacity); an example is discussed in Research in the news 8.1.

- *Census*: the enumeration of an entire population. Thus, if data are collected in relation to all units in a population, rather than in relation to a sample of units of that population, the data are treated as census data. The phrase '*the* census' typically refers to the complete enumeration of all members of the population of a nation state—that is, a national census. This form of enumeration currently occurs once every ten years in the UK, although there is some uncertainty at the time of writing about whether another census will take place. However, in a statistical context, like the term *population*, the idea of a census has a broader meaning than this.

Three sources of sampling bias can be identified (see Key concept 8.1 for an explanation of key terms).

1. *If a non-probability or non-random sampling method is used.* If the method used to select the sample is not random, it is likely that human judgement will affect the selection process, making some members of the population more likely to be selected. This source of bias can be eliminated through the use of probability/random sampling, which is described below.

2. *If the sampling frame is inadequate.* If the sampling frame is not comprehensive or is inaccurate or suffers from some other kind of deficiency, the sample that is derived cannot represent the population, even if a random/probability sampling method is employed.

3. *If some sample members refuse to participate or cannot be contacted—in other words, if there is non-response.* The problem with non-response is that those who agree to participate may differ in various ways from those who do not agree to participate. Some of the differences may be significant to the research question. If the data are available, it may be possible to check how far, when there is non-response, the resulting sample differs from the population. It is often possible to do this in terms of characteristics such as gender or age, or, in the case of something like a sample of university students, whether the sample's characteristics reflect the entire sample in terms of faculty membership. However, it is usually impossible to determine whether differences exist between the population and the sample after non-response in terms of 'deeper' factors, such as attitudes or patterns of behaviour.

 # Sampling error

In order to appreciate the implications of sampling error for achieving a representative sample, consider Figures 8.3–8.7. Imagine we have a population of 200 people and we want a sample of 50. Imagine as well that one of the variables of concern to us is whether people watch soap operas and that the population is equally divided between those who do and those who do not. This split is represented by the vertical line that divides the population into two halves (Figure 8.3). If the sample is representative we would expect our sample of 50 to be equally split in terms of this variable (Figure 8.4). If there is a small amount of sampling error, so that we have one person too many who does not watch soap operas and one too few who does, it will look like Figure 8.5. In Figure 8.6 we see a rather more serious degree of over-representation of people who do not watch soaps. This time there are three too many who do not watch them and three too few who do. In Figure 8.7 we have a very serious over-representation of people who do not watch

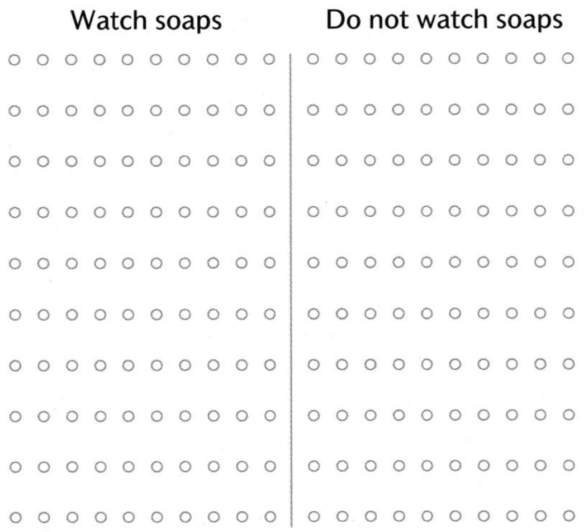

Figure 8.4
A sample with no sampling error

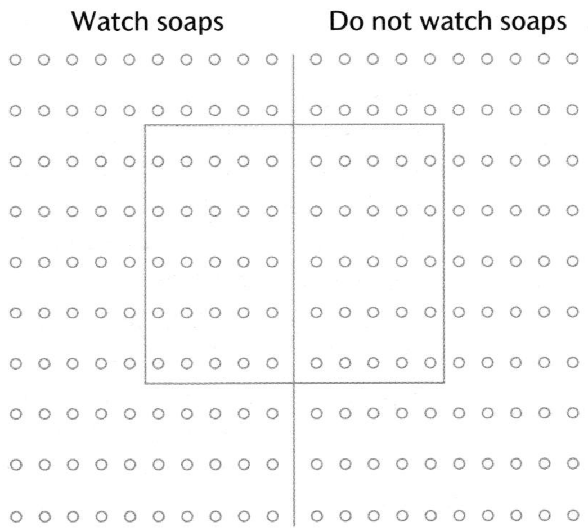

Watch soaps   Do not watch soaps

Figure 8.3
Watching soap operas in a population of 200

Watch soaps   Do not watch soaps

Figure 8.5
A sample with very little sampling error

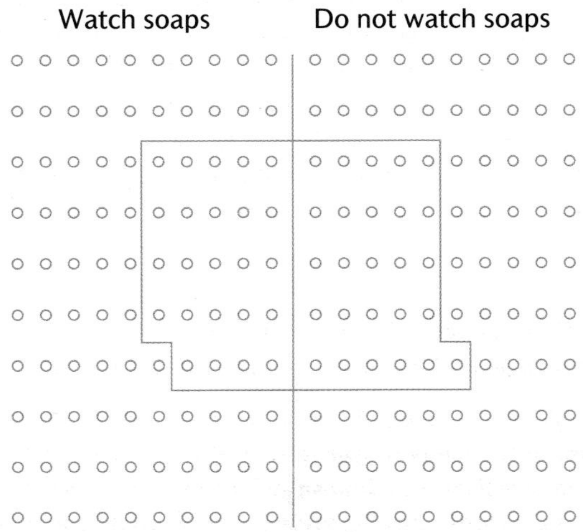

Watch soaps   Do not watch soaps

Figure 8.6
A sample with some sampling error

Watch soaps   Do not watch soaps

Figure 8.7
A sample with a lot of sampling error

Watch soaps   Do not watch soaps

soaps, because there are 35 people in the sample who do not watch them, which is much larger than the 25 who should be in the sample.

As suggested above, probability sampling does not and cannot eliminate sampling error. Even with a well-crafted probability sample, a degree of sampling error is likely to creep in. However, probability sampling stands a better chance than non-probability sampling of keeping sampling error in check so that it does not

end up looking like the outcome featured in Figure 8.7. Moreover, probability sampling allows the researcher to employ tests of statistical significance that permit inferences to be made about the sample from which the sample was selected. The term **inferential statistics** is used to refer to the tests that are used in inferring qualities of a population from data about a sample drawn randomly from that population. These will be addressed in Chapter 15.

Types of probability sample

Imagine that we are interested in levels of alcohol consumption among university students and the variables that relate to variation in levels of drinking. We might decide to conduct our research in a single nearby university. This means that our population will be all students in that university, which will in turn mean that we will be able to generalize our findings only to students of that university. We simply cannot assume that levels of alcohol consumption and their correlates will be the same in other universities. We might decide that we want our research to be conducted only on full-time students, so that part-time students are omitted. Imagine too that there are 9,000 full-time students in the university.

Simple random sample

The **simple random sample** is the most basic form of probability sample. With random sampling, each unit of the population has an equal probability of inclusion

in the sample. Imagine that we decide that we have enough money to interview 450 students at the university. This means that the probability of inclusion in the sample is

$$\frac{450}{9,000}, \text{ i.e. 1 in 20}$$

This is known as the *sampling fraction* and is expressed as

$$\frac{n}{N}$$

where n is the sample size and N is the population size.

The key steps in devising our simple random sample can be represented as follows.

1. Define the population. We have decided that this will be all full-time students at the university. This is our N and in this case is 9,000.

2. Select or devise a comprehensive sampling frame. It is likely that the university will have an office that keeps records of all students and that this will enable us to exclude those who do not meet our criteria for inclusion—e.g. part-time and distance learning students.

3. Decide your sample size (*n*). We have decided that this will be 450.

4. List all the students in the population and assign them consecutive numbers from 1 to *N*. In our case, this will be 1 to 9,000.

5. Using a table of random numbers, or a computer program that can generate random numbers, select *n* (450) different random numbers that lie between 1 and *N* (9,000).

6. The students to which the *n* (450) random numbers refer constitute the sample.

Two points are striking about this process. First, there is almost no opportunity for human bias to manifest itself. Students would not be selected on such subjective criteria as whether they looked friendly and approachable. The selection of whom to interview is entirely mechanical. Second, the process is not dependent on the students' availability. They do not have to be walking in the interviewer's proximity to be included in the sample. The process of selection is done without their knowledge. It is not until they are contacted by an interviewer that they know that they are part of a survey.

Step 5 mentions the possible use of a table of random numbers. These can be found in the appendices of many statistics books. The tables are made up of columns of five-digit numbers, such as:

```
09188
90045
73189
75768
54016
08358
28306
53840
91757
89415
```

The first thing to notice is that, since these are five-digit numbers and the maximum number that we can sample from is 9,000, which is a four-digit number, none of the random numbers seems appropriate, except for 09188 and 08358, although the former is larger than the largest possible number. The answer is that we should take just four digits in each number. Let us take the last four digits. This would yield the following:

```
9188
0045
3189
5768
4016
8358
8306
3840
1757
9415
```

However, two of the resulting numbers—9188 and 9415—exceed 9,000. We cannot have a student with either of these numbers assigned to him or her. The solution is simple: we ignore these numbers. This means that the student who has been assigned the number 45 will be the first to be

Tips and skills
Generating random numbers

The method described in the text for generating random numbers is what might be thought of as the classic approach. However, a far neater and quicker way is to generate random numbers on the computer. For example, the following website provides an online random generator which is very easy to use: **www.psychicscience.org/random.aspx** (accessed 26 September 2014). If we want to select 450 cases from a population of 9,000, specify 450 after 'Generate', the digit 1 after 'random integers between', and then 9000 after 'and'. You will also need to specify 'Unique Values' from a drop-down menu. This means that no random number will be selected more than once. Then simply click on GO and the 450 random numbers will appear in a box below OUTPUT. You can then copy and paste the random numbers into a document.

included in the sample; the student who has been assigned the number 3189 will be next; the student who has been assigned the number 5768 will be next; and so on.

However, this somewhat tortuous procedure may be replaced in some circumstances by using a *systematic sampling* procedure (see next section) and more generally can be replaced by enlisting the computer for assistance (see Tips and skills 'Generating random numbers').

Systematic sample

A variation on the simple random sample is the **systematic sample**. With this kind of sample, you select units directly from the sampling frame—that is, without resorting to a table of random numbers.

We know that we are to select 1 student in 20. With a systematic sample, we would make a random start between 1 and 20 inclusive, possibly by using the last two digits in a table of random numbers. If we did this with the ten random numbers above, the first relevant one would be 54016, since it is the first one where the last two digits yield a number of 20 or below, in this case 16. This means that the sixteenth student on our sampling frame is the first to be in our sample. Thereafter, we take every twentieth student on the list. So the sequence will go:

16, 36, 56, 76, 96, 116, etc.

This approach removes the need to assign numbers to students' names and then to look up names of the students whose numbers have been drawn by the random selection process. It is important to ensure, however, that there is no inherent ordering of the sampling frame, since this may bias the resulting sample. If there is some ordering to the list, the best solution is to rearrange it.

Stratified random sampling

In our imaginary study of university students, we might want our sample to exhibit a proportional representation of the different faculties to which students are attached. It might be that the kind of discipline a student is studying is viewed as relevant to a wide range of attitudinal features that are relevant to the study of drinking. Generating a simple random sample or a systematic sample *might* yield such a representation, so that the proportion of humanities students in the sample is the same as that in the student population and so on. Thus, if there are 1,800 students in the humanities faculty, using our sampling fraction of 1 in 20, we would expect to have 90 students in our sample from this faculty. However, because of sampling error, it is unlikely that this will occur and more likely that there will be a difference, for example 85 or 93 from this faculty.

Because it is almost certain that the university will include in its records the faculty to which students are attached, or may have separate sampling frames for each faculty, it will be possible to ensure that students are accurately represented in terms of their faculty membership. In the language of sampling, this means stratifying the population by a criterion (in this case, faculty membership) and selecting either a simple random sample or a systematic sample from each of the resulting strata. If there are five faculties we would have five strata with the numbers in each stratum being one-twentieth of the total for each faculty, as in Table 8.1. Table 8.1 also shows a hypothetical outcome of using a simple random sample, which results in a distribution of students across faculties that does not mirror the population all that well.

The advantage of stratified random sampling is clear: it ensures that the resulting sample will be distributed in the same way as the population in terms of the stratifying criterion. If you use a simple random or systematic sampling approach, you *may* end up with a distribution like that of the stratified sample, but it is unlikely. Two points are relevant here. First, you can conduct stratified sampling sensibly only when it is relatively easy to identify and allocate units to strata. If this is not possible or very difficult to do so, stratified sampling will not be feasible. Second, you can use more than one stratifying criterion. It may be that you would want to stratify by both faculty and gender or by both faculty and whether students are undergraduates or postgraduates. If it is feasible to identify students in terms of these stratifying criteria, it is possible to use pairs of criteria or several criteria (such as faculty membership plus gender plus undergraduate/postgraduate).

Stratified sampling is really feasible only when data are available that allow the ready identification of members of the population in terms of the stratifying criterion (or criteria). It is unlikely to be economical if the identification of population members for stratification purposes requires a great deal of work because there is no available listing in terms of strata.

Table 8.1
The advantages of stratified sampling

Faculty	Population	Stratified sample	Hypothetical simple random or systematic sample
Humanities	1,800	90	85
Social sciences	1,200	60	70
Pure sciences	2,000	100	120
Applied sciences	1,800	90	84
Engineering	2,200	110	91
TOTAL	9,000	450	450

Student experience
Probability sampling for a student project

Joe Thomson describes the sampling procedure that he and the other members of his team used for their study of students living in halls of residence at the University of East Anglia as a **stratified random sample**. The following description suggests that they employed a systematic sampling approach for finding students within halls.

> Stratified random sampling was used to decide which halls of residence each member of the research team would go to and obtain questionnaire responses. This sampling method was the obvious choice as it meant there could be no fixing/bias to which halls the interviewee would go to and also maintained the representative nature of the research.

> The stratified random sampling method known as the 'random walk process' was used when conducting the interviews. Each member of the research group was assigned a number between 4 and 8 as a sampling fraction gap: I was assigned the number 7 and 'Coleman house block 1' as my accommodation block. This meant that, when conducting my interviews, I would go to Coleman house and knock on the 7th door, and then the 14th door, adding 7 each time, until I had completed five interviews. If I encountered a lack of response from the 6th door, I would return to the first flat but add one each time to avoid periodicity. This sampling method was determined by the principles of standardization, reliability, and validity.

 To read more, go to the Online Resource Centre: www.oxfordtextbooks.co.uk/orc/brymansrm5e/

Multi-stage cluster sampling

In the example we have been dealing with, students to be interviewed are located in a single university. Interviewers will have to arrange their interviews with the sampled students, but, because they are all close together (even in a split-site university), they will not be involved in a lot of travel. However, imagine that we wanted a *national* sample of students. It is likely that interviewers would have to travel the length and breadth of the UK to interview the sampled students. This would add a great deal to the time and cost of doing the research. This kind of problem occurs whenever the aim is to interview a sample that is to be drawn from a widely dispersed population, such as a national population, or a large region, or even a large city.

One way of dealing with this potential problem is to employ **cluster sampling**. With cluster sampling, the primary sampling unit (the first stage of the sampling procedure) is not the units of the population to be sampled but groupings of those units. It is the latter groupings or aggregations of population units that are known as *clusters*. Imagine that we want a nationally representative sample of 5,000 students. Using simple random or systematic sampling would yield a widely dispersed sample, which would result in a great deal of travel for interviewers. One solution might be to sample universities and then students from each of the sampled universities. A probability sampling method would need to be employed at each stage. Thus, we might randomly sample ten universities from the entire population of universities, thus yielding ten clusters, and we would then interview 500 randomly selected students at each of the ten universities.

Now imagine that the result of sampling ten universities gives the following list:

- Glasgow Caledonian
- Edinburgh
- Teesside
- Sheffield
- University College Swansea
- Leeds Metropolitan
- University of Ulster
- University College London
- Southampton
- Loughborough

This list is fine, but interviewers could still be involved in a great deal of travel, since the ten universities are quite a long way from each other.

Research in focus 8.1
An example of a multi-stage cluster sample

For their study of social class in modern Britain, Marshall et al. (1988: 288) designed a sample 'to achieve 2,000 interviews with a random selection of men aged 16–64 and women aged 16–59 who were not in full-time education'.

- Sampling parliamentary constituencies
  - Parliamentary constituencies were ordered by standard region (there are eleven).
  - Constituencies were allocated to one of three population density bands within standard regions.
  - These subgroups were then reordered by political party voted to represent the constituency at the previous general election.
  - These subgroups were then listed in ascending order of percentage in owner-occupation.
  - 100 parliamentary constituencies were then sampled.
  - Thus, parliamentary constituencies were stratified in terms of four variables: standard region; population density; political party voted for in last election; and percentage of owner-occupation.
- Sampling polling districts
  - Two polling districts were chosen from each sampled constituency.
- Sampling individuals
  - Nineteen addresses from each sampled polling district were systematically sampled.
  - One person at each address was chosen according to a number of pre-defined rules.

One solution is likely to be to group all UK universities by standard region (see Research in focus 8.1 for an example of this kind of approach) and to sample randomly two standard regions. Five universities might then be sampled from each of the two lists of universities and then 500 students from each of the ten universities. Thus, there are separate stages:

- group UK universities by standard region and sample two regions;
- sample five universities from each of the two regions;
- sample 500 students from each of the ten universities.

In a sense, cluster sampling is always a multi-stage approach, because one always samples clusters first, and then something else—either further clusters or population units—is sampled.

Many examples of multi-stage cluster sampling entail stratification. We might, for example, want to stratify universities in terms of whether they are 'old' or 'new' universities—that is, those that received their charters after the 1991 White Paper for Higher Education, *Higher Education: A New Framework*. In each of the two regions, we would group universities along the old/new university

criterion and then select two or three universities from each of the two strata per region.

Research in focus 8.1 provides an example of a multi-stage cluster sample. It entailed three stages: the sampling of parliamentary constituencies, the sampling of polling districts, and the sampling of individuals. In a way, there are five stages, because addresses are sampled from polling districts and then individuals are sampled from each address. However, Marshall et al. (1988) present their sampling strategy as involving just three stages. Parliamentary constituencies were stratified by four criteria: standard region, population density, voting behaviour, and owner-occupation.

The advantage of multi-stage cluster sampling should be clear by now: it allows interviewers to be far more geographically concentrated than would be the case if a simple random or stratified sample were selected. The advantages of stratification can be capitalized upon because the clusters can be stratified in terms of strata. However, even when a very rigorous sampling strategy is employed, sampling error cannot be avoided, as the example in Research in focus 8.2 shows.

Research in focus 8.2
The 1992 British Crime Survey

The British Crime Survey (BCS) was a regular survey, funded by the Home Office, of a national sample drawn from the populations of England and Wales. The survey was conducted on eight occasions between 1982 and 2000 and then annually after 2001. In each instance, over 10,000 people were interviewed. The main object of the survey was to glean information on respondents' experiences of being victims of crime. There was also a self-report component in a sub-sample, who were interviewed on their attitudes to crime and asked to report on crimes they had committed. Before 1992, the BCS used the electoral register as a sampling frame. Relying on a register of the electorate as a sampling frame is not without problems in spite of appearing robust: it omits any persons who are not registered, a problem that was aggravated by the Community Charge (poll tax), which resulted in a significant amount of non-registration, as some people sought to avoid detection in order to avoid the tax. The Postcode Address File was employed as a sampling frame in 1992 and was used subsequently. Its main advantage over the electoral register as a sampling frame is that it is updated more frequently. It is not perfect, because the homeless will not be accessible through it. The BCS sample itself is a stratified multi-stage cluster sample. The sampling procedure produced 13,117 residential addresses. As with most surveys, there was some non-response, with 23.3 per cent of the 13,117 addresses not resulting in a 'valid' interview. Just under half of these cases were the result of an outright refusal. In spite of the fact that the BCS is a rigorously selected and very large sample, an examination of the 1992 survey by Elliott and Ellingworth (1997) shows that there is some sampling error. By comparing the distribution of survey respondents with the 1991 census, they show that certain social groups are somewhat under-represented, most notably owner-occupiers, households in which no car is owned, and male unemployed. However, Elliott and Ellingworth show that, as the level of property crime in postcode address sectors increases, the response rate (see Key concept 8.2) decreases. In other words, people who live in high-crime areas tend to be less likely to agree to be interviewed. How far this tendency affects the BCS data is difficult to determine, but the significance of this brief example is that, even when a high-quality sample is selected, the existence of sampling and non-sampling error cannot be discounted. The potential for a larger spread of errors when levels of sampling rigour fall short of a sample like that selected for the BCS is, therefore, considerable. The BCS became the Crime Survey for England and Wales in 2012.

The qualities of a probability sample

Probability sampling is a significant procedure in survey research because it allows inferences to be made from information about a random sample to the population from which it was extracted. In other words, we can generalize findings derived from a sample to the population. This is not to say that we treat the population data and the sample data as the same. If we take the example of the level of alcohol consumption in our sample of 450 students, which we will treat as the number of units of alcohol consumed in the previous seven days, we will know that the mean number of units consumed by the sample ($\bar{x}$) can be used to estimate the population mean (μ) but with known margins of error. The mean, or more properly the **arithmetic mean**, is the simple average.

In order to address this point it is necessary to use some basic statistical ideas. These are presented in Tips and skills 'Generalizing from a random sample to the population' and can be skipped if just a broad idea of sampling procedures is required.

Tips and skills
Generalizing from a random sample to the population

Let us say that the sample mean is 9.7 units of alcohol consumed (the average amount of alcohol consumed in the previous seven days in the sample). A crucial consideration here is: how confident can we be that the mean level of alcohol consumption of 9.7 units is likely to be found in the population, even when probability sampling has been

Figure 8.8
The distribution of sample means

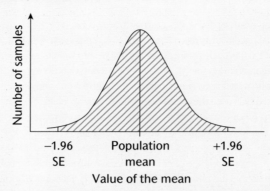

Notes: 95 per cent of sample means will lie within the shaded area. SE = standard error of the mean.

employed? If we take an infinite number of samples from a population, the sample estimates of the mean of the variable under consideration will vary in relation to the population mean. This variation will take the form of a bell-shaped curve known as a *normal distribution* (see Figure 8.8). The shape of the distribution implies that there is a clustering of sample means at or around the population mean. Half the sample means will be at or below the population mean; the other half will be at or above the population mean. As we move to the left (at or lower than the population mean) or the right (at or higher than the population mean), the curve tails off, implying that fewer and fewer samples generate means that depart considerably from the population mean. The variation of sample means around the population mean is the *sampling error* and is measured using a statistic known as the **standard error of the mean** (SE). This is an estimate of the amount that a sample mean is likely to differ from the population mean.

This consideration is important because sampling theory tells us that 68 per cent of all sample means will lie between + or −1 standard error from the population mean and that 95 per cent of all sample means will lie between + or − 1.96 standard errors from the population mean. It is this second calculation that is crucial, because it is at least implicitly employed by survey researchers when they report their statistical findings. They typically employ 1.96 standard errors as the crucial criterion in how confident they can be in their findings. Essentially, the criterion implies that you can be 95 per cent certain that the population mean lies within + or −1.96 sampling errors from the sample mean.

If a sample has been selected according to probability sampling principles, we know that we can be 95 per cent certain that the population mean will lie between the sample mean + or −1.96 multiplied by the standard error of the mean. This is known as the *confidence interval*. If the mean level of alcohol consumption in the previous seven days in our sample of 450 students is 9.7 units and the standard error of the mean is 1.3, we can be 95 per cent certain that the population mean will lie between

$$9.7 + (1.96 \times 1.3)$$

and

$$9.7 - (1.96 \times 1.3)$$

i.e. between 12.248 and 7.152.

If the standard error was smaller, the range of possible values of the population mean would be narrower; if the standard error was larger, the range of possible values of the population mean would be wider.

If a stratified sample is selected, the standard error of the mean will be smaller; this is because the variation between strata is essentially eliminated because the population will be accurately represented in the sample in terms of the stratification criterion or criteria employed. This consideration demonstrates the way in which stratification injects an extra increment of precision into the probability sampling process, since a possible source of sampling error is eliminated.

By contrast, a cluster sample without stratification exhibits a larger standard error of the mean than a comparable simple random sample. This occurs because a possible source of variability between students (i.e. membership of one university rather than another, which may affect levels of alcohol consumption) is disregarded. If, for example, some universities had a culture of heavy drinking in which a large number of students participated, and if these universities were not selected because of the procedure for selecting clusters, an important source of variability would have been omitted. It also implies that the sample mean would be on the low side, but that is another matter.

Sample size

As someone who is known as a teacher of research methods and a writer of books in this area, I often get asked questions about methodological issues. One question that is asked almost more than any other relates to the size of the sample—'how large should my sample be?' or 'is my sample large enough?' The decision about sample size is not straightforward: it depends on a number of considerations, and there is no one definitive answer. This is frequently a source of great disappointment to those who pose such questions. Moreover, most of the time decisions about sample size are affected by considerations of time and cost. Therefore, decisions about sample size invariably represent a compromise between the constraints of time and cost, the need for precision, and a variety of further considerations that will now be addressed.

Absolute and relative sample size

One of the most basic considerations is that, contrary to what you might have expected, it is the *absolute* size of a sample that is important and not its *relative* size. This means that a national probability sample of 1,000 individuals in the UK has as much validity as a national probability sample of 1,000 individuals in the USA, even though the latter has a much larger population. It also means that increasing the size of a sample increases the precision of a sample. This means that the 95 per cent confidence interval referred to in Tips and skills 'Generalizing from a random sample to the population' narrows. However, a large sample cannot *guarantee* precision, so that it is probably better to say that increasing the size of a sample increases

Tips and skills
Sample size and probability sampling

The issue of sample size is the matter that most often concerns students and others. This is an area where size really does matter—the bigger the sample, the more representative it is likely to be (provided the sample is randomly selected), regardless of the size of the population from which it is drawn. However, when doing projects, students clearly need to do their research with very limited resources. You should try to find out from your department whether there are any guidelines about whether samples of a minimum size are expected. If there are no such guidelines, you will need to conduct your mini-survey in such a way as to maximize the number of interviews you can manage or the number of postal questionnaires you can send out, given the amount of time and resources available to you. Also, in many if not most cases, a truly random approach to sample selection may not be open to you. The crucial point is to be clear about and to justify what you have done. Explain the difficulties that you would have encountered in generating a random sample. Explain why you really could not include any more in your sample of respondents. But, above all, do not make claims about your sample that are not sustainable. Do not claim that it is representative or that you have a random sample when it is clearly not the case that either of these is true. In other words, be frank about what you have done. People will be much more inclined to accept an awareness of the limits of your sample design than claims about a sample that are patently false. Also, it may be that there are lots of good features about your sample—the range of people included, the good response rate, the high level of cooperation you received from the firm. Make sure you play up these positive features at the same time as being honest about its limitations.

the *likely* precision of a sample. This means that, as sample size increases, sampling error decreases (see Tips and skills 'Sample size and probability sampling'). Therefore, an important component of any decision about sample size should be how much sampling error one is prepared to tolerate. The less sampling error one is prepared to tolerate, the larger a sample will need to be. Fowler (1993) warns against a simple acceptance of this criterion. He argues that in practice researchers do not base their decisions about sample size on a single estimate of a variable. Most survey research is concerned to generate a host of estimates—that is, estimates of the variables that make up the research instrument that is administered. He also observes that it is not normal for survey researchers to be in a position to specify in advance 'a desired level of precision' (Fowler 1993: 34). Moreover, since sampling error will be only one component of any error entailed in an estimate, the notion of using a desired level of precision as a factor in a decision about sample size is not realistic. Instead, to the extent that this notion does enter into decisions about sample size, it usually does so in a general rather than in a calculated way.

Time and cost

Time and cost considerations become very relevant in this context. In the previous paragraph it is clearly being suggested that the larger the sample size the greater the precision (because the amount of sampling error will be less). However, by and large, up to a sample size of around 1,000, the gains in precision are noticeable as the sample size climbs from low figures of 50, 100, 150, and so on upwards. After a certain point, often in the region of 1,000, the sharp increases in precision become less pronounced, and, although it does not

plateau, there is a slowing-down in the extent to which precision increases (and hence the extent to which the standard error of the mean declines). Considerations of sample size are likely to be profoundly affected by matters of time and cost at such a point, since striving for smaller and smaller increments of precision becomes an increasingly uneconomic proposition. As Hazelrigg (2004: 85) succinctly puts it: 'The larger the size of the sample drawn from a population the more likely ($\bar{x}$) converges to μ; but the convergence occurs at a decelerating rate (which means that very large samples are decreasingly cost efficient).'

Non-response

Considerations about sampling error do not end here. The problem of **non-response** should be borne in mind. Most sample surveys attract a certain amount of non-response (see Research in the news 8.1). Thus, it is likely that only some members of a sample will be contactable and of those who are contactable some will refuse to participate. This is more properly called 'unit non-response' to distinguish this kind of non-response from **item non-response**, which is when people (units) agree to participate but fail either deliberately or accidentally to answer specific questions (items) on a questionnaire. However, the term 'non-response' will be used here to refer to unit non-response. If it is our aim to ensure as far as possible that 450 students are interviewed and if we think that there may be a 20 per cent rate of non-response, it may be advisable to sample 550–60 individuals, on the grounds that approximately 90 will be non-respondents.

The issue of non-response, and in particular of refusal to participate, is of significance because it has been suggested by some researchers that response rates to surveys

Research in the news 8.1
The problem of non-response

In December 2006 an article in *The Times* reported that a study of the weight of British children had been hindered because many families declined to participate. The study was commissioned by the Department of Health and found that, for example, among those aged 10 or 11, 14 per cent were overweight and 17 per cent were obese. However, *The Times* writer notes that a report compiled by the Department of Health on the research suggests that such figures are 'likely systematically to underestimate the prevalence of overweight and obesity'. The reason for this bias is that parents were able to refuse to let their children participate, and those whose children were heavier were more likely to refuse. As a result, the sample was biased towards those who were less heavy. The authors of the report drew the inference about sampling bias because they noted that more children were recorded as obese in areas where there was a poorer response rate.

Source: **www.thetimes.co.uk/tto/news/uk/article1949951.ece** (accessed 9 October 2014)

(see Key concept 8.2) are declining in many countries. This implies that there is a growing tendency towards people refusing to participate in social survey research. In 1973 the American magazine *Business Week* carried an article ominously entitled 'The Public Clams Up on Survey Takers'. The magazine asked survey companies about their experiences and found considerable concern about declining response rates. Around the same time, in Britain, a report from a working party on the Market Research Society's Research and Development Committee in 1975 pointed to similar concerns among market research companies. An overview of non-response trends in the USA based on non-response rates for various continuous surveys suggests that there is a decline in the preparedness of households to participate in surveys (Groves et al. 2009). Further evidence comes from a study by Baruch (1999) of questionnaire-based articles published in 1975, 1985, and 1995 in five academic journals in the area of management studies. This article found an average (mean) response rate of 55.6 per cent, though with quite a large amount of variation around this average. The average response rate over the three years was 64.4 per cent in 1975, 55.7 per cent in 1985, and 48.4/52.2 per cent in 1995. Two percentages were provided for 1995 because the larger figure includes a journal that publishes a lot of research based on senior managers, who tend to produce a poorer response rate. Response rates were found that were as low as 10 per cent and 15 per cent.

An important question in connection with non-response is: how far should researchers go in order to boost their response rates? In Chapter 10, a number of steps that can be taken to improve response rates to postal questionnaires, which are particularly prone to poor response rates, are discussed. However, boosting response rates to interview-based surveys can prove expensive. Teitler et al. (2003) present a discussion of the steps taken to boost the response rate of a US sample that was hard to reach—namely, both parents of newly born children where most of the parents were not married. They found that, although there was evidence that increasing the response rate from an initial 68 per cent to 80 per cent meant that the final sample resembled more closely the population from which the sample had been taken, diminishing returns undoubtedly set in. In other words, the improvements in the characteristics of the sample necessitated a disproportionate outlay of resources. However, this is not to say that steps should not be taken to improve response rates. For example, following up respondents who do not initially respond to a postal questionnaire invariably results in an improved response rate at little additional cost. A survey of New Zealand residents by Brennan and Charbonneau (2009) provides strong evidence of the improvement in response rate that can be achieved by at least two follow-up mailings to respondents to postal questionnaire surveys, which tend to achieve lower response rates than comparable interview-based surveys. A chocolate sent with the questionnaire helps too, apparently!

Interesting findings in this connection derive from a national Web survey by Meterko et al. (2015) of healthcare leaders in the USA, which achieved a 95 per cent response rate. This very high response rate was achieved after four follow-ups of non-respondents. Of the healthcare leaders who participated, 29.7 per cent did so initially,

Key concept 8.2
What is a response rate?

The notion of a response rate is a common one in social survey research. When a survey is conducted, whether by structured interview or by self-administered questionnaire, invariably some people who are in the sample refuse to participate (referred to as non-response). The response rate is, therefore, the percentage of a sample that does, in fact, agree to participate. However, the calculation of a response rate is a little more complicated than this. First, not everyone who replies will be included: if a large number of questions are not answered by a respondent or if there are clear indications that he or she has not taken the interview or questionnaire seriously, it is better to employ only the number of usable interviews or questionnaires as the numerator. Similarly, it may be that not everyone in a sample turns out to be an appropriate respondent or can be contacted. Thus the response rate is calculated as follows:

$$\frac{\text{number of usable questionnaires}}{\text{total sample} - \text{unsuitable or uncontactable members of the sample}} \times 100$$

19.5 per cent after the first follow-up, 11.9 per cent after the second, 10.2 per cent after the third, and 28.8 per cent after the fourth. The researchers found that there was no statistical difference between respondents when comparing data from the five waves in terms of 'demographic characteristics, missing data, and distribution of responses across categories' (Meterko et al. 2015: 141). In other words, boosting the response rate at each stage did nothing to enhance the quality or nature of the data. The researchers show that their findings after the initial contact (when the response rate was just under 30 per cent) would have differed little from the findings after four follow-ups when the response rate was 95 per cent. This finding might seem to invite survey researchers not to bother to boost their response rates, but that is not the message that Meterko et al. seek to convey. They observe that there were some features of both their sample and the questionnaire that were distinctive and they therefore propose that the implications of different levels of response rates should always be considered on a case-by-case basis. However, they do suggest that their findings indicate that survey data deriving from surveys with relatively low response rates should not be automatically dismissed.

As the previously mentioned study of response rates by Baruch (1999) suggests, there is wide variation in the response rates that social scientists achieve when they conduct surveys. It is difficult to arrive at clear indications of what is expected from a response rate. Baruch's study focused on research in business organizations, and, as he notes, when senior managers are the focus of a survey, the response rate tends to be noticeably lower. In the survey component of the Cultural Capital and Social Exclusion (CCSE) project referred to in Research in focus 2.9, the initial main sample delivered a 53 per cent response rate (Bennett et al. 2009). The researchers decided to supplement this initial sample in various ways, one of which was to have an ethnic boost sample, mainly because the main sample did not include sufficient numbers of members of ethnic minorities. However, the response rate from the ethnic boost sample was substantially below that achieved for the main sample. The researchers write: 'In general, ethnic boosts tend to have lower response rates than cross-sectional surveys' (Thomson 2004: 10). There is a sense, then, that what might be anticipated to be a reasonable response rate varies according to the type of sample and the topics covered by the interview or questionnaire. While it is obviously desirable to do one's best to maximize a response rate, it is also important to be open about the limitations of a low response rate in terms of the likelihood that findings will be biased. In the future, it seems likely that, given that there will probably be limits on the degree to which a survey researcher can boost a response rate, more and more effort will go into refining ways of estimating and correcting for anticipated biases in findings (Groves 2006).

Heterogeneity of the population

Yet another consideration is the homogeneity and heterogeneity of the population from which the sample is to be taken. When a population is very heterogeneous, such as a whole country or city, a larger sample will be needed to reflect the varied population. When it is relatively homogeneous, such as a population of students or of members of an occupation, the amount of variation is less and therefore the sample can be smaller. The implication of this is that the greater the heterogeneity of a population, the larger a sample will need to be.

Kind of analysis

Finally, researchers should bear in mind the *kind of analysis* they intend to undertake. A case in point here is the **contingency table**. A contingency table shows the relationship between two variables in tabular form. It shows how variation in one variable relates to variation in another variable. To understand this point, consider the basic structure of a table in the study by Marshall et al. (1988) of social class in Britain. This research was referred to in Research in focus 8.1. The table is based on the 589 cohabiting couples (1,178 people) of the sample in which both partners are employed in paid work. The authors aim to show in the table how far couples are of the same or a different social class in terms of Goldthorpe's seven-category scheme for classifying social class. The result is a table in which, because each variable comprises 7 categories, there are 49 **cells** in the table (i.e. 7×7). In order for there to be an adequate number of cases in each cell, a fairly large sample was required. Imagine that Marshall et al. had conducted a survey on a much smaller sample in which they ended up with just 150 couples. If the same kind of analysis as Marshall et al. carried out was conducted, it would be found that these 150 couples would be very dispersed across the 49 cells of the table. It is likely that many of the cells would be empty or would have very small numbers in them, which would make it difficult to make inferences about what the table showed. In fact, quite a lot of the cells in Marshall et al.'s actual table have very small numbers in them (8 cells contain 1 or 0). This problem would have been even more pronounced if they had ended up with a much smaller sample of couples. Consequently, considerations of sample size should be sensitive to the kinds of analysis that will be subsequently required, such as the issue of the number of cells in a table. In a case such as this, a larger sample will be necessitated by the nature of the analysis to be conducted as well as the nature of the variables in question.

Types of non-probability sampling

The term 'non-probability sampling' is an umbrella term to capture all forms of sampling that are not conducted according to the principles of probability sampling. It is not surprising, therefore, that the term covers a wide range of different types of sampling strategy, at least one of which—the **quota sample**—is claimed by some practitioners to be almost as good as a probability sample. In this section we will cover three main types of non-probability sample: the **convenience sample**; the **snowball sample**; and the quota sample.

Convenience sampling

A convenience sample is one that is simply available to the researcher by virtue of its accessibility. Imagine that a researcher who lectures in education at a university is interested in the kinds of qualities that teachers look for in their head teachers. The researcher might administer a questionnaire to several classes of students, all of whom are teachers taking a part-time Master's degree in education. The chances are that the researcher will receive all or almost all of the questionnaires back, so that there will be a good response rate. The findings may prove quite interesting, but the problem with such a sampling strategy is that it is impossible to generalize the findings, because we do not know of what population this sample is representative. They are simply a group of teachers who are available to the researcher. They are almost certainly not representative of teachers as a whole—the very fact that they are taking this degree programme marks them off as different from teachers in general.

This is not to suggest that convenience samples should never be used. Let us say that our lecturer/researcher is developing a battery of questions that are designed to measure the leadership preferences of teachers. It is highly desirable to pilot such a research instrument before using it in an investigation, and administering it to a group that is not a part of the main study may be a legitimate way of carrying out some preliminary analysis of such issues as whether respondents tend to answer in identical ways to a question, or whether one question is often omitted when teachers respond to the questionnaire. For this kind of purpose, a convenience sample may be acceptable though not ideal. A second kind of context in which it may be at least fairly acceptable to use a convenience sample is when the chance presents itself to gather data from a convenience sample and it represents too good an opportunity to miss. The data will not allow definitive findings to be generated, because of the problem of generalization, but they could provide a springboard for further research or allow links to be forged with existing findings in an area.

It also perhaps ought to be recognized that convenience sampling probably plays a more prominent role than is sometimes supposed. Certainly, in the field of organization studies it has been noted that convenience samples are very common and indeed are more prominent than are samples based on probability sampling (Bryman 1989: 113–14). Social research is also frequently based on convenience sampling. Research in focus 8.3 contains an example of the use of convenience samples in social research. Probability sampling involves a lot of preparation, so that it is frequently avoided because of the difficulty and costs involved.

Research in focus 8.3
A convenience sample

Miller et al. (1998) were interested in theories concerning the role of shopping in relation to the construction of identity in modern society. Since many discussions of this issue have been concerned with shopping centres (malls), they undertook a mixed methods study in order to explore the views of shoppers at two London shopping centres: Brent Cross and Wood Green. One phase of the research entailed structured interviews with shoppers leaving the centres. The interviews were conducted mainly during weekdays in June and July 1994. Shoppers were chiefly questioned as they left the main exits, though some questioning at minor exits also took place. The authors tell us: 'We did not attempt to secure a quota [see the section on 'Quota sampling' below] or random sample but asked every person who passed by, and who did not obviously look in the other direction or change their path, to complete a questionnaire' (Miller et al. 1998: 55). Such a sampling strategy produces a convenience sample because only people who are visiting the centre, and who are therefore self-selected by virtue of their happening to choose to shop at these times, can be interviewed.

Snowball sampling

In certain respects, snowball sampling is a form of convenience sample, but it is worth distinguishing because it has attracted quite a lot of attention over the years. With this approach to sampling, the researcher makes initial contact with a small group of people who are relevant to the research topic and then uses these to establish contacts with others. I used an approach like this to create a sample of British visitors to Disney theme parks (Bryman 1999).

Research in focus 8.4 describes the generation of a snowball sample of marijuana users for what is often regarded as a classic study of drug use. Becker's comment on this method of creating a snowball sample is interesting: 'The sample is, of course, in no sense "random"; it would not be possible to draw a random sample, since no one knows the nature of the universe from which it would have to be drawn' (Becker 1963: 46). What Becker is essentially saying here (and the same point applies to my study of Disney theme park visitors) is that there is no accessible sampling frame for the population from which the sample is to be taken and that the difficulty of creating such a sampling frame means that a snowball sampling approach is the only feasible one. Moreover, even if one could create a sampling frame of marijuana users or of British visitors to Disney theme parks, it would almost certainly be inaccurate straight away, because this is a shifting population. People will constantly be becoming and ceasing to be marijuana users, while new theme park visitors are arriving all the time.

The problem with snowball sampling is that it is unlikely that the sample will be representative of the population, although the very notion of a population may be problematic in some circumstances. However, by and large, snowball sampling is used not within a quantitative research strategy, but within a qualitative one: both Becker's and my study were carried out using qualitative research. Concerns about external validity and the ability to generalize do not loom as large within a qualitative research strategy as they do in a quantitative research one (see Chapter 17). In qualitative research, the orientation to sampling is more likely to be guided by a preference for *purposive sampling* than by the kind of statistical sampling that has been the focus of this chapter (see Key concept 18.1). There is a much better 'fit' between snowball sampling and the purposive sampling strategy of qualitative research than with the statistical sampling approach of quantitative research. This is not to suggest that snowball sampling is irrelevant to quantitative research: when the researcher needs to focus upon or to reflect relationships between people, tracing connections through snowball sampling may be a better approach than conventional probability sampling (Coleman 1958).

Quota sampling

Quota sampling is comparatively rare in academic social research, but it is used intensively in commercial research, such as market research and political opinion polling. The aim of quota sampling is to produce a sample that reflects a population in terms of the relative proportions of people in different categories, such as gender, ethnicity, age groups, socio-economic groups, and region of residence, and in combinations of these categories. However, unlike a stratified sample, the sampling of individuals is not carried out randomly, since the final selection of people is left to the interviewer. Information about the stratification of the UK population or about certain regions can be obtained from sources like the census and from surveys based on probability samples such as the General Household Survey, British Social Attitudes, and Understanding Society.

Research in focus 8.4
A snowball sample: Becker's study of marijuana users

In an article first published in 1953, Becker (1963) reports on how he generated a sample of marijuana users. He writes:

> I conducted fifty interviews with marijuana users. I had been a professional dance musician for some years when I conducted this study and my first interviews were with people I had met in the music business. I asked them to put me in contact with other users who would be willing to discuss their experiences with me . . . Although in the end half of the fifty interviews were conducted with musicians, the other half covered a wide range of people, including laborers, machinists, and people in the professions.

(Becker 1963: 45–6)

Once the categories and the number of people to be interviewed within each category (known as *quotas* or *quota controls*) have been decided upon, it is then the job of interviewers to select people who fit these categories. The quotas will typically be interrelated. In a manner similar to stratified sampling, the population may be divided into strata in terms of, for example, gender, social class, age, and ethnicity (see Research in focus 8.5 for an example). Census data might be used to identify the number of people who should be in each subgroup. The numbers to be interviewed in each subgroup will reflect the population. Each interviewer will probably seek out individuals who fit several subgroup quotas. Accordingly, an interviewer may know that among the various subgroups of people he or she must find, and interview, five Asian, 25–34-year-old, lower-middle-class females in the area in which the interviewer has been asked to work (say, the Wirral). The interviewer usually asks people who are available to him or her about their characteristics (though gender will presumably be self-evident) in order to determine their suitability for a particular subgroup. Once a subgroup quota (or a combination of subgroup quotas) has been achieved, the interviewer will no longer be concerned to locate individuals for that subgroup.

The choice of respondents is left to the interviewer, subject to the requirement of all quotas being filled, usually within a certain time period. Those of you who have ever been approached on the street by a person toting a clipboard and interview schedule and have been asked about your age, occupation, and so on, before being asked a series of questions about a product or whatever, have almost certainly encountered an interviewer with a quota sample to fill. Sometimes, he or she will decide not to interview you because you do not meet the criteria required to fill a quota. This may be due to a quota already having been filled or to the criteria for exclusion meaning that a person with a certain characteristic you possess is not required.

A number of criticisms are frequently levelled at quota samples.

- Because the choice of respondent is left to the interviewer, the proponents of probability sampling argue that a quota sample cannot be representative. It may accurately reflect the population in terms of superficial characteristics, as defined by the quotas. However, in their choice of people to approach, interviewers may be unduly influenced by their perceptions of how friendly people are or by whether the people make eye contact with the interviewer (unlike most of us, who look at the ground and shuffle past as quickly as possible because we do not want to be bothered in our leisure time).

- People who are in an interviewer's vicinity at the times he or she conducts interviews, and are therefore

Research in focus 8.5
A quota sample: A study of Londoners following the July 2005 bombings

Between 18 and 20 July 2005, telephone interviews were carried out by a market research company (Market and Opinion Research International) for Rubin et al. (2005) to gauge the psychological effect of the London bombings of 7 July 2005 on Londoners. The company used **random digit dialling** (RDD) to produce London telephone numbers and then used quota sampling to select individuals aged 18 years and over to be interviewed. Quotas were set in terms of 'sex, age, working status, residential location, housing tenure, and ethnicity to make our sample representative of the demographic distribution of London as shown in the most recent census data' (Rubin et al. 2005: 1). The authors say that 11,072 people were contacted, of whom 1,059 proved to be ineligible. Then, 1,207 of the 10,013 eligible respondents agreed to participate but only 1,010 completed the interview, yielding a response rate of 10.1 per cent which the authors propose 'is not unusually low for a telephone survey using quota sampling' (2005: 3). The authors say that the application of the quota controls worked well because the impact of weighting their findings to reflect the demographic distribution of London was small. The findings show that the bombings caused 'substantial stress' and resulted in changes to people's travel plans. The authors were able to inject a longitudinal element into this research by securing agreement from 815 interviewees to be recontacted and seven months later they were able to re-interview 574 respondents (Rubin et al. 2007).

available to be approached, may not be typical. There is a risk, for example, that people in full-time paid work may be under-represented and that those who are included in the sample are not typical.

- The interviewer is likely to make judgements about certain characteristics in deciding whether to approach a person, in particular judgements about age. Those judgements will sometimes be incorrect—for example, when someone who is eligible to be interviewed, because a quota that he or she fits is unfilled, is not approached because the interviewer makes an incorrect judgement (for example, that the person is older than he or she looks). In such a case, a possible element of bias is being introduced.

- It has also been argued that the widespread use of social class as a quota control can introduce difficulties, because of the problem of ensuring that interviewees are properly assigned to class groupings (Moser and Kalton 1971).

- It is not permissible to calculate a standard error of the mean from a quota sample, because the non-random method of selection makes it impossible to calculate the range of possible values of a population.

All this makes the quota sample look a poor choice, and there is no doubt that it is not favoured by academic researchers. It does have some arguments in its favour, however.

- It is undoubtedly cheaper and quicker than an interview survey on a comparable probability sample. For example, interviewers do not have to spend a lot of time travelling between interviews.

- Interviewers do not have to keep calling back on people who were not available at the time they were first approached.

- Because calling back is not required, a quota sample is easier to manage. It is not necessary to keep track of people who need to be recontacted or to keep track of refusals. Refusals occur, of course, but it is not necessary (and indeed it is not possible) to keep a record of which respondents declined to participate.

- When speed is of the essence, a quota sample is invaluable when compared to the more cumbersome probability sample. Newspapers frequently need to know how a national sample of voters feel about a certain topic or how they intend to vote at that time. Similarly, researchers may need to know about the impact of a sudden event and again, a quota sample will be much faster.

- As with convenience sampling, quota sampling is useful for conducting development work on new measures or on research instruments. It can also be usefully

employed in relation to exploratory work from which new theoretical ideas might be generated.

- Although the standard error of the mean should not be computed for a quota sample, it frequently is. As Moser and Kalton (1971) observe, some writers argue that the use of a non-random method in quota sampling should not act as a barrier to such a computation because its significance as a source of error is small when compared to other errors that may arise in surveys (see Figure 8.9). However, they go on to argue that at least with random sampling the researcher can calculate the amount of sampling error and does not have to be concerned about its potential impact.

There is some evidence to suggest that, when compared to random samples, quota samples often result in biases. They under-represent people in lower social strata, people who work in the private sector and manufacturing, and people at the extremes of income, and they over-represent women in households with children and people from larger households. On the other hand, it has to be acknowledged that probability samples are often biased too—for example, it is often suggested that they under-represent men and those in employment (Marsh and Scarbrough 1990; Butcher 1994).

An issue that has received surprisingly little attention is the question of whether quota samples produce different findings from probability samples. Yang and Banamah (2013) selected a probability sample and a quota sample from the membership list of a university student society. For the quota sample, gender and educational level (Masters, PhD, etc.) were used as quotas. In the case of the probability sample, 22.5 per cent responded more or less immediately, increasing to 42.5 per cent after a first reminder, and to 67.5 per cent after a second and final reminder. The questionnaire had only a small number of questions covering such issues as religious participation, personal friendships, and mutual trust among members. The researchers found that statistically significant differences between the findings deriving from the two samples only became apparent when findings from the quota sample were compared to the findings after the second reminder. In other words, there were few if any statistically significant differences between the findings from the two samples when the quota sample was compared with the findings from those who had replied immediately or from this group with those who replied after one reminder. Yang and Banamah propose that these findings suggest that when a probability sample generates a low response rate, it is likely that it does not have a great advantage over an equivalent quota sample. Since response rates to surveys are declining, this finding is of some practical significance for survey researchers.

Sampling issues in online surveys

Surveys conducted over the Internet—either using online Web platforms or via email—have been a huge growth area since the late 1990s and their use is accelerating. For sampling purposes, a significant concern is that not everyone in any nation is online and has the technical ability to handle questionnaires online in either email or Web formats. Certain other features of online communications make the issue more problematic.

- Many people have more than one email address.
- Many people use more than one Internet service provider (ISP).
- A household may have one computer but several users.
- Internet users are a biased sample of the population, in that they tend to be better educated, wealthier, younger, and not representative in ethnic terms (Couper 2000).
- Few sampling frames exist of the general online population and most of these are likely to be expensive to acquire, since they are controlled by ISPs or may be confidential.

Such issues complicate the possibilities of conducting online surveys using probability sampling principles. For researchers who conduct research in organizations, the opportunities may be particularly good. In many organizations, most if not all non-manual workers are likely to be online and to be familiar with using email and the Internet. Thus surveys of samples of online populations can be conducted using essentially the same probability sampling procedures. Similarly, surveys of members of commercially relevant online groups can be conducted using these principles. An example of the use of a sampling frame to generate a probability sample is described in Research in focus 8.6. As Couper (2000: 485) notes of surveys of populations using probability sampling procedures:

> Intra-organizational surveys and those directed at users of the Internet were among the first to adopt this new survey technology. These restricted populations typically have no coverage problems . . . or very high rates of coverage. Student surveys are a particular example of this approach that are growing in popularity.

Thus, certain kinds of populations are less adversely affected by coverage problems and therefore render probability sampling in Internet surveys less problematic.

Tourangeau, Conrad, and Couper (2013: 13) note that there are several forms of probability sample in online surveys but suggest that 'surveys using probability sampling are likely to constitute a small minority of all Web surveys'. One of the most significant forms of online survey that is based on probability sampling is the pre-recruited online panel. An example is Germany's GESIS panel which comprises around 4,900 panel members of whom roughly two-thirds are online participants (**http://www .gesis.org/en/services/data-collection/gesis-panel/ sample-and-recruitment/**, accessed 21 October 2014). Initially, a random sample of the German population aged 18-70 was selected and all sample members who were prepared to be interviewed were interviewed using **computer-aided personal interviewing** (CAPI) to establish their willingness to be involved in the panel. Those who are willing to participate but who do not want or are unable to do so online are sent postal questionnaires.

Tips and skills
Using Internet surveys to supplement traditional postal questionnaire surveys

There is a growing tendency for researchers who conduct postal questionnaire surveys to offer their respondents the opportunity to complete their questionnaires online (Couper 2000). This can be done by indicating in the covering letter that goes out with the postal questionnaire that they can have the questionnaire emailed to them, or, if the questionnaire is accessible via the Web, they can be directed to the Web address. The latter is increasingly the more common option that is offered. The advantage of offering an **Internet survey** option is that some of the respondents may feel more comfortable completing the questionnaire online because they already spend a considerable amount of time online and it removes the need to return the questionnaire by post. There is the question of whether the mode of administration (postal as against online) influences the kinds of response received. This is an issue that has attracted a considerable amount of research (see Chapter 10).

Research in focus 8.6
Sampling for a mixed mode survey

Díaz de Rada and Domínguez-Álvarez (2014) conducted a self-administered questionnaire survey of emigrants from Andalusia who were resident abroad. A census of residents living abroad was used as a sampling frame. The population comprised 144,007 emigrés, from whom a systematic sample of 15,657 were selected. The researchers were aiming for a final sample (i.e. after non-response and not being able to contact some sample members) of at least 2,400. The sample members were contacted by post and were given three modes of answering the questionnaire: postal questionnaire, Web-based questionnaire, or computer-assisted telephone interviewing (CATI). Surveys that offer more than one means of answering questionnaires are known as 'mixed mode' surveys and are becoming an increasingly common part of the survey landscape. The initial response yielded 2,198 completed questionnaires; after a second set of questionnaires was sent out to non-responders, a final sample of 2,493 was achieved, a response rate of 18.9 per cent, though this is lower when some adjustments are made. The vast majority were sent by post (83.6 per cent), 14.4 per cent via the Internet, and the remainder were administered by telephone. Díaz de Rada and Domínguez-Álvarez argue that the high level of replying by postal questionnaire rather than using the Web is probably due to the fact that the questionnaire and a postage-paid reply envelope were sent with the letter. In order to complete the questionnaire online, the respondent had to take the trouble to power up the computer, go online, type in the link for the questionnaire which was shown on the letter, and enter an identification number. The authors feel that this sequence compared unfavourably to the immediacy of the postal questionnaire and resulted in a low level of response to the web-based questionnaire.

Hewson and Laurent (2008) suggest that, when there is no sampling frame, the main approach to generating an appropriate sample is to post an invitation to answer a questionnaire on relevant newsgroup message boards, to suitable mailing lists or on websites. The result will be a sample of unknown representativeness, and it is impossible to know what the response rate to the questionnaire is, since the size of the population is also unknown. However, if representativeness is not a significant concern for the researcher, the fact that it is possible to target groups that have a specific interest or form of behaviour makes such lists and sites an attractive means of contacting sample members.

A further issue in relation to sampling and sampling-related error is the matter of *non-response* (see Key concept 8.2). There is evidence that online surveys typically generate lower response rates than postal questionnaire surveys (Converse et al. 2008; Lozar Manfeda 2008; Research in focus 8.6). A meta-analysis of forty-five experimental comparisons of Web and other modes of survey administration (with email surveys included in the 'other survey modes' group) found that the former achieved on average an 11 per cent lower response rate (Manfreda et al. 2008). Response rates can be boosted by following two simple strategies.

1. Contact prospective respondents before sending them a questionnaire. This is regarded as basic 'netiquette'. Bosnjak et al. (2008) found that response rates to a Web-based panel survey could be enhanced by prenotifying prospec-

tive participants. They found that prenotifications sent by text (SMS) message were more effective than when sent by email but that a combination of both was more effective than text messages alone. However, prenotification by letter appears to be even more effective than by email (Tourangeau et al. 2013: 44).

2. As with postal questionnaire surveys, follow up non-respondents at least once.

One factor that may affect response rates is how far the topic is interesting or relevant to the sample members. Baumgartner and Morris (2010) achieved a respectable response rate of 37.9 per cent to a Web survey examining the influence of social networking sites as potential sources of news on students' engagement with the democratic process during the 2008 presidential campaign in the United States. Although the researchers found little evidence of social networking sites having an impact on political engagement, these sites play a significant role in young people's lives, and the fact that the survey was about them may have helped to give the survey a decent response rate.

Crawford et al. (2001) report the results of a survey of students at the University of Michigan that experimented with a number of possible influences on the response rate. Students in the sample were initially sent an email inviting them to visit the website, which allowed access, via a password, to the questionnaire. Some of those emailed were led to expect that the questionnaire would take 8–10 minutes to complete (in fact, it would take considerably longer); others were led to expect that it would take 20 minutes. Those led to believe it would take longer were less likely to accept the invitation, resulting in a lower response rate for this group. However, Crawford et al. also found that those respondents who were led to believe that the questionnaire would take only 8–10 minutes were *more* likely to give up on the questionnaire part of the way through, resulting in unusable partially completed questionnaires in most cases. Interestingly, they also found that respondents were most likely to abandon their questionnaires part of the way through when in the middle of completing a series of **open-ended questions**, suggesting that it is probably best to minimize the number of such questions in a Web survey.

Having a progress indicator with a Web survey can reduce the number of people who abandon the questionnaire part of the way through completion (Couper et al. 2001). A progress indicator is usually a diagrammatic representation of how far the respondent has progressed through the questionnaire at any particular point. Couper et al. also found that it took less time for respondents to complete related items (for example, a series of Likert items) when they appeared on a screen together than when they appeared singly. Respondents also seemed less inclined to omit related questions when they appeared together on a screen rather than singly.

However, it is important not to be too sanguine about some of these findings. One difficulty with many of them is that the findings are based on samples which derive from populations whose members are not as different from one another as would almost certainly be found in samples deriving from general populations. Another is that access to the Internet is still not universal, and there is evidence that those with Web access differ from those without both in terms of personal characteristics and attitudinally. Fricker et al. (2005) compared the administration of a questionnaire by Web survey and by telephone interview among a general US sample. They found that telephone interviewees were much more likely to complete the questionnaire (though it is possible that the same effect would have been noted if they had compared the Web mode with a self-administered mode). By contrast, telephone interviewees were more likely than in the Web administration to omit questions by saying they had 'no opinion', probably because online respondents were prompted to answer if they failed to answer a question.

Increasingly, *mixed mode surveys* which combine more than one method of administration have become standard practice among many survey researchers in both academic and commercial fields (De Leeuw and Hox 2011, 2015). There are many reasons for this trend and some of these will be touched on in Chapters 9 and 10, but one of the principal reasons is that declining response rates have led to inevitable concerns about how well samples cover the populations they are meant to reflect. Allowing potential respondents more than one mode of survey administration (as in Research in focus 8.6) increases the likelihood that the response rate will be enhanced (Blyth 2008). Web surveys occupy an increasingly significant role in this connection in that along with other media (such as mobile phones) they increase the range of survey administration opportunities that can be offered to respondents. There is a lingering concern that will also be touched on in the next two chapters: the problem of 'mode effects', whereby the findings that are produced from mixed mode surveys may be affected by the mode of administration, so that findings from one mode differ from those derived from another mode. One final point to register is that increasingly, survey researchers use post-survey adjustments to reduce the impact of problems such as non-response. This entails weighting samples that are achieved so that they better reflect the populations from which samples are taken (Tourangeau et al. 2013: 24–35). This area is beyond the scope of this book but it is important to appreciate the existence of such adjustments.

 # Limits to generalization

One point that is often not fully appreciated is that, even when a sample has been selected using probability sampling, any findings can be generalized only to the population from which that sample was taken. This is an obvious point, but it is easy to think that findings from a study have some kind of broader applicability. If we take our imaginary study of alcohol consumption among students at a university, any findings could be generalized only to that university. In other words, you should be very cautious about generalizing to students at other universities. There are many factors that may imply that the level of alcohol consumption is higher (or lower) than among university students as a whole. There may be a higher (or lower) concentration of pubs in the university's vicinity, there may be more (or fewer) bars on the campus, there may be more (or less) of a culture of drinking at this university, or the university may recruit a higher (or lower) proportion of students with disposable income. There may be many other factors too. Similarly, we should be cautious of over-generalizing in terms of locality. Lunt and Livingstone's (1992: 173) study of consumption habits was based on a postal questionnaire sent to '241 people living in or around Oxford during September 1989'. While the authors' findings represent a fascinating insight into modern consumption patterns, we should be cautious about assuming that they can be generalized beyond Oxford and its environs.

There could even be a further limit to generalization that is implied by the Lunt and Livingstone (1992) sample. They write that the research was conducted in September 1989. One issue that is rarely discussed in this context and that is almost impossible to assess is whether there is a time limit on the findings that are generated. Quite aside from the fact that we need to appreciate that the findings cannot (or at least should not) be generalized beyond the Oxford area, is there a point at which we have to say, 'well, those findings applied to the Oxford area then but things have changed and we can no longer assume that

they apply to that or any other locality'? We are, after all, used to thinking that things have changed when there has been some kind of prominent change. To take a simple example: no one would be prepared to assume that the findings of a study in 1980 of university students' budgeting and personal finance habits would apply to students in the early twenty-first century. Quite apart from changes that might have occurred naturally, the erosion and virtual dismantling of the student grant system has changed the ways students finance their education, including perhaps a greater reliance on part-time work, a greater reliance on parents, and the use of loans. But, even when there is no definable or recognizable source of relevant change of this kind, there is none the less the possibility (or even likelihood) that findings are temporally specific. Such an issue is impossible to resolve without further research.

Error in survey research

We can think of 'error' as being made up of four main factors (Figure 8.9).

1. *Sampling error*. See Key concept 8.1 for a definition. This kind of error arises because it is extremely unlikely that one will end up with a truly representative sample, even when probability sampling is employed.

2. We can distinguish what might be thought of as *sampling-related error*. This is error that is subsumed under the category *non-sampling error* (see Key concept 8.1) but that arises from activities or events that are related to the sampling process and that are connected with the issue of generalizability of findings. Examples are an inaccurate sampling frame and non-response.

3. There is also error that is connected with the design of the data collection instruments. We might call this *data-*

collection error. This source of error includes such factors as poor question wording in self-administered questionnaires or structured interviews; poor interviewing techniques; and flaws in the administration of research instruments.

4. Finally, there is *data-processing error*. This arises from faulty management of data, in particular errors in the *coding* of answers.

The third and fourth sources of error relate to factors that are not associated with sampling and instead relate much more closely to concerns about the validity of measurement, which was addressed in Chapter 7. However, the kinds of steps that need to be taken to keep these sources of error to a minimum in survey research will be addressed in Chapters 9–11.

Figure 8.9
Four sources of error in social survey research

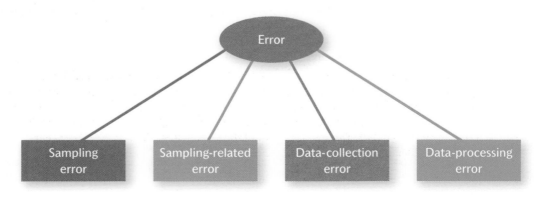

Key points

- Probability sampling is a mechanism for reducing bias in the selection of samples.
- Ensure you become familiar with key technical terms in the literature on sampling such as: representative sample; random sample; non-response; population; sampling error; etc.
- Randomly selected samples are important because they permit generalizations to the population and because they have certain known qualities.
- Sampling error decreases as sample size increases.
- Quota samples can provide reasonable alternatives to random samples, but they suffer from some deficiencies.
- Convenience samples may provide interesting data, but it is crucial to be aware of their limitations in terms of generalizability.
- Sampling and sampling-related error are just two sources of error in social survey research.
- Most of the same considerations involved in traditional survey sampling apply to sampling for online surveys.

Questions for review

- What do each of the following terms mean: population; probability sampling; non-probability sampling; sampling frame; representative sample; and sampling and non-sampling error?
- What are the goals of sampling?
- What are the main areas of potential bias in sampling?

Sampling error

- What is the significance of sampling error for achieving a representative sample?

Types of probability sample

- What is probability sampling and why is it important?
- What are the main types of probability sample?
- How far does a stratified random sample offer greater precision than a simple random or systematic sample?
- If you were conducting an interview survey of around 500 people in Manchester, what type of probability sample would you choose and why?
- A researcher positions herself on a street corner and asks 1 person in 5 who walks by to be interviewed. She continues doing this until she has a sample of 250. How likely is she to achieve a representative sample?

The qualities of a probability sample

- A researcher is interested in levels of job satisfaction among manual workers in a firm that is undergoing change. The firm has 1,200 manual workers. The researcher selects a simple random sample of 10 per cent of the population. He measures job satisfaction on a Likert scale comprising ten items. A high level of satisfaction is scored 5 and a low level is scored 1. The mean job satisfaction score is 34.3. The standard error of the mean is 8.58. What is the 95 per cent confidence interval?

Sample size

- What factors would you take into account in deciding how large your sample should be when devising a probability sample?
- What is non-response and why is it important to the question of whether you will end up with a representative sample?

Types of non-probability sampling

- Are non-probability samples useless?
- In what circumstances might you employ snowball sampling?
- 'Quota samples are not true random samples, but in terms of generating a representative sample there is little difference between them, and this accounts for their widespread use in market research and opinion polling.' Discuss.

Sampling issues in online surveys

- Do sampling problems render online social surveys too problematic to warrant serious consideration?
- Are response rates in online surveys worse or better than in traditional surveys?

Limits to generalization

- 'The problem of generalization to a population is not just to do with the matter of getting a representative sample.' Discuss.

Error in survey research

- 'Non-sampling error, as its name implies, is concerned with sources of error that are not part of the sampling process.' Discuss.

....

Online Resource Centre
www.oxfordtextbooks.co.uk/orc/brymansrm5e/

Visit the Online Resource Centre to enrich your understanding of sampling. Follow up links to other resources, test yourself using multiple choice questions, and gain further guidance and inspiration from the Student Researcher's Toolkit.

....

9
Structured interviewing

Chapter outline

Chapter guide

The structured interview is one of a variety of forms of research interview, but it is the one that is most commonly employed in survey research. The goal of the structured interview is for interviewing to be standardized so that differences between interviews in an investigation are minimized. There are many guidelines about how structured interviewing should be carried out so that variation in the conduct of interviews is small. The chapter explores:

- the reasons why the structured interview is a prominent research method in survey research; this issue entails a consideration of the importance of standardization to the process of measurement;

- the different contexts of interviewing, such as the use of more than one interviewer and whether the administration of the interview is in person or by telephone;

- various prerequisites of structured interviewing, including establishing rapport with the interviewee; asking questions as they appear on the interview schedule; recording exactly what is said by interviewees; ensuring there are clear instructions on the interview schedule concerning question sequencing and the recording of answers; and keeping to the question order as it appears on the schedule;

- problems with structured interviewing, including the influence of the interviewer on respondents and the possibility of systematic bias in answers (known as response sets); the feminist critique of structured interview, which raises a distinctive cluster of problems with the method, is also examined.

Introduction

The interview is a common occurrence in social life, because there are many different forms of interview. There are job interviews, media interviews, social work interviews, police interviews, appraisal interviews. And then there are research interviews, which are the kind of interview that will be covered in this and other chapters (such as Chapters 20 and 21). The different kinds of research interview share some common features, such as the eliciting of information by the interviewer from the interviewee and the operation of rules of varying degrees of formality or explicitness concerning the conduct of the interview.

In the research interview, the interviewer elicits from the interviewee or *respondent*, as he or she is frequently called in survey research, various kinds of information: the interviewee's own behaviour or that of others; attitudes; norms; beliefs; and values. There are many different types or styles of research interview, but the kind that is primarily employed in survey research is the structured interview, which is the focus of this chapter. Other kinds of interview will be briefly mentioned in this chapter but will be discussed in greater detail in later chapters.

 # The structured interview

The research interview is a prominent data-collection strategy in both quantitative and qualitative research. The survey is probably the chief context within which social researchers employ the structured interview (see Key concept 9.1) in connection with quantitative research, and it is this form of the interview that will be emphasized in this chapter. The **structured interview** is one of the two main ways of administering a survey research instrument, whose main forms are briefly outlined in Figure 8.2. This figure should be consulted as a background to this chapter and Chapter 10.

The reason why survey researchers typically prefer the structured interview is that it promotes standardization of both the asking of questions *and* the recording of answers. This feature has two closely related virtues: reducing error due to variation in the asking of questions, and greater accuracy in and ease of processing respondents' answers.

Reducing error due to interviewer variability

The standardization of both the asking of questions and the recording of answers means that, if the interview is properly executed, variation in people's replies will be due to 'true' or 'real' variation and not due to the interview context. To take a simple illustration, when we ask a question

 ## Key concept 9.1
What is a structured interview?

A structured interview, sometimes called a *standardized interview*, entails the administration of an interview schedule—a collection of questions designed to be asked by an interviewer. The aim is for all interviewees to be given exactly the same context of questioning. This means that each respondent receives exactly the same interview stimulus as any other. The goal of this style of interviewing is to ensure that interviewees' replies can be aggregated, and this can be achieved reliably only if those replies are in response to identical cues. Interviewers are supposed to read out questions exactly in the same words and in the same order as printed on the schedule. Questions are usually very specific and often offer the interviewee a fixed range of answers (this type of question is often called *closed, closed-ended, pre-coded,* or *fixed choice*).

Figure 9.1
A variable

Variation

Figure 9.2
A variable with little error

True variation

Variation due to error

Figure 9.3
A variable with considerable error

True variation

Variation due
to error

that is supposed to be an indicator of a concept, we want to keep error to a minimum. We can think of the answers to a question as constituting the values that a variable takes. These values, of course, exhibit variation. This could be the question on alcohol consumption among students that was a focus of Chapter 8 at certain points. Students will vary in the number of alcohol units they consume (as in Figure 9.1). However, some respondents may be inaccurately classified in terms of the variable. There are a number of possible reasons for this (see Thinking deeply 9.1).

Most variables will contain an element of error, so that it is helpful to think of variation as made up of two components: true variation and error. In other words:

variation = true variation + variation due to error

The aim is to keep the error component to a minimum (see Figure 9.2), since error has an adverse effect on the validity of a measure. If the error component is quite high (see Figure 9.3), validity will be jeopardized. The significance for error of standardization in the structured

Thinking deeply 9.1
Common sources of error in survey research

There are many sources of error in survey research in addition to those associated with sampling. This is a list of the principal sources of error:

1. a poorly worded question;

2. the way the question is asked by the interviewer;

3. misunderstanding on the part of the interviewee;

4. memory problems on the part of the interviewee;

5. the way the information is recorded by the interviewer;

6. the way the information is processed, either when answers are coded or when data are entered into the computer.

interview is that two sources of variation due to error—the second and fifth in Thinking deeply 9.1—are likely to be less pronounced, since the opportunity for variation in interviewer behaviour in these two areas (asking questions and recording answers) is reduced.

The significance of standardization and of thereby reducing interviewer variability is this: assuming that there is no problem with an interview question due to such things as confusing terms or ambiguity (an issue that will be examined in Chapter 11), we want to be able to say as far as possible that the variation that we find is true variation between interviewees and is not due to variation in the way a question was asked or the way the answers were recorded in the course of the administration of a survey by structured interview. Variability can occur in either of two ways. First, *intra-interviewer variability* occurs when an interviewer is not consistent in the way he or she asks questions and/or records answers. Second, when there is more than one interviewer, there may be *inter-interviewer variability*, whereby interviewers are not consistent with each other in the ways they ask questions and/or record answers. Needless to say, these two sources of variability are not mutually exclusive; they can coexist, compounding the problem even further. In view of the significance of standardization, it is hardly surprising that some writers prefer to call the structured interview a *standardized interview* (e.g. Oppenheim 1992) or *standardized survey interview* (e.g. Fowler and Mangione 1990).

Accuracy and ease of data processing

Like self-administered questionnaires, most structured interviews contain mainly questions that are variously referred to as *closed*, *closed-ended*, *pre-coded*, or *fixed-choice*. This issue will be covered in detail in Chapter 11. However, this type of question has considerable relevance to the current discussion. With the **closed-ended question**, the respondent is given a limited choice of possible answers. In other words, the interviewer provides respondents with two or more possible answers and asks them to select which one or ones apply. Ideally, this procedure will simply entail the interviewer placing a tick in a box by the answer(s) selected by a respondent or circling the selected answer or using a similar procedure. The advantage of this practice is that the potential for interviewer variability is reduced: there is no problem of whether the interviewer writes down everything that the respondent says or of misinterpretation of the reply given. If an *open* or *open-ended* question is asked, the interviewer may not write down everything said, may embellish what is said, or may misinterpret what is said.

However, the advantages of the closed-ended question in the context of survey research go further than this, as we will see in Chapter 11. One advantage that is particularly significant is that closed-ended questions greatly facilitate the processing of data. When an open-ended question is asked, the answers need to be sifted and *coded* in order for the data to be analysed quantitatively. Not only is this a laborious procedure, particularly if there is a large number of open-ended questions and/or of respondents; it also introduces the potential for another source of error, which is the sixth in Thinking deeply 9.1: it is quite likely that error will be introduced as a result of variability in the coding of answers. When open-ended questions are asked, the interviewer is supposed to write down as much of what is said as possible. Answers can, therefore, be in the form of several sentences. These answers have to be examined and then categorized, so that each person's answer can be aggregated with other respondents' answers to a certain question. A number will then be allocated to each category of answer, so that the answers can then be entered into a computer database and analysed quantitatively. This general process is known as coding and will be examined in greater detail in Chapter 11.

Coding introduces yet another source of error. First, if the rules for assigning answers to categories, collectively known as the **coding frame**, are flawed, the variation that is observed will not reflect the true variation in interviewees' replies. Second, there may be variability in the ways in which answers are categorized. As with interviewing, there can be two sources: *intra-rater variability*, whereby the person conducting the coding is inconsistent in the way he or she applies the rules for assigning answers to categories, and *inter-rater variability*, whereby if there is more than one person conducting the coding, they differ from each other in the way they apply the rules for assigning answers to categories. If either (or both) source(s) of variability occur, at least part of the variation in interviewees' replies will not reflect true variation and instead will be caused by error.

The closed-ended question sidesteps this problem neatly, because respondents allocate *themselves* to categories. The coding process is then a simple matter of attaching a different number to each category of answer and of entering the numbers into a computer database. This type of question is often referred to as pre-coded, because decisions about the coding of answers are typically undertaken as part of the design of the schedule—that is, before any respondents have actually been asked questions. There is very little opportunity for interviewers or coders to vary in the recording or the coding of answers. Of course, if some respondents misunderstand any terms in the alternative answers with which they are presented, or if the answers do not adequately cover the appropriate range of possibilities, the question will not provide a valid measure. However, that is a separate issue and one that will be returned to in Chapter 11. The chief point to absorb about closed-ended questions for the moment is that, when compared to open-ended questions, they reduce one potential source of error *and* are much easier to process for quantitative data analysis.

Other types of interview

The structured interview is by no means the only type of interview, but it is certainly the main type that is likely to be encountered in survey research and in quantitative research generally. Unfortunately, many different terms have been employed by writers on research methodology to distinguish the diverse forms of research interview. Key concept 9.2 represents an attempt to capture some of the major terms and types.

All the forms of interview outlined in Key concept 9.2, with the exception of the *structured interview* and the *standardized interview*, are primarily used in qualitative research, and it is in that context that they will be encountered again later in this book. They are rarely

Key concept 9.2
Major types of interview

- *Structured interview*. See Key concept 9.1.
- *Standardized interview*. See Key concept 9.1.
- *Semi-structured interview*. This is a term that covers a wide range of instances. It typically refers to a context in which the interviewer has a series of questions that are in the general form of an interview guide but is able to vary the sequence of questions. The questions are frequently somewhat more general in their frame of reference than the questions typically found in a structured interview schedule. Also, the interviewer usually has some latitude to ask further questions in response to what are seen as significant replies.
- *Unstructured interview*. The interviewer typically has only a list of topics or issues, often called an *aide-mémoire*, that are to be covered. The style of questioning is usually informal. The phrasing and sequencing of questions will vary from interview to interview.
- *Intensive interview*. This term is employed by Lofland and Lofland (1995) as an alternative term to the unstructured interview. Spradley (1979) uses the term 'ethnographic interview' to describe a form of interview that is also more or less synonymous with the unstructured interview.
- *Qualitative interview*. For some writers, this term seems to denote an unstructured interview (e.g. Mason 1996), but more frequently it is a general term that embraces interviews of both the semi-structured and unstructured kind (e.g. Rubin and Rubin 1995).
- *In-depth interview*. Like the term 'qualitative interview', this one sometimes refers to an unstructured interview but more often refers to both semi-structured and unstructured interviewing.
- *Focused interview*. This is a term devised by Merton et al. (1956) to refer to an interview using predominantly open-ended questions to ask interviewees questions about a specific situation or event that is relevant to them and of interest to the researcher.
- *Focus group*. This is the same as the focused interview, but interviewees discuss the specific issue in groups. See Key concept 21.1 for a more detailed definition.
- *Group interview*. Some writers see this term as synonymous with the focus group, but a distinction may be made between the latter and a situation in which members of a group discuss a variety of matters that may be only partially related.
- *Oral history interview*. This is an unstructured or semi-structured interview in which the respondent is asked to recall events from his or her past and to reflect on them. There is usually a cluster of fairly specific research concerns to do with a particular epoch or event, so there is some resemblance to a focused interview (see the section on 'Life history and oral history interviewing' in Chapter 20).
- *Life history interview*. This is similar to the oral history interview, but the aim of this type of unstructured interview is to glean information on the entire biography of each respondent (see the section on 'Life history and oral history interviewing' in Chapter 20).

used in connection with quantitative research, and survey research in particular, because the absence of standardization in the asking of questions and recording of answers makes respondents' replies difficult to aggregate and to process. This is not to say that they have no role at all. For example, as we will see in Chapter 11, the unstructured or semi-structured interview can have a useful role in relation to developing the fixed-choice alternatives which are presented to respondents in closed-ended questions.

 # Interview contexts

In an archetypal interview, an interviewer stands or sits in front of the respondent asking the latter a series of questions and writing down the answers. However, there are several possible departures from it, although this archetype is the most usual context for an interview.

More than one interviewee

In the case of group interviews or focus groups, there is more than one, and usually quite a few more than one, respondent or interviewee. Nor is this the only context in which more than one person is interviewed. McKee and Bell (1985), for example, interviewed couples in their study of the impact of male unemployment, while in my research on visitors to Disney theme parks, not just couples but often their children took part in the interview as well (Bryman 1999). However, it is very unusual for structured interviews to be used in connection with this kind of questioning. In survey research, it is almost always a single individual who is the object of questioning. Indeed, in survey interviews it is very advisable to discourage as far as possible the presence and intrusion of others during the course of the interview. Investigations in which more than one person is being interviewed tend to be exercises in qualitative research, though this is not always the case: Pahl's (1990) study of patterns of control of money among couples employed structured interviewing of couples and of husbands and wives separately.

More than one interviewer

This is a very unusual situation in social research, because of the considerable cost that is involved in dispatching two people to interview someone. Bechhofer et al. (1984) describe research in which two people interviewed individuals in a wide range of occupations. However, while their approach achieved a number of benefits for them, they used an unstructured interview approach that is typically employed in qualitative research, and they argue that the presence of a second interviewer is unlikely to achieve any added value to survey interviews.

In person or by telephone?

A third way in which the archetype may not be realized is that interviews may be conducted by telephone rather than face-to-face. While telephone interviewing is quite common in commercial fields such as market research, where it usually takes the form of **computer-assisted telephone interviewing** (CATI; see section on 'Computer-assisted interviewing' below), it is still customary to read reports of studies based on face-to-face interviews in academic research—but see Research in focus 8.5 for an example of a study based on telephone interviews.

There are several advantages of telephone over personal interviews.

- On a like-for-like basis, telephone interviews are far cheaper and quicker to administer because interviewers do not have to spend a great deal of time and money travelling between respondents. This factor will be even more pronounced when a sample is geographically dispersed, a problem that is only partially mitigated for personal interview surveys by strategies such as cluster sampling. Of course, telephone interviews take time and hired interviewers have to be paid, but the cost of conducting a telephone interview will still be lower than a comparable personal one. Moreover, the general efficiency of telephone interviewing has been enhanced with the advent and widespread use in commercial circles of computer-assisted telephone interviewing (CATI).

- The telephone interview is easier to supervise than the personal interview. This is a particular advantage when there are several interviewers, since it becomes easier to check on interviewers' transgressions in the asking of questions, such as rephrasing questions or the inappropriate use of probes. Interviews can be audio-recorded so that data quality can be assessed, but this raises issues that relate to data protection and confidentiality, so that this procedure has to be treated cautiously. Probes are stimuli introduced by the interviewer to elicit further information from the interviewee when the latter's response is inadequate, either because it fails to answer the question or because it answers the question but there is insufficient detail.

- Telephone interviewing has a further advantage, which is to do with evidence (which is not as clear-cut as one might want) that suggests that, in personal interviews, respondents' replies are sometimes affected by characteristics of the interviewer (for example, class, ethnicity) and indeed by his or her mere presence (implying that the interviewees may reply in ways they feel will be deemed desirable by interviewers). The remoteness of the interviewer in telephone interviewing removes this potential source of bias to a significant extent. The interviewer's personal characteristics cannot be seen, and the fact that he or she is not physically present may offset the likelihood of respondents' answers being affected by the interviewer.

Telephone interviewing suffers from certain limitations when compared to the personal interview.

- People who do not own or who are not contactable by telephone obviously cannot be interviewed by telephone. Since this characteristic is most likely to be a feature of poorer households, the potential for sampling bias exists. Also, many people choose to be ex-directory—that is, they have taken action for their telephone numbers not to appear in a telephone directory. Again, these people cannot be interviewed by telephone. One possible solution to this last difficulty is *random digit dialling*. With this technique, the computer randomly selects telephone numbers within a predefined geographical area. Not only is this a random process that conforms to the rules about probability sampling examined in Chapter 8; it also stands a chance of getting at ex-directory households. But it cannot, of course, gain access to those without a telephone at all.

- Respondents with hearing impairments are likely to find telephone interviewing much more difficult than personal interviewing.

- The length of a telephone interview is unlikely to be sustainable beyond 20–25 minutes, whereas personal interviews can be much longer than this (Frey 2004).

- The question of whether response rates (see Key concept 8.2) are lower with surveys by telephone interview than with surveys by personal interview is unclear, in that there is little consistent evidence on this question. However, there is a general belief that telephone interviews achieve slightly lower rates than personal interviews (Frey and Oishi 1995; Shuy 2002; Frey 2004).

- There is some evidence to suggest that telephone interviews fare less well when asking questions about sensitive issues, such as drug and alcohol use, income, tax returns, and health. However, the evidence is not entirely consistent on this point, though if many sensitive questions are to be asked, a personal interview may be preferable (Groves et al. 2009: 169; Shuy 2002).

- Developments in telephone communications, such as answerphones and other forms of call screening, and in mobile phones have almost certainly had an adverse effect on telephone surveys in terms of response rates and the general difficulty of getting access to respondents through conventional landlines. Households that rely exclusively on mobile phones are a particular difficulty.

- Telephone interviewers cannot engage in observation. This means that they are not in a position to respond to signs of puzzlement or unease on the faces of respondents when they are asked a question. In a personal interview, the interviewer may respond to such signs by restating the question or attempting to clarify the meaning of the question, though this has to be handled in a standardized way as far as possible. A further issue relating to the inability of the interviewer to observe is that, sometimes, interviewers may be asked to collect subsidiary information in connection with their visits (for example, whether a house is dilapidated). Such information cannot be collected when telephone interviews are employed.

- It is frequently the case that specific individuals in households or firms are the targets of an interview. In other words, simply anybody will not do. This requirement is likely to arise from the specifications of the population to be sampled, which means that people in a certain role or position or with particular characteristics are to be interviewed. It is probably more difficult to establish by telephone interview whether the correct person is replying.

- The telephone interviewer cannot readily employ visual aids such as show cards (see the section on 'Prompting' below), from which respondents might be asked to select their replies, or use diagrams or photographs.

- There is some evidence to suggest that the quality of data derived from telephone interviews is inferior to that of comparable face-to-face interviews. A series of experiments reported by Holbrook et al. (2003) on the mode of survey administration in the USA using long questionnaires found that respondents interviewed by telephone were more likely to engage in **satisficing** behaviour (see Key concept 9.3) such as expressing no opinion or 'don't know' (see Chapter 11 for more on this issue); answering in the same way to a series of linked questions; expressing socially desirable answers; being apprehensive about the interview; and being more likely to be dissatisfied with the time taken by the interviews (even though they were invariably shorter than in the face-to-face mode). Also, telephone interviewees tended to be less engaged with the interview process. While these results should be viewed with caution, since studies like these are bound to be affected by such factors as the use of a large questionnaire on a national sample, they do provide interesting food for thought.

One final issue to consider is that Skype and similar software such as Apple's Facetime offer the possibility of survey interviews that are hybrids of the face-to-face and telephone interviews. These platforms for conducting interviews do not seem to have been adopted by survey researchers, whereas they have begun to be used by qualitative researchers using semi-structured interviews (see Chapter 20).

Computer-assisted interviewing

Increasing use is being made of computers in the interviewing process, especially in commercial survey research of the kind conducted by market research and opinion polling organizations. There are two main formats for computer-assisted interviewing: computer-assisted personal interviewing (CAPI) and computer-assisted telephone interviewing (CATI). A very large percentage of telephone interviews is conducted with the aid of computers. Among commercial survey organizations, almost all telephone interviewing is of the CATI kind nowadays, and this kind of interview has become one of the most popular formats for such firms. The main reasons for the growing use of CAPI has been that the increased portability and affordability of laptop computers and tablets, and the growth in the number and quality of software packages that provide a platform for devising interview schedules, provide greater opportunity for them to be used in connection with face-to-face interviews. CAPI and CATI have not infiltrated academic survey research to the same degree that they have commercial survey research, although that picture is likely to change considerably because of the many advantages they possess. Indeed, the survey element of the mixed methods study Cultural Capital and Social Exclusion (see Research in focus 2.9) was administered by CAPI. In any case, many of the large data sets that are used for secondary analysis (see Chapter 14 for examples) derive from computer-assisted interviewing studies undertaken by commercial or large social research organizations.

With computer-assisted interviewing, the interview questions appear on the screen. As interviewers ask each question, they key in the appropriate reply using the keyboard (for open-ended questions) or a mouse (for closed-ended questions) and proceed to the next question. This process has the great advantage that, when **filter questions** (see Tips and skills 'Instructions for interviewers in the use of a filter question') are asked, whereby certain answers may be skipped as a result of a person's reply, the computer can be programmed to 'jump' to the next relevant question. This removes the possibility of interviewers inadvertently asking inappropriate questions or failing to ask ones that should be asked. As such, computer-assisted interviewing enhances the degree of control over the interview process and can therefore improve standardization of the asking and recording of questions. If the interviewer is out in the field all day, he or she can either take a storage device with the saved data to the research office or upload the data to a remote or cloud storage facility. It is possible that technophobic respondents may be a bit alarmed by the use of laptops or tablets, but, by and large, the use of computer-assisted interviewing seems destined to grow. However, there is very little evidence to suggest that the quality of data deriving from computer-assisted interviews is demonstrably superior to that obtained from comparable paper-and-pencil interviews (Couper and Hansen 2002).

There is evidence that professional interviewers generally like computer-assisted interviewing, often feeling that it improves the image of their occupation, though there are many who are concerned about the problems that might arise from technical difficulties and the inconvenience of correcting errors with a computer as opposed to with a pen. One issue that sometimes disconcerts interviewers is the fact that they can see only part of the schedule at any one time (Couper and Hansen 2002). One potential problem with CAPI and CATI is 'miskeying', where the interviewer clicks on the wrong reply. Whether this is more likely to occur than when the interviewer is using pen and paper is unknown. In the CCSE study, as noted in Research in focus 2.9, qualitative interviews were conducted with some of the survey respondents. In part this was done so that participants in the semi-structured interview phase could be asked about some of the answers they had given in the survey interview. As a result, the researchers found that sometimes the participant had been recorded as giving a particular answer that was in fact incorrect. An example is a respondent who had been recorded as indicating in the survey interview as preferring to eat out in Italian restaurants when in fact it should have been Indian ones (Silva and Wright 2008). As the researchers note, it is impossible to know how this error occurred, but miskeying is one possible reason.

Key concept 9.3
Satisficing in surveys

Drawing on Simon's (1960) notion of 'satisficing', which was referred to in the Guide to this book, Krosnick (1999) has proposed that survey respondents sometimes satisfice rather than **optimize**. Optimizing refers to expending effort to arrive at the best and most appropriate answer to a question. Precisely because of the effort required by optimizing, respondents sometimes satisfice, which means reducing the amount of effort required to answer the question so that 'Instead of generating the most accurate answers, respondents settle for merely satisfactory ones' (Krosnick 1999: 548). Examples of satisficing in answering survey questions include a tendency towards agreeing with statements ('yeasaying'—see the subsection on 'Acquiescence' below); opting for safe answers such as middle-points on answer scales (e.g. 'don't know' or 'neither agree nor disagree'); and not considering the full range of answers offered to a closed-ended question (e.g. selecting the last one). The principal implication of satisficing for question design is that the researcher will want to minimize the amount of effort required by respondents to answer questions.

Using mobile phones for interview surveys

The discussion of telephone interviewing and of CATI in the previous sections presumes that the medium is a landline. Since the ownership of mobile phones is so prevalent, they are likely to have a growing role in telephone surveys. Since lists of mobile-phone users are unlikely to be available in the way that telephone directories are, random digit dialing (RDD) is most likely to be employed by researchers seeking to interview by mobile phone. Alternatively, members of a panel may be given the option of which kind of device they would prefer to use when being interviewed by telephone.

ZuWallack (2009) reports the findings of some CATI projects conducted by mobile phone in the USA on health-related issues. The researchers found that many people hung up when contacted but that those respondents who persisted formed a useful complement to conventional landline telephone surveys because many of them were from groups often under-represented in such surveys, such as young adults and minorities. A large percentage of respondents lived in households without a landline, suggesting that, if the number of mobile-only households increases, mobile-phone surveys may become increasingly significant. ZuWallack also reports that the mobile-phone survey is more expensive than the equivalent landline CATI survey.

Lynn and Kaminska (2012) examined findings deriving from an experiment in Hungary comparing landline and mobile phone interviews and uncovered few significant differences in the findings. The authors were especially interested in whether interviewees were more likely to satisfice in one telephone mode rather than the other (see Key concept 9.3). They examined several indicators of satisficing behaviour (e.g. propensity to answer 'don't know') and found no statistically significant differences between landline and mobile phone interviews on these sources of error. They did find some evidence of less social desirability bias (see the section on this topic below) in mobile phone than landline interviews, which they suggest may be due to interviewees' ability to choose where interviews are located. Gundersen et al. (2013) used a mobile phone survey method to examine the health behaviour of a national sample of young adults aged 18–34 years in the USA who were contacted through RDD. They benchmarked their findings, which were on tobacco-related issues, against an established survey that contacted interviewees by both landline and mobile phones. Although the mobile phone response rate was lower than for landline interviewees, the findings regarding tobacco issues did not differ significantly between the two modes of administration. These findings are fairly reassuring about the potential of mobile phone surveys either as a stand-alone method or as a complement to landline surveys.

Conducting interviews

Issues concerning the conduct of interviews are examined here in a very general way. In addition to the matters considered here, there is clearly the important issue of how to word the interview questions themselves. This issue will be explored in Chapter 11, since many of the rules of question-asking relate to self-administered questionnaire techniques such as postal questionnaires as well as to structured interviews. One further general point to make here is that the advice concerning the conduct of interviews provided in this chapter relates to structured interviews. The framework for carrying out the kinds of interviewing conducted in qualitative research (such as unstructured and semi-structured interviewing and focus groups) will be handled in later chapters.

Know the schedule

Before interviewing anybody, an interviewer should be fully conversant with the schedule. Even if you are the only person conducting interviews, make sure you know it inside out. Interviewing can be stressful for interviewers; under pressure, standard interview procedures such as filter questions (see Tips and skills 'Instructions for interviewers in the use of a filter question') can cause interviewers to get flustered and miss questions out or ask the wrong questions. If two or more interviewers are involved, they need to be fully trained to know what is required of them and to know their way around the schedule. Training is especially important in order to reduce the likelihood of interviewer variability in the asking of questions, which is a source of error.

Introducing the research

Prospective respondents have to be provided with a credible rationale for the research in which they are being asked to participate and for giving up their valuable time. This aspect of conducting interview research is of particular significance at a time when response rates to survey research appear to be declining, though, as noted in Chapter 8, the evidence on this issue is the focus of some disagreement. The introductory rationale may be either spoken by the interviewer or written down. It comes in spoken form in such situations as when interviewers make contact with respondents on the street or when they 'cold call' respondents in their homes in person or by telephone. A written rationale will be required to alert respondents that someone will be contacting them in person or on the telephone to request an interview. Respondents will frequently encounter both forms—for example, when they are sent a letter and then when they ask the interviewer who turns up to interview them what the research is all about. It is important for the two accounts to be consistent, as this could be a test!

Introductions to research should typically contain the items of information outlined in Tips and skills 'Topics and issues to include in an introductory statement'. Since interviewers are the interface between the research and the respondent, they have an important role in maximizing the response rate for the survey. In addition the following points should be borne in mind.

- Interviewers should be prepared to keep calling back if interviewees are out or unavailable. This will require taking into account people's likely work and leisure habits—for example, there is no point in calling at home on people who work during the day. In addition, people living alone may be reluctant to answer the door when it is dark because of fear of crime.

- Be self-assured. You may get a better response if you presume that people will agree to be interviewed rather than that they will refuse.

- Reassure people that you are not a salesperson. Because of the tactics of certain organizations whose representatives say they are doing market or social research, many people have become very suspicious of people saying they would just like to ask you a few questions.

- Dress in a way that will be acceptable to a wide spectrum of people.

- Make it clear that you will be happy to find a time to suit the respondent.

Rapport

It is frequently suggested that it is important for the interviewer to achieve *rapport* with the respondent. This means that very quickly a relationship must be established that encourages the respondent to want (or at least be prepared) to participate in and persist with the interview. Unless an element of rapport can be established, some respondents may initially agree to be interviewed but then decide to terminate their participation because of the length of time the interview is taking or perhaps because of the nature of the questions being asked. While this suggestion essentially invites the interviewer to be friendly with respondents and to put them at ease, this quality should not be stretched too far. Too much rapport may result in the interview going on too long and the respondent suddenly deciding that too much time is being spent on it. Also, the mood of friendliness may result in the respondent answering questions in a way that is designed to please the interviewer. The achievement of rapport between interviewer and respondent is therefore a delicate balancing act. Moreover, it is probably somewhat easier to achieve in the face-to-face interview than in the telephone interview, since in the latter the interviewer is unable to offer obvious visual cues of friendliness such as smiling or maintaining good eye contact, which are also frequently regarded as conducive to gaining and maintaining rapport.

Tips and skills
Topics and issues to include in an introductory statement

There are several issues to include in an introductory statement to a prospective interviewee. The following list comprises the principal considerations.

- Make clear the identity of the person who is contacting the respondent.

- Identify the auspices under which the research is being conducted—for example, a university, a market research agency.

- Mention the source of any research funding, or, if you are a student doing an undergraduate or postgraduate dissertation or doing research for a thesis, make this clear.

- Indicate what the research is about in broad terms and why it is important, and give an indication of the kind of information to be collected.

- Indicate why the respondent has been selected—for example, selected by a random process.

- Make it clear that participation is voluntary.

- Reassure the respondent that he or she will not be identified or be identifiable in any way. This can usually be achieved by pointing out that data are anonymized when they are entered into the computer and that analysis will be conducted at an aggregate level.

- Provide reassurance about the confidentiality of any information provided.

- Provide the respondent with the opportunity to ask any questions—for example, provide a contact telephone number if the introduction is in the form of a written statement, or, if in person, simply ask if the respondent has any questions.

These suggestions are also relevant to the covering letter that accompanies postal questionnaires, except that researchers using this method also need to remember to include a stamped and addressed envelope!

Asking questions

It was earlier suggested that one of the aims of the structured interview is to ensure that each respondent is asked exactly the same questions. Recall that in Thinking deeply 9.1 it was pointed out that variation in the ways a question is asked is a potential source of error in survey research. The structured interview is meant to reduce the likelihood of this occurring, but it cannot guarantee that this will not occur, because there is always the possibility that interviewers will embellish or otherwise change a question when asking it. There is considerable evidence that this occurs, even among centres of social research that have a solid reputation for being rigorous in following correct methodological protocol (Bradburn and Sudman 1979). The problem with such variation in the asking of questions was outlined above: it is likely to engender variation in replies that does not reflect 'true' variation—in other words, error. Consequently, it is important for interviewers to appreciate the importance of keeping exactly to the wording of the questions they are charged with asking.

You might say: 'does it really matter?' In other words, surely small variations to wording cannot make a significant difference to people's replies? While the impact of variation in wording obviously differs from context to context and is in any case difficult to quantify exactly, experiments in question-wording suggest that even minor variations in wording can exert an impact on replies (Schuman and Presser 1981). Three experiments in England conducted by Social and Community Planning Research concluded that a considerable number of interview questions are affected by interviewer variability. The researchers estimated that, for about two-thirds of the questions that were considered, interviewers contributed to less than 2 per cent of the total variation in each question (M. Collins 1997). On the face of it, this is a small amount of error, but the researchers regarded it as a cause for concern.

The key point to emerge, then, is the importance of getting across to interviewers the importance of asking questions as they are written. There are many reasons why interviewers may vary question-wording, such as reluctance to ask certain questions, perhaps because of embarrassment (M. Collins 1997), but the general admonition to keep to the wording of the question needs to be constantly reinforced when interviewers are being trained. It also needs to be borne in mind for your own research.

Recording answers

An identical warning for identical reasons can be registered in connection with the recording of answers by interviewers, who should write down respondents' replies as exactly as possible. Not to do so can result in interviewers distorting respondents' answers and hence introducing error. Such errors are less likely to occur when the interviewer has merely to allocate respondents' replies to a category, as in a closed-ended question. This process can require a certain amount of interpretation on the part of the interviewer, but the error that is introduced is far less than when answers to open-ended questions are being written down (Fowler and Mangione 1990).

Clear instructions

In addition to instructions about the asking of questions and the recording of answers, interviewers need instructions about their progress through an interview schedule. An example of the kind of context in which this is likely to occur is in relation to *filter questions*. Filter questions require the interviewer to ask questions of some respondents but not others. For example, the question:

> For which political party did you vote at the last general election?

presumes that the respondent did in fact vote. This option can be reflected in the fixed-choice answers that are provided, so that one of these is a 'did not vote' alternative. However, a better solution is not to presume anything about voting behaviour but to ask respondents whether they voted in the last general election and then to filter out those who did not vote. The foregoing question about the political party voted for can then be asked of those who did in fact vote. Similarly, in a study of meals, there is no point in asking vegetarians lots of questions about eating meat. It will probably work out best to filter vegetarians out and then possibly ask them a separate series of questions. Tips and skills 'Instructions for interviewers in the use of a filter question' provides a simple example in connection with an imaginary study of alcohol consumption. The chief point to remember about this example is that it requires clear instructions for the interviewer. If such instructions are not provided, there is the risk that either respondents will be asked inappropriate questions (which can be irritating for them) or the interviewer will inadvertently fail to ask a

question (which results in missing information). In Tips and skills 'Instructions for interviewers in the use of a filter question', the contingent questions (1a and 1b) are indented and there is an arrow to indicate that a 'Yes' answer should be followed by question 1b and not question 2. Such visual aids can help to reduce the likelihood of errors by interviewers.

Question order

In addition to interviewers being warned about the importance of not varying the asking of questions and the recording of answers, they should be alerted to the importance of keeping to the order of asking questions. For one thing, varying the question order can result in certain questions being accidentally omitted, because the interviewer may forget to ask those that have been leapfrogged during the interview. Also, variation in question order may have an impact on replies: if some respondents have been previously asked a question that they should have been asked whereas others have not, a source of variability in the asking of questions will have been introduced and therefore a potential source of error.

Quite a lot of research has been carried out on the general subject of question order, but few if any consistent effects on people's responses that derive from asking questions at different points in a questionnaire or interview schedule have been unveiled. Different effects have been demonstrated on various occasions. A study in the USA found that people were less likely to say that their taxes were too high when they had been previously asked whether government spending ought to be increased in a number of areas (Schuman and Presser 1981: 32). Apparently, some people perceived an inconsistency between wanting more spending and lower taxes, and adjusted their answers accordingly. Research on crime victimization in the USA suggests that earlier questions may affect the salience of later issues (Schuman and Presser 1981: 45). Respondents were asked whether they had been victims of crime in the preceding twelve months. Some respondents had been previously asked a series of questions about their attitudes to crime, whereas others had not. Those who had been asked about their attitudes reported considerably more crime than those who had not been asked.

Mayhew (2000) provides an interesting anecdote on question order in relation to the British Crime Survey. Each wave of the BCS has included the question:

> Taking everything into account, would you say the police in this area do a good job or a poor job?

In 1988 this question appeared twice by mistake for some respondents! For all respondents it appeared early on, but for around half it also appeared later on in the context of questions on contact with the police. Of those given the question twice, 66 per cent gave the same rating, but

Tips and skills
Instructions for interviewers in the use of a filter question

Each of the following questions includes an instruction to the interviewer about how to proceed.

1. Have you consumed any alcoholic drinks in the last twelve months?

   No _____ (if **No** proceed to question 2)

   Yes _____

   1a. (*To be asked if interviewee replied* **Yes** *to question 1*)

   Which of the following alcoholic drinks do you consume most frequently?

   (Ask interviewee to choose the category that he or she drinks most frequently and tick one category only.)

   Beer _____

   Spirits _____

   Wine _____

   Liquors _____

   Other _____ specify _____

   1b. How frequently do you consume alcoholic drinks?

   (Ask interviewee to choose the category that comes closest to his or her current practice.)

   Daily _____

   Most days _____

   Once or twice a week _____

   Once or twice a month _____

   A few times a year _____

   Once or twice a year _____

2. (*To be asked if interviewee replied* **No** *to question 1*)

   Have you ever consumed alcoholic drinks?

   Yes _____

   No _____

22 per cent gave a more positive rating to the police and just 13 per cent gave a less favourable one. Mayhew suggests that, as the interview wore on, respondents became more sensitized to crime-related issues and more sympathetic to the pressures on the police.

However, it is difficult to draw general lessons from such research, at least in part because experiments in question order do not always reveal clear-cut effects of varying the order in which questions are asked, even in cases where effects might legitimately have been expected. There are two general lessons.

1. Within a survey, question order should not be varied (unless, of course, question order is the subject of the study!).

2. Researchers should be sensitive to the possible implications of the effect of early questions on answers to subsequent questions.

The following rules about question order are sometimes proposed.

- Early questions should be directly related to the topic of the research, about which the respondent has been informed. This removes the possibility that the respondent will be wondering at an early stage in the interview why he or she is being asked apparently irrelevant questions. This recommendation means that personal questions about age, social background, and so on should *not* be asked at the beginning of an interview.

- As far as possible, questions that are more likely to be salient to respondents should be asked early in the interview schedule, so that their interest and attention are more likely to be secured. This suggestion may conflict with the previous one, in that questions specifically on the research topic may not be obviously salient to respondents, but it implies that as far as possible questions relating to the research topic that are more likely to grab their attention should be asked at or close to the start of the interview.

- Sensitive questions or ones that may be a source of anxiety should be left till later. In fact, research should be designed to ensure that, as far as possible, respondents are not discomfited, but it has to be acknowledged that with certain topics this effect may be unavoidable.

- With a long schedule or questionnaire, questions should be grouped into sections, since this allows a better flow than skipping from one topic to another.

- Within each group of questions, general questions should precede specific ones. Tips and skills 'A sequence of questions on the topic of identity cards' provides an illustration of such a sequence, which follows the recommendations of Gallup (1947, cited in Foddy 1993: 61–2). The example is intended to demonstrate how the approach might operate in connection with identity cards, which have been an area of discussion and some controversy in the UK. The question order sequence is designed with a number of features in mind. It is designed to establish people's levels of knowledge of identity cards before asking questions about it and to distinguish those who feel strongly about it from those who do not. The second question (1a) is always open-ended, so that respondents' frames of references can be established with respect to the topic at hand. However, it seems likely that, if sufficient pilot research has been carried out, a closed-ended question could be envisaged, a point that applies equally to question (1c).

- A further aspect of the rule that general questions should precede specific ones is that it has been argued that, when a specific question comes before a general one, the aspect of the general question that is covered by the specific one is discounted in the minds of respondents because they feel they have already covered it. Thus, if a question about how people feel about the amount they are paid precedes a general question about job satisfaction, there are grounds for thinking that respondents will discount the issue of pay when responding about job satisfaction.

- It is sometimes recommended that questions dealing with opinions and attitudes should precede questions to do with behaviour and knowledge. This is because it is felt that behaviour and knowledge questions are less affected by question order than questions that tap opinions and attitudes.

- During the course of an interview, it sometimes happens that a respondent provides an answer to a question that is to be asked later in the interview. Because of the possibility of a question order effect, when the interviewer arrives at the question that appears already to have been answered, it should be repeated.

However, question order effects remain one of the more frustrating areas of structured interview and questionnaire design, because the evidence is inconsistent and because it is difficult to formulate generalizations or rules from the evidence that can be applied. A possible question order issue is discussed in Research in the news 9.1.

Tips and skills
A sequence of questions on the topic of identity cards

1. Have you heard of identity cards?

   Yes _____ No _____ (If **No**, go to question 2)

   1a. What are your views about identity cards?

   1b. Do you favour or not favour identity cards?

   Favour _____ Not favour _____

   1c. Why do you favour (not favour) identity cards?

   1d. How strongly do you feel about this?

   Very strongly   _____

   Fairly strongly   _____

   Not at all strongly   _____

Research in the news 9.1
A possible question order effect on the topic of fracking

On 13 August 2014, several newspapers reported the findings of a survey for the UK Government's Department of Energy and Climate Change (DECC) in connection with the extraction of shale gas through 'fracking'. The survey, known as the Public Attitudes Tracker, showed that 24 per cent supported fracking which was down from 29 per cent three months earlier. More interesting than the decline in support was the fact that the figure was published a day after a survey carried out for the shale gas industry which showed that 57 per cent of the sample believed that 'the UK should produce natural gas from shale' (**www.thetimes.co.uk/tto/environment/article4174476. ece**). Why the discrepancy? The newspapers highlighted two concerns: the context within which the questions were asked (essentially a question order issue), and the questions themselves.

The government survey asked about fracking as part of a general tracking survey of public attitudes to energy-related issues, so that shale gas extraction was just one of several areas being asked about. Respondents were provided with a sixty-three word explanation of what shale gas and fracking are and were then asked:

> Before today, how much, if anything, did you know about hydraulic fracturing for shale gas, otherwise known as 'fracking'?

They were asked to choose between one of four possible answers: 'knew a lot about it'; 'knew a little about it'; 'aware of it but did not really know what it was'; and 'never heard of it'. They were then asked whether they support or oppose its use and were given the following choices:

1. Strongly support
2. Support
3. Neither support nor oppose
4. Oppose
5. Strongly oppose
6. Don't know/no opinion

Almost half of the sample (47 per cent) replied that they neither support nor oppose fracking and 24 per cent were opposed.

Here is the question asked in a survey commissioned by UK Onshore Oil and Gas, a body that represents the industry:

> Natural gas from shale is found both onshore and offshore, typically a mile or more underground. For the rest of the survey please answer in relation to onshore shale only. Producing natural gas from shale uses a technique called hydraulic fracturing (often called fracking). This involves creating tiny fractures in the rock deep underground, freeing the gas. Fractures are created by pumping a fluid containing 99.5% water and sand and 0.5% approved non-hazardous chemicals down at high pressure. The British Geological Survey has estimated that the UK has 1,300 trillion cubic feet of natural gas from shale. If just 10% of this could be recovered, it would be enough to meet the UK's demand for natural gas for nearly 50 years or to heat the UK's homes for over 100 years. From what you know, do you think the UK should produce natural gas from shale?

Respondents were given a choice of 'Yes' or 'No' or 'Don't know', and 27 per cent chose the last option. There are several problems with the UKOOG question: it is almost certainly too long at 145 words; it did not provide a middle alternative for those with no opinion, leaving those with no opinion having to choose 'Yes' or 'No' or 'Don't know'; and it implies a solution to the UK's energy needs, thereby leading the respondent towards a positive answer.

However, a further consideration is that there may have been question order effect. The writer for *The Times* noted that the survey 'asked several questions about Britain's need for investment and energy security before asking the key question on fracking'. The questions entailed indicating level of agreement with each of the following statements:

- 'The UK needs to invest more in a whole range of new infrastructure, including housing, roads and railways, airport capacity and new energy sources'
- 'The UK needs to use a range of energy sources to meet the country's energy needs'
- 'Britain needs to be able to produce its own energy so it isn't reliant on gas from other countries'

The problem here is that respondents are being alerted to issues to do with the need for new energy sources and ones that are on home soil so they are primed for agreement rather than lack of agreement. It is impossible to know for certain whether the presence of these three questions prior to the actual shale gas question influenced respondents' answers but in view of the discrepancy between the two sets of findings, it is a possibility and represents a warning to consider question order effects when designing a questionnaire. One final consideration is that the two questions may not be as comparable as the newspaper writers implied. The DECC question asked about support and opposition whereas the UKOOG question asked for a 'Yes/No/Don't know' reply. 'Yes' and 'No' may not be (and almost certainly are not) equivalent to support and opposition. Also, the DECC question asks respondents to reply to a question about fracking whereas the question element of the UKOOG question asks about shale gas. It could be argued that since it has been mainly fracking that had been the object of media interest leading up to the surveys, which was often negative, it may be that it had more negative connotations in respondents' minds than shale gas extraction and this may have contributed to the lower level of support. The lesson is to think about your questions and what they really are asking.

Sources:

www.thetimes.co.uk/tto/environment/article4174476.ece

www.telegraph.co.uk/earth/energy/11028321/Support-for-fracking-has-declined-to-24-per-cent-energy-department-finds.html

Information about the DECC survey can be found at:
www.gov.uk/government/statistics/public-attitudes-tracking-survey-wave-10

and information about the UKOOG survey at:
www.ukoog.org.uk/about-ukoog/press-releases/131-new-survey-shows-57-of-britons-support-natural-gas-from-shale

Both of these URLs provide access to downloads that give more information about the surveys. All URLs were accessed 30 October 2014.

Probing

Probing is a highly problematic area for researchers employing a structured interview method. It frequently happens in interviews that respondents need help with their answers. One obvious case is where it is evident that they do not understand the question—they may either ask for further information or it is clear from what they say that they are struggling to understand the question or to provide an adequate answer. The second kind of situation the interviewer faces is when the respondent does not provide a sufficiently complete answer and has to be probed for more information. The problem in either situation is obvious: the interviewer's intervention may influence the respondent, and the nature of interviewers' interventions may differ. A potential source of variability in respondents' replies that does not reflect 'true' variation is introduced—that is, error.

Some general tactics with regard to probes are as follows.

- If further information is required, usually in the context of an open-ended question, standardized probes can be employed, such as 'Could you say a little more about that?' or 'Are there any other reasons why you think that?' or simply 'mmmm . . . ?' Probes have to be handled carefully. If they are not introduced in a consistent way or if they suggest a particular kind of answer to the interviewee, error will increase.

- If the problem is that when presented with a closed-ended question the respondent replies in a way that does not allow the interviewer to select one of the pre-designed answers, the interviewer should repeat the fixed-choice alternatives and make it apparent that the answer needs to be chosen from the ones that have been provided.

- If the interviewer needs to know about something that requires quantification, such as the number of visits to building societies in the last four weeks or the number of building societies in which the respondent has accounts, but the respondent resists this by answering in general terms ('quite often' or 'I usually go to the building society every week'), the interviewer needs to persist with securing a number from the respondent. This will usually entail repeating the question. The interviewer should not try to second-guess a figure on the basis of the respondent's reply and then suggest that figure to him or her, since the latter may be unwilling to disagree with the interviewer's suggested figure.

However, from the point of view of standardizing the asking of questions in surveys using structured interviewing, probing should be kept to a minimum (assuming it cannot be eliminated) because it introduces error. This occurs because it is impossible for interviewers to probe in a consistent manner and because interviewer effects are more likely to occur, whereby characteristics of the interviewer have an impact on the respondent's replies (Groves et al. 2009: 303–4).

Prompting

Prompting occurs when the interviewer suggests a possible answer to a question to the respondent. The key prerequisite here is that all respondents receive the same prompts. All closed-ended questions entail standardized prompting, because the respondent is provided with a list of possible answers from which to choose. An unacceptable approach to prompting would be to ask an open-ended question and to suggest possible answers only to some respondents, such as those who appear to be struggling to think of an appropriate reply.

During the course of a face-to-face interview, there are several circumstances in which it will be better for the interviewer to use 'show cards' rather than rely on reading out a series of fixed-choice alternatives. Show cards (sometimes called 'flash cards') display all the answers from which the respondent is to choose and are handed to the respondent at different points of the interview. Three kinds of context in which it might be preferable to employ show cards rather than to read out the entire set of possible answers are as follows.

- There may be a very long list of possible answers. For example, respondents may be asked which daily newspaper they each read most frequently. To read out a list of newspapers would be tedious, and it is probably better to hand the respondent a list of newspapers from which to choose.

- Sometimes, during the course of interviews, respondents are presented with a group of questions to which the same possible answers are attached. An example of this strategy is Likert scaling, which was discussed in Key concept 7.2. The components of a Likert scale are often referred to as *items* rather than as *questions*, since strictly speaking respondents are not being asked questions but are presented with statements to which they are asked to indicate their levels of agreement. See Research in focus 7.2 and 7.5 for examples. It would be excruciatingly dull to read out all five or seven possible answers for each item that comprises the scale. Also, it may be expecting too much of respondents to hear the answers once and then be required to keep the possible answers in their heads for the entire batch of questions to which they apply. A show card that can be used for the entire batch and to which respondents can constantly refer is an obvious solution. As was mentioned in Key concept 7.2, most Likert scales of this kind comprise five levels of agreement/disagreement, and it is this more conventional approach that is illustrated in Tips and skills 'A show card'.

- Some people are reluctant to divulge personal details such as their age or their income. One way of neutralizing the impact of such questioning is to present respondents with age or income bands with a letter or number attached to each band. They can then be asked to say which letter/number applies to them (see Tips and skills 'Another show card'). This procedure will obviously not be appropriate if the research requires *exact* ages or incomes. It may be extendable to sensitive areas such as number of sexual partners or sexual practices for the same kinds of reason.

Leaving the interview

Do not forget common courtesies like thanking respondents for giving up their time. But the period immediately after the interview is one in which some care is necessary, in that sometimes respondents try to engage the interviewer in a discussion about the purpose of the interview. Interviewers should resist elaboration beyond their standard statement, because respondents may communicate what they are told to others, which may bias the findings.

Tips and skills
A show card

Card 6

Strongly agree

Agree

Undecided

Disagree

Strongly disagree

Tips and skills
Another show card

Card 11

1. Below 20

2. 20–29

3. 30–39

4. 40–49

5. 50–59

6. 60–69

7. 70 and over

Student experience
The need for structure in a survey interview

Joe Thomson's survey research on students and their views of accommodation and facilities at his university was part of a team project. After he and other members of his team had piloted the interview schedule, they decided that it was not sufficiently structured. They felt that they needed to impose more structure and decided to use show cards (he refers to them by another common name, 'cue cards').

The group therefore used opportunistic sampling to test if the questionnaire would be successful when applied in a social setting, having to give the questionnaire to one person over the week. The following week the group discussed the issues they had encountered when carrying out the pilot questionnaire, raising amongst others the concern of not having a standard interview procedure, which would mean that certain biases could affect the results. Therefore the group decided they would use cue cards when giving the options in answer to the question, so as to avoid leading questions, etc. After these changes were implemented, the final version of the questionnaire was produced.

To read more, go to the Online Resource Centre: www.oxfordtextbooks.co.uk/orc/brymansrm5e/

Training and supervision

On several occasions, reference has been made to the need for interviewers to be trained. The standard texts on survey research and on interviewing practice tend to be replete with advice on how best to train interviewers. Such advice is typically directed at contexts in which a researcher hires an interviewer to conduct a large number or even all of the interviews. It also has considerable importance in research in which several interviewers (who may be either collaborators or hired interviewers) are involved in a study, since the risk of interviewer variability in the asking of questions needs to be avoided.

For many readers of this book who are planning to do research, such situations are unlikely to be relevant because they will be 'lone' researchers. You may be doing an undergraduate dissertation, or an exercise for a research methods course, or you may be a postgraduate conducting research for a Master's dissertation or for a thesis. Most people in such a situation will not have the luxury of being able to hire a researcher to do any interviewing (though you may be able to find someone to help you a little). When interviewing on your own, you must in a sense train yourself to follow the procedures and advice provided above. This is a very different situation from a large research institute or market research agency, which relies on an army of hired interviewers who carry out the interviews. Whenever people other than the lead researcher are involved in interviewing, they will need training and supervision in the following areas:

- contacting prospective respondents and providing an introduction to the study;
- reading out questions as written and following instructions in the interview schedule (for example, in connection with filter questions);
- using appropriate styles of probing;
- recording exactly what is said;
- maintaining an interview style that does not bias respondents' answers.

Fowler (1993) cites evidence that suggests that training of less than one full day rarely creates good interviewers.

Supervision of interviewers in relation to these issues can be achieved by:

- checking individual interviewers' response rates;
- tape-recording at least a sample of interviews;
- examining completed schedules to determine whether any questions are being left out or if they are being completed properly;
- call-backs on a sample of respondents (usually around 10 per cent) to determine whether they were interviewed and to ask about the interviewers' conduct.

Research in focus 9.1 provides an example of some of the ingredients of research involving multiple interviewers.

Research in focus 9.1
An example of research involving multiple interviewers

This example is taken from the study by Marshall et al. (1988) of social class in modern Britain (see Research in focus 8.1). The interviewing was carried out by a leading independent social research institute, Social and Community Planning Research (SCPR). The research aimed to achieve a sample of 2,000 respondents (1,770 was the number actually achieved; see Research in focus 8.1 for details of the sampling procedure).

> One hundred and twenty-three interviewers were employed on the survey. Six full-time briefing sessions were held, all of which were attended by a member of the Essex team, and interviewers were also given a full set of written instructions. The first three interviews conducted by each interviewer were subjected to an immediate thorough checking in order that critical comments, where appropriate, could be conveyed. During the course of fieldwork the work of interviewers was subject to personal recall. Ten per cent of issued addresses were re-issued for recall . . . In addition, 36 interviewers were accompanied in the field by supervisors.

(Marshall et al. 1988: 291)

Problems with structured interviewing

While the structured interview is a commonly used method of social research, certain problems associated with it have been identified over the years. These problems are not necessarily unique to the structured interview, in that they can sometimes be attributed to related methods, such as the self-administered questionnaire in survey research or even semi-structured interviewing in qualitative research. However, the structured interview is sometimes a focus for the identification of certain limitations, which are briefly examined below.

Characteristics of interviewers

There is evidence that interviewers' attributes can have an impact on respondents' replies, but, unfortunately, the literature on this issue does not lend itself to definitive generalizations. In large part, this ambiguity in the broader implications of experiments relating to the effects of interviewer characteristics is due to several problems, such as the problem of disentangling the effects of interviewers' different attributes from each other (race, gender, socio-economic status); the interaction between the characteristics of interviewers and the characteristics of respondents; and the interaction between any effects observed and the topic of the interview. Nonetheless, there is undoubtedly some evidence that effects due to characteristics of interviewers can be discerned.

The ethnicity of interviewers is one area that has attracted some attention. Schuman and Presser (1981) cite a study that asked respondents to nominate two or three of their favourite actors or entertainers. Respondents were much more likely to mention black actors or entertainers when interviewed by black interviewers than when interviewed by white ones. Schuman and Converse (1971) interviewed 619 black Detroiters shortly after Martin Luther King's assassination in 1969. The researchers found significant differences in the answers given between black and white interviewers in around one-quarter of the questions asked.

Although this proportion is quite disturbing, the fact that the majority of questions appear to have been largely unaffected does not give rise to a great deal of confidence that a consistent biasing factor is being uncovered. Similarly inconclusive findings tend to occur in relation to experiments with other sets of characteristics of interviewers. These remarks are not meant to play down the potential significance of interviewers' characteristics for measurement error, but to call attention to the limitations of drawing conclusive inferences about the evidence. All that needs to be registered at this juncture is that almost certainly the characteristics of interviewers have an impact on respondents' replies but that the extent and nature of the impact are unclear and likely to vary from context to context.

Response sets

Some writers have suggested that the structured interview is particularly prone to the operation among respondents of what Webb et al. (1966: 19) call 'response sets', which they define as 'irrelevant but lawful sources of variance'. This form of response bias is especially relevant to multiple-indicator measures (see Chapter 7), where respondents reply to a battery of related questions or items, of the kind found in a Likert scale (see Key concept 7.2). The idea of a response set implies that people respond to the series of questions in a consistent way but one that is irrelevant to the concept being measured. Two of the most prominent types of response set are known as 'acquiescence' (also known as 'yeasaying' and 'naysaying') and **social desirability** bias.

Acquiescence

Acquiescence refers to a tendency for some people consistently to agree or disagree with a set of questions or items. To illustrate this point, consider the study in Research in focus 7.5, which describes how a measure of organizational climate was validated. The measure was made up of seventeen underlying scales. One of these is 'Clarity of Organizational Goals', which is made up of five Likert items with respondents being asked to indicate the degree to which the statement is true or false. Imagine someone who replies 'Definitely true' to all five items. Four of the five items are in a positive direction so that indicating that these statements are definitely true would imply clarity of organizational goals (for example, 'People have a good understanding of what the organization is trying to do'). However, one of the five items is 'People aren't clear about the aims of the company'. If a respondent ticks 'Definitely true' to this item, he or she is implying an *absence* of clarity of organizational goals. So, if the respondent answers 'Definitely true' to all five items, we may be concerned that the answer to 'People aren't clear about the aims of the company' is inconsistent with the four other answers. One of the reasons why researchers who employ this kind of multiple-item measure use wordings that imply opposite stances (that is, some items implying a high level of clarity and others implying a low level of clarity) is to weed out those respondents who appear to be replying within the framework of an acquiescence response set.

Acquiescence is a form of satisficing behaviour in surveys (see Key concept 9.3).

Social desirability bias

The social desirability effect refers to evidence that some respondents' answers to questions are related to their perception of the social desirability of those answers. An answer that is perceived to be socially desirable is more likely to be endorsed than one that is not. This means that socially desirable forms of behaviour or attitudes tend to be over-reported and undesirable forms are under-reported. There is also evidence that the use of sensitive questions which are often the context within which socially desirable responding occurs can result in poorer response rates and item non-response (refusal to answer particular questions) (Tourangeau and Yan 2007). There are several strategies for checking and reducing the risk of socially desirable responding. One is not to use interviewers: there is some evidence that self-administered forms of answering are less prone to the problem, especially when the self-administration entails the mediation of a computer, as in computer-administered self-interviewing (Tourangeau and Yan 2007; Yeager et al. 2011). The other is to soften the asking of questions likely to produce social desirability bias. For example, Sudman and Bradburn (1982: 75) suggest question wording strategies such as 'Everybody does it'. An example might be: 'Even the calmest of car drivers occasionally loses their temper with inconsiderate motorists. Has this happened to you in the last month?'

In so far as these forms of response error go undetected, they represent sources of error in the measurement of concepts. However, it is important not to get carried away with such findings. We cannot be sure how prevalent these effects are, and to some extent awareness of them has led to measures to limit their impact on data (for example, by weeding out cases obviously affected by them or by instructing interviewers to limit the possible impact of the social desirability effect by not becoming overly friendly with respondents and by not being judgemental about their replies).

The problem of meaning

A critique of survey interview data and findings gleaned from similar techniques was developed by social scientists influenced by phenomenological and other interpretivist ideas of the kinds touched on in Chapter 2 (Cicourel 1964, 1982; Filmer et al. 1972; Briggs 1986; Mishler 1986). This critique revolves around what is often referred to in a shorthand way as the 'problem of meaning'. The kernel of the argument is that when humans communicate they do so in a way that not only draws on commonly held meanings but also simultaneously creates meanings. 'Meaning' in this sense is something that is worked at and achieved—it is not simply pre-given. Allusions to the problem of meaning in structured interviewing draw attention to the notion that survey researchers presume that interviewer and respondent share the same meanings of terms employed in the interview questions and answers. In fact, the problem of meaning implies that the possibility that interviewer and respondent may not be sharing the same meaning systems and hence imply different things in their use of words is simply sidestepped in structured interview research. The problem of meaning is resolved by ignoring it.

The feminist critique

The feminist critique of structured interviewing is difficult to disentangle from the critique launched against quantitative research in general, which was briefly outlined in Chapter 2. However, for many feminist social researchers the structured interview symbolizes more readily than other methods the limitations of quantitative research, partly because of its prevalence but also partly because of its nature. By 'its nature' is meant the fact that the structured interview epitomizes the asymmetrical relationship between researcher and subject that is seen as an ingredient of quantitative research: the researcher extracts information from the research subject and gives nothing in return. For example, standard textbook advice of the kind provided in this chapter implies that rapport is useful to the interviewer but he or she should guard against becoming too familiar. This means that questions asked by respondents (for example, about the research or about the topic of the research) should be politely but firmly rebuffed on the grounds that too much familiarity should be avoided and because the respondents' subsequent answers may be biased.

This is perfectly valid and appropriate advice from the vantage point of the canons of structured interviewing, with its quest for standardization and for valid and reliable data. However, from the perspective of feminism, when women interview women a wedge is hammered between them that, in conjunction with the implication of a hierarchical relationship between the interviewer and respondent, is incompatible with feminist values. An impression of exploitation is created, but exploitation of women is precisely what feminist social science seeks to fight against. Oakley (1981) found in her research on childbirth that she was frequently asked questions by her respondents. It was these questions that typified the problems of being a feminist interviewing women.

The dilemma of a feminist interviewer interviewing women could be summarised by considering the practical application of some of the strategies recommended in the textbooks for meeting interviewees' questions.

For example, these advise that such questions as 'Which hole does the baby come out of?' 'Does an epidural ever paralyse women?' and 'Why is it dangerous to leave a small baby alone in the house?' should be met with such responses from the interviewer as 'I guess I haven't thought enough about it to give a good answer right now', or 'a head-shaking gesture which suggests "that's a hard one" ' (Goode and Hatt [1952: 198]).

(Oakley 1981: 48)

Such advice still appears in textbooks concerned with survey research. For example, Groves et al. (2009: 305) supply the following advice:

1. Interviewers should refrain from expressing views or opinions on the topics covered by the survey instrument.

2. Interviewers should refrain from presenting any personal information that might provide a bias for inferring what their preferences or values might be that are relevant to the content of the interview.

3. Although a little informal chatting about neutral topics, such as the weather or pets, may help to free up communication, for the most part, interviewers should focus on the task.

This is in fact good advice from the point of view of reducing error that might arise from the interviewer influencing or biasing the interviewee's replies. As such, it is likely to reduce error arising from the influence of the interviewer.

Oakley's point is that to act according to such canons of textbook practice would be irresponsible for a feminist in such a situation. It was this kind of critique of structured interviewing and indeed of quantitative research in general that ushered in a period in which a great many feminist social researchers found qualitative research more compatible with their goals and norms. In terms of interviewing, this trend resulted in a preference for such forms of interviewing as unstructured and semi-structured interviewing and focus groups. These will be the focus of later chapters. However, as noted in Chapter 2, there has been some softening of attitudes towards the role of quantitative research among feminist researchers. For example, Walby and Myhill (2001) have shown how surveys of violence against women that are dedicated to uncovering such violence (rather than general crime surveys such as the BCS) reveal higher levels of violence than are often thought to occur. By paying greater attention to issues such as greater privacy in the interview and special training in sensitive interviewing, dedicated surveys in some countries have proved highly instructive about the causes and incidence of violence against women. Such research, which is based on structured interviewing, would not seem to be inconsistent with the goals of most feminist researchers and indeed may be of considerable significance for many women. Nonetheless, there is still a tendency for qualitative research to remain the preferred research strategy for many feminist researchers.

 ## Key points

- The structured interview is a research instrument that is used to standardize the asking and often the recording of answers in order to keep interviewer-related error to a minimum.

- The structured interview can be administered in person or over the telephone.

- Computer-assisted interviewing is growing in use in social research.

- Telephone interviews can be carried out using landlines or mobile telephones, and Skype can also be used.

- It is important to keep to the wording and order of questions when conducting survey research by structured interview.

- While there is some evidence that interviewers' characteristics can influence respondents' replies, the findings of experiments on this issue are somewhat equivocal.

- Response sets can be damaging to data derived from structured interviews and steps need to be taken to identify respondents exhibiting them.

- The structured interview symbolizes the characteristics of quantitative research that feminist researchers find distasteful: in particular, the lack of reciprocity and the taint of exploitation.

Questions for review

The structured interview

- Why is it important in interviewing for survey research to keep interviewer variability to a minimum?
- How successful is the structured interview in reducing interviewer variability?
- Why might a survey researcher prefer to use a structured rather than an unstructured interview approach for gathering data?
- Why do structured interview schedules typically include mainly closed-ended questions?

Interview contexts

- Are there any circumstances in which it might be preferable to conduct structured interviews with more than one interviewer present?
- 'Given the lower cost of telephone interviewing compared to face-to-face interviews, the former is generally preferable.' Discuss.
- 'The main reason for choosing computer-assisted interviewing over paper-and-pencil interviews is the greater ease with which filter questions can be asked and answered'. Discuss.
- What might be the principal reasons for choosing to interview members of a sample by mobile telephone rather than by landline telephone?

Conducting interviews

- Prepare an opening statement for a study of manual workers in a firm, to which access has already been achieved.
- To what extent is rapport an important ingredient of structured interviewing?
- How strong is the evidence that question order can significantly affect answers?
- How strong is the evidence that interviewers' characteristics can significantly affect answers?
- What is the difference between probing and prompting? How important are they and what dangers are lurking with their use?

Problems with structured interviewing

- What are response sets and why are they potentially important?
- What are the main issues that lie behind the critique of structured interviewing by feminist researchers?

 ### Online Resource Centre
www.oxfordtextbooks.co.uk/orc/brymansrm5e/

Visit the Online Resource Centre to enrich your understanding of structured interviewing. Follow up links to other resources, test yourself using multiple choice questions, and gain further guidance and inspiration from the Student Researcher's Toolkit.

10

Self-administered questionnaires

Chapter outline

Chapter guide

Questionnaires that are completed by respondents themselves are one of the main instruments for gathering data using a survey design, along with the structured interview that was covered in the previous chapter. Until the Internet became a platform for administering questionnaires, probably the most common form was the mail or postal questionnaire. The term 'self-administered questionnaire' is often preferred because it is somewhat more inclusive than 'postal questionnaire' as not all questionnaires are mailed. This chapter explores:

- the advantages and disadvantages of the questionnaire in comparison to the structured interview;

- how to address the potential problem of poor response rates, which is often a feature of the postal questionnaire;

- how questionnaires should be designed in order to make answering easier for respondents and less prone to error;
- online surveys and the possibilities of mixing modes of survey administration;
- the use of diaries as a form of self-administered questionnaire;
- experience and event sampling.

Introduction

In a very real sense, the bulk of the previous chapter was about questionnaires. The structured interview is in many respects a questionnaire that is administered by an interviewer. However, there is a tendency, which borders on a convention, to reserve the term 'questionnaire' for contexts in which a succession of usually closed-ended questions is completed by respondents themselves.

 ## Self-administered questionnaire or postal questionnaire?

The **self-administered questionnaire** is sometimes referred to as a *self-completion questionnaire*. The former term will be followed in this book. With a self-administered questionnaire, respondents answer questions by completing the questionnaire themselves. As a method, the self-administered questionnaire can come in several different forms. Probably the most prominent of these forms is the **postal** or **mail questionnaire**, whereby a questionnaire is sent through the post to the respondent. The latter, following completion of the instrument, is usually asked to return it by post; an alternative form of return is when respondents are requested to deposit their completed questionnaires in a certain location, such as a box in a school common room or in a supervisor's office in a firm. 'Postal' is used rather than mail to distinguish questionnaires that are sent out through the postal system from email questionnaires. The term 'self-administered questionnaire' also covers other forms of administration, such as when a researcher hands out questionnaires to all students in a class and collects them back after they have been completed. For example, Smith and McVie (2003) describe their use of such an instrument for their longitudinal cohort study of crime in relation to transformations during youth and adolescent development among a large sample of young people in Edinburgh. They write:

> In general, questionnaires were completed by a whole class under the supervision of one or two researchers. . . . Desks were spaced out as much as possible, and in most cases questionnaires were completed in exam-like conditions, with talking strongly discouraged, and little or no overlooking of others' questionnaires.
> (Smith and McVie 2003: 183)

In this case, we can see that the questionnaire is self-administered but is neither sent out nor returned through the postal system. This might be described as a 'supervised self-administered questionnaire'. 'Self-administered questionnaire' is, therefore, a more inclusive term than 'postal questionnaire'.

In this chapter, when points apply to more or less all forms of self-administered questionnaire, this term will be employed. When points apply specifically or exclusively to questionnaires sent through the post, the term 'postal questionnaire' will be used.

 ## Evaluating the self-administered questionnaire in relation to the structured interview

The self-administered questionnaire and the structured interview are very similar methods of social research. The obvious difference between them is that, with the self-administered questionnaire, there is no interviewer to ask the questions; instead, respondents must read each question themselves and answer the questions themselves. Beyond this obvious, but central, difference, they are remarkably similar. However, because there is no interviewer in the administration of the self-administered questionnaire, the research instrument has to be especially easy to follow and its questions have to be particularly easy to answer. After all, respondents cannot be trained in the way interviewers can be; nor do they know their way around a research instrument in the way a 'lone researcher' might.

As a result, self-administered questionnaires, as compared to structured interviews, tend to:

- have fewer open-ended questions, since closed-ended ones tend to be easier to answer;

- have easy-to-follow designs to minimize the risk that the respondent will fail to follow instructions for such things as filter questions or will inadvertently omit questions;

- be shorter, in order to reduce the likelihood of 'respondent fatigue': it is manifestly easier for a respondent who becomes tired of answering questions in a long questionnaire to consign it to a waste paper bin than it is for a respondent to terminate an interview.

Advantages of the self-administered questionnaire over the structured interview

Cheaper to administer

Interviewing can be expensive. The cheapness of the self-administered questionnaire is especially advantageous if you have a sample that is geographically dispersed. When this is the case, a postal questionnaire will be much cheaper, because of the time and cost of travel for interviewers. This advantage is obviously less pronounced in connection with telephone interviews, because of the lower costs of telephone charges relative to travel and time spent travelling. But, even in comparison to telephone interviewing, the postal questionnaire enjoys cost advantages.

Quicker to administer

Self-administered questionnaires can be sent out through the post or otherwise distributed in very large quantities at the same time. A thousand questionnaires can be sent out through the post in one batch, but, even with a team of interviewers, it would take a long time to conduct personal interviews with a sample of that size. However, it is important to bear in mind that the questionnaires may take several weeks to be returned. Also, it is invariably necessary to send out reminder letters and/or questionnaires to those who fail to return them initially.

Absence of interviewer effects

It was noted in Chapter 9 that various studies have demonstrated that characteristics of interviewers (and respondents) may affect the answers that people give. While the implications of this research are somewhat ambiguous, it has been suggested that characteristics such as ethnicity, gender, and the social background of interviewers may combine to bias the answers that respondents provide. Obviously, since there is no interviewer present when a self-administered questionnaire is being completed, interviewer effects are eliminated (see Research in focus 10.1). However, this advantage probably has to be regarded fairly cautiously, since few consistent patterns have emerged over the years from research to suggest what kinds of interviewer characteristics bias answers.

Probably of greater importance to the presence of an interviewer is the tendency for people to be more likely to exhibit social desirability bias when an interviewer is present. Research by Sudman and Bradburn (1982) suggests that postal questionnaires work better than personal interviews when a question carries the possibility of such bias. There is also a tendency for respondents to under-report activities that induce anxiety or about which they are sensitive. Research summarized by Tourangeau and Smith (1996) strongly suggests that respondents tend to report more drug use and alcohol consumption and a higher number of sexual partners and of abortions in self-administered questionnaires than in structured interviews.

The superiority of the self-administered questionnaire over the interview is also evident when questionnaires are administered via the Web. Tourangeau et al. (2013) carried out a meta-analysis (see Chapter 14) of studies that compared telephone interviews with equivalent Web-administered questionnaires. They found a greater propensity to report sensitive information in Web-administered questionnaires, implying that these may be less prone to social desirability bias than interviews.

No interviewer variability

Self-administered questionnaires do not suffer from the problem of interviewers asking questions in a different order or in different ways.

Convenience for respondents

Self-administered questionnaires are more convenient for respondents, because they can complete a questionnaire when they want and at the speed that they want to go.

Research in focus 10.1
Face-to-face interview or postal questionnaire: which is better at getting at the truth?

Preisendörfer and Wolter (2014) compared interviews and postal questionnaires in terms of which was more likely to get people to admit to having been convicted of a crime. The authors carried out two surveys: one using a face-to-face interview and the other a postal questionnaire. The two survey instruments were administered to addresses that related to people who had been identified as having been convicted of a criminal offence some years before the survey was carried out. The crimes were mainly minor offences. In the case of both surveys, the question about criminality was one of many questions and was phrased as follows:

> Have you ever—by penalty order or in a court case—been convicted under criminal law of a minor or more serious offense? By 'convicted under criminal law' we mean that the issue was handled by a public prosecutor.

> (Preisendörfer and Wolter 2014: 138)

Sixty-three per cent of the sample answered truthfully, but postal questionnaire respondents were more likely to be truthful than interviewees (67 per cent versus 58 per cent). This finding suggests that a self-administered questionnaire sent through the post may produce less socially desirable responding than an equivalent face-to-face interview. This study, which is an interesting case of testing for concurrent validity, also produced a fascinating finding, namely, that postal questionnaire respondents who returned their questionnaires fairly quickly produced more accurate answers than those who returned them late and after reminders. As the authors note, there is a growing debate among survey researchers about whether a high response rate is *necessarily* superior to a lower one in terms of producing high-quality data. Fricker and Tourangeau (2010), for example, have shown that the effort that often goes into reducing non-response can result in poorer quality data. Thus, Preisendörfer and Wolter's research contributes to an emerging debate about the relationship between response rates and data quality.

Disadvantages of the self-administered questionnaire in comparison with the structured interview

Cannot prompt

There is no one present to help respondents if they are having difficulty answering a question. It is always important to ensure that the questions that are asked are clear and unambiguous, but this is especially so with the self-administered questionnaire, since there is no interviewer to help respondents with questions they find difficult to understand and hence to answer. Also, great attention must be paid to ensure that the questionnaire is easy to complete; otherwise questions will be inadvertently omitted if instructions are unclear.

Cannot probe

There is no opportunity to probe respondents to elaborate an answer. Probing can be very important when open-ended questions are being asked. Interviewers are often trained to use probing to get more from respondents.

However, this problem largely applies to open-ended questions, which are not used a great deal in surveys by self-administered questionnaire.

Cannot ask many questions that are not salient to respondents

Questionnaire respondents are more likely than respondents in interviews to become tired of answering questions that are not very salient to them and that they perceive as boring. Because of the risk of a questionnaire being consigned to a waste paper bin, it is important to avoid including many questions that are likely to be non-salient in a self-administered questionnaire. When a research issue *is* likely to be salient to the respondent, a high response rate is feasible (Altschuld and Lower 1984). This means that, when questions are likely to be salient, the self-administered questionnaire may be a good choice for researchers, especially when the much lower cost is borne in mind.

Difficulty of asking other kinds of question

In addition to ensuring that you do not ask too many questions that are not salient to respondents, as previously suggested, it is also important to avoid asking more than a very small number of open-ended questions (because respondents frequently do not want to write a lot). Questions with complex structures, such as filters, should be avoided as far as possible (because respondents often find them difficult to follow).

Questionnaire can be read as a whole

Respondents are able to read the whole questionnaire before answering the first question. When this occurs, none of the questions asked is truly independent of the others. It also means that you cannot be sure that questions have been answered in the correct order. Also, the problem of question order effects (see Chapter 9) may arise. When the questionnaire is being answered in the context of a **Web survey**, it is possible to ensure that the respondent can view only a small number of questions at a time.

Do not know who answers

With postal questionnaires, you can never be sure whether the right person has answered the questionnaire. If a questionnaire is sent to a certain person in a household, it may be that someone else in that household completes the questionnaire. It is also impossible to have any control over the involvement of non-respondents (such as other members of a household) in the answering of questions. Similarly, if a questionnaire is sent to a manager in a firm, the task may simply be delegated to someone else. This advantage of the structured interview over the postal questionnaire does not apply when the former is administered by telephone, since the same problem applies. When a self-administered questionnaire is administered online (see the section below on 'Online social surveys'), there is the same problem of not knowing whether the right person has replied. Olson and Smyth (2014) examined a household survey in the United States and found that 18 per cent of respondents were not the ones who were supposed to have completed the questionnaire. There was a survey mode effect: 18.1 per cent of those households that received a postal questionnaire selected the wrong person, as against 20.3 per cent of households that answered via the Web. In addition, among those households that were supposed to deal with the questionnaire online but then were followed up by post, 14.4 per cent selected the wrong person, whereas among households contacted by post and then followed up online the corresponding figure was 20.4 per cent. The reasons for the wrong person answering the questionnaire were not necessarily to do with a deliberate subversion of the process; there may have been confusion about who was the correct person to nominate.

Cannot collect additional data

With a personal interview, interviewers might be asked to collect snippets of information about the home, school, firm, or whatever. This is not going to be possible in connection with a postal questionnaire, but if self-administered questionnaires are handed out in a school or firm, it is more feasible to collect such additional data.

Difficult to ask a lot of questions

As signalled above, because of the possibility of 'respondent fatigue', long questionnaires are rarely feasible. They may even result in a greater tendency for questionnaires not to be answered in the first place, since they can be offputting.

Not appropriate for some kinds of respondent

Respondents whose literacy is limited or whose facility with English is restricted will not be able to answer the questionnaire. The second of these difficulties cannot be entirely overcome when interviews are being employed, but the difficulties are likely to be greater with postal questionnaires.

Greater risk of missing data

Partially answered questionnaires are more likely, because of a lack of prompting or supervision, than in interviews. It is also easier for respondents actively to decide not to answer a question when on their own than when being asked by an interviewer. For example, questions that appear boring or irrelevant to the respondent may be especially likely to be skipped. If questions are not answered, this creates a problem of **missing data** for the variables that are created.

Lower response rates

One of the most damaging limitations is that surveys by postal questionnaire typically result in lower response rates (see Key concept 8.2) than comparable interview-based studies. The significance of a response rate is that, unless it can be proven that those who do not participate do not differ from those who do, there is likely to be the risk of bias. In other words, if, as is likely, there are differences between participants and refusals, it is probable that the findings relating to the sample will be affected. If a response rate is low, it is likely that the risk of bias in the findings will be greater.

Mangione (1995: 60–1) has provided the following classification of bands of response rate to postal questionnaires:

over 85%	excellent
70–85%	very good
60–69%	acceptable
50–59%	barely acceptable
below 50%	not acceptable

Tips and skills
Response rates

Response rates are important because the lower the response rate, the more questions are likely to be raised about the representativeness of the achieved sample. In a sense, this is likely to be an issue only with randomly selected samples. Postal questionnaire surveys in particular are often associated with low response rates, and, as Mangione's classification illustrates, according to some authorities a response rate of below 50 per cent is not acceptable. However, many published articles report the results of studies that are well below this level. In an examination of published studies in the field of organizational research in the years 1979–83, Mitchell (1985) found a range of response rates of 30–94 per cent. Therefore, if you achieve a low response rate, do not despair. Although such writers as Mangione (1995) regard response rates of 30 per cent as unacceptable, a great deal of published research achieves low response rates. The key point is to recognize and acknowledge the implications of the possible limitations of a low response rate. On the other hand, if your research is based on a convenience sample, ironically it could be argued that a low response rate is less significant. Many students find postal and other forms of self-administered questionnaire attractive because of their low cost and quick administration. The point of this discussion is that you should not be put off using such techniques because of the prospect of a low response rate.

Steps to improve response rates to postal questionnaires

Because of the tendency for postal questionnaire surveys to generate lower response rates than comparable structured interview surveys (and the implications this has for the external validity of findings), a great deal of thought and research has gone into ways of improving survey response. The following steps are frequently suggested.

- Write a good covering letter explaining the reasons for the research, why it is important, and why the recipient has been selected; mention sponsorship if any, and provide guarantees of confidentiality. The advice provided in Tips and skills 'Topics and issues to include in an introductory statement' (see Chapter 9) in connection with the kind of letter that might go out in advance of a respondent being asked to be interviewed can be followed to good effect.

- Postal questionnaires should always be accompanied by a stamped addressed envelope or, at the very least, return postage.

- Follow up individuals who do not reply at first, possibly with two or three further mailings. The importance of reminders cannot be overstated—they do work. My preferred approach has been to send out a reminder letter to non-respondents two weeks after the initial mailing, reasserting the nature and aims of the survey and suggesting that the person should contact a member of the research team or me to obtain a replacement copy of the questionnaire if the original one has been lost. Then, two weeks after that, all further non-respondents should be sent another letter along with a further copy of the questionnaire. These reminders have a demonstrable effect on the response rate. Some writers argue for further mailings of reminder letters to non-respondents. If a response rate is worryingly low, such further mailings would certainly be advisable.

- Unsurprisingly, shorter questionnaires tend to achieve better response rates than longer ones. However, this is not a clear-cut principle, because it is difficult to specify when a questionnaire becomes 'too long'. Also, the evidence suggests that the effect of the length of questionnaires on response rates cannot be separated very easily from the salience of the topic of the research for respondents and from the nature of the sample. Respondents may be highly tolerant of questionnaires that contain many questions on topics that interest them. Questionnaires measuring life satisfaction can result in response rates as high as 98 per cent (Diener, Inglehart, and Tay 2013).

- Clear instructions and an attractive layout improve postal questionnaire response rates. Dillman, Smyth, and Christian (2014) recommend darker and/or larger print for questions and lighter and/or smaller print for closed-ended answers. However, as well as attending to the aesthetics of the questionnaire, it is also crucial to ensure that there is consistency in the use of font types and embellishments. For example, if you use a larger print for questions, make sure you do that for all questions and that you do not use larger print for other elements of the questionnaire.

- Do not allow the questionnaire to appear unnecessarily bulky. Dillman et al. (2014) recommend printing the questionnaire in a booklet format or using the photocopier to reduce the size of the questionnaire to fit the booklet format. This format also gives the impression of a more professional approach.

- As with structured interviewing (see Chapter 9), begin with questions that are more likely to interest respondents. This advice is linked to the issue of salience, as discussed above, but has particular significance in the context of research that may have limited salience for the respondent.

- There is some disagreement about how much difference it makes to response rates when the researcher personalizes covering letters, by including the respondent's name and address, but Dillman et al. (2014) advocate that these details are supplied on covering letters and that each is individually signed.

- I am inclined to the view that, in general, postal questionnaires should comprise as few open-ended questions as possible, since people are often deterred by the prospect of having to write a lot of text. In fact, many writers on the subject recommend that open-ended questions are used as little as possible in self-administered questionnaires. However, I am not convinced that this suggestion applies equally to questionnaires that are completed online (see the section below on 'Online social surveys').

- Providing monetary incentives increases the response rate. These are more effective if the money comes with the questionnaire rather than if it is promised once the questionnaire has been returned. Apparently, respondents typically do not cynically take the money and discard the questionnaire! The evidence also suggests that quite small amounts of money have a positive impact on the response rate, but that larger amounts do not necessarily improve the response rate any further.

 # Designing the self-administered questionnaire

Do not cramp the presentation

Because of the well-known problem of low response rates to the postal questionnaire in particular, it is sometimes considered preferable to make the instrument appear as short as possible in order for it to be less likely to deter prospective respondents from answering. However, this is usually a mistake. As Dillman et al. (2014) observe, an attractive layout is likely to enhance response rates, whereas the kinds of tactics that are sometimes employed to make a questionnaire appear shorter than it really is—such as reducing margins and the space between questions—make it look cramped and therefore unattractive. Also, if questions are too close together, there is a risk they will be accidentally omitted, creating the problem referred to as 'item non-response' which results in missing data.

This is not to say that you should be ridiculously liberal in your use of space, as this does not necessarily provide for an attractive format either and may risk making the questionnaire look bulky. As with so many other issues in social research, a steady course needs to be steered between possible extremes.

Clear presentation

Far more important than making a self-administered questionnaire appear shorter than is the case is to make sure that its layout is easy on the eye, as Dillman et al. (2014) emphasize, and that it facilitates the answering of all questions that are relevant to the respondent. The recommendation of darker and/or larger print for questions and lighter and/or smaller print for closed-ended answers by Dillman et al. is an example of one consideration, but at the very least a variety of print styles (for example, different fonts, print sizes, bold, italics, and capitals) can enhance the appearance *but must be used in a consistent manner*. This last point means that you should ensure that you use one style for general instructions, one for headings, perhaps one for specific instructions (like 'Go to question 7'), one for questions, and one for closed-ended answers. Mixing print styles, so that one style is sometimes used for both general instructions and questions, can be very confusing for respondents.

Vertical or horizontal closed-ended answers?

Bearing in mind that most questions in a self-administered questionnaire are likely to be of the closed-ended kind, one consideration is whether to arrange the fixed answers vertically or horizontally. Very often, the nature of the answers will dictate a vertical arrangement because of their sheer length. Many writers prefer a vertical format whenever possible, because, in some cases where either arrangement is feasible, confusion can arise when a horizontal one is employed (Sudman and Bradburn 1982). Consider the following:

> What do you think of the Prime Minister's performance in his job since he took office?
> (*Please tick the appropriate response*)
>
> Very _____ Good _____ Fair _____ Poor _____ Very _____
> good   poor

There is a risk that, if the questionnaire is being answered in haste, the required tick will be placed in the wrong space—for example, indicating Good when Fair was the intended response. Also, a vertical format more clearly distinguishes questions from answers. To some extent, these potential problems can be removed through the sensible use of spacing and print variation, but they represent significant considerations. A further reason why vertical alignments can be superior is that they are probably easier to **code**, especially when pre-codes appear on the questionnaire. Very often, self-administered questionnaires are arranged so that to the right of each question are two columns: one for the column in which data relating to the question will appear in a data matrix; the other for all the pre-codes. The latter allows the appropriate code to be assigned to a respondent's answer by circling it for later entry into the computer. Thus, the choice would be between the formats presented in Tips and skills 'Closed-ended question with a horizontal format' and Tips and skills 'Closed-ended question with a vertical format'. In the second case, not only is there less ambiguity about where a tick is to be placed; the task of coding is easier. However, when there is to be a battery of questions with identical answer formats, as in a Likert scale, a vertical format will take up too much space. One way of dealing with this kind of questioning is to use abbreviations with an accompanying explanation. An example can be found in Tips and skills 'Formatting a Likert scale'.

Identifying response sets in a Likert scale

One of the advantages of using closed-ended questions is that they can be pre-coded, thus turning the processing of data for computer analysis into a fairly simple task (see Chapter 11 for more on this). However, some thought has to go into the scoring of the items of the kind presented in Tips and skills 'Formatting a Likert scale'. We might, for example, score question 23 as follows:

> Strongly agree = 5
>
> Agree = 4
>
> Undecided = 3
>
> Disagree = 2
>
> Strongly disagree = 1

Tips and skills
Closed-ended question with a horizontal format

What do you think of the Prime Minister's performance in his job since he took office?
(*Please tick the appropriate response*)

Very good _____ Good _____ Fair _____ Poor _____ Very poor _____ 5 4 3 2 1

Tips and skills
Closed-ended question with a vertical format

What do you think of the Prime Minister's performance in his job since he took office?
(*Please tick the appropriate response*)

Very good	_____	5
Good	_____	4
Fair	_____	3
Poor	_____	2
Very poor	_____	1

Tips and skills
Formatting a Likert scale

In the next set of questions, you are presented with a statement. You are being asked to indicate your level of agreement or disagreement with each statement by indicating whether you: Strongly Agree (SA), Agree (A), are Undecided (U), Disagree (D), or Strongly Disagree (SD).
(*Please indicate your level of agreement by circling the appropriate response*)

23. My job is like a hobby to me.
    SA   A   U   D   SD

24. My job is usually interesting enough to keep me from getting bored.
    SA   A   U   D   SD

25. It seems that my friends are more interested in their jobs.
    SA   A   U   D   SD

26. I enjoy my work more than my leisure time.
    SA   A   U   D   SD

These four items are taken from an eighteen-item Likert scale designed to measure job satisfaction (Brayfield and Rothe 1951).

Accordingly, a high score for the item (5 or 4) indicates satisfaction with the job and a low score (1 or 2) indicates low job satisfaction. The same applies to question 24. However, when we come to question 25, the picture is different. Here, agreement indicates a *lack* of job satisfaction. It is disagreement that is indicative of job satisfaction. We would have to reverse the coding of this item, so that:

   Strongly agree = 1

   Agree = 2

   Undecided = 3

   Disagree = 4

   Strongly disagree = 5

The point of including such items is to identify people who exhibit response sets, such as acquiescence (see Chapter 9). If someone were to agree with all eighteen items, when some of them indicated *lack* of job satisfaction, it is likely that the respondent is affected by a response set, and the answers are unlikely to provide a valid assessment of job satisfaction for that person. Another approach is to use 'distracter items'. Thomson and Phua (2012) developed a short version of the Brayfield-Rothe index of job satisfaction which they call the Brief Index of Affective Job Satisfaction. This index comprises just four of the eighteen items used in the original scale. All four items are positive, in the sense that agreement with all of them implies job satisfaction. This would seem to leave the

Brief Index vulnerable to response sets. However, the authors inserted three distracter items between the four Brief Index items: 'My job is unusual'; 'My job needs me to be fit'; and 'My job is time-consuming'. These distracter items act as what the authors call 'red herrings' that help to identify response set problems, like acquiescence.

Clear instructions about how to respond

Always be clear about how you want respondents to indicate their replies when answering closed-ended questions. Are they supposed to place a tick by or circle or underline the appropriate answer, or are they supposed to delete inappropriate answers? Also, in many cases it is feasible for the respondent to choose more than one answer—is this acceptable to you? If it is not, you should indicate this in your instructions, for example:

(*Please choose the one answer that best represents your views by placing a tick in the appropriate box.*)

If you do not make this clear and if some respondents choose more than one answer, you will have to treat their replies as if they had not answered. This possibility increases the risk of missing data from some respondents. If it is acceptable to you for more than one category to be chosen, you need to make this clear, for example:

(*Please choose all answers that represent your views by placing a tick in the appropriate boxes.*)

It is a common error for such instructions to be omitted and for respondents either to be unsure about how to reply or to make inappropriate selections.

Keep question and answers together

This is a simple and obvious, though often transgressed, requirement—namely, that you should never split a question so that it appears on two separate pages. A common error is to have some space left at the bottom of a page into which the question can be slotted but for the closed-ended answers to appear on the next page. Doing so increases the risk of the respondent forgetting to answer the question or providing an answer in the wrong group of closed-ended answers (a problem that is especially likely when a series of questions with a common answer format is being used, as with a Likert scale).

 # Online social surveys

There has been a massive growth in the online administration of surveys. There is a crucial distinction between surveys administered by email (email surveys) and surveys administered via the Web (Web surveys). In the case of the former, the questionnaire is sent via email to a respondent, whereas, with a Web survey, the respondent is directed to a website in order to answer a questionnaire. The Web survey has increasingly become the preferred choice largely because of the growing availability of software platforms for the design of questionnaires. They have also come to occupy a significant role in **mixed mode surveys**, which combine more than one mode of administration of a survey instrument and which were touched on in Chapter 9.

Email surveys

It is important to distinguish between **embedded** and **attached email questionnaire surveys**. In the case of the embedded questionnaire, the questions are to be found in the body of the email. There may be an introduction to the questionnaire followed by some marking that partitions the introduction from the questionnaire itself. Respondents have to indicate their replies using simple notations, such as an 'x', or they may be asked to delete alternatives that do not apply. If questions are open, they are asked to type in their answers. They then simply need to select the reply button to return their completed questionnaires to the researcher. With an attached questionnaire, the questionnaire arrives as an attachment to an email that introduces it. As with the embedded questionnaire, respondents must select and/or type their answers. To return the questionnaire, it must be attached to a reply email, although respondents may also be given the opportunity to fax or send the completed questionnaire by postal mail to the researcher (Sheehan and Hoy 1999).

The chief advantage of the embedded questionnaire is that it is easier for the respondent to return to the researcher and requires less computer expertise. Knowing how to read and then return an attachment requires some facility with handling online communication that is still not universally applicable. Also, the recipients' operating systems or software may present problems with reading attachments, while many respondents may refuse to open the attachment because of concerns about a virus. On the other hand, the limited formatting that is possible with most email software, such as using bold, variations in font size, indenting, and other features, makes the appearance of embedded questionnaires dull and featureless, although this limitation is rapidly changing. Furthermore, it is slightly easier for the respondent to type material into an attachment that uses well-known software such as Microsoft Word, since, if the questionnaire is embedded in an email, the alignment of questions and answers may be lost.

Dommeyer and Moriarty (2000) compared the two forms of email survey in connection with an attitude study. The attached questionnaire was given a much wider range of embellishments in terms of appearance than was possible with the embedded one. Before conducting the survey, undergraduate students were asked about the relative appearance of the two formats. The attached questionnaire was considered to be better looking, easier to complete, clearer in appearance, and better organized. The two formats were then administered to two random samples of students, all of whom were active email-users. The researchers found a much higher response rate with the embedded than with the attached questionnaire (37 per cent versus 8 per cent), but there was little difference in terms of speed of response or whether questions were more likely to be omitted with one format rather than the other. Although Dommeyer and Moriarty (2000: 48) conclude that 'the attached e-mail survey presents too many obstacles to the potential respondent', this study was conducted during early days in the life of online surveys. It may be that, as prospective respondents become more adept at using online communication methods and as viruses become less of a threat (for example, as virus-checking software improves in terms of accessibility and cost), the concerns that led to the lower response rate for the attached questionnaire will be less pronounced. Also, the researchers do not appear to have established a prior contact with the students before sending out the questionnaires; it may be that such an approach, which is frowned upon in the online community, may have been more negative in the case of the attached questionnaire format.

Web surveys

Web surveys operate by inviting prospective respondents to visit a website at which the questionnaire can be found and completed online. The Web survey has an important advantage over the email survey in that it can use a much wider variety of embellishments in terms of appearance (colour, formatting, response styles, and so on). Plate 10.1 presents part of the questionnaire from the gym survey from Chapter 15; it is in a Web survey format and is answered in the same way as in Tips and skills 'A completed and processed questionnaire' (see Chapter 15). With open-ended questions, the respondent is invited to type directly into a boxed area (for example, question 2 in Plate 10.1).

However, the advantages of the Web survey are not just to do with appearance. The questionnaire can be designed so that, when there is a filter question (for example, 'if yes go to question 12, if no go to question 14'), it skips automatically to the next appropriate question. This is a

Plate 10.1
Part of the gym survey in Web survey format

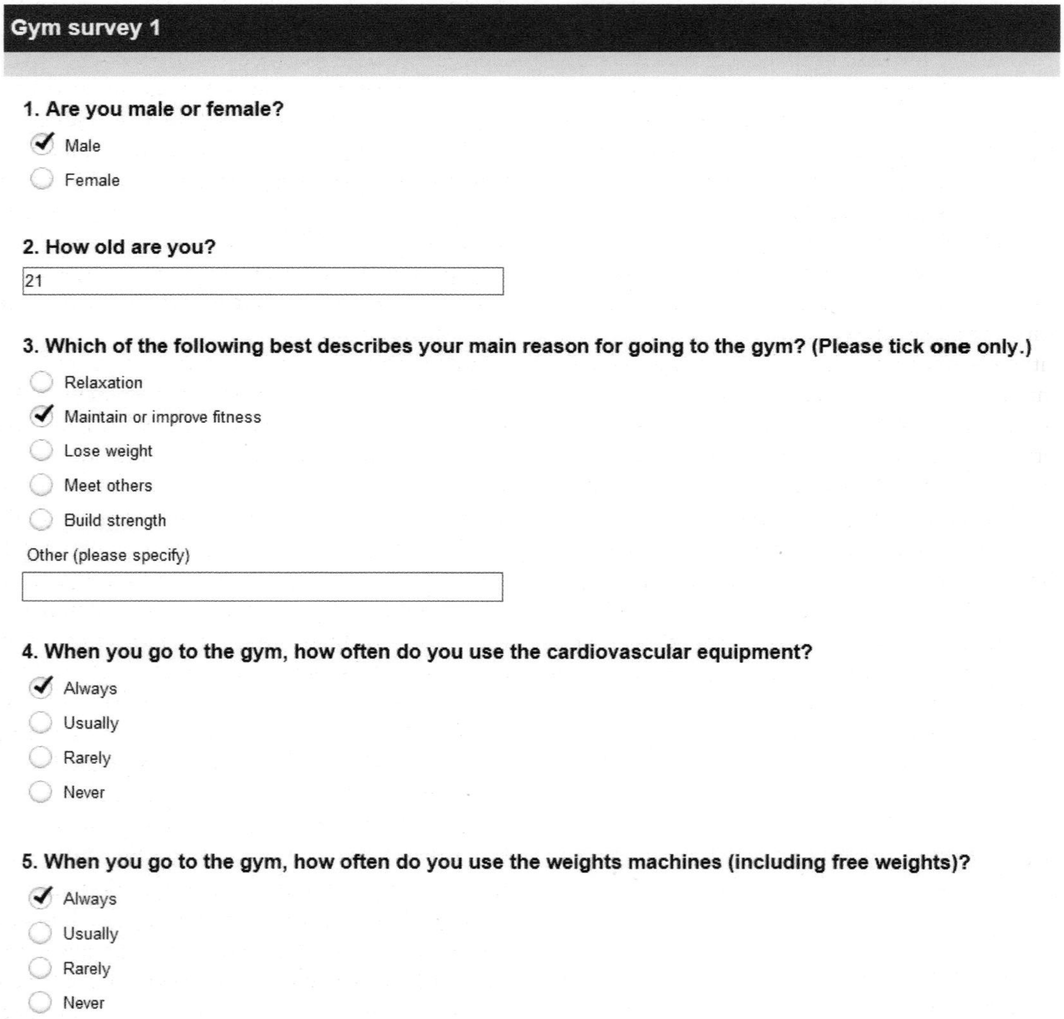

Gym survey 1

1. Are you male or female?

✓ Male

◯ Female

2. How old are you?

21

3. Which of the following best describes your main reason for going to the gym? (Please tick one only.)

◯ Relaxation

✓ Maintain or improve fitness

◯ Lose weight

◯ Meet others

◯ Build strength

Other (please specify)

4. When you go to the gym, how often do you use the cardiovascular equipment?

✓ Always

◯ Usually

◯ Rarely

◯ Never

5. When you go to the gym, how often do you use the weights machines (including free weights)?

✓ Always

◯ Usually

◯ Rarely

◯ Never

significant advantage over both postal and email-administered questionnaires, because it prevents respondents from inadvertently missing the question that follows on. The questionnaire can also be programmed so that only one question at a time appears on the screen or so that the respondent can scroll down and look at all questions in advance. Finally, respondents' answers can be automatically programmed to download into a database, thus eliminating the daunting coding of a large number of questionnaires. In order to produce a questionnaire with attractive features such as those in Plate 10.1, the researcher will have to use one of a growing number of software packages.

Plate 10.1 was created using Survey Monkey (**www .surveymonkey.com/MySurveys.aspx**, accessed 23 October 2014). With commercial websites such as these, you can design your questionnaire online and then create a Web address to which respondents can be directed in order to complete it. The questions in Plate 10.1 were created using the software's basic features, which are free of charge. There is a fee for using this software if more advanced features are required. The fee will be affected by the number of respondents who complete the questionnaire and the length of time that the questionnaire is active. Each respondent's replies are logged, and the entire data set can be retrieved once you decide the data-collection phase is complete. This means that there is no coding of replies (other than with open-ended questions) and no need to enter data into your software. Not only does this save time; it also reduces the introduction of errors during the processing of data.

Potential respondents need to be directed to the website containing the questionnaire. For example, in a Belgian study of attitudes towards immigrants, the researchers experimentally compared a Web and face-to-face interview survey (Heerwegh and Loosveldt 2008). The respondents were first-year men and women at the Katholieke Universiteit Leuven. They were emailed to request their participation in the Web survey and directed to the questionnaire. Two further emailings were conducted for those respondents who had not replied. Where there are possible problems to do with restricting who may answer the questionnaire, it may be necessary to set up a password system to filter out people for whom the questionnaire is not appropriate.

Use of mobile telephones as a platform for self-administered questionnaires

Although still very much in its infancy, there is growing interest in the potential of mobile phones and in particular smartphones as a means of administering self-administered questionnaires. The growth in the ownership of smartphones has begun to offer a new and potentially promising means of administration in addition to the Web, the subject of the previous section. It is too early for a comprehensive assessment of mobile phone questionnaires to be presented, but the following discussion outlines a small number of key points from the emerging literature.

On the face of it, questionnaires administered on mobile devices share many features with Web surveys whereby the respondent replies using a computer and keyboard. However, as Peytchev and Hill (2010) observe, smartphones and similar mobile devices differ from computers in three important ways: small screen size, navigation (mouse versus touchscreen or thumb wheel), and how information is inputted. Research by these authors suggests that Web surveys can be used with mobile phones but need to be adapted because features such as the small screen create difficulties for respondents, particularly when questions include a visual element. An early study in 2008 of a German sample's willingness to participate in a mobile phone survey found three factors were especially important: the perceived enjoyment of participating; attitudes towards participation (e.g. whether it is perceived to be exciting, absorbing, useful); and the perceived trustworthiness of the medium (e.g. anonymity, personal data not being misused) (Bosnjak et al. 2010). Such research provides pointers to factors that may be capable of being influenced in order to increase the likelihood of respondent participation.

An experiment conducted in Russia by Mavletova (2013) compared, in terms of data quality, a Web survey questionnaire completed using a computer with the same questionnaire administered using a mobile phone. The author found that the mobile format resulted in a lower level of completed questionnaires and fewer words being written in response to open-ended questions. However, in respect of other aspects of data quality, there were no or only very minor differences. Thus, there was no difference in primacy effects (whether answers to closed-ended questions that are higher on a list of answers are more likely to be selected); reporting levels in relation to sensitive questions; or in what the author calls 'non-substantive responses' (e.g. don't know, none of the above). Findings from a similar study in the Netherlands suggest no differences between mobile devices and computers in terms of the nature of the answers given, but when the questionnaire used for the experiment was answered using a mobile device, it took longer to complete and there was a lower response rate (de Bruijne and Wijnant 2013). Toepoel and Lugtig (2014) offered a mobile phone completion option to members of a Dutch Web panel and found few significant measurement differences between the two modes. However, Van Heerden et al. (2014) encountered several challenges in a South African study, one of which was problems with adapting the survey software to a smartphone context. A study of Russian respondents found that text/SMS (short message service) invitations to participate in a mobile Web survey were more effective than email invitations (Mavletova and Couper in press).

These findings are quite promising, but it is too early to be confident about the use of mobile phones as a means of administering Web surveys. Also, the significance of tablet computers (such as the iPad and Android tablets) raises the issue of whether these devices produce the same differences from computers as mobile phones. One early study which compared tablet administration with smartphone and Web administration revealed very few differences in findings between the studies, suggesting that tablets may prove to be a viable option (Wells et al. 2013).

One further development that we may see is the administration of questionnaires via text/SMS. It was noted in the previous paragraph that texts are being used as invitations to participate in Web surveys, but software is being developed for surveys to be administered and answered though texting. The possibilities are limited in that the questionnaire needs to be very short, but this may be appropriate for some kinds of research. Curran et al. (2013) report using a daily SMS survey to gauge sexual behaviour and pre-exposure prophylaxis among Kenyan men and women who were not infected by HIV. Four questions were asked daily for sixty days: whether the respondent had had sex the previous day, whether a condom was used, whether the respondent expected to have sex the following day, and whether the respondent had taken the prophylaxis the previous day.

 # Mixed mode surveys

Mixed mode surveys are becoming increasingly common ways of conducting surveys. They entail the use of two or more modes of administering a survey. They are not new. Survey researchers have often offered respondents the choice of whether to be interviewed or to complete a self-administered questionnaire, for example. Alternatively, surveys may sometimes be conducted so that some sets of questions are answered by interview and others by self-administered questionnaire.

The use of email and in particular Web surveys has increased the range of opportunities for mixed mode surveys and raises the prospect of research in which either of these media for distributing questionnaires might be combined with other media, such as postal questionnaires or face-to-face or telephone structured interviews (see Thinking deeply 10.1 for an example). Mixed modes of administering a survey raise the question of whether the mode of administration matters; in other words, do you get different results when you administer a questionnaire online from when you administer it offline (for example, by handing out a questionnaire or mailing it to respondents)? Obviously, it would not be desirable to aggregate data from two different modes of administration if part of the variation in respondents' replies could be attributed to the way they received and completed the questionnaire. Equally, researchers using solely a Web-based questionnaire need to know how far their findings are different from conventional modes of administration.

Experiments with different modes of administration are quite reassuring on this point, because the differences may not always be large. A study of self-reported illicit drug use among a large sample of US university students found that there were similar findings when the results from Web- and paper-based questionnaire surveys were compared (McCabe 2004). The sample had been randomly assigned to either of the two modes of administration. Denscombe (2006) compared paper and Web-based modes of administration of nearly identical questionnaires administered to young people at an East Midlands school. The questionnaire was concerned with perceptions of social issues. One batch of questions, which is explored in Denscombe's article, dealt with views about smoking. The findings confirmed McCabe's study in suggesting that there is little evidence that the mode of administration makes a significant difference to the findings. There was a lower incidence of self-reported smoking among those using the Web-based questionnaire than those using the paper one. However, given the large number of items compared for a mode effect in Denscombe's study, it was likely that a small number would be found to exhibit a mode effect, so it would be unwise to read too much into this particular finding.

Fleming and Bowden (2009) conducted a travel cost questionnaire survey by mail and the Web of visitors to Fraser Island, Australia. They found the results from

Thinking deeply 10.1
The GESIS Panel

The GESIS Panel is a panel for collecting social science data on a regular basis by self-administered questionnaire, with nearly 5,000 respondents participating. I invited the Founding Team Leader of the GESIS Panel, Michael Bosnjak, to provide a short account of its workings. I am a member of the panel's Scientific Quality Assurance Board. It might be argued that the panel is irrelevant to readers; it is inconceivable that they could set up a programme such as GESIS because of the huge costs and labour involved. However, the way in which the GESIS Panel operates will be interesting to readers, as this kind of survey context is becoming increasingly significant within the survey research community. It is also an interesting example of survey research in which the mixed mode approach is a core feature. A further point is that like many large-scale surveys of this kind, the data deriving from the GESIS panel are available for secondary analysis, an issue that will be taken up in Chapter 14. As the following account makes clear, researchers are also able to propose questions for inclusion in the questionnaire, though these requests are evaluated by the advisory board. Here is Michael Bosnjak's account of the GESIS panel and its significance.

Inferential statistics teaches us that we need a random probability sample to infer from a sample to the general population. In online survey research, however, volunteer access panels, in which respondents self-select themselves into the sample, dominate the landscape. Such panels are attractive, due to their low costs. Nevertheless, recent years have seen increasing numbers of debates about the quality, in particular about errors in the representativeness and measurement, of such volunteer access panels.

As an alternative, probability-based panels of the general population have been built recently, such as, for instance, the LISS Panel in the Netherlands, the ELIPSS Panel in France, and the German GESIS Panel (Blom et al. in press).

The GESIS Panel offers the academic social science community the possibility of collecting survey data within a probability-based, multi-topic panel free of charge. The data are representative of the German speaking population aged between 18 and 70 years. By the end of the recruiting phase in February 2014, the GESIS Panel encompassed about 5000 panellists. Academics from various social sciences fields, such as sociologists, psychologists, political scientists, economists, and criminologists at universities or non-commercial research institutes can submit study proposals. Upon approval by an independent reviewer board, data are being collected free of charge. GESIS Panel surveys take place on a bi-monthly basis and are split up into two self-administered survey modes (online and offline). At the beginning of each survey wave, about 65 per cent of the panellists are invited to participate online (web-based surveys) and about 35 per cent of the panellists are invited to participate offline (by postal mail). The reason for fielding parallel online and offline surveys is that Internet access is still not universal, and that a considerable proportion of Internet users tend to decline participating online.

Besides fielding a survey project, data collected within the GESIS Panel can be used by any academic researcher free of charge, e.g. to conduct secondary research.

www.gesis-panel.org (accessed 10 February 2015)

the two modes of administration to be similar and that, in particular, the estimates of the 'consumer surplus' (the amount the tourist would be willing to spend on the visit less the amount actually spent) were similar. In spite of the fact that there is some evidence of differences in response between modes of survey administration, mixing postal and Web questionnaires is often recommended as a survey approach (Van Selm and Jankowski 2006). On the other hand, the previously mentioned Belgian study of attitudes towards immigrants experimentally compared a Web and face-to-face interview survey (Heerwegh and Loosveldt 2008). The researchers found that the Web respondents were more likely to answer with 'don't know' answers, less likely to differentiate on rating scales (this means they made less use of the full range of possible response options), and more likely to fail to reply to individual questions or items in rating scales. These findings suggest not only that the two modes can produce different kinds of response, but also that data quality may be poorer in the Web mode. A similar kind of study involving US teachers found few differences in failure to respond to individual items other than with what the authors call 'fill-in-the-blank' questions (Wolfe et al. 2008). An example of this kind of question in this survey was when teachers were asked to estimate the average number of hours per week spent working on activities relating to teaching. With this kind of question, there was a much higher tendency towards non-response among Web respondents than among postal questionnaire ones. However, overall Wolfe et al. found differences in non-response at the level of the individual item or question to be very small.

Nonetheless, there is often a good case to be made for offering respondents an online option, but there is clearly a need to be aware of the limitations, such as possibly poorer data quality in Web surveys. There are grounds for caution when the survey in question is a mail questionnaire survey that offers respondents the option of responding through a Web-based questionnaire. Medway and Fulton (2012) conducted a meta-analysis of studies that examined the impact of offering a Web option and found a clear tendency for such surveys to produce *lower* response rates than those that do not provide such an option. The authors explain this possibly surprising finding by suggesting that the Web option increases the overall complexity of responding; introduces a break in the process of responding; and sometimes causes technical difficulties that result in respondents giving up. A covering letter might draw prospective respondents' attention to a Web-based option along with the necessary instructions for accessing it, so that those who prefer to work online are not put off responding to the questionnaire. However, the researcher has to be sensitive to the possibility of mode effects and potential problems of the kind described by Medway and Fulton.

Couper (2008) summarized the results of several studies that compared the use of open-ended questions in both Web and paper-based questionnaire surveys and found that the former were at least as good as the latter in terms of both quantity and quality of answers. In fact, in terms of the quantity written, the Web questionnaires were usually superior. More recently, Smyth et al. (2009) report that the quality of answers to open-ended questions in Web surveys can be enhanced by increasing the size of the space available for answers; drawing attention to the flexibility of the box into which answers are typed; and providing instructions that both clarify what is expected and motivate the respondent (such as pointing out the importance of their replies). A comparison of replies with an earlier equivalent paper-based questionnaire revealed that the quality of Web-based replies was superior in several different ways. Smyth et al. (2009) observe that, in recent years, the use of open-ended questions in surveys has declined because of the high costs of administering them and the poor quality of replies, but that, with growing evidence of their potential through a Web-based mode of administration, they may enjoy a renaissance, especially when it is borne in mind that there is no need to transcribe people's sometimes illegible handwriting.

These findings suggest that it is difficult to provide a definitive verdict on Web surveys compared to traditional forms of survey administration and on whether mixing survey modes represents a possible source of problems. It is difficult to separate out the particular formats that researchers use when experimenting with modes of administration from the modes themselves. It may be that, if they had displayed Web questions in a different manner, their findings would have been different. Further, Web surveys seem to work better than traditional survey forms in some respects but not in others. It is also difficult to separate mode effects from the fact that the respondents who opt for one mode rather than another will differ. Thus, in an online survey, respondents may be offered a mail option and it is possible that those who accept this alternative will differ from online respondents. Further, it may be possible to reduce mode effects. For example, Dillman et al. (2014), who are extremely in favour of mixed mode survey designs, propose making question and response formats and visual appearance as similar as possible (for example, ensuring a paper version of a questionnaire is visually similar to a corresponding Web one) across two or more modes to reduce mode effects. Mixing survey modes offers several advantages such as greater coverage (for example, people who do not have Web access may nonetheless be contactable by telephone) and superior response rates (for example, people who are disinclined to complete and return a mail questionnaire may find a Web questionnaire acceptable).

Tips and skills 'Advantages and disadvantages of online surveys compared to postal questionnaire surveys' summarizes the main factors to take into account when comparing online surveys with postal questionnaire surveys, and Table 10.1 compares the different methods of administering a survey.

Tips and skills
Advantages and disadvantages of online surveys compared to postal questionnaire surveys

This box summarizes the main advantages and disadvantages of online surveys compared to postal questionnaire surveys. The tally of advantages and disadvantages relates to both email and Web surveys. It should also be made clear that, by and large, online surveys and postal questionnaires suffer from one disadvantage relative to personal and telephone interviews—namely, that the researcher can never be certain that the person answering questions is who the researcher believes him or her to be.

Advantages

1. *Low cost.* Even though postal questionnaire surveys are cheap to administer, there is evidence that email surveys in particular are cheaper. This is in part due to the cost of postage, paper, envelopes, and the time taken to stuff covering letters and questionnaires into envelopes with postal questionnaire surveys. However, with Web surveys, there may be start-up costs associated with the software needed to produce the questionnaire.

2. *Faster response.* Online surveys tend to be returned considerably more quickly than postal questionnaires.

3. *Attractive formats.* With Web surveys, there is the opportunity to use a wide variety of stylistic formats for presenting questionnaires and closed-question answers. Also, automatic skipping when using filter questions and the possibility of immediate downloading of questionnaire replies into a database make this kind of survey quite attractive for researchers.

4. *Mixed administration.* Online surveys can be combined with postal questionnaire surveys so that respondents have the option of replying by post or online. Research reviewed in this chapter suggests that, although there is some evidence that the mode of administration can make some difference to the kinds of replies generated, in many cases that difference is not great.

5. *Unrestricted compass.* There are no constraints in terms of geographical coverage. The same might be said of postal questionnaire surveys, but online surveys eliminate the problems of sending respondents stamped addressed envelopes that can be used in their own countries.

6. *Fewer unanswered questions.* There is evidence that online questionnaires are completed with fewer unanswered questions than postal questionnaires, resulting in less missing data. However, there is also evidence of little difference in this regard between the two modes of administering surveys.

7. *Better response to open-ended questions.* To the extent that open-ended questions are used, they tend to be more likely to be answered online and to result in more detailed replies.

8. *Better data accuracy, especially in Web surveys.* Data entry is automated, so that the researcher does not have to enter data into a spreadsheet, and therefore errors in data entry are largely avoided.

Disadvantages

1. *Low response rate.* Typically, response rates to online surveys are lower than those for comparable postal questionnaire surveys.

2. *Restricted to online populations.* Only people who are available online can reasonably be expected to participate in an online survey. This restriction may gradually ease over time, but, since the online population differs in significant ways from the non-online population, it is likely to remain a difficulty. On the other hand, if online populations are the focus of interest, this disadvantage is unlikely to prove an obstacle.

3. *Requires motivation.* As online survey respondents must be online to answer the questionnaire, if they are having to pay for the connection they may need a higher level of motivation than postal questionnaire respondents. This suggests that the solicitation to participate must be especially persuasive.

4. *Confidentiality and anonymity issues.* It is normal for survey researchers to indicate that respondents' replies will be confidential and that they will be anonymous. The same suggestions can and should be made with respect to online surveys. However, with email surveys, since the recipient must return the questionnaire either embedded within the message or as an attachment, respondents may find it difficult to believe that their replies really are confidential and will be treated anonymously. In this respect, Web surveys may have an advantage over email surveys.

5. *Multiple replies.* With Web surveys, there is a risk that some people may mischievously complete the questionnaire more than once. There is less risk of this with email surveys.

Sources: Cobanoglu et al. (2001); Denscombe (2006); Dillman et al. (2014); Groves et al. (2009); Tse (1998); Kent and Lee (1999); Sheehan and Hoy (1999); **www.restore.ac.uk/orm/self-study.htm** (accessed 26 January 2015).

Table 10.1

The strengths of email and Web-based surveys in relation to face-to-face interview, telephone interview, and postal questionnaire surveys

Issues to consider	Mode of survey administration				
	Face-to-face interview	Telephone interview	Postal questionnaire	Email	Web
Resource issues					
Is the cost of the mode of administration relatively low?	✓	✓ ✓	✓ ✓ ✓	✓ ✓ ✓	✓ (unless access to low-cost software)
Is the speed of the mode of administration relatively fast?	✓	✓ ✓ ✓	✓ ✓ ✓	✓ ✓ ✓	✓ ✓ ✓
Is the cost of handling a dispersed sample relatively low?	✓ (✓ ✓ if clustered)	✓ ✓ ✓	✓ ✓ ✓	✓ ✓ ✓	✓ ✓ ✓
Does the researcher require little technical expertise for designing a questionnaire?	✓ ✓ ✓	✓ ✓ ✓	✓ ✓ ✓	✓ ✓	✓
Sampling-related issues					
Does the mode of administration tend to produce a good response rate?	✓ ✓ ✓	✓ ✓	✓	✓	✓
Is the researcher able to control who responds (i.e. the person at whom it is targeted is the person who answers)?	✓ ✓ ✓	✓ ✓ ✓	✓ ✓	✓ ✓	✓ ✓
Is the mode of administration accessible to all sample members?	✓ ✓ ✓	✓ ✓	✓ ✓ ✓	✓ (because of the need for respondents to be accessible online)	✓ (because of the need for respondents to be accessible online)
Questionnaire issues					
Is the mode of administration suitable for long questionnaires?	✓ ✓ ✓	✓ ✓	✓ ✓	✓ ✓	✓ ✓
Is the mode of administration suitable for complex questions?	✓ ✓ ✓	✓	✓ ✓	✓ ✓	✓ ✓
Is the mode of administration suitable for open questions?	✓ ✓ ✓	✓ ✓	✓	✓ ✓	✓ ✓
Is the mode of administration suitable for filter questions?	✓ ✓ ✓ (especially if CAPI used)	✓ ✓ ✓ (especially if CATI used)	✓	✓	✓ ✓ ✓ (if allows jumping)

(continued)

Table 10.1
(*Continued*)

Issues to consider	Mode of survey administration				
	Face-to-face interview	Telephone interview	Postal questionnaire	Email	Web
Does the mode of administration allow control over the order in which questions are answered?	✓✓✓	✓✓✓	✓	✓	✓✓
Is the mode of administration suitable for sensitive questions?	✓	✓✓	✓✓✓	✓✓✓	✓✓✓
Is the mode of administration less likely to result in non-response to some questions?	✓✓✓	✓✓✓	✓✓	✓✓	✓✓
Does the mode of administration allow the use of visual aids?	✓✓✓	✓	✓✓✓	✓✓	✓✓✓
Answering context issues					
Does the mode of administration give respondents the opportunity to consult others for information?	✓✓	✓	✓✓✓	✓✓✓	✓✓✓
Does the mode of administration minimize the impact of interviewers' characteristics (gender, class, ethnicity)?	✓	✓✓	✓✓✓	✓✓✓	✓✓✓
Does the mode of administration minimize the impact of the social desirability effect?	✓	✓✓	✓✓✓	✓✓✓	✓✓✓
Does the mode of administration allow control over the intrusion of others in answering questions?	✓✓✓	✓✓	✓	✓	✓
Does the mode of administration minimize the need for respondents to have certain skills to answer questions?	✓✓✓	✓✓✓	✓✓	✓ (because of the need to have online skills)	✓ (because of the need to have online skills)
Does the mode of administration enable respondents to be probed?	✓✓✓	✓✓✓	✓	✓✓	✓
Does the mode of administration reduce the likelihood of data entry errors by the researcher?	✓	✓	✓✓	✓	✓✓✓

Notes: Number of ticks indicates the strength of the mode of administration of a questionnaire in relation to each issue. More ticks correspond to more advantages in relation to each issue. A single tick implies that the mode of administering a questionnaire does not fare well in terms of the issue in question. Three ticks implies that it does very well, and two ticks implies that it is acceptable. This table has been influenced by the author's own experiences and the following sources:

Sources: Cobanoglu et al. (2001); Denscombe (2006); Dillman et al. (2014); Groves et al. (2009); Tse (1998); Kent and Lee (1999); Sheehan and Hoy (1999); **www.restore.ac.uk/orm/self-study.htm** (accessed 26 January 2015).

Diaries as a form of self-administered questionnaire

When the researcher is specifically interested in precise estimates of different kinds of behaviour, the diary warrants serious consideration, though it is still a relatively underused method. The term 'diary' has somewhat different meanings in social research (see Key concept 10.1). It is the first of the three meanings—what H. Elliott (1997) calls the 'researcher-driven diary'—that is the focus of attention here, especially in the context of its use in relation to quantitative research. When employed in this way, the researcher-driven diary functions in a similar way to the self-administered questionnaire. Equally, it could be said that the researcher-driven diary is an alternative method of data collection to observation. It can be thought of as the equivalent of structured observation (see Chapter 12) in the context of research questions that are framed in terms of quantitative research. With diary methods, observation takes place because the person who completes the diary observes his or her own behaviour.

Corti (1993) distinguishes between 'structured diaries' and 'free-text diaries'. Either may be employed by quantitative researchers. The research on gender and time use in Research in focus 10.2 is an illustration of the structured diary. The specific kind of diary employed in this research is often referred to as a 'time-use diary', in that it is designed so that diarists can record more or less contemporaneously the amount of time engaged in certain activities, such as food preparation, childcare, selfcare, eating, and so on. Estimates of the amount of time spent in different activities are often regarded as more accurate than questionnaire estimates, because the events are less subject to memory lapses or

to the tendency to round up or down (Fisher and Layte 2004). However, a time use diary is more intrusive than answering a questionnaire, and it could be argued that it causes changes in behaviour.

Crook and Light (2002) employed time-use diaries within a free-text format. University students were asked to keep a diary for a week of the different kinds of study and learning activity in which they engaged at different times of the day. The diaries were divided into fifteen-minute intervals, so that all students had to indicate for each interval 'details of their activity, location, and any study resources that might be in use' (Crook and Light 2002: 162). The various activities were grouped into three types: classes, private study, and social study (that is, study with a peer). They were able to show the very different patterns and amounts of study typically undertaken during a day.

Using free-text recording of behaviour carries the same kinds of problem as those associated with coding answers to structured-interview open-ended questions—namely, the time-consuming nature of the exercise and the risk of introducing error associated

Key concept 10.1
The diary in social research

There are three major ways in which the term 'diary' has been employed in the context of social research.

1. *The diary as a method of data collection.* Here the researcher devises a structure for the diary and then asks a sample of diarists to complete the instruments so that they record what they do more or less contemporaneously with their activities. H. Elliott (1997) refers to this kind of use of the diary as 'researcher-driven diary'. Such diaries can be employed for the collection of data within the context of both quantitative and qualitative research. Sometimes, the collection of data in this manner is supplemented by a personal interview in which the diarist is asked questions about such things as what he or she meant by certain remarks. This 'diary-interview', as it is often referred to (Zimmerman and Wieder 1977), is usually employed when diarists record their behaviour in prose form rather than simply indicating the amount of time spent on different kinds of activity.

2. *The diary as a document.* The diary in this context is written spontaneously by the diarist and not at the behest of a researcher but may be used as a source for analysis. Diaries in this sense are often used by historians but have some potential for social researchers working on issues that are of social scientific significance. As Scott (1990) observes, the diary in this sense often shades into autobiography. Blogs (Web logs), which represent what might be thought of as an online diary, may also be used as material on which an analysis might be conducted. Diaries as documents will be further addressed in Chapter 23.

3. *The diary as a log of the researcher's activities.* Researchers sometimes keep a record of what they do at different stages as an *aide-mémoire*. For example, the famous social anthropologist Malinowski (1967) kept an infamous log of his activities ('infamous' because it revealed his distaste for the people he studied and his inappropriate involvement with females). It has been suggested that blogs may be used in this way by researchers (Wakeford and Cohen 2008). This kind of diary often shades into the writing of field notes by ethnographers, about which more is written in Chapter 19.

Research in focus 10.2
A diary study to examine household structure and housework

Gershuny and Sullivan (2014) report the findings of a diary study that allowed them to examine the contributions to housework of all household members (not just couples) in four common household types. The four household types are: single mothers; couples with no children; non-parent not partnered adults; and couples with children. They conducted an analysis of the 2000/1 UK Time Use Survey which is part of the Eurostat Harmonised European Time Use Study (see Research in focus 10.3). Through an analysis of the data, Gershuny and Sullivan were able to demonstrate the differences between men and women in terms of the allocation of tasks, but also the contribution of others to the domestic division of labour. The research shows the ways in which various members of households both contribute to household work and provide the need for household work. For example, the authors show that 'children, and particularly girls, contribute not insignificant amounts to household work' (Gershuny and Sullivan 2014: 23) and there is the suggestion that when there is an elderly adult, it is on girls aged 13–17 that a considerable housework burden may fall.

with the coding of answers (see Chapter 11 for a discussion of these issues). However, the free-text approach is less likely to be problematic when diarists can be instructed about what is required and when the kinds of behaviour that are of interest are rather focused. It would be much more difficult to code free-text entries relating to general types of behaviour of the kind studied by Gershuny and Sullivan (2014; see Research in focus 10.2). Structured diaries particularly lend themselves to examining cross-cultural differences in time use—see Research in focus 10.3 for an example.

Corti (1993) recommends that the researcher preparing the diary should

- provide explicit instructions for diarists;
- be clear about the time periods within which behaviour is to be recorded—that is, day, twenty-four hours, week;
- provide a model of a completed section of a diary;
- provide checklists of 'items, events or behaviour' that can jog people's memory—but the list should not become too daunting in length or complexity;
- include fixed blocks of time or columns showing when the designated activities start and finish (for diaries of the kind used by Sullivan (1996), which show how people budget their time).

Research in focus 10.3
Harmonised European Time Use Surveys project

Time-use diaries offer great opportunities for cross-cultural studies. The Harmonised European Time Use Surveys (HETUS) project coordinates time-use diary studies among a wide range of European nations (see Fisher and Layte 2004). The data-collection process entails two diaries—one for a weekday and one for use on a weekend. The fieldwork covers a twelve-month period, so that the varied activities that take place over the period are covered. Diarists complete the instruments themselves and write in their own words what they were doing during each ten-minute interval during the day. These are later coded into clusters of activities. Diarists also supply information about whether anyone else was present and the location of the activity. For more information, see http://epp.eurostat.ec.europa.eu/cache/ITY_OFFPUB/KS-RA-08-014/EN/KS-RA-08-014-EN.PDF (accessed 23 October 2014).

The diary is mainly completed on paper, but increasingly diaries of this kind can be completed on computer. See Plate 10.2 for part of a sample one-day diary from the HETUS project.

Plate 10.2

Sample diary entry for the Harmonised European Time Use Surveys project

Adult example page 2/3

Time	What were you doing? *Record your main activity for each 10-minute period from 10.00 am to 13.00!* *Only one main activity on each line!* *Distinguish between travel and the activity that is the reason for travelling.*	What else were you doing? *Record the most important parallel activity.* *Indicate if you used, in the main or parallel activity, a computer or internet.* *You do not need to record the use of a computer or internet during working time.*	Where were you? *Record the location or the mode of transport* *e.g. at home, at friends' home, at school, at workplace, in restaurant, in shop, on foot, on bicycle, in car, on motorbike, on bus, …*	Were you alone or together with somebody you know? *Mark "yes" by crossing*					
				Alone	With other household members				Other persons that you know
					Partner	Parent	Household member up to 9 years	Other household member	
10.00-10.10	Work	Coffe break	Workplace	☐	☐	☐	☐	☐	☒
10.10-10.20				☒	☐	☐	☐	☐	☐
10.20-10.30				☒	☐	☐	☐	☐	☐
10.30-10.40				☒	☐	☐	☐	☐	☐
10.40-10.50				☒	☐	☐	☐	☐	☐
10.50-11.00				☒	☐	☐	☐	☐	☐
11.00-11.10				☒	☐	☐	☐	☐	☐
11.10-11.20				☒	☐	☐	☐	☐	☐
11.20-11.30				☒	☐	☐	☐	☐	☐
11.30-11.40	Lunch break: had lunch	Talked with colleagues	Canteen	☐	☐	☐	☐	☐	☒
11.40-11.50	--"--	--"--	--"--	☐	☐	☐	☐	☐	☒
11.50-12.00	--"--	--"--	--"--	☐	☐	☐	☐	☐	☒
12.00-12.10	Lunch break: went to the supermarket		On foot	☒	☐	☐	☐	☐	☐
12.10-12.20	Lunch break: bought food		Supermarket	☒	☐	☐	☐	☐	☐
12.20-12.30	Lunch break: went back to work		On foot	☒	☐	☐	☐	☐	☐
12.30-12.40	Work		Workplace	☒	☐	☐	☐	☐	☐
12.40-12.50				☒	☐	☐	☐	☐	☐
12.50-13.00				☒	☐	☐	☐	☐	☐

Time diary page as used in the Harmonised European Time Use Surveys. Taken from **http://ec.europa.eu/eurostat/ramon/statmanuals/files/KS-RA-08-014-EN.pdf** (page 110, accessed 26 January 2015).

Source: Eurostat. Reprinted with permission.

Advantages and disadvantages of the diary as a method of data collection

The studies that have been mentioned to illustrate the use of the diary also suggest its potential advantages.

- When fairly precise estimates of the frequency and/or amount of time spent in different forms of behaviour are required, the diary almost certainly provides more valid and reliable data than questionnaires.

- When information about the sequencing of different types of behaviour is required, the diary is likely to perform better than questionnaires or interviews.

- The first two advantages could be used to suggest that structured observation would be just as feasible, but structured observation is probably less appropriate for producing data on behaviour that is personally sensitive, such as sexual behaviour.

On the other hand, diaries may suffer from the following problems.

- They tend to be more expensive than personal interviews (because of the costs associated with recruiting diarists and of checking that diaries are being properly completed).

- Diaries can suffer from a process of attrition, as people decide they have had enough of the task of completing a diary.

- This last point raises the possibility that diarists become less diligent over time about their record keeping.

- There is sometimes failure to record details sufficiently quickly, so that memory recall problems set in.

However, diary researchers argue that the resulting data are more accurate than the equivalent data based on interviews or questionnaires.

Experience and event sampling

A variation on the diary method is **experience sampling**, also known as event sampling, which captures participants' feelings and affective state or their behaviour at the point at which they are prompted to complete the research instrument they have agreed to complete. With this method, participants are prompted to reply to questions about their behaviour and/or their affective states at particular points in time (or within a narrow timeframe). The method allows something approximating to real-time data about the occurrence and possibly intensity of the issue being asked about. Participants are usually prompted either at particular points in time (e.g. at the end of the working day, after eating breakfast) or at particular junctures (e.g. after receiving a telephone call, after a Facebook session). In addition, the participant might be prompted to complete the research instrument when a device that he or she carries around emits a sound. Experience/event sampling operates in a similar way to a diary in that participants record such things as their behaviour and their feelings or impressions in terms of a predetermined format at the appropriate juncture.

An experience sampling study of eighty-two Facebook users in the USA was conducted by Kross et al. (2013). The authors were interested in how far Facebook use influences subjective well-being. Initially, participants were administered questionnaires covering satisfaction with life, depression, self-esteem, and uses of Facebook. Then, over a fourteen-day period, participants were sent text messages five times per day at random times. Each text message included a link to an online questionnaire that included five questions concerning how the respondent was feeling; level of worry; feeling of loneliness; extent of use of Facebook since previous text message; and level of face-to-face interaction since last text message. The authors found that Facebook use was associated with lower levels of two subjective well-being variables: how people feel from one moment to another and their levels of satisfaction with their lives.

The chief advantages of the method over the traditional way of using a self-administered questionnaire is that the ensuing data tend to be more immediate (since participants reply *in situ*), less general (replies are not about feelings over a period of time), and less prone to memory distortions, though the data share most of the limitations associated with the diary method discussed above. Experience sampling tends to be more likely to be used than the diary for collecting data relating to participants' feelings and affects, whereas they are both employed for collecting information about behaviour.

Experience sampling may become more popular as people's familiarity with and use of smartphones increases, since they provide a very useful platform for prompting research participants to complete a research instrument and for completing and submitting answers. Hofmans et al. (2014) used smartphones to gather experience sampling data from fifty employees in a study of task characteristics and work effort. The employees were prompted with a beep, five times a day for five working days, to complete a small number of questions about their task at that time and their feelings about it. Beeps were not always responded to, so that there was an element of non-response, but the immediacy of the data that were received provides a significant alternative to conventional questionnaire answers. In this way, smartphones can be used both for the administration of prompts to answer questions and for the answering of the questions themselves.

 Key points

....

- Many of the recommendations relating to the self-administered questionnaire apply equally or almost equally to the structured interview, as has been mentioned on several occasions.

- Closed-ended questions tend to be used in survey research rather than open-ended ones. Coding is a particular problem when dealing with answers to open-ended questions.

- Structured interviews and self-administered questionnaires both have their respective advantages and disadvantages, but a particular problem with questionnaires sent by post is that they frequently produce a low response rate. However, steps can be taken to boost response rates for postal questionnaires.

- Presentation of closed-ended questions and the general layout constitute important considerations in preparing a self-administered questionnaire.

- The variety of ways in which questionnaires can be administered has increased with the arrival of online surveys, and this has led to a growing use of mixed modes of survey administration.

- The researcher-driven diary is a possible alternative to using questionnaires and interviews when the research questions are very specifically concerned with aspects of people's behaviour.

- Experience and event sampling operate in similar ways to a diary and are valuable ways of collecting data on behaviour.

Questions for review

Self-administered questionnaire or postal questionnaire?

- Are the self-administered questionnaire and the postal questionnaire the same thing?

Evaluating the self-administered questionnaire in relation to the structured interview

- 'The low response rates frequently achieved in research with postal questionnaires mean that the structured interview is invariably a more suitable choice.' Discuss.

- What steps can be taken to boost postal questionnaire response rates?

Designing the self-administered questionnaire

- Why are self-administered questionnaires usually made up mainly of closed-ended questions?

- Why might a vertical format for presenting closed-ended questions be preferable to a horizontal format?

Mixed mode surveys

- What is the significance of the distinction between email and Web surveys?

- Are there any special circumstances in which embedded email questionnaires will be more likely to be effective than attached questionnaires?

- Are mobile telephones and tablet computers a viable mechanism for conducting self-administered questionnaire research?

- 'The greater population coverage afforded by mixed modes of survey administration outweighs any limitations'. Discuss.

Diaries as a form of self-administered questionnaire

- What are the main kinds of diary used in the collection of social science data?

- Are there any circumstances when the diary approach might be preferable to the use of a self-administered questionnaire?

Online Resource Centre

www.oxfordtextbooks.co.uk/orc/brymansrm5e/

Visit the Online Resource Centre to enrich your understanding of self-administered questionnaires. Follow up links to other resources, test yourself using multiple choice questions, and gain further guidance and inspiration from the Student Researcher's Toolkit.

11

Asking questions

Chapter outline

Chapter guide

This chapter is concerned with the considerations that are involved in asking questions that are used in structured interviews and questionnaires of the kinds discussed in the two previous chapters. As such, it continues the focus upon survey research that began with Chapter 8. The chapter explores:

- the issues involved in deciding whether or when to use open- or closed-ended questions;
- the different kinds of question that can be asked in structured interviews and questionnaires;
- rules to bear in mind when designing questions;
- vignette questions in which respondents are presented with a scenario and are asked to reflect on the scenario;
- the importance of piloting questions;
- the possibility of using questions that have been used in previous survey research.

Introduction

To many people, how to ask questions represents the crux of considerations surrounding the use of social survey instruments such as the structured interview or the self-administered questionnaire. As the previous two chapters have suggested, there is much more to the design and administration of such research instruments than how best to phrase questions. However, there is no doubt that the issue of how questions should be asked is a crucial concern for the survey researcher, and it is not surprising that this aspect of designing survey instruments has been a major focus of attention over the years.

Open- or closed-ended questions?

One of the most significant considerations for many researchers is whether to ask a question in an open or closed format. This distinction was first introduced in Chapter 9. The issue of which of the two formats to use is relevant to the design of both structured interview research and self-administered questionnaire research.

With an **open-ended question** respondents are asked a question and can reply however they wish. With a **closed-ended question** they are presented with a set of fixed alternatives from which they have to choose an appropriate answer. All the questions in Tips and skills 'Instructions for interviewers in the use of a filter question' (in Chapter 9) are of the closed kind. So too are the Likert-scale items in Research in focus 7.2 and Tips and skills 'Formatting a Likert scale' (in Chapter 10); these form a particular kind of closed-ended question. What, then, are some of the advantages and limitations of these two types of question format?

Open-ended questions

Open-ended questions present both advantages and disadvantages to the survey researcher, though, as the following discussion suggests, the problems associated with the processing of answers to open-ended questions tend to mean that closed-ended questions are more likely to be used.

Advantages

Although survey researchers typically prefer to use closed-ended questions, open-ended questions do have certain advantages over closed-ended ones, as outlined in the list below.

- Respondents can answer in their own terms. They are not forced to answer in the same terms as those foisted on them by the response choices.

- They allow unusual responses to be derived. Replies that the survey researcher may not have contemplated (and that would therefore not form the basis for fixed-choice alternatives) are possible.

- The questions do not suggest certain kinds of answer to respondents. Therefore, respondents' levels of knowledge and understanding of issues can be tapped. The salience of issues for respondents can also be explored.

- They are useful for exploring new areas or ones in which the researcher has limited knowledge.

- They are useful for generating fixed-choice format answers. This is a point that will be returned to below.

Disadvantages

However, open-ended questions present problems for the survey researcher, as the following list reveals.

- They are time-consuming for interviewers to administer. Interviewees are likely to talk for longer than is usually the case with a comparable closed-ended question.

- Answers have to be 'coded', which is very time-consuming. Key concept 11.1 outlines the nature of coding and provides some considerations involved in its use. For each open-ended question it entails reading through answers, deriving themes that can be employed to form the basis for codes, and then going through the answers again so that the answers can be coded for entry into a computer spreadsheet. The process is essentially identical to that involved in **content analysis** and is sometimes called *post-coding* to distinguish it from *pre-coding*, whereby the researcher designs a coding frame in advance of administering a survey instrument and often includes the pre-codes in the questionnaire (as in Tips and skills 'Processing a closed-ended question'). However, in addition to being time-consuming, post-coding can be an unreliable process, because it can introduce the possibility of variability in the coding of answers and therefore of measurement error (and hence lack of validity). This is a form of data-processing error (see Figure 8.9). Research in focus 11.1 and 11.2 deal with aspects of coding open-ended questions.

- They require greater effort from respondents. Respondents are likely to talk for longer than would be the case for a comparable closed-ended question, or, in the case of a self-administered questionnaire, would need to write for much longer. Therefore, it is often suggested that open-ended questions have limited use in the context of self-administered questionnaires. Because of the greater effort involved, many prospective respondents may be put off by the prospect of having to write extensively, which may exacerbate the problem of low response rates with postal questionnaires in particular (see Chapter 10).

- In research based on structured interviews, there is the possibility of variability between interviewers in the recording of answers. This possibility can arise as a result of the difficulty of writing down verbatim what respondents say to interviewers. The obvious solution is to employ an audio-recorder. However, it is not always practicable to employ one—for example, in a noisy environment. Also, the transcription of recorded

Key concept 11.1
What is coding?

Coding is a key stage in quantitative research. Many forms of data that are of interest to social scientists are essentially in an unstructured form. Examples are: answers to open-ended questions in interviews and questionnaires; newspaper articles; television programmes; and behaviour in a school classroom. In order to quantify and analyse such materials, the researcher has to code them. Coding entails two main stages. First, the unstructured material must be categorized. For example, with answers to an open-ended question, this means that the researcher must examine people's answers and group them into different categories. Research in focus 11.1 provides some examples of this process. Second, the researcher must assign numbers to the categories that have been created. This step is a largely arbitrary process, in the sense that the numbers themselves are simply tags that will allow the material to be processed quantitatively. Thus, when Schuman and Presser (1981; see Research in focus 11.3) asked a question about the features of a job that people most prefer, answers were grouped into eleven categories: pay; feeling of accomplishment; control of work; pleasant work; security; opportunity for promotion; short hours; working conditions; benefits; satisfaction; other responses. Each of these eleven categories would then need to be assigned a number, such as: 1 for pay; 2 for feeling of accomplishment; 3 for control of work; 4 for pleasant work; etc.

There is an important distinction between *pre-coding* and *post-coding*. Many closed-ended questions in survey research instruments are **pre-coded** (see Tips and skills 'Processing a closed-ended question' for an example). This means that respondents are being asked to assign themselves to a category that has already had a number assigned to it. Post-coding occurs when answers to an open-ended question are being coded or when themes in newspaper articles concerned with a certain topic are being counted, as in content analysis (see Chapter 13).

When coding, three basic principles need to be observed (Bryman and Cramer 2011).

1. The categories that are generated must not overlap. If they do, the numbers that are assigned to them cannot be applied to distinct categories.

2. The list of categories must be complete and therefore cover all possibilities. If it is not, some material will not be capable of being coded. This is why coding a certain item of information, such as answers to an open-ended question, sometimes includes a category of 'other'.

3. There should be clear rules about how codes should be applied, so that the person conducting the coding has instructions about the kinds of answers that should be assigned to a particular code. Such rules are meant to ensure that those who are conducting the coding are consistent over time in how they assign the material to categories and, if more than one person is coding, are consistent with each other. The term 'coding frame' is often employed to describe the lists of codes that should be applied to unstructured data and the rules for their application. In content analysis and structured observation, the term **coding manual** is often preferred to describe the lists of codes for each item of information and the rules to be employed.

Quantitative data are also sometimes *recoded*. For example, if we have data on the exact age of each person in a sample, we may want to group people into age bands. The rationale for doing this is described in Chapter 15 and the procedure of recoding with a computer program is described in Chapter 16.

Coding also occurs in qualitative research, but the role it plays and its significance are different there from quantitative research. Coding in qualitative research is described in Chapter 24 and the procedure for coding with a qualitative data analysis computer program is described in Chapter 25.

Research in focus 11.1
Coding an open-ended question

Coding an open-ended question usually entails reading and rereading transcripts of respondents' replies and formulating distinct themes in their replies. A *coding frame* then needs to be designed that identifies the types of answer associated with each question and their respective codes (that is, numbers). A **coding schedule** may also be necessary to keep a record of rules to be followed in the identification of certain kinds of answer in terms of a theme. The numbers allocated to each answer can then be used in the computer processing of the data.

Livingstone et al. (2014) describe a survey that they conducted on children's perceptions of Internet risk. The survey was carried out using face-to-face interviews of over 25,000 European children aged 9 to 16 years who used the Internet. As with most surveys, the schedule comprised mainly closed-ended questions, but one question was open: 'What things on the Internet would bother people of your age?' Answers were written on a piece of paper which was then placed into an envelope that was sealed. This question was asked *before* the other questions that focused on risk, so that the children's replies to the open-ended question were not contaminated by other questions that had been asked. Just over one-third of the sample identified one or more risks. Livingstone et al. developed a coding scheme based on a pilot analysis of the verbatim comments. Coding was carried out by native speakers. Thus, the final coding scheme derived from an examination of some of the comments and a piloting of the scheme.

Up to three risks were coded for each child and each response was coded by two raters who coded independently of each other. The principal areas coded were:

- The type of risk, of which three types were identified and coded: content risk (for example, pornographic content, violent content); conduct risk from other young people (for example, bullying, hacking, insults); and contact risk from adults (for example, inappropriate contact from adults, grooming). Various other risks were coded, such as viruses and pop-ups.

- The type of platform on which the risk might occur (such as email, chat rooms, Facebook, Twitter).

- Emotions (such as fear, annoyance, disgust).

Cohen's kappa was calculated for inter-rater agreement for each of these (see Key concept 12.3). The level of agreement was generally quite high, though for 'Emotions' it was 0.63. The results show that the children identified a wide variety of risks and the researchers were able to show how these were connected in the children's minds to particular platforms.

Computers are increasingly being enlisted into the coding of open-ended questions. Akerlof et al. (2013) describe a postal questionnaire survey in which one of the questions was a closed-ended one which asked respondents whether they agreed that they personally have experienced global warming. Those who believed they had experienced it were asked an open-ended question: 'In what ways have you personally experienced global warming?' (Akerlof et al. 2013: 83–4). The authors used a computer to search for words and phrases that recurred. These were then developed into a coding schedule of twenty-eight variables. The schedule was then used by three raters to code thirty answers as a pilot exercise. Inter-rater agreement was generally high. The highest-rated personal experience was changes in the seasons. Fielding, Fielding, and Hughes (2013) have suggested that computer-assisted qualitative data analysis software (CAQDAS, which is covered in Chapter 25) can be helpfully used for coding answers to open-ended questions.

answers to open-ended questions is immensely time-consuming and adds additional costs to a survey. The problem of transcription is one continually faced by qualitative researchers using semi-structured and unstructured interviews (see Chapter 20).

Closed-ended questions

The advantages and disadvantages of closed-ended questions are in many respects implied in some of the considerations relating to open-ended questions.

Research in focus 11.2
Coding a very open-ended question

Foddy (1993) reports the results of an exercise in which he asked a small sample of his students 'Your father's occupation is (was) . . .' and requested three details: nature of business; size of business; and whether owner or employee. In answer to the size of business question, the replies were particularly variable in kind, including: 'big', 'small', 'very large', '3,000 acres', 'family', 'multinational', '200 people', and 'Philips'. The problem here is obvious: you simply cannot compare and therefore aggregate people's replies. In a sense, the problem is only partly to do with the difficulty of coding an open-ended question. It is also due to a lack of specificity in the question. If, instead, Foddy had asked 'How many employees are (were) there in your father's organization?', a more comparable set of answers should have been forthcoming. Whether his students would have known this information is, of course, yet another issue. However, the exercise does illustrate the potential problems of asking an open-ended question, particularly one like this that lacks a clear reference point for gauging size.

Advantages

Closed-ended questions offer the following advantages to researchers.

- It is easy to process answers. For example, the respondent in a self-administered questionnaire or the interviewer using a structured interview schedule will place a tick or circle an answer for the appropriate response. The appropriate code can then be almost mechanically derived from the selected answer, since the pre-codes are placed to the side of the fixed-choice answers. See Tips and skills 'Processing a closed-ended question' for an example, which is based on Tips and skills 'Closed-ended question with a vertical format' (see Chapter 10).

- Closed-ended questions enhance the comparability of answers. With post-coding there is always a problem of

knowing how far respondents' answers that receive a certain code are genuinely comparable. As previously noted, the assignment of codes to people's answers may be unreliable (see the sixth point in Thinking deeply 9.1). Checks are necessary to ensure that there is a good deal of agreement between coders and that coders do not change their coding conventions over time. Closed-ended questions essentially circumvent this problem.

- Closed-ended questions may clarify the meaning of a question for respondents. Sometimes, respondents may not be clear about what a question is getting at, and the availability of answers may help to clarify the situation for them.

- Closed-ended questions are easy for interviewers and/or respondents to complete. Precisely because interviewers

Tips and skills
Processing a closed-ended question

What do you think of the Prime Minister's performance in his job since he took office?

(Please tick the appropriate response)

Very good	____	5
Good	✓	(4)
Fair	____	3
Poor	____	2
Very poor	____	1

Research in focus 11.3
A comparison of results for a closed-ended and an open-ended question

Schuman and Presser (1981) conducted an experiment to determine how far responses to closed-ended questions can be improved by asking the questions first as open-ended questions and then developing categories of reply from respondents' answers. They asked a question about what people look for in work in both open and closed format. Different samples were used. They found considerable disparities between the two sets of answers (60 per cent of the open-format categories were not capable of being subsumed by the closed-format answers). They then revised the closed categories to reflect the answers they had received from people's open-ended answers. They readministered the open-ended question and the revised closed-ended question to two large samples of Americans. The question and the answers they received are as follows.

This next question is on the subject of work. People look for different things in a job. Which one of the following five things do you most prefer in a job? [closed-ended question]. What would you most prefer in a job? [open-ended question].

Closed-ended format		Open-ended format	
Answer	%	Answer involving . . .	%
Work that pays well	13.2	Pay	16.7
Work that gives a feeling of accomplishment	31.0	Feeling of accomplishment	14.5
Work where there is not too much supervision and you make most decisions yourself	11.7	Control of work	4.6
Work that is pleasant and people are nice to work with	19.8	Pleasant work	14.5
Work that is steady + little chance of being laid off	20.3	Security	7.6
	96% of sample		57.9% of sample
Other/DK/NA	4.0	Opportunity for promotion	1.0
		Short hours/lots of free time	1.6
		Working conditions	3.1
		Benefits	2.3
		Satisfaction/liking a job	15.6
		Other responses	18.3
	4.0% of sample		41.9% of sample

With the revised form for the closed-ended question, Schuman and Presser were able to find a much higher proportion of the sample whose answers to the open-ended question corresponded to the closed one. They argue that the new closed-ended question is superior to its predecessor and is also superior to the open-ended question. However, it is still disconcerting that only 58 per cent of respondents answering the open-ended question could be subsumed under the same categories as those answering the closed one. Also, the distributions are somewhat different: for example, twice as many respondents answer in terms of a feeling of accomplishment with the closed format than with the open one. Nonetheless, the experiment demonstrates the desirability of generating forced-choice answers from open-ended questions.

and respondents are not expected to write extensively and instead have to place ticks or circle answers, closed-ended questions are easier and quicker to complete.

- In interviews, closed-ended questions reduce the possibility of variability in the recording of answers in structured interviewing. If interviewers do not write down exactly what respondents say to them when answering questions, a source of bias and hence of invalidity is in prospect. Closed-ended questions reduce this possibility, though there is still the potential problem that interviewers may have to *interpret* what is said to them in order to assign answers to a category.

Disadvantages

However, closed-ended questions exhibit certain disadvantages.

- There is a loss of spontaneity in respondents' answers. There is always the possibility that they might come up with interesting replies that are not covered by the fixed answers that are provided. One solution to this possible problem is to ensure that an open-ended question is used to generate the categories (see Research in focus 11.3). Also, there may be a good case for including a possible response category of 'Other' and allowing respondents to indicate what they mean by using this category.
- It can be difficult to make forced-choice answers mutually exclusive. The fixed answers that respondents see

should not overlap. If they do overlap, the respondents will not know which one to choose and so will arbitrarily select one or the other or alternatively may tick both answers. If a respondent were to tick two or more answers when one is required, it would mean that you would have to treat the respondent's answer as missing data, since you would not know which of the ticked answers represented the true one. One of the most frequently encountered forms of this problem can be seen in the following age bands:

18–30

30–40

40–50

50–60

60 and over

In which band would a 40-year-old position him- or herself?

- It is difficult to make forced-choice answers exhaustive. All possible answers should really be catered for, although in practice this may be difficult to achieve, since this rule may result in excessively long lists of possible answers. Again, a category of 'Other' may be desirable to provide a wide range of answers.
- There may be variation among respondents in the interpretation of forced-choice answers. There is always a problem when asking any question that

Student experience
Closed-ended questions and quantitative data analysis

Joe Thomson and his fellow students who formed a team conducting research on students at their university favoured closed-ended questions because of the ease with which they could be analysed using SPSS, the software that is covered in Chapter 16. When they reviewed the interview schedule they had devised after it had been piloted, they focused on such issues as:

were there too many open- or closed-ended questions so not providing enough qualitative or quantitative data, or should the questions be on a dichotomous or ranking scale. As the results of the questionnaire were to be analysed using a data analysis computer program (SPSS), the group tended to favour closed-ended questions to give definite answers that could be correlated to show trends.

However, Sophie Mason, who was also a member of a team doing survey research at Joe's university, felt that the combination of closed and open-ended questions did offer certain advantages: 'By using both open- and closed-ended questions it was possible to gain the necessary statistics as well as opinions and experiences unique to each student.'

 To read more, go to the Online Resource Centre: www.oxfordtextbooks.co.uk/orc/brymansrm5e/

certain terms may be interpreted differently by respondents. If this is the case, then validity will be jeopardized. The presence of forced-choice answers can exacerbate this possible problem, because there may be variation in the understanding of key terms in the answers.

- Closed-ended questions may be irritating to respondents when they are unable to find a category that they feel applies to them.

- In interviews, a large number of closed-ended questions may make it difficult to establish rapport, because the respondent and interviewer are less likely to engage with each other in a conversation. The interview is more likely to have an impersonal feel to it. However, since the extent to which rapport is a desirable attribute of structured interviewing is somewhat difficult to determine (see Chapter 9), this is not necessarily too much of a problem.

Student experience
The dilemmas of open- and closed-ended questions

Joe Thomson encountered the classic dilemmas with the use of open- and closed-ended questions in the course of his research on students at the University of East Anglia. He writes:

As the results were analysed using SPSS, more closed-ended questions were asked, which I feel restrains scope and didn't give the interviewee a chance for personal expression through providing a specific range of answers. This was an issue that was decided would be overlooked, as the most important thing was that the results could be analysed and patterns drawn. Although open-ended questions provide more qualitative data, they are difficult to apply to any kind of scale and therefore are not easy to compare.

As he notes, closed-ended questions do not readily give respondents 'a chance for personal expression', but the data deriving from them are easier to analyse. On the other hand, open-ended questions may give richer qualitative data but it is less easy to analyse.

 To read more, go to the Online Resource Centre: www.oxfordtextbooks.co.uk/orc/brymansrm5e/

Types of questions

It is worth bearing in mind that when you are employing a structured interview or self-administered questionnaire, you will probably be asking several different types of question. There are various ways of classifying these, but here are some prominent types of question:

- *Personal factual questions.* These are questions that ask the respondent to provide *personal information*, such as age, education, occupation, marital status, income, and so on. This kind of question also includes questions about *behaviour*. Such factual questions may have to rely on the respondents' memories, as when they are asked about such things as frequency of church attendance, how often they visit the cinema, or when they last ate out in a restaurant.

- *Factual questions about others.* This type asks for personal information about others, sometimes in combination with the respondent. An example of such a question would be one about household income, which would require respondents to consider their own incomes in conjunction with those of their partners. Rosenfeld and Thomas's (2012) survey research on how couples meet in the Internet era asked respondents many questions about themselves and how they met their partners, but also asked questions about the partners, such as the partner's gender, ethnicity, religion, education, and political affiliation.

- *Informant factual questions.* Sometimes, we place people who are interviewed or who complete a questionnaire in the position of informants rather than of respondents answering questions about themselves. This kind of question can also be found in certain contexts, as when people are asked about such things as the size of the firm for which they work, who owns it, whether it employs certain technologies, and whether it has certain specialist functions. Such questions are essentially about characteristics of an entity of which they have knowledge, in this case, a firm. However, informant factual questions may also be concerned with behaviour. The measurement of abusive supervision in the research referred to in Research in the news 3.1 and Research in focus 7.4 entailed asking respondents about the behaviour of their supervisor, such as whether the supervisor 'puts me down in front of others'. There were five such items, and responses were on a five-point Likert scale from 'never' to 'very often'.

- *Questions about attitudes.* Questions about attitudes are very common in both structured interview and self-administered questionnaire research. The Likert scale is one of the most frequently encountered formats for measuring attitudes. As Voas (2014) points out, attitudes are often confused with beliefs and values. He proposes that an attitude is 'an everyday judgement, a normative view of a specific matter' (2014: 2.1).

- *Questions about beliefs.* Respondents are frequently asked about their beliefs, possibly religious and political beliefs. Another form of asking questions about beliefs is when respondents are asked whether they believe that certain matters are true or false—for example, a question asking whether the respondent believes the UK is better off as a result of being a member of the European Union. Alternatively, in a survey about crime, respondents might be asked to indicate whether they believe that the incidence of certain crimes is increasing.

- *Questions about normative standards and values.* Respondents may be asked to indicate what principles of behaviour influence them or they hold dear. The elicitation of such norms of behaviour is likely to have considerable overlap with questions about attitudes and beliefs, since norms and values can be construed as having elements of both.

- *Questions about knowledge.* Questions can sometimes be employed to 'test' respondents' knowledge in an area. For example, Sturgis, Allum, and Smith (2008) refer to a CATI survey conducted by a market research agency which asked respondents to indicate whether each of the following political knowledge questions is true or false:

  > 1. Britain's electoral system is based on proportional representation.
  > 2. MPs from different parties are on parliamentary committees.
  > 3. The Conservatives are opposed to the ratification of a constitution for the European Union.
  >
  > (Sturgis et al. 2008: 94)

Most structured interview schedules and self-administered questionnaires comprise more than one, and often several, of the types of question listed above. It is important to bear in mind the distinction between different types of question. There are a number of reasons for this.

- It is useful to keep the distinctions in mind because they force you to clarify in your own mind what you are asking about, albeit in rather general terms.

- An understanding of the different types of question will help to guard against asking questions in an inappropriate format. For example, a Likert scale is unsuitable for asking factual questions about behaviour.

- When building scales such as a Likert scale, do not mix different types of question. For example, attitudes and beliefs sound similar, and you may be tempted to use the same format for mixing questions about them. However, it is best not to do this and instead to have separate scales for attitudes and beliefs. If you mix them, the questions cannot really be measuring the same thing, so that measurement validity is threatened.

 # Rules for designing questions

Over the years, numerous rules (and rules of thumb) have been devised in connection with the 'dos' and 'don'ts' of asking questions in social science research. In spite of this, it is one of the commonest areas for making mistakes. There are three simple rules of thumb as a starting point; beyond that, the rules specified below act as a means of avoiding further pitfalls.

General rules of thumb

Always bear in mind your research questions

The questions that you will ask in your self-administered questionnaire or structured interview should always be geared to answering your research questions. This first rule of thumb has at least two implications. First, it means that you should make sure that you ask questions that relate to your research questions. Ensure, in other words, that the questionnaire questions you ask will allow your research questions to be addressed. You will definitely not want to find out at a late stage that you forgot to include some crucial questions. Second, it means that there is little point in asking questions that do not relate to your research questions. It is also not fair to waste your respondents' time answering questions that are of little value in your research.

What do you want to know?

Rule of thumb number two is to decide exactly what it is you want to know. Consider the seemingly harmless question:

Do you have a car?

What is this question seeking to tap? Is it car ownership? If it is car ownership, the question is inadequate, largely because of the ambiguity of the word 'have'. The question can be interpreted as: personally owning a car; having access to a car in a household; and 'having' a company car or a car for business use. Thus, an answer of 'yes' may or may not be indicative of car ownership. If you want to know whether your respondent owns a car, ask him or her directly about this matter. Similarly, there is nothing wrong with the question:

How many children do you have?

However, if what you are trying to address is the standard of living of a person or household, the crucial issue is how many are living at home.

How would *you* answer it?

Rule of thumb number three is to put yourself in the position of the respondent. Ask yourself the question and try to work out how *you* would reply. If you do this, there is at least the possibility that the ambiguity that is inherent in the 'Do you have a car?' question will manifest itself, and its inability to tap car ownership would become apparent. Let us say as well that there is a follow-up question to the previous one:

Have you driven the car this week?

Again, this looks harmless, but if you put yourself in the role of a respondent, it will be apparent that the phrase 'this week' is vague. Does it mean the last seven days or does it mean the week in which the questioning takes place, which will, of course, be affected by such things as whether the question is being asked on a Monday or a Friday? In part, this issue arises because the question designer has not decided what the question is about. Equally, however, a moment's reflection in which you put

yourself in the position of the respondent might reveal the difficulty of answering this question. Questions that are difficult to understand have several negative consequences for surveys, such as failure to complete the questionnaire, more 'nonsubstantive responses' (such as 'don't knows'), and more middle alternative responses (such as 'neither agree nor disagree'), according to research by Lenzner (2012).

Taking account of these rules of thumb and the following rules about asking questions may help you to avoid the more obvious pitfalls.

Specific rules when designing questions

Avoid ambiguous terms in questions

Avoid terms such as 'often' and 'regularly' as measures of frequency. They are very ambiguous, because respondents will operate with different frames of reference when employing them. Sometimes their use is unavoidable, but when there is an alternative that allows actual frequency to be measured, this will nearly always be preferable. So, a question such as:

How often do you usually visit the cinema?

Very often   _____

Quite often   _____

Not very often   _____

Not at all   _____

suffers from the problem that, with the exception of 'not at all', the terms in the response categories are ambiguous. Instead, try to ask about actual frequency, such as:

How frequently do you usually visit the cinema?
(Please tick whichever category comes closest to the number of times you visit the cinema)

More than once a week   _____

Once a week   _____

2 or 3 times a month   _____

Once a month   _____

A few times a year   _____

Once a year   _____

Less than once a year   _____

Alternatively, you might simply ask respondents about the number of times they have visited the cinema in the previous four weeks.

Words such as 'family' are also ambiguous, because people will have different notions of who makes up their family. As previously noted, words such as 'have' can also be sources of ambiguity.

It is also important to bear in mind that certain common words, such as 'dinner' and 'book', mean different things to different people. For some, dinner is a midday snack, whereas for others it is a substantial evening meal. Similarly, some people refer to magazines or to catalogues and brochures as books, whereas others work with a more restricted definition. In such cases, it will be necessary to define what you mean by such terms.

Avoid long questions

It is commonly believed that long questions are undesirable. In a structured interview the interviewee can lose the thread of the question, and in a self-administered questionnaire the respondent may be tempted to omit such questions or to skim them and therefore not give them sufficient attention. However, Sudman and Bradburn (1982) have suggested that this advice applies better to attitude questions than to ones that ask about behaviour. They argue that, when the focus is on behaviour, longer questions have certain positive features in interviews—for example, they are more likely to provide memory cues and they facilitate recall because of the time taken to complete the question. However, by and large, the general advice is to keep questions short.

Avoid double-barrelled questions

Double-barrelled questions are ones that in fact ask about two things. The problem with this kind of question is that it leaves respondents unsure about how best to respond. Take the question:

How satisfied are you with pay and conditions in your job?

The problem here is obvious: the respondent may be satisfied with one but not the other. Not only will the respondent be unclear about how to reply, but any answer that is given is unlikely to be a good reflection of the level of satisfaction with pay *and* conditions. Similarly:

How frequently does your husband help with cooking and cleaning?

suffers from the same problem. A husband may provide extensive help with cooking but be totally uninvolved in cleaning, so that any stipulation of frequency of help is going to be ambiguous and to create uncertainty for respondents.

The same rule applies to fixed-choice answers. In Research in focus 11.3, one of Schuman and Presser's (1981) answers is:

Work that is pleasant and people are nice to work with.

While there is likely to be a symmetry between the two ideas in this answer—pleasant work and nice people—there is no *necessary* correspondence between them.

Pleasant work may be important for someone, but he or she may be relatively indifferent to the issue of how pleasant their co-workers are. A further instance of a double-barrelled question is provided in Thinking deeply 11.1.

Double-barrelled questions are a fairly common feature of even quite well-known surveys. Timming (2009) has point out that there are several such questions in the Workplace Employment Relations Survey (WERS) of 2004. The questionnaire can be found at **www.gov.uk/government/publications/the-2004-workplace-employment-relations-survey-wers** (accessed 27 October 2014; this survey is referred to in Chapter 14). For example, one of the questions asks employees:

Overall, how good would you say managers at this workplace are at . . .

It then lists three areas and the respondent has to reply on a scale: very good, good, neither good nor poor, poor, very poor (there is also a 'Don't know' option). The three areas are:

Seeking the views of employees or employee representatives

Responding to suggestions from employees or employee representatives

Allowing employees or employee representatives to influence final decisions

In the case of each of these questions, the WERS researchers use the phrase 'employees or employee representatives'. Timming argues that respondents could hold quite different views for employees as against employee representatives regarding how good managers are in these three respects. Strictly speaking the researchers should ask separate questions with respect to *both* employees and employee representatives. Further, he identifies several other double-barrelled questions in the WERS questionnaire. Regarding one of the other double-barrelled questions, Forth et al. (2010: 58) in a reply to Timming's article argue that asking separate questions 'would arguably add little to the overall stock of knowledge emerging from WERS, yet would inevitably lengthen the questionnaire'. This is a reasonable point to make, and the point has been made several times in this book that all researchers have to wrestle with such practical considerations. However, the problem remains: respondents will be unsure how to reply to most double-barrelled questions.

Avoid very general questions

It is easy to ask a very general question when in fact what is wanted is a response to a specific issue. The problem with very general questions is that they lack a frame of reference. Thus:

How satisfied are you with your job?

Thinking deeply 11.1
Matching question and answers in closed-ended questions (and some double-barrelled questions too)

While the first edition of this book was being prepared, I was reading a novel whose publisher had inserted a feedback questionnaire within its pages. At one point in the questionnaire there is a series of Likert-style items regarding the book's quality. In each case, the respondent is asked to indicate whether the attribute being asked about is: poor; acceptable; average; good; or excellent. However, in each case, the items are presented as questions, for example:

Was the writing elegant, seamless, imaginative?

The problem here is that an answer to this question is 'yes' or 'no'. At most, we might have gradations of yes and no, such as: definitely; to a large extent; to some extent; not at all. However, 'poor' or 'excellent' cannot be answers to this question. The questions should have been presented as statements, such as:

Please indicate the quality of the book in terms of each of the following criteria:

The elegance of the writing:

Poor   _____

Acceptable   _____

Average   _____

Good   _____

Excellent   _____

Of course, I have changed the sense slightly here, because, as it is stated, a further problem with the question is that it is a double-barrelled question. In fact, it is 'treble-barrelled', because it actually asks about three attributes of the writing in one. The reader's views about the three qualities may vary. A similar question asks:

Did the plot offer conflict, twists, and a resolution?

Again, not only does the question imply a 'yes' or 'no', it actually asks about three attributes. How would you answer if you had different views about each of the three criteria?

It might be argued that the issue is a nit-picking one: someone reading the question obviously knows that he or she is being asked to rate the quality of the book in terms of each attribute. The problem is that we simply do not know what the impact might be of a disjunction between question and answer, so you may as well get the connection between question and answers right (and do not ask double- or treble-barrelled questions either!).

seems harmless but it lacks specificity. Does it refer to pay, conditions, the nature of the work, or all of these? If there is the possibility of such diverse interpretations, respondents are likely to vary in their interpretations too, and this will be a source of error. My favourite general question comes from Karl Marx's *Enquête ouvrière*, a questionnaire that was sent to 25,000 French socialists and others (though there is apparently no record of any being returned). The final (one-hundredth) question reads:

What is the general, physical, intellectual, and moral condition of men and women employed in your trade?

(Bottomore and Rubel 1963: 218)

Avoid leading questions

Leading or loaded questions are ones that appear to lead the respondent in a particular direction. Questions of the kind 'Do you agree with the view that . . .?' fall into this class of question. The obvious problem with such a question is that it suggests a particular reply to respondents, although invariably they do have the ability to rebut any implied answer. However, it is the fact that they might feel pushed in a certain direction that is undesirable. Such a question as:

Would you agree to cutting taxes further even though welfare provision for the most needy sections of the population might be reduced?

is likely to make it difficult for some people to answer in terms of fiscal probity. A possible leading question is suggested in Research in the news 9.1. But, once again, Marx is the source of a favourite leading question:

> If you are paid piece rates, is the quality of the article made a pretext for fraudulent deductions from wages?
> (Bottomore and Rubel 1963: 215)

Avoid questions that are actually asking two questions

The double-barrelled question is a clear instance of the transgression of this rule, but in addition there is the case of a question such as:

> Which political party did you vote for at the last general election?

What if the respondent did not vote? It is better to ask two separate questions:

> Did you vote at the last general election?
>
> Yes _____
>
> No _____
>
> If Yes, which political party did you vote for?

Another way in which more than one question can be asked is with a question like:

> How effective have your different job search strategies been?
>
> Very effective   _____
>
> Fairly effective   _____
>
> Not very effective   _____
>
> Not at all effective _____

The obvious difficulty is that, if the respondent has used more than one job search strategy, his or her estimation of effectiveness will vary for each strategy. A mechanism is needed for assessing the success of each strategy rather than forcing respondents to average out their sense of how successful the various strategies were.

Avoid questions that include negatives

The problem with questions with 'not' or similar formulations in them is that it is easy for the respondent to miss the word out when completing a self-administered questionnaire or to miss it when being interviewed. If this occurs, a respondent is likely to answer in the opposite way from the one intended. There are occasions when it is impossible to avoid negatives, but a question like the following should be avoided as far as possible:

> Do you agree with the view that students should not have to take out loans to finance higher education?

Instead, the question should be asked in a positive format. Questions with double negatives should be totally avoided, because it is difficult to know how to respond to them. Oppenheim (1966) gives the following as an example of this kind of question:

> Would you rather not use a non-medicated shampoo?

It is quite difficult to establish what an answer of 'yes' or 'no' would actually mean in response to this question.

One context in which it is difficult to avoid using questions with negatives is when designing Likert items. Since you may want to identify respondents who exhibit response sets and will therefore want to reverse the direction of your question asking (see Chapter 9), the use of negatives will be difficult to avoid.

Avoid technical terms

Use simple, plain language and avoid jargon. Do not ask a question like:

> Do you sometimes feel alienated from work?

The problem here is that many respondents will not know what is meant by 'alienated', and furthermore are likely to have different views of what it means, even if it is a remotely meaningful term to them.

Consider the following question:

> The influence of the TUC on national politics has declined in recent years.
>
> Strongly agree   _____
>
> Agree   _____
>
> Undecided   _____
>
> Disagree   _____
>
> Strongly disagree _____

The use of acronyms such as TUC can be a problem, because some people may be unfamiliar with what they stand for.

Does the respondent have the necessary knowledge?

There is little point in asking respondents lots of questions about matters of which they have no knowledge. It is very doubtful whether meaningful data about smartphone use could be extracted from respondents who have never used one.

Make sure that there is a symmetry between a closed-ended question and its answers

A common mistake is for a question and its answers to be out of phase with each other. Thinking deeply 11.1 describes such an instance.

Make sure that the answers provided for a closed-ended question are balanced

A fairly common error when asking closed-ended questions is for the answers that are provided to be unbalanced. For example, imagine that a respondent is given a series of options such as:

Excellent	____
Good	____
Acceptable	____
Poor	____

In this case, the response choices are balanced towards a favourable response. Excellent and Good are both positive; Acceptable is a neutral or middle position; and Poor is a negative response. In other words, the answers are loaded in favour of a positive rather than a negative reply, so that a further negative response choice (perhaps Very poor) is required.

Memory problems

Do not rely too much on stretching people's memories to the extent that the answers are likely to be inaccurate. It would be nice to have accurate replies to a question about the number of times respondents have visited the cinema in the previous twelve months, but it is highly unlikely that most will in fact recall events accurately over such a long space of time (other perhaps than those who have not gone at all or who have gone only once or twice in the preceding twelve months). It was for this reason that, in the similar question referred to above, the time frame was predominantly just one month.

Forced-choice rather than tick all that apply

Sometimes, when asking a question that allows the respondent to select more than one answer, there is an instruction that says something like 'Please tick all that apply'. An example might be a question that asks which of a list of sources of regular exercise the respondent has engaged in during the previous six months. The question might look something like this:

> **Which of the following sources of exercise have you engaged in during the last six months?**
> (Please tick *all* that apply)
>
> | | |
> |---|---|
> | Going to a gym | ☐ |
> | Sport | ☐ |
> | Cycling on the road | ☐ |
> | Jogging | ☐ |
> | Long walks | ☐ |
> | Other (please specify) | ☐ |

An alternative way of asking a question like this is to use a conventional forced-choice format, such as:

> **Have you engaged in the following sources of exercise during the last six months?**
>
> | | Yes | No |
> |---|---|---|
> | Going to a gym | ☐ | ☐ |
> | Sport | ☐ | ☐ |
> | Cycling on the road | ☐ | ☐ |
> | Jogging | ☐ | ☐ |
> | Long walks | ☐ | ☐ |
> | Other (please specify) | ☐ | ☐ |

It is easy to presume that these two ways of asking questions where there is the potential for more than one answer are equivalent. However, there is compelling evidence that the second of these two formats (the forced-choice one) is superior. Smyth et al. (2006) have shown that the forced-choice format results in more options being selected. As a result, Dillman et al. (2014) advocate the use of the forced-choice format for this kind of question situation.

Middle alternatives in attitude scales

One area of controversy over the years has been whether to offer a middle option in attitude rating scales and similar measuring devices. Examples are 'neither agree nor disagree', 'neither approve nor disapprove', and 'neither satisfied nor dissatisfied'. It is sometimes argued that middle alternatives play into the hands of respondents who satisfice, in that it might give them an option which does not require them to give significant thought or attention to their answer. On the other hand, *not to* supply a middle alternative may risk some respondents having to select a response that they do not in fact hold, e.g. selecting 'agree' when in fact they do not hold such an opinion. Also, it may be that the failure to include a middle alternative could result in greater item non-response and therefore missing data (Revilla, Saris, and Krosnick 2014). Sudman and Bradburn (1982) suggest that the evidence implies that the inclusion of the middle alterative does not affect the ratio of (say) agreement to disagreement relative to a question that excludes it. Sturgis, Roberts, and Smith (2014) found that for the vast majority of respondents the selection of a middle alternative was to do with not having an opinion on the issue and that therefore a middle alternative should always be offered to respondents; otherwise they will feel compelled to select a response that is not in tune with their actual position. As Sudman and Bradburn (1982) suggest, it is probably best to include middle alternatives unless there is a very good reason for not including them.

There is a similar debate relating to whether to offer 'don't know' alternatives. The reasons for and against

Tips and skills
Common mistakes when asking questions

Over the years, I have read many projects and dissertations based on structured interviews and self-administered questionnaires. I have noticed that a small number of mistakes recur. Here is a list of some of them.

- An excessive use of open-ended questions. Students sometimes include too many open-ended questions. While a resistance to closed-ended questions may be understandable, although not something I would agree with, open-ended questions are likely to reduce your response rate and will make your analysis more difficult. Keep the number to an absolute minimum.

- An excessive use of yes/no questions. Sometimes students include lots of questions that provide just a yes/no form of response. This is usually the result of lazy thinking and preparation. The world rarely fits into this kind of response. Take a question like:

  Are you satisfied with opportunities for promotion in the firm?

  Yes   ____

  No   ____

  This leaves out the possibility that respondents' feelings will not be a simple case of being satisfied or not. People vary in the intensity of their feelings about such things. So why not rephrase it as:

  How satisfied are you with opportunities for promotion in the firm?

  Very satisfied   ____

  Satisfied   ____

  Neither satisfied nor dissatisfied   ____

  Dissatisfied   ____

  Very dissatisfied   ____

- Students often fail to give clear instructions on self-administered questionnaires about how the questions should be answered. Specify whether you want a tick, something to be circled or deleted, or whatever. If only one response is required, make sure you say so—for example, 'tick the answer that comes closest to your view'.

- Be careful about letting respondents choose more than one answer. Sometimes it is unavoidable, but questions that allow more than one reply are often a pain to analyse. If you do want to ask a question for more than one answer, note the previous advice suggesting that a forced-choice format (which is less of a pain to analyse) tends to be superior to a 'tick all that apply' one.

- In spite of the fact that I always warn about the problems of overlapping categories, students still formulate closed answers that are not mutually exclusive. In addition, some categories may be omitted. For example:

  How many times per week do you typically use public transport?

  1–3 times   ____

  3–6 times   ____

  6–9 times   ____

  More than 10 times   ____

  Not only does the respondent not know where to answer if his or her answer might be 3 or 6 times; there is also no answer for someone who would want to answer 10.

- Students sometimes do not ensure the answers correspond to the question. For example:

  Do you regularly go to your gym?

  More than once a week   ____

  Once a week   ____

  2 or 3 times a month   ____

  Once a month   ____

The problem here is that the answer to the question is logically either 'yes' or 'no'. However, the student quite sensibly wants to gain some idea of frequency (something that I would agree with in the light of my second point in this list!). The problem is that the question and the response categories do not correspond. The student first needs to establish whether the respondent goes to a gym and then should ask a question about frequency, like:

How frequently do you go to your gym in any month?

More than once a week	____
Once a week	____
2 or 3 times a month	____
Once a month	____

- Students sometimes fail to provide a time frame (and one that is appropriate) with their questions. Thus, the question 'How much do you earn?' is hopeless because it fails to provide the respondent with a time frame. Is it per week, per month, or per annum? A further though separate problem is that respondents need to be told whether the figure required should be gross (i.e. before deductions for tax, national insurance, etc.) or net (i.e. after deductions). In view of the sensitivities surrounding a person's salary, it is often best not to ask the question this way but to provide instead a set of income bands on a show card (for example, below £10,000; £10,000–£19,999; £20,000–£29,999, etc.).

- Do remember the advice given in the text about the importance of using a format that makes it easy for respondents to answer and that also reduces the likelihood of them making mistakes in answering. While I was writing the previous edition of this book, I was given a card by someone who had carried out some work on my house. The card had to be sent to my local trading standards office. It contained a number of questions about my satisfaction with aspects of his work. At the end of the short questionnaire, the following question (or is it two questions?) was presented:

Please tick your age category

Under 50   O   60–64   O   65–74   O

75+   O   Male   O   Female   O

It is difficult to know where to start with this question. One obvious problem is that it seems to assume that nobody will be in the 50–59 age range. The second problem is that the answer categories for someone's age are wrapped around onto a second line. This is really not desirable. If your answer categories are to have a horizontal format, keep them on one line. If you cannot do that because of space problems, make the answers vertical. However, the most bizarre aspect is the way the categories Male and Female appear apparently on the same line as an age band. Also, they appear without a question! Do try to bear in mind the importance of good formatting and do remember that people can be aged between 50 and 59!

If you never committed any of these 'sins', you would be well on the way to producing a questionnaire that would stand out from the rest, provided you took into account the other advice I give in this chapter as well!

including the alternative are very similar to those relating to the inclusion of middle alternatives. A series of experiments conducted in the USA suggest that questions that appear later on in a questionnaire are more likely to result in 'don't know' being selected (Krosnick et al. 2002). This finding implies that as respondents become increasingly tired or bored as the questioning proceeds, they are prone to satisfice. One implication of this finding is that shorter questionnaires should definitely include the 'don't know' option. De Leeuw and Hox (2015) refer to a study that suggests that gentle probes administered either in telephone interviews or in Web questionnaires can reduce the number of 'don't know' answers, because when respondents elaborate on their reasons for opting for 'don't know', a more substantive answer is gleaned.

Vignette questions

A form of asking mainly closed-ended questions that has been used in connection with the examination of people's normative standards is the vignette technique. The technique essentially comprises presenting respondents with one or more scenarios and then asking them how they would respond when confronted with the circumstances of that scenario. Research in focus 11.4 describes a vignette that was employed in the context of a study of family obligations in Britain. The aim was to elicit respondents' normative judgements about how family members should respond to relatives who are in need and *who* should do the responding.

The vignette is designed to tease out respondents' norms concerning family obligations in respect of several

Research in focus 11.4
A vignette to establish family obligations

Jim and Margaret Robinson are a married couple in their early forties. Jim's parents, who live several hundred miles away, have had a serious car accident and they need long-term daily care and help. Jim is their only son. He and his wife both work for the Electricity Board and they could both get transfers so they could work near his parents.

Card E

(a) From the card, what should Jim and Margaret do?

Move to live near Jim's parents

Have Jim's parents move to live with them

Give Jim's parents money to help them pay for daily care

Let Jim's parents make their own arrangements

Do something else (SPECIFY)

Don't know

(b) In fact, Jim and Margaret are prepared to move and live near Jim's parents, but teachers at their children's school say that moving might have a bad effect on their children's education. Both children will soon be taking O-levels [predecessors to the current GCSE examinations].

What should Jim and Margaret do? Should they move or should they stay?

Move

Stay

(c) Why do you think they should move/stay?

Probe fully verbatim

(d) Jim and Margaret *do* decide to go and live near Jim's parents. A year later Jim's mother dies and his father's condition gets worse so that he needs full-time care.

Should Jim or Margaret give up their jobs to take care of Jim's father? *IF YES*: Who should give up their job, Jim or Margaret?

Yes, Jim should give up his job

Yes, Margaret should give up her job

No, neither should give up their jobs

Don't know/Depends

(Finch 1987: 108)

factors: the nature of the care (whether long- or short-term and whether it should entail direct involvement or just the provision of resources); the significance of geographical proximity; the dilemma of paid work and care; and the gender component of who should give up a job if that was deemed the appropriate course of action. There is a gradual increase in the specificity of the situation facing Jim and Margaret and therefore the respondent. Initially, we are not aware of whether Jim and Margaret are prepared to move; then we know they are; and then we learn they do in fact decide to move, which leads to the question of whether one of them should become a full-time carer.

Many aspects of the issues being tapped by the series of questions could be accessed through attitude items, such as:

> When a working couple decides that one of them should care for parents, the wife should be the one to give up her job.
>
> Strongly agree ____
>
> Agree ____
>
> Undecided ____
>
> Disagree ____
>
> Strongly disagree ____

The advantage of the vignette over such an attitude question is that it anchors the choice in a situation and as such reduces the possibility of an unreflective reply.

Finch (1987) also argues that, when the subject matter is a sensitive area (in this case, dealing with family relationships), there is the possibility that the questions may be seen as threatening by respondents. Respondents may feel that they are being judged by their replies. Finch argues that because the questions are about other people (and imaginary ones at that) there is some distance between the questioning and the respondent, which results in a less threatening context. However, it is hard to believe that respondents will not feel that their replies will at least in part be seen as reflecting on them, even if the questions are not about them as such.

One obvious requirement of the vignette technique is that the scenarios must be believable, so that considerable effort needs to go into the construction of credible situations. Finch points to some further considerations in relation to this style of questioning. It is more or less impossible to establish how far assumptions are being made about the characters in the scenario (such as their ethnicity) and what the significance of those assumptions might be for the validity and comparability of people's replies. It is also difficult to establish how far people's answers reflect their own normative views or indeed how they themselves would act when confronted with the kinds of choices revealed in the scenarios. However, in spite of these reservations, the vignette technique warrants serious consideration when the research focus is concerned with an area that lends itself to this style of questioning.

 # Piloting and pre-testing questions

It is always desirable to conduct a pilot study before administering a self-administered questionnaire or structured interview schedule to your sample. In fact, the desirability of piloting such instruments is not solely to do with trying to ensure that survey questions operate well; piloting also has a role in ensuring that the research instrument as a whole functions well. Pilot studies may be particularly crucial in relation to research based on the self-administered questionnaire, since there will not be an interviewer present to clear up any confusion. Also, with interviews, persistent problems may emerge after a few interviews have been carried out, and these can then be addressed. However, with self-administered questionnaires, since they are sent or handed out in large numbers, considerable wastage may occur before any problems become apparent.

Here are some uses of pilot studies in survey research.

- If the main study will include mainly closed-ended questions, open-ended questions can be asked in the

pilot to generate the fixed-choice answers. Glock (1988), for example, extols the virtues of conducting qualitative interviews in preparation for a survey for precisely this kind of reason.

- Piloting an interview schedule can provide interviewers with some experience of using it and can infuse them with a greater sense of confidence.

- If everyone (or virtually everyone) who answers a question replies in the same way, the resulting data are unlikely to be of interest because they do not form a variable. A pilot study allows such a question to be identified.

- In interview surveys, it may be possible to identify questions that make respondents feel uncomfortable and to detect any tendency for respondents' interest to be lost at certain junctures.

- Questions that seem not to be understood (more likely to be realized in an interview than in a self-administered questionnaire context) or questions that are often not answered should become apparent. The latter problem of questions being skipped may be due to confusing or threatening phrasing, poorly worded instructions, or confusing positioning in the interview schedule or questionnaire. Whatever the cause might be, such missing data are undesirable, and a pilot study may be instrumental in identifying the problem.

- Pilot studies allow the researcher to determine the adequacy of instructions to interviewers, or to respondents completing a self-administered questionnaire.

- It may be possible to consider how well the questions flow and whether it is necessary to move some of them around to improve this feature.

The pilot should not be carried out on people who might have been members of the sample that would be employed in the main study. One reason for this is that, if you are seeking to employ probability sampling, the selecting-out of a number of members of the population or sample may affect the representativeness of any subsequent sample. If possible, it is best to find a small set of respondents who are comparable to members of the population from which the sample for the main study will be taken.

Using existing questions

One final observation regarding the asking of questions is that you should also consider using questions that have been used by other researchers for at least part of your questionnaire or interview schedule. This may seem like stealing, and you would be advised to contact the researchers concerned regarding the use of questions they have devised. However, employing existing questions allows you to use questions that have in a sense been piloted for you. If any reliability and validity testing has taken place, you will know about the measurement qualities of the existing questions you use. A further advantage of using existing questions is that they allow you to draw comparisons with other research. This might allow you to indicate whether change has occurred or whether the findings apply to your sample. For example, if you are researching job satisfaction, using one of the standard job satisfaction scales would allow you to compare your findings with those of other researchers. Alternatively, using

the same questions as another researcher may allow you to explore whether the location of your sample appears to make a difference to the findings. While you need to be cautious about inferring too much from such comparisons between your own and other researchers' data, the findings can nonetheless be illuminating.

At the very least, examining questions used by others might give you some ideas about how best to approach your own questions, even if you decide not to use them as they stand. The use of existing questions is a common practice among researchers. For example, the researchers who developed the scale designed to measure attitudes to vegetarians (Research in focus 7.6) used several existing questions devised for measuring other concepts in which they were interested, such as measures of authoritarianism and political conservatism. These other measures had known properties in terms of their reliability and validity. Similarly, Walklate (2000: 194) describes how,

Tips and skills
Getting help in designing questions

When designing questions, as I suggested above, try to put yourself in the position of someone who has been asked to answer the questions. This can be difficult, because some (if not all!) of the questions may not apply to you—for example, if you are a young student doing a survey of retired people. However, try to think about how *you* would reply. This means concentrating not just on the questions themselves but also on the links between the questions. For example, do filter questions work in the way you expect them to? Then try the question out on some people you know, as in a pilot study. Ask them to be critical and to consider how well the questions connect to each other. Also, do look at the questionnaires and structured interview schedules that other experienced researchers have devised. They may not have asked questions on your topic, but the way they have asked the questions should give you an idea of what to do and what to avoid when designing such instruments.

in developing a survey instrument to be administered to possible victims of crime, she and her colleagues used 'tried and tested questions taken from pre-existing criminal victimization surveys amended to take account of our own more localized concerns'.

The UK Data Archive (UKDA), which aims to improve standards in UK survey research, has a very good 'Variable and question bank' providing access to questionnaires from major surveys (including the census) and associated commentary to assist survey design. It is freely available and can be found at **http://discover.ukdataservice. ac.uk/variables** (accessed 29 October 2014). The Variable and question bank includes questions from major surveys. They are presented in the context of the questionnaire in which they appeared and are accompanied by technical details. The search mechanism allows you to search for a particular questionnaire or to input keywords to find cases of the use of particular topics in questions.

 ## *Checklist*

Issues to consider for your structured interview schedule or self-administered questionnaire

○ Have you devised a clear and comprehensive way of introducing the research to interviewees or questionnaire respondents?

○ Have you considered whether there are any existing questions used by other researchers to investigate this topic that could meet your needs?

○ Do the questions allow you to answer all your research questions?

○ Could any questions that are not strictly relevant to your research questions be dropped?

○ Have you tried to put yourself in the position of answering as many of the questions as possible?

○ Have you piloted the questionnaire with some appropriate respondents?

○ If it is a structured interview schedule, have you made sure that the instructions to yourself and to anyone else involved in interviewing are clear (for example, with filter questions, is it clear which questions should be missed out)?

○ If it is a self-administered questionnaire, have you made sure that the instructions to respondents are clear (for example, with filter questions, is it clear which questions should be missed out)?

○ Are instructions about how to record responses clear (for example, whether to tick or circle or delete; whether more than one response is allowable)?

○ Have you included as few open-ended questions as possible?

○ Have you allowed respondents to indicate levels of intensity in their replies, so that they are not forced into 'yes' or 'no' answers where intensity of feeling may be more appropriate?

○ Have you ensured that each question and its answers do not span across more than one page?

○ Have socio-demographic questions been left until the end of the questionnaire?

○ Are questions relating to the research topic at or very close to the beginning?

○ Have you taken steps to ensure that the questions you are asking really do supply you with the information you need?

○ Have you taken steps to ensure that there are no:

　　○ Ambiguous terms in questions or response choices?

　　○ Long questions?

　　○ Double-barrelled questions?

　　○ Very general questions?

　　○ Leading questions?

　　○ Questions that are asking about two or more things?

　　○ Questions that include negatives?

　　○ Questions using technical terms?

○ Have you made sure that your respondents will have the requisite knowledge to answer your questions?

○ Is there an appropriate match between your questions and your response choices?

○ Have you made sure that your response choices are properly balanced?

○ Do any of your questions rely too much on your respondents' memory?

○ Have you ensured that there is a category of 'other' (or similar category such as 'unsure' or 'neither agree nor disagree') so that respondents are not forced to answer in a way that is not indicative of what they think or do?

If you are using a Likert-scale approach:

○ Have you included some items that can be reverse scored in order to minimize response sets?

○ Have you made sure that the items really do relate to the same underlying cluster of attitudes so that they can be aggregated?

○ Have you ensured that your response choices are exhaustive?

○ Have you ensured that your response choices do not overlap?

》 Key points

- While open-ended questions undoubtedly have certain advantages, closed-ended questions are typically preferable for a survey, because of the ease of asking questions and recording and processing answers.

- This point applies particularly to the self-administered questionnaire.

- Open-ended questions of the kind used in qualitative interviewing have a useful role in relation to the formulation of fixed-choice answers and piloting.

- It is crucial to learn the rules of question-asking to avoid some of the more obvious pitfalls.

- Remember always to put yourself in the position of the respondent when asking questions and to make sure you will generate data appropriate to your research questions.

- Piloting or pre-testing may clear up problems in question formulation.

Questions for review

Open- or closed-ended questions?

- What difficulties do open-ended questions present in survey research?
- Why are closed-ended questions frequently preferred to open-ended questions in survey research?
- What are the limitations of closed-ended questions?
- How can closed-ended questions be improved?

Types of question

- What are the main types of question that are likely to be used in a structured interview or self-administered questionnaire?

Rules for designing questions

- What is wrong with each of the following questions?

What is your annual salary?

Below £10,000	_____
£10,000–15,000	_____
£15,000–20,000	_____
£20,000–25,000	_____
£25,000–30,000	_____
£30,000–35,000	_____
£35,000 and over	_____

Do you ever feel alienated from your work?

All the time	_____
Often	_____
Occasionally	_____
Never	_____

How satisfied are you with the provision of educational services and social services in your area?

Very satisfied	_____
Fairly satisfied	_____
Neither satisfied nor dissatisfied	_____
Fairly dissatisfied	_____
Very dissatisfied	_____

What is your marital status?

Single	_____
Married	_____
Divorced	_____

Vignette questions

- In what circumstances are vignette questions appropriate?

Piloting and pre-testing questions

- Why is it important to pilot questions?

Using existing questions

● Why might it be useful to use questions devised by others?

Online Resource Centre

www.oxfordtextbooks.co.uk/orc/brymansrm5e/

Visit the Online Resource Centre to enrich your understanding of using and designing questions. Follow up links to other resources, test yourself using multiple choice questions, and gain further guidance and inspiration from the Student Researcher's Toolkit.

12

Structured observation

Chapter outline

Chapter guide

Structured observation is a method that is relatively underused in social research. It entails the direct observation of behaviour and the recording of that behaviour in terms of categories devised prior to the start of data collection. This chapter explores:

- the limitations of survey research for the study of behaviour;
- the different forms of observation in social research;
- the potential of structured observation for the study of behaviour;
- how to devise an observation schedule;
- different strategies for observing behaviour in structured observation;
- sampling issues in structured observation research, which are to do not just with people but also with the sampling of time and contexts;
- issues of reliability and validity in structured observation;
- field stimulations, whereby the researcher actively intervenes in social life and records what happens as a consequence of the intervention, as a form of structured observation;
- some criticisms of structured observation.

Introduction

Structured observation is a method for systematically observing the behaviour of individuals in terms of a schedule of categories. It is a technique in which the researcher employs explicitly formulated rules for the observation and recording of behaviour. One of its main advantages is that it allows behaviour to be observed directly, unlike in survey research, which allows behaviour only to be inferred. In surveys, respondents frequently report their behaviour, but there are good reasons for thinking that such reports may not be entirely accurate. Structured observation constitutes a possible solution in that it entails the direct observation of behaviour.

Problems with survey research on social behaviour

Chapters 8 through 11 have dealt with several aspects of survey research. In the course of outlining survey procedures, certain problems with the techniques with which it is typically associated have been identified. The deficiencies associated with the survey are often recognized by practitioners, who have developed ways of dealing with or at least of offsetting their impact to some degree. When survey techniques such as the structured interview or the self-administered questionnaire are employed in connection with the study of respondents' *behaviour*, certain characteristic difficulties are encountered, as identified in Tips and skills 'Problems with using survey research to investigate behaviour'. The list is by no means exhaustive but it does capture the main elements, some of which have been touched on in earlier chapters.

Tips and skills
Problems with using survey research to investigate behaviour

- *Problem of meaning.* People may vary in their interpretations of key terms in a question (see Thinking deeply 12.1).
- *Problem of omission.* When answering the question, respondents may inadvertently omit key terms in the question (see Thinking deeply 12.1).
- *Problem of memory.* Respondents may misremember aspects of the occurrence of certain forms of behaviour.
- *Social desirability bias.* Respondents may exhibit a tendency towards replying in ways that are meant to be consistent with their perceptions of the desirability of certain kinds of answer.
- *Question threat.* Some questions may appear threatening and result in a failure to provide an honest reply.
- *Interviewer characteristics.* Aspects of the interviewer may influence the answers provided.
- *Gap between stated and actual behaviour.* How people say they are likely to behave and how they actually behave may be inconsistent (see Thinking deeply 12.2).
- *Capacity to answer questions.* Some categories of research participant may lack the mental capacity to answer questions (for example, people with learning difficulties and sufferers of dementia).

Thinking deeply 12.1
Accurate reporting of behaviour and the problems of meaning and omission

Belson (1981) has conducted detailed studies of how people interpret questions designed to gauge attitudes and behaviour. One question about behaviour was embedded in a structured interview schedule administered to fifty-nine British adults and went as follows:

> When you turn on your television in the evening, do you generally go on viewing till the end of the evening or do you just watch one or two programmes?

(Belson 1981: 59)

Intensive interviews undertaken after the interviews had been carried out revealed that no respondents interpreted the question totally correctly. Twenty-five respondents arrived at incorrect interpretations; the rest were broadly correct but in varying degrees. A common problem was that the question was designed to refer to when the respondents themselves turned the television on. This was correctly interpreted by thirty-eight respondents, but fifteen interpreted the question to mean when the set was switched on—that is, not necessarily by the respondent (problem of meaning). Nine respondents appeared not to have taken any notice of the phrase 'when you turn on your television' (problem of omission). Ten failed to consider 'till the end of the evening' in their answers, while 'generally' spawned several interpretations. We see here problems of omission and meaning respectively.

Thinking deeply 12.2
Gap between stated and actual behaviour

This is one of the most infamous cases of problems of the gap between what people say they do (or are likely to do) and their actual behaviour. Questionnaires tap people's attitudes and reports of their behaviour, but one might legitimately question how well these relate to actual behaviour. A study of racial prejudice conducted by LaPiere (1934) illustrates this issue. He spent two years travelling with a young Chinese student and his wife to determine whether they were refused entry at hotels and restaurants. They twice crossed the USA. Of 66 hotels, they were refused entry once; of 184 restaurants and diners, none refused entry. LaPiere sought to eliminate himself as a possible contaminating influence by ensuring that he was not involved in gaining access to the various establishments and indeed seems to have sought to load the dice in favour of being turned away:

> Whenever possible I let my Chinese friend negotiate for accommodation . . . or sent them into a restaurant ahead of me. In this way I attempted to 'factor' myself out. We sometimes patronized high-class establishments after a hard and dusty day on the road and stopped at inferior auto camps when in our most presentable condition.

(LaPiere 1934: 232)

LaPiere then allowed six months to elapse and sent questionnaires to the hotels and restaurants they had visited. One of the questions asked: 'Will you accept members of the Chinese race as guests in your establishment?' Of the establishments that replied, 92 per cent of restaurants said no; and 91 per cent of hotels said no. LaPiere's simple though striking study clearly illustrates the gap that may exist between reports of behaviour and actual behaviour. It should also be noted that the question asked is somewhat unclear, a feature that is not usually remarked upon in connection with this widely cited study. 'Will you . . . ?' can be interpreted as asking the respondent to project into the future or to state the establishment's policy. Quite why the more obvious formulation of 'Do you . . .?' was not used is not clear, though it is unlikely that this point has a significant bearing on the findings and their implications for survey research.

See Thinking deeply 20.1 for more on this issue.

So why not observe behaviour?

An obvious solution to the problems identified is to observe people's behaviour directly rather than to rely on research instruments such as questionnaires to elicit such information. In this chapter, I am going to outline *structured observation* (see Key concept 12.1), also often called *systematic observation*.

Much like interviewing (see Key concept 9.2), there are many different forms of the observation approach in social research. Key concept 12.2 outlines some major ways of conducting observation studies in social research.

It has been implied that structured observation can be viewed as an alternative to survey methods of research. After all, in view of the various problems identified in Tips and skills 'Problems with using survey research to investigate behaviour', it would seem an obvious solution to observe people instead. However, structured observation has not attracted a large following and instead tends to be used in certain specific research areas, such as the behaviour of school teachers and pupils and interaction between them.

Central to any structured observation study will be the *observation schedule* or *coding scheme*. This specifies the categories of behaviour that are to be observed and how behaviour should be assigned to those categories. It is best to illustrate what this involves by looking at examples. One of the best-known schedules for the observation of classrooms is the Flanders Interaction Analysis Categories (FIAC), devised by Flanders (1970). This scheme was developed in the USA but has been employed fairly extensively in other countries. An observer

watches a classroom during a lesson and every three seconds allocates a category number to the type of activity that takes place in that three-second period. (See Figure 12.1 for the different types of activity in the FIAC scheme.) In other words, in each and every minute, the observer will write down twenty numbers, each of which will relate directly to the coding scheme. Figure 12.1

From such data a number of features can be derived. Teachers' styles can be compared in terms of such things as the relative emphasis upon teachers doing the talking and pupils talking or in terms of the amounts of silence or confusion that take place in their lessons. It also becomes possible to compare classes in terms of these categories. In fact, we tend to find, using the FIAC scheme, that two-thirds of time in the classroom is made up of talk. Of that talk, two-thirds derives from the teacher. It is helpful in bringing about an understanding of what happens in lessons and can be useful in developing information about which styles seem most effective. For example, are better exam results achieved by teachers who exhibit a high level of talking relative to that of pupils, or are teachers who allow more pupil talk more effective? The scheme can also be used in teacher training in order to help trainees to become aware of features of their teaching style, and possibly to begin to question its appropriateness.

It is interesting to think about how a scheme like this might be employed in connection with higher education teaching and in particular in tutorials and seminars. In the

---

Key concept 12.1
What is structured observation?

Structured observation, also called *systematic observation*, is a technique in which the researcher employs explicitly formulated rules for the observation and recording of behaviour. The rules inform observers about what they should look for and how they should record behaviour. Each person who is part of the research (we will call these people 'participants') is observed for a predetermined period of time using the same rules. These rules are articulated in what is usually referred to as an **observation schedule**, which bears many similarities to a structured interview schedule with closed-ended questions. The aim of the observation schedule is to ensure that each participant's behaviour is systematically recorded so that it is possible to aggregate the behaviour of all those in the sample in respect of each type of behaviour being recorded. The rules that constitute the observation schedule are as specific as possible in order to direct observers to exactly what aspects of behaviour they are supposed to be looking for. The resulting data resemble questionnaire data, in that the procedure generates information on different aspects of behaviour that can be treated as variables. Moreover, structured observation research is typically underpinned by a cross-sectional research design (see Key concept 3.6 and Figures 3.2 and 3.3).

Key concept 12.2
Major types of observation research

The following are the major forms of observational research in social research.

- *Structured observation*. See Key concept 12.1.

- *Systematic observation*. See Key concept 12.1.

- *Participant observation*. This is one of the best-known methods of social research. It is primarily associated with qualitative research and entails the relatively prolonged immersion of the observer in a social setting in which he or she seeks to observe the behaviour of members of that setting (group, organization, community, etc.) and to elicit the meanings they attribute to their environment and behaviour. Participant observers vary considerably in how much they participate in the social settings in which they locate themselves. See Key concept 19.1 and Chapter 19 generally for a more detailed treatment.

- *Non-participant observation*. This is a term that is used to describe a situation in which the observer observes but does not participate in what is going on in the social setting. Structured observers are usually non-participants in that they are in the social setting that is being observed but rarely participate in what is happening. The term can also be used in connection with unstructured observation.

- *Unstructured observation*. As its name implies, unstructured observation does not entail the use of an observation schedule for the recording of behaviour. Instead, the aim is to record in as much detail as possible the behaviour of participants with the aim of developing a narrative account of that behaviour. In a sense, most participant observation is unstructured, but the term unstructured observation is usually employed in conjunction with non-participant observation.

- *Simple observation and contrived observation*. Webb et al. (1966) write about forms of observation in which the observer is unobtrusive and is not observed by those being observed. With **simple observation**, the observer has no influence over the situation being observed; in the case of contrived observation, the observer actively alters the situation to observe the effects of an intervention. These two types of observation are invariably forms of non-participant observation and can entail either structured or unstructured observation.

Figure 12.1
FIAC categories

Teacher talk	Response	**1 Accepts feeling** (e.g. accepts and clarifies an attitude or the feeling tone of a pupil) **2 Praises or encourages** **3 Accepts or uses ideas of pupils**
	Initiation	**4 Asks questions** **5 Lecturing** **6 Giving direction** **7 Criticizing or justifying authority**
Pupil talk		**8 Pupil talk—response** **9 Pupil talk—initiation**
Silence		**10 Silence or confusion**

following imaginary scheme, the focus is on the teacher. The categories might be:

Tutor

1. asking question addressed to group;
2. asking question addressed to individual;
3. responding to question asked by member of group;
4. responding to comment by member of group;
5. discussing topic;
6. making arrangements;
7. silence.

Student(s)

8. asking question;
9. responding to question from tutor;
10. responding to comment from tutor;
11. responding to question from another student;
12. responding to comment from another student;
13. talking about arrangements.

We might want to code what is happening every five seconds. The coding sheet for a five-minute period in the tutorial might then look like Figure 12.2. In this grid, each cell represents a five-second interval so that a row

Figure 12.2

Coding sheet for imaginary study of university tutors

3	3	3	3	10	10	10	10	10	10	10	10
10	10	10	10	10	10	7	7	7	8	8	8
8	8	8	8	8	8	8	8	11	11	11	11
11	11	11	11	11	11	11	11	11	11	11	11
7	7	7	7	7	4	4	4	4	4	4	1

Note: Each cell represents a five-second interval and each row is one minute. The number in each cell refers to the code used to represent a category of behaviour that has been observed.

comprises twelve five-second intervals—that is, a minute. The numbers in each cell are the codes used to represent the classification of behaviour. Thus, the top left-hand cell has a 3 in it, which refers to a tutor responding to a question asked by a member of the group. We might try to relate the amount of time that the tutor is engaged in particular activities to such things as: number of students in the group; layout of the room; subject discipline; gender of tutor; age of tutor; and so on.

The observation schedule

Devising a schedule for the recording of observations is a crucial step in structured observation. The considerations that go into this phase are very similar to those involved in producing a structured interview schedule. The following considerations are worth taking into account.

- A clear focus is necessary. There are two aspects to this point. First, it should be clear to the observer exactly who or what (and possibly both) is to be observed. For example, if people are the focus of attention, the observer needs to know precisely who is to be observed. Also, the observer needs to know which if any aspects of the setting are to be observed and hence recorded. The second sense in which a clear focus is necessary is that observers need to know exactly which of the many things going on in any setting are to be recorded. Research in focus 12.1 describes the observation of individual children in a classroom using specified categories, modes, and time intervals.

- As with the production of a closed-ended question for a structured interview schedule or self-administered questionnaire, the forms taken by any category of

behaviour must be both mutually exclusive (that is, not overlap) and inclusive. Taking the earlier example of coding behaviour in a university tutorial, we might conceivably run into a problem of the thirteen categories not being exhaustive if a student knocks on the tutor's door and quickly asks him or her a question (perhaps about the tutorial topic if the student is from another of the tutor's groups). An observer unfamiliar with the ways of university life might well be unsure about whether this behaviour needs to be coded in terms of the thirteen categories or whether the coding should be temporarily suspended. Perhaps the best approach would be to have another category of behaviour to be coded that we might term 'interruption'. It is often desirable for a certain amount of unstructured observation to take place before the construction of the observation schedule and for there to be some piloting of it, so that possible problems associated with a lack of inclusiveness can be anticipated.

- The recording system must be easy to operate. Complex systems with large numbers of types of behaviour are undesirable because although observers need to be

Research in focus 12.1
Observing behaviour in English schools

Blatchford et al. (2003) conducted research into the impact of class size on pupil behaviour. They were interested in the possibility that, as class sizes increase, pupil inattentiveness also increases, resulting in difficult relationships between the children. The observational component of this research was based on children in large and small reception classes (age 4–5 years). The authors describe their approach as involving

> direct, i.e. on-the-spot, observations of selected children in terms of previously developed categories and in terms of 5-minute observation sheets divided into continuous 10-second time samples. The schedule was child-based in the sense that one child at a time was observed . . . The schedule involved categories that provided a description of time spent in three 'social modes'—when with their teachers, other children and when not interacting. Within each of these three modes sub-categories covered work, procedural, social and off-task activity . . . The aim was to observe [six randomly chosen] children in each class five times per day, for 3 days. In the event the average number of completed observation sheets per child was 14 . . . In terms of time there were 69 minutes of observation per child.

(Blatchford et al. 2003: 21–2)

Blatchford et al. (2003) emphasize the data relating to interaction between children and 'off-task' behaviour. The interaction between children was observed and coded in terms of the following categories: task; procedure (class organization and management); social; mucking about; aggressive; help; and unclear.

Research in focus 12.2
Observing jobs

Jenkins et al. (1975) report the results of an exploratory study to measure the nature of jobs. The research focused on several different types of job in a number of different types of organization. An observation schedule was devised to assess the nature of twenty aspects (dimensions) of the jobs in question. Most of the dimensions were measured through more than one indicator, each of which took the form of a question that observers had to answer on a six- or seven-point scale. These were then aggregated for each dimension. One dimension relates to 'Worker pace control' and comprises three observational indicators such as:

> How much control does the employee have in setting the pace of his or her work?

Another dimension was 'Autonomy', which comprised four items such as:

> The job allows the individual to make a lot of decisions on his or her own.

Most of the observers were university students. The procedure for conducting the observations was as follows: 'Each respondent was observed twice for an hour. The observations were scheduled so that the two different observations were separated by at least 2 days, were usually made at different times of the day, and were always made by two different observers' (Jenkins et al. 1975: 173).

trained, it is easy for an observer to become flustered or confused if faced with too many options.

- One problem is that observation schedules sometimes require the observer to interpret what is going on. For example, it might be difficult to distinguish between a student responding to a question raised by another student and discussing the tutorial topic. To the extent that it may be difficult to distinguish between the two, a certain amount of interpretation on the part of the observer may be required. If interpretation is required, there need to be clear guidelines for the observer, and considerable experience would be required (see Research in focus 12.2 for an illustration of a study in which a good deal of interpretation seems to have been necessary).

Strategies for observing behaviour

There are different ways of conceptualizing how behaviour should be recorded.

- We can record in terms of *incidents*. This means waiting for something to happen and then recording what follows from it. Essentially, this is what LaPiere (1934) did (see Thinking deeply 12.2), in that he waited for the Chinese couple to negotiate entry to each hotel or restaurant and then recorded whether they were allowed entry. I remember reading many years ago in a newspaper that someone placed a ladder over a pavement and then observed whether people preferred to go under the ladder or to risk life and limb in the face of oncoming traffic. A considerable number preferred the latter option, confirming the persistence of superstitious beliefs in an apparently secular society. Once again, an incident (someone approaching the ladder) triggered the observation. Observation of this kind is what Webb et al. (1966) would regard as an example of *contrived observation*, because the researchers fabricated the situation. The discussion later in this chapter of *field stimulations* provides further illustrations of this kind of research.

- We can observe and record in terms of *short periods* of time. This was the case with the research reported in Research in focus 12.1, where '5-minute observation sheets' were used. A slight variation on this theme can be found in the research reported in Research in focus 3.6. Children in St Helena were videotaped over a two-week period during their morning, lunchtime, and afternoon breaks. The tapes were then coded using

the Playground Behaviour Observation Schedule which is an instrument for recording the occurrence of 23 behaviours (e.g. games; fantasy play; character imitation; anti-social and pro-social behaviour) and their behaviour groupings (i.e. whether the behaviour was undertaken

by an individual, a pair, or with 3–5 or 6 or more children) . . . A separate Playground Behaviour Observation Schedule was completed for each 30-second segment.

(Charlton et al. 1998: 7)

- We can observe and record observations for quite *long periods* of time. The observer watches and records more or less continuously. The FIAC scheme adopts this strategy. Another example is the study of job characteristics in Research in focus 12.2, which entailed the observation of each worker on two occasions but for an hour on each occasion: 'The observation hour was structured so that the observer spent 10 min becoming oriented to the job, 30 min observing specific job actions, and 20 min rating the job in situ. The observers then typically spent an additional 15 min away from the job completing the observation instrument' (Jenkins et al. 1975: 174). This study is an example of what Martin and Bateson (2007) refer to as **continuous recording**, whereby the observer observes for extended periods, thus allowing the frequency and duration of the types of behaviour of interest to be measured. They contrast this approach with **time sampling**.

- *Time sampling* is a further approach to the observation of behaviour. An example here would be a study of schools known as the ORACLE (Observational Research and Classroom Learning Evaluation) project (Galton et al. 1980). In this research, eight children (four of each gender) in each class in which observation took place were observed for around four minutes but on ten separate occasions. A mechanical device made a noise every twenty-five seconds, and, on each occasion this occurred, the observer made a note of what the teacher or pupils were doing in terms of the observation schedule. The sampling of time periods was random.

 # Sampling

Just like survey research, structured observation necessitates decisions about sampling. However, with structured observation, sampling issues do not revolve solely around how to sample people.

Sampling people

When people are being sampled, considerations very similar to those encountered in Chapter 8 in respect of probability sampling apply. This means that the observer will

ideally want to sample on a random basis. In Croll and Moses's (1985) research on children with special educational needs, thirty-four classrooms from a number of different schools were selected for observation. All children were within the same age range. Initially, each teacher was interviewed to determine which children in his or her class were regarded as having special needs. In addition, tests of both reading ability and non-verbal reasoning were administered to children to identify those who appeared to have special needs, but who had not been identified by the teacher. Up to six children with special needs in each class were then randomly sampled as being the focus of structured observation; so too were four children who had not been identified as having special needs—these children acted as a kind of control group. In this way, 280 children were sampled, of whom 151 were identified as having special needs; the other 129 served as control participants. The teachers did not know exactly which children were being observed. Each child was observed for a few minutes, after which the observer proceeded to the next child to be observed in a predetermined random order. In the end, each child was observed for a total of two hours. This was made up of a large number of short observation periods. In the research reported in Research in focus 12.1, the six students in each class were selected randomly but with the stipulation that three boys and three girls would be sampled. In the study of job characteristics discussed in Research in focus 12.2, the individuals who were observed at work were randomly selected (Jenkins et al. 1975).

Sampling in terms of time

As implied by the idea of time sampling (see above), it is often necessary to ensure that, if certain individuals are sampled on more than one occasion, they are not always observed at the same time of the day. This means that, if particular individuals are selected randomly for observation on several different occasions for short periods, it is desirable for the observation periods to be randomly selected. For example, it would not be desirable for a certain pupil always to be observed at the end of the day. He or she might be tired, and this would give a false impression of that pupil's overall behaviour. In the research reported in Research in focus 12.1, each child was observed at separate times on three different days. As a result, the researchers' ratings of any child are unlikely to be distorted by unusual behaviour that he or she might exhibit on just one or two occasions.

Further sampling considerations

The sampling procedures mentioned so far conform to probability sampling principles, because it is feasible to construct a sampling frame for individuals. However, this is not always possible for different kinds of reason. Studies in public areas do not permit random sampling, because we cannot very easily construct a sampling frame of people walking along a street. Similarly, it is not feasible to construct a sampling frame of interactions. Reiss (1976), for example, has written about the difficulty of developing a random sample of encounters between police officers and the public. The problem with doing structured observation research on such a topic is that it does not lend itself to the specification of a sampling frame, and

therefore the researcher's ability to generate a probability sample is curtailed.

Considerations relating to probability sampling derive largely from concerns surrounding the external validity (or generalizability) of findings. Such concerns are not necessarily totally addressed by resorting to probability sampling, however. For example, if a structured observation study is conducted over a relatively short span of time, issues of the representativeness of findings are likely to arise. If the research was conducted in schools, observations conducted towards the end of the school year, when examinations are likely to preoccupy both teachers and students, may affect the results obtained compared to observations at a different point in the academic year. Consequently, consideration has to be given to the question of the timing of observation. This potential problem was dealt with in the ORACLE research by ensuring that teachers and each target pupil were observed on six occasions during each of the three school terms. Furthermore, how are the sites in which structured observation is to take place selected? Can we presume that they are themselves representative? Clearly, a random sampling procedure for the selection of schools may lessen any worries in this connection. However, in view of the difficulty of securing access to settings such as schools and business organizations, it is likely that the organizations to which access is secured may not be representative of the population of appropriate ones.

A further set of distinctions between types of sampling in structured observation have been drawn by Martin and Bateson (2007):

- *ad libitum* sampling, whereby the observer records whatever is happening at the time;
- **focal sampling**, in which a specific individual is observed for a set period of time; the observer records all examples of whatever forms of behaviour are of interest in terms of a schedule;
- **scan sampling**, whereby an entire group of individuals is scanned at regular intervals and the behaviour of all of them is recorded at that time—this sampling strategy allows only one or two types of behaviour to be observed and recorded; and
- **behaviour sampling**, whereby an entire group is watched and the observer records who was involved in a particular kind of behaviour.

Most structured observation research seems to employ the first two types: Flanders's FIAC scheme is an example of *ad libitum* sampling; the research by Galton et al. (1980), Croll and Moses (1985), Blatchford et al. (2003; see Research in focus 12.1), Jenkins et al. (1975; see Research in focus 12.2), and Buckle and Farrington (1994; see Research in focus 12.3) are illustrations of focal sampling.

Research in focus 12.3
A study of shoplifting

Buckle and Farrington (1994) report the results of a replication of an earlier study of shoplifting in a department store in Peterborough (Buckle and Farrington 1984). The replication was conducted in a similar store in Bedford. Customers were selected at random as they entered the store and were followed by two observers until they left. The observers recorded such details as cost of items bought; gender, race, and estimated age; and behaviour. In Peterborough 486 people formed the basis of the sample and in Bedford it was 502. Nine people shoplifted in Peterborough and six in Bedford. Shoplifters were more likely to be male and either under 25 (in Peterborough) or over 55 (in Bedford). Most shoplifters also purchased goods. Most shoplifting was of small items of relatively little monetary value. The sampling and observation strategies entailed random sampling of people followed by continuous recording for a short or long period depending on how long the person remained in the store.

Issues of reliability and validity

One writer has concluded that, when compared to interviews and questionnaires, structured observation 'Provides (a) more reliable information about events; (b) greater precision regarding their timing, duration, and frequency; (c) greater accuracy in the time ordering of variables; and (d) more accurate and economical reconstructions of large-scale social episodes' (McCall 1984: 277). This is a very strong endorsement for structured observation, but, as McCall notes, there are several issues of reliability and validity that confront practitioners. Some of these issues are similar to those faced by researchers when seeking to develop measures in social research in general (see Chapter 7) and in survey research in particular. However, certain concerns are specific to structured observation.

Reliability

Practitioners of structured observation have been concerned with the degree of *inter-observer consistency*. Essentially, this issue entails considering the degree to which two or more observers of the same behaviour agree in terms of their coding of that behaviour on the observation schedule. The chief mechanism for assessing this component of reliability is a statistic called *kappa* (see Key concept 12.3; *this box can be ignored if you feel unsure about addressing more complex statistical issues at this stage*).

A second consideration in relation to reliability is the degree of consistency in the application of the observation schedule over time—that is, *intra-observer consistency*. The procedures for assessing this aspect of reliability are broadly similar to those applied to the issue of inter-observer consistency. The study in Research in focus 12.2 addressed the issue of inter-observer consistency over

time and found that the measures fared even worse in this respect.

It is not easy to achieve reliability in structured observation. This is a point of some significance in view of the fact that validity presupposes reliability (see Chapter 7). Reliability may be difficult to achieve on occasions, because of the effects of such factors as observer fatigue and lapses in attention. However, this point should not be exaggerated, because the ORACLE researchers were able to achieve high levels of reliability for many of their measures, and indeed two critics of structured observation have written that 'there is no doubt that observers can be trained to use complex coding schedules with considerable reliability' (Delamont and Hamilton 1984: 32). (Using the Scott coefficient referred to in Key concept 12.3, it was found that the average inter-observer reliability level across the different components of pupil behaviour was 0.90.) The high levels of reliability may be due to the factors that are intrinsic to the school classroom and to the fact that there is a long tradition of structured observation research in schools, so that a fund of experience has been accumulated in this domain.

Validity

Measurement validity relates to the question of whether a measure is measuring what it is supposed to measure. The validity of any measure will be affected by:

- whether the measure reflects the concept it has been designed to measure (see Chapter 7), and
- error that arises from the implementation of the measure in the research process (see Chapter 9).

Key concept 12.3
Cohen's kappa

This box can be ignored if you feel unsure about addressing more complex statistical issues at this stage.

Cohen's kappa is a measure of the degree of agreement over the coding of items by two people. It could be applied to the coding of any textual information, as in the content analysis of newspaper articles or of answers to open-ended survey questions, as well as to the coding of observation. Much like Cronbach's alpha (see Key concept 7.4), by calculating Cohen's kappa you will end up with a coefficient that varies between 0 and 1. The closer the coefficient is to 1, the higher the agreement and the better the inter-observer consistency. A coefficient of 0.75 or above is considered very good; between 0.6 and 0.75, it is considered good; and between 0.4 and 0.6, it is regarded as fair. Croll (1986) refers to a very similar statistic, the Scott coefficient of agreement, which can be interpreted in an identical way.

The values of kappa in the study of job characteristics referred to in Research in focus 12.2 were mainly in the 'fair' category. The two items referred to in Research in focus 12.2 achieved kappa values of 0.43 and 0.54 respectively (Jenkins et al. 1975). These are not very encouraging and suggest that the coding of job characteristics was not very reliable. By contrast, the kappa coefficients for the various measures used in the observational research on pupils' engagement in class by Blatchford et al. (2009; Research in focus 12.1) ranged between 0.80 and 0.77, which indicates a high level of inter-observer consistency.

The first of these considerations means that in structured observation it is necessary to attend to the same kinds of issues concerning the checking of validity (assessing face validity, concurrent validity, and so on) that are encountered in research based on interviews and questionnaires. The second aspect of validity—error in implementation—relates to two matters in particular.

- Is the observation schedule administered as it is supposed to be? This is the equivalent of ensuring that interviewers using a structured interview schedule follow the research instrument and its instructions exactly as they are supposed to. If there is variability between observers or over time, the measure will be unreliable and therefore cannot be valid. Ensuring that observers have as complete an understanding as possible of how the observation schedule should be implemented is therefore crucial.

- Do people change their behaviour because they know they are being observed? This is an instance of what is known as the 'reactive effect' (Key concept 12.4). After all, if people adjust the way they behave because they know they are being observed (perhaps because they want to be viewed in a favourable way by the observer), their behaviour would be atypical. As a result, we could hardly regard the results of structured observation research as indicative of what hap-

pens in reality. As McCall (1984) notes, there is evidence that a reactive effect occurs in structured observation, but that by and large research participants become accustomed to being observed, so that the researcher essentially becomes less intrusive the longer he or she is present. Moreover, it should be borne in mind that frequently people's awareness of the observer's presence is offset by other factors. For example, teachers and students have many tasks to accomplish that reflect the demands of the classroom, so that the observer's ability to make a big impact on behaviour may be curtailed by the requirements of the situation. A study by Harvey et al. (2009) that entailed an evaluation of a programme to promote the use of insecticide-treated bed nets to reduce the incidence of malaria in the Peruvian Amazon illustrates this point. Four observers monitored sixty households in four rural villages continuously for twelve-hour periods. The observers informed the villagers they were observing that they must not interact with each other so that reactivity could be reduced. The observers recorded 339 instances of reactivity. At their most basic, these entailed salutations to the observer or interaction with the observer over matters unrelated to malaria prevention. On only two occasions was there evidence of reactivity that related to the study objectives. On these two occasions it was clear that the villagers changed their

Key concept 12.4
Reactive effect

Webb et al. (1966: 13) wrote about the 'reactive measurement effect', by which they meant that 'the research subject's knowledge that he is participating in a scholarly search may confound the investigator's data'. They distinguished four components of this effect.

1. *The guinea pig effect—awareness of being tested*. Examples are such effects as the research participant wanting to create a good impression or feeling prompted to behave in ways (or express attitudes) that would not normally be exhibited.

2. *Role selection*. Webb et al. argue that participants are often tempted to adopt a particular kind of role in research. An example is that there is a well-known effect in experimental research (but which may have a broader applicability) whereby some individuals seek out cues about the aims of the research and adjust what they say and do in line with their perceptions (which may of course be false) of those aims.

3. *Measurement as a change agent*. The very fact of a researcher being in a context in which no researcher is normally present may itself cause things to be different. For example, the fact that there is an observer sitting in the corner of a school classroom means that there is space and a chair being used that otherwise would be unoccupied. This very fact may influence behaviour.

4. *Response sets*. This is an issue that primarily relates to questionnaire and interview research and occurs when the respondent replies to a set of questions in a consistent but clearly inappropriate manner. Examples of this kind of effect are measurement problems such as social desirability bias and yeasaying and naysaying (consistently answering yes or no to questions or consistently agreeing or disagreeing with items regardless of the meaning of the question or item).

Reactive effects are likely to occur in any research in which participants know they are the focus of investigation. Webb et al. called for greater use of what they call *unobtrusive measures* or *non-reactive methods* that do not entail participants' knowledge of their involvement in research (see Key concept 14.3 for more information).

---

behaviour as a result of the observer's presence. Here is an example from the field notes of the observer concerned:

18:20: I put on my long-sleeved shirt because there are a lot of mosquitoes. The 33-year-old man enters his room and I see him return with his own long-sleeve shirt. I think he put it on because he saw me put on mine.

(Harvey et al. 2009: 14)

These findings are quite reassuring in suggesting that the reactive effect of observation is not as problematic as might be anticipated.

Field stimulations as a form of structured observation

Salancik (1979) has used the term **field stimulation** to describe a form of observation research that shares many of the characteristics of structured observation. Although he classifies field stimulations as a qualitative method, they are in fact better thought of as operating with a quantitative research strategy, since the researcher typically seeks to quantify the outcomes of his or her interventions. In terms of the classification offered in Key concept 12.2, it is in fact 'contrived observation'. A field stimulation, therefore, is a study in which the researcher directly intervenes in and/or manipulates a natural setting in order to observe what happens as a consequence of that intervention. However, unlike most structured observation, in a field stimulation participants do not know they are being studied.

Some field stimulations can take the form of an experimental design (see Chapter 3). An example is a study by Daniel (1968) of racial discrimination in Britain in the 1960s. Daniel undertook conventional attitude studies among immigrant groups to establish levels of discrimination. In addition, he developed 'situation tests' to back up his findings. For example, in one set of situation tests he examined discrimination in the area of accommodation. Sixty advertisements for accommodation to let were selected from a number of regions. Advertisements stipulating 'no coloureds' or 'Europeans only' were deliberately excluded. At the time, it was not illegal for landlords to place such instructions in their advertisements. Each landlord was approached by each of the following: a West Indian; a white Hungarian; and a white Englishman.

The applicants were presented with identical sets of characteristics, but they differed in terms of ethnicity. The applicant was requesting accommodation for a married couple with no children. In half of the applications (that is, thirty), the testers adopted 'professional roles'. In these roles they sought more expensive accommodation. In the other half, they adopted manual roles. In fifteen of the sixty cases, all three applicants got the same information (for example, let, still vacant). This means that discrimination occurred in the remaining forty-five cases (see Table 12.1).

Table 12.1
Daniel's (1968) situation test: the case of accommodation

Reaction to request for accommodation	No.
West Indian was told accommodation taken; both other applicants told it was vacant	38
West Indian was asked for higher rent than the others	4
West Indian and Hungarian were told accommodation let	2
West Indian and Hungarian were asked for higher rent	1
All applicants received the same information	15
TOTAL	60

Research in the news 12.1
A field stimulation on how to stimulate tips

An article on 10 May 2012 in *The Times* with the title 'Researchers Leave a Good Tip for Waitresses: Wear Red Lipstick' reported on some research that suggested that if restaurant waitresses want to maximize their tips, they should wear red lipstick. The story was based on a study by Guégen and Jacob (2012a) in three French restaurants in which diners were randomly assigned to one of seven waitresses who had been made up so that the only feature that distinguished them was whether they wore red, pink, brown, or no lipstick. Each waitress was observed for forty observational periods based on five days per week for eight weeks. A beautician made up the waitresses and did so in a way that limited the makeup variations between them to lipstick. Guégen and Jacob found no differences in tips according to the waitresses' lipstick when the person paying the bill was female. However, when males were paying the bill, there was a statistically significant difference between the waitresses in terms of whether a tip was given and the amount of the tip. In the red lipstick condition, 50.6 per cent of male customers gave tips to the waitress, but in the pink, brown, and no lipstick conditions the figures were 39.7 per cent, 34.5 per cent, and 30.3 per cent. Also, waitresses with red lipstick received on average much larger tips than waitresses in the three other conditions. For example, waitresses in the red lipstick condition received tips that were 50 per cent larger than waitresses who wore no lipstick. The journalist and the authors of the research suggest that the findings may be of practical significance for waitresses. Interestingly, another study by the same authors was picked up by the *Daily Mail*, which carried an item on 3 August 2012. This other study used a very similar field stimulation approach which found that waitresses who wore red were more likely to receive tips (Guégen and Jacob (2012b).

www.thetimes.co.uk/tto/science/biology/article3409883.ece

www.dailymail.co.uk/sciencetech/article-2183140/It-pays-scarlet-woman-Waitresses-wear-red-make-tips.html (both accessed 30 October 2014)

Daniel's research strongly suggests that, because the Hungarian was rarely discriminated against, it is colour rather than being a member of an ethnic minority as such that causes discrimination. Similar studies were conducted in relation to house purchase, employment, and car insurance. Interestingly, the researchers often found that these tests implied that discrimination was *greater* than had been indicated by the attitude surveys, presumably because it is difficult to know if you really have been discriminated against. A further example of a field stimulation can be found in Research in the news 12.1.

While such research provides some quite striking findings and gets around the problem of **reactivity** by not alerting research participants to the fact that they are being observed, as in the use of pseudo-patients in the study of mental hospitals (Rosenhan 1973), ethical concerns are sometimes raised, such as regarding the use of deception. Moreover, the extent to which an observation schedule can be employed is inevitably limited, because excessive use will blow the observer's cover. All that can usually be done is to engage in limited coding, in particular of the nature of the effect of the intervention, as in the LaPiere (1934) and Daniel (1968) studies, or to include a limited amount of further observation, as in the Rosenhan (1973) research.

 # Criticisms of structured observation

Although it is not extensively used in social research, structured observation has been quite controversial. Certain criticisms have been implied in some of the previous discussion of reliability and validity issues, as well as in connection with the issue of generalizability. However, certain other areas of criticism warrant further discussion.

- There is a risk of imposing a potentially inappropriate or irrelevant framework on the setting being observed. This point is similar to the problem of the closed-ended question in questionnaires. This risk is especially great if the setting is one about which little is known. One solution is for the structured observation to be preceded by a period of unstructured observation, so that appropriate variables and categories can be developed.

- Because it concentrates upon directly observable behaviour, structured observation is rarely able to get at intentions behind behaviour. Sometimes, when intentions are of concern, they are imputed by observers. Thus, in the FIAC scheme (see Figure 12.1), the category 'teacher praises or encourages' means imputing a motive to something that the teacher says. Similarly, Blatchford et al. (2009: 668) report that one of the categories of observation of pupil behaviour they employed in their study of the impact of teaching assistants on engagement in class was: '*Individual off-task (passive)*: target child is disengaged during task activity, for example, day dreaming.' Essentially, the problem is that structured observation does not readily allow the observer to get a grasp of the meaning of behaviour.

- There is a tendency for structured observation to generate lots of fragments of data. The problem here can be one of trying to piece them together to produce an overall picture, or one of trying to find general themes that link the fragments of data together. It becomes difficult, in other words, to see a bigger picture that lies behind the segments of behaviour that structured observation typically uncovers. It has been suggested, for example, that the tendency for structured observation studies of managers at work to find little evidence of planning in their everyday work (e.g. Mintzberg 1973) is due to the tendency for the method to fragment a manager's activities into discrete parts. As a result, something like planning, which may be an element in many managerial activities, becomes obscured from view (Snyder and Glueck 1980).

- It is sometimes suggested that structured observation neglects the context within which behaviour takes place. Delamont and Hamilton (1984), for example, note in connection with the ORACLE research that it was found that teachers' styles were related to their ages. However, they argue that such a finding can really be understood only 'if data are gathered on teacher careers and life histories of a kind eschewed by ORACLE' (1984: 9). Of course, were such data collected, this criticism would have little weight, but the tendency of structured observation researchers to concentrate on overt behaviour tends to engender this kind of criticism.

On the other hand . . .

It is clear from the previous section that there are undeniable limitations to structured observation. However, it also has to be remembered that, when overt behaviour is the focus of analysis and perhaps issues of meaning are less salient, structured observation is almost certainly more accurate and effective than getting people to report on their behaviour through questionnaires. Also, although the point was made in the previous section that the observation of behaviour often necessitates imputing meaning to it, that is not to say that imputing meaning is *always* involved. With most of the categories of behaviour used by Blatchford et al. (2009), little if any assignment of motive is required. Also, if video evidence is accumulated, the researcher has the opportunity to review the evidence in detail and not rush to a possibly snap decision about what is being observed. For example, Sampson and Raudenbush (1999) took video footage of Chicago streets to develop a measure of social disorder that included such indicators as alcohol consumption in public; sale of drugs; street prostitution; and fights between adults or hostile arguing.

It may also be that structured observation works best when accompanied by other methods. Since it can rarely provide reasons for observed patterns of behaviour, if it is accompanied by another method that can probe reasons, it is of greater use. Delamont (1976) in her research in a school found FIAC to be useful as a means of exploring differences in teaching style between teachers. However, she was able to get at some of the reasons for the quantitative differences that she discerned only because she had carried out some participant observation and semi-structured interviewing in various school classes. For example, she compared two Latin teachers who were similar in certain respects but differed in terms of 'the proportion of questioning to lecturing in their speech' (Delamont 1976: 108). These differences in teaching style reflected contrasting views about teaching and differences in personal demeanour. Blatchford (2005) reports that the structured observation data that were collected in the research reported in Research in focus 12.1 were part of a wider

study of the impact of variations in class size. The other methods employed were: termly questionnaires administered to teachers to gauge their estimates of how they allocated time in classrooms between different activities; end-of-year questionnaires administered to teachers asking them about their experiences of the impact of class size; and case studies of small and large classes comprising some semi-structured observation of events and semi-structured interviews with teachers and the head teacher.

In laboratory experiments in fields such as social psychology, observation with varying degrees of structure is quite commonplace, but in social research structured observation has not been frequently used. Perhaps one major reason is that, although interviews and questionnaires are limited in terms of their capacity to tap behaviour accurately, they do offer the opportunity to reveal information about both behaviour *and* attitudes and social backgrounds. In other words, they are more flexible and offer the prospect of being able to uncover a variety of correlates of behaviour (albeit reported behaviour), such as social background factors. They can also ask questions about attitudes and investigate explanations that people proffer for their behaviour. As a result, researchers using questionnaires are able to gain information about some factors that may lie behind the patterns of behaviour they uncover. Also, not all forms of behaviour are accessible to structured observation and it is likely that survey research, researcher-driven diaries (see Key concept 10.1). and experience sampling are the only likely means of gaining access to them. However, greater use of structured observation may result in greater facility with the method, so that reliable measures of the kind developed in areas like education might emerge.

Checklist

Structured observation research

○ Have you clearly defined your research questions?

○ Is the sample to be observed relevant to your research questions?

○ Can you justify your sampling approach?

○ Does your observation schedule indicate precisely which kinds of behaviour are to be observed?

○ Have your observation categories been designed so that there is no need for the observer to interpret what is going on?

○ Have you made sure that the categories of behaviour do not overlap?

○ Do all the different categories of behaviour allow you to answer your research questions?

○ Have you piloted your observation schedule?

○ Are the coding instructions clear?

○ Are the categories of behaviour inclusive?

○ Is it easy to log the behaviour as it is happening?

 ## Key points

- Structured observation is an approach to the study of behaviour that is an alternative to survey-based measures.
- It comprises explicit rules for the recording of behaviour.
- Structured observation has tended to be used in relation to a rather narrow range of forms of behaviour, such as that occurring in schools.
- It shares with survey research many common problems concerning reliability, validity, and generalizability.
- Reactive effects have to be taken into account but should not be exaggerated.
- Field stimulations represent a form of structured observation but suffer from difficulties concerning ethics.
- Problems with structured observation revolve around the difficulty of imputing meaning and ensuring that a relevant framework for recording behaviour is being employed.

 ## Questions for review

Problems with survey research on social behaviour

- What are the chief limitations of survey research with regard to the study of behaviour?

So why not observe behaviour?

- What are the chief characteristics of structured observation?
- To what extent does it provide a superior approach to the study of behaviour than questionnaires or structured interviews?

The observation schedule

- What is an observation schedule?
- 'An observation schedule is much like a self-administered questionnaire or structured interview except that it does not entail asking questions.' Discuss.
- Devise an observation schedule of your own for observing an area of social interaction in which you are regularly involved. Ask people with whom you normally interact in those situations how well they think it fits what goes on. Have you missed anything out?

Strategies for observing behaviour

- What are the main ways in which behaviour can be recorded in structured observation?

Sampling

- Identify some of the main sampling strategies in structured observation.

Issues of reliability and validity

- How far do considerations of reliability and validity in structured observation mirror those encountered in relation to the asking of questions in structured interviews and self-administered questionnaires?

- What is the reactive effect and why might it be important in relation to structured observation research?

Field stimulations as a form of structured observation

- What are field stimulations and what ethical concerns are posed by them?

Criticisms of structured observation

- 'The chief problem with structured observation is that it does not allow us access to the intentions that lie behind behaviour.' Discuss.

- How far do you agree with the view that structured observation works best when used in conjunction with other research methods?

. . . .

Online Resource Centre

www.oxfordtextbooks.co.uk/orc/brymansrm5e/

Visit the Online Resource Centre to enrich your understanding of structured observation. Follow up links to other resources, test yourself using multiple choice questions, and gain further guidance and inspiration from the Student Researcher's Toolkit.

. . . .

13
Content analysis

Chapter outline

Chapter guide

Content analysis is an approach to the analysis of documents and texts (which may consist of words and/or images and may be printed or online, written or spoken) that seeks to quantify content in terms of predetermined categories and in a systematic and replicable manner. It is a very flexible method that can be applied to a variety of different media. In a sense, it is not a research method in that it is an approach to the analysis of documents and texts rather than a means of generating data. However, it is usually treated as a research method because of its distinctive approach to analysis. This chapter explores:

- the kinds of research question to which content analysis is suited;
- how to approach the sampling of documents to be analysed;
- what kinds of features of documents or texts are counted;
- how to go about *coding*, which is the core of doing a content analysis;
- the using the Internet as an object of content analysis;
- the content analysis of visual images;
- the advantages and disadvantages of content analysis.

Introduction

Imagine that you are interested in the amount and nature of the interest shown by the mass media, such as newspapers, in a major news item such as Facebook security or superinjunctions. You might ask such questions as:

- When did news items on this topic first begin to appear?
- Which newspapers were fastest in generating an interest in the topic?
- Which newspapers have shown the greatest interest in the topic?
- At what point did media interest begin to wane?
- Have journalists' stances on the topic changed—for example, in terms of pro- versus anti-Facebook or pro- versus anti-superinjunctions?

If you want to know the answers to research questions such as these, you are likely to need to use content analysis to answer them.

Probably the best-known definition of content analysis is as follows:

> Content analysis is a research technique for the objective, systematic and quantitative description of the manifest content of communication.
>
> (Berelson 1952: 18)

Another well-known and apparently similar definition is:

> Content analysis is any technique for making inferences by objectively and systematically identifying specified characteristics of messages.
>
> (Holsti 1969: 14)

Both definitions contain a reference to two qualities: objectivity and being systematic. The former quality means that, as with something like an observation schedule (Chapter 12), rules are clearly specified in advance for the assignment of the raw material (such as newspaper stories) to categories. Objectivity in this sense is to do with the fact that there is transparency in the procedures for assigning the raw material to categories, so that the analyst's personal biases intrude as little as possible in the process. The content analyst is simply applying the rules in question. The quality of being systematic means that the application of the rules is done in a consistent manner so that bias is again suppressed. As a result of these two qualities, anyone could employ the rules and (hopefully) come up with the same results. The process of analysis is one that means that the results are not an extension of the analyst and his or her personal biases. The rules in question may, of course, reflect the researcher's interests and concerns, and therefore these might be a product of subjective bias, but the key point is that, once formulated, the rules should be capable of being applied without the intrusion of bias.

Berelson's definition also makes reference to 'quantitative description'. Content analysis is firmly rooted in the quantitative research strategy in that the aim is to produce quantitative accounts of the raw material in terms of the categories specified by the rules. The feature of quantification adds to the general sense of the systematic and objective application of neutral rules, so that it becomes possible to say with some certainty and in a systematic way that, for example, during a certain period in which it was potentially at the forefront of media attention, whether newspapers differed significantly in their coverage of a particular issue, such as Facebook security.

Two other elements in Berelson's definition are striking especially when contrasted with Holsti's. First, Berelson refers to 'manifest content'. This means that content analysis is concerned with uncovering the apparent content of the item in question: what it is clearly about. Holsti makes no such reference, alluding only to 'specified characteristics'. The latter essentially opens the door to conducting an analysis in terms of what we might term 'latent content'—that is, meanings that lie beneath the superficial indicators of content. Uncovering such latent content means interpreting meanings that lie beneath the surface. For example, Siegel et al. (2013) examined alcohol brand references in popular music in the USA in the years 2009–2011. In addition to the manifest content of brand references (brands and the types of alcohol referred to), the researchers coded references to latent meaning, such as whether the brands and alcohol type were referred to in a positive, negative, or neutral context and whether references to the consequences of alcohol use were positive, negative, or neutral. A related distinction is sometimes made between an emphasis on the text (in particular, counting certain words) and an emphasis on themes within the text, which entails searching for certain ideas within the text (Beardsworth 1980).

A second element in Berelson's definition not found in Holsti's is the reference to 'communication'. Berelson's (1952) book was about communication research, a field that has been especially concerned with newspapers, television, and other mass media. Holsti refers somewhat more generally to 'messages', which raises the prospect of a quite wide applicability of content analysis beyond the specific boundaries of the mass media and mass communications. Content analysis becomes applicable to many different forms of unstructured information, such as transcripts of semi- and unstructured interviews or answers to open-ended questions in surveys (e.g. Research in focus 11.1) and even qualitative case studies of organizations

Key concept 13.1
What is content analysis?

Content analysis is an approach to the analysis of documents and texts that seeks to quantify content in terms of predetermined categories and in a systematic and replicable manner.

Content analysis can be usefully contrasted with two other approaches to the analysis of the content of communication:

- *Semiotics.* The study/science of **signs**. An approach to the analysis of documents and other phenomena that emphasizes the importance of seeking out the deeper meaning of those phenomena. **Semiotics** is concerned to uncover the processes of meaning production and how signs are designed to have an effect upon actual and prospective consumers of those signs. This approach will be explored in Chapter 23.

- *Ethnographic content analysis.* A term employed by Altheide and Schneider (2013) to refer to an approach to documents that emphasizes the role of the investigator in the construction of the meaning of and in texts. It is also sometimes referred to as *qualitative content analysis*. As with most approaches that are described as ethnographic, there is an emphasis on allowing categories to emerge out of data and on recognizing the significance for understanding meaning in the context in which an item being analysed (and the categories derived from it) appeared. This approach will be explored in Chapter 23.

When the term 'content analysis' is employed in this chapter, it will be referring to quantitative content analysis as defined at the beginning of this Key concept—that is, the kind of analysis to which Berelson (1952) and Holsti (1969) refer.

(e.g. Research in focus 13.5). Nor is it necessary for the medium being analysed to be in a printed form. Research has been conducted on:

- the visual images (as well as the text) of women's and men's magazines to examine the degree to which messages about bodily appearance are gendered (Malkin et al. 1999);

- gender roles and deaths in animated films (2003; Colman et al. in press; see Research in the news 13.1);

- radio and television news programmes (see Research in focus 13.1 for an example);

- speeches, such as the Queen's Speech (John and Jennings 2010) and speeches in the European Parliament (Proksch and Slapin 2010);

- obituaries (Fowler and Bielsa 2007);

- alcohol brand references in the lyrics of popular songs (Siegel et al. 2013);

- discrimination narratives taken from sex discrimination cases (Bobbitt-Zeher 2011);

- social media posts and comments (Beullens and Schepers 2013);

- the content of websites and blogs (Davis et al. 2015).

However, there is little doubt that the main use of content analysis has been in the examination of printed texts and documents and of mass-media items in particular. In this regard, content analysis is one of a number of approaches to the examination of texts that have been developed over the years (see Key concept 13.1).

What are the research questions?

As with most quantitative research, it is necessary to specify the research questions precisely, as these will guide both the selection of the media to be content analysed and the coding schedule. If the research questions are not clearly articulated, there is a risk that inappropriate media will be analysed or that the coding schedule will

miss out key dimensions. Most content analysis is likely to entail several research questions. The research referred to in Research in focus 13.1 is concerned with 'the reporting of social science research in the British mass media'. In itself this is not very specific and hardly directs you to a clear specification of the media to be examined or the development of a coding schedule. However, like most researchers, Fenton et al. (1998) had certain specific research questions in mind, such as:

- How much social science research is reported?

- Do certain mass media report a disproportionate amount of social science research?

- In what locations does social science research tend to get reported (for example, special features rather than general news items)?

- Do some topics receive greater attention than others?

- Are certain social science disciplines favoured by the mass media?

Research in focus 13.1
An illustration of content analysis: social science research in the British mass media

Fenton et al. (1998) conducted a study using content analysis of the amount and nature of the reporting of social science research in the British mass media. A sample of eighty-one days of media coverage between 26 May 1994 and 31 March 1995 was taken. The authors state: 'Any media item that mentioned original research conducted by a social scientist or social scientific institution, whether domestic or foreign, was coded, along with any times in which a social scientist (as identified by the item) commented on social issues' (Fenton et al. 1998: 24). The media monitored comprised:

- 12 national newspapers—6 broadsheet and 6 tabloid newspapers; 5 of the 12 newspapers were Sunday papers;

- 4 local newspapers—1 costed and 1 free newspaper from each of Nottingham and Manchester;

- 5 magazines—2 weekly women's publications, 2 monthly women's publications, and 1 monthly men's publication;

- 13 national and local television news programmes covering all four terrestrial television channels broadcasting at the time;

- 6 weekly investigative journalism/social reportage television programmes;

- 5 weekly/daily television talk shows/magazine programmes;

- any prime time ad hoc television programmes deemed relevant;

- national radio news on both Radio 4 and Radio 5 Live;

- nine national Radio 4 investigative journalism/social reportage/studio talk shows and magazine programmes;

- local radio news in two regions: BBC Radio Nottingham and BBC GMR;

- local radio current affairs on BBC GMR Talkback.

The researchers uncovered 466 cases of research being reported. A further 126 news items were coded in which social scientists acted as pundits. The researchers included the cases of 'punditry' in many of their analyses, because the number of items in which social science research featured in news items was considerably smaller than they had envisaged.

Each news item was coded in terms of a number of features, such as:

- the source of the item (for example, which newspaper or television programme);

- the topic of the research;

- the social science discipline referred to in the news item;

- when no social science discipline was referred to, the 'inferred discipline';

- the professional status of the researcher;

- the main research method employed.

- Do the mass media tend to report research conducted by particular methods?
- What tends to prompt the reporting of social science research?
- Are researchers of a particular status (for example, professors) or from certain institutions (for example, prestigious universities) more likely to receive coverage than others?

Such questions seem to revolve around the questions of: *who* (gets reported); *what* (gets reported); *where* (does the issue get reported); *location* (of coverage within the items analysed); *how much* (gets reported); and *why* (does the issue get reported).

As with much content analysis, the researchers were just as interested in omissions in coverage as in what *does* get reported. For example, details about the status of the researcher(s) and about research methods were frequently omitted. Such omissions are in themselves potentially interesting, as they may reveal what is and is not important to reporters and their editors.

Another kind of issue that is frequently encountered in content analysis is one that was not a concern for the researchers looking at the reporting of social science research: How far does the amount of coverage of the issue change over time? This kind of research question is particularly asked by researchers who are keen to note trends in coverage to demonstrate ebbs and flows in media interest. Young and Dugas (2011) report some findings relating to the reporting of climate change in two major national newspapers in Canada. The reporting was examined in each of three time periods: 1988–9, 1998–9, and 2007–8. The authors say that newspaper coverage is especially important for climate change as there is evidence that newspapers are the public's main source of information. An electronic database of articles in the two newspapers was searched using keywords: 'climate change', 'global warming', 'greenhouse effect', or 'greenhouse gas'. The researchers' content analysis shows that, for example, claims that climate change is 'anthropogenically induced' (that is, caused by humans) declined substantially and progressively over the three time periods. They also show that some voices have become less prominent in terms of having a voice about climate change, such as university-based experts and government employees; by contrast, representatives of industry associations and of environmental groups have become more prominent. Young and Dugas (2011: 19) note that there has been a shift toward 'business-friendly narratives'. In this way, it was possible to identify various changes in the newspaper representation of climate change along several dimensions.

 # Selecting a sample

There are several phases in the selection of a sample for content analysis. Because it is a method that can be applied to many different kinds of document, the case of applying it to the mass media will be explored here. However, the basic principles have a broader relevance to a wide range of applications of content analysis.

Sampling media

Many studies of the mass media entail the specification of a research problem in the form of 'the representation of *X* in *Y*'. The *X* may be trade unions, food scares, crime, drink driving, or social science research; the *Y* may be mass media, songs, tweets, blogs, or speeches. If the focus is on the mass media, which media might be the focus? Will it be newspapers or television or radio or magazines? And, if newspapers, will it be all newspapers or tabloids or broadsheets? And, if both tabloids and broadsheets, will it be all of them and will it include Sunday papers? If it will be a sample of newspapers, including Sunday ones, will these be national or local or both? And will it include free newspapers? And, if newspapers, will all news items

be candidates for analysis—for example, would feature articles and letters to the editor be included?

The research reported in Research in focus 13.1 chose to cover a very wide variety of mass media, which is just as well, since the authors were not able to locate a very large number of appropriate items (news items covering social science research). More typically, researchers will opt for one or possibly two of the mass media and may sample within that type or types.

Sampling dates

Sometimes, the decision about dates is more or less dictated by the occurrence of a phenomenon. For example, Bligh et al. (2004) were keen to explore Weber's (1947) suggestion that charismatic leadership is most likely to emerge during a period of crisis. They examined the **rhetoric** of President George W. Bush's speeches before and after the terrorist attacks on the World Trade Center, the Pentagon, and Flight 73 on 11 September 2001. The authors found that not only did his speeches take on a more charismatic rhetoric compared to before the attacks, but that the media portrayal of Bush also tended to incorporate a more charismatic tone. In this case, a key date—9/11—was essentially a given, though there may be an important consideration in deciding at what point the content analysis should cease. The last of the speeches analysed was given on 11 March 2002, which raises the question of how long a charismatic style might be expected to continue following a crisis.

With a research question that entails an ongoing general phenomenon, such as the representation of social science research or crime, the matter of dates is more open. The principles of probability sampling outlined in Chapter 8 can readily be adapted for sampling dates. For example, Bobbitt-Zeher (2011) was interested in gender discrimination at the workplace and the parts that gender stereotypes and organizational variables play in its occurrence. To this end, she gained access to cases of sex discrimination in employment filed with the Ohio Civil Rights Commission between 1988 and 2003. She was especially interested in cases filed by women which were deemed to be 'probable cause' cases. There were 1,418 such cases from which Bobbitt-Zeher took a random sample of 219 cases.

One important factor is whether the focus will be on an issue that entails keeping track of representation as it happens, in which case the researcher may begin at any time and the key decision becomes when to stop, or whether it is necessary to go backwards in time to select media from one or more time periods in the past. Warde (1997) was interested in changes in the representation of food (what should be eaten and how it should be eaten) in the food columns of women's magazines. He writes:

> My primary sources were the five most widely read women's weekly magazines and the five most widely read monthly magazines in each of two twelve-month periods in 1967–8 and 1991–2. The magazines were sampled at the mid-point of the months of November, February, May and August in each year, in order to control for seasonal variation in the contents of food

Research in focus 13.2
Alcohol use on Facebook

Beullens and Schepers (2013) report a content analysis of 160 Belgian Facebook profiles to examine the representation of alcohol use on Facebook and friends' reactions to the postings with alcohol content. The sample was created by a researcher producing a Facebook profile and sending friend requests to 166 college students who were informed that he was looking for participants for his research. Two research questions drove the study.

RQ1: How is alcohol use depicted on Facebook?
RQ2: How do peers react to alcohol-related content on Facebook?

(Beullens and Schepers 2013: 498)

A coding scheme was created that coded the profiles and status updates at three levels: the profile (such as total number of photographs); the personal/profile photographs (all photographs that included alcohol); and status updates (all text provided it referred to alcohol use). For example, one of the variables at the second level is 'Evaluation of use' which is coded as follows:

(1) Positive: the picture shows alcohol use in a positive context, e.g., a picture showing someone proposing a toast to someone with a smile on his or her face

(2) Negative: the picture shows alcohol use in a negative context, e.g., a picture showing someone looking disapprovingly at a drunk person

(3) Neutral: the picture shows alcohol use in a neutral context, e.g., no explicit emotion on face

(4) Unknown: impossible to discern based on the picture, e.g., when no face is shown

(Beullens and Schepers 2013: 499)

A random sample of twenty profiles was tested for inter-rater reliability using Cohen's kappa (see Key concept 12.3). Most variables exhibited a high level of inter-rater reliability of .90 or above; only two were lower than this but both of those were above .80. In terms of the 'Evaluation of use' variable, alcohol use was portrayed in a positive light in 72 per cent of photographs and neutral in 23 per cent. The remaining 5 per cent were either negative or unknown. Among the authors' other findings are that photographs that portrayed alcohol use positively and which showed a brand logo were significantly more likely to receive Facebook 'likes' than others.

columns. . . . From the selected magazines I drew a systematic sample of recipes. This produced 114 recipes in the earlier year, 124 in the later period, which, given their random selection, should be sufficient to make some generalizations about recipes and any changes over time.

(Warde 1997: 44–5)

Three points stand out in this passage. First, there is the concern with being able to establish change by tracking back in time to earlier issues of the mass medium being analysed. Second, Warde wanted to ensure that the magazines were selected from four different points in each of the two twelve-month periods in order to ensure that seasonal factors did not overly influence the findings. If he had selected magazines just from November, there might have been a preoccupation with Christmas fare, while findings from magazines from a summer

month might have been affected by the greater availability of certain foods, such as particular fruit. A decision was made to cover the four seasons in order to reduce the impact of such factors. Third, there is a clear concern to enhance the representativeness of the recipes and therefore the generalizability of the findings by using a probability sampling method in the form of a systematic sample (see Chapter 8).

A further issue is to ensure that certain kinds of objects of analysis are not over-represented. Random or systematic sampling will help in this regard, but when this is not feasible, alternative steps may be necessary. For example, for the research discussed in Research in focus 13.2, the authors write that because they 'wanted to avoid the over-representation of frequent and active Facebook users, for each profile the 20 last status updates were coded' (Beullens and Schepers 2013: 498).

 # What is to be counted?

Obviously, decisions about what should be counted in the course of a content analysis are bound to be profoundly affected by the nature of the research questions under consideration. With content analysis different kinds of 'units of analysis' can be considered. The following kinds of units of analysis are frequently encountered and can be used as guides to the kinds of objects that might be the focus of attention. However, what you would actually *want* or *need* to count will be significantly dictated by your research questions.

Significant actors

Particularly in the context of mass-media news reporting, the main figures in any news item and their characteristics are often important items to code. These considerations are likely to result in such persons as the following being recorded in the course of a content analysis.

- What kind of person has produced the item (for example, general or specialist news reporter)?

- Who is or are the main focus of the item (for example, politician, expert, government spokesperson, or representative of an organization)?

- Who provides alternative voices (for example, politician, expert, government spokesperson, representative of an organization, or person in the street)?

- What was the context for the item (for example, interview, release of a report, or an event such as an outbreak of hostilities or a minister's visit to a hospital)?

In the case of the content analysis of the reporting of social science research in the mass media (see Research in focus 13.1), the significant actors included:

- the author of the item (for example, type of correspondent);

- the type of item (for example, in the case of the press, whether the research was reported in a general article, feature article, or some other context);

- the details of the researcher who was most prominent in the item (for example, personal details, status, and whether he or she was acting as a researcher or pundit in the context of the item);

- what prompted the item (for example, launch of a report, a new research initiative, or a conference);

- the details of the main (if any) commentators on the research;

- any other actors.

The chief objective in recording such details is to map the main protagonists in news reporting in an area and to begin to reveal some of the mechanics involved in the production of information for public consumption.

Words

While it may seem a dull activity, the counting of the frequency with which certain words occur is sometimes undertaken in content analysis. However, the use of some words rather than others can often be of some significance, because it can reveal the predilection for sensationalizing certain events. Bailey, Giangola, and Boykoff (2014) examined the incidence of what they call 'epistemic markers' (words or expressions that imply uncertainty) in the media reporting of climate change. They compared two US newspapers with two comparable Spanish newspapers for the years 2001 and 2007. These two years are significant because reports from the Intergovernmental Panel on Climate Change (IPCC) appeared during the two years. They searched for words and expressions concerning such things as activities leading to uncertain outcomes (e.g. predicting, estimating); quantitative indications of uncertainty (e.g. probability, likelihood); hedging verbs (e.g. believe); challenges to the IPCC and its reports (e.g. challenge, debate); references to opponents of climate change ideas (e.g. deniers); and 'modifiers' (e.g. controversial). While words alone *can* be of interest, when coding the articles 'context was always considered before a term was marked as "epistemic"' (Bailey et al. 2014: 202). Epistemic markers were found to be clearly more frequent in US than in Spanish news items in both years and increased over the two years for both countries. The authors point out that the latter is striking because scientific understanding of climate change and of the role of humans in connection with climate change strengthened during this period.

Computer-assisted content analysis

Tips and skills 'Counting words in electronic news reports' discusses the use of computer-assisted (or automated) content analysis (CACA) in the context of electronic newspapers. Some examples of content analysis that emphasize words can be found in Research in focus 13.3. These two boxed features bring out the growing role that can be played by CACA. Most obviously, CACA can be used to count the frequency of words or phrases in a body of text (as in Research in focus 13.3). It offers considerable advantages over manual methods, such as no problems of inter- or intra-rater reliability; key-word-in-context (KWIC) output can be easily generated which can aid the interpretation of words and their frequencies; it can establish co-occurrences of words and phrases; and it can handle a large body of textual material quickly. However, it has its limitations such as lack of a capacity to handle nuances; difficulty of providing a comprehensive list of words or phrases to be searched for; and a risk of focusing too much on frequencies to the exclusion of interpretation and meaning (Bligh and Kohles 2014).

In the examination by Bligh et al. (2004) of the content of President George W. Bush's speeches before and after the terrorist attacks of 9/11 the authors wanted to establish whether there was a shift in their

Tips and skills
Counting words in electronic news reports

The growing availability of the printed news media in electronic form, such as CD-ROM and electronic databases, greatly facilitates the search for and counting of keywords in this kind of context. Most of the main UK newspapers and many overseas ones are available in electronic format either through their own websites or through a website such as British Media Online (www.wrx.zen.co.uk/britnews.htm, accessed 31 October 2014), which acts as a launch pad for a host of different electronic newspapers. The newspapers can then usually be searched for keywords and phrases. You will probably need a password (for example, Athens authentication) to access them, especially if you are seeking to access them away from your university or college.

Further, some simple analyses can be conducted using LexisNexis. This database comprises newspaper articles from a wide variety of newspapers. For example, Beardsworth and Bryman (2004) used LexisNexis Professional to search this database for the years 1985 to 2002 for the incidence of keywords relating to BSE, such as: Bovine Spongiform Encephalopathy; BSE; CJD; and Creutzfeldt-Jakob Disease. They chart the number of reports using at least one of these terms in each newspaper per annum. Their analysis shows how there was a small surge of media reporting around 1990 and then a huge 'spike' in the mid-1990s, when it attracted a great deal of media interest, and then a trailing-off in the incidence of reporting. They also show how the statistics for beef and veal consumption in the UK display a corresponding pattern. This article demonstrates the use of a simple counting procedure that can be quite revealing and that is greatly facilitated by the availability of electronic (and in this case online) mass media. However, caution is needed in the use of LexisNexis. Deacon (2007) has drawn attention to several drawbacks in its use relative to conventional manual searching. For example, he notes that there is considerable loss of information because the visual elements of media reporting are not included and because news articles are treated in isolation and not in relation to other news articles.

Research in focus 13.3
Computerized keyword analysis

Seale et al. (2006) report the results of a study in which he retrieved all postings on a single day (20 April 2005) to online forums of the two most prevalent websites in the UK concerned with breast and prostate cancer. Keywords in this research were words that occur with unusual frequency compared with other words in the corpus that is analysed. In this case, Seale and his colleagues were interested in keyword frequency in the breast cancer postings as compared to the prostate cancer postings. The search for keywords was undertaken with specialist software called *Wordsmith*: www.lexically.net/wordsmith/ (accessed 6 November 2014).

Seale et al. (2006: 2582) then 'used this quantitative information to facilitate an interpretive, qualitative analysis focusing on the meanings of word clusters associated with keywords'. Thus, Seale and his colleagues use this quantitative analysis of words as a springboard for a more probing qualitative examination of the links between the words. They found that men with prostate cancer were more likely to use words associated with research (for example, 'study'), treatment (for example, 'radical prostatectomy'), and tests and diagnosis (for example, 'biopsy') compared to women discussing breast cancer. By contrast, women discussing breast cancer were more likely to use keywords associated with feelings (for example, 'scared') and people (for example, 'family') and also to use 'superlatives' (for example, 'amazing').

In a later study, the same analytic approach was applied to postings in April 2005 to Internet forums concerning breast cancer, prostate cancer, and sexual health (Seale et al. 2010). The analysis was compared to a parallel examination of qualitative interviews with people discussing their experiences of breast and prostate cancer and their sexual health concerns (a total of 140 interviews). The authors report that what they call the 'orientation' of the two formats differed. In interviews, there was an emphasis on the reporting of the past, presumably because the interview format encouraged narratives about the past experience of the illness. This is a focus that has been a particular feature of studies of health and illness that have been influenced by **narrative analysis** and the notion of 'illness narratives' (see the section on 'Narrative analysis' in Chapter 24). The Internet postings tended to be about the exchange of information and support and therefore dealt more directly with the immediate experience of illness. Seale et al. propose that this means that the Internet postings provide superior access to the experience of illness as the accounts are not produced for the benefit of an interviewer. The Internet postings also come across as more spontaneous and as allowing greater freedom for issues to be raised that relate to the sufferer's experience (for example, the frequent discussion of chocolate among breast cancer postings), whereas the interviewer's influence was very evident (for example, 'relationship' or 'relationships' were used in questions 622 times). The authors argue that the tendency for interviewers to seek to elicit narratives about the illness and with particular issues in mind tends to militate against direct expressions of illness experiences, although the ability to probe, which can yield significant data, is something missing in the postings. Seale et al. argue that, while they are not flawless as sources of data about illness, particularly for research into sensitive topics where there are concerns about the truthfulness of reports in interviews, Internet postings about illness experiences warrant serious consideration, especially when the time and cost involved in sampling, conducting, and transcribing qualitative interviews are borne in mind.

charismatic tone. They used CACA to do this. It involved using software called DICTION, which at the time meant using version 5.0. The program analyses passages using pre-existing dictionaries that have already been set up and allows the creation of dictionaries created by users for their own needs. The procedure allowed Bligh et al. to establish that there was a change in President Bush's speeches before and after the crisis. Information about DICTION can be found at: **www.**

dictionsoftware.com/diction-overview/ (accessed 18 December 2014)

The website describes the software as follows:

DICTION is a computer-aided text analysis program ... that uses a series of dictionaries to search a passage for five semantic features—Activity, Optimism, Certainty, Realism and Commonality—as well as thirty-five sub-features. DICTION uses predefined dictionaries and can use up to thirty custom dictionaries built with words that the user has defined, such as topical or negative words, for particular research needs.

DICTION uses dictionaries (word-lists) to search a text for these qualities:

- **Certainty**—Language indicating resoluteness, inflexibility, and completeness and a tendency to speak ex cathedra.
- **Activity**—Language featuring movement, change, the implementation of ideas and the avoidance of inertia.
- **Optimism**—Language endorsing some person, group, concept or event, or highlighting their positive entailments.
- **Realism**—Language describing tangible, immediate, recognizable matters that affect people's everyday lives.
- **Commonality**—Language highlighting the agreed-upon values of a group and rejecting idiosyncratic modes of engagement.

Another kind of CACA is automated sentiment analysis. Greaves et al. (in press) used a combination of quantitative and qualitative content analysis to examine tweets aimed at NHS hospitals (this study is discussed in Chapter 23 in the section on 'Social media'). Most of the quantitative content analysis was carried out manually but in addition Greaves et al. used automated sentiment analysis. They used software designed by TheySay Ltd. (**www.theysay.io/sentiment-analysis-api/**, accessed 18 December 2014) 'to produce an overall sentiment score for each tweet of positive, negative or neutral' (Greaves et al. in press).

CACA allows the removal of certain concerns to do with human bias and cognitive limitations associated with traditional manual content analysis (although at a cost, as outlined previously). As the software improves and becomes able to perform more tasks, it seems reasonable to assume that its use will increase. It is also worth pointing out that some of the basic word counting and KWIC functions can be performed using CAQDAS software of the kind discussed in Chapter 25, so if you want to try out CACA and are familiar with CAQDAS, it may be worth trying it out there. Also, both DICTION and TheySay software permit free trials.

Subjects and themes

Frequently in a content analysis the researcher will want to code text in terms of certain subjects and themes. Essentially, what is being sought is a categorization of the phenomenon or phenomena of interest. For example, in the case of the content analysis of the reporting of social science research in the British mass media, Fenton et al. (1998) were concerned to classify the main social science discipline that formed the backcloth to the research being reported (Research in focus 13.1). This entailed a

classification into one of seven types: sociology; social policy; economics; psychology; business and management; political science; and interdisciplinary. Research drawing on other social science disciplines was not included in the study. Another topic was the methodology of the research being reported, which resulted in research being classified in terms of such categories as survey/mail questionnaire; interview; ethnography; and, of course, content analysis.

However, while such categorizations are often relatively straightforward, when the process of coding is thematic, a more interpretative approach needs to be taken. At this point, the analyst is searching not just for manifest content but for latent content as well. It becomes necessary to probe beneath the surface in order to ask deeper questions about what is happening. In the investigation of social science research in the mass media discussed in Research in focus 13.1, each reported study was classified in terms of the subject area of the research (Fenton et al. 1998). Sixty-two categories were employed and were grouped into seven main areas: UK and overseas economy; UK and overseas government politics and policy; social integration and control; health; demographics; social analysis—general; and lifestyles. A further example is a study by de Grosbois (2012) of corporate social responsibility (CSR) reporting on hotel groups' websites. The websites of the 150 largest hotel companies were searched for content relating to CSR. This search included online content of such things as annual reports and sustainability reports. Five CSR themes and 33 CSR-related goals were used as a framework. The five themes were: environmental goals; employment quality; diversity and accessibility; society/community well-being; and economic prosperity. The 33 CSR-related goals were directly connected to the five themes. Thus, there were eight goals relating to the 'employment quality' theme, such as 'create a safe and healthy work environment', 'provide a work/life balance', 'provide fair wages and benefits', and 'provide opportunities for career advancement'. Each theme and goal was coded in terms of whether there was evidence of the hotel group being committed to it. Each goal was also coded in terms of whether there was evidence of initiatives at the corporate level and at the individual property level, and also whether the group reported progress towards the attainment of the goal at the corporate level and at the individual property level. In addition, the different methods of communication were coded (such as whether there was a separate CSR report).

Dispositions

A further level of interpretation is likely to be entailed when the researcher seeks to demonstrate a disposition in the texts being analysed. For example, it may be that the researcher wants to establish whether journalists, in the reporting of an issue in the news media, are favourably inclined or hostile towards an aspect of it, such as their stances on the government's handling of a food scare crisis. In the case of the study by Fenton et al. (1998; see Research in focus 13.1) of the reporting of social science research, each item was coded in terms of whether the editorial commentary on the research was positive, negative, or merely descriptive. In many cases, it was necessary to infer whether the editorial commentary was implicitly positive or negative if there were no manifest indications of such value positions. Such an analysis entails establishing whether a judgemental stance can be discerned in the items being coded and, if so, the nature of the judgement. Similarly, in the examination of climate change reporting in US and Spanish newspapers referred to above (in the section on 'Words'), Bailey et al. (2014) categorized the tone of epistemic markers as negative or as neutral.

Another way in which dispositions may be revealed in content analysis is through the coding of ideologies, beliefs, or principles. For example, for her content analysis of discrimination narratives, Bobbitt-Zeher (2011) coded narratives in terms of whether there was evidence of gender stereotyping. In doing so, she used a distinction between descriptive and prescriptive stereotyping, with the former being 'expressions of how women in general are assumed to be and expressions indicating that women's traits are incompatible with a particular job', whereas prescriptive discrimination refers to 'expressions that a particular woman worker violates gender assumptions' (Bobbitt-Zeher 2011: 770). She found the former mode of stereotyping to be the more common: it was found in 44 per cent of narratives against 8 per cent for the other mode. In the remaining 48 per cent of narratives, no stereotyping was found in the majority (37 per cent) and the rest were categorized as 'other'.

Coding

As much of the foregoing discussion has implied, coding is a crucial stage in the process of doing a content analysis. There are two main elements to a content analysis coding scheme: designing a coding schedule and designing a coding manual. To illustrate these processes, imagine a student interested in crime reporting in a local newspaper. The student chooses to focus on the reporting of crimes that are subject to court proceedings and where the victim is a person rather than an organization. To simplify the issue we will just have the following variables:

1. nature of the offence;
2. gender of perpetrator;
3. social class of perpetrator;
4. age of perpetrator;
5. gender of victim;
6. social class of victim;
7. age of victim;
8. depiction of victim;
9. position of news item.

Content analysts would normally be interested in a much larger number of variables than this, but a simple illustration like this can be helpful for getting across the operation of a coding schedule and a coding manual. Also, it is quite likely that the student would want to record the item so that the details of more than one offender and more than one victim can be included. In other words, very often a crime will entail multiple perpetrators and/

or victims, so that the details of each of the key figures (age, gender, occupation, depiction of victim) would need to be recorded. However, to keep the illustration simple, just one perpetrator and victim is assumed.

Coding schedule

The coding schedule is a form onto which all the data relating to an item being coded will be entered. Figure 13.1 provides an example of a coding schedule. The schedule is very much a simplification in order to facilitate the discussion of the principles of coding in content analysis and of the construction of a coding schedule in particular.

Each of the columns in Figure 13.1 is a dimension that is being coded. The column headings indicate the dimension to be coded. The blank cells on the coding form are the places in which codes are written. One form would be used for each media item that was coded. The codes can then be transferred to a computer data file for analysis with a software package such as SPSS (see Chapter 16).

Coding manual

On the face of it, the coding schedule in Figure 13.1 seems very bare and does not appear to provide much information about what is to be done or where. This is where the coding manual comes in. The coding manual is a statement of instructions to coders that also includes all the possible categories for each dimension being coded. It provides: a list of all the dimensions; the different

Figure 13.1
Coding schedule

Case number	Day	Month	Year	Nature of offence I	Gender of perpetrator	Occupation of perpetrator	Age of perpetrator	Gender of victim	Occupation of victim	Age of victim	Depiction of victim	Nature of offence II	Position of news item

categories subsumed under each dimension; the numbers (that is, *codes*) that correspond to each category; and guidance on what each dimension is concerned with and any factors that should be taken into account in deciding how to allocate any particular code to each dimension. Figure 13.2 provides the coding manual that might correspond to the coding schedule in Figure 13.1. A coding manual includes all the dimensions that would be employed in the coding process, indications of the guidance for coders, and the lists of categories that were created for each dimension.

The coding manual includes the occupation of both the perpetrator and the victim. It uses Goldthorpe's social class categorization and is based on the summary by Marshall et al. (1988: 22). To this scheme have been added three further categories that might be used in newspapers: unemployed; retired; and housewife. There is also a category of 'other'. The offences are categorized in terms of those used by the police in recording crimes notified to them according to Home Office rules. Much finer distinctions could be used, but, since the student may not be planning to examine a large sample of news items, broader categories might be preferable. These categories have the further advantage of being comparable to the Home Office data. Recorded crime statistics have been criticized for their lack of reliability and validity (see Chapter 14), but the comparison between such data and the reporting of crime in local newspapers would be potentially illuminating.

The coding schedule and manual permit two offences to be recorded when an incident entails more than one offence. If there are more than two, the student has to make a judgement concerning the most significant offence. The student should also treat as the first offence the main one mentioned in the article.

The coding manual is crucial because it provides coders with complete listings of all categories for each dimension they are coding and guidance about how to interpret the dimensions. It is on the basis of these lists and guidance that a coding schedule of the kind presented in Figure 13.1 will be completed. Even if you are a lone researcher, such as a student conducting a content analysis for a dissertation or thesis, it is important to spend a lot of time providing yourself with instructions about how to code. While you may not face the problem of **inter-rater reliability**, the issue of **intra-rater reliability** is still significant for you (see the section below on 'Potential pitfalls in devising coding schemes').

Plates 13.1 and 13.2 provide examples of the kind of article that might appear. Both are from the *Nottingham Evening Post*.

The coding of the incidents would be filled in on coding schedules, as shown in Figure 13.1, and the data from each form would then be entered as a row of data in a computer program such as SPSS.

The coding of the incident in Plate 13.1 would appear as in Figure 13.3; the data entered on the computer would appear as follows:

123 27 12 02 1 1 17 46 1 17 –1 3 16 2

Note that the news item in Plate 13.2 contains a second offence, which has been coded as 16 under 'Nature of offence II'. Figure 13.4 contains the form that would be completed for the item in Plate 13.2. The following row of data would be created:

301 04 07 03 1 1 17 24 1 5 –1 3 0 2

Forms like these would be completed for each news item within the chosen period or periods of study.

Potential pitfalls in devising coding schemes

There are several potential dangers in devising a content analysis coding scheme, and they are very similar to the kinds of consideration that are involved in the design of structured interview and structured observation schedules.

- *Discrete dimensions.* Make sure that your dimensions are entirely separate; in other words, there should be no conceptual or empirical overlap between them. For example, in the research presented in Research in focus 13.1, it is necessary to be clear about the difference between the

Figure 13.2
Coding manual

Nature of offence I

1. Violence against the person
2. Sexual offences
3. Robbery
4. Burglary in a dwelling
5. Burglary other than in a dwelling
6. Theft from a person
7. Theft of pedal cycle
8. Theft from shops
9. Theft from vehicle
10. Theft of motor vehicle
11. Vehicle interference and tampering
12. Other theft and handling stolen goods
13. Fraud and forgery
14. Criminal damage
15. Drug offences
16. Other notifiable offences

Gender of perpetrator

1. Male
2. Female
3. Unknown

Occupation of perpetrator

1. I   Higher grade professionals, administrators, and officials; managers in large establishments; large proprietors
2. II   Lower-grade professionals, administrators, and officials; higher-grade technicians; managers in small business and industrial establishments; supervisors of nonmanual employees
3. IIIa   Routine nonmanual employees in administration and commerce
4. IIIb   Personal service workers
5. IVa   Small proprietors, artisans, etc., with employees
6. IVb   Small proprietors, artisans, etc., without employees
7. IVc   Farmers and smallholders; self-employed fishermen
8. V   Lower-grade technicians, supervisors of manual workers
9. VI   Skilled manual workers
10. VIIa   Semi-skilled and unskilled manual workers (not in agriculture)

11. VIIb   Agricultural workers
12.   Unemployed
13.   Retired
14.   Housewife
15.   Student
16.   Other
17.   Unknown

Age of perpetrator

Record age (−1 if unknown)

Gender of victim

1. Male
2. Female
3. Unknown
4. Organization (if victim is an organization as in fraud cases)

Occupation of victim

Same as for occupation of perpetrator

(if not applicable, code as 99)

Age of victim

Record age (−1 if unknown; −2 if not applicable)

Depiction of victim

1. Victim responsible for crime
2. Victim partly responsible for crime
3. Victim not at all responsible for crime
4. Not applicable

Nature of offence II (code if second offence mentioned in relation to the same incident; code 0 if no second offence)

Same as for Nature of offence I

Position of news item

1. Front page
2. Inside
3. Back page

Plate 13.1
Reporting a crime in local newspapers I

Dogs fighting led to assault

Owner guilty of chain attack and cruelty

By SEAN KENNY

IT began with a fight between two dogs — but ended when one owner faced assault and animal cruelty charges.

Conrad Aaron Martin, 46, of Leybourne Drive, Bestwood, attacked a dog and its owner with a chain when they met while out for a morning walk, Nottingham magistrates heard.

He was out with his English and Staffordshire bull terrier cross, on May 27 on the Hucknall Embankment in Bestwood when his pet met Rocco Lamagna's German shepherd dog, Lupo, out for his morning walk.

The terrier locked his teeth around Lupo's front leg and Mr Lamagna, of Bestwood, asked Martin to control his dog.

But, the court was told, Martin replied: "I'm going to kill you... and your dog."

Mr Lamagna told the court: "He got a massive chain and hit me and the dog with it.

"I tried to bend over my dog, I couldn't do anything. My dog was bleeding from his eye."

Mr Lamagna told the court he had not taken his dog along that route since the incident.

Talking to the *Post* after the trial, Mr Lamagna said: "The attack was totally unexpected.

"I'd just come out of hospital and was taking Lupo for a walk when his dog went for mine."

Mr Lamagna controlled his dog and tried to protect him: "Lupo's eye was bleeding and I tried to cover him to stop him getting bitten again.

"The vet's bill cost me £65.

"I used to walk Lupo down there all the time, but I never go there now."

Denied

The court heard that after Mr Lamagna reported the attack to the police, investigations led to an identity parade being organised.

Mr Lamagna immediately picked out Martin, the court was told.

Martin had denied the charges of assault and cruelty to animals, but was found guilty.

He told the court: "There's nothing I wouldn't do to defend my dog."

Magistrate Mrs Ann Allison said: "We accept Mr Lamagna was certain when he picked you out at the identity parade."

Martin has two previous convictions for affray whilst walking his dog, in November and December last year.

His sentence will be decided by the crown court.

FIGHT VICTIMS: Rocco Lamagna and his dog Lupo.   C241202SO7-1

Source: From *Nottingham Evening Post*, 27 December 2002, p. 13. Reprinted with kind permission of the publisher.

Plate 13.2
Reporting a crime in local newspapers II

Landlords hit out as pub attacker avoids jail

PUB ASSAULT: Injured landlord Paul Buxton and, left, his assailant Tom Turton

Disgust at 'lenient' sentence

ANGRY licensees have blasted the "deplorable" sentence given to a violent customer.

Tom Turton, 24, poked his thumbs into landlord Paul Buxton's eyes after being asked to leave the Lady Bay pub in Trent Boulevard.

Turton, of Fourth Avenue, Sherwood Rise, was ordered to do 200 hours community service by Nottingham magistrates after admitting common assault. He was also told to pay £170 compensation and £55 costs.

The sentence has outraged members of the West Bridgford Pubwatch scheme, of which Mr Buxton is a member.

Letter

Today they were sending a letter to the Chairman of the Magistrates Bench which reads: "We are writing to express our disgust at the leniency of the sentence given to the accused Tom Turton. What kind of message are we giving out here?"

The landlords described the handling of the case, including numerous adjournments, as "deplorable".

The Pubwatch group is also taking legal advice about whether to appeal against the decision.

Alan Merryweather, the Pubwatch vice-chairman who runs the Test Match Inn in West Bridgford, said: "I don't know what guidelines the magistrates have, but Turton should have got a six month custodial sentence.

"We feel that reflects the severity of the injuries."

Assaulted landlord Paul Buxton said: "I don't think his sentence was stiff enough.

"He needs a short, sharp shock — but the message that's gone out is smack a landlord and you'll get away with it.

"No-one should go to work and get punched or poked in the eyes."

Magistrates heard that on Sunday, March 9, Turton had spent all afternoon and evening drinking in the Lady Bay pub, downing six or seven pints of lager.

At closing time, he became enraged when Mr Buxton jokingly told him to leave.

Dennis Quinn, prosecuting, told the court: "He deliberately stuck both thumbs in each of Mr Buxton's eyes.

"Mr Buxton said he could feel the thumbs in his eye sockets."

The landlord suffered cuts to the rear of his eyes. It has left him with occasional blurred vision and needing eye drops, but there will be no lasting damage.

Mr Turton was the first person to be banned from all 22 pubs within the West Bridgford Pubwatch.

Sundeep Soor, in mitigation, said it was Turton's first violent offence and he was very remorseful".

ANGRY: Mr Buxton with the letter sent to magistrates and, above, the Lady Bay pub

Graham Hooper, Justices Clerk at Nottingham Magistrates' Court, said the maximum penalty for common assault is a £5,000 fine or six months in prison.

He added: "When a licensee or someone going about their business serving the public is assaulted that's seen as a fact which makes the offence more serious.

"But magistrates are required to look at the circumstances of the offender and consider each case on its merits."

Source: From *Nottingham Evening Post*, 4 July 2003, p. 13. Reprinted with kind permission of the publisher.

Figure 13.3

Completed coding schedule for news item in Plate 13.1

Case number	Day	Month	Year	Nature of offence I	Gender of perpetrator	Occupation of perpetrator	Age of perpetrator	Gender of victim	Occupation of victim	Age of victim	Depiction of victim	Nature of offence II	Position of news item
123	27	12	02	1	1	17	46	1	17	−1	3	16	2

Figure 13.4

Completed coding schedule for news item in Plate 13.2

Case number	Day	Month	Year	Nature of offence I	Gender of perpetrator	Occupation of perpetrator	Age of perpetrator	Gender of victim	Occupation of victim	Age of victim	Depiction of victim	Nature of offence II	Position of news item
301	04	07	03	1	1	17	24	1	5	−1	3	0	2

social science discipline and the topic of the featured research, even though they have a similar ring.

- *Mutually exclusive categories.* Make sure that there is no overlap in the categories supplied for each dimension. If the categories are not mutually exclusive, coders will be unsure about how to code each item.

- *Exhaustive categories.* For each dimension, all possible categories should be available to coders.

- *Clear instructions.* Coders should be clear about how to interpret what each dimension is about and what factors to take into account when assigning codes to each category. Sometimes, these will have to be very elaborate. Coders should have little or no discretion in how to allocate codes to units of analysis.

- *Clarity about the unit of analysis.* For example, in the study of social science research in the mass media (see Research in focus 13.1), the authors found it necessary to operate with a clear distinction between the media item (e.g. a newspaper article) and the social science research being reported. Thus some of the data recorded were to do with the media item; other data recorded were to do with the research being referred to. The researchers content analysed up to three social science research profiles per media item, because often the media reporting of research referred to more than one investigation. For example, in Davis's (2003) examination of sex-role stereotyping of cartoon characters in commercial cartoons shown between children's programmes, 167 cartoons were sampled. However, it was the *characters* in those cartoons that provided the units of analysis,

so that characteristics of the 478 characters were coded and analysed. Similarly, in the imaginary study of the media reporting of crime in the local press, more than one offence per media item could be recorded. You need to be clear about the distinction between the media item (e.g. a newspaper article) and the topic being coded (an offence). In practice, a researcher is interested in both but needs to keep the distinction in mind.

In order to be able to enhance the quality of a coding scheme, it is highly advisable to pilot early versions of the scheme. Piloting will help to identify difficulties in applying the coding scheme, such as uncertainty about which category to employ when considering a certain dimension or discovering that no code is available to cover a particular case. Piloting will also help to identify any evidence that one category of a dimension tends to subsume an extremely large percentage of items. If this occurs, it may be necessary to consider breaking that category down so that it allows greater discrimination between the items being analysed.

The reliability of coding is a further potential area of concern. Coding must be done in a consistent manner. As with structured observation, coding must be consistent between coders (*inter-rater reliability*), and each coder must be consistent over time (*intra-rater reliability*). An important part of piloting the coding scheme will be testing for consistency between coders and, if time permits, intra-rater reliability. The process of gauging reliability is more or less identical to that briefly covered in the context of structured observation in Key concept 12.3.

The Internet as object of content analysis

Websites, social media posts and similar virtual documents are potential sources of data in their own right and can be regarded as potential material for both quantitative and qualitative content analysis of the kind discussed in this chapter and Chapter 23. Research in focus 13.4 presents an example of such analysis.

However, there are clearly difficulties with using websites as sources of data in this way. The four criteria for assessing the quality of documents (J. Scott 1990) discussed in Chapter 23 may be applied to websites. In addition to the issues raised there, the following additional observations are worth considering:

- You will need to find the websites relating to your research questions. This is likely to mean trawling the Web using a search engine such as Google. However, any search engine provides access to only a portion of the Web. While this means that the use of several search engines is preferable when seeking out appropriate websites, it has to be recognized that not only will they allow access to just a portion of the available websites but also they may be a biased sample.

- Related to this point, seeking out websites on a topic can only be as good as the keywords that are employed in the search process. The researcher has to be very patient to try as many relevant keywords as possible (and combinations of them—known as Boolean searches) and may be advised to ask other people (librarians, supervisors, and so on) whether the most appropriate ones are being used.

- New websites are continually appearing and others disappearing. Researchers basing their investigations on websites need to recognize that their analyses may be based on websites that no longer exist and that new ones may have appeared since data collection was terminated.

- Websites are also continually changing, so that an analysis may be based upon at least some websites that have been quite considerably updated. Thus, while the hotels in de Grosbois's (2012) investigation still have websites, the specific content of those websites that were used in their study may no longer be available and is likely to be significantly different from the content that can be obtained currently.

- The analysis of websites is a new field that is very much in flux. New approaches are being developed at a rapid rate. Some draw on traditional ways of interpreting

Research in focus 13.4
Conducting a content analysis of websites

The reporting of organizations' environmental performance has become increasingly significant as concerns about our ecology and environment have grown. Jose and Lee (2007: 309) conducted a content analysis of the websites of the world's 200 largest corporations to examine the

> content of corporate environmental disclosures with respect to the following seven areas: environmental planning considerations, top management support to the institutionalization of environmental concerns, environmental structures and organizing specifics, environmental leadership activities, environmental control, external validations of certifications of environmental programs, and forms of corporate disclosures.

In fact, only 140 companies' websites could be analysed, mainly due to the absence of relevant statements. Environmental statements were coded in terms of the presence of the various indicators that the researchers developed. One set of findings related to the philosophical underpinnings of the statements. Here, there are three interesting findings. First, 64 per cent of the 140 companies depict environmental performance in terms of sustainable development. Secondly, 58 per cent take an 'integrated management' approach whereby issues of environmental performance are suffused through the organization's structures and processes. Thirdly, only 40 per cent adopt a life-cycle approach in which products are deemed to be a company's responsibility from initial inception to the point where it is terminally expended. Overall, one of the key findings is that the evidence suggests that the growing focus on environmental responsibility is not totally driven by regulation; in other words, at least so far as their public statements are concerned, companies are going beyond their countries' regulatory frameworks.

documents such as discourse analysis and qualitative content analysis. Others have been developed specifically in relation to the Web, such as the examination of hyperlinks between websites and their significance (Schneider and Foot 2004).

Most researchers who use documents as the basis for their work have to confront the issue that it is difficult to determine the universe or population from which they are sampling. Therefore, the problems identified here and in Chapter 23 are not unique to websites. However, the rapid growth and speed of change in the Web accentuate these kinds of problems for social researchers, who are likely to feel that the experience is like trying to hit a target that not only continually moves but is in a constant state of metamorphosis. The crucial issue is to be sensitive to the limitations of the use of websites as material that can be analysed, as well as to the opportunities they offer.

In addition, it is important to bear in mind the four quality criteria recommended by J. Scott (1990) in connection with documents (see Chapter 23). Scott's suggestions invite us to consider quite why a website is constructed. Why is it there at all? Is it there for commercial reasons? Does it have an axe to grind? In other words, we should be no less sceptical about websites than about any other kind of document.

One further point to register is that, just like most documents, websites can be subjected to both qualitative and quantitative forms of analysis. The studies referred to above have involved quantitative content analysis, but qualitative content analysis of the kind covered in Chapter 23 is also feasible (see Research in focus 13.3).

Yet another kind of document that has been subjected to analysis is the blog (Web log). Boepple and Thompson (2014) conducted a quantitative content analysis of twenty-one healthy living blogs, that is, blogs in which the authors write about what they take to be their healthy living regime. The blogs in the sample were those which had received a blogging award relating to health; of those which had won an award, those with the largest numbers of pageviews were selected. The authors coded information about the blogger and four categories of information: 'appearance variables, thin appearance ideal variables, disordered food/nutrition variables and health variables' (Boepple and Thompson 2014: 364), as well as information in the 'About Me' sections of the blogs. The researchers found, for example, that five bloggers used very negative language about being fat or overweight and four invoked admiration for being thin. Boepple and Thompson draw the important conclusion that the blogs comprise messages that are 'potentially problematic' for anyone changing their behaviour on the basis of advice contained in them. As they put it: 'Much of the content emphasizes appearance, thin appearance ideals, and disordered messages about food/nutrition' (Boepple and Thompson 2014: 365).

The examination of postings to chatrooms and discussion forums has become a particularly fertile data source for socials scientists with interests in health and health-related issues (see Research in focus 13.3). As Seale et al. (2010) argue (see the second study in Research in focus 13.3), the rationale for their use is compelling because they provide access to the immediacy of the experience of illness and because they are 'given' data and as such are not influenced by an interviewer, obviating the need for a full interview-based study. However, they also observe that there are some problems with a reliance on such postings: access to and facility with the Internet is highly variable; those who submit postings may differ in significant ways from those who do not (quite aside from the issue of access to and facility with the Internet); the researcher cannot probe the individuals concerned; and only a limited number of research questions can be answered with the materials provided by postings, whereas qualitative interviews can be tailored to answer a host of different kinds of question. Health and health-related

Tips and skills
Referring to websites

There is a growing practice in academic work that, when referring to websites, you should include the date you consulted them. This convention is very much associated with the fact that websites often disappear and frequently change, so that, if subsequent researchers want to follow up your findings, or even to check on them, they may find that they are no longer there or that they have changed. Citing the date you accessed the website may help to relieve any anxieties about someone not finding a website you have referred to or finding it has changed. This does mean, however, that you will have to keep a running record of the dates you accessed the websites to which you refer.

topics are by no means the only context for content analysis of online communities. Davis et al. (2015) conducted an analysis of postings that followed a blog post concerning a cyberbullying suicide by a 15-year-old named Amanda Todd. There were 1,094 comments of which 482 contained stories about being bullied. Of the 482 stories, 12 per cent were about cyberbullying, 75 per cent about traditional bullying, and the rest comprised a mixture of both. Davis et al. analysed the stories for themes in the form of the reasons given for being bullied. The most common reason was to do with the victim's physical appearance. The researchers also coded the coping strategies developed by the victims and the perceived effectiveness of the strategies. The researchers conclude that their findings imply that with both types of bullying the victims 'are often targeted because they do not conform in one way or another to mainstream norms and values' (2015: 371).

The arrival of 'Big Data' opportunities in the form of social networking venues such as Facebook and Twitter are likely to mean a proliferation of approaches to the Internet as an object of content analysis in the future. One of the challenges for the content analyst when faced with such Big Data opportunities is how to reduce the population of tweets or posts to a manageable size. This issue is taken up in Chapter 23 in the context of the qualitative content analysis of documents, but the suggestions there are relevant to quantitative content analysis too. An example is a content analysis by Humphreys et al. (2014)

of the kinds of personal information disclosed on Twitter. The authors collected an initial sample of users and they then searched friends of this initial sample. They did this by taking the median number of friends of all users and searching for that median number of all members of the initial sample. They collected a second sample of tweets and in total collected 101,069 tweets. It is worth noting that they were also interested in how the tweets were submitted (for example, through its website or by text message). They then took a random sample of 1,050 Web and 1,050 text message tweets, though both figures declined slightly when non-English tweets were excluded. The authors found that not only do Twitter users share information about themselves, they frequently share information about others too.

Social networking does not necessarily generate large populations of cases that have to be narrowed down through sampling. For example, Ledford and Anderson (2013) examined the response to the use of Facebook by the US drug company, Novartis, to recall some batches of Excedrin, a headache medication. The company used Facebook as a means of disseminating the recall and the researchers examined Facebook posts to establish how consumers interacted on Facebook as they sought information and support about what was happening. The researchers collected posts for the ten days after the recall, producing 49 posts by the company and 655 posts by users. While this is a significant number of posts, the researchers chose to code all of the posts.

 ## Content analysis of visual materials

As is noted in Chapter 19, there is a growing interest in visual materials among social researchers. Content analysis can be applied to visual materials of various kinds, and the principles articulated in earlier sections of this chapter apply to this kind of material too. The use of images in websites and social networking sites is also potentially interesting. Kapidzic and Herring (2015) analysed 400 photographs on a chat site used by teenagers. One of their research questions was:

> RQ1: What differences, if any, are there in distance, behavior, and dress in the profile pictures that male teens and female teens post for self-presentation?
>
> (Kapidzic and Herring 2015: 963)

To this end, all images were coded in terms of distance (close, intermediate, or far); behaviour (looking away, which the authors call 'affiliation'; straight at camera, referred to as 'seduction'; down at camera, referred to as 'submission'; sideways at camera/head tilted, referred to as 'offer'; or other); and dress (fully dressed, revealingly dressed, partially dressed, or not applicable). The

behaviour variable exhibited particularly clear gender differences, with females being far more likely to look straight at the camera and males being more likely to look away, look down at the camera, or look sideways at the camera or with head tilted. Kapidzic and Herring note that these differences are similar to what is found in face-to-face interaction which leads them to propose: 'It seems that the teens who posted profile pictures to the chat site...have internalized the societal message that women should be submissive and sexually alluring and men should be powerful and emotionally remote' (Kapidzic and Herring 2015: 969). As regards dress, males were more likely to be fully or partially dressed, females were more likely to be revealingly dressed. A further example of the content analysis of visual content can be found in Research in the news 13.1.

The content analysis of visual materials has to be carried out with the same principles in mind as those presented above. In other words, the researcher still needs to attend to such issues as the nature of the unit of analysis; sampling; reliability and validity; and deciding what is to be counted.

Research in the news 13.1
Psycho versus *Finding Nemo*

An article in *The Times* on 17 December 2014 appeared with the intriguing title 'Cartoons more brutal than Psycho'. The opening paragraph reads:

> Forget about *Psycho's* shower scene; if you want grisly suspense just watch the first five minutes of *Finding Nemo*. And do you think Tarantino is violent? Then pity Snow White's stepmother who, scientists note, 'was struck by lightning, forced off a cliff and crushed by a boulder while being chased by seven vengeful dwarves'.

The author, Tom Whipple, who is *The Times*' science correspondent, then goes on to explain that a 'study in the *British Medical Journal* has found that major characters are far more likely to die—and often die badly—in cartoons meant for children than they are in films made for adults'.

The study in question turns out to be by Colman et al. (2014). It compared the all-time top-grossing (at the box office) animated films aimed at children with the two highest-grossing adult North American films released in the same year as each animated film. The date range of the 45 animated films was from 1937 (*Snow White and the Seven Dwarfs*) to 2013 (*Frozen*). The comparison group of adult films comprised 90 cases. Whipple quotes the authors' conclusion that 'children's animated films, rather than being innocuous alternatives to the gore and carnage typical of American films, are in fact hotbeds of murder and mayhem' (Colman et al. 2014). The statistical analysis of the comparison shows:

- a significantly greater risk of the death of an important character in animated movies than adult ones (two-thirds versus a half);
- causes of death differ between the two types of films (e.g. gunshot more likely in adult films, but animal attack more likely in animated films);
- important characters were at greater risk of murder in animated films;
- the victims of the first death differ (e.g. parents of the main protagonist are more likely to die in animated than in adult films);
- deaths of main characters occur earlier in animated films.

Colman et al. argue that their findings are significant because of the considerable amount of animation consumed by children nowadays; the large number of murders of key characters means that children may experience trauma and need to be consoled by parents.

www.thetimes.co.uk/tto/news/uk/article4299280.ece (accessed 17 December 2014)

Advantages of content analysis

Content analysis has several advantages, which are outlined below.

- Content analysis is a very transparent research method. The coding scheme and the sampling procedures can be clearly set out so that replications and follow-up studies are feasible. It is this transparency that often causes content analysis to be referred to as an objective method of analysis.

- It can allow a certain amount of longitudinal analysis with relative ease. Several of the studies referred to above allow the researcher to track changes in frequency over time (Warde 1997; Bligh et al. 2004; Bailey et al. 2014). The time periods can have long spans, such as Warde's (1997) analysis of women's magazines over two time periods more than twenty years apart, or quite short time spans, such as the research by Bligh et al. (2004) on President Bush's speeches in the months before and after 9/11.

- Content analysis is often referred to favourably as an *unobtrusive method*, a term devised by Webb et al. (1966) to refer to a method that does not entail participants in a study having to take the researcher into account (see Key concept 14.3). It is therefore a *non-reactive method* (see Key concepts 12.4 and 14.3). However, this point has to be treated with a little caution. It is certainly the case that, when the focus of a content analysis is upon things such as newspaper articles or television programmes, there is no reactive effect. Newspaper articles are obviously not written in the knowledge that a content analysis may one day be carried out on them. On the other hand, if the content analysis is being conducted on documents such as interview transcripts or ethnographies (see Research in focus 13.5), while the process of content analysis does not itself introduce a reactive effect, the documents may have been at least partly influenced by such an effect.

- The unobtrusiveness of content analysis can be significant for many students. For students conducting research for an undergraduate or postgraduate project (perhaps for a dissertation), content analysis has the advantage that it does not usually require them to undergo the same level of ethical scrutiny that is common for students selecting methods that require research participants. This is not to suggest that students should select research methods on the basis that they can avoid increasingly difficult ethical surveillance regimes, particularly given the arguments in Chapters 1 and 4 about the need to tailor research methods to research questions. However, it does point to a consideration that is worth bearing in mind when thinking about how to approach a student research project.

- Content analysis is a highly flexible method. It can be applied to a wide variety of different kinds of unstructured textual information. While content analysis is often associated with the analysis of mass-media outputs, it has a much broader applicability than this. Research in focus 13.5 presents an illustration of a rather unusual but none the less interesting application of content analysis.

- Content analysis can allow information to be generated about social groups to which it is difficult to gain access. For example, most of our knowledge of the social backgrounds of elite groups, such as senior clergy, company directors, and top military personnel, derives from content analyses of such publications as *Who's Who* and *Burke's Peerage* (Bryman 1974).

Student experience
The significance of the transparency of content analysis

For her research on the front covers of women's magazines, Sarah Hanson felt that the transparency of the research method she had chosen was significant. She writes:

> My supervisor, Kristin, influenced my research methods a lot, as, having never done a study quite so large before, I needed a good way to organize my research and writing. By introducing Bryman's *Social Research Methods* (Second Edition) and the chapter on Content Analysis into my dissertation, I was able to do a lot of research within a controlled environment; my total word count for the research in my appendix tables was over 2,000 words. Content analysis allows for many different types of research and data collection to be easily carried out and studied, allowing you to work methodically throughout the decoding and analysis. By including content analysis in my dissertation, it allowed for easy reference throughout the text and allowed the marker to see the 'mathematical' workings, providing proof of how I came to my final conclusions.

It is nice to know one's work has an impact!

 *To read more, go to the Online Resource Centre: **www.oxfordtextbooks.co.uk/orc/brymansrm5e/***

Research in focus 13.5
A content analysis of qualitative research on the workplace

Hodson (1996: 724) reports the results of a content analysis of 'book-length ethnographic studies based on sustained periods of direct observation'. There is an excellent website in connection with the Workplace Ethnography Project, which can be found at **www.sociology.ohio-state.edu/rdh/Workplace-Ethnography-Project.html** (accessed 6 November 2014).

Ethnography, which will be explored in detail in Chapter 19, entails a long period of participant observation in order to understand the culture of a social group. Hodson's content analysis concentrated on ethnographic studies of workplaces that had been published in book form (that is, published articles were excluded because they rarely included sufficient detail). Thousands of case studies were assessed for possible inclusion in the sample. The sample was made up of studies from different countries. According to the Workplace Ethnography Project website (**www.sociology.ohio-state.edu/rdh/Workplace-Ethnography-Project.html**, accessed 6 November 2014), the current and probably final tally is described as follows: 'The study generated 204 ethnographic cases. These cases were derived from 156 separate books since the observations reported in some books allowed the coding of multiple cases.'

In Hodson (1996) each case was coded in terms of one of five types of workplace organization (craft, direct supervision, assembly line, bureaucratic, and worker participation). This was the independent variable. Various dependent variables and 'control' variables (variables deemed to have an impact on the relationships between independent and dependent variables) were also coded.

Here are two of the variables and their codes.

WORKERS:

Job satisfaction
1 = very low; 2 = moderately low; 3 = average; 4 = high; 5 = very high

Autonomy
1 = none (the workers' tasks are completely determined by others, by machinery or by organizational rules); 2 = little (workers occasionally have the chance to select among procedures or priorities); 3 = average (regular opportunities to select procedures or set priorities within definite limits); 4 = high (significant latitude in determining procedures and setting priorities); 5 = very high (significant interpretation is needed to reach broadly specified goals)

(Hodson 1996: 728)

Hodson's findings suggest that some pessimistic accounts of worker participation schemes (for example, that they do not genuinely permit participation and do not necessarily have a beneficial impact on the worker) are incomplete. A more detailed treatment of this research can be found in Hodson (1999). Since this 1996 publication, many others have been published in major journals, including the article on social fulfilment at the workplace (Hodson 2004), which was referred to in Chapter 4.

Not only does the website provide a list of publications deriving from the project (including downloadable pdf files of most of the articles) and all the coding information; you can also download the data into SPSS, which is the software that will be covered in Chapter 16.

Disadvantages of content analysis

Like all research techniques, content analysis suffers from certain limitations, which are described below.

- A content analysis can only be as good as the documents on which the practitioner works. Scott (1990) recommends assessing documents in terms of such criteria as authenticity (that the document is what it purports to be); credibility (whether there are grounds for thinking that the contents of the document have been or are distorted in some way); and representativeness (whether the documents examined are representative of all possible relevant documents, as, if certain kinds of document are unavailable or no longer exist, generalizability will be jeopardized). These kinds of consideration will be especially important to bear in mind when a content analysis is being conducted on documents such as letters. These issues will be explored in further detail in Chapter 23.

- It is almost impossible to devise coding manuals that do not entail some interpretation on the part of coders. Coders must draw upon their everyday knowledge as participants in a common culture in order to be able to code the material with which they are confronted (Cicourel 1964; Garfinkel 1967). To the extent that this occurs, it is questionable whether it is justifiable to assume a correspondence of interpretation between the persons responsible for producing the documents being analysed and the coders (Beardsworth 1980).

- Particular problems are likely to arise when the aim is to impute latent rather than manifest content. In searching for positive and negative portrayals of alcohol use (Research in focus 13.2) or inferring a social science discipline (Research in focus 13.1), the potential for an invalid conjecture being made is magnified.

- It is difficult to ascertain the answers to 'why?' questions through content analysis. For example, Beullens and Schepers (2013; see Research in focus 13.2) found that the presence of an alcohol brand logo in a photograph made a difference to whether a posting received a 'like'. Why? Beullens and Schepers (2013: 501) propose that the reason is to do with 'a general positive attitude toward alcohol use', but this is and can only be a speculation in the absence of further evidence. Similarly, Fenton et al. (1998) found that sociology was only the fourth most common discipline to be referred to when social science research was being reported (see Research in focus 13.1). However, Fenton et al. also inferred subject disciplines when they were not referred to explicitly by journalists. Sociology was by far the most frequent *inferred* discipline. While this is an interesting finding, the reasons for it can only be speculated about (Fenton et al. 1998). Sometimes, users of content analysis have been able to shed some light on 'why?' questions raised by their investigations by conducting additional data-collection exercises. Such exercises might include qualitative content analysis (Research in focus 13.3) and/or interviews with journalists and others (e.g. Fenton et al. 1998).

- Content analytic studies are sometimes accused of being atheoretical. The emphasis on measurement in content analysis can easily result in an accent being placed on what is measurable rather than on what is theoretically significant. However, content analysis is not necessarily atheoretical. Beullens and Schepers (2013) relate their findings to theories of alcohol use and of media effects. Fenton et al. (1998) conducted their content analysis within an overall approach that stressed the importance of studying the mass communication process from inception to reception and the importance of power and contestation within that process. Hodson's (1996) content analysis of workplace ethnographies was underpinned by theoretical ideas deriving from the work of influential writers such as Blauner (1964) and Edwards (1979) concerning developments in modes of workplace organization and their impacts on workers' experiences.

Checklist

Content analysis

....

  ◯   Have you clearly defined your research questions?

  ◯   Is the population of documents to be content analysed relevant to your research questions?

  ◯   Can you explain and justify your sampling approach?

○ Have you made sure that your dimensions do not overlap?

○ Have you made sure that the categories used for each of your dimensions do not overlap?

○ Are the categories you use for each dimension exhaustive?

○ Do all the dimensions help you to answer your research questions?

○ Have you piloted your coding schedule?

○ Are the coding instructions clear?

○ If your research is based on the mass media, can you justify the time span of your coverage?

○ Are you clear about the unit of analysis?

» Key points

- Content analysis is very much located within the quantitative research tradition of emphasizing measurement and the specification of clear rules that exhibit reliability.
- While traditionally associated with the analysis of mass-media content, it is in fact a very flexible method that can be applied to a wide range of phenomena.
- It is crucial to be clear about your research questions in order to be certain about your units of analysis and what exactly is to be analysed.
- You also need to be clear about what is to be counted.
- The coding schedule and coding manual are crucial stages in the preparation for a content analysis.
- Content analysis is not just concerned with textual material, in that visual materials may also be the focus of attention.
- Content analysis becomes particularly controversial when it is used to seek out latent meaning and themes.

? Questions for review

- To what kinds of documents and media can content analysis be applied?
- What is the difference between manifest and latent content? What are the implications of this distinction for content analysis?

What are the research questions?

- Why are precise research questions especially crucial in content analysis?
- With what general kinds of research questions is content analysis concerned?

Selecting a sample

- What special sampling issues does content analysis pose?

What is to be counted?

- What kinds of things might be counted in the course of doing a content analysis?
- To what extent do you need to infer latent content when you go beyond counting words?

Coding

- Why is coding so crucial in content analysis?
- What is the difference between a coding schedule and a coding manual?
- What potential pitfalls need to be guarded against when devising coding schedules and manuals?

The Internet as object of analysis

- In what ways might the analysis of websites pose particular difficulties that are less likely to be encountered in the analysis of non-electronic documents?

Content analysis of visual materials

- Do visual materials present special problems for content analysis?

Advantages of content analysis

- 'One of the most significant virtues of content analysis is its immense flexibility in that it can be applied to a wide variety of documents.' Discuss.

Disadvantages of content analysis

- To what extent does the need for coders to interpret meaning undermine content analysis?
- How far are content analysis studies atheoretical?

Online Resource Centre
www.oxfordtextbooks.co.uk/orc/brymansrm5e/

Visit the Online Resource Centre to enrich your understanding of content analysis. Follow up links to other resources, test yourself using multiple choice questions, and gain further guidance and inspiration from the Student Researcher's Toolkit.

14

Using existing data

 Chapter outline

 Chapter guide

This chapter explores the possibilities associated with the analysis of data that have been collected by others. There are four main types discussed in this chapter:

- the secondary analysis of data collected by other researchers;
- the quantitative analysis of data that have been supplied in published or otherwise circulated sources;
- the secondary analysis of official statistics—that is, statistics collected by government departments in the course of their work or specifically for statistical purposes;
- so-called 'Big Data'.

This chapter explores:

- the advantages and disadvantages of carrying out secondary analysis of data collected by other researchers, particularly in view of many data sets being based on large, high-quality investigations that are invariably beyond the means of students;
- how to obtain such data sets;
- the analysis of data supplied in such outputs as journal articles;
- the potential of official statistics in terms of their reliability and validity;
- the growing recognition of the potential of official statistics after a period of neglect as a result of criticisms levelled at them;
- the notion that official statistics are a form of *unobtrusive method*—that is, a method that is not prone to a reaction on the part of those being studied to the fact that they are research participants;
- the emerging possibilities associated with Big Data, in particular in the form of social media outputs.

Introduction

With the exception of the previous chapter, the focus in this part of the book has been on the collection of primary data such as by a questionnaire survey. The use of these methods can be very time-consuming, which raises the question of whether it might be possible to use existing data. To a significant extent, this is precisely what content analysis—the focus of the previous chapter—entails. With content analysis, the data (newspaper articles, cartoons, television programmes, etc.) already exist, although of course the raw materials for a content analysis still have to be harvested. In this chapter, I will examine four other contexts in which data already exist and which can be worked on by the researcher:

1. the secondary analysis of data that have been collected by other researchers (see Key concept 14.1)—I will emphasize large, high-quality surveys that invariably operate on a continuous basis;

2. meta-analysis—the analysis of large numbers of quantitative studies;

3. the secondary analysis of data that have been collected by government departments in the course of their business (official statistics);

4. Big Data—the analysis of the large volumes of data that are generated through media such as Facebook and Twitter.

Secondary analysis of other researchers' data

There are several reasons why secondary analysis should be considered a serious alternative to collecting new data. These advantages of secondary analysis have been covered by Dale et al. (1988), from which I have borrowed most of the following observations. In considering the various advantages of secondary analysis, I have in mind the particular needs of the lone student conducting a small research project as an undergraduate or a more substantial piece of work as a postgraduate. However, this emphasis should definitely not be taken to imply that secondary analysis is relevant only to students. Quite the contrary: secondary analysis should be considered by all social researchers, and, indeed, the Economic and Social Research Council (ESRC) requires applicants for research grants who are proposing to collect new data to demonstrate that relevant data are not already available in the UK Data Archive (see the subsection below on 'Accessing the UK Data Archive').

My reason for emphasizing the prospects of secondary analysis for students is simply based on my personal experience that they tend to assume that any research they carry out has to entail the collection of primary data. Unless you are advised otherwise by your supervisor or by any documentation supplied by your department or university, it is worth giving serious consideration to doing a secondary analysis, because it will allow you to spend more time on the analysis and interpretation of data. Moreover, you simply will not be in a position to produce a

Key concept 14.1
What is secondary analysis?

Secondary analysis is the analysis of data by researchers who will probably not have been involved in the collection of those data, for purposes that may not have been envisaged by those responsible for the data collection. Secondary analysis may entail the analysis of either quantitative data (Dale et al. 1988) or qualitative data (Corti et al. 1995), but it is with the former that we will be concerned in this chapter. The distinction between primary and secondary analysis is not always clear-cut. If a researcher is involved in the collection of survey data and analyses some of the data, with the analysis resulting in some publications, but then some time later decides to rework the data, it is not entirely clear how far the latter is primary or secondary analysis. Typically, secondary analysis entails the analysis of data that others have collected, but, as this simple scenario suggests, this need not necessarily be the case. In this chapter, the term 'secondary analysis' is relevant to the discussion of the analysis of research data (usually survey data) already collected by others and to the analysis of official statistics such as those to do with crime or unemployment.

data set of comparable quality, because of the lack of time and resources likely to be available to you. Further, as the next section on the advantages of secondary analysis suggests, you may be able to conduct analyses that would be inconceivable if you relied on data you collected yourself.

Advantages of secondary analysis

Secondary analysis offers numerous benefits to students carrying out a research project. These are outlined below.

- *Cost and time.* As noted at the outset, secondary analysis offers the prospect of having access to good-quality data for a tiny fraction of the resources involved in carrying out a data-collection exercise yourself. Numerous data sets are available from the UK Data Archive, which is located at the University of Essex. You do not even have to go to Colchester yourself to search for data. The Archive has a very good website, which can be searched in a variety of ways, such as keywords (as discussed below in the subsection on 'Accessing the UK Data Archive').

- *High-quality data.* Many of the data sets that are employed most frequently for secondary analysis are of extremely high quality. By this I mean several things. First, the sampling procedures were rigorous, in most cases resulting in samples that are as close to being representative as one is likely to achieve. While the organizations responsible for these studies suffer the same problems of survey non-response as anybody else, well-established procedures are usually in place for following up non-respondents and thereby keeping this problem to a minimum. Second, the samples are often national samples or at least cover a wide variety of regions of Great Britain or the UK. The degree of geographical spread and the sample size of such data sets are invariably attained only in research that attracts quite substantial resources. It is certainly inconceivable that student projects could even get close to the coverage that such data sets attain. Third, many data sets have been generated by experienced researchers, and, in the case of some of the large data sets, such as the British Social Attitudes (BSA) survey (see Research in focus 14.1), Understanding Society (formerly the British Household Panel Survey or BHPS; see Research in focus 14.1), GESIS (see Thinking deeply 10.1), and the European Social Survey (ESS—see Research in focus 2.4), the data are gathered by social research organizations that have developed structures and control procedures to check on the quality of the emerging data.

- *Opportunity for longitudinal analysis.* Partly linked to the last point is the fact that secondary analysis can offer the opportunity for longitudinal research, which, as noted in Chapter 3, is rather rare in the social sciences because of the time and cost involved. Sometimes, as with Understanding Society, a panel design has been employed, and it is possible to chart trends and connections over time. Such data are sometimes analysed cross-sectionally, but there are obviously opportunities for longitudinal analysis as well. Also, with data sets such as the Understanding Society and the BSA surveys, where similar data are collected over time, usually because certain interview questions are recycled each year, trends (such as shifting opinions or changes in behaviour) can be identified over time. With such data sets, respondents differ from year to year, so that causal inferences over time cannot be readily established, but nonetheless it is still possible to gauge trends. In the case of cohort studies, there is the opportunity to establish how members of a sample born around the same time are similar to or different from each other. An example of such a case is discussed in Research in the news 14.1.

- *Subgroup analysis.* When large samples are the source of data, there is the opportunity to study what can often be quite sizeable subgroups. Very often, in order to study specialized categories of individuals, small localized studies are the only feasible way forward because of costs. Large data sets can frequently yield quite large nationally representative samples. For example, Arber and Gilbert (1989) used the 1980 General Household Survey (GHS), a large household survey that became known as the General Lifestyle Survey but which was discontinued in 2012, to isolate a sample of over 4,500 elderly people living in private households. In 1980, respondents aged 65 and over were asked various questions about their ability to perform certain tasks. This information was used to compile a disability index. Levels of disability could then be related to patterns of caring for the elderly. As Arber and Gilbert (1989: 75) observe: 'The large sample size, high response rate (82 per cent) and representative nature of the sample size make the GHS a valuable data source to complement, extend and systematically test findings and theoretical ideas derived from small, qualitative and localised studies.' While the data did not address the elderly in institutional care, the survey nonetheless provides a valuable source of high-quality data on the elderly. It is easy to see how a wide range of different subgroups could be identified for similar kinds of analysis.

- *Opportunity for cross-cultural analysis.* Cross-cultural research has considerable appeal at a time when social scientists are more attuned to the processes associated with globalization and to cultural differences. It is easy

Research in focus 14.1
Religion in Britain and the 'believing without belonging' thesis

'Believing without belonging', as the phrase implies, is meant to suggest that religion has not declined in modern British society in terms of the extent to which religious beliefs are held; rather, the phrase suggests that it is allegiance to institutional religion that has declined, in that religious beliefs are still fairly robust. This thesis was explored by Voas and Crockett (2005), who conducted secondary analyses of both the BHPS and the BSA survey. For the BHPS analysis, the authors looked at waves 1 (1991) and 9 (1999–2000), focusing on three questions that are asked:

1. A question asking whether the respondent views him- or herself as belonging to any religion and, if so, which one. This is used to indicate a person's religious affiliation.

2. A question asking how often the respondent attends religious services or meetings. This is commonly used as an indicator of participation.

3. A question asking each respondent how much difference religious beliefs make to his or her life. Respondents answer on a scale: no difference; little difference; some difference; great difference. This question is taken to indicate strength of belief and its significance in the respondent's life.

The findings lead Voas and Crockett (2005: 15) to suggest that 'religious decline is principally the result of differences between generations: each age cohort is less religious than the last'. Also, the same data do not support the 'believing without belonging' thesis: if anything, religious belief is declining faster than belonging. They explored the BSA data, which could be examined over a much longer period (1983–2002). The data were examined as a continuous time series for each year for which there were data on religious affiliation and belief. They show that the dominant effect was a cohort effect; that is, each cohort (five cohorts were distinguished) was less religious (in terms of affiliation, attendance, and belief) than the previous one. Overall, then, these longitudinal data suggest that the 'believing without belonging' thesis cannot be supported empirically.

to forget that many findings should not be taken to apply to countries other than that in which the research was conducted. However, cross-cultural research presents barriers to the social scientist. There are obvious barriers to do with the cost and practical difficulties of doing research in a different country, especially when language and cultural differences are likely to be significant. The secondary analysis of comparable data from two or more countries provides one possible model for conducting cross-cultural research. In order for a cross-cultural analysis to be conducted, some coordination is necessary so that the questions asked are comparable. The research on egalitarian attitudes by Röder and Mühlau (2014) described in Research in focus 2.4 provides an example of such coordination. The authors describe the process as follows:

Data were extracted from rounds 2 and 4 of the European Social Survey (ESS) collected in 2004 and 2008. These are two rounds for which measures of gender egalitarianism are included. The ESS is designed to allow cross-national analyses by ensuring that the questions are understood in the same way by respondents in different countries and languages, and is a high-quality data set where the sampling design approximates a simple random sample and has a relatively high response rate.

Röder and Mühlau (2014: 905)

Röder and Mühlau's results derived from a secondary analysis of the data from twenty-seven of the thirty-three nations involved in the research. Opportunities for such cross-cultural analysis appear to be increasing. For example, core questions used in the Labour Force Survey (LFS) are also used in equivalent surveys conducted by EU member states.

- *More time for data analysis.* Precisely because data collection is time-consuming, the analysis of data is often squeezed. It is easy to perceive data collection as the difficult phase and to take the view that the analysis of data is relatively straightforward. This is not the case. Working out what to make of your data is no easy matter and requires considerable thought and often a preparedness to consider learning about unfamiliar techniques of data analysis. While secondary analysis

Research in the news 14.1
Gender and religion

On 21 January 2015, both the *Daily Mail* and *The Times* ran articles referring to research showing that women were more likely to believe in God and the afterlife than men. Both articles were in large part prompted by the consecration the following week of the first female Church of England bishop. The source of the information on which the articles were based was a secondary analysis of data from the 1970 British Cohort Study (BCS70). For example, *The Times* reporter notes that 'almost two thirds of women in their early forties believe in some sort of afterlife compared with only a third of men'. The information for the two newspaper articles seems to derive from a news feed from the UCL Institute for Education in London, which currently carries out and manages the research (**www.ioe.ac.uk/newsEvents/110639.html**).

www.dailymail.co.uk/news/article-2919058/Women-likely-believe-God-afterlife-Two-thirds-faith-compared-half-men.html

www.thetimes.co.uk/tto/faith/article4329058.ece

All URLs accessed 21 January 2015.

invariably entails a lot of data management—partly so that you can get to know the data and partly so that you can get it into a form that you need (see the section below on 'Limitations of secondary analysis')—the fact that you are freed from having to collect fresh data means that your approach to the analysis of data can be more considered than it might otherwise have been.

- *Reanalysis may offer new interpretations.* It is wrong to think that, once a set of data has been analysed, the data have in some sense been drained of further insight. What, in other words, could possibly be gained by going over the same data that someone else has analysed? In fact, data can be analysed in so many different ways that it is very unusual for the range of possible analyses to be exhausted. Several possibilities can be envisaged. A secondary analyst may decide to consider the impact of a certain variable on the relationships between variables of interest. Such a possibility may not have been envisaged by the initial researchers. Second, the arrival of new theoretical ideas may suggest analyses that could not have been considered by the original researchers. In other words, the arrival of such new theoretical directions may prompt a reconsideration of the relevance of the data. Third, an alternative method of quantitative data analysis may be employed which offers the prospect of a rather different interpretation of the data. Fourth (and related to the last point), new methods of quantitative data analysis are continuously emerging. Disciplines such as statistics and econometrics are continually developing new techniques of analysis, while some techniques are being developed within the social

sciences themselves. As awareness of such techniques spreads, and their potential relevance is recognized, researchers become interested in applying them to new data sets.

- *The wider obligations of the social researcher.* For all types of social research, research participants give up some of their time, usually for no reward. It is not unreasonable that the public should expect that the data that they participate in generating should be mined to its fullest extent. However, much social research is chronically under-analysed. Primary researchers may feel they want to analyse only data relating to central research questions or may lose interest as a new set of research questions interpose themselves into their imagination. Making data available for secondary analysis enhances the possibility that fuller use will be made of data.

Limitations of secondary analysis

The foregoing list of the benefits of secondary analysis sounds almost too good to be true. In fact, there are few limitations, but the following warrant some attention.

- *Lack of familiarity with data.* When you collect your own data, you are likely to be very familiar with the structure and contours of your data, but with data collected by others, a period of familiarization is necessary. You have to get to grips with the range of variables, the ways in which the variables have been coded, and various aspects of the organization of the data. The period of familiarization can be quite substantial with large complex data sets and should not be under-estimated.

- *Complexity of the data.* Some of the best-known data sets that are employed for secondary analysis, such as Understanding Society, are very large in the sense of having large numbers of both respondents and variables. The sheer volume of data can present problems with the management of the information at hand, and, again, a period of acclimatization may be required. Also, some of the most prominent data sets that have been employed for secondary analysis are known as *hierarchical* data sets, such as the GHS and the Understanding Society. The difficulty here is that the data are collected and presented at the level of both the household and the individual, as well as at other levels. The secondary analyst must decide which level of analysis is going to be employed. If the decision is to analyse individual-level data, the individual-level data must then be extracted from the data set. Different data will apply to each level. Thus, at the household level, the GHS provides data on such variables as number of cars and consumer durables, while, at the individual level, data on income and employment can be found. Dale (1987), who was interested in life-cycle stages, employed household-level data from the 1979 GHS to develop a typology of life-cycle stages, which included fourteen categories and various correlates of the various categories such as net disposable household income.

- *No control over data quality.* Secondary analysis offers students and others the opportunity to examine data of far higher quality than they could collect themselves. This point applies mainly to data sets such as the Understanding Society (see Research in focus 3.10), the BCS (see Research in the news 7.1), the NCDS (see Research in focus 3.11), and the European Social Survey (Research in focus 2.4). While the quality of data should never be taken for granted, in the case of such data sets it is reasonably assured; that is not to say, though, that the data will necessarily meet all of a prospective secondary analyst's needs, since data may not have been collected on an aspect of a topic that would have been of considerable interest. With other data sets, somewhat more caution may be necessary in connection with data quality, although certain fundamental checks on quality are usually made by archives in which data are deposited.

- *Absence of key variables.* Because secondary analysis entails the analysis of data collected by others for their own purposes, it may be that one or more key variables may not be present. You may, for example, want to examine whether a relationship between two variables holds even when one or more *other* variables are taken into account. Such an analysis is known as **multivariate**

analysis, which will be discussed in Chapter 15. The inability to examine the implications or otherwise of a theoretically important variable can be frustrating and can arise when, for example, a theoretical approach that has emerged since the collection of the data suggests its importance. Obviously, when researchers collect primary data themselves, the prospect of this happening should be less pronounced.

Accessing the UK Data Archive

The UK Data Archive at the University of Essex is likely to be your main source of quantitative data for secondary analysis, although it is possible that some of your lecturers will have data sets that they can put at your disposal. The best route for finding out about data held at the Archive is to examine its online catalogue. Access to this catalogue can be obtained by going to the UK Data Archive home page at **http://ukdataservice.ac.uk/** (accessed 7 January 2015), or by going directly to the UK Data Service catalogue search page at **http://ukdataservice.ac.uk/get-data.aspx** (accessed 7 January 2015).

I searched for any studies with the keyword 'risk' in the title. I clicked on the GO button. This resulted in 929 studies being found (see Plate 14.1). This allows you to examine the documentation relating to any promising candidates for analysis and even to order the data set concerned. The information provided typically gives a description of the study, along with a variety of particulars: sponsors; sampling details; method of data collection; main topics of the survey; and information about publications deriving from the study. It also informs you whether there are special conditions relating to access. With the one I chose, which was SN 5357—Public Risk Perceptions, Climate Change and the Reframing of UK Energy Policy in Britain, 2005, was the first on the list and I was told: 'The depositor has specified that registration is required and standard conditions of use apply.' When there are special conditions, they normally involve signing an undertaking form. To order the data, you need to have set up an account, which will have resulted in your being given a user name and password that will allow you to download data. You will need to find out if there is an administrative charge for receiving the data, but it is likely that, if you are a student at or a member of staff in a UK institution of higher education, there will be no charge or perhaps a nominal one. Online documentation is available through the website for the chosen study (for example, a user guide). It should also be noted that Study SN 5357 is the source of the survey component of a mixed methods study (Bickerstaff et al. 2008) referred to in Chapter 27. Plate 14.2 presents some of the information that was displayed on the Data Service page for this study.

Plate 14.1

Results of a search of the UK Data Archive

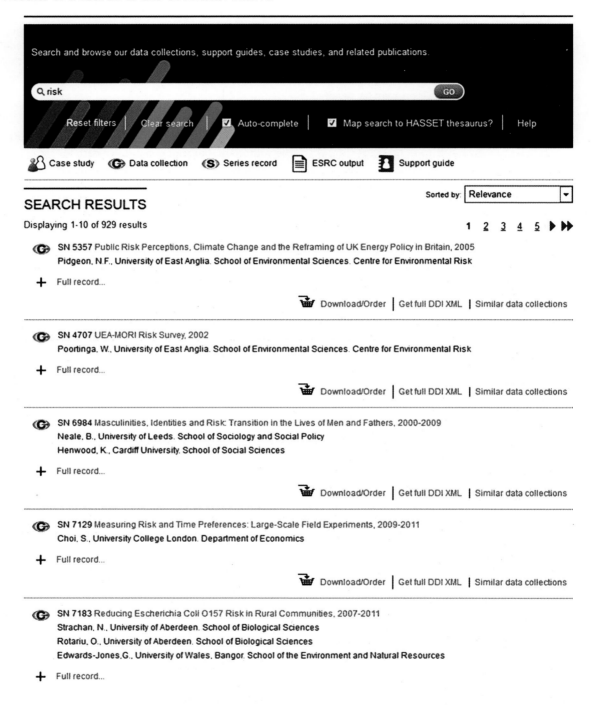

Information about searching for qualitative data for the purpose of conducting a secondary analysis can be found in Chapter 24. Qualitative data can also be searched for through the UK Data Service).

A useful starting point for many if not most of the most popular data sets that can be accessed through the UK Data Service can be found at: **http://ukdataservice.ac.uk/ get-data/key-data.aspx** (accessed 7 January 2015).

Plate 14.2
Description and documentation for the chosen data

ABSTRACT ⌃

The project consisted of undertaking a comprehensive empirical survey of public opinion towards future energy options for the UK, with a particular emphasis on attitudes towards nuclear power when placed in the context of climate change.

The survey questionnaire consisted of 4 main sections. The first main section looked at climate change and nuclear power from a broad perspective, comparing these two with a range of other environmental and energy-related issues at different global/local scales. This section also examined attitudes towards various options for generating electricity. The second section specifically considered attitudes towards nuclear power. The third section examined attitudes towards climate change in more detail. Sections two and three contain a number of standardised questions that were aimed to measure general attitudes towards nuclear power and climate change, the perceived risks and benefits of the two issues, as well as questions on ambivalence, attitudinal certainty, and trust in risk regulation. In addition, the two sections contain a number of issue-specific questions. The fourth and final section of the questionnaire looked specifically at attitudes towards the reframing of nuclear power as a solution to climate change. This section contains questions that were designed to compare the risks of climate change with the risks of nuclear power, and attitudes towards different energy futures and options of electricity generation that might help to prevent climate change, using a split-sample technique.

Although there are a range of one-off or tracker surveys and risk perception studies available that have asked about energy generation, nuclear energy, and climate change separately, the value of the current instrument is that it generates a database which allows responses to be compared across all three sets of issues. In addition there is no comparable existing survey which asks, in a comprehensive way, about the reframing question.

Main Topics:
The main topics covered were: energy futures; nuclear power; climate change; environmental issues; risk perception.

COVERAGE, UNIVERSE, METHODOLOGY ⌃

Dates of fieldwork:	01 October 2005 - 06 November 2005
Country:	Great Britain
Spatial units:	Government Office Regions
Universe:	National
	Members of the general public, aged 15 years and over in Great Britain during 2005
Time dimensions:	Cross-sectional (one-time) study
Sampling procedures:	Quota sample; Multi-stage stratified random sample
Number of units:	1,491
Method of data collection:	Face-to-face interview
Weighting:	Data are weighted to age, sex, working status using 2001 census data (Variable= @WEIGHT0)

KEYWORDS ⌃

AGE	ATTITUDES	CHILDREN
CLIMATE CHANGE	ECONOMIC ACTIVITY	ECONOMIC GROWTH
ELECTRIC POWER GENERATION	ENERGY POLICY	ENERGY RESOURCES
ENGLAND	ENVIRONMENTAL CHANGES	ENVIRONMENTAL DEGRADATION
ENVIRONMENTAL ISSUES	FUTURE	GENDER
NUCLEAR ENERGY	NUCLEAR POWER STATIONS	PERCEPTION
POLLUTION	PUBLIC OPINION	QUALIFICATIONS
RADIOACTIVE WASTES	REGULATIONS	RENEWABLE ENERGY
RENEWABLE RESOURCES	RISK	SCOTLAND
SOCIAL CLASS	TRUST	VOTING INTENTION
WALES		

Table 14.1

Large data sets suitable for secondary analysis

Title	Data set details	Topics covered
1970 British Cohort Study (BCS70)	An irregular survey of 17,200 people born in a single week in 1970. Data have since been collected at ages 5, 10, 16, 26, 30, 34, 38, and 42. Although this is a longitudinal survey, there is also a cross-sectional element in that it is supplemented by a sample that includes immigrants who came to Britain before age 16 but were born in the same week. See **www.cls.ioe.ac.uk** (accessed 9 January 2015).	Health; physical development; economic and social circumstances; variety of attitudes.
British Crime Survey (BCS); now Crime Survey for England and Wales	An irregular survey of a randomly selected sample of people questioned by structured interview. It began in 1982 and was carried out in 1984, 1988, 1992, and then biennially between 1992 and 2000 and annually from 2001. The 2001–2 BCS had a target sample of 36,000 individuals. For the 2013–14 survey, around 50,000 households were invited to participate. See **www.crimesurvey.co.uk/** (accessed 9 January 2015).	Experience of and attitudes to crime; fear of crime; risk of crime.
British Household Panel Survey (BHPS); now Understanding Society – The UK Household Longitudinal Study	A panel study that began as the BHPS in 1991 and was conducted annually by interview and questionnaire with a national representative sample of around 10,000 individuals in just over 5,000 households. The same individuals were interviewed each year. The BHPS was replaced in 2010–11 by the Understanding Society survey, which is based on a much larger panel of 40,000 households and which incoprorates the households that made up the BHPS. See **www.understandingsociety.ac.uk** (accessed 9 January 2015).	Household organization; labour market behaviour; income and wealth; housing; health; socio-economic values.
British Social Attitudes (BSA) Survey	More or less annual survey since 1983 of a multi-stage stratified random sample of over 3,000 respondents aged 18 and over. Each survey comprises an hour-long interview and a self-administered questionnaire. See **www.natcen.ac.uk/our-research/research/british-social-attitudes/** (accessed 9 January 2015).	Wide range of areas of social attitudes and behaviour. Some areas are core ones asked annually; others are asked irregularly.
European Social Survey (ESS)	A coordinated survey conducted every other year since 2001 across Europe. Samples are selected randomly and different modes of administration of the questionnaire are employed (telephone, Web, face-to-face). See **www.europeansocialsurvey.org/about/index.html** (accessed 9 January 2015).	Attitudes, beliefs, and behaviour in over thirty European countries.
Living Costs and Food Survey (LCFS)	The new name for the Expenditure and Food Survey, which began in April 2001 and which combined and replaced the FES and NFS. Data are based on households, which are asked to complete diaries of expenditure and income over a two-week period. In addition, face-to-face interviews are conducted by CAPI. It is part of the IHS.	Areas formerly covered by FES and NFS.
Family Expenditure Survey (FES)	Annual interviews from 1957 with members of around 10,000 households who kept diary records of expenditure and income over a two-week period. It was replaced by the Expenditure and Food Survey in 2001.	Family expenditure and income.
General Household Survey (GHS)/General Lifestyle Survey (GLF)	Based on annual interviews since 1971 with members aged over 16 in over 8,000 randomly sampled households. No surveys were carried out in 1997–8, when the GHS was reviewed, or in 1999–2000, when it was revamped. Following this hiatus, the GHS was resumed on an annual basis but closed in January 2012.	Standard issues such as education and health asked each year, plus additional items that vary annually. Huge variety of questions relating to social behaviour and attitudes.
Integrated Household Survey (IHS)	Incorporating the LCFS and the Annual Population Survey, this survey began in 2009. It comprises a set of core questions and modules from other continuous surveys carried out by the Office for National Statistics (ONS): Labour Force Survey, General Lifestyle Survey, Living Costs and Food Survey, English Housing Survey, and Life Opportunities Survey. For a short period, it also included the ONS Opinions Survey, but this module has now been dropped. The survey generates estimates at the local authority level.	See: Labour Force Survey, General Lifestyle Survey, Living Costs and Food Survey, and ONS Opinions Survey.

(continued)

Table 14.1
(*Continued*)

Title	Data set details	Topics covered
Labour Force Survey (LFS)	Biennial interviews, 1973–83, and annual interviews, 1984–91, comprising a quarterly survey of around 15,000 addresses per quarter and an additional survey in March–May; since 1991 a quarterly survey of around 60,000 addresses. Since 1998, core questions are also administered in member states of the European Union.	Hours worked; job search methods; training; personal details such as nationality and gender.
Millennium Cohort Study	Study of 19,000 babies and their families born between 1 September 2000 and 31 August 2001 in England and Wales, and between 22 November 2000 and 11 January 2002 in Scotland and Northern Ireland. Data were collected by interview with parents when babies were 9 months and around 3 years old. Since then, surveys have been conducted at ages 5 and 7 years old. See **www.cls.ioe.ac.uk** (accessed 9 January 2015).	Continuity and change in each child's family and its parenting environment; important aspects of the child's development.
National Child Development Study (NCDS)	Irregular but ongoing study of all 17,000 children born in Great Britain in the week of 3–9 March 1958. Since 1981 comprises interview and questionnaire. There have been six waves of data collection: in 1965 (when members were aged 7 years), in 1969 (age 11), in 1974 (age 16), in 1981 (age 23), in 1991 (age 33), in 1999–2000 (age 41–2), in 2004 (age 46), in 2008–9 (age 50–1), and in 2013 (age 55). See **www.cls.ioe.ac.uk** (accessed 9 January 2015).	Physical and mental health; family; parenting; occupation and income; housing and environment.
National Food Survey (NFS)	First set up in 1940, this survey entailed interviews with a representative sample of households, and diary records for one week. In 1998 data were collected from both sources from 6,000 households. It was replaced by the Expenditure and Food Survey in 2001.	Nature of household; food shopping; meals.
Opinions and Lifestyle Survey; formerly ONS Omnibus Survey and ONS Opinions Survey	This ONS-run survey involves the collection of interview data eight times a year following a period when data were collected monthly and before that eight times per year. The Opinions and Lifestyle Survey merges the ONS Opinions Survey and the LFS.	Core questions each year about respondents, plus modules (asked on behalf of participating organizations) on topics that change annually concerning e.g. food safety; eating behaviour; personal finance; sports participation.
Workplace Employment Relations Survey (WERS)	This survey was carried out in 1980, 1984, 1990, 1998, 2004, and 2011. Workplaces of ten or more employees were sampled, and interviews carried out with managers, worker representatives, and employees.	Pay determination; recruitment and training; equal opportunities; workplace change; work attitudes; management organization; employee representation.

Table 14.1 lists several large data sets that are accessible to students and would repay further investigation in terms of their potential use in the context of research questions in which you might be interested. Further information about these data sets can be found via the UK Data Service or by using Google or any other search engine to look for them.

In discussing secondary analysis in this chapter, I have tended to emphasize large data sets such as the BHPS. However, it is worth bearing in mind that the UK Data Archive holds data deriving from a wide range of studies. If you enter 'Research methods' as your search term when searching the catalogue, one of the studies that comes up is a content analysis of journal articles that combine quantitative and qualitative research (SN 5077). This is a study that I conducted in 2003–4 and that forms the basis for much of Chapter 27. However, this is in no sense a large data set like the ones that have been the focus of attention for much of the previous discussion. It is also worth keeping a look-out for interesting good-quality studies that may not be archived. As mentioned in Chapter 13, the data from the Workplace Ethnography Project (Research in focus 13.5) can be easily downloaded and could form the basis of a very interesting secondary analysis project for someone with interests in areas such as the sociology of work.

Meta-analysis

Meta-analysis involves summarizing the results of a large number of quantitative studies and conducting various analytical tests to show whether or not a particular variable has an effect. This provides a means whereby the results of large numbers of quantitative studies of a particular topic can be summarized and compared. The aim of this approach is to establish whether or not a particular variable has a certain effect by comparing the results of different studies. Meta-analysis thus involves pooling the results from various studies in order to estimate an overall effect by correcting the various **sampling** and **non-sampling errors** that may arise in relation to a particular study. A meta-analysis lies between two kinds of activity covered in this book: doing a literature review of existing studies in an area in which you are interested (the focus of Chapter 5), and conducting a secondary analysis of other researchers' data. It differs from the secondary analysis of other researchers' data in that with meta-analysis, you do not work on the raw data collected by the original researchers. Instead, you use information supplied in the outputs of research in an area in order to estimate the effect of a variable of interest.

With a meta-analysis, the researcher works on data supplied in articles and other outputs, such as correlation coefficients which are covered in Chapter 15.

Meta-analysis relies on all the relevant information being available for each of the studies examined. Since not all the same information relating to methods of study and sample size may be included in published papers, meta-analysis is not always feasible. Meta-analysis is vulnerable to what is known as the **file drawer problem**. This occurs when a researcher conducts a study, finds that the independent variable does not have the intended effect, but has difficulty publishing his or her findings. As a result, it is often suggested that the findings are simply filed away in a drawer. If the file drawer problem has occurred in a field of research, the findings of a meta-analysis will be biased in favour of the independent variable being found to have a certain effect, as some of the findings that contradict that effect will not be in the public domain. There may also be a bias against smaller studies because it is much easier to demonstrate a statistically significant effect when samples are large. Whether the key findings of a study are statistically significant is often taken to mean

Research in focus 14.2
A meta-analysis of research testing intergroup contact theory

Pettigrew and Tropp (2006) carried out a meta-analysis of research testing intergroup contact theory—the notion that intergroup prejudice declines when there is the potential for intergroup contact, which has an affinity with the theories mentioned in Research in focus 2.2. They specified clear criteria as to whether a study could be could be included in their meta-analysis, such as that only research dealing with 'contact between members of discrete groups' would be included (Pettigrew and Tropp 2006). The search process involved the following steps:

1. Searching several databases using 54 search terms.

2. An examination of the bibliographies of all studies produced through the database searchers and an examination of the bibliographies of previous meta-analyses in the field.

3. Personal letters written to researchers in the field requesting conference papers and any other material.

4. Emails to networks of researchers requesting relevant work.

This search process and the application of the inclusion criteria yielded 526 studies, based on 713 samples (some papers report the results of more than one study). The typical study is a questionnaire/survey study based on reports of contact with the group to which one does not belong (referred to as the 'out-group'). Around 30 per cent were quasi-experiments or true experiments. Interestingly, experiments were found to show a larger effect than surveys, but generally the authors conclude that their results 'clearly indicate that intergroup contact typically reduces intergroup prejudice' (Pettigrew and Tropp 2006: 766). The researchers checked for the possibility of a file drawer problem but concluded that their findings suggested that there was 'minimal publication bias' (2006: 754).

that an effect has been demonstrated and this probably increases the likelihood of publication. However, findings that fail to achieve statistical significance are less likely to be published and because it is more difficult to come up with statistically significant findings when samples are small, this may mean a bias against smaller-scale studies.

The file drawer problem clearly presents a problem to meta-analysts but it should be borne in mind that practitioners have developed techniques that allow checks to be made on the likelihood of the problem existing for a body of research. Research in focus 14.2 provides an example of a meta-analytic study.

 # Official statistics

The use and analysis of official statistics for purposes of social research has been a very controversial area for many years. Agencies of the state, in the course of their business, are required to keep a running record of their areas of activity. When these records are aggregated, they form the official statistics in an area of activity. Thus, in Great Britain, the police compile data that form the crime rate (also known as 'notifiable crimes recorded by the police') and data are collected on unemployment based on those claiming unemployment related benefits (also known as the 'claimant count'). These are just two high-profile sets of statistics that can be categorised as 'official statistics'. Such statistics are frequently the cause of headlines in the mass media—for example, if there has been a sharp increase in the level of recorded crime or unemployment. But they would also seem to offer considerable potential for social researchers.

We could imagine such official statistics offering the social researcher certain advantages over some other forms of quantitative data, such as data based on surveys.

- The data have already been collected. Therefore, as with other kinds of secondary analysis of data, considerable time and expense may be saved. Also, the data may not be based on samples, so that a complete picture can be obtained.

- Since the people who are the source of the data are not being asked questions that are part of a research project, the problem of reactivity will be much less pronounced than when data are collected by interview or questionnaire.

- There is the prospect of analysing the data both cross-sectionally and longitudinally. When analysing the data cross-sectionally, we could examine crime rates (and indeed the incidence of specific crimes) in terms of such standard variables as social class, income, ethnicity, age, gender, and region. Such analyses allow us to search for the factors that are associated with crime or unemployment. Also, we can analyse the data over time. Precisely because the data are compiled over many years, it is possible to chart trends over time and perhaps to relate these to wider social changes.

- There is the prospect as well of cross-cultural analysis, since the official statistics from different nation states can be compared for a specific area of activity. After all, a sociological classic of the stature of Durkheim's *Suicide* (Durkheim 1952) was the result of a comparative analysis of official statistics on suicide in several countries.

However, readers who recall Research in the news 7.1 will already be on their guard. The official statistics concerned with an area of social life such as crime can be very misleading, because they record only those individuals who are processed by the agencies that have the responsibility for compiling the statistics. Crime and other forms of deviance have been a particular focus of attention and concern among critics of the use of official statistics. Figure 14.1 illustrates, in connection with crime and the crime rate, the kinds of factor that can lead to concern.

If we take a criminal offence as the starting point (step 1), we can consider the factors that might or might not result in its becoming part of the crime rate. An offence might become a candidate for inclusion in the crime rate as a result of either of two events (it might be that others can be envisaged but these two represent major possibilities). First, the crime may be seen by a member of the public or a member of the public may be a victim of a crime (step 2). However, a crime has to be recognized as such before it will be reported to the police (step 3). Even if it is recognized as a criminal offence, the member of the public (even if he or she is a victim) may choose not to bring the crime to the notice of the police. This means that, if a criminal act goes unnoticed, or is noticed but not recognized as criminal, or is noticed and recognized as criminal but not reported to the police, it will not enter the official statistics. Step 4 is the reporting of the crime to the police. Even then the crime may not be entered into the crime statistics, because the police have considerable discretion about whether to proceed with a conviction and may choose to let the person off with a warning (step 6). They may be influenced by such factors as the severity of the crime, the perpetrator's previous record, the perpetrator's demeanour or suggestions of contrition, or their volume of work at the time.

Figure 14.1
The social construction of crime statistics: eight steps

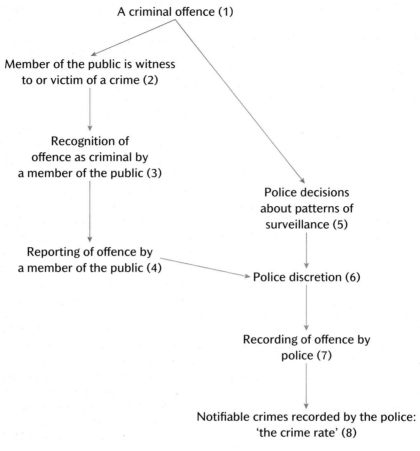

Source: adapted from a figure in Beardsworth et al. (n.d.)

Alternatively, a crime may be observed by the police as a result of their patterns of surveillance, which is a product of decisions about how best to deploy police officers (step 5). Once again, the crime may not become part of the crime rate because of the operation of police discretion. Thereafter, once the police exercise discretion in such a way as to lead them to seek a prosecution (step 6), the offence is recorded (step 7) and it becomes a 'notifiable crime recorded by the police' and as such part of the crime rate (step 8).

What are the implications of this process for the crime rate and for criminal statistics generally? For one thing, it means that a substantial amount of crime undoubtedly goes unrecorded as a result of: not coming to the attention of members of the public; not being recognized as criminal; not being reported; decisions regarding police surveillance that may result in some crimes being given lower priority; and the operation of police discretion. This undercurrent of unrecorded crime is frequently referred

to as 'the dark figure' (Coleman and Moynihan 1996). Similarly, suicide statistics almost certainly fail to record many potential cases for inclusion and may even include a small number that are not in fact suicides (as a result of problems of deciding whether the 'victim' was involved in an accident or intended to commit suicide). It may be difficult to determine whether someone is the victim of suicide when there is no suicide note. Moreover, those responsible for concluding whether a death is a suicide or not may come under considerable pressure not to record it as such, possibly because of feelings of potential stigma or because of religious taboos concerning suicide. To push the point even further, the deficiencies of official statistics do not relate just to areas of deviant behaviour such as crime and suicide. For example, the 'claimant count', which is used to gain a picture each month of the level of unemployment, may misrepresent the 'real' level of unemployment: people who are unemployed but who do not claim benefits or whose claim is disallowed will not be counted in the statistics, while those who form part of the claimant count but who work in part of what is known as the 'black' or 'informal' economy (and who therefore are not really unemployed) *will* be included in the unemployment statistics.

Increasingly, official statistics and summaries of them are available via the Internet. The Office for National Statistics is a good springboard for access to a wide variety of official statistics and can be accessed at **www.statistics. gov.uk/default.asp** (accessed 8 January 2015).

Reliability and validity

Issues of reliability and validity seem to loom large in these considerations. Reliability seems to be jeopardized because definitions and policies regarding the phenomena to be counted vary over time. For example, the UK Government Home Office or police service policies may mean that more resources are to be put into surveillance of a certain area of crime, such as drugs or drink-driving. Moreover, as part of a crackdown, it may be that police officers are less likely to operate their discretion in such a way as to result in perpetrators being let off with a warning. The problem for the reliability of the crime statistics is that variations over time in levels of a particular crime may be due not to variations in the level of transgression but to variations in the propensity to expend resources on surveillance and to proceed with prosecution. Also, there may be changes over time in the definitions of crime or in the propensity of victims to proceed with a complaint. Such changes will clearly affect the degree to which fluctuations in the rate of

occurrence of certain crimes reflect 'real' fluctuations in the incidence of those crimes or other factors (that is, variations over time in surveillance, operation of discretion, definition, propensity to report, and other factors). A further factor that can impair the reliability of crime statistics is 'fiddling' by police officers (see Research in the news 7.1 and Thinking deeply 14.1). To the extent that such factors operate, the reliability of the crime data will be adversely affected, and, as a result, validity will be similarly impaired.

Also, the problems with official statistics extend to the examination of the variables with which the crime rate is associated. For example, it might be assumed that, if an examination of regional differences demonstrates that the crime rate varies by the chief ethnic or social class composition of an area, this implies that ethnic status and social class are themselves related to crime. There are two problems with drawing such an inference. First, there is an analytic difficulty known as the **ecological fallacy** (see Key concept 14.2). Second, aside from the problem of the ecological fallacy, we would still be faced with an issue that is related to the matter of validity. Variations between ethnic groups or social classes may be a product of factors other than variations between ethnic groups and social classes in their propensity to commit crimes. The variations may be due to such factors as variations in the likelihood of members of the public reporting a crime when the perpetrator is of one ethnic group or class rather than others; variations in the surveillance activities of the police so that areas with a high concentration of members of one ethnic group or class rather than others are more likely to be the focus

Thinking deeply 14.1
Fiddling the crime figures

An article in *The Times* (Leake 1998) reported that there was growing evidence that senior police officers frequently massage the crime statistics for their forces. The author argued that many officers deliberately 'lose' crimes in order to make their detection rates look better. As a result, crime rates are often lower than they should be. The article cites the following methods of suppressing crimes:

- classifying multiple burglaries—for example, in a block of flats in one day—as a single incident;
- cataloguing multiple credit card or cheque card frauds as a single offence;
- excluding common assaults, when people are not seriously injured, from the figures for violent crime;
- excluding drug offences where people admit to offending but are only cautioned.

These methods of reducing the crime rate will adversely affect reliability, because it is not possible to compare the figures over different time periods because of variations over time in the propensity to massage the data. Validity will be similarly affected, in part because measurement validity presupposes reliability (see Chapter 7) and also because the figures cannot be regarded as providing a picture of the true level of crime.

Key concept 14.2
What is the ecological fallacy?

The ecological fallacy is the error of assuming that inferences about individuals can be made from findings relating to aggregate data. Coleman and Moynihan (1996) provide the example of the relationship between ethnicity and crime. They observe that findings showing a higher incidence of crime in regions with high concentrations of ethnic minorities have been used to imply that members of such minority groups are more likely to commit crimes. However, research on this issue in the 1960s suggested that in fact members of ethnic minority groups were less likely to offend. The fallacy can arise for several reasons—for example, it may not be the members of the minority groups who are responsible for the high levels of offending.

of activity; variations between ethnic groups or social classes in the propensity of police officers to exercise discretion; and problems for the police of learning about and investigating certain crimes that are themselves related to ethnicity or class (for example, white-collar crime). Similarly, as Douglas (1967) observes in connection with suicide statistics, it is quite likely that variations between ethnic and religious groups in suicide rates may be a product at least in part of variations in the predilection of the families of suicide victims to put pressure on official figures such as coroners not to treat a death as a suicide.

Condemning and resurrecting official statistics

In the 1960s, in particular, there was a torrent of criticism of various kinds of official statistics, especially those connected with crime and deviance. So entrenched was the belief that official statistics were of dubious value to social researchers that the view took root that they were virtually worthless. Instead, it was recommended that social researchers should turn their attention to the investigation of the organizational processes that produce the various deficiencies identified by the various writers. In the words of the writers of one influential article, rates of crime and other forms of deviance 'can be viewed as indices of organizational processes rather than as indices of certain forms of behavior' (Kitsuse and Cicourel 1963: 137). The effect of this view was to consign official statistics to the sidelines of social research so that they became an object of research interest rather than a potential source of data, although research based on official statistics continued in certain quarters. Also, official statistics, because they are a by-product of the activities of state agencies, are often not tailored to the needs of social researchers. In other words, it may be that the

definitions of apparently similar or identical terms (such as unemployment or socio-economic class) employed by those responsible for compiling official statistics may not be commensurate with the definitions employed by social researchers.

An important article by Bulmer (1980) questioned the relative neglect of official statistics by British sociologists in particular and represented a turning point in the views of many researchers towards this source of data (Levitas and Guy 1996). Bulmer argued that the critique of official statistics had largely revolved around the elaboration of criticisms surrounding statistics relating to crime and deviance. He observes that these are subject to special well-known problems and it would be wrong to generalize these problems to the full range of official statistics. Many official statistics may be flawed in certain respects, but the flaws are not necessarily as pronounced as those to do with crime and deviance. Moreover, the flaws in many of the official statistics not concerned with crime and deviance are probably no worse than the errors that occur in much measurement deriving from methods such as surveys based on questionnaires and structured interviews. Indeed, some forms of official statistics are probably very accurate by almost any set of criteria, such as statistics relating to births, marriages, and deaths.

Bulmer also argues that, so far as some of the key variables in social research are concerned, the distance between the definitions employed by the compilers of official statistics and those employed by social researchers is not as great as is sometimes supposed. However, he notes that the case of social class is somewhat different. The development of the Registrar General's classification of social class groupings seems to have taken little notice of the schemes devised by sociologists, such as the influential Hall–Jones and Hope–Goldthorpe approaches. However, Bulmer notes that the Registrar General's classification nonetheless helpfully brings out clear divergences of socio-economic position between the groupings it comprises and is frequently employed by social researchers to make precisely this point. Bulmer points to the fact that data deriving from official statistics that show pronounced social class differences in mortality are extremely important and of considerable significance to medical and other sociologists. The data are not without problems and detractors, but there is a considerable willingness to use the statistics. The same applies to Inland Revenue data based on estate duties that have been employed to examine wealth distribution.

A further criticism of the rejection of various forms of official statistics is that it implies that quantitative data compiled by social researchers are somehow error free or at least superior. However, as we have seen in previous chapters, while social researchers do their best to reduce the amount of error in their measurement of key concepts (such as through the standardization of the asking of questions and the recording of answers in survey research), it is not the case that the various measures that are derived are free of error. All social measurement is prone to error; what is crucial is taking steps to keep that error to a minimum. Therefore, to reject official statistics because they contain errors is misleading if in fact all measurement in social research contains errors. The problem here is that some official statistics are particularly prone to error, such as those relating to crime and deviance.

However, even here some caution is necessary. While data deriving from the British Crime Survey (now called the Crime Survey for England and Wales) may be employed to show that only a proportion of all crimes are notified to the police (see Research in the news 7.1), it would be wrong to conclude that the survey is an error-free yardstick. Coleman and Moynihan (1996) point to several measurement errors that are likely to afflict the BCS. For example, there is evidence to suggest that the BCS results in an overestimation of serious incidents through a process known as 'forward telescoping'. This means that serious incidents that are outside the recall period of twelve months (the period about which respondents are questioned) are erroneously considered to have occurred during that period. In other words, people have a tendency to believe that serious crimes of which they have been victims, but that occurred more than twelve months previously, actually occurred during the recall period. Coleman and Moynihan (1996) also point to errors arising from factors such as concealment in the course of interviewing. For example, there is some evidence to suggest that women are more likely to report sexual offences and domestic violence to the police (step 4 in Figure 14.1) than to a survey interviewer. In other words, dismissing official statistics on crime on the basis of survey evidence of the kind generated by the BCS is not without problems because the BCS is not free of error itself.

Following Bulmer's (1980) statement of the issue, the wholesale rejection of official statistics by many social researchers has been tempered. While there is widespread recognition and acknowledgement that problems remain with certain forms of official statistics (in particular those relating to crime and deviance), each set of statistics has to be evaluated for the purposes of social research on its own merits.

Official statistics as a form of unobtrusive method

One of the most compelling and frequently cited cases for the continued use of official statistics is that they can be considered a form of unobtrusive measure, although nowadays many writers prefer to use the term **unobtrusive method** (Lee 2000). This term is derived from the notion of 'unobtrusive measure' coined by Webb et al. (1966). In a highly influential book, Webb et al. argued that social researchers are excessively reliant on measures of social phenomena deriving from methods of data collection that are prone to *reactivity* (see Research in focus 3.3 and Key concept 12.4, where this idea is introduced). This means that, whenever people know that they are participating in a study (which is invariably the case with methods of data collection such as structured interviewing, self-administered questionnaire, and structured observation), a component of their replies or behaviour is likely to be influenced by their knowledge that they are being investigated. In other words, their answers to questions or the behaviour they exhibit may be untypical.

Official statistics fit fairly squarely in the second of the four types of unobtrusive measures outlined in Key concept 14.3. As noted in the box, this second grouping covers a very wide range of sources of data, which includes statistics generated by organizations that are not agencies of the state. This is a useful reminder that potentially interesting statistical data are frequently compiled by a wide range of organizations. An interesting use of such data is described in Research in focus 14.3. However, social researchers do not make a great deal of use of such data, and it is relevant that the author referred to in the research presented in Research in focus 14.3 is an economist. There may be greater potential for searching out and mining statistical data produced by organizations that are relatively independent of the state.

Key concept 14.3
What are unobtrusive methods?

An unobtrusive method is 'any method of observation that directly removes the observer from the set of interactions or events being studied' (Denzin 1970). Webb et al. (1966) distinguished four main types.

1. *Physical traces.* These are the 'signs left behind by a group' and include such things as graffiti and trash.

2. *Archive materials.* This category includes statistics collected by governmental and non-governmental organizations, diaries, the mass media, and historical records.

3. *Simple observation.* This refers to 'situations in which the observer has no control over the behavior or sign in question, and plays an unobserved, passive, and nonintrusive role in the research situation' (Webb et al. 1966: 112).

4. *Contrived observation.* This is the same as simple observation, but the observer either actively varies the setting in some way (but without jeopardizing the unobtrusive quality of the observation) or employs hidden hardware to record observations, such as video cameras.

Official statistics would be subsumed under Category 2, as would content analysis of media content of the kind described in Chapter 13. However, a content analysis like that described in Research in focus 13.5 would not be considered an example of an unobtrusive measure, because the material being content analysed (workplace ethnographies) derives from studies in which the data were generated in an obtrusive fashion. Structured observation of the kind covered in Chapter 12 will typically not fall into Categories 3 and 4, because the observer is usually known to those being observed. A study by Rosenhan (1973), which used pseudo-patients in the study of mental hospitals, is an example of contrived observation because the pseudo-patients were not known to be researchers and they actively varied the situation by their own behaviour. The Daniel (1968) study described in Table 12.1 is also an example of contrived observation, because the 'actors' were not known to be researchers and by applying for rented accommodation they were actively varying the situation.

It is important to realize that Webb et al. (1966) were not intending that unobtrusive methods should supplant conventional methods. Instead, they argued that the problem they were identifying was the almost exclusive reliance upon methods that were likely to be affected by reactivity. Webb et al. argued for greater **triangulation** (see Key concept 17.4) in social research, whereby conventional (reactive) and unobtrusive (non-reactive) methods would be employed in conjunction. For example, they wrote that they were providing an inventory of unobtrusive methods 'because they demonstrate ways in which the investigator may shore up reactive infirmities of the interview and questionnaire' (Webb et al. 1966: 174). In more recent years, many writers have preferred the term 'unobtrusive method' to 'unobtrusive measure' (e.g. Lee 2000), perhaps because the latter term is too suggestive of a quantitative research approach alone.

It is worth noting that unobtrusive methods encapsulate at least two kinds of ways of thinking about the process of capturing data. First, many so-called unobtrusive methods are in fact *sources* of data, such as graffiti, diaries, media articles, and official statistics. Such sources require analysis in order to be rendered interesting to a social scientific audience. Second, while documents of various kinds warrant being called 'unobtrusive' sources of data, in the sense that they have not been produced at the behest of a researcher (and are therefore not *reactive*), that should not be taken to mean that they are unproblematic. They are invariably produced for a purpose (albeit not specifically for research purposes) with an end in mind. Third, it includes *methods* of data collection, such as simple and contrived observation. While the data generated by such methods of data collection also require analysis, the data have to be produced by the methods. The data are not simply out there awaiting analysis in the way in which diaries or newspaper articles are (although, of course, a great deal of detective work is often necessary to unearth such sources). This means that neither of the terms 'unobtrusive methods' or 'unobtrusive measures' captures the variety of forms terribly well.

Lee (2000) has developed a classification of unobtrusive methods that differs slightly from that of Webb et al. (1966). He distinguishes the following kinds of data.

1. *Found data.* This category corresponds more or less exactly to *physical traces*.

2. *Captured data*. This category comprises both *simple observation* and *contrived observation*.

3. *Retrieved data: running records*. Records concerned with births, marriages, and deaths are prominent cases of this kind of record, whereby records can be examined over quite long periods so that changes can be explored. Lee also includes in this category personal advertisements such as marriage announcements and dating advertisements, as well as job advertisements.

4. *Retrieved data: personal and episodic records*. With this category, Lee has in mind three kinds of data: **personal documents** (letters, diaries, memoirs), visual images in the mass media (for example, newspaper photographs and picture postcards), and 'documents produced through "institutional discovery" procedures' (Lee 2000: 87) (for example, reports of inquiries into the factors that led to a disaster).

5. Lee also distinguishes *records produced through the Internet*, especially the various forms of computer-mediated communication, such as email and various kinds of message boards and chat rooms. In the years since Lee wrote, blogs (Web logs) might be added to this list.

Many of these different kinds of data are encountered elsewhere in this book—for example, personal documents in Chapter 23 and computer-mediated communications (including 'Big Data') in Chapters 13 and 23. Each of the different types that Webb et al. and Lee distinguish poses distinctive questions in terms of such issues as the reliability of the evidence and the ethical problems involved.

Research in focus 14.3
Using unofficial statistics? The case of New York taxi cab drivers

Following his informal observation on the behaviour of New York taxi drivers (cabbies), Camerer (1997) was interested in testing two different theories about the relationship between the number of hours a cabby works and average hourly earnings. One theory—the law of supply—predicted that cabbies would want to work more when their average hourly earnings would be high (for example, during bad weather or on working days when more business people are around) rather than when they are low. The second theory—daily income targeting—suggests that cabbies set themselves an income target for the day and once that target is attained they stop work for the day. On good days (when hourly wages are higher) this theory simply means they will stop earlier. Camerer obtained taximeter readings from the New York Taxi and Limousine Commission. The data allowed 3,000 observations of cabbies' behaviour for 1988, 1990, and 1994. Tips are not recorded, so a guess had to be made about likely levels in this area. The data provided unequivocal support for the daily income targeting theory, but further analysis revealed a difference between newer and more experienced drivers: the former behaved in line with income targeting theory; the more experienced drivers were much more varied and generally their behaviour were closer to the law of supply theory, though not entirely in conformity with it. Overall, if cabbies obeyed the law of supply, their mean incomes would rise by around 15 per cent.

Big Data

Big Data is a very difficult term to define and pin down, not least because the nature of the kinds of information it refers to are themselves rapidly changing. It is usually taken to refer to extremely large sources of data that are not immediately amenable to conventional ways of handling them. The term has been used in connection with such things as the vast amounts of data that retailers collect about us and our spending habits when we use loyalty cards. So far as social researchers are concerned, the main Big Data context that has provided a focus of attention is social media (especially Twitter and Facebook). The studies referred to in Chapter 13 by Humphreys et al. (2014)

who examined the personal information revealed on Twitter, by Ledford and Anderson (2013) who examined the response to the use of Facebook by a drug company, and by Greaves et al. (in press) that analysed the contents of tweets aimed at NHS hospitals (also discussed in Chapter 23 in the section on 'Social media') are examples of the use of Big Data by social scientists.

This is very much a field in flux both in terms of the nature and forms of Big Data that have arisen and may appear and also in terms of the uses that are made of the data and the techniques applied to them. Consequently, much of this section is tentative and even limited in terms of its relevance as new forms of Big Data and new approaches emerge. What I do in this section is to provide a flavour of the range of areas to which Big Data analyses have been applied.

Tinati et al. (2014) suggest that there has been a tendency for researchers using Big Data to have approached the sheer volume of data it offers by reducing it, resulting in smaller-scale analyses that do not take advantage of the full potential of the data. This is usually done either by concentrating on a reduced sample of users, such as a focus on only the largest US police departments in the study by Lieberman, Koetzle, and Sakiyama (2013) of police departments' use of Facebook, or taking a sample of tweets or posts usually for content analysis, such as the study by Humphreys et al. (2014). Tinati et al. (2014: 665) argue that such research is 'methodologically limited because social scientists have approached Big Data with methods that cannot explore many of the particular qualities that make it so appealing to use: that is, the scale, proportionality, dynamism and relationality'. There seems to be a distinction here between two types of Big Data analysis, at least so far as social media contexts are concerned: studies that are concerned with the *content* of social media postings (which may or may not entail sampling) and studies that are concerned to reveal aspects of the *structure and process* of social media activity. The Big Data studies that appear in Chapters 13 and 23 are principally concerned with content, so in this section I will draw attention to two studies that emphasize the features referred to by Tinati et al.

- Tinati et al. (2014: 668) developed a tool 'that enables the metrics, dynamics and content of Twitter information flows and network formation to be explored in real-time or via historical data'. They focus in particular on the role of Twitter in political activism. For example, they collected tweets relating to the protest against the introduction of tuition fees in English universities using the hashtag #feesprotest. The collection comprised 12,831 tweets sent by 4,737 users in the period 8 October to 21 November 2011. The tool allows them to show the patterns of information flows both before and during the protest in terms of the numbers of retweeted messages which reveal the most influential users and their location in networks of users. It also reveals changes over time in the popularity of users. The research shows an interest in content too, as the researchers point out a shift in content from 'calls to participation' such as:

[Wed 02 Nov 2011 20:40:49] *"RT @michaeljohnroberts: There is a march of 10000 students to the city of London on November 15th come! #barricades #feesprotest"*
(Tinati et al. 2014: 673)

to an emphasis on the police and intimations of heavy-handed tactics, such as:

[Sat 05 Nov 2011 20:27:52] *"RT @Witness: More disgusting police behaviour. We need to think about #feesprotest and how to defend ourselves. #abca"*
(Tinati et al. 2014: 673)

They also show that there are individuals who, though not generators of content themselves, play a significant role in the flow of information by being significant retweeters. One individual was especially influential but in a restricted way, in that the retweeted messages tended to be about the organization of the protest. Influential retweeters could achieve their significance either by being quick to retweet or by having a retweeting approach that diffused tweets with a variety of content.

- Procter et al. (2013) secured access to a corpus of tweets relating to the riots that took place in the UK in August 2011. They focus in particular on the use made of Twitter for securing support for a 'clean-up' in the aftermath. Thus, one Twitter account which was categorized as belonging to a celebrity and with over one and a half million followers tweeted 'Visit **www.riot cleanup.co.uk** for info on how and where to help if you can. #riotcleanup' (quoted in Procter et al. 2013: 202). The authors were able to categorize the Twitter accounts that were involved in terms of the type of actor associated with the account (for example, journalists, celebrities, bloggers). They also created a timeline for the number of tweets over the period. In addition, the researchers were interested in the role of rumour and created a timeline of tweets over a very short time period relating to a (false) rumour that rioters were going to attack Birmingham Children's Hospital. While the data suggest that tweeting and retweeting did play a role in the propagation of a rumour, Twitter was also used to challenge the rumour, for example: '#birminghamriots brmb radio and chief medical officer have confirmed Birmingham children's hospital has NOT been hit by riots' (quoted in Procter et al. 2013: 206).

Big Data are an attractive source of material for social scientists. The sources are non-reactive in that they have not been generated at the behest of a researcher. They offer the opportunity to work on large amounts of data, though this is clearly both a strength and a challenge. Research based on Big Data that focus on the content of communication may well be within the competence of many students and early career researchers. However, studies emphasizing the structure and process of social media communications should be not be embarked upon in an unguarded way. Many of the studies—like Tinati et al. (2014) and Procter et al. (2013)—are the results of collaborations between social scientists and computer specialists. Consequently, I would recommend caution if this kind of study is being considered. However, content-based studies of tweets and Facebook posts are definitely feasible.

 ## Key points

- Secondary analysis of existing data offers the prospect of being able to explore research questions of interest to you without having to go through the process of collecting the data yourself.
- Very often, secondary analysis offers the opportunity of being able to employ high-quality data sets that are based on large and reasonably representative samples.
- Secondary analysis presents few disadvantages.
- The analysis of official statistics may be thought of as a special form of secondary analysis but one that is more controversial because of unease about the reliability and validity of certain types of official data, especially those relating to crime and deviance.
- The problems associated with official data relating to crime and deviance should not be generalized to all official statistics. Many forms of official statistics are much less prone to the kinds of errors that are detectable in relation to crime and deviance data, but there remains the possible problem of divergences of definition between compilers of such data and social researchers.
- Official statistics represent a form of unobtrusive method and enjoy certain advantages (especially lack of reactivity) because of that.
- Big Data are a new form of data that can be the focus of a secondary analysis but that present some challenges to researchers.

 ## Questions for review

- What is secondary analysis?

Other researchers' data

- Outline the main advantages and limitations of secondary analysis of other researchers' data.
- Examine recent issues of one of the British sociology journals, such as *Sociology*. Locate an article that uses secondary analysis. How well do the advantages and limitations you outlined fit this article?
- Does the possibility of conducting a secondary analysis apply only to quantitative data produced by other researchers?

Meta-analysis

- For which kinds of studies is meta-analysis suitable and what advantages might it have over a narrative review of such studies?

Official statistics

- Why have many social researchers been sceptical about the use of official statistics for research purposes?
- How justified is their scepticism?
- What reliability and validity issues do official statistics pose?
- What are unobtrusive methods or measures? What is the chief advantage of such methods?

Big Data

- How might Big Data be of use to the social researcher?
- How might you be able to use Big Data in a research project of your own?

Online Resource Centre

www.oxfordtextbooks.co.uk/orc/brymansrm5e/

Visit the Online Resource Centre to enrich your understanding of secondary analysis and official statistics. Follow up links to other resources, test yourself using multiple choice questions, and gain further guidance and inspiration from the Student Researcher's Toolkit.

15
Quantitative data analysis

 Chapter outline

 Chapter guide

In this chapter, some of the basic but nonetheless most frequently used methods for analysing quantitative data analysis will be presented. In order to illustrate the use of the methods of data analysis, a small imaginary set of data based on attendance at a gym is used. It is the kind of small research project that would be feasible for most students doing undergraduate research projects for a dissertation or similar exercise. The chapter explores:

- the importance of *not* leaving considerations of how you will analyse your quantitative data until after you have collected all your data; you should be aware of the ways in which you would like to analyse your data from the earliest stage of your research;

- the distinctions between the different kinds of variable that can be generated in quantitative research; knowing how to distinguish types of variables is crucial so that you appreciate which methods of analysis can be applied when you examine variables and relationships between them;

- methods for analysing a single variable at a time (*univariate analysis*);

- methods for analysing relationships between variables (*bivariate analysis*);

- the analysis of relationships between three or more variables (*multivariate analysis*).

Introduction

In this chapter, some very basic techniques for analysing quantitative data will be examined. Chapter 16 will introduce the ways in which these techniques can be implemented using sophisticated computer software known as IBM SPSS Statistics. The formulae that underpin the techniques to be discussed will not be presented here, since the necessary calculations can easily be carried out by using SPSS. Two chapters cannot do justice to these topics, and readers are advised to move as soon as possible on to books that provide more detailed and advanced treatments (e.g. Bryman and Cramer 2011).

Before beginning this exposition of techniques, I would like to give you advance warning of one of the biggest mistakes that people make about quantitative data analysis:

> I don't have to concern myself with how I'm going to analyse my survey data until after I've collected my data. I'll leave thinking about it till then, because it doesn't impinge on how I collect my data.

This is a common error that arises because quantitative data analysis looks like a distinct phase that occurs after the data have been collected (see, for example, Figure 7.1, in which the analysis of quantitative data is depicted as a late step—number 9—in quantitative research).

Quantitative data analysis is indeed something that occurs typically at a late stage in the overall process and is also a distinct stage.

However, that does not mean that you should not be considering how you will analyse your data until then. In fact, you should be fully aware of what techniques you will apply at a fairly early stage—for example, when you are designing your questionnaire, observation schedule, coding frame, or whatever. The two main reasons for this are as follows.

1. You cannot apply just any technique to any variable. Techniques have to be appropriately matched to the types of variables that you have created through your research. This means that you must be fully conversant with the ways in which different types of variable are classified.

2. The size and nature of your sample are likely to impose limitations on the kinds of techniques you can use (see the section on 'Kind of analysis' in Chapter 8).

In other words, you need to be aware that decisions that you make at quite an early stage in the research process, such as the kinds of data you collect and the size of your sample, will have implications for the sorts of analysis that you will be able to conduct.

 # A small research project

This discussion of quantitative data analysis will be based upon an imaginary piece of research carried out by an undergraduate marketing student for a dissertation. The student in question is interested in the area of leisure in modern society and in particular, because of her own enthusiasm for leisure clubs and gyms, the ways in which such venues are used and people's reasons for joining them. She has a hunch that they may be indicative of a 'civilizing process' and uses this theory as a framework for her findings (Rojek 1995: 50–6). The student is also interested in issues relating to gender and body image and suspects that men and women will differ in their reasons for going to a gym and the kinds of activities in which they engage in the gym. She also suspects that these factors will vary by age.

The student secures the agreement of a gym close to her home to contact a sample of its members by post. The gym has 1,200 members and she decides to take a simple random sample of 10 per cent of the membership (that is, 120 members). She sends out postal questionnaires to members of the sample with a covering

letter testifying to the gym's support of her research. She would have preferred to contact the members of her sample online so that they could complete the questionnaire online, but the gym was unwilling to pass on members' email addresses. However, she does offer research participants the option of completing the questionnaire online, so that this is in effect a mixed mode survey (postal and Web), although most of those who reply opt for the postal questionnaire version. One thing she wants to know is how much time people spend on each of the three main classes of activity in the gym: cardiovascular equipment, weights equipment, and exercises. She defines each of these carefully in the covering letter and asks members of the sample to keep a note of how long they spend on each of the three activities on their next visit. They are then requested to return the questionnaires to her in a prepaid reply envelope. She ends up with a sample of ninety questionnaires—a response rate of 75 per cent.

Part of the questionnaire is presented in Tips and skills 'A completed and processed questionnaire' and has been

Tips and skills
A completed and processed questionnaire

Question		Code

1. Are you male or female (please tick)?

    Male ✓   Female ___   ①2

2. How old are you?

    <u>21</u> years   21

3. Which of the following best describes your *main* reason for going to the gym? (please tick *one* only)

Relaxation	___	1
Maintain or improve fitness	✓	②
Lose weight	___	3
Meet others	___	4
Build strength	___	5
Other (please specify)	___	6

4. When you go to the gym, how often do you use the cardiovascular equipment (jogger, step machine, bike, rower)? (please tick)

Always	✓	①
Usually	___	2
Rarely	___	3
Never	___	4

5. When you go to the gym, how often do you use the weights machines (including free weights)? (please tick)

Always	✓	①
Usually	___	2
Rarely	___	3
Never	___	4

6. How frequently do you usually go to the gym? (please tick)

Every day	___	1
4–6 days a week	___	2
2 or 3 days a week	✓	③
Once a week	___	4
2 or 3 times a month	___	5
Once a month	___	6
Less than once a month	___	7

7. Are you usually accompanied when you go to the gym or do you usually go on your own? (please tick *one* only)

On my own	✓	①
With a friend	___	2
With a partner/spouse	___	3

8. Do you have sources of regular exercise other than the gym?

Yes ____   No ✓____   1 ②

*If you have answered **No** to this question, please proceed to question* **9**

8a If you have replied **Yes** to question **8**, please indicate the *main* source of regular exercise
in the last six months from this list. (please tick *one* only)   ⓪

Sport   ____   1

Cycling on the road   ____   2

Jogging   ____   3

Long walks   ____   4

Other (please specify)   ____   5

9. During your last visit to the gym, how many minutes did you spend on the cardiovascular equipment
(jogger, step machine, bike, rower)?

33 minutes   33

10. During your last visit to the gym, how many minutes did you spend on the weights machines (including
free weights)?

17 minutes   17

11. During your last visit to the gym, how many minutes did you spend on other activities (e.g. stretching
exercises)?

5 minutes   5

completed by a respondent and coded by the student. The entire questionnaire runs to four pages, but only twelve of the questions are provided here. Many of the questions (1, 3, 4, 5, 6, 7, 8, and 8a) are pre-coded, and the student simply has to circle the code to the far right of the question under the column 'code'. With the remainder of the questions, specific figures are requested, and she simply transfers the relevant figure to the code column.

Missing data

The data for all ninety respondents are presented in Tips and skills 'Gym survey data'. Each of the twelve questions is known for the time being as a variable number (var00001, etc.). The variable number is a default number that is imposed by SPSS, the statistical package that is described in Chapter 16. Each variable number corresponds to a question in Tips and skills 'A completed and processed questionnaire' (i.e. var00001 is question 1, var00002 is question 2, etc.). An important issue arises in the management of data as to how to handle 'missing data'. Missing data arise when respondents fail to reply to a question—either by accident or because they do not

want to answer the question. Thus, respondent 24 has failed to answer question 2, which is concerned with age. This has been coded as a zero (0) and it will be important to ensure that the computer software is notified of this fact, since it needs to be taken into account during the analysis. Also, question 8a has a large number of zeros; this is because many people did not answer it because they had been filtered out by the previous question (that is, they do not have other sources of regular exercise). These have also been coded as zero to denote missing data, though strictly speaking their failure to reply is more indicative of the question not being applicable to them. Note also that there are zeros for var00010, var00011, and var00012. However, these do *not* denote missing data but show that the respondent spends zero minutes on the activity in question. Everyone has answered questions 9, 10, and 11, so there are in fact no missing data for these variables. If there had been missing data, it would be necessary to code missing data with a number that could not also be a true figure. For example, nobody has spent 99 minutes on these activities, so this might be an appropriate number, as it is easy to remember and could not be read by the computer as anything other than missing data.

Tips and skills
Gym survey data

var00001	var00002	var00003	var00004	var00005	var00006	var00007	var00008	var00009	var00010	var00011	var00012
1	21	2	1	1	3	1	2	0	33	17	5
2	44	1	3	1	4	3	1	2	10	23	10
2	19	3	1	2	2	1	1	1	27	18	12
2	27	3	2	1	2	1	2	0	30	17	3
1	57	2	1	3	2	3	1	4	22	0	15
2	27	3	1	1	3	1	1	3	34	17	0
1	39	5	2	1	5	1	1	5	17	48	10
2	36	3	1	2	2	2	1	1	25	18	7
1	37	2	1	1	3	1	2	0	34	15	0
2	51	2	2	2	4	3	2	0	16	18	11
1	24	5	2	1	3	1	1	1	0	42	16
2	29	2	1	2	3	1	2	0	34	22	12
1	20	5	1	1	2	1	2	0	22	31	7
2	22	2	1	3	4	2	1	3	37	14	12
2	46	3	1	1	5	2	2	0	26	9	4
2	41	3	1	2	2	3	1	4	22	7	10
1	25	5	1	1	3	1	1	1	21	29	4
2	46	3	1	2	4	2	1	4	18	8	11
1	30	3	1	1	5	1	2	0	23	9	6
1	25	5	2	1	3	1	1	1	23	19	0
2	24	2	1	1	3	2	1	2	20	7	6
2	39	1	2	3	5	1	2	0	17	0	9
1	44	3	1	1	3	2	1	2	22	8	5
1	0	1	2	2	4	2	1	4	15	10	4
2	18	3	1	2	3	1	2	1	18	7	10
1	41	3	1	1	3	1	2	0	34	10	4
2	38	2	1	2	5	3	1	2	24	14	10
1	25	2	1	1	2	1	2	0	48	22	7
1	41	5	2	1	3	1	1	2	17	27	0
2	30	3	1	1	2	2	2	0	32	13	10
2	29	3	1	3	2	1	2	0	31	0	7
2	42	1	2	2	4	2	1	4	17	14	6
1	31	2	1	1	2	1	2	0	49	21	2
2	25	3	1	1	2	3	2	0	30	17	15
1	46	3	1	1	3	1	1	3	32	10	5
1	24	5	2	1	4	1	1	2	0	36	11
2	34	3	1	1	3	2	1	4	27	14	12
2	50	2	1	2	2	3	2	0	28	8	6
1	28	5	1	1	3	2	1	1	26	22	8
2	30	3	1	1	2	1	1	4	21	9	12
1	27	2	1	1	2	1	1	3	64	15	8
2	27	2	1	2	4	2	1	4	22	10	7
1	36	5	1	1	3	2	2	0	21	24	0
2	43	3	1	1	4	1	2	0	25	13	8
1	34	2	1	1	3	2	1	1	45	15	6
2	27	3	1	1	2	1	1	4	33	10	9
2	38	2	1	3	4	2	2	0	23	0	16
1	28	2	1	1	3	3	1	2	38	13	5
1	44	5	1	1	2	1	2	0	27	19	7
2	31	3	1	2	3	2	2	0	32	11	5
2	23	2	1	1	4	2	1	1	33	18	8
1	45	3	1	1	3	1	1	2	26	10	7
2	34	3	1	2	2	3	2	0	36	8	12
1	27	3	1	1	2	3	1	3	42	13	6

(continued)

var00001	var00002	var00003	var00004	var00005	var00006	var00007	var00008	var00009	var00010	var00011	var00012
2	40	3	1	1	2	2	1	4	26	9	10
2	24	2	1	1	2	1	1	2	22	10	9
1	37	2	1	1	5	2	2	0	21	11	0
1	22	5	1	1	4	1	1	1	23	17	6
2	31	3	1	2	3	1	1	4	40	16	12
1	37	2	1	1	2	3	2	0	54	12	3
2	33	1	2	2	4	2	2	0	17	10	5
1	23	5	1	1	3	1	1	1	41	27	8
1	28	3	1	1	3	3	2	0	27	11	8
2	29	2	1	2	5	2	1	2	24	9	9
2	43	3	1	1	2	1	2	0	36	17	12
1	28	5	1	1	3	1	1	1	22	15	4
1	48	2	1	1	5	1	1	4	25	11	7
2	32	2	2	2	4	2	2	0	27	13	11
1	28	5	1	1	2	2	2	0	15	23	7
2	23	2	1	1	5	1	1	4	14	11	5
2	43	2	1	2	5	1	2	0	18	7	3
1	28	2	1	1	4	3	1	2	34	18	8
2	23	3	1	1	2	1	2	0	37	17	17
2	36	1	2	2	4	2	1	4	18	12	4
1	50	2	1	1	3	1	1	2	28	14	3
1	37	3	1	1	2	2	2	0	26	14	9
2	41	3	1	1	2	1	1	4	24	11	4
1	26	5	2	1	5	1	1	1	23	19	8
2	28	3	1	1	4	1	2	0	27	12	4
2	35	2	1	1	3	1	1	1	28	14	0
1	28	5	1	1	2	1	1	2	20	24	12
2	36	2	1	1	3	2	2	0	26	9	14
2	29	3	1	1	4	1	1	4	23	13	4
1	34	1	2	2	4	2	1	0	24	12	3
1	53	2	1	1	3	3	1	1	32	17	6
2	30	3	1	1	4	1	2	0	24	10	9
1	43	2	1	1	2	1	1	2	24	14	10
2	26	5	2	1	4	1	1	1	16	23	7
2	44	1	1	1	4	2	2	0	27	18	6
1	45	1	2	2	3	3	2	0	20	14	5

Types of variable

One of the things that might strike you when you look at the questions is that the kinds of information that you receive varies by question. Some of the questions call for answers in terms of real numbers: questions 2, 9, 10, and 11. Questions 1 and 8 yield either/or answers and are therefore in the form of dichotomies. The rest of the questions take the form of lists of categories, but there are differences between these too. Some of the questions are in terms of answers that are rank ordered: questions 4, 5, and 6. Thus we can say in the case of question 6 that the category 'Every day' implies greater frequency than '4–6 days a week', which in turn implies

greater frequency than '2 or 3 days a week', and so on. However, in the case of questions 3, 7, and 8a, the categories are *not* capable of being rank ordered. We cannot say in the case of question 3 that 'relaxation' is more of something than 'maintain or improve fitness' or 'lose weight'.

These considerations lead to a classification of the different types of variable that are generated in the course of research. The four main types are:

- *Interval/ratio variables.* These are variables where the distances between the categories are identical across the range of categories. In the case of variables var00010 to var00012, the distance between the categories is 1 minute. Thus, a person may spend 32 minutes on cardiovascular equipment, which is 1 minute more than someone who spends 31 minutes on this equipment. That difference is the same as the difference between someone who spends 8 minutes and another who spends 9 minutes on the equipment. Interval/ratio variables are regarded as the highest level of measurement because they permit a wider variety of statistical analyses to be conducted on them than with the other types of variable. Further, they typically allow more powerful analyses to be conducted. There is, in fact, a distinction between interval and ratio variables, in that the latter are interval variables with a fixed zero point. However, since most interval variables exhibit this quality in social research (for example, income, age, number of employees, revenue), they are not being distinguished here.

- *Ordinal variables.* These are variables whose categories can be rank ordered (as in the case of interval/ratio variables) but the distances between the categories are not equal across the range. Thus, in the case of question 6, the difference between the category 'every day' and '4–6 days a week' is not the same as the difference between '4–6 days a week' and '2 or 3 days a week', and so on. Nonetheless, we can say that 'every day' is more frequent than '4–6 days a week', which is more frequent than '2 or 3 days a week', etc. You should also bear in mind that, if you subsequently group an interval/ratio variable such as var00002, which refers to people's ages, into categories (e.g. 20 and under;

21–30; 31–40; 41–50; 51 and over), you are transforming it into an ordinal variable.

- *Nominal variables.* These variables, also known as *categorical variables*, comprise categories that cannot be rank ordered. As noted previously, we cannot say in the case of question 3 that 'relaxation' is more of something than 'maintain or improve fitness' or 'lose weight'.

- *Dichotomous variables.* These variables contain data that have only two categories (for example, gender). Their position in relation to the other types is slightly ambiguous, as they have only one interval. They therefore can be considered as having attributes of the other three types of variable. They look as though they are nominal variables, but because they have only one interval they are sometimes treated as ordinal variables. However, it is probably safest to treat them for most purposes as if they were ordinary nominal variables.

The four main types of variable and illustrations of them from the gym survey are provided in Table 15.1.

Multiple-indicator (or multiple-item) measures of concepts, such as Likert scales (see Key concept 7.2), produce strictly speaking ordinal variables. However, many writers argue that they can be treated as though they produce interval/ratio variables, because of the relatively large number of categories they generate. For a brief discussion of this issue, see Bryman and Cramer (2011), who distinguish between 'true' interval/ratio variables and those produced by multiple-indicator measures (2011: 71–3).

Figure 15.1 provides guidance about how to identify variables of each type.

Table 15.1

Types of variable

Type	Description	Examples in gym study	Variable Name in SPSS (see Chapter 16)
Interval/ratio	Variables where the distances between the categories are identical across the range	var00002 var00010 var00011 var00012	age cardmins weimins othmins
Ordinal	Variables whose categories can be rank ordered but the distances between the categories are not equal across the range	var00004 var00005 var00006	carduse weiuse frequent
Nominal	Variables whose categories cannot be rank ordered; also known as *categorical*	var00003 var00007 var00009	reasons accomp exercise
Dichotomous	Variables containing data that have only two categories	var00001 var00008	gender othsourc

Figure 15.1

Deciding how to categorize a variable

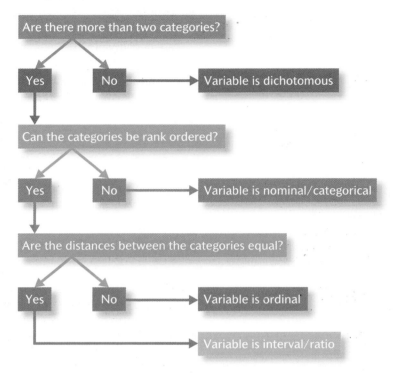

Univariate analysis

Univariate analysis refers to the analysis of one variable at a time. In this section, the commonest approaches will be outlined.

Frequency tables

A **frequency table** provides the number of people and the percentage belonging to each of the categories for the variable in question. It can be used in relation to all of the different types of variable. An example of a frequency table is provided for var00003 in Table 15.2. Notice that nobody chose two of the possible choices of answer—'meet others' and 'other'—so these are not included in the table. The table shows, for example, that 33 members of the sample go to the gym to lose weight and that they represent 37 per cent (percentages are often rounded up and down in frequency tables) of the entire sample. The procedure for generating a frequency table with SPSS is described in Chapter 16.

If an interval/ratio variable (e.g. people's ages) is to be presented in a frequency table format, it is invariably the case that the categories will need to be grouped. When grouping in this way, take care to ensure that the categories you create do not overlap (for example, like

this: 20–30, 30–40, 40–50, etc.). An example of a frequency table for an interval/ratio variable is shown in Table 15.3: it provides a frequency table for var00002, which is concerned with the ages of those visiting the gym. If we did not group people in terms of age ranges, there would be thirty-four different categories, which is too many to take in. By creating five categories, we make the distribution of ages easier to comprehend. Notice

Table 15.2

Frequency table showing reasons for visiting the gym

Reason	n	%
Relaxation	9	10
Maintain or improve fitness	31	34
Lose weight	33	37
Build strength	17	19
TOTAL	90	100

Table 15.3

Frequency table showing ages of gym members

Age	n	%
20 and under	3	3
21–30	39	44
31–40	23	26
41–50	21	24
51 and over	3	3
TOTAL	89	100

Figure 15.3

Pie chart showing the main reasons for visiting the gym (SPSS output)

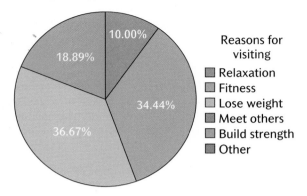

that the sample totals 89 and that the percentages are based on a total of 89 rather than 90. This is because this variable contains one missing value (respondent 24). The procedure for grouping respondents with SPSS is described in Chapter 16.

Diagrams

Diagrams are among the most frequently used methods of displaying quantitative data. Their chief advantage is that they are relatively easy to interpret and understand. If you are working with nominal or ordinal variables, the *bar chart* and the *pie chart* are two of the easiest methods to use. The bar chart shown in Figure 15.2 uses the same data as that presented in Table 15.2. Each bar represents the number of people falling into each category. This figure was produced with SPSS. The

procedure for generating a bar chart with SPSS is described in Chapter 16.

Another way of displaying the same data is through a pie chart, like the one in Figure 15.3. This also shows the relative size of the different categories but brings out as well the size of each slice relative to the total sample. The percentage that each slice represents of the whole sample is also given in this diagram, which was also produced with SPSS. The procedure for generating a pie chart with SPSS is described in Chapter 16.

If you are displaying an interval/ratio variable, like var00002, a *histogram* is likely to be employed. Figure 15.4, which was also generated by SPSS, uses the same data and categories as Table 15.3. As with the bar chart, the bars represent the relative size of each of the

Figure 15.2

Bar chart showing the main reasons for visiting the gym (SPSS output)

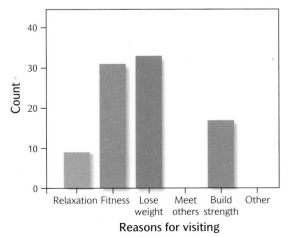

Figure 15.4

Histogram showing the ages of gym visitors (SPSS output)

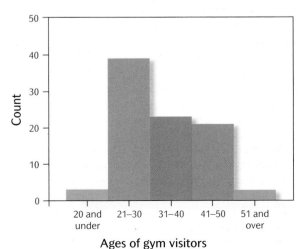

age bands. However, note that, with the histogram, there is no space between the bars, whereas there is a space between the bars of a bar chart. Histograms are produced for interval/ratio variables, whereas bar charts are produced for nominal and ordinal variables. The procedure for generating a histogram with SPSS is described in Chapter 16.

Measures of central tendency

Measures of central tendency encapsulate in one figure a value that is typical for a **distribution of values**. In effect, we are seeking out an average for a distribution, but, in quantitative data analysis, three different forms of average are recognized.

- *Arithmetic mean*. This is the average as we understand it in everyday use—that is, we sum all the values in a distribution and then divide by the number of values. Thus, the arithmetic mean (or more simply the *mean*) for var00002 is 33.6, meaning that the average age of gym visitors is nearly 34 years of age. The mean should be employed only in relation to interval/ratio variables, though it is not uncommon to see it being used for ordinal variables as well.

- *Median*. The **median** is the mid-point in a distribution of values. Whereas the mean is vulnerable to **outliers** (extreme values at either end of the distribution), which will exert considerable upwards or downwards pressure on the mean, by taking the mid-point of a distribution the median is not affected in this way. The median is derived by arraying all the values in a distribution from the smallest to the largest and then finding the middle point. If there is an even number of values, the median is calculated by taking the mean of the two middle numbers of the distribution. In the case of var00002, the median is 31. This is slightly lower than the mean, in part because some considerably older members (especially respondents 5 and 10) inflate the mean slightly. The median can be used in relation to both interval/ratio and ordinal variables.

- *Mode*. The **mode** is the value that occurs most frequently in a distribution. The mode for var00002 is 28. The mode can be employed in relation to all types of variable.

The procedure for generating the mean, median, and mode with SPSS is described in Chapter 16.

Measures of dispersion

The amount of variation in a sample can be just as interesting as providing estimates of the typical value of a distribution. For one thing, it becomes possible to draw contrasts between comparable distributions of values. For example, is there more or less variability in the amount of

time spent on cardiovascular equipment as compared to weights machines?

The most obvious way of measuring dispersion is by the **range**. This is simply the difference between the maximum and the minimum value in a distribution of values associated with an interval/ratio variable. We find that the range for the two types of equipment is 64 minutes for the cardiovascular equipment and 48 minutes for the weights machines. This suggests that there is more variability in the amount of time spent on the former. However, like the mean, the range is influenced by outliers, such as respondent 60 in the case of var00010.

Another **measure of dispersion** is the **standard deviation**, which is essentially the average amount of variation around the mean. Although the calculation is somewhat more complicated than this, the standard deviation is calculated by taking the difference between each value in a distribution and the mean and then dividing the total of the differences by the number of values. The standard deviation for var00010 is 9.9 minutes and for var00011 it is 8 minutes. Thus, not only is the average amount of time spent on the cardiovascular equipment higher than for the weights equipment; the standard deviation is greater too. The standard deviation is also affected by outliers, but, unlike the range, their impact is offset by dividing by the number of values in the distribution. The procedure for generating the standard deviation with SPSS is described in Chapter 16.

A type of figure that has become popular for displaying interval/ratio variables is the *boxplot* (see Figure 15.5). This form of display provides an indication of both central tendency (the median) and dispersion (the range). It also indicates whether there are any outliers. Figure 15.5 displays a boxplot for the total number of minutes users spent during their last gym visit. There is an outlier—case number 41, who spent a total of 87 minutes in the gym. The box represents the middle 50 per cent of users. The upper line of the box indicates the greatest use of the gym within the 50 per cent and the lower line of the box represents the least use of the gym within the 50 per cent. The line going across the box indicates the median. The line going upwards from the box goes up to the person whose use of the gym was greater than any other user, other than case number 41. The line going downwards from the box goes down to the person whose use of the gym was lower than that of any other user. Boxplots are useful because they display both central tendency and dispersion. They vary in their shape depending on whether cases tend to be high or low in relation to the median. With Figure 15.5, the box and the median are closer to the bottom end of the distribution, suggesting less variation among gym users below the median. There is more variation above the median. The procedure for generating boxplots using SPSS is described in Chapter 16.

Figure 15.5

A boxplot for the number of minutes spent on the last visit to the gym

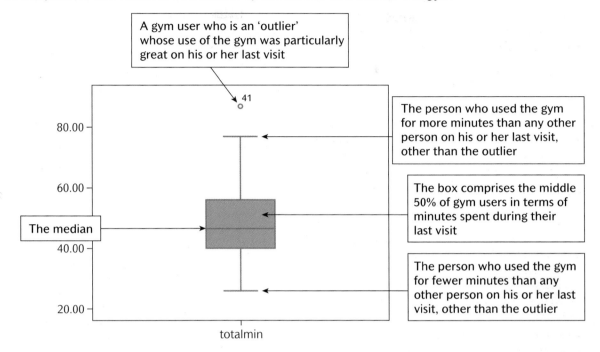

Bivariate analysis

Bivariate analysis is concerned with the analysis of two variables at a time in order to uncover whether or not the two variables are related. Exploring relationships between variables means searching for evidence that the variation in one variable coincides with variation in another variable. A variety of techniques is available for examining relationships, but their use depends on the nature of the two variables being analysed. Figure 15.6 is an attempt to portray the main types of bivariate analysis according to the types of variable involved.

Relationships, not causality

An important point to bear in mind about all of the methods for analysing relationships between variables is that it is precisely **relationships** that they uncover. As was noted in Chapter 3 in relation to cross-sectional designs, this means that you cannot infer that one variable causes another. Indeed, there are cases when what appears to be a causal influence working in one direction actually works in the other way. An interesting example of this problem of causal direction will be presented much later

in the book in Chapter 27. The example shows that Sutton and Rafaeli (1988) expected to find a causal relationship between the display of positive emotions (for example, smiling, or friendliness on the part of checkout staff) in retail outlets and sales in those outlets. In other words, the display of positive emotions was deemed to have a causal influence on levels of retail sales. In fact, the relationship was found to be the other way round: levels of retail sales exerted a causal influence on the display of emotions (see Research in focus 27.7 for more detailed explanation of this study).

Sometimes, we may feel confident that we can infer a causal direction when a relationship between two variables is discerned—for example, if we find that age and voting behaviour are related. It is impossible for the way people vote to influence their age, so, if we do find the two variables to be related, we can infer with complete confidence that age is the independent variable. It is not uncommon for researchers, when analysing their data, to draw inferences about causal direction based on their assumptions about the likely causal direction among related variables, as Sutton and Rafaeli (1988) did in their

Figure 15.6
Methods of bivariate analysis

	Nominal	Ordinal	Interval/ratio	Dichotomous
Nominal	Contingency table + chi-square (χ^2) + Cramér's V	Contingency table + chi-square (χ^2) + Cramér's V	Contingency table + chi-square (χ^2) + Cramér's V If the interval/ratio variable can be identified as the dependent variable, compare means + eta	Contingency table + chi-square (χ^2) + Cramér's V
Ordinal	Contingency table + chi-square (χ^2) + Cramér's V	Spearman's rho (ρ)	Spearman's rho (ρ)	Spearman's rho (ρ)
Interval/ratio	Contingency table + chi-square (χ^2) + Cramér's V If the interval/ratio variable can be identified as the dependent variable, compare means + eta	Spearman's rho (ρ)	Pearson's r	Spearman's rho (ρ)
Dichotomous	Contingency table + chi-square (χ^2) + Cramér's V	Spearman's rho (ρ)	Spearman's rho (ρ)	phi (ϕ)

study. Although such inferences may be based on sound reasoning, they can only be inferences, and there is the possibility that the real pattern of causal direction is the opposite of that which is anticipated.

Contingency tables

Contingency tables are probably the most flexible of all methods of analysing relationships in that they can be employed in relation to any pair of variables, though they are not the most efficient method for some pairs, which is the reason why the method is not recommended in all the cells in Figure 15.6. A contingency table is like a frequency table but it allows two variables to be simultaneously analysed so that relationships between the two variables can be examined. It is normal for contingency tables to include percentages, since these make the tables easier to interpret. Table 15.4 examines the relationship between two variables from the gym survey: gender and reasons for visiting the gym. The percentages are *column percentages*—that is, they calculate the number in each **cell** as a percentage of the total number in that column. Thus, to take the top left-hand cell, the three men who go to the gym for relaxation are 7 per cent of all 42 men in the sample. Users of contingency tables often present the presumed independent variable (if one can in fact be presumed) as the column variable and the presumed dependent variable as the row variable. In this case, we are presuming that gender influences reasons for going to the gym. In fact, we know that going to the gym cannot

influence gender. In such circumstances, it is column rather than row percentages that will be required. The procedure for generating a contingency table with SPSS is described in Chapter 16.

Contingency tables are generated so that patterns of association can be searched for. In this case, we can see clear gender differences in reasons for visiting the gym. As our student anticipated, females are much more likely than men to go to the gym to lose weight. They are also somewhat more likely to go to the gym for relaxation. By

Table 15.4
Contingency table showing the relationship between gender and reasons for visiting the gym

Reasons	Gender			
	Male		Female	
	No.	%	No.	%
Relaxation	3	7	6	13
Fitness	15	36	16	33
Lose weight	8	19	25	52
Build strength	16	38	1	2
TOTAL	42		48	

Note: $\chi^2 = 22.726$ $p < 0.0001$.

contrast, men are much more likely to go to the gym to build strength. There is little difference between men and women in terms of fitness as a reason.

Pearson's *r*

Pearson's *r* is a method for examining relationships between interval/ratio variables. The chief features of this method are as follows:

- the coefficient will almost certainly lie between 0 (zero or no relationship between the two variables) and 1 (a perfect relationship)—this indicates the *strength* of a relationship;
- the closer the coefficient is to 1, the stronger the relationship; the closer it is to 0, the weaker the relationship;
- the coefficient will be either positive or negative—this indicates the *direction* of a relationship.

To illustrate these features consider Tips and skills 'Imaginary data from five variables to show different types of relationship' and the scatter diagrams in Figures 15.7–15.10, which look at the relationship between pairs of interval/ratio variables. The scatter diagram for variables 1 and 2 is presented in Figure 15.7 and shows a perfect **positive relationship**, which would have a Pearson's *r* correlation of 1. This means that, as one variable increases, the other variable increases by the same amount and that no other variable is related to either of them. If the correlation was below 1, it would mean that variable 1 is related to at least one other variable as well as to variable 2.

The scatter diagram for variables 2 and 3 (see Figure 15.8) shows a perfect **negative relationship**, which would have a Pearson's *r* correlation of −1. This means that, as one variable increases, the other variable decreases and that no other variable is related to either of them.

If there was no or virtually no correlation between the variables, there would be no apparent pattern to the markers in the scatter diagram. This is the case with the relationship between variables 2 and 5. The correlation is virtually zero at −0.041. This means that the variation in each variable is associated with other variables than the ones present in this analysis. Figure 15.9 shows the appropriate scatter diagram.

If a relationship is strong, a clear patterning to the variables will be evident. This is the case with variables 2 and 4, whose scatter diagram appears in Figure 15.10. There is clearly a positive relationship, and in fact the Pearson's *r* value is +0.88 (usually, positive correlations are presented without the + sign). This means that the variation in the two variables is very closely connected, but that there is some influence of other variables in the extent to which they vary.

Going back to the gym survey, we find that the correlation between age (var00002) and the amount of time

Tips and skills
Imaginary data from five variables to show different types of relationship

Variables 1	2	3	4	5
1	10	50	7	9
2	12	45	13	23
3	14	40	18	7
4	16	35	14	15
5	18	30	16	6
6	20	25	23	22
7	22	20	19	12
8	24	15	24	8
9	26	10	22	18
10	28	5	24	10

Figure 15.7
Scatter diagram showing a perfect positive relationship

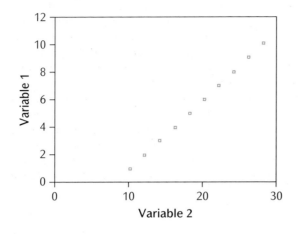

Figure 15.9
Scatter diagram showing two variables that are not related

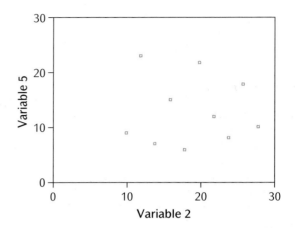

Figure 15.8
Scatter diagram showing a perfect negative relationship

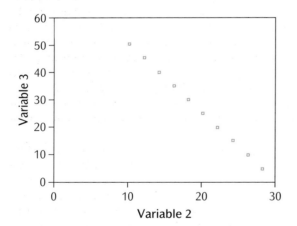

Figure 15.10
Scatter diagram showing a strong positive relationship

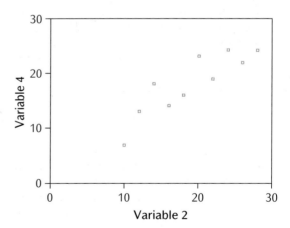

spent on weights equipment (var00011) is −0.27, implying a weak negative relationship. This suggests that there is a tendency such that, the older a person is, the less likely he or she is to spend much time on such equipment, but that other variables clearly influence the amount of time spent on this activity.

In order to be able to use Pearson's r, the relationship between the two variables must be broadly *linear*—that is, when plotted on a scatter diagram, the values of the two variables approximate to a straight line (even though they may be scattered, as in Figure 15.10) and do not curve. Therefore, plotting a scatter diagram before using

Pearson's r is important, in order to determine that the nature of the relationship between a pair of variables does not violate the assumptions being made when this method of correlation is employed.

If you square a value of Pearson's r, you can derive a further useful statistic—namely the *coefficient of determination*, which expresses how much of the variation in one variable is due to the other variable. Thus, if r is −0.27, r^2 is 0.0729. We can then express this as a percentage by multiplying r^2 by 100. The product of this exercise is 7 per cent. This means that just 7 per cent of the variation in the use of cardiovascular equipment is accounted for by age.

The coefficient of determination is a useful adjunct to the interpretation of correlation information.

The procedures for using SPSS to generate Pearson's *r* and scatter diagrams are described in Chapter 16.

Spearman's rho

Spearman's rho, which is often represented with the Greek letter ρ, is designed for the use of pairs of ordinal variables, but is also used, as suggested by Figure 15.6, when one variable is ordinal and the other is interval/ratio. It is exactly the same as Pearson's *r* in terms of the outcome of calculating it, in that the computed value of rho will be either positive or negative and will vary between 0 and 1. If we look at the gym study, there are three ordinal variables: var00004, var00005, and var00006 (see Table 15.1). If we use Spearman's rho to calculate the correlation between the first two variables, we find that the correlation between var00004 and var00005—frequency of use of the cardiovascular and weights equipment—is low at 0.2. A slightly stronger relationship is found between var00006 (frequency of going to the gym) and var00010 (amount of time spent on the cardiovascular equipment), which is 0.4. Note that the latter variable is an interval/ratio variable. When confronted with a situation in which we want to calculate the correlation between an ordinal and an interval/ratio variable, we cannot use Pearson's *r*, because both variables must be at the interval/ratio level of measurement. Instead, we must use Spearman's rho (see Figure 15.6). The procedure for generating Spearman's rho with SPSS is described in Chapter 16.

Phi and Cramér's *V*

Phi (φ) and **Cramér's *V*** are two closely related statistics. The phi coefficient is used for the analysis of the relationship between two dichotomous variables. Like Pearson's *r*, it results in a computed statistic that varies between 0 and + or −1. The correlation between var00001 (gender) and var00008 (other sources of regular exercise) is 0.24, implying that males are somewhat more likely than females to have other sources of regular exercise, though the relationship is weak.

Cramér's *V* uses a similar formula to phi and can be employed with nominal variables (see Figure 15.6). However, this statistic can take on only a positive value, so that it can give an indication only of the strength of the relationship between two variables, not of the direction. The value of Cramér's *V* associated with the analysis presented in Table 15.4 is 0.50. This suggests a moderate relationship between the two variables. Cramér's *V* is usually reported along with a contingency table and a **chi-square test** (see the subsection 'The chi-square test' below). It is not normally presented on its own. The procedure for generating phi and Cramér's *V* with SPSS is described in Chapter 16.

Comparing means and eta

If you need to examine the relationship between an interval/ratio variable and a nominal variable, and if the latter can be relatively unambiguously identified as the independent variable, a potentially fruitful approach is to compare the means of the interval/ratio variable for each subgroup of the nominal variable. As an example, consider Table 15.5, which presents the mean number of minutes spent on cardiovascular equipment (var00010) for each of the four categories of reasons for going to the gym (var00003). The means suggest that people who go to the gym for fitness or to lose weight spend considerably more time on this equipment than people who go to the gym to relax or to build strength.

This procedure is often accompanied by a test of association between variables called **eta**. This statistic expresses the level of association between the two variables and, like Cramér's *V*, will always be positive. The level of eta (η) for the data in Table 15.5 is 0.48. This suggests a moderate relationship between the two variables.

Table 15.5

Comparing subgroup means: time spent on cardiovascular equipment by reasons for going to the gym

Time	Reasons				
	Relaxation	Fitness	Lose weight	Build strength	Total
Mean number of minutes spent on cardiovascular equipment	18.33	30.55	28.36	19.65	26.47
n	9	31	33	17	90

Eta-squared expresses the amount of variation in the interval/ratio variable that is due to the nominal variable. In the case of this example, eta-squared is 22 per cent. Eta is a very flexible method for exploring the relationship between two variables, because it can be employed when one variable is nominal and the other interval/ratio. Also, it does not make the assumption that the relationship between variables is linear. The procedure for comparing means and for generating eta with SPSS is described in Chapter 16.

 ## Multivariate analysis

Multivariate analysis entails the simultaneous analysis of three or more variables. This is quite an advanced topic, and it is recommended that readers examine a textbook on quantitative data analysis for an exposition of techniques (e.g. Bryman and Cramer 2011). There are three main contexts within which multivariate analysis might be employed.

Could the relationship be spurious?

In order for a relationship between two variables to be established, not only must there be evidence that there is a relationship but the relationship must be shown to be *non-spurious*. A **spurious relationship** exists when there appears to be a relationship between two variables, but the relationship is not real: it is being produced because each variable is itself related to a third variable. For example, if we find a relationship between income and voting behaviour, we might ask: could the relationship be an artefact of age (see Figure 15.11)? The older one is, the more one is likely to earn, while age is known to influence voting behaviour. If age were found to be producing the apparent relationship between income and voting behaviour, we would conclude that the relationship is spurious. In this case, the variable of age would be known as a **confounding variable**.

An interesting possible case of a spurious relationship was highlighted in a very short report in *The Times* (1 October 1999, p. 2) of some medical findings. The article noted that there is evidence to suggest that women on hormone replacement therapy (HRT) have lower levels of heart disease than those not on this form of therapy. The article cites Swedish findings that suggest that the relationship may be due to the fact that women who choose to start the therapy are 'thinner, richer and healthier' than those who do not. These background factors would seem to affect both the likelihood of taking HRT *and* the likelihood of getting heart disease. A further illustration in connection with a health-related issue comes from another *Times* article (Hawkes 2003), which reports a relationship among men between frequency of shaving and likelihood of a heart attack or stroke. The reason appears to be that each of the variables (frequency of shaving and vulnerability to a heart attack or stroke) is affected by lifestyle and hormonal factors.

Could there be an intervening variable?

Let us say that we do not find that the relationship is spurious; we might ask *why* there is a relationship between two variables. For example, it is well known that there is a relationship between people's incomes and their voting behaviour. One possibility is that people of different incomes vary in their political attitudes, which in turn has implications for their voting behaviour. Political attitudes are thus an **intervening variable**:

income → political attitudes → voting behaviour

An intervening variable allows us to answer questions about the bivariate relationship between variables. It suggests that the relationship between the two variables is not a direct one, since the impact of people's income on their voting behaviour is viewed as occurring via their political attitudes. Intervening variables are sometimes called *mediating variables*.

Could a third variable moderate the relationship?

We might ask a question such as: does the relationship between two variables hold for men but not for women? If it does, the relationship is said to be moderated by gender. We might ask in the gym study, for example, if the relationship between age and whether visitors have other sources of regular exercise (var00008) is moderated by gender. This would imply that, if we find a pattern relating age to other sources of exercise, this pattern

Figure 15.11
A spurious relationship

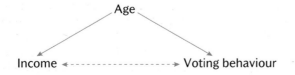

Table 15.6

Contingency table showing the relationship between age and whether or not gym visitors have other sources of regular exercise (%)

Other source of exercise	Age		
	30 and under	31–40	41 and over
Other source	64	43	58
No other source	36	57	42
n	42	23	24

Table 15.7

Contingency table showing the relationship between age and whether or not gym visitors have other sources of regular exercise for males and females (%)

Other source of exercise	Gender					
	Male			Female		
	30 and under	31–40	41 and over	30 and under	31–40	41 and over
Other source	70	33	75	59	50	42
No other source	30	67	25	41	50	58
n	20	9	12	22	14	12

will vary by gender. Table 15.6 shows the relationship between age and other sources of exercise. In this table, age has been broken down into just three age bands to make the table easier to read. The table suggests that the 31–40 age group is less likely to have other sources of regular exercise than the 30 and under and 41 and over age groups. However, Table 15.7, which breaks the relationship down by gender, suggests that the pattern for males and females is somewhat different. Among males, the pattern shown in Table 15.6 is very pronounced, but for females the likelihood of having other sources of exercise declines with age. It would seem that the relationship between age and other sources of exercise is a **moderated relationship** because it is moderated by gender. This example illustrates the way in which contingency tables can be used for multivariate analysis. However, there is a wide variety of other techniques (Bryman and Cramer 2011: Chapter 10). The procedure for conducting such an analysis with SPSS is described in Chapter 16.

 # Statistical significance

One difficulty with working on data deriving from a sample is that there is often the lingering worry that, even though you have employed a probability sampling procedure (as in the gym survey), your findings will not be generalizable to the population from which the sample was drawn. As we saw in Chapter 8, there is always the possibility that **sampling error** (difference between the population and the sample that you have selected) has occurred, even when probability sampling procedures have been followed. If this happens, the sample will be unrepresentative of the wider population and therefore any findings will be invalid. To make matters worse, there is no feasible way of finding out whether or not they do in fact apply to the population! What you can do is provide an indication of how confident you can be in your findings. This is where **statistical significance** and the various tests of statistical significance come in.

We need to know how confident we can be that our findings can be generalized to the population from which that sample was selected. Since we cannot be absolutely certain that a finding based on a sample will also be found in the population, we need a technique that allows us to establish how confident we can be that the finding exists in the population and what risk we are taking in inferring that the finding exists in the population. These two elements—confidence and risk—lie at the heart of tests of statistical significance (see Key concept 15.1). However, it is important to appreciate that tests of statistical significance can be employed only in relation to samples that have been drawn using probability sampling. The process of inferring findings from a probability sample to the population from which it was selected is known as **statistical inference**.

In Chapter 8 (see Tips and skills 'Generalizing from a random sample to the population'), in the context of the discussion of the standard error of the mean, we began to get an appreciation of the ideas behind statistical significance. For example, we know that the mean age of the gym sample is 33.6. Using the concept of the standard error of the mean, we can calculate that we can be 95 per cent confident that the population mean lies between 31.72 and 35.47. This suggests that we can determine in broad outline the degree of confidence that we can have in a sample mean.

In the rest of this section, we will look at the tests that are available for determining the degree of confidence we can have in our findings when we explore relationships between variables. All of the tests have a common structure.

- *Set up a null hypothesis.* A **null hypothesis** stipulates that two variables are not related in the population—for example, that there is *no* relationship between gender and visiting the gym in the population from which the sample was selected.

- *Establish the level of statistical significance that you find acceptable.* This is essentially a measure of the degree of risk that you might reject the null hypothesis (implying that there *is* a relationship in the population) when you should support it (implying that there is no relationship in the population). Levels of statistical significance are expressed as probability levels—that is, the probability of rejecting the null hypothesis when you should be confirming it. See Key concept 15.2 on this issue. The convention among most social researchers is that the maximum level of statistical significance that is acceptable is $p < 0.05$, which implies that there are fewer than 5 chances in 100 that you could have a sample that shows a relationship when there is not one in the population.

- *Determine the statistical significance of your findings* (that is, use a statistical test like chi-square—see the subsection 'The chi-square test' below).

- If your findings are statistically significant at the 0.05 level—so that the risk of getting a relationship as strong as the one you have found, when there is *no* relationship in the population, is no higher than 5 in 100—you would *reject* the null hypothesis. Therefore, you are implying that the results are unlikely to have occurred by *chance*.

There are in fact two types of error that can be made when inferring statistical significance. These errors are known as Type I and Type II errors (see Figure 15.12). A Type I error occurs when you reject the null hypothesis when it should in fact be confirmed. This means that your results have arisen by chance and you are falsely concluding that there is a relationship in the population when there is not one. Using a $p < 0.05$ level of significance

Key concept 15.1
What is a test of statistical significance?

A test of statistical significance allows the analyst to estimate how confident he or she can be that the results deriving from a study based on a randomly selected sample are generalizable to the population from which the sample was drawn. When examining statistical significance in relation to the relationship between two variables, it also tells us about the risk of concluding that there is in fact a relationship in the population when there is no such relationship in the population. If an analysis reveals a statistically significant finding, this does not mean that the finding is intrinsically significant or important. The word 'significant' seems to imply importance. However, statistical significance is solely concerned with the confidence researchers can have in their findings. It does not mean that a statistically significant finding is substantively significant.

Key concept 15.2
What is the level of statistical significance?

The level of statistical significance is the level of risk that you are prepared to take that you are inferring that there is a relationship between two variables in the population from which the sample was taken when in fact no such relationship exists. The maximum level of risk that is conventionally taken in social research is to say that there are up to 5 chances in 100 that we might be falsely concluding that there is a relationship when there is not one in the population from which the sample was taken. This means that, if we drew 100 samples, we are recognizing that as many as 5 of them might exhibit a relationship when there is not one in the population. Our sample might be one of those 5, but the risk is fairly small. This significance level is denoted by $p < 0.05$ (p means *probability*). If we accepted a significance level of $p < 0.1$, we would be accepting the possibility that as many as 10 in 100 samples might show a relationship where none exists in the population. In this case, there is a greater risk than with $p < 0.05$ that we might have a sample that implies a relationship when there is not one in the population, since the probability of our having such a sample is greater when the risk is 1 in 10 (10 out of 100 when $p < 0.1$) than when the risk is 1 in 20 (5 out of 100 when $p < 0.05$). Therefore, we would have greater confidence when the risk of falsely inferring that there is a relationship between two variables is 1 in 20, as against 1 in 10. But, if you want a more stringent test, perhaps because you are worried about the use that might be made of your results, you might choose the $p < 0.01$ level. This means that you are prepared to accept as your level of risk a probability of only 1 in 100 that the results could have arisen by chance (that is, due to sampling error). Therefore, if the results, following administration of a test, show that a relationship is statistically significant at the $p < 0.05$ level, but *not* the $p < 0.01$ level, you would have to confirm the null hypothesis.

means that we are more likely to make a Type I error than when using a $p < 0.01$ level of significance. This is because with 0.01 there is less chance of falsely rejecting the null hypothesis. However, in doing so, you increase the chance of making a Type II error (accepting the null hypothesis when you should reject it). This is because you are more likely to confirm the null hypothesis when the significance level is 0.01 (1 in 100) than when it is 0.05 (1 in 20).

The chi-square test

The chi-square (χ^2) test is applied to contingency tables like Table 15.4. It allows us to establish how confident we can be that there is a relationship between the two variables in the population. The test works by calculating for each cell in the table an expected frequency or value—that is, one that would occur on the basis of chance alone.

Figure 15.12
Type I and Type II errors

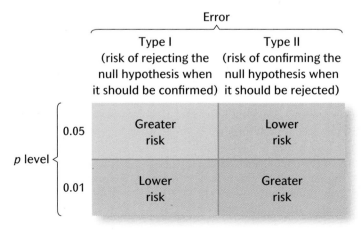

The chi-square value, which in Table 15.4 is 22.726, is produced by calculating the differences between the actual and expected values for each cell in the table and then summing those differences (it is slightly more complicated than this, but the details need not concern us here). The chi-square value means nothing on its own and can be meaningfully interpreted only in relation to its associated level of statistical significance, which in this case is $p < 0.0001$. This means that there is only 1 chance in 10,000 of falsely rejecting the null hypothesis (that is, inferring that there is a relationship in the population when there is no such relationship in the population). You could be extremely confident that there is a relationship between gender and reasons for visiting the gym among all gym members, since the chance that you have obtained a sample that shows a relationship when there is no relationship among all gym members is 1 in 10,000.

Whether or not a chi-square value achieves statistical significance depends not just on its magnitude but also on the number of categories of the two variables being analysed. This latter issue is governed by what is known as the 'degrees of freedom' associated with the table. The number of degrees of freedom is governed by the simple formula:

Number of degrees of freedom
= (number of columns − 1)(number of rows − 1).

In the case of Table 15.4, this will be $(2 - 1)(4 - 1)$—that is, 3. In other words, the chi-square value that is arrived at is affected by the size of the table, and this is taken into account when deciding whether the chi-square value is statistically significant or not. The procedure for chi-square in conjunction with a contingency table with SPSS is described in Chapter 16.

Correlation and statistical significance

Examining the statistical significance of a computed correlation coefficient, which is based on a randomly selected sample, provides information about the likelihood that the coefficient will be found in the population from which the sample was taken. Thus, if we find a correlation of −0.62, what is the likelihood that a relationship of at least that size exists in the population? This tells us if the relationship could have arisen by chance.

If the correlation coefficient r is −0.62 and the significance level is $p < 0.05$, we can reject the null hypothesis that there is no relationship in the population. We can infer that there are only 5 chances in 100 that a correlation of at least −0.62 could have arisen by chance alone. You *could* have 1 of the 5 samples in 100 that shows a

relationship when there is not one in the population, but the degree of risk is reasonably small. If, say, it was found that $r = -0.62$ and $p < 0.1$, there could be as many as 10 chances in 100 that there is no correlation in the population. This would *not* be an acceptable level of risk for most purposes. It would mean that in as many as 1 sample in 10 we might find a correlation of −0.62 or above when there is not a correlation in the population. If $r = -0.62$ and $p < 0.001$, there is only 1 chance in 1,000 that no correlation exists in the population. There would be a very low level of risk if you inferred that the correlation had not arisen by chance.

Whether a correlation coefficient is statistically significant or not will be affected by two factors:

1. the size of the computed coefficient; and
2. the size of the sample.

This second factor may appear surprising. Basically, the larger a sample, the more likely it is that a computed correlation coefficient will be found to be statistically significant. Thus, even though the correlation between age and the amount of time spent on weights machines in the gym survey was found to be just −0.27, which is a fairly weak relationship, it is statistically significant at the $p < 0.01$ level. This means that there is only 1 chance in 100 that there is no relationship in the population. Because the question of whether or not a correlation coefficient is statistically significant depends so much on the sample size, it is important to realize that you should always examine *both* the correlation coefficient *and* the significance level. You should not examine one at the expense of the other.

This treatment of correlation and statistical significance applies to both Pearson's r and Spearman's rho. A similar interpretation can also be applied to phi and to Cramér's V. SPSS automatically produces information regarding statistical significance when Pearson's r, Spearman's rho, phi, and Cramér's V are generated.

Comparing means and statistical significance

A test of statistical significance can also be applied to the comparison of means that was carried out in Table 15.5. This procedure entails treating the total amount of variation in the dependent variable—amount of time spent on cardiovascular equipment—as made up of two types: variation *within* the four subgroups that make up the independent variable, and variation *between* them. The latter is often called the *explained variance* and the former the *error variance*. A test of statistical significance for the comparison of means entails relating the two types of variance to form what is known as the F statistic. This statistic expresses the amount of explained variance in relation to the amount of error variance. In the case of the data in Table 15.5, the resulting *F* statistic is statistically significant at the $p < 0.001$ level. This finding suggests that there is only 1 chance in 1,000 that there is no relationship between the two variables among all gym members. SPSS produces information regarding the *F* statistic and its statistical significance if the procedures described in Chapter 16 are followed.

Checklist
Doing and writing up quantitative data analysis

○ Have you answered your research questions?

○ Have you made sure that you have presented only analyses that are relevant to your research questions?

○ Have you made sure that you have taken into account the nature of the variable(s) being analysed when using a particular technique (that is, whether nominal, ordinal, interval/ratio, or dichotomous)?

○ Have you used the most appropriate and powerful techniques for answering your research questions?

○ If your sample has *not* been randomly selected, have you made sure that you have not made inferences about a population (or at least, if you have done so, have you outlined the limitations of making such an inference)?

○ If your data are based on a cross-sectional design, have you resisted making unsustainable inferences about causality?

○ Have you remembered to code any missing data?

○ Have you commented on all the analyses you present?

○ Have you gone beyond univariate analysis and conducted at least some bivariate analyses?

○ If you have used a Likert scale with reversed items, have you remembered to reverse the coding of them?

Key points

● You need to think about your data analysis before you begin designing your research instruments.

● Techniques of data analysis are applicable to some types of variable and not others. You need to know the difference between nominal, ordinal, interval/ratio, and dichotomous variables.

● You need to think about the kinds of data you are collecting and the implications your decisions will have for the sorts of techniques you will be able to employ.

● Become familiar with computer software like SPSS before you begin designing your research instruments, because it is advisable to be aware at an early stage of difficulties you might have in presenting your data in SPSS.

● Make sure you are thoroughly familiar with the techniques introduced in this chapter and when you can and cannot use them.

● The basic message, then, is not to leave these considerations until your data have been collected, tempting though it may be.

● Do not confuse statistical significance with substantive significance.

Questions for review

- At what stage should you begin to think about the kinds of data analysis you need to conduct?
- What are missing data and why do they arise?

Types of variable

- What are the differences between the four types of variable outlined in this chapter: interval/ratio; ordinal; nominal; and dichotomous?
- Why is it important to be able to distinguish between the four types of variable?
- Imagine the kinds of answers you would receive if you administered the following four questions in an interview survey. What kind of variable would each question generate: dichotomous; nominal; ordinal; or interval/ratio?

  1. Do you enjoy going shopping?

     Yes   ____

     No   ____

  2. How many times have you shopped in the last month? Please write in the number of occasions below.

     ____

  3. For which kinds of items do you most enjoy shopping? Please tick one only.

     Clothes (including shoes)   ____

     Food   ____

     Things for the house   ____

     Presents   ____

     Entertainment (CDs, videos, etc.)   ____

  4. How important is it to you to buy clothes with designer labels?

     Very important   ____

     Fairly important   ____

     Not very important   ____

     Not at all important   ____

Univariate analysis

- What is an outlier and why might one have an adverse effect on the mean and the range?
- In conjunction with which measure of central tendency would you expect to report the standard deviation: the mean; the median; or the mode?

Bivariate analysis

- Can you infer causality from bivariate analysis?
- Why are percentages crucial when presenting contingency tables?
- In what circumstances would you use each of the following: Pearson's r; Spearman's rho; phi; Cramér's V; eta?

Multivariate analysis

- What is a spurious relationship?
- What is an intervening variable?
- What does it mean to say that a relationship is moderated?

Statistical significance

● What does statistical significance mean and how does it differ from substantive significance?

● What is a significance level?

● What does the chi-square test achieve?

● What does it mean to say that a correlation of 0.42 is statistically significant at $p < 0.05$?

Online Resource Centre

www.oxfordtextbooks.co.uk/orc/brymansrm5e/

Visit the Online Resource Centre to enrich your understanding of quantitative data analysis. Follow up links to other resources, test yourself using multiple choice questions, and gain further guidance and inspiration from the Student Researcher's Toolkit.

16

Using IBM SPSS statistics

Chapter guide

Chapter guide

In order to implement the techniques that you learned in Chapter 15, you would need to do either of two things: learn the underlying formula for each technique and apply your data to it, or use computer software to analyse your data. The latter is the approach chosen in this book for two main reasons.

- It is closer to the way in which quantitative data analysis is carried out in real research nowadays.
- It helps to equip you with a useful transferable skill.

You will be learning IBM SPSS Statistics, which is the most widely used package of computer software for doing this kind of analysis. It is relatively straightforward to use. I will be continuing to refer to the techniques introduced in Chapter 15 and will continue to use the gym survey as an example.

This chapter largely operates in parallel to Chapter 15, so that you can see the links between the techniques learned there and the use of SPSS to implement them.

Introduction

This chapter aims to provide a familiarity with some basic aspects of SPSS for Windows, which is possibly the most widely used computer software for the analysis of quantitative data for social scientists. SPSS, which originally was short for Statistical Package for the Social Sciences, has been in existence since the mid-1960s and over the years has undergone many revisions, particularly since the arrival of personal computers. It is now known as IBM SPSS Statistics and the version that was used in preparing this chapter was Release 22. The gym survey used in Chapter 15 will be employed to illustrate SPSS operations and methods of analysis. The aim of this chapter is to introduce ways of using SPSS to implement the methods of analysis discussed in Chapter 15.

SPSS operations will be presented in **bold**, for example, **Variable Name:** and **Analyze**. Names given to variables in the course of using SPSS will be presented in ***bold italics***, e.g. ***gender*** and ***reasons***. Labels given to values or to variables are also in bold but not in italic, e.g. **reasons for visiting** and **male**. Tips and skills 'Basic operations in SPSS' presents a list summarizing these terms. One further element in the presentation is that a right-pointing arrow ($\rightarrow$) will be used to denote 'click once with the left-hand button of your mouse'. This action is employed to make selections and similar activities.

Tips and skills
Basic operations in SPSS

- The **SPSS Data Editor**. This is the sphere of SPSS into which data are entered and subsequently edited and defined. It is made up of two screens: the **Data Viewer** and the **Variable Viewer**. You move between these two viewers by selecting the appropriate tab at the bottom of the screen.

- The **Data Viewer**. This is the spreadsheet into which your data are entered. When you start up SPSS, the **Data Viewer** will be facing you.

- The **Variable Viewer**. This is another spreadsheet, but this one displays information about each of the variables and allows you to change that information. It is the platform from which you provide for each variable such information as: the variable name; a variable label; and value labels (as described below in this list).

- The **Output Viewer**. When you perform an analysis or produce a diagram (called a 'chart' in SPSS), your output will be deposited here. The **Output Viewer** superimposes itself over the **Data Editor** after an analysis has been performed or a chart generated.

- A **Variable Name**. This is the name that you give to a variable, e.g. ***gender***. The name must be no more than eight characters. Until you give a variable a name, it will be referred to as *var00001*, etc. When the variable has been given a name, it will appear in the column for that variable in the **Data Viewer**. Variable names are generated from the **Variable Viewer**.

- A **Variable Label**. This is a label that you can give to a variable but which is not restricted to eight characters. Spaces can be used, e.g. **reasons for visiting**. The label will appear in any output you generate. Variable labels are generated from the **Variable Viewer**.

- A **Value Label**. This is a label that you can attach to a code that has been used when entering data for all types of variables other than interval/ratio variables. Thus, for var00001, we would attach the label **male** to 1 and **female** to 2. When you generate output, such as a frequency table or chart, the labels for each value will be presented. This makes the interpretation of output easier. Value labels are generated from the **Variable Viewer**.

- **Missing Values** . . . When you do not have data for a particular variable when entering data for a case, you must specify how you are denoting missing values for that variable. Missing values are generated from the **Variable Viewer**.

- **Recode**. A procedure that allows codes or numbers to be changed. It is especially helpful when you need to combine groups of people—for example, when producing age bands.

- **Compute** . . . A procedure that allows you to combine two or more variables to form a new variable.
- **Analyze**. This is the point on the menu bar above the **Data Viewer** from which you choose (via a drop-down menu) which method of analysis you want to select. Note that, whenever an item on a menu appears with a right-pointing arrowhead after it, this means that, if you select that option, a further menu will follow on.
- **Graphs**. This is the point on the menu bar above the **Data Viewer** from which you choose (via a drop-down menu) which type of chart you want to use.
- **Chart Editor**. When you produce a graph, you can edit it with the **Chart Editor**. To activate this editor, double-click anywhere in the graph. A small chart editor window will appear and your main graph will appear opaque until you exit the Editor. From the Editor, you can make various changes and enhancements to your graph.

Getting started in SPSS

Beginning SPSS

To start SPSS, double-click on the **IBM SPSS Statistics** icon on your computer screen. If there is no icon, → the Start button in the bottom left-hand corner of your screen. From the menu of programs, → **SPSS Inc**. A follow-on menu will appear, from which you should select **IBM SPSS Statistics 22**. When SPSS loads, you *may* be faced with an opening dialog box with the title 'What do you want to do?' and a list of options. Many users prefer to disable this opening box. It is not important in relation to the following exposition, so → **Cancel**. You will then be faced with the **SPSS Data Editor**. This is made up of two components: **Data View** and **Variable View**. In the following discussion, these two screens are referred to as the **Data Viewer** and the **Variable Viewer**. You move between these two viewers by selecting the appropriate tab at the bottom of the screen. The **Data Viewer** is in the form of a spreadsheet grid into which you enter your data. The columns represent *variables*—in other words, information from the responses given by each person in the gym study sample. Until data are entered and names are given to variables, each column simply has **var** as its heading. The rows represent *cases*, which can be people (as in the example you will be working through) or any unit of analysis. Each block in the grid is referred to as a 'cell'. Note also that when the data are in the SPSS spreadsheet, they will look different; for example, 1 will be 1.00.

Entering data in the Data Viewer

To input the data into the **Data Viewer**, make sure that the top left-hand cell in the grid is highlighted (see Plate 16.1). If it is not highlighted, simply click once in that cell. Then, type the appropriate figure for that cell. If you were entering data from the gym survey, the figure would be 1 (the first value shown in the gym survey data from Chapter 15). This number goes directly into that cell and into the box beneath the toolbar. As an alternative to using the mouse, many people find it easier to use the arrow keys on their keyboard to move from cell to cell. If you make a mistake at any point, simply click once in the cell in question, type in the correct value, and click once more in that cell. When you have finished, you should end up in the bottom right-hand cell of what will be a perfect rectangle of data. Plate 16.2 shows the **Data Viewer** with the data from the gym survey entered (though only part of the set of data is visible, in that only the first thirty-one respondents are visible). The first row of data contains the coded answers from the completed questionnaire in Chapter 15 (see Tips and skills 'A completed and processed questionnaire').

In order to proceed further, you will find that SPSS works in the following typical sequence for defining variables and analysing your data.

1. You make a selection from the menu bar at the top of the screen, e.g. → **Analyze.**

2. From the menu that will appear, make a selection, e.g. → **Descriptive Statistics**.

3. This will bring up a *dialog box* into which you will usually inform SPSS of what you are trying to do—e.g. which variables are to be analysed.

4. Very often, you then need to convey further information and to do this you have to → a button that will bring up what is called, following Bryman and Cramer (2011), a *sub-dialog box*.

Plate 16.1
The SPSS Data Viewer

Each row represents a case

Each column represents a variable

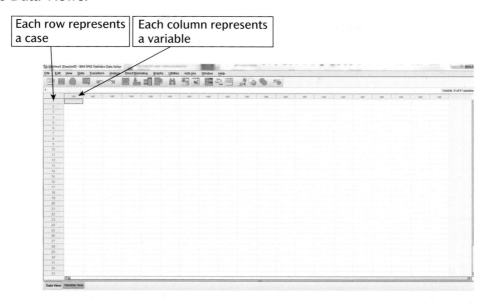

Plate 16.2
The Data Viewer with 'gym study' data entered

This row shows the data for the first person who completed the Gym Survey questionnaire

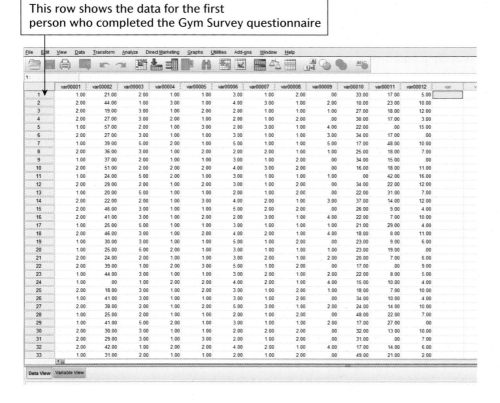

	var00001	var00002	var00003	var00004	var00005	var00006	var00007	var00008	var00009	var00010	var00011	var00012
1	1.00	21.00	2.00	1.00	1.00	3.00	1.00	2.00	.00	33.00	17.00	5.00
2	2.00	44.00	1.00	3.00	1.00	4.00	3.00	1.00	2.00	10.00	23.00	10.00
3	2.00	19.00	3.00	1.00	2.00	2.00	1.00	1.00	1.00	27.00	18.00	12.00
4	2.00	27.00	3.00	2.00	1.00	2.00	1.00	2.00	.00	30.00	17.00	3.00
5	1.00	57.00	2.00	1.00	3.00	2.00	3.00	1.00	4.00	22.00	.00	15.00
6	2.00	27.00	3.00	1.00	1.00	3.00	1.00	1.00	3.00	34.00	17.00	.00
7	1.00	39.00	5.00	2.00	1.00	5.00	1.00	1.00	5.00	17.00	48.00	10.00
8	2.00	36.00	3.00	1.00	2.00	2.00	2.00	1.00	1.00	25.00	18.00	7.00
9	1.00	37.00	2.00	1.00	1.00	3.00	1.00	2.00	.00	34.00	15.00	.00
10	2.00	51.00	2.00	2.00	2.00	4.00	3.00	2.00	.00	16.00	18.00	11.00
11	1.00	24.00	5.00	2.00	1.00	3.00	1.00	1.00	1.00	.00	42.00	16.00
12	2.00	29.00	2.00	1.00	2.00	3.00	1.00	2.00	.00	34.00	22.00	12.00
13	1.00	20.00	5.00	1.00	1.00	2.00	1.00	2.00	.00	22.00	31.00	7.00
14	2.00	22.00	2.00	1.00	3.00	4.00	2.00	1.00	3.00	37.00	14.00	12.00
15	2.00	46.00	3.00	1.00	1.00	5.00	2.00	2.00	.00	26.00	9.00	4.00
16	2.00	41.00	3.00	1.00	2.00	2.00	3.00	1.00	4.00	22.00	7.00	10.00
17	1.00	25.00	5.00	1.00	1.00	3.00	1.00	1.00	1.00	21.00	29.00	4.00
18	2.00	46.00	3.00	1.00	2.00	4.00	2.00	1.00	4.00	18.00	8.00	11.00
19	1.00	30.00	3.00	1.00	1.00	5.00	1.00	2.00	.00	23.00	9.00	6.00
20	1.00	25.00	5.00	2.00	1.00	3.00	1.00	1.00	1.00	23.00	19.00	.00
21	2.00	24.00	2.00	1.00	1.00	3.00	2.00	1.00	2.00	20.00	7.00	6.00
22	2.00	39.00	1.00	2.00	3.00	5.00	1.00	2.00	.00	17.00	.00	9.00
23	1.00	44.00	3.00	1.00	1.00	3.00	2.00	1.00	2.00	22.00	8.00	5.00
24	1.00	.00	1.00	2.00	2.00	4.00	2.00	1.00	4.00	15.00	10.00	4.00
25	2.00	18.00	3.00	1.00	2.00	3.00	1.00	2.00	1.00	18.00	7.00	10.00
26	1.00	41.00	3.00	1.00	1.00	3.00	1.00	2.00	.00	34.00	10.00	4.00
27	2.00	38.00	2.00	1.00	2.00	5.00	3.00	1.00	2.00	24.00	14.00	10.00
28	1.00	25.00	2.00	1.00	1.00	2.00	1.00	2.00	.00	48.00	22.00	7.00
29	1.00	41.00	5.00	2.00	1.00	3.00	1.00	1.00	2.00	17.00	27.00	.00
30	2.00	30.00	3.00	1.00	1.00	2.00	2.00	2.00	.00	32.00	13.00	10.00
31	2.00	29.00	3.00	1.00	3.00	2.00	1.00	2.00	.00	31.00	.00	7.00
32	2.00	42.00	1.00	2.00	2.00	4.00	2.00	1.00	4.00	17.00	14.00	6.00
33	1.00	31.00	2.00	1.00	1.00	2.00	1.00	2.00	.00	49.00	21.00	2.00

5. You then provide the information in the sub-dialog box and then go back to the dialog box. Sometimes, you will need to bring up a further sub-dialog box and then go back to the dialog box.

When you have finished going through the entire procedure, → **OK**. The toolbar beneath the menu bar allows shortcut access to certain SPSS operations.

Defining variables: variable names, missing values, variable labels, and value labels

Once you have finished entering your data, you need to define your variables. The following steps will allow you to do this:

1. → the **Variable View** tab at the bottom of the **Data Viewer** (opens the **Variable Viewer** shown in Plate 16.3).

2. To provide a variable name, click on the current variable name (e.g. *var00003*) and type the name you want to give it (e.g. *reasons*). Remember that this name must be no more than eight characters and you *cannot* use spaces.

3. You can then give your variable a more detailed name, known in SPSS as a variable label. To do this, → the cell in the **Label** column relating to the variable for which you want to supply a variable label. Then, simply type in the variable label (i.e. **reasons for visiting**).

4. Then you will need to provide 'value labels' for variables that have been given codes. The procedure generally applies to variables that are not interval/ratio variables. The latter, which are numeric variables, do not need to be coded (unless you are grouping them in some way). To assign value labels, → in the **Values** column relating to the variable you are working on. A small button with three dots on it will appear. → the button. The **Value Labels** dialog box will appear (see Plate 16.4). → the box to the right of **Value** and begin to define the value labels. To do this, enter the value (e.g. **1**) in the area to the right of **Value:** and then the value label (e.g. **relaxation**) in the area to the right of **Label:**. Then → **Add**. Do this for each value. When you have finished → **OK**.

5. You will then need to inform SPSS of the value that you have nominated for each variable to indicate a missing value. In the case of *reasons*, the value is 0 (zero). To assign the missing value, → the cell for this variable in the **Missing** column. Again, → the button that will appear with three dots on it. This will generate the **Missing Values** dialog box (see Plate 16.5). In the **Missing Values** dialog box, enter the missing value (**0**) below **Discrete missing values** and then → **OK**.

In order to simplify the following presentation, *reasons* will be the only variable for which a variable label will be defined.

Plate 16.3
The Variable Viewer

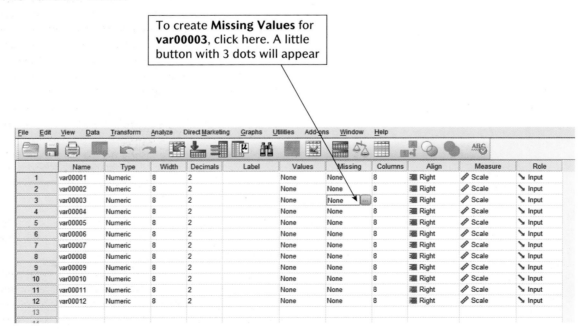

To create **Missing Values** for **var00003**, click here. A little button with 3 dots will appear

Plate 16.4
The Value Labels dialog box

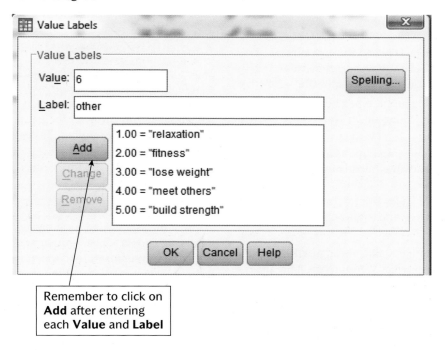

Remember to click on **Add** after entering each **Value** and **Label**

Plate 16.5
The Missing Values dialog box

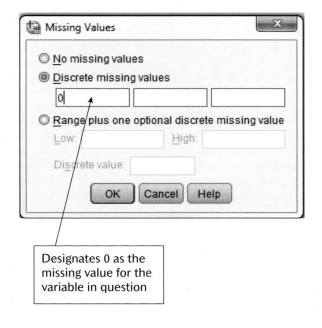

Designates 0 as the missing value for the variable in question

Recoding variables

Sometimes you need to recode variables—for example, when you want to group people. You would need to do this in order to produce a table like Table 15.3 for an interval/ratio variable such as **var00002**, which we will give the variable name *age*. SPSS offers two choices: you can recode *age* so that it will be changed in the **Data Viewer**, or you can keep *age* as it is and create a new variable. This latter option is desirable whenever you want to preserve the variable in question as well as create a new one. Since we may want to carry out analyses involving *age* as an interval/ratio variable, we will recode it so that a new variable, which we will call *agegp*, for *age* groups, will be created. The aim of the following operations is to create a new variable—*agegp*—which will comprise five age bands, as in Table 15.3.

1. From the menu bar, → **Transform** → **Recode** → **Into Different Variables** . . . [opens the **Recode into Different Variables** dialog box shown in Plate 16.6]

2. → *age* → ⊡ [puts *age* in **Numeric Variable** -> **Output Variable:** box] → box beneath **Output Variable Name:** and type *agegp* → **Change** [puts *agegp* in the **Numeric Variable** -> **Output Variable:** box] → **Old and New**

Values . . . [opens **Recode into Different Variables: Old and New Values** sub-dialog box shown in Plate 16.7]

3. → the circle by **System- or user-missing** and by **System-missing** under **New Value**, if you have missing values for a variable, which is the case for this variable → **Add**

4. → circle by **Range, LOWEST through value:** and type **20** in the box → box by **Value** under **New Value** and type **1** → **Add** [the new value will appear in the **Old -> New:** box]

5. → first box by **Range:** and type **21** in box after **through** type **30** → box by **Value** under **New Value** and type **2** → **Add**

6. → first box by **Range:** and type **31** in box after **through** type **40** → box by **Value** under **New Value** and type **3** → **Add**

7. → first box by **Range:** and type **41** in box and after **through** type **50** → box by **Value** under **New Value** and type **4** → **Add**

8. → circle by **Range, value through HIGHEST** and type **51** in the box → box by **Value** in **New Value** and type **5** → **Add** → **Continue** [closes the **Recode into Different Variables: Old and New Values** sub-dialog box shown in Plate 16.7 and returns you to the **Recode into Different Variables** dialog box shown in Plate 16.6]

9. → **OK**

The new variable *agegp* will be created and will appear in the **Data Viewer**. You would then need to generate **value labels** for the five age bands and possibly a **variable label** using the approach described above.

Computing a new variable

A person's total amount of time spent in the gym is made up of three variables: *cardmins*, *weimins*, and *othmins*. If we add these up, we should arrive at the total number of minutes spent on activities in the gym. In so doing, we will create a new variable *totalmin*. To do this, this procedure should be followed:

1. → **Transform** → **Compute** . . . [opens the **Compute Variable** dialog box shown in Plate 16.8]

2. under **Target Variable:** type *totalmin*

3. from the list of variables at the left, → *cardmins* ▸ [puts *cardmins* in box beneath **Numeric Expression:**] → **+ button** → *weimins* ▸ [puts *weimins* after + sign] → **+** button → *othmins* ▸ [puts *othmins* after + sign]

4. → **OK**

The new variable *totalmin* will be created and will appear in the **Data Editor**.

Now at last, we can begin to analyse the data!

Plate 16.6

The Recode into Different Variables dialog box

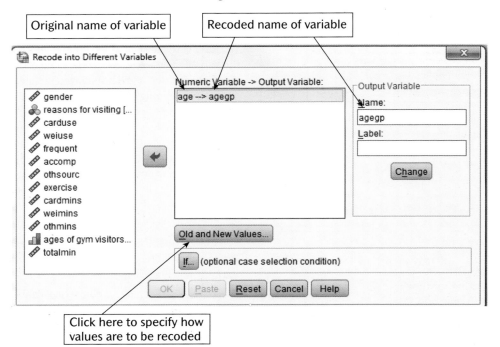

Plate 16.7
The Recode into Different Variables: Old and New Values sub-dialog box

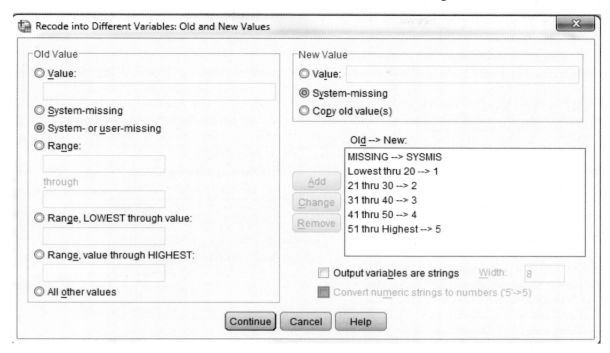

Plate 16.8
The Compute Variable dialog box

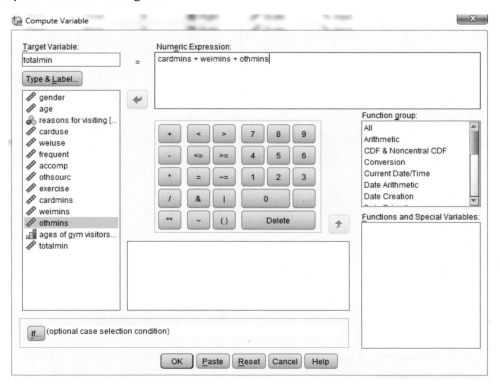

Data analysis with SPSS

Generating a frequency table

To produce a frequency table like the one in Table 15.2:

1. → **Analyze** → **Descriptive Statistics** → **Frequencies** . . . [opens the **Frequencies** dialog box shown in Plate 16.9]

2. → **reasons for visiting** → ▸ [puts **reasons for visiting** in **Variable[s]:** box]

3. → **OK**

The table will appear in the **Output Viewer** (see Plate 16.10).

Plate 16.9
The Frequencies dialog box

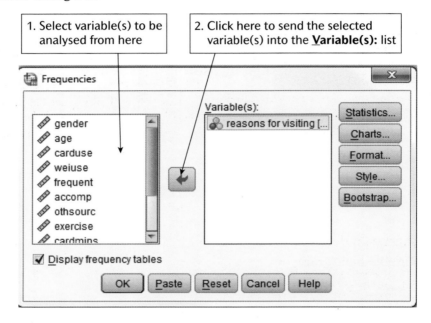

1. Select variable(s) to be analysed from here

2. Click here to send the selected variable(s) into the **Variable(s):** list

Plate 16.10
The Output Viewer with Frequency table

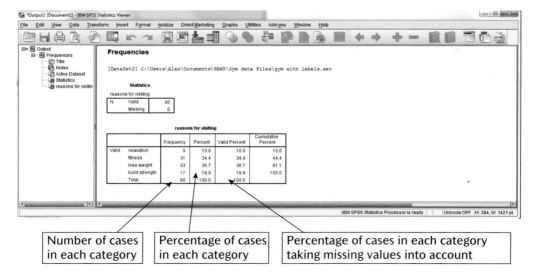

Number of cases in each category

Percentage of cases in each category

Percentage of cases in each category taking missing values into account

Note that in the **Frequencies** dialog box, variables that have been assigned labels will appear in terms of their variable labels, but those that have not been assigned labels will appear in terms of their variable names. This is a feature of all dialog boxes produced via **Analyze** and **Graphs** as discussed in the next subsections.

Generating a bar chart

To produce a bar chart like the one in Figure 15.2:

1. → **G**raphs → **C**hart Builder . . . [opens **Chart Builder** dialog box shown in Plate 16.11]

2. → **Bar** below **C**hoose from: and then → the simple bar format in the top left-hand corner of the **Gallery** and drag and drop it into the area above it. Then → *age* and drag and drop in the same way as for a bar chart.

3. → **reasons for visiting** from below **V**ariables: and drag and drop into area marked in blue **X-Axis?**

4. → **OK**

Generating a pie chart

To produce a pie chart like the one in Figure 15.3:

1. → **G**raphs → **C**hart Builder . . . [opens the **Chart Builder** dialog box shown in Plate 16.12] → **Pie/Polar** below **C**hoose from: and then → the pie chart format in the top left-hand corner of the **Gallery** and drag and drop it into the area above it.

2. → **reasons for visiting** from below **V**ariables: and drag and drop into area marked in blue **Slice by?**

3. → **OK**

In order to include percentages, as in Figure 15.3, *double-click* anywhere in the chart in order to bring up the **Chart Editor**. The chart will appear in the **Chart Editor** and the main figure will become opaque. Then → **Elements** and then → **Show D**ata Labels. This will place percentages in each slice as a default. If you want the frequencies, → **Count** in the **Properties** sub-dialog box that appears simultaneously (see Plate 16.12).

Plate 16.11
Creating a bar chart with the Chart Builder

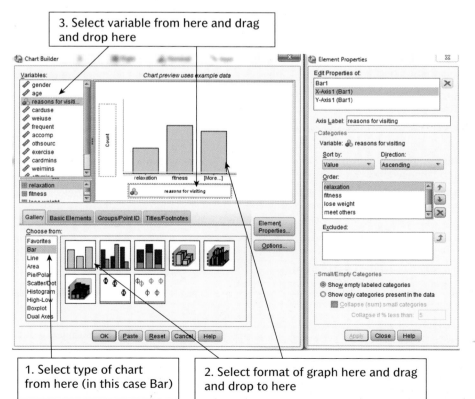

Plate 16.12

Creating a pie chart with the Chart Builder and Properties box

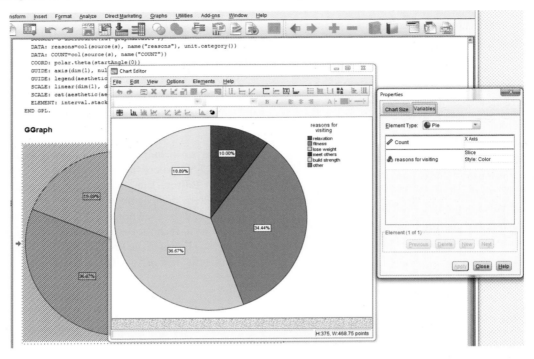

Your chart will be in colour, but, if you have access only to a monochrome printer, you can change your pie chart into patterns, which allows the slices to be clearer. This can be done through the **Chart Editor**.

Generating a histogram

In order to generate a histogram for an interval/ratio variable such as *age*, → **Graphs** → **Chart Builder** . . . [opens the **Chart Builder** dialog box shown in Plate 16.12] → **Histogram** below **Choose from:** and then → the histogram format you prefer from the **Gallery** and drag and drop it into the area above it. Then → *age* and drag and drop it in the same way as for a bar chart. This procedure will generate a histogram whose age bands are defined by the software. By double-clicking on the diagram, the histogram can be edited using the **Chart Editor**.

Generating the arithmetic mean, median, standard deviation, range, and boxplots

To produce the mean, median, standard deviation, and the range for an interval/ratio variable like *age*, these steps should be followed:

1. → **Analyze** → **Descriptive Statistics** → **Explore** . . . [opens the **Explore** dialog box]

2. → *age* → ▣ to the left of **Dependent List:** [puts *age* in the **Dependent List:** box] → **Statistics** under **Display** → **OK**

The output will also include the 95 per cent confidence interval for the mean, which is based on the standard error of the mean. The output can be found in Table 16.1. If you select **Plots** . . . , the **Explore: Plots** sub-dialog box will come up and you can elect to generate a histogram. To do this, you will need to select either **Both** or **Plots** under **Display** on the **Explore** dialog box. In addition, selecting **Both** or **Plots** will produce two further types of figure, one of which is a boxplot, which was covered in Chapter 15.

Generating a contingency table, chi-square, and Cramér's *V*

In order to generate a contingency table, like that in Table 15.4, along with a chi-square test and Cramér's *V*, follow this procedure: → **Analyze** → **Descriptive Statistics** → **Crosstabs** . . . [opens the **Crosstabs** dialog box shown in Plate 16.13]

Table 16.1
Explore output for *age* (SPSS output)

Explore

Case Processing Summary

	Cases					
	Valid		Missing		Total	
	N	Percent	N	Percent	N	Percent
age	89	98.9%	1	1.1%	90	100.0%

Descriptives

			Statistic	Std. Error
age	Mean		33.5955	.94197
	95% Confidence	Lower Bound	31.7235	
	Interval for Mean	Upper Bound	35.4675	
	5% Trimmed Mean		33.3159	
	Median		31.0000	
	Variance		78.971	
	Std. Deviation		8.88656	
	Minimum		18.00	
	Maximum		57.00	
	Range		39.00	
	Interquartile Range		14.00	
	Skewness		.446	.255
	Kurtosis		-.645	.506

1. → **reasons for visiting** → ⮕ by **Row[s]** [**reasons for visiting** will appear in the **Row[s]:** box] → *gender* → ⮕ by **Column[s]:** [*gender* will appear in the **Column[s]:** box] → **Cells** . . . [opens **Cross-tabs: Cell Display** sub-dialog box shown in Plate 16.14]

2. Make sure **Observed** in the **Counts** box has been selected. Make sure **Column** under **Percentages** has been selected. If either of these has not been selected, simply click at the relevant point. → **Continue** [closes **Crosstabs: Cell Display** sub-dialog box and returns you to the **Crosstabs** dialog box shown in Plate 16.13]

3. → **Statistics** . . . [opens the **Crosstabs: Statistics** sub-dialog box shown in Plate 16.15]

4. → **Chi-square** → **Phi and Cramér's *V*** → **Continue** [closes **Crosstabs: Statistics** sub-dialog box and returns you to the **Crosstabs** dialog box shown in Plate 16.13]

5. → **OK**

The resulting output can be found in Table 16.2.

If you have a table with two dichotomous variables, you would use the same sequence of steps to produce phi.

Generating Pearson's *r* and Spearman's rho

To produce Pearson's *r* in order to find the correlations between *age*, *cardmins*, and *weimins*, follow these steps:

1. → **Analyze** → **Correlate** → **Bivariate** . . . [opens **Bivariate Correlations** dialog box shown in Plate 16.16]

2. → *age* → ⮕ → *cardmins* → ⮕ → *weimins* → ⮕ [*age*, *cardmins*, and *weimins* should now be in the **Variables:** box] → **Pearson** [*if* not already selected] → **OK**

The resulting output is in Table 16.3.

To produce correlations with Spearman's rho, follow the same procedure, but, instead of selecting **Pearson**, you should → **Spearman** instead.

Generating scatter diagrams

Scatter diagrams, known as **scatterplots** in SPSS, are produced in the following way. Let us say that we want to plot the relationship between *age* and *cardmins*. There

Table 16.2

Contingency table for *reasons for visiting* by *gender* (SPSS output)

Crosstabs

Case Processing Summary

	Cases					
	Valid		Missing		Total	
	N	Percent	N	Percent	N	Percent
reasons for visiting * gender	90	100.0%	0	0.0%	90	100.0%

reasons for visiting * gender Crosstabulation

			gender		Total
			Male	Female	
reasons for visiting	relaxation	Count	3	6	9
		% within gender	7.1%	12.5%	10.0%
	fitness	Count	15	16	31
		% within gender	35.7%	33.3%	34.4%
	lose weight	Count	8	25	33
		% within gender	19.0%	52.1%	36.7%
	build strength	Count	16	1	17
		% within gender	38.1%	2.1%	18.9%
Total		Count	42	48	90
		% within gender	100.0%	100.0%	100.0%

Chi-Square Tests

	Value	df	Asymp. Sig. (2-sided)
Pearson Chi-Square	22.726[a]	3	.000
Likelihood Ratio	25.805	3	.000
Linear-by-Linear Association	9.716	1	.002
N of Valid Cases	90		

a. 2 cells (25.0%) have expected count less than 5. The minimum expected count is 4.20.

Interprets the Pearson Chi-Square values for information about chi-square

Symmetric Measures

		Value	Approx. Sig.
Nominal by Nominal	Phi	.503	.000
	Cramer's V	.503	.000
N of Valid Cases		90	

Shows the strength of the relationship between the variables

Shows the level of statistical significance of the computed value of Cramér's *V*

Plate 16.13

The Crosstabs dialog box

Select and place here the variable that will make up the rows. This will be the dependent variable if it is possible and legitimate to make a claim about likely causality

Select and place here the variable that will make up the columns. This will be the independent variable if it is possible and legitimate to make a claim about likely causality

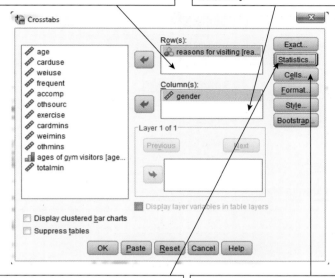

Click here to bring up the **Crosstabs: Statistics** sub-dialog box (Plate 16.15) in order to select chi-square and other measures of association that often accompany contingency tables

Click here to bring up the **Crosstabs: Cell Display** sub-dialog box (Plate 16.14) to select the kinds of information that will be included in each cell, such as column percentages

Plate 16.14

The Crosstabs: Cell Display sub-dialog box

Select **Observed** to show the number of cases in each cell in the table

Select **Column** for the percentage of cases of each category of a column variable

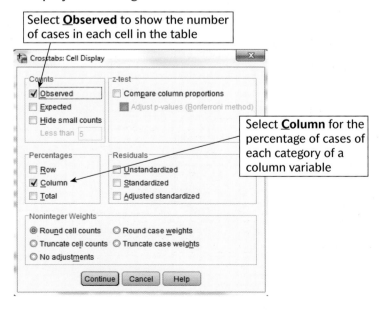

Plate 16.15
The Crosstabs: Statistics sub-dialog box

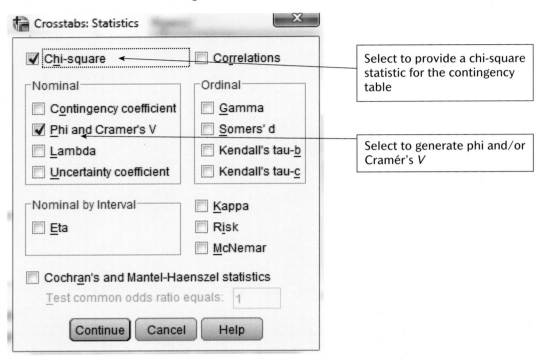

Table 16.3
Correlations output for *age*, *weimins*, and *cardmins* (SPSS output)

Correlations

		age	cardmins	weimins
age	Pearson Correlation	1	−.109	−.273**
	Sig. (2-tailed)		.311	.010
	N	89	89	89
cardmins	Pearson Correlation	−.109	1	−.161
	Sig. (2-tailed)	.311		.130
	N	89	90	90
weimins	Pearson Correlation	−.273**	−.161	1
	Sig. (2-tailed)	.010	.130	
	N	89	90	90

** Correlation is significant at the 0.01 level (2-tailed).

Correlations of $p < 0.05$ are 'flagged' with asterisks

Shows number of cases involved in the calculation of a correlation, less any cases for which there are missing values for either or both variables

Shows strength of relationship between variables as indicated by Pearson's *r*

Shows level of statistical significance of computed value of Pearson's *r*

Plate 16.16
The Bivariate Correlations dialog box

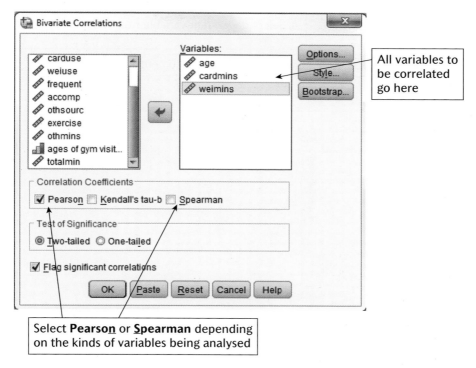

is a convention that, if one variable can be identified as likely to be the independent variable, it should be placed on the *x* axis—that is, the horizontal axis. Since *age* is bound to be the independent variable, we would follow these steps:

1. → **Graphs** → **Chart Builder** [opens the **Chart Builder** dialog box shown in Plate 16.17]

2. → **Scatter/Dot** from below **Choose from:**. Then select, from the scatter diagram formats, the basic format which is in the top left-hand corner and drag and drop into the area above the scatter diagram formats

3. → *cardmins* and drag and drop into area designated **Y-Axis?** and → *age* and drag and drop into area designated **X-Axis?** (see Plate 16.17)

A default scatter diagram is shown in Figure 16.1. The scatter diagram can then be edited by bringing up the **Chart Editor** by double-clicking with the left-hand button anywhere in the diagram. For example, the type and size of the markers can be changed by clicking anywhere in the chart in the **Chart Editor**. This brings up a **Properties** sub-dialog box, which allows a variety of changes to the appearance of the diagram, such as colour and the nature of the points on the plot.

Comparing means and eta

To produce a table like Table 15.5, these steps should be followed:

1. → **Analyze** → **Compare Means** → **Means** . . . [opens the **Means** dialog box shown in Plate 16.18]

2. → *cardmins* → ▶ to the left of **Dependent List:** [puts *cardmins* in the **Dependent List: box**] → **reasons for visiting** → ▶ to the left of **Independent List:** [puts **reasons for visiting** in the **Independent List:box**]→ **Options** . . . [opens the **Means: Options** sub-dialog box]

3. → **Anova table and eta** underneath **Statistics for First Layer** → Continue [closes the **Means: Options** sub-dialog box and returns you to the **Means** dialog box shown in Plate 16.18] → **OK**

Generating a contingency table with three variables

To create a table like that in Table 15.7, you would need to follow these steps:

1. → **Analyze** → **Descriptive Statistics** → **Crosstabs** . . . [opens the **Crosstabs** dialog box shown in Plate 16.13]

Plate 16.17
Creating a scatter diagram with the Chart Builder

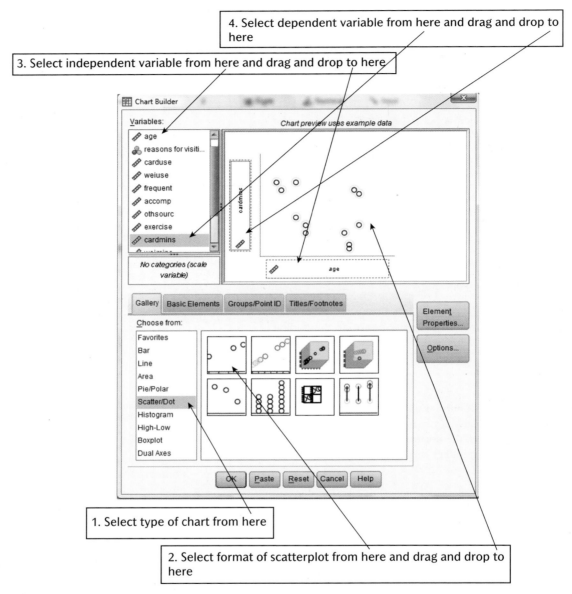

4. Select dependent variable from here and drag and drop to here

3. Select independent variable from here and drag and drop to here

1. Select type of chart from here

2. Select format of scatterplot from here and drag and drop to here

2. → *othsourc* → **Independent List:** by **Row[s]** [*othsourc* will appear in the **Row[s]:** box]

3. → *age3* [this is the name we gave when we created a new variable with *age* recoded into three categories] → **Independent List:** by **Column[s]:** [*age3* will appear in the **Column[s]:** box] → *gender* → **Independent List:** beneath **Previous** [*gender* will appear in the box underneath **Layer 1 of 1**] → **Cells** [opens **Crosstabs: Cell Display** sub-dialog box shown in Plate 16.14]

4. Make sure **Observed** in the **Counts** box has been selected. Make sure **Column** under **Percentages** has been selected. If either of these has not been selected, simply click at the relevant point. → **Continue** [closes **Crosstabs: Cell Display** sub-dialog box and returns you to the **Crosstabs** dialog box shown in Plate 16.13]

5. → **OK**

The resulting table will look somewhat different from Table 15.7 in that gender will appear as a row rather than as a column variable.

Figure 16.1

Scatter diagram showing the relationship between *age* and *cardmins* (SPSS output)

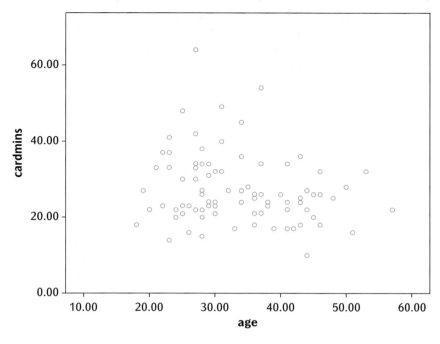

Plate 16.18

The Means dialog box

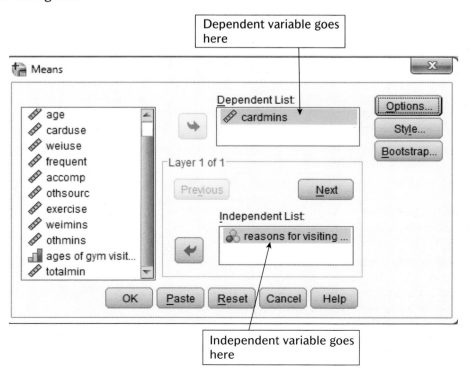

Further operations in SPSS

Saving your data

You will need to save your data for future use. To do this, make sure that the **Data Editor** is the active window. Then,

→ **File** → **Save As...**

The **Save Data As** dialog box will then appear. You will need to provide a name for your data, which will be placed after **File name:** We called the file 'gym study'. You also need to decide where you are going to save the data—for example, onto a memory stick. To select the destination drive, → the downward pointing arrow to the left of **Look in** and then select the drive and folder into which you want to place your data. Then → **Save**.

Remember that this procedure saves your data *and* any other work you have done on your data—for example, value labels and recoded variables. If you subsequently use the data again and do more work on your data, such as creating a new variable, you will need to save the data again or the new work will be lost. SPSS will give you a choice of renaming your data, in which case you will have two files of data (one with the original data and one with any changes), or keeping the same name, in which case the file will be changed and the existing name retained.

Retrieving your data

When you want to retrieve the data file you have created, → **File** → **Open** . . . The **Open File** dialog box will appear. You then need to go to the location in which you have deposited your data to retrieve the file containing your data and then → **Open** → **Data** . . . A shortcut alternative to this procedure is to → the first button on the toolbar (it looks like an open file), which brings up the **Open File** dialog box.

Printing output

To print all the output in the **SPSS Output Viewer**, make sure that the **Output 1—SPSS Viewer** is the active window and then → **File** → **Print** . . . The **Print** dialog box will appear and then → **OK**. To print just some of your output, hold down the Ctrl button on your keyboard and click once on the parts you want to print. The easiest way to do this is to select all the elements you want in the output summary in the left-hand segment of the **Output Viewer** shown in Plate 16.10. Then bring up the Print dialog box. When the **Print** dialog box appears, make sure **Selection** under **Print range** has been selected. The third button on the toolbar (which appears as a printer) provides a shortcut to the **Print** dialog box.

Key points

- SPSS can be used to implement the techniques learned in Chapter 15, but learning new software requires perseverance and at times the results obtained may not seem to be worth the learning process.

- But it is worth it—it would take you far longer to perform calculations on a sample of around 100 than to learn the software.

- If you find yourself moving into much more advanced techniques, the time saved is even more substantial, particularly with large samples.

- It is better to become familiar with SPSS before you begin designing your research instruments, so you are aware of difficulties you might have in presenting your data in SPSS at an early stage.

Questions for review

Getting started in SPSS

- Outline the differences between variable names, variable labels, and value labels.

- In what circumstances might you want to recode a variable?

- In what circumstances might you want to create a new variable?

Data analysis with SPSS

Using the gym survey data, create:

- a frequency table for *exercise*;
- a bar chart and pie chart for *exercise* and compare their usefulness;
- a histogram for *cardmins*;
- measures of central tendency and dispersion for *cardmins*;
- a contingency table and chi-square test for *exercise* and *gender*;
- Pearson's r for *age* and *cardmins*;
- Spearman's rho for *carduse* and *weiuse*;
- a scatter diagram for *age* and *cardmins*;
- a comparing means analysis for *totalmin* and **reasons for visiting**.

Online Resource Centre
www.oxfordtextbooks.co.uk/orc/brymansrm5e/

Visit the Online Resource Centre to enrich your understanding of using SPSS for Windows. Follow up links to other resources, test yourself using multiple choice questions, and gain further guidance and inspiration from the Student Researcher's Toolkit.

Part **Three**

Qualitative Research

Part Three of this book is concerned with qualitative research. Chapter 17 sets the scene by presenting the main features of this research strategy. Chapter 18 explores the distinctive approach that qualitative researchers take towards sampling. Chapter 19 deals with ethnography and participant observation, which are among the main ways of collecting qualitative data. Chapter 20 is concerned with the kind of interviewing that is carried out in qualitative research. Chapter 21 addresses the focus group method, which is an increasingly popular technique that allows groups of people to be interviewed. Chapter 22 explores two approaches to the study of language in social research: conversation analysis and discourse analysis. Chapter 23 explores the types of documents with which qualitative researchers tend to be concerned and discusses the approaches to examining them. Chapter 24 examines different approaches to qualitative data analysis and offers advice on how it can be carried out. Chapter 25 shows you how to use computer software in the form of NVivo to conduct the kind of analysis discussed in Chapter 24.

These chapters will provide you with the essential tools for doing qualitative research. They will take you from the very general issues to do with the generic features of qualitative research to the very practical issues of conducting your own observational studies or interviews and analysing your own data.

17

The nature of qualitative research

Chapter outline

Chapter guide

Qualitative research is a research strategy that usually emphasizes words rather than quantification in the collection and analysis of data. As a research strategy it is broadly inductivist, constructionist, and interpretivist, but qualitative researchers do not always subscribe to all three of these features. This chapter outlines the main features of qualitative research and as such explores:

- the main steps in qualitative research: delineating the sequence of stages in qualitative research is more controversial than with quantitative research, because it exhibits less codification of the research process;

- the relationship between theory and research;

- the nature of concepts in qualitative research and their differences from concepts in quantitative research;

- how far reliability and validity are appropriate criteria for qualitative researchers and whether alternative criteria that are more tailored to the research strategy are necessary;

- the main preoccupations of qualitative researchers: five areas are identified in terms of an emphasis on seeing through the eyes of research participants; description and context; process; flexibility and lack of structure; and concepts and theory as outcomes of the research process;

- some common criticisms of qualitative research;

- the main contrasts between qualitative and quantitative research;

- the stance of feminist researchers on qualitative research.

Introduction

I began Chapter 7 by noting that *quantitative* research had been outlined in Chapter 2 as a distinctive research strategy. Much the same kind of general point can be registered in relation to *qualitative* research. In Chapter 2 it was suggested that qualitative research differs from quantitative research in several ways. Most obviously, qualitative research tends to be concerned with words rather than numbers, but three further features were particularly noteworthy:

1. an inductive view of the relationship between theory and research, whereby the former is generated out of the latter (though see the section below on '**Abductive** reasoning' as a qualification of this view);

2. an epistemological position described as interpretivist, meaning that, in contrast to the adoption of a natural scientific model in quantitative research, the stress is on the understanding of the social world through an examination of the interpretation of that world by its participants; and

3. an ontological position described as constructionist, which implies that social properties are outcomes of the interactions between individuals, rather than phenomena 'out there' and separate from those involved in its construction.

As Bryman and Burgess (1999) observe, although there has been a proliferation of writings on qualitative research since the 1970s, stipulating what it is and is not as a distinct research strategy is by no means straightforward. They propose three reasons for this state of affairs.

1. As a term, 'qualitative research' is sometimes taken to imply an approach to social research in which quantitative data are not collected or generated. Many writers on qualitative research are critical of such a rendition of qualitative research, because (as we will see) the distinctiveness of qualitative research does not reside solely in the absence of numbers.

2. Qualitative research has comprised different traditions and stances over the years (see Thinking deeply 17.1). Moreover, research is still conducted and published that fits well with the earliest of the stages identified by Denzin and Lincoln (2005b) as described in Thinking deeply 17.1. For example, Venkatesh's (2008) popular ethnography of drugs gangs in Chicago, while displaying some characteristics of experimental writing (Stage 5), has many of the features associated with the first two stages.

3. Sometimes, qualitative research is discussed in terms of the ways in which it differs from quantitative research. A potential problem with this tactic is that it means that qualitative research ends up being addressed in terms of what quantitative research is *not*.

Thinking deeply 17.1
The eight moments of qualitative research

Denzin and Lincoln (2005b) have suggested that in North America qualitative research has progressed through a number of stages. It is not clear why the stages are presented as relating only to North America, but the distinctions are worth drawing attention to because they relate closely to the suggestion that there are different traditions of qualitative research. The significance of the stages seems to have declined in their later writings, so that in the most recent edition of Denzin and Lincoln's *Handbook of Qualitative Research* (2011), it occupies a mere footnote and has been reduced to eight stages. Nonetheless, the classification warrants attention because it is thought-provoking (Denzin and Lincoln 2011).

1. *The traditional period*. The early twentieth century up to the Second World War. This phase takes in the work of social anthropologists and the Chicago School. It refers to in-depth studies of 'slices of life' that portrayed those who were studied as strange or alien. It was heavily imbued with positivism.

2. *Modernist phase*. Post–Second World War to early 1970s. During this period, qualitative researchers built on the work of the traditional period but at the same time sought to enhance the rigour of qualitative enquiries and began to reflect on the nature of their craft. These investigations also showed a tendency towards positivism.

3. *Blurred genres*. 1970–86. This was a period when a variety of epistemological and ontological approaches, as well as theoretical ideas, were being explored as plausible bases for qualitative enquiries. According to Denzin and Lincoln, we see in this period a continued proclivity towards positivism, but with the beginnings of an interpretivist self-consciousness, influenced by Geertz's (1973a) insistence that qualitative researchers are involved in interpretations of the interpretations of those on whom they conduct their investigations.

4. *Crisis of representation*. Mid-1980s onwards. Most of the key writings associated with this moment occurred in the 1980s. It refers to a period in which qualitative social researchers in general (though much of the writing stemmed initially from social anthropology) developed greater self-awareness concerning in particular the fact that their accounts of their fieldwork are just one way of representing reality and that, moreover, their representations are heavily influenced by their social locations. The 'crisis of representation', then, is the recognition that the researcher's written work has limited scientific authority. These ideas will be encountered again in the section on 'Writing ethnography' in Chapter 19.

The next three phases refer to 'a triple crisis' stemming from the fourth moment above.

5. *Postmodern period of experimental ethnographic writing*. Mid-1990s. Heavily influenced by **postmodernism** (see Key concept 17.1), work under this heading is characterized by an awareness of the different ways of representing research participants (often referred to as 'the other') when writing up findings. Qualitative researchers tried different ways of representing the people on whom they conduct their investigations.

6. *Post-experimental enquiry*. 1995–2000. This period is associated mainly with the emergence of AltaMira Press, a publisher of qualitative research that encourages experimental and interdisciplinary writing. It describes itself as having a 'focus on interdisciplinary work, breaking long-standing boundaries' (**https://rowman.com/ Altamira**, accessed 18 November 2014).

7. *The methodologically contested present*. 2000–4. This refers to a period in which there was considerable disagreement about how qualitative research should be conducted and the directions it should be heading. It was very much associated with the arrival of such journals as *Qualitative Inquiry* and *Qualitative Research*, which provide forums for these debates. While Denzin and Lincoln (2005b) date this period as 2000–4, there is a great deal of evidence to suggest that the contestation of methodological differences have not abated. One of the areas that has been a focus of the ongoing debates has been the issue of research quality criteria in relation to qualitative studies.

8. *The fractured future*. Lincoln and Denzin (2005: 1123) also speculate about what the immediate future holds: 'Randomized field trials . . . will occupy the time of one group of researchers while the pursuit of a socially and culturally responsive, communitarian, justice-oriented set of studies will consume the meaningful working moments of the other.'

This timeline of phases is useful because it highlights the difficulty of characterizing 'qualitative research'. Denzin and Lincoln's 'moments' have to be treated with some caution. First, it has to be borne in mind that work that could be depicted in terms very similar to the first two phases continues to be conducted. Indeed, many of the qualitative investigations that serve as illustrations in Part Three are of this type. Although qualitative researchers may be more self-conscious nowadays about their influence on the research process and the significance of how they write, many qualitative studies are still characterized by realism, at least to some degree. Second, Denzin and Lincoln's later phases are associated too much with particular events—the arrival of a new publisher or new journals—which looks strange when viewed in relation to the several decades with which the earlier moments are associated. Third, their eighth and final moment seems to be concerned with a rift in social research in general rather than within qualitative research as such.

Silverman (1993) has been particularly critical of accounts of qualitative research that do not acknowledge the variety of forms that the research strategy can assume. In other words, writers such as Silverman are critical of attempts to specify the nature of qualitative research as a general approach (see also Thinking deeply 17.1). However, unless we can talk to a certain degree about the nature of qualitative research, it is difficult to see how it is possible to refer to qualitative research as a distinctive research strategy. In much the same way that in Chapter 7 it was recognized that quantitative researchers employ different research designs, in writing about the characteristics of qualitative research we will need to be sensitive to the different orientations of qualitative researchers. Without at least a sense of what is common to a set of many if not most studies that might be described as qualitative, the very notion of qualitative research would be rendered problematic. Yet it is clear that, for many social scientists, it is a helpful and meaningful category that can be seen in a variety of ways. Examples are: the arrival of specialist journals, such as *Qualitative Sociology*, *Qualitative Research*, *Ethnography*, and *Qualitative Inquiry*; texts on qualitative research (e.g. Seale 1999; Silverman 2010); a *Handbook of Qualitative Research* (Denzin and Lincoln 1994, 2000, 2005a, 2011); and a series of books on different facets of qualitative research (the Sage Qualitative Research Methods Series).

Several reasons might be proposed for the unease among some writers concerning the specification of the nature of qualitative research. Two reasons might be regarded as having particular importance. First, qualitative research incorporates several diverse research methods that differ from each other considerably. The following are the main research methods associated with qualitative research.

- *Ethnography/participant observation*. While some caution is advisable in treating ethnography and participant observation as synonyms, in many respects they refer to similar if not identical approaches to data collection in which the researcher is immersed in a social setting for some time in order to observe and listen with a view to gaining an appreciation of the culture of a social group. It has been employed in such social research classics as Whyte's (1955) study of street corner life in a slum community and Gans's (1962) research on a similar group in the throes of urban redevelopment.

- *Qualitative interviewing*. This is a very broad term to describe a wide range of interviewing styles (see Key concept 9.2 for an introduction). Moreover, qualitative researchers employing ethnography or participant observation typically engage in a substantial amount of qualitative interviewing.

- Focus groups (see Key concept 9.2).

Key concept 17.1
What is postmodernism?

As noted in the main text, postmodernism is extremely difficult to pin down. Part of the problem is that, as an approach, postmodernism is at least two things. One is that it is an attempt to get to grips with the nature of modern society and culture. The other, which is the more relevant aspect for this book, is that it represents a way of thinking about and representing the nature of the social sciences and their claims to knowledge. In particular, it is a distinctive sensitivity regarding the representation of social scientific findings. Postmodernists tend to be deeply suspicious of notions that imply that it is possible to arrive at a definitive version of any reality. Reports of findings are viewed as versions of an external reality, so that the key issue becomes one of the plausibility of those versions rather than whether they are right or wrong in any absolute sense. Postmodernists have probably been most influential in qualitative research when discussing the nature of ethnographic accounts and questioning the ethnographer's implicit claim to have provided a definitive account of a society. This thinking can be discerned in Van Maanen's (1988) implicit critique of 'realist tales' as he called them (see the section on 'Writing ethnography' in Chapter 19).

For postmodernists, there can be no sense of an objective reality out there waiting to be revealed to and uncovered by social scientists. That reality is always going to be accessed through narratives in the form of research reports that provide representations. With this shift in orientation came an interest in the language employed in research reports, such as written ethnographies, to reveal the devices researchers use to convey the definitiveness of their findings (Delamont and Atkinson 2004). Postmodernists tend to emphasize the notion of reflexivity (see Key concept 17.6), which posits the significance of the researcher for the research process and consequently the tentativeness of any findings presented in a research report (since the researcher is always implicated in his or her findings).

- Language-based approaches to the collection of qualitative data, such as **discourse analysis** and **conversation analysis**.
- The collection and qualitative analysis of **texts** and documents.

Each of these approaches to data collection will be examined in Part Three. The picture with regard to the very different methods and sources that comprise qualitative research is made somewhat more complex by the fact that a multimethod approach is frequently employed. As noted above, researchers employing ethnography or participant observation frequently conduct qualitative interviews. However, they also often collect and analyse texts and documents as well. Thus, there is considerable variability in the collection of data among studies that are typically deemed to be qualitative. Quantitative research also subsumes several different methods of data collection, but the inclusion of methods concerned with the analysis of language as a form of qualitative research implies somewhat greater variability.

A second reason why there is some resistance to a delineation of the nature of qualitative research is that the connection between theory and research is somewhat more ambiguous than in quantitative research. With the latter research strategy, theoretical issues drive the formulation of a research question, which in turn drives the collection and analysis of data. Findings then feed back into the relevant theory. This is rather a caricature, because what counts as 'theory' is sometimes little more than the research literature relating to a certain issue or area. In qualitative research, theory is supposed to be an outcome of an investigation rather than something that precedes it. However, some writers, like Silverman (1993: 24), have argued that such a depiction of qualitative research is 'out of tune with the greater sophistication of contemporary field research design, born out of accumulated knowledge of interaction and greater concern with issues of reliability and validity'. This is particularly the case with conversation analysis, an approach to the study of language that will be examined in Chapter 22. However, qualitative research is more usually regarded as denoting an approach in which theory and categorization emerge out of the collection and analysis of data. The more general point being made is that such a difference within qualitative research may account for the unease about depicting the research strategy in terms of a set of stages.

 # The main steps in qualitative research

The sequence outlined in Figure 17.1 provides a representation of how the qualitative research process can be visualized. In order to illustrate the steps, a published study by Foster (1995) of crime in communities will be used. This study was previously encountered in Research in focus 2.6.

- *Step 1. General research question(s)*. The starting point for Foster's (1995) study of crime in communities, particularly ones that contain predominantly public housing, is the high levels of crime in poorer areas. To the extent that it is a focus of attention, it is frequently assumed that communities with high levels of crime tend to have low levels of social control. But Foster argues that we know very little about how informal social control operates in such communities and what its significance for crime is. She also notes that council estates are frequently presumed to be crime prone but that there is little evidence on 'the diversity in experience and attitudes of residents within individual estates' (Foster 1995: 563). It would be easy to presume that, to the extent that council estates are prone to high crime levels, they exhibit low levels of social control. Thus Foster formulates a general set of concerns revolving around council estates and their crime proneness and the possible role and dynamics of social control in the

process. She also notes that some writers have suggested that the propensity to crime in council estates may be in part attributed to flaws in the design of the estates.

- *Step 2. Selection of relevant site(s) and subjects*. The research was conducted on a London council estate (with the fictitious name 'Riverside'), which had a high level of crime and which exhibited the kinds of housing features that are frequently associated with a propensity to crime. Relevant research participants, such as residents, were identified.

- *Step 3. Collection of relevant data*. Foster describes her research as 'ethnographic'. She spent eighteen months 'getting involved in as many aspects of life there as possible from attending tenant meetings, the mothers and toddlers group, and activities for young people, to socializing with some of the residents in the local pub' (Foster 1995: 566). Foster also tells us that 'extended interviews' were conducted with forty-five residents of Riverside (and another London estate, but the majority were from Riverside) and twenty-five 'officials', such as police and housing officers. Foster's account of her research methods suggests that she is likely to have generated two types of data: fieldwork notes, based on her ethnographic observation of life in the community, and detailed notes (and most probably transcripts) of interviews undertaken.

Figure 17.1

An outline of the main steps of qualitative research

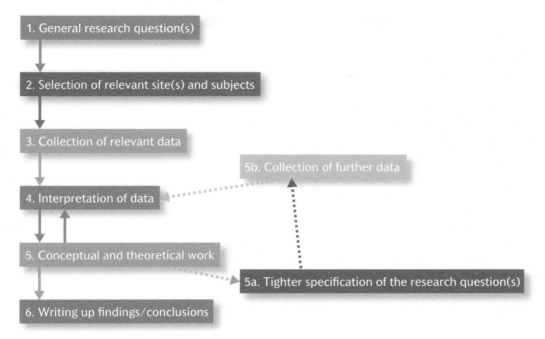

Step 4. *Interpretation of data*. One of the key findings to emerge from the data is the fact that, in spite of Riverside having a high crime rate, it is not perceived as a problem in this regard by Riverside residents. For example, she quotes from an interview with an elderly tenant: 'They used to say that they couldn't let the flats [apartments] here . . . but I mean as far as muggings or anything like that you don't hear of nothing like that even now' (Foster 1995: 568). Instead, housing problems loomed larger in the minds of residents than crime. She also found that 'hidden economy' crimes were prevalent on the estate and that much crime was tolerated by residents. She also observes that, contrary to expectations about estates like Riverside, there was clear evidence of informal social control mechanisms at work, such as shaming practices.

Step 5. *Conceptual and theoretical work*. No new concepts seem to emerge from Foster's research, but her findings enable her to tie together some of the elements outlined above under Step 1. For example, she writes:

Crime then need not be damaging *per se* providing other factors cushion its impact. On Riverside these included support networks in which tenants felt that someone was watching out for their properties and provided links with people to whom they could turn if they were in trouble. Consequently while generalized fears about crime remained prevalent, familiarity and support went some way to reducing the potential for hostile encounters.

(Foster 1995: 580)

It is this step, coupled with the interpretation of data, that forms the study's findings.

Steps 5a. *Tighter specification of the research question(s), and 5b. Collection of further data*. There is no specific evidence from Foster's account that she followed a process in which she collected further data after she had built up early interpretations of her data. When this occurs, as it sometimes does in research within a grounded theory framework, there can be an interplay between interpretation and theorizing, on the one hand, and data collection, on the other. Such a strategy is frequently referred to as an *iterative* one. Foster does write at one point that some residents and officials were interviewed twice and in some cases even three times in the course of her research. This raises the possibility that she was re-interviewing certain individuals in the light of her emerging ideas about her data, but this can only be a speculation. (See also Thinking deeply 17.2 for further discussion of the development of research questions in qualitative research.)

Thinking deeply 17.2
Research questions in qualitative research

Research questions in qualitative research are stated with varying degrees of explicitness. Sometimes, the research question is embedded within a general statement of the orientation of an article.

Brannen, O'Connell, and Mooney (2013) examined how dual earner families with young children integrated meal times and food preparation into their busy lives. They write:

> We sought to understand how employed parents (mothers) fitted food and eating into their working family lives and how habitual practices of eating together and eating meals were influenced by the timetables of other family members.
>
> (Brannen et al. 2013: 420)

Others opt for a more explicit treatment of research questions.

Hine was interested in the ways in which parents participated in discussions of how to handle headlice in an online parenting forum. She was especially interested in how parents justified their handling of headlice and in particular the extent to which they drew on scientific understanding when providing justifications. She specified several research questions:

- What resources do participants in online discussions about headlice draw upon, and in particular what part does science play? What forms of authority are held to be convincing?
- What notions of risk do participants express, and how are these made accountable?
- To what extent are the resources advanced by participants in discussion bound to identities held to be salient in this specific context?
- How do the dynamics of advice-giving in this context relate to conventional notions of medical and scientific expertise and/or to new relations of expertise such as apomediation that may be occasioned by the Internet? (Hine 2014: 578)

As noted in Chapter 1, in their study of senior managers who retired early, Jones et al. (2010) stated their research questions explicitly though they were not formatted to stand out in the same way:

> to what extent do our respondents construct a new balance of activities? Do respondents construct new discourses of everyday life? Does the move by respondents into leisure retirement create new tensions in other parts of their lives?
>
> (Jones et al. 2010: 105)

The researchers went on to investigate these research questions by collecting qualitative data from semi-structured interviews. The formulation of research questions in qualitative research, much as in quantitative research, is closely connected to the relevant literature. The research questions will be to a significant extent prompted and stimulated by the literature. The key points to consider are what it is you want to find out about and why it is important to know the answer. The literature will be central to both considerations.

Not all qualitative researchers agree about the importance of research questions at the outset of an investigation. Some exponents of grounded theory (see Key concept 17.2) advocate a more open-ended strategy of beginning with a blank slate. As such, the literature becomes significant at later stages of helping to inform theoretical ideas as they emerge from the data and as a way of contextualizing the significance of the findings. There is considerable disagreement over the desirability of deferring a literature review. Dunne (2011) advocates a reflexive approach to reviewing the literature in grounded theory whereby the researcher reflects on the ways in which the literature may have influenced and moulded his or her understanding of the field. The literature review is such an expected element of social science writing that not to include one risks alienating reviewers or examiners. Also, the literature review serves some useful purposes (as outlined in Chapter 5), such as making sure that you are not reinventing the wheel and learning from other researchers' methodological and other lapses of judgement, so there are practical risks associated with deferring contact with the literature.

- *Step 6. Writing up findings/conclusions.* There is no real difference between the significance of writing up in quantitative research and qualitative research, so that exactly the same points made in relation to Step 11 in Figure 7.1 apply here. An audience has to be convinced about the credibility and significance of the interpretations offered. Researchers are not and cannot be simply conduits for the things they see and the words they hear. The salience of what researchers have seen and heard has to be impressed on the audience. Foster does this by making clear to her audience that her findings have implications for policies regarding estates and crime and for our understanding of the links between housing, community, and crime. A key point to emerge from her work, which she emphasizes at several points in the article and hammers home in her concluding section, is that being an insider to Riverside allowed her to see that a community that may be regarded by outsiders as having a high propensity towards crime should not be presumed to be seen in this way by members of that community.

Two particularly distinctive aspects of the sequence of steps in qualitative research are the highly related issues of the links between theory and concepts with research data. It is to these issues that we now turn.

Theory and research

Most qualitative researchers when writing about their craft emphasize a preference for treating theory as something that emerges out of the collection and analysis of data. As will be seen in Chapter 24, practitioners of **grounded theory**—a frequently cited approach to the analysis of qualitative data—especially stress the importance of allowing theoretical ideas to emerge out of one's data. But some qualitative researchers argue that qualitative data can and should have an important role in relation to the *testing* of theories as well. Silverman (1993), in particular, has argued that in more recent times practitioners of qualitative research have become increasingly interested in the testing of theories and that this is a reflection of its growing maturity. Certainly, there is no reason why qualitative research cannot be employed in order to test theories that are specified in advance of data collection. In any case, much qualitative research entails the testing of theories in the course of the research process. So, in Figure 17.1, the loop back from Step 5a, 'Tighter specification of the research question(s)', to Step 5b, 'Collection of further data', implies that a theoretical position may emerge in the course of research and may spur the collection of further data to test that theory. This alternation between testing emerging theories and collecting data is a particularly distinctive feature of grounded theory. It is presented as a dashed line in Figure 17.1, because it is not as necessary a feature of the process of qualitative research as the other steps.

Key concept 17.2
What is grounded theory?

Grounded theory has been defined as 'theory that was derived from data, systematically gathered and analysed through the research process. In this method, data collection, analysis, and eventual theory stand in close relationship to one another' (Strauss and Corbin 1998: 12). Thus, two central features of grounded theory are that it is concerned with the development of theory out of data and that the approach is iterative, or recursive, as it is sometimes called, meaning that data collection and analysis proceed in tandem, repeatedly referring back to each other.

As the discussion in this chapter shows, the two originators of the approach—Glaser and Strauss—eventually disagreed on the path on which Strauss was taking grounded theory. A further complication is that there is a lack of agreement on what grounded theory is. To some writers it is a distinct method or approach to qualitative research in its own right; to others, it is an approach to the generation of theory. It is this second view of grounded theory that is taken in this chapter. Grounded theory is not a theory—it is an approach to the generation of theory out of data. Usually, 'data' is taken to refer to qualitative data, but grounded theory can be used in connection with different kinds of data. One final complication is that, although it has just been suggested that grounded theory is a strategy for generating theory out of data, in many cases, reports that use a grounded theory approach generate concepts rather than theory as such.

One key point that is implied by Figure 17.1 is that the typical sequence of steps in qualitative research entails the generation of theories rather than the testing of theories that are specified at the outset. Silverman (1993) is undoubtedly correct that pre-specified theories *can be* and sometimes *are* tested with qualitative data, but the generation of theory tends to be the preferred approach.

Concepts in qualitative research

A central feature of Chapter 7 was the discussion of concepts and their measurement. For most qualitative researchers, developing measures of concepts will not be a significant consideration, but concepts are very much part of the landscape in qualitative research. However, the way in which concepts are developed and used tends to be different from that implied in quantitative research. Blumer's (1954) distinction between 'definitive' and

Research in focus 17.1
The emergence of a concept in qualitative research: the case of emotional labour

Hochschild's (1983) idea of emotional labour—labour that 'requires one to induce or suppress feelings in order to sustain the outward countenance that produces the proper state of mind in others' (1983: 7)—has become a very influential concept in the sociology of work and in the developing area of the sociology of emotions. Somewhat ironically for a predominantly qualitative study, Hochschild's initial conceptualization appears to have emerged from a questionnaire she distributed to 261 university students. Within the questionnaire were two requests: 'Describe a real situation that was important to you in which you experienced a deep emotion' and 'Describe as fully and concretely as possible a real situation that was important to you in which you either changed the situation to fit your feelings or changed your feelings to fit the situation' (1983: 13). Thus, although a self-administered questionnaire was employed, the resulting data were qualitative. The data were analysed in terms of the idea of emotion *work*, which is the same as emotional labour but occurs in a private context. Emotional labour is essentially emotion work that is performed as part of one's paid employment. In order to develop the idea of emotional labour, Hochschild looked to the world of work. The main occupation she studied was that of flight attendant. Several sources of data on emotional labour among flight attendants were employed. She gained access to Delta Airlines, a large American airline, and in the course of her investigations she:

- watched sessions for training attendants and had many conversations with both trainees and experienced attendants during the sessions;
- interviewed various personnel, such as managers in various sections, and advertising agents;
- examined Delta advertisements spanning thirty years;
- observed the flight attendant recruitment process at Pan American Airways, since she had not been allowed to do this at Delta;
- conducted 'open-ended interviews lasting three to five hours each with thirty flight attendants in the San Francisco Bay Area' (Hochschild 1983: 15).

In order to forge a comparison with a contrasting occupational group that is nonetheless also involved in emotional labour, Hochschild also interviewed five debt-collectors. In her book, she explores such topics as the human costs of emotional labour and the issue of gender in relation to it. It is clear that Hochschild's concept of emotional labour began as a somewhat imprecise idea that emerged out of a concern with emotion work and that was gradually developed in order to address its wider significance. The concept has been picked up by other qualitative researchers in the sociology of work. For example, Leidner (1993) explored through ethnographic studies of a McDonald's restaurant and an insurance company the ways in which organizations seek to 'routinize' the display of emotional labour.

sensitizing concepts captures aspects of the different ways in which concepts are thought about.

Blumer (1954) argued stridently against the use of definitive concepts in social research. The idea of definitive concepts is typified by the way in which, in quantitative research, a concept, once developed, becomes fixed through the elaboration of indicators. For Blumer, such an approach entailed the application of a straitjacket on the social world, because the concept in question comes to be seen exclusively in terms of the indicators that have been developed for it. Fine nuances in the form that the concept can assume or alternative ways of viewing the concept and its forms are sidelined. In other words, definitive concepts are excessively concerned with what is common to the phenomena that the concept is supposed to incorporate rather than with variety. Instead, Blumer (1954: 7) recommended that social researchers should recognize that the concepts they use are sensitizing concepts in that they provide 'a general sense of reference and guidance in approaching empirical instances'. For Blumer, then, concepts should be employed in such a way that they give a very general sense of what to look for and act as a means for uncovering the variety of forms that the phenomena to which they refer can assume. In providing

a critique of definitive concepts, it is clear that Blumer had in mind the concept-indicator model described in Chapter 7. In other words, his views entailed in large part a critique of quantitative research and a programmatic statement that would form a springboard for an alternative approach that nowadays we would recognize as qualitative research.

Blumer's distinction is not without problems. It is not at all clear how far a very general formulation of a concept can be regarded as a useful guide to empirical enquiry. If it is too general, it will simply fail to provide a useful starting point because its guidelines are too broad; if too narrow, it is likely to repeat some of the difficulties Blumer identified in relation to definitive concepts. However, his general view of concepts has attracted some support, because his preference for not imposing preordained schemes on the social world chimes with that of many qualitative researchers. As the example in Research in focus 17.1 suggests, the researcher frequently starts out with a broad outline of a concept, which is revised and narrowed during the course of data collection. For subsequent researchers, the concept may be taken up and revised as it is employed in connection with different social contexts or in relation to different research questions.

 # Reliability and validity in qualitative research

In Chapters 3 and 7 it was noted that reliability and validity are important criteria in establishing and assessing the quality of quantitative research. However, there has been some discussion among qualitative researchers concerning the relevance of these criteria for qualitative research. Moreover, even writers who do take the view that the criteria are relevant have considered the possibility that the meanings of the terms need to be altered. For example, the issue of measurement validity almost by definition seems to carry connotations of measurement. Since measurement is not a major preoccupation among qualitative researchers, the issue of validity would seem to have little bearing on such studies. As foreshadowed briefly in Chapter 3, a number of different stances have been taken by qualitative researchers in relation to these issues.

Adapting reliability and validity for qualitative research

One stance is to assimilate reliability and validity into qualitative research with little change of meaning other than playing down the salience of measurement issues. Mason (1996: 21), for example, argues that reliability, validity, and generalizability (which is the main component of external validity—see Chapter 3) 'are different kinds

of measures of the quality, rigour and wider potential of research, which are achieved according to certain methodological and disciplinary conventions and principles'. She sticks very closely to the meaning of these criteria in quantitative research, where they have been largely developed. Thus, validity refers to whether 'you are observing, identifying, or "measuring" what you say you are' (Mason 1996: 24). LeCompte and Goetz (1982) and Kirk and Miller (1986) also write about reliability and validity in relation to qualitative research but invest the terms with a somewhat different meaning from Mason. LeCompte and Goetz write about the following.

- *External reliability*, by which they mean the degree to which a study can be replicated. This is a difficult criterion to meet in qualitative research, since, as LeCompte and Goetz recognize, it is impossible to 'freeze' a social setting and the circumstances of an initial study to make it replicable in the sense in which the term is usually employed (see Chapter 7). However, they suggest several strategies that can be introduced in order to approach the requirements of external reliability. For example, they suggest that a qualitative researcher replicating ethnographic research needs to adopt a similar social role to that adopted by the original researcher. Otherwise what a researcher conducting a replication sees and hears will not be comparable to the original research.

- *Internal reliability*, by which they mean whether, when there is more than one observer, members of the research team agree about what they see and hear. This is a similar notion to *inter-rater consistency* (see Key concept 7.3).

- *Internal validity*, by which they mean whether there is a correspondence between researchers' observations and the theoretical ideas they develop. LeCompte and Goetz argue that this tends to be a strength of qualitative research, particularly ethnographic research, because the prolonged participation in the social life of a group over a long period of time allows the researcher to develop congruence between concepts and observations.

- *External validity*, which refers to the degree to which findings can be generalized across social settings. LeCompte and Goetz argue that, unlike internal validity, external validity represents a problem for qualitative researchers because of their tendency to employ case studies and small samples.

As this brief treatment suggests, qualitative researchers have tended to employ the terms reliability and validity in very similar ways to quantitative researchers when seeking to develop criteria for assessing research.

Alternative criteria for evaluating qualitative research

An alternative position is that qualitative studies should be judged or evaluated according to quite different criteria from those used by quantitative researchers. Lincoln and Guba (1985) and Guba and Lincoln (1994) propose that it is necessary to specify terms and ways of establishing and assessing the quality of qualitative research that provide an alternative to reliability and validity. They propose two primary criteria for assessing a qualitative study: *trustworthiness* and *authenticity*.

Trustworthiness

Trustworthiness is made up of four criteria, each of which has an equivalent criterion in quantitative research:

1. *credibility*, which parallels internal validity;
2. *transferability*, which parallels external validity;
3. *dependability*, which parallels reliability;
4. *confirmability*, which parallels objectivity.

A major reason for Guba and Lincoln's unease about the simple application of reliability and validity standards to qualitative research is that the criteria presuppose that

a single absolute account of social reality is feasible. In other words, they are critical of the view (described in Chapter 2 as *realist*) that there are absolute truths about the social world that it is the job of the social scientist to reveal. Instead, they argue that there can be more than one and possibly several accounts.

Credibility

The significance of this emphasis on multiple accounts of social reality is especially evident in the trustworthiness criterion of *credibility*. After all, if there can be several possible accounts of an aspect of social reality, it is the feasibility or credibility of the account that a researcher arrives at that determines its acceptability to others. Establishing the credibility of findings entails both ensuring that research is carried out according to the principles of good practice *and* submitting research findings to the members of the social world who were studied in order to obtain confirmation that the investigator has correctly understood that social world. This latter technique is often referred to as **respondent validation** or *member validation* (see Key concept 17.3). Another technique that Guba and Lincoln recommend is **triangulation** (see Key concept 17.4).

Transferability

Because qualitative research typically entails the intensive study of a small group, or of individuals sharing certain characteristics (that is, depth rather than the breadth that is a preoccupation in quantitative research), qualitative findings tend to be oriented to the contextual uniqueness and significance of the aspect of the social world being studied. As Lincoln and Guba (1985: 316) put it, whether findings 'hold in some other context, or even in the same context at some other time, is an empirical issue'. Instead, qualitative researchers are encouraged to produce what Geertz (1973a) calls **thick description**—that is, rich accounts of the details of a culture. Lincoln and Guba argue that a thick description provides others with what they refer to as a database for making judgements about the possible transferability of findings to other milieux.

Dependability

As a parallel to reliability in quantitative research, Lincoln and Guba propose the idea of dependability and argue that, to establish the merit of research in terms of this criterion of trustworthiness, researchers should adopt an 'auditing' approach. The idea is to keep an **audit trail** which entails ensuring that complete records are kept of all phases of the research process—problem formulation, selection of research participants, fieldwork notes, interview transcripts, data analysis decisions, and so on—in an accessible manner. Peers would then act as auditors,

Key concept 17.3
What is respondent validation?

Respondent validation, which is also sometimes called member validation, is a process whereby a researcher provides the people on whom he or she has conducted research with an account of his or her findings. The aim of the exercise is to seek corroboration or otherwise of the account that the researcher has arrived at. Respondent validation has been particularly popular among qualitative researchers, because they frequently want to ensure that there is a good correspondence between their findings and the perspectives and experiences of their research participants. There are several different forms of respondent validation.

- The researcher provides each research participant with an account of what he or she has said to the researcher in an interview and conversations, or of what the researcher observed by watching that person in the course of an observational study. For example, Bloor (1978, 1997) reports that he carried out observations of ear, nose, and throat (ENT) consultants concerning their approaches to making decisions about the assessment of patients. He submitted a report to each consultant on his or her practices.

- The researcher feeds back to a group of people or an organization his or her impressions and findings in relation to that group or organization. Bloor (1997) says that, for his research on therapeutic communities, he conducted group discussions (which were audio-recorded) with community members to gauge reactions to draft research reports.

- The researcher feeds back to a group of people or an organization some of his or her writings that are based on a study of that group or organization (for example, articles, book chapters). Ball (1984) asked teachers in a school in which he had conducted ethnographic research to comment on draft articles and chapters, and similarly Willis (1977) asked the young working-class males who were the focus of his ethnography to comment on draft chapters, as did Skeggs (1994) for her parallel study of young working-class women (see Research in focus 19.7 for further details).

In each case, the goal is to seek confirmation that the researcher's findings and impressions are congruent with the views of those on whom the research was conducted and to seek out areas in which there is a lack of correspondence and the reasons for it. However, the idea is not without practical difficulties.

- Respondent validation may prompt defensive reactions and even censorship on the part of research participants.

- Bloor (1997: 45) observes that, because some approaches to enquiry may result in research participants developing relationships with the researcher of 'fondness and mutual regard', there may be a reluctance to be critical.

- It is questionable whether research participants can validate a researcher's analysis, since this entails inferences being made for an audience of social science peers. This means that, even though the first two methods of respondent validation may receive a corroborative response, the researcher still has to make a further leap, through the development of concepts and theories, in providing a social science frame for the resulting publications. If the third method of respondent validation is employed, it is unlikely that the social scientific analyses will be meaningful to research participants. Hobbs (1993) fed back some of his writings on entrepreneurship in London's East End to his informants, and it is clear that they made little sense of what he had written. Similarly, Skeggs (1994: 86) reports: ' "Can't understand a bloody word it says" was the most common response' (see Research in focus 19.7 for further details of this study).

possibly during the course of the research and certainly at the end to establish how far proper procedures are being and have been followed. This would include assessing the degree to which theoretical inferences can be justified. Auditing has not become a popular approach to enhancing the dependability of qualitative research. A rare example is a study of behaviour at an American 'swap meet', where second-hand goods are bought and sold (Belk et al. 1988). A team of three researchers collected data over four days through observation, interviews, photography, and video-recording. The researchers conducted several trustworthiness tests, such as respondent validation and triangulation. But, in addition, they submitted their draft manuscript and entire data set to three peers, whose task

Key concept 17.4
What is triangulation?

Triangulation entails using more than one method or source of data in the study of social phenomena. The term has been employed somewhat more broadly by Denzin (1970: 310) to refer to an approach that uses 'multiple observers, theoretical perspectives, sources of data, and methodologies', but the emphasis has tended to be on methods of investigation and sources of data. One of the reasons for the advocacy by Webb et al. (1966) of a greater use of unobtrusive methods was their potential in relation to a strategy of triangulation (see Key concept 14.3). Triangulation can operate within and across research strategies. It was originally conceptualized by Webb et al. (1966) as an approach to the development of measures of concepts, whereby more than one method would be employed in the development of measures, resulting in greater confidence in findings. As such, triangulation was very much associated with quantitative research. However, triangulation can also take place within a qualitative research strategy. In fact, ethnographers often check out their observations with interview questions to determine whether they might have misunderstood what they had seen. Bloor (1997) reports that he tackled the process of death certification in a Scottish city in two ways: interviewing clinicians with a responsibility for certifying causes of deaths, and asking the same people to complete dummy death certificates based on case summaries he had prepared. Increasingly, triangulation is also being used to refer to a process of cross-checking findings deriving from both quantitative and qualitative research (Deacon et al. 1998). Triangulation represents just one way in which it may be useful to think about the integration of these two research strategies and is covered in Chapter 27 in the context of mixed methods research.

'was to criticize the project for lack of sufficient data for drawing its conclusions if they saw such a void' (Belk et al. 1988: 456). The study highlights some problems associated with the auditing idea. One is that it is very demanding for the auditors, bearing in mind that qualitative research frequently generates extremely large data sets, and it may be that this is a major reason why it has not become a pervasive approach to validation.

Confirmability

Confirmability is concerned with ensuring that, while recognizing that complete objectivity is impossible, the researcher can be shown to have acted in good faith; in other words, it should be apparent that he or she has not overtly allowed personal values or theoretical inclinations to sway the conduct of the research and the findings deriving from it. Lincoln and Guba propose that establishing confirmability should be one of the objectives of auditors.

Authenticity

In addition to these four trustworthiness criteria, Lincoln and Guba suggest criteria of *authenticity*. These criteria raise a wider set of issues concerning the broader political impact of research. These are the criteria:

- *Fairness*. Does the research fairly represent different viewpoints among members of the social setting?
- *Ontological authenticity*. Does the research help members to arrive at a better understanding of their social milieu?
- *Educative authenticity*. Does the research help members to appreciate better the perspectives of other members of their social setting?
- *Catalytic authenticity*. Has the research acted as an impetus to members to engage in action to change their circumstances?
- *Tactical authenticity*. Has the research empowered members to take the steps necessary for engaging in action?

The authenticity criteria are thought-provoking but have not been influential, and their emphasis on the wider impact of research is controversial. They have certain points of affinity with **action research** (see Key concept 17.5), which by and large has not been a popular form of social research, though it has had some impact in fields like organization studies and education. The emphasis on practical outcomes differentiates it from most social research.

Key concept 17.5
What is action research?

There is no single type of action research, but broadly it can be defined as an approach in which the action researcher and members of a social setting collaborate in the diagnosis of a problem and in the development of a solution based on the diagnosis. It can take a variety of forms, from the action researcher being hired by a client to work on the diagnosis to and solution of a problem, to working with a group of individuals who are identified as needing to develop a capacity for independent action. The collection of data is likely to be involved in the formulation of the diagnosis of a problem and in the emergence of a solution. In action research, the investigator becomes part of the field of study. Action research can involve the collection of both quantitative and qualitative data. Gibson (2004: 5) describes a Canadian project that was interested in the social and cultural factors that have an impact on the prevention and treatment of tuberculosis (TB) among 'foreign-born and aboriginal populations'. The idea for the project came from a nurse in a TB clinic who garnered support from the groups most affected by the disease. An advisory committee, which drew its membership from the local community in a province of Alberta, as well as from government and academic constituencies, was formed. Two representatives from each of the ten distinct socio-cultural communities were recruited and acted as research associates. Following training, they collected data through interviews and analysed some of the resulting data. Interviews were conducted in relation to four groups: TB sufferers; people on prophylaxis; people who refused prophylaxis; and 'those with a more distant history of TB in their country of origin or on aboriginal reserves' (Gibson 2004: 5). The research associates, members of the advisory committee, and academic staff analysed the interview data. The findings revealed that, while the health care system deals well with active TB cases, it is less effective in relation to prevention in communities at risk. They also revealed that health professionals often fail to identify TB because it is not prevalent in Western nations. The advisory group then produced a plan to disseminate its findings and developed other initiatives including 'an information video, a community education nurse position, and TB fact sheet in their various languages' (Gibson 2004: 5).

Action research is more common in some social science areas than others. It is especially common in fields such as business and management research, education, and social policy. It is sometimes dismissed by academics for lacking rigour and for being too partisan in approach. However, it is advocated by some researchers because of its commitment to involving people in the diagnosis of and solutions to problems rather than imposing on them solutions to predefined problems.

Action research should not be confused with *evaluation research* (Key concept 3.5), which usually denotes the study of the impact of an intervention, such as a new social policy or a new innovation in organizations. The research referred to in Research in focus 17.5 was conducted broadly with an evaluation research frame of reference in that it was concerned to evaluate the impact of the introduction of performance appraisal in British universities.

Recent discussions about quality criteria for qualitative research

The main point of discussing Lincoln and Guba's ideas is that they differ from such writers as LeCompte and Goetz in seeking criteria for appraising qualitative research that represent a departure from those employed by quantitative researchers. The issue of research quality in relation to qualitative investigations has become a contested area in recent years, with several schemes of criteria being proposed as possible alternatives to reliability and validity and to schemes like Lincoln and Guba's list. For example, Yardley (2000) proposed the following four criteria:

- *Sensitivity to context*: sensitivity not just to the context of the social setting in which the research is conducted but also to potentially relevant theoretical positions and ethical issues.

- *Commitment and rigour*: substantial engagement with the subject matter, having the necessary skills, and thorough data collection and analysis.

- *Transparency and coherence*: research methods clearly specified, a clearly articulated argument, and a reflexive stance (see Key concept 17.6 on **reflexivity**).

- *Impact and importance*: having an impact on and significance for theory, practitioners, and the community on which the research is conducted.

Key concept 17.6
What is reflexivity?

Reflexivity has several meanings in the social sciences. The term is employed by ethnomethodologists to refer to the way in which speech and action are constitutive of the social world in which they are located; in other words, they do more than merely act as indicators of deeper phenomena (see Chapter 22). The other meaning of the term carries the connotation that social researchers should be reflective about the implications of their methods, values, biases, and decisions for the knowledge of the social world they generate. Relatedly, reflexivity entails a sensitivity to the researcher's cultural, political, and social context. As such, 'knowledge' from a reflexive position is always a reflection of a researcher's location in time and social space. This notion is especially explicit in Pink's (2001) formulation of a reflexive approach to the use of visual images (see the section on 'The rise of visual ethnography' in Chapter 19) and in Plummer's (2001) delineation of a reflexive approach to life histories (see the section on 'Life history and oral history interviewing' in Chapter 20).

There has been evidence of a growing reflexivity in social research in the form of a profusion of books that collect together inside stories of the research process that detail the nuts and bolts of research as distinct from its often sanitized portrayal in research articles. An early volume edited by P. Hammond (1964) paved the way for many imitators (e.g. Bell and Newby 1977; Bryman 1988b; Townsend and Burgess 2009a), and the confessional tales referred to in Chapter 19 are invariably manifestations of this development. Therefore, the rise of reflexivity largely predates the growing awareness of postmodern thinking since the late 1980s. What distinguishes the reflexivity that has followed in the wake of postmodernism is a greater awareness and acknowledgement of the role of the researcher as part and parcel of the construction of knowledge. In other words, the reflexive attitude within postmodernism is highly critical of the notion that the researcher is someone who extracts knowledge from observations and conversations with others and then transmits knowledge to an audience. The researcher is viewed as implicated in the construction of knowledge through the stance that he or she adopts in relation to what is observed and through the ways in which an account is transmitted in the form of a text. This understanding entails an acknowledgement of the implications and significance of the researcher's choices as both observer and writer.

However, reflexivity is a notoriously slippery concept. Lynch (2000) has complained that too often it is assumed that a reflexive position is somehow superior to an unreflexive one. The case for the superiority of reflexivity is rarely made. Moreover, he points out that the term has different meanings. One of these is methodological reflexivity, which comes closest to the kind of reflexivity that is being referred to in this chapter. However, this meaning has a number of sub-meanings, three of which are especially prominent in methodological writings.

1. *Philosophical self-reflection*: an introspection involving 'an inward-looking, sometimes confessional and self-critical examination of one's own beliefs and assumptions' (Lynch 2000: 29).

2. *Methodological self-consciousness*: taking account of one's relationships with those whom one studies.

3. *Methodological self-criticism*: the confessional style of ethnographic writing (see Chapter 19), but Lynch notes that the injunction to be self-critical that is associated with such ethnographic writing is much more pervasive in academic disciplines.

The term 'reflexivity' has to be used with a degree of caution, as Lynch's discussion implies.

When compiling these criteria, Yardley had in mind health researchers who are likely to emphasize the impact of a study; this probably accounts for the presence of the last of these four criteria—impact and importance—which has some affinities with Lincoln and Guba's authenticity criteria.

Perhaps in response to the proliferation of lists of qualitative research criteria and also because of the lack of agreed criteria, Spencer et al. (2003) produced an extremely comprehensive list (see Thinking deeply 17.3). This list of quality criteria draws on the schemes that already existed at the time of their research and also on consultations with researchers in various fields. These consultations were in the form of semi-structured interviews and focus groups with practising researchers and writers on social research methods. In fact, I was one of the interviewees and also a focus group participant.

Thinking deeply 17.3
Using checklists for appraising quality in qualitative research?

Spencer et al. (2003) were commissioned to produce a report for the UK government's Cabinet Office that aimed to provide a framework for assessing the quality of evaluation research studies that derived from qualitative investigations. Although their report focused upon evaluation research (see Key concept 3.5), they drew on considerations relating more generally to qualitative research, so that their scheme has a general relevance.

The authors produced what is probably the most comprehensive list of criteria around. Here are the criteria that they suggest should be used when appraising the quality of a qualitative research study. In the case of each criterion, the original wording has been used.

1. How credible are the findings?
2. Has knowledge/understanding been extended by the research?
3. How well does the evaluation address its original aims and purposes?
4. Scope for drawing wider influences—how well is this explained?
5. How clear is the basis of the evaluative appraisal?
6. How defensible is the research design?
7. How well defended is the sample design/target selection of cases/documents?
8. Sample composition/case inclusion—how well is the eventual coverage described?
9. How well was the data collection carried out?
10. How well has the approach to, and formulation of, the analysis been conveyed?
11. Contexts of data sources—how well are they retained and portrayed?
12. How well has diversity of perspective and content been explored?
13. How well has detail, depth and complexity (richness?) of the data been conveyed?
14. How clear are the links between data, interpretation and conclusions—i.e. how well can the route to any conclusions be seen?
15. How clear and coherent is the reporting?
16. How clear are the assumptions/theoretical perspectives/values that have shaped the form and output of the evaluation?
17. What evidence is there of attention to ethical issues?
18. How adequately has the research process been documented?

Each of these eighteen criteria comes with 'quality indicators' that are designed to help in the appraisal of a study. What is not clear is how such a framework should be used. It has the appearance of a checklist, but, as Spencer et al. (2003: 90) note, there is resistance within the qualitative research community to the possibly rigid application of any list of criteria that a checklist would entail. The researchers found that the idea of checklists of quality criteria was generally regarded rather negatively by interviewees. In fact, Spencer et al. do not promote their framework as a checklist, noting various concerns about the use of checklists in qualitative research, such as the risk of their becoming too prescriptive or being applied too rigidly. However, the fact that the authors do not treat their framework as a checklist does not mean that it cannot or should not be used in that way. Indeed, around the same time that Spencer and her colleagues published their report, Michael Quinn Patton, a leading qualitative evaluation researcher, published online a list of criteria that *was* designed to be used as a checklist—see: http://www.wmich.edu/sites/default/files/attachments/u350/2014/qualitativeevalchecklist.pdf (accessed 29 May 2015). The full report by Spencer *et al.* can be found at:

www.civilservice.gov.uk/wp-content/uploads/2011/09/a_quality_framework_tcm6-38740.pdf (accessed 12 November 2014).

There has been a proliferation of schemes for appraising and/or thinking about quality criteria for qualitative research. These schemes often include similar criteria to those produced by Spencer et al. but repackage them in various ways. For example, Tracy (2010) stipulates eight criteria:

1. Worthy topic—the topic is relevant, interesting, significant, etc.

2. Rich rigour—rich data is supplied in abundance and appropriately

3. Sincerity—the researcher is reflexive (see Key concept 17.6) about values and biases and is transparent in approach

4. Credibility—the researcher implements practices such as thick descriptions, triangulation (see Key concept 17.4), and respondent validation (see Key concept 17.3)

5. Resonance—the research has an affecting impact on readers

6. Significant contribution—the research makes an impact in terms of such outcomes as theory, practice, and morality

7. Ethical—the researcher considers and engages in ethical practices

8. Meaningful coherence—the research addresses what it claims to address, uses appropriate methods, and links research questions, literature, findings and interpretations.

These eight criteria cover similar ground to the Spencer et al. scheme but bundle them together differently. The notion of 'resonance' is possibly the main element that is not explicitly outlined in their scheme. Stige, Malterud, and Midtgarden (2009) have also produced a list of what appear to be criteria for qualitative research and which cover similar ground to the criteria proposed by Spencer et al. and by Tracey. However, Stige et al. argue that the items they outline should be thought of as an agenda for dialogue about qualitative research rather than as strict criteria around which there is a consensus. Thus, these authors are inviting us to think about qualitative research quality criteria differently.

The fact that qualitative researchers have been seeking to make progress in formulating quality criteria appropriate to their approach does not mean that this necessarily has an impact on the reception of their research. Pratt (2008) has shown that many qualitative researchers believe that their work continues to be judged by criteria associated with validity and reliability (introduced in Chapter 3), which tend to be viewed as more appropriate to quantitative research. This tendency has implications for the nature of the research that does get published in academic journals, in that it gives an advantage to those researchers working within a quantitative research tradition. In other words, although qualitative researchers have sought to develop what they deem to be appropriate criteria, the impact on the evaluation of research is not as great as might be expected.

Between quantitative and qualitative research criteria

Hammersley (1992a) lies midway between the preference for adapting quantitative research criteria and the preference for alternative quality criteria when assessing the quality of qualitative investigations. He proposes that validity is an important criterion but reformulates it. For Hammersley, validity means that an empirical account must be plausible and credible and should take into account the amount and kind of evidence used in arriving at a set of findings. Hammersley's position shares with realism (see Key concept 2.3) the notion that there is an external social reality that can be accessed by the researcher. However, he simultaneously shares with the critics of the empirical realist position the rejection of the notion that such access is direct and in particular that the researcher can act as a mirror on the social world, reflecting its image back to an audience. Instead, the researcher is always engaged in representations or constructions of that world. The plausibility and credibility of a researcher's 'truth claims' then become the main considerations in evaluating qualitative research. Hammersley's *subtle realist* position, as he calls it, entails recognizing that we can never be absolutely certain about the truth of any account, since we have no completely incontrovertible way of gaining direct access to the reality on which it is based. Therefore, he argues, 'we must judge the validity of claims [about truth] on the basis of the adequacy of the evidence offered in support of them' (1992a: 69). This means that an account can be held to be 'valid or true if it represents accurately those features of the phenomena that it is intended to describe, explain or theorise' (1992a: 69).

Hammersley also suggests *relevance* as an important criterion of qualitative research. Relevance is taken to be assessed from the vantage point of the importance of a topic within its substantive field or its contribution to the literature on that field. Hammersley also discusses the question of whether the concerns of practitioners (that is, people who are part of the social setting being investigated and who are likely to have a vested interest in the research question and the implications of findings deriving from it) might be an aspect of considerations of relevance. In this way, his approach touches on the kinds of consideration that are addressed by Guba and Lincoln's authenticity criteria (Lincoln and Guba 1985; Guba and Lincoln 1994). However, he recognizes that the kinds of research questions and findings that might be of interest to practitioners and researchers are likely to be different. Practitioners are likely to be interested in research that helps them to understand or address problems with which they are confronted. These may not be at the forefront of a researcher's set of preoccupations. However, there may be occasions when researchers can combine the two and may even be able to use this capability as a means of securing access to organizations in which they wish to conduct research (see Chapter 19 for a further discussion of access issues).

Overview of the issue of quality criteria

There is a recognition that a simple application of the quantitative researcher's criteria of reliability and validity to qualitative research is not desirable, but writers vary in the degree to which they propose a complete overhaul of those criteria. Nor do the three positions outlined above—adapting quantitative research criteria, developing alternative criteria, and Hammersley's subtle realism—represent the full range of possible stances on this issue (Hammersley 1992a; Seale 1999). To a large extent, the differences between the three positions reflect divergences in the degree to which a realist position is broadly accepted or rejected. Writers on qualitative research who apply the ideas of reliability and validity with little if any adaptation broadly position themselves as realists—that is, as saying that social reality can be captured by qualitative researchers through their concepts and theories. Lincoln and Guba reject this view, arguing instead that qualitative researchers' concepts and theories are representations and that there may, therefore, be other equally credible representations of the same phenomena. In terms of the axis with realism at one end and anti-realism at the other, Hammersley's position occupies a middle ground in that, while acknowledging the existence of social phenomena that are part of an external reality, he disavows any suggestion that it is possible to reproduce that reality. Most qualitative researchers nowadays probably operate around the midpoint on this realism axis, though without necessarily endorsing Hammersley's views. Typically, they treat their accounts as one of a number of possible representations rather than as definitive versions of social reality. They also bolster those accounts through some of the strategies advocated by Lincoln and Guba, such as thick descriptions, respondent validation exercises, and triangulation.

To a certain extent, traditional quantitative research criteria have made something of a comeback since the late 1990s. One issue is to do with the perception of qualitative research. For one thing, to reject notions such as reliability and validity could be taken by some constituencies (such as funding bodies) as indicative of a lack of concern with rigour, which is not a desirable impression to project. Consequently, there has been evidence of increased concern with such issues. Armstrong et al. (1997) report the result of an exercise in what they call 'inter-rater reliability', which involved the analysis by six experienced researchers of a focus group transcript. The transcript related to research concerned with links between perceptions of disability and genetic screening. The focus group was made up of sufferers of cystic fibrosis (CF), and the participants were asked to discuss genetic screening. The raters were asked to extract prominent themes from transcripts, which is one of the main ways of analysing qualitative data (see Chapter 24). They tended to identify similar themes but differed in how themes were 'packaged'. One theme that was identified was 'visibility'. This theme was identified in transcripts by all raters and refers to the invisibility of genetic disorders. The CF sufferers felt disadvantaged relative to other disabled groups because of the invisibility of their disorder and felt that the public were more sympathetic to and more inclined to recognize visible disabilities. However, some raters linked it to other issues: two linked it with stigma; one to problems of managing invisibility. In a sense the results are somewhat inconclusive, but they are relevant to this discussion because they reveal an interest in reliability on the part of qualitative researchers. A similar exercise is described in Research in focus 17.2.

Research in focus 17.2
Reliability for qualitative researchers

Gladney et al. (2003) report the findings of an exercise in which two multidisciplinary teams of researchers were asked to analyse qualitative interviews with eighty Texas school students. The interviews were concerned with reflections on violence on television; reasons for violence among some young people; and reasons for some young people *not* being violent. One group of raters read interview transcripts of the interviews; the other group listened to the audio-taped recordings. Thus, the dice were slightly loaded in favour of different themes being identified by the two groups. In spite of this there was remarkable consistency between the two groups in the themes identified. For example, in response to the question 'Why are some young people violent?', Group One identified the following themes: family/parental influence; peer influence; social influence; media influence; and coping. Group Two's themes were: the way they were raised; media influence; appearance; anger, revenge, protection; and environmental or peer influence. Such findings are quite reassuring and are interesting because of their clear concern with reliability in a qualitative research context. Exercises such as this can be viewed as a form of what Lincoln and Guba (1985) call *auditing*.

Student experience
Thinking about reliability

Hannah Creane was concerned about the reliability of her categorization of her qualitative data and enlisted others to check out her thinking.

> There was a slight concern when I was grouping data together that my categorization was of an arbitrary nature, and so I could be making assumptions and theorizing on the basis of highly subjective categories. However, I tried to make sure that all the categories I used were relevant, and I checked them over with other people to make sure they made sense in relation to the research and the questions I was dealing with.

To read more, go to the Online Resource Centre: www.oxfordtextbooks.co.uk/orc/brymansrm5e/

The main preoccupations of qualitative researchers

As was noted in Chapter 7, quantitative and qualitative research can be viewed as exhibiting a set of distinctive but contrasting preoccupations. These preoccupations reflect epistemologically grounded beliefs about what constitutes acceptable knowledge. In Chapter 2, it was suggested that at the level of epistemology, whereas quantitative research is profoundly influenced by a natural science approach to what should count as acceptable knowledge, qualitative researchers are more influenced by interpretivism (see Key concept 2.4). This position can itself be viewed as the product of the confluence of three related stances: Weber's notion of *Verstehen*; symbolic interactionism; and phenomenology. In this section, five distinctive preoccupations among qualitative researchers will be outlined and examined.

Seeing through the eyes of the people being studied

An underlying premise of many qualitative researchers is that the subject matter of the social sciences (that is, people and their social world) does differ from the subject matter of the natural sciences. A key difference is that the objects of analysis of the natural sciences (atoms, molecules, gases, chemicals, metals, and so on) cannot attribute meaning to events and to their environment. However, people *do*. This argument is especially evident in the work of Schutz and can particularly be seen in the passage quoted in Chapter 2 in the section on 'Interpretivism', where Schutz draws attention to the fact that, unlike the objects of the natural sciences, the objects of the social sciences—people—are capable of attributing meaning to their environment. Consequently, many qualitative researchers have suggested that a methodology is required for studying people that reflects these differences between people and the objects of the natural sciences. As a result, many qualitative researchers express a commitment to viewing events and the social world through the eyes of the people that they study. The social world must be interpreted from the perspective of the people being studied, rather than as though they were incapable of their own reflections on the social world. The epistemology underlying qualitative research has been expressed by the authors of one widely read text as involving two central tenets: '(1) . . . face-to-face interaction is the fullest condition of participating in the mind of another human being, and (2) . . . you must participate in the mind of another human being (in sociological terms, "take the role of the other") to acquire social knowledge' (Lofland and Lofland 1995: 16).

It is not surprising, therefore, that many researchers make claims in their reports of their investigations about having sought to take the views of the people they studied as the point of departure. This tendency reveals itself in frequent references to empathy and seeing through others' eyes. Here are some examples.

- Pearson conducted an ethnography of football fans and writes that he wanted 'to access the intersubjective "life-world" (Husserl, 1931) of the supporter groups, spending time with them and trying to understand their behaviour, motivations and their interpretations of the world around them' (2012: 13).

- Benson writes that in her ethnographic study of British expatriates in rural France, she chose to emphasize the 'worldview' of her participants and to focus on 'understanding...their everyday lives in their own terms' (2011: 17).

- In the opening sentence of their book, which is based on an ethnographic study of the work of itinerant technical contractors in the USA, Barley and Kunda (2004: ix) write: 'As ethnographers, our agenda is to depict the world of technical contracting from the perspective of those who live in it.' They go on to claim that their work 'is the story of contracting told from the participants' perspectives' (2004: 30).

- For their research on teenaged girls' views on and experiences of violence, Burman et al. (2001: 447) 'sought to ground the study in young women's experiences of violence, hearing their accounts and privileging their subjective views'.

Student experience
Importance of seeing through research participants' eyes

Rebecca Barnes was attracted to qualitative research for her research on violence in same-sex relationships because there had been only quantitative research in this area and because she wanted to understand the phenomenon in her research participants' own words.

I chose a qualitative research design for a number of reasons. First, I was aware that very little qualitative research exists in my field of research, and at the time that I started my research, I could not find any comprehensive qualitative studies of woman-to-woman partner abuse in the UK. Thus, I wanted my research to contribute towards filling this gap, on a national and international level. I also chose a qualitative research design because I wanted to achieve an in-depth understanding of the experiences of woman-to-woman partner abuse that women reported in their own words and using their own frames of reference. I also set out to achieve a more textured analysis of the dynamics of abuse and the different impacts that being abused has upon women, and how these may change over time.

To read more, go to the Online Resource Centre: www.oxfordtextbooks.co.uk/orc/brymansrm5e/

This preference for seeing through the eyes of the people studied is often accompanied by the closely related goal of seeking to probe beneath surface appearances. By taking the position of the people you are studying, the prospect is raised that they might view things differently from the way an outsider with little direct contact might have expected. This stance reveals itself in:

- Foster's (1995) research on a high-crime community, which was not perceived as such by its inhabitants;
- Skeggs's (1994: 74) study of young working-class women, showing that they were not 'ideological dupes of both social class and femininity';
- Armstrong's (1993: 11) quest in his research on football hooliganism to 'see beyond mere appearances' and his finding that, contrary to the popular view, hooligans are not a highly organized group led by a clearly identifiable group of ringleaders;
- O'Reilly's (2000) ethnography of British expatriates on the Costa del Sol in Spain, in which she shows how the widely held view that this group is deeply dissatisfied with their lives in the sun and long to return is by no means an accurate portrayal in terms of how they view themselves and their situation.
- Michel's (2014) long-term ethnography of investment bankers showing that rather than treating participative forms of organization and decision-making as an opportunity for reducing work pressures, they used them as a platform for greater work intensification.

The empathetic stance of seeking to see through the eyes of one's research participants is very much in tune with interpretivism and demonstrates well the epistemological links with phenomenology, symbolic interactionism, and *Verstehen*. However, it is not without practical problems. For example: the risk of 'going native' and losing sight of what you are studying (see Key concept 19.3); the problem of how far the researcher should go, such as the potential problem of participating in illegal or dangerous activities, which could be a risk in research such as that engaged in by Pearson (2012) who admits that in the course of his study of football fans he witnessed many offences being committed and when in his covert role committed some offences himself; and the possibility that the researcher will be able to see through the eyes of only some of the people who form part of a social scene but not others, such as only people of the same gender. These and other practical difficulties will be addressed in the chapters that follow.

Abductive reasoning

Precisely because in much qualitative research the perspectives of those one is studying are the empirical point of departure, many writers argue that the kind of reasoning involved is better described not as inductive reasoning but as *abductive* reasoning (e.g. N. Blaikie 2004a; Charmaz 2006). With **abduction** the researcher grounds a theoretical understanding of the contexts and people he or she is studying in the language, meanings, and perspectives that form their worldview. The crucial step in abduction is that, having described and understood the world from his or her participants' perspectives, the researcher must come to a social scientific account of the social world as seen from those perspectives. Further, in arriving at a social scientific account the researcher must not lose touch with the world as it is seen by those whose voices provided the data. On the face of it, this looks like an inductive logic, and indeed there is an element of induction in this process, but what distinguishes abduction is that the theoretical account is grounded in the worldview of those one researches. Abduction is broadly inductive in approach but is worth distinguishing by virtue of its reliance on explanation and understanding of participants' worldviews.

Description and the emphasis on context

Qualitative researchers are much more inclined than quantitative researchers to provide a great deal of descriptive detail when reporting their findings. This is not to say that they are exclusively concerned with description. They *are* concerned with explanation, and indeed the extent to which qualitative researchers ask 'why?' questions is frequently understated. For example, Skeggs (1997: 22) has written that her first question for her research on young working-class women was 'why do women, who are clearly not just victims of some ideological conspiracy, consent to a system of class and gender oppression which appears to offer few rewards and little benefit?' (see Research in focus 19.7 for further details of this study).

Many qualitative studies provide a detailed account of what goes on in the setting being investigated and often seem to be full of apparently trivial details. However, these details are frequently important for the qualitative researcher, because of their significance for their subjects and also because the details provide an account of the context within which people's behaviour takes place. This is what Geertz (1973a) had in mind when he recommended the provision of **thick descriptions** of social settings, events, and often individuals. As a result of this emphasis on description, qualitative studies are often full of detailed information about the social worlds being examined. On the surface, some of this detail may appear irrelevant, and, indeed, there is a risk of the researcher becoming too embroiled in descriptive detail. Lofland

and Lofland (1995: 164–5), for example, warn against the sin of what they call 'descriptive excess' in qualitative research, whereby the amount of detail overwhelms or inhibits the analysis of data.

One of the main reasons why qualitative researchers are keen to provide descriptive detail is that they typically emphasize the importance of the contextual understanding of social behaviour. This means that behaviour, values, or whatever is being examined must be understood in context. This recommendation means that we cannot understand the behaviour of members of a social group other than in terms of the specific environment in which they operate. In this way, behaviour that may appear odd or irrational can make sense when we understand the particular context within which that behaviour takes place. The emphasis on context in qualitative research goes back to many of the classic studies in social anthropology, which often demonstrated how a particular practice, such as the magical ritual that may accompany the sowing of seeds, made little sense unless we understand the belief systems of that society. This descriptive detail is what provides the mapping of context in terms of which behaviour is understood. The propensity for description can also be interpreted as a manifestation of the naturalism that pervades much qualitative research (see Key concept 3.4), because it places a premium on detailed, rich descriptions of social settings.

Conducting qualitative research in more than one setting can be helpful in identifying the significance of context and the ways in which it influences behaviour and ways of thinking. Research in focus 17.3 provides an illustration of a multiple-case study that demonstrates this potential.

Emphasis on process

Qualitative research tends to view social life in terms of processes. This tendency reveals itself in a number of different ways. One of the main ways is that there is often a concern to show how events and patterns unfold over time. As a result, qualitative evidence often conveys a strong sense of change and flux. As Pettigrew (1997: 338) usefully puts it, process is 'a sequence of individual and collective events, actions, and activities unfolding over time in context'. Qualitative research that is based in ethnographic methods is particularly associated with this emphasis on process. It is the element of participant observation, a key feature of ethnography, that is especially instrumental in generating this feature.

Ethnographers are typically immersed in a social setting for a long time—frequently years. Consequently, they are able to observe the ways in which events develop over time or the ways in which the different elements of a social system (values, beliefs, behaviour, and so on)

Research in focus 17.3
Contextual understanding in an ethnographic study of three schools

Swain (2004) conducted an ethnographic study of three junior schools in the UK in the late 1990s. Ethnography is discussed in Chapter 19. Because it compared findings from three schools, this was a multiple-case study, which drew on the strengths of using a comparative design in that it was possible to explore the significance of context across the three schools. The schools were different in terms of the social characteristics of the pupils they recruited: Highwoods Independent's pupils were mainly upper middle class; pupils at Petersfield Junior were predominantly middle class; and Westmoor Abbey Junior's pupils were mainly working class (the school names are pseudonyms). Swain (2004: 169) describes his data-collection methods as involving non-participant observation of pupils in lessons and around the school and 'loosely structured interviews' with pupils based on 'nominated friendship groups'. In this article, Swain was interested in the ways in which boys construct what it means to be masculine in the school and draws primarily on data collected on boys rather than on girls. Swain shows that masculinity was inseparable from the achievement of status among school peer groups and that the body was the means of expressing masculinity. The significance of context emerges in connection with Swain's account of how the body was used to convey masculinity in the three schools: at Highwoods, sport was the medium through which the body expressed masculinity; at Westmoor Abbey, the emphasis was macho and frequently took on a violent tone; and, at Petersfield, it was speed and strength (predominantly in the playground rather than on the sports field). Context reveals itself in the different resources in the three schools that students must draw upon to perform masculinity.

interconnect. Such findings can inject a sense of process by seeing social life in terms of streams of interdependent events and elements (see Research in focus 17.4 for an example).

This is not to say, however, that ethnographers are the only qualitative researchers who inject a sense of process into our understanding of social life. This can also be achieved through semi-structured and unstructured interviewing, by asking participants to reflect on the processes leading up to or following on from an event. For example, Krause and Kowalski (2013) were interested in the processes through which young adults aged 26 to 31 years acquire romantic or sexual partners in New York and Berlin. They did this by asking their interviewees how they got together with their current partners or most recent 'dates'. Interviewees were probed for 'the details, turning points and key decisions' as well as 'other stories of courtship' (Krause and Kowalski 2013: 25). Interviewees were asked to provide 'concrete stories in as much detail as possible in order to target the practice of courtship as it unfolds in the everyday' (2013: 25). As a result, the researchers were able to build up accounts of the process of getting together and to compare interviewees from the two cities in this respect. For example, Krause and Kowalski found greater intentionality in the process of getting together in New York than in Berlin.

Thus, process may be investigated in real time through participant observation (see Research in focus 17.4 for an example) or, as in the examples described in the previous paragraph, it may be arrived at through retrospective interviewing or by constructing a processual account through the examination of documents.

Research in focus 17.4
Process and flexibility in the ethnographic study of a restaurant

Demetry (2013: 583) conducted an ethnography of what she describes as 'the kitchen of a high-end restaurant' in the USA. The observation period lasted six months and she observed for four hours at a time once or twice a week, varying the timing of her observations. In addition, she conducted interviews with staff at all levels. Part of the way through her data collection period, the head chef (Matt) left and was replaced with a slightly older man (Paul) who had something of a culinary reputation. With the change of head chef came a change of regime, with a shift from an informal atmosphere of camaraderie to a more professional one with an emphasis on following regulations and being more business-like in the kitchen. The change in managerial regime gave Demetry the opportunity to examine its impact on the kitchen, something that she describes as a 'natural ethnographic experiment'. She notes, for example, how speech patterns and discourse changed and how, contrary to what might be expected, cooks 'negotiated their new occupational demands by symbolically reconstructing their shared past under Matt as inferior to Paul's organization' (Demetry 2013: 600). However, when Paul was away, the kitchen staff reverted to Matt's ways, as revealed in a telling field note:

> The lack of a head chef is obvious everywhere. Pots, pans, and towels are scattered throughout the kitchen. Certainly Paul would not have put up with this mess. Music is also playing in the background. Several times through the night the cooks mention how the kitchen feels like how when Matt was here. Tracy nostalgically notes, 'This is how every day used to be. People are casually talking with each other. Grayson is dancing and cussing as loudly as ever.' Ben adds, 'Paul not being here is about the same [as when Matt was here].' . . . Indeed, the dirty and corny jokes common under Matt returned.

(field note quoted in Demetry 2013: 600)

Demetry shows how time and space were organized in a different way across the two regimes even though the temporal and spatial template of the kitchen and the restaurant was unchanged. This ethnographic case study provides interesting insights into the ways in which the change process is played out in work settings. Demetry was fortunate in being able to study a process—the change process—in real time because she was in the right place at the right time, but she was also concerned to reveal another kind of process, namely the group culture of the kitchen as 'a process where reoccurring patterns of interaction within a group create culture' (2013: 581). In addition, this study demonstrates the significance of the attribute of flexibility in qualitative research, namely, that Demetry was able to capitalize on a fortunate event and weave it into her ethnography.

Flexibility and limited structure

Many qualitative researchers are disdainful of approaches to research that entail the imposition of predetermined formats on the social world. This position is largely to do with the preference for seeing through the eyes of the people being studied. After all, if a structured method of data collection is employed, since this is bound to be the product of an investigator's reflections about the object of enquiry, certain decisions must have been made about what he or she expects to find and about the nature of the social reality that would be encountered. Therefore, the researcher is limited in the degree to which he or she can genuinely adopt the worldview of the people being studied. Consequently, most qualitative researchers prefer a research orientation that entails as little prior contamination of the social world as possible. To do otherwise risks imposing an inappropriate frame of reference on people. Keeping the structure of data-collection instruments to a minimum enhances the opportunity of genuinely revealing research participants' perspectives. Also, in the process, aspects of people's social world that are particularly important to them, but that might not even have occurred to a researcher unacquainted with it, are more likely to be forthcoming. As a result, qualitative research tends to be a strategy that tries not to restrict areas of enquiry too much and to ask fairly general rather than specific research questions (see Thinking deeply 17.2). For example, Dacin, Munir, and Tracey (2010: 1399) justify their selection of a qualitative research approach to investigate whether Cambridge University dining rituals serve to perpetuate the British class system on the grounds that it 'allowed us to build our understanding of the properly contextualized experiences of those involved in the dining ritual, rather than imposing a particular framework upon them'.

Because of the preference for an unstructured approach to the collection of data, qualitative researchers adopt methods of research that do not require the investigator to develop highly specific research questions in advance and therefore to devise instruments specifically for those questions to be answered. Ethnography, with its emphasis on participant observation, is particularly well suited to this orientation. It allows researchers to submerge themselves in a social setting with a fairly general research focus in mind and gradually to formulate a narrower emphasis by making as many observations of that setting as possible. They can then formulate more specific research questions out of their collected data. Similarly, interviewing is an extremely prominent method in the qualitative researcher's armoury, but it is not the kind of interview we encountered in the course of most of Chapter 9—namely, the structured interview. Instead, qualitative researchers prefer less structured approaches to interviewing, as we will see in Chapter 20. Blumer's (1954) argument for sensitizing rather than definitive concepts (that is, the kind employed by quantitative researchers), as discussed above in the section on 'Concepts in qualitative research', is symptomatic of the preference for a more open-ended, and hence less structured, approach.

An advantage of the unstructured nature of most qualitative enquiry (that is, in addition to the prospect of gaining access to people's worldviews) is that it offers the prospect of flexibility. The researcher can change direction in the course of his or her investigation much more easily than in quantitative research, which tends to have a built-in momentum once the data collection is under way: if you send out hundreds of postal questionnaires and realize after you have started to get some back that there is an issue that you would have liked to investigate, you are not going to find it easy to retrieve the situation. Structured interviewing and structured observation can involve some flexibility, but the requirement to make interviews as comparable as possible for survey investigations limits the extent to which this can happen. O'Reilly (2000) has written that her research on the British on the Costa del Sol shifted in two ways over the duration of her participant observation: from an emphasis on the elderly to expatriates of all ages; and from an emphasis on permanent residents to less permanent forms of migration, such as tourism. These changes in emphasis occurred because of the limitations of just focusing on the elderly and on permanent migrants, since these groups were not necessarily as distinctive as might have been supposed. Similarly, Kathleen Gerson has explained that, in her research on changing forms of the family, she conducted an early interview with a young man who had been brought up in his early years in a traditional household that underwent a considerable change during his childhood. This led her to change her focus from an emphasis on family structures to processes of change in the family (Gerson and Horowitz 2002). See Research in focus 17.4 for a further illustration of the significance of flexibility for qualitative research.

Concepts and theory grounded in data

This issue has already been addressed in much of the exposition of qualitative research above. For qualitative researchers, concepts and theories are usually inductively arrived at from the data that are collected (see Research in focus 17.1 and 17.5).

Research in focus 17.5
Emerging concepts

In the late 1980s and early 1990s, most UK universities were in the throes of introducing staff appraisal schemes for both academic and academic-related staff. Staff appraisal is employed to review the appraisee's performance and activities over a period of usually one or two years. Along with some colleagues, I undertook an evaluation of staff appraisal schemes in four universities (Bryman et al. 1994). The research entailed the collection of both quantitative and qualitative data within the framework of a comparative research design. The qualitative data were derived from large numbers of interviews with appraisers, appraisees, senior managers, and many others. In the course of conducting the interviews and analysing the subsequent data we became increasingly aware of a cynicism among many of the people we interviewed. This attitude revealed itself in several ways, such as: a view that appraisal had been introduced just to pacify the government; a belief that nothing happened of any significance in the aftermath of an appraisal meeting; the view that it was not benefiting universities; and a suggestion that many participants in the appraisal process were just going through the motions. As one of the interviewees said in relation to this last feature: 'It's like going through the motions of it [appraisal]. It's just get it over with and signed and dated and filed and that's the end of it' (quoted in Bryman et al. 1994: 180).

On the basis of these findings, it was suggested that the attitudes towards appraisal and the behaviour of those involved in appraisal were characterized by *procedural compliance*, which was defined as 'a response to an organizational innovation in which the technical requirements of the innovation . . . are broadly adhered to, but where there are substantial reservations about its efficacy and only partial commitment to it, so that there is a tendency for the procedures associated with the innovation to be adhered to with less than a total commitment to its aims' (Bryman et al. 1994: 178).

The critique of qualitative research

In a similar way to the criticisms that have been levelled at quantitative research mainly by qualitative researchers, a parallel critique has been built up of qualitative research. Some of the more common criticisms follow.

Qualitative research is too subjective

Quantitative researchers sometimes criticize qualitative research as being impressionistic and subjective. By these criticisms they usually mean that qualitative findings rely too much on the researcher's often unsystematic views about what is significant and important, and also upon the close personal relationships that the researcher frequently strikes up with the people studied. Precisely because qualitative research often begins in a relatively open-ended way and entails a gradual narrowing-down of research questions or problems, the consumer of the writings deriving from the research is given few clues as to why one area was the chosen area upon which attention was focused rather than another. By contrast, quantitative researchers point to the tendency for the problem

formulation stage in their work to be more explicitly stated in terms of such matters as the existing literature on that topic and key theoretical ideas.

Difficult to replicate

Quantitative researchers also often argue that these tendencies are even more of a problem because of the difficulty of replicating a qualitative study, although replication in the social sciences is by no means a straightforward matter regardless of this particular issue (see Chapter 7). Precisely because it is unstructured and often reliant upon the qualitative researcher's ingenuity, it is almost impossible to conduct a true replication, since there are hardly any standard procedures to be followed. In qualitative research, the investigator him- or herself is the main instrument of data collection, so that what is observed and heard and also what is the focus of the data collection are very much products of his or her preferences. There are several possible components of this criticism: what qualitative researchers (especially perhaps in ethnography) choose to emphasize while in the field is a product of what strikes them as significant, whereas other researchers may focus on other issues; the responses of participants (people being observed or interviewed) to qualitative researchers is likely to be affected by the characteristics of the researcher (personality, age, gender, and so on); and, because of the unstructured nature of qualitative data, interpretation will be influenced by the subjective leanings of a researcher. Therefore, it is difficult to replicate qualitative findings. The difficulties ethnographers experience when they revisit grounds previously trodden by another researcher (often referred to as a 'restudy') do not inspire confidence in the replicability of qualitative research (Bryman 1994).

Problems of generalization

It is often suggested that the scope of the findings of qualitative investigations is restricted. When participant observation is used or when qualitative interviews are conducted with a small number of individuals in a certain organization or locality, critics argue that it is impossible to know how the findings can be generalized to other settings. How can just one or two cases be representative of all cases? In other words, can we treat Atkinson's (2006) research on the Welsh National Opera as representative of all opera companies, or Armstrong's (1998) research on Sheffield United supporters as representative of all football supporters, or Demetry's (2013) study of a high-end restaurant in the USA as generalizable to all such establishments? In the case of research based on interviews rather than participation, can we treat interviewees who have not been selected through a probability procedure or even quota sampling as representative? Are the female intravenous drug-users of A. Taylor's study (1993) typical of all members of that category or are the young working-class women of Skeggs's study (1994; see Research in focus 19.7) typical?

The answer in all these cases is, of course, emphatically 'no'. A case study is not a sample of one drawn from a known population. Similarly, the people who are interviewed in qualitative research are not meant to be representative of a population, and indeed, in some cases, such as that of female intravenous drug-users, it may be more or less impossible to enumerate the population in any precise manner. Instead, the findings of qualitative research are to generalize to theory rather than to populations. It is 'the cogency of the theoretical reasoning' (J. C. Mitchell 1983: 207), rather than statistical criteria, that is decisive in considering the generalizability of the findings of qualitative research. In other words, it is the quality of the theoretical inferences that are made out of qualitative data that is crucial to the assessment of generalization. As noted in Chapter 3, this view of generalization is called

'analytic generalization' by Yin (2009) and 'theoretical generalization' by J. C. Mitchell (1983).

However, not all writers on the issue of generalization in relation to qualitative research (and case study research in particular) accept this view. M. Williams (2000: 215) has argued that, in many cases, qualitative researchers are in a position to produce what he calls *moderatum* generalizations—that is, ones in which aspects of the focus of enquiry (a group of drug-users, a group of football hooligans, a strike) 'can be seen to be instances of a broader set of recognizable features'. In addition, Williams argues that not only is it the case that qualitative researchers *can* make such generalizations but in fact they often *do* make them. Thus, when generating findings relating to the hooligans who follow a certain football club, a researcher will often draw comparisons with findings by other researchers relating to comparable groups. Indeed, the researcher may also draw comparisons and linkages with still other groups: followers of other professional sports teams or violent groups that are not linked to sport. When forging such comparisons and linkages, the researcher is engaging in *moderatum* generalization. *Moderatum* generalizations will always be limited and somewhat more tentative than statistical generalizations associated with probability sampling (see Chapter 8), but they do permit a modicum of generalization and help to counter the view that generalization beyond the immediate evidence and the case is impossible in qualitative research.

These three criticisms reflect many of the preoccupations of quantitative research that were discussed in Chapter 7. A further criticism that is often made of qualitative research, but that is perhaps less influenced by quantitative research criteria, is the suggestion that qualitative research frequently lacks transparency in how the research was conducted.

Lack of transparency

It is sometimes difficult to establish from qualitative research what the researcher actually *did* and how he or she arrived at the study's conclusions. For example, qualitative research reports are sometimes unclear about such matters as how people were chosen for observation or interview. This deficiency contrasts sharply with the sometimes laborious accounts of sampling procedures in reports of quantitative research. However, it does not seem plausible to suggest that outlining in some detail the ways in which research participants are selected smacks of quantitative research criteria. Readers have a right to know how research participants were selected and why they were sampled in a particular way. The process of qualitative data analysis is often similarly unclear (Bryman and Burgess 1994a). It is often not obvious how the analysis was conducted—in other words, what the researcher was actually doing when the data were analysed and therefore how the study's conclusions were arrived at. These areas of insufficient transparency are increasingly being addressed by qualitative researchers. It is striking that when O'Cathain et al. (2008) examined issues of quality in mixed methods research in the health services field, the qualitative methods were less likely to be described fully (and sometimes not at all) than the quantitative components.

Is it always like this?

This was a heading that was employed in Chapter 7 in relation to quantitative research, but it is perhaps less easy to answer in relation to qualitative research. To a large extent, this is because qualitative research is less codified than quantitative research—that is, it is less influenced by strict guidelines and directions about how to go about data collection and analysis. As a result, accounts of qualitative research are frequently less prescriptive in tone than those encountered in connection with quantitative research. Instead, they often exhibit more of a descriptive tenor, outlining the different ways qualitative researchers have gone about research or suggesting alternative ways of conducting research or analysis based on the writer's own experiences or those of others. To a large extent, this picture is changing, in that there is a growing number of books that seek to make clear-cut recommendations about how qualitative research should be carried out.

However, if we look at some of the preoccupations of qualitative research that were described above, we can see certain ways in which there are departures from the practices that are implied by these preoccupations. One of the main departures is that qualitative research is sometimes a lot more focused than is implied by the suggestion that the researcher begins with a general research question and narrows it down so that theory and concepts are arrived at during and after the data collection. There is no *necessary* reason why qualitative research cannot be employed to investigate a specific research problem. For example, as noted in Chapters 2 and 3, the study by Hughes et al. (2011) of inter-group relations in three Northern Ireland communities was concerned to provide insight into the usefulness of two contrasting theories of the quality of inter-ethnic relations (contact and conflict theories). This study exhibits multiple-case study design (see Chapter 3), with an emphasis on a comparison of the three cases. However, qualitative research is sometimes very open-ended and relatively unfocused. As noted in Thinking deeply 17.2, some grounded theory practitioners advocate beginning with a blank slate so that theoretical ideas emerge out of the data. However, grounded theory practitioners are not alone in this approach, for it is by no means uncommon for qualitative researchers to begin with a general focus. For example, Barley and Kunda's (2004) ethnography of technical contractors does not appear to have any research questions but seeks instead to shed light on the world of these contractors and to demonstrate the implications of some of their findings for issues in the sociology of work. There seems, then, to be a continuum in qualitative research, with studies at one end presenting highly specific research questions and at the other end studies with almost no specificity at the outset about what the researcher intends to find out about (although such specificity may emerge—see Research in focus 19.5 for an example). In between, there is considerable variety in the extent to which the qualitative research process is influenced at the outset by specific research questions or objectives.

A further way in which qualitative research differs from the standard model is in connection with the notion of a lack of structure in approaches to collecting and analysing data. As will be seen in Chapter 22, techniques such as conversation analysis entail the application of a highly codified method for analysing talk. Moreover, the growing use of computer-assisted qualitative data analysis software (**CAQDAS**), which will be the subject of Chapter 25, is leading to greater transparency in the procedures used for analysing qualitative data. This greater transparency may be producing greater codification in qualitative data analysis than has previously been the case.

Some contrasts between quantitative and qualitative research

Several writers have explored the contrasts between quantitative and qualitative research by devising tables that allow the differences to be brought out (e.g. Halfpenny 1979; Bryman 1988a; Hammersley 1992b). Table 17.1 attempts to draw out the chief contrasting features.

- *Numbers vs Words*. Quantitative researchers are often portrayed as preoccupied with applying measurement procedures to social life, while qualitative researchers are seen as using words in the presentation of analyses of society.

- *Point of view of researcher vs Point of view of participants*. In quantitative research, the investigator is in the driving seat. The set of concerns that he or she brings to an investigation drives the investigation. In qualitative research, the perspective of those being studied—what they see as important and significant—provides the point of orientation.

- *Researcher is distant vs Researcher is close*. This dimension is to do with the relationship between researchers and their research participants. In quantitative research, researchers are uninvolved with their participants and in some cases, as in research based on postal questionnaires or on hired interviewers, may have no contact with them at all. Sometimes, this lack of a relationship with participants is considered desirable by quantitative researchers, because they feel that their objectivity might be compromised if they become too involved with the people they study. The qualitative researcher seeks close involvement with the people being investigated, so that he or she can genuinely understand the world through their eyes.

- *Theory and concepts tested in research vs Theory and concepts emergent from data*. Quantitative researchers typically bring a set of concepts to bear on the research instruments being employed, so that theoretical work precedes the collection of data, whereas in qualitative research concepts and theoretical elaboration emerge out of data collection.

- *Static vs Process*. Quantitative research is frequently depicted as presenting a static image of social reality with its emphasis on relationships between variables. Change and connections between events over time tend not to surface, other than in a mechanistic fashion. Qualitative research is often depicted as attuned to the unfolding of events over time and to the interconnections between the actions of participants of social settings.

- *Structured vs Unstructured*. Quantitative research is typically highly structured, so that the investigator is able to examine the precise concepts and issues that are the focus of the study; in qualitative research the approach is invariably unstructured, so that the possibility of getting at actors' meanings and of concepts emerging out of data collection is enhanced.

- *Generalization vs Contextual understanding*. Whereas quantitative researchers want their findings to be generalizable to the relevant population, the qualitative researcher seeks an understanding of behaviour, values, beliefs, and so on in terms of the context in which the research is conducted.

- *Hard, reliable data vs Rich, deep data*. Quantitative data are often depicted as 'hard' in the sense of being robust and unambiguous, owing to the precision offered by measurement. Qualitative researchers claim, by contrast, that their contextual approach and their often prolonged involvement in a setting engender rich data.

- *Macro vs Micro*. Quantitative researchers are often depicted as involved in uncovering large-scale social trends and connections between variables, whereas qualitative researchers are seen as being concerned with small-scale aspects of social reality, such as interaction.

- *Behaviour vs Meaning*. It is sometimes suggested that the quantitative researcher is concerned with people's behaviour and the qualitative researcher with the meaning of action.

- *Artificial settings vs Natural settings*. Whereas quantitative researchers conduct research in a contrived context, qualitative researchers investigate people in natural environments.

However, while these contrasts depict reasonably well the differences between quantitative and qualitative research, they should not be viewed as constituting hard-and-fast distinctions. Qualitative research can be employed to test theories, while quantitative research is often a good deal more exploratory than is typically assumed. Indeed, the section on 'Reverse operationism' in Chapter 7 implies that in quantitative research concepts

Table 17.1

Some contrasts between quantitative and qualitative research

Quantitative	Qualitative
Numbers	Words
Point of view of researcher	Points of view of participants
Researcher distant	Researcher close
Theory testing	Theory emergent
Static	Process
Structured	Unstructured
Generalization	Contextual understanding
Hard, reliable data	Rich, deep data
Macro	Micro
Behaviour	Meaning
Artificial settings	Natural settings

often emerge out of the data that are collected. Also, it is by no means always appropriate to characterize qualitative researchers as collecting their data in natural (rather than artificial) settings. This may be an appropriate depiction of research based on participant observation, but a lot of qualitative research involves interviewing and interviews do not constitute natural settings, even though the interviews tend to be less structured than in survey research. Further, quantitative and qualitative research are not so far apart that they cannot be combined, as is explained in the discussion in Chapter 27 of mixed methods research.

 # Some similarities between quantitative and qualitative research

It is also worth bearing in mind the ways in which quantitative and qualitative research are *similar* rather than different. Hardy and Bryman (2004) have pointed out that, although there clearly are differences between quantitative and qualitative research, it should also be recognized that there are similarities too. They draw attention to the following points:

- *Both are concerned with data reduction*. Both quantitative and qualitative researchers collect large amounts of data. These large amounts of data represent a problem for researchers, because they then have to distil the data in order to produce findings. By reducing the amount of data, they can then begin to make sense of the data. In quantitative research, the process of data reduction takes the form of statistical analysis—something like a mean or a frequency table is a way of reducing the amount of data on large numbers of people. In qualitative data analysis, as will be seen in Chapter 24, qualitative researchers develop concepts out of their often rich data.

- *Both are concerned with answering research questions*. Although the nature of the kinds of research questions asked in quantitative and qualitative research are typically different (more specific in quantitative research, more open-ended in qualitative research), they are both fundamentally concerned with answering questions about the nature of social reality.

- *Both are concerned with relating data analysis to the research literature*. Both quantitative and qualitative researchers are typically concerned to relate their findings to points thrown up by the literature relating to the topics on which they work. In other words, the researcher's findings take on significance in large part when they are related to the literature.

- *Both are concerned with variation*. In different ways, both quantitative and qualitative researchers seek to uncover and then to represent the variation that they uncover. This means that both groups of researchers are keen to explore how people (or whatever the unit of analysis is) differ and to explore some of the factors connected to that variation, although, once again, the *form* that the variation takes differs.

- *Both treat frequency as a springboard for analysis*. In quantitative research, frequency is a core outcome of collecting data, as the investigator typically wants to reveal the relative frequency with which certain types of behaviour occur or how many newspaper articles emphasize a certain issue. In qualitative research, issues of frequency arise in the fact that, in reports of findings in publications, terms like 'often' or 'most' are commonly employed. Also, when analysing qualitative data, the frequency with which certain themes occur commonly acts as a catalyst for which ones tend to be emphasized when writing up findings.

- *Both seek to ensure that deliberate distortion does not occur*. Very few social researchers nowadays subscribe to the view that it is possible to be an entirely objective and dispassionate student of social life. Further, sometimes researchers can be partisan (see Chapter 6). However, that does not imply that 'anything goes'. In particular, researchers seek to ensure that 'wilful bias' (Hammersley and Gomm 2000) or what Hardy and Bryman (2004: 7) call 'consciously motivated misrepresentation' does not occur.

- *Both argue for the importance of transparency*. Both quantitative and qualitative researchers seek to be clear about their research procedures and how their findings were arrived at. This allows others to judge the quality and importance of their work. In the past, it has sometimes been suggested that qualitative researchers could be opaque about how they went about their investigations, but increasingly transparency surfaces as an expectation.

- *Both must address the question of error*. In Chapter 9, the significance of error for quantitative research (or, more specifically, survey research) and steps that can be taken to reduce its likelihood were introduced. For the quantitative researcher, error must be reduced as far as possible so that variation that is uncovered is real variation and not the product of problems with how questions are asked or how research instruments are administered. In qualitative research, the investigator seeks to reduce error by ensuring that, for example, there is a good fit between his or her concepts and the evidence that has been amassed.

- *Research methods should be appropriate to the research questions*. This point is not addressed by Hardy and Bryman (2004), but a further issue is that both groups of researchers seek to ensure that, when they specify research questions, they select research methods and approaches to the analysis of data that are appropriate to those questions.

These tend to be rather general points of similarity, but they are an important corrective to any view that portrays the two strategies as completely different. There *are* differences between quantitative and qualitative research but that is not to say that there are no points of similarity.

 # Feminism and qualitative research

A further dimension that could have been included in the section on 'Some contrasts between quantitative and qualitative research' is that, in the view of some writers, qualitative research is associated with a feminist sensitivity, and that, by implication, quantitative research is viewed by many feminists as incompatible with feminism. This issue was briefly signposted in Chapter 2. The link between feminism and qualitative research is by no means a cut-and-dried issue, in that, although it became something of an orthodoxy among some writers, it has not found favour with all feminists. Indeed, there are signs at the time of writing that views on the issue are changing.

The notion that there is an affinity between feminism and qualitative research has at least two main components to it: a view that quantitative research is inherently incompatible with feminism, and a view that qualitative research provides greater opportunity for a feminist sensitivity to come to the fore. Quantitative research is frequently viewed as incompatible with feminism for the following reasons.

- According to Mies (1993), quantitative research suppresses the voices of women either by ignoring them or by submerging them in a torrent of facts and statistics.

- The criteria of valid knowledge associated with quantitative research are ones that turn women, when they are the focus of research, into objects. This means that women are again subjected to exploitation, in that knowledge and experience are extracted from them with nothing in return, even when the research is conducted by women (Mies 1993).

- The emphasis on controlling variables further exacerbates this last problem, and indeed the very idea of control is viewed as a masculine approach.

- The use of predetermined categories in quantitative research results in an emphasis on what is already known and consequently in 'the silencing of women's own voices' (Maynard 1998: 18).

- The criteria of valid knowledge associated with quantitative research also mean that women are to be researched in a value-neutral way, when in fact the goals of feminist research should be to conduct research specifically *for* women.

- It is sometimes suggested that the quest for universal laws is inconsistent with feminism's emphasis on the situated nature of social reality, which is seen as embedded in the various social identities (based on gender, ethnicity, sexual orientation, class, and so on) that are unique to individuals (Miner-Rubino et al. 2007).

By contrast, qualitative research has been viewed by many feminists as either more compatible with feminism's central tenets or as more capable of being adapted to those tenets. Thus, in contrast to quantitative research, qualitative research allows:

- women's voices to be heard;

- exploitation to be reduced by giving as well as receiving in the course of fieldwork;

- women *not* to be treated as objects to be controlled by the researcher's technical procedures; and

- the emancipatory goals of feminism to be realized. For example, Skeggs (2001: 429) has observed that one of the earliest principles on which feminist research was based was that it should 'alleviate the conditions of oppression'.

How qualitative research achieves these goals will be addressed particularly in relation to the next four chapters, since the issues and arguments vary somewhat from one method to the other. Skeggs (2001: 429–30) argues that the political goals of feminist research led to a preference for qualitative research 'to focus on women's experience and to listen and explore the shared meanings between women with an aim to reformulate traditional research agendas'. However, there are risks with this prioritization of women's experience. In feminist standpoint epistemology, a perspective that places a particular emphasis on experience from the standpoint of women, this prioritization is especially pronounced. However, as Letherby (2003: 46) has suggested, this position 'can and has been used to replace male supremacy with female supremacy and [to] support binary oppositions'. She suggests that, for many analysts, this is likely to be viewed as an unhelpful position to take.

Student experience
Feminism and the research relationship

For Erin Sanders, the prospect of using a feminist approach drawing on qualitative research was attractive in terms of her personal value commitments. However, as this passage shows, she recognized that there are dilemmas and that the issue of feminist research being less exploitative than other approaches should not be exaggerated.

> A number of ethical questions emerged re interviewing sex workers. Because I was employing feminist methodologies . . . I wanted to truly engage with the women that I spoke to, rather than employing a more positivist methodology that would mandate a sense of distance. I felt that feminist methodologies would allow a more balanced research experience—and would enable me to share information about myself to help offset the inherent power imbalance in the research relationship. However, it became evident to me that, employing a variety of 'traditional' feminist methodologies, there was still a power differential. I had hoped to avoid exploiting the women I interviewed for my own personal gain, but I am not sure that this actually happened. I'm not sure that it is ever possible to overcome the power imbalance in the research relationship, especially when I, as a 'White', 'Western' woman, research an 'Other'. From an ethical perspective, it seems to me that the research relationship fosters an exploitative relationship in a number of ways, and I will have to seriously consider how (or if) I can avoid these in future.

To read more, go to the Online Resource Centre: **www.oxfordtextbooks.co.uk/brymansrm5e/**

In fact, the issue of qualitative research as providing the opportunity for a feminist approach has somewhat different aspects when looking at ethnography, qualitative interviewing, and focus groups—the topics of Chapters 19–21. However, it ought also to be recognized that there has been a softening of attitude among some feminist writers towards quantitative research in recent years. Examples of this softening are as follows.

- There is a recognition that many of the worst excesses of discrimination against women might not have come to light so clearly were it not for the collection and analysis of statistics revealing discrimination (Maynard 1994; Oakley 1998). The very presence of factual evidence of this kind has allowed the case for equal opportunities legislation to be made much more sharply, although, needless to say, there is much more that still needs to be done in this field.

- Quantitative research can be enlisted as an aid to implementing social change for feminists. Miner-Rubino et al. (2007) suggest that knowing about the distribution of attitudes and behaviour in a sample can be used to establish the most appropriate course of action for social change.

- J. Scott (2010) has observed that one reason why qualitative research has often been preferred among many feminist researchers is that they have tended to be interested in women's experiences. Qualitative research is well attuned to such study. However, this represents only part of the picture when it comes to understanding inequalities, because investigating the experience of gender inequality and discrimination neglects the wider picture of the wider social structures in which those experiences are embedded. Also needed is large-scale quantitative evidence of the extent and form of gender inequality and discrimination. Scott shows how survey evidence can do this. For example, discussing one set of data, she shows that, 'although overall there has been a decrease in the downward mobility of women across childbirth, if women have longer breaks out of the work force or return after childbirth to a part-time job, the occupational penalties in terms of downward mobility have *increased* over time' (J. Scott 2010: 229). Such evidence can be of considerable significance from a feminist perspective, even though in itself it does not address women's experiences. What is crucial is that the research questions that drive a feminist quantitative project are informed by a feminist perspective.

- As Jayaratne and Stewart (1991) and Maynard (1994, 1998) have pointed out, at the very least it is difficult to see why feminist research that combines quantitative and qualitative research would be incompatible with the feminist cause.

- There has also been a recognition of the fact that qualitative research is not *ipso facto* feminist in orientation. If, for example, ethnography provided for a feminist sensitivity, we would expect fields like social anthropology, which have been virtually founded on the approach, to be almost inherently feminist, which is patently not the case (Reinharz 1992: 47–8). If this is so, the question of appropriate approaches to feminist research would seem to reside in the *application* of methods rather than something that is inherent in them. Consequently, some writers have preferred to write about *feminist researchpractice* rather than about *feminist methods* (Maynard 1998: 128).

These issues will be returned to in Chapters 19–21.

Key points

- There is disagreement over what precisely qualitative research is.
- Qualitative research does not lend itself to the delineation of a clear set of linear steps.
- It tends to be a more open-ended research strategy than is typically the case with quantitative research.
- Theories and concepts are viewed as outcomes of the research process.
- There is considerable unease about the simple application of the reliability and validity criteria associated with quantitative research to qualitative research. Indeed, some writers prefer to use alternative criteria that have parallels with reliability and validity.
- Most qualitative researchers reveal a preference for seeing through the eyes of research participants.
- Several writers have depicted qualitative research as having a far greater affinity with a feminist standpoint than quantitative research can exhibit.

Questions for review

- What are some of the difficulties with providing a general account of the nature of qualitative research?
- Outline some of the traditions of qualitative research.
- How compelling is Denzin and Lincoln's (2005b) marking-out of distinct 'moments' in the history of qualitative research?
- What are some of the main research methods associated with qualitative research?

The main steps in qualitative research

- Does a research question in qualitative research have the same significance and characteristics as in quantitative research?

Theory and research

- Is the approach to theory in qualitative research inductive or deductive?

Concepts in qualitative research

- What is the difference between definitive and sensitizing concepts?

Reliability and validity in qualitative research

- How have some writers adapted the notions of reliability and validity to qualitative research?
- Why have some writers sought alternative criteria for the evaluation of qualitative research?
- Evaluate Lincoln and Guba's (1985) criteria.
- Would it be useful to develop quality criteria into checklists?
- What is respondent validation?
- What is triangulation?
- Can checklists be valuable for appraising the quality of qualitative studies?

The main preoccupations of qualitative researchers

- Outline the main preoccupations of qualitative researchers.
- How do these preoccupations differ from those of quantitative researchers, which were considered in Chapter 7?

The critique of qualitative research

- What are some of the main criticisms that are frequently levelled at qualitative research?
- To what extent do these criticisms reflect the preoccupations of quantitative research?

Is it always like this?

- Can qualitative research be employed in relation to hypothesis testing?

Some contrasts between quantitative and qualitative research

- 'The difference between quantitative and qualitative research revolves entirely around the concern with numbers in the former and with words in the latter.' How far do you agree with this statement?

Some similarities between quantitative and qualitative research

- Does it make sense to describe quantitative and qualitative research as being characterized by both differences *and* similarities?

Feminism and qualitative research

- Why have many feminist researchers preferred qualitative research?
- Is there no role for quantitative research in relation to feminist research?

Online Resource Centre

www.oxfordtextbooks.co.uk/orc/brymansrm5e/

Visit the Online Resource Centre to enrich your understanding of the nature of qualitative research. Follow up links to other resources, test yourself using multiple choice questions, and gain further guidance and inspiration from the Student Researcher's Toolkit.

18

Sampling in qualitative research

 ## *Chapter outline*

 ## *Chapter guide*

This chapter outlines the main ways of sampling in qualitative research. Whereas, in survey research, there is an emphasis on probability sampling, qualitative researchers tend to emphasize *purposive sampling*, which places the investigator's research questions at the heart of the sampling considerations. This chapter explores:

- the significance of a consideration of levels of sampling;
- the nature of purposive sampling and the reasons for its emphasis among many qualitative researchers;
- theoretical sampling, which is a key ingredient of the grounded theory approach, and the nature of theoretical saturation, which is one of the main elements of this sampling strategy;
- the importance of not assuming that theoretical and purposive sampling are the same thing;
- the generic purposive sampling approach as a means of distinguishing theoretical sampling from purposive sampling in general;
- the use of more than one sampling approach in qualitative research.

Introduction

In much the same way that, in quantitative research, the discussion of sampling revolves around **probability sampling**, discussions of sampling in qualitative research tend to revolve around the notion of **purposive sampling** (see Key concept 18.1). This type of sampling is to do with the selection of units (which may be people, organizations,

Key concept 18.1
What is purposive sampling?

Purposive sampling is a non-probability form of sampling. The researcher does not seek to sample research participants on a random basis. The goal of purposive sampling is to sample cases/participants in a strategic way, so that those sampled are relevant to the research questions that are posed. Very often, the researcher will want to sample in order to ensure that there is a good deal of variety in the resulting sample, so that sample members differ from each other in terms of key characteristics relevant to the research question. Because it is a non-probability sampling approach, purposive sampling does not allow the researcher to generalize to a population. Although a purposive sample is not a random sample, it is not a convenience sample either (see Chapter 8 on convenience sampling). A convenience sample is simply available by chance to the researcher, whereas in purposive sampling the researcher samples with his or her research goals in mind. In purposive sampling, sites, such as organizations, and people (or whatever the unit of analysis is) within sites are selected because of their relevance to the research questions. The researcher needs to be clear in his or her mind what the criteria are that will be relevant to the inclusion or exclusion of units of analysis (whether the 'units' are sites, people, or something else). Examples of purposive sampling in qualitative research are theoretical sampling (see Key concept 18.3) and snowball sampling (see Research in focus 18.2 for an example). In quantitative research, quota sampling is a form of purposive sampling procedure.

documents, departments, and so on), with direct reference to the research questions being asked. The idea is that the research questions should give an indication of which units need to be sampled. Research questions are likely to provide guidelines as to what categories of people (or whatever the unit of analysis is) need to be the focus of attention and therefore sampled. In this chapter, purposive sampling will serve as the master concept around which different sampling approaches in qualitative research can be distinguished.

Probability sampling may be used in qualitative research, though it is more likely to occur in interview-based rather than in ethnographic qualitative studies. There is no obvious rule of thumb that may be used to help the qualitative researcher in deciding when it might be appropriate to employ probability sampling, but two criteria might be envisaged. First, if it is important for the qualitative researcher to be able to generalize to a wider population, probability sampling is likely to be a more compelling sampling approach. This might occur when the audience for one's work is one for whom generalizability in the traditional sense of the word is important. Second, if the research questions do not suggest that particular categories of people (or whatever the unit of analysis is) should be sampled, there may be a case for sampling randomly.

However, probability sampling is rarely used in qualitative research. In many cases, it is not feasible, because of the constraints of ongoing fieldwork and also because it can be difficult to map 'the population' from which a random sample might be taken—that is, to create a sampling frame. However, the reason why qualitative researchers rarely seek to generate random samples is not due to these technical constraints but because, like researchers basing their investigations on qualitative interviewing, they typically want to ensure that they gain access to as wide a range of individuals relevant to their research questions as possible, so that many different participant perspectives and ranges of activity are the focus of attention.

Levels of sampling

Writers on sampling in qualitative research sometimes provide lists of the different sampling approaches that may be found (see Key concept 18.2 for some of the main types). While these are useful, they sometimes intermingle two different levels of sampling, an issue that is particularly relevant to the consideration of sampling in qualitative research based on single-case study or multiple-case study designs. With such research designs, the researcher must first select the case or cases; subsequently, the researcher must sample units within the case. When sampling contexts or cases, qualitative researchers have a number of principles of purposive sampling on which to draw. To a significant extent, the ideas and principles behind these were introduced in Chapter 3 in connection with the different types of case, particularly following Yin's (2009) classification. An example is a study by Savage et al. (2005) of the ways in which people retain a sense of place in the face of growing globalization. The authors sampled four areas in the Greater Manchester area and then sampled households within each of the four areas. In fact, in this research there are three levels of sampling. First, the authors justify their selection of Manchester as a site for the examination of globalization and a sense of local belonging by showing that it 'exemplifies the tensions and ambivalences of globalization itself' (Savage et al. 2005: 14). In terms of the categorization of types of case presented in Chapter 3, Manchester is therefore an exemplifying case. Subsequently, there were two levels of sampling: of contexts and then of participants.

1. *Sampling of context.* The researchers 'selected four contrasting residential areas in and around Manchester, whose residents had different combinations of economic and/or cultural capital and we deliberately did not seek to examine those in poor or working-class areas' (Savage et al. 2005: 15). The four sampled areas—Cheadle, Chorlton, Ramsbottom, and Wilmslow—were therefore purposively selected in line with the researchers' focus on local belonging in an era of globalization. Each is an exemplifying case in its own right, since the four areas 'were chosen to exemplify different kinds of social mix' (Savage et al. 2005: 17). The areas were sampled on the basis of statistical data and the researchers' 'local investigations'. We see here a common strategy when sampling for multiple-case studies: sampling for both heterogeneity (the different social mixes of the four areas) and homogeneity (all within Greater Manchester and therefore a common heritage).

2. *Sampling of participants.* Savage et al. write that they sought to generate a sample within each area that exemplified the population under consideration. Using the electoral register as a sampling frame, they sampled one in three of certain streets and then arranged interviews with individuals in households. They interviewed 186 people across the four areas using a semi-structured interview guide, achieving a 34 per cent response rate. Their sampling strategy allowed them to examine similarities and differences among interviewees within each area and between areas.

Key concept 18.2
Some purposive sampling approaches

The following is a list of some prominent types of purposive sample that have been identified by writers such as Patton (1990) and Palys (2008):

1. *Extreme or deviant case sampling.* Sampling cases that are unusual or that are unusually at the far end(s) of a particular dimension of interest.

2. *Typical case sampling.* Sampling a case because it exemplifies a dimension of interest.

3. *Critical case sampling.* Sampling a crucial case that permits a logical inference about the phenomenon of interest—for example, a case might be chosen precisely because it is anticipated that it might allow a theory to be tested.

4. *Maximum variation sampling.* Sampling to ensure as wide a variation as possible in terms of the dimension of interest.

5. *Criterion sampling.* Sampling all units (cases or individuals) that meet a particular criterion.

6. *Theoretical sampling.* See Key concept 18.3.

7. *Snowball sampling.* See Research in focus 18.2.

8. *Opportunistic sampling.* Capitalizing on opportunities to collect data from certain individuals, contact with whom is largely unforeseen but who may provide data relevant to the research question.

9. *Stratified purposive sampling.* Sampling of usually typical cases or individuals within subgroups of interest.

The first three purposive sampling approaches are ones that are particularly likely to be employed in connection with the selection of cases or contexts. The others are likely to be used in connection with the sampling of individuals as well as cases or contexts.

The sampling of areas and then participants is a common strategy in qualitative research. It can be seen in the research by Butler and Robson (2001), covered in Research in focus 2.1, which entailed sampling three London areas and then interviewees within each. In this way, there were two levels of purposive sampling: of contexts/cases (that is, the areas) and of 'gentrifiers'. It can also be seen in Swain's (2004) ethnographic study of friendship groups in schools that was examined in Research in focus 17.3. In this research, it was important for him to study the construction of masculinity in schools of contrasting socio-economic background. Since his research question implied that the construction of masculinity draws on the cultural resources that are available in a setting, it was important to demonstrate the operation of this process of social construction by exploring different social settings, since the cultural resources would be different in each setting. Because friendship groups were likely to be important contexts within which masculinities were constructed and reinforced, the sampling of students for interview was implemented by drawing on nominated friendship groups. In this research, there were two levels of sampling—of contexts/cases (that is, the schools) and then of participants (that is, of students). See Research in focus 3.17 for two further examples.

 # Purposive sampling

Most sampling in qualitative research entails purposive sampling of some kind. What links the various kinds of purposive sampling approach is that the sampling is conducted with reference to the research questions, so that units of analysis are selected in terms of criteria that will allow the research questions to be answered. This term is explained in Key concept 18.1.

In order to contextualize the discussion, I will draw on two useful distinctions that have been employed in relation to purposive sampling. First, Teddlie and Yu (2007) distinguish a sampling approach that they refer to as sequential sampling, which implies a distinction between sequential and non-sequential approaches. Non-sequential approaches to sampling might be termed 'fixed sampling strategies'. With a sequential approach, sampling is an evolving process in that the researcher usually begins with an initial sample and gradually adds to the sample as befits the research questions. Units are selected by virtue of their relevance to the research questions, and the sample is gradually added to as the investigation evolves. With a fixed purposive sampling strategy, the sample is more or less established at the outset of the research, and there is little or no adding to the sample as the research proceeds. The research questions guide the sampling approach, but the sample is more or less fixed early on in the research process.

Second, Hood (2007) distinguishes between a priori and contingent sampling approaches. A purposive sampling approach is contingent when the criteria for sampling units of analysis evolve over the course of the research. The research questions again guide the sampling of participants, but the relevant sampling criteria shift over the course of the research as the research questions change or multiply. With an a priori purposive sample, the criteria for selecting participants are established at the outset of the research. The criteria will again be ones that are designed to answer the research questions, but the criteria do not evolve as the research progresses.

Theoretical sampling

One form of purposive sampling is **theoretical sampling** (see Key concept 18.3), advocated by Glaser and Strauss (1967) and Strauss and Corbin (1998) in the context of an approach to qualitative data analysis that they developed known as grounded theory. In Glaser and Strauss's view, because of its reliance on statistical rather than theoretical criteria, probability sampling is not appropriate to qualitative research. Theoretical sampling is meant to be an alternative strategy. As they put it: 'Theoretical sampling is done in order to discover categories and their properties and to suggest the interrelationships into a theory. Statistical sampling is done to obtain accurate evidence on distributions of people among categories to be used in descriptions and verifications' (Glaser and Strauss 1967: 62). What distinguishes theoretical sampling from other sampling approaches is the emphasis on the selection of cases and units with reference to the quest for the generation of a theoretical understanding. Figure 18.1 outlines the main steps in theoretical sampling.

In grounded theory, you carry on collecting data (observing, interviewing, collecting documents) through theoretical sampling until theoretical saturation (see Key concept 18.4) has been achieved. This means that successive interviews/observations have both formed the basis for the creation of a category and confirmed its importance; that there is no need to continue with data collection in relation to that category or cluster of categories; and that instead, the researcher should move on and generate hypotheses out of the categories that are building up and then move on to collecting data in relation to these hypotheses. As Charmaz (2006) puts it, when new data no

Figure 18.1
The process of theoretical sampling

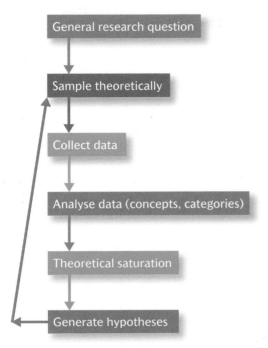

longer stimulate new theoretical understandings or new dimensions of the principal theoretical categories, the relevant categories are saturated. Proponents of grounded theory argue that there is a great deal of redundancy in statistical sampling. For example, committing yourself to interviewing x per cent of an organization's members may mean that you end up wasting time and resources because you could have confirmed the significance of a concept and/or its connections with other concepts by using a much smaller sample. Instead, grounded theory advocates that you sample in terms of what is relevant to and meaningful for your theory. The key is to ensure that you sample so as to test your emerging theoretical ideas. The approach is supposed to be an iterative one—that is, one in which there is a movement backwards and forwards between sampling and theoretical reflection, but it may be that the researcher feels that his or her categories achieve theoretical saturation (see Key concept 18.4) at a relatively early stage. For example, for their research on organization dress, which is referred to in Research in focus 20.7, Rafaeli et al. (1997: 14) initially used a stratified random sampling approach (discussed in Chapter 8) but then evaluated their data 'after completing interviews with the 20 individuals selected and concluded that, because we had reached theoretical saturation (Glaser and Strauss 1967), no additional interviews were necessary'.

Key concept 18.3
What is theoretical sampling?

According to Glaser and Strauss (1967: 45), theoretical sampling 'is the process of data collection for generating theory whereby the analyst jointly collects, codes, and analyzes his data and decides what data to collect next and where to find them, in order to develop his theory as it emerges. The process of data collection is *controlled* by the emerging theory, whether substantive or formal.' This definition conveys a crucial characteristic of theoretical sampling—namely, that it is an ongoing process rather than a distinct and single stage, as it is, for example, in probability sampling. Moreover, it is important to realize that it is not just people who are the 'objects' of sampling, as can be seen in a more recent definition: 'Data gathering driven by concepts derived from the evolving theory and based on the concept of "making comparisons," whose purpose is to go to places, people, or events that will maximize opportunities to discover variations among concepts and to densify categories in terms of their properties and dimensions' (Strauss and Corbin 1998: 201). For Charmaz (2000: 519), theoretical sampling is a 'defining property of grounded theory' and is concerned with the refinement of the theoretical categories that emerge in the course of analysing data that have been collected, rather than boosting sample size. Theoretical sampling differs from generic purposive sampling, which is outlined below, in that its practitioners emphasize using it to provide a springboard for the generation of theory and the refinement of theoretical categories. It is iterative in the sense that it is not a one-off but an ongoing process that entails several stages. In terms of the distinction proposed by Teddlie and Yu (2007), it is a sequential sampling approach; in terms of Hood's distinction, it is a contingent sampling approach. It emphasizes **theoretical saturation** (see Key concept 18.4) as a criterion for deciding when to cease collecting new data on a particular theoretical idea and to move on to the investigation of some ramifications of the emerging theory.

Key concept 18.4
What is theoretical saturation?

The key idea is that you carry on sampling theoretically until a category has been saturated with data. 'This means, until (*a*) no new or relevant data seem to be emerging regarding a category, (*b*) the category is well developed in terms of its properties and dimensions demonstrating variation, and (*c*) the relationships among categories are well established and validated' (Strauss and Corbin 1998: 212). In the language of grounded theory, a category operates at a somewhat higher level of abstraction than a concept in that it may group together several concepts that have common features denoted by the category. Saturation does not mean, as is sometimes suggested, that the researcher develops a sense of déjà vu when listening to what people say in interviews but that new data no longer suggest new theoretical insights or no longer suggest new dimensions of theoretical categories.

The use of theoretical saturation as a criterion for deciding when to cease further sampling does not necessarily imply that a theoretical sampling approach has been employed. This is confirmed by the quotation from Rafaeli et al., where there is no suggestion of an iterative movement between sampling and theory development. What we see here is an approach that is more redolent of what I call below a generic purposive sampling approach than of theoretical sampling.

A theoretical sampling approach that is more in tune with Glaser and Strauss's (1967) idea of theoretical sampling is provided by Finch and Mason's (1990) account of their Family Obligations Project (see Research in focus 18.1). The chief virtue of theoretical sampling is that the emphasis is upon using theoretical reflection on data as the guide to whether more data are needed. It therefore places a premium on theorizing rather than the statistical adequacy of a sample, which may be a limited guide to sample selection in many instances. However, O'Reilly and Parker (2013) argue that the notion of theoretical saturation has become overused in qualitative research in generic ways that do not respect the true meaning of the term or the diversity of qualitative research methods. Crucially, they distinguish between **data saturation**, which is when sampling continues until no new findings are generated, and theoretical saturation, which involves continuing to sample until conceptual categories are fully developed and relationships between them are accounted for. This latter usage is integral to grounded theory, which will be examined in greater detail in the context of qualitative data analysis in Chapter 24. O'Reilly and Parker are also critical of the lack of transparency that surrounds the notion of saturation, as researchers rarely explain in a transparent way how this was achieved. Further, in the context of inductive research, they suggest that data saturation may be an unrealistic target, as the number of themes emerging from a data set is potentially limitless.

The ideas of theoretical sampling and theoretical saturation will be encountered again when grounded theory is examined in greater detail in the context of qualitative data analysis in Chapter 24.

Generic purposive sampling

Hood (2007: 152) has usefully pointed out that there is a tendency among many writers and researchers to 'identify all things qualitative with "grounded theory"'. This is particularly the case with the notion of theoretical sampling, which is often treated as synonymous with purposive sampling when in fact it is one form of purposive sampling (see Key concept 18.3). Hood usefully contrasts grounded theory with what she calls a 'generic inductive qualitative model', which is relatively open-ended and emphasizes the generation of concepts and theories but does not entail (among other things) the iterative style of grounded theory. Sampling considerations are particularly prominent in this contrast between grounded theory and the generic inductive qualitative model. Whereas, as we have seen, theoretical sampling is a sequential sampling process whereby sampling is conducted in order to develop theoretical categories and inferences, in the generic inductive qualitative model, sampling is conducted purposively but not necessarily with regard to the generation of theory and theoretical categories. I am going to call this sampling approach *generic purposive sampling*, a category that incorporates several of the sampling strategies identified in Key concept 18.2, though not theoretical sampling. Generic purposive sampling may be employed in a sequential or in a fixed manner and the criteria for selecting cases or individuals may be formed a priori (for example, socio-demographic criteria) or be contingent or a mixture of both. In most of the examples discussed in this book, generic purposive sampling is fixed and a priori. However, the criteria employed are ones that are informed by the research

Research in focus 18.1
Theoretical sampling in a study of family obligations

Finch and Mason's (1990: 26) Family Obligations Project was a study of 'patterns of support, aid and assistance . . . between adult kin' in Manchester. Initially, survey research, using a structured interview, was conducted and yielded nearly 1,000 completed interviews. A sample of these interviewees was then approached to be interviewed by semi-structured interview. The initial sample for this phase of the investigation was selected purposively—that is, with specific target subgroups in mind. These were divorced and/or remarried people and also the youngest group at the time of the survey (18–24 years of age). Their rationale for this purposive selection is as follows: 'Since fieldwork was principally to be concerned with understanding the process of negotiation between relatives, we decided that it would be much more useful to focus upon individuals who might currently or recently have been involved in processes of negotiation and renegotiation of family relationships' (1990: 33).

Finch and Mason sampled five at a time from the total of each of these subgroups who were willing to be interviewed again (112 in the divorced/remarried subgroup and 117 young adults). Individuals were sampled using random numbers. In addition, the authors wanted to interview the kin groups of individuals from the initial social survey as providing examples of 'negotiations between relatives over issues concerning financial or material support' (1990: 38). They decided to conduct two further interviews with the focal person in a negotiation over family obligations and one interview with each of that person's relatives. However, the sampling strategy was based on the selection not of individuals as cases but of *situations*. In order to make the data comparable, they searched out individuals and their kin who had been identified in the survey—for example, as having moved back into their parents' home following a divorce. A further element in their sampling strategy was that the authors 'tried to keep an eye on the range of experiences that [they] were studying, and to identify any obvious gaps' (1990: 43). As a result of this ongoing 'stocktaking exercise', as they call it, they identified certain gaps in their data: men, because by and large they were the focus of interviews as part of kin networks rather than initial **key informants** in their own right; unemployed people, particularly because of high levels at the time of the research; ethnic minorities; social classes I, IV, and V; widows and widowers; and stepchildren and stepgrandparents. As Finch and Mason's experience shows, the process of theoretical sampling is not only one that gives priority to theoretical significance in sampling decisions, but is also one that forces researchers to sharpen their reflections on their findings during the fieldwork process.

---

questions. When using a generic purposive sampling approach with respect to the selection of cases or contexts, the researcher establishes criteria concerning the kinds of cases needed to address the research questions, identifies appropriate cases, and then samples from those cases that have been identified. When contexts are being sampled, as in the examples cited above in the work of Butler and Robson (2001), Swain (2004), and Savage et al. (2005), it is common for some form of generic purposive sampling to be employed. In the case of the study by Savage et al., each of the four sampled areas had to be predominantly middle class but had to vary in terms of social mix. These were criteria specified at the outset that determined the sampling of areas. In Swain's (2004) ethnographic research, the three schools were selected to reveal variation in terms of two criteria: type of school (state versus fee-paying) and the social characteristics of the intake.

Generic purposive sampling (or variations of it) is often employed in relation to the selection of participants.

The initial sample that provided the basis for the twenty participants in the study by Jones et al. (2010) that was referred to several times in Chapter 1 (see in particular Table 1.1) was generated by searching in the databases of several organizations for senior managers who had taken early retirement. Thus, two criteria appear to have been established from the outset on an a priori basis—being a senior manager and an early retiree. For her study of new forms of mediated communication and their implications for interaction, Rettie (2009) focused upon mobile phone communication. She conducted semi-structured interviews with thirty-two UK adults who spent at least £15 per month on their mobile phones. For their study of the meaning of work–life balance issues for trade union representatives in two sectors (retailing and media), Rigby and O'Brien-Smith (2010) selected a purposive sample based on three criteria: representatives were at each of three levels (national officials, full-time officials, and lay representatives); union respondents were at 'better organised workplaces' (2010: 206); and there was variety in the geographical location of the representatives who were interviewed. Finally, for the research referred to in Research in focus 20.8, the authors purposively sampled employees from each of six quite different organizations. They write: 'We aimed for diversity in terms of age, organization and occupation, and approximately equal numbers of men and women. Our assumption was that this would maximize the likelihood of accessing variation and highlight any common core of experience more than a homogeneous sample would' (Bosley et al. 2009: 1499). What we see in all these examples is a quest for appropriate samples in terms of the research questions in which the researcher is interested.

Generic purposive sampling in a mixed methods context

Sometimes, when conducting a mixed methods investigation involving both quantitative and qualitative research, the findings from a survey might be used as the basis for the selection of a purposive sample. For example, in a study of social policy researchers in the UK, a Web survey was conducted that sought respondents' views on a wide variety of issues concerning criteria for evaluating the quality of social policy research (Sempik et al. 2007; Bryman et al. 2008). Respondents were asked whether they would be prepared to be interviewed by telephone so that issues could be probed more deeply and other issues that had not been explored in the Web survey could be addressed. Of the 251 respondents who replied to the online questionnaire, 90 agreed to be interviewed. On the basis of their replies, 28 of the 90 respondents were interviewed by telephone using a semi-structured interview approach. The 28 interviewees were selected to reflect a variety of orientations to social policy research and to the evaluation of research quality. For example, one criterion was derived from where the respondent stood on the issue of whether he or she felt that social policy research should contribute to policy and practice or to knowledge or to a combination of both. This sampling strategy allowed interviewees to be selected purposively in terms of criteria that were central to the main topic of the research—the appraisal of research quality.

Another example is the study by Brannen et al. (2013), referred to in Chapter 17, of the ways in which dual earner

Student experience
Purposive sampling for a student project

Several of the students who completed questionnaires about their investigations used a form of purposive sampling when they were conducting qualitative research. Isabella Robbins provided a particularly detailed account of how she went about purposive sampling of mothers for her study of decision-making in relation to childhood vaccinations and the reasons for some of her choices. Her sampling strategy entailed a generic purposive sampling approach.

> Recruitment of participants was planned to take place in my own locality, for the pragmatic reason of fitting in the collection of fieldwork with my own complex obligations. I planned to recruit mothers with contrasting socio-economic profiles, the reason being, to help make key comparisons and test and develop theoretical propositions. My plan was to recruit twenty mothers from working-class and twenty mothers from middle-class profiles in order to yield approximately forty interviews. I acknowledge that assigning the profile of class is problematic, and even more so for women whose working status is interrupted by motherhood. Their socio-economic profiles were assigned based on the mothers' current or previous job using the National Statistics Socio-Economic Classification (NS-SEC) schema.

> Vaccination rates are known to differ in terms of socio-demographic profiles. In line with this, I gained access to parent and toddler groups in identifiable working-class and middle-class areas of Nottingham . . . Mothers were recruited through Parent and Toddler groups in areas with socio-economic profiles. Names of the groups and their organizers were identified from a local council publication, supplemented by other publications offering information regarding services offered to parents and children in the locality.

One of the features that is striking about this account is that Isabella employed statistics about vaccination rates as a springboard for her choices of criteria of whom to interview.

To read more, go to the Online Resource Centre: www.oxfordtextbooks.co.uk/orc/brymansrm5e/

families with young children integrated meal times and food preparation into their busy lives. The researchers selected interviewees by following up respondents to the UK's National Diet and Nutrition Survey. The authors write:

> We selected households from NDNS according to a number of criteria: a range of households with higher and lower incomes, and a roughly equal distribution of children by gender and age.
>
> (Brannen et al. 2013: 420)

In this way, quantitative data are used essentially as a sampling frame from which to purposively sample people from whom qualitative data will be collected.

Snowball sampling

Snowball sampling is a technique in which the researcher initially samples a small group of people relevant to the research questions, and these sampled participants propose other participants who have had the experience or characteristics relevant to the research. These participants will then suggest others and so on. As noted in Chapter 8, it is sometimes (though rarely) used in survey research when probability sampling is more or less impossible. It is also sometimes recommended when networks of individuals are the focus of attention (Coleman 1958). In fact, Noy (2008) points out that snowball sampling is frequently presented as a strategy to be employed when probability sampling is impossible or not feasible—for example, when trying to sample populations that are hard to reach because of the absence of a sampling frame. This is often how it is represented in discussions of its use in survey research and sometimes in qualitative research too (see Research

in focus 8.4). However, Noy observes from his studies of Israeli backpackers and of Israeli semi-professional male drivers that one advantage the technique offers is that it is able simultaneously to capitalize on and to reveal the connectedness of individuals in networks. Snowball sampling was employed in my study of visitors to Disney theme parks and by Scheper-Hughes in her ethnography of the illicit trade in organs (see Research in focus 18.2).

The sampling of informants in ethnographic research is sometimes a combination of opportunistic sampling and snowball sampling. Much of the time ethnographers are forced to gather information from whatever sources are available to them. Very often they face opposition or at least indifference to their research and are relieved to glean information or views from whoever is prepared to divulge such details. Also, the difficulty of finding appropriate participants frequently leads to the adoption of such a strategy. For example, Benson (2011: 17) writes of her approach to sampling British expatriates in rural France that on a previous visit to the area in which she conducted fieldwork, she had encountered a family who were very co-operative and who, in addition to acting as participants, introduced her to friends and acquaintances in the area. However, although she was very occasionally able to approach Britons who had been overheard talking in restaurants, she soon realized that 'there were very few public places where the British in the Lot regularly congregated' (2011: 17). As a result, she writes:

> Over time, my initial participants would introduce me to their friends or recommend people I could approach. In this way, I established myself within a wide network of Britons living in the Lot.
>
> (Benson 2011: 17)

Research in focus 18.2
A snowball sample

For her study of a highly sensitive and covert area—the global trade in organs—Scheper-Hughes (2004: 31) describes her sampling approach as follows (although using the term 'she', Scheper-Hughes is referring to herself):

> Using the traditional method of 'snowballing'—one patient, one surgeon, one hospital, one mortuary, one eye bank leading to the next—she begins to uncover a string of clues that will eventually take her from Brazil to Argentina and Cuba, and from South Africa to Israel, the West Bank and Turkey, and from Moldova in Eastern Europe to the Philippines in Southeast Asia. Finally, the clues lead her back to transplant units in Baltimore, Philadelphia and New York City.

> Through this sampling procedure, she was able to interview a diversity of people involved in the organs trade—transplant surgeons, nurses, procurement specialists, police officers, health ministers, and so on as well as kidney donors in several countries, kidney hunters, kidney buyers, and organ brokers. In addition, she was able to observe many of the transactions that took place.

Student experience
Snowball sampling for a student project

Jonathan Smetherham used snowball sampling for his ethnographic study of a non-governmental organization in rural Nicaragua. He writes:

> Snowball sampling was used as I was living amongst the community for 7 weeks & contacts would be made almost every day through my activities as a volunteer. By spending time talking to local residents, I would be introduced to others and made aware of further areas of the community that I would benefit from visiting.

 To read more, go to the Online Resource Centre: www.oxfordtextbooks.co.uk/orc/brymansrm5e/

Similarly, A. Taylor (1993: 16) has written in connection with her study of female drug-users that her research participants were

> eventually obtained by a mix of 'snowballing techniques' . . . and my almost continuous presence in the area. . . . Rather than ask to be introduced or given names of others I could contact, when I met a woman I would spend as much time with her as she would allow, participating in her daily round, and through this come to meet others in her social circle. My continued presence in the area also led other women drug users to approach me when I was alone . . . In addition, the drug worker in the area would mention my presence and interest to women with whom he came in contact and facilitate introductions where possible.

 # Sample size

One of the problems that the qualitative researcher faces is that it can be difficult to establish at the outset how many people will be interviewed if theoretical considerations guide selection. It is impossible to know, for example, how many people should be interviewed before theoretical saturation has been achieved. This is not helped by the fact that the criteria for recognizing or establishing when or whether saturation has been achieved are rarely articulated in detail (Guest et al. 2006). Also, as an investigation proceeds, it may become apparent that groups will need to be interviewed who were not anticipated at the outset. Morse (2004a) gives the example of a study of sudden infant death syndrome, which was initially to focus on parents but which, as a result of interviews with them, had to be broadened to include professionals. This necessity arose because parents' accounts flagged the importance of there being uncertainty about which groups of professionals had primary responsibility in such circumstances. With probability sampling, such considerations can be specified, taking into account the size of the population and time and cost constraints.

As a rule of thumb, however, the broader the scope of a qualitative study and the more comparisons between groups in the sample that are required, the more interviews will need to be carried out (Warren 2002; Morse 2004b). Taking the second of these two criteria, if several comparisons are likely to be wanted—between males and females, different age groups, different types of research participants in terms of locally relevant factors—a larger sample is likely to be necessary. Also, in a study of the experience of relationship breakdown, fewer respondents are likely to be necessary if the emphasis is on those who have been formally married as opposed to the more general category of being in a relationship. Nonetheless, Warren (2002: 99) remarks that, for a qualitative interview study to be published, the minimum number of interviews required seems to be between 20 and 30. This suggests that, although there is an emphasis on the importance of sampling purposively in qualitative research, minimum levels of acceptability operate, although there are almost certainly exceptions to Warren's rule (for example, very intensive interviews of the kind conducted in life story interviews, where there may be just one or two interviewees). By no means all practitioners would agree with Warren's figure. Gerson and Horowitz (2002: 223) write that 'fewer than 60 interviews cannot support convincing conclusions and more than 150 produce too much material to analyse effectively and expeditiously'. However, Adler and Adler (2012) advise a range between 12 and 60 and a mean of 30. The differences between these various authors suggest how difficult it can be to try to specify minimum sample sizes (see also Guest et al. (2006) and Mason (2010) for other summaries of some researchers' suggestions on this issue). The size of sample that is able to support convincing conclusions is likely to vary somewhat from situation to situation in purposive sampling terms, and qualitative researchers have to recognize that they are engaged in a delicate balancing act:

> In general, sample sizes in qualitative research should not be so small as to make it difficult to achieve data saturation, theoretical saturation, or informational redundancy. At the same time, the sample should not be so large that it is difficult to undertake a deep, case-oriented analysis.
>
> (Onwuegbuzie and Collins 2007: 289)

Given the ranges of opinion about appropriate sample sizes, it is not surprising that, when Mason (2010) examined the abstracts of doctoral theses derived from interview-based qualitative research in Great Britain and Ireland, he found that the 560 theses varied in sample size from 1 to 95, with a mean of 31 and a median of 28. The difference between the mean and median suggests that the mean is being inflated by some rather large samples. Mason refers to a study (an online paper whose link no longer worked when I tried to access it) that reviewed 50 research articles based on grounded theory, which found sample sizes to vary between 5 and 350.

It is also likely that the orientation of the researchers and the purposes of their research will be significant. Crouch and McKenzie (2006) make a virtue of small sample sizes by arguing that samples of fewer than 20 increase the qualitative researcher's chances of getting close involvement with their participants in interview-based studies and generating fine-grained data, features that were significant for their study of long-term cancer survivors. What is crucial is to justify rigorously any sample size. In other words, rather than rely on others' impressions of suitable sample sizes in qualitative research, it is almost certainly better to be clear about the sampling method you employed, why you used it, and why the sample size you achieved is appropriate. It may be that the reason why you feel that a sample of a certain size is adequate is because you feel you have achieved theoretical saturation, a term that, while strongly linked to grounded theory, is often used by researchers operating within a variety of approaches. If saturation is the criterion for sample size, specifying minima or maxima for sample sizes is pointless. Essentially, the criterion for sample size is whatever it takes to achieve saturation. The problem is that, as several writers observe (e.g. Guest et al. 2006; Mason 2010), saturation is often *claimed* but not justified or explained (Bowen 2008). See Thinking deeply 18.1 for more on this issue. Also, even when saturation *is* the criterion for deciding sample size, if this

Thinking deeply 18.1
Saturation and sample size

As noted in the main text, it is very difficult to know in advance how many interviews you need to conduct if theoretical saturation (see Key concept 18.4) is employed as a principle for assessing the adequacy of a sample. Further, the criteria for deciding when theoretical saturation has been achieved are more or less absent. In response to these conundrums, Guest et al. (2006) conducted some experiments with data they had collected from in-depth interviews with women in two West African countries. They had conducted and transcribed sixty interviews. They analysed the process of what they call 'data saturation', which means the number of interviews 'needed to get a reliable sense of thematic exhaustion and variability within [their] data set' (Guest et al. 2006: 65). Interestingly, they found that, by and large, data saturation was achieved once around twelve transcripts had been thematically analysed. Taking the transcripts from just one of the two West African countries, by the time twelve interviews had been examined, 92 per cent of the codes used for this batch of transcripts had been generated. Also, the codes generally did not require significant revision after twelve interviews, implying that saturation of categories was arrived at quite quickly. However, as the authors note, their sample was relatively homogenous (women at high risk of contracting HIV), and the research was narrow in scope (how these women discuss sex). Consequently, it may be that saturation was achieved at an earlier point than with qualitative studies drawing on more heterogeneous samples and with broad research foci. The experiment is instructive in terms of implying that research based on qualitative interviews can be based on quite small samples, when theoretical saturation is used as a criterion for deciding on the adequacy of the sample. Further work could undertake similar experiments with different samples and topics.

means that a sample size is very small it may lack integrity, as suggested by the rules of thumb proposed above by Adler and Adler (2012), Gerson and Horowitz (2002), and Warren (2002). When this occurs, the researcher may be advised to boost the sample to achieve a sample size of greater credibility.

Drawing on several of these issues, Bryman (2012) proposed the following five considerations to be taken into account when deciding how large a sample should be:

1. Saturation: if it is a consideration (as it is in many qualitative studies), this will necessarily be a factor in when to decide that data collection can cease. However, the researcher needs to be clear whether it is *theoretical* saturation or *data* saturation that is the criterion.

2. The minimum requirements for an adequate sample—though, as noted above, there is considerable variation among writers concerning what this figure might be.

3. The style or theoretical underpinnings of the research: some approaches to enquiry such as the life story method and conversation analysis tend to be associated with smaller samples on which the researcher carries out an intensive analysis.

4. The heterogeneity of the population from which the sample is drawn: in the case of a heterogeneous population, a larger sample may be required in order to reflect its inherent variability.

5. Research questions: these vary in scope and specificity, so that those that are broad and quite general may require larger samples in order to address the theoretical and empirical reach of the questions.

These five factors are meant to provide some guidelines in deciding on a sample size. However, it is also crucial to remember to provide a robust justification for the sampling decisions you make in terms of both the sampling approach and the resulting sample size.

Related to the issue of sample size is that you need to be sure that you do not generalize inappropriately from your data. Onwuegbuzie and Leech (2010) observe that for the most part there are two kinds of generalization that may be inferred from a qualitative study. One is analytic generalization, which is much the same as theoretical generalization (J. C. Mitchell 1983). These two terms were encountered in Chapters 3 and 17. The other they call 'case-to-case transfer', which refers to making generalizations from one case to another case that is broadly similar. This is more or less the same as the notion of *moderatum* generalization (M. Williams 2000), which was referred to in Chapter 17. Generalization to a population may be legitimate when a probability sampling procedure has been employed. Onwuegbuzie and Leech analysed all 125 empirical articles that had been published in the *Qualitative Report*, an academic journal that has been in publication since 1990. They found that 29.6 per cent of the articles contained generalizations that illegitimately went beyond the sample participants. In other words, just under one-third of articles made inferences to a population beyond the study's participants. As the authors note, when this occurs, there is an inconsistency between the design of the research and the interpretations that are made about the resulting data. There is clearly a lesson here about the need to appreciate what you can and cannot infer from a sample of any kind, something that applies to sampling in quantitative research too.

 # Not just people

Sampling is not just about people but also about sampling other things. Principles of purposive sampling can be applied to such things as documents, in much the same way that probability sampling can be applied to different kinds of phenomena to generate a representative sample. However, there is another dimension to sampling in qualitative research that is worth bearing in mind. This is to do with needing to sample the different contexts within which interviewing or observation take place. Writing about ethnographic research, Hammersley and Atkinson (1995) mention time and context as needing to be considered in the context of sampling. Attending to *time* means that the ethnographer must make sure that people or events are observed at different times of the day and different days of the week. To do otherwise risks drawing inferences about certain people's behaviour or

about events that are valid only for mornings or for weekdays rather than weekends. It is impossible to be an ethnographer all the time for several reasons: need to take time out to write up notes; other commitments (work or domestic); and body imperatives (eating, sleeping, and so on). When the group in question operates a different cycle from the ethnographer's normal regime (such as night shifts in a hospital or going to nightclubs), the requirement to time sample may necessitate a considerable change of habit.

It can also be important to sample in terms of *context*. People's behaviour is influenced by contextual factors, so that it is important to ensure that such behaviour is observed in a variety of locations. For example, one of the important features of research on football fans is that they are not full-time fans. In order to understand their culture and lives, such writers as Armstrong (1993, 1998), Giulianotti (1995), and Pearson (2009, 2012; Research in focus 19.2) had to ensure that they interacted with them not just around the time of football matches, but also in a variety of contexts (pubs, general socializing), which also meant at different times. Pearson (2012) contrasts his experiences as a participant observer of supporters of both Blackpool and Manchester United football clubs and notes that one significant difference was that he did not live in the same area as fans of the former club whereas he did live in the Manchester area. He writes:

I was now able to gain data about their behaviour outside the immediacy of the football match. Living locally gave me access to a wider and more varied life-world of some of the individuals . . . This gave me a much better idea of how their behaviour around football changed from their behaviour in other contexts.

(Pearson 2012: 31)

The opportunity for ethnographers to observe people's behaviour in different contexts is clearly significant in view of the salience of contextual understanding to the qualitative researcher's epistemological stance (see Chapter 17).

 # Using more than one sampling approach

Purposive sampling often involves more than one of the approaches outlined above. For example, it is quite common for snowball sampling to be preceded by another form of purposive sampling. In effect, the process entails sampling initial participants without using a snowball approach and then using these initial contacts to broaden out through a snowballing method. Thus, in their study of the role of power in the branding of a tourist destination—the Gold Coast in Australia—Marzano and Scott (2009) initially purposively sampled key stakeholders in the branding process. These were individuals who had key roles in the agencies responsible for and with an interest in the branding of this tourist destination. As a result of the snowballing process, people such as senior managers in hotels and theme parks were also identified and became candidates for inclusion in the research, which was conducted by semi-structured interview. Similarly, Vasquez and Wetzel (2009) report the results of a study of racial identities among two US ethnic groups. When collecting data on one of these groups—Potawatomi Indians—the researchers collected data from an initial group of interviewees who had been selected by virtue of their formal positions in the life of Potawatomi Nation. These are described as 'elected officials, directors of key programmes, and community members' (Vasquez and Wetzel 2009: 1560). Thereafter, snowball sampling took over to broaden out the scope of the research, with 113 individuals being interviewed. In both of these studies, individuals were initially selected because they occupied a position relevant to the investigation, and this primary sample was then used to suggest further relevant participants to expand the research. In both cases, a generic purposive sample (based on individuals who met a criterion—occupancy of structural positions relevant to the research) was selected, and then a snowballing approach was used.

A further sense in which more than one sampling approach may be employed is when researchers appear to aim for an element of both purposiveness and representativeness in their approach. As an example, Savage et al. (2005) used an electoral register to sample one in three of certain streets and then arranged interviews with individuals in households. Their search was for interviewees who would exemplify the social make-up of each of the four Manchester areas. Similarly, Butler and Robson (2001) aimed to interview seventy-five 'gentrifiers' in each of three London areas and used the electoral register to locate individuals who could be identified as appropriate to their research. They write: 'we believe that our respondents are largely representative of the middle-class populations in each of our areas' (Butler and Robson 2001: 2148). For her study of hair salons and barbers referred to in Research in focus 2.3, R. S. Cohen (2010) constructed an initial sample by listing all salons in the city by postcode and interviewing at least one person in each establishment. There was then a second stage, which was more suggestive of purposive sampling, where data derived from the survey were employed to select interviewees from four categories of salon that were relevant to the research questions and that had not been sufficiently covered in the first sampling stage: 'salons containing chair-renting, chain-salons, barbershops, and salons with primarily ethnic minority clients' (R. S. Cohen 2010: 204).

There is evidence of a quest for both purposiveness and a degree of representativeness (or at least exemplification) in these three studies. With the work of both Savage et al. and Butler and Robson, the purposiveness reveals itself mainly in the search for areas with appropriate characteristics; in the case of Cohen's research, the purposiveness reveals itself in the boosting of the sample with additional interviewees likely to be relevant to the research questions. At the same time, there is a strong sense of wanting to generate a sample with at least a semblance of representativeness. This is quite an interesting development, since sampling in qualitative research, as we have seen, is primarily associated with purposive sampling. At the same time, it raises an interesting question that may at least in part lie behind the use of representativeness in these studies. Given that, when you sample purposively, in many cases several individuals (or whatever the unit of analysis is) will be eligible for inclusion, how do you decide which one or ones to include? In other words, if my research questions direct me to select a subsample that has criteria *a* and *b* and another subsample that has criteria *a* and *c*, so that I can compare them, how do I choose between the individuals who meet each of the two pairs of criteria? Sampling for at least a modicum of representativeness, as these researchers appear to have done, may be one way of making such a decision.

 ## Key points

- Purposive sampling is the fundamental principle for selecting cases and individuals in qualitative research.

- Purposive sampling places the investigation's research questions at the forefront of sampling considerations.

- It is important to bear in mind that purposive sampling will entail considerations of the levels at which sampling needs to take place.

- It is important to distinguish between theoretical sampling and the generic purposive sampling approach, as they are sometimes treated synonymously.

- Theoretical saturation is a useful principle for making decisions about sample size, but there is evidence that it is often claimed rather than demonstrated.

- There is considerable disagreement about what is an acceptable minimum sample size.

Questions for review

- How does purposive sampling differ from probability sampling and why do many qualitative researchers prefer to use the former?

Levels of sampling

- Why might it be significant to distinguish between the different levels at which sampling can take place in a qualitative research project?

Purposive sampling

- Why is theoretical sampling such an important facet of grounded theory?

- How does theoretical sampling differ from the generic purposive sampling approach?

- Why is theoretical saturation such an important ingredient of theoretical sampling?

- What are the main reasons for considering the use of snowball sampling?

Sample size

- Why do writers seem to disagree so much on what is a minimum acceptable sample size in qualitative research?

- To what extent does theoretical sampling assist the qualitative researcher in making decisions about sample size?

Not just people

- Why might it be important to remember in purposive sampling that it is not just people who are candidates for consideration in sampling issues?

Using more than one sampling approach

- How might it be useful to select people purposively following a survey?

Online Resource Centre
www.oxfordtextbooks.co.uk/orc/brymansrm5e/

Visit the Online Resource Centre to enrich your understanding of sampling in qualitative research. Follow up links to other resources, test yourself using multiple choice questions, and gain further guidance and inspiration from the Student Researcher's Toolkit.

19

Ethnography and participant observation

Chapter outline

Chapter guide

Ethnography and participant observation entail the extended involvement of the researcher in the social life of those he or she studies. However, the former term is also frequently taken to refer to the written output of that research. This chapter explores:

- the problems of gaining access to different settings and some suggestions about how such problems might be overcome;
- the issue of whether a covert role is practicable and acceptable;
- the role of key informants for the ethnographer;
- the different kinds of roles that ethnographers can adopt in the course of their fieldwork;
- the role and different types of field notes in ethnography;
- issues involved in bringing ethnographic research to an end;
- the growing use of online ethnography;
- the role of visual materials, which have attracted increased attention in recent years, in ethnography;
- the controversy about the nature of feminist ethnography;
- key issues raised by discussions about the writing of ethnography;
- the changing meanings of 'ethnography'.

Introduction

Discussions about the merits and limitations of participant observation have been a fairly standard ingredient in textbooks on social research for many years. However, for some time writers on research methods have preferred to write about **ethnography** rather than **participant observation**. It is difficult to date the point at which this change of terminology (though it is more than just this) occurred, but sometime in the 1970s 'ethnography' began to become the preferred term. Before that, the term 'ethnography' was primarily associated with social anthropological research, whereby the investigator visits a (usually) foreign land, gains access to a group (for example, a tribe or village), spends a considerable amount of time (often many years) with that group with the aim of uncovering its culture, watches and listens to what people say and do, engages people in conversations to probe specific issues of interest, takes copious **field notes**, and returns home to write up the fruits of his or her labours.

Key concept 19.1 represents an attempt to deal with some of these issues of terminology and to arrive at a working definition of ethnography. The seven bullet points at the end of Key concept 19.1 that make up the definition of ethnography featured there could be viewed as a simple process of joining a group, watching what goes on, making some notes, and writing it all up. In fact, ethnography is nowhere nearly as straightforward

as this implies. This chapter will outline some of the main decision areas that confront ethnographers, along with some of the many contingencies they face. However, it is not easy to generalize about the ethnographic research process in such a way as to provide definitive recommendations about research practice. As prefigured at the end of the previous chapter, the diversity of experiences that confront ethnographers and the variety of ways in which they deal with them does not readily permit clear-cut generalizations. The following comment in a book on ethnography makes this point well:

> Every field situation *is* different and initial luck in meeting good informants, being in the right place at the right time and striking the right note in relationships may be just as important as skill in technique. Indeed, many successful episodes in the field do come about through good luck as much as through sophisticated planning, and many unsuccessful episodes are due as much to bad luck as to bad judgement.
>
> (Sarsby 1984: 96)

However, this comment should not be taken to imply that forethought and an awareness of alternative ways of doing things are irrelevant. It is with this kind of issue that the rest of this chapter will be concerned. Issues to do with the conduct of interviews by ethnographers will be reserved for Chapter 20.

Key concept 19.1
What are ethnography and participant observation?

Definitions of ethnography and participant observation are often difficult to distinguish. Both draw attention to the fact that the participant observer/ethnographer immerses him- or herself in a group for an extended period of time, observing behaviour, listening to what is said in conversations both between others and with the fieldworker, and asking questions. It is possible that the term 'ethnography' is sometimes preferred because 'participant observation' seems to imply just observation, though in practice participant observers do more than just observe. Typically, participant observers and ethnographers will gather further data through interviews and the collection of documents. It may be, therefore, that the apparent emphasis on observation in the term 'participant observation' has meant that an apparently more inclusive term would be preferable, even though in fact it is generally recognized that the method entails a wide range of methods of data collection and sources. Ethnography is also sometimes taken to refer to a study in which participant observation is the prevalent research method but that also has a specific focus on the culture of the group in which the ethnographer is immersed.

However, the term 'ethnography' has an additional meaning, in that it frequently simultaneously refers to both a method of research of the kind outlined above *and* the written product of that research. Indeed, 'ethnography' frequently denotes both a research process and the written outcome of the research. For example, consider the opening sentences of A. Taylor's (1993) book on female drug-users.

> This book provides an account of the lives and experiences of a group of female intravenous drug users in Glasgow. It is based on fifteen months' participant observation of the women in their own setting and on in-depth interviews carried out at the end of the observation period. It is the first full ethnographic account of the lifestyle of female drug users.
>
> (A. Taylor 1993: 1)

It is worth noting the following features.

- The book is subtitled *An Ethnography of a Female Injecting Community*. The term 'ethnography' therefore seems to apply both to the method of investigation and to the book itself. This is underlined by the phrase 'the first full ethnographic account'.
- The mention of the main data-collection methods as participant observation *and* interviewing suggests that the ethnographic research comprises these two techniques of data collection but that interviewing is viewed as something separate from participant observation. In fact, participant observers frequently conduct interviews in the course of their research.
- The passage draws on several qualitative research motifs encountered in Chapter 17, such as the preference for seeing through the eyes of the people being studied (reference to 'lives and experiences') and a naturalistic stance ('in their own setting').

In this book, ethnography will be taken to mean a research method in which the researcher:

- is immersed in a social setting for an extended period of time;
- makes regular observations of the behaviour of members of that setting;
- listens to and engages in conversations;
- interviews informants on issues that are not directly amenable to observation or that the ethnographer is unclear about (or indeed for other possible reasons);
- collects documents about the group;
- develops an understanding of the culture of the group and people's behaviour within the context of that culture;
- and writes up a detailed account of that setting.

Thus, ethnography is being taken to include participant observation and is also taken to encapsulate the notion of ethnography as a written product of ethnographic research.

Tips and skills
Micro-ethnography

If you are doing research for an undergraduate project or Master's dissertation, it is unlikely that you will be able to conduct a full-scale ethnography. Ethnographic research usually entails long periods of time in the field in an organization, as part of a community, or in the company of a group. Nevertheless, it may be possible to carry out a form of *micro-ethnography* (Wolcott 1990b). This would involve focusing on a particular aspect of a topic. For example, if you are interested in call centres, you might focus on the way staff manage to interact and discuss work problems in spite of continuously receiving calls and being monitored. A relatively short period of time (from a couple of weeks to a few months) could be spent in the organization—on either a full-time or a part-time basis—to study such a tightly defined topic.

Access

One of the key and yet most difficult steps in ethnography is gaining access to a social setting that is relevant to the research problem in which you are interested. The way in which access is approached differs along several dimensions, one of which is whether the setting is relatively open or relatively closed (Bell 1969). Hammersley and Atkinson (1995) make a similar distinction when they refer to 'public' settings as opposed to ones that are not public (see also Lofland and Lofland 1995). Closed, non-public settings are likely to be organizations of various kinds, such as firms, schools, cults, social movements, and so on. The open/public setting is likely to be everything else—that is, research involving communities, gangs, drug-users, and so on.

Overt versus covert ethnography

One way to ease the access problem is to assume a *covert* role—in other words, not to disclose the fact that you are a researcher. This strategy removes the need to negotiate access to organizations or to explain why you want to intrude into people's lives and make them objects of study. Seeking access is often a fraught business, and the adoption of a covert role removes some of the difficulties. These two distinctions—the open/public versus closed setting and the overt versus covert role—suggest, following Bell (1969), a fourfold distinction in forms of ethnography. For each of the four types, Figure 19.1 contains examples that have been encountered in earlier chapters or that will be mentioned in this one.

Figure 19.1
Four forms of ethnography

	Open/public setting	Closed setting
Overt role	*Type 1* • Taylor's (1993) study of intravenous drug users • Foster's (1995) study of a high-crime community • Giulianotti's (1995) research on football hooligans • Benson's (2011) research on British expatriates living in rural France • Whyte's (1955) classic study of street corner life in a Boston slum area • O'Reilly's (2000) research on the British living on Spain's Costa del Sol • Hodkinson's (2002) study of goths • Pearson's (2012) ethnography of Manchester United fans	*Type 2* • Leidner's (1993) studies of a McDonald's restaurant and an insurance firm • Wacquant's (2004) research in a Chicago boxing gym • Mears's (2011) study of fashion models • Khan's (2011) research at an elite US high school at which he was employed • Atkinson's (2006) ethnography of the Welsh National Opera • Sampson's (2013) study of international seafarers • Sallaz's (2009) research while employed in a South African casino • Kellogg's (2011) ethnography of the implementation of a new practice in three US hospitals • Demetry's (2013) ethnography of a restaurant • Michel's (2014) long-term ethnography of two investment bank departments • O'Brien's (2010) participant observation research as a female bouncer in night clubs
Covert role	*Type 3* • Patrick's (1973) study of a violent Glasgow gang • Pearson's (2009, 2012) study of Blackpool football fans • Brotsky and Giles's (2007) online ethnography of a pro-anorexia community • Banks's (2012, 2014) online participant observation in the 'advantage play' gambling subculture	*Type 4* • Holdaway's (1982, 1983) study of a police force in which he was already a policeman • Lowe's (2011) research on the Integrated Special Branch while a Detective Sergeant • Lloyd's (2012) research while employed in a call centre in Middlesbrough • Sallaz's (2009) research while employed in a Nevada casino • Research by Mattley (2006) on working for a sex fantasy phone line • Research by Hobbs et al. (2003) on bouncers (see also Winlow et al. 2001)

Note: This figure is a development of a table in Bell (1969).

Three points should be registered about Figure 19.1. First, the distinction between the open/public setting versus the closed setting is not a hard-and-fast one. Sometimes, gaining access to groups can have a near-formal quality, such as having to pacify a gang leader's anxieties about your goals. Also, organizations sometimes create contexts that have a public character, such as the meetings that are arranged for members or prospective recruits by social movements such as religious cults or political movements.

Secondly, the overt versus covert distinction also has problems. For example, while an ethnographer may seek access through an overt route, there may be many people with whom he or she comes into contact who will not be aware of the ethnographer's status as a researcher. Cassidy's (2014: 172) ethnographic research in London betting shops was not covert but she notes that 'it is possible that some of the people I observed in shops were unaware of the reason for my presence'. Similarly, writing about her participant observation research as a female bouncer in clubs, O'Brien (2010) observes that she did not try to conceal her identity as a researcher but the clubs' clientele and most staff were unaware of her research. Also, some ethnographers move between the two roles (see Research in focus 19.1).

Another interesting case is provided by Glucksman (1994), who in the 1970s left her academic post to work on a factory assembly line in order to shed light on the reasons why feminism appeared not to be relevant to working-class women. In a sense, she was a covert observer, but her motives for the research were primarily political, and she says that, at the time she was undertaking the research, she had no intention of writing the book that subsequently appeared and that was published under a pseudonym (Cavendish 1982). After the book's publication, it was treated as an example of ethnographic research. Was she an overt or a covert observer (or neither or both)? Whichever description applies, this is an interesting case of what might be termed *retrospective ethnography*.

A third point to note about Figure 19.1 is that entries are more numerous in the Types 1 and 2 cells than in the Types 3 and 4 cells. This reflects the fact that ethnographers are far more likely to adopt an overt role than a covert one. There are several reasons for this situation. As Key concept 19.2 reveals, the reasons for the preference of most ethnographers for an overt role are to do with practical and ethical considerations, but the latter predominate in most researchers' thinking. Because of the ethical problems that beset covert research (and indeed some of the practical difficulties), the bulk of the discussion of access issues that follows will focus upon ethnographers seeking to employ an overt role.

Research in focus 19.1
An example of the perils of covert observation: the case of field notes in the lavatory

Ditton's (1977) research on 'fiddling' in a bakery provides an interesting case of the practical difficulties of taking notes during covert observation as well as an illustration of an ethnographer who shifted from covert to overt observation partly because of those difficulties:

> Nevertheless, I *was* able to develop personal covert participant-observation skills. Right from the start, I found it impossible to keep everything that I wanted to remember in my head until the end of the working day. . . . and so had to take rough notes as I was going along. But I was stuck 'on the line', and had nowhere to retire to privately to jot things down. Eventually, the wheeze of using innocently provided lavatory cubicles occurred to me. Looking back, all my notes for that third summer were on Bronco toilet paper! Apart from the awkward tendency for pencilled notes to be self-erasing from hard toilet paper. . . . my frequent requests for 'time out' after interesting happenings or conversations in the bakehouse and the amount of time I was spending in the lavatory began to get noticed. I had to pacify some genuinely concerned workmates, give up totally undercover operations, and 'come out' as an observer—albeit in a limited way. I eventually began to scribble notes more openly, but still not in front of people when they were talking. When questioned about this, as I was occasionally, I coyly said that I was writing things down that occurred to me about 'my studies'.
>
> (Ditton 1977: 5)

In terms of the distinctions in Figure 19.1, Ditton moved from a Type 4 to a Type 2 form of ethnography.

Key concept 19.2
What is the value of the covert role in ethnography?

Advantages

- *The problem of securing access is greatly reduced.* Adopting a covert role largely gets around the access problem, because the researcher does not have to seek permission to gain entry to a social setting or organization.

- *Reactivity is not a problem.* Using a covert role reduces reactivity (see Key concept 12.4), because participants do not know the person conducting the study is a researcher. Therefore, they are less likely to adjust their behaviour because of the researcher's presence.

Disadvantages

- *The problem of taking notes.* As Ditton (1977; see Research in focus 19.1) discovered, it is difficult and probably in some circumstances impossible to take notes when people do not realize you are conducting research. Notes are very important to an ethnographer, and it can be risky to rely exclusively on your memory. None the less, when in a covert role, the participant observer has no choice. For his covert research on Blackpool FC supporters, Pearson (2012: 28; see also Research in focus 19.2) writes that he tried to write up the bulk of his observations as soon as possible after a match but he acknowledges that 'much useful data was almost certainly forgotten'.

- *The problem of not being able to use other methods.* Ethnography usually entails the use of several methods, but if the researcher is covert it is difficult to steer conversations in a certain direction for fear of detection and it is essentially impossible to engage in interviewing.

- *Anxiety.* The covert ethnographer is under constant threat of having his or her cover blown. Ethnography can be a stressful research method, and the worries about detection can add to those anxieties. Moreover, if the ethnographer *is* found out, the whole research project may be jeopardized.

- *Ethical problems.* Covert observation transgresses two important ethical tenets: it does not provide participants with the opportunity for informed consent (whereby they can agree or disagree to participate on the basis of information supplied to them) and it entails deception. It can also be taken to be a violation of the principle of privacy. Also, many writers take the view that, in addition to being potentially damaging to research participants, it can also harm the practice of research because of fears about social researchers being identified by the public as snoopers or voyeurs if they are found out. Ethical issues are considered in greater detail in Chapter 6.

However

- As the main text points out, in some circumstances the overt/covert distinction may be a matter of degree.

- Also, a covert participant observer may reveal *some* aspects of his or her true identity. While Mattley (2006: 144) describes herself as having been a covert participant observer when she worked for and conducted ethnographic research on a sex fantasy phone line, she writes: 'I decided that I would be open about who I am, but not why I wanted to be hired.' Part of the way through the research, her supervisor suggested she should do a study of the callers. She asked the owner of the business about whether she could do this and he agreed, declining her offer to let him read anything she wanted to write about the work prior to publication. As he graphically put it: 'I hate to read that fucking stuff, I trust you, you won't fuck me over' (Mattley 2006: 146). However, with respect to her callers, Mattley was still a covert participant observer.

Access to closed settings

As Van Maanen and Kolb (1985: 11) observe, 'gaining access to most organizations is not a matter to be taken lightly but one that involves some combination of strategic planning, hard work and dumb luck'. In selecting a particular social setting to act as a case study in which to conduct an ethnographic investigation, the researcher may employ several criteria. These criteria should be determined by the general research area in which he or she is interested. Very often a number of potential cases (and sometimes very many) will be relevant to your research problem. You may choose a certain case because of its 'fit' with your research questions, but there are no guarantees of success, as Van Maanen and Kolb's remark suggests. Sometimes, sheer perseverance pays off. Leidner (1993) was determined that one of the organizations in which she conducted ethnographic research on the routinization of service work should be McDonald's. She writes:

> I knew from the beginning that I wanted one of the case studies to be of McDonald's. The company was a pioneer and exemplar of routinized interaction, and since it was locally based, it seemed like the perfect place to start. McDonald's had other ideas, however, and only after tenacious pestering and persuasion did I overcome corporate employees' polite demurrals, couched in terms of protecting proprietary information and the company's image.
>
> (Leidner 1993: 234–5)

This kind of determination is necessary whenever you want to study a specific organization, such as a particular religious sect or social movement. Rejection is likely to require a complete rethink.

However, with many research questions, several potential cases are likely to meet your criteria. Organizational researchers have developed a range of tactics, many of which may seem rather unsystematic in tone, but they are worth drawing attention to.

- Use friends, contacts, colleagues, and academics to help you gain access; provided the organization is relevant to your research question, the route should not matter.

- Try to get the support of someone within the organization who will act as your champion. This person may be prepared to vouch for you and the value of your research. Such people are placed in the role of 'sponsors'.

- Usually you will need to get access through top management/senior executives. Even though you may secure a certain level of agreement lower down the hierarchy, you will usually need clearance from the top management. Such senior people act as 'gatekeepers'.

- Offer something in return (for example, a report). This strategy carries risks in that it may turn you into a cheap consultant and may invite restrictions on your activities, such as insistence on seeing what you write. However, it helps to create a sense of being *trustworthy*. Some writers on research methodology do not recommend this approach, although it is commonplace among researchers on formal organizations.

- Provide a clear explanation of your aims and methods and be prepared to deal with concerns. Suggest a meeting at which you can deal with worries and provide an explanation of what you intend to do in terms that can readily be understood by others.

- Be prepared to negotiate—you will want complete access, but it is unlikely you will be given *carte blanche*.

- Be reasonably honest about the amount of people's time you are likely to take up. This is a question you will almost certainly be asked if you are seeking access to commercial organizations and probably to many not-for-profit ones too.

Access to open/public settings

Gaining access to public settings is beset with problems, many of which are similar in nature to gaining access to closed settings. An example of the difficulties that await the researcher is one of Whyte's (1955) early encounters in the field in his classic case study *Street Corner Society*, when he was trying to make contacts during his early days in the field in Boston's North End. The following incident occurred in a hotel bar:

> I looked around me again and now noticed a threesome: one man and two women. It occurred to me that here was a maldistribution of females which I might be able to rectify. I approached the group and opened with something like this: 'Pardon me. Would you mind if I join you?' There was a moment of silence while the man stared at me. He then offered to throw me downstairs. I assured him that this would not be necessary and demonstrated as much by walking right out of there without any assistance.
>
> (Whyte 1955: 289)

Sometimes, ethnographers will be able to have their paths smoothed by individuals who act as both sponsor and gatekeeper. In Whyte's case, the role played by 'Doc' has become the stuff of legend, and there is a temptation to seek out your Doc when attempting to gain access to a group. Indeed, when Gans (1962) decided to conduct ethnographic research in an area that was adjacent to the part of Boston on which Whyte had carried out his research, he visited Whyte 'to find out how [he] could meet a "Doc"' (Gans 1968: 311). Research in the news 19.1 describes a researcher's chance meeting that led to opportunities to collect data.

In seeking to gain access to one group of football hooligans, Giulianotti (1995) actively sought out someone who could adopt the gatekeeping role for him, but in gaining access to a second group he was able to draw upon existing acquaintances who could ease his entrée into the group. We see here two common methods of gaining access to groups—via gatekeepers and via acquaintances who then act as sponsors. In seeking access to access to animal rights activists, Upton (2011) consciously used a gatekeeper strategy. He was able to gain access to monthly meetings of one group, and at his first meeting he met

Research in the news 19.1
Model student

This was the title of a quite lengthy article in *The Sunday Times Magazine* on 4 December 2011 about Ashley Mears, who had just published a book (Mears 2011) based on her ethnography of the world of the fashion model (**http://www.thesundaytimes.co.uk/sto/Magazine/Interviews/article829778.ece**, accessed 20 November 2014).

The article's opening sentences set the scene and provide an insight into the significance of 'dumb luck' (as Van Maanen and Kolb 1985: 11) call it:

> For many 23-year-old women being approached in a New York Starbucks by a modelling scout and told 'you've got a great look and could be making a fortune' would be a dream come true. For sociology graduate Ashley Mears, looking for a subject for her thesis on gender politics, it was a blessing of another kind . . ..Mears decided to go undercover as a model to study a world widely regarded as glamorous.
>
> (Lamb 2011: 42)

She signed on with a New York agency and later one in London. Mears had previously worked as a model during summer breaks while at college (Mears 2011, 2013). In the *Sunday Times* article, she is quoted as saying that she told people with whom she came into contact that she intended to use her experiences as a model as research material for a doctorate but says 'I don't think they got it'. She successfully sought permission from managerial staff to keep a record of her observations (Mears 2011). Her data collection comprised taking field notes whenever she could and interviewing other models, agents, and clients.

To describe her approach to ethnography, she borrows from Wacquant (2004) the term 'observant participation' which 'allows researchers to engage in the same rhythms, rates of movement, and emotional and physical sensations of the people about whom we are most curious' (2013: 22). What is crucial to observant participation is that the body is central to ethnographic work in the sense that it has to be 'right' for the world being observed. Mears points out that she had to keep herself in good shape so that she maintained the 'look' that had brought her to attention in the first place. When her look was no longer deemed suitable, her research access would be curtailed. Fortunately for Mears, this did not happen until she had already collected a great deal of research material.

'Emma' who he believed might be convinced to act as a gatekeeper. Although initially unenthusiastic about Upton's research, she did provide some contacts and as a result he was able to observe some protest demonstrations. Ethnographers may seek to gain access by offering something in return or may be asked to offer something in return, which is sometimes referred to as a 'research bargain' by writers on research method. Sallaz (2009) managed to secure access to a casino in South Africa in part because the person who was acting as gatekeeper wanted him to be his 'eyes and ears' in the casino, though in fact Sallaz developed various ways of not meeting his 'obligations'.

'Hanging around' is another common access strategy. It typically entails either loitering in an area until you are noticed or gradually becoming incorporated into or asking to join a group. The second of these was roughly the approach Whyte (1955) was taking, which nearly led to an encounter with a staircase. Wolf (1991) employed a hanging-around strategy in gaining access to outlaw

bikers in Canada. On one occasion he met a group of them at a motorcycle shop and expressed an interest in 'hanging around' with them, but he tried to move too quickly in seeking information about and access to them and was forced to abandon his plans. Eventually, a hanging-around strategy resulted in him being approached by the leader of a biker group (Rebels MC), who acted as his sponsor. In order to bring this off, Wolf ensured that he was properly attired. Attention to dress and demeanour can be a very important consideration when seeking access to either public or closed settings.

As these anecdotes suggest, gaining access to social settings is a crucial first step in ethnographic research, in that, without access, your research plans falter. It is also fraught with difficulties and in certain cases with danger—for example, when the research is likely to be on groups engaged in violent or criminal activities. Therefore, this discussion of access strategies can be only a starting point in knowing what kinds of approach can be considered.

Research in focus 19.2
Access to football supporters

Pearson (2012) carried out an ethnography of football fans which is, in a sense, three ethnographies. First, he carried out covert participant observation of supporters of Blackpool Football Club between 1995 and 1998 (see also Pearson 2009). He was known to other supporters as a student pursuing a degree in law, but his status as an academic researcher was unknown to them. His approach was to meet up with them in the pub before a match or sometimes on entering the stadium, and to meet up with them afterwards for a drink. He attended seventy-eight matched but notes that because he did not live in the area, he was unable to observe the supporters outside of a football context. For away games, he would travel back with supporters. He chose Blackpool FC as his research site because of its relative proximity to Lancaster, where he was a student, and because of its reputation for hooliganism problems. He seems to have been able to gradually insinuate himself into the supporters' world by being recognized as a regular 'fan' (he is actually a Manchester United supporter, about which see the last paragraph of this account). Pearson played up his knowledge and understanding of the game and of the club and was able to integrate into their world.

Second, Pearson carried out a participant observation study of England fans between 1998 and 2006 mainly at away matches. This research was more intensive than the Blackpool research in one particular sense, namely, that it entailed sustained and concentrated observation from the departure lounge of the airport to the return flight; when attending tournaments, the observation would last several days. It also differed because each period of observation was with a different group of supporters from previously. Pearson seems to have largely been a covert participant observer in this research too.

Third, in 2001, Pearson began participant observation with Manchester United fans at their away matches in European competitions, but this changed in 2007 when his research broadened to matches in the domestic competitions. Because he is from Manchester and a supporter possessed of much background knowledge about United and its supporters, Pearson was able to integrate with the fans he wanted to observe and associate with. However, in the same year, while at a United away game in Kiev, he came into contact with a group of fans known as the Red Brigade which, 'provided an excellent focus for an ethnography of carnival fans' (2012: 30). After he gradually became acquainted with many members of this group, he asked them in 2009 if he could focus on their activities. Their agreement meant that he was able to interview many Red Brigade participants and make note of conversations for the next two seasons. Prior to this, he had to rely almost entirely on observations recorded after they had happened. This move to overt participant observation meant that he was less constrained in terms of the recording of data. Also, he was able to associate with them beyond the environment of football, and therefore to establish how their behaviour changed when they were observed outside football.

Ongoing access

But access does not finish when you have made contact and gained an entrée to the group. You still need access to *people*. Simply because you have gained access to an organization does not mean that you will have an easy passage through the organization. Securing access is in many ways an ongoing activity. It is likely to prove a problem in closed contexts such as organizations.

- People will have suspicions about you, perhaps seeing you as an instrument of top management (it is very common for members of organizations to believe that researchers are placed there to check up on them). When Sharpe (2000: 366) began research on prostitu-

tion in a red light area, she was quickly depicted as being 'anything from a social worker to a newspaper reporter with hidden cameras and microphones'. When conducting her research on the British on the Costa del Sol, O'Reilly (2000) was suspected of being from the Department of Social Security and of being a tax inspector.

- People will worry that what they say or do may get back to bosses or to colleagues in work organizations and to peers in other kinds of environment. Van Maanen (1991a) notes from his research on the police that, if you conduct ethnographic research among officers, you are likely to observe activities that may be deeply discrediting and even illegal. Your credibility among police officers will be determined by your reac-

Student experience
The need for persistence

Getting access to organizations can be very difficult. This is likely to be the case for researchers wanting to conduct qualitative research based on interviews, as well as for participant observers. Gareth Matthews's account of trying to gain access to employers and managers of hospitality organizations suggests that this can be difficult and that it is necessary to allow a considerable amount of time.

> I needed to gain access to employers and managers of 40 hospitality establishments while I was living in Brighton. Therefore, I wrote a letter to around 200 employers, which included a description of my research aims and a rough idea as to the content of the interview questions. The letter ended by saying something along the lines of 'I will telephone early next week to try to arrange an appropriate time for the interview'. The following Monday, I telephoned all these businesses, asking to speak to the manager or employer and, referring to the letter, I requested an interview.

> This strategy was not really a success. First, as I did not know the names of the individual managers and employers, not many of the people I spoke to had opened or read the letter, as it was addressed to the 'manager'. Second, while some of those in small businesses had read the letter, and were relatively easy to get hold of on the phone, it was extremely difficult to speak to the managers of large hotels—partly because there are, of course, numerous 'managers' in these organizations.

> In the end, it proved useful to draw up a spreadsheet with all the relevant data on each business—under 'name of business', 'address', 'telephone number', etc.—and to record the responses at particular times when I telephoned. This was a good way, first, to narrow down the list by deleting those who refused to be interviewed and, second, to keep track of when I had been told the manager/employer would be likely to be around to speak to.

> I had some success with this approach, but I also found that it worked well simply to walk around Brighton asking managers and employers for interviews 'on the spot'. It seemed that, when not given the easy choice of arranging or postponing the interview (which they often subsequently forgot anyway), managers/employers were more likely to agree there and then, or to ask me to come back later on the same day.

> It is also worth noting that both these strategies were far more successful in the winter than in the summer, which is unsurprising considering how busy hospitality businesses are during the holiday months.

Gareth's last point suggests that it is important to be sensitive to the nature of the organizations to which you are seeking to gain access.

 To read more, go to the Online Resource Centre: www.oxfordtextbooks.co.uk/orc/brymansrm5e/

---

tions to situations and events that are known to be difficult for individuals.

- If people have these worries, they may go along with your research but in fact sabotage it, engaging in deceptions, misinformation, and not allowing access to 'back regions' (Goffman 1956).

There are three things you can do to smooth the path of ongoing access.

- Play up your credentials. Use your past work and experience; your knowledge of the organization and/or its sector; your understanding of their problems.

- Pass tests. Do not be judgemental when things are said to you about informal activities or about the organization; make sure information given to you does not get back to others, whether bosses or peers. For example, when researching gang members in a poor community, Horowitz (Gerson and Horowitz 2002; see Research in focus 19.5) writes that she was frequently told 'confidential' stories (which turned out to be fictional) to determine whether she could keep a secret.

- You may need a role. If your research involves quite a lot of participant observation, the role will be part of your position in the organization; otherwise, you will need to construct a 'front', by your dress, by your explanations about what you are doing there, by helping out occasionally with work or offering advice. Be consistent—do not behave ambiguously or inconsistently.

Similar considerations apply to research in public settings.

- Make sure you have thought about ways in which people's suspicions can be allayed. You will need a 'front', as Ditton (1977; Research in focus 19.1) had when referring to 'his studies'. Similarly, Giulianotti (1995) simply said that he was doing research on football supporters for a book.

- Be prepared for checks of either competence or credibility. Upton (2011) describes an episode when he was asked in front of other animal rights protestors where he stood on animal rights and animal testing. He answered that he was able to see both sides and admitted that he did believe in animal testing in medical experiments, explaining that a chemotherapy treatment that would have been tested on animals helped to prolong the life of his father, who was suffering from gallbladder cancer, by eight months. His frankness appears to have been reassuring and was almost certainly more effective than a glib answer of support. O'Brien (2010) conducted participant observation research as a female bouncer in several clubs. She felt that sometimes the male bouncers used 'overtly sexualised behaviour' towards her as a means of testing her suitability for the work.

- Be prepared for changes in circumstances. Both Giulianotti (1995) and Armstrong (1993) found that sudden newspaper exposés of football hooliganism or evidence of police infiltration could engender worries that they were not what or who they said they were.

Key informants

One aspect of having sponsors or gatekeepers who smooth access for the ethnographer is that they may become **key informants** in the course of the subsequent fieldwork. The ethnographer relies a lot on informants, but certain informants may become particularly important to the research. They often develop an appreciation of the research and direct the ethnographer to situations, events, or people likely to be helpful to the progress of the investigation. Whyte's (1955) study is again an extreme example of this development. Whyte reports Doc as saying to him at one point: 'You tell me what you want to see, and we'll arrange it. When you want some information, I'll ask for it, and you listen. When you want to find out their philosophy of life, I'll start an argument and get it for you. If there's something else you want to get, I'll stage an act for you' (Whyte

1955: 292). Doc was also helpful in warning Whyte that he was asking too many questions, when he told him to 'go easy on that "who," "what," "why," "when," "where," stuff' (Whyte 1955: 303). A. Taylor (1993) says that her participant observation was of fifty female drug-users and that intensive interviews were carried out with twenty-six women, but that eight of the women were key informants. Gatekeepers often have a role as key informants at least initially; thus, in Benson's (2011) research on British migrants to rural France, a family with which she had initial contact helped her to identify a wider range of people to see.

Key informants can clearly be of great help to the ethnographer and frequently provide a support that helps with the stress of fieldwork. However, it also needs to be borne in mind that working with a key informant can carry risks in that the ethnographer may develop an excessive reliance on the key informant, and, rather than seeing social reality through the eyes of members of the social setting, the researcher may be seeing it through the eyes of the key informant.

In addition, the ethnographer will encounter many people who will act as informants. Their accounts may be solicited or unsolicited (Hammersley and Atkinson 1995). Some researchers prefer the latter, because of its greater spontaneity and naturalism. Very often, research participants develop a sense of the kinds of events the ethnographer wants to see or encounters that it would be beneficial to be present at. Armstrong (1993) says that, while doing research on 'The Blades', a group of supporters of Sheffield United Football Club who were engaged in hooligan activity (see Chapter 17 for other references to this research), he would sometimes get tip-offs:

> 'We're all gonna' Leeds in a couple o' weeks. . . . four coaches, Pond Street, town centre. If you're serious about this study you'll be down there on one of 'em.' I often travelled on the same coach as Ray [an informant]; he would then sit with me at matches and in pubs and point out Blades, giving me background information. Sometimes he would start conversations with Blades about incidents which he knew I wanted to know about and afterwards would ask 'Did you get all that down then?'. . . . There was never one particular informant; rather, there were many Blades I could ring up and meet at any time, who were part of the core and would always welcome a beer and a chat about 'It', or tell me who I 'ought to 'ave a word wi'.
>
> (Armstrong 1993: 24–5)

Such unsolicited sources of information are attractive to ethnographers because of their relative spontaneity, although, as Hammersley and Atkinson (1995: 130–1) observe, they may on occasions be staged for their benefit. Solicited accounts can occur in two ways: by interview (see Chapter 20) or by casual questioning during conversations (though in ethnographic research the boundary between an interview and a conversation is not clear-cut, as Burgess (1984) makes clear). When the ethnographer needs specific information concerning an issue that is not amenable to direct observation or that is not cropping up during 'natural' conversations, solicited accounts are likely to be the only way forward.

 # Roles for ethnographers

Related to the issue of ongoing access (or relationships in the field, as it is sometimes called) is the question of the kind of role the ethnographer adopts in relation to the social setting and its members. Several schemes have been devised by writers on research methods to describe the various roles that can be and have been adopted by ethnographers (Gold 1958; Gans 1968; Adler and Adler 1987). These classifications usually focus on the degree of involvement of the ethnographer in the social world he or she is researching.

Figure 19.2 attempts to bring together some of the underlying features of these classifications of ethnographers' roles. It distinguishes six roles which are best thought of as ideal-typical forms (Weber 1947). It is reasonably exhaustive and most ethnographic roles can be incorporated more or less under each type. The six roles are arrayed in terms of levels of participation in the life and core activities of the group or social context being investigated. There is a tendency, which is apparent from the descriptions of the roles, for those that entail higher levels of participation and involvement to exhibit a greater reliance on observation rather than interviewing and/or examination of documents; with lower levels of participation, there is a reversal with a greater reliance on interviewing and/or documents and a lesser reliance on observation. Michel's research on investment banking (Research in the news 19.2) involved both participant and non-participant observation.

Each role carries its own advantages and risks. The roles of full member (covert and overt) and participating observer carry the risk of over-identification and hence of 'going native' (see Key concept 19.3), but offer the opportunity to get close to people and thereby glean a more complete and intense understanding of their culture and values. Which role is adopted is only partly a matter of choice. Not everyone has the physical credentials to be a full member as a bouncer (Winlow et al. 2001), a goth (Hodkinson 2002), or a fashion model (Mears 2011; see Research in the news 19.1). Equally, the kind of access associated with being a full member would be very unlikely for someone like Gusterson (1996; see Thinking deeply 19.5) for his study of a nuclear weapons laboratory. Also, the ethnographer's research questions are likely to be relevant in that they may not require an intensive examination of a particular social context.

Ethnographers often move between these roles at different times during the life cycle of their research. Skeggs (1994) appears to have begun her research as a participating observer. She was supplementing her grant with some part-time teaching and gradually got to know her students—a group of young working-class women (eventually there were eighty-three of them) whom she realized were very relevant to the doctoral research with a strong feminist orientation that she was planning.

> Over a period of three years [during 1980–3] I did the research by spending as much time as I could with the young women . . . . I traced the trajectories of the young women through the educational system and asked them for biographical details . . . I also conducted formal and informal interviews and meetings with family members, friends, partners and college teachers . . . .. Obviously, it was physically impossible to do intensive participant observation with all eighty-three of them all of the time, so during the three years, I concentrated on different groups at different times.
>
> (Skeggs 1994: 72, 73)

Skeggs adds that the 'time spent doing the ethnography was so intense that the boundary between my life inside and outside the research dissolved' (1994: 73). Subsequently, she 'followed the women's progress through further interviews in 1985, 1989 and 1992' (1994: 73). As such, it is likely that she would have moved into something closer to the role of a non-participating observer with interaction. Even if it were possible to adopt a single ethnographic role over the entire course of a project, it is likely that it would be undesirable: there would be a lack of flexibility in handling situations and people, and risks of excessive involvement (and hence of going native) or detachment would loom large. The issue of the kind of role(s) the ethnographer adopts is of considerable significance, because it has implications for field relationships in the various situations that are encountered.

Further, the kind of role adopted by an ethnographer is likely to have implications for his or her capacity to penetrate the surface layers of an organization. One of the strengths of organizational ethnography is that it offers the prospect of being able to find out what an organization is 'really' like, as opposed to how it formally depicts itself. For example,

Figure 19.2

Field roles and participation in ethnographic research

Participation and involvement	Type and description of role	Example studies
High	**Covert full member.** Full membership of group but the researcher's status as a researcher is unknown. In closed settings such as organizations, the researcher works as a paid employee for the group. The employment may be extant or something that takes place after a decision to do the research has been arrived at. In the case of open settings such as communities, the researcher moves to the area for a significant length of time or employs a pre-existing identity or location as a means of becoming a full member for the purposes of research.	Pearson's (2009, 2012) covert participant observation study of Blackpool FC supporters (see Research in focus 19.2): 'Whilst it was possible to avoid committing some individual offences, a refusal to commit crimes on a regular basis would have aroused suspicions and reduced research opportunities. As a result, I committed 'minor' offences (which I tentatively defined as those which would not cause direct physical harm to a research subject) on a weekly basis as part of the research routine. My strategy was to commit only the offences which the majority of the research subjects were committing and that I considered necessary to carry out the research. Furthermore, whilst I would commit lesser offences with regularity I would, if possible, avoid more serious ones' (Pearson 2009: 246-7).
		Research by Winlow et al. on bouncers: 'As our researcher became more conversant with the environment, acting like a bouncer became almost second nature and the covert role relatively easy to sustain. He was after all not just pretending to be one of them, he actually was. He was being paid to be a bouncer, and with the job came involvement in virtually every violent incident that occurred in his place of employment during the research period . . .. The fact that being a bouncer involves dealing with violence means that our ethnographer was not able to lurk on the periphery and observe' (Winlow et al. 2001: 544, 546).
		Mattley's study of telephone sex line work: 'in 1993 I got a job working for a phone fantasy line, and conducted covert participant observation' (Mattley 2006: 142).
		Banks's (2012, 2014) covert virtual ethnography of 'advantage play', a form of online gambling: 'Data are derived from both the researcher's participation in advantage play and the covert participant observation of an online forum frequented by advantage players, over an eighteen-month period . . .. Participation in advantage play and participant observation was largely unstructured in nature, being built in and around the researcher's normal working and social practices . . .. Over an eighteen-month period, extensive field notes were developed through participation, participant observation, personal exchanges and discussions through website message boards, instant messaging services, email and short message services (Banks 2012: 175, 176)
	Overt full member. Full membership of group but the researcher's status as a researcher is known. In other respects, same as Covert Full Member.	Khan's (2011, 2014) ethnography of an elite high school in the United States. 'Ethnography is a method wherein the scholar imbeds himself in the relations under study, spending long periods of time with research subjects. For me, it meant getting a job at St. Paul's School . . .I moved into an apartment on campus, coached the tennis and squash teams, taught, advised students in a dorm, and . . . observed the daily life of the school. After my years at St. Paul's, I returned many times, and I sought out alumni to interview and discuss some of the things I'd learned' (Khan 2014: 103).
		Hodkinson's participant observation study of goths and their culture and lifestyle. 'I had been an enthusiastic participant in the goth scene since the beginning of [the 1990s], but in 1996 my personal involvement became one part of an extensive research project . . . I adopted a multi-method ethnographic approach, which included participant observation, in-depth interviews, media analysis and even a questionnaire . . .in some respects my insider status was actually enhanced, as the project was built around an intensified attendance of clubs, gigs and festivals across Britain . . . Participation on internet discussion groups and other goth internet facilities widened the scope of my research . . .' (Hodkinson 2002: 4-5).
		Mears's (2011, 2013) ethnography of the world of the fashion model (see Research in the news 19.1). 'Two and a half years would be spent in participant observation, or, more like "observant participation," [a term borrowed from Wacquant 2004: 6] working for both agencies in the full range of modeling work, including five Fashion Weeks, hundreds of castings, and dozens of jobs in every type of modeling work – catwalk shows, magazine shoots in studios and outdoors . . ., catalog shoots, and fittings in the showrooms of Seventh Avenue, New York . . .. I sat beside bookers at their table in the office, drank with them at their favorite pubs, and hung out with them backstage at fashion shows. As I was nearing the end of the participant observation phase . . . and withdrawing from modeling work, I formally interviewed a sample of bookers, managers, and accountants . . .' (Mears 2013: 18, 19).

Figure 19.2
(Continued)

Participation and involvement	Type and description of role	Example studies
	Participating observer. Participates in group's core activities but not as a full member. In closed settings such as organizations, the researcher works for the concern possibly on an occasional basis and sometimes as part of a research bargain to gain entry or to gain acceptance; in open settings, the researcher is a regular in the vicinity and is involved fully in the principal activities.	Anderson's study, conducted in the 1970s, of Jelly's, a bar in Chicago, in order to understand the social lives of street corner black men: 'an understanding of the setting came to me in time, especially as I participated more fully in the life of the corner . . .As the ethnography progressed, I felt increasingly included in the activities of the group members, especially the regulars. I felt this inclusion especially during times when the group members would call my name in a familiar manner . . .People seemed more at ease with me, as I did with them . . .. But probably the most important thing about my getting the trust of the men was my continued presence at Jelly's' (Anderson 2006: 45, 48, 54).

Zilber's study of a rape crisis centre in Israel over a nineteen-month period: 'I spent at least two days per week in the center, observing board and staff meetings, volunteer gatherings, and weekend get-togethers. I also participated in the training course and served as a volunteer, answering calls and meeting with victims of sexual assaults. In addition to keeping a detailed field diary, I recorded meetings and daily discussions, which were later transcribed. For ethical reasons, I did not observe support sessions held by phone or in person. I used indirect sources—mainly volunteers' stories and the activity log—to learn about this aspect of the organization's life' (Zilber 2002: 239). In addition, she conducted 36 interviews with centre members and analysed organizational documents.

Foster's study of Riverside, a London housing estate that was the focus of an intervention to improve perceptions of the estate and to reduce crime on Riverside and on some other estates: 'The fieldwork on the London estate was conducted between April 1987 and June 1990. Over that period I spent 18 months on Riverside getting involved in as many aspects of life there as possible from attending tenant meetings, the mothers and toddlers group, and activities for young people, to socializing with some of the residents in the local pub. I adopted an overt role and made initial contact with the Tenants Association. As my contacts developed I visited a small number of households on a regular basis and gradually extended my associations from the initial tenant group to other residents by 'snowball' techniques, asking people to introduce me to others they knew on the estate. I also accompanied survey researchers conducting interviews for the 'after' survey. In addition to my detailed observations I conducted extended interviews with 45 residents . . . on the two London estates (the majority of which were on Riverside) and 25 'officials' including police officers and housing staff' (Foster 1995: 566).

Sampson's (2013) ethnographic research on international seafarers. In April 1999, she boarded her first cargo ship. 'Contrary to my fears, the crew of Swedish and Filipino seafarers welcomed me into their lives and for forty-two days I lived and worked alongside them, painting the ship with them, venturing ashore to the seamen's bars with them, laughing with them, even dancing and singing with them.' (2013: 1-2). Since then she has undertaken further shipboard research on a variety of other ships.

Goffman's (2009, 2014) ethnography of men in a poor black neighbourhood in Philadelphia who are wanted by the police. Following an initial entrée through contacts, Goffman secured a foothold in the neighbourhood: 'Between January 2002 and August 2003, I conducted intensive observation "on the block," spending most of my waking hours hanging out on Chuck's back porch steps, or along the alley way between his block and Mike's block, or on the corner across from the convenience store. In the colder months, we were usually indoors at Chuck's and a few other houses in the area. I also went along to lawyers' offices, court, the probation and parole office, the hospital, and local bars and parties. By 2004, some of the young men were in county jails and state prisons; for the next four years I spent between two and six days a week on 6th street and roughly one day a week visiting members of the group in jail and prison. I also kept in touch by phone and through letters' (Goffman 2009: 342). |

Figure 19.2
(Continued)

Participation and involvement	Type and description of role	Example studies
	Partially participating observer. Same as Participating Observer, but observation is not necessarily the main data source. Interviews and documents can be as significant as observation and sometimes more significant as sources of data.	For her research on McDonald's, in addition to interviewing, Leidner attended management training classes and was then placed in a franchised restaurant: 'The manager of the franchise arranged for me to be trained to serve customers; once trained, I worked without pay for half a dozen shifts , or a total of about twenty-eight hours of work . . .. I also spent long hours hanging around the crew room, where I talked informally with workers . . .and listened as workers talked with each other about their experiences and their reactions to those experiences' (Leidner 1993: 16).
		Búriková and Miller's study of fifty Slovak au pairs in London in which the first-named author 'spent nearly every day of her year in London in the direct company of au pairs . . .. Most of the au pairs spent the day in isolation looking after children and cleaning houses. Not surprisingly, they welcomed the presence of a fellow Slovak who could assist in these tasks. Zuzana's study often developed into more general friendships in which she shared a wide variety of experiences and confidences' (Búriková and Miller 2010: 3). In addition, all fifty au pairs were interviewed and the researchers, who were both interested in material culture studies, 'paid particular attention to the details of how exactly they decorate their rooms within the family house' (Búriková and Miller 2010: 3).
		O'Brien's research on 'doorwork' whereby she worked as a female bouncer at a number of clubs: 'Our project . . .focused in five major cities and included interviews with fifty female bouncers and interviews with key stakeholders including police and local authority licensing officers, night club operators and security firm directors (O'Brien 2010: 119). In addition, she worked as a bouncer which meant among other things 'vetting customers at the point of entry and managing violent and disorderly customers inside venues' (2010: 119). She also writes that her 'own immersion in this occupational setting was limited: I worked only twelve shifts' (2010: 120) and that she had participated in courses for door supervisors.
	Minimally participating observer. Observes but participates minimally in group's core activities. Observer interacts with group members but observation may or may not be the main source of data. When it is not the main source of data, interviews and documents play a prominent role.	Fine's study of the work of restaurant cooks: 'I conducted participant observation in four restaurants in the Twin Cities metropolitan area, spending a month observing and taking notes in each kitchen during all periods in which the restaurant was open.. .. In each restaurant, I interviewed all full-time cooks, a total of thirty interviews . . .. At no time did I "cook," but occasionally, when a need existed, I served as an extra pair of hands, occasionally peeling potatoes or destringing celery. Generally I would sit or stand in a corner of the kitchen and take notes, conversing with the cooks or servers in slow periods' (Fine 1996: 93, 94).
		Venkatesh's study of the Black Kings, a Chicago gang, led by J.T. who befriended him: 'I realized that if I truly wanted to understand the complicated lives of black youth in inner-city Chicago, I only had one good option: to accept J.T.'s counsel and hang out with people' (Venkatesh 2008: 22). However, for one day only, Venkatesh crossed the line and became gang leader for a day. However, it would be unwise to suggest that he became a Full Member on that day because he was unwilling to engage in a physical confrontation on behalf of the Black Kings, when one was expected, and instead opted for a more intellectualized solution of the problem.
		Michel's (2014) ethnography of Wall Street bankers (see Research in the news 19.2). 'The banks allowed observation for two years. In year one, I observed five to seven days a week (80–120 hours), mirroring bankers' schedules, and then at least three days aeek. To balance my deep familiarity with investment banking, I chose the observer as my primary role, jotting down notes . . .. As participant, I helped with minor tasks, a standard practice . . .that allowed me to ask otherwise intrusive questions' Michel 2014: 519). In addition, she has carried out numerous interviews for this long-term ethnography.

Figure 19.2
(Continued)

Participation and involvement	Type and description of role	Example studies
		Kellogg (2011) conducted ethnographic research in three US hospitals to examine the introduction of a new practice and its aftermath (see the second study in Research in focus 3.18). She writes: 'At Advent and Bayshore, I spent fifteen months following residents in surgery as they did their daily work . . .. I followed residents as they visited patients twice daily on rounds, I scrubbed in on surgeries, and I slept overnight in family waiting rooms next to the resident call rooms so that I could get up with residents in the middle of the night. I regularly ate breakfast, lunch, and dinner with residents, fraternized with them in the residents' lounges, and attended resident parties and weekly drinking evenings . . .My work at Calhoun was based primarily on interviews . . .I observed a good deal of everyday life at Calhoun by spending time with groups of two or three residents outside of interviews in the surgical resident lounge and hospital cafeteria' (Kellogg 2011: 14-15, 16). Kellogg clearly did not participate in the core activity (surgery) but her close involvement in the work and leisure lives of her participants means that she is probably closest to the Minimally Participating Observer role, but at Calhoun she was a Non-Participating Observer with Interaction.
		Demetry's (2013) study of a 'high-end' restaurant in the US (see Research in focus 17.4). 'I observed the kitchen of a high-end restaurant in a suburb of a Midwestern city for approximately six months, varying my day and time of observation. Each observation lasted approximately four hours and I visited once or twice a week. In addition, I conducted formal interviews with all core organizational members (cooks, chefs, and managers) and informal interviews with peripheral workers (valet, waiters/waitresses, and dishwashers) . . .. I was frequently in the way of the cooks as they skillfully crisscrossed the space and awkwardly placed in the direct line of waiters and waitresses, making it impossible for me to stand in any one spot for long. Nevertheless, as my time in the kitchen passed, I became more like an actor within the space. Soon, I was no longer simply "observing," but also a direct participant . . .Matt would use me as a "go-to" to relay messages, and carry dishes and utensils from cook to cook' (Demetry: 583, 584).
	Non-participating observer with interaction. Observes (sometimes minimally) but does not participate in group's core activities. Interaction with group members occurs, but often tends to be through interviews which, along with documents, tend to be the main source of data.	Gambetta and Hammill's study of taxi drivers and their fares in Belfast and New York (see Thinking Deeply 19.1). In the Belfast part of their study, the authors write that in addition to interviews: 'We sat in the dispatch office of five different taxi companies and observed the dispatcher and the interaction between the drivers; we also drove around with five drivers while they were working' (Gambetta and Hammill 2005: 21).
		Gusterson's study of a nuclear weapons laboratory (see Thinking deeply 19.5). The top-secret nature of the work meant that the primary sources of data were interviews and documents. However, he was given access to open areas: 'although I was not allowed to wander freely around the areas where people do classified work, it was not entirely off-limits to me. Two of the laboratories' three cafeterias were open to the public and I often ate lunch and met with laboratory employees in them' (Gusterson 1996: 33).
		Research by Prichard et al. (2014; see also Turnbull et al. 2012) on the introduction of a computer decision support system (CDSS) in three NHS call centres (see Research in focus 27.9). 'The study used an ethnographic approach. Researchers undertook 491 hours of nonparticipant observation and 64 interviews. Overt observation was conducted to provide a detailed, nuanced description of the design, development, management and use of the CDSS in each setting. There were opportunities to talk informally with staff and observation was purposively structured to capture activity at different times of the day/days of the week, covering all or part of a shift depending on the setting' (Prichard et al. 2014: 813). In addition, 'Interviews were conducted with call handlers, supervisors and managers, clinical staff and key stakeholders around each organization' (Prichard et al. 2014: 814).

Low

Research in the news 19.2
Long-term ethnography

It is not often that research published in an academic sociology journal makes the front page of the *Financial Times* but that is precisely what happened to Alexandra Michel (2014) when her findings were reported in an article entitled 'Workaholic ex-bankers impose their long-hours culture on new colleagues' on 22 March 2014 (**www.ft.com/cms/s/0/3c26b148-ae9c-11e3-aaa6-00144feab7de.html#axzz3JcLy4UoA**, accessed 20 November 2014). The lead paragraph tells the story well: 'Bankers' punishing hours are no longer merely of concern to the families of financiers—the fallout of their all-consuming office culture is spreading as they take their hard-driving ways to new workplaces'. The article informs the reader that the findings derive from a 'forthcoming survey' by a former banker at Goldman Sachs. In fact, the article derives from an ongoing ethnographic study begun twelve years earlier at two investment banking departments (Michel 2011; 2014). Michel's participants are four cohorts of two per bank which joined the banks in the first and second years of Michel's research. Her data collection comprised the following:

1. Participant and non-participant observation for two years. Michel observed bankers so that their schedules were mirrored in her observation. In the first year this was five to seven days per week or 80–120 hours and in the second year three days per week. She was more of an observer than a participant but she did help with minor tasks. At the time of this writing, she had completed 7,000 hours of observation.

2. Semi-structured formal interviews. In the first and second years, Michel conducted 136 such interviews lasting 30–45 minutes. She was not allowed to audio-record them so took detailed notes after each interview. During the subsequent ten years, she conducted around 600 longer interviews with each of the 'focal bankers' on two or more occasions.

3. Informal interviews. These have been on themes as they emerged in Michel's research and have been with such people as clients and bankers' friends and family members. So far, there have been 200 of these.

4. Documents. These have included bankers' yearly performance reviews and documents about training and selection.

In the article that attracted the attention of the *Financial Times*, Michel analyses the implications of the banks' practices that promote participation in decision-making and autonomy. She shows that contrary to what might be expected, the loosening of the reins associated with participative work practices resulted in an intensification of work leading to a self-inflicted overload. At the extreme, this sometimes resulted in deteriorating performance due to the inability of the bankers' bodies to cope with the intensity of the work. Moreover, when they left the two banks, they transported their work practices with them and imposed them on others as well as themselves.

Michael Humphreys conducted ethnographic research in the UK headquarters of a US bank referred to pseudonymously as Credit Line (Humphreys and Watson 2009). He was aware of the firm's commitment to corporate social responsibility but became increasingly conscious that, although people working in the organization were publicly enthusiastic about its ethical stance, many were privately sceptical about the firm's actual commitment. For example, he quotes one employee (Charity) as saying:

> My problem is that, in this organization, corporate social responsibility is a sham—it's just rhetoric—I mean how can we call ourselves responsible when we give credit cards to poor people and charge them 30 per cent APR [annual percentage rate] just because they are high risk?
> (quoted in Humphreys and Watson 2009: 50)

For employees to divulge such private views which cast doubt on the integrity of their organization, the ethnographer will probably need to become something of a confidant, since it requires the organizational participants to be confident about sharing their private views which could lead to them being censured by senior managers.

Active or passive?

A further issue that is raised about any situation in which the ethnographer participates is the degree to which he or she should be or can be an active or a passive participant (Van Maanen 1978). Even when the ethnographer is in a predominantly non-observing role, there may be contexts in which either participation is unavoidable or

Key concept 19.3
What is 'going native'?

'Going native' refers to a plight that sometimes afflicts ethnographers when they lose their sense of being a researcher and become wrapped up in the worldview of the people they are studying. The prolonged immersion of ethnographers in the lives of the people they study, coupled with the commitment to seeing the social world through their eyes, lie behind the risk and actuality of going native. Going native is a potential problem for several reasons but especially because the ethnographer can lose sight of his or her position as a researcher and therefore find it difficult to develop a social scientific angle on the collection and analysis of data. When Hobbs (1988: 6) writes in connection with his fieldwork on entrepreneurship in London's East End that he 'often had to remind himself that [he] was not in a pub to enjoy [himself] but to conduct an academic inquiry, and repeatedly woke up the following morning with an incredible hangover facing the dilemma of whether to bring it up or write it up', he may have been on the brink of going native.

However, it should not be assumed that going native is an inevitable risk associated with ethnography or indeed that it is the only risk to do with how participant observers relate to the social situations in which they find themselves. Lee-Treweek (2000) carried out research on auxiliary carers in two homes for the elderly. She describes how in one of these homes she had an almost completely opposite reaction to going native. She disliked the home and appears to have found the staff unappealing because of their lack of sympathy for and their uncaring approach to the elderly people for whom they were responsible. None the less, she felt that she 'was gathering good data, despite [her] feelings of being an outsider' (Lee-Treweek 2000: 120). The lesson of this story is that going native is not an inevitable accompaniment to ethnography.

Wacquant (2009) is relatively sanguine about the idea of going native. He describes his position as 'go native, but *go native armed*' (2009: 145). What he means by this is not losing one's perspective as (in his case) a sociologist and therefore making sure that the full arsenal of theoretical and methodological skills of a discipline are brought to bear on the field site. To quote him again:

> Go ahead, go native, but come back a sociologist. In my case, the concept of habitus served as both a bridge to enter the factory of pugilistic know-how and methodically parse the texture of the work(ing) world of the pugilist, and as a shield against the lure of the subjectivist rollover of social analysis into narcissistic story-telling.
>
> (Wacquant 2009: 145)

It is precisely the difficulty of avoiding this 'subjectivist rollover' that has been behind the warnings about going native.

a compulsion to become involved in a limited way may be felt, resulting in the ethnographer becoming a minimally participating observer (see Figure 19.2). For example, Fine's (1996) research on the work of chefs in restaurants was carried out largely by semi-structured interview. In spite of his limited participation, he found himself involved in washing up in the kitchens to help out during busy periods. In many instances, the researcher has no choice. Researchers who do ethnographic research on the police, for example, unless they are covert observers like Holdaway (1982) or take steps to become police officers like Rubinstein (1973), are unlikely to be able to be active participants beyond offering fairly trivial assistance. An example of this can be found in an incident reported in Punch's field notes in connection with his research on the police in Amsterdam:

> Tom wanted to move the cars which were blocking the narrow and busy street in front of the station, and said sternly to the suspect, but with a smile at me behind his back, 'You stay here with your hands up and don't try anything because this detective here [pointing at me] is keeping an eye on you.' I frowned authoritatively.
>
> (Punch 1979: 8)

Punch travelled with the officers in their cars, but he wore civilian clothes and employed as a 'front' the role of a plain-clothes policeman. On the other side of the coin, in taking the job of a bouncer, the participant observer is not

Research in focus 19.3
Active ethnography and illegal activity

In the context of his study of entrepreneurship (a euphemism for several kinds of legal and illegal activity) among East Enders in London, Hobbs (1988: 7, 15) admits he engaged in illegal activities:

> A refusal, or worse still an enquiry concerning the legal status of the 'parcel', would provoke an abrupt conclusion to the relationship. Consequently, I was willing to skirt the boundaries of criminality on several occasions, and I considered it crucial to be willingly involved in 'normal' business transactions, legal or otherwise. I was pursuing an interactive, inductive study of an entrepreneurial culture, and in order to do so I had to display entrepreneurial skills myself. . . . [My] status as an insider meant that I was afforded a great deal of trust by my informants, and I was allowed access to settings, detailed conversations, and information that might not otherwise have been available.

going to have the luxury of deciding whether to become involved in fights, since these are likely to an ingredient of the role (Winlow et al. 2001).

Sometimes, ethnographers may *feel* they have no choice but to get involved, because a failure to participate actively might indicate to members of the social setting a lack of commitment and lead to a loss of credibility. Ryan (2009) conducted research on commercial cleaning in Australia and found that being prepared to help cleaners with some of their tasks helped to build up his credibility and made them more prepared to be interviewed by him. In the course of her study of a restaurant, Demetry (2013; see Research in focus 17.4) found it difficult to find a suitable point at which to observe, partly because she would often get in the way of the various staff as they frantically moved around trying to fulfil their roles in satisfying diners' needs. She began to do more than observe and would relay messages, carry dishes, and

even on one occasion assisted with meal preparation. She hints at one point that this may have helped to establish rapport during the period that the first chef was in charge. Participation in group activities can lead to dilemmas on the part of ethnographers, especially when the activities in which they actively take part (or might do so) are illegal or dangerous (see Research in focus 19.3). On the other hand, many writers counsel against active participation in criminal or dangerous activities (Polsky 1967). Both Armstrong (1993) and Giulianotti (1995) refused to participate in fights while doing research into football hooliganism. Pearson (2012: 33) admits that when in his covert role (see Research in focus 19.2) he sometimes committed offences. We see here a strong argument against covert research on criminals or those involved in dangerous activities, since it will be much more difficult for someone in such a role not to participate.

Field notes

Because of the frailties of human memory, ethnographers have to take notes based on their observations. These should be fairly detailed summaries of events and behaviour and the researcher's initial reflections on them. The notes need to specify key dimensions of whatever is observed or heard. There are some general principles.

- Write down notes, however brief, as quickly as possible after seeing or hearing something interesting.

- Write up full field notes at the very latest at the end of the day and include such details as location, who is involved, what prompted the exchange or whatever, date and time of the day, and so on.

- Nowadays, people may prefer to use a digital recorder to record initial notes, but this may create a problem of needing to transcribe a lot of speech. However, see Tips and skills 'Dealing with digitally voice-recorded field notes'.

- Notes must be vivid and clear—you should not have to ask at a later date 'what did I mean by that?'

- It is valuable to write some personal reflections about your own feelings about occasions and people. Such notes may be helpful for formulating a reflexive account of fieldwork. Czarniawska (2007) provides a lot of field notes in connection with a study in Warsaw

Tips and skills
Dealing with digitally voice-recorded field notes

Improvements in voice recognition software may make transcription unnecessary when a digital recording is made of spoken field notes. For example, at the time of writing there are free apps from Dragon, a company that specializes in such software, that can be downloaded through the iTunes Store onto an iPhone or iPad and will produce a document based on your speech. This document can be saved and later printed out. It would require close checking for errors of translation from voice to the written word.

of what she calls Big City Management. She sought to shadow a finance director (as well as several others on different occasions) who was uncooperative, and these notes are revealing as much for the self-doubt and anxiety about her research skills that crept in as for the substantive findings conveyed.

- There is likely to be considerable value in including initial analytic thoughts about what is observed and heard. These may be useful for acting as a springboard for theoretical elaboration of the data.

- You need to take copious notes, so, if in doubt, write it down. The notes may be of different types, as will now be discussed.

Obviously, it can be very useful to write your notes straight away—that is, as soon as something interesting happens. However, wandering around with a notebook and pencil in hand and continuously scribbling notes down may make people self-conscious. It may be necessary, therefore, to develop strategies of taking small amounts of time out, though hopefully without generating the anxieties Ditton (1977) appears to have engendered (see Research in focus 19.1).

Strategies for taking field notes are affected by the degree to which the ethnographer enters the field with clearly delineated research questions. As noted in Chapter 17, most qualitative research adopts an approach of beginning with general research questions (as specifically implied by Figure 17.1), but there is considerable variation in the degree to which this is the case. Obviously, when there is some specificity to a research question, ethnographers have to orient their observations to that research focus, but at the same time maintain a fairly open mind so that the element of flexibility that is a strength of qualitative research is not eroded. Ditton (1977; Research in focus 19.1) provides an illustration of a very open-ended approach when he writes that his research 'was not set up to answer any empirical questions' (1977: 11). Similarly, reflecting on his

ethnography of tattooists in the USA, Sanders (2009) writes that he was not motivated to conduct this study in order to answer a research question; instead, he writes: 'Concepts, theories, research questions, hypotheses, and other abstract intellectual scaffolding arise from the experiences I share with people in the field and the things they tell me' (Sanders 2009: 65). Armstrong (1993: 12) writes in connection with his research on football hooliganism that his research 'began without a focus' and that as a result 'he decided to record everything'. As a result, a typical Saturday 'would result in thirty sides of notes handwritten on A4 paper'. This period of open-ended observation usually cannot be maintained for long, because of the temptation to try to record the details of absolutely everything, which can be very tiresome. Usually the ethnographer will begin to narrow down the focus of his or her research and to match observations to the emerging research focus. This approach is implied by the sequence suggested by Figure 17.1, and can be seen in the account by Anderson (2006; see Thinking deeply 19.1). For these reasons, ethnographers frequently try to narrow down their focus of interest and to devise specific research questions or relate their emerging findings to the social scientific literature (see Research in focus 19.5).

For most ethnographers, the main equipment with which they will need to supply themselves in the course of observation will be a note pad and a pen. A recording device such as a digital voice recorder can be another useful addition to the participant observer's hardware, but, as suggested above, it is likely to result in a big increase in the amount of transcription (though see Tips and skills 'Dealing with digitally voice-recorded field notes' above) and is possibly more obtrusive than writing notes. Most ethnographers report that after a period of time they become less conspicuous to participants in social settings, who become familiar with their presence. Speaking into a recording device may rekindle an awareness of the ethnographer's presence. Also, in gatherings it may be difficult to use, because of the impact of extraneous noise.

Thinking deeply 19.1
Research questions in ethnographic research

As I noted in Chapter 17, research questions in qualitative research, and in ethnographic research in particular, are usually open-ended, though the extent to which this is the case varies a great deal. Elijah Anderson (2006) has provided a fascinating account of the background to his participant observation research into the lives of black street corner men in Chicago in the 1970s (Anderson 1978). This study was undertaken by focusing on the lives and habits of clients of Jelly's—a drinking establishment that acted as both a bar and a store for the sale of alcoholic drinks. Anderson says that, at the outset of his fieldwork, he 'had absolutely no idea where the research would lead' and had in mind 'no explicit sociological problem or question' (2006: 40). Indeed, he writes that 'this open-ended approach was a conscious act', arguing that to go in with a pre-designed set of issues 'could preclude certain lines of enquiry that might prove valuable later' (2006: 40). Gradually, the research questions emerged: 'Why did men really come to and return to Jelly's corner? What did they seek to gain? What was the nature of the social order there? What was the basis for their social ranking?' (2006: 46). Similarly, Mears, whose ethnography of the world of fashion modelling is discussed in Research in the news 19.1, has written: 'I didn't know my theoretical questions or analytic foci until spending considerable time in the field' (2011: 264).

Anderson's open-ended strategy can be interestingly contrasted with a study of taxi drivers in New York and Belfast whose data are described as 'of an ethnographic kind' (Gambetta and Hamill 2005: 18). The researchers were fundamentally interested in the sociological study of trust and sought to explore how taxi drivers establish whether prospective passengers that they might pick up are trustworthy. Taxi drivers are very vulnerable in many ways: the passenger may not pay, or worse may rob the driver, or even worse may rob and assault the driver. Therefore, they are forced to make more or less instant decisions about whether someone who hails them is trustworthy. Their hypothesis is worth quoting: '*drivers screen passengers looking for reliable signs of trust- or distrust-warranting properties*, in the sense that they look for signs that are too costly for a mimic to fake but affordable for the genuine article' (Gambetta and Hamill 2005: 11; emphasis in original).

To investigate this explicit research question, Gambetta and Hamill (2005: 18) conducted 'partially structured interviews and participant observation with drivers, dispatchers, and passengers'. Unlike Anderson's initially open-ended strategy, where research questions emerged in the course of the study, Gambetta and Hamill collected their data to examine the validity of their research question, which they also refer to as a hypothesis. Their findings are presented in order to shed light on this research question, and new research questions do not appear to have emerged in the course of the study.

I have an impression that an open-ended approach of the kind used by Anderson is seen less frequently than in the past. That is not to say that researchers veer towards the explicit formulation that we see in Gambetta and Hamill's study but that there is a greater tendency towards explicitness nowadays. I suspect that this is often to do with the expectations of research funding bodies when deciding whether to fund investigations and perhaps also to do with the expectations of journals. It may also be to do with the expectations of committees that review the ethical integrity of proposed projects, because securing ethical clearance forces researchers to be explicit about what they intend to do and why. However, this is an impression only—maybe it could be called a hypothesis!

Photography can be an additional source of data and helps to stir the ethnographer's memory, but it is likely that some kinds of research (especially involving crime and deviance) will render the taking of photographs unworkable.

Types of field notes

Some writers have found it useful to classify the types of field notes that are generated in the process of conducting an ethnography. The following classification is based

Research in focus 19.4
Taking field notes: encounters with doctors and patients in a medical school training programme

In the context of his research in a medical school, P. Atkinson (1981: 131–2) provides an account that strongly implies that ethnographers need to be flexible in their note-taking tactics:

> I found that my strategies for observation and recording changed naturally as the nature of the social scene changed. Whenever possible I attempted to make rough notes and jottings of some sort whilst I was in the field. Such notes were then amplified and added to later in the day when I returned to the office. The quantity and type of on the spot recording varied across recurrent types of situation. During 'tutorials', when one of the doctors taught the group in a more or less formal manner, or when there was some group discussion. . . . then it seemed entirely natural and appropriate to sit among the students with my notebook on my knee and take notes almost continuously. At the other extreme, I clearly did not sit with my notebook and pen whilst I was engaged in casual conversations with students over a cup of coffee. Whereas taking notes is a normal thing to do, taking notes during a coffee break chat is not normal practice. . . . Less clear cut was my approach to the observation and recording of bedside teaching. On the whole I tried to position myself at the back of the student group and make occasional jottings: main items of information on the patients, key technical terms, and brief notes on the shape of the session (for example, the sequence of topics covered, the students who were called on to perform, and so on).

Research in focus 19.5
Narrowing the focus of an ethnography

Ruth Horowitz has written (Gerson and Horowitz 2002) about the process of narrowing down the focus of her research on groups on the margins of society. As she puts it, she tends to be interested in such questions as:

> 'What is really going on' in such groups and communities? How do people make sense of their social worlds? How do they strike a balance between group membership and wider social participation? And finally, what limits and what helps create the social worlds of the people?
>
> (Gerson and Horowitz 2002: 202)

In her early research on young people in a very poor community in Chicago, she used these general research questions to guide her data collection but 'began to focus on specifying the sociological issues only after some time in the field' (Gerson and Horowitz 2002: 202). She found a great deal of variety in the ambitions, orientations, patterns of interaction, attitudes towards street life, and behaviour in different settings among the young people she observed. Horowitz began to ask questions about how well the world of these young people fitted with two prominent models used to explain the worlds of the poor. Her research questions about the degree of fit between these models and her data led her to conclude that the models 'failed to account for young people's creativity or for the struggles they mounted and the choices that they made in the face of great obstacles' (Gerson and Horowitz 2002: 202).

on the similar categories suggested by Adler and Adler (2009), Sanjek (1990) and Lofland and Lofland (1995).

- *Mental notes*—particularly useful when it is inappropriate to be seen taking notes (for example, during the coffee breaks referred to by Atkinson in Research in focus 19.4).

- *Jotted notes* (also called *scratch notes*)—very brief notes written on pieces of paper or in small notebooks to jog one's memory about events that should be written up later. Lofland and Lofland (1995: 90) refer to these as being made up of 'little phrases, quotes, key words, and the like'. Adler and Adler (2009: 227) refer to these as 'writing down the facts of what was happening'. They need to be jotted down inconspicuously, preferably out of sight, since detailed note taking in front of people may make them self-conscious. These are equivalent to the 'rough notes and jottings' that Atkinson refers to in Research in focus 19.4.

- *Full field notes*—detailed notes, made as soon as possible, which will be your main data source. They should be written at the end of the day or sooner if possible. Write as promptly and as fully as possible. Write down information about events, people, conversations, and so on. Write down initial ideas about interpretation. Record impressions and feelings. When Atkinson (in Research in focus 19.4) refers to notes in which he 'amplified and added to' the jottings made during the day, he was producing full field notes. An example of a full field note is provided in Research in focus 19.6. For Adler and Adler (2009) a key facet of this exercise is developing a conceptualization of one's observations. They call these 'analytic notes'; such notes entail reflections about patterns in the observations.

- *Methodological notes.* Adler and Adler (2009) also use a separate file of notes in which they record observations about methodological decisions, experiences in the field, and 'barriers and breakthroughs'.

Field notes are often to do with the ethnographer as well as with the social setting being observed. It is frequently in field notes that the ethnographer's presence is evident.

We see this in the field note in Research in focus 19.6, when the ethnographer—Demetry—is motioned to the dining table by the manager so that she can see the head chef at work. Precisely because they record the quotidian as observed and experienced by ethnographers, it is here that ethnographers come to the surface. In the finished work—the ethnography in the sense of a written account of a group and its culture—the ethnographer is frequently written out of the picture (Van Maanen 1988). A major difference here is that field notes, except for brief passages such as those taken from Demetry's work, are invariably for personal consumption at least initially (Coffey 1999), whereas the written ethnography is for public consumption and has to be presented as a definitive account of the social setting and culture in question. Allowing the ethnographer to surface in the text risks conveying a sense of the account as an artifice rather than an authoritative chronicle. This issue will be addressed in further detail below.

There is also an issue of how far the ethnographer should aim to be comprehensive in how much is recorded. Wolfinger (2002) has observed that, if the ethnographer does not seek to be comprehensive, his or her background expectations are likely to influence what is or is not recorded. He suggests that the ethnographer may be particularly inclined to make a note of events that stand out and what is taken to stand out is likely to be influenced by other events that have been observed or by the ethnographer's expectations of what is likely to happen. In

Research in focus 19.6
A field note: observing a restaurant

Demetry's (2013) ethnographic research on a high-end restaurant in the United States was briefly mentioned above and discussed in Research in focus 17.4. One of the chief elements in this study is that there was a change of head chef part of the way through the study which inaugurated a change in work regime. During the first day of her time at the restaurant (during the first regime), Demetry recorded the following field note:

> The dining room of Tatin has an inviting atmosphere: one is greeted by beige and light-green color tones and a roaring fireplace. Soft lighting bathes the room, and classical music plays quietly in the background encouraging one to relax and unwind. Two swinging doors with glass window cut-outs lead to the kitchen. I walk into the kitchen to find the TOTAL opposite of the relaxing dining room ambiance. Rap music is blaring, and cooks in jeans and T-shirts are nodding their heads as they work separately at their stations. The manager motions me to the 'dining table'—a small nook across from the hotline set up similar to the tables on the other side of the swinging doors. Inside sits Matt, the head chef, typing on a white Mac laptop, surrounded by stacks of mail and clothing draped all over the table.

> (Demetry 2013: 586)

As Demetry points out, the field note brings out the relaxed, informal ambience created by the first head chef (Matt) and the use that he made of music as a means of reinforcing that atmosphere.

the case of the field note in Research in focus 19.6, the loud rap music seems to have had a considerable impact on Demetry's immediate impression of the restaurant's ambience, as she is clearly surprised by it.

Sometimes, field notes may seem to describe incidents that are so mundane that they seem barely worth recording. For example, the following field note is taken from Watts's (2008) study of train travel. The idea of 'mobile ethnography' has garnered interest as social geographers and sociologists have become increasingly interested in studying people on the move and in the research methods that might be employed. She travelled on the same train service once a week over three weeks. In her field note she writes:

> Nothing seems to happen. . . . I want to write that something happens. But nothing happens. A man reads a book, then reads a newspaper. A woman fidgets and sniffs. . . . A cloud catches me and I drift off, dreaming of

my destination. . . . I am drifting into reverie, the flashing light, the tiredness, the endless munching of crisps from nearby, the reading, reading . . . the juddering, the rolling of the carriage, the white light of Cornwall. I am travelling outside the train, through the fields, as though the carriage were air on which I was carried, blown along.

> (Watts 2008: 713)

The sense of boredom is unmistakable and hardly seems worth recording. However, quite apart from providing insight into her own experience of train travel, Watts also reveals the tediousness of the experience of train travel for others. While she reports some things that did happen, they are not striking or colourful. As a result, ethnographers in such circumstances have to be on their guard to allow the dullness of the experience to come through but not to get sucked into the boredom so that they lose sight of recording it in their field notes.

Bringing ethnographic research to an end

Knowing when to stop is not an easy or straightforward matter in ethnography. Because of its unstructured nature and the absence of specific hypotheses to be tested (other than those that might emerge during data collection and analysis), there is a tendency for ethnographic research to lack a sense of an obvious end point. But clearly it does come to an end! It may be that there is an almost natural end to the research, such as when a strike that is being observed comes to a conclusion, but this is a fairly rare occurrence. Mears's research in which she was a fashion model (see Research in the news 19.1) effectively came to an end when she was informed in an email that she was no longer going to be booked by the fashion agency. Sometimes, the rhythms of the ethnographer's occupational career or personal and family life will necessitate withdrawal from the field. Such factors include the end of a period of sabbatical leave; the need to submit a doctoral thesis by a certain date; or research funding drawing to a close. As regards family and personal commitments, for example, Taylor (1993) writes that one of the factors that were instrumental in her departure from the field was an illness of her youngest son that lasted many months.

Moreover, ethnographic research can be highly stressful for many reasons: the nature of the topic, which may place the fieldworker in stressful situations (as in research on crime); the marginality of the researcher in the social setting and the need constantly to manage a front; and the prolonged absence from one's normal life that is often necessary. The ethnographer may feel that he or she has simply had enough. A further possibility that may start to bring fieldwork to a close is that the ethnographer may

begin to feel that the research questions on which he or she has decided to concentrate are answered, so that there are no new data worth generating. Altheide (1980: 310) has written that his decision to leave the various news organizations in which he had conducted ethnographic research was often motivated by 'the recurrence of familiar situations and the feeling that little worthwhile was being revealed', a kind of data saturation (see Chapter 18).

The reasons for bringing ethnographic research to a close can involve a wide range of factors from the personal to matters of research design. Whatever the reason, disengagement has to be *managed*. This means that promises must be kept, so that, if you promised a report to an organization as a condition of entry, that promise should not be forgotten. It also means that ethnographers must provide good explanations for their departure. Members of a social setting always know that the researcher is a temporary fixture, but over a long period of time, and especially if there was genuine participation in activities within that setting, people may forget that the ethnographer's presence is temporary. The farewells have to be managed and in an orderly fashion. Also, the ethnographer's *ethical* commitments must not be forgotten, such as the need to ensure that persons and settings are anonymized—unless, of course, as sometimes happens, there has been an agreement that the nature of the social setting can be disclosed.

Michael Humphreys, in his research on Credit Line, went even further in his desire for organizational participants to remain anonymous (Humphreys and Watson 2009). He became aware that the gulf between the company's public position on corporate social responsibility and the private views of many staff about that position presented him with an ethical dilemma in that he clearly needed to protect their anonymity so that they would not get into trouble with the firm. The words of 'Charity' were quoted earlier in the chapter, but Charity is not a pseudonym, the usual tactic used by researchers to preserve the identity of their informants. 'Charity' is a composite person rather than a real person. Her views and words are in fact an aggregation of those of several employees who expressed identical or similar positions.

Can there be a feminist ethnography?

This heading is in fact the title of a widely cited article by Stacey (1988). It is a rebuttal of the view that there is and/or can be a distinctively feminist ethnography that both draws on the distinctive strengths of ethnography and is informed by feminist tenets of the kind outlined at the end of Chapter 17. Reinharz (1992) sees feminist ethnography as significant in terms of feminism, because:

- it documents women's lives and activities, which were previously largely seen as marginal and subsidiary to men's;

- it understands women from their perspective, so that the tendency that 'trivializes females' activities and thoughts, or interprets them from the standpoint of men in the society or of the male researcher' (Reinharz 1992: 52), is militated against; and

- it understands women in context.

Similarly, Skeggs (2001: 430) has observed that ethnography, 'with its emphasis on experiences and the words, voice and lives of the participants', has been viewed by many feminist researchers as being well suited to the goals of feminism. Reinharz's principles lay behind Mattley's (2006) choice of participant observation for collecting data on working for a sex fantasy phone line in order to explore the notion of emotional labour (see Research in focus 17.1 for a brief discussion of the emergence of this concept). She writes:

> I knew that as a feminist my goals were to understand the phone workers' experiences, to document their experiences using their own words and perspectives, and to understand how their emotional labor was a part of their work context. I also knew that understanding their experiences from their own point of view was important to challenge the dominant sociological view of sex workers as deviants, which has most often been written by male sociologists.
>
> (Mattley 2006: 143)

However, such commitments and practices go only part of the way. Of great significance to feminist researchers is the question of whether the research allows for a non-exploitative relationship between researcher and researched. One of the main elements of such a strategy is that the ethnographer does not treat the relationship as a one-way process of extracting information from others, but actually provides something in return.

Skeggs's (1994, 1997) account of her ethnographic research on young women represents an attempt to address this issue of a non-exploitative relationship when women conduct ethnographic research on other women (see Research in focus 19.7). J. Stacey (1988: 23), however, argues, on the basis of her fieldwork experience, that the various situations she encountered as a feminist ethnographer placed her

> in situations of inauthenticity, dissimilitude, and potential, perhaps inevitable betrayal, situations that I now believe are inherent in fieldwork method. For no matter how welcome, even enjoyable the fieldworker's presence may appear to 'natives', fieldwork represents an intrusion and intervention into a system of relationships, a system of relationships that the researcher is far freer to leave.

Stacey also argues that, when the research is written up, it is the feminist ethnographer's interpretations and judgements that come through and that have authority. Skeggs responds to this general charge against feminist ethnography by acknowledging in the case of her own study that her academic career was undoubtedly enhanced by the research, but argues that Stacey's views construe women as victims. Instead, she argues:

> The young women were not prepared to be exploited; just as they were able to resist most things which did not promise economic or cultural reward, they were able to resist me. . . . They enjoyed the research. It provided resources for developing a sense of their self-worth. More importantly, the feminism of the research has provided a framework which they use to explain that their individual problems are part of a wider structure and not their personal fault.
>
> (Skeggs 1994: 88)

Similarly, Reinharz (1992: 74–5) argues that, although ethnographic fieldwork relationships may sometimes *seem* manipulative, a clear undercurrent of reciprocity often lies beneath them. The researcher, in other words, may offer help or advice to her research participants, or she may be

Research in focus 19.7
A feminist ethnography

A study by Skeggs (1997: 1) refers to 'the 83 White working-class women of this longitudinal ethnographic study, set in the North West of England' and writes that it was

> based on research conducted over a total period of 12 years including three years' full-time, in-the-field participant observation. It began when the women enrolled on a 'caring' course at a local college and it follows their trajectories through the labour market, education and the family.

The elements of a distinctively feminist ethnography can be seen in the following comments:

- This ethnography was 'politically motivated to provide space for the articulations and experiences of the marginalized' (Skeggs 1997: 23).

- The 'study was concerned to show how young women's experience of structure (their class and gender positioning) and institutions (education and the media) framed and informed their responses and how this process informed constructions of their own subjectivity' (Skeggs 1994: 74). This comment, like the previous one, reflects the commitment to documenting women's lives and allowing their experiences to come through, while also pointing to the significance of the understanding of women in context, to which Reinharz (1992) refers.

Skeggs also feels that the relationship with the women was not an exploitative one. For example, she writes that the research enabled the women's 'sense of self-worth' to be 'enhanced by being given the opportunity to be valued, knowledgeable and interesting' (Skeggs 1994: 81). She also claims she was able to 'provide a mouthpiece against injustices' and to listen 'to disclosures of violence, child abuse and sexual harassment' (Skeggs 1994: 81).

exhibiting reciprocity by giving a public airing to normally marginalized voices (although the ethnographer is always the mouthpiece for such voices and may be imposing a particular 'spin' on them). Moreover, it seems extreme to abandon feminist ethnography on the grounds that the ethnographer cannot fulfil all possible obligations simultaneously. Indeed, this would be a recipe for the abandonment of all research, feminist or otherwise. What is also crucial is transparency—transparency in the feminist ethnographer's dealings with the women she studies and transparency in the account of the research process, both of which are a great strength in Skeggs's work. Nonetheless, it is clear that the question of whether there is or can be a feminist ethnography is a matter of ongoing debate.

The rise of online ethnography

Ethnography may not seem to be an obvious method for collecting data on Internet use. The image of the ethnographer is that of someone who visits communities and organizations. The Internet seems to go against the grain of ethnography, in that it seems a decidedly placeless space. In fact, as Hine (2000) has observed, conceiving of the Internet as a place—a cyberspace—has been one strategy for an ethnographic study of the Internet, and from this it is just a short journey to the examination of communities in the form of online communities or virtual communities. In this way, our concepts of place and space that are constitutive of the way in which we operate in the real world are grafted onto the Internet and its use. A further issue is that ethnography entails participant observation, but in cyberspace what is the ethnographer observing and in what is he or she participating?

The methods and sources of data associated with online ethnography have sometimes been used as adjuncts to conventional ethnographies of communities. Both Hine (2008) and Garcia et al. (2009) have observed that there is a growing tendency and need for online ethnographers to take into account offline worlds, because even the most committed Internet user has a life beyond the computer. This development means taking into account how the members of the online communities that tend to be the focus of ethnographic studies have lives offline and that the two will have implications for the other. There is a corollary to this observation that, as the Internet becomes increasingly embedded in people's lives, practitioners of what might be thought of as conventional ethnography (in the sense of the ethnographic study of non-virtual lives and communities) increasingly have to take into account individuals' engagements with the Internet. For example, Pearson (2012) found that there were numerous football Internet forums, notably message boards, that were relevant to his research. At the time he was writing one of his chapters, Red Cafe, the largest of the Manchester United forums, had 840 users online and the second largest had 679. These forums provide a platform for supporters to discuss footballing issues and often for participants to arrange to meet up. In view of the significance of these forums, they had to be included within Pearson's ethnography. The message board associated with Manchester United's Red Brigade had a particular significance for his research. This forum provided an opportunity for supporters to discuss plans for football trips and meeting up. This study serves as an example of the way in which offline and online ethnography cannot be treated as separately as was formerly the case. Similarly, Hallett and Barber (2014: 314) have described how in two separate conventional ethnographies of 'physical spaces' they found themselves increasingly '*pulled* into online spaces because that was where our participants were' (emphasis in original). In one of the studies—an ethnography of two men's hair salons—the authors had planned a conventional ethnography based on observations and interviews to explore the ways in which beauty was reimagined in the context of masculinity. It gradually became apparent that the Internet was important for the men and was a source of information for them about salons. One of the salons refused to allow clients to be interviewed and so the researchers turned to Yelp.com reviews. It soon became apparent that the reviews provided 'insight into how clients invoked masculine identities while simultaneously discussing their manicures, pedicures, hair coloring, and haircuts' (Hallett and Barber 2014: 320). Similarly, earlier online ethnographies tended to emphasize people's involvement and participation in online worlds to the relative exclusion of offline worlds, perhaps because the relative newness of the Internet and its lack of reach into everyday life during those days meant that the virtual could be treated as a relatively autonomous domain.

Early ethnographic research in connection with the Internet often entailed the use of semi-structured interviews which were administered online (e.g. Markham 1998). As the use of the Internet has changed, there has been a burgeoning of online discussion groups and these have increasingly become a focus of attention for researchers wanting to conduct online ethnographic research. Internet-based ethnographies have increasingly come to focus on these online communities. Examples can be found in Research in focus 19.8 and 19.9.

Studies of online communities invite us to consider the nature of the Internet as a domain for investigation, but they also invite us to consider the nature and the adaptability of our research methods. In the examples discussed in this section, the question of what is and is not ethnography is given a layer of complexity. But these studies are also cases of using Internet-based research methods to investigate Internet use. Future online ethnographic investigations of issues unrelated to the Internet will give a clearer indication of the possibilities that the method offers.

There has been considerable debate regarding the status of 'lurking' in online ethnography. This practice is disliked by members of online communities and can result in censure from participants who are often able to detect the practice. Hine (2008) has also suggested that a sole reliance on lurking without participation risks omitting crucial experiential aspects of the understanding of online communities (Hine 2008). However, she was able to use a non-participative approach to an online community to good effect in her examination of the use of science in discussions of headlice in an online parenting community (Hine 2014). This study's research questions were referred to in Thinking deeply 17.2. Hine gained permission from the administrators of the Mumsnet forum to examine discussion threads relating to headlice and their treatment, but she did not contact participants to the discussions or participate herself. Her study shows, among other things, that while scientific knowledge was often introduced into discussions, it was not privileged over personal experience and was sometimes given less credibility.

Online ethnographers sometimes lurk as a prelude to their fieldwork in order to gain an understanding of the setting prior to their participation. Even when ethnographers lurk in this way, ethical issues arise (see Chapter 6), while it has been suggested that 'ethnographers will get a more authentic experience of an online setting if they jump straight into participation' (Garcia et al. 2009: 60). The presence or absence of participation distinguishes a purely documentary qualitative analysis (such as a thematic analysis of postings without participation, as in Hine's case and Research in focus 23.9) from a virtual or online ethnographic study (such as a thematic analysis of postings with participation, as in Research in focus 19.9). In the case of the study reported in Research in focus 19.8, the researcher moved from a purely documentary analysis in the first phase to an online ethnography in the second. Mkono and Maxwell (2014) write that a passive, lurking approach is the most common one in tourism-related studies of online communities.

Research in focus 19.8
Participant observation in cyberspace

J. P. Williams (2006) conducted participant observation research into straightedge, a youth subculture that emerged out of punk and that is associated with a lifestyle that is largely free of drugs, alcohol, and promiscuous sex and is committed to a vegetarian and often vegan diet. It is also associated with distinctive music that is heavily influenced by punk music. Williams notes that, since the emergence of the Internet, straightedge adherents have emerged who exhibit only limited participation in local music scenes and, he suggests, who might not otherwise have been adherents at all. Williams was interested in the struggle in online discussions to present an authentic straightedge identity in the face of these two major and different patterns of adherence. To this end, he focused his attention on an online straightedge discussion forum, which, he suggests, has the characteristics of an online community. There were two phases to this ethnography. In the first, he read forum threads without contributing to them. The first message of each thread was analysed using ethnographic content analysis (see Chapter 23). As a result of this work, he became increasingly aware of a conflict among contributors over what was an authentic straightedge self. He used the themes that emerged from this analysis to inform the second phase of the research in which, over a period of two years, he initiated discussions within the forum. He writes:

> I started threads that asked participants about their affiliation with straightedge, their understandings of subcultural rules, their opinions about mainstream culture, and so on. By monitoring the threads daily, I could guide conversations, bring them back on track when participants strayed off topic, and ask follow-up questions based on initial responses.

(J. P. Williams 2006: 181)

Prior to doing this, he had announced himself as a researcher who was analysing textual conversations. In addition, Williams conducted online synchronous interviews with nine key informants who were purposively sampled by virtue of the nature of their participation, with the website administrator, with several individuals who were regular contributors, and with some who were frequent contributors who then quit. Through this research, Williams was able to show that the online forums have had a significant impact on the straightedge community and on how its adherents position themselves in terms of a sense of identity.

Research in focus 19.9
Covert participant observation in cyberspace

Brotsky and Giles (2007) report some findings and experiences relating to the first author's covert participation study of the 'pro-ana' community—in essence a community of people who are supportive of eating disorders such as and most notably anorexia nervosa. She identified twelve pro-ana websites and obtained membership of the various discussion contexts each website hosted—forums, email discussion lists, chatrooms, and so on. Brotsky fabricated a plausible persona in terms of age, sex, height, eating disorder (anorexia), and weight (current, past, and intended). The authors write that Brotsky

> began by introducing herself as an authentic pro-ana sympathsizer who was hoping to establish virtual relationships with like-minded individuals, and continued to participate as naturally as possible across the course of the investigation. As the investigation unfolded, connections were made and close relationships developed through ongoing conversations with participants. . . . [She] successfully acquired membership of 23 separate groups across 12 websites, including discussion forums, chatrooms, blog sub-communities, online journal/diary sites, and e-mail-group affiliations.

(Brotsky and Giles 2007: 98)

Through this study, the authors were able to identify the sources of support offered within the communities and group identities (such as whether anorexia was viewed as a lifestyle or illness).

The study of communities has been a major feature of online ethnography. These are often represented as online communities, though how far they constitute communities in the traditional sense (especially since community participation is highly fluid) is a matter of debate. Thinking deeply 19.2 distinguishes four types of online community study. It is likely that which of the four types is employed is not entirely a matter of choice. For example, hostility to outsiders and in particular to researchers may make a researcher inclined to lurk or to participate covertly, as suggested by Brotsky and Giles (2007; see Research in focus 19.9). Another possibility is that the nature of the community being studied may have implications for the approach taken. For example, Kozinets (2010) draws a distinction between online ethnographies of online communities and ethnographies of communities online. The former involve the study of communities that have a largely online existence, such as his research on online discussion forums of knowledgeable coffee enthusiasts (Kozinets 2002). Kozinets uses the term **netnography** to refer to the ethnographic study of online (or predominantly online) communities (see Key concept 19.4). A more recent example of a community with an exclusively online existence is Banks's (2012, 2014) covert online ethnography of the 'advantage play' subculture, whose participants seek to use mathematical techniques to reduce the risks inherent in various forms of online gambling by taking advantage of technical weaknesses in the implementation of gambling

Thinking deeply 19.2
Four types of online community study

As noted in the main text, the study of online communities has been a particularly prominent area for qualitative researchers. This often involves the examination of online discussion groups, such as online support groups and discussion boards. As also noted in the main text, the study of such documents and online ethnography can shade into each other with this kind of research. There are four prominent types of online interaction study employed by qualitative researchers. All four types entail a considerable degree of immersion in the postings, but Type 1 is the least likely of the four to be viewed as a form of online ethnography, as the researcher largely occupies a position as external observer.

Type 1. Study of online communities only, with no participation
Such a study typically entails solely the examination of blogs, discussion groups, listservs, etc., without any participation or intervention on the part of the researcher(s). Typically, it takes the form of 'lurking' and conducting an analysis without the authors of the materials being aware of the researcher's(s') presence.

Examples: C. F. Sullivan (2003; see Research in focus 23.9); Sanders (2005); Hine (2014); Wu and Pearce (2014; see Research in focus 19.4); Janta et al. (2014); Goodman and Rowe (2014).

Type 2. Study of online communities only, with some participation
A study of this type will typically entail the examination of discussion groups, forums, listservs, etc., but with some participation or intervention on the part of researcher(s). The researcher is not passive and instead intervenes (overtly or covertly) in the ongoing Internet-mediated postings and discussions. A variant of this type in a context which is not an online discussion forum occurs when the ethnography participates in an online subculture.

Examples: Kozinets (2002); Brotsky and Giles (2007; Research in focus 19.9); Banks (2012, 2014).

Type 3. Study of online communities plus online or offline interviews
Same as Type 2, but in addition the researcher interviews some of the people involved in the online interaction. The interviews may be online or offline.

Examples: Kanayama (2003); J. P. Williams (2006; see Research in focus 19.8).

Type 4. Study of online communities plus offline research methods (in addition to online or offline interviews)
Same as Type 3, but in addition there is active participation of the researcher(s) in the offline worlds of those being studied, such as attending gatherings, as well as interviews (which may be online or offline).

Examples: Kendall (1999); Kozinets (2001).

Key concept 19.4
What is netnography?

One of the most significant approaches to conducting ethnographic research on online communities is *netnography*, which has been developed by Kozinets (2002, 2010). Netnography is a form of ethnography because it entails the researcher's immersion in the online worlds under investigation; it is an essentially naturalistic method; and it relies considerably on observation, though often supported by forms of online interview. It is tailored to the examination of communities that have an exclusively online existence, although it can play a role in relation to communities that have both an online and an offline existence. With cases where a community has both an online and offline presence, the offline element needs to be examined through a conventional ethnographic approach. In a sense, the term 'netnography' and the package of methods and sensitivities with which Kozinets invests the term represent a helpful bringing together of a variety of terms and procedures associated with ethnographic approaches to Internet phenomena. For example, Mkono and Maxwell (2014) regard such terms as 'online ethnography', 'webnography', and 'virtual ethnography' as synonyms for netnography. Thus far, netnographies have tended to focus on areas of research associated with marketing and retailing, such as branding and the response to new products.

An example of a self-proclaimed netnography is Wu and Pearce's (2014) examination of the approach's potential in relation to the study of new tourist markets in a digital era. They take the example of recreational vehicle tourists and examine Chinese tourists' experiences of this form of tourism in Australia. The authors conducted a search for appropriate travel blogs posted on two sites (Qyer.com and Sina.com) in January 2013. They found 107 blogs but these were whittled down to 37 by focusing only on 'rich detailed blogs posted by mainland Chinese' (Wu and Pearce 2014: 467). Because the blogs were written in an open-access manner, permission was not sought from the bloggers to quote and process their words. The blogs were manually coded and themes were developed to reveal the motivations for this form of tourism. However, in addition, because routes were included in the blogs, it was possible to examine typical routes taken and calculate distances travelled.

products. Banks became an advantage player and was a covert participant observer of an online forum for eighteen months. The study shows how participants seek to manage risk, not just of losing money, but of being fleeced by gambling sites that take the gambler's stake but closes down its operations before paying out.

The ethnographic study of communities online entails research into communities that have a predominantly offline existence. An example is Kozinets's study of *Star Trek* fans, for which he became a very active member of fan clubs, attended conventions, and (for the online component) examined newsgroup postings and Web pages and engaged in email exchanges (Kozinets 2001). The relevance of this distinction is that Type 4 studies are feasible only in connection with the study of communities online that have a clear offline presence.

The rise of visual ethnography

One of the most striking developments in qualitative research in recent years has been the growth of interest in the use of visual materials. The use of such materials in social research is by no means new; for example, social anthropologists have for many decades made use of photographs of the tribes and villages in which they resided. It was not uncommon in the late nineteenth century and the early twentieth to encounter articles that made use of photographs in the *American Journal of Sociology*. However, from around the time of the First World War, their use fell away. One factor in this loss of interest in the use of photographs is likely to have been a feeling that their inclusion was inconsistent with the discipline's growing scientific pretensions. However, in recent years, there has been a clear sense that the use of visual materials in social research has entered a new phase of interest that can be discerned in the number of books that appeared around the turn of the millennium in this area (Banks 2001; Pink 2001; Rose 2001).

Thinking deeply 19.3
Two stances on the role of visual images in ethnography

Pink (2001) draws an important distinction between two positions on visual materials. The traditional framework is a *realist* one (see Key concept 2.3 on realism) in which the photograph or video recording simply captures an event or setting that then becomes a 'fact' for the ethnographer to interpret along with his or her other data. The image and what it represents are essentially unproblematic and act as a window on reality. This has been the dominant frame within which visual resources have been produced and analysed. Researchers who employ photographs to illustrate their work or as adjuncts to their field notes typically operate within a realist frame of reference that treats the image as relatively unproblematic (see Research in focus 19.10 and Thinking deeply 19.4 for examples). In contrast, Pink draws attention to a position that she calls *reflexive*, which entails an awareness of and sensitivity to the ways in which the researcher as a person has an impact on what a photograph reveals. This sensitivity requires a grasp of the way that one's age, gender, background, and academic proclivities influence what is photographed, how it is composed, and the role that informants and others may have played in influencing the resulting image.

Photographs did not disappear completely from the outputs of social scientists, of course. Particularly in book-length monographs, photographs could sometimes be found. For example, Blauner's (1964) well-known book on alienated work under different technological conditions contained several photographs that were used to illustrate each of the technologies. Of particular significance is that the photographs were accompanied by quite detailed captions that informed readers of what they were seeing in the images. These photographs were presented as having uncontested meanings, which was very much in tune with the realist stance on visual images (see Thinking deeply 19.3 on the distinction between realist and reflexive approaches to visual materials and Thinking deeply 19.4 for more on issues relating to Blauner's use of photographs).

A distinction can be made between the use of visual materials that are *extant* and those that are produced more or less exclusively for the purposes of research. The former will be featured in Chapter 23 and take the form of such artefacts as people's collections of photographs and images in newspapers and magazines. In this chapter I will be emphasizing research-driven visual images, and my main focus will be upon photographs. Visual images that are research-driven may be taken either by the researcher or by the research participants themselves. In either case, the images may be used as a basis for what is often referred to as **photo-elicitation**, whereby the researcher uses the images as a springboard for discussion with the producers of the photographs concerning the meaning and significance of the images (see Research in focus 19.11 for an example). Wright et al. (2010) equipped

African Caribbean young people who had been excluded from school with disposable cameras and instructed them to take photographs of family and friends who had been sources of support. The researcher wanted to understand how the young people managed their transition into adulthood. The images tended to be of events and contexts that were significant at that particular juncture of their lives and that were therefore significant for the development of their personal identities. The authors argue that the use of a visual research approach helped to empower these marginalized young people and to reduce some of the power distance between the researchers and their participants. Photo-elicitation is often employed in connection with extant images too, and this point will be addressed further in Chapter 23.

The distinction between extant and research-driven visual materials is not an entirely satisfactory one. For example, when research participants are asked to discuss items in their photograph collections, this is similar to asking participants to take photographs and then to discuss the images that are taken. However, in order to restrict the discussion of documents in Chapter 23 only to items that have *not* been produced for research purposes, the distinction is required.

Although the term 'visual ethnography' is becoming increasingly popular (e.g. Pink 2001, 2013), it is sometimes used in a way that does not imply the kind of sustained immersion in a social setting that has been taken in this chapter to be a feature of ethnography. Sometimes, the term is used to include interviews of the kind covered in Chapter 20 in which visual materials figure prominently. However, in order to avoid splitting visual resources and

Thinking deeply 19.4
Copyright and photographs

An interesting fairly early use of photographs can be found in Blauner's (1964) influential book on work in four different technological conditions. Blauner used photographs to illustrate each of the four technologies and the kinds of work with which each was associated. They are very memorable photographs, which were accompanied by a detailed description of the work beneath the image. I wanted to include a photograph very similar to the one in Plate 19.1 to demonstrate Blauner's use of photographs to illustrate assembly-line work in the automobile industry in the USA in the 1950s and early 1960s. Blauner's photograph had the title 'Subdivided jobs and restricted freedom' and was accompanied by a description of employees' work and the following comment:

> These men perform the identical tasks shown above all day long and may fasten from eight hundred to one thousand wheels in eight hours. The movement of the cars along the conveyor belt determines the pace of their work and kept them close to their stations, virtually 'chained' to the assembly line.

(Blauner 1964: 112)

Plate 19.1
The automobile assembly line

Copyright DaimlerChrysler Corporation, used with permission.

Thus, Blauner used the image to illustrate the work of assembly-line workers and was operating very much within a realist view of the role of the photograph. I write above that Plate 19.1 is 'very similar', because it proved impossible to track the owner of the image. In Blauner's book the image he used is described as 'Courtesy of the Chrysler Corporation'. However, Chrysler's archivists could not find the photograph and therefore could not provide us with permission to use it. However, they were kind enough to allow me to use the image in Plate 19.1. This anecdote demonstrates some of the difficulties with the use of photographs in general and of older ones in particular. Sometimes, authors and publishers include photographs even when they are unable to track down the copyright owner and usually cover themselves with a general statement such as 'Every effort has been made to find the owner of the copyright but if anyone believes they are the copyright owner please contact the publisher'. This option was not available to us, because the print quality of the photographs in Blauner's book was poor.

research methods across too many chapters, I have located the discussion of their use in qualitative research in this chapter.

In the discussion that follows, I will emphasize photographs, mainly because they are the visual medium that has received the greatest attention. There are several ways in which photographs have been employed by qualitative researchers.

- As an *aide-mémoire* in the course of fieldwork, in which context the images essentially become components of the ethnographer's field notes. This is how I used images in my own work (see Research in focus 19.10).

- As sources of data in their own right and not simply as adjuncts to the ethnographer's field notes (see Research in focus 19.12).

- As prompts for discussion by research participants. Sometimes the photographs may be extant, and this kind of context will be examined in Chapter 23. Alternatively, the discussions may be based on photographs taken by the ethnographer or by research participants (see Research in focus 19.11) more or less exclusively for the purposes of the investigation. In the case of photographs that are taken by research participants and that form the basis for an interview or discussion, Pink (2004: 399) writes: 'By working with informants to produce images that are meaningful for them we can gain insights into their visual cultures and into what is important for them as individuals living in particular localities.'

Pink (2001) draws attention to two different ways in which visual images have been conceptualized in social research. She calls these the *realist* and *reflexive* approaches (see Thinking deeply 19.3). The latter approach is frequently collaborative, in the sense that research participants may be involved in decisions about what photographs should be taken and then how they should be interpreted. Further, there is a recognition of the fluidity of the meaning of images, implying that they can never be fixed and will always be viewed by different people in different ways. Thus, in Pink's research on Spanish bullfighters, the images she took of bullfights were interpreted by enthusiasts in terms of the performative qualities of the bullfighter. UK viewers of the images employed a different interpretative frame to do with animal rights and cruelty. Further examples of the use of visual resources in ethnographic contexts can be found in Thinking deeply 19.3 and Research in focus 19.12.

The various examples of the use of visual materials give a sense that they have great potential for ethnographers and qualitative researchers more generally. Their growing popularity should not entice readers into thinking that visual methods should necessarily be incorporated into their investigations: their use must be relevant to the research questions being asked. For her research on the body work landscape in South Florida, Wolkowitz (2012; Research in focus 19.12) was interested in what she terms the growth of the 'body work economy'—that is, turning the body into an object to be worked on for profit. She recognizes that statistical data can document aspects of this process but argues that the photographs are better at demonstrating the clustering of body work establishments in the location; the photographs also provide readers with the raw material for considering the adequacy of the researcher's inferences.

As sources of data, visual research methods require an ability on the part of the researcher to 'read' images in a manner that is sensitive to the context in which they were generated; the potential for multiple meanings that may need to be worked through with research participants; and, where the researcher is the source of the images, the significance of his or her own social position. In other words, the analyst of visual materials needs to be sceptical about the notion that a photograph provides an unproblematic depiction of reality. In addition, researchers

Research in focus 19.10
Researching Disneyization

I have been intrigued by something that I call 'Disneyization', which refers to the process by which the principles associated with the Disney theme parks have permeated many aspects of modern society and economy. In my book on Disneyization (Bryman 2004) I included several photographs that I felt illustrated quite well the processes I was describing. In addition to serving this role, the photographs were very helpful in acting as reminders of contexts that revealed the process of Disneyization for me. This was especially the case with an article I wrote on the Disneyization of McDonald's (Bryman 2003). At one point in this article I discussed the rather bizarre case of a themed McDonald's in Chicago that employed a rock 'n' roll narrative. I had visited Chicago a year previously to give a paper at the American Sociological Association conference and took the opportunity to take some photographs of the restaurant. These images were very helpful in remembering the restaurant, although I did not use them for illustrative purposes in either the book or the article. One of the images is presented here—Plate 19.2 shows the restaurant's exterior against the Chicago skyline.

Plate 19.2
Disneyization in pictures: a themed McDonald's

Research in focus 19.11
Photographs in a study of the experience of homelessness

Radley et al. (2005) were interested in the ways in which homeless people visualize their lives. They were especially interested in how their lives are visualized in the context both of their hostels and the streets of London. Following an initial interview, twelve homeless people were each given disposable cameras and asked to take photographs 'that represented their experience of being a homeless person. They were told that photographs could be of key times in their day, of typical activities and spaces, or of anything else that portrayed their situation' (Radley et al. 2005: 277). The films were developed shortly after the photographs had been taken, and the participants were interviewed shortly after that. On each occasion, participants were asked about all the photographs and which ones best expressed their experience of being a homeless person. This approach to interviewing—namely, asking people to discuss photographs and their meaning and significance for them—is often referred to as the technique of *photo-elicitation*. Plates 19.3 and 19.4 provide examples of the kinds of photograph that were taken. The photograph in Plate 19.3 was taken by Rose (the names are pseudonyms) and shows the entrance to her day centre. For Rose, this photograph had significance because it is where she is welcomed and welcomes others and where she is given the opportunity to move between her two worlds—as someone who sleeps rough at night but who during the day is able to mix with others with more conventional lives in terms of having jobs and homes. The photograph in Plate 19.4 was taken by Mary, who, unlike Rose, did not sleep rough at night, as she made use of a hostel that was in fact close to Rose's day centre. For Mary, this

Plate 19.3
Images of homelessness

Copyright Alan Radley, Darrin Hodgetts, and Andrea Cullen. Reproduced with thanks.

photograph took on significance because it 'shows us a community of friends who share not only a place [referred to as The Wall situated on Vauxhall Bridge Road] but also an activity—drinking' (Radley et al. 2005: 283; note how the faces are pixelated to protect the individuals in the photographs). The photographs and the discussions of them by the participants provide insights into the experience of homelessness and how the homeless navigate an identity in a world in which homelessness is on the fringes of society.

Plate 19.4
Images of homelessness

Copyright Alan Radley, Darrin Hodgetts, and Andrea Cullen. Reproduced with thanks.

Research in focus 19.12
Photographs and the body work landscape of South Florida

Wolkowitz (2012) has used photographs in a loosely ethnographic context in documenting the growth of what she calls the 'body work economy' in South Florida. Over several visits to the region, Wolkowitz has taken numerous digital photographs and has collected relevant photographs taken by others relating to 'places where body work goes on' (2012: para. 3.5). The process began as the equivalent of taking written notes to record observations, but Wolkowitz writes that she became increasingly aware of 'not only the ubiquity of body work enterprises as a feature of the landscape, but also their size, self-presentation (modest, grand, welcoming, forbidding), the apparent seamlessness of their integration into the consumer services sector, and the explicitness of their focus on the body' (Wolkowitz 2012: para 3.5). Her photographs show a variety of locations of different sizes and contexts (beauty service establishments, general medical facilities, specialist medical treatment centres, gyms, tattoo studios), some workers involved in the industries, and some of those targeted by the businesses. Plate 19.5 contains an example of the kinds of photographs that were taken of the medical establishments that featured in her research. The photographs are supplemented with interviews with health care workers and managers, and others. She uses the photographs as a means of establishing 'a vivid picture of how body work as a social phenomenon is changing in its appearance and scale' (2012: para 7.2), how these establishments are clustered in the region, and how the body is being commodified in contemporary capitalism.

Plate 19.5
Using visual images in the study of the body landscape of South Florida

Copyright Carol Wolkowitz. Reproduced with thanks.

will usually include non-visual research methods (such as interviews) in their investigations. This leads to the question of the relative significance of words and images in the analysis of data and the presentation of findings. Since words are the traditional medium, it is easy to slip into seeing the visual as ancillary.

However, at the same time, Pink (2004) reminds us that visual research methods are never purely visual. As Pink points out, they are usually accompanied by other (often traditional) research methods such as interviewing and observation. Second, the visual is almost always accompanied by the non-visual—words—that are the medium of expression for both the research participants and the researchers themselves.

Finally, visual research methods raise especially difficult issues of ethics, an area that is explored in Chapter 6. The Visual Sociology Group, a study group of the British Sociological Association (BSA), has provided a statement of ethical practice for researchers using visual research methods: **www.visualsociology. org.uk/BSA_VS_ethical_statement.pdf** (accessed 30 November 2014).

This is a useful statement, which draws on the BSA's *Statement of Ethical Practice*, referred to in Chapter 6. Here are some statements of ethical practice that are recommended:

> Researchers may want to discuss the status of the images with participants in order to clearly explain the dissemination strategy of the research project. In certain circumstances, the researcher(s) may want to create a written or verbal contract guaranteeing the participants ownership of the images produced. Under UK law copyright can be waived by participants and given to the researcher(s); however it is recommended that researchers read the current legislation or seek legal advice if taking this option (please note that the date of the creation of the image affects the legal status).

> As far as possible participation in sociological research should be based on the freely given informed consent of those studied. This implies a responsibility on the sociologist to explain in appropriate detail, and in terms meaningful to participants, what the research is about, who is undertaking and financing it, why it is being undertaken, and how it is to be disseminated and used. Here again clarity about the status and ownership of visual data will benefit the participants and the reputation of the discipline.

As these points reveal, there is a special sensitivity to the use of visual materials, such as photographs, in that the subjects who appear in them may have their images widely disseminated. It is important, therefore, to ensure that permission is gained from those whose images appear and that they are fully aware of the implications of that agreement. If you are considering using visual research methods, you should consult the Visual Sociology Group's statement of ethical practice.

 # Writing ethnography

The term 'ethnography' is interesting, because it refers both to a method of social research and to the finished product of ethnographic research. In other words, it is both something that is carried out in doing research and something that one reads. Since around the mid-1980s, the production of ethnographic texts has become a focus of interest in its own right associated with what Denzin and Lincoln (2005b: 20) call 'the postmodern period of experimental ethnographic writing' (see Thinking deeply 17.1). This means that there has been a growth of interest not just in how ethnography is carried out in the field but also in the **rhetorical** conventions employed in the production of ethnographic texts.

Ethnographic texts are designed to convince readers of the *reality* of the events and situations described, and the plausibility of the ethnographer's explanations. The ethnographic text must not simply present a set of findings: it must provide an 'authoritative' account of the group or culture in question. In other words, the ethnographer must convince us that he or she has arrived at an account of social reality that has strong claims to truth.

The ethnographic text is permeated by stylistic and rhetorical devices whereby the reader is persuaded to enter into a shared framework of facts and interpretations, observations and reflections. The ethnographer typically works within a writing strategy that is imbued with **realism**. This simply means that the researcher presents an authoritative, dispassionate account that represents an external, objective reality. Van Maanen (1988) called ethnographic writing that conforms to these characteristics *realist tales*, but he distinguished two other types:

1. *Realist tales*—apparently definitive, confident, and dispassionate third-person accounts of a culture and of the behaviour of members of that culture. This is the most prevalent form of ethnographic writing.

2. *Confessional tales*—personalized accounts in which the ethnographer is fully implicated in the data-gathering and writing-up processes. These are warts-and-all accounts of the trials and tribulations of doing ethnography. They have become more prominent since the 1970s and reflect a growing emphasis on reflexivity in qualitative research in particular. Several of the sources referred to in this chapter include or are confessional tales (e.g. Mears 2011, 2013; Pearson 2009, 2012; Wacquant 2004). However, confessional tales are more concerned with detailing how research was carried out than with presenting findings. Very often the confessional tale is told in one context (such as an invited chapter in a book of similar tales), but the main findings are written up as realist tales.

3. *Impressionist tales*—accounts that place a heavy emphasis on 'words, metaphors, phrasings, and. . . . the expansive recall of fieldwork experience' (Van Maanen 1988: 102). There is a heavy emphasis on stories of dramatic events that provide 'a representational means of cracking open the culture and the fieldworker's way of knowing it' (Van Maanen 1988: 102).

Van Maanen (2011) has since revised his characterization of ethnographic writing, suggesting that increasingly confessional tales are routinely incorporated within standard ethnographies rather than largely appearing as distinct chapters or appendices. He also distinguishes:

1. *Structural tales*—accounts that link observation of the quotidian to wider 'macro' issues in society at large. Burawoy's (1979) ethnography of a factory, which was heavily influenced by labour process theory, is an example, as is Sallaz's (2009) ethnography of casinos in Las Vegas and South Africa which links his findings concerning the work conditions of casino workers to the wider regulatory environments operating in the two countries.

2. *Poststructural tales*—accounts that suggest that reality is a 'fragile social construction subject to numerous lines of sight and interpretation' (Van Maanen 2011: 248). This is done by peering behind the scenes of a manifest reality and suggesting that things are not quite what they seem. Van Maanen proposes that a good example of this type of tale is Fjellman's (1992) deconstructive account of what lies behind many of the design features of Disney World in Florida in terms of the corporation's manipulation of visitors' perceptions and wallets.

3. *Advocacy tales*—accounts that are profoundly motivated by a sense that something is wrong and that the ethnographer wants to lay that bare for all to see. Examples are Gusterson's (1996) ethnography of a nuclear weapons laboratory, Khan's (2011) ethnography of an elite United States high school in which he shows how privilege and cultural capital are interlinked and are perpetuated over generations, and Goffman's (2014) account of the injustices faced by black men in a poor Philadelphia ghetto.

Adler and Adler (2008) have provided a categorization of genres of ethnographic writing that builds, at least in part, on an earlier version of Van Maanen categorization of types of ethnographic writing (Van Maanen 1988). They distinguish four genres:

1. *Classical ethnography*—realist tales that are accessible and aim to provide a persuasive account of a setting. The discussion of research methods often takes on the style of a confessional tale. The literature review is often used to show a gap in previous research on the topic area. Hodkinson's (2002) study of goths (discussed in Figure 19.2) provides an example of this genre.

2. *Mainstream ethnography*—also realist tales, but oriented to a wider constituency of social scientists rather than just other qualitative researchers. It tends to be deductive in approach, and, although Adler and Adler do not put it this way, it has many of the trappings of a positivist style of representation. Mainstream ethnographies draw explicitly on an established literature and tend to be explicit about the research questions that drove the investigation. The research methods are laid out in a formal and specific manner. Zilber's (2002) study of a rape crisis centre in Israel, with its explicit focus on contributing to institutional theory, provides a good example, as does Maitlis and Lawrence's (2007) study of three British orchestras, which uses the literature on sensegiving in organizations as its *raison d'être*.

3. *Postmodern ethnography*—the ethnographer/writer is overtly insinuated into the writing and indeed often within the data and findings themselves. Postmodern ethnographies often take the form of auto-ethnographies, in which the text is heavily personalized and the overall approach intensely reflexive. Mears's (2011) ethnography of the world of the fashion model (see Research in the news 19.1) and Wacquant's (2004) ethnography of the world of boxing have some of these features though neither would necessarily accept the label of 'postmodern'.

4. *Public ethnography*—in fact a form of ethnography that has existed for decades, the public ethnography is written with a general audience in mind. It is usually written in an accessible style and fairly light on the discussion of previous literature, and the presentation of the research methods is brief. Examples of this genre are Venkatesh's (2008) study of a Chicago gang (see Figure 19.2), Khan's (2011) ethnography of an elite high school in the United States, Goffman's (2014) study of the experiences of black men in a Philadelphia ghetto who are wanted for criminal offences, and Búriková and Miller's (2010) study of Slovak au pairs in London. Public ethnographies are more likely to be in book than article format.

It should also be appreciated that any ethnography may well contain elements of more than one category in these classifications. Thus, although Hodkinson's (2002) ethnography of goths has been classified above as a classical ethnography in Adler and Adler's scheme, it has elements of a postmodern ethnography in the way in which the author/researcher himself crops up in the text on a number of occasions. As such, these various ways of portraying modes of writing and representation in ethnography are best thought of as tendencies within ethnographies rather than as descriptions of them.

The changing nature of ethnography

Ethnography has been very much in flux since the end of the twentieth century. The arrival of new forms or modes of ethnography such as visual ethnography and virtual/online ethnography along with a growing interest in alternative forms of writing ethnography give a sense of a vibrant and highly flexible approach. At the same time, concerns are sometimes voiced that the term 'ethnography' is used loosely and that many so-called ethnographies are not obviously ethnographic in the traditional sense of involving a period of prolonged participant observation in a social setting (see Thinking deeply 19.5). There is a further suggestion that the traditional ethnography is in decline. Zickar and Carter (2010) have argued that workplace ethnographies, which have in the past been a rich vein of research (see Research in focus 13.5), have declined in use. One reason is possibly to do with the pressures

on researchers nowadays. They write: 'The time commitment of traditional ethnographic research is intense and would require a reorganization of academic rewards and tenure policies given that ethnographic research often does not get published until 7 to 10 years after the original fieldwork began' (Zickar and Carter 2010: 312). This trend may be behind Emerson's (1987) suggestion that many ethnographers do not spend sufficient time in the field nowadays (see Thinking deeply 19.5). It implies that, if they do conduct ethnographic research at all, qualitative researchers are more likely to have relatively brief sojourns as fieldworkers so that their work may be closer to what Wolcott (1990b) calls 'micro-ethnographies' (see Tips and skills 'Micro-ethnographies'). For inclusion in the Workplace Ethnography Project (see Research in focus 13.5), an ethnography had to have been conducted for at

Thinking deeply 19.5
When is a study ethnographic?

There is some debate about when it is appropriate to refer to a qualitative investigation as an ethnography. In fact, one gets the impression that ethnography is almost a matter of degree. For writers like Emerson (1987) and Wolcott (1990b), some immersion in the field is the touchstone of ethnography, with Emerson arguing that too often ethnographers do not spend enough time in the field. Indeed, my account of ethnography in Key concept 19.1 entails immersion in a social setting.

However, ethnographers are rarely purely participant observers, in that they invariably conduct interviews or examine documents, a point that raises the question of when it is appropriate to refer to a qualitative study as ethnographic. There may be circumstances when the requirement of immersion needs to be relaxed. A striking case in point is Gusterson's (1996: ix) 'ethnographic study of a nuclear weapons laboratory' in the USA. Because of the top-secret nature of work at this establishment and its sheer scale, participant observation in the conventional sense of prolonged immersion in the field was not possible. Gusterson (1996: 32) writes: 'I decided to mix formal interviews and the collection of documentary sources with a strategy of participant observation adapted to the demands and limitations of my own fieldwork situation. . . . I relied less on participant observation than most anthropologists in the field.' However, he did seek out as many employees as he could muster and he lived in the community in which the laboratory was located, participating in many of their core activities. While a study such as this may not exhibit the characteristics of a conventional ethnography of a workplace—because this option was not available to the researcher—Gusterson's determination to live among members of the community and to see the development of nuclear weapons through the eyes of those who worked there through interviews provides the investigation with many of the right ingredients. What the study also suggests, along with the discussions of writers such as Emerson (1987) and Wolcott (1990b), is that whether a qualitative study is ethnographic is a matter of degree.

least six months' duration in the workplace concerned. It is interesting to contrast this requirement with DeSoucey's (2010) account of her ethnographic fieldwork. In terms of the classification in Figure 19.2, she was a non-participating observer with interaction. She writes in connection with her case study of the controversy surrounding *foie gras* and its production in France:

> I collected primary data during four months of ethnographic fieldwork at 10 foie gras farms and 7 production facilities . . . a Parisian gourmet food exposition, local outdoor markets . . . tourist offices, foie gras museums, ships, restaurants, and a hotel management school.
>
> (DeSoucey 2010: 436)

Here we have an ethnographic study that over a four-month period collected data from nineteen organizations plus unspecified numbers of markets, tourist offices, museums, and restaurants, implying that it is unlikely that prolonged immersion in any setting took place.

The constraints on modern qualitative researchers to which Zickar and Carter refer may also have produced a tendency for the term 'ethnographic' to have broadened to include studies that include little or no participant observation. Research methods such as qualitative interviewing are flexible and are less disruptive of the work and personal lives of both researchers and research participants. Given both the growing diversity of forms/modes of ethnography and a tendency towards a stretching of the kind of investigation to which the term 'ethnography' refers (with prolonged participant observation no longer a *sine qua non*), it may be that the term is losing its original meaning.

One factor that may lie behind the apparently growing tendency towards ethnographies of shorter duration is that, as Van Maanen (2011) has observed, more and more such studies are 'multi-site' (Marcus 1998). This term can be employed in two connections. One is that the tendency towards global flows of people means that increasingly ethnographers have to follow their subjects across sites. An example is Scheper-Hughes's (2004) ethnography of the illegal traffic in organs (see Research in focus 18.2). We are given an insight into the multi-sited nature of her research when she writes:

> My basic ethnographic method—'follow the bodies!'— brought me to police morgues, hospital mortuaries, medical-legal institutes, intensive care units, emergency rooms, dialysis units, surgical units, operating rooms, as well as to police stations, jails and prisons, mental institutions, orphanages and court rooms in North and South America, Europe, the Middle East, Africa and Asia.
>
> (Scheper-Hughes 2004: 32)

The other is that there has been a growing tendency towards multiple-case study ethnographies of the kind discussed in Chapter 3. Several of the ethnographic studies that have been discussed in this chapter were conducted in two or more locations (Leidner 1993; Fine 1996; Swain 2004; Kellogg 2009, 2011; Gambetta and Hammill 2005; Maitlis and Lawrence 2007; Pearson 2012; Sallaz 2009). The decision to study more than one site almost inevitably means that the duration at each location is shorter than in single-site research, given the career and personal constraints on ethnographers.

» *Key points*

- The term 'ethnography' refers to both a method and the written product of research based on that method.

- The ethnographer is typically a participant observer who also uses non-observational methods and sources such as interviewing and documents.

- The ethnographer may adopt an overt or covert role, but the latter carries ethical difficulties.

- The method of access to a social setting will depend in part on whether it is a public or closed one.

- Key informants frequently play an important role for the ethnographer, but care is needed to ensure that their impact on the direction of research is not excessive.

- There are several different ways of classifying the kinds of role that the ethnographer may assume. These roles are not necessarily mutually exclusive.

- Field notes are important for prompting the ethnographer's memory and form much of the data for subsequent analysis.

- Feminist ethnography has become a popular approach to collecting data from a feminist standpoint, but there have been debates about whether there really can be a feminist ethnography.

- There has been growing interest in the use of online ethnography in the form of such things as the study of online communities.

- Visual materials such as photographs and video have attracted considerable interest among ethnographers in recent years, not just as adjuncts to data collection but as objects of interest in their own right.

- The consideration of different ways of writing up ethnographic research has become a topic of interest in its own right.

- The nature of ethnography and what is taken to be an ethnography has changed over the years.

 # Questions for review

- Is it possible to distinguish ethnography and participant observation?

- How does participant observation differ from structured observation?

- To what extent do participant observation and ethnography rely solely on observation?

Access

- 'Covert ethnography obviates the need to gain access to inaccessible settings and therefore has much to recommend it.' Discuss.

- Examine some articles in British sociology journals in which ethnography and participant observation figure strongly. Was the researcher in an overt or covert role? Was access needed to closed or open settings? How was access achieved?

- Is access to closed settings necessarily more difficult to achieve than to open settings?

- Does the problem of access finish once access to a chosen setting has been achieved?

- What might be the role of key informants in ethnographic research? Is there anything to be concerned about when using them?

Roles for ethnographers

- Why might it be useful to classify participant observer roles?

- What is meant by going native?

- Should ethnographers be active or passive in the settings in which they conduct research?

Field notes

- Why are field notes important for ethnographers?

- Why is it useful to distinguish between different types of field notes?

Bringing ethnographic research to an end

- How do you decide when to complete the data-collection phase in ethnographic research?

Can there be a feminist ethnography?

- What are the main ingredients of feminist ethnography?

- Assess Stacey's argument about whether feminist ethnography is possible in the light of Skeggs's research or any other ethnographic study that describes itself, or can be seen, as feminist.

The rise of online ethnography

- How does ethnography need to be adapted in order to collect data on the use of the Internet?

- Are ethnographies of the Internet really ethnographic?

The rise of visual ethnography

- What kinds of roles can visual materials play in ethnography?
- Do photographs provide unproblematic images of reality?

Writing ethnography

- How far is it true to say that ethnographic writing is typically imbued with realism?
- What forms of ethnographic writing other than realist tales can be found?

The changing nature of ethnography

- What factors lie behind some of the changing meanings of 'ethnography'?

Online Resource Centre

www.oxfordtextbooks.co.uk/orc/brymansrm5e/

Visit the Online Resource Centre to enrich your understanding of ethnography and participant observation. Follow up links to other resources, test yourself using multiple choice questions, and gain further guidance and inspiration from the Student Researcher's Toolkit.

20

Interviewing in qualitative research

 ## Chapter outline

 ## Chapter guide

This chapter is concerned with the interview in qualitative research. The term 'qualitative interview' is often used to capture the different types of interview that are used in qualitative research, and this is the term that I will use as a shorthand way of categorizing the different forms. Such interviews tend to be less structured than the kind of interview associated with survey research, which was discussed in Chapter 9 in terms of structured interviewing. This chapter is concerned with individual interviews in qualitative research; the focus group method, which is a form of interview but with several people, is discussed in Chapter 21. The two forms of qualitative interviewing discussed in this chapter are unstructured and semi-structured interviewing. The chapter explores:

- the differences between structured interviewing and qualitative interviewing;

- the main characteristics of and differences between unstructured and semi-structured interviewing; this entails a recognition that the two terms refer to extremes and that in practice a wide range of interviews with differing degrees of structure lie between the extremes;
- how to devise and use an interview guide for semi-structured interviewing;
- the different kinds of question that can be asked in an interview guide;
- the importance of recording and transcribing qualitative interviews;
- life history and oral history interviewing;
- the significance of qualitative interviewing in feminist research;
- the use of the Internet as a platform for conducting qualitative interviews, including the use of Skype;
- the advantages and disadvantages of qualitative interviewing relative to participant observation.

Introduction

The interview is probably the most widely employed method in qualitative research. Of course, ethnography usually involves a substantial amount of interviewing, which undoubtedly contributes to the widespread use of the interview by qualitative researchers. However, it is the flexibility of the interview that makes it so attractive. Since ethnography entails an extended period of participant observation, which is very disruptive for researchers because of the sustained absence(s) required from work and/or family life, research based mainly on interviews is a highly attractive alternative for the collection of qualitative data. Interviewing, the transcription of interviews, and the analysis of transcripts are all very time-consuming, but can be more readily accommodated into researchers' personal lives.

In Key concept 9.2, several different types of interview were briefly outlined. The bulk of the types outlined there—other than the structured interview and the standardized interview—are ones associated with qualitative research. *Focus groups* and *group interviewing* will be examined in the next chapter, and the remaining forms of interview associated with qualitative research will be explored at various points in this chapter. In spite of the proliferation of terms describing types of interview in qualitative research, the two main types are the **unstructured interview** and the **semi-structured interview**. Researchers sometimes use the term 'qualitative interview' to capture these two types of interview. There is clearly the potential for considerable confusion here, but the types and definitions offered in Key concept 9.2 are meant to provide some consistency of terminology.

Differences between the structured interview and the qualitative interview

Qualitative interviewing is usually very different from interviewing in quantitative research in several ways.

- Qualitative interviewing tends to be much less structured than interviewing in quantitative research. In quantitative research, the interview is structured to maximize the reliability and validity of measurement of key concepts because the researcher has a clearly specified set of research questions to be investigated. The structured interview is designed to answer these questions. Instead, in qualitative interviewing, initial research ideas are more open-ended and there is an emphasis on interviewees' own perspectives.

- In qualitative interviewing, there is greater interest in the interviewee's point of view; in quantitative research, the interview reflects the researcher's concerns. This contrast is a direct outcome of the previous one.

- In qualitative interviewing, 'rambling' or going off at tangents is often encouraged—it gives insight into what the interviewee sees as relevant and important;

in quantitative research, it is usually regarded as a nuisance and discouraged.

- In qualitative interviewing, interviewers can depart significantly from the interview guide. They can ask new questions that follow up interviewees' replies and can vary the order and even the wording of questions. In quantitative interviewing, none of these things should be done, because they will compromise the standardization of the interview process and hence the reliability and validity of measurement.

- Consequently, qualitative interviewing tends to be flexible, responding to the direction in which interviewees take the interview and perhaps adjusting the emphases in the research as a result of significant issues emerging in the course of interviews (see Research in focus 20.3 for an example). By contrast, quantitative interviews are typically inflexible, because of the need to standardize the way in which each interviewee is dealt with.

- In qualitative interviewing, the researcher wants rich, detailed answers; in structured interviewing, the interview is supposed to generate answers that can be **coded** and processed quickly.

- In qualitative interviewing, interviewees may be interviewed on more than one and sometimes even several occasions (see Research in focus 20.3 for an example). In structured interviewing, unless the research is longitudinal, the person will be interviewed on one occasion only.

Research in focus 20.1
Unstructured interviewing

Rayburn and Guittar (2013) describe how they carried out interviews with homeless people in Orlando, Florida, in order to gain an understanding of how they cope with the stigma associated with their situation. Their interviewing approach, which was broadly unstructured, is described as follows:

> During the interviews, participants discussed any aspects of their lives they wanted, for as long as they wanted. Although we prepared guiding questions, we tried not to lead participants in any particular direction during the interview. The main aim of interviews and focus groups was to generally inquire about sobriety, homelessness, and what it was like to live at a facility for homeless people, and through this, themes of stigma management emerged.

(Rayburn and Guittar 2013: 164)

Student experience
The advantages of semi-structured interviewing

The relatively unstructured nature of the semi-structured interview and its capacity to provide insights into how research participants view the world was important to Hannah Creane. Hannah was attracted to it because she was concerned not to 'pigeon-hole' people while she was researching childhood.

> The aim of my study was to explore the generational changes within childhood. I decided to interview nine people of several different generations about their childhood experiences, their opinions on the concept and construction of childhood, and their thoughts on childhood today. I chose to use semi-structured interviews because of the fact that they would allow me to gain the research I wanted without pigeon-holing the response of those I was interviewing.

To read more, go to the Online Resource Centre: www.oxfordtextbooks.co.uk/orc/brymansrm5e/

Conducting a qualitative interview

However, qualitative interviewing varies a great deal in the approach taken by the interviewer. The two major types were mentioned at the beginning of the chapter.

1. The almost totally *unstructured interview*. Here the researcher uses at most an *aide-mémoire* as a brief set of prompts to him- or herself to deal with a certain range of topics. There may be just a single question that the interviewer asks, and the interviewee is then allowed to respond freely, with the interviewer simply responding to points that seem worthy of being followed up. Unstructured interviewing tends to be very similar in character to a conversation (Burgess 1984). See Research in focus 20.1 for an illustration of an unstructured interview style.

2. A *semi-structured interview*. The researcher has a list of questions or fairly specific topics to be covered, often referred to as an **interview guide**, but the interviewee has a great deal of leeway in how to reply. Questions may not be asked exactly in the way outlined on the schedule. Questions that are not included in the guide may be asked as the interviewer picks up on interviewees' replies. But, by and large, all the questions will be asked and a similar wording will be used from interviewee to interviewee. Research in focus 20.2 and 20.3 provide examples of these features.

In both cases, the interview process is *flexible*. Also, the emphasis must be on how the interviewee frames and understands issues and events—that is, what the interviewee views as important in explaining and understanding

events, patterns, and forms of behaviour. Thus, Leidner (1993: 238) describes the interviewing she carried out in a McDonald's restaurant as involving a degree of structure, but adds that the interviews also 'allowed room to pursue topics of particular interest to the workers'. There is a growing tendency for semi-structured and unstructured interviewing to be referred to collectively as *in-depth interviews* or as *qualitative interviews*. The kinds of interviewing carried out in qualitative research are typical also of **life history interviewing** and **oral history interviewing**, which are examined in a section below.

The two different types of interview are extremes, and there is quite a lot of variability between them (the example in Research in focus 20.2 seems somewhat more structured than that in Research in focus 20.3, for example, though both are illustrative of semi-structured interviewing), but most qualitative interviews are close to one type or the other. In neither case does the interviewer slavishly follow a schedule, as is done in quantitative research interviewing; but in semi-structured interviews the interviewer does follow a script to a certain extent. The choice of whether to veer towards one type rather than the other is likely to be affected by a variety of factors.

- Researchers who are concerned that the use of even the most rudimentary interview guide will not allow genuine access to the worldviews of members of a social setting or of people sharing common attributes are likely to favour an unstructured interview.

Research in focus 20.2
Semi-structured interviewing

Lupton (1996) was interested in investigating people's food preferences, and to this end her research entailed thirty-three semi-structured interviews conducted by four female interviewers (of whom she was one) living in Sydney in 1994. She writes:

> Interviewees were asked to talk about their favourite and most detested foods; whether they thought there was such a thing as 'masculine' or 'feminine' foods or dishes; which types of foods they considered 'healthy' or 'good for you' and which not; which types of foods they ate to lose weight and which they avoided for the same reason; memories they recalled about food and eating events from childhood and adulthood; whether they liked to try new foods; which foods they had tasted first as an adult; whether there had been any changes in the types of food they had eaten over their lifetime; whether they associated different types of food with particular times, places or people; whether they ever had any arguments about food with others; whether they themselves cooked and if they enjoyed it; whether they ate certain foods when in certain moods and whether they had any rituals around food.

(Lupton 1996: 156, 158)

Research in focus 20.3
Flexibility in semi-structured interviewing

Mazmanian, Orlikowski, and Yates (2013) describe a study of knowledge professionals' use of mobile email devices, such as the BlackBerry. Interviews were conducted with forty-eight participants in two rounds of interviews. The interviews were 'open-ended conversations covering a broad and evolving set of questions' (2013: 1340). The authors write:

> As interesting themes emerged in one interview, we incorporated these into our conversations in subsequent interviews. We began our interviews by asking participants to describe their jobs and organizational positions, as well as the nature of their work and communication practices. We then asked participants to describe in detail their activities during the prior day, from waking up to going to sleep. We were specifically interested in where, when, and why they engaged with their mobile email device to get their work done. This chronological narrative provided a structure to the interview, but we encouraged elaborations and digressions as people recounted and reflected on their communicative choices, actions, experiences, and outcomes.
>
> (Mazmanian et al. 2013: 1340)

Flexibility is apparent in this passage in two senses. First, the interview would often take its lead from participants in that their 'elaborations and digressions' were followed through. Second, the interview evolved as the research progressed: the researchers included 'interesting themes' that emerged in early interviews into later interviews. The evolving nature of the interview is also apparent in the researchers' discussion of some of the questions asked:

> Specific questions ranged from 'When do you first check the device in the day?' to 'On what occasions do you find the device to be useful/not useful? Why?' As it became clear that participants—although predominantly positive about their choice to use the mobile email devices—were also claiming a sense of compulsion to use them, we began to probe more deeply for these tensions. For example, we asked questions such as 'When you receive a message, how soon do you feel you have to respond? Why?' and 'Would you ever come to work without checking your emails from home? Why/why not?'
>
> (Mazmanian et al. 2013: 1340–1)

Some months later, a sub-sample of these participants were re-interviewed using a more structured instrument.

- If the researcher is beginning the investigation with a fairly clear focus, rather than a very general notion of wanting to do research on a topic, it is likely that the interviews will be semi-structured ones, so that the more specific issues can be addressed.

- If more than one person is to carry out the fieldwork, in order to ensure some comparability of interviewing style, it is likely that semi-structured interviewing will be preferred. See Research in focus 20.2 and 20.3 for examples.

- If you are doing multiple-case study research, you are likely to need some structure in order to ensure cross-case comparability. All my qualitative research on different kinds of organization has entailed semi-structured interviewing, and it is not a coincidence that this is because most of it has been multiple-case study research (e.g. Bryman et al. 1994; see Research in focus 17.5; Bryman, Gillingwater, and McGuinness 1996).

Preparing an interview guide

The idea of an interview guide is much less specific than the notion of a structured interview schedule. The term typically refers to a list of issues to be addressed or questions to be asked in semi-structured interviewing. What is crucial is that the questioning allows interviewers to glean research participants' perspectives on their social world and that there is flexibility in the conduct of the interviews. The latter is as much if not more to do with the conduct of the interview than with the nature of the interview guide as such. Figure 20.1 presents guidelines that suggest the series of steps in formulating questions for an interview guide in qualitative research.

In preparing for qualitative interviews, Lofland and Lofland (1995: 78) suggest asking yourself the question 'Just what about this thing is puzzling me?' This can be applied to each of the research questions you have generated or it may be a mechanism for generating some research questions. They suggest that your puzzlement can be stimulated by various activities: random thoughts in different contexts, which are then written down as quickly as possible; discussions with colleagues, friends, and relatives; and, of course, the existing literature on the topic. The formulation of the research question(s) should not be so specific that alternative avenues of enquiry that might arise during the collection of fieldwork data are closed off. Such premature closure of your research focus would be inconsistent with the general orientation of qualitative research (Figure 17.1), with the emphasis on the worldview of the people you will be interviewing, and with the approaches to qualitative data analysis such as **grounded theory** that emphasize the importance of not starting out with too many preconceptions (see Chapter 24). Gradually, an order and structure will begin to emerge in your meanderings around your research question(s) and will form the basis for your interview guide.

You should also consider 'What do I need to know in order to answer each of the research questions I'm interested in?' This means generating an appreciation of what the interviewee sees as significant and important in relation to each of your topic areas. Thus, your questioning must cover the areas that you need to cover in order to address your research questions but from the perspective of your interviewees. This means that, even though qualitative research is predominantly unstructured, it is rarely so unstructured that the researcher cannot at least specify a research focus. After you have developed your list of interview questions, reflect on them to satisfy yourself that they really do cover the range of issues that you need to address.

Some basic elements in the preparation of your interview guide will be:

- create a certain amount of order on the topic areas, so that your questions about them flow reasonably well,

Figure 20.1
Formulating questions for an interview guide

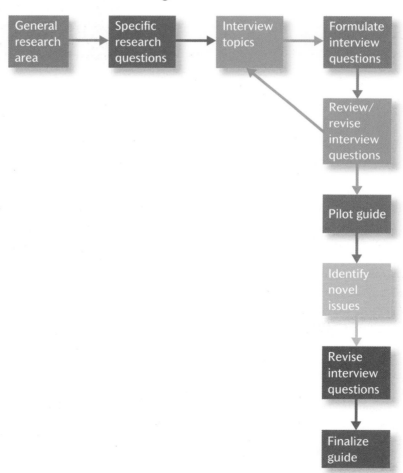

but be prepared to alter the order of questions during the actual interview;

- formulate interview questions or topics in a way that will help you to answer your research questions (but try not to make them too specific);

- try to use a language that is comprehensible and relevant to the people you are interviewing;

- just as in interviewing in quantitative research, do not ask leading questions;

- remember to ensure that you ask or record 'facesheet' information of a general kind (name, age, gender, etc.) and a specific kind (position in company, number of years employed, number of years involved in a group, etc.), because such information is useful for contextualizing people's answers.

There are some practical details to attend to before the interview.

- Make sure you are familiar with the setting in which the interviewee works or lives. This will help you to understand what he or she is saying in the interviewee's own terms.

- Make sure you have a compelling answer to questions that the interviewee might ask about your reasons for wanting to examine the topic that you are addressing, why it is important, why he or she was selected to be interviewed, and so on.

- Get hold of a good-quality recording machine and microphone. Qualitative researchers nearly always record and then transcribe their interviews (see the section on 'Recording and transcription' below). A good microphone is highly desirable, because many interviews are let down by poor recording. Also, make sure you are thoroughly familiar with the operation of the equipment you use before beginning your interviews.

- Make sure as far as possible that the interview takes place in a setting that is quiet (so there is no or little outside noise that might affect the quality of the recording) and private (so interviewees do not have to worry about being overheard).

- Prepare yourself for the interview by cultivating as many as possible of the criteria of a quality interviewer suggested by Kvale (1996) (see Tips and skills 'Criteria of a successful interviewer'). What underpins a lot of the desirable qualities of the qualitative interviewer specified by Kvale is that he or she must be a good *listener*, which entails being active and alert in the interview. An inability to listen may mean failing to pick up on a really important point or asking an irritatingly

Student experience
On not leading interviewees

As noted in the list of bullet points concerning the preparation of an interview guide, it is important not to lead interviewees. Gareth Matthews describes how he was concerned not to lead the employers and managers in firms in the hospitality industry to focus on migrant workers. He wanted any discussion of migrant workers to come naturally from them. Here is how he went about it.

Also, I wanted to explore the nature of employers' recruitment decisions in terms of their perceptions of skill/ attributes/attitudes that exist in the external labour market in both British workers and migrant workers, though without making it overly obvious that this was a primary line of enquiry. Therefore, while I did not want to mask the research aims from interviewees, I also did not want to alert them to focus on migrants, as I felt that this would prejudice their responses (I found that, in the first few interviews, employers were generally quite suspicious and, accordingly, quite defensive when speaking about these matters).

Therefore, I found it easier to focus on the notion of 'skill shortages' in the hospitality industry, by referring to the published information that points to a crisis in the sector with regards to finding workers with the appropriate attributes. This tended to [elicit] a detailed response on the nature of skills and the perceptions of British workers with regards to these skills. It was then easier to turn the discussion towards a focus on employers' recruitment of migrant workers and their perceptions of the attributes embodied in these workers vis-à-vis British workers. Also, this discussion made it possible to explore employers' perceptions of particular groups of migrant workers, and led to some very interesting (though worrying) findings with regards to employers' use of race and nationality as distinctive categories when making recruitment decisions.

 To read more, go to the Online Resource Centre: www.oxfordtextbooks.co.uk/orc/brymansrm5e/

Tips and skills
Interviewing for the first time

The prospect of doing your first interview can be daunting. Also, it is easy to make some fundamental mistakes when you begin interviewing. A study of American postgraduates' experiences of a lengthy interview training course showed that novice interviewers were easily thrown off by a number of events or experiences in the course of the interview (Roulston et al. 2003). Their findings suggest five challenges that are worth bearing in mind when approaching your first interview(s).

1. *Unexpected interviewee behaviour or environmental problems*. These inexperienced interviewers were easily discomforted by responses or behaviour on the part of interviewees or by problems such as noise in the vicinity of the interview. When you go into the interview, bear in mind that things may not go according to plan. Interviewees sometimes say things that are very surprising and some like to startle or even shock interviewers. Equally, there can be many distractions close to where the interview takes place. You clearly cannot plan for or have control over these things, but you can bear in mind that they might happen and try to limit their impact on you and on the course of the interview.

2. *Intrusion of own biases and expectations*. Roulston et al. report that some of the trainees were surprised when they read their transcripts how their own biases and expectations were evident in the ways they asked questions and followed up on replies.

3. *Maintaining focus in asking questions*. Students reported that they sometimes had difficulty probing answers, asking follow-up questions, and clarifying questions in a way that did not lose sight of the research topic and what the questions were getting at.

4. *Dealing with sensitive issues*. Some students asked questions that caused interviewees to become upset, and this response could have an adverse impact on the course of the interview. However, most students felt that they coped reasonably well with such emotionally charged situations.

5. *Transcription*. Many reported finding transcription difficult and time-consuming—more so than they had imagined.

There are, of course, many other possible issues that impinge on first-time interviewers. Many do not go away either, no matter how experienced you become. It is very difficult to know how to deal with some of these contingencies, but it is worth bearing in mind that they arise and that their impact may be greatest when you begin interviewing.

pointless question later in the interview. The list of qualities is also underpinned by a need for the interviewer to be *flexible* when appropriate (see also the section on 'Flexibility in the interview' later). It is also important to be *non-judgemental* as far as possible. Try not to indicate agreement or disagreement with the interviewee. He or she may even try to get you to respond to his or her views. Be careful about doing this, as it may distort later answers.

- Interviewing is very demanding, and students who are new to the method sometimes do not appreciate fully the personal issues involved. It is worth conducting some pilot interviews, not just to test how well the interview flows but in order to gain some experience. As Tips and skills 'Interviewing for the first time' shows, it is better to be prepared for some of the unexpected contingencies that can arise in the course of an interview.

After the interview, make notes about:

- how the interview went (was interviewee talkative, cooperative, nervous, well-dressed/scruffy, etc.?);
- where the interview took place;
- any other feelings about the interview (did it open up new avenues of interest?);
- the setting (busy/quiet, many/few other people in the vicinity, new/old buildings, use of computers).

Kinds of questions

The kinds of questions asked in qualitative interviews vary considerably. Kvale (1996) has suggested nine different kinds of question. Most interviews will contain virtually all of them, although interviews that rely on lists

Tips and skills
Criteria of a successful interviewer

Kvale (1996) has proposed a very useful list of ten criteria of a successful interviewer.

- *Knowledgeable*: is thoroughly familiar with the focus of the interview; pilot interviews of the kind used in survey interviewing can be useful here.

- *Structuring*: gives purpose for interview; rounds it off; asks whether interviewee has questions.

- *Clear*: asks simple, easy, short questions; no jargon.

- *Gentle*: lets people finish; gives them time to think; tolerates pauses.

- *Sensitive*: listens attentively to what is said and how it is said; is empathetic in dealing with the interviewee.

- *Open*: responds to what is important to interviewee and is flexible.

- *Steering*: knows what he or she wants to find out.

- *Critical*: is prepared to challenge what is said—for example, dealing with inconsistencies in interviewees' replies.

- *Remembering*: relates what is said to what has previously been said.

- *Interpreting*: clarifies and extends meanings of interviewees' statements, but without imposing meaning on them.

To Kvale's list I would add the following.

- *Balanced*: does not talk too much, which may make the interviewee passive, and does not talk too little, which may result in the interviewee feeling he or she is not talking along the right lines.

- *Ethically sensitive*: is sensitive to the ethical dimension of interviewing, ensuring that the interviewee appreciates what the research is about, its purposes, and that his or her answers will be treated confidentially.

---

of topics are likely to follow a somewhat looser format. Kvale's nine types of question are as follows.

1. *Introducing questions*: 'Please tell me about when your interest in X first began?'; 'Have you ever . . . ?'; 'Why did you go to . . . ?'.

2. *Follow-up questions*: getting the interviewee to elaborate his or her answer, such as 'What do you mean by that?' or even 'Yeeees?' See Research in focus 20.4 for an example when the interviewer's simple interjection—'No'—invites further information. Kvale suggests that repeating significant words in an answer can stimulate further explanation.

3. *Probing questions*: following up what has been said through direct questioning, such as 'Could you say some more about that?'; 'You said earlier that you prefer not to X. Could you say what kinds of things have put you off X?'; 'In what ways do you find X disturbing?' In Research in focus 20.4, in the second interview sequence from the research by Jones et al. (2010) the interviewer asks 'Uh huh. But I mean, you have been retired for ten years, haven't

you?' In effect, the interviewer is trying to get the interviewee to explain how he could have been retired for ten years and yet still not know what his plans were.

4. *Specifying questions*: 'What did you do then?'; 'How did X react to what you said?'; 'What effect did X have on you?' See Research in focus 20.4 for an example from the Savage et al. (2005) study—'if you move, where would you like to move to?' In Research in focus 20.3, the question 'When you receive a message, how soon do you feel you have to respond? Why?' is of this type.

5. *Direct questions*: 'Do you find it easy to keep smiling when serving customers?'; 'Are you happy with the way you and your husband decide how money should be spent?' Such questions are perhaps best left until towards the end of the interview, in order not to influence the direction of the interview too much. In Research in focus 20.3 the question 'Would you ever come to work without checking your emails from home? Why/why not?' is of this type, and in Research in focus 20.4, the question 'would you ever consider going back to work?' is a further example.

Research in focus 20.4
Using a semi-structured interview

It can be difficult in qualitative interviews to get people to expand further on their answers. The following sequence between the interviewer (Int) and interviewee (R), which is from the study of early retirees by Jones et al. (2010) that was referred to on several occasions in Chapter 1, is interesting in this regard.

Int   Yes, would you ever consider going back to work?

R   Not at the moment, well I suppose it depended what was on offer, the big problem is, I did actually consider, or I considered and was considered for a directorship at Lloyds Insurance Company, so I went down and spoke to them, and I said to Diane [wife] before I went, it's like two days every month, you know you get paid thirty thousand a year, which is very nice, but it's two days every month and you've got to be there, which means if we went away for five weeks, we're sort of knackered and you've got to build all your holidays around it, so anyway went for the interview, I didn't get it but on the other hand I wasn't that enthusiastic about it.

Int   No.

R   But if I could actually do something I don't know, fundraising or something like that, and got paid for it, I wouldn't mind doing that, on my own terms and when it suits me, but I don't think I'd want to go back full time or consultancy (Jones et al. 2010: 111).

The striking feature of this exchange is the way in which the interviewer's simple interjection—'No'—draws out a further set of reflections that qualify somewhat the interviewee's previous remark. As such it acts as what Kvale calls a follow-up question. In the following exchange, there is an interesting use of a probing question:

R   I'd like to find out what we want to do. I think the hardest thing we've got is both of us don't know what we want.

Int   Uh huh. But I mean, you have been retired for ten years, haven't you?

R   Ten years, yeah but we still don't know what we want to do. We're drifting, I suppose—nicely, no problems on that, but we haven't got anything . . . we keep on saying, we've got the money, what do we want to spend it on? We don't know. It's always been that we don't know what we want to do; we don't know whether we want to buy a house. We do look at them and say we don't want another house. We don't really want another car—can't be bothered about that. I should give my car away! And things like that, so . . . no, we don't know what we want to do (Jones et al. 2010: 113).

The interviewer is clearly paying close attention to what is being said because he or she picks up on the respondent's claimed lack of post-retirement direction and as a result seeks clarification of the interviewee's reply. There is a risk that the interviewer could be viewed as being judgemental ('how on earth can you not have decided what you want to be doing with your retirement after ten years?') but the comment is handled skilfully and, as it happens, productively in that the interviewee expands significantly on the earlier answer.

The following exchange is taken from an interview with an inhabitant of Chorlton in Greater Manchester for the study by Savage et al. (2005) of globalization and a sense of place that was referred to in Chapter 18:

In what ways do you think the area is changing?
I think it is becoming more trendy. Round the corner we have two wine bars that have opened in the last few years, two expensive clothes shops, very good for young people and just various things. Lots of restaurants.

Do you think it is good or bad?
Yes, I like it, it reminds me of London and places I've lived in. In a way I would quite like to be living in London, I can't afford that, but that type of feel about it, I would like it to be a bit more cosmopolitan.

If you move, where would you like to move to?
Well my ideal sort of place would be somewhere by the sea that is fairly town-like, somewhere like Brighton, sort of London with the sea, or somewhere where the architecture is really nice, Cambridge or Oxford (Savage et al. 2005: 96).

This provides a useful example of the use of what Kvale calls 'specifying questions', particularly in the second and third questions, which encourage the interviewee to amplify his or her original response with some more specific detail.

6. *Indirect questions*: 'What do most people round here think of the ways that management treats its staff?', perhaps followed up by 'Is that the way you feel too?', in order to get at the individual's own view.

7. *Structuring questions*: 'I would now like to move on to a different topic.'

8. *Silence*: allow pauses to signal that you want to give the interviewee the opportunity to reflect and amplify an answer.

9. *Interpreting questions*: 'Do you mean that your leadership role has had to change from one of encouraging others to a more directive one?'; 'Is it fair to say that what you are suggesting is that you don't mind being friendly towards customers most of the time, but when they are unpleasant or demanding you find it more difficult?' For the research referred to in Research in focus 20.8, the interviewer 'sought to verify her interpretations during the course of each interview by offering tentative summaries and inviting participants to challenge or confirm her understanding' (Bosley et al. 2009: 1499).

As this list suggests, one of the main ingredients of the interview is listening—being attentive to what the interviewee is saying or even not saying. It means that the interviewer is active without being too intrusive—a difficult balance. But it also means that, just because the interview is being recorded (the generally recommended practice whenever it is feasible), the interviewer cannot take things easy. In fact, an interviewer must be very attuned and responsive to what the interviewee is saying and doing. This is also important because something like body language may indicate that the interviewee is becoming anxious about a line of questioning. An ethically sensitive interviewer will not want to place undue pressure on the person he or she is talking to and will need to be prepared to cut short that line of questioning if it is clearly a source of concern.

It is also likely that the kinds of questions asked will vary in terms of the different stages of a qualitative interview.

Charmaz (2002) distinguishes three types of questions in this connection. She was in fact writing in the context of interviewing for a project guided by grounded theory (see Chapter 24), but her suggestions have a more general applicability. She distinguishes:

- *Initial open-ended questions*: 'What events led to . . . ?'; 'What was your life like prior to . . . ?'; 'How far is this organization typical of others you have worked in?'

- *Intermediate questions*: 'How did you feel about . . . when you first learned about it?'; 'What immediate impacts did . . . have on your life?'; 'What do you like most/least about working in this organization?'

- *Ending questions*: 'How far have your views about . . . changed?; 'What advice would you give now to someone who finds that he or she must get experience . . . ?'; 'If you had your time again, would you choose to work for this organization?'

Most questions are likely to be of the intermediate kind in any interview guide, and in practice there is likely to be overlap between the three kinds. None the less, this is a useful distinction to bear in mind.

Remember as well that in interviews you are going to ask about different kinds of things, such as:

- values—of interviewee, of group, of organization;

- beliefs—of interviewee, of others, of group;

- behaviour—of interviewee, of others;

- formal and informal roles—of interviewee, of others;

- relationships—of interviewee, of others;

- places and locales;

- emotions—particularly of the interviewee, but also possibly of others;

- encounters;

- stories.

Tips and skills
Interviewees and distance

Sometimes you may need to contact interviewees who are a long way from you—perhaps even abroad. While interviewing in qualitative research has traditionally taken place face-to-face, it may be that time, money, and convenience mean that you will need to interview people who are a long way away in a less personal context. There are two possibilities. One is telephone interviewing. The cost of a telephone interview is much less than the cost involved in travelling long distances and the results of studies comparing face-to-face and telephone interviews are quite reassuring. A second possibility is to use Skype or something like the iPhone's Facetime facility. Another possibility is the online interview, in which the interview is conducted by email or by some form of conference software. These possibilities are discussed further in the next section.

Try to vary the questioning in terms of types of question (as suggested by Kvale's nine types outlined above) *and* the types of phenomena you ask about. One final bit of advice when formulating interview questions is to bear in mind some of the principles for asking questions in surveys, as outlined in Chapter 11. Some of the principles outlined there apply equally well to qualitative interviewing, in particular, avoiding questions that are too complex; are double-barrelled; are leading; or use difficult or unfamiliar terms.

Vignette questions in qualitative interviews

Although there may be times when you want to ask fairly general questions, these are frequently best avoided. Mason (2002) counsels against the use of general questions, arguing that, when they are used, interviewees usually ask the interviewer to clarify what is meant by or to contextualize the question. As an alternative, vignette questions may be used as one way of asking specific questions. This type of question was previously encountered in Chapter 9 in the context of survey research. In qualitative research, they can be used to ground interviewees' views and accounts of behaviour in particular situations (Barter and Renold 1999). By presenting interviewees with concrete and realistic scenarios, researchers can elicit how certain contexts mould behaviour. R. Hughes (1998) employed the technique in a study of perceptions of HIV risk among drug injectors. This is a field of research in which context has been shown to be important, because injectors' willingness to engage in risky behaviour is influenced by situational factors. A scenario was produced that presented risk behaviour scenarios that two hypothetical drug injectors have to address. The vignette helped to reveal the kinds of behaviour interviewees felt that injectors *should* engage in (such as protected sex) and how they felt the hypothetical injectors *would* behave (such as unprotected sex in particular situations). Hughes argues that such an approach is particularly valuable with sensitive topics of this kind and for eliciting a range of responses to different contexts. Jenkins et al. (2010) also employed the vignette technique with drug-users but with a much larger sample of seventy-eight, of whom fifty-nine were re-interviewed twelve weeks later. This longitudinal element allowed changes in orientation to drugs over time to be charted. In fact, just over one-third of those interviewed a second time showed a marked change of perspective.

Using photographs in qualitative interviews

A further way in which questioning in qualitative interviews may be grounded is through the use of photographs. The use of photographs in interviews was explored in the context of visual ethnography in Chapter 19 but is briefly covered here to present some further thoughts in the specific context of interviewing. The use of photographs in this way is often referred to as *photo-elicitation*, which has been defined as 'the simple idea of inserting a photograph into a research interview' (Harper 2002: 13). Photographs that are part of the interviewee's collection (see Research in focus 20.5 for an example) or ones that he or she has taken for the purpose of the research may be used as a stimulus for questioning. Yet another use can be discerned in the study entitled 'Masculinities, Identities and Risk: Transition in the Lives of Men as Fathers' that is part of the Timescapes programme of research (see Research in focus 3.12). In addition to using some of the fathers' own photographs, Henwood, Shirani and Finn (2011) presented fathers who joined the research in 2008 with historical photographs depicting fatherhood and masculinity. Five images were used, going from Victorian times through the 1950s to the present day. Interviewees were asked to discuss their reactions to the photographs and to consider what was being represented and how it relates to them. One of the fathers talks about how he can relate much more to one of the more recent images:

> Marcus That's more where I see myself being.
> I So you think we've moved, changed, the representation's got more what?
> Marcus I think maybe it's got more tactile and more emotional and less functional. (Henwood et al. 2011: 337)

In this way, the researchers are able to use these historical photographs as an anchor to address perceptions of fatherhood and masculine identity.

Harper argues that using photographs (or indeed other visual media) in interviews may serve several useful roles:

- Images may help to ground the researcher's interview questions. The kinds of things in which social researchers are interested are often quite difficult for others to relate to. Using a photograph may help to provide both parties to the interview with a meaningful context for their discussion.

- Stimulating interviewees to engage visually with familiar settings and objects may help them to think in different ways about things that they take for granted.

- The use of photographs may stimulate the interviewee to remember people or events or situations that might otherwise have been forgotten.

However, Harper cautions that using photographs in qualitative interviews does not necessarily result in superior interviews. He cites the case of a study he conducted of farmers in the USA. The research sought to understand farmers' perspectives on a host of issues such as how they

Research in focus 20.5
A photo-elicitation study of inter-racial families

Twine (2006) discusses her use in several different countries of photo-elicitation interviews designed to explore racial consciousness in inter-racial families. In one study, she used family photographs to explore, with 'white mothers of African-descent children', issues of cultural identity and the practices through which identity is generated, and how racial identities shift over time. The photographs were explored in terms of what was important about them to the interviewee. The photographs in tandem with the interviews allowed Twine to reveal that the images of apparent familial and racial harmony occluded an underlying opposition to the inter-racial partnership that was created. This opposition was found on both sides of the family. However, the use of both the photographs and the interview generated a balanced account in which the discord was tempered by considerable harmony. Referring to the particular photo-elicitation interview that is the focus of her article, Twine (2006: 507) writes: 'photo-interview combined with my analysis of the photographs brought into sharp relief the emphasis that I had placed on conflicts, tensions and racial troubles while not considering the degree of social cohesion that existed.' Twine argues that the photographs provided an opportunity and pretext for the interviewees to reflect on the struggles of the past in relation to the present and to reframe their understanding of the significance of the photographs. What emerges is a balanced account of harmony and disharmony and of change in relationships in connection with the life course.

defined the land and the animals they nurtured and their views of such things as changes in farming technology. However, Harper writes that the photographs he took 'did not evoke deep reflections on the issues I was interested in' and 'did not *break the frame* of farmers' normal views' (Harper 2002: 20; emphasis in original). He suggests that the photographs may have been too familiar in appearance to farmers, in that they possibly resembled images that regularly appear in farming magazines. Harper found that, when he subsequently took aerial photographs and used historical ones, farmers were more reflective in their interviews. This experience from a leading exponent of visual research methods reminds us that there is no way of guaranteeing interesting data in qualitative investigations and suggests that a preparedness to experiment when things do not go quite according to plan can pay dividends.

Using a mobile interview approach

The emergence around the beginning of this century of the so-called 'new mobilities' paradigm was meant to draw attention to the significance of the fact that people are increasingly on the move and that traditionally, the social sciences have used research methods and concepts that failed adequately to reflect this development (see, for example, Sheller and Urry 2006). As a result, there has been growing interest in focusing on and developing methods for the study of people on the move. The study

by Watts (2008), which was referred to in Chapter 19, is an illustration of this focus.

One methodological development that has a bearing on the qualitative interviewing is the use of mobile interviews in which people are interviewed as they move around their environments. The 'walking interview' is one type of mobile interview and was used by Clark and Emmel (2010: 1) as a 'way of understanding senses of places and neighbourhood attachment, and the extent to which social networks are contextualised and reproduced spatially'. Clark and Emmel believe that this kind of interview has a number of advantages over static interviews because it increases interviewees' control over the direction of the interview; focuses more on what they see as important to them in their neighbourhoods; helps to connect experiences and contexts more closely, stimulating reflections on those connections; may elicit reflections that would not otherwise have arisen; and is more closely related to people's everyday lives. The idea is to get participants to reflect on the meaning of places to them—their memories, which places they go to or do not go to, people they know in each location, what they like or dislike about the area, etc. Clark and Emmel used a digital recorder but note that a video record might provide more detailed information as it can include routes taken. However, as they point out, a video recording may make people too self-conscious. Increasingly, GPS data are likely to be capable of being related to the routes taken.

In addition to collecting observational data, Ferguson (in press) accompanied social workers on their way to their clients. Interviews were conducted and audio-recorded en route either on foot or in the car. Ferguson points out that these interviews provided him with information about the clients and their situation, about the social workers' plans for the meeting, about how they felt about the case at that particular time, and about how they were feeling at the point of arrival. He notes too that the journey in the car provided social workers with the chance to prepare themselves for what could sometimes be difficult meetings. In addition, there was the opportunity to capture social workers' thoughts afterwards about how the meeting had gone and their feelings about the clients.

Mobile interviews, then, provide opportunities for social researchers to tap into the fact that their participants are frequently on the move and to reflect that movement in the kinds of data collected. It is striking in both of the examples referred to above that the fact of movement provides opportunities for the collection of data that are unlikely to be accessible through conventional static methods.

Using an interview guide: an example

Research in focus 20.6 is taken from an interview from a study of visitors to Disney theme parks (Bryman 1999). The study was briefly mentioned in Chapter 8 as an example of a snowball sampling procedure. The interviews were concerned to elicit visitors' interpretations of the parks that they had visited. The interview is with a man who was in his sixties and his wife who was two years younger. They had visited Walt Disney World in Orlando, Florida, and were very enthusiastic about their visit.

The sequence begins with the interviewer asking what would be considered a 'direct question' in terms of Kvale's

Research in focus 20.6
Part of the transcript of a semi-structured interview

Interviewer OK. What were your views or feelings about the presentation of different cultures, as shown in, for example, Jungle Cruise or It's a Small World at the Magic Kingdom or in World Showcase at Epcot?

Wife Well, I thought the different countries at Epcot were wonderful, but I need to say more than that, don't I?

Husband They were very good and some were better than others, but that was down to the host countries themselves really, as I suppose each of the countries represented would have been responsible for their own part, so that's nothing to do with Disney, I wouldn't have thought. I mean some of the landmarks were hard to recognize for what they were supposed to be, but some were very well done. Britain was OK, but there was only a pub and a Welsh shop there really, whereas some of the other pavilions, as I think they were called, were good ambassadors for the countries they represented. China, for example, had an excellent 360 degree film showing parts of China and I found that very interesting.

Interviewer Did you think there was anything lacking about the content?

Husband Well I did notice that there weren't many black people at World Showcase, particularly the American Adventure. Now whether we were there on an unusual day in that respect I don't know, but we saw plenty of black Americans in the Magic Kingdom and other places, but very few if any in that World Showcase. And there was certainly little mention of black history in the American Adventure presentation, so maybe they felt alienated by that, I don't know, but they were noticeable by their absence.

Interviewer So did you think there were any special emphases?

Husband Well thinking about it now, because I hadn't really given this any consideration before you started asking about it, but thinking about it now, it was only really representative of the developed world, you know, Britain, America, Japan, world leaders many of them in technology, and there was nothing of the Third World there. Maybe that's their own fault, maybe they were asked to participate and didn't, but now that I think about it, that does come to me. What do you think, love?

Wife Well, like you, I hadn't thought of it like that before, but I agree with you.

(1996) nine question types. The initial reply is very bland and does little more than reflect the interviewees' positive feelings about their visit to Disney World. The wife acknowledges this when she says 'but I need to say more than that, don't I?' Interviewees frequently know that they are expected to be expansive in their answers. This sequence occurred around halfway through the interview, so the interviewees were primed by then into realizing that more details were expected. There is almost a tinge of embarrassment that the answer has been so brief and not very illuminating. The husband's answer is more expansive but not particularly enlightening.

There then follows the first of two important prompts by the interviewer. The husband's response is more interesting in that he now begins to answer in terms of the possibility that black people were under-represented in attractions such as the American Adventure, which tells the story of America through tableaux and films via a debate between two audio-animatronic figures—Mark Twain and Benjamin Franklin. The second prompt yields further useful reflection, this time carrying the implication that Third World countries are under-represented in World Showcase in the Epcot Centre. The couple are clearly aware that it is the prompting that has made them provide these reflections when they say: 'Well thinking about it now, because I hadn't really given this any consideration before you started asking about it' and 'Well, like you, I hadn't

thought of it like that before'. This is the whole point of prompting—to get the interviewee to think more about the topic and to provide the opportunity for a more detailed response. It is not a leading question, since the interviewees were not being asked 'Do you think that the Disney company fails to recognize the significance of black history (or ignores the Third World) in its presentation of different cultures?' There is no doubt that it is the prompts that elicit the more interesting replies, but that is precisely their role.

Recording and transcription

The point has already been made on several occasions that, in qualitative research, the interview is usually audio-recorded and transcribed whenever possible (see Tips and skills 'Why you should record and transcribe interviews'). Qualitative researchers are frequently interested not just in *what* people say but also in the *way* that they say it. If this aspect is to be fully woven into an analysis, it is necessary for a complete account of the series of exchanges in an interview to be available. Also, because the interviewer is supposed to be alert to what is being said—following up interesting points made, prompting and probing where necessary, drawing attention to any inconsistencies in the interviewee's answers—it is best if he or she is not distracted by having to concentrate on getting down notes on what is said.

Tips and skills
Why you should record and transcribe interviews

With approaches that entail detailed attention to language, such as conversation analysis and discourse analysis (see Chapter 22), the recording of conversations and interviews is to all intents and purposes essential. However, researchers who use qualitative interviews and focus groups (see Chapter 21) also tend to record and then transcribe interviews. Heritage (1984: 238) suggests that the procedure of recording and transcribing interviews has the following advantages.

- It helps to correct the natural limitations of our memories and of the intuitive glosses that we might place on what people say in interviews.

- It allows more thorough examination of what people say.

- It permits repeated examinations of interviewees' answers.

- It opens up the data to public scrutiny by other researchers, who can evaluate the analysis that is carried out by the original researchers (that is, a **secondary analysis**).

- It therefore helps to counter accusations that an analysis might have been influenced by a researcher's values or biases.

- It allows the data to be reused in other ways from those intended by the original researcher—for example, in the light of new theoretical ideas or analytic strategies.

However, it has to be recognized that the procedure is very time-consuming. It also requires good equipment, usually in the form of a good-quality recording device and microphone but also, if possible, a transcription machine. Also, recording equipment may be offputting for interviewees.

Tips and skills
Audio-recording interviews digitally

For years, the cassette tape recorder was the accepted medium for recording interviews and focus group sessions. Increasingly, researchers use digital audio-recording devices, which can be played back on a computer with the appropriate software or a smartphone. The chief advantage of a digital recording is that it is far superior, not least because the familiar 'hiss' that can usually be heard when playing back cassette tapes is eliminated. It is also possible to enhance the recordings so that background noise is filtered out. As a result of the superior sound quality, it is easier to transcribe interviews and also mistakes due to mishearing are less likely. Digital recordings can be easily backed up and played back again and again to listen to a portion that may be unclear without increasing any risk to the recording.

One further advantage is that it may be possible to use voice-recognition (voice-to-text) software to transcribe the interviews. This represents a massive saving on time. The problem is that, although such software is improving all the time, interviews are not an ideal medium for such software because the software needs to be 'trained' to recognize a voice. An interview comprises as least two voices and a project will comprise usually many interviewees, which makes the process of 'training' difficult. Some researchers have adapted to the use of speech-recognition software and the difficulty of getting interviewees voice-trained for the software by using their own voice to speak back all the recording into the microphone, so that their speech alone is processed by the software. They use a headset to listen to the recording and simultaneously speak what is said into the microphone, though it is necessary to keep on stopping and starting the recording that is being listened to. However, speech-recognition software is improving and using the Dragon app with iPhone and iPad can be surprisingly effective for turning speech into text.

Digital recordings are not without disadvantages. One is obviously the cost of the recording device. Second, digital audio files, for example .wav ones, are huge, so that they require a lot of disk space for storage. Third, there are competing formats for both digital files and voice-to-text software, which can cause compatibility problems.

Attending to such issues as using a high-quality microphone and seeking out a venue with as little extraneous noise as possible are also important to recording quality.

As with just about everything in conducting social research, there is a cost (other than the financial cost of recording equipment and software), in that the use of a recorder can disconcert respondents, who may become self-conscious or alarmed at the prospect of their words being preserved. Most people agree for interviews to be recorded, though it is not uncommon for a small number to refuse (see Research in focus 20.7). When faced with refusal, it is best to go ahead with the interview, as it is likely that useful information will still be forthcoming. This advice also applies to cases of a malfunction in recording equipment (again see Research in focus 20.7). Among those who do agree to be recorded, there will be some who will not get over their alarm at being confronted with a microphone. As a result, some interviews may not be as interesting as you might have hoped. In qualitative research, there is often quite a large amount of variation in the amount of time that interviews take.

For example, in Chattoe and Gilbert's (1999) study of budgeting in what they call 'retired households', the twenty-six interviews they carried out lasted between thirty minutes and three hours; in the research in Research in focus 20.7, the twenty interviews varied between forty-five minutes and three hours. It should not be assumed that shorter interviews are necessarily inferior to longer ones, but very short ones that are a product of interviewee non-cooperation or anxiety about being recorded are likely to be less useful—though it is not being suggested that this applies to these researchers' shorter interviews. When an interview has produced very little of significance, it may not be worth the time and cost of transcription. Thankfully, such occasions are relatively rare. If people do agree to be interviewed, they are usually cooperative and loosen up after initial anxiety about the microphone, so that even short interviews can be revealing.

Research in focus 20.7
Getting it taped and transcribed: an illustration of two problems

Rafaeli et al. (1997) conducted semi-structured interviews with twenty female administrators in a university business school in order to study the significance of dress at the workplace. They write:

> Everyone we contacted agreed to participate. Interviews took place in participants' offices or in a school lounge and lasted between 45 minutes and three hours. We recorded and transcribed all but two interviews: 1 participant refused to be taped, and the tape recorder malfunctioned during another interview. For interviews not taped, we recorded detailed notes. We assured all participants that their responses would remain confidential and anonymous and hired an outside contractor to transcribe the interviews.
>
> (Rafaeli et al. 1997: 14)

Even though, overall, this interview study was highly successful, generating eighteen interviews that were recorded and transcribed, it does show two kinds of problems qualitative interviewers can face—namely, refusals to be recorded and hardware malfunctions. It also suggests that it may be useful not to rely exclusively on hardware and to take notes in the course of an interview so that you will at least have notes if the hardware malfunctions.

Tips and skills
Transcribing interviews

If you are doing research for a project or dissertation, you may not have the resources to pay for professional transcription, and, unless you are an accurate touch typist, it may take a lot longer than the suggested five to six hours per hour of speech. However, the important thing to bear in mind is that you must allow sufficient time for transcription and be realistic about how many interviews you will be able to transcribe in the time available.

The problem with transcribing interviews is that it is very time-consuming. It is best to allow around five to six hours for **transcription** for every hour of speech. Also, transcription yields vast numbers of pages, which you will need to wade through when analysing the data. For example, Wright, Nyberg, and Grant (2012) report that the thirty-six semi-structured interviews they carried out with managers or external consultants with a responsibility for sustainability issues lasted between 50 and 120 minutes each and produced over 1,000 pages of transcript. It is clear, therefore, that, while transcription has the advantage of keeping intact the interviewee's (and interviewer's) words, it does so by piling up the amount of text to be analysed. It is no wonder that writers like Lofland and Lofland (1995) advise that the analysis of qualitative data is not left until all the interviews have been completed and transcribed. To delay may give the researcher the impression that he or she faces a monumental task. Also, there

are good grounds for making analysis an ongoing activity, because it allows the researcher to be more aware of emerging themes that he or she may want to ask about in a more direct way in later interviews (see Research in focus 20.3 for an example). The preference for ongoing analysis is also recommended by advocates of approaches to qualitative data analysis such as grounded theory (see Chapter 24).

It is easy to think that transcription is a relatively unproblematic translation of the spoken into the written word. However, given the reliance on transcripts in qualitative research based on interviews, the issue should not be taken lightly. Transcribers need to be trained in much the same way that interviewers do. Moreover, even among experienced transcribers, errors can creep in. Poland (1995) has provided some fascinating examples of mistakes in transcription that can be the result of many different factors (mishearing, fatigue,

Student experience
Handling large amounts of qualitative data

Rebecca Barnes found that she collected a large amount of data as a result of transcribing her recordings of semi-structured interviews, but help was at hand! She writes:

> The sheer amount of data which I had collected (40 transcripts, averaging 30 pages each) was at first quite overwhelming, but using NVivo made it much more manageable.

To read more, go to the Online Resource Centre: www.oxfordtextbooks.co.uk/orc/brymansrm5e/

Tips and skills
Conventions when using direct quotations from an interview

When transcribing an interview, it is important that the written text reproduces exactly what the interviewee said, word for word. For this reason, if there are parts of the interview that you cannot hear properly on the audio-recording, do not be tempted to guess or make them up; instead indicate in your transcript that there is a missing word or phrase—for example, by using the convention {???}. This helps to give the reader confidence in your data-collection process. However, people rarely speak in fully formed sentences, they often repeat themselves and they may have verbal 'tics' in the form of a common word or phrase that is often repeated either through habit or just because they like it! So when it comes to writing up your research, when you will probably wish to quote directly from the interview transcripts, you may want to edit out some of these digressions for the sake of length and ease of understanding. However, you must make sure that you do not paraphrase the words of the speaker and then claim these as the actual words that were spoken, because this is misleading, and there is always the possibility that someone reading your work might suspect that people did not really speak in such a fluent way. The use of certain conventions when quoting from an interview transcript helps to overcome these problems.

- Use quotation marks to indicate that this is a direct quotation or indicate this by consistently setting them out so they stand out from the main body of text—for example, by indenting them or by using a different font, in a similar way to how you would quote at length from a book. This makes it immediately apparent to the reader that this is a direct quotation and it enables you to differentiate between your presentation of the data and your analysis of it.

- If it is appropriate in relation to ethical considerations (see Chapter 6), indicate who is speaking in the quotation, either introducing the speaker before the quotation by saying something like 'As John put it', or 'Anne explained her reasons for this', or attribute the quotation to the interviewee immediately afterwards—for example, by writing his or her pseudonym or [Interviewee 1] in square brackets.

- If you wish to quote the first sentence from a section of speech and then a sentence or two further on from the transcript, use the convention of three consecutive dots to indicate the break point.

- If an interviewee omits a word from a sentence that is a grammatical omission or if the interviewee refers to a subject in a way that does not make its meaning clear and you need to provide the readers with more contextual information so that they can understand the quotation, use the convention of square brackets in which you insert the words you have added.

- Finally, one of the most difficult things about presenting interview data as part of your analysis is that it can take some effort and perseverance to create a smooth flow to the text because of the switches between your 'voice', as the researcher, and the 'voices' of the interviewees, which can make the text seem quite fragmented. For this reason it is important to introduce direct quotations before you present them and then take a sentence or two of your analysis to explain in your own words how you have interpreted them. In this way you construct a narrative that guides the reader through your data and shows why you have chosen the particular quotations you have as illustrative of particular themes or concepts.

carelessness). For example, one transcript contained the following passage:

> I think unless we want to become like other countries, where people have, you know, democratic freedoms . . .

But the actual words on the audiotape were:

> I think unless we want to become like other countries, where people have no democratic freedoms . . .

(Poland 1995: 294)

Steps clearly need to be taken to check on the quality of transcription.

It is also worth bearing in mind that it may not always be feasible to record interviews. Grazian (2003) conducted his ethnographic research into the manufacture of authentic blues music in Chicago blues clubs. He started out using a cassette recorder to record interviews with musicians and members of the audience but gave up. He writes that one of the reasons for giving up on the use of tape recorders was: 'I was observing settings where the combination of loud music and chattering customers made the level of background noise extremely high, and thus a recording device would have proved useless' (Grazian 2003: 246).

Flexibility in the interview

One further point to bear in mind is that you need to be flexible in your approach to interviewing in qualitative research. This advice is not just to do with needing to be responsive to what interviewees say to you and following up interesting points that they make. Such flexibility *is* important and is an important reminder that, with semi-structured interviewing, you should not turn the interview into a structured interview but with open-ended questions. Flexibility is important in such areas as varying the order of questions, following up leads, and clearing up inconsistencies in answers. Flexibility is important in other respects, such as coping with audio-recording equipment breakdown and refusals by interviewees to allow a recording to take place (see Research in focus 20.7). A further element is that interviewers often find that, as soon as they switch off their recording equipment, the interviewee continues to reflect on the topic of interest and sometimes will say more interesting things than in the interview. It is usually not feasible to switch the machine back on again, so try to take some notes either while the person is talking or as soon as possible after the interview.

Tips and skills
Transcribing sections of an interview

Sometimes interviews or at least large portions of them are not very useful, perhaps because interviewees are reticent or what they say is not relevant to your research. There seems little point in transcribing material that you know is unlikely to be fruitful. This is a common experience among qualitative interviewers. Gerson and Horowitz (2002: 211) observe that some qualitative interviews are 'uninspiring and uninteresting', so, if you do find some interviews or portions of them that are not terribly illuminating, you may not be alone in this respect. It may be that, for some of your interviews, it would be better to listen to them closely first, at least once or more usually twice, and then transcribe only those portions that you think are useful or relevant. However, this may mean that you miss certain things or that you have to go back to the recordings at a later stage in your analysis to try and find something that emerges as significant only later on.

Student experience
The advantage of transcribing your own interviews

Rebecca Barnes chose to transcribe the recordings of her semi-structured interviews herself. She writes:

> I tape-recorded all interviews, and I then transcribed all the tapes myself. I chose to transcribe the interviews myself because, whilst it was an arduous and very time-consuming task, it offered great benefits in terms of bringing me closer to the data, and encouraging me to start to identify key themes, and to become aware of similarities and differences between different participants' accounts.

To read more, go to the Online Resource Centre: www.oxfordtextbooks.co.uk/orc/brymansrm5e/

Such 'unsolicited accounts' can often be the source of revealing information or views (Hammersley and Atkinson 1995). This is certainly what Parker found in connection with his research on three British organizations—a National Health Service District Health Authority, a building society, and a manufacturing company—which was based primarily on semi-structured interviews: 'Indeed, some of the most valuable parts of the interview took place after the tape had been switched off, the closing intimacies of the conversation being prefixed with a silent or explicit "well, if you want to know what I really think . . .". Needless to say, a visit to the toilet to write up as much as I could remember followed almost immediately' (Parker 2000: 236).

Tips and skills
Keep the recorder going

Since interviewees sometimes 'open up' at the end of the interview, perhaps just when the recording device has been switched off, there are good grounds for suggesting that you should keep it switched on for as long as possible. So, when you are winding the interview down, don't switch off the audio-recorder immediately.

Student experience
Comments after the interview

Tips and skills 'Keep the recorder going' suggests that valuable material may be lost if you stop recording as soon as the formal interview is over. This has also been suggested by Warren et al. (2003) and was mentioned by Hannah Creane.

> One of the main issues which arose for me was that often after I had completed my interview and stopped recording, other things were said that were relevant to the interview and were often very interesting, and so unfortunately not all these points were always in my findings.

Hannah mentioned this point when dealing with the issue of whether she had encountered any ethical difficulties in her research. This is interesting, because it raises the question of the ethical status of post-interview remarks. From the interviewee's point of view, they could be regarded as 'off the record'. One way of dealing with the ethics of post-interview remarks would be to ask the interviewee whether it is all right to use them for the research once proceedings have finally come to an end.

To read more, go to the Online Resource Centre: www.oxfordtextbooks.co.uk/orc/brymansrm5e/

Telephone interviewing

Telephone interviewing is quite common in survey research but has not been used a great deal in qualitative research. It is likely to have certain benefits when compared to face-to-face qualitative interviewing. One of these inevitably is cost, since it will be much cheaper to conduct qualitative interviews by telephone, just as it is with survey interviewing. It is likely to be especially useful for dispersed groups and when interviewer safety is a consideration. Further, it may be that asking sensitive questions by telephone will be more effective, since interviewees may be less anxious about answering when the interviewer is not physically present.

There is some evidence that there are few differences in the kinds of answers given to questions asked by telephone rather than in person (referred to as 'mode effects' in the survey literature—see Chapter 10). Sturges and Hanrahan (2004) were conducting a study of visitors' and correctional officers' views concerning visiting jail inmates in California. Because of some difficulties associated with conducting the study, some respondents had to be interviewed by phone. This allowed a comparison of responses between the telephone and face-to-face interviews. Fifteen visitors were interviewed face-to-face and nineteen by telephone. Nine prison officers were interviewed—six face-to-face and three by telephone. Sturges and Hanrahan (2004: 113) concluded there were no noticeable differences between the responses given in that there were 'similarities in the quantity, nature and depth of responses'. Similarly, Irvine et al. (2013) conducted a small number of semi-structured interviews on the topic of mental health and employment. Some interviews were face-to-face and some were by telephone. Unlike Sturges and Hanrahan, the researchers found that, with the former mode of interviewing, interviewees tended to talk for longer. Interestingly, Irvine et al. also found differences between the two modes in the behaviour of the interviewer. For example, the interviewer was more likely in face-to-face interviews to give vocalized responses to show that she understood what was being said (such as 'yeah' and 'mm hm'). She was also more likely not to finish fully her questions or the questions were less likely to be grammatically correct in the face-to-face mode. However, Vogl (2013) interviewed 112 German children by semi-structured interview twice—once face-to-face and once by telephone. Her research suggests that mode effects are very slight in that differences in duration, number of pauses, requests for clarification, children's share of the number of words uttered, number of 'don't know' replies, and responses to sensitive questions were very similar between the two modes. Overall, the various studies of mode effects for telephone and face-to-face qualitative interviewing are fairly reassuring and suggest that concerns about data quality in the telephone mode are not as great as sometimes feared.

Certain issues about the use of telephone interviewing in qualitative research need to be borne in mind. Most obviously, it will not be appropriate to some groups of interviewees, such as those with no or limited access to telephones. Second, it is unlikely to work well with interviews that are likely to run on for a long time. It is much easier for the interviewee to terminate a telephone interview than one conducted in person. This is especially significant for qualitative interviews, which are often time-consuming for interviewees. Third, it is not possible to observe body language to see how interviewees respond in a physical sense to questions. Body language may be important because of the interviewer's ability to discern such things as discomfort, puzzlement, or confusion. It should also be borne in mind that there can be technical difficulties with recording interviews. Special equipment is needed, and there is always the possibility that the line will be poor. Fourth, the interviewer is unable to collect potentially illuminating observational material about such things as the setting (local area, type of building, whether lot of people are around, etc.) that may be illuminating. Fifth,

it is far less likely that the interviewer will be able to leave the recorder running (see Tips and skills 'Keep the recorder running') in a telephone interview.

My colleagues and I used qualitative telephone interviews for a study of social policy researchers (Sempik et al. 2007; Bryman et al. 2008). The interviews were designed to allow us to probe more deeply into researchers' views about research quality in the field of social policy following the use of an online questionnaire. We found that interviewees were quite expansive in their replies, and there were no significant recording problems. No comparison with in-person interviews of the kind conducted by Sturges and Hanrahan was carried out, but the comprehensive replies suggested that the method can generate detailed and considered replies of the kind typically sought by qualitative researchers. When the saving of time and travel costs is taken into account, given that the interviewees were widely dispersed in the UK, the method can certainly be regarded as very efficient when viewed in relation to the large volume of data collected.

A useful toolkit and examination of interviewing by telephone in qualitative research based in part on a comparison of Irvine's use of the two modes can be found at **eprints.ncrm.ac.uk/1576/1/14-toolkit-phone-inter views.pdf** (accessed 4 December 2014). At the same time, it is important to bear in mind the possibility of mode effects in view of the fact that there is a growing tendency to mix different modes of qualitative interview. For example, in a study of 'lad cultures' in higher education institutions, Phipps and Young (2015) conducted personal interview with twenty-one participants. Of these, five were conducted in person, ten via Skype, and a further six by email. If the mixing of modes of administration grows, there will be greater need in the future to assess the nature and significance of mode effects in qualitative interviewing.

Life history and oral history interviewing

Two special forms of the kind of interview associated with qualitative research are *life history* and *oral history* interviews. The former is generally associated with the **life history method**, where it is often combined with various kinds of personal documents such as diaries, photographs, and letters. This method is often referred to alternatively as the *biographical method*. A life history interview invites the subject to look back in detail across his or her entire life course. It has been depicted as documenting 'the inner experience of individuals, how they interpret, understand, and define the world around them' (Faraday and Plummer 1979: 776). However, the life history method is very much associated with the life history interview, which is a kind of unstructured interview covering the totality of an individual's life. Thomas and Znaniecki, who are among the pioneers of the approach as a result of their early use of it in relation to Polish immigrants to the USA, regarded it as 'the *perfect* type of sociological material' (quoted in Plummer 1983: 64). Their use, in particular, of a solicited autobiography that was written for them by one Polish peasant is regarded as an exemplification of the method.

However, in spite of Thomas and Znaniecki's endorsement, while there was a trickle of studies using the approach over the years (a table in Plummer 1983 points to twenty-six life histories dating from Thomas and Znaniecki's research in the 1910s up until the publication of Plummer's book), until the 1990s it was not a popular approach. It has tended to suffer because of an erroneous treatment of the life in question as a sample of one and hence of limited generalizability. However, it has certain clear strengths from the perspective of the qualitative researcher: its unambiguous emphasis on the point of view of the life in question and a clear commitment to the processual aspects of social life, showing how events unfold and interrelate in people's lives. The terms *life history* and *life story* are sometimes employed interchangeably, but R. L. Miller (2000: 19) suggests that the latter is an account someone gives about his or her life and that a life history dovetails a life story with other sources, such as diaries and letters (of the kind discussed in Chapter 23).

An example of the life history interview approach is provided by O. Lewis (1961: xxi) in the context of his research on the Sánchez family and their experiences of a Mexican slum:

> In the course of our interviews I asked hundreds of questions of [the five members of the Sánchez family] . . . While I used a directive approach to the interviews, I encouraged free association, and I was a good listener. I attempted to cover systematically a wide range of subjects: their earliest memories, their dreams, their hopes, fears, joys, and sufferings; their jobs; their relationship with friends, relatives, employers; their sex life; their concepts of justice, religion, and politics; their knowledge of geography and history; in short, their total world view of the world. Many of my questions stimulated them to express themselves on subjects which they might otherwise never have thought about.

Miller (2000) distinguishes between certain aspects of life history interviews. One distinction has to do with age and life course effects. The former relates to the ageing process, in the sense of biological ageing and its effects and manifestations; life course effects are the patterned features associated with the stages of the life course. Miller also points to the need to distinguish cohort effects, which are the unique clusters of experiences associated with a specific generation.

An interesting use of the life history method is the research by Laub and Sampson (2004) in connection with the study referred to in Research in focus 3.13 (see also Research in focus 27.4). They approached their reconstruction of the lives of the fifty-two delinquents from the original study in two ways. First, they developed a form of life history calendar that provided their sample with a framework within which they could pinpoint major turning points in their lives, such as marriage, job change, and divorce. Second, they also conducted interviews that invited the fifty-two men to reflect on their life course. They write:

> Of particular interest were the questions regarding the participant's assessment of his own life, specifically whether he saw improvement or a worsening since childhood, adolescence, or young adulthood and the self-evaluation of turning points in one's own life course and the relationship to criminal activity and various life course transitions (e.g., marriage, divorce, military service, residential change, and the like). . . . By drawing on the men's own words, narratives helped us unpack mechanisms that connect salient life events across the life course, especially regarding personal choice and situational context.
>
> (Laub and Sampson 2004: 93, 94)

Through the collection of these data, the researchers were able to enhance their understanding of the significance of turning points in an individual's life that influence the likelihood of continued involvement in or desistance from crime.

R. L. Miller (2000) suggests there has been a resurgence of interest and Chamberlayne et al. (2000) argue that there has been a recent 'turn to biographical methods'. To a large extent, the revival of the approach derives from a growth of interest in the role and significance of agency in social life. The revival is largely associated with the growing use of life story interviews and especially those that are often referred to as *narrative interviews*. Moreover, the growing use of such interviews has come to be associated less and less with the study of a single life (or indeed just one or two lives) and increasingly with the study of several lives (see Research in focus 24.7).

Plummer (2001) draws a useful distinction between three types of life story:

1. *Naturalistic life stories*. These are life stories that occur whenever people reminisce or write autobiographies or diaries, or when job applicants write out letters of application and are interviewed.

2. *Researched life stories*. These are life stories that are solicited by researchers with a social scientific purpose in mind. Most research based on life history/story interviews, like that of Squire (2000), are of this kind.

3. *Reflexive and recursive life stories*. Such life stories recognize that the life story is always a construction in which the interviewer is implicated.

R. Atkinson (2004) observes that the length of the typical life story interview varies considerably but suggests that it usually comprises two or three sessions of between one hour and one-and-a-half hours each. He has provided a catalogue of questions that can be asked and divides these into groups. The following list of categories and sample questions are taken from Atkinson (1998: 43–53):

- *Birth and family of origin*. For example: 'How would you describe your parents?'
- *Cultural settings and traditions*. For example: 'Was your family different from others in the neighbourhood?'
- *Social factors*. For example: 'What were some of your struggles as a child?'
- *Education*. For example: 'What are your best memories of school?'
- *Love and work*. For example: 'How did you end up in the type of work you do or did?'
- *Historical events or periods*. For example: 'Do you remember what you were doing on any of the really important days in our history?'

- *Retirement*. For example: 'What is the worst part of being retired?'
- *Inner life and spiritual awareness*. For example: 'What are the stresses of being an adult?'
- *Major life themes*. For example: 'What are the crucial decisions in your life?'
- *Vision of the future*. For example: 'Is your life fulfilled yet?'
- *Closure questions*. For example: 'Do you feel that you have given a fair picture of yourself?'

One final point about the life history interview is that, while it has been presented in this section as a stand-alone technique, the increased interest in its use cannot be detached from the growth of interest in and use of narrative analysis (see Chapter 24). Life history interviewing is often seen as one of the springboards for producing data that can be viewed through a narrative lens. **Narrative analysis** focuses attention on people's stories concerning sequences of events that permeate their lives (see Chapter 24 for a discussion of narrative analysis). Life history interviewing can be a significant tool in eliciting such accounts. See Research in focus 20.8 and 24.7 for examples.

An **oral history interview** is usually somewhat more specific in that the subject is asked to reflect upon

Research in focus 20.8
Constructionism in a life history study of occupational careers

In an article on the concept of the occupational career by Bosley, Arnold, and Cohen (2009), an explicitly constructionist stance was taken. Rather than viewing careers as a relatively fixed series of stages through which people progress, Bosley et al. researched careers as social constructions that are contingent on a series of experiences and on other individuals who influence the occupational directions that people take. As the authors put it: 'career is seen as social practice, constituted by actors themselves in and through their relationships with others, and as they move through time and space. It is an iterative and on-going process' (2009: 1498). The authors employed a life story method in which twenty-eight employees were interviewed (see Chapter 18 for a brief mention of the sampling method). The interviews 'elicited participants' accounts of their careers from school-leaving to present day. Describing encounters with helpers in the context of preceding and subsequent events enabled participants to recall and identify significant career helpers and the role played by helpers in shaping their careers' (2009: 1499). For each interviewee, a narrative account was generated that portrayed each interviewee's career in terms of contacts, relationships, and encounters that shaped his or her career direction. Out of these narratives, the authors forged a typology of career shaping roles: adviser, informant, witness, gatekeeper, and intermediary. Each role is associated with a different kind of impact on employees' career trajectories and decision-making. The authors write: 'shaping encounters served as a vehicle through which participants negotiated with and navigated through the structural environments in which they were situated' (2009: 1515). The constructionism associated with this research lies in its emphasis on interviewees, and the events and people that were significant in the course and direction of their careers.

specific events or periods in the past. The emphasis is less upon the individual and his or her life than on the particular events in the past. It too is sometimes combined with other sources, such as documents. The chief problem with the oral history interview (which it shares with the life history interview) is the possibility of bias introduced by memory lapses and distortions (Grele 1998). On the other hand, oral history testimonies have allowed the voices to come through of groups that are typically marginalized in historical research (a point that also applies to life history interviews), either because of their lack of power or because they are typically regarded as unexceptional (Samuel 1976). Bloor (2002) has shown how oral history testimonies, collected in 1973 and 1974, of Welsh miners' experiences of pit life could be used to facilitate an understanding of how they sought collectively to make an impact on their health in the pits and to improve safety. Bloor draws lessons from these testimonies for social policies at the time he was writing.

 # Feminist research and interviewing in qualitative research

Unstructured and semi-structured interviewing have become prominent methods of data gathering within a feminist research framework. In part, this is a reflection of the preference for qualitative research among many feminist researchers, but it also reflects a view that the kind of interview with which qualitative research is associated allows many of the goals of feminist research to be realized. Indeed, the view has been expressed that, 'whilst several brave women in the 1980s defended quantitative methods, it is nonetheless still the case that not just qualitative methods, but the in-depth face-to-face interview has become the paradigmatic "feminist method"' (Kelly et al. 1994: 34). This comment is enlightening because it implies that it is not simply that qualitative research is seen by many writers and researchers as more consistent with a feminist position than quantitative research, but that, specifically, qualitative interviewing is seen as especially appropriate. The point being made here is not necessarily that such interviewing is somehow more in tune with feminist values than, say, ethnography (especially since it is often an ingredient of ethnographic research). Instead, it could be that the intensive and time-consuming nature of ethnography means that, although it has great potential as an approach to feminist research (see Chapter 19), qualitative interviewing is often preferred because it is usually less invasive in these respects.

However, it is specifically interviewing of the kind conducted in qualitative research that is seen as having potential for a feminist approach, not the structured interview with which social survey research is associated. Why might one type of interview be consistent with a sensitivity to feminism and the other not? In a frequently cited article, Oakley (1981) outlines the following points about the standard survey interview.

- It is a one-way process—the interviewer extracts information or views from the interviewee.

- The interviewer offers nothing in return for the extraction of information. For example, interviewers using a structured interview do not offer information or their own views if asked. Indeed, they are typically advised not to do such things because of worries about contaminating respondents' answers.

- The interviewer–interviewee relationship is a form of hierarchical or power relationship. Interviewers arrogate to themselves the right to ask questions, implicitly placing their interviewees in a position of subservience or inferiority.

- The element of power is also revealed by the fact that the structured interview seeks out information from the perspective of the researcher.

- Because of these points, the standard survey interview is inconsistent with feminism when women interview other women. This view arises because it is seen as indefensible for women to 'use' other women in these ways.

Instead of this framework for conducting interviews, feminist researchers advocate one that establishes:

- a high level of rapport between interviewer and interviewee;

- a high degree of reciprocity on the part of the interviewer;

- the perspective of the women being interviewed;

- a non-hierarchical relationship.

In connection with the reciprocity that she advocates, Oakley noted, for example, that, in her research on the transition to motherhood, she was frequently asked questions by her respondents. She argues that it was ethically indefensible for a feminist not to answer when faced with questions of a certain kind with which she was confronted (see the subsection on 'The feminist critique' in Chapter 9 for an illustration of this point). For Oakley, therefore, the qualitative interview was viewed as a means of resolving the dilemmas that she encountered as a feminist interviewing other women. However, as noted in previous chapters, while this broad adherence to a set of principles for interviewing in feminist research continues, it has been tempered by a greater recognition of the possible value of quantitative research.

An interesting dilemma that is perhaps not so easily resolved is the question of what feminist researchers should do when their own 'understandings and interpretations of women's accounts would either not be shared by some of them [i.e. the research participants], and/or represent a form of challenge or threat to their perceptions, choices and coping strategies' (Kelly et al. 1994: 37). It is the first type of situation that will be examined here, at least in part, because, while it is of particular significance to feminist researchers, its implications are somewhat broader. It raises the tricky question of how far the commitment of seeing through the eyes of the people you study can and/or should be stretched. Two examples are relevant here. Reinharz (1992: 28–9) cites the case of an American study by Andersen (1981), who interviewed twenty 'corporate wives'; they came across as happy with their lot and were supportive of feminism only in relation to employment discrimination. Andersen interpreted their responses to her questions as indicative of 'false consciousness'—in other words, she did not really believe her interviewees. When Andersen wrote an article on her findings, the women wrote a letter rejecting her account, affirming that women can be fulfilled as wives and mothers. A similar situation confronted Millen (1997: 4.6) when she interviewed thirty-two British female scientists using 'semi-structured, in-depth individual interviewing'. As she puts it:

There was a tension between my interpretation of their reported experience as sex-based, and the meaning the participants themselves tended to attribute to their experience, since the majority of respondents did not analyse these experiences in terms of patriarchy or sex–gender systems, but considered them to be individualised, or as 'just something that had to be coped with'. . . . From my external, academically privileged vantage point, it is clear that sexism pervades these professions, and that men are assumed from the start by other scientists to be competent scientists of status whilst women have to prove themselves, overcome the barrier of their difference before they are accepted. These women, on the other hand, did not generally view their interactions in terms of gendered social systems. There is therefore a tension between their characterisation of their experience and my interpretation of it.

(Millen 1997: 5.6, 5.9)

Three interesting issues are thrown up by these two accounts. First, how can such a situation arise? This is an issue that pervades qualitative research that makes claims to reveal social reality as viewed by members of the setting in question. If researchers are genuinely seeing through others' eyes, the 'tension' to which Millen refers should not arise. However, it clearly can and does, and this strongly suggests that qualitative researchers are more affected by their own perspectives and research questions when collecting and analysing data than might be expected from textbook accounts of the research process. Second, there is the question of how to handle such a 'tension'—that is, how do you reconcile the two accounts? Andersen's (1981) solution was to reinterpret her findings in terms of the conditions that engender the contentment she uncovered. Third, given that feminist research is often concerned with wider political goals of emancipation, a tension

Student experience
Feminism and the choice of semi-structured interviews

The potential of the semi-structured interview for feminist researchers as a means of allowing women's voices to be heard and in their own words was important to Erin Sanders in the context of her research on sex workers in Thailand.

My feminist background influenced my decision to employ feminist research methods. I used in-depth, semi-structured interviews because I wanted the women I interviewed to be able to express their ideas and their thoughts in their own way—I wanted their voices and their stories to be heard, rather than my own words and ideas directing their thoughts.

To read more, go to the Online Resource Centre: www.oxfordtextbooks.co.uk/orc/brymansrm5e/

between participants' worldviews and the researcher's position raises moral questions about the appropriateness of imposing an interpretation that is not shared by research participants themselves. Such an imposition could hardly be regarded as consistent with the principle of a non-hierarchical relationship in the interview situation.

Therefore, while qualitative interviewing has become a highly popular research method for feminist researchers because of its malleability into a form that is in tune with the principles of feminism, interesting questions are raised in terms of the relationship between researchers' and participants' accounts. Such questions are significant generally for the conduct of qualitative research.

Qualitative research using online personal interviews

The issues involved in conducting online personal interviews for qualitative research are essentially the same as those to do with conducting online focus groups. In particular, the researcher must decide whether the interviews should take place in synchronous or asynchronous mode (see the discussion of this distinction in Chapter 21). The factors involved in deciding which to use are also largely the same, although issues to do with variable typing speed or computer-related knowledge among focus group participants will not apply.

Although online interviews run the risk relative to face-to-face interviews that the respondent is somewhat more likely to drop out of the exchange (especially in asynchronous mode like email, since the interviews can sometimes be very protracted), Mann and Stewart (2000: 138–9) suggest that in fact a relationship of mutual trust can be built up. This kind of relationship can make it easier for a longer-term commitment to the interview to be maintained, but also makes it easier for the researcher to go back to his or her interviewees for further information or reflections, something that is difficult to do with the face-to-face personal interview. The authors also suggest that it is important for interviewers to keep sending messages to respondents to reassure them that their written utterances are helpful and significant, especially since interviewing through the Internet is still an unfamiliar experience for most people.

A further issue for the online personal interviewer to consider is whether to send all the questions at once or to interview on the basis of a question followed by a reply. The problem with the former tactic is that respondents may read all the questions and then reply only to those that they feel interested in or to which they feel they can make a genuine contribution, so that asking one question at a time is likely to be more reliable. Bampton and Cowton (2002) report their experiences of conducting email interviews by sending questions in small batches. They argue that this approach took pressure off interviewees to reply quickly, gave them the opportunity to provide considered replies (although the authors recognize that there may have been a loss of spontaneity), and gave the interviewers greater opportunity to respond to interviewees' answers.

There is evidence that prospective interviewees are more likely to agree to participate if their agreement is solicited prior to sending them questions and if the researcher uses some form of self-disclosure, such as directing the person being contacted to the researcher's website, which contains personal information, particularly information that might be relevant to the research issue (Curasi 2001; O'Connor and Madge 2001). The argument for obtaining prior agreement from interviewees before sending them questions to be answered is that unsolicited emails, often referred to as 'spamming', are regarded as a nuisance among online users and receiving them can result in an immediate refusal to take the message seriously.

Curasi (2001) conducted a comparison in which twenty-four online interviews carried out through email correspondence (and therefore asynchronous) were contrasted with twenty-four parallel face-to-face interviews. The interviews were concerned with shopping on the Internet. She found the following:

- Face-to-face interviewers are better able than online interviewers to maintain rapport with respondents.

- Greater commitment and motivation are required for completing an online interview, but, because of this, replies are often more detailed and considered than with face-to-face interviews.

- Online interviewers are less able to have an impact on whether the interview is successful or not because they are more remote.

- Online interviewees' answers tend to be more considered and grammatically correct because they have more time to ponder their answers and because they can tidy them up before sending them. Whether this is a positive feature is debatable: there is the obvious advantage of a 'clean' transcript, but there may be some loss of spontaneity which Gibson (2010) found in connection with her research when she compared email and face-to-face interviews.

- Follow-up probes can be carried out in online interviews, as well as in face-to-face ones.

On the other hand, Curasi also found that the worst interviews in terms of the amount of detail forthcoming were from online interviews. It may be that this and the other differences are to do with the fact that, whereas a qualitative face-to-face interview is *spoken*, the parallel online interview is *typed*. The full significance of this difference in the nature of the respondent's mode of answering has not been fully appreciated.

It is very clear from many of the discussions about online interviews by email that a significant problem for many interviewers is that of keeping respondents involved in the interview when questions are being sent one or two at a time. Respondents tend to lose momentum or interest. However, Kivits (2005) has shown that recontacting interviewees on regular occasions and adopting an accessible and understanding style can not only help to maintain momentum for many interviewees but also bring some who have lost interest or forgotten to reply back into the research.

Some researchers have combined different types of interview in a single investigation. In addition to examining email and other forms of Internet-based communications for their study of online social support in the UK, Nettleton et al. (2002) interviewed fifty-one people involved in these communications. The interviewees were all approached by email after they had submitted relevant postings in the various lists that were being studied. In addition, some interviewees had responded to postings submitted by the research group. Some of these interviews were conducted face-to-face, some on the telephone, and still others online. One of the online interviews was with a woman in her 60s with myalgic encephalomyelitis (ME). She brings across the importance of online social support for someone with this condition:

> The mailing list MECHAT . . . in particular has been a real lifeline. I check mail several times a day. I have been able to discuss things with people who understand . . . important as ME is an especially misunderstood illness . . . make new friends and share experiences and laughter . . . It is a real comfort if any trauma or upset occurs—death or illness of a loved one, relapse, relationship problems, or even just thoughtless remarks from folks who do not understand ME, which we would otherwise have to bear alone.
>
> (Nettleton et al. 2002: 183)

Evans, Elford, and Wiggins (2008) employed both face-to-face and synchronous online interviews in a study of gay men and HIV. They found that the online interviews lasted longer and produced considerably fewer words. They also found that there was considerably more variation in both interview length and number of words in the face-to-face context.

An interesting issue with asynchronous personal interviews is whether it is appropriate to describe them as interviews at all and indeed whether they are experienced by research participants as interviews. Since the process of answering questions in an **asynchronous online interview** entails writing, particularly if there is minimal interaction with the researcher, it may be experienced by the 'interviewee' as more akin to answering open-ended questions in a self-administered questionnaire. This does not apply to the kind of online interview described in the next section, however.

Student experience
Using the Internet for supplementary data

Isabella Robbins wanted to interview mothers whose children had been vaccinated and those whose children had not been vaccinated. However, she found it difficult to find mothers in the latter group. This passage shows how she enlisted the Internet to help her to find supplementary data on mothers' decision-making in relation to the preference not to vaccinate their children, but it is also interesting and significant for her reliance on data saturation (see Key concept 18.4).

> Recruitment of mothers was fairly straightforward in terms of the mothers who said they had vaccinated. However, recruiting mothers who had not vaccinated proved to be problematic. Essentially, because childhood vaccination is a moral issue, these mothers were careful about who they talked to about their resistance. They were a hard to get at community. With time running out I decided to use Internet message boards—from women/mothers forums—in order to supplement my data. This data helped to confirm that I had reached saturation. No new themes came out from it, but it provided some additional rich data.

To read more, go to the Online Resource Centre: www.oxfordtextbooks.co.uk/orc/brymansrm5e/

Using Skype

Thus far, most of the discussion of online personal interviewing assumes that the exchange is conducted entirely in a textual context. However, the webcam and Skype may offer further possibilities for synchronous online personal interviews. Skype is available for use on many smartphones and tablets, as well as conventional computers. It makes the online interview similar to a telephone interview, in that although it is mediated by Internet technology, it is also similar to an in-person interview, since those involved in the exchange are able to see each other. Some researchers have begun to report and reflect on their experiences of using Skype in this way and the early indications are broadly positive (Deakin and Wakefield 2014; Hanna 2012; Weinmann et al. 2012). These early impressions suggest that the obvious advantage of Skype (or similar software, such as FaceTime) over telephone interviewing, namely that it allows a visual element that is akin to a face-to-face interview, is borne out. In addition researchers' early impressions suggest several other advantages:

- The Skype interview is more flexible than the face-to-face interview, in that last-minute adjustments to the scheduling of the interview can be easily accommodated.

- There are obvious time and cost savings in that the need to travel to the interview is removed, which is a particular advantage with geographically dispersed samples.

- The convenience of being interviewed by Skype may actually encourage some people to agree to be interviewed when they might otherwise have declined.

- There are fewer concerns about the safety of both parties to an interview, particularly when the interview is being conducted at night.

- There seems little evidenced that the interviewer's capacity to secure rapport is significantly reduced in comparison with face-to-face interviews.

There are some limitations that warrant mention too:

- There are potential technological problems with the use of Skype and similar platforms. Not everyone has the necessary Wifi connection and familiarity with Skype is by no means universal.

- Skype can be prone to fluctuations in the quality of the connection (and sometimes outages) which can make the flow of the interview less than smooth. Breaking up of speech can result in poor recordings of the interview, which makes transcription difficult if not impossible at times.

- One of the principal advantages of the online interview is lost, because the respondent's answers need to be transcribed, as in traditional qualitative interviewing.

- Although it is clearly advantageous for interviewers and interviewees to see each other, so that visual cues can be picked up, responses may be affected by visual characteristics of the interviewer, such as gender, age, and ethnic group.

- There is some evidence that prospective Skype interviewees are more likely than face-to-face interviewees to fail to be present for an interview.

- A study of German youth conducted in 2011 found that it was harder to secure agreement to participate in Skype interviews than in telephone interviews (Weinmann et al. 2012).

Interviewing via Skype clearly has great potential and it may be that some of the difficulties reported above will gradually become less pronounced as familiarity with the software increases and Wifi connections improve.

Qualitative interviewing versus participant observation

The aim of this section is to compare the merits and limitations of interviewing in qualitative research with those of participant observation. These are probably the two most prominent methods of data collection in qualitative research, so there is some virtue in assessing their strengths, a debate that was first begun many years ago (Becker and Geer 1957; Trow 1957). In this section, interviewing is being compared to participant observation rather than ethnography, because the latter invariably entails a significant amount of interviewing. So too does participant observation, but in this discussion I will be following the principle that I outlined in Key concept 19.1—namely, that the term will be employed to refer to the specifically observational activities in which the participant observer engages. As noted in Key concept 19.1, the term 'ethnography' is being reserved for the wide range of data-collection activities in which ethnographers engage—one of which is participant observation—along with the written account that is a product of those activities.

Advantages of participant observation in comparison to qualitative interviewing

The following is an examination of the ways in which participant observation exhibits advantages over qualitative interviewing.

Seeing through others' eyes

As noted in Chapters 2 and 17, seeing through others' eyes is one of the main tenets of qualitative research, but, on the face of it, the participant observer would seem to be better placed for gaining a foothold on social reality in this way. The researcher's prolonged immersion in a social setting would seem to make him or her better equipped to see as others see. The participant observer is in much closer contact with people for a longer period of time; also, he or she participates in many of the same kinds of activity as the members of the social setting being studied. Research that relies on interviewing alone is likely to entail much more fleeting contacts, though qualitative interviews can last many hours, and re-interviewing is not unusual.

Learning the native language

Becker and Geer (1957) argued that the participant observer is in the same position as a social anthropologist visiting a distant land, in that in order to understand a culture the language must be learned. However, it is not simply the formal language that must be understood in the case of the kinds of social research in which a participant observer in a complex urban society engages. It is also very often the 'argot'—the special uses of words and slang—that is important to penetrate that culture. Such an understanding is arrived at through the observation of language use.

The taken for granted

The interview relies primarily on verbal behaviour, and, as such, matters that interviewees take for granted are less likely to surface than in participant observation, where such implicit features in social life are more likely to be revealed as a result of the observer's continued presence.

Ability to observe behaviour

Whereas the interviewer who is interested in behaviour has to rely on verbal self-reports of behaviour or reports of the behaviour of others, participant observation offers the opportunity to observe behaviour directly. However, because not all behaviour will be accessible to participant observers (for example, if the observer's gender makes it difficult to observe certain areas of behaviour), they are frequently forced to interview in order to glean information about such difficult-to-access areas or types of behaviour.

Deviant and hidden activities

Much of what we know about criminal and deviant subcultures has been gleaned from participant observation. These are areas that insiders are likely to be reluctant to talk about in an interview context alone. Understanding is again likely to come through prolonged interaction. Many of the examples in Chapter 19 entailed participant observation of criminal or deviant worlds, such as drug taking, violent gangs, pilferage, illegal commerce, and hooliganism. Ethnographers conducting participant observation are more likely to place themselves in situations in which their continued involvement allows them gradually to infiltrate such social worlds and to insinuate themselves into the lives of people who might be sensitive to outsiders. For similar reasons, participant observers have found that they are able to gain access to areas such as patterns of resistance at work or to groups of people who support a generally despised ideology, such as extreme right-wing racist groups.

Sensitivity to context

The participant observer's extensive contact with a social setting allows the context of people's behaviour to be mapped out fully. The participant observer interacts with people in a variety of different situations and possibly roles, so that the links between behaviour and context can be forged.

Encountering the unexpected and being flexible

It may be that, because of the unstructured nature of participant observation, it is more likely to uncover unexpected topics or issues. Except with the most unstructured forms of interview, the interview process is likely to entail some degree of closure as the interview guide is put together, which may blinker the researcher slightly. Also, participant observation may be more flexible because of the tendency for interviewers to instil an element of comparability (and hence an element of structure) in their questioning of different people. Ditton's (1977) decision at a very late stage in the data-collection process to focus on pilferage in the bakery in which he was a participant observer is an example of this feature (see Research in focus 19.1).

Naturalistic emphasis

Participant observation has the potential to come closer to a naturalistic emphasis, because the qualitative researcher confronts members of a social setting in their natural environments. Interviewing, because of its nature as a disruption of members' normal flow of events, even when it is at its most informal, is less amenable to this feature.

Embodied nature of experience

Participant observation entails an embodied approach to collecting data that largely eludes the qualitative interviewer. Coming to understand how those being studied experience their social world and their meaning systems entails the use of the participant observer's body as an element in the collection of data. This is more apparent and more relevant in some studies than in others and can be seen in Wacquant's (2004) research in and on a boxing gym, in which the decision to become a boxer required an embodied approach to appreciate the rigours of the craft. Similarly, O'Brien (2010) describes how as a female bouncer she had to decide which women should be searched for inappropriate possessions such as drugs; this meant learning and using signifiers of class and culture, but O'Brien also had to then physically search the women, an activity that she found uncomfortable performing. However, ethnographers may not be able to overcome the limitations of their bodies in this connection. Parreñas (2011) worked as a hostess in a number of clubs in Tokyo to gain some insight into the experience but reports in a footnote: 'I was an inept hostess, as acting feminine did not come naturally to me. I was also considered one of the less attractive hostesses, being much older and bigger than my co-workers' (Parreñas 2011: 284). However, she also reports that this ineptitude did bring with it the advantage that it meant she was not seen as a threat to the business of her co-workers so that they were much more prepared to 'show [her] the ropes' (2011: 284).

Advantages of qualitative interviewing in comparison to participant observation

The following is an examination of the ways in which qualitative interviewing exhibits advantages over participant observation.

Issues resistant to observation

It is likely that there is a wide range of issues that are simply not amenable to observation, so that asking people about them represents the only viable means of finding out about them within a qualitative research strategy. For example, for their research on the gendered management of household finances, Bisdee et al. (2013—see Research in focus 3.9) were interested in the role of ageing in relation to this issue. However, although the observation of couples' household financial management is not impossible to envisage, it is not really sensible or feasible to carry out participant observation in relation to something like this, which is clearly highly episodic.

Reconstruction of events

Qualitative research frequently entails the reconstruction of events by asking interviewees to think back over how a certain series of events unfolded in relation to a current situation. Research on careers by Bosley et al. (2009—see Research in focus 20.8) shows how the researchers, through life history interviews, encouraged their participants to reflect backwards on their careers. This questioning procedure allowed the researchers to bring out key turning points and the roles of various other individuals in their career development. Similarly, in the research on knowledge workers' use of mobile email devices by Mazmanian et al. (2013—see Research in focus 20.3), one sequence of interviewing entailed getting participants to describe their previous day from waking to going to sleep in order to bring out the role of these devices in their lives in a relatively unprompted way. This reconstruction of events is something that cannot be accomplished through participant observation alone. See Research in focus 20.9 for a further example of the use of the interview to elicit a reconstruction of events.

Ethical considerations

There are certain areas that could be observed—albeit indirectly through hidden hardware like a microphone—but that would raise ethical considerations. The research by McKeganey and Barnard (1996; see Research in focus 20.9) on prostitution furnishes an example of this. One of the areas they were especially interested in was negotiations between prostitutes and their clients over the use of condoms in the light of the spread of HIV/AIDS infection. It is not inconceivable that such transactions could have been observed with the aid of hidden hardware and it is possible that some prostitutes would have agreed to being wired up for this purpose. However, clients would not have been party to such agreements, so that ethical principles of informed consent and invasion of privacy would have been transgressed (see Key concept 6.1). As a result, the researchers relied on interview accounts of such negotiations or of prostitutes' stances on the matter (see Research in focus 20.9), as well as the views of a small number of clients.

Reactive effects

The question of reactive effects is by no means a straightforward matter. As with structured observation (see Chapter 12), it might be anticipated that the presence of a participant observer would result in reactive effects (see Key concept 12.4). People's knowledge of the fact that they are being observed may make them behave less naturally. However, participant observers, like researchers using structured observation, typically find that people become accustomed to their presence

Research in focus 20.9
Information through interviews: research on prostitution

McKeganey and Barnard (1996) have discussed their strategies for conducting research into prostitutes and their clients. Their research was based in a red-light area in Glasgow. Their approach was largely that of non-participating observer with interaction (see Figure 19.2), in that their research was based primarily on interviews with prostitutes and their clients, as well as some (frequently accidental) observation of interactions and overheard conversations. The interviews they conducted were especially important in gaining information in relation to such areas as how the prostitutes had moved into this line of work; permitted and prohibited sex acts; links with drug use; experience of violence; and the management of identity. In the following passage, a prostitute reconstructs her movement into prostitution:

I was 14 and I'd run away from home. I ended up down in London where I met a pimp. . . . He'd got me a place to stay, buying me things and everything and I ended up sleeping with him as well. . . . One night we got really drunk and stoned and he brought someone in. . . . [Then] after it happened I thought it was bad, I didn't like it but at least I was getting paid for it. I'd been abused by my granddad when I was 11 and it didn't seem a million miles from that anyway.

(McKeganey and Barnard 1996: 25)

and begin to behave more naturally the longer they are around. Indeed, members of social settings sometimes express surprise when participant observers announce their imminent departure when they are on the verge of disengagement. Interviewers clearly do not suffer from the same kind of problem, but it could be argued that the unnatural character of the interview encounter can also be regarded as a context within which reactive effects may emerge. Participant observation also suffers from the related problem of observers disturbing the very situation being studied, because conversations and interactions will occur in conjunction with the observer that otherwise would not happen. This is by no means an easy issue to resolve and it seems likely that both participant observation and qualitative interviewing set in motion reactive effects but of different kinds.

Less intrusive in people's lives

Participant observation can be very intrusive in people's lives in that the observer is likely to take up a lot more of their time than in an interview. Qualitative interviews can sometimes be very long, and re-interviewing is not uncommon, but the impact on people's time will probably be less than having to take observers into account on a regular basis, though it is likely that this feature will vary from situation to situation. Participant observation is likely to be especially intrusive in terms of the amount of people's time taken up when it is in organizational settings. In work organizations, there is a risk that the rhythms of work lives will be disrupted.

Longitudinal research easier

One of the advantages of participant observation is that it is inherently longitudinal, because the observer is present in a social setting for a period of time. As a result, change and connections between events can be observed. However, there are limits to the amount of time that participant observers can devote to being away from their normal routines. Consequently, participant observation does not usually extend much beyond two to three years in duration. When participant observation is conducted into an area of research that is episodic rather than requiring continued observation, a longer time period may be feasible. Armstrong's (1993) research on football hooliganism entailed six years of participant observation, but, since football hooligans are not engaged full-time in this area of activity, the research did not require the researcher's continued absence from his work and other personal commitments. Interviewing can be carried out within a longitudinal research design somewhat more easily because repeat interviews may be easier to organize than repeat visits to participant observers' research settings, though the latter is not impossible (e.g. Burgess 1987, who revisited the comprehensive school in which he had conducted participant observation). Following up interviewees on several occasions is easier than returning to research sites on a regular basis.

Greater breadth of coverage

In participant observation, the researcher is invariably constrained in his or her interactions and observations to

Thinking deeply 20.1
A debate about ethnography and interviewing

When I was writing the fourth edition of this book, I considered removing this section which has been an ever-present since the first edition. I felt it was looking dated—it does after all have its origins in a debate from around sixty years ago! However, I decided not to go ahead—and decided not to do so for this edition either—because the debate has in a sense resurfaced though in a different guise. Jerolmack and Khan (2014) write that research based on interviews and survey research suffers from what they call 'the attitudinal fallacy', which is the inappropriate inferring of behaviour from verbal accounts. This is of course a reprise of the issues raised in Thinking deeply 12.2 regarding the gap between what people say they do and what they actually do, and indeed Lapiere (1934) is cited by them. Jerolmack and Khan lump together qualitative interviewing and survey research as methods that solely produce verbal accounts; simultaneously, they are critical of the lumping together of qualitative interviewing and ethnography on the grounds that ethnography 'routinely attempts to explain' the issue of the inconsistency between attitudes and behaviour whereas the interview study 'regularly disregards the problem' (Jerolmack and Khan 2014: 180). Jerolmack and Khan do *not* argue that interview-based studies (and surveys) are worthless, but they do argue that if the researcher seeks to draw inferences about situated behaviour they are inappropriate because unlike in ethnography, behaviour is not directly studied. Of course, ethnographers do interview in the course of their work (as Khan [2011] did in the study of an elite US high school in the US), but it is the fact that ethnography 'prioritizes the observation of social action . . . within the real-world rather than a research context' (Jerolmack and Khan 2014: 202) that distinguishes it.

The journal in which this article was published invited several leading writers to comment on it (as well as a response by Jerolmack and Khan). The comments are from several different standpoints with some suggesting that the attitudinal fallacy problem is over-stated, for example, because research suggests that there is often a fairly good correspondence between accounts and actual behaviour, or that it has to be remembered that not all potential sites of action are amenable to observation (Cerulo 2014). In addition, Lamont and Swidler, two leading qualitative researchers, have separately written an article that provides a spirited defence of the interview in the face of Jerolmack and Khan's paper and other recent examples of what they call 'methodological tribalism'. They argue that focusing on the issue of the correspondence between attitude and behaviour is too restricted and that it is important to focus on what qualitative interviews can be used for. They point to the significance of the fact that in interviews:

- 'comparison across contexts, situations, and kinds of people' (Lamont and Swidler 2014: 158) can be relatively easily accommodated, allowing an in-depth understanding with systematically crafted breadth of coverage to answer research questions;

- data about the emotional side of human experience that is not necessarily apparent in people's behaviour can be gleaned;

- people can be invited to reflect on their behaviour in a variety of situations whereas the ability to vary situational differences in ethnography is limited.

Thus, the critics of positions such as that of Jerolmack and Khan are quick to remind us of the merits of interviews and the importance of tailoring research method to research questions (though this is apparent in Jerolmack and Khan's article too). The basic point about the significance of ethnography for understanding behaviour is important to bear in mind when drawing inferences about behaviour from interview-based research.

a fairly restricted range of people, incidents, and localities. Participant observation in a large organization, for example, is likely to mean that knowledge of that organization far beyond the confines of the department or section in which the observation is carried out is likely not to be very extensive. Interviewing can allow access to a wider variety of people and situations.

Specific focus

As noted in Chapter 17, qualitative research sometimes begins with a specific focus, and indeed Silverman (1993) has been critical of the notion that it should be regarded as an open-ended form of research. Qualitative interviewing would seem to be better suited to such a situation, since the interview can be directed at that focus and its associated research questions. Thus, the research by my colleagues and myself on the police had a very specific research focus in line with its Home Office funding—namely, conceptions of leadership among police officers (Bryman, Stephens, and A Campo 1996). The bulk of the data gathering was in two police forces and entailed interviewing police officers at all levels using a semi-structured interview guide. Because it had such a clear focus, it was more appropriate to conduct the research by interview rather than participant observation, since issues to do with leadership notions may not crop up on a regular basis, which would make observation an extravagant method of data collection.

Overview

When Becker and Geer (1957: 28) proclaimed in the mid-twentieth century that the 'most complete form of the sociological datum . . . is the form in which the participant observer gathers it', Trow (1957: 33) reprimanded them for making such a universal claim and argued that 'the problem under investigation properly dictates the methods of investigation'. The latter view is very much the one taken in this book. Research methods are appropriate to researching some issues and questions but not others. The discussion of the merits and limitations of participant observation and qualitative interviews is meant to draw attention to some of the considerations that might be taken into account if there is a choice between one or the other in a study.

Equally, and to repeat an earlier point, the comparison is a somewhat artificial exercise, because participant observation is usually carried out as part of ethnographic research, and as such it is usually accompanied by interviewing as well as other methods. In other words, participant observers frequently buttress their observations with methods of data collection that allow them access to important areas that are not amenable to observation. However, the aim of the comparison was to provide a kind of balance sheet in considering the strengths and limitations of a reliance on either participant observation or qualitative interview alone. Its aim is to draw attention to some of the factors that might be taken into account in deciding how to plan a study and even how to evaluate existing research. See Thinking deeply 20.1 for a resurfacing of this kind of debate.

Checklist
Issues to consider for your qualitative interview

- ○ Have you devised a clear and comprehensive/informative way of introducing the research to interviewees?

- ○ Does your interview guide clearly relate to your research questions?

- ○ Have you piloted the guide with some appropriate respondents?

- ○ Have you thought about what you will do if your interviewee does not turn up for the interview?

- ○ Does the guide contain a good mixture of different kinds of questions, such as probing, specifying, and direct questions?

- ○ Have you ensured that interviews will allow novel or unexpected themes and issues to arise?

- ○ Is your language in the questions clear, comprehensible, and free of unnecessary jargon?

- ○ Are your questions relevant to the people you are proposing to interview?

- ○ Does your interview guide include requests for information about the interviewee, such as his or her age, work experience, position in the firm?

- ○ Have your questions been designed to elicit reflective discussions so that interviewees are not tempted to answer in 'yes' or 'no' terms?

- ○ Do your questions offer a real prospect of seeing the world from your interviewees' point of view rather than imposing your own frame of reference on them?

- ○ Are you familiar with the setting(s) in which the interviews will take place?

○ Are you thoroughly familiar with and have you tested your recording equipment?

○ Have you thought about how you will present yourself in the interview, such as how you will be dressed?

○ Have you thought about how you will go about putting into operation the criteria of a good interviewer?

» Key points

- Interviewing in qualitative research is typically of the unstructured or semi-structured kind.
- In qualitative research, interviewing may be the sole method in an investigation or may be used as part of an ethnographic study, or indeed in tandem with another qualitative method.
- Qualitative interviewing is meant to be flexible and to seek out the worldviews of research participants.
- If an interview guide is employed, it should not be too structured in its application and should allow some flexibility in the asking of questions.
- The qualitative interview should be recorded and then transcribed.
- Interviewing in qualitative research can exhibit a variety of forms, such as life history and oral history interviewing.
- The qualitative interview has become an extremely popular method of data collection in feminist studies.
- Conducting personal interviews online has become a viable alternative to face-to-face interviews in many instances.
- Whether to use participant observation or qualitative interviews depends in large part on their relative suitability to the research questions being addressed. However, it must also be borne in mind that participant observers invariably conduct some interviews in the course of their investigations.

? Questions for review

- Outline the main types of interview employed by qualitative researchers.

Differences between the structured interview and the qualitative interview

- How does qualitative interviewing differ from structured interviewing?

Asking questions in the qualitative interview

- What are the differences between unstructured and semi-structured interviewing?
- Could semi-structured interviewing stand in the way of flexibility in qualitative research?
- What are the differences between life history and oral history interviews?
- What kinds of consideration need to be borne in mind when preparing an interview guide?
- What kinds of question might be asked in an interview guide?
- What kinds of skills does the interviewer need to develop in qualitative interviewing?
- Why is it important to record and transcribe qualitative interviews?
- What role might vignette questions play in qualitative interviewing?

Life and oral history interviewing

- What are the main kinds of life history interview and what are their respective uses?
- Why might the life history interview be significant for a researcher employing a narrative analysis approach?

Feminist research and interviewing in qualitative research

- Why has the qualitative interview become such a prominent research method for feminist researchers?
- What dilemmas might be posed for feminist researchers using qualitative interviewing?

Qualitative research using online personal interviews

- Can online personal interviews really be personal interviews?
- To what extent does the absence of direct contact mean that the online interview cannot be a true interview?
- Can Skype be used as an alternative to face-to-face personal interviews?

Qualitative interviewing versus participant observation

- Outline the relative advantages and disadvantages of qualitative interviewing and participant observation.
- Does one method seem more in tune with the preoccupations of qualitative researchers than the other?

Online Resource Centre

www.oxfordtextbooks.co.uk/orc/brymansrm5e/

Visit the Online Resource Centre to enrich your understanding of interviewing in qualitative research. Follow up links to other resources, test yourself using multiple choice questions, and gain further guidance and inspiration from the Student Researcher's Toolkit.

21

Focus groups

Chapter outline

Chapter guide

The focus group method is an interview with several people on a specific topic or issue. It has been used extensively in market research but has only relatively recently made inroads into social research. This chapter explores:

- the possible reasons for preferring focus group interviews to individual interviews;
- how focus groups should be conducted in terms of such features as the need for recording, the number and size of groups, how participants can be selected, and how direct the questioning should be;
- the significance of interaction between participants in focus group discussions;
- the prospects of conducting focus groups online;
- some practical difficulties with focus group sessions, such as the possible loss of control over proceedings and the potential for unwanted group effects.

Introduction

We are used to thinking of the interview as something that involves an interviewer and one interviewee. Most textbooks reinforce this perception by concentrating on individual interviews. The **focus group** technique is a method of interviewing that involves more than one, usually at least four, interviewees. Essentially it is a group interview. Some authors draw a distinction between focus group techniques and group interview techniques. Three reasons are sometimes put forward to suggest a distinction.

- Focus groups typically emphasize a specific theme or topic that is explored in depth, whereas group interviews often span very widely.

- Sometimes group interviews are carried out so that the researcher is able to save time and money by carrying out interviews with a number of individuals simultaneously. Focus groups are not carried out for this reason.

- The focus group practitioner is invariably interested in the ways in which individuals discuss a certain issue *as members of a group*, rather than simply as individuals. In other words, with a focus group the researcher will be interested in such things as how people respond to each other's views and build up a view out of the interaction that takes place within the group.

However, the distinction between the focus group method and the group interview is by no means clear-cut, and the terms are frequently used interchangeably. Nonetheless, the definition proposed in Key concept 21.1 provides a starting point.

Most focus group researchers undertake their work within the traditions of qualitative research. This means that they are explicitly concerned to reveal how the group participants view the issues with which they are confronted; therefore, the researcher will aim to provide a fairly unstructured setting for the extraction of their views and perspectives. The person who runs the focus group session is usually called the **moderator** or facilitator, and he or she will be expected to guide each session but not to be too intrusive.

Another general point about the focus group method is that, while it has been gaining in popularity since the 1980s, it is by no means a new technique. It has been used for many years in market research, where it is employed for such purposes as testing responses to new products and advertising initiatives. In fact, there is a large literature within market research to do with the practices that are associated with focus group research and their implementation (e.g. Calder 1977).

Key concept 21.1
What is the focus group method?

The focus group method is a form of group interview in which there are several participants (in addition to the moderator/facilitator); there is an emphasis in the questioning on a particular fairly tightly defined topic; and the accent is upon interaction within the group and the joint construction of meaning. As such, the focus group contains elements of two methods: the group interview, in which several people discuss a number of topics; and what has been called a focused interview, in which interviewees are selected because they 'are known to have been involved in a particular situation' (Merton et al. 1956: 3) and are asked about that involvement. The focused interview may be administered to individuals or to groups. Thus, the focus group method appends to the focused interview the element of interaction within groups as an area of interest and is more focused than the group interview.

 # Uses of focus groups

What are the uses of the focus group method? In many ways its uses are bound up with the uses of qualitative research in general, but, over and above these, the following points can be registered.

- The original idea for the focus group—the focused interview—was that people who were known to have had a certain experience could be interviewed in a relatively unstructured way about that experience. The bulk of the discussion by Merton et al. (1956) of the notion of the focused interview was in terms of

individual interviews, but their book also considered the extension of the method into group interview contexts. Subsequently, the focus group has become a popular method for researchers examining the ways in which people in conjunction with one another interpret the general topics in which the researcher is interested. One of the best-known studies using the method in the context of a social scientific topic is Morgan and Spanish's (1985) study of the ways in which people organize knowledge about health issues. Their special interest was the question of people's knowledge about who has heart attacks and why they have them. Thus, the emphasis was on how focus group participants make sense of the causation of heart attacks in terms of the knowledge they have picked up over the years. However, a major impetus for the growing use of focus groups has been their intensive use in media and cultural studies. The growing emphasis in these fields is on what is known as 'audience reception'—how audiences respond to television and radio programmes, films, newspaper articles, and so on (McGuigan 1992; Fenton et al. 1998: Chapter 1). An influential study in this context was Morley's (1980) research on *Nationwide*, a British news programme shown in the early evening that was popular in the 1970s. Morley organized focus groups made up of specific categories of people (for example, managers, trade unionists, students) and showed them recordings of the programme. He found that the different groups arrived at somewhat divergent interpretations of the programmes they had watched, implying that meaning does not reside solely in the programmes but also in the ways in which they are watched and interpreted. This research and the increasing attention paid to audience reception set in motion a growth of interest in the use of the focus group method for the study of audience interpretations of cultural and media **texts**.

- The technique allows the researcher to develop an understanding about *why* people feel the way they do. In a normal individual interview the interviewee is often asked about his or her reasons for holding a particular view, but the focus group approach offers the opportunity of allowing people to probe each other's reasons for holding a certain view. This can be more interesting than the sometimes predictable question-followed-by-answer approach of conventional interviews. For one thing, an individual may answer in a certain way during a focus group, but, as he or she listens to others' answers, he or she may want to qualify or modify a view; or alternatively may want to voice agreement to something that he or she probably would not have thought of without the opportunity of hearing the views of others. These possibilities mean that focus groups may also be very helpful in the elicitation of a variety of views in relation to a particular issue.

- In focus groups, participants are able to bring to the fore issues in relation to a topic that they deem to be important and significant. This is clearly an aim of individual interviews too, but, because the moderator has to relinquish a certain amount of control to the participants, the issues that concern them can surface. This is clearly an important consideration in the context of qualitative research, since the viewpoints of the people being studied are an important point of departure.

- In conventional one-to-one interviewing, interviewees are rarely challenged; they might say things that are inconsistent with earlier replies or that patently could not be true, but we are often reluctant to point out such deficiencies. In a focus group, individuals will often argue and challenge each other's views. This means that the researcher may end up with more realistic accounts of what people think, because they are forced to think about and possibly revise their views.

- The focus group offers the researcher the opportunity to study the ways in which individuals collectively make sense of a phenomenon and construct meanings around it. It is a central tenet of theoretical positions such as symbolic interactionism that the process of understanding and interpreting social phenomena is not undertaken by individuals in isolation from each other. Instead, it is something that occurs in interaction and discussion with others. In this sense, therefore, focus groups reflect the processes through which meaning is constructed in everyday life and to that extent can be regarded as more naturalistic (see Key concept 3.4 on the idea of naturalism) than individual interviews (S. Wilkinson 1998).

- The use of focus groups by feminist researchers has grown considerably in recent years, and S. Wilkinson (1998, 1999b) has argued that it has great potential in this regard. Its appeal to feminist researchers is its compatibility with the ethics and politics of feminism. As we have seen in previous chapters, feminist researchers tend to be suspicious of research methods that may be exploitative and create a power relationship between the female researcher and the female respondent. Wilkinson observes that the risk of this occurring is reduced in a focus group because participants are able to take over much of the direction of the session from the moderator. They may even subvert the goals of the session in ways that could be of considerable interest to the moderator. As a result, participants' points of view are much more likely to be revealed than in a traditional interview. This kind of argument has been extended to suggest focus groups may have a further role in allowing the voices of highly marginalized groups of women to surface. Madriz (2000: 843) argues that, for a group such as lower-socio-economic-class women of colour, focus groups constitute a relatively rare opportunity for them to 'empower themselves by making sense of their experience of vulnerability and subjugation'.

 # Conducting focus groups

There are a number of practical aspects of the conduct of focus group research that require some discussion.

Recording and transcription

As with interviewing for qualitative research, the focus group session will work best if it is recorded and subsequently transcribed. The following reasons are often used to explain this preference.

- One reason is the simple difficulty of writing down not only exactly what people say but also who says it. In an individual interview you might be able to ask the respondent to hold on while you write something down, but to do this in the context of an interview involving several people would be extremely disruptive.

- The researcher will be interested in who expresses views within the group, such as whether certain individuals seem to act as opinion leaders or dominate the discussion. This also means that there is an interest in ranges of opinions within groups; for example, in a session, does most of the range of opinion derive from just one or two people or from most of the people in the group?

- A major reason for conducting focus group research is the fact that it is possible to study the processes whereby meaning is collectively constructed within each session (as mentioned in the previous section). It would be very difficult to do this by taking notes, because of the need to keep track of *who* says what (see also previous point). If this element is lost, the dynamics of the focus group session would also be lost, and a major rationale for doing focus group interviews rather than individual ones would be undermined.

- Like all qualitative researchers, the focus group practitioner will be interested in not just what people say but *how* they say it—for example, the particular language that they employ. There is every chance that the nuances of language will be lost if the researcher has to rely exclusively on notes.

Transcribing focus group sessions is more complicated and hence more time-consuming than transcribing traditional interview recordings. This is because you need to take account of *who* is talking in the session, as well as what is said. This is sometimes difficult, since people's voices are not always easy to distinguish. Also, people sometimes talk over each other, which can make transcription even more difficult. In addition, it is extremely important to ensure that you equip yourself with a very high-quality microphone, which is capable of picking up voices, some of which may be quite faint, from many directions. Focus group transcripts always seem to have more missing bits because of lack of audibility than transcripts from conventional interviews.

How many groups?

How many groups do you need? Table 21.1 provides data on the number of groups and other aspects of the composition of focus groups in several studies based on this method (it follows a similar table in Deacon, Pickering, Golding, and Murdock, 1999, in the view that this is a helpful way of providing basic information on this issue). As Table 21.1 suggests, there is a good deal of variation in

 ## Tips and skills
Transcription of a focus group interview

In Tips and skills 'Transcribing sections of an interview' (see Chapter 20), I pointed out that it may not always be desirable or feasible to transcribe the whole of the interview. The same applies to focus group research, which is often more difficult and time-consuming to transcribe than personal interview recordings because of the number of speakers who are involved. The suggestions I made in Chapter 20 in relation to transcribing sections of an interview therefore apply equally well to focus group recordings.

Table 21.1
Composition of groups in focus group research

Authors	Morgan and Spanish (1985)	Schlesinger et al. (1992)	Kitzinger (1993, 1994)	Lupton (1996)	Macnaghten and Jacobs (1997)	Fenton et al. (1998)	Silva and Wright (2005); Silva et al. (2009); Bennett et al. (2009)	Warr (2005)	Wiles (2014)
Area of research	Lay health beliefs concerning heart attacks	The responses of women to watching violence	Audience responses to media messages about AIDS	Responses to controversies concerning diet and health	Public understanding of and identification with sustainable development	Audience responses to reporting of social science research	Cultural tastes and activities; each focus group was allocated a pair of topics specific to that group	Expectations regarding intimate relationships in socio-economically disadvantaged contexts	Perceptions of trust in GPs among patients with specific conditions
Number of groups	9	14	52	12	8 (each group had 2 sessions)	14	25	8	6
Size range of groups	4–5	5–9	Not specified but appears to be 3–9 or 3–10	3–5	6–10	4–6	2–8	4–9	4–10
Average (mean) size of groups	4.4	6.6	6.75	4.1	Approximately 8	5	5.7	Not clear	6.3
Stratifying criteria (if any)	None mentioned, but all participants needed to be aged 35–50 and those who had experienced a heart attack were excluded	Experience of violence, Scottish/English ethnicity, social class	None, but groups made up of specific groups (e.g. civil engineers, retirement club members, male prostitutes)	Gender	Age, ethnicity, gender, occupation, retired, rural/urban location	Gender, education, occupation (private/public sector)	Gender; urban/rural; occupation; ethnicity; age; employed/unemployed	Gender	Specific conditions: chronic pain; mental health; visual impairment; Parkinson's Disease
Natural groups?	No, but all participants were mature university students	Some	Yes	Yes	No	Some	No	Most	No

the numbers of groups used in the studies referred to, with a range from six to fifty-two. However, there seems to be a tendency for the range to be mainly from eight to fifteen.

It is unlikely that just one group will meet the researcher's needs, since there is the possibility that the responses are particular to that one group. Equally, there are strong arguments for saying that too many groups will be a waste of time. Calder (1977) proposes that, when the moderator reaches the point that he or she is able to anticipate fairly accurately what the next group is going to say, then there are probably enough groups already. This notion is very similar to the data saturation criterion that was introduced in Key concept 18.4. In other words, once new themes are no longer emerging there seems little point in continuing, and so it would be appropriate to bring data collection to a halt. For their study of audience discussion programmes, Livingstone and Lunt (1994: 181) used data saturation as a criterion: 'The number of focus groups was determined by continuing until comments and patterns began to repeat and little new material was generated.' When this point of saturation is reached, as an alternative to terminating data collection, there may be a case for moving on to an extension of the issues that have been raised in the focus group sessions.

One factor that may affect the number of groups is whether the researcher feels that the kinds and range of views are likely to be affected by socio-demographic factors such as age, gender, class, and so on. Many focus group researchers like to use stratifying criteria such as these to ensure that groups with a wide range of features will be included. If so, a larger number of groups may be required to reflect the criteria. In connection with the research described in Research in focus 21.1, Kitzinger (1994) writes that a large number of groups was preferred, not because of concerns about the representativeness of the views gleaned during the sessions, but in order to capture a diversity of perspectives. However, it may be that high levels of diversity are not anticipated in connection with some topics, in which case a large number of groups could represent an unnecessary expense.

One further point to bear in mind when considering the number of groups is that a larger number will increase the complexity of your analysis. For example, Schlesinger et al. (1992: 29; see Table 21.1) report that the fourteen audio-recorded sessions they organized produced over 1,400 pages of transcription. This pile of paper was accumulated from discussions in each group of an average of one hour for each of the four screenings of violence that session participants were shown. Although this means that the sessions were longer than is normally the case, it does demonstrate that the amount of data to analyse can be very large, even though a total of fourteen sessions may not sound a lot to someone unfamiliar with the workings of the method.

Research in focus 21.1
Focus group in action: AIDS in the Media Research Project

Focus group research on the representation of AIDS in the mass media was part of a larger project on this topic. The focus groups were concerned with the examination of the ways in which 'media messages are explored by audiences and how understandings of AIDS are constructed. We were interested not solely in what people thought but in *how* they thought and *why* they thought as they did' (Kitzinger 1994: 104).

Details of the groups are in Table 21.1. Since one goal of the research was to emphasize the role of interaction in the construction of meaning, it was important to provide a platform for enhancing this feature. Accordingly, 'instead of working with isolated individuals, or collections of individuals drawn together simply for the purposes of the research, we elected to work with pre-existing groups—people who already lived, worked or socialized together' (Kitzinger 1993: 272).

As a result, the groups were made up of such collections of people as a team of civil engineers working on the same site, six members of a retirement club, intravenous drug-users, and so on. The sessions themselves are described as having been 'conducted in a relaxed fashion with minimal intervention from the facilitator—at least at first' (Kitzinger 1994: 106). Each session lasted approximately two hours and was audio-recorded.

Size of groups

How large should groups be? Morgan (1998a) suggests that the typical group size is six to ten members, although the numbers in the groups cited in Table 21.1, which admittedly are not randomly selected, imply that this calculation is slightly high in terms of both the range and the mean. One major problem faced by focus group practitioners is people who agree to participate but who do not turn up on the day. It is almost impossible to control for 'no-shows' other than by consciously over-recruiting, a strategy that is sometimes recommended (e.g. S. Wilkinson 1999a: 188).

The question of 'no-shows' aside, Morgan (1998a) recommends smaller groups when participants are likely to have a lot to say on the research topic. This is likely to occur when participants are very involved in or emotionally preoccupied with the topic. He also suggests smaller groups when topics are controversial or complex and when gleaning participants' personal accounts is a major goal. Morgan (1998a: 75) recommends larger groups when involvement with a topic is likely to be low or when the researcher wants 'to hear numerous brief suggestions'. However, I am not convinced that larger groups are necessarily superior for topics in which participants have little involvement, since it may be more difficult to stimulate discussion in such a context. Larger groups may make it even more difficult if people are reticent about talking about a topic about which they know little or have little experience. A topic such as media representations of social science research, which most people are unlikely to have much interest in or even to have thought about, could easily have resulted in a wall of silence in large groups (Fenton et al. 1998; see Table 21.1). Barbour (2007) proposes a maximum of eight for most purposes. She argues that larger groups will be less suited to the interest among most social researchers in participants' interpretations and the ways in which views are constructed in the course of focus group sessions. Also, she suggests that larger groups can be a challenge for moderators in terms of responding to participants' remarks in the course of sessions and also at the analysis stage because of practical difficulties such as recognizing the different voices in audio-recordings of the sessions. Peek and Fothergill (2009) provide confirmation of the likelihood that, in many contexts, smaller groups will be preferable (see Research in focus 21.4 for more on this research). They report that those focus groups that included between three and five participants 'ran more smoothly than the larger group interviews that we conducted' (Peek and Fothergill 2009: 37). By contrast, they found that the management of larger focus groups that varied between six and fifteen members was considerably more taxing. It was harder to entice more reticent members to speak up. Also, in the smaller groups, there seemed to be greater opportunity for disagreement and diversity of opinion, perhaps because there was less of a tendency for one person to dominate proceedings.

Level of moderator involvement

How involved should the moderator/facilitator be? In qualitative research, the aim is to glean participants' perspectives. Consequently, the approach should not be intrusive and structured. Therefore, there is a tendency for researchers to use a fairly small number of very general questions to guide the focus group session. There is a further tendency for moderators to allow quite a lot of latitude to participants, so that the discussion can range fairly widely. If the discussion goes off at a total tangent it may be necessary to refocus the participants' attention, but even then it may be necessary to be careful, because what appear to be digressions may in fact reveal something of interest to the group participants. The advantage of allowing a fairly free rein to the discussion is that the researcher stands a better chance of getting access to what people see as important or interesting. On the other hand, too much irrelevant discussion may prove too unproductive, especially in the commercial environment of market research. It is not surprising, therefore, that, as S. Wilkinson (1999a) observes, some writers on focus

Tips and skills
Number of focus groups

Focus groups take a long time to arrange, and it takes a long time to transcribe the recordings that are made. It is likely that students will not be able to include as many focus group sessions for projects or dissertations as the studies cited in this chapter. You will, therefore, need to make do with a smaller number of groups in most instances. Make sure you are able to justify the number of groups you have chosen and why your data are still significant.

groups perceive the possibility that participants come to take over the running of a session from the moderator as a problem and offer advice on how to reassert control (e.g. Krueger 1988).

One way in which the moderator may need to be involved is in responding to specific points that are of potential interest to the research questions but that are not picked up by other participants. In the extract in Research in focus 21.2 from the study of the reception of media representations of social science research from Fenton et al. (1998), a group of men who have been in higher education and are in private-sector employment begin to talk about the differences between the natural and the social sciences.

It is interesting to see the way in which a consensus about the social sciences is built up in this discussion with a particular emphasis on the lack of control in social research and on the supposed subjectivity of interpretation when compared to the 'pure' sciences. On other occasions, a little nudge from the moderator may be required when a particularly interesting point is not followed up by other participants. An example of this is provided in Research in focus 21.3, which is from the same research, but this time the focus group is made up of women in private-sector employment and whose education is up to

GCSE level. They are talking about a news item reporting research on victims of crime but that includes a number of detailed case studies of individual experiences of being a victim.

On this occasion, the moderator's intervention usefully allows the discussion to bring out the kinds of attributes that make for an easy and interesting media item on this topic. In particular, the participants feel that they can appreciate the media representation of social science research when it is something they can relate to and that an important way of doing this is the ability to use people's personal experiences as a lens through which the research can be viewed.

Clearly, the moderator has to straddle two positions: allowing the discussion to flow freely and intervening to bring out especially salient issues, particularly when group participants do not do so. This is not an easy dilemma to resolve, and each tactic—intervention and non-intervention—carries risks. The best advice is to err on the side of minimal intervention—other than to start the group on a fresh set of issues—but to intervene when the group is struggling in its discussions or when it has not alighted on something that is said in the course of the session that appears significant for the research topic. Kandola (2012) usefully recommends tactics to

Research in focus 21.2
Extract from a focus group showing no moderator involvement

In the following extract, three focus group participants engage in a discussion with no intervention or involvement on the part of the moderator. The participants are discussing how people view media reporting of social science research.

R1 Essentially with the pure sciences I get an end result. Whereas with the social sciences it's pretty vague because it's very, very subjective.

R2 I suppose for me the pure sciences seem to have more control of what they are looking at because they keep control of more. Because with social sciences there are many different aspects that could have an impact and you can't necessarily control them. So it seems more difficult to pin down and therefore to some extent controversial.

R3 Pure science is more credible because you've got control over test environments, you've got an ability to test and control factually the outcome and then establish relationships between different agents or whatever. I think in social science it's always subject to interpretation. . . . I think if you want to create an easy life and be unaccountable to anybody, to obtain funding and spend your time in a stress-free way then one of the best things to do is to work in funded research and one of the best areas to do it in is in social science.

(Fenton et al. 1998: 127)

Research in focus 21.3
Extract from a focus group showing some moderator involvement

In the following extract, three focus group participants engage in a discussion with only a little intervention or involvement on the part of the moderator. The participants are discussing how people view media reporting of social science research.

R1	That was easy and interesting.
[Moderator]	Why interesting? Why easy?
R2	Because it affects all of us.
R1	It was actually reading about what had happened to people. It wasn't all facts and figures. I know it was, but it has in the first sentence, where it says 'I turned the key and experienced a sinking feeling'. You can relate to that straight away. It's how you'd feel.
R3	She's in a flat and she hears noises—it's something that everyone does. Being on their own and they hear a noise.

(Fenton et al. 1998: 129)

keep the discussion flowing, such as acknowledging what has been said, summarizing and stimulating reflection on what has been said, and allowing adequate time for participants to speak. Equally, she recommends that the moderator should avoid certain forms of intervention, notably agreeing or disagreeing, expressing personal opinions, and interrupting. She also cautions against the use of bodily responses like frowning, looking distracted, fidgeting, and shaking one's head (nodding is recommended, though I would recommend caution here as nodding can be interpreted by participants as agreement).

One of the challenges for focus group moderators is ensuring that there is a good level of participation among members. Getting equal participation is unrealistic but it is clearly preferable for all group members to participate to a reasonable degree. Kandola suggests writing comments that arise in the course of a discussion onto a flipchart. However, she cautions that as far as possible, participants' own language should be employed when making such notes so that the researchers' own understandings are not imposed.

The role of moderator is not just to do with asking questions and ensuring that the discussion flows well. It is also to do with controlling events in the discussion. If participants begin to talk at the same time, as often happens when a discussion really 'takes off', it will make the

audio-recording of the session impossible to decipher. The moderator has an important role in reminding participants to talk one at a time (see Research in focus 21.9 for an example). Also, it is well known that some participants have a tendency to monopolize discussions and that some participants are very reticent about talking. The moderator can have an important role in encouraging the latter to speak, perhaps by asking whether those who have not said much would like to take the opportunity to contribute.

Selecting participants

Who can participate? Anyone for whom the topic is relevant can logically be an appropriate participant. Sometimes, certain topics do not require participants of a particular kind, so that there is little if any restriction on who might be appropriate. This is a fairly unusual situation and normally some restriction is required. For example, for their research on the organization of knowledge about heart attacks, Morgan and Spanish (1985: 257) recruited people in the 35–50 age range, since they 'would be likely to have more experience with informal discussions of our chosen topic', but they excluded anyone who had had a heart attack or who was uneasy about discussing the topic. Research in focus 21.4 describes various recruitment strategies used by researchers.

Research in focus 21.4
Recruiting focus group participants

Peek and Fothergill (2009) have outlined the strategies they used in recruiting participants for focus groups studies in three North American contexts: with parents, children, and teachers in two urban day-care centres; with Muslim Americans following 9/11; and experiences of children and young people after the Hurricane Katrina flooding of New Orleans. They used three approaches:

- What they call *researcher-driven recruitment*, whereby the researcher, with the support of an organization with an interest in the research, uses email, letters, flyers, and telephone calls to solicit interest in participation.

- *Key informant recruitment*, which entails stakeholder organizations actively assisting in the recruitment of participants. For example, in the Hurricane Katrina study, a schoolteacher smoothed the path for the researchers to make contact with 'middle school students'.

- *Spontaneous recruitment*, which arises when individuals volunteer to participate having heard about the research through others. An example is when people see someone being interviewed and ask to join in.

Similar strategies seem to have been at work in the focus groups that formed part of the CCSE research on cultural tastes and activities (Research in focus 2.9, 21.6, and 21.9). The authors write that 'group formation involved a variety of processes of access negotiation, via community groups, businesses, professional organisations, and drew on established personal and professional networks' (Silva and Wright 2005: 3). For example, to recruit the Pakistani groups, a community centre was approached, and, to secure working-class pensioners, a church acted as a source. At the same time, relevant businesses were approached for employment- or work-related groups.

More often, as Table 21.1 suggests, a wide range of people is required, but they are organized into separate groups in terms of stratifying criteria, such as age, gender, education, occupation, and having or not having had a certain experience. Participants for each group can then be selected randomly or through some kind of snowball sampling method. The aim is to establish whether there is any systematic variation in the ways in which different groups discuss a matter. For example, drawing on findings from their research into the responses of women to viewing violence, Schlesinger et al. (1992) derived a similar kind of conclusion. They showed their fourteen groups (see Table 21.1) four items: an episode of *Crimewatch UK* featuring some violence; an episode of *EastEnders* in which violence was incidental; a television drama, *Closing Ranks*, featuring marital violence; and the Hollywood movie *The Accused*, which contains an extremely vivid rape scene. Drawing on their findings concerning the groups' responses to these showings, the authors concluded:

> in general, the salience in any particular programme of ethnicity, class, or gender or a lived experience such as violence is greatest for those *most directly involved* and diminishes in importance with social distance. Having a particular experience or a particular background does

significantly affect the interpretation of a given text. The four programmes screened are obviously open to various readings. However, on the evidence, *how* they are read is fundamentally affected by various socio-cultural factors and by lived experience.

> (Schlesinger et al. 1992: 168; emphases in original)

A slight variation on this approach can be seen in Kitzinger's (1994) study of reactions to media representations of AIDS (see Research in focus 21.1 and Table 21.1). Her groups were made up of people in a variety of different situations. Some of these were what she calls 'general population groups' (for example, a team of civil engineers working on the same site), but others were made up of groups that might have a special interest in AIDS (for example, male prostitutes, intravenous drug users). However, the general point is that focus group practitioners often try to discern patterns of variation by putting together groups with particular attributes.

A further issue is whether to select people who are unknown to each other or to use natural groupings (for example, friends, co-workers, students on the same course). Some researchers prefer to exclude people who know each other on the grounds that pre-existing styles of interaction or status differences may contaminate the session. Not all writers accept this rule of thumb.

Some prefer to select natural groups whenever possible. Kitzinger (1994; Research in focus 21.1 and Table 21.1) used groups made up of people who knew each other. The reason was that she wanted the discussions to be as natural as possible, and she felt that this quality would be enhanced through the use of members of what she calls 'pre-existing groups'. Holbrook and Jackson (1996) report that, for their research on shopping centres, they initially tried to secure participants who did not know each other, but this strategy did not result in anybody coming forward. They then sought out participants from various clubs and social centres in the vicinity of the two North London shopping centres that were the focus of their research. They argue that, in view of their interest in research questions concerning shopping in relation to the construction of identity and how it relates to people's sense of place, recruiting people who knew each other was a highly appropriate strategy.

However, opting for a strategy of recruiting people entirely from natural groups is not always feasible, because of difficulties of securing participation. Fenton et al. (1998: 121), in the context of their research on the representation of social science research (Table 21.1), report that they preferred to recruit 'naturally occurring groups' but that 'this was not always achievable'. Morgan (1998a) suggests that one problem with using natural groups is that people who know each other well are likely to operate with taken-for-granted assumptions that they feel do not need to be brought to the fore. He suggests that, if it is important for the researcher to bring out such assumptions, groups of strangers are likely to work better.

Asking questions

The focus group researcher also has to consider to what extent there should be a set of questions that must be addressed during each session. This issue is similar to the considerations about how unstructured an interview should be in qualitative interviewing (see Chapter 20). Some researchers prefer to use just one or two very general questions to stimulate discussion, with the moderator intervening as necessary along the lines outlined above. For example, in their research on knowledge about heart attacks, Morgan and Spanish (1985) asked participants to discuss just two topics. One topic was 'who has heart attacks and why?'; here participants were encouraged to talk about people they knew who had had attacks. The second topic was 'what causes and what prevents heart attacks?'

However, other researchers prefer to inject somewhat more structure into the organization of the focus group sessions. An example of this is the research on the viewing of violence by women by Schlesinger et al. (1992; see Table 21.1). For example, in relation to the movie *The Accused*, the reactions of the audiences were gleaned through 'guiding questions' under five main headings, the first three of which had several more specific elements.

- Initially, the participants were given the opportunity to discuss the film in terms of such issues as perceived purpose of the film; gratifications from the film; and realism and storyline.

- The questioning then moved on to reactions to the characters such as Sarah Tobias (the woman who is raped); the three rapists; the female lawyer; and the male lawyers.

- Participants were then asked about their reactions to scenes such as the rape; the female lawyer's decision to change from not supporting Sarah Tobias's case to supporting it; and the winning of the case.

- Participants were asked about their reactions to the inclusion of the rape scene.

- Finally, they were asked about how they perceived the film's value, in particular whether the fact that it is American made a difference to their reactions.

While the research by Schlesinger et al. (1992) clearly contained quite a lot of specific questions to be addressed, the questions themselves were fairly general and were designed to ensure that there was some comparability between the focus group sessions in terms of gauging participants' reactions to each of the four programmes that were shown. Moreover, there was ample opportunity for moderators to react to points made in the course of the sessions. The authors write that 'due allowance was made for specific issues raised within a given group' (Schlesinger et al. 1992: 28). Moreover, the early questions were designed to generate initial reactions in a relatively open-ended way. Such a general approach to questioning, which is fairly common in focus group research, allows the researcher to navigate the channel between, on the one side, addressing the research questions and ensuring comparability between sessions, and, on the other side, allowing participants to raise issues they see as significant and in their own terms.

Clearly, there are different questioning strategies and approaches to moderating focus group sessions. Most seem to approximate to the research by Fenton et al. depicted in Research in focus 21.3, which lies in between the rather open-ended approach employed by Morgan and Spanish (1985) and the somewhat more structured one used by Schlesinger et al. (1992). Similarly, Macnaghten and Jacobs (1997; see Table 21.1) employed a 'topic guide' and grouped the topics to be covered into areas of discussion. Their middle-of-the-road approach in terms of the degree to which the questioning was structured can be seen in the following passage, in which a group of working women reveal a cynicism about governments and experts regarding the reality of environmental problems, a tendency that could also be seen in most of the other groups, which similarly preferred to rely on their own sensory experience (in this passage 'F' is 'female'):

F	They only tell us what they want us to know. And that's just the end of that, so we are left with a fog in your brain, so you just think—what have I to worry about? I don't know what they're on about.
Mod	So why do Government only tell us what they want us to hear?
F	To keep your confidence going. (All together)
Mod	So if someone provides an indicator which says the economy is improving you won't believe it?
F	They've been saying it for about ten years, but where? I can't see anything!
F	Every time there's an election they say the economy is improving.

(Macnaghten and Jacobs 1997: 18)

In this passage, we see an emphasis on the topic to be addressed but a capacity to pick up on what the group says. A rather structured approach to focus group questioning was used in a cross-national study of young Europeans' 'orientations to the present and future, with respect to their "careers" as partners, parents and workers' (Smithson and Brannen 2002: 14). The countries involved were Ireland, Norway, Portugal, Sweden, and the UK. Three hundred and twelve people participated in the research, but the number of groups and the number of participants in them varied considerably by country. The somewhat more structured approach to questioning can be seen in the fact that there were nineteen topic areas, each of which had several questions. For example, for the topic of 'jobs':

- What do you want from a job?
- What is important when you look for a job?
- Do you think it is important to support yourself?
- How do you expect to do that (job/state/spouse/other way)?
- Do you think it is different for women and men of your age?
- Do you expect to be in paid employment in five years' time/ten years' time? (Brannen et al. 2002: 190)

The more structured approach to questioning that seems to have occurred with these groups may have been the result of the demands of ensuring comparability between the sessions conducted in the different nations.

There is probably no one best way, and the style of questioning and moderating is likely to be affected by various factors, such as the nature of the research topic (for example, if it is one that the researcher already knows a lot about, a modicum of structure is feasible) and levels of interest and/or knowledge among participants in the research (for example, a low level of participant interest may require a somewhat more structured approach). Kandola (2012) recommends asking for examples and further elaboration as a means of stimulating further discussion that may allow amplification of key points. The sensitivity of the topic may be a further consideration where several open-ended questions may be needed to act as 'icebreakers' (see Research in focus 21.5). Whichever strategy of questioning is employed, the focus group researcher should generally be prepared to allow at least some discussion that departs from the interview guide, since such debate may provide new and unexpected insights. A more structured approach to questioning might inhibit such spontaneity, but it is unlikely to remove it altogether.

Beginning and finishing

It is recommended that focus group sessions begin with an introduction, whereby the moderators thank people for coming and introduce themselves, the goals of the research are briefly outlined, the reasons for recording the session are given, and the format of the focus group session is sketched out. It is also important to present some of the conventions of focus group participation, such as: only one person should speak at a time (perhaps explaining the problems that occur with recordings when people speak over each other); that all data will be treated confidentially and anonymized; that the session is open, and everyone's views are important; and the amount of time that will be taken up. During the introduction phase, focus group researchers also often ask participants to fill in forms providing basic socio-demographic information about themselves, such as age, gender, occupation, and where resident. Participants should then be encouraged to introduce themselves and to write out their first names on a card placed in front of them, so that everyone's name is known.

At the end, moderators should thank the group members for their participation and explain very briefly what will happen to the data they have supplied. If a further session is to be arranged, steps should be taken to coordinate this.

Research in focus 21.5
Questioning in a focus group

Warr's (2005) study was concerned with notions of intimacy among predominantly socio-economically disadvantaged people in New Zealand. Most of her participants were aged between 18 and 29 years. Her questioning strategy was to begin with what she calls an 'icebreaker', which entailed asking participants about a popular movie that was on release at the time. Such an opening can be useful in stimulating initial thoughts on issues of intimacy, given the frequency with which relationships are emphasized in movies. This icebreaker was followed by the following questions:

'How do you know when you've in love?' 'How do you know when someone is in love with you?' 'In getting to know people, who makes the first move?' and 'How do you learn about sex and love?' To conclude, I would request participants to imagine the future in terms of whether they expected to settle down with someone, get married, or have children. The theme list posed very broad questions for discussion so there was plenty of scope for participants to pursue the topics in undirected ways and to introduce other issues as required.

(Warr 2005: 156)

This approach clearly entailed using broad questions or topics as a means of stimulating discussion.

Group interaction in focus group sessions

Kitzinger (1994) has observed that reports of focus group research frequently do not take into account interaction within the group. This is surprising, because it is precisely the operation of social interaction and its forms and impact that distinguishes the focus group from the individual interview. Yet, as Kitzinger observes, very few publications based on focus group research cite or draw inferences from patterns of interaction within the group. Wilkinson reviewed over 200 studies based on focus groups and published between 1946 and 1996. She concluded: 'Focus group data is most commonly presented as if it were one-to-one interview data, with interactions between group participants rarely reported, let alone analysed' (S. Wilkinson 1998: 112).

In the context of her research on AIDS in the mass media, Kitzinger (1994) drew attention to two types of interaction in focus groups: complementary and argumentative interactions. The former bring out the elements of the social world that provide participants' own frameworks of understanding. The discussion in Research in focus 21.2 illustrates the agreement that emerges about the differences between the natural and the social sciences in people's minds. The discussion demonstrates broad agreement between the participants concerning such issues as the lack of control and the subjective nature of interpretation. Such a view is an emergent product of the interaction, with each participant building on the preceding remark. A similar sequence can be discerned in the following passage, which is taken from Morgan and Spanish's (1985: 414) research on heart attack victims:

No. 1   But I think maybe what we're saying here is that there's no one cause of heart attacks, there's no one type of person, there's probably umpteen different types of heart attacks and causes coming from maybe smoking, maybe obesity, maybe stress, maybe design fault, hereditary, overwork, change in life style. Any of these things in themselves could be . . .

No. 2   And when you start putting them in combination [unclear] be speeding up on yourself.

No. 3   Yeah, you may be really magnifying each one of these particular things.

No. 2   Yeah, and depending on how, and in each person that magnification is different. Some people can take a little stress without doing any damage, some people can take a little smoking, a little drinking, a little obesity, without doing any damage. But you take a little of each of these and put them together and you're starting to increase the chances of damage. And any one of these that takes a magnitude leap increases the chances.

This sequence brings out the consensus that emerges around the question of who has heart attacks and why. No. 1 summarizes several factors that have been discussed; No. 2 then introduces the possible significance of some of these factors existing in combination; No. 3 agrees about the importance of combinations of factors; and No. 2 summarizes the position of the group on the salience of combinations of factors, raising at the same time the possibility that for each person there are unique combinations that may be responsible for heart attacks.

Munday (2006) suggests that the capacity of focus group research to highlight the emergence of a consensus as well as the mechanics of that consensus makes it a potent tool for research into collective identity. She gives the example of her research on social movements and in particular a focus group with members of a Women's Institute (WI). For example, she asked the group about the movie *Calendar Girls*, based on the nude calendar made by Rylestone WI members some years previously. Munday writes that she asked the question because she felt it might encourage them to discuss the traditional image of WIs as staid and stuffy. Instead, the women chose to discuss the Rylestone WI and its members, such as the impact that the calendar's notoriety had on its members. At a later stage, the following interaction ensued:

Alice   It might appeal more to the younger ones than perhaps the older members don't you think?... Although I suppose they were middle-aged ladies themselves.

Jane   Oh yes.

Mar   Oh yes they were yes.

Jane   They weren't slim and what have you.

Mary   Oh no no.

Jane   ( )

Mary   No they were quite well . . .

Jane   They were.

Mary   Weren't they?

June   I mean it was very well done because you never saw anything you wouldn't want to.

(Munday 2006: 100)

Munday argues that the discussion of the movie did not revolve around dispelling the traditional image of WIs, but instead on dispelling a traditional image of older women, while at the same time recognizing that the women's respectability was not compromised. Thus, a sense of collective identity surrounding gender emerged that was different from how the researcher had anticipated the discussion would develop.

However, as Kitzinger (1994) suggests, arguments in focus groups can be equally revealing. She suggests that moderators can play an important role in identifying differences of opinion and exploring with participants the factors that may lie behind them. Disagreement can provide participants with the opportunity to revise their opinions or to think more about the reasons why they hold the view that they do. By way of illustration, a passage from Schlesinger et al. (1992; see Table 21.1) is presented. The group is made up of English Afro-Caribbean women with no experience of violence. The debate is concerned with the rape scene in *The Accused* and reveals a misgiving that its inclusion may actually be exploiting sexual violence:

Speaker 1   I think . . . that they could've explained it. They could easily leave that rape scene.

Speaker 2   But it's like that other film we watched. You don't realise the full impact, like, the one we were watching, the first one [*Crimewatch*], until you've got the reconstruction.

Speaker 3   Yeah, but I think with that sort of film, it would cause more damage than it would good, I mean, if someone had been raped, would you like to have [to] sit through that again?

(Schlesinger et al. 1992: 151–2)

The debate then continues to consider the significance of the scene for men:

Speaker 1   But you wouldn't miss anything, would you? What would you? All right, if you didn't watch that particular part, would you miss anything? You could still grasp it couldn't you?

Speaker 2   You could still grasp it but the enormous effect that it's had on us at the moment, it wouldn't be as drastic . . . without those.

Speaker 1   Yeah, but I'm thinking how would men see it? . . .

Speaker 3   That's what I'm saying, how would they view that scene?

Speaker 4   They couldn't believe it either, I mean, they didn't—they didn't think they were doing any wrong.

Speaker 1   Men would sit down and think, 'Well, she asked for it. She was enjoying it and look, the men around enjoyed it.'

(Schlesinger et al. 1992: 152)

One factor, then, that seems to be behind the unease of some of the women about the inclusion of the vivid rape scene is that it may be enjoyed by men, rather than being found repulsive, and that they would identify with the onlookers in the film. This account has come about because of the discussion that is stimulated by disagreement within the group and allows a rounded account of women's reactions to the scene to be forged. As Kitzinger (1994) argues, drawing attention to patterns of interaction within focus groups allows the researcher to determine how group participants view the issues with which they are confronted in their own terms. The posing of questions by and agreement and disagreement among participants helps to elicit their own stances on these issues. The resolution of disagreements also helps to force participants to express the grounds on which they hold particular views.

As Warr's (2005) research on intimacy found, focus groups frequently reveal a mixture of agreement and disagreement among participants (see Table 21.1 and Research in focus 21.5 for more on this research as well as Research in focus 21.6 for an example of a disagreement in a focus group). This feature allows the researcher to draw out the tensions associated with people's private beliefs in relation to wider public debates and expectations. This was of particular significance for Warr's interest in intimacy, because of the difficulties involved in resolving disagreements about what is and is not appropriate in matters of love and sex. Warr argues that focusing on areas of agreement and disagreement in focus groups can be a useful starting point for the interpretation and analysis of the qualitative data that derive from them. However, Wiles's (2014) focus group study of trust in GPs seems, from the many sequences of discussion supplied, to be characterized by high levels of agreement about the kinds of factors that make patients trust their GPs. The following, which is taken from a group of participants with visual impairment and which is discussing the importance of communication skills, is fairly representative:

Norma:	And I think that's the most important thing of all, really, is a doctor that will listen to you, and talk to you. That is really important; that's the start.
Beryl:	And they mustn't talk down to you. They've got to be on the same level. I mean I don't want the doctor that's going to sit in the chair and say 'I'm a doctor and I know everything and you're nothing'.
Elizabeth:	They talk to you.
Beryl:	I think they've got to be on the same level all the time.
Margaret:	Some doctors are rather abrupt, and that puts you off right away.
Rose:	Yeah, so you want them to listen to you, to allow you to talk.
Beryl:	And not use long words that I do not understand.
Arthur:	Well you've got to interject then, if they use a long word you've got to say, 'explain what you mean'.
Beryl:	Well I've always done that, and asked for simpler words.
Elizabeth:	Well that will depend on the attitude of the doctor. If he's abrupt, you cannot interrupt him. You are already, when he's abrupt when you go in, you're already intimidated.

(Wiles 2014: no page number)

While interaction and disagreements are distinctive characteristics of focus groups compared to individual interviews, it is also the case that they add a layer of complexity to the analysis of the ensuing qualitative data. Most of the principles and approaches for data analysis that will be identified in Chapter 24 can and should be usefully applied to the analysis of focus group data. In addition, Barbour (2007) recommends seeking out patterns within focus group data—for example, showing how particular interpretations are associated with individuals in different positions or with certain social characteristics. This might involve seeking out intra-group or inter-group patterns, depending on whether each group is made up of similar individuals or different ones or a mixture of both.

Morgan (2010) argues that focus group data that emphasize group interaction are not necessarily superior to those that do not. This is clearly a different position from that proposed by Kitzinger (1994). He argues that it all depends on what the researcher wishes to demonstrate. Sometimes, quoting what individuals have said can be more effective than passages of interaction, if what the researcher wants to show is an often repeated position. Quoting sequences of interaction might be less effective in making the point and also uses up far more words, which may be a consideration when there is a tight word limit. One situation that Morgan refers to as almost always warranting emphasizing interaction is when a new topic is introduced and this very rapidly stimulates a series of responses from a variety of focus group participants. The emerging consensus or dispute in this situation is clearly very significant to participants and warrants being quoted in detail.

Research in focus 21.6
Disagreement in a focus group

In the following extract from the CCSE research, three focus group participants engage in a discussion with no intervention or involvement by the moderator, David, after his initial question. The participants are discussing Tupac Shakur, a rap singer.

David	Who would be more the kind of modern artists you would listen to . . . ?
Yousuf	Tupac. Tupac Shakur. I'm not into that Hindi or nothing. R&B and Hip Hop unless you recommend to me it like to me it's Tupac.
Moin	I think Tupac, the way he sings his songs and jumps around is a thug and I don't really appreciate him.
Kamran	Who?
Moin	Tupac Shakur, Machiavelli he calls himself. You see a lot of women jumping up and down, flashy cars, he is singing about his life experience, no that doesn't do anything for me. I would rather listen to some Bollywood songs.

(Silva and Wright 2005: 10)

On the face of it, this exchange from a focus group of Pakistani working-class participants may seem unexceptional, but Silva and Wright report that Yousuf played very little further part in the session after the suggestion that he proffered had been undermined by Moin and to some extent by Kamran claiming not to have heard of Tupak. This is one of the risks of focus groups—namely, that, although they can capitalize on diversity of perspectives, sometimes disagreement may be difficult to deal with and may be offputting to some participants. Should the moderator, David, have intervened to quell the disagreement? Probably not: disagreements about taste are common in everyday life, and he could not really have anticipated Yousuf's unusual response.

Online focus groups

In a similar way to qualitative interviews, there has been a growth in the use of online focus groups, where there is a fundamental distinction between **synchronous** and **asynchronous online focus groups**. With the former, the focus group is in real time, so that contributions are made more or less immediately after previous contributions (whether from the moderator or from other participants) among a group of participants, all of whom are simultaneously online. Contributions can be responded to as soon as they are typed (and with some forms of software, the contributions can be seen as they are being typed). As Mann and Stewart (2000) observe, because several participants can type in a response to a contribution at the same time, the conventions of normal turn-taking in conversations are largely sidelined.

With asynchronous groups, focus group exchanges are not in real time. Email is one form of asynchronous communication that has been used (see Research in focus 21.7 for an example). For example, the moderator might ask a question and then send the email containing it to focus group participants. The latter will be able to reply to the moderator and to other group members at some time in the future. Such groups get around the time zone problem and are probably easier than synchronous groups for participants who are not skilled at using the keyboard. However, the risk of dropouts is greater.

One of the advantages of both types of online focus groups stems from the possibility of using a 'captive population' of people who are already communicating with each other, unlike face-to-face focus groups that are brought together for the purpose of the focus group meeting. This means researchers are often able to take advantage of pre-existing social groups of people who are already communicating with one another online (Stewart and Williams 2005). Online focus groups also enable geographical distances to be overcome. International focus groups can enable cross-cultural discussions at a relatively low cost. However, setting up a time and place

Research in focus 21.7
An early asynchronous focus group study

Adriaenssens and Cadman (1999) report their experiences of conducting a market research exercise to explore the launch of an online share-trading platform in the UK. Participants were in two groups: one group of active shareholders (twenty participants) and a second group of passive shareholders (ten participants). They were identified through the MORI Financial Services database as 'upmarket shareholders who were also Internet users' (1999: 418–19). The participants who were identified were very geographically spread, so online focus groups were ideal. Questions were emailed to participants in five phases with a deadline for returning replies, which were then copied anonymously to the rest of the participants. The questions were sent in the body of the email, rather than as attachments, to solve problems of software incompatibility. After each phase, a summary document was produced and circulated to participants for comment, thus injecting a form of respondent validation into the project. The researchers found it difficult to ensure that participants kept to the deadlines, which in fact were rather tight, although it was felt that having a schedule of deadlines that was kept to as far as possible was helpful in preventing dropouts. The researchers felt that the group of active shareholders was too large to manage and suggest groups of no more than ten participants.

for synchronous online focus group discussions between international participants may be problematic because of time zone differences, making it hard to find a time that is convenient to everyone (Stewart and Williams 2005).

Conferencing software is used for synchronous groups and is often used for asynchronous groups as well. This may mean that focus group participants will require access to the software, which can be undesirable if the software needs to be loaded onto their computers. Participants may not feel confident about loading the software, and there may be compatibility problems with particular machines and operating systems. Research in focus 21.8 provides an example of the use of this kind of software in an online focus group study.

Selecting participants for online focus groups is potentially difficult, not least because they must normally have access to the necessary hardware and software. One possibility is to use questionnaires as a springboard for identifying possible participants, while another possibility is to contact them by email, this being a relatively quick and economical way of contacting a large number of possible participants. For their study of users of a parenting website, O'Connor and Madge (see Research in focus 21.8) secured their online focus group participants through a Web survey.

The requisite number of participants is affected by the question of whether the online focus group is being conducted synchronously or asynchronously. Mann and Stewart (2000) advocate that, with the former type, the group should not be too large, because it can make it difficult for some people to participate, possibly because of limited keyboard skills, and they recommend groups

of between six and eight participants. Also, moderating the session can be more difficult with a large number. In asynchronous mode, such problems do not exist, and very large groups can be accommodated—certainly much larger ones than could be envisaged in a face-to-face context, although Adriaenssens and Cadman (1999) suggest that large groups can present research management problems.

Before starting the focus group, moderators are advised to send out a welcome message introducing the research and laying out some of the ground rules for the ongoing discussion. There is evidence that participants respond more positively if the researchers reveal something about themselves (Curasi 2001). This can be done in the opening message or by creating links to personal websites.

One problem with the asynchronous focus group is that moderators cannot be available online twenty-four hours a day, although it is not inconceivable that moderators could have a shift system to deal with this limitation. This lack of continuous availability means that emails or postings may be sent and responded to without any ability of the moderator to intervene or participate. This feature may not be a problem, but could become so if offensive messages were being sent or if it meant that the discussion was going off at a complete tangent from which it would be difficult to redeem the situation. Further, because focus group sessions in asynchronous mode may go on for a long time, perhaps for several days or even weeks, there is a greater likelihood of participants dropping out of the study. A further problem arises from response rates, which may be lower than for face-to-face focus groups (Stewart and Williams 2005). Even though it is relatively easy for the researcher to contact a large number of possible respondents using email, the response rates of those wishing to participate in an online focus group has been found to be quite low (between 5 and 20 per cent). Further reservations have been expressed about the lack of non-verbal data obtained from online focus groups, such as facial expression. Underhill and Olmstead (2003) compared data from synchronous online focus groups with parallel data from conventional face-to-face ones and found little difference in terms of data quantity or quality. By contrast, Brüggen and Willems (2009) found that when they compared synchronous online focus group findings with those deriving from face-to-face ones in a market research area, the traditional mode of delivery yielded data of superior depth. Abrams et al. (2015) compared the quality of data deriving from two face-to-face, two

Research in focus 21.8
A synchronous focus group study

O'Connor and Madge (2001, 2003; see also Madge and O'Connor 2002) employed conferencing software in connection with a virtual focus group study of the use of online information for parents. The research was specifically concerned with one UK parenting website (**www.babyworld.co.uk**, accessed 8 December 2014). Initially, the researchers set up a **Web survey** (see later in the chapter for information about this technique) on the use of this website. When respondents sent in their questionnaire, they were thanked for their participation and asked to email the researchers if they were prepared to be interviewed in depth. Of the 155 respondents who returned questionnaires, 16 agreed to be interviewed. Interviewees were sent the software to install on their own machines. The researchers tried to ensure that each group was asked more or less the same questions, so the researchers worked in pairs whereby one cut and pasted questions into the discussion (or otherwise typed questions) and the other acted as a focus group moderator by thinking about the evolution of the discussion and about when and how to intervene. For each session, the researchers introduced themselves and asked participants to do likewise. In addition, they had placed descriptions and photographs of themselves on a website to which participants were directed. An important part of the process of building rapport was the fact that both of the researchers were mothers. One of the findings reported is that the greater anonymity afforded by the Internet gave participants greater confidence to ask embarrassing questions, a finding that has implications for online focus groups. This can be seen in the following extract:

Amy: I feel better askign BW [Babyworld] than my health visitor as they're not goign to see how bad I am at housekeeping!!!

Kerry: I feel the same. Like the HV [health visitor] is judging even though she says she isn't

Kerry: Although my HV has been a life line as I suffer from PND [post natal depression]

Amy: Also, there are some things that are so little that you don't want to feel like you're wasting anyone's time. Askign the HV or GP might get in the way of something mreo important, whereas sending an email, the person can answer it when convenient

Amy: My HV is very good, but her voice does sound patronising. I'msure she doesn't mean it, but it does get to me . . .

Kerry: Being anon means that you don't get embarrassed asking about a little point or something personal.

(O'Connor and Madge 2001: 10.4)

It is striking that this brief extract reveals a good flow without intervention by the researchers. It contains several misspellings and mistakes (for example, 'I'msure'), but these are retained to preserve the reality of the interaction. The researchers did not have to transcribe the material because it was already in textual form. Also, the fact that participants appear to relish the anonymity of the Internet as a source of information has implications for online focus groups, because it may be that participants find it easier to ask naive questions or to make potentially embarrassing comments than in face-to-face focus groups.

Tips and skills
Advantages and disadvantages of online focus groups and personal interviews compared to face-to-face focus groups and interviews in qualitative research

Here is a summary of the main advantages and disadvantages of online focus groups and personal interviews compared to their face-to-face counterparts. The two methods are combined because the tally of advantages and disadvantages applies more or less equally well to both of them.

Advantages

- Online interviews and focus groups are extremely cheap to conduct compared to comparable face-to-face equivalents. They are likely to take longer, however, especially when conducted asynchronously.
- Interviewees or focus group participants who would otherwise normally be inaccessible (for example, because they are located in another country) or hard to involve in research (for example, very senior executives, people with almost no time for participation) can more easily be involved.
- Large numbers of possible online focus group participants can be contacted by email.
- Interviewees and focus group participants are able to reread what they (and, in the case of focus groups, others) have previously written in their replies. This does not apply to the online audio-visual medium.
- People participating in the research may be better able to fit the interviews into their own time.
- People participating in the research do not have to make additional allowances for the time spent travelling to a focus group session.
- The interviews do not have to be audio-recorded, thus eliminating interviewee apprehension about speaking and being recorded. This does not apply to the online audio-visual medium, which requires recording.
- There is no need for transcription. This represents an enormous advantage because of the time and cost involved in getting recorded interview sessions transcribed. This advantage does not apply to the online audio-visual medium.
- As a result of the previous point, the interview transcripts can be more or less immediately entered into a computer-assisted qualitative data analysis software (CAQDAS) program of the kind introduced in Chapter 25.
- The transcripts of the interviews are more likely to be accurate, because the problems that may arise from mishearing or not hearing at all what is said do not arise. This is a particular advantage with focus group discussions, because it can be difficult to establish who is speaking and impossible to distinguish what is said when participants speak at the same time. This advantage does not apply to the online audio-visual medium.
- Focus group participants can employ pseudonyms so that their identity can be more easily concealed from others in the group. This can make it easier for participants to discuss potentially embarrassing issues or to divulge potentially unpopular views. The ability to discuss sensitive issues generally may be greater in electronic than face-to-face focus groups and individual interviews. This advantage does not apply to the online audio-visual medium.
- In online focus groups, shy or quiet participants may find it easier than in face-to-face contexts to come to the fore.
- Equally, in focus groups overbearing participants are less likely to predominate, but in synchronous groups variations in keyboard skills may militate slightly against equal participation.
- Participants are less likely to be influenced by such characteristics as the age, ethnicity, or appearance (and possibly even gender if pseudonyms are used) of other participants in a focus group. This advantage does not apply to the online audio-visual medium.
- Similarly, interviewees and focus group participants are much less likely to be affected by characteristics of interviewers or moderators respectively, so that interviewer bias is less likely. This advantage may not apply to the online audio-visual medium.

- When interviewees and participants are online at home, they are essentially being provided with an 'anonymous, safe and non-threatening environment' (O'Connor and Madge 2001: 11.2), which may be especially helpful to vulnerable groups.

- Similarly, researchers are not confronted with the potentially discomfiting experience of having to invade other people's homes or workplaces, which can themselves sometimes be unsafe environments.

Disadvantages

- The balance of evidence tends to show that face-to-face focus groups yield data of superior quality compared to online ones.

- Only people with access to online facilities and/or who find them relatively straightforward are likely to be in a position to participate.

- It can be more difficult for the interviewer/moderator to establish rapport and to engage with interviewees. However, when the topic is of interest to participants, this may not be a great problem.

- It can be difficult in asynchronous interviews to retain over a longer term any rapport that has been built up.

- Probing is more difficult though not impossible. Curasi (2001) reports some success in eliciting further information from respondents, but it is easier for interviewees to ignore or forget about the requests for further information or for expansion on answers given. This problem is less likely to apply to the online audio-visual medium.

- Asynchronous interviews may take a very long time to complete, depending on participants' cooperativeness.

- With asynchronous interviews and focus groups, there may be a greater tendency for participants to discontinue their involvement than is likely to be the case with face-to-face contexts.

- There is less spontaneity of response, since interviewees can reflect on their answers to a much greater extent than is possible in a face-to-face situation. However, this can be construed as an advantage in some respects, since interviewees are likely to give more considered replies (though some commentators see the ability to provide more considered replies a disadvantage; see Adriaenssens and Cadman 1999). The problem of spontaneity may not apply to the online audio-visual medium.

- There may be a tendency for refusal to participate to be higher in online personal interviews and from possible online focus group participants.

- The researcher cannot be certain that the people who are interviewed are who they say they are (though this issue may apply on occasion to face-to-face interviews as well). This problem is less likely to apply to the online audio-visual medium.

- Turn-taking conventions between interviewer/moderator and interviewee/focus group participant are more likely to be disrupted. This problem is less likely to apply to the online audio-visual medium.

- In synchronous focus groups, variations in keyboard skills may make equal levels of participation difficult. This problem does not apply to the online audio-visual medium.

- Participating from home in online interviews and focus groups requires considerable commitment from interviewees and participants if they have to install software onto their computers and remain online for extended periods of time, thereby incurring expense if they have a contract with an Internet Service Provider whereby their use of broadband is limited (though it is possible to offer remuneration for such costs).

- The interviewer/moderator may not be aware that the interviewee/participant is distracted by something and in such circumstances will continue to ask questions as if he or she had the person's full attention.

- Online connections may be lost, so research participants need to know what to do in case of such an eventuality.

- Interviewers/moderators cannot capitalize on body language or other forms of non-verbal data that might suggest puzzlement, or in the case of focus groups a thwarted desire to contribute to the discussion. This problem is less likely to apply to the online audio-visual medium.

Sources: Clapper and Massey (1996); Adriaenssens and Cadman (1999); Tse (1999); Mann and Stewart (2000); Curasi (2001); O'Connor and Madge (2001); Sweet (2001); Davis et al. (2004); Evans et al. (2008); Hewson and Laurent (2008); Abrams et al. (2015); www.restore.ac.uk/orm/interviews/intcontents.htm (accessed 8 December 2014).

online audio-visual (that is using software such as Skype as a medium of delivery), and two online text-only focus groups. It was found that face-to-face focus groups produced considerably more topic-related data. Coders rated the face-to-face and online audio-visual face-to-face focus groups as having superior data richness to online text-only ones, and the latter were also found to be inferior in terms of numbers of words produced. The balance of evidence, then, still seems to favour the traditional focus group environment, but the online audio-visual mode fares reasonably well and may prove a viable alternative in the future as environments such as Skype become more familiar.

Online focus groups are unlikely to replace their face-to-face counterparts. Instead, they are likely to be employed in connection with certain kinds of research topic and/or sample. As regards the latter, dispersed or inaccessible people are especially relevant to online focus group research. As Sweet (2001) points out, relevant topics are likely to be ones involving sensitive issues and ones concerned with Internet use—for example, the studies discussed in Research in focus 21.7 and 21.8.

In Tips and skills 'Advantages and disadvantages of online focus groups and personal interviews compared to face-to-face focus groups and interviews in qualitative research' the discussion of online focus groups is combined with a discussion of online personal interviews, which were discussed in Chapter 20, since most of the elements in the balance sheet of advantages and disadvantages are the same.

Limitations of focus groups

Focus groups clearly have considerable potential for research questions in which the processes through which meaning is jointly constructed are likely to be of particular interest. Indeed, it may be that, even when this is not a prominent emphasis, the focus group method may be appropriate and even advantageous, since it allows participants' perspectives—an important feature of much qualitative research (see Chapter 17)—to be revealed in ways that are different from individual interviews (for example, through discussion, participants' questions, arguments, and so on). It also offers considerable potential for feminist researchers. What, then, might be its chief limitations?

- The researcher probably has less control over proceedings than with the individual interview. By no means all writers on focus groups perceive this as a disadvantage, and indeed feminist researchers often see it as an advantage. Kamberelis and Dimitriadis (2005) note that some focus group researchers value the method because it provides greater opportunity than most other methods for research participants to have some 'ownership' of the interview and the research process more generally. However, the question of control raises issues for researchers of how far they can allow participants to 'take over' the running of a focus group. There is clearly a delicate balance

Student experience
The challenges of focus groups

For her research around the topic of childhood obesity with mothers of young children, Samantha Vandermark conducted two focus groups of six people per group. She clearly found moderating the groups challenging:

> Organisation of the focus groups was a primary difficulty, not only in terms of getting the right demographic for my samples but getting all of the mothers in one place at one time to conduct the focus group. My skills as an interviewer and moderator were tested as the mothers often tended to lose focus on the questions and shift conversation onto broader topics; I had to ensure that I used my initiative to adapt the questions according to the flow of conversation, keeping the questions relevant and the respondents interested.

This experience demonstrates that it is important to remain very active in a focus group session so that you do not lose control over the proceedings.

To read more, go to the Online Resource Centre: www.oxfordtextbooks.co.uk/orc/brymansrm5e/

between how involved moderators should be and how far a set of prompts or questions should influence the conduct of a focus group, as some of the earlier discussions have suggested. What is not clear is the degree to which it is appropriate to surrender control of a focus group to its participants, especially when there is a reasonably explicit set of research questions to be answered, as is commonly the case, for example, in funded research.

- The data are difficult to analyse. A huge amount of data can be very quickly produced. Developing a strategy of analysis that incorporates themes in both what people say and patterns of interaction is not easy. Also, focus group recordings are particularly prone to inaudible elements, which affects transcription. However, studies such as those of Morgan and Spanish (1985) and Kitzinger (1994) demonstrate that the examination of group interaction can be used to show how issues of thematic interest arise in the course of discussion.

- They are difficult to organize. Not only do you have to secure the agreement of people to participate in your study; you also need to persuade them to turn up at a particular time. Small payments, such as book or store tokens, are sometimes made to induce participation, but nonetheless it is common for people not to turn up. As a result, it is a common practice in focus group circles to over-recruit for each session on the grounds that at least one or two people will not turn up.

- The recordings are probably more time-consuming to transcribe than equivalent recordings of individual interviews, because of variations in voice pitch and the need to take account of who says what. For example, Bloor et al. (2001) suggest that a focus group session lasting one hour can take up to eight hours to transcribe, which is longer than would be likely in connection with an equivalent personal interview.

- There are problems with focus groups that are not encountered in individual interviews, most notably the tendency for two or more participants to speak at the same time. It is usually very difficult and often impossible to make sense of and therefore transcribe the portions of recordings where this has occurred. Moderators can ask participants not to speak at the same time, but in my experience it is difficult to prevent this from occurring in spite of constant warnings (see Research in focus 21.9 for an example).

Research in focus 21.9
Speaking at the same time in a focus group

Like Research in focus 21.6, this extract is taken from one of the twenty-five focus groups that were part of the CCSE project (see Research in focus 2.9). This is a group of unskilled and semi-skilled workers discussing museum visiting:

[All talking at once]

Stephanie   Please, please, I know I'm being like a schoolteacher . . .

Bill   No, no, we're all ears 'Miss'!

[General laughter]

Stephanie   Will you all shut up!

Tel   I don't think I would go to the [museum] in Swansea because it wouldn't be as good as the one in London. And please 'Miss' I need to piss.

Stephanie   All right then but no running in the corridors and make sure you wash your hands afterwards.

[General laughter]

(Silva and Wright 2005: 7)

The moderator, Stephanie, has clearly had problems stopping this group talking at the same time. She very cleverly turns it into a joke by likening herself to a schoolteacher, even telling them to shut up. The group seems to enter into the spirit of the joke but whether she was able to stop participants from talking over each other, thereby making audio-recording more or less impossible, is another question.

- There are possible problems of group effects. This includes the obvious problem of dealing with reticent speakers and with those who hog the stage! Krueger (1998: 59) suggests in relation to the problem of overly prominent participants that the moderator should make clear to the speaker and other group participants that other people's views are definitely required; for example, he suggests saying something like 'That's one point of view. Does anyone have another point of view?' As for those who do not speak very much, it is recommended that they are actively encouraged to say something. Also, as the well-known Asch experiments showed, an emerging group view may mean that a perfectly legitimate perspective held by just one individual may be suppressed (Asch 1951). There is also evidence that, as a group comes to share a certain point of view, group members come to think uncritically about it and to develop almost irrational attachments to it (Janis 1982). It is not known how far such group effects have an adverse impact on focus group findings, but they cannot be entirely ignored. It would be interesting to know how far agreement among focus group participants is more frequently encountered than disagreement (I have a hunch that it is), since the effects to which both Asch and Janis referred would lead us to expect more agreement than disagreement in focus group discussions.

- Related to this last issue is the fact that, in group contexts, participants may be more prone to expressing culturally expected views than in individual interviews. Morgan (2002) cites the case of a study in which group interviews with boys discussing relationships with girls were compared with individual interviews with them on the same topic. In the latter they expressed a degree of sensitivity that was not present in the group context, where more macho views tended to be forthcoming. This suggests that, in the group interviews, the boys were seeking to impress others and were being influenced by peer group norms. However, this does not render the group interview data questionable, because it may be precisely the gulf between privately and publicly held views that is of interest.

- Madriz (2000) proposes that there are circumstances when focus groups may not be appropriate, because of their potential for causing discomfort among participants. When such discomfort might arise, individual interviews will be preferable. Situations in which unease might be occasioned are: when intimate details of private lives need to be revealed; when participants may not be comfortable in each other's presence (for example, bringing together people who are in a hierarchical relationship to each other); and when participants are likely to disagree profoundly with each other.

 Checklist

Issues to consider for your focus group

○ Have you devised a clear and comprehensive way of introducing the research to participants?

○ Do the questions or topics you have devised allow you to answer all your research questions?

○ Have you piloted the guide with some appropriate respondents?

○ Have you devised a strategy for encouraging respondents to turn up for the focus group meeting?

○ Have you thought about what you will do if some participants do not turn up for the session?

○ Have you ensured that sessions will allow novel or unexpected themes and issues to arise?

○ Is your language in the questions clear and comprehensible?

○ Are your questions relevant to the people who are participating in the focus groups?

○ Have your questions been designed to elicit reflective discussions so that participants are not tempted to answer in 'yes' or 'no' terms?

○ Have your questions been designed to encourage group interaction and discussion?

○ Do your questions offer a real prospect of seeing the world from your interviewees' point of view rather than imposing your own frame of reference on them?

○ Are you familiar with the setting(s) in which the session will take place?

○ Are you thoroughly familiar with and have you tested your recording or audio-visual equipment?

○ Have you thought about how you will present yourself in the session, such as how you will be dressed?

○ Have you devised a strategy for dealing with silences?

○ Have you devised a strategy for dealing with participants who are reluctant to speak?

○ Have you devised a strategy for dealing with participants who speak too much and hog the discussion?

○ Do you have a strategy for how far you are going to intervene in the focus group discussion?

○ Do you have a strategy for dealing with the focus group if the discussion goes off in a tangent?

○ Have you tested out any aids that you are going to present to focus group participants (for example, visual aids, segments of film, case studies)?

 ## Key points

- The focus group is a group interview that is concerned with exploring a certain topic.
- The moderator generally tries to allow a relatively free rein to the discussion. However, there may be contexts in which it is necessary to ask fairly specific questions, especially when cross-group comparability is an issue.
- An important aspect of the focus group is the joint production of meaning among participants.
- Focus group discussions need to be recorded and transcribed.
- There are several issues concerning the recruitment of focus group participants—in particular, whether to use natural groupings and whether to employ stratifying criteria.
- Group interaction is an important component of discussions.
- Focus groups can be carried out online but this poses some challenges.
- Some writers view focus groups as being well suited to a feminist standpoint.

Questions for review

- Why might it be useful to distinguish between a focus group and a group interview?

Uses of focus groups

- What advantages might the focus group method offer in contrast to an individual qualitative interview?
- Evaluate the argument that the focus group can be viewed as a feminist method.

Conducting focus groups

- How involved should the moderator be?
- Why is it necessary to record and transcribe focus group sessions?
- Are there any circumstances in which it might be a good idea to select participants who know each other?
- What might be the advantages and disadvantages of using an interview guide in focus group sessions?

Group interaction in focus group sessions

- Why might it be important to treat group interaction as an important issue when analysing focus group data?

Online focus groups

- What is the significance of the distinction between synchronous and asynchronous focus groups?
- How different is the role of the moderator in online, as against face-to-face, focus groups?

Limitations of focus groups

- Does the potential for the loss of control over proceedings and for group effects damage the potential utility of the focus group as a method?
- How far do the greater problems of transcription and difficulty of analysis undermine the potential of focus groups?
- To what extent are focus groups a naturalistic approach to data collection?

....

Online Resource Centre

www.oxfordtextbooks.co.uk/orc/brymansrm5e/

Visit the Online Resource Centre to enrich your understanding of focus groups. Follow up links to other resources, test yourself using multiple choice questions, and gain further guidance and inspiration from the Student Researcher's Toolkit.

....

22

Language in qualitative research

Chapter outline

Chapter guide

This chapter is concerned with two approaches to the examination of language: conversation analysis and discourse analysis. For the practitioners of these approaches, language is an object of interest in its own right and not simply a resource through which research participants communicate with researchers. This chapter explores:

- the roots of conversation analysis in ethnomethodology;
- some of its rules and principles;
- the assumptions of discourse analysis;
- some of its analytic strategies;
- points of difference between the two approaches;
- features of a variant of discourse analysis called critical discourse analysis.

Introduction

Language is bound to be significant for social researchers. It is, after all, through language that we ask people questions in interviews and through which questions are answered. Understanding language categories has been an important component of research involving participant observation, because knowing how words are used and the meanings of specific terms in the local vernacular (often called 'argot') is frequently viewed as crucial to an appreciation of how the social world being studied is viewed by its members.

In this chapter, however, two approaches will be examined that treat language as their central focal points: **conversation analysis** (CA) and **discourse analysis** (DA). What is crucial about these approaches is that, unlike traditional views of the role of language in social research, they treat language as a topic rather than as a resource (admittedly a cliché). This means that language is treated as significantly more than a medium through which social research is conducted (such as asking questions in interviews). It becomes a focus of attention in its own right. While CA and DA do not exhaust the range of possibilities for studying language as a topic, they do represent two of the most prominent approaches. Each has developed a technical vocabulary and set of techniques. This chapter will outline some of their basic ingredients and draw attention to some contrasting features.

 # Conversation analysis

Conversation analysis (CA) is the fine-grained analysis of talk as it occurs in interaction in naturally-occurring situations. The talk is recorded and transcribed so that a detailed analysis can be carried out. These analyses are concerned with uncovering the underlying structures of talk in interaction and as such with the achievement of order through interaction. The roots of CA lie in **ethnomethodology**, a sociological position developed in the USA under the general tutelage of Harold Garfinkel and Harvey Sacks, though it is the latter with whom CA is most associated. Ethnomethodology takes as its basic focus of attention 'practical, common-sense reasoning' in everyday life and as such is fundamentally concerned with the notion of social life as an accomplishment. Social order is seen not as a pre-existing force constraining individual action, but as something that is worked at and accomplished in and through interaction. Contrary to what its name implies, ethnomethodology is *not* a research methodology; it is the study of the methods employed in everyday life though which social order is accomplished. As Garfinkel (1967: vii) put it in his inimitable style:

> in contrast to certain versions of Durkheim that teach that the objective reality of social facts is sociology's fundamental principle, the lesson is taken instead, and used as a study policy, that the objective reality of social facts *as* an ongoing accomplishment of the concerted activities of daily life, with the ordinary, artful ways of that accomplishment being by members known, used, and taken for granted, is, for members doing sociology, a fundamental phenomenon.

Two ideas are particularly central to ethnomethodology and find clear expression in CA: indexicality and reflexivity. The former means that the meaning of an act, which in CA essentially means spoken words or utterances including pauses and sounds, depends upon the conversational context in which it is used. Reflexivity means that spoken words are constitutive of the social world in which they are located; in other words, the principle of reflexivity in ethnomethodology means that talk is not a 'mere' representation of the social world, so that it does much more than just stand for something else. In these ways, ethnomethodology fits fairly squarely with two aspects of qualitative research—the predilection for a contextual understanding of action (see Chapter 17) and an ontological position associated with constructionism (see Chapter 2).

In the years following its initial introduction into sociology, ethnomethodological research split into two camps. One entailed drawing on traditional social research methods, albeit in perhaps a somewhat altered form, and on ethnography in particular (e.g. Cicourel 1968). The other, which is mainly associated with Sacks and his co-workers (e.g. Sacks et al. 1974), sought to conduct fine-grained analyses of talk in naturally-occurring situations. Moreover, it is not just talk in itself that is the object of interest but talk as it occurs in and through social interaction. CA concerns itself with the organization of such talk in the context of interaction. In order to conduct such investigations, a premium was placed on the recording of naturally-occurring conversations and their transcription for the purpose of intensive analysis of the sequences of interaction revealed in the subsequent transcripts. As such, CA is a multifaceted approach—part theory, part method of data acquisition, part method of analysis. The preference for the analysis of talk gleaned from naturally-occurring situations suggests that CA chimes with another preoccupation among qualitative researchers—namely, a commitment to naturalism (see Key concept 3.4).

As the above definition and discussion of CA suggest, CA takes from ethnomethodology a concern with the production of social order through and in the course of social interaction but takes conversation as the basic form through which that social order is achieved. The element of indexicality is also evident, in that practitioners of CA argue that the meaning of words is contextually grounded, while the commitment to reflexivity is revealed in the view that talk is constitutive of the social context in which it occurs.

Conversation analysts have developed a variety of procedures for the study of talk in interaction. Psathas (1995: 1) has described them as 'rigorous, systematic procedures' that can 'provide reproducible results'. Such a framework smacks of the commitment to the codification of procedures that generate valid, reliable, and replicable findings that are a feature of quantitative research. It is not surprising, therefore, that CA is sometimes described as having a positivist orientation. Thus, a cluster of features that are broadly in tune with qualitative research (contextual, naturalistic, studying the social world in its own terms and without prior theoretical commitments) are married to traits that are resonant of quantitative research. However, the emphasis on context in CA is somewhat different from the way in which contextual understanding is normally conceptualized in qualitative research. For CA practitioners, context refers to the specific here-and-now context of immediately preceding talk, whereas for most qualitative researchers it has a much wider set of resonances, which have to do with an appreciation of such things as the culture of the group within which action occurs. In other words, for most qualitative researchers action is to be understood in terms of the values, beliefs, and typical modes of behaviour of that group. This is precisely the kind of attribution from which CA practitioners are keen to refrain. It is no wonder, therefore, that such writers as Silverman (1993) find it difficult to fit CA into broad descriptions of the nature of qualitative research.

Assumptions of conversation analysis

An initial route into CA often begins with the analyst noticing something striking about the way that a speaker says something. This recognition then generates an emphasis on what that turn of phrase or whatever might be 'doing'—that is, what functions it serves. Clayman and Gill (2004) give the example, which was first noticed by Harvey Sacks, of the way in which children often begin a question by saying 'You know what, daddy [or whoever]?' when among adults. Their question invariably produces the reply 'What?' and thereby allows the child to find a slot in a sequence of conversation or to inaugurate such a sequence. The use of this strategy reflects children's desire to insinuate themselves in conversations as legitimate participants and indeed to be able to initiate sequences of the talk.

Once such a focus has been identified, conversation analysts typically follow certain basic assumptions. Heritage (1984, 1987) has proposed three such assumptions:

1. *Talk is structured*. Talk comprises invariant patterns— that is, it is structured. Participants are implicitly aware of the rules that underpin these patterns. As a result, conversation analysts avoid inferring the motivations of speakers from what they say or ascribing their talk to personal characteristics. Such information is unnecessary, since the conversation analyst is oriented to the underlying structures of action, as revealed in talk.

2. *Talk is forged contextually*. Action is revealed in talk and as such talk must be analysed in terms of its context. This means that what someone says must be examined in terms of the talk that preceded it and that therefore talk is viewed as exhibiting patterned sequences.

3. *Analysis is grounded in data*. Conversation analysts shun prior theoretical schemes and instead argue that characteristics of talk and of the constitutive nature of social order in each empirical instance must be induced out of data.

Heritage (1987: 258) has written: 'it is assumed that social actions work *in detail* and hence that the specific details of interaction cannot simply be ignored as insignificant without damaging the prospects for coherent and effective analyses.' This assumption represents a manifesto for the emphasis on fine-grained details (including length of pauses, prolongation of sounds, and so on) that is the hallmark of CA.

Transcription and attention to detail

As the third of the three assumptions associated with CA implies, the approach requires the analyst to produce detailed transcripts of natural conversation. Consider the portion of transcript in Research in focus 22.1, which contains some of the basic notational symbols employed in CA (see Tips and skills 'Basic notational symbols in conversation Analysis' for an explanation of some of these).

The attention to detail in the sequence in Research in focus 22.1 is very striking and represents a clear difference from the way in which talk is normally treated by social researchers—for example, in their transcription conventions when analysing qualitative interviews. But what is significant in this sequence of talk? Silverman (1994) draws two main inferences from this sequence. First, *P* initially tries to deflect any suggestion that there might be a special reason that she needs a test. As a result, the disclosure that she has been engaging in potentially risky behaviour is delayed. Second, *P*'s use of 'you' depersonalizes her behaviour. Silverman (1994: 75) argues

Research in focus 22.1
Conversation analysis in action showing a question and answer adjacency pair

Silverman (1994: 72) provides the following extract from a conversation between an HIV counsellor (*C*) at a clinic and a patient (*P*):

1. *C* Can I just briefly ask why: you thought about having
2. an HIV test done:
3. *P* .hh We:ll I mean it's something that you have these
4. I mean that you have to think about these da: ys, and
5. I just uh: m felt (0.8) <u>you</u>—you have had sex with
6. several people and you just don't want to go on (.)
7. not k<u>n</u>owing.

Tips and skills
Basic notational symbols in conversation analysis

.hh	h's preceded by a dot indicate an intake of breath. If no dot is present, it means breathing out.
We:ll	A colon indicates that the sound that occurs directly before the colon is prolonged. More than one colon means further prolongation (e.g. : : : :).
(0.8)	A figure in parentheses indicates the length of a period of silence, usually measured in tenths of one second. Thus, (0.8) signals eight-tenths of a second of silence.
<u>you</u> and k<u>n</u>owing	An underline indicates an emphasis in the speaker's talk.
(.)	Indicates a very slight pause.
↑↓	Indicates a change of pitch in an upwards (↑) or downwards (↓) direction.
[	Square brackets indicate overlapping talk, i.e. two or more speakers talk at the same time.
=	Refers to a continuation of talk

A full list of CA notation can be found at:
http://homepages.lboro.ac.uk/~ssca1/notation.htm (accessed 9 December 2014).

that sequences like these show how 'people receiving HIV counselling skilfully manage their talk about delicate topics'. The hesitations are designed by patients to establish that issues like these are not the subject of normal conversation; the rather general replies to questions are meant to indicate that the speaker is not the kind of person who will immediately launch into a discussion about difficult sexual matters with a stranger. Silverman (1994: 76) suggests that the notion that the hesitancy and depersonalization on the part of *P* is to do with her embarrassment about talking about sex is 'severely limited' and that instead we find that 'the production and management of delicate topics is skilfully and co-operatively organized between professionals and clients'.

This analysis shows how attention to fine details is an essential ingredient of CA work. Pauses and emphases are not to be regarded as incidental in terms of what the speaker is trying to achieve; instead, they are part of 'the specific details of interaction [that] cannot simply be ignored as insignificant', as Heritage put it in the quotation above.

Some basic tools of conversation analysis

The gradual accumulation of detailed analyses of talk in interaction has resulted in a recognition that there are recurring features of the ways in which it is organized. These features represent tools that can be applied to sequences

Tips and skills
Don't collect too much data

If you are doing a project based on CA, do not be tempted to collect too much data. The real work of CA goes into the painstaking analysis that its underlying theoretical stance requires. It may be that just one or two portions of transcribed text will allow you to address your research questions using the technique.

of conversation. The following tools are presented merely to provide a flavour of the ways in which CA proceeds.

Turn-taking

One of the fundamental ideas in CA is the notion that one way in which order is achieved in everyday conversation is through **turn-taking**. This is a particularly important tool of conversation analysis, because it illustrates that talk depends on shared codes. If such codes did not exist, there would not be smooth transitions in conversation. In other words, there must be codes for indicating the ends of utterances.

Hutchby and Wooffitt (1998: 47) summarize this model as indicating that: '(1) turn-taking occurs; (2) one speaker tends to talk at a time; and (3) turns are taken with as little gap or overlap between them as possible'. This is not to say that turn-taking 'errors' do not occur. They manifestly do, as the discussion of *repair mechanisms* below suggests. One of the ways in which turn-taking is revealed is through the examination of **adjacency pairs**, which are the focus of the next section.

Adjacency pairs

The idea of the adjacency pair draws attention to the well-attested tendency for some kinds of activity as revealed in talk to involve two linked phases: a question followed by an answer, as in Research in focus 22.1; an invitation followed by a response (accept/decline); or a greeting followed by a returned greeting. The first phase invariably implies that the other part of the adjacency pair will be forthcoming—for example, that an invitation will be responded to. The second phase is of interest to the conversation analyst not just because it becomes a springboard for a response in its own right but because compliance with the putative normative structure of the pairing indicates an appreciation of how one is supposed to respond to the initial phase. In this way, 'intersubjective understandings' are continuously reinforced (Heritage 1987: 259–60). This is not to imply that the second phase will *always* follow the first; indeed, the response to a failure to comply with the expected response has itself been the focus of attention by conversation analysts.

Preference organization

While it is true to say that the second phase in an adjacency pair is always anticipated, some responses are clearly preferential to others. An example is that, when an invitation or a request is proffered, acceptance does not have to be justified, whereas a refusal does have to be justified. A further example is that, when an attempt to be self-deprecating is provided, it will be met with disagreement rather than agreement. In each case, the former (acceptance, disagreement) is the *preferred response* and the latter (refusal, agreement) is the *dispreferred response*. Therefore, the preference structure is discovered by the conversation analyst through the response to an initial statement.

Speakers' awareness of the preference organization of such pairings has implications for the structure of a conversation. For example, Potter (1996: 59) contrasts a sequence in which an offer is met with a straightforward preferred response of acceptance—'thank you'—with the sequence in Research in focus 22.2, in which an invitation is declined (the dispreferred response).

Potter argues that this kind of response by A is fairly typical of invitation rejections, which are, of course, dispreferred responses. Potter draws attention to several features that contrast strikingly with the unequivocal 'thank you' associated with the case of acceptance. For example, A delays the start of his or her response and fills it with 'hehh'. Also, the rejection is 'softened' by A saying that he or she does not 'think' he or she can make it and is accompanied by an explanation for failing to provide the preferred response. Moreover, Potter follows the admonition not to make inferences about speakers' motivations by observing that the notion of a preference structure is a feature of the talk and not of the motivations of the participants. After all, it may be that A would actually have preferred to accept the invitation but was prevented from doing so by a prior commitment. The key point is that the participants recognize the preference structure of this kind of adjacency pairing, and this affects the form of their response (that is, hesitancy, acknowledgement of the invitation, and providing an explanation) in the case of declining the offer or an unelaborated (or barely elaborated) response in the case of acceptance.

Research in focus 22.2
Conversation analysis in action: a dispreferred response

1. *B*: Uh if you'd care to come over and visit a little while
2. this morning I'll give you a cup of <u>coffee</u>.
3. *A*: hehh
4. Well
5. that's awfully sweet of you,
6. I don't think I can make it this morning. hh uhm
7. I'm running an ad in the paper and—and uh I have to
8. stay near the phone (Atkinson and Drew 1979: 58; quoted in Potter 1996: 59)

Accounts

A feature of the sequence in Research in focus 22.2 is that from line 7 onwards *A* formulates an account of why it is that the invitation cannot be accepted. As Potter observes, the account does two things: it establishes a reason for declining the invitation and depicts *A* as constrained by circumstances. The important feature to note in the treatment of accounts in CA is that they are analysed in context—that is, the form that they assume is handled as being occasioned by what precedes it (an invitation). Unlike the traditional view of accounts in sociology, a CA view of *A*'s account is to stress the importance of depicting it as allowing the invitation to be construed in a positive light even though it cannot be accepted, thereby not jeopardizing the relationship between the two parties. Moreover, in CA, accounts are not unusual phenomena to be deployed when things go wrong but are intrinsic to talk in a variety of situations. What is also striking about this sequence as an account is that it is in essence simply a description of a state of affairs (having an advertisement in the paper and as a result needing to stay close to the telephone in case there are calls). The factual nature of the account further allows the relationship between the two parties to be unharmed by *A*'s dispreferred response.

Repair mechanisms

Of course, things do go wrong in conversations, as occurs when turn-taking conventions are not followed so that there is overlapping of people talking. Silverman (1993: 132) notes several repair mechanisms, such as:

- when someone starts to speak before someone else has finished, the initial speaker stops talking before completing his or her turn;

- when a turn transfer does not occur at an appropriate point (for example, when someone does not respond to a question), the speaker may speak again, perhaps reinforcing the need for the other person to speak (for example, by reinforcing the question).

The crucial point to note about such repair mechanisms is that they allow the rules of turn-taking to be maintained in spite of the fact that they have been breached.

Overview

This review of CA can only scratch the surface of an approach that has developed a sophisticated way of studying talk in interaction. It has sometimes been suggested that it fails to capture body movements, but in recent times video recordings have supplemented its toolkit of methods (e.g. Heath et al. 2010). Also, there has been a growing use of CA in connection with the examination of talk in institutional settings such as organizations and mediation sessions. CA can sometimes look as though its practitioners take an arbitrary piece of talk and theorize about it or that they 'cherry-pick' a sequence to fit a point they wish to make. However, as Wilkinson and Kitzinger (2008) make clear, there are several steps involved in the process: becoming aware of a feature of conversations that appears striking; bringing together possible exemplars of that conversational feature; uncovering the most striking of these exemplars; subjecting the clearest examples to a detailed analysis; examining those cases that are less clear; and conducting an analysis of deviant conversational cases. In other words, the examples of talk that appear in a publication based on CA and the points made about them are actually the end point of a rigorous process of analysis.

The insistence of conversation analysts that it is important to locate understanding in terms of sequences of talk, and therefore to avoid making extraneous inferences about the meanings of that talk, marks CA as representing a different approach from much qualitative research. As we have seen in previous chapters, qualitative researchers often claim (perhaps erroneously from the perspective of CA) that they seek to achieve understanding from the perspective of those being studied. Conversation analysts claim to do this only in so far as that understanding can be revealed in the specific contexts of talk. To import elements that are not specifically grounded in the here and now of what has just been said during a conversation risks implanting an understanding that is not grounded in participants' own terms (Schegloff 1997).

Two points seem relevant here. First, this is a somewhat limiting stance, in that it means that the attribution of motives and meanings as a result of an in-depth understanding of a culture is illegitimate. While a [interpre]tative understanding of social action carries t[he risk] of misunderstanding, an approach that prohibits [such] speculation is potentially restrictive. Second, CA is [con]textual in that it locates understanding in the sequences of talk. However, for the participants of an exchange, much of their talk is informed by their mutual knowledge of contexts. The analyst is restricted from taking those additional components of the context into account if they are not specifically part of the organization of talk. Again, this admonition seems to restrict the analyst more than is desirable in many circumstances and to consign CA to a range of research questions that are amenable solely to the location of meaning in talk alone. On the other hand, CA reduces the risk about making unwarranted speculations about what is happening in social interaction and has contributed much to our understanding of the accomplishment of social order, which is one of the classic concerns of social theory.

Discourse analysis

Unlike CA, DA is an approach to language that can be applied to forms of communication other than talk. As such, it can be and has been applied to texts, such as newspaper articles, and is in this respect more flexible than CA. Moreover, in DA there is much less of an emphasis on naturally-occurring talk, so that talk in research interviews can be a legitimate target for analysis. However, DA should not be treated as being totally in opposition or contradistinction to CA, since it incorporates insights from it. In addition, DA incorporates insights from the work of continental philosophers such as Michel Foucault (1926–84), for whom 'discourse' was a term that denoted the way in which a particular set of linguistic categories relating to an object and the ways of depicting it frame the way we comprehend that object. The discourse forms a version of it. Moreover, the version of an object comes to *constitute* it. For example, a certain discourse concerning mental illness comes to make up our concepts of what mentally ill persons are like, the nature of their illness, how they should be treated, and who is legitimately entitled to treat them. The discourse then becomes a framework for the justification for the power of practitioners concerned with the mentally ill and for their treatment regimes. In this way, a discourse is much more than language as such: it is constitutive of the social world that is a focus of interest or concern. Foucault took a broad-brush historical approach to the study of discourse. Discourse analysts, in incorporating insights from CA, generate more fine-grained analyses of talk and texts than was a feature of Foucault's approach.

Unlike CA, which by and large reveals a uniformity based on an orthodoxy associated with certain classic statements concerning its core practices (e.g. Sacks et al. 1974), there are several different approaches that are labelled as DA (Potter 1997). The version to be discussed in this section is one that has been of special interest to social researchers and is associated with such writers as Gilbert and Mulkay (1984); Potter and Wetherell (1987, 1994); Billig (1992); and Potter (1997). This version of DA (see Key concept 22.1) has been described as exhibiting two distinctive features at the level of **epistemology** and **ontology** (Potter 1997).

1. It is *anti-realist*; in other words, it denies that there is an external reality awaiting a definitive portrayal by the researcher and it therefore disavows the notion that any researcher can arrive at a privileged account of the aspect of the social world being investigated. Some discourse analysts, however, adopt a stance that is closer to a realist position, but most seem to be anti-realist in orientation.

2. It is *constructionist*; in other words, the emphasis is placed on the versions of reality propounded by members of the social setting being investigated and on the fashioning of that reality through their renditions of it (see Key concept 2.6). More specifically, the constructionist emphasis implies a recognition that discourse entails a selection from many viable renditions and that in the process a particular depiction of reality is built up.

Key concept 22.1
What is discourse analysis?

There is no one version of discourse analysis (DA). The version described in the main body of this section is one that has been of particular interest to social scientists and that can be applied to both naturally-occurring and contrived forms of talk and to texts. According to Potter (1997: 146), DA 'emphasizes the way versions of the world, of society, events and inner psychological worlds are produced in discourse'. Language is depicted in discourse analysis as constituting or producing the social world; it is not simply a means of understanding that world, as it is in most quantitative and qualitative research methods.

In the next section, a variant of discourse analysis—**critical discourse analysis**—will be discussed. Critical discourse analysis, which is very influenced by the work of Michel Foucault, seeks to link language and its modes of use to the significance of power and social difference in society.

Thus, discourse is not simply a neutral device for imparting meaning. People seek to accomplish things when they talk or when they write; DA is concerned with the strategies they employ in trying to create different kinds of effect. This version of DA is therefore action-oriented—that is, a way of getting things done. This is revealed in three basic discourse-analytic questions:

- What is this discourse doing?
- How is this discourse constructed to make this happen?
- What resources are available to perform this activity?

(Potter 2004: 609)

Research questions in DA tend to be fairly open-ended at least initially and then narrowed down. Writing about their research on mealtimes among families and how food was discursively constructed during and in relation to those occasions, Wiggins and Potter (2008) say that, following initial scrutiny of transcripts, they decided to focus on evaluation during mealtimes, such as:

1.   (0.8)
2. Simon: mm↑mm: (0.2) that's
3.   ↑lovely
4.   (0.6)

(Wiggins and Potter 2008: 84)

This narrowed focus led them to be guided by research questions such as: 'how are food evaluations used by speakers in mealtime interaction?' and 'what are the different forms of food evaluations and what actions are they involved with?' (Wiggins and Potter 2008: 80).

The action orientation of DA (what is the discourse doing?) is usefully revealed in a study of the first few moments of telephone calls to a National Society for the Prevention of Cruelty to Children (NSPCC) helpline. Through an analysis of these call openings, Potter and

Hepburn (2004) show that these first few moments perform certain actions:

- They are the springboard for the caller specifying the details of his or her concerns.
- They seek to establish that the child protection officer who receives the call is someone who, as an expert, can verify the caller's concerns.
- The caller makes it clear that he or she is concerned but not so concerned or certain about the status of the situation as to contact the police.
- The child protection officer is able to treat the report as serious without having to presuppose the truth or seriousness of the report.

Through an analysis of these brief moments of conversation, the flow of discourse achieves a number of objectives for both parties and is therefore action. Similarly, Wiggins and Potter (2008) note that the 'mmm' that appears in the brief sequence above appeared quite frequently in their transcripts. They depict these 'mmm's as expressions of gustatory delight that occur within sequences of verbal interaction; as evaluations of food that occur within verbal interaction; and as expressions of embodiment within verbal interaction. In other words, the simple and recurring 'mmm' accomplishes several tasks within verbal interaction.

In addition, DA shares with CA a preference for locating contextual understanding in terms of the situational specifics of talk. As Potter (1997: 158) puts it, discourse analysts prefer to avoid making reference in their analyses to what he refers to as 'ethnographic particulars' and argues that instead they prefer 'to see things as things that are worked up, attended to and made relevant in interaction rather than being external determinants'. However, some DA practitioners are less wedded to this principle than conversation analysts, in that they sometimes show a greater preparedness to make reference to 'ethnographic particulars'. For example, the research referred to in Research in focus 22.3 by O'Grady et al. (2014) concentrates on short interactional sequences but the authors add that DA 'was complemented by ethnographic approaches that included interviews at the clinical site and an extended interview with the participating surgeon, so as to bring the perspective of the medical profession to bear on our interpretation of the data' (O'Grady et al. 2014: 68). However, in the case of the study by Wiggins and Potter (2008) of conversations during mealtimes, there is a close link with the preferences of CA practitioners to keep the analysis located within ongoing conversational sequences, and indeed it employs CA notation to present the material examined. However, a preference for using CA notation and using its insights is not necessarily associated with an aversion to reference to ethnographic particulars, as O'Grady et al. used CA notation too.

Discourse analysts resist the idea of codifying their practices and indeed argue that such a codification is probably impossible. Instead, they prefer to see their style of research as an 'analytic mentality' and as 'a craft skill, more like bike riding or chicken sexing than following the recipe for a mild chicken rogan josh' (Potter 1997: 147–8). One useful point of departure for DA research that has been suggested by Gill (1996) following Widdicombe (1993) is to treat the way that something is said as being 'a solution to a problem' (Widdicombe 1993: 97; quoted in Gill 1996: 146). She also suggests adopting a posture

Research in focus 22.3
Discourse analysis in action: solving a problem

O'Grady et al. (2014) used DA to examine how trust is accomplished in surgical consultations in a gastro-intestinal clinic in Australia. The authors had access to a corpus of twenty-eight consultations, but in this article they focus on one as an illustration of the process of building trust. The case in point is a woman aged 56 who is accompanied by her niece. She has had an inguinal hernia operation and is seeking a second opinion because the pain she experienced prior to the operation has worsened. The patient's confidence in the medical profession is low and the article shows how the doctor, through a variety of discursive moves, gradually seeks to build up trust in him and the process. The building of trust is reinforced towards the end of the consultation when the doctor decides that the three of them will construct a letter to the referring doctor:

> 359 Doctor: = Um let me write a letter (.) while you (.) listen you help me write the letter.

> (O'Grady et al. 2014: 77)

The following sequence, which addresses the patient's weight gain, is quite instructive:

> Letter Extract 2
> 364 Doctor: As far as the weight gain's concerned (.) a::h (.) there's been an increase of (.) inverted commas (.) three dress sizes (.) close inverted commas (.) stop (.) new paragraph Mrs Bada a:hh looks (.) despairing (.) stop < That's a (.) an ex (.) an explanation isn't it>

> 365 Niece: Yeah.

> 366 Patient: (hhh hh)

> 367 Doctor: Um () very uncomfortable and er self-conscious about being inverted commas (.) seven months pregnant (.) close inverted commas

> 368 Niece: [chuckles].

> 369 Patient: [chuckles].(O'Grady et al. 2014: 78)

O'Grady et al. point out that at turns 364 and 367, the doctor dictates the same words the patient and her niece had employed. This, coupled with the element of humour that he injects, reinforces that he has been listening and wants to reduce the patient's embarrassment about gaining weight. At the same time, the reference to looking 'despairing' introduces an element of empathy which reinforces that he takes the patient's concerns very seriously. As the authors argue, while the building up of trust has been a gradual process in this encounter, the 'co-constructed consultation letter' is a 'final means to strengthen trust' (O'Grady et al. 2014: 79).

Tips and skills
Using existing material

As some of the examples of DA show, you may well be able to employ the technique to illuminate issues of interest to you on materials that are in the public domain, such as speeches. In many cases, these will be available in electronic form. This means that you do not have to put a lot of effort into the collection of data, though it will still be necessary to seek out the materials. Instead, you can give greater emphasis to analysing the materials using the DA approach. See Research in focus 22.4 for an example.

of 'sceptical reading' (Gill 2000). This means searching for a purpose lurking behind the ways that something is said or presented. Gill has also proposed that DA can be usefully thought of as comprising four main themes, which are outlined in Thinking deeply 22.1.

The bulk of the exposition of DA that follows is based on two studies: research on scientists' discourse and research on the use of numbers in a television programme on cancer. In the case of the former, we will see that attention to scientists' discourse is a solution to problems of how to represent their practices in formal and informal settings; the study of the television programme demonstrates that the examination of discourse reveals how claims about facts can be boosted or undermined through the use of a language of quantification. A further element to be sensitive to is that, as Gill (1996), following Billig (1991), suggests, what is said is always a way of *not* saying something else. In other words, either total silence on a topic, or formulating an argument in a conversation or article in one way rather than in another way, is crucial to seeing discourse as a solution to a problem. As we will see, the silences about aspects of their procedures in the scientists' published papers are significant for conveying a sense of the fixed, neutral nature of their findings; in the case of the television programme, conveying a quantitative argument in one way rather than in another way is crucial to undermining the credibility of claims about success in the treatment of cancer.

Thinking deeply 22.1
Four themes in discourse analysis

Gill (2000) has drawn attention to four prominent themes in DA.

1. *Discourse is a topic*. This means that discourse is a focus of enquiry itself and not just a means of gaining access to aspects of social reality that lie behind it. This view contrasts with a traditional research interview in which language is a way of revealing what interviewees think about a topic or their behaviour and the reasons for that behaviour.

2. *Language is constructive*. This means that discourse is a way of constituting a particular view of social reality. Moreover, in rendering that view, choices are made regarding the most appropriate way of presenting it, and these will reflect the disposition of the person responsible for devising it.

3. *Discourse is a form of action*. As Gill (2000: 175) puts it, language is viewed 'as a practice in its own right'. Language is a way of accomplishing acts, such as attributing blame, presenting oneself in a particular way, or getting an argument across. Moreover, a person's discourse is affected by the context that he or she is confronting. Thus, your account of your reasons for wanting a job may vary according to whether you are addressing interviewees in a job interview, members of your family, or friends. See Research in focus 22.4 for an example of discourse as a form of action.

4. *Discourse is rhetorically organized*. This means that DA practitioners recognize that discourse is concerned with 'establishing one version of the world in the face of competing versions' (Gill 2000: 176). In other words, there is a recognition that we want to persuade others when we present a version of events.

Research in focus 22.4
Discourse as action

On several occasions, it has been noted that, for DA practitioners, discourse is a form of action. Discourse is performative—it does things. An example is provided by a DA-informed examination by O'Reilly et al. (2009) of the decision letters written by representatives of Research Ethics Committees (RECs) to researchers who apply for ethical clearance to conduct health-related research. The authors write: 'We argue that RECs use texts not only to do their own accountability, using a range of discursive devices to display the quality of their own work and the resulting decisions, but also to establish the accountability of applicants for the quality of their applications' (O'Reilly et al. 2009: 248). They note four ways in which accountability is performed in the letters:

1. Referring to the *process behind the decision*. The letters often draw attention to the rigorous discussion and thought that went into the REC's decision, with such wording as 'considered carefully' and 'discussed the protocol at great length'.

2. *Holding the applicants accountable*. This tactic entails the decision letter making it clear that, when ethical issues are raised about the application, it is the applicant who is accountable for the REC's decision, not the REC. This justifies the REC's decision and the demands for revision that it makes.

3. Reference to the REC's *specialist expertise*. Requests or instructions for revision of applications or for declining applications often draw attention to the specific expertise of particular REC members.

4. Invoking *external authorities*. Here, a decision is legitimated by reference to an applicant's failure to conform to official guidelines. An example is the following statement concerning an application that was given a provisional outcome but that was later accepted: 'For the storage of samples, patient information sheets and consent forms should conform to the current MRC publication on Human Tissue and Biological Samples for use in Research—Operational and Ethical guidelines. These are available from the MRC website, **www.mrc.ac.uk**' (quoted in O'Reilly et al. 2009: 256).

This study shows that accountability is performed first in the obvious sense that the REC accounts for its decision but also in the sense that it deflects blame for what are disappointing decisions for applicants onto the applicants themselves.

Potter and Wetherell (1994) suggest that there are two tendencies within the kind of DA work being discussed in this chapter, although they acknowledge that the distinction is somewhat artificial. One is the identification of 'the general resources that are used to construct discourse and enable the performance of particular actions' (1994: 48–9), which is concerned with identifying **interpretative repertoires**. The other is concerned to identify 'the detailed procedures through which versions are constructed and made to look factual' (1994: 49). I will now explore these two strands of DA.

Uncovering interpretative repertoires

In order to illustrate the idea of an interpretative repertoire, an influential study of scientists by Gilbert and Mulkay (1984) will be employed. This research is outlined in Research in focus 22.5. Gilbert and Mulkay noticed a difference between the ways in which the scientists presented their work in formal contexts, most notably scientific papers, and in informal contexts, such as in interviews with the researchers. Such differences went far beyond predictable differences in tone of presentation, in that they also related to such areas as the depiction of the ways in which the findings emerged. For example, Gilbert and Mulkay noted an instance in which a scientific paper portrayed a model as emerging out of the data, whereas in the research interview the rendition is one of reinterpreting the model, which in turn suggested seeing the existing data from a different perspective, which in turn suggested a new series of experiments. Similarly, Gilbert and Mulkay found that the sections of the scientific papers that described the experimental methodology portrayed the procedures in terms that implied they were neutral operations that were largely independent of the scientist and could be replicated by anyone. In the research interviews, however, the scientists emphasized the operation of practical skills that are the product of

Research in focus 22.5
Discourse analysis in action: the study of interpretative repertoires in scientists' discourse

Gilbert and Mulkay's (1984) research on scientists' discourse is concerned with the field of bioenergetics and in particular with the process whereby scientists working in this area come to understand a mechanism they dubbed 'oxidative phosphorylation'. The main source of Gilbert and Mulkay's data was interviews with thirty-four researchers in this field. The interviews lasted between two-and-a-half and three hours on average. The authors describe the process of analysing the resulting data as follows:

> The interviews were tape-recorded and transcribed in full. We then read through the transcripts and copied those pages which included material relating to the topics which interested us. The passages from the interviews concerning each topic were placed together in 'topic files', so that we had convenient access to all the material on, for instance, consensus or diagrams and pictorial representations. We aimed to make each file as inclusive as possible so that no passage which could be read as dealing with a particular topic was omitted from its file.
>
> (Gilbert and Mulkay 1984: 19)

In addition, the authors drew on further sources, such as privately circulated letters written by leading authorities in the field; the main articles in the field; and copies of the chief textbooks in the field. Through an examination of the ways in which textbooks and articles on the one hand explained the research process and accounts of how research was done provided by the scientists themselves, Gilbert and Mulkay were able to build up a picture of the differences between the *empiricist repertoire* and the *contingent repertoire* (see main text).

experience and developing a 'feel' for experimental work. As one scientist put it:

> How could you write it up? It would be like trying to write a description of how to beat an egg. Or like trying to read a book on how to ski. You'd just get the wrong idea altogether. You've got to go and watch it, see it, do it. There's no substitute for it. These are *practical* skills. We all know that practical skills are not well taught by bits of paper.
>
> (Quoted in Gilbert and Mulkay 1984: 53; emphasis in original)

Gilbert and Mulkay argue that in the formal context of the scientific paper an *empiricist repertoire* prevailed. This concept was derived from 'the observation that the texts of experimental papers display certain recurrent stylistic, grammatical, and lexical features which appear to be coherently related' (1984: 55–6). The empiricist repertoire was revealed in such features as an emphasis on procedural routines in the conduct of experiments, such that the findings appear as an inevitable, logical outcome; no mention of theoretical commitments on the part of authors; and an impersonal writing style with little or no mention of the authors' role in the production of the findings. By contrast, in the informal milieu of the research interview, a *contingent repertoire* was in operation. In this context, 'scientists presented their actions and beliefs as heavily dependent on speculative insights, prior

intellectual commitments, personal characteristics, indescribable skills, social ties and group membership' (1984: 56). In other words, when describing their research within a contingent repertoire, scientists were much less likely to present their findings as the inevitable outcome of their experimental engagement with natural phenomena and were therefore far more likely to acknowledge their own role in the production of scientific findings. Gilbert and Mulkay then go on to show that, when scientists disagree with the positions of other scientists, they describe their own work within an empiricist repertoire, in which their own findings take on the character of natural inevitability through the following of proper procedure, but other scientists' work is described within a contingent repertoire, which shows up their competitors' errors as the product of prejudices, theoretical commitments, bias, and so on.

The notion of the interpretative repertoire is interesting because it brings out the idea that belief and action take place within templates that guide and influence the writer or speaker. The two repertoires discussed by Gilbert and Mulkay by no means exhaust the range of possibilities: Potter and Wetherell (1987), for example, suggest that a community repertoire was used in the context of a riot in Bristol in 1980 to cast light on events and beliefs. In the process, the police were cast in the role of *agents provocateurs* rather than as keepers of the peace. What is particularly striking about Gilbert and Mulkay's research, however, is that the two repertoires are employed by scientists but in different contexts (in formal or informal contexts, and whether describing their own or competitors' procedures). In a similar vein, Billig's (1992: 149) research on the ways in which people talk about the royal family suggested that, when referring to the role of newspapers in providing information about its members, two positions were frequently held and deployed on different occasions: 'the papers as the sources of lies and the papers as the source of knowledge'. Such a recognition of the almost simultaneous use of different repertoires brings to the fore the 'dilemmatic' nature of thinking in these and other environments (Billig et al. 1988).

Producing facts

As with the exposition of interpretative repertoires in DA, in this section a study will be employed as a lens through which to view the practice of discourse analytic research.

The emphasis will be on the resources that are employed in conveying allegedly factual knowledge. The researchers were especially interested in the role of what they call *quantification rhetoric*, by which is meant the ways in which numerical and non-numerical statements are made to support or refute arguments. The interest in this issue lies in part in the importance of quantification in everyday life and in part in the tendency for many social scientists to make use of this strategy themselves (John 1992). The specific focus of the research was upon a television programme shown on Channel 4 in April 1988 and entitled *Cancer: Your Money or your Life* (Potter et al. 1991; Potter and Wetherell 1994). The programme claimed to show that the huge amounts of money donated by the public to cancer charities are doing little to 'cure' the disease. The details of the materials used in the research and an outline of the process of analysis are provided in Research in focus 22.6. Research in focus 22.7 provides a key part of the transcript of the television programme itself.

Research in focus 22.6
Discourse analysis in action: producing facts through quantification rhetoric

The study of the representation of facts in the television programme *Cancer: Your Money or your Life* (Potter et al. 1991; Potter and Wetherell 1994) used a variety of different sources:

- a video recording of the programme;
- the observations of one of the members of the team making the programme, who acted as a participant observer while it was being made;
- drafts of the script, shooting schedules, and recordings of editing sessions;
- the entire interviews with the various people interviewed for the programme (such as cancer research specialists and heads of charities);
- research interviews with some of the latter people;
- research interviews with some of the people involved in making the programme.

One of the phases of the analysis entailed the 'coding' of the various sources that had been collected. The authors tell us:

> We made a list of about a dozen keywords and phrases that related to the sequence—percentage, cure rates, death rates, 1 per cent, etc.—and then ran through each of the interview and interaction files, looking for them with a standard word-processor . . . Whenever we got a 'hit' we would read the surrounding text to see if it had relevance to our target sequence. When it did we would copy it across to an already opened coding file . . . noting the transcript page numbers at the same time. If we were not sure if the sequence was relevant we copied it anyway, for, unlike the sorts of coding that take place in traditional content analysis, the coding is not the analysis itself but a preliminary to make the task of analysis manageable.
>
> (Potter and Wetherell 1994: 52)

A prominent sequence used in the research is provided in Research in focus 22.7.

Research in focus 22.7
Sequence from the study of the television programme *Cancer: Your Money or your Life*

The following sequence occurred roughly halfway through the television programme *Cancer: Your Money or Your Life*, following interviews with cancer scientists who cast doubt on whether their research, much of it funded by charities, results in successful treatment:

Commentary   The message from these scientists is clear—exactly like the public—they hope their basic research will lead to cures in the future—although at the moment they can't say how this will happen. In the meantime, their aim is to increase scientific knowledge on a broad front and they're certainly achieving this. But do their results justify them getting so much of the money that has been given to help fight cancer? When faced with this challenge the first thing the charities point to are the small number of cancers which are now effectively curable.

[on screen: DR NIGEL KEMP CANCER RESEARCH CAMPAIGN]

Kemp   The outlook for individuals suffering from a number of types of cancer has been totally revolutionized. I mean for example—children suffering from acute leukaemia—in old days if they lived six months they were lucky—now more than half the children with leukaemia are cured. And the same applies to a number of other cancers—Hodgkin's Disease in young people, testicular tumours in young men, and we all know about Bob Champion's success [Champion was a prominent jockey who contracted testicular cancer, made a much-heralded recovery, won the Grand National, and even had a movie made about him]. (Potter and Wetherell 1994: 52–3)

At this point a table showing the annual incidence of thirty-four types of cancer begins to scroll on the screen. The total incidence is 243,000 and the individual incidences range from placenta (20) to lung (41,400). The three forms of cancer mentioned by Kemp and their levels of incidence are highlighted in yellow: childhood leukaemia (350), testis (1,000), and Hodgkin's Disease (1,400). The programme continues while the table is scrolling.

Commentary   But those three curable types are amongst the rarest cancers—they represent around 1 per cent of a quarter of a million cases of cancers diagnosed each year. Most deaths are caused by a small number of very common cancers.

Kemp   We are well aware of the fact that erm once people develop lung cancer or stomach cancer or cancer of the bowel sometimes—the outlook is very bad and aaa obviously one is frustrated by the sss relatively slow rate of progress on the one hand but equally I think there are a lot of real opportunities and and positive signs that advances can be made—even in the more intractable cancers. (Potter and Wetherell 1994: 53)

In proceeding with an analysis of their data, such as the portions of transcript in Research in focus 22.7, Potter and Wetherell employed several devices.

Looking for rhetorical detail

Attention to rhetorical detail entails a sensitivity to the ways in which arguments are constructed. Thus, during the editing of the film, the programme-makers' discourse suggested they were looking for ways to provide a convincing argument for their case that cancer remains largely intractable in spite of the money spent on it. The programme-makers very consciously devised the strategy outlined in the section on 'Using variation as a lever' below of playing down the numerical significance of those cancers that *are* amenable to treatment. Moreover, Potter et al. (1991) point out that one element of their argumentative strategy is to employ a tactic they call a 'preformulation', whereby a possible counter-argument is discounted in the course of presenting an argument, as when the commentary informs us: 'When faced with this challenge the first thing the charities point to are the small number of cancers which are now effectively curable.' Research in focus 22.8 examines a further rhetorical device that is employed in making a persuasive argument.

Research in focus 22.8
The extreme case formulation: the social construction of the asylum-seeker

Discourse analysts have examined a variety of different rhetorical strategies through which arguments are formulated. One interesting form is the *extreme case formulation*. Potter (1996: 187) gives the example of someone who returns an item of clothing to a dry cleaner claiming that it has damaged the clothing; the customer might emphasize the significance of the claim by suggesting that the item is not simply new but 'brand new'. An interesting use of the concept can be found in connection with a study of letters to newspapers written by members of the general public in connection with 'asylum-seekers', who were the focus of considerable controversy during the period the letters were written (March to September 2001). The researchers point to a 'striking predominance' of two rhetorical strategies in the discourse surrounding asylum-seekers, of which the extreme case formulation was one (Lynn and Lea 2003: 446). Examples, with the extreme case formulation elements underlined, are:

> Perhaps if they learned to say no now and again instead of accepting <u>every freebie</u> that comes their way any resentment would melt away. (*Sun*)

> Asylum-seekers who are genuine should have <u>no qualms</u> about being held in a reception centre. (*Daily Mail*)

> A solution to the problem of dispersing asylum-seekers is staring us in the face—namely, billet them free of charge on white liberals. That would have the advantage of both dispersing asylum-seekers widely and to areas with no social deprivation. White liberals will, of course, be <u>only too happy to welcome them into their homes</u>. Indeed it is most odd that they have not been queuing up to offer their services. (*Independent*)

The extreme case formulation allows the writer to convey a position that is hostile to asylum-seekers and that simultaneously justifies that position. In essence, it acknowledges that a possibly extreme position is being presented that is unsympathetic to asylum-seekers and that might even be viewed as racist, but uses the extreme case formulation in order to legitimize the position. It forms an important ingredient in the social construction of the asylum-seeker as someone who is unfairly advantaged relative to UK citizens and who is a possible threat to the social order.

Rhetorical analysis is a mode of analysis that is often used in its own right. Researchers interested in rhetorical analysis emphasize the ways in which arguments are constructed either in speech or in written texts and the role that various linguistic devices (such as metaphor, analogy, and irony) play in the formulation of arguments. In their study of the decision letters produced by RECs (see Research in focus 22.4), O'Reilly et al. (2009) noted several rhetorical constructions in the letters. They noted the use of third-person terms (for example, 'the Committee'), which were employed to give a sense of an authoritative and official judgement. The authors also note that the letters are rhetorically organized to negate alternative versions of ethical practice, thereby privileging the REC rendering.

Using variation as a lever

The authors draw attention to the phrase '1 per cent of a quarter of a million' (see Research in focus 22.7), because it incorporates two quantitative expressions: a relative expression (a percentage) and an absolute frequency (quarter of a million). The change of the register of quantification is important, because it allows the programme-makers to make their case about the low cure levels (just 1 per cent) compared with the large number of new cases of cancer. They could have pointed to the absolute number of people who are cured, but the impact would have been less. Also, the 1 per cent is not being contrasted with 243,000 but with a quarter of a million. Not only does this citation allow the figure to increase by 7,000; a quarter of a million sounds larger.

Reading the detail

Discourse analysts incorporate the CA preference for attention to the details of discourse. For example, Potter and Wetherell suggest that the description of the three 'curable cancers' as 'amongst the rarest cancers' is deployed to imply that these are atypical cancers, so that it is unwise to generalize to all cancers from experiences with them.

Looking for accountability

Discourse analysts draw on CA practitioners' interest in and approach to accounts. The programme-makers were concerned to be accountable for the position they took, and Potter and Wetherell's (1994: 61) transcript of an editing session suggests they were keen to ensure they could defend their inference about the 1 per cent. From the point of view of both CA and DA, the extracts presented in Research in focus 22.6 can and should be regarded as accounts. The editing session notes suggest that it is the credibility of the account that was of concern to the programme-makers. For DA practitioners, the search for accountability entails attending to the details through which accounts are constructed.

Cross-referencing discourse studies

Potter and Wetherell suggest that reading other discourse studies is itself an important activity. First, it helps to sharpen the analytic mentality at the heart of DA. Second, other studies often provide insights that are suggestive for one's own data. Potter and Wetherell indicate that they were influenced by a study of market traders by Pinch and Clark (1986). This research showed that a kind of quantification rhetoric was often being used by the traders (though Pinch and Clark did not use this term) in order to convey a sense of value (such as selling a pen with a pencil). It appeared that something similar was occurring when the table was being scrolled whereby the large number of cancers and the long list of types were being contrasted with the small number (three) of curable ones. Similarly, the 'extreme case formulation' in the context of asylum-seekers discussed in Research in focus 22.7 could be compared to uses of this rhetorical device in other contexts and studies.

 # Critical discourse analysis

Critical discourse analysis (CDA) emphasizes the role of language as a power resource that is related to ideology and socio-cultural change. It draws in particular on the theories and approaches of Foucault (e.g. 1977), who sought to uncover the representational properties of discourse as a vehicle for the exercise of power through the construction of disciplinary practices, such as individual subjectivity and the operation of rules and procedures that enable the construction of disciplinary practices that facilitate the construction of the self-disciplining subject. The notion of 'discourse' is therefore defined more broadly than in fine-grained approaches, as this summary by Phillips and Hardy (2002: 3) illustrates:

> We define a discourse as an interrelated set of texts, and the practices of their production, dissemination, and reception, that brings an object into being . . . In other words, social reality is produced and made real through discourses, and social interactions cannot be fully understood without reference to the discourses that give them meaning. As discourse analysts, then, our task is to explore the relationship between discourse and reality.

Thus, CDA practitioners are more receptive than discourse analysts to the idea of a pre-existing material reality that constrains individual agency.

Discourses are conceived of as drawing on and influencing other discourses; so, for example, the discourse of globalization might affect discourses on new technology, free trade and liberalism, or corporate social responsibility. CDA involves exploring why some meanings become privileged or taken for granted and others become marginalized. In other words, discourse does not just provide an account of what goes on in society; it is also a process whereby meaning is created. Power is typically central to or at least acts as a background 'given' to CDA research as practitioners seek to reveal why some discourses are privileged over others and the role of power in relation to them. This involves asking 'who uses language, how, why and when' (van Dijk 1997: 2), to which might be added 'and to what effect?'

Analysis of a particular *discursive event* is usually carried out according to a 'three-dimensional' framework, which proceeds as follows:

> (i) examination of the actual content, structure, and meaning of the text under scrutiny (the *text dimension*);
> (ii) examination of the form of discursive interaction used to communicate meaning and beliefs (the *discursive practice dimension*); and (iii) consideration of the social context in which the discursive event is taking place (the *social practice dimension*).

> (Grant et al. 2004: 11)

A further key concept within CDA is the notion of *intertextuality*. This notion draws attention to connections between texts so that any text that is being subjected to scrutiny is considered in relation to other related texts. Like discourse analysts, CDA practitioners tend to prefer naturally-occurring data on which to perform their analyses. In deciding how to select texts for analysis, Phillips and Hardy propose several considerations but the first—'What texts are the most important in constructing the object of analysis?' (2002: 75)—is probably the first and overriding

Research in focus 22.9
A critical discourse analysis of the 2003 GM Nation? debate

Attar and Genus (2014) use CDA to examine the GM Nation? debate that took place in the UK in 2003 concerning the possible introduction of genetically modified crops and their commercialization. The authors' research questions provide a strong sense of the concerns of CDA practitioners and especially of the significance of power:

> (a).what are the effects of texts in creating, sustaining and transforming ideologies? (b). how are these ideological effects embedded in the organisation and, in particular, the framing of the GM Nation? public debate; and (c). how are they implicated in the deliberations of the participants?

> (Attar and Genus 2014: 242)

Their data comprise transcripts of public meetings and emails and comments on the website **www.gmnation. co.uk**, which is no longer accessible. The authors analysed the documents with specific reference to the discursive strategies used in legitimating (and therefore justifying) arguments. The research shows that the principal rationalization strategy used was what Fairclough calls 'rationalization' and which he defines as: 'Legitimation by reference to the utility of institutionalized action, and to the knowledges society has constructed to endow them with cognitive validity' (2003: 98). Attar and Genus use the following quotation, which was posted on the GM Nation? website, as an illustration:

> Opposing GM crops is both irrational and financial lunacy. There is no evidence that GM crops have had any harmful effects whatsoever, and they pose no more danger than any natural genetic mutations. Unfortunately the people opposed to GM crops know little about the science and want to make Britain a scientific and commercial backwater. If people want to grow food uneconomically and produce less healthy products, then they certainly have the right to do so. However such people should not try to impose their views on the rest of us.

> (quoted in Attar and Genus 2014: 247)

Attar and Genus argue that their research shows that the debate reproduced the 'ideological discourse of neo-liberal economics' which 'emphasises free markets, wealth accumulation by individuals and a restricted role for the state and citizens to intervene in economic affairs' (2014: 248). Thus, while GM Nation? allowed a debate to be opened up, that debate was framed and structured by the discourse of neo-liberal economics. Analysis in terms of intertextuality revealed that the participants to the debate came from entrenched positions that were not meant to achieve consensus.

consideration. Unlike many discourse analysts, however, CDA practitioners are much more favourably inclined towards orienting the analysis of discourse to its context and indeed, for many, doing so is a prerequisite. As Phillips and Hardy put it: 'if we are to understand discourses and their effects, we must also understand the context in which they arise' (2002: 4). Example of the use of CDA can be found in Research in focus 22.9 and 23.11.

Overview

As the discussion has emphasized on several occasions, DA draws on insights from CA. Particularly when analysing strings of talk, DA draws on conversation analytic insights into the ways in which interaction is realized in and through talk in interaction. The CA injunction to focus on the talk itself and the ways in which intersubjective meaning is accomplished in sequences of talk is also incorporated into DA. This is not easy to achieve, and, when one reads articles based on DA, it sometimes seems as though the practitioners come perilously close to invoking speculations that do not seem to be directly discernible in the sequences being analysed—that is, speculations about 'ethnographic particulars' and hence about motives.

Sometimes, there is a more explicit recognition of the potential contribution of an appreciation of the ethnographic context. Edley and Wetherell (1997) report findings relating to a study conducted within a DA framework. The data were gathered from discussions held in three-person groups with 17–18-year-old boys in a UK school. The focus of the article was upon the construction of masculinity as it emerged in the course of the group discussions. However, one of the authors carried out observations within the school. This ethnographic research 'led to the identification of divisions within friendship groups in the sixth form as a major participant concern connected with formulations of masculinity within the school' (Edley and Wetherell 1997: 207). One of the key components of the friendship structure was the division between rugby players and the rest. Edley and Wetherell show that an important component of the construction of masculinity during talk among the non-players is their antipathy towards the rugby players. In other words, they defined their masculinity in contradistinction to the concepts of masculinity associated with the rugby players. However, the key point is that the periods of ethnographic observation at least in part informed the discourse analytic interpretation of the sequences of talk that had been recorded. Such research suggests that the proscription concerning the recourse to ethnographic particulars is honoured more by some discourse analysts than others. It is easy to see why: attention to ethnographic details may alert the analyst to nuances and understandings that are not directly entrenched in the flow of discourse.

DA is in certain respects a more flexible approach to language in social research than CA in that it is not solely concerned with the analysis of naturally-occurring talk, since practitioners also use various kinds of documents and research interviews in their work, although some practitioners follow the CA preference for using naturally-occurring data. Also, DA permits the intrusion of understandings of what is going on that are not specific to the immediacy of previous utterances. It is precisely this to which conversation analysts object, as when Schegloff (1997: 183) writes about DA: 'Discourse is too often made subservient to contexts not of its participants' making, but of its analysts' insistence.' For their part, discourse analysts sometimes object to the restriction that this injunction imposes, because it means that conversation analysts 'rarely raise their eyes from the next turn in the conversation, and, further, this is not an entire conversation or sizeable slice of social life but usually a tiny fragment' (Wetherell 1998: 402). Thus, for discourse analysts, such

phenomena as interpretative repertoires are very much part of the context within which talk occurs, whereas in CA they are inadmissible evidence. But it is here that we see the dilemma for the discourse analyst, for, in seeking to admit a broader sense of context (such as attention to interpretative repertoires in operation) while wanting to stick close to the conversation analysts' distaste for ethnographic particulars, they are faced with the uncertainty of just how far to go in allowing the inclusion of conversationally extraneous factors.

The anti-realist inclination of many DA practitioners has been a source of controversy, because the emphasis on representational practices through discourses sidelines any notion of a pre-existing material reality that can constrain individual agency. Reality becomes little more than that which is constituted in and through discourse. This lack of attention to a material reality that lies behind and underpins discourse has proved too abstracted for some social researchers and theorists. For example, writing from a critical realist position (see Key concept 2.3), Reed (2000) has argued that discourses should be examined in relation to social structures, such as power relationships, that are responsible for the occasioning of those discourses. Attention would additionally be focused on the ways in which discourses then work through existing structures. Discourse is thereby conceived as a 'generative mechanism' rather than as a self-referential sphere in which nothing of significance exists outside it. Reed (2000: 529) provides an interesting example of such an alternative view:

> Discourses—such as the quantitatively based discourses of financial audit, quality control and risk management—are now seen as the generative mechanisms through which new regulatory regimes 'carried out' by rising expert groups—such as accountants, engineers and scientists—become established and legitimated in modern societies. What they represent is less important than what they do in facilitating a radical re-ordering of pre-existing institutional structures in favour of social groups who benefit from the upward mobility which such innovative regulatory regimes facilitate.
>
> (Reed 2000: 529)

As this passage suggests, while many DA practitioners are anti-realist, an alternative, realist position in relation to discourse is feasible. Such an alternative position is perhaps closer to the classic concerns of the social sciences than an anti-realist stance.

Many of these studies refer to their analysis of language using the term 'discourse'. However, the extensive use of this term brings its own problems, because what different researchers understand the term 'discourse' to mean varies considerably, and so does their approach to analysis. There is thus a danger, noted by Alvesson and Kärreman (2000), that the term 'discourse analysis' is too broad to be meaningful, with authors treating the term as though it has a clear, broadly agreed-upon meaning that, just from reading this chapter, you will be able to see it does not. Hence 'discourse sometimes comes close to standing for everything, and thus nothing' (Alvesson and Kärreman 2000: 1128). However, the important thing to remember is that understanding how language is used is viewed by some researchers as crucial to understanding the social world, and the approaches examined in this chapter provide some tools through which language can be explored as a focus of attention in its own right.

 ## Key points

- CA and DA approaches take the position that language is itself a focus of interest and not just a medium through which research participants communicate with researchers.
- CA is a systematic approach to conversation that locates action in talk.
- In CA, talk is deemed to be structured in the sense of following rules.
- Practitioners of CA seek to make inferences about talk that are not grounded in contextual details that are extraneous to talk.
- DA shares many features with CA but there are several different versions of it.
- DA can be applied to a wider variety of phenomena than CA, which is concerned just with naturally-occurring talk.
- Discourse is conceived of as a means of conveying meaning.
- DA practitioners display a greater inclination to relate meaning in talk to contextual factors.

 ## Questions for review

- In what ways does the role of language in conversation and discourse analysis differ from that which is typical in most other research methods?

Conversation analysis

- In what ways is CA fundamentally about the production of social order in interaction? Why are audio-recording and transcription crucial in CA?
- What is meant by each of the following: turn-taking; adjacency pair; preference organization; account; repair mechanism?
- How do the terms in the previous question relate to the production of social order?
- Evaluate Schegloff's (1997) argument that CA obviates the need to make potentially unwarranted assumptions about participants' motives.

Discourse analysis

- What does it mean to say that DA is anti-realist and constructionist?
- What is an interpretative repertoire?
- What techniques are available to the discourse analyst when trying to understand the ways in which facts are presented through discourse?
- What are the chief points of difference between CA and DA?

Critical discourse analysis

- What is distinctive about CDA?
- What key questions might a CDA practitioner ask in seeking to reveal the meaning of discourses surrounding something like climate change?
- Why is the notion of intertextuality important to CDA practitioners?

Online Resource Centre
www.oxfordtextbooks.co.uk/orc/brymansrm5e/

Visit the Online Resource Centre to enrich your understanding of the examination of language in qualitative research. Follow up links to other resources, test yourself using multiple choice questions, and gain further guidance and inspiration from the Student Researcher's Toolkit.

23
Documents as sources of data

Chapter outline

Chapter guide

The term 'documents' covers a very wide range of different kinds of source. This chapter aims to reflect that variability by examining a wide range of different documentary sources that have been or can be used in qualitative research. In addition, the chapter touches on approaches to the analysis of such sources. The chapter explores:

- personal documents in both written form (such as diaries and letters) and visual form (such as photographs);
- official documents deriving from the state (such as public inquiries);
- official documents deriving from private sources (such as documents produced by organizations);
- mass-media outputs;
- virtual outputs, such as Internet resources;
- the criteria for evaluating each of the above sources;
- qualitative content analysis and semiotics as two approaches to the analysis of documents.

Introduction

This chapter will be concerned with a fairly heterogeneous set of sources of data, such as letters, diaries, autobiographies, newspapers, magazines, websites, blogs, and photographs. The emphasis is placed on documents that have not been produced at the request of a social researcher—instead, the objects that are the focus of this chapter are simply 'out there' waiting to be assembled and analysed. The fact that documents are available for the social researcher to work on does not necessarily render them somehow less time-consuming or easier to deal with than primary data that need to be collected or even that documents are unproblematic. On the contrary, the search for documents relevant to your research can often be a frustrating and highly protracted process. Moreover, once they are collected, considerable interpretative skill is required to ascertain the meaning of the materials that have been uncovered. Further, documents themselves are often implicated in chains of action that are a potential focus of attention in their own right.

Documents of the kind referred to in this chapter are materials that:

- can be read (though the term 'read' has to be understood in a somewhat looser fashion than is normally the case when we come to visual materials, such as photographs);
- have not been produced specifically for the purpose of social research;
- are preserved so that they become available for analysis; and
- are relevant to the concerns of the social researcher.

Documents have already been encountered in this book, albeit in a variety of contexts or guises. For example,

the kinds of source upon which content analysis is often carried out are documents, such as newspaper articles. However, the emphasis in this chapter will be upon the use of documents in qualitative research. A further way in which documents have previously surfaced was in the brief discussion in Key concept 14.3, which noted that archive materials are one form of unobtrusive method. Indeed, this points to an often-noted advantage of using documents of the kind discussed in this chapter—namely, they are non-reactive. This means that, because they have not been created specifically for the purposes of social research, the possibility of a reactive effect can be largely discounted as a limitation on the validity of data.

In discussing the different kinds of documents used in the social sciences, J. Scott (1990) has usefully distinguished between personal documents and official documents and has further classified the latter in terms of private as opposed to state documents. These distinctions will be employed in much of the discussion that follows. A further set of important distinctions made by Scott relate to the criteria for assessing the quality of documents. Scott suggests four criteria (1990: 6).

1. *Authenticity*. Is the evidence genuine and of unquestionable origin?

2. *Credibility*. Is the evidence free from error and distortion?

3. *Representativeness*. Is the evidence typical of its kind, and, if not, is the extent of its untypicality known?

4. *Meaning*. Is the evidence clear and comprehensible?

This is an extremely rigorous set of criteria against which documents might be assessed, and frequent reference to them will be made in the following discussion.

 ## Personal documents

This section discusses the nature of and issues involved in using a variety of kinds of personal documents that individuals produce and that are often used in social research.

Diaries, letters, and autobiographies

Diaries and letters have been used a great deal by historians but have not been given a great deal of attention by social researchers, who have tended to employ them as sources when they have been specifically elicited from their authors. The researcher-driven diary has been used as a method of data collection in both quantitative and

qualitative research. A similar approach can be employed in relation to letters: for example, Ang (1985) placed an advertisement in a Dutch women's magazine asking readers to write to her about their reactions to and feelings about the American television series *Dallas*. She received forty-two letters in response to this advertisement. However, the kinds of diary and letter that are the focus of this chapter are ones that have not been solicited by a researcher, i.e. they are extant. Research in focus 23.1 and 23.2 provide examples of the use of personal documents in social research in both historical and more contemporary contexts.

Research in focus 23.1
Using historical personal documents: the case of Augustus Lamb

Dickinson (1993) provides an interesting account of the use of historical personal documents in the case of Augustus Lamb (1807–36), who was the only child of Lady Caroline Lamb and William Lamb, the second Viscount Melbourne. It is possible that Augustus suffered throughout his short life from epilepsy, though he seems to have suffered from other complaints as well. Dickinson was drawn to him because of her interest in nineteenth-century reactions to people with mental handicaps who were not institutionalized. In fact, Dickinson doubts whether the term 'mental handicap' is applicable to Augustus and suggests the somewhat milder description of having learning difficulties. The chief sources of data are 'letters from family and friends; letters to, about and (rarely) from Augustus' (Dickinson 1993: 122). These letters were found in collections at the Hertfordshire County Office, the British Museum, and Southampton University Library. Other sources used include the record of the post-mortem examination of Augustus and extracts from the diary of Augustus' resident tutor and physician for the years 1817–23. Dickinson employs these materials to demonstrate the difficulty of arriving at a definitive portrayal of what Augustus was like. At the same time, she shows the difficulties that people around him experienced in coming to terms with his conditions, in large part because of the difficulty they experienced in finding a vocabulary that was consistent with his high social status.

It is likely that the potential of letters in historical and social research is or will be fairly limited to a certain time period. As J. Scott (1990) observes, letter writing became a significant activity only after the introduction of an official postal service and in particular after the penny post in 1840. The emergence of the telephone as a prevalent form of communication may have limited the use of letter writing, and it is likely that the emergence of email communication, especially in so far as emails are not kept in electronic or printed form, is likely to mean that the role of letters has been declining for some time and may continue to do so.

Whereas letters are a form of communication with other people, diarists invariably write for themselves, but, when written for wider consumption, diaries are difficult to distinguish from another kind of personal document—the autobiography. Like letters and diaries, autobiographies can be written at the request of a researcher, particularly in connection with life history studies (see Chapter 20). When used in relation to the life history or biographical method, letters, diaries, and autobiographies (whether solicited or unsolicited) either can be the primary source of data or may be used to complement another source of data, such as life history or life story interviews.

When we evaluate personal documents, the *authenticity* criterion is clearly of considerable importance. Is the purported author of the letter or diary the real author? In the case of autobiographies, this has become a growing problem in recent years as a result of the increasing use of 'ghost' writers by the famous. None the less,

Research in focus 23.2
Using contemporary personal documents

Jacobs (1967) analysed 112 suicide notes written by adults and adolescents in the Los Angeles area who had committed suicide. The notes were acquired in the course of a study of attempts by adolescents to commit suicide. The author writes that he was impressed with the 'rational and coherent character' of the notes (1967: 62) and attempts what he describes as a 'phenomenological' analysis of them. This analysis entailed attending to 'the conscious deliberations that take place before the individual is able to consider and execute the act of suicide' (1967: 64). Jacobs found that the notes fell into six groups, such as notes referring to an illness, a category that in turn was of two types: those in which the writers begged for forgiveness and those in which they did not.

autobiographies can be used to good effect. Pasquandrea (2014) conducted a discursive analysis of the autobiographical writings of Louis Armstrong, the famous jazz trumpeter (1901–71). The written works included two autobiographies, an anthology of his writings, and a long interview with Armstrong. For example, Pasquandrea shows that Armstrong presented the inability of some of his peers to read and write music in quite different ways and that he did this in order to produce certain kinds of effect on the reader, such as whether particular musicians were to be depicted in a positive or negative light. Sometimes the inability to read or write music is presented as a virtue and at other times as negative. However, the issue of the influence of others in the writing process is relevant here too, as it is clear that the original draft of one of the autobiographies (which is in an archive) was heavily edited.

The same may apply to other documents. For example, in the case of Augustus Lamb (Research in focus 23.1), Dickinson (1993: 126–7) notes that there are 'only three letters existing from Augustus himself (which we cannot be certain were written in Augustus's own hand, since the use of amanuenses was not uncommon)'. This remark raises the question of how far Augustus was in fact the author of the entirety of the letters, especially in the light of his learning difficulties. Turning to the issue of *credibility*, J. Scott (1990) observes that there are at least two major concerns with respect to personal documents: the factual accuracy of reports and whether they do in fact report the true feelings of the writer. The case of Augustus Lamb, in which clear differences were found in views about him and his condition, suggests that the notion that there might be a definitive factually accurate account is problematic. Scott recommends a strategy of healthy scepticism regarding the sincerity with which the writer reports his or her true feelings. Famous people may be fully aware that their letters or diaries will be of considerable interest to others and may, therefore, have one eye firmly fixed on the degree to which they really reveal themselves in their writings, or alternatively ensure that they convey a 'front' that they want to project.

Letters written by famous people have to be treated with similar caution, since they can frequently be exercises in reputation building. In the case of the suicide notes analysed by Jacobs (1967) (see Research in focus 23.2), although the notes themselves were found to be rational and coherent, it is likely that the individuals themselves were in a highly distressed state, so that it is not clear how far their true feelings were being revealed.

Representativeness is clearly a major concern for these materials. Since literacy was far lower in earlier times, letters, diaries, and autobiographies are likely to be the preserve of the literate and by and large the middle class. Moreover, since boys were often more likely to receive an education than girls, the voices of women tend to be under-represented in these documents. Women were also less likely to have had the self-confidence and encouragement to write diaries and autobiographies. Therefore, such historical documents are likely to be biased in terms of authorship. A further problem is the selective survival of such documents as letters. Why do any survive at all and what proportion are damaged, lost, or thrown away? We do not know, for example, how representative the 112 suicide notes analysed by Jacobs (1967; see Research in focus 23.2) are. Quite aside from the fact that only a relatively small percentage of suicide victims leave notes, it may be that notes are sometimes destroyed by family members. Similarly, we do not know why 'Charlie Mac's' Civil War letters survived (whereas presumably those written by other soldiers did not) nor whether some of his letters did not survive (see Research in focus 23.3). The question of *meaning* is often rendered problematic by such things as damage to letters and diaries and the use by authors of abbreviations or codes that are difficult to decipher. Also, as J. Scott (1990) observes, letter-writers may leave much unsaid in their communications, because they share with their recipients common values and assumptions that are not revealed.

Visual objects

There is a growing interest in the visual in social research, a point that was highlighted in Chapter 19. The photograph is the most obvious manifestation of this trend, in that, rather than being thought of as incidental to the research process, photographs are becoming objects of interest in their own right (see Thinking deeply 23.1). Once again, there is a distinction between photographs and other visual objects that are produced as part of fieldwork, as discussed in Chapter 19, and those that are extant (which are the focus of attention here). One of the main ways in which photographs may be of interest in social research is in terms of what they reveal about families. As J. Scott (1990) observes, many family photographs are taken as a record of ceremonial occasions (weddings, christenings) and of recurring events such as Christmas, annual holidays, and wearing a new uniform at the start of the new school year. Scott refers to a distinction between three types of home photograph: *idealization*, which is a formal pose—for example, the wedding photograph or a photograph of the family in its finery; *natural portrayal*, which entails capturing actions as they happen, though there may be a contrived component to the photograph; and *demystification*, which entails capturing an image of the subject in an untypical (and often embarrassing) situation. Scott suggests that it is necessary to be aware of these different types in order not to be exclusively concerned

Research in focus 23.3
Comparing military blogs and Civil War letters and diaries

It is tempting to think that the century-and-a-half that separates a soldier writing a military blog and the letters and diary of a soldier in the American Civil War will be far apart in tone and content. Shapiro and Humphreys (2013) compare the military blog of 'Dadmanly', who was in the US army for just over four years beginning in August 2004 and who served in Iraq for eighteen months, with the letters and diaries of 'Charlie Mac', who joined the Union Army in 1862. The latter's writings continued until April 1865 and have been compiled in an anthology. There are clear differences: for example, Dadmanly wrote for a general audience the vast majority of whom he would never know, whereas Charlie Mac wrote primarily for members of his large family, although he seems to have anticipated that his letters might have a wider readership. Although Dadmanly's blog posts were clearly written for a general audience, Charlie Mac's letters were written in a way that suggests he anticipated that they would be handed around to others. There are various common elements. Both writers show a desire to reassure family and friends about their safety and well-being. Both expressed opinions about the progress of their respective wars and offered political comments about them; both wrote in large part to maintain relationships with their families; and for both of them, writing was therapeutic in dealing with the personal experience of war. Shapiro and Humphreys see the comparison as significant because it suggests that although the contexts of writing are very different in these two instances, there are continuities between them that suggest that we should be wary of assuming that new media formats necessarily imply changes in communication content.

with the superficial appearance of the images and so that we can probe beneath that surface. He writes:

> There is a great deal that photographs do not tell us about their world. Hirsch [1981: 42] argues, for example, that 'The prim poses and solemn faces which we associate with Victorian photography conceal the reality of child labour, women factory workers, whose long hours often brought about the neglect of their infants, nannies sedating their charges with rum, and mistresses diverting middle class fathers.'
>
> (J. Scott 1990: 195)

As Scott argues, this means not only that the photograph must not be taken at its face value when used as a research source; it is also necessary to have considerable additional knowledge of the social context to probe beneath the surface. In fact, one might wonder whether the photograph in such a situation can be of any use to a researcher at all. The researcher does not need the photograph to uncover the ills that formed the underbelly of Victorian society; its only purpose seems to be to suggest that there is a gap between the photographic image and the underlying reality. A similar kind of point is made by Sutton in Research in focus 23.4.

Scott sees the issue of *representativeness* as a particular problem for the analyst of photographs. As he suggests, the photographs that survive the passage of time—for example, in archives—are unlikely to be representative.

They are likely to have been subject to all sorts of hazards, such as damage and selective retention. The example provided in Research in focus 23.4 of photographs of visits to Disney theme parks suggests that the process of discarding photographs may be systematic. The other problem relates to the issue of what is *not* photographed, as suggested by the quotation by Hirsch, and Sutton's suggestion that unhappy events at Disney theme parks may not be photographed at all. A sensitivity to what is not photographed can reveal the 'mentality' of the person(s) behind the camera. This is the point that Sutton is making: the absence of photographs depicting less happy experiences at the parks suggests something about how the prospect of a visit to a Disney theme park is viewed and therefore tells us something about the reach of an influential corporation in the culture industry. What is clear is that the question of representativeness is much more fundamental than the issue of what survives, because it points to the way in which the selective survival of photographs may be constitutive of a reality that family members (or others) seek to fashion. As in Sutton's example, that very manufactured reality may then become a focus of interest for the social researcher in its own right.

The real problem for the user of photographs is that of recognizing the different ways in which the image may be comprehended. Blaikie (2001) found some fascinating photographs in the local museums of the Northern

Thinking deeply 23.1
What are the roles of photographs in social research?

Photographs may have a variety of roles in relation to social research. While Chapter 19 and the present chapter discuss them in relation to qualitative research, there is no reason why they cannot be employed in quantitative research, and some researchers have used them in this connection. For example, photographs could be the focus of content analysis or might be employed as prompts in connection with structured interviewing or an experiment. However, the growing interest in photographs and visual materials more generally has tended to come from qualitative researchers. There is an important distinction between the use of *extant* photographs that have not been produced for the research and *research-generated* photographs that have been produced by the researcher or at the researcher's request. Three prominent roles have been:

1. *Illustrative.* Photographs may have a role whereby they do little more than illustrate points and therefore enliven what might otherwise be a rather dry discussion of findings. In some classic reports of their findings by anthropologists, photographs seemed to have such a limited role. Gradually, some anthropologists began to experiment with forms of ethnography in which photographs had a more prominent position.

2. *As data.* Photographs may be viewed as data in their own right. When they are research-generated photographs, they become essentially part of the researcher's field notes (see Research in focus 19.10 for an example). When they are extant photographs, they become the main source of data about the field in which the researcher is interested. The examples in the text of this section by Sutton (1992; Research in focus 23.4) and Blaikie (2001) are examples of this kind of use.

3. *As prompts.* Photographs may be used as prompts to entice people to talk about what is represented in them. Both research-generated photographs (see Research in focus 19.10) and extant photographs may be used in this way. Sometimes, research participants may volunteer the use of their photographs for this kind of use. For example, Riches and Dawson (1998) found that, in interviews with bereaved parents, unsolicited photographs of their deceased children were often shown. These photographs were frequently shown by the parents to others, so that their use in interviews merged with their existing practices for handling their grief. In this case, the photographs were extant ones. Research in focus 19.11 provides an illustration of the use of photographs of the research-generated kind, in that they were taken at the instigation of the researchers who were interested in the experience of homelessness.

Research in focus 23.4
Photographs of the Magic Kingdom

Sutton (1992) has noted a paradox about people's visits to Disney theme parks. On the one hand, the Magic Kingdom is supposed to be 'the happiest place on Earth', with employees ('cast members') being trained to enhance the experience. However, it is clear that some people do not enjoy themselves while visiting a park. The time spent in queues, in particular, was a gripe for Sutton, as it often is for other visitors ('guests') (Bryman 1995). Nonetheless, people expect their visit to be momentous and therefore take along their cameras (and increasingly camcorders, though Sutton does not make this point). Sutton argues that photographs distort people's memories of their visit. They take pictures that support their anticipation that the Disney theme parks are happy places, and, when they return home, they 'discard photographs that remind them of unpleasant experiences and keep photographs that remind them of pleasant experiences' (Sutton 1992: 283). In other words, positive feelings are a post-visit reconstruction that are substantially aided by one's photographs. As a result, Sutton argues, the photographs provide not accurate recollections of a visit but distorted ones.

Isles of Orkney and Shetland. These photographs derived from the work of local photographers and donated family albums. As Blaikie (2001: 347) observes, in the images themselves and the ways in which they are represented by the museums, the 'apparently raw "reality" of island culture has already been appropriated and ordered'. The problem for the researcher is then one of coming to terms with the image and what it can be taken to mean. As he notes, is the image of a crofter standing by his home suggestive of respectability or of poverty? Also, however the image is construed, should it be seen as having had the function for the photographer of providing a social commentary, or of depicting a disappearing way of life, or of merely providing an image with no obvious subtext? Any or a combination of these different narratives may be applicable, so does this mean that the photograph is a highly limited form of document for the social researcher? While acknowledging the diversity of interpretations that can be bestowed on the images he examined, Blaikie argues that, in his case, they provide a perspective on the emergence of modernity and the sense of loss of a past life, especially

in terms of the ways in which they were organized by the museums. Coming to this kind of understanding requires a sensitivity to the contextual nature of images and the variety of interpretations that can be attributed to them.

A related issue concerns the tendency in everyday discourse to give photographs special credibility and to presume that their meaning is transparent. Sayings such as 'a picture is worth a thousand words' or 'the camera never lies' are examples of a tendency to valorize images in this way. An illustration of the way in which such views can be misleading can be seen in relation to the photograph in Plate 23.1 taken on 9 July 1937 outside Lord's cricket ground on the opening day of the Eton–Harrow annual match. This image is widely viewed as a capsule statement of Britain's divided class system. For example, in an article in *The Times* on 16 January 2015, the journalist Philip Collins wrote an article on the class-bound nature of Britain's education system. The middle portion of the photograph is included (though not commented on at any point) with the caption: 'The class-bound way we educate our children is

Plate 23.1
Toffs and toughs

Copyright: Jimmy Sime/Hulton Archive Getty Images.

economic suicide' (**http://www.thetimes.co.uk/tto/opinion/columnists/article4324673.ece**, accessed 19 January 2015). The meaning and significance of the photograph are treated as givens and not requiring comment or elaboration. The photograph is known as 'toffs and toughs' and is presumed to show two Etonian boys in uniform standing outside Lord's being looked upon with some bemusement by three working-class 'toughs'. However, a discussion of this photograph by Ian Jack, a *Guardian* journalist, shows that this widely held view is extremely misleading. Quite aside from the fact that the two public school boys were from Harrow, not Eton, they had dressed for a special party that the parents of one of them were organizing following the cricket match that the boys were attending. This was not standard uniform. The boys were waiting for a car to arrive to take them to the party and it was late, possibly accounting for the boys apparently ignoring the 'toughs' and staring into the distance because they were looking out for their transport. Further, the two boys were not 'toffs'—the father of one of them was a professional soldier. Nor were the three boys 'toughs'. They attended a local Church of England school and had been to the dentist that day. They had decided to hang around at Lord's in order to make some money by carrying bags or opening car doors and were indeed successful in that respect. Also, as Jack notes, the boys are not unkempt—they are simply wearing open-necked shirts and informal clothes typical of working-class boys of their day. By contrast, the two Harrow pupils were in special garb rather than what was typical of public-school boys of their day. This fascinating story provides some insight into the reasons why an unquestioning stance on photographs is something that should be discouraged. Ian Jack's article can be found at: **http://moreintelligentlife.com/content/ian-jack/5-boys?page=full#_** (accessed 3 June 2014).

Official documents deriving from the state

The state is the source of a great deal of information of potential significance for social researchers. It produces a great deal of statistical information, some of which was touched on in Chapter 14. In addition to such quantitative data, the state is the source of a great deal of textual material of potential interest, such as Acts of Parliament and official reports.

Thompson et al. (2013) use UK Government policy documents from the period 2002–11 to show how East London was positioned as a problem area and how this narrative was deployed as a justification for locating the 2012 Olympic Games in London. The documents included: several House of Commons sources (the London Olympic Bid, a publication on the funding and legacy of the Olympic Games and the Paralympic Games); Department for Culture, Media, and Sport sources (such as a publication on making the most of the Games and a framework for the evaluation of the Games's impacts and legacy); a British Olympic Association publication on London; a statement on the Olympic legacy by the boroughs involved; and a spatial development strategy report by the Greater London Authority. The authors quote from the House of Commons report on the funding and legacy of the Games: 'Public money is being used to transform the Olympic Park, a contaminated wasteland, into a cleansed zone ready for development' (quoted in Thompson et al. 2013: 3.3). The depiction of the area as one of deprivation was coupled with a narrative of an area in which community sport was in decline and where being out of work had become a way of life. The London 2012 Olympics were presented as a cornerstone of the transformation and regeneration of East London. Thompson et al. use their analysis of these documents as a means of demonstrating the tying of a neoliberal rhetoric to the justification of the massive investment involved.

Similar kinds of materials but in a different context were employed by Abraham (1994) in connection with his research on the medical drug Opren. The research was concerned with the role of interests and values in scientists' evaluations of the safety of medicines. The author describes his sources as 'publicly available transcripts of the testimonies of scientists, including many employed in the manufacture of Opren, Parliamentary debates, questions and answers in *Hansard*, and leaflets, letters, consultation papers and other documentation disposed by the British regulatory authority in respect of its duties under the 1968 British Medicines Act' (Abraham 1994: 720). Abraham's research shows that there were inconsistencies in the scientists' testimonies, suggesting that interests play an important role in such situations. He also uses his findings to infer that the notion of a scientific ethos, which has been influential in the sociology of science, has limited applicability in areas of controversy in which interests come to the surface.

In terms of J. Scott's (1990) four criteria, such materials can certainly be seen as authentic and as having meaning (in the sense of being clear and comprehensible to the researcher), but the two other standards require somewhat greater consideration. The question of credibility raises the issue of whether the documentary source is biased. This is exactly the point of Abraham's (1994) research. In other words, such documents can be interesting precisely because of the biases they reveal. Equally, this point suggests that caution is necessary in attempting to treat them as depictions of reality. The issue of representativeness is complicated in that materials like these are in a sense unique, and it is precisely their official or quasi-official character that makes them interesting in their own right. There is also, of course, the question of whether the case itself is representative, but in the context of qualitative research this is not a meaningful question, because no case can be representative in a statistical sense. The issue is one of establishing a cogent theoretical account and possibly examining that account in other related or similar contexts.

Official documents deriving from private sources

This is a very heterogeneous group of sources, but one type that has been used a great deal is company documents. Companies (and indeed organizations generally) produce many documents. Some of these are in the public domain, such as annual reports, mission statements, press releases, advertisements, and public relations material in printed form and on the Internet. Other documents are not (or may not be) in the public domain, such as company newsletters, organizational charts, minutes of meetings, memos, internal and external correspondence, manuals for new recruits, and so on. Such materials are often used by organizational ethnographers as part of their investigations, but the difficulty of gaining access to some organizations means that many researchers have to rely on public-domain documents alone. Even if the researcher is an insider who has gained access to an organization, it may well be that certain documents that are not in the public domain will not be available to him or her. For his study of ICI, Pettigrew (1985; see Research in focus 3.16) was allowed access to company archives, so that, in addition to interviewing, he was allowed to examine 'materials on company strategy and personnel policy, documents relating to the birth and development of various company OD [organizational development] groups, files documenting the natural history of key organizational changes, and information on the recruitment and training of internal OD consultants, and the use made of external OD consultants' (Pettigrew 1985: 41).

Such information can be very important for researchers conducting case studies of organizations using such methods as participant observation or (as in Pettigrew's case) qualitative interviews. Other writers have relied more or less exclusively on documents. The study of the film director Alfred Hitchcock by Kapsis (1989) employed a combination of personal documents (notably correspondence) and official documents, such as production notes and publicity files.

Such documents need to be evaluated using Scott's four criteria. As with the materials considered in the previous section, documents deriving from private sources such as companies are likely to be authentic and meaningful (in the sense of being clear and comprehensible to the researcher), though this is not to suggest that the analyst of documents should be complacent. Issues of credibility and representativeness are likely to exercise the analyst of documents somewhat more.

People who write documents are likely to have a particular point of view that they want to get across. An interesting illustration of this simple observation is provided by a study of company documentation by Forster (1994). In the course of a study of career development issues in a major British retail company (referred to pseudonymously as TC), Forster carried out an extensive analysis of company documentation relating primarily to human resource management issues, as well as interviews and a questionnaire survey. Because he was able to interview many of the authors of the documents about what they had written, 'both the accuracy of the documents and their authorship could be validated by the individuals who had produced them' (Forster 1994: 155). In other words, the authenticity of the documents was confirmed, and it would seem that credibility was verified as well. However, Forster also tells us that the documents showed up divergent interpretations among different groupings of key events and processes:

> One of the clearest themes to emerge was the apparently incompatible interpretations of the same events and processes amongst the three sub-groups within the company—senior executives, HQ personnel staff and regional personnel managers. . . . These documents were not produced deliberately to distort or obscure events or processes being described, but their effect was to do precisely this.
>
> (Forster 1994: 160)

Research in focus 23.5
Remembering the moon landings

Goodings, Brown, and Parker (2013) examined visitor feedback relating to a special exhibition about the Apollo moon landings at the National Space Centre in Leicester in the UK. Visitors were encouraged to write 'memory cards' which were deposited on a wall at the exhibit. Over 400 cards were analysed; the authors stated that they 'were looking at the internal structure of the brief accounts on the cards, what they defined at important and relevant, how they constructed a personal narrative, and the meanings that were accorded to the historical event' (Goodings et al. 2013: 271). The authors identified three broad narratives associated with remembering the moon landings. These narratives were formed by producing a set of themes 'that loosely organised the accounts offered on individual cards' (Goodings et al. 2013: 271). The themes were: an association of the moon landings with the writer's sense of 'my generation'; a recollection of watching the landings on television; and the sense of a new future associated with the landing but which NASA (National Aeronautical and Space Administration) in the USA actively managed.

In other words, members of the different groupings expressed through the documents certain perspectives that reflected their positions in the organization. Consequently, although authors of the documents could confirm the content of those documents, the latter could not be regarded as 'free from error and distortion', as J. Scott (1990: 6) puts it. Therefore, documents cannot be regarded as providing objective accounts of a state of affairs. They have to be interrogated and examined in the context of other sources of data. As Forster's case suggests, the different stances that are taken up by the authors of documents can be used as a platform for developing insights into the processes and factors that lie behind divergence. In this instance, the documents are interesting in bringing out the role and significance of subcultures within the organization.

Issues of representativeness are likely to loom large in most contexts of this kind. Did Forster have access to a totally comprehensive set of documents? It could be that some had been destroyed or that he was not allowed access to certain documents that were regarded as sensitive.

Kapsis (1989) employed a wide variety of documents (correspondence, speeches, publicity files, etc.) relating to the Hollywood director, Alfred Hitchcock, in his study of how Hitchcock's reputation was created. Hitchcock or possibly others may have chosen not to deposit documents that were less than favourable to his image. Since Kapsis's article is concerned with reputation building and particularly with the active part played by Hitchcock and others in the construction of his reputation as a significant film-maker, the part played by documents that might have been less than supportive of this reputation would be of considerable importance. This is not to say that such documents necessarily exist but that doubts are bound to surface whenever there is uncertainty about the representativeness of sources. Similarly, while the findings relating to Research in focus 23.5 are highly instructive about the ways in which the moon landings are remembered both nostalgically and with a recognition of disappointment about what followed, issues of representativeness might arise in terms of whether the narratives described apply to all visitors and whether all memory cards were available to the researchers.

Mass-media outputs

Newspapers, magazines, television programmes, films, and other mass media are potential sources for social scientific analysis. Of course, we have encountered these kinds of source before when exploring content analysis in Chapter 13. In addition to mass-media outputs being explored using a quantitative form of data analysis such as content analysis, such sources can also be examined so that their qualitative nature is preserved. Typically, such analysis entails searching for themes in the sources that are examined, but see the section below on 'Interpreting documents' for a more detailed examination of this issue.

Vincent et al. (2010) conducted a textual analysis of English newspapers' narratives about the England football team's participation in the 2006 World Cup in Germany. They examined *The Times*, *Daily Telegraph*, *Daily Mail*, *Daily Mirror*, and *The Sun*, as well as those newspapers'

Sunday publications (which included the now defunct *News of the World*), for the duration of the competition. The authors propose that in contrast to the competition's official slogan of 'a time to make friends', the newspapers fuelled a patriotic fervour in which they drew on often invented traditions and motifs from English history. For example, they show how the notion of a 'lionheart spirit', associated with the famous lions on the England shirt and with King Richard I, known as 'the Lionheart', produced frequent allusions to lions and roaring, such as the *Daily Mirror*'s 'Let's Roar! The Hearts of Our Nation are with You' and the *Sun*'s 'England Lionheart Wayne Rooney is Fired Up and Ready to Roar'. An 'us and them' rhetoric was also projected by allusions to English fair play and the propensity of others to cheat (diving, feigning injury, etc.). The theme of xenophobia and fair play surfaced again when England were ejected from the competition in a match against Portugal. Not only did the newspapers turn their sights on Rooney's then Manchester United team-mate Cristiano Ronaldo for his role in getting him sent off, but it was time to turn on the England manager and in a way that surfaced his foreignness. The quotation from the *Daily Mail* is illustrative:

> The most disgracefully prepared team in England's World Cup history was managed by a money-grabbing charlatan . . . all Sven Göran Eriksson deserves is to go back up his fjord to the land of winter darkness, hammer throwers and sexual promiscuity from where he came. We've sold our birthright down the fjord to a nation of seven million skiers and hammer throwers who spend half their lives in darkness.
>
> (quoted in Vincent et al. 2010: 218)

Thus, this research brings out the themes of English identity, invented traditions, and globalization. It also showed that although these themes cropped up in all the newspapers that were included in the analysis, the more lurid xenophobic allusions tended to be found in the popular press. A quantitative content analysis of the kind examined in Chapter 13 might have been able to bring out aspects of this set of findings, but the use of a more fine-grained analysis allows a greater sensitivity to the nature and content of specific themes.

Authenticity is sometimes difficult to establish in the case of mass-media outputs. While the outputs can usually be deemed to be genuine, the authorship of articles is often unclear (for example, editorials, some magazine articles), so that it is difficult to know whether the account can be relied upon as being written by someone in a position to provide an accurate version. Credibility is frequently an issue, but in fact, as the examples used in this section show, it is often the uncovering of error or distortion that is the objective of the analysis. Representativeness is rarely an issue for analyses of newspaper or magazine articles, since the corpus from which a sample has been drawn is usually ascertainable, especially when a wide range of newspapers is employed, as in the study by Vincent et al. (2010). Finally, the evidence is usually clear and comprehensible but may require considerable awareness of contextual factors, such as the need for Wagg to be sensitive to the history of Manchester United and its significance for the club's supporters (see Research in focus 23.6).

Research in focus 23.6
Cristiano Ronaldo and the football fanzine

Fanzines can provide interesting alternative insights, as they are often positioned by their contributors as providing an alternative worldview to mainstream commentators and media. In that vein, Wagg (2010) notes that during his stay at Manchester United in the years 2003–2009 and particularly towards the end of that period, Cristiano Ronaldo was widely hailed as a player of great talent and as equivalent in footballing stature to United idols, such as George Best. However, Wagg also observes that Ronaldo was not regarded with the same fondness by *Red Issue*, a Manchester United fanzine, one of whose contributors described him when he was close to a move to Real Madrid as a 'preening, perma-tanned, posturing, petulant prick' (2010: 920). Wage argues that the reason for the author's displeasure was not just the nature of Ronaldo's participation in securing his lucrative departure to Spain, but his failure to display the appropriate markers of being a Mancunian who inhabited a niche defined by place and class. He also shows that among Portuguese migrants living in the same area and who follow Manchester United, the view of Ronaldo was more positive, a stance that Wagg attributes to the fact that they too are seeking to prosper in a global economy and to take up the international opportunities it proffers.

Virtual documents

Websites, online discussion groups, blogs, email, social networking sites, etc. are potential sources of data in their own right and can be regarded as potential material for both quantitative and qualitative content analysis. Several examples in this book have drawn on this kind of material:

- The growing use (noted in Chapter 19) of online forums as a means of collecting data and contacting people by researchers alongside conventional ethnography, such as Pearsons's (2012) research on Manchester United's Red Brigade, Williams's (2006) use of online forums dedicated to straightedge alongside conventional ethnography (Research in focus 19.8), and Hallett and Barber's (2014) research on men's hair salons;

- Brotsky and Giles's (2007) covert participant observation study of 'pro-ana' discussion groups (Research in focus 19.9);

- the various studies using online community discussion group data referred to in Thinking deeply 19.2;

- Hine's (2014) research on headlice in an online parenting discussion group (see Thinking deeply 17.2);

- Attar and Genus's (2014) critical discourse analysis of the GM Nation? debate, which included emails and comments on the website (Research in focus 22.9);

- Shapiro and Humphreys's comparison of military blogs and American Civil War letters and diaries (Research in focus 23.3);

- Beullens and Schepers's (2013) content analysis of Belgian Facebook profiles to examine the representation of alcohol use (Research in focus 13.2);

- Kapidzic and Herring's (in press) analysis of photographs on a teenagers' chat site referred to in Chapter 13.

Websites

Sillince and Brown (2009), for example, examined the websites of all English and Welsh police constabularies between October 2005 and March 2006. The websites were analysed to explore how the constabularies' organizational identities as displayed in the websites were rhetorically constructed. Through a rhetorical analysis of such documents, Sillince and Brown (2009) show that organizational identity was rhetorically constructed through core themes:

1. the constabulary as effective or ineffective;

2. the constabulary as part of the community or as apart from the community;

3. the constabulary as progressive or not progressive.

Within each of these three organizational identity constructions Sillince and Brown identified distinctive rhetorical manœuvres. Thus, with the last of the three themes, the identification of the constabulary as progressive or not progressive was often placed within a wider narrative of improvement, particularly from being not progressive to being progressive. Of particular theoretical significance is the investigation's finding on the basis of the analysis that organizational identity is not unitary but is often conflicting and ambiguous and is designed to support claims to legitimacy for both internal and external audiences.

However, as noted in Chapter 13 (in the section on 'The Internet as object of content analysis'), there are clearly difficulties with using websites as sources of data in this way and the issues highlighted there are equally applicable in this context. It is worth reviewing these points once again.

In addition, it is important to bear in mind the four quality criteria recommended by J. Scott (1990) in connection with documents. Scott's suggestions invite us to consider

Tips and skills
Referring to websites

There is a growing practice in academic work that, when referring to websites, you should include the date you consulted them. This convention is very much associated with the fact that websites often disappear and frequently change, so that, if subsequent researchers want to follow up your findings, or even to check on them, they may find that they are no longer there or that they have changed. Citing the date you accessed the website may help to relieve any anxieties about someone not finding a website you have referred to or finding it has changed. This does mean, however, that you will have to keep a running record of the dates you accessed the websites to which you refer.

quite why a website is constructed. Why is it there at all? Is it there for commercial reasons? Does it have an axe to grind? In other words, we should be no less sceptical about websites than about any other kind of document.

Blogs

Yet another kind of document that has been subjected to analysis is the blog (Web log). We have already encountered an example of the use of a blog as data in Research in focus 23.3 and in Key concept 19.4. Sometimes, blogs may be difficult to distinguish from websites and their analysis. For example, in the case of Research in focus 23.7, it was noted that the researchers included within their purview a headmaster's blog that was linked to the school's website. Further examples of examinations of blogs are provided in Research in focus 23.8 and in Key concept 19.4.

Chatrooms, discussion forums, and online communities

As noted in Chapter 13, postings to chatrooms, discussion forums, and online communities of different kinds can be a fertile source of data for researchers. Collectively, these

are often referred to as studies of online interaction and sometimes, when it is appropriate, as studies of online communities. An example can be found in Research in focus 23.10. Such data might be gleaned in real time, in which case they are closer to a form of observation, or they may be archived interactions, in which case they are forms of document. When the documents are postings to online discussion groups, as in Research in focus 23.9 (see also the study by Hine referred to in Thinking deeply 17.2), some further considerations come into play. Sometimes the researcher may read and analyse the various postings without any participation. This can often lead to accusations of 'lurking', where the researcher simply reads without participation and without announcing his or her presence and which is sometimes regarded as being ethically dubious. On other occasions, the researcher may be a participant and in such circumstances the research is much closer to online ethnography. These considerations demonstrate that the analysis of online documents and virtual/online ethnography easily shade into each other. The examination of posts to online communities shades into and is largely inseparable from online ethnography, which was discussed in Chapter 19, and in particular from netnography (see Key concept 19.4).

Research in focus 23.7
Conducting a qualitative content analysis of websites

Brooks and Waters (2015) noted that the theme of internationalization is a common one in British higher education, with its emphasis on having a global reach and attracting overseas students. They argue that much the same applies to schools where parents are often concerned that their children acquire what the authors call 'global capital', but they suggest that little is known about the extent to which this is a focus for schools. They analysed websites, prospectuses, and other public documents relating to thirty 'elite' schools with sixth forms in England. The sample comprised 'influential' private schools, 'high-performing' private schools, and 'high-performing' state schools. Documents relating to ten schools of each type were the focus of the analysis, which they describe as follows:

> We were interested to explore the extent to which certain themes were mentioned and/or represented (e.g. HE destinations outside the UK, international pupils, trips and expeditions abroad), and used a detailed grid to record this information. We also explored, in a more discursive manner, the way in which these various themes were constructed in the websites and elsewhere.

> (Brooks and Waters 2015)

The authors found that while internationalism was significant for the schools, this theme was less prominent than providing a strong sense of the 'Englishness' or 'Britishness' of the school and its offerings, such as the following taken from one school's website:

> While [Influential Private 10] provides a distinctively British education, our programmes include extensive international links with a group of schools around the world through which exchange of educational practice and ideas and cross-cultural encounter can be developed over the long term.

> (quoted in Brooks and Waters 2015)

This research then uses websites (including a headmaster's blog for at least one of the schools) and other documents to reveal some interesting tensions in the ways in which elite schools represent themselves.

Research in focus 23.8
Conducting a thematic analysis of gap year travel blogs

Snee (2013) was interested in how representations of cultural difference were portrayed in 'gap year' narratives. She used sought out blogs containing the phrase 'gap year' using two blog search engines (Google Blog Search and Technorati) and also searched some websites which seemed to be associated with the blogs she uncovered through this search. She selected those whose author was from the UK and whose gap year was taken overseas, was sandwiched between school and university, and included more than a couple of posts. Initially, she uncovered 700 blogs but these were narrowed down to 39 because she sought a balance in terms of both gender and the type of gap year. These blogs form her data, along with interviews with nine of the bloggers. The interviews indicated that bloggers wrote up their experiences in this format because it was more convenient than an email to large numbers of people and in order to provide 'a record of their travels' (Snee 2013: 147), suggesting that blogs are very much a modern form of diary. Her inductive analysis of the blogs yielded four themes:

1. The bloggers drew on common representations of the exotic qualities of the places they visited in order to portray their destinations. For example: 'We sailed to White Haven Beach which is just like on the postcards; white sands and light blue sea' (Jo, quoted in Snee 2013: 149).

2. Bloggers often convey a sense of feeling out of place in these exotic locations. This sense of feeling out of place arose either from an awareness of the bloggers' physical differences or from cultural factors. For example, one of the bloggers came to realize that by standing with her arms crossed in Uganda she had in fact been rude according to the local cultural traditions.

3. Through their interaction with local people and their physical environment, gap year bloggers often displayed a sensitivity to local customs and to the complexity of the locations in which they were travelling. For example, one blogger expressed his unease at the lack of respect shown by some tourists at Ayers Rock (Uluru) in Australia by clambering over it.

4. There is often a narrative of the danger, risk, and sometimes irritations associated with the local environment. There are complaints about the quality of driving in Delhi, lack of concern for safety in Ecuador, and the frightening quality of Rio de Janeiro. These involve implicit and sometimes explicit comparisons with the UK.

As Snee notes, the themes deriving from the blogs reveal a tension:

> On one hand, there is a desire to learn about and understand the local, reflect on global issues and experience what places are 'really like' . . . . On the other hand, established discourses are reproduced of an 'Other' that is exoticized, romanticized, or even criticized.
>
> (Snee 2013: 158)

Snee has produced a useful toolkit for doing analyses of blogs: **eprints.ncrm.ac.uk/1321/2/10-toolkit-blog-analysis.pdf** (accessed 10 December 2014).

Social media

Social media are another area where virtual documents may be found and subjected to analysis. This is a research area that is in its infancy and which has tended to be associated with the examination of so-called 'Big Data' (e.g. Procter, Vis, and Voss 2013). For a researcher intending to use social media posts for a thematic analysis a major challenge is likely to be how to sample from the vast array of possible documents. However, we have already seen from the quantitative content analysis reported in Research in focus 13.2 how such an investigation might be feasible. Greaves

et al. (in press) were interested in the frequency of tweets relating to acute NHS hospitals in England and also in their content, especially in relation to care quality. They write:

> We prospectively collected tweets aimed at NHS hospitals from the Twitter streaming application-programming interface (API) for a year. We identified tweets aimed at NHS hospitals by using 'mentions', where a tweet includes the '@username' of a Twitter user.
>
> (Greaves et al. in press)

The authors searched hospital trust websites to determine which ones were on Twitter and found 75 out of 166

Research in focus 23.9
Conducting a thematic analysis of online discussion postings

Postings on websites have been a fertile source of data for many researchers. Sullivan (2003) analysed postings to two online US listservs that offered online support to cancer sufferers. One group offered support for ovarian cancer and the other for prostate cancer. The point about the choice of these two groups is that their respective diseases are gender-specific and therefore the researcher was able to explore gender differences in support. The postings were submitted to a thematic analysis (see Chapter 24). Differences between the two sets of postings were discerned. The postings to the prostate cancer support group tended to be of a technical nature, focusing a great deal on information giving and requesting. For example, one patient wrote:

> Around the 11th week of estramustine (Emcyt) (+ vinblastine) I had my first bona fide side effect (apart from some fatigue and muscle cramping): my nipples have enlarged, and possibly the breasts a bit, although I may just be focusing on existing fat. Does anyone with experience know if they continue to enlarge (obviously not forever) and if the sensitivity (some, not great) increases or just stays constant?

> (quoted in Sullivan 2003: 94)

The ovarian cancer postings were more likely to deal with personal experiences and comments, such as:

> those feelings sound SOOOO familiar that I had to gulp hard reading your post—it came very close to home. There were times when I felt that way even though I was finished with chemo and not facing a recurrence that I knew of!

> (quoted in Sullivan 2003: 89)

that had a Twitter presence. They collect 198,499 tweets covering the period 17 April 2012 to 26 June 2013. They randomly selected 1,000 tweets for a quantitative content analysis which entailed a more nuanced qualitative content analysis as well. Care quality was a theme in just 11.3 per cent of tweets. Within the theme of care quality there were three subthemes. The first, 'patient experience', was itself made up of three sub-themes: staff interaction (e.g. 'Home from [@named hospital] after a weeks stay . . . we feel blessed to have been cared for by such an amazing team. Thank you [named ward] x'); environment/facilities (e.g. '[@named hospital] Your a&e department is absolutely filthy it makes the hospital visit even more unpleasant. #unsatisfactory'); and timeliness/access (e.g. '[@named hospital] where the waiting time is ridiculous waited 3hr yesterday, 3lots of bloods took, 2hrs so far today for a blood test again!'). The other two themes relating to care quality were 'effective care' (e.g. [@named hospital] my nan is on [named ward].I'm appalled at the care! I'm a nurse and would never treat my patients like that. The CQC will enjoy my complaint') and 'safe care' (e.g. '#tweetsfromhospbed [@named hospital] I think I'll have to report him, needs more training on drugs before serious mistake hate to do it though'). All of the quotations above are taken from Greaves et al. (in press). The most frequently encountered theme related to fundraising.

A few points are worth registering about this study. First, in the interests of confidentiality, all of the quotations have anonymized people and hospitals and wards. Second, the authors note that when compared to a study of reviews of hospital care deposited on review websites, there was far more frequent mention of technical aspects of care. Greaves et al. (in press) speculate that this may be due to the fact that tweets have to be brief (maximum of 140 characters). This suggests a possible limitation of tweets as documents to be content analysed (either quantitatively or qualitatively), namely that their brevity acts as a constraint on what can be written and therefore on what can be inferred from a content analysis. Third, the decision to sample randomly is a sensible way forward when the population of relevant tweets is so large (nearly 200,000). An alternative might be to use purposive sampling, but that would require a great deal of reading through of a large body of tweets to establish whether they meet the criteria being employed. Theoretical sampling could be used as an alternative approach, since the researcher would be able to break off from reading the tweets once the saturation of theoretical categories had been achieved.

Another possibility that might be considered and could also be used in connection with quantitative content analysis is suggested by Schneider (in press), who was interested in how the Canadian Toronto police present themselves through Twitter. Schneider used search terms to identify both appropriate Twitter accounts and tweets. At the time of his research, he was faced with 105,801 tweets from Canadian Toronto Police Service Twitter accounts. Using an ethnographic content analysis approach, Schneider identified certain useful themes from an initial examination of tweets. One of the themes identified was 'police professionalism', and in order to flesh out this notion he used search terms to create a data set of tweets associated with this concept. Using the term 'professional' yielded 124 tweets but as Schneider notes, this term can mean different things. He then sought out tweets that related to each of the different facets of professionalism. One of these is the idea that police officers are apolitical enforcers of the law. Pursuing this idea produced 34 tweets. The same process was undergone with each of the other key terms that he wanted to develop. Tweets were selected according to a theoretical sampling procedure,

i.e. on the basis of their theoretical relevance and with the goal of saturation in mind. As a result, he was able to narrow down the number of tweets to a reasonable size that would be suitable for the kind of close scrutiny associated with qualitative forms of content analysis. One of Schneider's (in press) research questions was 'how does the use of Twitter contribute to the development and expansion of police presentational strategies?' Through his ethnographic content analysis, he shows that officers use Twitter on official accounts but often in off-duty activities (such as attending a sporting event) giving an impression of being engaged in police work, creating a form of organizational publicity that seeks to enhance the public's trust in the police.

Unsurprisingly, Facebook has also been subjected to this kind of analysis. An example using ethnographic content analysis can be found in Research in focus 23.13.

 # The reality of documents

An issue that has attracted attention only relatively recently and that has implications for the interpretation of documents (the focus of the next section) is that of the status of documents. It is clearly tempting to assume that documents reveal something about an underlying social reality, so that the documents that an organization generates (minutes of meetings, newsletters, mission statements, job definitions, and so on) are viewed as representations of the reality of that organization. In other words, we might take the view that such documents tell us something about what goes on in that organization and will help us to uncover such things as its culture or ethos. According to such a view, documents are windows onto social and organizational realities.

However, some writers have expressed scepticism about the extent to which documents can be viewed in these terms. Rather than viewing documents as ways of gaining access to an underlying reality, writers like Atkinson and Coffey (2011) argue that documents should be viewed as a distinct level of 'reality' in their own right. Atkinson and Coffey propose that documents should be examined in terms of, on the one hand, the context in which they were produced and, on the other hand, their implied readership. When viewed in this way, documents are significant for what they were supposed to accomplish and who they are written for. They are written in order to convey an impression, one that will be favourable to the authors and those whom they represent. Moreover, any document should be viewed as linked to other documents, because invariably they refer to and/or are a response to

other documents. Other documents form part of the context or background to the writing of a document. Atkinson and Coffey refer to the interconnectedness of documents as *inter-textuality*.

The minutes of a meeting in an organization might be the kind of document that would interest a social scientist. On the face of it, they are a record of such things as issues raised at the meeting; the discussion of those issues; views of the participants; and actions to be taken. As such, they might be deemed interesting for a social researcher for their capacity to reveal such things as the culture of the organization or section responsible for the minutes, its preoccupations, and possible disputes among the meeting participants. However, precisely because the minutes are a document that is to be read not only by participants but also by others (members of other departments or of other organizations, or in the case of a public-sector organization the minutes may be accessed by the public under the Freedom of Information Act), they are likely to be written with prospective scrutiny by others in mind. Disagreements may be suppressed and actions to be taken may reflect a desire to demonstrate that important issues are to be addressed rather than because of a genuine desire for acting on them. Also, the minutes are likely to be connected either explicitly or implicitly to other documents of that organization—such as previous minutes, mission statements, job definitions, organizational regulations—and to various documents external to the organization (for example, legislation). Further, following Atkinson and Coffey's suggestions, the minutes should be examined for the ways in which language is employed to convey the messages that are contained.

Atkinson and Coffey's central message is that documents have a distinctive ontological status, in that they form a separate reality, which they refer to as a 'documentary reality', and should not be taken to be 'transparent representations' of an underlying organizational or social reality. They go on to write: 'We cannot . . . learn through written records alone how an organization actually operates day by day. Equally, we cannot treat records—however "official"—as firm evidence of what they report' (Atkinson and Coffey 2011: 79).

Thus, documents need to be recognized for what they are—namely, texts written with distinctive purposes in mind, and not as simply reflecting reality. This means that, if the researcher wishes to employ documents as a means of understanding aspects of an organization and its operations, it is likely that he or she will need to buttress an analysis of documents with other sources of data. First, if we want to treat documents as telling us something about an underlying reality, we will need to employ other sources of data regarding that reality and the contexts within which the documents are produced (see Research in focus 23.9 for an example). These other sources are likely to be significant for developing a contextual understanding of the documents and their significance. We can see this with the study by O'Reilly et al. of REC letters presented in Research in focus 22.4. As the authors note: 'Regardless of what has happened during the REC meeting, the decision letter goes on to create its own "documentary reality"' (O'Reilly et al. 2009: 257). The letter has a life of its own and requires for its understanding other documents (such as REC guidelines and final decision outcomes) and the backcloth of an increasingly tight regime of ethical practice in the social sciences.

Second, a document is rhetorically designed to 'do something'. As Prior (2008) observes, documents are typically viewed by social researchers as resources to be worked on and for their substantive meaning to be revealed, perhaps using techniques introduced in this chapter and in Chapters 13 and 24. At the same time, documents are written to get something done and as such are parts of chains of action

---

Research in focus 23.10
Documents and disaster

Diane Vaughan (1996) wrote a highly regarded book on the *Challenger* accident, which occurred in January 1986 when the Space Shuttle *Challenger* burst into flames just after its launch. Vaughan had been interested in what she calls the 'dark side' of organizations and wanted to use this dreadful incident as a case study for understanding the chain of individual and organization factors that preceded and led to the decision to launch the shuttle in spite of evidence of possible problems. A huge report was written by the Presidential Commission that was appointed to investigate the accident. This report might have been considered sufficient to provide insights into the issues in which she was interested, but Vaughan also examined various other sources: an archive of NASA documents; other investigations of the accident; US House of Representatives hearing transcripts; transcripts of 160 interviews with people involved with *Challenger* conducted by government investigators; risk-assessment documents that were solicited by Vaughan under the US Freedom of Information Act; and numerous interviews conducted by Vaughan herself (Vaughan 2004).

However, as Vaughan (2006) points out, examining documents such as Presidential Commission reports can be extremely illuminating about the kinds of issues that they emphasize and the kinds of ways in which the issues are framed. Vaughan (2006) examined three Commission Reports: the *Challenger* report; the *Columbia* Accident Investigation Board report, which dealt with another space shuttle disaster that took place in February 2003; and the 9/11 Commission report. She shows that each report was shaped by a dominant frame, and these were respectively an 'accident investigation frame'; a 'sociological frame'; and an 'historical/war frame' (2006: 304). Further, she notes that the 9/11 report located causation in what she calls 'regulatory failure' (2006: 300), which is to do with problems with the activities of the agencies charged with upholding national security. An effect of that attribution of causation is to absolve the President and to some extent US foreign policy of responsibility. This examination of documents in their own right implies that they can tell us about such things as how those responsible for reporting officially on major incidents construe the background and causal precedents of those incidents. As such, the reports are interesting as much for where responsibility is *not* perceived as lying. As Atkinson and Coffey remind us, what these reports cannot tell us is what actually led up to them.

that are potential research topics in their own right. An example that is relevant here is the examination by Fincham et al. (2011) of 100 suicide case files. The suicide notes that form part of the files can be analysed for their meaning (as in Research in focus 23.2) but Fincham et al. propose that these documents offer more than this. They write:

> The notes are social documents that use other persons and objects to extend the deceased person beyond death by affecting the way the bereaved will remember them as and the objects and practices they will remember them by. Thus the notes can be considered agents that have the ability to change the living as persons.
>
> (Fincham et al. 2011: 100–1).

The authors found, for example, that suicide notes included a wide range of practical issues to be attended to such as funeral preferences and instructions about resuscitation. Thus, the suicide note turns out to be significant not just for its content in terms of revealing such things as the victim's state of mind or reasons, but for the agency with which the writer invests them. This orientation represents a shift in how documents are regarded for research purposes. For many researchers, content will continue to be the main focus of attention, but it is also important to be attuned to the significance of documents in terms of the parts they play and are intended to play in organizations and social life in general (see Research in focus 23.10).

Interpreting documents

Although it means straying into areas that are relevant to the next chapter, this section will briefly consider the question of how you interpret documents. Two possible approaches are outlined: qualitative content analysis and semiotics. In addition to these, discourse analysis, which was covered in Chapter 22, has been employed as an approach for analysing documents. Research in focus 23.11 provides an example of the use of critical discourse analysis in relation to the interpretation of one kind of document reviewed in this chapter—newspaper articles.

Research in focus 23.11
Using critical discourse analysis to interpret newspaper articles

Critical discourse analysis was introduced in Chapter 22 as an approach to the examination of language and its use that can be applied to a variety of different materials. Teo (2000) employed it in relation to news reporting in Australian newspapers. Teo's focus of interest was the ways in which racism surfaced or was neutralized in two of the main Sydney newspapers. He emphasized in particular nine articles to do with 5T, a young Vietnamese gang that was relatively openly involved in drug-dealing in a suburb of Sydney. Critical discourse analysis was a suitable approach to interpreting these documents because of its capacity to provide insights into the way in which language use produces and legitimates racism in the press. As Teo observes, the 'critical' element in critical discourse analysis invites attention to the ideological basis of a discourse that naturalizes and thereby renders acceptable stances such as racism. He notes a variety of mechanisms that are employed to convey a particular position with regard to racism and the police service's war on drugs. For example, Teo refers to the linguistic device that he refers to as *generalization*, which occurs when a cluster of characteristics of an identified group of individuals is extended (that is, generalized) to a wider set of individuals. For example, he finds:

> In the newspaper discourse under analysis, we observe a *generalization* of the crimes of the *5T* . . . to a progressively wider group of people (Vietnamese, Southeast Asians and Asians). References to 'Vietnamese' and 'Asian' appears so consistently and frequently in relation to criminal activities of the *5T* that it becomes almost an endemic part of the drug culture of Australia.
>
> (Teo 2000: 16)

Examples quoted include: 'three Vietnamese men gunned down', 'the tall youth of Asian appearance', and 'five other youths of Asian appearance' (Teo 2000: 17). Here, then, the use of a critical discourse analysis approach to these documents provides a means of gaining insight into the ideological foundations of racism.

Qualitative content analysis

This is probably the most prevalent approach to the qualitative analysis of documents. It comprises a searching-out of underlying themes in the materials being analysed and can be discerned in several of the studies referred to earlier in this chapter, such as Vincent et al. (2010), Wagg (2010), Snee (2013), and Goodings et al. (2013). The processes through which the themes are extracted is sometimes not specified in detail. The extracted themes are usually illustrated—for example, with brief quotations from a newspaper article or magazine. For example, Snee identified four themes through her analysis of gap year blogs (see Research in focus 23.8). These themes were arrived at inductively and reveal the main elements of thematic analysis, which is examined in Chapter 24. She illustrates the second of the four themes referred to in Research in focus 23.8—'feeling out of place'—through several quotations from blogs, one of which is striking because the travel was in a Western country and reveals some of the typos that often appear:

> We were slightly nervour [nervous] about travelling on teh [the] subway esp[ecially] later in the evening. However it wasnt too bad despite getting a few looks and for a whi;e [while] travelling in a carriage where we were the only white people out of 20 or so people (Hugo).
>
> (quoted in Snee 2013: 151)

Research in focus 23.12 provides a further example of a thematic analysis that illustrates some of its ingredients.

Altheide and Schneider (2013) have outlined an approach that they call **ethnographic content analysis** (which they contrast with quantitative content analysis of the kind outlined in Chapter 13). Altheide's approach (which he refers to as ECA) represents a degree of codification of certain procedures that might be viewed as typical of the kind of qualitative content analysis on which many of the studies referred to so far are based. He describes his approach as differing from traditional quantitative content analysis in that the researcher is constantly revising the themes or categories that are distilled from the examination of documents. As he puts it:

> ECA follows a recursive and reflexive movement between concept development–sampling–data collection–data coding–data analysis–interpretation. The aim is to be systematic and analytic but not rigid. Categories and variables initially guide the study, but others are allowed and expected to emerge during the study, including an orientation to *constant discovery* and *constant comparison* of relevant situations, settings, styles, images, meanings, and nuances.
>
> (Altheide and Schneider 2013: 26; emphases in original)

Research in focus 23.12
Discerning themes in newspaper articles concerning the harms of alcohol

Wood et al. (2014) carried out a qualitative content analysis of articles addressing the harms associated with alcohol consumption in seven UK and three Scottish national newspapers from January 2005 to just after the passing in May 2012 of legislation to impose a minimum unit price on alcohol in Scotland. The authors searched two electronic databases—Nexis UK and Newsbank—using the search terms 'alcohol and/or pricing'. Following the exclusion of articles that did not make a reference to minimum unit pricing, 403 articles were included in the analysis. The process is described as follows:

> To develop a coding frame, a random selection of 100 articles were read to identify key themes around alcohol and create thematic categories in the initial coding frame. Using the principles of grounded theory, further batches of 20 articles were read and coded until no new categories emerged. At this point we assessed we had reached 'saturation', having identified all relevant thematic categories . . . . Coding of articles was conducted over a 10-week period by three coders . . . working together in close collaboration, with the first coder . . . checking and validating each others' coding . . . . All text was re-read and re-coded to discover patterns and anomalous ideas.
>
> (Wood et al. 2014: 579–80)

Five themes were identified: the extent of harm on people other than drinkers themselves; harms being diffused throughout society; the economic cost to society at large; the harm associated with social disorder and crime; and the harm to families. As Wood et al. observe, their qualitative content analysis reveals how the newspapers framed the debate about minimum unit pricing to the public.

Thus, with ECA there is much more movement back and forth between conceptualization, data collection, analysis, and interpretation than is the case with the kind of content analysis described in Chapter 13. Quantitative content analysis typically entails applying predefined categories to the sources; ECA employs some initial categorization, but there is greater potential for refinement of those categories and the generation of new ones. In addition, ECA emphasizes the context within which documents are generated, so that a study of newspaper reporting of a certain issue requires an appreciation of news organizations and the work of journalists (Altheide and Schneider 2013). Research in focus 23.13 presents an ethnographic content analysis of Facebook postings relating to the 2011 Vancouver riot.

Research in focus 23.13
Using ethnographic content analysis in a study of Facebook postings relating to the 2011 Vancouver riot

Schneider and Trottier (2012) conducted an ethnographic content analysis of the role of Facebook in the 2011 Vancouver riot, when a major public disturbance was occasioned by the Stanley Cup ice hockey game on 15 June 2011 (see also Altheide and Schneider 2013: 105–14). The researchers examined a Facebook page of photographs taken of the riot and 12,587 postings on the main Facebook 'wall' of the page. As with Schneider's (in press) Twitter study, all the postings were saved into a pdf file, although a Word file could also be used. This is a useful step in order to ensure that the documents are preserved and because they can be easily searched. In fact, Altheide and Schneider recommend doing initial searches for key words and phrases as a means of creating a familiarity with the data and for a sense of the frequency of key terms. They give the example of a protocol created for the word 'criminal', which appeared 402 times in the document but in a variety of contrasting ways and contexts. Four interesting elements in the protocol are as follows:

- The type of crime: this means indicating what crimes are identified in a post (e.g. arson, vandalism, breach of the peace).
- The theme: this takes the form of specifying whether the posting conveys the riot in a positive or negative light. Altheide and Schneider give as examples contrasts between criminal or non-criminal and whether those involved were real sports fans or otherwise.
- The perspective: this includes such things as whether the posting is pro-authority and whether it reveals a strong regional identity (e.g. pro-Vancouver).
- The language: the researchers propose considering whether the discourse adopts a criminal justice stance.

The analysis allows the researchers to 'provide insight into everyday members' assumptions and expectations as they pertain to "law and order"' (Altheide and Schneider 2013: 111), such as whether the police and their activities are supported rather than the rioters, and beliefs about the criminal justice system. One theme that surfaced in Schneider and Trottier (2012) was the role of Facebook itself in providing photographs and accounts of the activities of rioters and their stupidity in not realizing how they opened themselves up to prosecution. As one post put it:

> these people are so stupid!! LOL dont they realize everyone has cameras and will sell you out for a nickel!! AHAHAHAHAHAHAHAHAH!!! yea post those pics, people will recognize you, give your name . . . its gunna be a kina "wheres waldo" game for locals to play. LETS SEE HOW MANY NAMES WE GET!! A photo says a million things but all the police want is a name.
>
> (quoted in Schneider and Trottier 2012)

The iterative nature of the ECA process is apparent in Altheide and Schneider's (2013: 112) proposal that the goal is to keep searching with an open mind for 'emergent patterns' in the data, making notes as you go along on the key themes, and as 'themes continue to emerge, the researcher can then move from open coding (e.g. "criminal") to more specific coding (e.g. activities, actions, etc.).'

Altheide and Schneider (2013) describe the steps involved in ECA as requiring the researcher to:

1. generate a research question;

2. become familiar with the context within which the documents were/are generated;

3. become familiar with a small number of documents (6–10) and consider what the unit of analysis is (e.g. whether it is articles or incidents, of which there may be several in an article);

4. generate some categories that will guide the collection of data and draft a protocol for collecting the data in terms of the generated categories—the protocol is very similar to the kind of instrument (coding schedule) used to conduct a quantitative content analysis (see Figure 13.1);

5. test the protocol by using it for collecting data from a number of documents;

6. revise the protocol and select further cases to sharpen it up;

7. establish your sampling strategy which, Altheide and Schneider suggest, will usually entail theoretical sampling;

8. collect data, which means filling the empty spaces in the protocol for the item under consideration (there will be a protocol for each case) with notes that address each area that needs to be addressed—the researcher is essentially summarizing each case in terms of the areas that the protocol needs to address;

9. conduct data analysis, which includes refining and developing categories;

10. make notes about extreme cases and differences between cases;

11. combine the summaries of cases, drawing attention to extremes and typical cases;

12. bring together findings and interpretation in the writing up.

The process is highly iterative with a movement back and forth between coding/categorization and data collection. It draws on some elements of grounded theory, most notably theoretical sampling, coding, and constant comparison (see Chapter 24). Qualitative content analysis as a strategy of searching for themes in one's data lies at the heart of the coding approaches that are often employed in the analysis of qualitative data and as such will be encountered again in the next chapter.

Semiotics

Semiotics is invariably referred to as the 'science of signs'. It is an approach to the analysis of symbols in everyday life and as such can be employed in relation not only to documentary sources but also to all kinds of other data because of its commitment to treating phenomena as texts. The main terms employed in semiotics are:

- the **sign**—that is, something that stands for something else; the sign is made up of the *signifier* and the *signified*;
- the *signifier* is the thing that points to an underlying meaning (the term *sign vehicle* is sometimes used instead of *signifier*);
- the *signified* is the meaning to which the signifier points;
- a **denotative** *meaning* is the manifest or more obvious meaning of a signifier and as such indicates its function;
- a *sign-function* is an object that denotes a certain function;
- a **connotative** *meaning* is a meaning associated with a certain social context that is in addition to its denotative meaning;
- *polysemy* refers to a quality of signs—namely, that they are always capable of being interpreted in many ways;
- the *code* is the generalized meaning that interested parties may seek to instil in a sign; a code is sometimes also called a *sign system*.

Semiotics is concerned to uncover the hidden meanings that reside in texts as broadly defined. Consider, by way of illustration, the curriculum vitae (CV) in academic life. The typical CV that an academic will produce contains such features as personal details; education; previous and current posts; administrative responsibilities and experience; teaching experience; research experience; research grants acquired; and publications. We can treat the CV as a system of interlocking signifiers that signify, at the level of denotative meaning, a summary of the individual's experience (its sign function) and, at the connotative level, an indication of an individual's value, particularly in connection with his or her prospective employability. Each CV is capable of being interpreted in different ways, as anyone who has ever sat in on a short-listing meeting for a lectureship can testify, and is therefore polysemic, but there is a code whereby certain attributes of CVs are seen as especially desirable and are therefore less contentious in terms of the attribution of meaning. Indeed, applicants for posts know this latter point and devise their CVs to amplify the desired qualities so that the CV becomes an autobiographical practice for the presentation of self, as Miller and Morgan (1993) have suggested.

Research in focus 23.14 provides an illustration of a study from a semiotic perspective of Disneyland as a text.

Research in focus 23.14
A semiotic Disneyland

Gottdiener (1982; 1997: 108–15) has proposed that Disneyland in Los Angeles, California, can be fruitfully analysed through a semiotic analysis. In so doing, he was treating Disneyland as a text. One component of his analysis is the notion that Disneyland's meaning 'is revealed by its oppositions with the quotidian—the alienated everyday life of residents of L.A.' (1982: 148). He identifies through this principle nine *sign systems* that entail a contrast between the park and its surrounding environment: transportation; food; clothing; shelter; entertainment; social control; economics; politics; and family. Thus, the first of these sign systems—transportation—reveals a contrast between the Disneyland visitor as pedestrian (walk in a group; efficient mass transportation, which is fun) and as passenger (car is necessary; poor mass transportation; danger on the congested freeways). A further component of his analysis entails an analysis of the connotations of the different 'lands' that make up the park. He suggests that each land is associated as a signifier with signifiers of capitalism, as follows:

- Frontierland—predatory capital
- Adventureland—colonialism/imperialism
- Tomorrowland—state capital
- New Orleans—venture capital
- Main Street—family capital (Gottdiener 1982: 156).

The chief strength of semiotics lies in its invitation to the analyst to try to see beyond and beneath the apparent ordinariness of everyday life and its manifestations. The main difficulty one often feels with the fruits of a semiotic analysis is that, although we are invariably given a compelling exposition of a facet of the quotidian, it is difficult to escape a sense of the arbitrariness of the analysis provided. However, in all probability this sensation is unfair to the approach, because the results of a semiotic analysis are probably no more arbitrary than any interpretation of documentary materials or any other data, such as a thematic, qualitative content analysis of the kind described in the previous section. Indeed, it would be surprising if we were not struck by a sense of arbitrariness in interpretation, in view of the principle of polysemy that lies at the heart of semiotics.

Checklist
Evaluating documents

Can you answer the following questions about the document being examined?

○ Who produced the document?

○ Why was the document produced?

○ Was the person or group that produced the document in a position to write authoritatively about the subject or issue?

○ Is the material genuine?

○ Did the person or group have an axe to grind, and if so can you identify a particular slant?

○ Is the document typical of its kind, and if not is it possible to establish how untypical it is and in what ways?

○ Is the meaning of the document clear?

○ Can you corroborate the events or accounts presented in the document?

○ Are there different interpretations of the document from the one you offer, and if so what are they and why have you discounted them?

» Key points

- Documents constitute a very heterogeneous set of sources of data, which include personal documents, official documents from both the state and private sources, and the mass media.

- Such materials can be the focus of both quantitative and qualitative enquiry, but the emphasis in this chapter has been upon the latter.

- Documents of the kinds considered may be in printed, visual, digital, or indeed any other retrievable format.

- Criteria for evaluating the quality of documents are: authenticity; credibility; representativeness; and meaning. The relevance of these criteria varies according to the kind of document being assessed.

- The different kinds of virtual documents provide a rich and varied source of documents for the researcher to analyse.

- There are several ways of analysing documents within qualitative research. In this chapter we have covered qualitative content analysis and semiotics.

? Questions for review

- What is meant by the term 'document'?
- What are Scott's four criteria for assessing documents?

Personal documents

- Outline the different kinds of personal documents.
- How do they fare in terms of Scott's criteria?
- What might be the role of personal documents in relation to the life history or biographical method?
- What uses can family photographs have in social research?

Official documents deriving from the state

- What do the studies by Abraham (1994) and Thompson et al. (2013) suggest in terms of the potential for social researchers of official documents deriving from the state?
- How do such documents fare in terms of Scott's criteria?

Official documents deriving from private sources

- What kinds of documents might be considered official documents deriving from private sources?
- How do such documents fare in terms of Scott's criteria?

Mass-media outputs

- What kinds of documents are mass-media outputs?
- How do such documents fare in terms of Scott's criteria?

Virtual documents

- Do Internet documents and other virtual outputs raise special problems in terms of assessing them from the point of view of Scott's criteria?

- How do the different kinds of virtual documents differ from each other in terms of their potential for research and the challenges they pose?

The reality of documents

- In what sense can documents provide evidence on which social researchers can draw as data?

Interpreting documents

- How does qualitative content analysis differ from the kind of content analysis discussed in Chapter 13?

- What is a sign? How central is it to semiotics?

- What is the difference between denotative meaning and connotative meaning?

....

Online Resource Centre

www.oxfordtextbooks.co.uk/orc/brymansrm5e/

Visit the Online Resource Centre to enrich your understanding of the use of documents as sources of data. Follow up links to other resources, test yourself using multiple choice questions, and gain further guidance and inspiration from the Student Researcher's Toolkit.

....

24

Qualitative data analysis

Chapter outline

Chapter guide

Because qualitative data deriving from interviews or participant observation typically take the form of a large corpus of unstructured textual material, they are not straightforward to analyse. Moreover, unlike quantitative data analysis, clear-cut rules about how qualitative data analysis should be carried out have not been developed. In this chapter, some general approaches to qualitative data analysis will be examined, along with coding, which is the main feature of most of these approaches. The chapter explores:

- *analytic induction* as a general strategy of qualitative data analysis;

- *grounded theory* as a general strategy of qualitative data analysis; this is probably the most prominent of the general approaches to qualitative data analysis; the chapter examines its main features, processes, and outcomes, along with some of the criticisms that are sometimes levelled at the approach;

- *coding* as a key process in grounded theory and in approaches to qualitative data analysis more generally; it is the focus of an extended discussion in terms of what it entails and some of the limitations of a reliance on coding;

- *thematic analysis* as a strategy which is often influenced by grounded theory and which is often highly dependent on coding as a means of identifying themes in the data;
- the criticism that is sometimes made of coding in relation to qualitative data—namely, that it tends to fragment data; the idea of *narrative analysis* is introduced as an approach to data analysis that is gaining a growing following and that does not result in data fragmentation;
- the possibility of conducting a secondary analysis of other researchers' qualitative data;
- the synthesis of findings deriving from qualitative studies.

Introduction

One of the main difficulties with qualitative research is that it very rapidly generates a large, cumbersome database because of its reliance on prose in the form of such media as field notes, interview transcripts, or documents. Miles (1979) has described qualitative data as an 'attractive nuisance', because of the attractiveness of its richness but the difficulty of finding analytic paths through that richness. The researcher must guard against being captivated by the richness of the data collected, so that there is a failure to give the data wider significance for the social sciences. In other words, it is crucial to guard against failing to carry out a true analysis. This means that you must protect yourself against the condition Lofland (1971: 18) once called 'analytic interruptus'.

Finding a path through the thicket of prose that makes up your data is not an easy matter and is baffling to many researchers confronting such data for the first time. 'What do I do with it now?' is a common refrain. Unlike the analysis of quantitative data, there are few well-established and widely accepted rules for the analysis of qualitative data. Although learning the techniques of quantitative data analysis may seem painful at the time, they do give you an unambiguous set of rules about how to handle your data. You still have to interpret your analyses, but at least there are relatively clear rules for getting to that point. Qualitative data analysis has not reached this degree of codification of analytic procedures, and many writers would argue that this is not necessarily desirable anyway (see Bryman and Burgess 1994b on this point). What *can* be provided are broad guidelines (see Okely 1994), and it is in the spirit of this suggestion that this chapter has been written.

This chapter has five main sections.

1. *General strategies of qualitative data analysis.* In this section, I consider two approaches to data analysis—**analytic induction** and **grounded theory**.

2. *Basic operations in qualitative data analysis.* This section entails a focus on **coding**, which is central to grounded theory and thematic analysis in particular.

3. Thematic analysis. This approach has emerged as a general, though not terribly well defined, approach to qualitative data analysis that has become a common description used by qualitative researchers to summarize how they went about their task. Grounded theory often entails the search for themes and equally when conducting qualitative data analysis, researchers invariably use the basic operations of qualitative data analysis, many of which were developed in the context of grounded theory.

4. Narrative analysis, which is an approach to qualitative data analysis, is to a certain extent different in style from the emphasis on coding that can be seen in both grounded theory and thematic analysis.

Analytic induction, grounded theory, thematic analysis, and narrative analysis are probably the most frequently cited general strategies for doing qualitative data analysis, though others do exist (e.g. R. Williams 1976; Hycner 1985). By a general strategy of qualitative data analysis, I simply mean a framework that is meant to guide the analysis of data. As we will see, one of the ways in which qualitative and quantitative data analysis sometimes differ is that, with the latter, analysis invariably occurs after your data have been collected. However, approaches such as grounded theory (and analytic induction) are often described as *iterative*—that is, there is a repetitive interplay between the collection and analysis of data. This means that analysis starts after some of the data have been collected, and the implications of that analysis then shape the next steps in the data-collection process. Consequently, while grounded theory and analytic induction are described as strategies of analysis, they can also be viewed as strategies for the *collection* of data.

In addition, this chapter will cover:

5. Secondary analysis of qualitative data.

6. Synthesizing qualitative studies.

In the next chapter, the use of computers in qualitative data analysis will be outlined.

Analytic induction

The main steps in analytic induction are outlined in Figure 24.1. Analytic induction (see Key concept 24.1) begins with a rough specification of a research question, proceeds to a hypothetical explanation of that problem, and then continues on to the collection of data (examination of cases). If a case that is inconsistent with the hypothesis is encountered, the hypothesis is *either* redefined so as to exclude the deviant or negative case *or* reformulated and further data are collected. If the latter path is chosen, if a further deviant case is found, the analyst must choose again between reformulation or redefinition.

Figure 24.1
The process of analytic induction

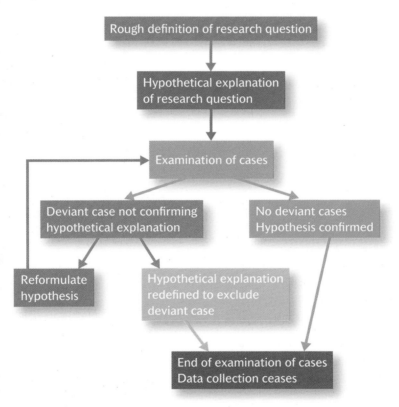

 ## Key concept 24.1
What is analytic induction?

Analytic induction is an approach to the analysis of data in which the researcher seeks universal explanations of phenomena by pursuing the collection of data until no cases that are inconsistent with a hypothetical explanation (deviant or negative cases) of a phenomenon are found.

As this brief outline suggests, analytic induction is an extremely rigorous method of analysis, because encountering a single case that is inconsistent with a hypothesis is sufficient to necessitate further data collection or a reformulation of the hypothesis. The alternative of reformulating the hypothetical explanation must not be regarded as a soft option, as is shown by Katz's (1982) study of poverty lawyers in Chicago. Katz was interested in finding some characteristics that distinguished those who stayed on for some time as lawyers to help the poor (in spite of the lower pay and status associated with such work) from those whose tenure was brief. He writes that 'the definition of the explanandum [the phenomenon to be explained] was changed from staying two years, to desiring to stay two years, to desiring to stay in a frustrating place, to involvement in a frustrating place, to involvement in an insignificant status . . .' (Katz 1982: 200). Each shift necessitated a reanalysis and reorganization of his data. The rigours of analytic induction have not endeared the approach to qualitative researchers, and most of the examples used in textbooks to illustrate it derive from the 1940s and early 1950s (Bryman and Burgess 1994a: 4). Katz's work is unusual in being relatively recent. Bloor (1978) used a version of analytic induction in a study of doctors' decisions about whether to recommend an adenotonscillectomy. His approach notably diverged from the sequence described in Figure 24.1 in that a specific hypothesis was not formulated. An account using Bloor's approach can be found in Johnson (1998).

Two further problems with analytic induction are worth noting. First, the final explanations that analytic induction arrives at specify the conditions that are *sufficient* for the phenomenon occurring but rarely specify the *necessary* conditions. This means that analytic induction may find out why people of certain characteristics or in certain circumstances become drug addicts (the focus of one major analytic induction study by Lindesmith 1947), but it does not allow us to say why those particular people became addicts rather than others in the same situation with the same characteristics. Second, it does not provide useful guidelines (unlike grounded theory) as to how many cases need to be investigated before the absence of negative cases and the validity of the hypothetical explanation (whether reformulated or not) can be confirmed.

 # Grounded theory

Grounded theory (see Key concept 17.2) has become one of the most widely used frameworks for analysing qualitative data. The book that is the chief wellspring of the approach, *The Discovery of Grounded Theory: Strategies for Qualitative Research* by Barney G. Glaser and Anselm L. Strauss (published in 1967), must be one of the most widely cited books in the social sciences. However, providing a definitive account of the approach is by no means a straightforward matter for the following reasons.

- Glaser and Strauss developed grounded theory along different paths after the publication of the above book. Glaser felt that the approach to grounded theory that Strauss was promoting (most notably in Strauss 1987, and Strauss and Corbin 1990) was too prescriptive and emphasized too much the development of concepts rather than of theories (Glaser 1992). However, because of the greater prominence of Strauss's writings, his version is largely the one followed in the exposition below. There is, however, considerable controversy about what grounded theory is and entails (Charmaz 2000). It is not uncommon for users of grounded theory to indicate whether the version that they are following is the Glaserian or the Straussian approach.

- Straussian grounded theory has changed a great deal over the years. This is revealed in a constant addition to the tool chest of analytic devices that is revealed in his writings.

- Some writers have suggested that grounded theory is honoured more in the breach than in the observance, implying that claims are often made that grounded theory has been used but that evidence of this being the case is at best uncertain (Bryman 1988a: 85, 91; Locke 1996; Charmaz 2000). Sometimes the term is employed simply to imply that the analyst has grounded his or her theory in data, so that grounded theory is more or less synonymous with an **inductive** approach. Grounded theory is more than this and refers to a set of procedures that are described below. Referencing academic publications is often part of a tactic of persuading readers of the legitimacy of one's work (Gilbert 1977), and this process can be discerned in the citation of grounded theory whereby reference to grounded theory's seminal publications is employed as a signal that a grounded theory approach has been used. Alternatively, researchers sometimes appear to have used just one or two features of grounded theory but refer without qualification to their having used the approach (Locke 1996).

Simply using one or two grounded theory features of the kind discussed in the next section does not make a grounded theory (Walsh et al. 2015). Against such a background, writing about what is and what is not grounded theory is not an easy matter.

It is not going to be possible to describe here grounded theory in all its facets; instead, its main features will be outlined. In order to organize the exposition, I find it helpful to distinguish between *tools* and *outcomes* in grounded theory.

Tools of grounded theory

Some of the tools of grounded theory have been referred to in previous chapters. Their location is indicated in the list that follows.

- *Theoretical sampling*—see Key concept 18.3.
- *Coding*—the key process in grounded theory, whereby data are broken down into component parts, which are given names. It begins soon after the collection of initial data. As Charmaz (2000: 515) puts it: 'We grounded theorists code our emerging data as we collect it. . . . Unlike quantitative research that requires data to fit into *preconceived* standardized codes, the researcher's interpretations of data shape his or her emergent codes in grounded theory' (emphasis in original). In grounded theory, different types or levels of coding are recognized (see the section on 'Coding in grounded theory' below).
- *Theoretical saturation*—see Key concept 18.4. Theoretical saturation is a process that relates to two phases in grounded theory: the coding of data (implying that you reach a point where there is no further reason to review your data to see how well they fit with your concepts or categories) and the collection of data (implying that, once a concept or category has been developed, you may wish to continue collecting data to determine its nature and operation but then reach a point where new data are no longer illuminating the concept).
- *Constant comparison*—an aspect of grounded theory that was prominent in Glaser and Strauss (1967) and that is often referred to as a significant phase by practitioners, but that seems to be an implicit, rather than an explicit, element in more recent writings. It refers to a process of maintaining a close connection between data and conceptualization, so that the correspondence between concepts and categories with their indicators is not lost. More specifically, attention to the procedure of **constant comparison** enjoins the researcher constantly to compare phenomena being

coded under a certain **category** so that a theoretical elaboration of that category can begin to emerge. Glaser and Strauss advised writing a *memo* (see the subsection below on 'Memos') on the category after a few phenomena had been coded. Constant comparison also entails being sensitive to contrasts between the categories that are emerging.

Coding in grounded theory

Coding is one of the most central processes in grounded theory. It entails reviewing transcripts and/or field notes and giving labels (names) to component parts that seem to be of potential theoretical significance and/or that appear to be particularly salient within the social worlds of those being studied. As Charmaz (1983: 186) puts it: 'Codes . . . serve as shorthand devices to *label*, *separate*, *compile*, and *organize* data' (emphases in original). Coding in this context is a different process from coding in relation to quantitative data, such as survey data. With the latter, coding is a means of preparing data for quantitative data analysis, whereas in grounded theory, and indeed in approaches to qualitative data analysis that do not subscribe to grounded theory, it is an important first step in the generation of theory. Coding in grounded theory is also more tentative than in relation to the generation of quantitative data, where there is a tendency to think in terms of data and codes as fixed. Coding in qualitative data analysis tends to be in a constant state of potential revision and fluidity. The data are treated as potential indicators of concepts, and the indicators are *constantly compared* (see the section on 'Tools of grounded theory' above) to see which concepts they best fit with. As Strauss (1987: 25) put it: 'Many indicators (behavioral actions/events) are examined comparatively by the analyst who then "codes" them, naming them as indicators of a class of events/behavioral actions.'

Grounded theory practitioners tend to view coding as a progression through a series of stages. Two different ways of representing and classifying this progression have been developed. One has been developed by Strauss and Corbin (1990) and the other by Charmaz (2006; Thornberg and Charmaz 2014). The latter scheme is influenced by Glaser's preference for delaying the point at which concepts become fixed. Both schemes represent the process as involving three types of code or coding, which may also be viewed as stages or levels of coding, but the types are not equivalent. Each scheme can be viewed as a mechanism for allowing concepts and theories to be progressively elaborated. Table 24.1 outlines the three types of coding associated with each approach and provides examples.

Table 24.1

Two approaches to the progressive elaboration of concepts and theories in grounded theory

Strauss and Corbin approach (with an example derived from a study of stress triggers in adolescent girls' lives by Haraldsson et al. 2011)	Charmaz approach (with an example derived from a study of victims of school bullying by Thornberg et al. 2013)
Open coding: 'the process of breaking down, examining, comparing, conceptualizing and categorizing data' (Strauss and Corbin 1990: 61); this process of coding yields concepts, which are later to be grouped and turned into categories.	*Initial coding*: 'When researchers conduct initial coding . . ., they compare data with data; stay close to and remain open to exploring what they interpret is happening in the data; construct and keep their codes short, simple, precise and active; and move quickly but carefully through the data' (Thornberg and Charmaz 2014: 156). Often entails the assignment of codes per line of text.
Example: 'each event and situation related by the informant that corresponded to the aim of the study was labelled with a code. These codes were then compared, and those with a similar content were grouped into categories that were labelled at a higher level of abstraction' (Haraldsson et al. 2011: 63).	Example: 'First, we conducted an initial coding in which codes were constructed by comparing data segments and using analytical questions such as "What is happening in the data? How do the participants explain bullying? What does the data suggest? What category does this specific datum indicate?". . . This step involved naming words, lines and segments of data' (Thornberg et al. 2013: 313).
Axial coding: 'a set of procedures whereby data are put back together in new ways after open coding, by making connections between categories' (Strauss and Corbin 1990: 96). This is done by linking codes to contexts, to consequences, to patterns of interaction, and to causes.	*Focused coding*: 'As a result of doing initial coding, the researcher will eventually "discover" the most significant or frequent initial codes that make the most analytical sense. In focused coding . . ., the researcher uses these codes, identified or constructed as focused codes, to sift through large amounts of data' (Thornberg and Charmaz 2014: 158). 'Focused coding requires decisions about which initial codes make the most analytic sense to categorize your data incisively and completely' (Charmaz 2006: 57–8).
Example: 'In the axial coding, the categories were developed by searching for a relationship between and within them by constantly going back and forth between the categories and the data. A coding paradigm (Strauss and Corbin 1998) was used when putting questions to the data about conditions, context, actions/strategies and consequences, as illustrated by the following examples: ". . . everybody is not focused on doing their very best in all subjects, but I feel that I want to do it (strategy) in order to feel satisfied with myself and this is where our views may not be compatible . . . . We fight (actions) and then it is difficult to concentrate (consequence) . . . but when I am very busy (condition) I cannot help her and then she gets angry and mum says (context) that—you can help her, you have got the time. But I have not and, well, the situation becomes awkward (consequence)"' (Haraldsson et al. 2011: 63).	Example: 'In the second step, we carried out focused coding. The most significant and frequent codes from the initial coding were compared to each other to synthesize the large amounts of data into more elaborated categories. "Victimising" identified as the core concept of the study as well as a set of other focused codes now delimited and guided the coding work' (Thornberg et al. 2013: 313).
Selective coding: 'the procedure of selecting the core category, systematically relating it to other categories, validating those relationships, and filling in categories that need further refinement and development' (Strauss and Corbin 1990: 116). A *core category* is the central issue or focus around which all other categories are integrated. It is what Strauss and Corbin call the storyline that frames an analytical account of the phenomenon of interest.	*Theoretical coding*: 'theoretical codes specify possible relationships between categories you have developed through your focused coding . . . . Theoretical codes are integrative; they lend form to the focused codes you have collected . . . . these codes not only conceptualize how your substantive codes are related, but also move your analytic story in a theoretical direction' (Charmaz 2006: 63). At this stage, the researcher may incorporate ideas from the existing literature to enhance the story that is being developed.
Example: 'In the selective coding, theoretical selection was utilized to compare the different categories and to test, by means of existing and/or new data, how the descriptions of the phenomenon belonging to each category were related and how they could be explained in order to develop and test for core categories (i.e. categories of central importance for the understanding and explanation of the underlying social processes). During the analysis process, memos were continuously written to support the development of the model' (Haraldsson et al. 2011: 63).	Example: 'We explored and analysed how the core concept ["Victimising"] and our other constructed codes or concepts were related to each other and integrated them into a grounded theory by using theoretical codes . . . . Examples of theoretical codes that we used because . . . they earned their way into the analysis in terms of fitting with the data and with our previously generated codes, were process, phases, self-concept, external–internal, strategy and mutual interaction. Moreover, during the analysis, pre-existing theoretical concepts from literature, such as social construction, stigma and labelling, were used as sensitising concepts (Blumer 1969) or analytical tools (Charmaz 2006 . . .), because we found them relevant—they fitted with our data and codes' (Thornberg et al. 2013: 313).

Strauss and Corbin (1990) distinguish between three types of coding practice: *open coding, axial coding,* and *selective coding.* Each relates to a different point in the elaboration of categories in grounded theory. The notion of axial coding has been controversial because it is sometimes perceived as closing off too quickly the open-endedness and exploratory character of coding in qualitative data analysis. The nature of each of the three types of coding are further outlined in Table 24.1 along with an example by Haraldsson et al. (2011), which is a study of the social processes that engender stress among adolescent girls. The data derive from in-depth interviews with fourteen 17-year-old girls in a Swedish school. The research followed the Strauss and Corbin approach and yielded two **core categories**, that is, categories which form the hub of the storyline that the other categories are related to. The two core categories were 'responsibility' and 'encounter' and it was the interaction between them that typically triggered stress among the participants. The researchers identified four forms of such interaction, which were derived from whether 'responsibility' was voluntary or forced and whether the encounter was characterized by closeness or distance. In the most recent edition of Strauss and Corbin (1990), the authors seem to place far less emphasis on the open/axial/selective coding distinction to the extent that they now refer mainly to open coding in relation to the coding process (Corbin and Strauss 2015). Open coding is viewed as the springboard for the generation of grounded theory. Since the authors' distinction between different types of coding is well established, I have retained its use is this chapter.

Pidgeon and Henwood (2004) provide a useful example of the move from initial coding to axial coding based on Henwood's study of adult mother–daughter relationships. Sixty interviews with mother–daughter dyads were conducted. They write:

> The initial coding led to the development of a long and varied, but highly unwieldy, list of instances under the label 'relational closeness'. The attributes that had been coded onto the card were initially glossed as attaching global value to the relationship. However, closer reading and comparison of the individual instances indicated a much more mixed view of the emotional intensity of the relationships, ranging from a welcome but painful sense of gratitude and debt to a stance of hypersensitivity and a desire to flee from a relationship which involved 'confinement' or 'smothering'. The inextricable link between the two concepts resulting from this subdivision was retained and coded through their respective labels 'Closeness' and 'Overcloseness'. This link then became a key stimulus and focus for conceptual development and reflection.
>
> (Pidgeon and Henwood 2004: 638)

Charmaz (2006) prefers to distinguish between three main types of coding which can also be viewed as different phases of coding: *initial coding, focused* or *selective coding* and *theoretical coding.* Initial coding tends to be very detailed and can often entail a code per line of text to provide initial impressions of the data. It is crucial at this stage to be open-minded and to generate as many new ideas and hence codes as necessary to encapsulate the data. Focused coding entails emphasizing the most common codes and those that are seen as most revealing about the data. This means that some, if not many, initial codes will be dropped. New codes may be generated by combining initial codes. The data are then re-explored and re-evaluated in terms of these selected codes. Theoretical coding is the point at which the codes deriving from the previous stage are brought together to provide a theoretical understanding of the object of interest. Theoretical codes are an antidote to the data fragmentation associated with initial and focused coding and are the point at which the researcher instils a theoretical coherence and understanding of his or her data. The nature of each of the three types of coding are further outlined in Table 24.1 along with an example by Thornberg et al. (2013; see also Thornberg and Charmaz 2014). This is a study of victims of bullying at school and in particular their perceptions of their experiences and its effects on them. Data were derived from semi-structured interviews with twenty-one Swedish students (nine at secondary school and 12 at university). The coding process allowed the researchers to build a model of the underlying process of victimizing, which was found to evolve through four stages: 'initial attacks', followed by 'double victimizing' (the bullying activities of others and the victims' responses, which often reinforce the activities of bullies), followed by 'bullying exit', and finally 'the after-effects of bullying'.

Although there are differences in the way in which the phases of the coding process is supposed to occur in grounded theory according to its practitioners, there is a basic understanding of it as involving a movement from generating codes that stay close to the data to more selective and theoretically elaborate ways of conceptualizing the phenomenon of interest.

Outcomes of grounded theory

The following are the products of different phases of grounded theory.

- *Concept(s)*—refers to labels given to discrete phenomena; concepts are referred to as the 'building blocks of theory' (Strauss and Corbin 1998: 101). Concepts are produced through *open coding.*

- *Category, categories*—a **category** is a concept that has been elaborated so that it is regarded as representing real-world phenomena. As noted in Key concept 18.4, a category may subsume two or more concepts. As such, categories are at a higher level of abstraction than concepts. A category may become a *core category* around which the other categories pivot. Research in focus 24.1 provides a good example of the emergence of a core category.

- *Properties*—attributes or aspects of a category.

- *Hypotheses*—initial hunches about relationships between concepts.

- *Theory*—according to Strauss and Corbin (1998: 22): 'a set of well-developed categories . . . that are systematically related through statements of relationship to form a theoretical framework that explains some relevant social . . . or other phenomenon'. Since the inception of grounded theory, writings have pointed to two types or levels of theory: *substantive theory* and *formal theory*. The former relates to theory in a certain empirical instance or substantive area, such as occupational socialization. A formal theory is at a higher level of abstraction and has a wider range of applicability to several substantive areas, such as socialization in a number of spheres, suggesting that higher-level processes are at work. The generation of formal theory requires data collection in contrasting settings.

The different elements—the processes and outcomes—of grounded theory can be portrayed as in Figure 24.2. As with all diagrams, this is a representation, and it is particularly so in the case of grounded theory, because the existence of different versions of the approach does not readily permit a more definitive rendition. Also, it is difficult to get across diagrammatically the iterative nature of grounded theory—in particular its commitment to the idea that data collection and analysis occur in parallel. This is partly achieved in the diagram through the presence of arrows pointing in both directions in relation to certain steps. The figure implies the following.

- The researcher begins with a general research question (step 1).

- Relevant people and/or incidents are theoretically sampled (step 2).

- Relevant data are collected (step 3).

Research in focus 24.1
Categories in grounded theory

Orona's (1997) study of sufferers of Alzheimer's disease and in particular of their relatives exemplifies many features of grounded theory. Orona began her research with an interest in the decision-making process that led relatives to place sufferers in a home. She gradually realized from coding her interview transcripts that this was not as crucial a feature for relatives as she had anticipated, not least because many of them simply felt they had no choice. Instead, she was slowly struck by the significance for relatives of the 'identity loss' sufferers were deemed to experience. This gradually became her core category. She conducted further interviews in order to flesh this notion out and reread existing transcripts in the light of it. The link between indicators and category can be seen in relatives' references to the sufferer as 'gone', 'different', 'not the same person', and as a 'stranger'. Orona was able to unearth four major themes that emerged around the process of identity loss. The theme of 'temporality' was particularly significant in Orona's emerging theoretical reflections and was revealed in such comments in transcripts as:

> It was the *time of the year* when nobody goes in the yard anyway . . .
>
> At the *beginning* . . .
>
> It got much worse *later on.*
>
> *More and more*, he was leaning on me.
>
> *Before* she would never have been like that.
>
> She *used* to love coffee.

(Orona 1997: 179–80)

In other words, such comments served as indicators that allowed the category 'temporality' to be built up. The issue of temporality was significant in Orona's emerging analysis, because it related to the core category of identity loss. Relatives sought to help sufferers maintain their identities. However, gradually, with the passage of time, crucial events meant that the relatives could no longer deny sufferers' identity loss.

Figure 24.2

Processes and outcomes in grounded theory

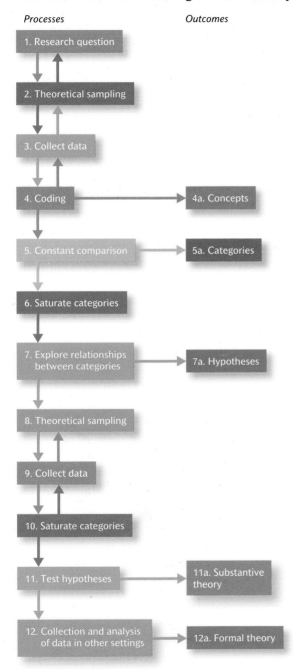

- Through a constant comparison of indicators and concepts (step 5) categories are generated (step 5a). The crucial issue is to ensure that there is a fit between indicators and concepts.
- Categories are saturated during the coding process (step 6).
- Relationships between categories are explored (step 7) in such a way that hypotheses about connections between categories emerge (step 7a).
- Further data are collected via theoretical sampling (steps 8 and 9).
- The collection of data is likely to be governed by the theoretical saturation principle (step 10) and by the testing of the emerging hypotheses (step 11), which leads to the specification of substantive theory (step 11a). See Research in focus 24.2 for an illustration.
- The substantive theory is explored using grounded theory processes in relation to different settings from that in which it was generated (step 12), so that formal theory may be generated (step 12a). A formal theory will relate to more abstract categories, which are not specifically concerned with the research area in question (for example, chronically ill men or relatives of sufferers of Alzheimer's disease).

Step 12 is relatively unusual in grounded theory, because researchers typically concentrate on a certain setting, although the investigation described in Research in focus 24.3 did examine other settings to explore the emerging concepts. A further way in which formal theory can be generated is through the use of existing theory and research in comparable settings.

Concepts and categories are perhaps the key elements in grounded theory. Indeed, it is sometimes suggested that, as a qualitative data analysis strategy, grounded theory works better for generating categories than for generating theory. In part, this may be because studies purporting to use the approach often generate grounded *concepts* rather than grounded theory as such. Concepts and categories are nonetheless at the heart of the approach, and key processes such as coding, theoretical sampling, and theoretical saturation are designed to guide their generation.

Memos

One aid to the generation of concepts and categories is the *memo*. Memos in grounded theory are notes that researchers might write for themselves and for those with whom they work concerning such elements of grounded theory as coding or concepts. They serve as reminders about what is meant by the terms being used and provide the building blocks for a certain amount of reflection.

- Data are coded (step 4), which may at the level of open coding generate concepts (step 4a).
- There is a constant movement backwards and forwards between the first four steps, so that early coding suggests the need for new data, which results in the need to sample theoretically, and so on.

Research in focus 24.2
Grounded theory in action

Charmaz's (1997) research is concerned with the identity dilemmas of men who have chronic (but not terminal) illnesses. She outlines very clearly the chief steps in her analysis.

- Interviews with men and a small number of women.
- Exploring the transcripts for gender differences.
- Searching for themes in the men's interviews and published personal accounts (for example, autobiographies). An example is the notion of 'accommodation to uncertainty', as men find ways of dealing with the unpredictable paths of their illnesses.
- Building 'analytic categories from men's definitions of and taken-for-granted assumptions about their situations' (1997: 39). Of particular significance in her work is the idea of 'identity dilemmas'—that is, the ways in which men approach and possibly resolve the assault on their traditional self-images in terms of masculinity. She shows that men often used strategies to re-establish earlier selves, so that for many audiences their identity (at least in their own eyes) could be preserved.
- Further interviews designed to refine the categories.
- Rereading personal accounts of chronic illness with a particular focus on gender.
- Reading a new group of personal accounts.
- Making 'comparisons with women on selected key points' (1997: 39).

Charmaz provides a substantive theory that helps to explain the importance of notions of masculinity for the carving-out of an identity for chronically ill men.

Research in focus 24.3
Grounded theory in a study of visitor experiences of museums

Goulding (2009) has discussed the way in which she implemented grounded theory in the context of a study of how visitors experience museums, particularly so-called 'living' museums that seek to recreate the UK's industrial heritage. The approach she took was closer to Glaser's than to Strauss's version of grounded theory. Initially, she selected an open-air museum and interviewed the director and then conducted observations of parties of visitors, noting how they handled the attractions and exhibits. While these relatively unstructured observations were illuminating in terms of how visitors responded to the attractions, they did not generate insights into motivations, so Goulding conducted interviews with visitors to shed light on such things as their expectations and their perceptions of the exhibits. She conducted a line-by-line analysis of the interview transcripts, which generated a huge number of codes and words. She reduced this vast array of codes to themes that helped to understand her data, and this produced seven concepts, such as the stimulation of nostalgia, the desire for education, and the experience of alienation in the present. Each of these concepts had distinctive properties or dimensions. For example, the stimulation of nostalgia was encapsulated in such things as a sense of retreat from the present and a 'rose-tinted' recollection of the past. However, Goulding felt that she had not saturated her concepts, so she collected new data in two new comparable but different sites. The same data-collection approach was taken as with the original site but no new concepts were generated. However, the new data did allow her to reinforce her concepts and to produce a categorization of three types of visitor to such museums: existential, purist, and social. For example, existential visitors tended to exhibit high levels of the stimulation of nostalgia (one of the seven concepts derived from the data), which was apparent from their position with regard to such codes as 'selective recall', 'rose-tinted remembrance', a 'rejection of the present', and an 'ability to distort the past'.

Research in focus 24.4
A memo

In the course of research into the bus industry that I carried out with colleagues in the early 1990s (Bryman et al. 1996), we noticed that the managers we interviewed frequently referred to the notion that their companies had *inherited* features that derived from the running of those companies before deregulation. They often referred to the idea of inheriting characteristics that held them back in trying to meet the competitive environment they faced in the 1990s. As such, inheritance is what Strauss (1987) calls an 'in vivo code' (one that derives from the natural language of people in the social context being studied), rather than what he calls 'sociologically constructed codes', which are labels employing the analyst's own terminology. The following memo outlines the concept of inheritance, provides some illustrative quotations, and suggests some properties of the concept.

Memo for inheritance

Inheritance: many of our interviewees suggest that they have inherited certain company traits and traditions from the period prior to deregulation (i.e. pre-1985). It is a term that many of them themselves employed to denote company attributes that are not of their choosing but have survived from the pre-deregulation period. The key point about inheritance is that the inherited elements are seen by our interviewees as hindering their ability to respond to the changing environment of the post-deregulation era.

Inherited features include:

- expensive and often inappropriate fleets of vehicles and depots;
- the survival of attitudes and behaviour patterns, particularly among bus drivers, which are seen as inappropriate to the new environment (e.g. lack of concern for customer service) and which hinder service innovation;
- high wage rates associated with the pre-deregulation era; means that new competitors can enter the market while paying drivers lower wages.

Sample comments:

'We *inherited* a very high cost structure because of deregulation. 75% of our staff were paid in terms of conditions affected by [rates prior to deregulation]' (Commercial Director, Company B).

'I suppose another major weakness is that we are very tied by conditions and practices we've *inherited*' (Commercial Director, Company G).

'We have what we've *inherited* and we now have a massive surplus of double decks . . . We have to go on operating those' (Managing Director, Company B).

Managing Director of Company E said the company had inherited staff who were steeped in pre-deregulation attitudes, which meant that 'we don't have a staff where the message is "the customer is number one". We don't have a staff where that is emblazoned on the hearts and minds of everyone, far from it.'

Pre/post-deregulation: interviewee makes a contrast between the periods before and after deregulation to show how they've changed. This shows in a sense the *absence* of inherited features and their possible impact; can refer to how the impact of possibly inherited features was negated or offset. For example, *X* referring to the recent end of the 3-week strike: 'there was no way we were going to give in to this sort of thing, this sort of blackmail. We just refused to move and the trade unions had never experienced that. It was all part of the change in culture following deregulation . . .'.

Inheriting constraints: such as staff on high wage rates and with inappropriate attitudes.

Inheriting surplus capacity: such as too many buses or wrong size.

Memos are potentially very useful to researchers in helping them to crystallize ideas and not to lose track of their thinking on various topics. An illustration of a memo from research in which I was involved is provided in Research in focus 24.4.

Finding examples of grounded theory that reveal all its facets and stages is very difficult, and it is unsurprising that many expositions of grounded theory fall back on the original illustrations provided in Glaser and Strauss (1967). Many studies show some of its ingredients but not others. Research in focus 24.1 provides an illustration by one of Strauss's students that incorporates some key grounded theory features.

Criticisms of grounded theory

In spite of the frequency with which it is cited and the frequent lip service paid to it, grounded theory is not without limitations, of which the following can be briefly registered.

- Bulmer (1979) has questioned whether, as prescribed by the advocates of grounded theory, researchers can suspend their awareness of relevant theories or concepts until quite a late stage in the process of analysis. Social researchers are typically sensitive to the conceptual armoury of their disciplines, and it seems unlikely that this awareness can be put aside. Indeed, nowadays it is rarely accepted that theory-neutral observation is feasible. In other words, it is generally agreed that what we 'see' when we conduct research is conditioned by many factors, one of which is what we already know about the social world being studied (both in terms of social scientific conceptualizations and as members of society). Also, many writers might take the view that it is desirable that researchers are sensitive to existing conceptualizations, so that their investigations are focused and can build upon the work of others.

- Related to this first point is that, in many circumstances, researchers are required to spell out the possible implications of their planned investigation. For example, a lecturer making a bid for research funding or a student applying for funding for postgraduate research is usually required to demonstrate how his or her research will build upon what is already known or to demonstrate that he or she has a reasonably tightly defined research question, something that is also frequently disdained in grounded theory.

- There are practical difficulties with grounded theory. The time taken to transcribe recordings of interviews, for example, can make it difficult for researchers, especially when they have tight deadlines, to carry out a genuine grounded theory analysis with its constant interplay of data collection and conceptualization.

- It is debatable whether grounded theory in many instances really results in *theory*. As previously suggested, it provides a rigorous approach to the generation of concepts, but it is often difficult to see what theory, in the sense of an explanation of something, is being put forward. Moreover, in spite of the frequent lip service paid to the generation of formal theory, most grounded theories are substantive in character; in other words, they pertain to the specific social phenomenon being researched and not to a broader range of phenomena (though, of course, they *may* have such broader applicability).

- In spite of the large amount written on grounded theory, but perhaps because of the many subtle changes in its presentation, grounded theory is still vague on certain points, such as the difference between concepts and categories. For example, while Strauss and Corbin (1998: 73) refer to theoretical sampling as 'sampling on the basis of emerging *concepts*' (emphasis added), Charmaz (2000: 519) writes that it is used to 'develop our emerging *categories*' (emphasis added). The term 'categories' is increasingly being employed rather than concepts, but such inconsistent use of key terms is not helpful to people trying to understand the overall process.

- Grounded theory is very much associated with an approach to data analysis that invites researchers to fragment their data by coding the data into discrete chunks. In the eyes of some writers, this kind of activity results in a loss of a sense of context and of narrative flow (Coffey and Atkinson 1996).

- The presence of competing accounts of the ingredients of grounded theory does not make it easy to characterize it or to establish how to use it. This situation has been made even more problematic by Charmaz's (2000) suggestion that most grounded theory is objectivist and that an alternative, constructionist (she calls it *constructivist*) approach is preferable. She argues that the grounded theory associated with Glaser, Strauss, and Corbin is objectivist in that it aims to uncover a reality that is external to social actors. She offers an alternative, constructionist version that 'assumes that people create and maintain meaningful worlds through dialectical processes of conferring meaning on their realities and acting within them. . . . Thus, social reality does not exist independent of human action' (Charmaz 2000: 521). This position contrasts with earlier grounded theory texts that 'imply that categories and concepts inhere within the data, awaiting the researcher's discovery. . . . Instead, a constructivist approach recognizes that the categories, concepts, and theoretical level of an analysis emerge from the researcher's interaction within the field and questions about the data' (Charmaz 2000: 522). One difficulty is that the two meanings of constructionism referred to in Key concept 2.6 seem to be conflated. Charmaz's first quotation above refers to constructionism as an ontological position in relation to social objects and categories; the second is a reference to constructionism in relation to the nature of knowledge of the social world. It is certainly fair to suggest that Glaser, Strauss, and Corbin in their various writings neglect the role of the researcher in the generation of knowledge, but it is not clear that they are indifferent to the notion that social reality exists independently of social actors. Strauss was, after all, the lead author of the study discussed in Chapter 2 (in the subsection on 'Constructionism') concerning the hospital as a negotiated order, which was used as an illustration of constructionism (Strauss et al. 1973). Also, Orona's (1997) account of her grounded theory analysis of sufferers of

Alzheimer's disease is described in a commentary on the research by Strauss and Corbin (1997: 172) as a 'textbook exemplification' of the approach. Yet this study is concerned with the subjective experience of the disease (an interpretivist approach) and with the *construction* of identity in everyday life.

Nonetheless, grounded theory probably represents the most influential general strategy for conducting qualitative data analysis, though how far the approach is followed varies from study to study. What can be said is that many of its core processes, such as coding, memos, and the very idea of allowing theoretical ideas to emerge out of one's data, have been hugely influential. Indeed, it is striking that one of the main developments in qualitative data analysis since the early 1990s—computer-assisted qualitative data analysis (CAQDAS)—has implicitly promoted many of these processes, because the software programs have often been written with grounded theory in mind (Richards and Richards 1994).

 # Coding

Coding is the starting point for most forms of qualitative data analysis, although some writers prefer to call the process *indexing* rather than coding. The principles involved have been well developed by writers on grounded theory and others. Some of the considerations in developing codes, some of which are derived from Lofland and Lofland (1995), are as follows.

- Of what general category is this item of data an instance?
- What does this item of data represent?
- What is this item of data about?
- Of what topic is this item of data an instance?
- What question about a topic does this item of data suggest?
- What sort of answer to a question about a topic does this item of data imply?
- What is happening here?
- What are people doing?
- What do people say they are doing?
- What kind of event is going on?

Steps and considerations in coding

The following steps and considerations need to be borne in mind in preparation for and during coding.

- *Code as soon as possible.* It is well worth coding as you go along, as grounded theory suggests. This may sharpen your understanding of your data and help with theoretical sampling. Also, it may help to alleviate the feeling of being swamped by your data, which can happen if you defer analysis entirely until the end of the data collection period. At the very least, you should ensure that, if your data collection involves recording interviews, you begin transcription at a relatively early stage.

- *Read through your initial set of transcripts, field notes, documents, etc.,* without taking any notes or considering an interpretation; perhaps at the end jot down a few general notes about what struck you as especially interesting, important, or significant.

- *Do it again.* Read through your data again, but this time begin to make marginal notes about significant remarks or observations. Make as many as possible. Initially, they will be very basic—perhaps key words used by your respondents, names that you give to themes in the data. When you do this you are *coding*— generating an index of terms that will help you to interpret and theorize in relation to your data.

- *Review your codes.* Begin to review your codes, possibly in relation to your transcripts. Are you using two or more words or phrases to describe the same phenomenon? If so, remove one of them. Do some of your codes relate to concepts and categories in the existing

Tips and skills
Coded text from the Disney project

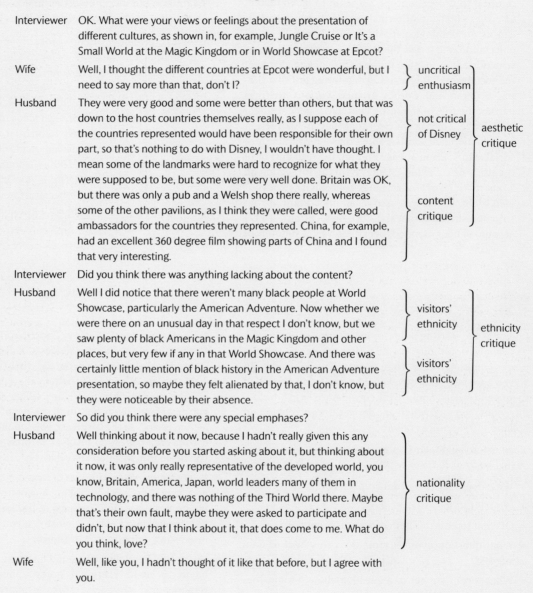

Interviewer	OK. What were your views or feelings about the presentation of different cultures, as shown in, for example, Jungle Cruise or It's a Small World at the Magic Kingdom or in World Showcase at Epcot?	
Wife	Well, I thought the different countries at Epcot were wonderful, but I need to say more than that, don't I?	uncritical enthusiasm
Husband	They were very good and some were better than others, but that was down to the host countries themselves really, as I suppose each of the countries represented would have been responsible for their own part, so that's nothing to do with Disney, I wouldn't have thought. I	not critical of Disney } aesthetic critique
	mean some of the landmarks were hard to recognize for what they were supposed to be, but some were very well done. Britain was OK, but there was only a pub and a Welsh shop there really, whereas some of the other pavilions, as I think they were called, were good ambassadors for the countries they represented. China, for example, had an excellent 360 degree film showing parts of China and I found that very interesting.	content critique
Interviewer	Did you think there was anything lacking about the content?	
Husband	Well I did notice that there weren't many black people at World Showcase, particularly the American Adventure. Now whether we were there on an unusual day in that respect I don't know, but we saw plenty of black Americans in the Magic Kingdom and other	visitors' ethnicity } ethnicity critique
	places, but very few if any in that World Showcase. And there was certainly little mention of black history in the American Adventure presentation, so maybe they felt alienated by that, I don't know, but they were noticeable by their absence.	visitors' ethnicity
Interviewer	So did you think there were any special emphases?	
Husband	Well thinking about it now, because I hadn't really given this any consideration before you started asking about it, but thinking about it now, it was only really representative of the developed world, you know, Britain, America, Japan, world leaders many of them in technology, and there was nothing of the Third World there. Maybe that's their own fault, maybe they were asked to participate and didn't, but now that I think about it, that does come to me. What do you think, love?	nationality critique
Wife	Well, like you, I hadn't thought of it like that before, but I agree with you.	

literature? If so, might it be sensible to use these instead? Can you see any connections between the codes? Is there some evidence that respondents believe that one thing tends to be associated with or caused by something else? If so, how do you characterize and therefore code these connections?

* *Consider more general theoretical ideas in relation to codes and data.* At this point, you should be beginning

to generate some general theoretical ideas about your data. Try to outline connections between concepts and categories you are developing. Consider in more detail how they relate to the existing literature. Develop hypotheses about the linkages you are making and go back to your data to see if they can be confirmed.

* Remember that *any item or slice of data can and sometimes should be coded in more than one way.*

- *Do not worry about generating what seem to be too many codes*—at least in the early stages of your analysis; some will be fruitful and others will not—the important thing is to be as inventive and imaginative as possible; you can worry about tidying things up later.

- *Keep coding in perspective.* Do not equate coding with analysis. It is part of your analysis, albeit an important one. It is a mechanism for thinking about the meaning of your data *and* for reducing the vast amount of data with which you are confronted (Huberman and Miles 1994). You must still interpret your findings, which means attending to issues such as the significance of your coded material for the lives of the people you are studying, forging interconnections between codes, and reflecting on the overall importance of your findings for the research questions and the research literature that have driven your data collection.

Turning data into fragments

The coding of such materials as interview transcripts has typically entailed writing marginal notes on them and gradually refining those notes into codes. In this way, portions of transcripts become seen as belonging to certain names or labels. This process used to be accompanied by cutting and pasting in the literal sense of using scissors and paste. It entailed cutting up one's transcripts into files of chunks of data, with each file representing a code. The process of cutting and pasting is useful for data retrieval, though it is always important to make sure that you have ways of identifying the origins of the chunk of text (for example, name, position, date). Word-processing programs allow this to be done in a way that does not rely on your DIY skills so much. Nowadays CAQDAS software is increasingly being used to perform these tasks (see Chapter 25).

As Coffey and Atkinson (1996) observe, following Strauss and Corbin's account (1990) of grounded theory, codes should not be thought of purely as mechanisms for the fragmentation and retrieval of text. In other words, they can do more than simply manage the data you have gathered. For example, if we ask about the properties and interconnections between codes, we may begin to see that some of them may be dimensions of a broader phenomenon. An instance of this is shown in the next chapter (see especially Figure 25.1): 'ethnicity critique' came to be seen as a dimension of 'ideology critique', along with 'class critique' and 'gender critique'. In this way, we can begin to map the more general or formal properties of concepts that are being developed.

Problems with coding

One of the most commonly mentioned criticisms of the coding approach to qualitative data analysis is the possible problem of losing the context of what is said. By plucking chunks of text out of the context within which they appeared, such as an interview transcript, the social setting can be lost.

A second criticism of coding is that it results in a fragmentation of data, so that the narrative flow of what people say is lost (Coffey and Atkinson 1996). Sensitivity to this issue has been heightened by a growing interest in **narrative analysis** since the late 1980s (see the section on 'Narrative analysis' below). Riessman (1993) became concerned about the fragmentation of data that results from coding themes when she came to analyse data she had collected through structured interviews on divorce and gender. She writes:

> Some [interviewees] developed long accounts of what had happened in their marriages to justify their divorces. I did not realize these were narratives until I struggled to code them. Applying traditional qualitative methods, I searched the texts for common thematic elements. But some individuals knotted together several

Tips and skills
Too many codes

The initial coding of a large corpus of data can generate an alarming number of codes. Charmaz (2004), for example, recommends as a first stage in coding for grounded theory 'line by line coding', whereby virtually every line in a transcript or other source of data will have a code attached to it. She argues that this process means that the qualitative researcher does not lose contact with his or her data and the perspectives and interpretations of those being studied. However, this process will almost certainly result in a proliferation of codes. This should not be alarming. What the analyst of qualitative data needs to do is ask questions about what these codes have in common, so that they can be combined into higher-order and more abstract codes, or whether any can be discarded if they seem to cover the same phenomena.

themes into long accounts that had coherence and sequence, defying easy categorization. I found myself not wanting to fragment the long accounts into distinct thematic categories. There seemed to be a common structure beneath talk about a variety of topics. While I coded one interview, a respondent provided language for my trouble. As I have thought about it since, it was a 'click moment' in my biography as a narrative researcher.

(Riessman 1993: vi)

Riessman's account is interesting because it suggests several possibilities: that coding fragments data; that some forms of data may not be suited to coding; and that researchers can turn narrative analysis on themselves, since what Riessman provides in this passage is precisely a narrative. Interest in narrative analysis has been growing for some time, and in large part this trend parallels the rebirth of interest in the life history approach (see Chapter 20). Nonetheless, the use of coding is unlikely to decline in prominence, because of several factors: its widespread

acceptance in the research community; the fact that not all analysts are interested in research questions that lend themselves to the elicitation of narratives; the influence of grounded theory and its associated techniques; and the growing use and acceptance of computer software for qualitative data analysis, which frequently invites a coding approach.

Regardless of which analytical strategy you employ, what you must not do is simply say: 'this is what my subjects said and did—isn't that incredibly interesting'. It may be interesting, but your work can acquire significance only when you theorize in relation to it. Sometimes, researchers are wary of this—they worry that, in the process of interpretation and theorizing, they may fail to do justice to what they have seen and heard; that they may contaminate their subjects' words and behaviour. This is a risk, but it has to be balanced against the fact that your findings acquire significance only when you have reflected on, interpreted, and theorized your data. You are not there as a mere mouthpiece.

Thematic analysis

One of the most common approaches to qualitative data analysis entails what is often referred to as **thematic analysis**. However, unlike strategies such as grounded theory or critical discourse analysis, this is not an approach that has an identifiable heritage or that has been outlined in terms of a distinctive cluster of techniques. Indeed, the search for themes is an activity that can be discerned in many if not most approaches to qualitative data analysis, such as grounded theory, critical discourse analysis, qualitative content analysis, and narrative analysis. Also,

for some writers a theme is more or less the same as a code, whereas for others it transcends any one code and is built up out of groups of codes. Key concept 24.2 provides some criteria for identifying what a theme is.

This does not appear to be a promising start, because, although qualitative researchers often claim to have employed thematic analysis, it is not an identifiable approach. Indeed, it did not appear as a separate section in the first two editions of this book! Yet, as a simple exercise while writing this section, I did a search on 25 March 2014

Key concept 24.2
What is a theme?

In spite of its apparent frequency of use in the analysis of qualitative data, thematic analysis is an underdeveloped procedure in that there are few specifications of its steps or ingredients. This has changed over time (e.g. Ryan and Bernard 2003; Braun and Clarke 2006), but, even so, what actually constitutes a theme is often not spelled out. By and large, we can say that a theme is:

- a category identified by the analyst through his/her data;
- that relates to his/her research focus (and quite possibly the research questions);
- that builds on codes identified in transcripts and/or field notes;
- and that provides the researcher with the basis for a theoretical understanding of his or her data that can make a theoretical contribution to the literature relating to the research focus.

of the SSCI via the Web of Science for 'thematic analysis' for the years 2000–14 inclusive and came up with 3,356 hits. The vast majority of these derived from references in abstracts to the article being based on 'thematic analysis'. This figure represents a large increase on the corresponding figure of 1,184 in the previous edition of this book for the 2000–10 period and for the third edition when for the 2000–7 period, 400 hits were produced. Here are some relatively recent accounts of the use of thematic analysis:

1. Jones et al. (2010: 109), in their study of early retirement referred to at several points in Chapter 1, write that 'a thematic analysis was undertaken whereby an initial coding scheme was developed and indexing undertaken through constant comparison within and between cases. Transcripts were coded by author two and categories developed and refined in an iterative process'.

2. Ferguson (in press), in his observational and interview-based study of social workers and their clients (see Chapter 20), writes: 'Cross-case comparative analysis enabled the drawing-out of themes, which could be illustrated by detailed case studies'.

3. Brooks and Waters (2015; see Research in focus 23.7) write of their qualitative content analysis of websites of elite schools in the UK: 'We were interested to explore the extent to which certain themes were mentioned and/or represented (e.g. HE [higher education] destinations outside the UK, international pupils, trips and expeditions abroad), and used a detailed grid to record this information. We also explored, in a more discursive manner, the way in which these various themes were constructed in the websites and elsewhere'.

4. Wood et al. (in press; see Research in focus 23.12) write of their qualitative content analysis of the representation of alcohol in the UK news: 'To develop a coding frame, a random selection of 100 articles were read to identify key themes around alcohol and create thematic categories in the initial coding frame. . . . Written summaries of thematic categories and the constant comparative method . . . informed the interpretation of the data across the articles to consider what the key messages were and how they were framed.'

5. Bagguley and Hussain (in press) write of their interviews with young South Asian women about higher education in the UK: 'In the analysis, we have reconstructed the key themes from these texts through a thematic analysis of the young women's views and experiences, in particular, when these have emerged as relevant, similarities and differences with respect to ethnic origins and religion have been highlighted and discussed in more detail.'

One general strategy for assisting a thematic analysis of qualitative data is provided by Framework, which was developed at the National Centre for Social Research in the UK. Framework is described as a 'matrix based method for ordering and synthesising data' (Ritchie et al. 2003: 219). The idea is to construct an index of central themes and subthemes, which are then represented in a matrix that resembles an SPSS spreadsheet with its display of cases and variables. The themes and subthemes are essentially recurring motifs in the text that are then linked to the data. The themes and subthemes derive from a thorough reading and rereading of the transcripts or field notes that make up the corpus of data. The grid is then applied to the data, which are organized initially into core themes, and the data are then displayed in terms of subthemes within the matrix and for each case. If we take the Disney project data described in Chapter 23, one of the main themes that was identified was 'Ideological critique'. This theme can be viewed as having a number of subthemes—class critique; ethnicity critique; gender critique; and nationality critique. Figure 24.3 is a matrix that draws on the coded text in Tips and skills 'Coded text from the Disney project' and that would be used for representing the data on the theme 'Ideological critique'. The four subthemes are presented, and the idea is to place brief snippets from the data into the appropriate cell. Thus, the passage in Tips and skills 'Coded text from the Disney project' provides the data for the insertion of some material into two of the cells for Interviewee 4. It also specifies the location within the transcript of the snippet(s) that are included in the cell. Ritchie et al. advise that, when inserting material into cells, the researcher should:

1. indicate where in the transcript the fragment comes from (I have used the question number);

2. keep the language of the research participant as far as possible;

3. try not to insert too much quoted material; and

4. use abbreviations in cells so that cells do not become too full.

As its name implies, this approach is meant to supply a framework for the thematic analysis of qualitative data and provides one way of thinking about how to manage themes and data. It does not tell the user how to identify themes; this process is likely to reflect the analyst's awareness of recurring ideas and topics in the data. Recent versions of the software discussed in Chapter 25—QSR NVivo—have been developed to support the Framework approach. See: **www.natcen.ac.uk/our-expertise/methods-expertise/qualitative/framework/** (accessed 22 December 2014).

Figure 24.3
The Framework approach to thematic analysis

Theme: Ideological critique

	Class critique	Ethnicity critique	Gender critique	Nationality critique
Interviewee 1				
Interviewee 2				
Interviewee 3				
Interviewee 4		'saw plenty of black Americans' in MK 'but few if any in that World Showcase'. 'Little mention of black history' (Q14)		World Showcase 'only really representative of the developed world' (Q14)
Interviewee 5				

When searching for themes, Ryan and Bernard (2003) recommend looking for:

- *repetitions:* topics that recur again and again. This is probably one of the most common ways in which themes are identified. For example, Green, Steinbach, and Datta (2012: 276) write that when they reviewed interview transcripts derived from their research on Londoners' transport choices, they 'were struck by the frequency of references to responsibilities and the moral significance of transport choices';

- *indigenous typologies or categories:* local expressions that are either unfamiliar or used in an unfamiliar way;

- *metaphors and analogies:* the ways in which participants represent their thoughts in terms of metaphors or analogies (they give the example of people describing their marriage as like 'the Rock of Gibraltar');

- *transitions:* the ways in which topics shift in transcripts and other materials;

- *similarities and differences:* exploring how interviewees might discuss a topic in different ways or differ from each other in certain ways, or exploring whole texts such as transcripts and asking how they differ;

- *linguistic connectors:* examining the use of words such as 'because' or 'since', because such terms point to causal connections in the minds of participants;

- *missing data:* reflecting on what is *not* in the data by, for example, asking questions about what interviewees omit in their answers to questions;

- *theory-related material:* using social scientific concepts as a springboard for themes.

Repetition is probably one of the most common criteria for establishing that a pattern within the data warrants being considered a theme. Repetition may refer to recurrence within a data source (for example, an interview transcript or document) or, as is more often the case, across data sources (for example, a corpus of interview transcripts or documents). However, repetition *per se* is an insufficient criterion for something to warrant being labelled a theme. Most importantly, it must be relevant to the investigation's research questions or research focus. In other words, simply because quite a large number of people who have been interviewed say much the same thing does not mean it warrants being considered a theme. Further, Owen (1984) suggests considering any evidence of the forcefulness with which any recurring topic is conveyed as a criterion for whether it should be considered a theme. In spoken speech, forcefulness might be identified through inflections; in documents, through italicized text or references to emphasis. The identification of a theme is a stage or two further on from coding data in terms of initial or open codes (Braun and Clarke 2006). It requires the researcher to reflect on the initial codes that have been generated and to gain a sense of the continuities and linkages between them.

While thematic analysis lacks a clearly specified series of procedures, there is a growing sense of a core set of procedures that are outlined in the next section. These core procedures can be used in relation to several of the different ways of analysing qualitative data covered in this book, such as grounded theory, narrative analysis, critical discourse analysis, and qualitative content analysis, and in relation to a wide variety of kinds of qualitative material. This set of procedures has also been employed in relation to the systematic review of qualitative research (see the subsection below on 'Thematic synthesis'). It is this flexibility—the fact that it can be deployed in such different contexts—that probably accounts for the popularity of thematic analysis, in spite of the absence of a codification of its core procedures.

Bazeley (2013) is cautious about thematic analysis, arguing that researchers who claim to have used it are frequently vague about how themes were 'identified' or how themes 'emerged' from the data. She argues that it is important not just to specify themes that have been identified but to justify why they are important and significant. Simply presenting the themes accompanied by some illustrative quotations is insufficient. The researcher needs to go further by showing how the themes are significant, for example by showing how they relate to other themes, what their implications are, and how

they relate to other literature. The researcher also needs to present the process whereby the themes were identified. Having an audit trail of key decisions relating to coding, theme identification, and conceptualization, as well as an evidence base for those decisions, is likely to help this aspect of the justification of how themes were arrived at.

Thematic analysis as the basis for a generic approach to qualitative data analysis

In much the same way that I proposed in Chapter 18 that there is a generic purposive sampling approach that incorporates the core steps involved but which transcends the minor differences between the different purposive sampling strategies, it is possible to identify a generic qualitative data analysis approach. In large part, this account draws on thematic analysis as the guiding set of principles (especially Braun and Clarke 2006; Clarke and Braun 2013) but it also incorporates insights from other writers, most notably Attride-Stirling (2001), Gioia, Corley, and Hamilton (2012), Ritchie et al. (2003), and Thomas (2006). The steps run roughly as follows:

1. *Read through at least a sample of the materials to be analysed.* Initially, the researcher needs to become thoroughly acquainted with the body of material (which

Student experience
Thematic analysis of transcripts

Several of the students who had conducted qualitative research using interviews mentioned forms of analysis that were indicative of adopting a thematic approach. Rebecca Barnes writes that she sought to 'identify key themes', while Erin Sanders writes that she 'transcribed the interviews verbatim—and used NVivo to code the transcripts—looking for emerging and relevant themes'.

Once Samantha Vandermark had completed and transcribed her focus groups with mothers of young children, she

began a qualitative thematic analysis. I read through the transcripts line by line, noting down themes as I saw them appear in the data, for example if a mother openly spoke about the negative impact of fast food chains on childhood health, I would note this down as 'Causes—fast food'. At the bottom of each page I would then note down the main themes that had come from that page's conversation. From this initial, detailed analysis I looked again at the themes that had been pulled out, and started to conglomerate these into wider thematic categories that would represent overall segments of conversation from within the focus groups. Finally, I used the electronic copies of my transcripts to piece together the segments of data which represented each theme, and developed my qualitative analysis through analysing in detail what the mothers said about these themes and what they might signify in terms of wider social attitudes and norms.

 To read more, go to the Online Resource Centre: www.oxfordtextbooks.co.uk/orc/brymansrm5e/

Student experience
Combining memos with thematic analysis

Isabella Robbins used memos as a means of elaborating her thematic analysis of her data. Her memos formed part of her discussions with her supervisor.

> I developed analytic memos, on each interview completed, throughout the data-collection period. These along with full verbatim transcripts and message board data were put into NVivo. I had ideas about the thematics before I used NVivo, so at the beginning a pen and paper were used in conjunction with NVivo. The themes that I was pulling from the data were consistent, and this felt reassuring. My supervisors were also involved with the analysis, in that I would report back with analytic memos and we discussed emerging themes, and I developed ideas and analysis from there.

 To read more, go to the Online Resource Centre: www.oxfordtextbooks.co.uk/orc/brymansrm5e/

may be transcripts, field notes, documents, images). This may be just a sample of the materials or it may be the entire corpus, but either way a process of familiarization is a crucial first step.

2. *Begin coding the materials.* The researcher develops his or her thinking about the data. The coding that takes place at this stage is likely to be at the level of open coding or initial coding, so that there is likely to be a proliferation of codes. The researcher is involved in a process of giving names to what are usually small portions of text.

3. *Elaborate many of the codes into themes.* At this stage, the researcher seeks to reduce the number of codes and to search for common elements in codes so that they can be raised to the level of higher-order codes or themes. At this stage, it is wise to begin writing summaries of what is meant by the codes/themes in the form of memos. The researcher provides names for the codes and themes.

4. *Evaluate the higher-order codes or themes.* For some writers this stage means seeking to combine the codes from Stage 3 into even higher-order codes but for others it entails searching for sub-themes or dimensions among the codes. Whichever course is taken is likely to depend on the level of abstraction to which codes and themes have been developed at Stage 3. Again, writing memos is likely to have an important role.

    4a. *Give names or labels to the themes and their sub-themes (if there are any).* At this stage, the researcher may refer to the literature that relates to the focus of the study but the crucial issue is to develop names that adequately reflect the codes that underpin them and allow the researcher to capture the data. The researcher needs to satisfy him- or herself that the names capture well large portions of the data and

provide genuine insight into the data. The names can at this stage be considered *concepts*.

5. *Examine possible links and connections between concepts and/or how the concepts vary in terms of features of the cases.* The researcher might want to consider whether the concepts are related in a sequence, such as a temporal sequence, or to examine whether the intensity of some of the concepts varies in terms of what is known about the cases that produced the data (such as women versus men, or mature students versus younger students). Some writers propose the construction of networks of themes and sub-themes to portray the interconnections (Attride-Stirling 2001; Grogan et al. 2013).

6. *Write up the insights from the previous stages to provide a compelling narrative about the data.* Remember, the themes that you derive are not intrinsically interesting and important. You have to make the case that they are interesting and important. Writing up is the focus of Chapter 28 and the insights there will be relevant to this consideration. It is crucial to tie your themes to your research question(s) and to the literature that relates to your research focus.

    6a. *Make sure you justify your themes.* OK, you uncovered *x* themes. Why are they important and significant? This means ensuring that you draw inferences about the themes' interconnections with each other and their implications. Ensure that in your write-up, the themes are related to the research literature on your topic. Also, ensure that you justify how you arrived at the themes, which means a transparent account of the process of reading through transcripts, documents, etc. and the ways in which themes were identified in relation to the coding of the data.

Research in focus 24.5
A thematic analysis of body image

Grogan et al. (2013) were interested in how women relate to their clothes and their body image. Twenty women aged between 18 and 45 years were accompanied on a shopping trip in which they were looking for a dress. The researchers audio-recorded their comments as they tried on the dresses and as they chose the one they eventually purchased. The participants were also subjected to a body scan and were photographed. The resulting images were used as visual aids in semi-structured interviews that were carried out after the fitting to understand participants' feelings about the dress and how it fitted them. The researchers write that they carried out a thematic analysis of transcripts but that this was 'broadly informed' by grounded theory procedures. First of all, the researchers carried out line-by-line coding 'to identify initial categories' (2013: 383). Then they used axial coding whereby they 'combined similar and related categories and investigated the relationships between them' (2013: 383). This was followed by selective coding 'to confirm and verify the categories and to make changes where necessary' (2013: 383). This sequence was performed on eleven of the transcripts on the basis of which a model of the main themes and sub-themes and their interconnections was produced. This model was then checked against the remaining nine transcripts after discussion among the research team. The model comprises four themes: functional aspects of clothes fit; body confidence and clothes fit; clothes dimensions and size coding; and the slim hourglass ideal. Each theme was made up of sub-themes; for example, the theme 'functional aspects of clothes fit' was made up of three sub-themes:

- 'Clothes should emphasise most attractive features'. For example, one participant, Ellie, said while trying on dresses that she prefers 'something that pulls in at the waist' (quoted in Grogan et al. 2013: 383).

- 'Clothes should hide disliked parts of the body'. For example, Mary said of her chosen dress that she liked it 'Because it's a bit flattering for my tummy, otherwise it would stick out a bit, so I think it's good' (quoted in Grogan et al. 2013: 384).

- 'Clothes should not expose breasts, thighs or underwear'. An example is Anna, who said while trying on her dress: 'My boobs [breasts] weren't on show, my bra wasn't on show, and my bum [buttocks] wasn't, you know, my bum and my tum [stomach] were fairly covered up' (quoted in Grogan et al. 2013: 384—text in square brackets is in the original).

In their discussion of their findings, the researchers systematically relate their findings to existing research on body image.

While these stages have been numbered, they do not necessarily follow a strict sequence. In qualitative data analysis there is a constant interplay between conceptualization and reviewing the data. Also, the stages merge in some studies. However, the stages are meant to provide a rough indication of the principal elements in thematic analysis and an indication of how they interconnect.

Research in focus 24.5 provides an example of thematic analysis related to body image.

Narrative analysis

Narrative analysis is an approach to the elicitation and analysis of data that is sensitive to the sense of temporal sequence that people, as providers of accounts (often in the form of stories) about themselves or events by which they are affected, detect in their lives and surrounding episodes and inject into their accounts. With narrative analysis, the focus of attention shifts from 'what actually happened?' to 'how do people make sense of what happened?' The last point can be expanded to 'how do people make sense of what happened and to what effect?', because stories are nearly always told with a purpose in mind—there is an intended effect. Proponents of narrative analysis argue that most approaches to the collection and analysis of data neglect the fact that people perceive their lives in terms of continuity and process and that attempts to understand social life that are not attuned to this feature neglect the perspective of those being studied. Life history research (see Chapter 20) has been a prominent setting for the application of narrative analysis (see Research in focus 20.8 for an example), but its use can be much broader than this. Mishler (1986: 77), for example, has argued for greater interest in 'elicited personal narratives'. In his view, and that of many others, the answers that people provide, in particular in qualitative interviews, can be viewed as stories that are potential raw material for a narrative analysis. In other words, narrative analysis relates not just to the life span but also to accounts relating to episodes and to the interconnections between them.

Some researchers apply narrative analysis to interview accounts. For example, in her account of her 'click moment' as a narrative researcher (quoted above in the subsection on 'Problems with coding'), Riessman describes how she applied narrative analysis to conventional interview transcript material and then began to uncover the stories her interviewees were telling her. In this case, Riessman was applying a narrative approach to materials that had been gathered in a conventional way for conventional purposes. Other researchers start out with the intention of conducting a narrative analysis and deliberately ask people to recount stories (e.g. R. L. Miller 2000). Thus, while stories can arise out of answers to questions that are not designed to elicit a narrative, certain kinds of question are especially likely to elicit them. Riessman (2004) suggests that a question such as 'tell me what happened', followed up with 'and then what happened?', is much more likely to provide a narrative account than 'when did X happen?' While some narrative researchers prefer simply to start people off by asking them to tell their story about an event, Riessman argues that it is usually necessary to keep asking follow-up questions to stimulate the flow of details and impressions. For example, in her study of divorce, she often asked 'Can you remember a time when . . . ?' and then followed it up with 'What happened that makes you remember that particular moment in your marriage?' Chase (2011) suggests that what distinguishes the use of interviews in a narrative inquiry context from conventional qualitative interviewing is that there is a deliberate attempt to elicit stories rather than an exclusive focus on interviewees' experiences. Brannen observes that people will sometimes break into the telling of stories in the course of a standard qualitative interview and that they therefore 'engage with this mode to some extent under the conditions of their own choosing' (2013: 5.1). However, Brannen shows that even when there is a deliberate attempt to elicit narratives, they will not necessarily be forthcoming. She contrasts narrative interviews with two Irish immigrants as part of a study of change and continuity in fatherhood. One interviewee slipped easily into the narrative mode, but the other rejected the narrative mode. The interviewer had to proceed in the latter case by coaxing out 'small stories' in response to specific questions. The general attempt to produce an account of his life by asking 'Can you just tell me the story of your life? You can start where you want' was totally unsuccessful.

There are, then, two distinct ways of thinking about narrative analysis: for some researchers it is an approach to analysing different kinds of data; for others, it is this, but, in addition, the researcher deliberately seeks to stimulate the telling of stories. The example provided in Research in focus 24.6 is an example of the former; Research in focus 24.7 is an example of the purposeful elicitation of stories.

Coffey and Atkinson (1996) argue that a narrative should be viewed in terms of the functions that the narrative serves for the teller. The aim of narrative interviews is to elicit interviewees' reconstructed accounts of connections between events and between events and contexts. A narrative analysis entails seeking out the forms and functions of narrative. R. L. Miller (2000) proposes that narrative interviews in life story or biographical research are far more concerned with eliciting the interviewee's perspective as revealed in the telling of the story of his or her life or family than with the facts of that life. There is a concern with how that perspective changes in relation to different contexts. The interviewer is very much a part of the process in that he or she is fully implicated in the construction of the story for the interviewee. Research in focus 24.6 provides an example of the application of a narrative analysis approach to an environment that demonstrates its potential beyond the life story context. In this case, the author explores competing narratives in accounting for the failed implementation of an IT system in a British hospital.

Narrative analysis, then, is an approach to the analysis of qualitative data that emphasizes the stories that people employ to account for events. It would be wrong to view narrative analysis primarily in terms of qualitative interviewing in spite of the focus on it in the account presented here. Narrative analysis can be employed in relation to documents too, and as such it provides a potential strategy for analysing such sources in addition to those covered in Chapter 23. For example, E. M. Davis (2008) conducted a narrative analysis of documents concerning breast cancer produced by the National

Research in focus 24.6
An example of organizational narratives in a hospital

Brown (1998) examined the competing narratives involved in the aftermath of the introduction of a hospital information support system (HISS) at a British hospital trust referred to as 'The City'. The information technology (IT) implementation was largely seen as unsuccessful because of cost over-runs and the absence of clear clinical benefits. Drawing on his unstructured and semi-structured interviews with key actors regarding the IT implementation and its aftermath, Brown presents three contrasting narratives: the ward narrative, the laboratory narrative, and the implementation team's narrative, thereby presenting the perspectives of the main groups of participants in the implementation.

The three contrasting narratives provide a very clear sense of the organization as a political arena in which groups and individuals contest the legitimacy of others' interpretations of events. Thus, 'the representations of each group's narrative are described as vehicles for establishing its altruistic motives for embarking on the project, and for attributing responsibility for what had come to be defined as a failing project to others' (Brown 1998: 49).

Thus, while the three groups had similar motivations for participating in the initiative, largely in terms of the adoption of an ethic of patient care, they had rather different latent motivations and interpretations of what went wrong. In terms of the former, whereas the ward narrative implied a latent motivation to save doctors' and nurses' time, the laboratory team emphasized the importance of retaining the existing IT systems, and the implementation team placed the accent on the possible advantages for their own careers, in large part by the increased level of dependence on their skills. In terms of the contrasting narratives of what went wrong, the ward narrative was to do with the failure of the implementation team to coordinate the initiative and meet deadlines, and the laboratory team emphasized the tendency for the implementation team not to listen or communicate. For their part, the implementation team's diagnosis was to do with the ward staff failing to communicate their needs, lack of cooperation from the laboratory staff, and poorly written software.

Research in focus 24.7
Constructing narratives about anorexia

O'Shaughnessy, Dallos, and Gough (2013) wanted to convey the accounts of women suffering from anorexia nervosa with a particular focus on the stories they use to represent their condition and experiences of it. Four women being treated for anorexia were identified and data were collected from them in three phases: a life story interview; a semi-structured interview and a member validation exercise (see Key concept 17.3). The life story interview asked a single question designed to elicit a life story narrative:

> I am interested in hearing about the life experiences of women living with anorexia. I would like you to tell me the story of your life, all the events and experiences which are important to you; start wherever you like. Please take as much time as you need, I'll listen and I won't interrupt.
>
> (O'Shaughnessy et al. 2013: 47)

In the semi-structured interviews, participants were prompted to reflect on their responses to the life story interview and to elaborate on their answers as well as to explore aspects not covered there. This process was also designed to allow the researchers to examine the narratives in terms of Labov's (1982) framework for analysing the structure of narratives and to evaluate the degree to which the interviews revealed narrative strategies, especially ones with defensive overtones. The member validation process entailed feeding each participant's narrative account back to her for validation. In addition to using the Labov scheme, the researchers made notes about the tone of the interviews. The interviews lasted between forty-five minutes and two hours.

In the article, the researchers present each interview in terms of the six elements that make up the Labov framework. In addition, they searched for narrative themes that were shared by the life story accounts. Five such themes were identified. Two examples of the shared narrative themes may be useful. First, O'Shaughnessy et al. identified a 'lonely story' which was to do with both a quest for and an anxiety about being connected with others. For example, one of the four women, Jessica, a twenty-one-year-old, says at one point:

> Erm (pause), erm (pause). I've never had a boyfriend, erm, although I would like one . . . But, although I say that, I wouldn't—I don't think like . . . I mean I do—I would—I do have moments when I want one to cuddle or something like that you know? Erm . . . but, I don't know if I could allow myself to have that affection, or allow myself to—or allow someone else to get close to me. Erm . . . I don't know, so . . . I don't know, really, if it'll ever happen. But . . . I can still dream on (laughs). Erm . . . er . . . I haven't really got any friends.
>
> (quoted in O'Shaughnessy et al. 2013: 53)

Another narrative theme is 'a fearful and threatening world' whereby the participants express anxiety about their past and present lives. Jessica is quoted in this connection too:

> Even when . . . I don't know why but . . . even now, erm . . . when I go to the supermarket with mum, she says 'oh, I'll just be over there' or something or, you know and . . . erm . . . she'll be . . . er . . . I'll go back there and then she's not there and I'll just feel this horrible, horrible panic . . . like . . . it's horrible, I don't why I feel like it. But I just feel like . . . so panicky . . . that I can't find her and (pause) . . . erm . . . No, I don't know why . . . Yeah, I don't know why. I don't know where that came from either (laughs). But, yeah . . . I just feel like . . . erm . . . I just don't want to lose her . . . so . . . Yeah.
>
> (quoted in O'Shaughnessy et al. 2013: 54)

The authors also noted aspects of narratives that were absent. For example, they note that narratives about hospitalization for anorexia were largely absent, suggesting that this omission in itself is a defensive strategy.

Cancer Institute in the USA. Davis (2008: 68) employed six dimensions of narrative to analyse the discourse surrounding breast cancer in these documents: 'characters, setting, events, audience, causal relations, and themes'. She uncovered 'a robust narrative focused on an ideal of women who can be treated successfully and who can look forward to recovery from breast cancer. The narrative demonstrates a generally consistent set of underlying values and expectations' (E. M. Davis 2008: 68). She calls this an early cancer narrative, which comprises six elements that form a narrative plot:

1. *Presymptomatic.* The woman is diligent about checking herself.

2. *Symptomatic.* The woman responds quickly and in a medically appropriate way to the discovery of an abnormality.

3. *Diagnosis.* Tests are conducted, and, if cancer is diagnosed, the woman becomes a patient. A doctor will administer the appropriate treatment.

4. *Treatment.* The woman becomes informed about her treatment(s) and their side effects and communicates regularly about her condition and concerns with her doctor.

5. *Recovery.* The patient improves both physically and emotionally, while maintaining communication with her doctor.

6. *Post-recovery.* The patient returns to her previous life before the onset of cancer.

Underlying this narrative are two core themes: risk (all women are at risk of the disease) and control (medical treatments are crucial to the control of the disease). In addition, Davis points to a contradiction within the narrative: on the one hand, breast cancer is a temporary nuisance; on the other hand, it is a lifelong issue for women.

As Riessman (2008) observes, narratives may relate to quite long periods of time (such as an entire life story or to an extended period of time, as in many illness narratives or in relation to an occupational career, as in Research in focus 20.8) or to a specific event. In relation to the latter, she gives the example of stories of acts of resistance, as provided somewhat unusually in answers to open-ended questions employed in the course of a structured interview survey of 430 people in New Jersey concerning how 'they experience, interpret, and use law' (Ewick and Silbey 2003: 1338). One of the strategies of resistance identified

Student experience
The use of narrative interviews

Isabella Robbins adopted a narrative interview approach for her study of parents' decision-making in connection with vaccination of their children. She did this by encouraging them to tell stories about the vaccinations.

In order to capture what I considered to be complex decision-making routes for some people contemplating childhood vaccination, I employed qualitative in-depth interviews as my main methodological route. In these interviews mothers were invited to explain how they came to their decisions regarding childhood vaccination. They were encouraged to tell the story of their child's/children's vaccination/s, and I took opportunities to follow up their talk. This narrative approach was supplemented towards the end of the interviews by inviting the mothers to respond to a series of informal vignettes, designed to elicit material relevant to foreshadowed and emerging themes.

  To read more, go to the Online Resource Centre: www.oxfordtextbooks.co.uk/orc/brymansrm5e/

was 'rule literalness', which refers to people using organizations' rules to their own ends in order to circumvent or bend those rules as a means of resistance. An example is that of Michael Chapin, who was arrested and fined $500 for driving without insurance and was forced to pay in cash. It was later found that he had been arrested in error and the charges against him were dismissed. He refused to accept a cheque as a refund:

> Then they try to write me a check for my money back and I wouldn't accept it. I made a big stink. I said I want my cash back. I gave you cash, I want cash back . . . I said I don't care what you have to do. I don't care if you have to print the money up. I want cash money. You didn't trust me for a check and I don't trust you either. I made them open the safe. [The judge] came back to see what I was yelling at the clerk, telling her I want my money.

(Ewick and Silbey 2003: 1353–4)

In this case, the story relates to a specific incident rather than something that occurs over an extended period of time.

As an approach to the analysis of qualitative data, narrative analysis has not gone uncriticized. Bury (2001), while noting the growing interest in *illness narratives* (stories that people tell about the causes of, in particular, chronic illnesses they and/or others experience and the impacts the illnesses have on their and others' lives), argues that there has been a tendency for narrative researchers to treat uncritically the stories that they are told. For example, he suggests that the frequent recourse in illness narratives to coping with and normalizing chronic illness may in large part be to do with an attempt to convince the audience (for example, an interviewer or the reader of a book about someone's struggle with illness) of competence. It may, therefore, have more to do with signalling that one is not a failure in a society in which failure is frowned upon. Thus a narrative of coping with adversity in the form of a chronic illness may have more to do with wanting to be seen as a fully functioning member of society than a realistic account of coming to terms with a medical condition. However, as Bury recognizes, the social conditions that prompt such narratives and the forms that the narratives take are themselves revealing. In drawing attention to the motives that may lie behind illness narratives, he is seeking not to undermine narrative analysis but to draw attention to the issue of what it is that narratives are supposed to be revealing to the researcher.

One further issue is that narrative analysis has splintered into a number of different approaches that nonetheless share certain common assumptions. For example, Phoenix, Smith, and Sparkes (2010) draw a distinction between analyses that focus on the content and structure of stories and those that emphasize how the stories are conveyed. The latter entails attending to such things as stories as performances or the rhetorical devices used to convey them. As Riessman (2008: 11) has observed: 'Narrative analysis refers to a family of methods for interpreting texts that have in common a storied form. As in all families, there is conflict and disagreement among those holding different perspectives.' The presence of different ways of practising narrative analysis does not represent a criticism of the approach, but it does suggest that, for students interested in applying it to their data, there is a good deal of groundwork that needs to be done in terms of sorting out what kind of narrative analysis they are conducting.

Secondary analysis of qualitative data

One final point to bear in mind is that this discussion of qualitative data analysis may have been presumed to be solely concerned with the analysis of data in which the analyst has played a part in collecting. However, secondary analysis of qualitative data has become a growing focus of discussion and interest. While the secondary analysis of quantitative data has been on the research agenda for many years (see Chapter 14), similar use of qualitative data has only recently come to the fore. The general idea of secondary analysis was addressed in Key concept 14.1.

There is no obvious reason why qualitative data cannot be the focus of secondary analysis, though it is undoubtedly the case that such data do present certain challenges that are not fully shared by quantitative data. The possible grounds for conducting a secondary analysis are more or less the same as those associated with quantitative data (see Chapter 14). In the context of qualitative data, it is possible that a secondary analysis will allow the researcher to mine data that were not examined by the primary investigators or that new interpretations may be possible (see Research in focus 24.8 for an example).

With such considerations in mind, Qualidata, an archival resource centre, was created in the UK in 1994. The centre was not a repository for qualitative data; instead, it was concerned with 'locating, assessing and documenting qualitative data and arranging their deposit in suitable public archive repositories' (Corti et al. 1995). It is now called QualiBank and can be found at: **http://discover.ukdataservice.ac.uk/QualiBank** (accessed 23 December 2014).

QualiBank acknowledges certain difficulties with the reuse of qualitative data, such as the difficulty of making settings and people anonymous and the ethical problems involved in such reuse, associated with promises of confidentiality. Also, Hammersley (1997) has suggested that reuse of qualitative data may be hindered by the secondary analyst's lack of an insider's understanding of the social context within which the data were produced. This possible difficulty may hamper the

Research in focus 24.8
A secondary analysis of qualitative data from the *Affluent Worker* study

Savage (2005) examined the field notes collected by researchers in the course of the *Affluent Worker* study in the 1960s (see, e.g., Goldthorpe et al. 1968). This was an important project that explored questions concerning social class and work in Great Britain in this period. The findings in the monographs that emerged from the study emphasized the quantitative data collected from the social survey, and little use was made of the qualitative data that were collected in the course of the interviews. These qualitative data were deposited with Qualidata. Savage re-examined some of the essentially qualitative field note data that were collected. Savage argues that, although a huge amount of qualitative data was generated through the *Affluent Worker* studies, very little of it made its way into publication. Instead the researchers focused on aspects of their data that could be quantified, so that 'a huge amount of evocative material was "left on the cutting room floor"' (Savage 2005: 932). Savage uses the field notes, which contain many verbatim quotations from respondent interviews, to argue that rereading the field notes with a contemporary understanding of issues of money, power, and status indicates that the respondents had different understandings of class from Goldthorpe et al. that the researchers did not pick up on, and this difference in understanding affected how the data were interpreted. Savage shows that many of the affluent workers struggled with the notion of 'class identity' and that the kinds of views that they held about class and related matters were not as different from other working-class groups as the authors' inferences about their survey data implied. He shows how the interpretation of the data is affected by the researcher, in that the differences between his views of the data and those of the original researchers may in part be to do with different perspectives that are brought to bear on those data. This example of the secondary analysis of qualitative data indicates that new light can be shed on old data, but it also raises interesting methodological issues, in this case concerning how to disentangle inferences about change from the impact of looking at old data through new conceptual lenses.

interpretation of data but would seem to be more of a problem with ethnographic field notes than with interview transcripts. Such problems even seem to afflict researchers revisiting their own data many years after the original research had been carried out (Mauthner et al. 1998: 742). There are also distinctive ethical issues deriving from the fact that the original researcher(s) may not have obtained the consent of research participants for the analysis of data by others. This is a particular problem with qualitative data in view of the fact that it invariably contains detailed accounts of contexts and people that can make it difficult to conceal the identities of institutions and individuals in the presentation of raw data (as opposed to publications in which such concealment is usually feasible). Nonetheless, in spite of certain practical difficulties, secondary analysis offers rich opportunities, not least because the tendency for qualitative researchers to generate large and unwieldy sets of data means that much of the material remains underexplored.

 # Synthesizing qualitative studies

There has been growing interest among qualitative researchers in how to synthesize qualitative studies that relate to a particular research domain. The idea of arriving at a synthesis is the equivalent of conducting a meta-analysis of quantitative studies. Conducting syntheses of qualitative research in a domain allows a sense of what is known in that domain to be established in a rigorous way, and can therefore act as a springboard for moving future research forward.

One of the principal problems facing someone considering doing a synthesis of qualitative studies is that there are several different approaches and the field does not seem to be close to alighting on a preferred option (Paterson 2012; Timulak 2014). The list of possibilities includes conducting a quantitative synthesis of qualitative studies by using content analysis (see Research in focus 13.5 for an example). It is not possible to cover all of the approaches to qualitative synthesis in this book, but I will mention two of the more prominent approaches—**meta-ethnography** and **thematic synthesis**.

Meta-ethnography

Meta-ethnography is used to achieve an interpretative synthesis of qualitative research and other secondary sources, thus providing a counterpart to meta-analysis in quantitative research (Noblit and Hare 1988). It can be used to synthesize and analyse information about a phenomenon that has been extensively studied, such as lay experiences of diabetes (see Research in focus 24.9). However, this is where the similarity ends, because meta-ethnography 'refers not to developing overarching generalizations but, rather, translations of qualitative studies into one another' (Noblit and Hare 1988: 25). Noblit and Hare base their approach on the idea that all social science explanation is comparative, involving the researcher in a process of translating existing studies into his or her own worldview, and through this

he or she creates a reading of other people's readings about a subject. Meta-ethnography involves a series of seven phases that overlap and repeat as the synthesis progresses.

1. *Getting started.* This involves the researcher identifying an intellectual interest that the qualitative research might inform by reading interpretative accounts.

2. *Deciding what is relevant to the initial interest.* Unlike positivists, interpretative researchers are not concerned with developing an exhaustive list of studies that might be included in the review. Instead the primary intent is to determine what accounts are likely to be credible and interesting to the intended audience for the synthesis.

3. *Reading the studies.* This involves the detailed, repeated reading of the studies, rather than moving to analysis of their characteristics.

4. *Determining how the studies are related.* This stage entails 'putting together' the various studies by determining the relationships between them and the metaphors used within them.

5. *Translating the studies into one another.* This phase is concerned with interpreting the meaning of studies in relation to each other: are they directly comparable or 'reciprocal' translations (so that the concepts used by each study are translated one-by-one into concepts used by the others); do they stand in opposition to each other as 'refutational' translations; or do they, taken together, represent a line of argument that is neither 'reciprocal' nor 'refutational'?

6. *Synthesizing translations.* The researcher compares the different translations and shows how they relate to each other. This may involve grouping them into different types.

7. *Expressing the synthesis.* This involves translating the synthesis into a form that can be comprehended by the audience for which it is intended.

Crucial to understanding this approach is that the synthesis is focused primarily on the interpretations and explanations offered by studies that are included, rather than on the data that these studies are based on. Meta-ethnography thus translates the interpretations of one study into the interpretations of another one. Although the name of the approach implies that it is to do with the synthesis of ethnographic studies, it is typically applied to groups of studies that are qualitative in character rather than just ethnographies.

Lee et al. (in press) examined several meta-ethnographies, one of which is the example in Research in focus 24.9, and found that there was often considerable variation in how the stages were implemented. One of their conclusions was that collaborative work is extremely important for conducting meta-ethnography since it allows different interpretations of studies to surface and be debated and reconciled. This feature may hinder its appropriateness to a student dissertation, although it may be feasible for group projects. The very time-consuming nature of the process which Lee et al. experienced may constitute a further barrier.

Thematic synthesis

Thematic synthesis essentially applies thematic analysis to existing studies in a particular domain. Although thematic synthesis tends to be thought of as a method for synthesizing qualitative studies, it can be used in such a way as to include quantitative studies too (Kavanagh et al. 2012), but to simplify this presentation, the focus will be on its use in relation to qualitative synthesis.

In line with the procedures outlined in Table 5.1, the researcher has to specify a clear research question (often called a 'review question'), search for studies that meet the criteria implied by the research question, eliminate those studies that are not eligible in terms of the criteria, appraise the quality of the studies, and eliminate those studies that do not pass the expected quality criteria or take the quality assessment into account when presenting

Research in focus 24.9
A meta-ethnography of lay experiences of diabetes

Campbell et al. (2003) report their approach to conducting a meta-ethnography of studies within the medical sociology field of lay experiences of diabetes and diabetes care. A search came up with ten articles based on qualitative research that addressed this area. Three were excluded for quite different reasons: one turned out not to be based on qualitative research; the evidence in another was appraised as being too weak to warrant inclusion; and the findings of the third paper turned out to be in one of the seven papers that would be included. The seven papers could be grouped into three 'clusters': response to diabetes and treatment; how patients and practitioners differ in perceptions of the disease; and the connections between beliefs about the causes of diabetes and how the people with diabetes managed the disease. One of the themes to emerge among the four articles in the first of these three clusters was the link between control and 'strategic cheating'. Campbell et al. note that one study noted the significance of people's sense of control of the disease, which they accomplished through managing it strategically. Such people are referred to as 'copers'. Another study made a similar distinction between those who felt they were in control of their diet and those described as 'buffeted' by it. Their stance on this issue affected their perception of diabetes, with the former group having a less negative image of it. Some people were able to manage their diet strategically in a flexible way, which was sometimes perceived as 'cheating without guilt'. These reflections were then linked to findings across the two other studies in this group. The authors write:

> Looking across these four studies it would seem that strategic cheating, departing from medical advice in a thoughtful and intelligent way, in order to achieve a balance between the demands of diabetes and the way the person wants to live their life, was associated with a feeling of confidence, less guilt, acceptance of the diabetes and improved glucose levels.

(Campbell et al. 2003: 678)

In addition, six concepts were found from the seven studies to be significant for the diabetes sufferers in terms of helping them to achieve a balance between controlling the disease and also having some control over their lives—for example, the need to adopt a less subservient approach to medical practitioners. Interestingly, the authors were able to derive insights from their meta-ethnography that were not present in any of the articles.

the synthesis. Once the final group of studies to be synthesized has been arrived at, there are three principal stages in the implementation of a synthesis (Thomas and Harden 2008; Thomas, Harden, and Newman 2012):

1. *Coding the text in the studies.* The very first thing to do is to identify what the findings are, which is not as straightforward as it might seem. It might refer to what the participants in each of the component studies reported or to the researchers' inferences and conclusions. Then coding can begin. As with thematic analysis, this initial coding stage typically entails line-by-line coding. The reviewers examine each line of text for what it is saying and label what they take to be its significance for the research question. In the case of the qualitative studies in the systematic review referred to in Table 5.1, the authors write that they took 'study findings to be all of the text labelled as "results" or "findings" in study reports' (Thomas and Harden 2008: 4). These were entered into NVivo (see Chapter 25) and treated as qualitative data to be analysed thematically. Initially, the researchers carried out line-by-line coding of the findings. For example, they developed a code called 'bad food = nice, good food = awful' and show that in one of the eight studies the following were coded this way. Examples of coded text are:

> *'All the things that are bad for you are nice and all the things that are good for you are awful.'* (Boys, year 6) [[56], p74]
>
> *'All adverts for healthy stuff go on about healthy things. The adverts for unhealthy things tell you how nice they taste.'* [[56], p75]
>
> *Some children reported throwing away foods they knew had been put in because they were 'good for you' and only ate the crisps and chocolate.* [[56], p75]
>
> (Thomas and Harden 2008: 6; italics in original)

Thus, findings that were coded in preparation for synthesis could be quotations from interview transcripts, as in the first two quotations, or quotations from researchers' presentations of their findings, as in the third quotation. The bracketed numbers refer to the publications in which the quotations appeared and the page numbers.

2. *Generating descriptive themes.* The codes produced at the first stage are organized into higher-order themes by combining the many codes that will have been produced through line-by-line coding. Thomas et al. (2012) say that some thematic syntheses will stop at this stage if they have provided adequate answers to the review question. Other syntheses will progress to . . .

3. *Generating analytic themes.* This stage, if it occurs at all, entails drawing together the themes generated at the previous stage into what Thomas et al. call 'new conceptualisations and explanations' that transcend the primary studies on which the codes and descriptive themes were based. The authors suggest considering each descriptive theme and asking how each one addresses the review question.

Thematic synthesis is at its strongest when it provides compelling answers to the review question through descriptive or, more likely, analytic themes. As Thomas and Harden (2008) make clear, generating analytic themes is controversial as it is so reliant on the impressions and ingenuity of the researcher, but without such a leap, thematic synthesis runs the risk of synthesizing studies but offering little in the way of new insights.

Research in focus 24.10 provides an example of thematic synthesis examining doctors' use of evidence-based medicine.

Research in focus 24.10
A thematic synthesis of studies of doctors' use of evidence-based medicine

Swennen et al. (2013) conducted a thematic synthesis of qualitative studies investigating the barriers and facilitators to doctors' use of evidence-based medicine (EBM). They initially identified 1,211 studies but this was finally narrowed down to thirty studies after applying eligibility and quality criteria. The researchers' approach corresponds quite well to the three stages outlined by Thomas and Harden (2008):

1. *Coding the text in the studies.* Two members of the research team 'independently read all text of results paragraphs, line by line, and interpreted the content of each text fragment' (Swennen et al. 2013: 1385). In addition, each fragment was coded in terms of whether it was a barrier or facilitator, or as 'undecided' if it was not possible to identify the outcome. This process produced 189 labels or codes to do with EBM.

2. *Generating descriptive themes.* The 189 labels were grouped into eight descriptive themes to do with 'different aspects of EBM'. The researchers used a theoretical saturation approach to the generation of the themes, of which there were eight.

3. *Generating analytic themes.* The researchers 'looked for similarities and differences of content, outcomes, and context within and between the descriptive themes' and in a search for 'new interpretative explanations on doctors' barriers and facilitators for EBM, they sorted and rearranged the descriptive themes into analytic themes' which 'go beyond the results and conclusions of the primary studies' (Swennen et al. 2013: 1385). These analytic themes were made up of subthemes.

At the last stage, the researchers produced five analytic themes as follows (with illustrative quotations):

* Individual mind-set. 'A fear by some surgeons that evidence will somehow be used against them' (a quotation from one of the synthesized papers and which derives from an interpretation by the author(s) of that paper and which is associated with the subtheme of 'Attitude towards EBM').

* Professional group norms. 'We [residents] have staff surgeons who dismiss most randomized controlled trials that don't agree with their approach by saying that the surgeons who published the paper must not be as technically adept as them' (a quotation from one of the synthesized papers and which derives from a quotation by a research participant and is associated with the sub-theme of 'Culture towards change').

* EBM competencies. 'Because of the time constraint, you wouldn't be able to look through the literature and get the right papers with the minimal amount of time' (a quotation from one of the synthesized papers and which derives from a quotation by a research participant and is associated with the sub-theme of 'Searching best evidence').

* Balance between confidence and critical reflection. 'While peer-reviewed written sources may have theoretical influence, [we] . . . found that, in practice, "opinion leadership" and personal contact provide the real stimulus' (a quotation from one of the synthesized papers and which derives from a quotation by the author(s) of that paper and is associated with the sub-theme of 'Information seeking behaviour').

* Managerial collaboration. 'The incorporation of EBM into daily practice is time-consuming, however, and it can therefore be at odds with management requirements. The general opinion is that management should do more to facilitate the search for state-of-the-art knowledge, but that such searching is also the responsibility of the individual physician' (a quotation from one of the synthesized papers and which derives from an interpretation by the author(s) of that paper).

This study provides an explicit application of thematic synthesis to a body of literature. At the same time, it provides a good illustration of thematic analysis itself.

❯❯ *Key points*

....

* The collection of qualitative data frequently results in the accumulation of a large volume of information.

* Qualitative data analysis is not governed by codified rules in the same way as quantitative data analysis.

* There are different approaches to qualitative data analysis, of which grounded theory is probably the most prominent.

* Coding is a key process in most qualitative data analysis strategies, but it is sometimes accused of fragmenting and decontextualizing text.

- Narrative analysis is an approach that emphasizes the stories that people tell in the course of interviews and other interactions with the qualitative researcher and that has become a distinctive strategy in its own right for the analysis of qualitative data.

- Secondary analysis of qualitative data is becoming a more prominent activity than in the past.

- Approaches to the synthesis of qualitative studies are being developed.

Questions for review

- What is meant by suggesting that qualitative data are an 'attractive nuisance'?

General strategies of qualitative data analysis

- What are the main ingredients of analytic induction?

- What makes it a rigorous method?

- What are the main ingredients of grounded theory?

- What is the role of coding in grounded theory and what are the different types of coding?

- What is the role of memos in grounded theory?

- Charmaz (2000: 519) has written that theoretical sampling 'represents a defining property of grounded theory'. Why do you think she feels this to be the case?

- What are some of the main criticisms of grounded theory?

Basic operations in qualitative data analysis

- Is coding associated solely with grounded theory?

- What are the main steps in coding?

- To what extent does coding result in excessive fragmentation of data?

Thematic analysis

- How far is there a codified scheme for conducting thematic analysis?

- How does the Framework approach help with a thematic analysis?

- What are the chief ways of identifying themes in qualitative data?

Narrative analysis

- To what extent does narrative analysis provide an alternative to data fragmentation?

- How does the emphasis on stories in narrative analysis provide a distinctive approach to the analysis of qualitative data?

- Can narrative analysis be applied to all kinds of qualitative interview?

- What is a narrative interview and how far does it differ from other kinds of qualitative interview?

Secondary analysis of qualitative data

- How feasible is it for researchers to analyse qualitative data collected by another researcher?

Synthesizing qualitative studies

- To what extent does thematic synthesis entail an application of the principles of thematic analysis?

Online Resource Centre

www.oxfordtextbooks.co.uk/orc/brymansrm5e/

Visit the Online Resource Centre to enrich your understanding of qualitative data analysis. Follow up links to other resources, test yourself using multiple choice questions, and gain further guidance and inspiration from the Student Researcher's Toolkit.

25

Computer-assisted qualitative data analysis: using NVivo

Chapter outline

Chapter guide

One of the most significant developments in qualitative research since the middle of the 1980s is the emergence of software designed to assist in the analysis of qualitative data. This software is often referred to as computer-assisted (or computer-aided) qualitative data analysis software (CAQDAS). CAQDAS removes the clerical tasks associated with the manual coding and retrieving of data. There is no industry leader among the different programs. This chapter introduces NVivo, a widely-used CAQDAS package. This chapter explores:

- some of the debates about the desirability of CAQDAS;
- how to set up your research materials for analysis with NVivo;
- how to code using NVivo;
- how to retrieve coded text;
- how to create memos;
- basic computer operations in NVivo.

Introduction

One of the most notable developments in qualitative research in recent years has been the arrival of computer software that facilitates the analysis of qualitative data. **Computer-assisted qualitative data analysis software**, or CAQDAS as it is conventionally abbreviated, has been a growth area in terms of both the proliferation of programs that perform such analysis and the numbers of people using them. The term and its abbreviation were coined by Lee and Fielding (1991).

Most of the best-known programs are variations on the code-and-retrieve theme. This means that they allow the analyst to code text while working at the computer and to retrieve the coded text. Thus, if we code a large number of interviews, we can retrieve all those sequences of text to which a code (or combination of codes) was attached. This means that the computer takes over manual tasks associated with the coding process referred to in the previous chapter. Typically, the analyst would:

- go through a set of data marking sequences of text in terms of codes (coding); and
- for each code, collect together all sequences of text coded in a particular way (retrieving).

The computer takes over the physical task of writing marginal codes, making photocopies of transcripts or field notes, cutting out all chunks of text relating to a code, and pasting them together. CAQDAS does not automatically do these things: the researcher must still interpret the data, code, and then retrieve the data, but the computer takes over the manual labour involved (wielding scissors and pasting small pieces of paper together, for example).

Is CAQDAS like quantitative data analysis software?

One of the comments often made about CAQDAS is that it does not and cannot help with decisions about the coding of textual materials or about the interpretation of findings (Sprokkereef et al. 1995; Weitzman and Miles 1995). However, this situation is no different from quantitative data analysis software. In quantitative research, the investigator sets out the crucial concepts and ideas in advance rather than generating them out of his or her data. Also, it would be wrong to represent the use of quantitative data analysis software such as SPSS as purely mechanical: once the analyses have been conducted, it is still necessary to interpret them. Indeed, the choice of variables and the techniques of analysis are areas in which a considerable amount of interpretative expertise is required. Creativity is required by both forms of software.

CAQDAS differs from the use of quantitative data analysis software largely in terms of the environment within which it operates.

No industry leader

With quantitative data analysis, SPSS is both widely known and widely used. It is not the only statistical software used by social researchers, but it is certainly dominant. It has competitors but SPSS is close to being the industry leader. No parallel situation exists with regard to CAQDAS.

In this chapter, we will introduce one of the best-known packages—**NVivo**.

Advice on qualitative data analysis software can be found at: **onlineqda.hud.ac.uk/Which_software/ what_packages_are_available/index.php** (accessed 16 July 2014).

Lack of universal agreement about the usefulness of CAQDAS

Unlike quantitative data analysis, in which the use of computer software is both widely accepted and to all intents and purposes a necessity, among qualitative data analysts its use is by no means universally embraced. There are several concerns.

- Some writers are concerned that the ease with which coded text can be quantified, either within qualitative data analysis packages or by importing coded information into quantitative data analysis packages such as SPSS, will mean that the temptation to quantify findings will prove irresistible. As a result, there is a concern that qualitative research will then be colonized by the reliability and validity criteria of quantitative research (Hesse-Biber 1995).
- It has been suggested that CAQDAS reinforces the tendency for the code-and-retrieve process that underpins most approaches to qualitative data analysis to result in a fragmentation of the textual materials on which researchers work (Weaver and Atkinson 1994). As a result, the narrative flow of interview

transcripts and events recorded in field notes may be lost.

- It has also been suggested that the fragmentation process of coding text into chunks that are then retrieved and put together into groups of related fragments risks decontextualizing data (Buston 1997; Fielding and Lee 1998: 74). Having an awareness of context is crucial to many qualitative researchers and the prospect of this element being sidelined is unattractive.

- Catterall and Maclaran (1997) have argued that CAQDAS is not very suitable for focus group data because the code and retrieve function tends to result in a loss of the communication between participants. Many writers view the interaction that occurs in focus groups as an important feature of the method (Kitzinger 1994).

- Stanley and Temple (1995) have suggested that most of the coding and retrieval features are achievable through word-processing software. They show how this can be accomplished using Microsoft Word. The advantage of using such software is that it does not require a lengthy period of getting acquainted with it.

- Researchers working in teams may experience difficulties in coordinating the coding of text when different people are involved in this activity (Sprokkereef et al. 1995).

- Coffey, Holbrook, and Atkinson (1994) have argued that the style of qualitative data analysis enshrined in most CAQDAS software (including NVivo) is resulting in the emergence of a new orthodoxy. This arises because these programs presume a certain style of analysis—one based on coding and retrieving text—that owes a great deal to grounded theory. Coffey et al. argue that the emergence of a new orthodoxy is inconsistent with the growing experimentation with a variety of representational modes in qualitative research.

On the other hand, several writers are enthusiastic about CAQDAS software on a variety of grounds:

- Most obviously, CAQDAS can make the coding and retrieval process faster and more efficient.

- It has been suggested that new opportunities are offered. For example, Mangabeira (1995) has argued on the basis of her experience that her ability to relate her coded text to what are often referred to as 'facesheet variables' (socio-demographic and personal information, such as age, title of job, number of years in school education) offered new opportunities in the process of analysing her data. Thus, CAQDAS may be helpful in the development of explanations.

- It is sometimes suggested that CAQDAS enhances the transparency of the process of qualitative data analysis. It is often noted that the ways in which qualitative

data are analysed are unclear in reports of findings (Bryman and Burgess 1994b). CAQDAS may force researchers to be more explicit and reflective about the process of analysis.

- CAQDAS invites the analyst to think about codes that are developed in terms of 'trees' of interrelated ideas. This can be a useful feature, in that it urges the analyst to consider possible connections between codes.

- Writers such as Silverman (1985) have commented on the tendency towards anecdotalism in much qualitative research—that is, the tendency to use quotations from interview transcripts or field notes but with little sense of the prevalence of the phenomenon they are supposed to exemplify. CAQDAS invariably offers the opportunity to count such things as the frequency with which a form of behaviour occurred or a viewpoint was expressed in interviews. However, some qualitative researchers perceive risks in the opportunity offered for quantification of findings, as discussed above.

- Paulus, Lester, and Britt (2013) analysed a number of textbooks on qualitative research and note that sometimes the attitude to CAQDAS is overly cautious, emphasizing its limitations rather than its advantages. They propose that this cautionary approach is based on an outdated understanding of what the software can and cannot do and they urge researchers to embrace the affordances of this new technology. They also note that some of the textbook authors, writing within a more positivist frame, have suggested that CAQDAS increases the rigour of qualitative data analysis.

To use or not to use CAQDAS? If you have a very small data set, it is probably not worth the time and trouble navigating your way around new software; on the other hand, if you think you may use it on a future occasion, making the effort may be worthwhile. It is also worth bearing in mind that learning new software does provide you with useful skills that may be transferable on a future occasion. If you do not have easy access to CAQDAS, it is likely to be too expensive for your personal purchase. By and large, I feel it is worthwhile, but you need to bear in mind some of the factors mentioned above in deciding whether or not to use it. It is also striking that the bulk of the references are pre-2000; see also the discussion of CAQDAS debates at: **onlineqda.hud.ac.uk/Intro_CAQDAS/software_debates.php** (accessed 16 July 2014). In large part, this is because CAQDAS has become more accepted and because the main parameters of the debate have not changed significantly.

The rest of this chapter provides an introduction to NVivo. It is based on my study of visitors to Disney theme parks, where I used NVivo as a tool to assist me in the process of qualitative data analysis.

Learning NVivo

This explanation of NVivo and its functions addresses just its most basic features. There may be features not covered here that you would find useful in your own work, so try to explore it. There is a very good Help facility, and tutorials have been included to assist learners. As in Chapter 16, → signifies 'click once with the left-hand button of your mouse'—that is, select.

On opening NVivo, you will be presented with a welcome screen (see Plate 25.1). This screen shows any existing NVivo projects and is the springboard for either opening one of the existing projects or starting a new one. If you are starting a new project, as in the example that follows, → **File** → **New**. The **New Project** dialog box appears and you are asked to provide a **Title** for your project. For this exercise, the title 'Disney Project1' was chosen. You are also asked to give a **Description** of

the project, but this is optional. When you have done this, → **OK.**

You then need to import the documents you want to code. In this case, the documents are interview transcripts from the project on visitors to Disney theme parks, referred to in Chapter 24. Other kinds of documents can be imported, such as field notes. NVivo 10 can accept documents in both rich text and Word formats. To import the documents, → **Internals** (below **Sources** at the top of the **Navigation view**) → **External Data** tab on the **Ribbon** → **Documents** button on the **Find bar** [opens the **Import Internals** dialog box] → **Browse.** . . to locate the documents that are to be imported → the documents to be imported (you can hold down the Ctrl key to select several documents or if you want to select all of them hold down the Ctrl key and tap the A key) → **Open.** (See Plate 25.2

Plate 25.1
The opening screen

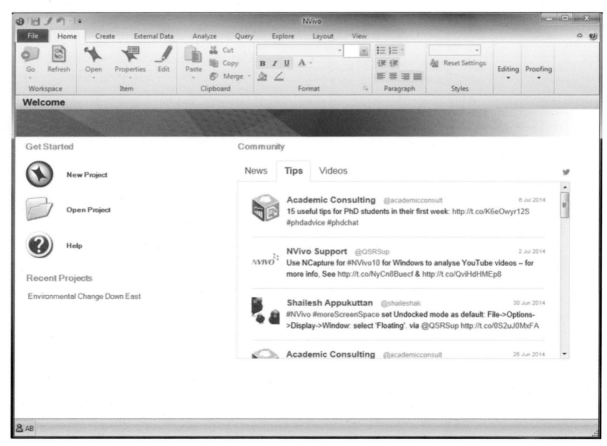

Plate 25.2

Stages in importing documents into NVivo

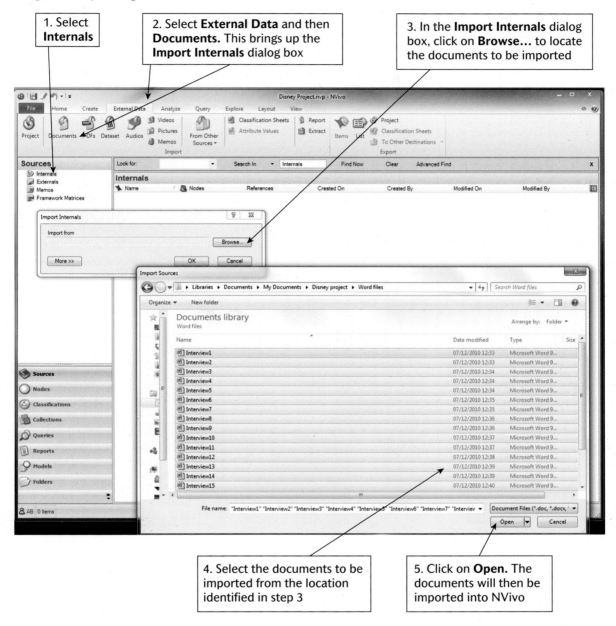

1. Select **Internals**

2. Select **External Data** and then **Documents.** This brings up the **Import Internals** dialog box

3. In the **Import Internals** dialog box, click on **Browse...** to locate the documents to be imported

4. Select the documents to be imported from the location identified in step 3

5. Click on **Open.** The documents will then be imported into NVivo

for the series of steps.) The documents will then be visible in the **Document Viewer**. Once the documents have been imported, they can be read and edited. All you need to do is double-click on the 📄 icon to the left of each interview in the Viewer.

Coding

Coding your data is one of the key phases in the whole process of qualitative data analysis. For NVivo, coding is accomplished through *nodes* (see Key concept 25.1).

Key concept 25.1
What is a node?

NVivo's Help system in earlier releases defined coding as 'the process of marking passages of text in a project's documents with *nodes*' (emphasis added). Nodes are, therefore, the route by which coding is undertaken. In turn, a node is defined in the latest release as 'a collection of references about a specific theme, place, person or other area of interest'. When a document has been coded, the node will incorporate references to those portions of documents in which the code appears. Once established, nodes can be changed or deleted.

There are several ways of going about the coding process in NVivo. The approach I took in relation to the coding of the Disney Project was to follow these steps:

1. I read through the interviews both in printed form and in the **Document Viewer** (see Plate 25.3).

2. I worked out some codes that seemed relevant to the documents.

3. I went back into the documents and coded them using NVivo.

An alternative strategy is to code while browsing the documents.

Creating nodes

The nodes that I used that were relevant to the passage in Tips and skills 'Coded text from the Disney project' (Chapter 24) are presented in Figure 25.1. Prior to NVivo 9 and 10, when creating a node, the researcher chose between creating a 'free node' or a 'tree node'. The latter is a node that is organized in a hierarchy of connected nodes, whereas free nodes were not organized in this way. This distinction was dropped in NVivo 9, and the software now assumes that a hierarchically-organized node is being created. Two points are crucial to note here for users of earlier releases of the software. First, the tendency now is not

Plate 25.3
The NVivo Workspace

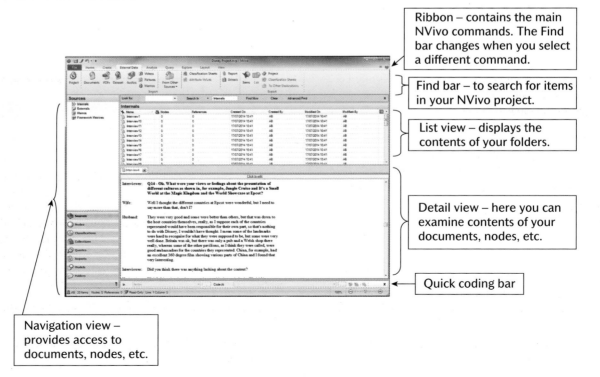

Ribbon – contains the main NVivo commands. The Find bar changes when you select a different command.

Find bar – to search for items in your NVivo project.

List view – displays the contents of your folders.

Detail view – here you can examine contents of your documents, nodes, etc.

Quick coding bar

Navigation view – provides access to documents, nodes, etc.

Figure 25.1

Nodes used in the Disney project

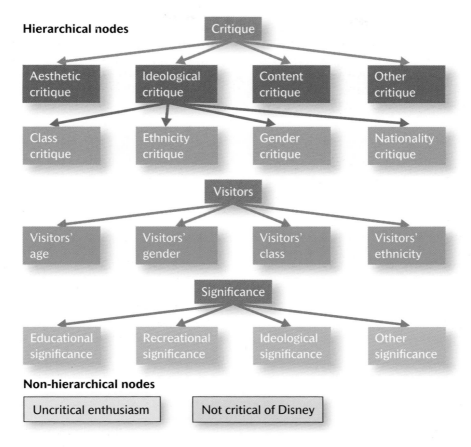

Non-hierarchical nodes

| Uncritical enthusiasm | Not critical of Disney |

to refer to 'tree nodes' but to treat them as hierarchically organized nodes. Second, free nodes (that is, nodes that are not hierarchically organized) can still be created—they are simply nodes without 'children', to use the latest NVivo terminology.

Notice that there are three groups of *hierarchically organized nodes* and two *non-hierarchically organized nodes* in Figure 25.1. The nodes can be created in the following way.

Creating a non-hierarchically organized node

This sequence of steps demonstrates how to create the non-hierarchically organized node *not critical of Disney*.

1. While in the **Document Viewer** [the term used to describe the general screen shown in Plate 25.3] → **Create** in the Ribbon

2. → **Node** in the **Find bar** [opens the **New Node** dialog box—see Plate 25.4]

3. Enter the node **Name** [*not critical of Disney*] and a **Description** (this is optional)

4. → **OK**

Creating hierarchically organized nodes

To create a hierarchically organized node, the initial process is exactly the same as with a non-hierarchically organized node. I will explain how to create the hierarchically organized node *Class critique*, which is a child of the hierarchically organized node *Ideological critique*, which is itself a child of the hierarchically organized node *Critique* (see Figure 25.1). The following steps will generate this node.

1. While in the **Document Viewer** → **Create** in the Ribbon

2. → **Node** in the **Find bar** [opens the **New Node** dialog box—see Plate 25.5]

Plate 25.4
Stages in creating a non-hierarchically organized node

1. Select **Create**

2. Select **Node**

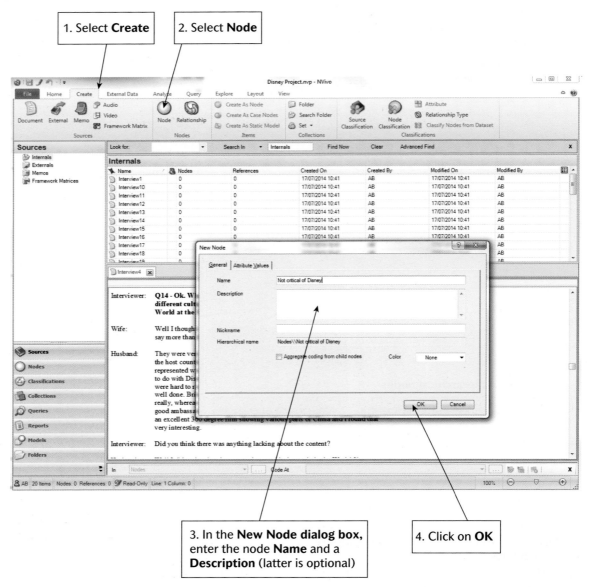

3. In the **New Node dialog box,** enter the node **Name** and a **Description** (latter is optional)

4. Click on **OK**

3. Enter the node **Name** [*critique*] and a **Description** (the latter is optional)

4. → **OK**

5. → *Critique* in the list of nodes in the List viewer

6. → **Node** in the **Find bar** [opens the **New Node** dialog box—see Plate 25.5]

7. Enter the node **Name** [*Ideological critique*] and a **Description** (the latter is optional). This node will form a child of the hierarchically organized node [make sure

that in Hierarchical name it reads **Nodes\\Critique**, as this will mean it is a child of **Critique**]. See Plate 25.5.

8. → *Ideological critique* in the list of nodes in the List viewer

9. → **Node** in the **Find bar** [opens the **New Node** dialog box—see Plate 25.5]

10. Enter the node **Name** [*Class critique*] and a **Description** (the latter is optional). This node will form a child of the hierarchically organized node [make sure that in

Plate 25.5

Stages in creating a hierarchically organized node

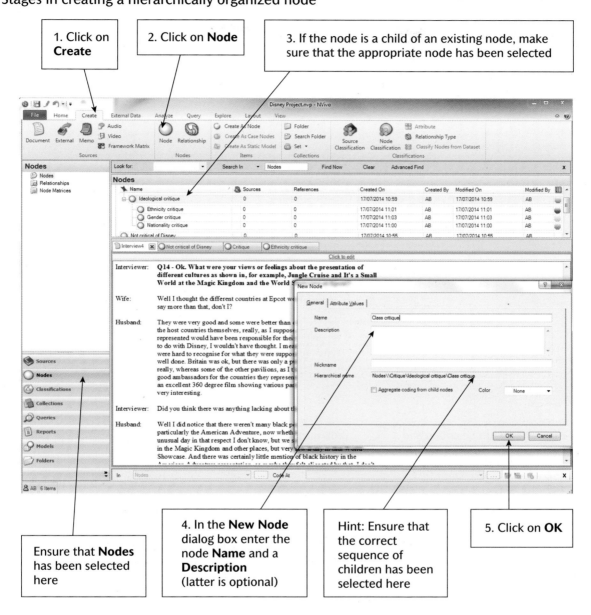

1. Click on **Create**

2. Click on **Node**

3. If the node is a child of an existing node, make sure that the appropriate node has been selected

Ensure that **Nodes** has been selected here

4. In the **New Node** dialog box enter the node **Name** and a **Description** (latter is optional)

Hint: Ensure that the correct sequence of children has been selected here

5. Click on **OK**

Hierarchical name it reads **Nodes\\Critique\Ideological critique**, as this will mean it is a child of **Ideological critique**, which is itself a child of **Critique**]. See Plate 25.5.

11. → **OK**

Applying nodes in the coding process

Coding is carried out by applying nodes to segments of text. Once you have set up some nodes (and do remember you can add and alter them at any time), assuming that you are looking at a document in the viewer, you can highlight the area of the document that you want to code and then right-click on the mouse while holding the cursor over the highlighted text. Then, → **Code Selection** → **Code Selection at New Node. . . .** This opens the **New Node** dialog box. You can then create a new node in the manner outlined in the previous sections.

Plate 25.6
Using drag and drop to code

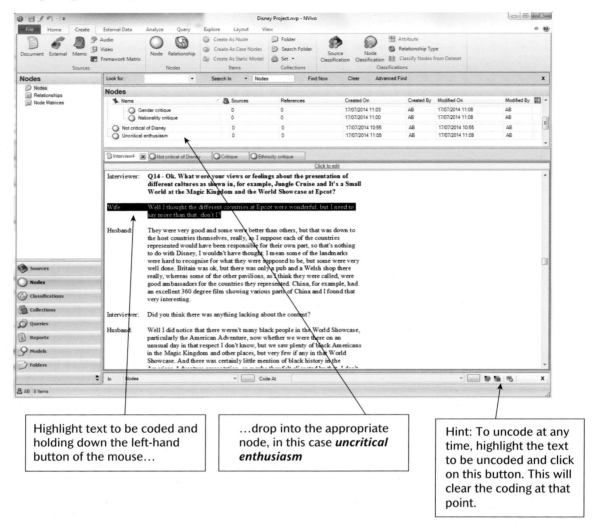

Highlight text to be coded and holding down the left-hand button of the mouse…

…drop into the appropriate node, in this case *uncritical enthusiasm*

Hint: To uncode at any time, highlight the text to be uncoded and click on this button. This will clear the coding at that point.

If the code you want to use has been created, one of the easiest ways of coding in NVivo 10 is to drag and drop text into an existing code (see Plate 25.6). To do this, highlight the text to be coded and then, holding down the left-hand button, drag the text over to the appropriate node in the **List view**.

Another way is to highlight the text you want to code, right-click over the highlighted text, → **Code Selection** → **Code Selection at Existing Nodes**, which opens the **Select Project Items** dialog box (see Plate 25.7). Tick the node(s) you want to use. Thus, in the example in Plate 25.7, the tick by *Uncritical enthusiasm* will code the highlighted text at that node. If you also wanted to use a hierarchically organized node, you would need to find the appropriate parent in the list of nodes within the List

view and then click on the plus to the left of it. To *uncode* at any point, simply highlight the passage to be uncoded, and → the button with a red cross in it 🗑 in the Quick coding bar (see Plate 25.3). Alternatively, right-click on the highlighted text and → **Uncode**.

Coding stripes

It is very helpful to be able to see the areas of text that have been coded and the nodes applied to them. NVivo has a useful aid to this called *coding stripes*. Selecting this facility allows you to see multicoloured stripes that represent portions of coded text and the nodes used. Overlapping codes do not represent a problem.

To activate coding stripes, → **View** in the **Ribbon** and then → **Coding Stripes** in the **Find** bar → **Nodes**

Plate 25.7
Coding in NVivo

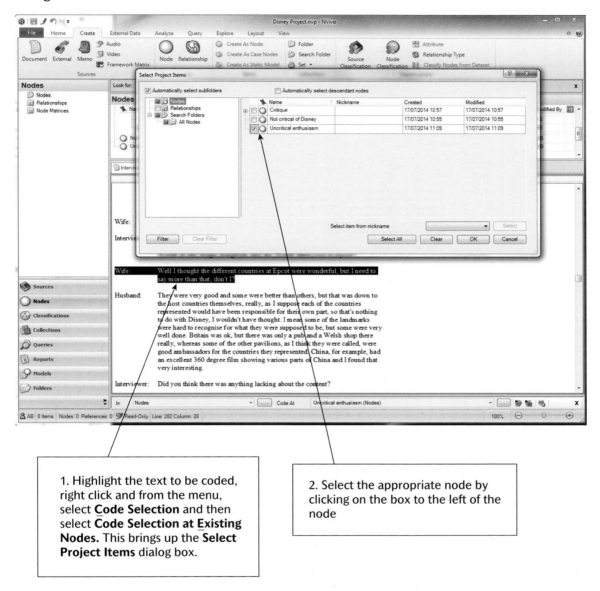

1. Highlight the text to be coded, right click and from the menu, select **Code Selection** and then select **Code Selection at Existing Nodes.** This brings up the **Select Project Items** dialog box.

2. Select the appropriate node by clicking on the box to the left of the node

Recently Coding. Plate 25.8 shows these stripes. We can see that some segments have been coded at two or more nodes—such as *visitors' ethnicity* and *ethnicity critique*. All the nodes that have been used are clearly displayed.

Searching text

Once you have coded your data, however preliminary that may be, you will want to conduct searches of your data at some point. A typical instance is that you are likely to want to retrieve all occurrences in your documents of a particular node. NVivo allows you very rapidly to trawl through all your documents so that you will end up with all text that was coded at a particular node in all of your documents. This is very easy to do in NVivo.

To search for occurrences of a single node

These steps describe how to conduct a search for sequences of text that have been coded in terms of the node *Ethnicity critique*. The stages are outlined in Plate 25.9.

Plate 25.8
Coding stripes

1. While in the **Document Viewer → Nodes** in the **Navigation view**. This will bring up your list of nodes in the **List view.**

2. If you cannot find the parents of *Ethnicity critique* → on the little box with a + sign ⊞ ⬡ to the left of *Critique* [this brings up a list of all branches of the node *Critique*].

3. → on the + sign ⊞ ⬡ to the left of *Ideological critique* [this brings up a list of all branches of the node *Ideological critique*].

4. Double-click on *Ethnicity critique.*

5. All instances of coded text at the node *Ethnicity critique* will appear at the bottom of the screen, as in Plate 25.9.

To search for text coded in terms of a non-hierarchically organized node, the process is simpler, in that you just double-click on the relevant **Free Nodes** to generate all the text coded at that node.

To search for the intersection of two nodes

This section is concerned with searching for sequences of text that have been coded at two nodes: *aesthetic critique* and *not critical of Disney*. This type of search is known as a 'Boolean search'. It will locate text coded in terms of the two nodes together (that is, where they intersect), *not* text coded in terms of each of the two nodes. The following steps need to be followed:

1. In the **Document Viewer**, → **Queries** in the **Navigation view**

2. → **Query** on the **Find** bar

3. → 🔍 [opens the **Coding Query** dialog box in Plate 25.10]

4. → **Coding Criteria** tab

5. → **Ad**v**anced, tab**

6. In the **Define more criteria**: panel, → **Coded at** from the drop-down menu

Plate 25.9

Stages in retrieving text from a hierarchically organized node

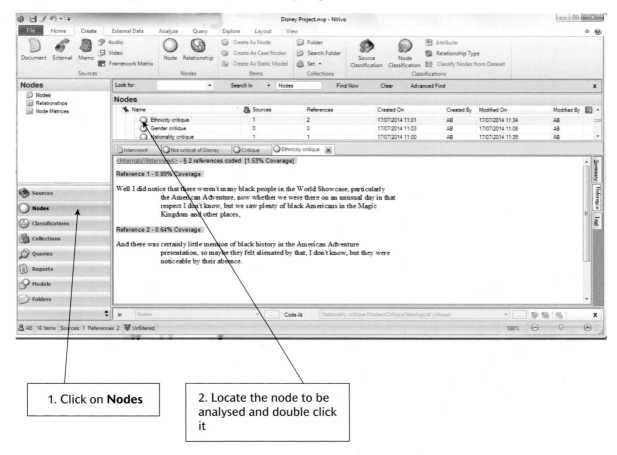

1. Click on **Nodes**

2. Locate the node to be analysed and double click it

7. → **Select**. You then need to choose the two nodes to be analysed from the **Select Project Items** dialog box.

8. → Once the nodes have been selected, → **OK** which returns you to the **Coding Query** dialog box, and in the **Coding Query** dialog box → **Add to List**

9. Make sure **AND** has been selected immediately below **Define more criteria**:

10. → **Run**

To search for specific text

NVivo can also perform searches for specific words or phrases, often referred to as 'strings' in computer jargon. For example, to search for **Magic Kingdom**, the following steps would need to be taken:

1. → **Home** on the **Ribbon**

2. → 🔍 [opens the **Find Content** dialog box in Plate 25.11]

3. Insert **Magic Kingdom** to the right of **Text**

4. To the right of **Look in**, make sure **Text** has been selected

5. → **Find Next**

Text searching can be useful for the identification of possible in vivo codes—those that derive from the natural language of people in the social context being studied (as described in Research in focus 24.4). You would then need to go back to the documents to create nodes to allow you to code in terms of any in vivo codes.

Output

To find the results of coding at a particular node, → the **Nodes** button in the bottom left. This will bring up your node structure. Find the node that you are interested in and simply double-click on that node. This will bring up all text coded at that node along with information about which interview(s) the text comes from.

Plate 25.10

The Coding Query dialog box (searching for the intersection of two nodes)

2. Select **Query**

3. Select **Coding**. This brings up the **Coding Query** dialog box.

4. Select the **Coding Criteria tab**

5. Select the **Advanced** tab

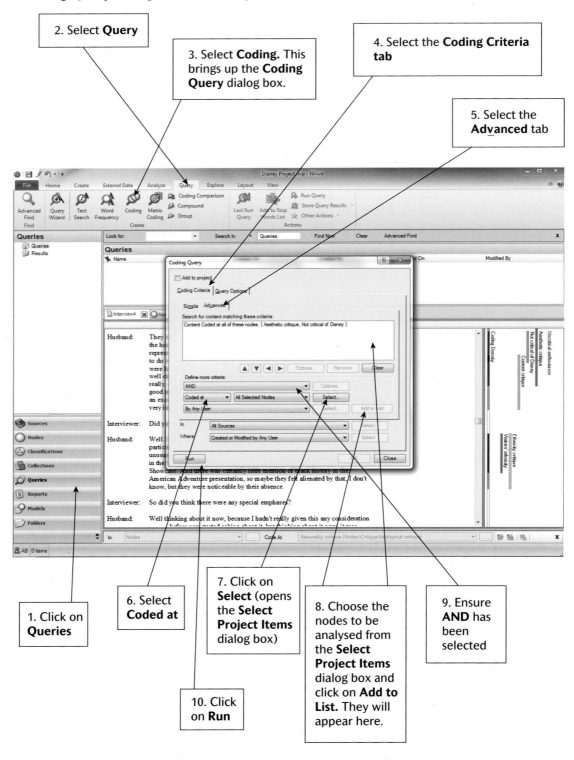

7. Click on **Select** (opens the **Select Project Items** dialog box)

6. Select **Coded at**

1. Click on **Queries**

8. Choose the nodes to be analysed from the **Select Project Items** dialog box and click on **Add to List.** They will appear here.

9. Ensure **AND** has been selected

10. Click on **Run**

Plate 25.11
The Find Content dialog box

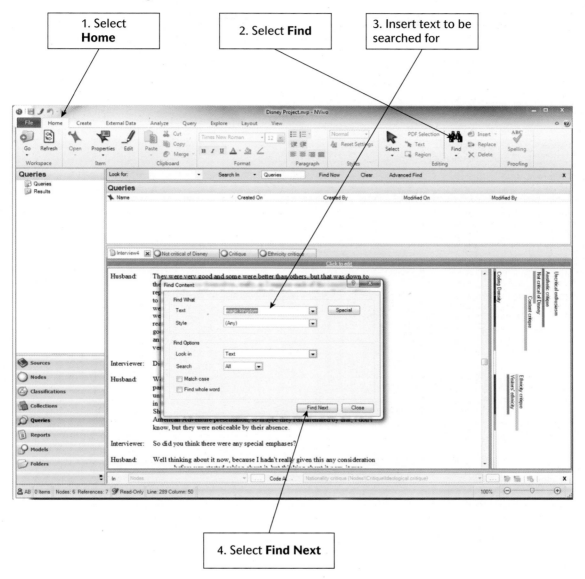

1. Select **Home**

2. Select **Find**

3. Insert text to be searched for

4. Select **Find Next**

Memos

In Chapter 24, it was noted that one feature of the grounded theory approach to qualitative data analysis is the use of memos in which ideas and illustrations might be stored. Memos can be easily created in NVivo. The following steps, which are outlined in Plate 25.12, should be followed:

1. In the **Navigation View**, → **Sources**

2. Under **Sources** → **Memos**

3. → **Create** tab on the **Find bar** and then

4. → **Memo** [opens the **New Memo** dialog box shown in Plate 25.12]

5. To the right of **Name**, type in a name for the memo (e.g. **gender critique**). You can also provide a brief description of the document in the window to the right of Description, as in Plate 25.12

6. → **OK**

Plate 25.12
Stages in creating a memo

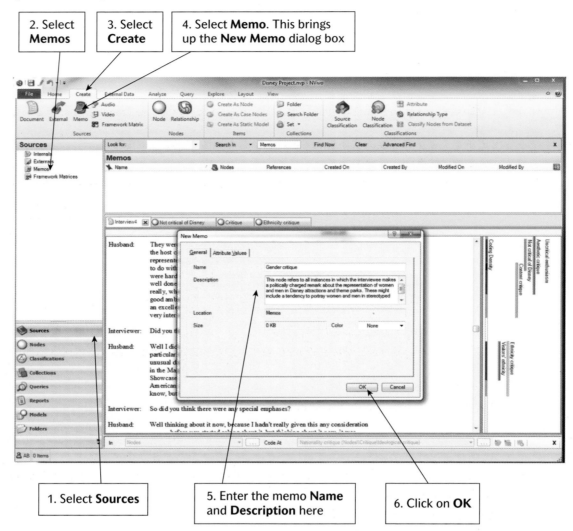

2. Select **Memos**

3. Select **Create**

4. Select **Memo**. This brings up the **New Memo** dialog box

1. Select **Sources**

5. Enter the memo **Name** and **Description** here

6. Click on **OK**

Saving an NVivo project

When you have finished working on your data, you will need to save it for future use. To do this, on the menu bar at the top, → **File** → **Save**. This will save all the work you have done. You will then be given the opportunity to exit NVivo or to create or open a project without worrying about losing all your hard work.

Opening an existing NVivo project

To retrieve a project you have created, at the Welcome screen, → **File** → **Open.** This opens the **Open Project** dialog box. Search for and then select the project you want to work on. Then → **Open.**

Final thoughts

As with the chapter on SPSS (Chapter 16), a short chapter such as this can provide help only with the most basic features of the software. In so doing, I hope that it will have given students who may be uncertain about whether CAQDAS is for them an impression of what the software is like and a sense of its capabilities. Some readers may decide it is not for them and that the tried-and-tested cut and paste will do the trick, but the software warrants serious consideration because of its power and flexibility.

Some useful online help in the use of NVivo can be found at the Online QDA website and the CAQDAS Networking Project website at: **http://onlineqda.hud.ac.uk/** (accessed 17 July 2014) **http://caqdas.soc.surrey.ac.uk/** (accessed 17 July 2014)

 ## Key points

- CAQDAS does not and cannot help with decisions about how to code qualitative data or how to interpret findings.
- CAQDAS can make many if not most of the clerical tasks associated with the manual coding and retrieving of data easier and faster.
- If you have a very small data set, it is probably not worth the time and trouble navigating your way around a new software program.
- If you have a larger data set, or are intending to use the software skills that you acquire on other research projects in the future, CAQDAS can be an invaluable tool.

 ## Questions for review

Is CAQDAS like quantitative data analysis software?

- What are the main points of difference between CAQDAS and quantitative data analysis software such as SPSS?
- Why is CAQDAS controversial?
- To what extent does CAQDAS help with qualitative data analysis?

Learning NVivo

- What is a node?
- What is the difference between a non-hierarchically organized node and a hierarchically organized node?
- What is an in vivo code?
- Do nodes have to be set up in advance?
- In NVivo, what is the difference between a document and a memo?
- How do you go about searching for a single node and for the intersection of two nodes?
- Why might it be useful to display coding stripes?
- How do you search for specific text?

 ## Online Resource Centre
www.oxfordtextbooks.co.uk/orc/brymansrm5e/

Visit the Online Resource Centre to enrich your understanding of computer-assisted qualitative data analysis using NVivo. Follow up links to other resources, test yourself using multiple choice questions, and gain further guidance and inspiration from the Student Researcher's Toolkit.

Part Four
Mixed Methods Research and Writing Up

In Part Four we will explore areas that transcend the quantitative/qualitative distinction. Chapter 26 invites readers to consider how useful the distinction is. This may seem a perverse thing to do, since the book has been organized around the quantitative/qualitative distinction. However, the aim is to show that the distinction is not a hard-and-fast one. Chapter 27 considers the different ways in which quantitative and qualitative research can be combined. Such combinations are referred to as *mixed methods research*. Chapter 28 examines issues relating to the writing-up of social research and explores some features of good writing in quantitative, qualitative and mixed methods research.

These chapters draw together certain issues from previous parts of the book but also address others that have been raised already but this time are discussed in much greater depth.

26

Breaking down the quantitative/ qualitative divide

Chapter outline

Chapter guide

This chapter is concerned with the degree to which the quantitative/qualitative divide should be regarded as a hard-and-fast one. It shows that, while there are many differences between the two research strategies, there are also many examples of research that transcend the distinction. One way in which this occurs is through research that combines quantitative and qualitative research, which is the focus of Chapter 27. The present chapter is concerned with points of overlap between them. This chapter explores:

- aspects of qualitative research that can contain elements of the natural science model;
- aspects of quantitative research that can contain elements of interpretivism;
- the idea that research methods are more independent of epistemological and ontological assumptions than is sometimes supposed;

- ways in which aspects of the quantitative/qualitative contrast sometimes break down;
- studies in which quantitative and qualitative research are employed in relation to each other, so that qualitative research is used to analyse quantitative research and vice versa;
- the use of quantification in qualitative research.

Introduction

With this book structured so far around the distinction between quantitative and qualitative research, it might appear perverse to raise at this stage the prospect that the distinction might be overblown. The distinction has been employed so far for two main reasons.

1. There *are* differences between quantitative and qualitative research in terms of research strategy, and many researchers and writers on research methodology perceive this to be the case.

2. The distinction is a useful means of organizing research methods and approaches to data analysis.

However, while epistemological and ontological commitments may be associated with certain research methods—such as the often-cited links between a natural science epistemology (in particular, positivism) and social survey research, or between an interpretivist epistemology (for example, phenomenology) and qualitative interviewing—the connections are not deterministic. In other words, while qualitative interviews may often reveal a predisposition towards or a reflection of an interpretivist and constructionist position, this is not always the case (see Research in focus 26.1). This means that the connections that were posited in Chapter 2 between epistemology and ontology, on the one hand, and research method, on the other, are best thought of as tendencies rather than as definitive connections. Such connections were implied by the suggestion that within each of the two research strategies—quantitative and qualitative—there is a distinctive mix of epistemology, ontology, and research methods (see Table 2.1). However, we cannot say that the use of a structured interview or self-administered questionnaire *necessarily* implies a commitment to a natural scientific model or that ethnographic research *must* mean an interpretivist epistemology. We should not be surprised at this: after all, quantitative research teaches us that it is rarely the case that we find perfect associations between variables. We should not be surprised, therefore, that the practice of social research similarly lacks absolute determinism.

Research in focus 26.1
Using qualitative research to test a hypothesis

Adler and Adler (1985) were concerned to explore the issue of whether participation in athletics in higher education in the USA is associated with higher or lower levels of academic achievement, an issue on which the existing literature was inconsistent. The first author was a participant observer for four years of a basketball programme in a university, and both authors carried out 'intensive, taped interviews' with players. The authors' findings do lead them to conclude that athletic participation is likely to result in lower academic achievement. This occurs because the programme participants gradually drift from idealistic goals about their academic careers, and a variety of factors lead them to become increasingly detached from academic work. For example, one student is quoted as saying: 'If I was a student like most other students I could do well, but when you play the calibre of ball we do, you just can't be an above-average student. What I strive for now is just to be an average student. . . . You just can't find the time to do all the reading' (Adler and Adler 1985: 247). This study shows how, although qualitative research is typically associated with generating theories, it can also be employed for testing them.

It is striking that, although the Adler and Adler study is broadly interpretivist in epistemological orientation, with its emphasis on how college athletes view their social situation, the findings have objectivist, rather than constructionist, overtones. When the authors describe the students' academic performance as 'determined less by demographic characteristics and high school experiences than by the structure of their college experiences' (Adler and Adler 1985: 249), they are suggesting a social world that is 'out there' and that has a formal, objective quality. It is an example of qualitative research in the sense that there is no quantification or very little of it, but it does not have *all* the other features outlined in Table 2.1.

Research methods are much more free-floating than is sometimes supposed. A method of data collection such as participant observation can be employed in such a way that it is in tune with the tenets of constructionism, but equally it can be used in a manner that reveals an objectivist orientation. Also, it is easy to under-emphasize the significance of practical considerations in the way in which

social research is conducted (though look again at Figure 2.3). Conducting a study of drug-dealers by postal questionnaire may not be totally impossible, but it is unlikely to succeed in terms of yielding valid answers to questions.

In the rest of this chapter I will examine a variety of ways in which the contrast between quantitative and qualitative research should not be overdrawn.

 # The natural science model and qualitative research

One of the chief difficulties with the links that are frequently forged between issues of epistemology and matters of research method is that they often entail a characterization of the natural sciences as necessarily or inherently positivist in orientation. There are three notable difficulties here.

1. There is no agreement on the epistemological basis of the natural sciences. As noted in Chapter 2, positivism is but one version of the nature of the natural sciences, *realism* being one alternative account (Bhaskar 1975).

2. If we assume that the practices of natural scientists are those that are revealed in their written accounts of what they do (and most of the discussions of the nature of the natural sciences do assume this), we run into a problem because studies by social researchers of scientists' practices suggest that there is often a disparity between their work behaviour and their writings. It is useful to recall in this connection the research by Gilbert and Mulkay (1984) cited in Chapter 22 (see the section on 'Uncovering interpretative repertoires'), which suggested that the ways in which scientists talked about their work frequently revealed a different set of practices from those inscribed in their articles.

3. As Platt (1981) has argued, the term 'positivist' has to be treated in a circumspect way, because, while it does refer to a distinctive characterization of scientific enquiry (see Key concept 2.2), it is also frequently employed in a polemical way. When employed in this manner, it is rarely helpful, because the term is usually a characterization (a negative one) of the work of others rather than of one's own work.

Quite aside from the difficulty of addressing the natural science model and positivism, there are problems with associating them solely with quantitative research. Further, qualitative research frequently exhibits features that one would associate with a natural science model. This tendency is revealed in several ways:

- *Empiricist overtones*. Although empiricism (see Key concept 2.1) is typically associated with quantitative research, many writers on qualitative research display an equal emphasis on the importance of direct contact with social reality as the springboard for any investigation. Thus, writers on qualitative research frequently stress the importance of direct experience of social settings and fashioning an understanding of social worlds via that contact. The very idea that theory is to be grounded in data (see Chapter 24) seems to constitute a manifesto for empiricism, and it is unsurprising, therefore, that some writers claim to detect 'covert positivism' in qualitative research. Another way in which empiricist overtones are revealed is in the suggestion that social reality must be studied from the vantage point of research participants but that the only way to gain access to their interpretations is through extended contact with them, implying that meaning is accessible to the senses of researchers. The empiricism of qualitative research is perhaps most notable in conversation analysis, which was examined in Chapter 22. This is an approach that takes precise transcriptions of talk as its starting point and applies rules of analysis to such data. The analyst is actively discouraged from engaging in speculations about intention or context that might derive from an appreciation of the ethnographic particulars of the social setting.

- *A specific problem focus*. As noted in Chapter 17 in connection with the research by Hughes et al. (2011), qualitative research can be employed to investigate quite specific, tightly defined research problems.

- *Hypothesis- and theory-testing*. Following on from the last point, qualitative researchers typically discuss hypothesis- and theory-testing in connection with hypotheses or theories generated in the course of conducting research, as in analytic induction or grounded theory. However, there is no obvious reason why this cannot occur in relation to previously specified hypotheses or theories (an example of the use of qualitative research to test an hypothesis is provided in Research in focus 26.1). In fact, one of the best-known and most frequently cited articles on participant observation was written to show how to design a study using this method, 'which seeks to discover hypotheses as well as to test them' (Becker 1958: 652). The somewhat infamous research by Festinger et al. (1956) on a millenarian religious cult is a classic study that used participant observation, a technique associated with qualitative research, to test a theory. The theory had to do with the ways in which people respond when a belief that they zealously endorse is disconfirmed. The authors argued that it is possible to imagine a number of conditions that, if met, could result in the belief being held *more* fervently than previously after the belief had been shown to be flawed. When the authors learned of a local religious cult that believed that the end of the world was imminent, they felt that this group would provide an ideal opportunity for finding out how people respond to the falsification of a cherished belief. The researchers and some hired observers pretended to be converts and became members of the group. This membership afforded the opportunity for first-hand observation of levels of conviction and commitment among the cult's adherents and therefore for testing the theory. Clearly assuming that the prediction would not in fact come true, the researchers gathered data before the fateful day about members' levels of conviction and behaviour and then afterwards on their adaptation to the thwarted prophecy. This research violates certain ethical principles that were addressed in Chapter 6.

- *Realism.* Realism (Key concept 2.3) is one way in which the epistemological basis of the natural sciences has been construed. It has entered into the social sciences in a number of ways, but one of the most significant of these is Bhaskar's (1989) notion of **critical realism**. This approach accepts neither a constructionist nor an objectivist ontology and instead takes the view that the 'social world is reproduced and transformed in daily life' (Bhaskar 1989: 4). Social phenomena are produced by mechanisms that are real, but that are not directly accessible to observation and are discernible only through their effects. For critical realism the task of social research is to construct hypotheses about such mechanisms and to seek out their effects. Critical realists occupy a middle position between positivism and postmodernism by claiming that an entity can exist independently of our knowledge of it, while also asserting that access to the social world is always mediated

Research in focus 26.2
Critical realist ethnography

A critical realist stance was employed by Porter (1993, 2002) in connection with an ethnographic study in a large Irish hospital in which the author was employed for three months as a staff nurse. Porter's interest was in the possible role of racism in this setting. He suggests that racism and professionalism were in operation such that the latter tempered the effects of the former in the context of interactions between doctors and nurses. Thus, racism and professionalism were conceptualized as generative structures—that is, mechanisms—that could be productive of certain kinds of effect. Two hypotheses were proposed: racism would play some part in the relationships between white staff and those from 'racialized minorities' and the 'occupational situation would affect the way in which racism was expressed' (Porter 1993: 599). Porter found that racism was not a significant factor in relationships between members of racialized minorities and the other staff. However, racism did manifest itself behind the backs of the racialized minorities in the form of racist remarks. Racism did not intrude into work relationships, because of the operation of the greater weight given to people's achievements and performance (such as qualifications and medical skills) rather than to their ascriptive qualities (that is, 'race') when judging members of professions. The emphasis on values associated with professionalism counteracted the potential role of those associated with racism. In part, this was due to the way in which black or Asian doctors made a point of emphasizing their knowledge and qualifications during interaction so that their professional credentials were confirmed. Thus, 'racism can be seen as a tendency that is realised in certain circumstances, but exercised unrealised in others' (Porter 1993: 607). In terms of critical realism, one possible structural mechanism (racism) was countered by the operation of another structural mechanism (professional ideology). On certain occasions, the tension between these two mechanisms would surface—for example, when a Muslim doctor proceeded to conduct his religious observances on his knees in the middle of a hospital unit (Porter 2002).

and thus subjective. Critical realists also believe in the notion of material entities that are said to be real if they have an effect on behaviour. In addition to the empirical domain of observable events, there is a real domain 'in which generative mechanisms capable of producing patterns of events reside' (Tsang and Kwan 1999: 762). Porter's (1993) critical realist ethnography is interesting in this connection (see Research in focus 26.2), because it demonstrates the use of ethnography in connection with an epistemological position that derives from the natural sciences. It also relates to the previous point in providing a further illustration of hypothesis-testing qualitative research.

In addition, writers on qualitative research sometimes distinguish stances on qualitative research that contain elements of both quantitative and qualitative research. R. L. Miller (2000), in connection with an examination of life history interviews (see Chapter 20), distinguishes three approaches to such research. One of these, which he calls 'neo-positivist', uses 'pre-existing networks of concepts . . . to make theoretically based predictions concerning people's experienced lives' (R. L. Miller 2000: 12). Therefore, one approach to the life history method, which is associated with qualitative rather than quantitative research, would seem to entail a theory-testing approach to the collection and analysis of qualitative data. A further illustration is Charmaz's (2000) suggestion that two approaches to grounded theory can be distinguished: objectivist and constructionist (she uses the term 'constructivist'). She argues that, in spite of the differences that developed between Glaser (1992) and Strauss (e.g. Strauss and Corbin 1998), both held to the view of an objective, external reality. In other words, in the eyes of both the major writers on grounded theory, there is a social world beyond the researcher, whose job it is to reveal its nature and operation.

Quantitative research and interpretivism

Qualitative research would seem to have a monopoly on the ability to study meaning. Its proponents essentially claim that it is only through qualitative research that the world can be studied through the eyes of the people who are studied. As Platt (1981: 87) observes, this contention seems rather at odds with the widespread study of attitudes in social surveys based on interviews and questionnaires. In fact, it would seem that quantitative researchers frequently address meanings. An example is the well-known concept of 'orientation to work' associated with the *Affluent Worker* research in the 1960s, which sought to uncover the nature and significance of the meanings that industrial workers bring with them to the workplace (Goldthorpe et al. 1968). Similarly, survey research by Stewart et al. (1980: 112) showed that clerks should not be treated as a unitary category and that 'the *meaning* of clerical work will not be the same for all engaged in it' (emphasis added).

The widespread inclusion of questions about attitudes in social surveys suggests that quantitative researchers are interested in matters of meaning. It might be objected that survey questions do not really tap issues of meaning because they are based on categories devised by the designers of the interview schedule or questionnaire. Two points are relevant here. First, in the absence of respondent validation exercises, the notion that qualitative research is more adept at gaining access to the point of view of those being studied than quantitative research is invariably assumed rather than demonstrated. Qualitative researchers frequently claim to have tapped into participants' worldviews because of, for example, their extensive participation in the daily round of those they study, the length of time they spent in the setting being studied, or the lengthy and intensive interviews conducted. However, the explicit demonstration that interpretative understanding has been accomplished—for example, through respondent validation (see Key concept 17.3)—is rarely undertaken. Second, if the design of attitude questions is based on prior questioning that seeks to bring out the range of possible attitudinal positions on an issue, as in the research discussed in Research in focus 11.3, attitudinal questions may be better able to gain access to meaning.

Also, as Marsh (1982) has pointed out, the practice in much survey research of asking respondents the reasons for their actions implies that quantitative researchers are frequently concerned to uncover issues of meaning. For example, she cites Brown and Harris's (1978) research, which was based on a survey on the relationship between critical life events (such as loss of a job, death of husband) and depression. In this research, exploring the meaning of critical life events for respondents was a notable feature of the questioning. As Marsh (1982: 115) puts it, 'it is the *meaning* that these events have for the subjects that gives them their causal force in provoking an onset' (emphasis added). Examples such as these further point to the possibility that the gulf between quantitative and qualitative research is not as wide as is sometimes supposed.

Quantitative research and constructionism

It was noted in Chapter 2 that one keynote feature of constructionism is a concern with issues of representation, as these play an important role in the construction of the social world. Qualitative content analysis has played an important role in developing such an understanding, just as discourse analysis has in relation to the social construction of events and meanings in newspaper reports and television programmes. However, it is easy to forget that conventional quantitative content analysis can also be useful in this way.

An example of its use is Lantz and Booth's (1998) research on the social construction of the notion of a breast cancer epidemic (see Research in focus 2.7). As Research in focus 2.7 makes clear, much of their understanding of the representation of breast cancer derived from a qualitative content analysis of magazine articles, but they also employed a quantitative content analysis. For example, a content analysis of the photographs of women linked to each article revealed that 80 per cent are apparently of women who are below the age of 50. Also, 85 per cent of the anecdotes and case stories related to women in this age group. This emphasis on younger women creates the impression that this is the age group that is at risk. This finding allowed Lantz and Booth to make an interesting connection between relative youth and lifestyles and behaviour that are conducive to breast cancer; this connection is consistent with the 'blame the victim' theme that is conveyed (see Research in focus 2.7). In fact, fewer than 20 per cent of new cases of breast cancer are in women under 50, and the mean age at diagnosis is 65. Thus, the quantitative content analysis of the articles in terms of the ages of the women who are focused upon is inconsistent with the actual age of women when first diagnosed with the disease. In this way, content analysis played an important part in revealing the social construction of the perception of breast cancer.

More generally, this example shows how quantitative research can play a significant role in relation to a constructionist stance.

Research methods and epistemological and ontological considerations

If we review the argument so far, it is being suggested that:

- there are differences between quantitative and qualitative research in terms of their epistemological and ontological commitments, *but*
- the connection between research strategy, on the one hand, and epistemological and ontological commitments, on the other, is not deterministic. In other words, there is a *tendency* for quantitative and qualitative research to be associated with the epistemological and ontological positions outlined in Chapter 2 (for example, in Table 2.1), but the connections are not perfect.

However, some writers have suggested that research methods carry with them a cluster of epistemological and ontological commitments such that to elect to use a self-administered questionnaire is more or less simultaneously and inevitably to select a natural science model and an objectivist worldview. Similarly, the use of participant observation is often taken to imply a commitment to interpretivism and constructionism. Such a view implies that research methods are imbued with specific clusters of epistemological and ontological commitments and can be seen in comments of the following kind: 'the choice and adequacy of a method embodies a variety of assumptions regarding the nature of knowledge and the methods through which that knowledge can be obtained, as well as a set of root assumptions about the nature of the phenomena to be investigated' (Morgan and Smircich 1980: 491). The difficulty with such a view is that, if we accept that there is no perfect correspondence between research method and matters of epistemology and ontology, the notion that a method is inherently or necessarily indicative of certain wider assumptions about knowledge and the nature of social reality begins to founder.

In fact, research methods are much more 'free-floating' in terms of epistemology and ontology than is often supposed. This can be particularly demonstrated by reference to historical and other studies of social research. For example, Snizek (1976) examined 1,434 articles published in sociology journals between 1950 and 1970. He based his analysis on Ritzer's (1975) suggestion that sociology is underpinned by three **paradigms**, a term that will be briefly explored again in Chapter 27 (see Key concept 27.1). Two of the paradigms—the 'social factist' and the 'social definitionist' paradigms—correspond roughly to quantitative and qualitative research respectively. Snizek was unable to uncover an unambiguous pattern linking the grounding of an article in either of these two paradigms with the research methods used. Similarly, Platt's (1986) historical research on American sociology has suggested that the connection that is often forged between functionalism, which itself is often associated with positivism, and the social survey is greatly exaggerated. Her research suggested that 'the two originated independently, and that leading functionalists had no special propensity to use surveys and leading surveyors no special propensity for functionalism' (Platt 1986: 527). Moreover, Platt's general conclusion from her research on the use of research methods in American sociology between 1920 and 1960 is very revealing:

research methods may on the level of theory, when theory is consciously involved at all, reflect intellectual *bricolage* or *post hoc* justifications rather than the consistent working through of carefully chosen fundamental assumptions. Frequently methodological choices are steered by quite other considerations, some of a highly practical nature, and there are independent methodological traditions with their own channels of transmission. . . . In many cases general theoretical/methodological stances are just stances: slogans, hopes, aspirations, not guidelines with clear implications that are followed in practice.

(Platt 1996: 275; emphasis in original)

Platt's conclusion again suggests that the notion that research methods reflect or reveal certain assumptions about knowledge and social reality has to be questioned. When the use of research methods in practice is examined, while tendencies may be discernible that link them to certain assumptions, the connections are not absolute.

A further aspect of the way in which research methods are more autonomous than is sometimes supposed can be seen in the fact that the methods associated with both quantitative and qualitative research are often employed together within a single piece of research. This issue is the focus of Chapter 27.

 # Problems with the quantitative/ qualitative contrast

The contrasts between quantitative and qualitative research that were drawn in Chapter 17 suggest a somewhat hard-and-fast set of distinctions and differences (see in particular Table 17.1). However, there is a risk that this kind of representation exaggerates the differences between them. A few of the distinctions will be examined to demonstrate this point.

Behaviour versus meaning

The distinction is sometimes drawn between a focus on behaviour and a focus on meanings. However, quantitative research frequently involves the study of meanings in the form of attitude scales (such as the Likert scaling technique) and other techniques. Qualitative researchers may feel that the tendency for attitude scales to be preformulated and imposed on research participants means that they do not really gain access to meanings. The key point being made here is that at the very least quantitative researchers frequently *try* to address meanings. Also, somewhat ironically, many of the techniques

with which quantitative research is associated, most notably survey research based on questionnaires and interviews, have been shown to relate poorly to people's actual behaviour (see, for example, Thinking deeply 12.2). Moreover, looking at the other side of the divide, qualitative research frequently, if not invariably, entails the examination of behaviour in context. Qualitative researchers often want to interpret people's behaviour in terms of the norms, values, and culture of the group or community in question. In other words, quantitative and qualitative researchers are typically interested in both what people do and what they think, but they go about the investigation of these areas in different ways. To complicate things further, Jerolmack and Khan (2014) have pointed out that much qualitative research, in particular studies based on interviews, does not in fact address behaviour directly (see Thinking deeply 20.1). Therefore, the degree to which the 'behavior versus meaning' contrast coincides with quantitative and qualitative research should not be overstated. See Thinking deeply 26.1 for further consideration of this point.

Thinking deeply 26.1
Quantitative and qualitative research and the study of class identities

One of the problems with the quantitative/qualitative contrast is that sometimes there is a tendency to polarize or exaggerate their respective capacities. The 'behaviour versus meaning' issue is an illustration of that tendency. Another interesting example can be discerned in relation to the use of surveys to investigate class identities. Savage et al. (2001) conducted in-depth interviews with residents in the Manchester area to explore the nature of class identities at the end of the twentieth century. The interviews show that there is an ambivalence about class identities: people's sense of class identity is weak but class is nonetheless relevant to them. The authors depict class as a resource that is drawn upon to forge identity. In the abstract to the article, the authors make an interesting remark: 'sociologists should not assume that there is any necessary significance in how respondents define their class identity in surveys' (Savage et al. 2001: 875). Payne and Grew (2005) queried the implication that a qualitative research approach to the study of class identities might be superior to that deriving from surveys. They point out that such a view often arises because of the greater spontaneity and hence apparent naturalness of qualitative interviewing. Payne and Grew (2005: 907) suggest that these features are often exaggerated by sociologists, who also 'over-estimate the degree of rapport and shared meaning with their respondents'. Further, Sturridge (2007: 211) has argued that quantitative research in the form of the survey can have an important role in the study of class identities, namely 'to look at who expresses a sense of class identity and how this sense of class identity relates to other identities. This is the major strength which large-scale surveys have in the field, they are able to provide a social mapping of who expresses a sense of class belonging.' Sturridge conducted a secondary analysis of data from the 2003 British Social Attitudes Survey to explore class identities. In line with her comments about the opportunities that surveys afford, she found that a sense of working-class identity continues to be salient for some social groups and that men are much more likely to express this awareness. She also found that for some groups a sense of belonging to the working class is construed in terms of class opposition and that this reflects workplace orientations and experiences.

These reflections and findings suggest that there is a tendency to overstate the differences between quantitative and qualitative research in terms of certain inherent capacities and that this may result in a neglect of certain issues and research questions. In this instance, the view that survey research has little to offer the study of class identities could result in its potential to address important issues on this topic not being exploited.

Theory and concepts tested in research versus theory and concepts emergent from data

A further related point is that the suggestion that theory and concepts are developed prior to undertaking a study in quantitative research is something of a caricature that is true only up to a point. It reflects a tendency to characterize quantitative research as driven by a theory-testing approach. However, while experimental investigations probably fit this model well, survey-based studies are often more exploratory than this view implies. Although concepts have to be measured, the nature of their interconnections is frequently not specified in advance. Quantitative research is far less driven by a hypothesis-testing strategy than is frequently supposed. The analysis of quantitative survey data is often more exploratory than is generally appreciated and consequently offers opportunities for the generation of theories and concepts. As one American survey researcher has commented in relation to a large-scale survey he conducted in the 1950s, but which has much relevance today: 'There are so many questions which might be asked, so many correlations which can be run, so many ways in which the findings can be organized, and so few rules or precedents for making these choices that a thousand different studies could come out of the same data' (J. A. Davis 1964: 232).

The common depiction of quantitative research as solely an exercise in testing preformulated ideas fails to appreciate the degree to which findings frequently suggest new departures and theoretical contributions. Reflecting on his career in survey research, Glock provides the following example based on his research on the correlates of variation in church involvement in an American sample:

> It occurred to me and my collaborators that one or both of two things might be happening. The results might simply be a reflection of the fact that women, older persons, the familyless, and the less well-to-do have more time on their hands to become involved in the Church. Alternatively or in addition, it could be that these people become involved as a compensation for being deprived, relative to their counterparts, of access to the rewards of the larger society. The data, having suggested these explanations, did not afford a means to test them . . . Subsequently, I had the opportunity to test the theory with new data.
>
> (Glock 1988: 45–6)

Therefore, the suggestion that, unlike an interpretivist stance, quantitative research is solely concerned with the testing of ideas that have previously been formulated (such as hypotheses) fails to recognize the creative work that goes into the analysis of quantitative data and into the interpretation of findings. Equally, as noted earlier, qualitative research can be used in relation to the testing of theories.

Numbers versus words

Even perhaps this most basic element in the distinction between quantitative and qualitative research is not without problems. Qualitative researchers sometimes undertake a limited amount of quantification of their data. Silverman (1984, 1985) has argued that some quantification of findings from qualitative research can often help to uncover the generality of the phenomena being described. While observing doctor–patient interactions in National Health Service and private oncology clinics, Silverman quantified some of his data in order to bring out the differences between the two types of clinic. Through this exercise he was able to show that patients in private clinics were able to have a greater influence over what went on in the consultations. However, Silverman warns that such quantification should reflect research participants' own ways of understanding their social world.

In any case, it has often been noted that qualitative researchers engage in 'quasi-quantification' through the use of terms such as 'many', 'often', and 'some'. All that is happening in cases of the kind described by Silverman is that the researcher is injecting greater precision into estimates of frequency.

Artificial versus natural

The artificial/natural contrast referred to in Table 17.1 can similarly be criticized. It is often assumed that, because much quantitative research employs research instruments that are applied to the people being studied (questionnaires, structured interview schedules, structured observation schedules, and so on), it provides an artificial account of how the social world operates. Qualitative research is often viewed as more naturalistic (see Key concept 3.4 on naturalism). Ethnographic research in particular would seem to exhibit this quality, because the participant observer studies people in their normal social worlds and contexts—in other words, as they go about normal activities. However, when qualitative research is based on interviews (such as semi- and unstructured interviewing and focus groups), the depiction 'natural' is possibly less appropriate. Interviews still have to be arranged and interviewees have to be taken away from activities that they would otherwise be engaged in, even when the interviewing style is of the more conversational kind. We know very little about interviewees' reactions to and feelings about being interviewed. Phoenix (1994) reports on the responses of interviewees to in-depth interviews in connection with two studies—one concerned with mothers under the age of 20 and the other with the social identities of young people. While many of her interviewees apparently quite enjoyed being interviewed, it is equally clear that they were conscious of the fact that they had been engaged in interviews rather than conversations. This is revealed by the tendency in the replies quoted by Phoenix for some of the interviewees to disclose that they were aware that the experience was out of the ordinary. In the study of social identities, one black young woman is reported as saying that she liked the interview and added: 'I had the chance to explain how I feel about certain things and I don't really get the opportunity to do that much.' And another interviewee said it was a 'good interview' and added: 'I have never talked so much about myself for a long time, too busy talking about kids and their problems' (Phoenix 1994: 61). The interviews were clearly valuable in allowing to surface the perspectives of people whose voices are normally silent, but the point being made here is that the view that the methods associated with qualitative research are naturalistic is to exaggerate the contrast with the supposed artificiality of the research methods associated with quantitative research.

As noted in Chapter 21, focus group research is often described as more natural than qualitative interviewing because it emulates the way people discuss issues in real life. Natural groupings are often used to emphasize this element. However, whether this is how group participants view the nature of their participation is unclear. In particular, when it is borne in mind that people are sometimes strangers, have to travel to a site where the session takes place, are paid for their trouble, and frequently discuss topics they rarely if ever talk about, it is not hard to take the view that the naturalism of focus groups is assumed rather than demonstrated.

In participant observation, the researcher can be a source of interference that renders the research situation less natural than it might superficially appear to be. Whenever the ethnographer is in an overt role, a certain amount of reactivity is possible—even inevitable. It is difficult to estimate the degree to which the ethnographer represents an intrusive element that has an impact on what is found, but once again the naturalism of such research is often assumed rather than demonstrated, although it is admittedly likely that it will be less artificial

than the methods associated with quantitative research. However, when the ethnographer also engages in formal interviewing (as opposed to casual conversations), the naturalistic quality is likely to be less pronounced.

These observations suggest that there are areas and examples of studies that lead us to question the degree to which the quantitative/qualitative contrast is a rigid one. This is not to suggest that the contrast is unhelpful, but that we should be wary of assuming that in writing and talking about quantitative and qualitative research we are referring to two absolutely divergent and inconsistent research strategies.

 # The mutual analysis of quantitative and qualitative research

One further way in which the barriers between quantitative and qualitative research might be undermined is by virtue of developments in which each is used as an approach to analyse the other.

A qualitative research approach to quantitative research

There has been a growing interest in the examination of the writings of quantitative researchers using some of the methods associated with qualitative research. In part, this trend can be seen as an extension of the growth of interest among qualitative researchers in the writing of ethnography, which can be seen in such work as Van Maanen (1988) and P. Atkinson (1990). The attention to quantitative research is very much part of this trend, because it reveals a concern in both cases with the notion that the written account of research not only constitutes the presentation of findings but is also an attempt to persuade the reader of the credibility of those findings. This is true of the natural sciences too; for example, in relation to the research by Gilbert and Mulkay (1984) discussed in Chapter 22, it was shown how the scientists employed an empiricist repertoire when writing up their findings. This writing strategy was used to show how proper procedures were followed in a systematic and linear way. However, Gilbert and Mulkay demonstrated that, when the scientists discussed in interviews how they did their research, it is clear that the process was suffused with the influence of factors to do with their personal biographies.

One way in which a qualitative research approach to quantitative research is manifested is through what Gephart (1988: 9) has called 'ethnostatistics', by which is meant 'the study of the construction, interpretation,

and display of statistics in quantitative social research'. Gephart shows that there are a number of ways in which the idea of ethnostatistics can be realized, but it is with just one of these—approaching statistics as rhetoric—that I will be concerned here. Directing attention to the idea of statistics as rhetoric means becoming sensitive to the ways in which statistical arguments are deployed to bestow credibility on research for target audiences. More specifically, this means examining the language used in persuading audiences about the validity of research. Indeed, the very use of statistics itself can be regarded as a rhetorical device because the use of quantification means that the researcher can endow findings with the appearance of a natural science and thereby achieve greater legitimacy and credibility by virtue of that association (McCartney 1970; John 1992).

A quantitative research approach to qualitative research

In Chapter 13, the research by Hodson (1996), which was based on the content analysis of workplace ethnographies, was presented (see Research in focus 13.5). Essentially, Hodson's approach was to apply a quantitative research approach—in the form of content analysis—to outputs of qualitative research. This is an approach that may have potential in other areas of social research in which ethnography has been a popular method, and as a result a good deal of ethnographic evidence has been built up. Hodson (1999) suggests that the study of social movements may be one such field; religious sects and cults may be yet another. Hodson's research is treated as a solution to the problem of making comparisons between ethnographic studies in a given area. One approach to synthesizing related qualitative studies is meta-ethnography (see Chapter 24), which is a qualitative research approach to such aggregation (Noblit and Hare 1988). However, whereas the practice of meta-ethnography is meant to be broadly in line with the goals of qualitative research, such as a commitment to interpretivism and a sensitivity to the social context, Hodson's approach is one that downplays contextual factors in order to explore relationships between variables that have been abstracted out of the ethnographies.

Certain key issues need to be resolved when conducting analyses of the kind carried out by Hodson. One relates to the issue of conducting an exhaustive literature search for suitable studies for possible inclusion. Hodson chose to analyse books, rather than articles, because of the limited amount of information that can usually be included in the latter. Even then, criteria for the inclusion of a book needed to be stipulated. Hodson (1999: 22) employed three: 'The criteria for inclusion were (*a*) the book had to be based on ethnographic methods of observation over a period of at least 6 months, (*b*) the observations had to be in a single organization, and (*c*) the book had to focus on at least one clearly identified group of workers . . .'. The application of these criteria resulted in the exclusion of 279 out of 365 books. A second crucial area relates to the coding of the studies, which was briefly covered in Research in focus 13.5. Hodson stresses the importance of

having considerable knowledge of the subject area, adopting clear coding rules, and pilot testing the coding schedule. In addition, he recommends checking the reliability of coding by having 10 per cent of the documents coded by two people. The process of coding was time-consuming, in that Hodson calculates that each book-length ethnography took forty or more hours to code.

This approach has many attractions, not the least of which is the impossibility of a quantitative researcher being able to conduct investigations in such a varied set of organizations. Also, it means that more data of much greater depth can be used than can typically be gathered by quantitative researchers. It also allows hypotheses deriving from established theories to be tested, such as the 'technological implications' approach, which sees technologies as having impacts on the experience of work (Hodson 1996). However, the loss of a sense of social context is likely to be unattractive to many qualitative researchers.

Of particular significance for this discussion is the remark that 'the fundamental contribution of the systematic analysis of documentary accounts is that it creates an analytic link between the in-depth accounts of professional observers and the statistical methods of quantitative researchers' (Hodson 1999: 68). In other words, the application of quantitative methods to qualitative research may provide a meeting ground for the two research strategies.

 # Quantification in qualitative research

The 'numbers versus words' contrast is perhaps the most basic in many people's minds when they think about the differences between quantitative and qualitative research. After all, it relates to the very terms used to denote the two approaches, which seem to imply the presence and absence of numbers. However, it is not the case that there is a complete absence of quantification in qualitative research. As we will see in the next chapter, when qualitative researchers incorporate research methods associated with quantitative research into their investigations, a certain amount of quantification is injected into the research.

Quite aside from the issue of mixed methods research, three observations are worth making about quantification in the analysis and writing-up of qualitative data.

Thematic analysis

In Chapter 24 it was observed that one of the commonest approaches to qualitative data analysis is undertaking a search for themes in transcripts or field notes. However, as Bryman and Burgess (1994b: 224) point out, the

criteria employed in the identification of themes are often unclear. One possible factor that these authors suggest may be in operation is the frequency of the occurrence of certain incidents, words, phrases, and so on that denote a theme. In other words, a theme is more likely to be identified the more times the phenomenon it denotes occurs in the course of coding. This process may also account for the prominence given to some themes over others when writing up the findings. In other words, a kind of implicit quantification may be in operation that influences the identification of themes and the elevation of some themes over others. In fact, Ryan and Bernard (2003) recommend the search for 'repetitions' as one of the ways in which themes may be identified.

Quasi-quantification in qualitative research

Qualitative researchers engage in 'quasi-quantification' through the use of terms such as 'many', 'frequently', 'rarely', 'often', and 'some'. In order to be able to make

Thinking deeply 26.2
Counting in qualitative research

Hannah and Lautsch (2011) have examined a number of articles from the field of management research in order to identify what seem to be the principal reasons for engaging in quantification. They identify four types of counting:

1. Autonomous counting. With autonomous counting, the goal is to generate counts that will represent important reasons in their own right. It allows authors to summarize a large part of their data and so identify patterns that would otherwise be hard to discern.

2. Supplementary counting. This type is subsidiary to the main qualitative findings that are presented but adds an additional dimension to them. It allows further development of the qualitative findings.

3. Corroborative counting. The aim here is to use counting to corroborate qualitative findings and as such is very much in tune with a triangulation approach (see Key concept 17.4 and Chapter 27). For example, a researcher might combine a quantitative and a qualitative content analysis, using the former to confirm the latter findings.

4. Credentialing counting. This fourth type of counting entails using counts to enhance the credibility of qualitative research findings by providing quantitative summaries of aspects of the research process, such as number of interviews, number of months spent conducting observation, number of pages of field notes or interview transcripts, length of interviews or focus groups, or number of meetings attended.

The fourth type is not particularly helpful in that it is extremely common for qualitative researchers to supply such information even whether they are wedded to maintaining a qualitative emphasis. Hannah and Lautsch (2011: 17) usefully suggest that counting is best avoided when qualitative researchers feel it is important for them 'to gain access to the perspectives of insiders' since counting may distance them from participants' perspectives or when they 'wish to pursue unexpected findings during an inductive data collection process' since counting may inhibit their responsiveness to unexpected aspects of their data.

While Hannah and Lautsch consider research in the management field in arriving at this classification, there is no reason to think that it does not have a broader applicability in the social sciences.

such allusions to quantity, the qualitative researcher should have some idea of the relative frequency of the phenomena being referred to. However, as expressions of quantities, they are imprecise, and it is often difficult to discern why they are being used at all. The alternative would seem to be to engage in a limited amount of quantification when it is appropriate, such as when an expression of quantity can bolster an argument. Thinking deeply 26.2 summarizes the main reasons that qualitative researchers engage in quantification. This point leads directly on to the next section.

Combating anecdotalism through limited quantification

One of the criticisms that is sometimes levelled at qualitative research is that the evidence in the publications on which it is based is often anecdotal, giving the reader little guidance as to the prevalence of the issue to which the anecdote refers. The widespread use of brief sequences of conversation, snippets from interview transcripts, and accounts of encounters between people provides little sense of the prevalence of whatever such items of evidence are supposed to indicate. There is the related risk that a particularly striking statement by someone or an unexpected activity may have more significance attached to it than might be warranted in terms of its frequency.

Perhaps at least partly in response to these problems, qualitative researchers sometimes undertake a limited amount of quantification of their data. We can see this feature in Silverman's (1984, 1985) research on oncology clinics, which was referred to earlier. Gabriel (1998) describes how he studied organizational culture in a variety of organizations by collecting stories about the organizations during interviews. Computers and information technology were a particular focus of the stories elicited. Altogether 377 stories were collected in the course of 126 interviews in 5 organizations. Gabriel shows that the stories were of different types, such as: comic stories (which were usually a mechanism for disparagement of others);

epic stories (survival against the odds); tragic stories (undeserved misfortune); gripes (personal injustices); and so on. He counted the number of each type: comic stories were the most numerous at 108; then epic stories (82); tragic stories (53); gripe stories (40); and so on. Themes in the stories were also counted, such as whether they involved a leader, a personal trauma, an accident, and so forth. In all these cases, the types of stories and the themes could have been treated in an anecdotal way, but the use of such simple counting conveys a clear sense of their relative prevalence.

Exercises like these can be used to counter the suggestion that is sometimes made that the approach to presenting qualitative data can be too anecdotal, so that readers are given too little sense of the *prevalence* of certain beliefs or a certain form of behaviour. All that is happening in such cases is that the researcher is injecting greater precision into estimates of frequency than can be derived from quasi-quantification terms. Moreover, it is not inconceivable that there might be greater use of

limited amounts of quantification in qualitative research in the future as a result of the growing use of computers in qualitative data analysis (CAQDAS). Most of the major software programs include a facility that allows the analyst to produce simple counts of such things as the frequency with which a word or a coded theme occurs. In many cases, they can also produce simple cross-tabulations—for example, relating the occurrence of a coded theme to gender. Writing when CAQDAS was used far less than it is today, Ragin and Becker (1989: 54) concluded their review of the impact of personal computers (referred to as 'microcomputers') on sociologists' 'analytic habits' with the following remark: 'Thus, the microcomputer provides important technical means for new kinds of dialogues between ideas and evidence and, at the same time, provides a common technical ground for the meeting of qualitative and quantitative researchers.' The greater use of quantification by qualitative researchers may turn out to be one of the more significant areas for this 'meeting'.

 ## Key points

- There are differences between quantitative and qualitative research but it is important not to exaggerate them.

- The connections between epistemology and ontology, on the one hand, and research methods, on the other, are not deterministic.

- Qualitative research sometimes exhibits features normally associated with a natural science model.

- Quantitative research aims on occasions to engage with an interpretivist stance.

- Research methods are more autonomous in relation to epistemological commitments than is often appreciated.

- The artificial/natural contrast that is often an element in drawing a distinction between quantitative and qualitative research is frequently exaggerated.

- A quantitative research approach can be employed for the analysis of qualitative studies and a qualitative research approach can be employed to examine the rhetoric of quantitative researchers.

- Some qualitative researchers employ quantification in their work.

 ## Questions for review

- What is the nature of the link between research methods and epistemology?

The natural science model and qualitative research

- Are the natural sciences positivistic?

- To what extent can some qualitative research be deemed to exhibit the characteristics of a natural science model?

Quantitative research and interpretivism

- To what extent can some quantitative research be deemed to exhibit the characteristics of interpretivism?

Quantitative research and constructionism

- To what extent can some quantitative research be deemed to exhibit the characteristics of constructionism?

Research methods and epistemological and ontological considerations

- How far do research methods necessarily carry epistemological and ontological implications?

Problems with the quantitative/qualitative contrast

- Outline some of the ways in which the quantitative/qualitative contrast may not be as hard and fast as is often supposed.

The mutual analysis of quantitative and qualitative research

- What might some of the implications of Gilbert and Mulkay's (1984) concepts of interpretative repertoires be for the qualitative analysis of quantitative research?
- Assess the significance of ethnostatistics.
- Assess the significance of Hodson's research.

Quantification in qualitative research

- How far is quantification a feature of qualitative research?
- What, if anything, is lost when qualitative data are quantified?

Online Resource Centre

www.oxfordtextbooks.co.uk/orc/brymansrm5e/

Visit the Online Resource Centre to enrich your understanding of the issues involved in breaking down the quantitative/qualitative divide. Follow up links to other resources, test yourself using multiple choice questions, and gain further guidance and inspiration from the Student Researcher's Toolkit.

27

Mixed methods research: combining quantitative and qualitative research

Chapter outline

Chapter guide

This chapter is concerned with mixed methods research—that is, research that combines quantitative and qualitative research. While this may seem a straightforward way of resolving and breaking down the divide between the two research strategies, it is not without controversy. Moreover, there may be practical difficulties associated with mixed methods research. This chapter explores:

- arguments against the combination of quantitative and qualitative research; two kinds of argument are distinguished and are referred to as the embedded methods argument and the paradigm argument;

- the suggestion that there are two versions of the debate about the possibility of combining quantitative and qualitative research: one that concentrates on methods of research and another that is concerned with epistemological issues;

- the different ways in which mixed methods research has been carried out;

- the need to recognize that mixed methods research is not inherently superior to research that employs a single research strategy.

Introduction

So far throughout the book an emphasis has been placed upon the strengths and weaknesses of the research methods associated with quantitative and qualitative research. One possible response to this kind of recognition is to propose combining them. After all, such a strategy would seem to allow the various strengths to be capitalized upon and the weaknesses offset. However, not all writers on research methods agree that such mixing is either desirable or feasible. On the other hand, it is probably the case that the amount of mixed methods research has been increasing since the early 1980s. Therefore, in discussing the combination of quantitative and qualitative research, this chapter will be concerned with three main issues:

1. an examination of the arguments against fusing quantitative and qualitative research;

2. the different ways in which quantitative and qualitative research have been combined;

3. an assessment of mixed methods research, which asks whether it is necessarily superior to investigations relying on just one research strategy and whether there are any additional problems deriving from it.

The term **mixed methods research** is used as a simple shorthand to stand for research that combines quantitative and qualitative research within a single project. Of course, there is research that, for example, combines structured interviewing with structured observation or ethnography with semi-structured interviewing. However, these instances of the combination of research methods are associated with just one research strategy. By mixed methods research I am referring to research that combines research methods that cross the two research strategies. Indeed, mixed methods research has become something of a growth industry since the first edition of this book. Since *Social Research Methods* was first published in 2001, mixed methods research has become an increasingly used

Thinking deeply 27.1
Stages in the development of mixed methods research

Creswell and Plano Clark (2011) have suggested that mixed methods research has proceeded through five stages.

1. A *formative period* during which various writers took tentative steps towards and lay the foundations for mixed methods approaches. This stage corresponds roughly to a period spanning the 1950s through to the early 1980s.

2. A *paradigm debate period* during the 1970s and 1980s that responded to qualitative researchers' insistence that their style of investigation was based on different epistemological and ontological foundations from quantitative research. Because of this insistence, quantitative and qualitative research were viewed as not capable of integration. During this period, a number of writers challenged this view, arguing that mixed methods investigations were feasible and potentially could lead to superior findings. I am placed in this period, because in my book *Quantity and Quality in Social Research* (Bryman 1988a) I 'reviewed the debate and established connections between the two traditions' (Creswell and Plano Clark 2011: 23).

3. A *procedural development period* beginning in the late 1980s and progressing into the twenty-first century that is concerned with how mixed methods studies could be designed. Morgan (1998b), whose work is referred to below, belongs to this period. I am also in this period, because in Bryman (1988a) I 'addressed the reasons for combining quantitative and qualitative research' (Creswell and Plano Clark 2011: 23).

4. An *advocacy and expansion* period that began in the present century and is concerned with the recognition of and development of mixed methods research as a distinctive approach, even as a movement. The arrival of a separate handbook for mixed methods researchers (Tashakkori and Teddlie 2003, 2010) and of the *Journal of Mixed Methods Research* are indicative of this development.

5. A *reflective* period that began around 2005 in which many authors assessed the state of mixed methods research, glimpsed into its future, and in some cases launched critiques of its state and direction.

and accepted approach to conducting social research (for an account of its history, see Thinking Deeply 27.1). It has been the focus of a specialist handbook that has gone into a second edition (Tashakkori and Teddlie 2003, 2010) and specialist journals, such as the *Journal of Mixed Methods Research*, have begun publication. When I examined articles based on mixed methods research published in the period 1994–2003, I found a threefold increase over that period (Bryman 2008a). Just after I finished writing the second edition of this book, I conducted research specifically to do with the nature of mixed methods research (Bryman 2006a, 2006b). I have organized the section on 'Approaches to mixed methods research' around some of my findings from that research project.

The argument against mixed methods research

The argument against mixed methods research tends to be based on either and sometimes both of two kinds of argument:

1. the idea that research methods carry epistemological commitments, and

2. the idea that quantitative and qualitative research are separate paradigms.

These two arguments will now be briefly reviewed.

The embedded methods argument

This first position, which was outlined in Chapter 26, implies that research methods are ineluctably rooted in epistemological and ontological commitments. This view of research methods can be discerned in statements such as the following:

> every research tool or procedure is inextricably embedded in commitments to particular versions of the world and to knowing that world. To use a questionnaire, to use an attitude scale, to take the role of participant observer, to select a random sample, to measure rates of population growth, and so on, is to be involved in conceptions of the world which allow these instruments to be used for the purposes conceived.
>
> (J. A. Hughes 1990: 11)

According to such a position, the decision to employ, for example, participant observation is not simply about how to go about data collection but a commitment to an epistemological position that is inimical to positivism and that is consistent with interpretivism.

This kind of view of research methods has led some writers to argue that mixed methods research is not feasible or even desirable. An ethnographer may collect questionnaire data to gain information about a slice of social life that is not amenable to participant observation, but this does not represent an integration of quantitative and qualitative research, because the epistemological positions in which the two methods are grounded constitute irreconcilable views about how social reality should be studied. J. K. Smith (1983: 12, 13), for example, argues that each of the two research strategies 'sponsors different procedures and has different epistemological implications' and therefore counsels researchers not to 'accept the unfounded assumption that the methods are complementary'. Smith and Heshusius (1986: 8) criticize the integration of research strategies, because it ignores the assumptions underlying research methods and transforms 'qualitative inquiry into a procedural variation of quantitative inquiry'.

The chief difficulty with the argument that writers such as Smith present is that, as was noted in Chapter 26, the idea that research methods carry with them fixed epistemological and ontological implications is very difficult to sustain. They are capable of being put to a wide variety of tasks.

The paradigm argument

The paradigm argument is closely related to the previous one. It conceives of quantitative and qualitative research as **paradigms** (see Key concept 27.1) in which epistemological assumptions, values, and methods are inextricably intertwined and are incompatible between paradigms (e.g. Guba 1985; Morgan 1998b). Therefore, when researchers combine participant observation with a questionnaire, they are not really combining quantitative and qualitative research, since paradigms are incommensurable—that is, they are incompatible: the integration is only at a superficial level and within a single paradigm.

The problem with the paradigm argument is that it rests, as does the embedded methods one, on contentions about the interconnectedness of method and epistemology in particular that cannot—in the case of social research—be demonstrated. Moreover, while Kuhn (1970) certainly argued that paradigms are incommensurable, it is by no means clear that quantitative and qualitative research are in fact paradigms. As suggested in Chapter 26, there are areas of overlap and commonality between them.

Key concept 27.1
What is a paradigm?

Kuhn's (1970) highly influential use of the term 'paradigm' derives from his analysis of revolutions in science. A paradigm is 'a cluster of beliefs and dictates which for scientists in a particular discipline influence what should be studied, how research should be done, [and] how results should be interpreted' (Bryman 1988a: 4). Kuhn depicted the natural sciences as going through periods of revolution, whereby normal science (science carried out in terms of the prevailing paradigm) is increasingly challenged by anomalies that are inconsistent with the assumptions and established findings in the discipline at that time. The growth in anomalies eventually gives way to a crisis in the discipline, which in turn occasions a revolution. The period of revolution is resolved when a new paradigm emerges as the ascendant one and a new period of normal science sets in. An important feature of paradigms is that they are *incommensurable*—that is, they are inconsistent with each other because of their divergent assumptions and methods. Disciplines in which no paradigm has emerged as pre-eminent, such as the social sciences, are deemed pre-paradigmatic, in that they feature competing paradigms. One of the problems with the term is that it is not very specific: Masterman (1970) was able to discern twenty-one different uses of it by Kuhn. Nonetheless, its use is widespread in the social sciences (e.g. Ritzer 1975; Guba 1985).

Two versions of the debate about quantitative and qualitative research

There seem to be two different versions of the nature of quantitative and qualitative research, and these two different versions have implications in writers' minds about whether the two can be combined.

- An *epistemological version*, as in the embedded methods argument and the paradigm argument, sees quantitative and qualitative research as grounded in incompatible epistemological principles (and ontological ones too, but these tend to be given less attention). According to this version of their nature, mixed methods research is not possible.

- A *technical version*, which is the position taken by most researchers whose work is mentioned in the next section, gives greater prominence to the strengths of the data-collection and data-analysis techniques with which quantitative and qualitative research are each associated and sees these as capable of being fused.

There is a recognition that quantitative and qualitative research are each connected with distinctive epistemological and ontological assumptions, but the connections are not viewed as fixed and inevitable. Research methods are perceived, unlike in the epistemological version, as autonomous. A research method from one research strategy is viewed as capable of being pressed into the service of another. Indeed, in some instances, as will be seen in the next section, the notion that there is a 'leading' research strategy in a mixed methods investigation may not even apply in some cases.

The technical version of the nature of quantitative and qualitative research essentially views the two research strategies as compatible. As a result, mixed methods research becomes both feasible and desirable. It is in that spirit that we now turn to a discussion of the ways in which quantitative and qualitative research can be combined.

Classifying mixed methods research in terms of priority and sequence

As interest in mixed methods research has grown, various ways of classifying it have arisen. One approach is in terms of the purposes of mixed methods studies and the roles that the quantitative and qualitative components play in such studies (see also Bryman 2006a, 2008b). However, a further approach has been to classify mixed

Figure 27.1
Classifying mixed methods research in terms of priority and sequence

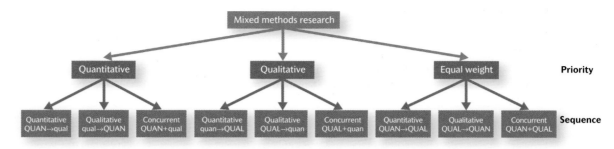

Note: Capitals and lower case indicate priority; arrows indicate sequence; + indicates concurrent.

methods studies in terms of two criteria (e.g. Morgan 1998b):

- *The priority decision*. How far is a qualitative or a quantitative method the principal data-gathering tool or do they have equal weight?

- *The sequence decision*. Which method precedes which? In other words, does the qualitative method precede the quantitative one or vice versa, or is the data collection associated with each method concurrent?

These criteria yield nine possible types (see Figure 27.1). In this classification, upper case indicates priority—for example, QUAL indicates that the qualitative component was the main data-collection approach; lower

case indicates a more subsidiary role—for example, qual. Arrows refer to the sequence—for example, QUAN→qual means that the collection of quantitative data was the main data-collection approach and that the collection of these quantitative data was undertaken before the qualitative data, which occupy a subsidiary role. The + simply means that the quantitative and the qualitative data were collected more or less concurrently. One difficulty with this and related classifications that embellish it is that it is not always easy to establish issues of priority and sequence when reading the report of a study. However, it is useful as a way of thinking about fundamental aspects of the design of mixed methods studies.

 # Types of mixed methods design

Writers on mixed methods research have drawn on several of the distinctions outlined in the previous section to distinguish between different types of mixed methods design. Several different ways of distinguishing them have been put forward by various writers but the one provided by Creswell and Plano Clark (2011) is probably the most commonly employed. They distinguish six designs, of which the four presented in Figure 27.2 are the most commonly referred to.

The convergent parallel design entails the simultaneous collection of quantitative and qualitative data which typically have equal priority. The resulting analyses are then compared and/or merged to form an integrated whole. This kind of design tends to be associated with triangulation exercises whereby the researcher aims to compare two sets of findings and also situations in which the researcher aims to offset the weaknesses of both

quantitative and qualitative research by capitalizing on the strengths of both. For example, Bregoli (2013) was interested in whether the strength of a tourist destination brand is stronger when stakeholders in that brand co-ordinate their brand activities. She collected quantitative data through an online questionnaire sent to stakeholders in tourism organizations in Edinburgh and qualitative data from semi-structured interviews with representatives of tourism organizations and from documents. She writes: 'Results were merged by comparing them and were interpreted and discussed by stating the degree to which they converged, diverged, or related' (Bregoli 2013: 216).

The exploratory sequential design entails the collection of qualitative data prior to the collection of quantitative data. It is associated with investigations in which the researcher wants to generate hypotheses or hunches, which

Figure 27.2
Four basic mixed methods designs

(a) Convergent parallel design

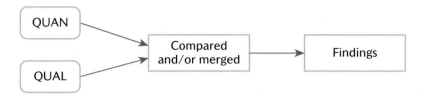

(b) Exploratory sequential design

(c) Explanatory sequential design

(d) Embedded design

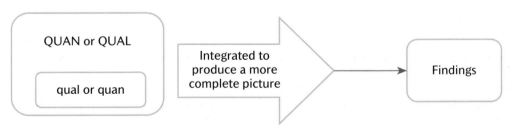

Note: based on Creswell and Plano Clark (2011).

can then be tested using quantitative research, and with investigations in which the aim is to develop research instruments such as questionnaire questions, which can then be used in a quantitative investigation. Another purpose is to follow up qualitative findings with quantitative research which allows the scope and generalizability of the qualitative findings to be assessed. Although Creswell and Plano Clark depict the qualitative element as typically having

priority within this design, this is not always the case, such as when it has a largely handmaiden role in relation to the quantitative research. In fact, I would argue that typically the quantitative component has priority. I have tried to convey this in Figure 27.2(b). The research by Capstick and Pidgeon (2014) provides a good example of an exploratory sequential design and is described in some detail in the subsection on 'Instrument development' below.

The explanatory sequential design entails the collection and analysis of quantitative data followed by the collection and analysis of qualitative data in order to elaborate or explain the quantitative findings. The need for such an approach can arise when the researcher feels that the broad patterns of relationships uncovered through quantitative research require an explanation which the quantitative data on their own are unable to supply or when further insight into the quantitative findings is required. Here again, although Creswell and Plano Clark depict the quantitative element as having priority within this design, this is not always the case, such as when the explanation or elaboration to be provided by the qualitative findings is especially significant for the study's research questions. The research described in Research in focus 27.6 provides an example of the use of this design.

The embedded design can have either quantitative or qualitative research as the priority approach but draws on the other approach as well within the context of a study.

The need for an embedded design can arise when the researcher needs to enhance either quantitative or qualitative research with the other approach. The phasing of the data collection may be simultaneous or sequential. The need for the design arises when the researcher feels that quantitative (or qualitative) research alone will be insufficient for understanding the phenomenon of interest. For example, the researcher may be interested in examining a research question principally using quantitative research but have a subsidiary research question that is best addressed through qualitative research. See Research in focus 27.9 for an example of the use of this design.

One of the issues that should emerge from this brief exposition of the different types of mixed methods design is that the choice of design is closely bound up with the anticipated use(s) of a mixed methods approach in the eyes of the researcher. Thus the choice of mixed methods design should be undertaken in tandem with an expectation of the role that mixed methods research will play.

Approaches to mixed methods research

This section will be structured in terms of a classification I derived from conducting a content analysis of empirical articles in refereed journals in the social sciences (Bryman 2006a, 2006b; see Research in focus 27.1 for a brief description of this research). The classification has been changed slightly from the one presented in my earlier publications.

A content analysis of articles based on mixed methods research

One component of the research on mixed methods research described in Research in focus 27.1 was a content analysis of journal articles reporting the findings of mixed methods research. Journal articles do not encapsulate all possible contexts in which projects reporting mixed methods research might be found. Conference papers and books are other possible sites. However, journal articles are a major form of reporting findings and have the advantage that, in most cases, the peer review process provides a quality control mechanism. By contrast, conference papers and books are sometimes not peer reviewed. The approach to gleaning a sample was to search the Social Sciences Citation Index (SSCI) for articles in which relevant keywords or phrases such as 'quantitative' and 'qualitative', or 'multi(-)method', or 'mixed method', or 'triangulation' appeared in the title, keywords, or abstract. This means that the sample comprises articles that to some degree foreground the fact

Research in focus 27.1
Mixed methods research on mixed methods research

In 2003–4 I worked on a fellowship funded by the Economic and Social Research Council that focused on mixed methods research. There were two main components: a content analysis on articles reporting the findings of mixed methods research and interviews with mixed methods researchers. With the first component I was interested in the ways that quantitative and qualitative research are combined in published journal articles (Bryman 2006a). With the second component, I conducted semi-structured interviews with twenty mixed methods researchers because I was keen to glean an inside view of the research process. The findings from the two components of this project will be used for discussing mixed methods research in the rest of this chapter.

Thinking deeply 27.2
Ways of combining quantitative and qualitative research

Drawing on a content analysis of articles deriving from mixed methods research, Bryman (2006a) identified the following ways in which quantitative and qualitative research are combined.

1. *Triangulation* or greater validity—refers to the traditional view that quantitative and qualitative research might be combined to triangulate findings in order that they may be mutually corroborated. If the term was used as a synonym for integrating quantitative and qualitative research, it was not coded as triangulation.

2. *Offset*—refers to the suggestion that the research methods associated with both quantitative and qualitative research have their own strengths and weaknesses so that combining them allows the researcher to offset their weaknesses to draw on the strengths of both.

3. *Completeness*—refers to the notion that the researcher can arrive at a more comprehensive account of the area of enquiry in which he or she is interested if both quantitative and qualitative research are employed.

4. *Process*—quantitative research provides an account of structures in social life but qualitative research provides a sense of process.

5. *Different research questions*—this is the argument that quantitative and qualitative research can each answer different research questions, but this item was coded only if authors explicitly stated that they were doing this.

6. *Explanation*—one of the two research methods is used to help explain findings generated by the other.

7. *Unexpected results*—refers to the suggestion that quantitative and qualitative research can be fruitfully combined when one generates surprising results that can be understood by employing the other.

8. *Instrument development*—refers to contexts in which qualitative research is employed to develop questionnaire and scale items, for example, so that better wording or more comprehensive closed answers can be generated.

9. *Sampling*—refers to situations in which one approach is used to facilitate the sampling of respondents or cases.

10. *Credibility*—refers to suggestions that employing both approaches enhances the integrity of findings.

11. *Context*—refers to cases in which the combination is rationalized in terms of qualitative research providing contextual understanding coupled with either generalizable, externally valid findings or broad relationships among variables uncovered through a survey.

12. *Illustration*—refers to the use of qualitative data to illustrate quantitative findings, often referred to as putting 'meat on the bones' of 'dry' quantitative findings.

13. *Utility* or improving the usefulness of findings—refers to a suggestion, which is more likely to be prominent among articles with an applied focus, that combining the two approaches will be more useful to practitioners and others.

14. *Confirm and discover*—this entails using qualitative data to generate hypotheses and using quantitative research to test them within a single project.

15. *Diversity of views*—this includes two slightly different rationales—namely, combining researchers' and participants' perspectives through quantitative and qualitative research respectively and uncovering relationships between variables through quantitative research while also revealing meanings among research participants through qualitative research.

16. *Enhancement* or building upon quantitative/qualitative findings—this entails a reference to making more of or augmenting either quantitative or qualitative findings by gathering data using a qualitative or quantitative research approach.

17. *Other/unclear*.

18. *Not stated*.

that the study is based on both quantitative and qualitative research. During the search, the emphasis was on uncovering articles in five fields: sociology; social psychology; human, social and cultural geography; management and organizational behaviour; and media and cultural studies. The analysis was restricted to a ten-year period of 1994–2003. Judgements about whether articles fell within the purview of the investigation, in terms of whether they could be regarded as deriving from the five fields, were made on the basis of the journal title or information supplied in abstracts. In this way, a sample of 232 articles was generated and content analysed.

A major focus of the content analysis was on the rationales proffered for combining quantitative and qualitative research. A coding scheme was developed for classifying the rationales given by authors of articles. This coding scheme was based on an extensive review of the kinds of reasons that are frequently given in both methodological writings and research articles for combining quantitative and qualitative research. The scheme provided for the rationales is outlined in Thinking Deeply 27.2. These can be thought of as ways of combining quantitative and qualitative research.

When coding each article, a distinction was made between *rationale* and *practice*. First, the rationale given by authors for combining the two approaches to data collection and/or analysis was coded. For this exercise, the reasons that had been given before the findings were presented were typically examined and coded. Then, the ways in which quantitative and qualitative research were actually combined were coded. In doing so, the coding reflected authors' reflections on what they felt had been gleaned from combining quantitative and qualitative research and any ways in which the two were combined that were not reflected in authors' accounts. This is what is meant by *practice*. The purpose of distinguishing between these two ways of thinking about the justification for mixed methods research was that authors' accounts of why they intended to combine quantitative and qualitative research might differ from how they actually combined them in practice.

Table 27.1 shows the number of articles classified in terms of each category of rationale and practice and their respective percentages of all 232 articles. The percentages add up to over 100 per cent in the case of both rationale and practice because any article could be coded in terms of two or more categories. Interestingly, the number and percentage of articles within each category are usually higher for practice than for rationale. This occurs for two reasons. One is that the number of articles where the rationale is not stated falls from just over one-quarter to nearly zero. Second, researchers seem to find more uses for mixed methods research than they envisaged at the outset.

Table 27.1
Mixed methods research in practice

Category	Rationale	Practice
	Number of articles (% of all 232 cases)	
Triangulation	29 (12.5)	80 (34.5)
Offset	7 (3)	4 (1.7)
Completeness	31 (13)	67 (28.9)
Process	5 (2.2)	6 (2.6)
Different research questions	13 (5.6)	10 (4.3)
Explanation	13 (5.6)	32 (13.8)
Unexpected results	0	2 (0.9)
Instrument development	18 (7.8)	21 (9.1)
Sampling	31 (13.4)	43 (18.5)
Credibility	2 (0.9)	5 (2.2)
Context	8 (3.4)	10 (4.3)
Illustration	4 (1.7)	53 (22.8)
Utility	2 (0.9)	2 (0.9)
Confirm and discover	9 (3.9)	15 (6.5)
Diversity of views	26 (11.2)	35 (15.1)
Enhancement	73 (31.5)	121 (52.2)
Other/unclear	8 (3.4)	14 (6.1)
Not stated	62 (26.7)	1 (0.4)

Source: based on Bryman (2006a).

The bulk of the rest of this chapter will present some examples of each of these rationales for conducting mixed methods research. Some of the examples are ones that were in the sample on which the content analysis was based, but others are not. In the latter category, I have included books, which were not included in the sample. Each of the rationales may be thought of as an approach to conducting mixed methods research.

Approaches to combining quantitative and qualitative research in mixed methods research

This section of the chapter provides illustrations of each of the ways of combining quantitative and qualitative research in mixed methods research using the classification presented in Thinking Deeply 27.2 (see also Table 27.1). Each of the rationales outlined in the previous section can be thought of as an approach to mixed methods research. This applies rather less obviously to two of the rationales—credibility and utility—but these have been included for the sake of completeness.

Triangulation

The idea of triangulation has been previously encountered in Key concept 17.4. When applied to mixed methods research, it implies that the results of an investigation employing a method associated with one research strategy are cross-checked against the results of using a method associated with the other research strategy. It is an adaptation of the argument by such writers as Webb et al. (1966) that confidence in the findings deriving from a study using a quantitative research strategy can be enhanced by using more than one way of measuring a concept.

An illustration of a study using a triangulation approach as well as other rationales for doing mixed methods research is the Cultural Capital and Social Exclusion (CCSE) study referred to in Research in focus 2.9. Silva and Wright (2008: 3) write that the qualitative interviews were conducted to 'check and correct the quantitative data' and make the survey data more robust. In the CCSE study, the researchers took the relatively unusual step of asking each sampled interviewee about many of the answers they had given in the questionnaire in order to see whether the two kinds of answer corresponded. More often, researchers conducting a triangulation exercise compare the quantitative and qualitative findings in aggregate. For example, Bickerstaff et al. (2008) conducted research into people's perceptions of climate change and radioactive waste against a backdrop of a great deal of debate at the UK policy level concerning energy, which to a significant extent has the potential to frame perceptions. The researchers drew on two sources of data: a national interview survey based on a quota sample of 1,547 adults, and one focus group discussion in each of four towns (Cromer, Norwich, Heysham, and Liverpool) with each group meeting twice. The authors suggest that the two sets of findings were consistent when they write that the focus group discussions 'revealed a profoundly negative set of responses to the idea of radioactive waste and in this way support the findings of the national survey' (Bickerstaff et al. 2008: 153).

A triangulation exercise may be planned or unplanned. In other words, at the outset, a researcher may plan to conduct mixed methods research in order to establish whether the quantitative and qualitative findings corroborate each other; alternatively, the possibility of comparing the quantitative and the qualitative findings may arise once the data have been collected. Thus, in the study of the foot and mouth disease outbreak covered in Research in focus 2.8 and 27.3, the researchers did not obviously build a triangulation strategy into their plans but note at one point that 'both in the questionnaire survey and the focus groups people expressed high concern about FMD and its possible consequences' (Poortinga et al. 2004: 86). At another point the authors write: 'The perceived causes of the FMD outbreak in the focus groups overlapped largely the three factors that were identified in the questionnaire survey' (Poortinga et al. 2004: 87). It is striking that the authors use the word 'largely' here, suggesting that there was not a perfect correspondence. This occurred because the three perceived causes—farming practices, regulation, and market forces—were also found in the focus group data, but the factors were discussed by group members in combination. As such, there is an element of what is described in Thinking Deeply 27.2 as 'enhancement'. This is not uncommon when a triangulation approach to mixed methods research is employed: the two sets of data correspond to each other but not perfectly, thus requiring a certain degree of qualification.

When looking at these examples, it is clear that the findings were broadly consistent. However, when a triangulation exercise is undertaken, the possibility of a failure to corroborate findings always exists. This raises the issue of what approach should be taken to inconsistent results.

In the course of their research into media reporting of social science research (Research in focus 27.2), Fenton et al. (1998) found that their data revealed an inconsistency between some of the quantitative and qualitative data: the former (methods 2 and 3) suggested that journalists and social scientists enjoyed broadly consensual relationships with regard to the reporting of social science research in the media, but the qualitative findings (methods 4 and 5) suggested greater collision of approaches and values. Rather than opt for one set of findings as providing the more accurate view, the data were re-examined. For example, Deacon et al. show that a major component of the apparent discrepancy has to do with the tendency for social scientists who are answering survey questions about coverage of their own research (method 3) to reply in terms of a feeling of relief that it was not as bad as expected. However, in interviews (method 4), social scientists tend to make much more of what Deacon et al. call 'war stories'—that is, memorable and often highly wounding encounters with the media. Such encounters were not being depicted in the interviews as typical, but their general feelings about media coverage of social science research appeared to have been highly influenced by their bruising encounters. Thus, in general, the questionnaires revealed that social scientists were relatively pleased with the reporting of their research, but, when they were encouraged to reflect on specific problems in the past, the drift of their replies became more negative.

Offset

Offset was rarely encountered. It implies that the weaknesses of a quantitative or a qualitative method can be offset by including a qualitative or a quantitative method

Research in focus 27.2
Research methods used in a study of the reporting of social science research in the mass media

In their research on the reporting of social science research in the British mass media, Fenton et al. (1998; see also Deacon et al. 1998) employed several quantitative and qualitative methods:

1. content analysis of news and current affairs coverage (local and national newspapers, TV, and radio) (592 items); see Research in focus 13.1 for more on this aspect of the research;

2. postal questionnaire survey of social scientists' views about media coverage and their own practices (674 respondents);

3. postal questionnaire survey of social scientists who had received media coverage as identified in the content analysis (123 respondents);

4. semi-structured interviews with social scientists who had received coverage as identified in the content analysis (20 interviews);

5. semi-structured interviews with journalists identified in the content analysis (34 interviews);

6. semi-structured interviews with representatives of funding bodies and government (27 interviews);

7. tracking of journalists at conferences (3 conferences);

8. focus group analysis of audience reception of media items (13 focus groups); see Chapter 21 for more on this aspect of the research.

that has its own strengths. In the preamble to her account of mixed methods research on the benefits of adult learning, Hammond (2005: 240) has suggested that 'each approach has its own limitations or "imperfections," which can be compensated for by using an alternative method'. Similarly, the authors of the study referred to in Research in focus 27.8 write that the combination of methods helped 'to reduce the biases associated with each method and therefore improve our understanding of the cultural forces involved in child development' (Harkness et al. 2006: 78). One of the mixed methods research practitioners that I interviewed (see Research in focus 27.1) was explicit on this point:

> it seems to me that the only way you can begin to get close to the kind of methods that are reliable in natural scientific or engineering work is to use every tool you've got. You know, our tools are so inadequate and the material to which we're applying them is so slippery that you've got to use everything you have.

Completeness

Completeness indicates that a more complete answer to a research question or set of research questions can be achieved by including both quantitative and qualitative methods. It implies that the gaps left by one method (for example, a quantitative one) can be filled by another (for

example, a qualitative one). One of its most common forms is when ethnographers employ structured interviewing or possibly a self-administered questionnaire, because not everything they need to know about is accessible through participant observation. This kind of need can arise for several reasons, such as the need for information that is not accessible to observation or to qualitative interviewing (for example, systematic information about social backgrounds of people in a particular setting), or the difficulty of gaining access to certain groups of people. For her research on the processes whereby people became Moonies (members of the Unification Church) in Britain, Barker (1984) relied mainly on participant observation and in-depth interviewing. However, she also conducted a number of questionnaire surveys of members. Sometimes, this was done to test hypotheses she had begun to formulate, but often it was undertaken in order to acquire information on respondents' social class backgrounds and religious experiences prior to their becoming Moonies. Such information was not accessible through participant observation.

A further example relates to the study of dress fit and body image that was used as an illustration of thematic analysis in Research in focus 24.5. In addition to the qualitative research described there, Grogan et al. administered a body image questionnaire to their participants.

For example, Research in focus 24.5 refers to one of the themes that were derived—clothes should hide disliked parts of the body. Because a body image questionnaire had been administered, the authors were able to infer that this theme was most likely to be expressed by those women who were least satisfied with their body image as indicated by the questionnaire. The three women who had the highest satisfaction scores tended to be less concerned about this theme. However, the comment by 'Mary' in Research in focus 24.5 takes on significance in this context because although she expressed a concern about her 'tum', she was in fact the person who had the highest body satisfaction score. Thus, even when someone is broadly satisfied with her body image, there can still be a lingering concern. The quantitative evidence therefore provides valuable contextual information that helps with the understanding of the qualitative findings and as such provides a more complete picture.

Lockyer (2006) employed a mixed methods approach for her study of humour. She was interested in the controversies that can arise in relation to humour. There were various components to her mixed methods examination of humour, including: a quantitative content analysis of readers' letters of complaint in *Private Eye* about offence caused to them concerning humour in the magazine; an examination of the discursive practices used in the magazine for managing complaints; a detailed linguistic analysis of some of the letters; libel cases brought against the magazine; and semi-structured interviews with *Private Eye* journalists. Lockyer argues that the chief benefit of using a mixed methods approach is that a comprehensive portrait of humour in this magazine (and the controversies surrounding that humour) is forthcoming. Thus, the content analysis provided a necessary overview of the issue, such as the topics that are particularly likely to produce complaints, while the examination of discursive strategies for managing complaints identified some of the rhetorical strategies used to do this (such as suggesting that the reader lacks a sense of humour). The intensive linguistic examination of some letters, which were selected from those that had been content analysed, showed the ways in which the criticism of humour is initiated. Lockyer shows, for example, that readers rarely baldly state that they have been caused offence and that they often provide a preamble to their letters that establishes that they greatly value *Private Eye* and thereby help to head off objections to their letters. Lockyer argues that humour is a complex social phenomenon, largely because of the ambiguities and controversies with which it is often, if not invariably, imbued. She suggests that complex objects of social scientific analysis such as this require a variety of research tools to arrive at a comprehensive understanding.

A further example is provided by the investigation described in Research in focus 2.8 and Research in focus 27.3.

Process

One of the contrasts suggested by Table 17.1 is that, whereas quantitative research tends to bring out a static picture of social life, qualitative research is more processual. The term 'static' can easily be viewed in a rather negative light. In fact, it is very valuable on many occasions to uncover regularities, and it is often the identification of such regularities that allows a processual analysis to proceed. A mixed methods research approach offers the prospect of being able to combine both elements. For example, both Lacey (1976) and Ball (1981) conducted ethnographic studies of schools, in which the chief purpose was to explore processes of selection and socialization. However, in addition both researchers employed sociometric questionnaires to examine pupils' friendship patterns. Such questionnaires ask respondents to indicate those people with whom they interact and the frequency of interaction. The use of these research instruments allowed the stability of pupils' friendship patterns to be explored. The study by Laub and Sampson in Research in focus 27.4 provides an illustration of the use of mixed methods research in terms of regularities and process.

A further illustration is a study by Holdsworth (2006) of university students' experiences of student life in terms of their residential status (whether living away from home or at home). For the quantitative data, undergraduates at four higher educational institutions around Greater Merseyside were contacted by email or by electronic bulletin board to complete a web-based questionnaire. Ten per cent of eligible students (3,282) completed the questionnaire. Qualitative interviews were then carried out with a sample of students who had signalled in their questionnaire responses that they were prepared to be interviewed. Interviewees were purposively sampled on the basis of answers they had given concerning such issues as gender, their residential status, and whether they were paying fees. In addition, six focus groups were conducted with prospective year 13 students at local schools and colleges. Holdsworth's theoretical framework for analysing her data was strongly influenced by the work of Bourdieu and in particular his concept of 'habitus'. The quantitative findings point strongly to clear differences in the student experience between those living at home and those living away. A thematic analysis of the interviews was designed 'to explore how students' habitus facilitates the process of fitting in and how the experience of leaving home is part of that process' (Holdsworth 2006: 505). Thus, while the quantitative data provide insight into broad differences between students, the qualitative data are used to explore the processes that lie behind the differences in experience revealed by the survey findings.

Research in focus 27.3
Mixed methods research and foot and mouth disease

In Research in focus 2.8, a mixed methods study (Poortinga et al. 2004) that was carried out at the height of the foot and mouth disease (FMD) outbreak in the UK was introduced as an example of a study that implies that quantitative and qualitative research can be combined. It was introduced at that point to illustrate the possibility of a mixed methods investigation.

The main rationale for the use of mixed methods research was in terms of completeness, in that the authors argue that a more comprehensive picture would be generated. In addition, the survey allowed focus group participants to be purposively sampled. In terms of rationale, therefore, following the categories outlined in Thinking Deeply 27.2, completeness and sampling are the main uses of their mixed methods research. In terms of practice, six uses of mixed methods research could be discerned:

1. *Illustration*. The authors write that the focus group data were 'used to illustrate findings from the questionnaire' (Poortinga et al. 2004: 61).

2. *Completeness*. They write that the focus groups 'provided valuable additional information, especially on the reasons, rationalizations and arguments behind people's understanding of the FMD issue'.

3. *Triangulation*. Focus group findings 'reinforce' questionnaire findings (for example, few worried about health impacts on people) and reveal concern about government policies in the handling of FMD rather than the disease itself. This implies that there was also an element of *enhancement*, as the qualitative findings augmented the quantitative ones by clarifying the nature of concern about the disease.

4. *Explanation*. The authors suggest that, in Bude, the high trust ratings of local sources of information and the low trust ratings of government 'may well be a judgement of where these sources are thought to stand in this debate. . . . the focus groups suggested that trust judgements might reflect the extent to which sources are believed to protect people and their interests' (Poortinga et al. 2004: 88).

5. *Sampling*. As previously noted, the survey allowed the focus group participants to be purposively sampled.

6. *Enhancement*. This occurs on several occasions in this article. See the section on 'Enhancement' for more on this aspect.

Different research questions

The research referred to in Research in focus 27.2 is an example of a research project in which quantitative and qualitative research were used in order to answer different research questions.

- Questions about coverage, such as: how much coverage is there of social science research? What gets covered? Where? (method 1).

- Questions about the production of media items, such as: what kinds of attributes do journalists look for when thinking about whether to write an item on social science research? (methods 5 and 7).

- Questions about social scientists' attitudes to the media reporting of research in general (method 2) and to the reporting of their own research (methods 3 and 4). In addition, the research addressed social scientists' practices with regard to media coverage. Method 4 was designed to allow the findings deriving from method 3 to be elaborated and more fully understood.

- Questions about reception, such as: how do readers/viewers interpret media reporting of social science research? (method 8).

- Questions about the communication environment, such as: what are the policies of universities, government departments, and funding bodies concerning the media reporting of research? (method 6).

This form of mixed methods research entails making decisions about which kinds of research question are best answered using a quantitative research method and which by a qualitative research method and about how best to interweave the different elements, especially since the outcomes of mixing methods are rarely predictable.

Similarly, in my investigation of mixed methods research which is referred to in Research in focus 27.1,

Research in focus 27.4
Mixed methods research in the study of juvenile delinquency

An unusual instance of mixed methods research is the study referred to in Research in focus 3.13. Although the main data generated by Glueck and Glueck for this longitudinal study of juvenile delinquents in the USA were quantitative, a great deal of qualitative data were also collected (for example, interviews with research participants and their families). For their secondary analysis of the quantitative data that Glueck and Glueck had compiled, Laub and Sampson (1998: 220) were concerned to uncover 'the main predictors of desistance from criminal careers over time'. They used the qualitative data to compile a life history analysis that, when merged with the quantitative findings, would 'provide a more complete portrait of criminal offending over the life course' (Laub and Sampson 1998: 221). With the life history analysis of the qualitative data, Laub and Sampson were concerned to explore changes over the life course and how environmental factors interacted with change over time for each person examined.

The results of the secondary quantitative analysis were used to identify suitable candidates for the in-depth analysis required by the life history study. For example, the quantitative data demonstrated that job stability predicted desistence from crime. Accordingly, they selected for the life history study cases where there was a combination of high job stability and no arrest in adult life; cases where there was a combination of low job stability and arrest in adult life; and cases that were inconsistent with the pattern of job stability and desistence being related. The same was done for marital attachment, as the quantitative data showed that being married was associated with desistence. The authors write:

> our qualitative analysis was consistent with the hypothesis that the major turning points in the life courses of men who refrained from crime and deviance in adulthood were stable employment and good marriages. At the same time, we found that persistence in criminal behavior in adulthood often was the result of a developmental process of 'cumulative disadvantage' in which the negative influences of structural disadvantages (e.g., dropping out of school, having a criminal record or a dishonorable discharge from the military) persist throughout adult development.
>
> (Laub and Sampson 2004: 86)

In this way, the qualitative data were able to extend and amplify the quantitative findings. The cases that were inconsistent with the general pattern were used to enhance the explanation: for example, the qualitative data suggested that alcohol abuse could offset the positive impact of marital attachment or job stability on desistence.

Laub and Sampson followed up fifty-two of the original participants at the age of 70. One reason was that they felt that Glueck and Glueck had emphasized 'behavioral continuity' and, as a result, the qualitative data in particular were not suited to examining 'behavioral change in the lives of the participants' (Laub and Sampson 2004: 90). This is an interesting instance of the way in which the assumptions of researchers have an impact on the kinds of data that are collected. The researchers decided to conduct life history interviews with the fifty-two men for various reasons. Most notably, it would allow them to shed light on how involvement in and/or desistence from crime over time was related to their personal circumstances as well as to the wider social context. They elicited life history narratives for those who maintained an involvement in crime, those who desisted, and those who were in and out of criminal activity. The key contribution that these new qualitative data provided was the significance of turning points in their interviewees' lives:

> Changes in crime were associated in the narratives with a number of themes, including aging, employment, marriage, military service, excessive drinking, and personal choice. Of all the themes we have investigated, marriage turned up again and again in the narratives as a turning point. One former delinquent stated, 'If I hadn't met my wife at the time I did, I'd probably be dead.'
>
> (Laub and Sampson 2004: 95)

The significance of marriage as a turning point prompted the researchers to return to their quantitative data and to examine its importance. Their reanalysis of the data confirmed the importance of turning points and of marriage in particular.

I had in mind different research questions for each of the two components of that investigation. With the content analysis, I wanted to know about the kinds of mixed methods research that are carried out in terms of issues such as:

- What kinds of research methods are employed in mixed methods research?
- Does the amount of mixed methods research vary by discipline?
- What are the reasons given for conducting mixed methods research?

In the interviews, I wanted to glean the perspectives of mixed methods researchers concerning current practice and the contingencies that they faced in their own investigations. I was especially interested in questions such as:

- Do mixed methods researchers see the approach as generating distinctive problems that are separate from the quantitative and qualitative components?
- How did they feel about the state of mixed methods research?
- Did they experience problems of integrating the quantitative and the qualitative data?

Research in focus 27.5 provides a further example of the linking of different research questions with particular research methods.

Research in focus 27.5
Mixed methods research in a study of political advertising

Parmelee et al. (2007) drew on evidence that young voters had felt alienated from the political advertising of the US presidential candidates (George W. Bush and John Kerry) during the election campaign of 2004. Their overarching research question was to explain how and why the political advertising had failed to engage young adults. They formulate three sub-questions to tackle this issue:

- How does the interaction between audience-based and media-based framing contribute to college students' interpretations of the messages found in political advertising?
- To what extent do those interpretations match the framing found in the ads from the 2004 US presidential election?
- How can political ads be framed better to engage college students?

(Parmelee et al. 2007: 187)

Media-based frames refer to the ways in which the mass media frame the perception and salience of issues in such situations; audience-based frames are the prior cognitive structures members of audiences bring to bear on their interpretation of media items. Focus groups were employed to examine the first and third research questions. There were four groups with 5, 6, 7, and 14 18–28-year-olds. A mixture of quantitative content analysis and focus groups was employed in relation to the second question. As the authors put it:

Qualitative focus groups of college students examined how young voters interpret the salience of political advertising to them, and a quantitative content analysis of more than 100 ads from the 2004 presidential race revealed why focus group participants felt so alienated by political advertising.

(Parmelee et al. 2007: 184)

In this study, the research methods are very explicitly tied to the *different research questions*. The authors were able to *triangulate* the two sets of findings. They write that the content analysis data 'helped to confirm findings from the focus groups as well as explain why focus group participants felt so alienated by political advertising' (2007: 190). Both sets of data confirmed that the advertising had failed to address the needs of young adults (for example, by emphasizing issues such as pensions) and tended to make negative remarks about opposition candidates, which the young people disliked. They also write that 'the qualitative and quantitative methods were integrated in a way so that each could shore up the weaknesses of the other, as well as provide confirmation and elaboration' (2007: 196). Here we see a suggestion of what is referred to in Thinking Deeply 27.2 as *offset* but also elements of *triangulation* ('confirmation') and *enhancement* ('elaboration'). For example, the content analysis confirmed complaints from the focus groups regarding the negative tone of the advertising but at the same time some participants liked the negativity when it was laced with humour.

Explanation

A problem that frequently confronts quantitative researchers is how to explain relationships between variables. One strategy is to look for what is called an intervening variable, which is influenced by the independent variable but which in turn has an effect on the dependent variable. Thus, if we find a relationship between ethnicity and occupation, we might propose that education is one factor behind the relationship, implying:

ethnicity → education → occupation

This sequence implies that the variable ethnicity has an impact on people's education (for example, how much education people of different ethnic groups tend to undergo), which in turn has implications for the kinds of jobs that people of different ethnic groups attain. An alternative approach might be to seek to explore the relationship further by carrying out a qualitative study.

An example is provided by research on HIV-related risk behaviour among drug injectors by Barnard and Frischer (1995). Quantitative data from survey interviews with 503 injectors in Glasgow revealed that 'females report significantly higher levels of needle sharing, sexual activity and AIDS awareness than their male counterparts. Furthermore, women who are co-habiting with sexual partners who are themselves injectors are particularly likely to report high levels of risk behaviour and also AIDS awareness' (Barnard and Frischer 1995: 357). What are the factors that produced this pattern of relationships between gender, risk behaviour, and co-habitation? Semi-structured interviews with seventy-three injectors in Glasgow were also conducted. The authors suggest that the relationships between these variables 'can be explained by the tendency for women to be in sexual relationships with men who themselves inject and with whom they are unlikely to use condoms' (Barnard and Frischer 1995: 360). Once again, we see an instance of light being shed on relationships between variables derived from quantitative research by a related qualitative one.

In the research by Bickerstaff et al. (2008) on climate change and radioactive waste, the survey evidence suggested strongly that concerns about risk were far greater about radioactive waste than for climate change. The focus groups helped the researchers to explain this finding. The focus group participants tended to view climate change as something that would occur somewhere else and would not have an impact on their daily lives. Also, whereas 'climate change lacked a deeply affective cultural imagery' (Bickerstaff et al. 2008: 152), the focus group participants were able to draw on a rich stock of images

Research in focus 27.6
Using an explanatory sequential design in a study of childhood obesity

Bilinski, Duggleby, and Rennie (2013) used an explicit explanatory sequential design in order to explore research questions relating to the incidence of obesity among school children in a rural area in Canada (Saskatchewan) because the increase in obesity among school children in such areas has been greater than that of adults. Quantitative data were collected from 9-to-12-year-olds. These data derived from a questionnaire that students and their parents completed about their health and health-related behaviour. In addition, Body Mass Index data were collected on each child. Qualitative interviews were then conducted with those students who agreed to be interviewed when completing their questionnaires and their parents in order to 'explore the cultural meaning of health' (Bilinski et al. 2013: 6). These qualitative findings allowed the researchers to elaborate and explain their quantitative findings. They write:

> For example, although the quantitative data identified that many children (34%) were an unhealthy weight with a significantly higher prevalence of unhealthy weights in boys, the qualitative data discovered that neither weight status nor gender influenced children's beliefs about health. That is, both boys and girls, and children of healthy and unhealthy weight status, described themselves as healthy, had similar beliefs about health, and emphasized that happiness was the most important dimension to their health.

(Bilinski et al. 2013: 8)

These findings imply that the high incidence of obesity among these research participants is at least in part to do with beliefs about health and weight. As the authors recognize, the findings have implications for intervention strategies, but the main point to register from a methodological point of view is that way in which this sequential design allowed an explanation and elaboration of the quantitative findings through the collection of related qualitative data.

concerning the nuclear industry in the UK that was to do with errors, the control of the technology, and possible problems of waste getting into the wrong hands. Research in focus 27.6 presents a further example of the use of an explanation approach to doing mixed methods research.

Unexpected results

The outcomes of research are not always easy to anticipate, and sometimes researchers are presented with puzzling surprises. When this occurs, employing a research method associated with the research strategy that was not used initially can be helpful. One context in which this might occur is when qualitative research is used as a salvage operation, when an anticipated set of results from a quantitative investigation fails to materialize (Weinholtz et al. 1995). Research in focus 27.7 provides an interesting illustration of this use of mixed methods research.

Research in focus 27.7
Using mixed methods research to solve a puzzle: the case of displayed emotions in convenience stores

An example of combining quantitative and qualitative research to solve a puzzle is Sutton and Rafaeli's (1988) study of the display of emotions in organizations. Following a traditional quantitative research strategy, based on their examination of studies like Hochschild (1983), Sutton and Rafaeli formulated a hypothesis suggesting a positive relationship between the display of positive emotions to retail shoppers (smiling, friendly greeting, eye contact) and the level of retail sales. In other words, we would expect that, when retail staff are friendly and give time to shoppers, sales will be better than when they fail to do so. Sutton and Rafaeli had access to data that allowed this hypothesis to be tested. The data derived from a study of 576 convenience stores in a national retail chain in the USA. Structured observation of retail workers provided the data on the display of positive emotions, and sales data provided information for the other variable. The hypothesis implied that there would be a positive relationship—that is, stores in which there was a more pronounced display of positive emotions would report superior sales. When the data were analysed, a relationship was confirmed, but it was found to be negative; that is, stores in which retail workers were *less* inclined to smile, be friendly, and so on tended to have better sales than those in which such emotions were in evidence. This was the reverse of what the authors had anticipated that they would uncover. Sutton and Rafaeli (1992: 124) considered restating their hypothesis to make it seem that they had found what they had expected, but fortunately resisted the temptation! Instead, they conducted a qualitative investigation of four case study stores to help understand what was happening. This involved a number of methods: unstructured observation of interactions between staff and customers; semi-structured interviews with store managers; brief periods of participant observation; casual conversations with store managers, supervisors, executives, and others; and data gathered through posing as a customer in stores. The stores were chosen in terms of two criteria: high or low sales and whether staff typically displayed positive emotions. The qualitative investigation suggested that the relationship between the display of positive emotions and sales *was* negative, but that sales were likely to be a cause rather than a consequence of the display of emotions. This pattern occurred because, in stores with high levels of sales, staff were under greater pressure and encountered longer queues at checkouts. Staff therefore had less time and inclination for the pleasantries associated with the display of positive emotions. The quantitative data were then reanalysed with this alternative interpretation in mind and it was supported.

Thus, instead of the causal sequence being

Display of positive emotions → Retail sales

it was

Retail sales → Display of positive emotions

This exercise also highlights the main difficulty associated with inferring causal direction from a cross-sectional research design.

Research in focus 27.8
Mixed methods research in a cross-cultural investigation

Harkness et al. (2006) provide an interesting example of mixed methods research in relation to a seven-nation investigation of research into cultural context of children's development in home and school and transition from home to school. The seven nations were: Australia, Italy, the Netherlands, Poland, Spain, Sweden, and the USA.

Sixty families per nation were recruited, with the target children stratified in age groups up to age 8. Data were gathered from parents through semi-structured interviews and week-long diaries dealing with their child's activities. These provided the qualitative component of the study. Parents also completed several questionnaires to do with areas such as: sources of advice and support; child's temperament; child's first contact with school; and child's qualities related to school success.

The combination of quantitative and qualitative research served several purposes for the researchers. It provided the opportunity for *triangulation*, whereby they were able to test their central hypothesis that 'parents structure and participate in activities with their children that resonate with their cultural beliefs' through both quantitative and qualitative findings (Harkness et al. 2006: 68). Another key contribution of their mixed methods approach was that the qualitative findings informed the *instrument development* by developing measures in the questionnaires, so that these 'would be reliable and valid for the various cultural sites' (Harkness et al. 2006: 69).

A somewhat different form of this category of mixed methods research occurs when researchers are interested in generating data that will allow them to address a specific research question or hypothesis but at the same time want to leave open the possibility of coming up with unanticipated findings. Usually, the quantitative research methods are deployed to address a specific hypothesis, while the usually more open-ended qualitative methods are designed to allow novel, unexpected findings to emerge. In the cross-cultural study described in Research in focus 27.8, the authors were concerned to address the hypothesis that 'parents structure and participate in activities with their children in ways that resonate with their cultural beliefs' (Harkness et al. 2006: 68). While both the quantitative and the qualitative research methods were seen as relevant to this hypothesis, the qualitative component threw up some unexpected findings. One of these was a cultural practice that had not been documented previously. The authors call this 'Swedish parent–child co-sleeping'. The researchers noted through interviews and informal home visits that, among Swedish families, children were spending a large amount of their night-times sleeping in their parents' bedrooms. This finding prompted the researchers to ask specific questions about this practice in later interviews, and questionnaires were devised to glean further details. The authors write: 'Close analysis of the Swedish co-sleeping findings, using both qualitative and quantitative methods, provided a new way to access Swedish cultural models of the child and the family, particularly in relation to cultural ideas about

gender and equality' (Harkness et al. 2006: 75). Also, the finding encouraged the researchers in the other countries to ask explicit questions about children and night-time behaviour.

This category of mixed methods research is more or less impossible to plan for. It essentially provides the quantitative researcher with an alternative either to reconstruct a hypothesis or to file the results away (and probably never to look at them again) when findings are inconsistent with a hypothesis. There may also be instances in which a quantitative study could shed light on puzzling findings drawn from a qualitative investigation.

Instrument development

The in-depth knowledge of social contexts acquired through qualitative research can be used to inform the design of survey questions for structured interviewing and self-administered questionnaires. Pope and Mays (1995) point out that semi-structured interviewing took place before a British national survey on sexual attitudes and lifestyles (Wellings et al. 1994), so that the most appropriate sexual terms to be used in the survey questions could be decided. The interviews revealed considerable misunderstanding about many terms. Livingstone (2006) reports that the findings deriving from focus groups with children concerning their use of the Internet were used to inform the content of questions concerning online privacy in a subsequent questionnaire survey. The Cultural Capital and Social Exclusion (CCSE) researchers report that their questionnaire was 'informed by the evidence of cultural tastes and practices derived from a prior discussion of 25 focus groups' (Silva et al. 2009: 302; see also Table 21.1). An example of the use of mixed methods research in the context of instrument development in a cross-cultural study can be found in Research in focus 27.8.

A further example is provided by a study of climate change scepticism by Capstick and Pidgeon (2014). The authors carried out five focus groups with each group meeting twice. The first focus group was quite wide-ranging and the second more specific with an emphasis on a then-recent conference on climate change, media reporting, and policy issues. A thematic analysis was undertaken and the resulting themes tended to revolve around either of two major categories of scepticism. First, 'scientific/physical scepticism' was associated with such themes as scientific expertise, evidence, severity of change, and scientific impropriety. Second, 'social/behavioural scepticism' was associated with such themes as political responses, communication, and climate change fatigue. For example, one focus group participant is quoted as saying in relation to the theme of scepticism about the severity of change: 'I don't think there's many people in society who don't believe there is a problem, I think what they all struggle to believe is the extent of the problem' (quoted in Capstick and Pidgeon 2014: 392). Then the authors carried out a survey of a nationally representative quota sample. The survey was concerned not just with scepticism but with climate change issues more generally, but the authors write that they developed twenty questionnaire items 'to measure climate change scepticism utilising the dual framework developed in the qualitative phase' (Capstick and Pidgeon 2014: 394). In other words, the findings deriving from the qualitative data were used to prepare the questions in the survey that related to climate change scepticism. The twenty items were in the form of Likert items on a five-point scale of 'strongly agree' to 'strongly disagree'. For example, one of two items addressing scepticism about the severity of change was: 'The effects of climate change are likely to be catastrophic' and was reverse-coded to reflect scepticism. The data were submitted to a factor analysis (see Key concept 7.6) which showed a slightly more complex underlying structure to the twenty items in that the analysis produced three factors: response scepticism (scepticism about the effectiveness of responses to climate change), 'folk psychology scepticism' (scepticism associated with beliefs about people's preparedness to change their behaviour), and 'epistemic scepticism' (acceptance of the evidence for climate change or lack of such acceptance). The researchers then combined the two sets of findings to suggest that there are two major elements to climate change scepticism—epistemic scepticism and response

scepticism—while recognizing that there were minor aspects of both the quantitative and the qualitative data that could not fully be incorporated into this dichotomy.

Sampling

One way in which quantitative research can prepare the ground for qualitative research is through the selection of people to be interviewed. This can occur in several ways. In the case of the research on the reporting of social science research in the British mass media (see Research in focus 27.2), a content analysis of media content (method 1) was used as a source of data in its own right. However, it also served as a means of identifying journalists who had reported relevant research (method 5). In addition, replies to questions in the general survey of social scientists (method 2) were used to help identify two groups of social scientists—those with particularly high and those with low levels of media coverage of their research—who would then be interviewed with a semi-structured approach (method 4).

Another example is a study of mental well-being among members of a multinational IT company in England by Thøgersen-Ntoumani and Fox (2005). The authors sent email invitations to all members of the company to complete a questionnaire on the Web (see Chapter 10 for the use of Web-based survey research). A 33 per cent response rate was achieved. At the end of the questionnaire, respondents were asked whether they were prepared to be interviewed. The questionnaire comprised various measures, such as a Satisfaction with Life Scale, an assessment of physical activity, and the Brayfield–Rothe job satisfaction scale, which allowed respondents to be classified in terms of their being at risk or in need in terms of their mental well-being. An analysis of the questionnaire data resulted in four categories of employee being generated: self-assured; exercising happy; unhappy; and physically unhappy. Individuals were then selected to be interviewed using a semi-structured guide on the basis of their membership of the four categories of employee generated from the analysis of the survey data, although gender and age were also considered in the selection of who should be interviewed. With both these studies, quantitative data deriving from a survey were used as criteria for the sampling of individuals to be interviewed. The surveys provided the data for generic purposive sampling of the interviewees.

Jamieson (2000) reports that for a study of offending she administered a self-administered questionnaire to a sample of young men in which they reported criminal offences. On the basis of their replies, equal numbers of young men were interviewed using a qualitative interview in each of three categories: those who did not offend; those who had offended but not recently; and persistent offenders. A similar use of mixed methods research can be seen in the example in Research in focus 27.3. Laub and Sampson (1998) in the study described in Research in focus 27.4 used quantitative data on criminal activity as a means of selecting people for further study. Similarly, the CCSE researchers purposively sampled individuals for the qualitative interview phase of the research on the basis of their replies to questionnaires (see the subsection on 'Generic purposive sampling in a mixed methods context' in Chapter 18).

Credibility

When credibility is the rationale for mixed methods research, the emphasis tends to be upon the symbolic virtues of the approach in terms of its capacity to bestow legitimacy on the research and its outputs. Milkman (1997: 192), for example, has suggested in the context of her research on a General Motors factory that the promise that she 'would produce "hard", quantitative data through survey research was what secured [her] access', even though she had no experience in this method. Milkman preferred a qualitative approach, relying mainly on semi-structured interviews with a variety of individuals and stakeholders in the factory, but she clearly felt that including a quantitative component, in this case a survey, would secure the access she needed.

In this example, the researcher uses mixed methods research to gain credibility in the eyes of the organization in which she wanted to conduct her fieldwork. Sometimes mixed methods research is conducted because it is believed to have greater credibility among audiences. These may be audiences of different kinds, such as dissertation supervisors; dissertation examiners; research funding agencies; policy-makers; and potential readers. For example, Rocheleau (1995) included a questionnaire in conjunction with a qualitative study in the field of political ecology because she and her research team felt that the survey data would be more familiar and acceptable to policy-makers. She admits that the inclusion of the questionnaire in the research was 'cynical', as she puts it, because in fact she and her team felt that the qualitative data would be far more insightful. Similarly, when I conducted interviews with mixed methods researchers, some of my interviewees confessed that they sometimes used mixed methods research because they felt it would be more likely to get funded (Bryman 2007b). For example, one interviewee said:

> And also . . . and I don't know how true this is, but I think there's been a general perception . . . that the ESRC had . . . undergone quite a quantitative turn and that there was a concern about the lack of quantitative research [a] concern about lack of quantitative skills and that they particularly kind of favoured projects that

used mixed methods or had a strong quantitative component. And so, I tend to use them because strategically I think it's a good idea.

In other words, in the view of this interviewee, mixed methods research was more likely to be funded because it was perceived as having greater credibility among those responsible for funding social science research.

Context

The typical circumstance for this approach to mixing methods was for a qualitative study to provide the context for understanding broad-brush quantitative findings. An example is provided by research reported by Phillipson et al. (1999). The research was concerned with older people's experiences of community life in three English urban areas: Bethnal Green, Wolverhampton, and Woodford. Each of these areas had been the focus of earlier research on this general topic in the 1940s or 1950s. As such, this multiple-case study research introduced a longitudinal element by allowing comparisons to be drawn with previous findings. A questionnaire survey of around 200 older people in each of these three locations was conducted and was designed to explore the extent of change since the earlier studies and such issues as experiences of assistance from neighbours. Qualitative interviews were conducted with sixty-two older people who had participated in the survey. In the qualitative interviews, questions were asked partly to allow contrasts with the earlier investigations but also in order to 'provide a context for the information about social networks gleaned from the survey' (Phillipson et al. 1999: 723). For example, at one point the authors present some statistical findings concerning whether people could find something they liked about their area. Most (79 per cent) could find something they liked, but this varied quite a lot, with Woodford residents being more likely than Bethnal Green ones to be able to mention a feature they liked. However, the qualitative interviews provided insights into what it was about the areas that people liked. For example, having a community feeling was viewed positively, with one elderly woman in Woodford saying: 'More like a village. Everybody knows everyone else. It is very friendly' (Phillipson et al. 1999: 723). The authors note that Bethnal Green residents were especially likely to mention having roots in an area as being of particular significance, as when one woman said: 'It's my home, my roots are here now. It's what I'm used to . . . living here and working here for so many years' (Phillipson et al. 1999: 724). In this example, the qualitative findings allow the quantitative data to be contextualized. We understand the statistical data better because we have an appreciation of the nature of the areas in which the surveys were conducted and the motives and preferences of their members.

Illustration

Sometimes, mixed methods researchers find it useful to employ little vignettes from their qualitative findings to illustrate some of their quantitative findings. Quantitative data can often seem remote and cold, while some rich interview material can be employed to put some flesh on the bare bones of such data. An example of the use of mixed methods research in this way can be discerned from the CCSE research referred to in Research in focus 2.9 and above. The researchers used the survey data to establish dimensions on which respondents differed in terms of their cultural activities and taste. Sometimes, they employ passages from their interview transcripts to illustrate positions in relation to the dimensions. For example, the researchers found that, of all the areas of cultural tastes, visual art differentiates people more than any other. The authors use the case of Margaret, who has a moderate engagement with visual art and for whom it is merely decorative around the house.

> Margaret   . . . if I put that boat picture up there like that wouldn't do anything for my kitchen . . . I'm sort of trying to get things that would suit my kitchen you know and that does . . . you know, you have . . . It took me about three or four days to get those pictures for in here [pointing to framed pictures of flowers on the wall]. Do you know what I mean; I just didn't go out and get the first thing that I saw.
>
> (Bennett et al. 2009: 124)

In this passage, 'that boat picture' is a painting by J. M. W. Turner—*The Fighting Temeraire Tugged to her Last Berth to be Broken Up* (1838)—which interviewees were asked to discuss. A rather different position in relation to visual art is revealed by Cynthia, who has close connections with the art world:

> Cynthia   A great friend who was in the art world . . . she was a 19th century expert and through her, I got to like [name] . . . and we've got one picture of his and that has gone up mad in value as you can imagine, wonderful. . . . But the ones I really like, Turner . . . he was actually a friend of my father's and I was taken to see his studios and things like that and I've got quite a lot of not original [inaudible] tiny little thing when he scribbled something to my father, but that's about all.
>
> (Bennett et al. 2009: 125)

It is striking that Cynthia is a great deal more confident discussing art as well as knowledgeable about the art world and some of its key players. She and Margaret represent different positions in relation to this differentiating aspect of cultural taste. Illustration was also a feature of the research reported in Research in focus 27.3.

Utility

For some writers and researchers, mixed methods research is preferred because it is felt that it is more likely to generate findings that will have utility. This is more likely to be a concern among researchers in fields with a strong disposition towards findings having practical benefits. For example, one of my interviewees said of mixed methods research: 'The main reason I use it and the main reason I will probably always put it on grant applications is because of the issues around needing to . . . generate data that's . . . suitable for policy-makers.' This interviewee went on to add: 'I think by doing both methods, it enables you . . . to speak to kind of policy audiences and to speak to academic audiences.' By way of further illustration of utility as a rationale for mixed methods research, Pernice (1996) conducted both quantitative and qualitative research on unemployed people in New Zealand. She found that the questionnaire data revealed that most members of the sample wanted a job. However, qualitative data gleaned from interviews revealed a more complex set of attitudes with regard to intentions towards employment. Many spoke about alternatives to paid employment that they were considering and also revealed in interviews a more nuanced set of attitudes towards employment than was being (or could be) revealed through the questionnaires. Pernice (1996: 348) argues that not only was her understanding of unemployment enhanced through mixed methods research, but also, 'if only quantitative approaches are taken, our understanding of unemployment will not be deep enough to formulate effective solutions'.

Confirm and discover

The most common form of this rationale for mixed methods research is that the inferences that are derived from a qualitative study are then subsequently tested with quantitative research. An example is a study by Tripp et al. (2002) of revenge in the workplace. Initially, eighty-eight working MBA students in the USA were asked to give an account of two incidents in which the student or someone else had sought to gain revenge against another person. The revenge episodes were examined to establish the activities involved in taking revenge. The overriding finding was that there should be symmetry between the initial episode and the revenge. This symmetry has two elements: symmetry of consequences—the revenge should do the same amount of harm as the original wrongdoing; and symmetry of method—the way in which revenge is exacted should resemble that involved in the initial harm that was done. Drawing on this distinction, the researchers conducted a second study, using an experimental design, to test their prediction, which emerged out of the qualitative study, that 'the symmetry of consequences will influence individual judgments of revenge [and] symmetry of method should shape individual judgments about revenge' (Tripp et al. 2002: 972–3). In fact, the experiment did not entirely support these expectations. When revenge is symmetric in terms of consequences, the experiment showed that the vengeful act is viewed more positively. This was in line with the researchers' expectations. However, symmetry of method operated in a manner contrary to their expectations: vengeful acts were viewed *more* harshly when they were symmetric with the original harmful act.

Diversity of views

Sometimes, researchers want to gather two kinds of data: qualitative data that will allow them to gain access to participants' perspectives; and quantitative data that will allow them to explore specific issues in which they are interested. When this occurs, they are seeking to explore an area in both ways, so that they can both adopt an unstructured approach to data collection in which participants' meanings are the focus of attention and investigate a specific set of issues through the more structured approach of quantitative research. An example of this is Milkman's (1997) study of a General Motors car manufacturing plant in the USA.

She was interested in the nature of the labour process in the late twentieth century and whether new factory conditions were markedly different for car production workers from the negative portrayals of such work in the 1950s and early 1960s (e.g. Blauner 1964). As such, she was interested in the meaning of industrial work. She employed semi-structured interviews and focus groups with car production workers to elicit data relevant to this aspect of her study. However, in addition she had some specific interests in a 'buyout' plan that the company's management introduced in the mid-1980s after it had initiated a variety of changes to work practices. The plan gave workers the opportunity to give up their jobs for a substantial cash payment. In 1988 Milkman carried out a questionnaire survey of workers who had taken up the company's buyout offer. These workers were surveyed again the following year and in 1991. The reason for the surveys was that Milkman had some very specific interests in the buyout scheme, such as the reasons for workers taking the buyout, how they had fared since leaving General Motors, how they felt about their current employment, and differences between social groups (in particular, different ethnic groups) in current earnings relative to those at General Motors.

A further example is the research on school size differences that was referred to in Research in focus 12.1. One of the aims of this study was the exploration of the relationships between class size and various aspects of classrooms. As noted in Research in focus 12.1 and elsewhere in Chapter 12, Blatchford and his colleagues collected quantitative data, drawing on structured observation of classrooms and questionnaires. The data that were generated reflected the preoccupations of the research team.

However, Blatchford (2005) reports that they also wanted to capture teachers' experiences and to that end conducted semi-structured interviews and conducted detailed case studies of particular classes. Further, the various qualitative findings relating to the differences between large and small classes influenced later questionnaires that were developed (a case of 'instrument development').

Enhancement

In the Poortinga et al. (2004) article on the foot and mouth disease (FMD) crisis (see Research in focus 2.8 and 27.3), enhancement occurs on several occasions. For example, as noted in the section on triangulation, the authors note that their focus group data regarding the perceived causes of the outbreak were more or less the same as the causes identified in their questionnaire survey, but they also qualified this assertion. Another example is when they note another correspondence between their quantitative and their qualitative data: 'The findings of the focus groups reinforce those of the questionnaire regarding general concern' (Poortinga et al. 2004: 78). However, they then go on to note that the picture from the focus groups is slightly more complex than if one relies on the survey data alone, and they quote a focus group participant to exemplify this point:

> In terms of health impacts, people were worried that rotting carcasses of culled animals, which in some cases were not put onto a funeral pyre immediately, would spread various diseases, and also because of toxins being emitted from the fires. That is, people were more concerned about health risks arising from *government policy measures and handling of FMD* than about the *disease itself.*

> I think a lot of people are genuinely concerned about the fires, the toxins coming out in the fires, that became quite an issue. And that is one of those things that we probably won't know if there is any kind of come back on it, we probably won't know for a few years and that is quite a concern. (Norwich, Male)
>
> (Poortinga et al. 2004: 78; emphasis in original)

In the study by Bickerstaff et al. (2008), the survey evidence suggested that the causes of climate change (car use, energy use, and so on) were more likely to be seen as beneficial to respondents themselves and to society than causes of radioactive waste (for example, nuclear power production). The focus group data elaborated the causal inferences that were being made in the surveys. For example, when talking about energy-consuming facets of modern life such as transport and heating, focus group participants tended to emphasize the benefits rather than the risks. The adverse effects of these on the environment were regarded as unavoidable features of modernity. Research in focus 27.9 provides another example of enhancement.

Research in focus 27.9
Enhancement and completeness in a mixed methods study of NHS non-clinical call-handlers

Turnbull et al. (2012) wanted to identify the skills and expertise needed by non-clinical call-handlers who are faced with taking calls in which they have to make an assessment of the caller's needs with the support of a computer decision support system (CDSS). They used a mixed methods embedded design with a qualitative research emphasis. Qualitative data were collected in each of three settings: 999, an emergency telephone service administered by an Ambulance Trust; an urgent care service run by the same trust; and an out-of-hours service for GPs. Three forms of qualitative data were collected: non-participant observation in the three settings comprising just under 500 hours of observation; semi-structured interviews with call-handlers and others, such as managers; and examination of documents concerning the skills and qualifications believed to be important for call-handlers. The quantitative component comprised a survey of call-handlers 'to provide further data on the skills that call-handlers perceived to be important' and 'aspects not fully captured' by the qualitative component 'including call-handlers' qualifications, demographic characteristics, previous work experience and work aspirations' (Turnbull et al. 2012: 235). Thus, the quantitative data were collected to allow the researchers to both extend their qualitative data and to provide a more complete account than could be gleaned from the qualitative data alone. For example, at one point, Turnbull et al. observe that the qualitative evidence suggests that call-handlers develop what they call 'pseudo-clinical expertise', something that many of them enjoyed. For example the following observation was made at the 999 centre:

> The call-handler says "we've all got our bits of knowledge . . . someone's husband has diabetes, someone else knows about asthma". They can ask each other for advice and learn from their experiences. She describes a call about a baby who was fitting. Prior to the CDSS, advice included removing some layers of clothes, sponging with cold water and opening windows. But this call-handler still advises "right well, undo the top buttons of her cardigan and open a window". The call-handler merges her advice with the CDSS to offer what she thinks is the best advice.
>
> (Turnbull et al. 2012: 238)

The authors then immediately refer to a table presenting survey data that amplifies this point:

> The survey suggests that call-handlers rated the use of informal knowledge from friends, family, and colleagues less highly than other key competencies . . ., reflecting their awareness that this is not formally sanctioned, but nonetheless they acknowledge its place in their work.
>
> (Turnbull et al. 2012: 238)

Thus, the mixed methods nature of this study allowed the authors to build on their qualitative findings by making regular references to their survey findings when they allowed an enhancement of the qualitative evidence or supplied some gaps in the qualitative evidence.

Quality issues in mixed methods research

There can be little doubt that mixed methods research is becoming far more common than when I first started writing about it (Bryman 1988a; see Thinking Deeply 27.3). Two particularly significant factors in prompting this development are:

1. a growing willingness to think of research methods as techniques of data collection or analysis that are not as

burdened by epistemological and ontological baggage as is sometimes supposed, and

2. a softening in the attitude towards quantitative research among feminist researchers, who had previously been highly resistant to its use (see Chapter 17 for a discussion of this point).

Thinking deeply 27.3
Are the paradigm wars over?

The period during which many commentators viewed quantitative and qualitative research as based on incompatible assumptions is often referred to as the 'paradigm wars' (Hammersley 1992c; Oakley 1999) or the 'paradigm debate' (Creswell and Plano Clark 2011). The growing popularity of mixed methods research would seem to signal the end of the paradigm wars, as it is sometimes represented as having given way to pragmatism. Many of the contributors to Tashakkori and Teddlie's (2003, 2010) *Handbook* appear to be committed to a pragmatist position. However, there are signs that the paradigm wars have not entirely disappeared but have resurfaced in slightly different ways (Bryman 2008). One of these is the growing fondness for systematic reviews of the literature, particularly in areas of the social sciences with a strong applied focus (see Key concept 5.1 and Research in focus 5.2). Several writers have noted that the proponents of systematic review advocate its use in terms of principles that are very much associated with quantitative research and its positivist foundations. They tend to attribute to it qualities such as reliability, replicability, transparency of procedures, and greater comprehensiveness, and suggest that it is more objective (Hammersley 2001; MacLure 2005). These attributes have strong affinities with quantitative research. In contrast, the critics of systematic review tend to emphasize what systematic review does *not* do and what traditional narrative reviews are capable of achieving. The critics of systematic review highlight features of systematic review that are associated with qualitative research and its interpretivist foundations. They tend to emphasize the significance of interpretation in narrative literature reviews and the importance of understanding and locating findings within the entire study of which the findings are a part. They also suggest that systematic review neglects intertextuality—the links between studies and their findings—whereas it is standard practice in a literature review to explore such links. The key point to register at this point is that this debate has several of the hallmarks of the paradigm arguments.

Other factors are doubtless relevant, but these two developments seem especially significant. However, it is important to appreciate that mixed methods research is not intrinsically superior to mono-method or mono-strategy research. It is tempting to think that mixed methods research is more or less inevitably superior to research that relies on a single method on the grounds that more and more varied findings are inevitably 'a good thing'. Indeed, social scientists sometimes display such a view (Bryman 2006b).

However, several points must be borne in mind. These reflections are influenced by writings concerned with indicators of quality in mixed methods research (e.g. Bryman et al. 2008; O'Cathain et al. 2008). Rather than include all possible quality criteria that can or have been applied to mixed methods research (e.g. O'Cathain 2010), the approach taken here is to emphasize criteria that recur in discussions of quality in connection with mixed methods research (Bryman 2014).

1. Mixed methods research, like mono-method research, must be competently designed and conducted. Poorly conducted research will yield suspect findings, no matter how many methods are employed.

2. Just like mono-method or mono-strategy research, mixed methods research must be appropriate to the research questions with which you are concerned. There is no point collecting more data simply on the basis of a belief that 'more is better'. Mixed methods research has to be dovetailed to research questions, just as all research methods must be. It is, after all, likely to consume considerably more time and financial resources than research relying on just one method.

3. It is best to be explicit about why you have conducted mixed methods research. Providing a rationale for its use gives the reader a better sense of the relationship between the research questions and the research methods and also what the use of two or more methods was meant to achieve in terms of the overall project.

4. Try not to think of mixed methods research as made up of separate components. It is best to consider how the quantitative and qualitative components are related to each other from the outset. There is a feeling among many writers that many so-called mixed methods projects are not really mixed at all because the researchers do not integrate their quantitative and qualitative findings. This is particularly evident when researchers present and discuss their quantitative and qualitative findings separately rather than bringing the evidence together. I will return to this issue in Chapter 28.

5. Make sure that you provide a sufficiently detailed account of all the methodological details of the research for both the quantitative and the qualitative components. Sometimes researchers provide more detail concerning one element or give only a surface treatment of both. So, make sure that information about sampling, design and administration of research instruments, analysis of the data, and the like are provided for both components. Also, ensure that you have justified the decisions that you have made in connection with these issues.

6. As awareness of the different types of mixed methods design has spread, there is a growing expectation that the researcher stipulates the kind of design he or she is using and the reasons for that choice. The section on 'Types of mixed methods design' above provides an outline of the basic types of design.

In other words, mixed methods research should not be considered as an approach that is universally applicable or as a panacea. It *may* provide a better understanding of a phenomenon than if just one method had been used. It may also frequently enhance our confidence in our own or others' findings—for example, when a triangulation exercise has been conducted. It may even serve a tactical purpose of enhancing the credibility of an application for research funding or a publication, especially when it is borne in mind that some writers believe that mixed methods research has become methodologically fashionable (Sandelowski 2003). However, as I have tried to suggest with these final reflections, mixed methods research is subject to the same (or at least very similar) considerations and constraints as any research method or design.

On the other hand, Molina-Azorín (2012) compared the mixed methods articles published between 1980 and 2006 in *Strategic Management Journal* with an equivalent set of mono-method articles from the same journal. He found that mixed methods articles were noticeably more likely to be cited that the mono-method articles. For example, eight years after publication the mean number of citations of a mixed methods article was around 6 but the equivalent number of citations of mono-method articles was around 3.5. Citations refer to references to a particular article in other articles. The number of citations is sometimes treated as an indicator of the impact of a piece of work within its field. Molina-Azorín's findings suggest that mixed methods articles typically make a greater impact than their mono-method counterparts.

Checklist

Issues to consider when planning, conducting, and writing up mixed methods research

○ Have you made sure you have all the necessary skills in advance for undertaking all the components of a mixed methods project?

○ Have you planned the project as a mixed methods one and not as a project with separate components?

○ Have you built integration of the quantitative and qualitative elements into your plans from the outset?

○ Are you clear in your own mind about why you are doing a mixed methods study? (Do not assume that doing mixed methods research is inherently superior.)

○ When writing up the research, have you made clear your rationale(s) for doing a mixed methods study?

○ Have you shown clearly how the research methods you intend to use (if a proposal) or have used (when writing up) relate to your research questions?

○ Have you integrated your quantitative and qualitative findings? Have you shown how they are mutually informative and not treated them as separate?

○ Have you demonstrated what is gained by doing mixed methods research?

◯ Have you provided details about how you conducted the quantitative and qualitative components (sampling, instrument design and implementation, analysis, etc.) and have you justified the decisions you made in these areas?

◯ Have you made clear the nature of mixed methods research design that you have employed?

 ## Key points

....

- While there has been a growth in the amount of mixed methods research, not all writers support its use.

- Objections to mixed methods research tend to be the result of a view that there are epistemological and ontological impediments to the combination of quantitative and qualitative research.

- There are several different ways of combining quantitative and qualitative research and of representing mixed methods research.

- The outcomes of combining quantitative and qualitative research can be planned or unplanned.

- Mixed methods research is not necessarily superior to mono-method research.

Questions for review

....

- What is mixed methods research?

The argument against mixed methods research

- What are the main elements of the embedded methods and paradigm arguments in terms of their implications for the possibility of mixed methods research?

Two versions of the debate about quantitative and qualitative research

- What are the main elements of the technical and epistemological versions of the debate about quantitative and qualitative research? What are the implications of these two versions of the debate for mixed methods research?

Approaches to mixed methods research

- What is the significance of priority and sequence as ways of classifying mixed methods research?
- What are the chief ways in which quantitative and qualitative research have been combined?
- Why might it be useful to distinguish between them?
- What is the logic of triangulation?
- Traditionally, qualitative research has been depicted as having a preparatory role in relation to quantitative research. To what extent do the different forms of mixed methods research reflect this view?

Quality issues in mixed methods research

- Why has mixed methods research become more prominent?
- Is mixed methods research necessarily superior to mono-method research?
- To what extent does the rise of mixed methods research suggest that the paradigm wars are over?
- Are there quality considerations that apply specifically to mixed methods research?

Online Resource Centre

www.oxfordtextbooks.co.uk/orc/brymansrm5e/

Visit the Online Resource Centre to enrich your understanding of mixed methods research. Follow up links to other resources, test yourself using multiple choice questions, and gain further guidance and inspiration from the Student Researcher's Toolkit.

28

Writing up social research

Chapter outline

Chapter guide

It is easy to forget that one of the main stages in any research project, regardless of its size, is that it has to be written up. Not only is this how you will convey your findings, but being aware of the significance of writing is crucial, because your audience must be persuaded about the credibility and significance of your research. This chapter presents some of the characteristics of the writing-up of social research. The chapter explores:

- why writing, and especially good writing, is important to social research;
- using examples, how quantitative, qualitative, and mixed methods research are written up;
- the expectations and conventions of writing for academic audiences.

Introduction

The aim of this chapter is to examine some of the strategies that are employed in writing up social research. Initially, we will explore the question of whether quantitative and qualitative research reveal divergent approaches. As we will see, the similarities are sometimes more striking than the differences, but the main point of this chapter is to present some principles of good practice that can be developed and incorporated into your own writing. This is an important issue, since people sometimes find writing up research more difficult than carrying it out. Also, many people treat the writing-up stage as relatively unproblematic. No matter how well research is conducted, others (that is, your readers) have to be convinced about the credibility of the knowledge claims you are making. Good writing is, therefore, very much to do with developing your style so that it is *persuasive*

Key concept 28.1
What is rhetoric?

The study of rhetoric is fundamentally concerned with the ways in which attempts to convince or persuade an audience are formulated. We often encounter the term in a negative context, such as 'mere rhetoric' or the opposition of 'rhetoric and reality'. However, rhetoric is an essential ingredient of writing, because when we write our aim is to convince others about the credibility of our knowledge claims. To suggest that rhetoric should somehow be suppressed makes little sense, since it is in fact a basic feature of writing. The examination of rhetorical strategies in written texts based on social research is concerned with the identification of the techniques in those texts that are designed to convince and persuade.

and *convincing*. Flat, lifeless, uncertain writing does not have the power to persuade and convince. It is useful to examine the **rhetorical** strategies that social researchers use in order to convince readers of the value of their work when writing up their findings (see Key concept 28.1 on rhetoric).

This chapter will review some of the ways in which social research is written up in order to provide some basic ideas about structuring your own written work if you have to produce something like a dissertation.

Writing up your research

It is easy to neglect the writing stage of your work because of the difficulties that you may have encountered in getting your research under way. But—obvious though this point is—your dissertation has to be written. Your findings must be conveyed to an audience, something that all of us who carry out research have to face. The first bit of advice is . . .

Start early

It is easy to take the view that the writing-up of your research findings is something that you can think about after you have collected and analysed your data. There is, of course, a grain of truth in this view, in that you could hardly write up your findings until you know what they are, which is something that you can know only once you have gathered and analysed your data. However, there are good reasons for beginning writing early on, since you might want to start thinking about such issues as how best to present and justify the research questions that are driving your research or how to structure the theoretical and research literature that will have been used to frame your research questions. Students often underestimate the time that it will take to write up their research, so it is a good idea to allow plenty of time for this; this is especially important if you are expecting your

supervisor to read and comment on an early draft, since you will need to allow him or her a reasonable amount of time for this. A further reason why it is advisable to begin writing earlier rather than later is an entirely practical one: many people find it difficult to get started and employ (probably unwittingly) procrastination strategies to delay the inevitable. This tendency can result in the writing being left until the last minute and consequently rushed. Writing under this kind of pressure is not ideal. How you represent your findings and conclusions is a crucial stage in the research process. If you do not provide a convincing account of your research, you will not do justice to it.

Be persuasive

This point is crucial. Writing up your research is not simply a matter of reporting your findings and drawing some conclusions. Writing up your research will contain many other features, such as referring to the literature on which you drew, explaining how you did your research, and outlining how you conducted your analysis. But above all, you must be *persuasive*. This means that you must convince your readers of the credibility of your conclusions. Simply saying 'this is what I found; isn't it interesting' is not enough. You must persuade your readers

Student experience
Writing up is difficult

Several of the students mentioned that they found writing up difficult. Gareth Matthews comments that he 'found this stage the most difficult'. Isabella Robbins admits that writing the chapters presenting her findings was 'the most difficult task of the PhD process'. Having enough time for writing up is a common refrain in their responses to questionnaires. Sarah Hanson's advice is:

> The only problem with a writing project of this size is time. As it is always against you, start early, and be organized, do one thing at a time. Work chronologically. Lecturers and markers like to see that you have gone on a journey of exploration into an interesting world and at the end have come out with something worthwhile that has changed your thinking and will hopefully challenge theirs.

To read more, go to the Online Resource Centre: **www.oxfordtextbooks.co.uk/orc/brymansrm5e/**

that your findings and conclusion are significant and that they are plausible.

Get feedback

Try to get as much feedback on your writing as possible and respond positively to the points anyone makes about your drafts. Your supervisor is likely to be the main source of feedback, but institutions vary in what supervisors are allowed to comment on. Provide your supervisor with drafts of your work to the fullest extent that regulations will allow. Give him or her plenty of time to provide feedback. Other students will want your supervisor to comment on their work, and, if he or she feels rushed, the comments may be less helpful. Also, you could ask others on the same degree programme to read your drafts and comment on them. They may ask you to do the same. Their comments may be very useful, but, by and large, your supervisor's comments are the main ones you should seek out.

Avoid sexist, racist, and disablist language

Remember that your writing should be free of sexist, racist, and disablist language. The British Sociological Association provides very good general and specific advice about this issue, which can be found at: **www.britsoc.co.uk/equality** (accessed 5 January 2015).

Structure your writing

It may be that you have to write a dissertation of around 10,000–15,000 words for your degree. How might it be structured? The following is typical of the structure of a dissertation.

Title page

You should examine your institution's rules about what should be entered here.

Tips and skills
Non-sexist writing

One of the biggest problems (but by no means the only one) when trying to write in a non-sexist way is avoiding complex his/her formulations. The easiest way of dealing with this is to write in the plural in such circumstances. Consider, for example: 'I wanted to give each respondent the opportunity to complete the questionnaire in his or her own time and in a location that was convenient for him or her.' This is a rather tortuous sentence and, although grammatically correct, it could be phrased more helpfully as: 'I wanted to give respondents the opportunity to complete their questionnaires in their own time and in a location that was convenient for them.'

Acknowledgements

You might want to acknowledge the help of various people, such as gatekeepers who gave you access to an organization, people who have read your drafts and provided you with feedback, or your supervisor for his or her advice.

List of contents

Your institution may have recommendations or prescriptions about the form this should take.

An abstract

A brief summary of your dissertation. Not all institutions require this component, so check on whether it is required. Journal articles usually have abstracts, so you can draw on these for guidance on how to approach this task.

Introduction

The following are some points to consider when writing an introduction.

- You should explain what you are writing about and why it is important. Saying simply that it interests you because of a long-standing personal interest is not enough.

- You might indicate in general terms the theoretical approach or perspective you will be using and why.

- You should also at this point outline your research questions. In the case of dissertations based on qualitative research, it is likely that your research questions will be rather more open-ended than is the case with quantitative research. But do try to identify some research questions. A totally open-ended research focus is risky and can lead to the collection of too much data, and, when it comes to writing up, it can result in a lack of focus.

- The opening sentence or sentences are often the most difficult of all. Becker (1986) advises strongly against opening sentences that he describes as 'vacuous' and 'evasive'. He gives the example of 'This study deals with the problem of careers', and adds that this kind of sentence employs 'a typically evasive manœuvre, pointing to something without saying anything, or anything much, about it. *What* about careers?' (Becker 1986: 51). He suggests that such evasiveness often occurs because of concerns about giving away the plot. In fact, he argues, it is much better to give readers a quick and clear indication of what is going to be presented to them and where it is going.

Literature review

See Chapter 5 for more detailed advice on how to go about writing this chapter of your dissertation. Research questions are sometimes outlined here rather than in the Introduction.

Research methods

The term 'research methods' is meant here as a kind of catch-all for several issues that need to be outlined: your research design; your sampling approach; how access was achieved if relevant; the procedures you used (such as, if you sent out a postal questionnaire, did you follow up non-respondents); the nature of your questionnaire, interview schedule, participant observation role, observation schedule, coding frame, or whatever (these will usually appear in an appendix, but you should comment on such things as your style of questioning or observation and why you asked the things you did); problems of non-response; note taking; issues of ongoing access and cooperation; coding matters; and how you proceeded with your analysis. When discussing each of these issues, you should describe and justify the choices that you made, such as why you used a postal questionnaire rather than a structured interview approach, or why you focused upon that particular population for sampling purposes, or, if you conducted a case study, why the particular case is appropriate. Also, it is important to ensure that your account of your research method is comprehensive.

Writing about the management and criminal justice fields respectively, Zhang and Shaw (2012) and Fox and Jennings (2014) have noted that a common problem with articles that are submitted to journals is that the methods section is incomplete. The reader should not be left wondering what your sampling approach is or suddenly wonder when reading your results how you came to have data about a particular issue. Zhang and Shaw (2012) write that it is important to remember when writing the methods section what they call the 'three Cs': completeness; clarity (transparency about what you did and how you went about it); and credibility (justifying your methodological decisions).

Results

In this chapter you present the bulk of your findings. If you intend to have a separate Discussion chapter, it is likely that the results will be presented with little commentary in terms of the literature or the implications of your findings. If there will be no Discussion chapter, you will need to provide some reflections on the significance of your findings for your research questions and for the literature. Bear these points in mind.

- Remember not to include *all* your results. You should present and discuss only those findings that relate to your research questions. This requirement may mean a rather painful process of leaving out many findings,

Tips and skills
The importance of an argument

One of the things that students find most difficult about writing up the argument. The writing-up of research should be organized around an research process from problem formulation, through literature review to the discussion and conclusion. Too often, students make a series of of those points is to the overall argument that they are trying to present is and try to organize your writing to support and enhance it. That will think in terms of seeking to tell a story about your research and your fin material that may mean that your readers will lose the thread of your ar clear argument, you are very vulnerable to the 'so what?' question. Ask yourself: 'What is the key point or message that I want my readers to take away with them when they have finished reading my work?' If you cannot answer that simple question satisfactorily (and it may be worth trying it out on others), almost certainly you do not have an argument. The argument is a thread that runs through your dissertation (see Figure 28.1 for an illustration of this). One way in which the sense of an argument can be enhanced is by providing some signposts of where you intend to go in your dissertation and why. I will say more about this in the section on 'Academic writing' at the end of this chapter.

but it is necessary so that the thread of your argument is not lost (see Tips and skills 'The importance of an argument').

- Your writing should point to particularly salient aspects of the tables, graphs, or other forms of analysis you present. Do not just summarize what a table shows; you should direct the reader to the component or components of it that are especially striking from the point of view of your research questions. Try to ask yourself what story you want the table to convey and relay that story to your readers.

- Another sin to be avoided is simply presenting a graph or table or a section of the transcript of a semi-structured interview or focus group session without any comment whatsoever, because the reader is left wondering why you think the finding is important.

- When reporting quantitative findings, it is quite a good idea to vary wherever possible the method of presenting results—for example, provide a mixture of diagrams and tables. However, you must remember the lessons of Chapter 15 concerning the methods of analysis that are appropriate to different types of variable.

- A particular problem that can arise with qualitative research is that students find it difficult to leave out large parts of their data. As one experienced qualitative researcher has put it: 'The major problem we face in qualitative inquiry is not to get data, but to get rid of it!' (Wolcott 1990a: 18). He goes on to say that the 'critical task in qualitative research is not to accumulate all the data you can, but to "can" [i.e. get rid of] most of the data you accumulate' (Wolcott 1990a: 35). You have to recognize that much of the rich data you accumulate will have to be discarded. If you do not do this, the sense of an argument in your work is likely to be lost. There is also the risk that your account of your findings will appear too descriptive and lack an analytical edge. This is why it is important to use research questions as a focus and to orient the presentation of your findings to them. It is also important to keep in mind the theoretical ideas and the literature that have framed your work. The theory and literature that have influenced your thinking will also have shaped your research questions.

- If you are writing a thesis—for example, for an MPhil or PhD degree—it is likely that you will have more than one and possibly several chapters in which you present your results. You should indicate which research question or questions are being addressed in the chapter and provide some signposts about what will be included in the chapter. In the conclusion of the chapter, you should make clear what your results have shown and draw out any links that might be made with the next results chapter.

[redacted]

[redacted] argument in a dissertation

[redacted]		Commonly used phrases in formulating an argument
[redacted]uction		This dissertation is concerned with… This dissertation will explore/examine… There has been a growth of interest in X to which this dissertation will make a contribution. The growing adoption of … has attracted a lot of interest in the mass media but there is a dearth of research into its actual use.
Literature review		X has attracted a great deal of interest in recent years. In particular, [name1 year] has argued/suggested/noted… According to [name2 year] the concept of Y can be usefully employed to illuminate X because… Recent research on X has shown that… …although the findings are somewhat inconsistent. Therefore, much of the existing research suggests… By contrast, [name3 year] found/argued/suggested… One area of controversy in the literature about X revolves around the question of… In this dissertation, I will build on [name3]'s suggestion that… In exploring this issue, the following research questions are proposed:…
Research methods	A	Research method1 was employed to answer the research questions because/in order to… The sampling approach entailed a purposive sampling approach because… The research followed [name3]'s approach to studying X by… Questionnaires were administered by postal mail in order to… A mixed methods approach was taken so that it would be possible to…
Results/ findings	R G U M	In exploring the research questions, three main themes were identified… The findings suggest that… Interviewees differed in their perspectives on X in two key respects… As Table 7 shows, women were more likely than men to… No statistically significant relationship between variable4 and variable15 was uncovered (see Table 4) which suggests that... This theme is exemplified by Interviewee23's comment that… By contrast, Interviewee12 pointed out that…
Discussion	E N T	The aim of this study was to… The findings reported in Table 4 failed to provide empirical support for Hypothesis 2 in that… The thematic analysis strongly suggests that the concept of Y is very significant for an understanding of… The findings provide clear evidence that [name2]'s concept of Y can be usefully employed to extend our understanding of X because… Overall, these findings confirm/fail to provide support for the suggestion that… Four main themes relating to the research questions emerged. These themes have implications for the investigation of X… The themes derived from the semi-structured interviews helped to explain the correlation between variable4 and variable9 by suggesting that…
Conclusion		In conclusion, these findings suggest that [name2]'s concept of Y can provide a useful springboard for the investigation of X because… A key finding of this research for [name2]'s Z theory is that… The failure to confirm Hypothesis 2 implies that [name3]'s concept of Y is of questionable utility, since it would be expected that… The concepts that have been used to research X have been shown to be of some utility but the results are somewhat mixed in that… Through this research it has been demonstrated that… The main contribution(s) of this research is (are)… Taking a mixed methods approach proved beneficial because… The implications of these findings for the study of X are that… In conclusion, it is proposed that future research should concentrate on/not rely so much on… On the basis of the findings generated by this study, it is concluded that… One limitation of this study is that…

X refers to a topic or area (e.g. mobile phones, recycling)
Y refers to a concept (e.g. cultural capital, quasi-subject)
Z refers to a theory (e.g. actor network theory, risk society)

Student experience
Do not try to write up everything

You will not be able to write up everything that you have found. Sophie Mason recognized this. She writes:

> The great quantity of data meant that I had to use my own judgement as to what data was the most relevant to the aims of the research. I also had to be careful to use visual aids when using complicated statistics to emphasize the importance of the results.

Rebecca Barnes writes:

> Because so many important and interesting issues have emerged in the analysis of my data, I have had to be selective; I have chosen to do justice to a smaller number of themes, rather than resorting to superficial coverage of a larger number of themes.

 *To read more, go to the Online Resource Centre: **www.oxfordtextbooks.co.uk/orc/brymansrm5e/***

Student experience
The importance of research questions, theory, and the literature in writing up findings

Several students mentioned how important it was for them to keep in mind their research questions and the theory and literature that were driving their research while writing up. For one thing, they help the student to decide which findings to include or to emphasize when writing up. Rebecca Barnes writes:

> I chose to have three chapters of my thesis that reported my findings, and I chose the themes that I would include in each of these chapters. These were not, however, set in stone, and have changed in a number of respects from when I first started to plan the writing-up. Each of these chapters addresses one of my main research questions or aims.

Erin Sanders writes:

> First I wrote down the main points and ideas I wanted to get across—and how my findings related to [my] research question.'

Hannah Creane's writing-up of her findings was geared to her research questions.

> I grouped together questions and responses that concerned similar aspects within the childhood debate and formed three main chapters: What makes a child a child?; Childhood past times; and The child today. Within these chapters I interwove themes that emerged from the data and seemed to be present in most responses.

For Gareth Matthews the theoretical debates about the labour process were crucial:

> This has allowed me to frame my thesis theoretically, and to lay the foundations for a discussion of my empirical findings.

 *To read more, go to the Online Resource Centre: **www.oxfordtextbooks.co.uk/orc/brymansrm5e/***

Discussion

In the Discussion, you reflect on the implications of your findings for the research questions that have driven your research. In other words, how do your results illuminate your research questions? If you have specified hypotheses, the discussion will revolve around whether the hypotheses have been confirmed or not, and, if not, you might speculate about some possible reasons for and implications of their refutation.

Conclusion

The main points here are as follows.

- A Conclusion is not the same as a summary. However, it is frequently useful to bring out in the opening paragraph of the Conclusion your argument thus far. This will mean relating your findings and your discussion of them to your research questions. Thus, your brief summary should be a means of hammering home to your readers the significance of what you have done.

- You should make clear the implications of your findings for your research questions.

- You might suggest some ways in which your findings have implications for theories relating to your area of interest.

- You might draw attention to any limitations of your research with the benefit of hindsight, but it is probably best not to overdo this element and provide examiners with ammunition that might be used against you!

- It is often valuable to propose areas of further research that are suggested by your findings.

- Two things to avoid are engaging in speculations that take you too far away from your data, or that cannot be substantiated by the data, and introducing issues or ideas that have not previously been brought up.

Appendices

In your appendices you might want to include such things as your questionnaire, coding frame, or observation schedule, letters sent to sample members, and letters sent to and received from gatekeepers where the cooperation of an organization was required.

References

Include here all references cited in the text. For the format of the References section you should follow whichever one is prescribed by your department. Nowadays, the format is usually a variation of the Harvard method (see Chapter 5), such as the one employed for this book.

Finally

Remember to fulfil any obligations you entered into, such as supplying a copy of your dissertation, if, for example, your access to an organization was predicated on providing one, and maintaining the confidentiality of information supplied and the anonymity of your informants and other research participants.

Student experience
Structure of the dissertation or thesis

Some of the students wrote up their work with a similar structure to the one that has been outlined in this section. Sophie Mason writes:

> The research project was written in various stages and split into several different sections; these were as follows: Introduction and Aims, Literature Review, Research Design and Data Gathering, Data Analysis and Research Findings, Conclusions and Recommendations, Appendix and Bibliography.

Erin Sanders writes:

> I wrote it in order, introduction, literature review, research design, findings, discussion, and conclusion. I took each section as if it were an essay in and of itself, and attempted to break it down into chunks so as not to get lost in a long document.

To read more, go to the Online Resource Centre: www.oxfordtextbooks.co.uk/orc/brymansrm5e/

Tips and skills
Proof reading your dissertation

Before submitting your dissertation, make sure that it is spell-checked and check it for grammatical and punctuation errors. There are many useful guides and handbooks that can be used for this purpose. It may also be useful to ask someone else, such as a friend or family member, to proof read your work in case there are errors that you have missed. As well as being an important presentational issue, this will affect the ease with which your written work can be read and understood. It therefore has the potential to affect the quality of your dissertation significantly.

Writing up quantitative, qualitative, and mixed methods research

In the next three sections, research-based articles that have been published in journals are examined to detect some helpful features. One is based on quantitative research, one on qualitative research, and the third on mixed methods research. The presentation of the quantitative and the qualitative research articles raises the question of whether practitioners of the two research strategies use different writing approaches. It is sometimes suggested that they do, though, when I compared two articles based on research in the sociology of work, I found that the differences were less pronounced than I had anticipated on the basis of reading the literature on the topic (Bryman 1998). One difference that I have noticed is that, in journals, quantitative researchers often give more detailed accounts of their research design, research methods, and approaches to analysis than qualitative researchers. This is surprising, because, in books reporting their research, qualitative researchers provide detailed accounts of these areas. Indeed, the chapters in Part Three of this book rely heavily on these accounts. Wolcott (1990a: 27) has also noticed this tendency: 'Our [qualitative researchers'] failure to render full and complete disclosure about our data-gathering procedures give our methodologically oriented colleagues fits. And rightly so, especially for those among them willing to accept our contributions if we would only provide more careful data about our data.' Being informed that a study was based on a year's participant observation or a number of semi-structured interviews is not enough to gain an acceptance of the claims to credibility that a writer might be wishing to convey.

Writing up quantitative research

To illustrate some of the characteristics of the way quantitative research is written up for academic journals, I will take the article by Kelley and De Graaf (1997). I am not suggesting that this article is exemplary or representative, but rather that it exhibits some features that are often regarded as desirable qualities in terms of presentation and structure. The article is based on a secondary analysis of survey data on religion in fifteen nations and was accepted for publication in one of the most prestigious journals in sociology—the *American Sociological Review*, which is the official journal of the American Sociological Association. The vast majority of published articles in academic journals undergo blind refereeing of articles submitted. This means that an article will be read by two or three peers, who comment on the article and give the editor(s) a judgement about its merits and hence whether it is worthy of publication. Most articles submitted are rejected. With very prestigious journals, it is common for in excess of 90 per cent of articles to be rejected. It is unusual for an article to be accepted on its first submission. Usually, the referees suggest areas that need revising, and the journal's editors will expect the author (or authors) to respond to that feedback. Revised versions of articles are usually sent back to the referees for further comment, and this process may result in the author having to revise the draft yet again. It may even result in rejection. Therefore, an article like Kelley and De Graaf's is not just the culmination of a research process, but is also the outcome of a feedback process. The fact that it has been accepted for publication, when many others have been rejected, testifies to its merits as having met the standards of the journal. That is not to say it is perfect, but the refereeing process is an indication that it does possess certain crucial qualities.

Structure

The article has the following components, aside from the abstract:

1. introduction;
2. theory;
3. data;
4. measurement;
5. methods and models;
6. results;
7. conclusion.

Introduction

Right at the beginning of the introduction, the opening four sentences attempt to grab our attention, to give a clear indication of where the article's focus lies, and to provide an indication of the probable significance of the findings. This is what the authors write:

> Religion remains a central element of modern life, shaping people's world-views, moral standards, family lives, and in many nations, their politics. But in many Western nations, modernization and secularization may be eroding Christian beliefs, with profound consequences that have intrigued sociologists since Durkheim. Yet this much touted secularization may be overstated—certainly it varies widely among nations and is absent in the United States (Benson, Donahue, and Erickson 1989: 154–7; Felling, Peters, and Schreuder 1991; Firebaugh and Harley 1991; Stark and Iannaccone

1994). We explore the degree to which religious beliefs are passed on from generation to generation in different nations.

(Kelley and De Graaf 1997: 639)

This is an impressive start, because, in just over 100 words, the authors have set out what the article is about and its significance. Let us look at what each sentence achieves.

- The first sentence locates the article's research focus as addressing an important aspect of modern society that touches on many people's lives.

- The second sentence notes that there is variety among Western nations in the importance of religion and that the variations may have 'profound consequences'. But this sentence does more than the first sentence: it also suggests that this is an area that has been of interest to sociologists. To support this point, one of sociology's most venerated figures—Émile Durkheim—is mentioned. The motives for citing the work of others is considered in Thinking deeply 28.1.

- The third sentence suggests that there is a problem with the notion of secularization, which has been a research focus for many sociologists of religion. Several fairly recent articles are cited to support the authors' contention that there is a possibility that secularization is being exaggerated by some commentators. In this sentence, the authors are moving towards a rationale for their article that is more in terms of sociological concerns than pointing to social changes, which are the main concern of the two opening sentences.

- Then in the fourth sentence the authors set up their specific contribution to this area—the exploration of the passing-on of religious beliefs between generations.

So, by the end of four sentences, the contribution that the article is claiming to make to our understanding of religion in modern society has been outlined and situated within an established literature on the topic. This is quite a powerful start to the article, because the reader knows what the article is about and the particular case the authors are making for their contribution to the literature on the subject.

Theory

In this section, existing ideas and research on religious socialization are presented. The authors point to the impact of parents and other people on children's religious beliefs, but they then assert that 'a person's religious environment is also shaped by factors other than their own and their parents' religious beliefs, and hence is a potential cause of those beliefs' (Kelley and De Graaf 1997: 641). This suggestion is then justified, which prompts

the authors to argue that 'prominent among these "unchosen" aspects of one's religious environment is birthplace' (1997: 641). Kelley and De Graaf's ruminations on this issue lead them to propose the first of three hypotheses. It stipulates that contextual factors have an impact on religious beliefs. This leads the authors to suggest in two related hypotheses that, in predominantly secular societies, family background will have a greater impact on a person's religious beliefs than in predominantly devout societies, because in the former, devout parents and other family members are more likely to seek to isolate children from secular influences. However, in devout societies this insulation process is less necessary and the influence of national factors will be greater. Thus, we end up with very clear research questions, which have been arrived at by reflecting on existing ideas and research in this area.

Data

In this section, the authors outline the data they drew on for their research, which came from the 1991 'Religion' module of the International Social Survey Programme. The authors' exposition entails a general outline of the data sets. The sampling procedures are outlined along with sample sizes and response rates.

Measurement

In this section, Kelley and De Graaf explain how the main concepts in their research were measured. The concepts were: *religious belief* (the questionnaire items used are in Research in focus 7.3); *parents' church attendance*; *secular and religious nations* (that is, the scoring procedure for indicating the degree to which a nation was religious or secular in orientation on a five-point scale); *other contextual characteristics of nations* (for example, whether a former Communist nation or not); and *individual characteristics* (for example, age and gender).

Methods and models

This is a very technical section, which outlines the different ways in which the relationships between the variables might be conceptualized and the implications of using different multivariate analysis approaches for the ensuing findings.

Results

The authors provide a general description of their findings and then consider whether the hypotheses *are* supported. In fact, it turns out the hypotheses are supported. The significance of other contextual characteristics of nations and individual differences are separately explored.

Thinking deeply 28.1
Motives for citing the work of others

Why do we academic writers cite the work of others? Some of the reasons have been hinted at in this and earlier chapters. Erikson and Erlandson (2014) have proposed that there are four main motives to cite. It is not clear how they arrived at their classification of motives but it is worth examining for its comprehensive coverage. The four main categories are:

1. **Argumentation**. This is the traditional motive and occurs when the researcher wants to support a certain position. There are five sub-categories:

   - Positioning the paper in relation to existing approaches. This delimits the scope of the paper.
   - Using a citation to support the author's arguments.
   - Using a citation to establish a criticism of the cited authors' work.
   - Including a cited work because the cited author is a key figure or the journal is a very prestigious one.
   - Indicating further reading in cases when 'the scope of the paper is limited' (Erikson and Erlandson 2014: 630).

2. **Social alignment.** This motive for the citation of a paper is associated with the author's sense of his or her location within a field. Three sub-categories are identified:

   - Expectations within a field regarding the appropriate number of citations and the appropriate kind of cited item (for example, books rather than journal articles or vice versa).
   - Whether the author wants to give the impression that he or she is 'mainstream and safe or avant garde' (Erikson and Erlandson 2014: 631).
   - The authors refer to 'effort compensation', as when a paper is cited even though it is not relevant, so that the citation compensates the author for the effort involved—especially if it was dull.

3. **Mercantile agreement**. An item is cited so that the author gains credit. Erikson and Erlandson identify five sub-categories:

   - Giving credit to the work of the cited author.
   - Demonstrating that the author knows the field well.
   - Citing an item in the hope that it will lead to a reciprocal citation.
   - Citing one's own publications in order to publicize and promote them.
   - Trying to make a favourable impression on an editor or reviewers by referring to certain theories or authors or including a larger number of references.

4. **Data**. Cited sources are used as data by the author. This is a different context from the other three in that it 'is limited to papers in which the main purpose is to analyse the writings of others, particularly in review papers or meta-analytic studies' (Erikson and Erlandson 2014: 629).

The first three categories of motive are particularly relevant to the kind of situation discussed here, namely, when the researcher intends to present a discussion of the literature that will frame and relate to his or her own research. The main reason for including this elaboration of citation motives here is to sensitize readers to their own motives for including a citation.

Conclusion

In this final section, Kelley and De Graaf return to the issues that have been driving their investigation. These are the issues they had presented in the Introduction and Theory sections. They begin the section with a strong statement of their findings: 'The religious environment of a nation has a major impact on the beliefs of its citizens: People living in religious nations acquire, in proportion to the orthodoxy of their fellow citizens, more orthodox beliefs than those living in secular nations' (Kelley and De Graaf 1997: 654). They then reflect on the implications of the confirmation of their hypotheses for our understanding of the process of religious socialization and religious beliefs. They also address the implications of their findings for certain theories about religious beliefs in modern society, which were outlined in their Theory section:

> Our results also speak to the long-running debate about US exceptionalism (Warner 1993): They support the view that the United States is unusually religious. . . .Our results do not support Stark and Iannaccone's (1994) 'supply-side' analysis of differences between nations which argues that nations with religious monopolies have substantial unmet religious needs, while churches in religiously competitive nations like the United States do a better job of meeting diverse religious needs.
>
> (Kelley and De Graaf 1997: 655)

The final paragraph spells out some inferences about the ways in which social changes have an impact on levels of religious belief in a nation. The authors suggest that factors such as modernization and the growth of education depress levels of religious belief and that their impact tends to result in a precipitous rather than a gradual fall in levels of religiosity. In their final three sentences, they go on to write about societies undergoing such change:

> The offspring of devout families mostly remain devout, but the offspring of more secular families now strongly tend to be secular. A self-reinforcing spiral of secularization then sets in, shifting the nation's average religiosity ever further away from orthodoxy. So after generations of stability, religious belief declines abruptly in the course of a few generations to the modest levels seen in many Western nations.
>
> (Kelley and De Graaf 1997: 656)

It might be argued that these reflections are somewhat risky, because the data from which the authors derive their findings are cross-sectional, in research design terms, rather than longitudinal. They are clearly extrapolating from their scoring of the fifteen nations in terms of levels of modernization to the impact of social changes on national levels of religiosity. However, these final sentences make for a strong conclusion, which itself might form a springboard for further research.

Lessons

What lessons can be learned from Kelley and De Graaf's article? To some extent, these have been alluded to in the course of the above exposition, but they are worth spelling out.

- There is a clear attempt to grab the reader's attention with strong opening statements, which also act as signposts to what the article is about.
- The authors spell out clearly the rationale of their research. This entails pointing to the continued

significance of religion in many societies and to the literature on religious beliefs and secularization.

- The research questions are spelled out in a very specific way. In fact, the authors present hypotheses that are a highly specific form of research question. As noted in Chapter 7, by no means all quantitative research is driven by hypotheses, even though outlines of the nature of quantitative research often imply that it is. Nonetheless, Kelley and De Graaf chose to frame their research questions in this form.
- The nature of the data, the measurement of concepts, the sampling, the research methods employed and the approaches to the analysis of the data are clearly and explicitly summarized in sections 3, 4, and 5.
- The presentation of the findings in section 6 is oriented very specifically to the research questions that drive the research.
- The conclusion returns to the research questions and spells out the implications of the findings for them and for the theories examined in section 2. This is an important element. It is easy to forget that you should think of the research process as closing a circle in which you must return unambiguously to your research questions. There is no point inserting extraneous findings if they do not illuminate your research questions. Digressions of this kind can be confusing to readers, who might be inclined to wonder about the significance of the extraneous findings.

We also see that there is a clear sequential process moving from the formulation of the research questions through the exposition of the nature of the data and the presentation of the findings to the conclusions. Each stage is linked to and follows on from its predecessor. The structure used by Kelley and De Graaf is based on a common one employed in the writing-up of quantitative research for academic journals in the social sciences. Sometimes there is a separate Discussion section that appears between the Results and the Conclusion. Another variation is that issues of measurement and analysis appear in the same section as the one dealing with research methods, but perhaps with distinct subheadings.

Writing up qualitative research

Now we will look at an example of a journal article based on qualitative research. Again, I am not suggesting that the article is exemplary or representative, but that it exhibits some features that are often regarded as desirable qualities in terms of presentation and structure. The article is one that has been referred to in previous chapters, in particular Chapter 1 (see especially Table 1.1): a study of retired senior managers by Jones et al. (2010). The study is based on semi-structured interviews and was published in *Sociology*, a leading British journal published on behalf of the British Sociological Association.

Structure

The structure runs as follows:

1. introduction;
2. background;
3. methods;
4. findings;
5. discussion;
6. conclusion.

What is immediately striking about the structure is that it is not dissimilar to Kelley and De Graaf's (1997). Nor should this be all that surprising. After all, a structure that runs

Introduction → Literature review → Research design/ methods → Results → Discussion → Conclusions

is not obviously associated with one research strategy rather than the other. As with Kelley and De Graaf's article, we will examine the writing in terms of the article's structure.

Introduction

The first five sentences provide an immediate sense of what the article is about and where its focus lies:

> Many commentators argue that we are in the midst of a profound restructuring of social life that operates at both a global level (Held et al. 1999) and at the level of what has been described as the institutionalized life course (Kohli 1986; Phillipson 2002). This has given impetus to those who claim that modernity has been rearranged around the key organizing principle of reflexive individualization, which has unintended side effects as assumptions of functional differentiation and the 'better calibration of ends with means' break down (Beck et al. 2003; Latour 2003). These transformations have had both positive and negative impacts on retirement and later life (Phillipson and Smith 2005). In the UK this has led to a decline in the proportion of older people living in poverty and increasing numbers of retired people being fit and healthy and benefiting from occupational pensions (Hills 2004; Thane 2000). But there also appears to be a concomitant increase in inequalities in old age (Brewer et al. 2006).
>
> (Jones et al. 2010: 104)

Like Kelley and De Graaf's, this is a strong introduction. We can look again at what each sentence achieves.

- The first sentence makes clear that the research is concerned with issues to do with the study of the nature of modernity in relation to the life course.

- The third sentence provides us with the specific research focus—the study of retirement and later life— and makes a claim for our attention by suggesting that this is a topic that is very salient to issues to do with the transformations identified in the first two sentences. It is striking that by this point some key social theorists, such as Beck and Latour, have been referred to as well as some significant literature relating to retirement and the nature of modernity.

- The fourth sentence relates the theoretical issues briefly outlined in the first three sentences to what the authors take to be an important social trend relating to retirement and later life.

- The fifth sentence is attention-grabbing in that it brings the suggestion of an interesting contrast—increasing fitness and health in later life but at the same time growing inequalities.

After around 170 words, the reader has a clear idea of the focus of the research and how its empirical emphasis on retirement connects with significant sociological and social concerns. The remainder of the Introduction outlines the theoretical issues that provide the rationale for the article. Towards the end of this section, the authors helpfully provide the reader with a link between their review of the relevant theories and the focus of the article: 'This article therefore utilizes the prism of second modernity to address the ways in which retirement, *for some*, is actively constructed as a lifestyle option or choice as opposed to forms of retirement constructed around financial need and fitting in with a normal stage in the life course' (Jones et al. 2010: 105, emphasis in original). They then proceed in the same paragraph to outline the nature of the research on which the article is based and the research questions that drove the data collection and analysis. These research questions can be found in Table 1.1.

Background

In this section, the literature on retirement is reviewed. This review is helpfully organized into two sections. The first—'Reasons for Taking Early Retirement: Timing, Choice and Compulsion'—reviews the literature on early retirement in particular. The second—'Later Life and Reflexivity'—also includes an assessment of relevant literature, but further draws attention to a potentially interesting contrast between commentators who have suggested that retirement is often associated with isolation and those who have suggested that it is associated with a complex set of accommodations in which notions of self and identity are frequently realigned.

Methods

In this section, the authors outline:

- who was to be studied and why;
- how respondents were recruited—this includes a table showing some of the socio-demographic characteristics of each sample member (age, years since retirement, previous job title, and gender);
- the semi-structured interviewing approach—no rationale for using this method is given at this point, but at the end of the first section the authors signalled that their research approach was designed to uncover the meanings and experiences of early retirement for retirees;
- the number of people interviewed and the context in which the interviews took place;
- the approach to analysing the interview transcripts (thematic analysis) and the use of CAQDAS.

Findings

This section begins by saying that three themes emerged from the analysis. The themes are briefly outlined and then there are subsections for each of them in which the findings relating to each theme are elaborated. For example, one of the themes is 'Third age identities and the quasi-subject', which, the authors point out, has affinities with the writings of such theorists as Beck in positing the growing significance of a reflexive quasi-subject, with a fluid rather than fixed identity, and of an emphasis on spontaneity. They note that interviewees varied in their responses to the new and varied opportunities offered by their early retirement between those who embraced their new situation and those who felt at a loss to know how best to respond. For all of the three themes there is considerable use of passages from the interview transcripts. Thus, as an example of someone who embraces a positive and fluid view of retirement, 'interview 16' contains the following passage, which is quoted:

> I was looking for the ability to do things when you want to do them; to be able to go out for the day on the day you wanted to, the day the sun was shining and not at the weekend when it was pouring with rain. (pause) I do enjoy writing, I enjoy lecturing and things like that, and workshops and things like that, so I was really looking at various things and my wife being a lecturer is also interested in those sort of things, and we work together on that.
>
> (quoted in Jones et al. 2010: 112)

Thinking deeply 28.2 looks in greater detail into the use of verbatim quotations in social science publications.

Discussion

This section outlines the findings in the context of some of the literature that was covered in the first two sections of the article. In other words, the authors draw the significance of their findings in relation to the theoretical issues and literature that they had previously examined. There is also a subsection in which the authors draw attention to the limitations of the study. They note in particular the fact that theirs is a purposive sample that was deliberately selected to include people who had chosen to take early retirement and who were likely to have the resources to enjoy third age lifestyles. As such, it cannot be generalized to retirees who do not meet these criteria.

Conclusion

In this section, the authors return to many of the ideas and themes that drove their research. For example, at one point the authors assess the implications of their findings for some of the main concepts that drove the investigation, such as the notion of a reflexive quasi-subject:

> the respondents gave accounts of the experience of and expectations for early retirement that resonated with the concept of a reflexive, individualized, quasi-subject. Retirement was not associated with old age and was related to the opening up of new and multiple lifestyle choice where the emphasis was on spontaneity and more fluid forms of identity. The positive up-beat accounts of third age lifestyles were, however, balanced by concerns about status. Respondents in this study appeared to wish to maintain their social status in line with that achieved during their work careers.
>
> (Jones et al. 2010: 116)

In their final paragraph the authors make clear what they regard as the principal contribution of their research, which revolves around the notion of a 'generational habitus' in retirement—'an emphasis on individuality, choice, and self-expression' (Jones et al. 2010: 105) among retirees of a particular era—which they propose warrants further attention.

Lessons

As with Kelley and De Graaf's article, it is useful to review some of the lessons learned from this examination of the article by Jones et al.

- Just like the illustration of quantitative research writing, there are strong opening sentences, which grab our attention and give a clear indication of the nature and content of the article.

- The rationale of the research is clearly identified; it mainly revolves around identifying the theoretical credentials of the research in terms of a stream of theorizing associated with notions of modernity, individuality, and identity.

- Research questions are specified but they are somewhat more open-ended than in Kelley and De Graaf's article, which is in keeping with the general orientation of qualitative researchers. The research questions revolve around the issue of new constellations of choice and self-expression among retirees.

- The research design and methods are outlined and an indication is given of the approach to analysis. The section in which these issues are discussed demonstrates greater transparency than is sometimes the case with articles reporting qualitative research.

- The presentation and discussion of the findings are geared to the broad research questions that motivated the researchers' interest in modernity and retirement.

Thinking deeply 28.2
Using verbatim quotations from interviews

It is striking that, in presenting their findings, Jones et al. (2010) use verbatim quotations to reinforce the points they are making (as they do with 'interview 16' above). They do so by including the quotations as they go along to reinforce or illustrate points they are making about the themes they extracted from their data. This is quite a common approach to the use of verbatim interview quotations. However, I have noticed in certain US publications in particular a slightly different approach that I suspect is very much associated with what Adler and Adler (2008) call 'mainstream ethnography' (see Chapter 19). Here, the tone and mode of presenting the findings is very formal and conforms to traditional, mainstream expectations of what a research article should comprise. In particular, there is a 'definite harkening to a more positivistic style' in the presentation of findings, which is associated with a 'generic and impersonal' use of quotations (Adler and Adler 2008: 13, 14). One way in which this is revealed in some US journals is that verbatim quotations are presented in a formal manner in tables rather than *en passant*. An example can be found in Table 28.1, which is taken from Maitlis and Lawrence's (2007) multiple-case study ethnography of three British orchestras. The article was published in a leading journal and adopts the mainstream ethnography frame. This can be discerned in the more formalistic tone than is usually encountered in the other writing frames identified by Adler and Adler. The article is about how 'sensegiving' takes place in organizations—that is, how leaders and others frame perceptions for others. One of the key themes identified was the competence of the leader, and this theme had three components (referred to as 'first-order concepts'). Maitlis and Lawrence used a table to provide 'representative quotations' for each of the three components (see Table 28.1). This style of presenting quotations has become noticeably popular in some leading journals. I suspect the reasons are that the provision of a table provides a sense of something equivalent to the more commonly encountered table summarizing the results of a statistical procedure; it provides a more formal style in keeping with the prevalent tone of such journals; and possibly it gives less of a sense that the quotations are anecdotal or 'cherry-picked'.

Corden and Sainsbury (2006) conducted research into qualitative researchers' use of such quotations. They found that researchers employ verbatim quotations for interview transcripts for a variety of reasons, such as to illustrate a point; to give voice to participants; to provide evidence; or to deepen readers' understanding. When Corden and Sainsbury examined a wide range of publications in the social policy field, they found a wide variety of approaches to the use of quotations. There was a great deal of variety in how those quoted are referred to and in editing conventions, such as the removal of 'er' and 'erm' and of false starts, as well whether pauses or laughter are indicated. Thus, there is a wide variety of practice in the use of verbatim quotations. Corden and Sainsbury recommend that researchers should decide which approach they want to use and why and be able to justify the choice made if necessary.

Table 28.1

The use of verbatim interview quotations in a table

	Data supporting the theme 'perceptions of a lack of leader competence'	
Associated first-order concepts		Representative quotations
Poor organizational decision process	2.1	'[The associate leader] expressed concern over the lack of information from the office and wondered whether enough was being done to seek out potential leaders to work with the orchestra.' (minutes, BSO orchestra committee meeting) (BSO5)
	2.2	Commenting on the appointment decision process for an orchestra leader: 'It's one incredible grey area. Nobody seems to know what's happening with that and no one seems to know whose responsibility it is. . . . Eventually, the principals just made it so clear that basically they weren't happy [that the appointment was not made]. . . . But we have a theory that he may have promised the guy the job first, and got himself into a pickle.' (interview, BSO orchestra committee member) (BSO5)
	2.3	Commenting on a decision not to terminate a player, a LSO player board member commented: 'There was a decision over this player. The vote was taken and it went against the wishes of the chairman, and he said, "Well okay, we'll call a council of principals meeting". . . . Most of the principals are more than happy to sit on the fence. They've got a hard enough job. They don't want to put their oar in and stir things up, so of course the vote went the other way. Now I think that's a misuse of power, if you like. You're widening the goal posts and moving them at the same time. I was more than a little pissed off about that because it didn't seem to be fair. What was the point of having a [board]?' (interview, LSO player board member) (LSO5)
Poor outcomes of leader decision making	2.4	'Programming is [the senior producer]—you couldn't ask for better repertoire. [The senior producer] is very successful. He has organized some very good programmes and concerts.' (interview, BSO player) (BSO1)
	2.5	'Looking back on all this, I would say that those judgments [of the chief executive] were fatally flawed for our organization on two counts: [the principal conductor's] availability and commitment, and his financial cost.' (interview, PSO player director) (PSO2)
	2.6	'It was like lambs to the slaughter. The contract [the principal conductor] was offered should never have been accepted.' (interview, PSO deputy CEO) (PSO2)
	2.7	'If you look at the main [home city] concerts, something has happened there, and we've lost our thread, because we had three distinct series. . . . So I think the [PSO], represented by the board and the senior management, has a duty to make sure that the repertoire actually fulfils the artistic strategy.' (interview, PSO player chairman-elect) (PSO1)
Lack of leader expertise	2.8	'[We need] someone who knows what they're doing, who has sufficient commercial grasp to know the effect of what they're doing, and appreciates the need to create a programme for [the PSO home city] that will also apply in [other regional towns]. It's that thorough vision that is lacking at the moment, causing all sorts of orchestral problems.' (interview, PSO finance director) (PSO1)
	2.9	'You have someone here [the chief executive] who has no understanding of orchestras at all.' (observation, musicians' union representative, PSO players meeting with musicians' union) (PSO6)

Source: Maitlis and Lawrence (2007: 67); reproduced with permission.

The links with specific items in the literature are clearly outlined.

- The discussion and conclusion elaborate on the significance of the results for the research questions. They also explore the implications of this investigation into early retirement for the theoretical issues that guided the article's opening two sections. In the final paragraph, there is a clear and succinct statement of the article's major theoretical contributions.

Writing up mixed methods research

Partly because interest in and the practice of mixed methods research has gained momentum only in relatively recent times, it has few writing conventions, so that it is difficult to say what an exemplary or model mixed methods research journal article might look like. To a certain extent, it is bound to borrow some of the conventions associated with writing up quantitative and qualitative research in terms of needing to start out with a research focus in the sense of a research problem and/or some research questions. Creswell and Tashakkori (2007: 108), the former editors of the *Journal of Mixed Methods Research*, have suggested that 'good original/empirical mixed methods articles' should be:

- 'well-developed in both quantitative and qualitative components' (Creswell and Tashakkori 2007: 108); and

- 'more than reporting two distinct "strands" of quantitative and qualitative research; these studies must also integrate, link, or connect these "strands" in some way' (Creswell and Tashakkori 2007: 108).

They actually add a third feature of good mixed methods articles—namely, that they contribute to the literature on mixed methods research in some way. This seems a rather tall order for many writers and researchers, so that I would tend to emphasize the other two features.

The first implies that the quantitative and the qualitative components of a mixed methods article should be at the very least competently executed. This means that, in terms of the fundamental criteria for conducting good quantitative and good qualitative research, mixed methods research should conform to both quantitative and qualitative research criteria. In terms of writing, it means that, for each of the components, it should be clear what

the research questions were, how the sampling was done, what the data-collection technique(s) was or were, and how the data were analysed.

The second feature implies that a good mixed methods article will be more than the sum of its parts. This issue relates to a tendency that has been identified by some writers (e.g. Bryman 2007c; O'Cathain et al. 2007) for some mixed methods researchers not to make the best use of their quantitative and qualitative data, in that they often sometimes do not link the two sets of findings so as to extract the maximum yield from their study. As Creswell and Tashakkori (2007: 108) put it:

> The expectation is that, by the end of the manuscript, conclusions gleaned from the two strands are integrated to provide a fuller understanding of the phenomenon under study. Integration might be in the form of comparing, contrasting, building on, or embedding one type of conclusion with the other.

To some extent, when writing up the results from a mixed methods study, researchers might make it easier for themselves to get across the extra yield associated with their investigations if they make clear their rationales for including both quantitative and qualitative components in their overall research strategy. The issue of rationales for conducting mixed methods research is one that was addressed in Chapter 27 (especially Thinking deeply 27.2).

Tips and skills
Do not separate your quantitative from your qualitative findings

I have noticed that some students who conduct mixed methods investigations treat their quantitative and qualitative findings as separate domains, so that they present one set and then the other. In PhD theses and Master's dissertations, this can take the form of separate chapters labelled something like 'survey findings' and 'qualitative interview findings'. This may not be a problem if the two (or more) sets of findings are then integrated with each other in the Discussion sections or chapters. However, treating findings in this way can encourage a view of the quantitative and the qualitative findings as separate spheres and may therefore militate against integration, which, as writers such as Creswell and Tashakkori (2007) imply, is increasingly an expectation in mixed methods studies. Instead, try to think of the quantitative and the qualitative findings thematically across the two sets of results, so that the findings are presented in terms of substantive issues rather than in terms of different methods.

Creswell and Plano Clark (2011: 258–9) provide an example outline structure of a mixed methods dissertation or thesis that derives from a doctoral dissertation submitted at the University of Nebraska-Lincoln. The thesis has separate chapters for the qualitative and then the quantitative results, which is different from the kind of structure proposed by the authors for a mixed methods journal article. This separation of the presentation of the two sets of findings may have been appropriate for the research on which this thesis was based, but I feel uneasy about any implication that it might be a model structure, though Creswell and Plano Clark do not suggest that it is. Separating the quantitative and qualitative findings may sometimes be appropriate—for example, when the overall research project is designed to answer rather separate research questions—but as a general principle I do not think it is advisable.

Further advice on writing up mixed methods research can be found in suggestions in Creswell and Plano Clark's (2011: 264) delineation of a structure for a mixed methods journal article. They suggest that the structure should be along the following lines.

- *Introduction*. This would include such features as: a statement of the research problem or issue; an examination of the literature on the problem/issue; an examination of the problems with the prior literature, which might include indicating why a mixed methods approach would be beneficial, perhaps because much of the previous research is based mainly on just quantitative or qualitative research; and the specific research questions.
- *Methods*. This would include such features as: indicating the rationale for the mixed methods approach; the type of mixed methods design (see Figure 27.2); data-collection and data-analysis methods; and indications of how the quality of the data can be judged.
- *Results*. The quantitative and the qualitative findings might be presented either in tandem or sequentially, but, if the latter, they would need to be merged together in the Discussion.
- *Discussion*. Summarize and explain results, emphasizing the significance of the mixed methods nature of the research and what is gained from the presence of both quantitative and qualitative findings; draw attention to any limitations of the investigation; and possibly suggest avenues for future research.

In terms of the overall structure, Creswell and Plano Clark's (2011) suggestions are more or less the same as for an article based on quantitative research or an article based on qualitative research (see the respective sections on the two types above). It is in the need to outline the mixed methods nature of the research and to bring the two sets of findings together that the distinctiveness of mixed methods writing can be discerned.

An example of mixed methods writing

Many of these features can be seen in the study of the foot and mouth disease (FMD) crisis by Poortinga et al. (2004). This article has been previously encountered in Research in focus 2.8 and 27.3. It may be worth looking back at these two accounts as a reminder of the study. The following examination of the writing of this article is organized in terms of its structure.

Introduction

The article begins with a very strong and clear statement of the focus of the article and its methodological leanings:

Thirty years of empirical work on public perceptions have generated an impressive body of findings on attitudes to the consequences, benefits and institutional profiles of a range of important risk issues . . . However, much of the available research tends to have been conducted when the risk issues studied are not particularly salient in public debate. Although there is some evidence from opinion polling, risk perception studies are rarely conducted during a major risk crisis. The present study examines public attitudes to risk and its management during one such crisis: the 2001 Foot and Mouth Disease (FMD) epidemic in Britain. A mixed method study design was employed, specifically a quantitative survey conducted at the height of the epidemic followed up by qualitative focus groups comprising individuals who had participated in the survey. Recent studies have shown that combining different research methods can provide a more comprehensive view on risk issues than can any one methodology alone.

(Poortinga et al. 2004: 73–4)

This opening passage accomplishes the following:

- It locates the study immediately in the literature on risk.
- It provides a justification for conducting the study on and at the time of the FMD crisis.
- It identifies itself as a mixed methods study *and* provides a rationale for a mixed methods approach.

The authors then go on to outline the structure of the article so that the reader has a route map for what is to come.

The British 2001 foot and mouth crisis

The authors outline the origins of the crisis, its timing, its extent, and its effects. As a result, the reader is left with a clear understanding of the nature of the FMD crisis.

Government policy, trust, and public reactions to the FMD epidemic

This section provides a justification for the researchers' emphasis on the significance of trust in the government and its policies and draws attention to related literature on the topic. For example, the authors draw attention to a study of trust in relation to another food-related crisis in Britain, the BSE crisis:

Losing trust, as occurred to the British government over the BSE (mad cow) crisis in the mid-1990s, may have far-reaching consequences (Slovic, 1993), as people become suspicious about new government policy interpreted in the light of earlier experiences, perhaps turning elsewhere for information and advice. So, it is vitally important to have some gauge of public response. Not only regarding perceptions of the FMD crisis as an event within society, but also as a test case of the impacts of government policy and industry responsiveness in the UK in the wake of the BSE crisis.

(Poortinga et al. 2004: 75)

The authors then outline the nature of their study in broad-brush terms, pointing out that it comprised a survey and focus groups. The authors explain that they emphasized in their research four aspects of FMD and its management (see the subsection on 'Results' below) and that they were also keen to examine how perceptions of these aspects differed between the two communities (see Research in focus 2.8).

Methodology

The discussion of the research design and research methods is divided into three sections.

1. *Study locations.* The two communities—Bude and Norwich—are examined, along with a justification for using these two communities, where the authors write that they wanted 'to find out more about differences in attitudes between communities that were differentially affected by the epidemic' (Poortinga et al. 2004: 75).

2. *The questionnaire survey.* The authors explain how and when the questionnaires were distributed in Bude and Norwich. They outline the kinds and formats of the questions that were asked. They provide the response rates for the two surveys and examine the comparability of the ensuing samples.

3. *Focus groups.* The authors explain that the focus group participants were selected from the questionnaire survey samples. They provide data on the numbers of participants and of focus groups, when they took place, and how long the sessions lasted. The topics for discussion are also summarized.

Results

The findings are organized into four numbered sections, each of which deals with one of the four aspects of FMD and its management that were indicated earlier in the article: public risk perceptions of FMD; blame; government handling of the FMD crisis; and trust in information about FMD. It is striking that, when presenting data for each of the four aspects of FMD, the authors present both the quantitative and the qualitative findings, examining how the two interrelate. For example, when discussing the first of the four aspects—public risk perceptions of FMD—they begin by presenting some questionnaire data about respondents' levels of concern about FMD. These questionnaire data derive from Likert items that asked about levels of agreement with statements such as 'My main concerns about FMD are to do with the possible impacts on the health and welfare of animals'. A table is

presented showing mean levels of agreement with this and five other items, with the data being presented for the whole sample, as well as for Bude and Norwich separately. The authors then present the focus group findings, noting that the 'findings of the focus groups reinforce those of the questionnaire regarding general concern' (Poortinga et al. 2004: 78). The focus groups found, though, that participants were deeply concerned about the slaughter of animals and the rotting carcasses, whereas the questionnaires did not pick up this point. The possible health effects of these rather than of the disease itself was a concern (the survey and the focus group results both suggest that there was a low level of concern about the direct health effects of FMD).

Discussion

The Discussion section begins by outlining the rationale for the mixed methods study and what has been gleaned from it:

> The aim of this mixed methodology study was to investigate public reactions to the FMD epidemic, support for government policies to get FMD under control, and trust in information about FMD. More specifically, a quantitative survey and qualitative focus groups were conducted to examine how two separate communities that were affected to different degrees by the epidemic responded to the crisis. In this study, the focus groups were mainly used to illustrate the findings of the questionnaire. The focus groups provided valuable additional information, especially on the reasons, rationalizations and arguments behind people's understanding of the FMD issue.
>
> (Poortinga et al. 2004: 86)

Thus, the authors restate the mixed methods nature of the investigation and the rationale for the different components. They then proceed to provide a detailed summary of the main findings in which they relate them to other crises, such as the BSE crisis, and to existing literature on crisis management. They reflect in some detail on the differences between responses in Bude and Norwich. The final paragraph provides a very strong concluding statement:

> In conclusion, the combination of a questionnaire survey and a focus group study gave a comprehensive view on people's perceptions and responses to the 2001 FMD epidemic. The unique aspect of this study is that it has captured perceptions *during* the FMD crisis. Although it only gives a snapshot of public attitudes to risk and its management, it provided a vivid picture of people's perceptions and debates on FMD at the height of the epidemic. Further research may provide insight in the dynamics and the long-term effects of the disease. Some studies have shown that risk perception can be related

to the amount of press coverage that is given to that particular risk (Renn et al. 1992). Additional studies may provide answers on how a range of different drivers, such as the media, policy measures, and local and individual events (see e.g. Pidgeon et al. 2003) take on various levels of importance for people's reaction to a crisis such as FMD. Taken as a whole, this study suggests that risk perceptions of a crisis are embedded in both local and national social contexts.

(Poortinga et al. 2004: 89; emphasis in original)

This final paragraph is significant and well crafted for several reasons:

- The first sentence restates the mixed methods nature of the study and that its primary rationale was to provide a 'comprehensive' overview of the topic.

- The major contribution of the research—that it was conducted in the course of the crisis—is suggested to the reader in the second sentence.

- The third sentence provides a brief indication of a limitation of the study ('only gives a snapshot') but then invites the reader not to dwell on this limitation by suggesting that the research 'provided a rich description'.

- The next three sentences suggest future potentially fruitful avenues for enquiry.

- The last sentence provides a final message for readers to take away with them—namely, that 'risk perceptions

of a crisis are embedded in both local and national social contexts'.

This is a very strong final and concluding paragraph that leaves readers in no doubt about what the authors believe is the major contribution of their findings and that reminds readers of the significance of the fact that it is a mixed methods study.

One striking feature is that in terms of structure and overall approach the article is quite similar to the quantitative and the qualitative research articles previously examined. Indeed, it was noted that the structure and approach of the qualitative research article were not dissimilar to those of the quantitative one. These similarities can be attributed to the fact that there are general conventions about how findings should be written up for academic audiences, and these conventions act as a template for, and to some extent constrain, much academic writing. What *is* distinctive about the article by Poortinga et al. is their inclination to make as much of the mixed methods status and context of their research as possible, as recommended in the guidelines suggested by Creswell and Plano Clark (2011).

While attention to the writing-up of mixed methods research is an area that is in its infancy, the suggestions of writers such as Creswell and Tashakkori (2007) and Creswell and Plano Clark (2011), mentioned above, along with strong exemplars such as the article by Poortinga et al., provide helpful pointers to the ways in which this task should be approached.

Student experience
Writer's block

Sometimes when writing we feel as though the words will not come out. Rebecca Barnes writes that, when this happened to her, it usually meant that she needed to return to her data to work out what exactly she was trying to say.

> There have been frustrating times when I have been unsure of what to write and have spent many hours staring at a largely blank computer screen. I have now realized that when I experience this, it is usually because I need to return to the data and spend more time planning what I want to say, how, and why it matters.

Isabella Robbins's response to similar problems was to try to write every day:

> Sometimes just getting words on the page is difficult. I have set myself the task of writing 1,000 words a day, no matter how incoherent they are. I can usually achieve this. I have tried to put the thesis into the realm of 'good enough' and 'the last part of my research training' rather than it being 'something exceptional'.

 To read more, go to the Online Resource Centre: www.oxfordtextbooks.co.uk/orc/brymansrm5e/

Academic writing

When you reach the point that you have to write up your own research, remember that academic writing is a technical form of writing. It has its own conventions, many of which have been covered in this chapter. It is important to follow the guidelines that you have been given by your university, but also to become acquainted with the conventions of academic writing. It is a precise form of writing, and readers can be very unforgiving about vagueness and a failure to incorporate the expected components of academic writing (Research in the news 28.1 presents some tips from editors of academic journals). It is also a form of writing which requires that

you justify most of your key decisions and assertions. You may select a certain theoretical perspective as your point of departure, but you need to justify why that is an appropriate theory. Similarly, do not simply assert your research questions and the focus of your research—you need to demonstrate why those research questions and the focus of your research are important and significant, and this means justifying them. Also, you need to justify the methods that you have employed. This means that you need to justify your research design, your sampling approach, your data collection methods, and your approach to data analysis.

Research in the news 28.1
Tips from editors about how to publish in an academic journal

This is almost certainly stretching the idea of 'research in the news' but on 3 January 2015, the *Guardian* published an article in which journal editors from several disciplines gave their view about what you need to do in order to get an article accepted in an academic journal. Many of the suggestions are specific to journal publishing (such as making sure you pick the right journal) but several others have a broader applicability to academic writing and are relevant to students. I would particularly emphasize the following:

1. 'Focus on a story that progresses logically, rather than chronologically.' This means planning the flow of what you are going to write before starting your writing.

2. 'Don't try to write and edit at the same time.' Doing this may adversely affect your ability to write creatively.

3. 'Don't bury your argument like a needle in a haystack.' The editor who made this point wrote: '[the] argument should appear in your abstract and in the very first paragraph (even the first line) of your paper. Don't make us hunt for your argument as for a needle in a haystack…Oh, and make sure your argument runs all the way through the different sections of the paper and ties together the theory and empirical material.' This is basically about making sure you have an argument that runs through your paper (see Figure 28.1) and ensuring that it is apparent.

4. 'Ask a colleague to check your work.' For you as a student, this is likely to mean setting up reciprocal arrangements whereby you and your fellow students give each other feedback and also ensuring that you respond to feedback from your supervisor.

5. 'Don't over-state your methodology.' The editor who wrote this gives the example of ethnography which she says is 'trendy' but 'a couple of interviews in a café do not constitute ethnography. Be clear—early on—about the nature and scope of your data collection.' This raises the issue of when a qualitative study can be regarded as ethnographic (see Thinking deeply 19.5), but it is mainly about ensuring transparency about your research methods and not claiming more from them than is legitimate.

6. One of the editors also wrote about the importance of responding positively and creatively to comments you receive as feedback.

These tips echo many of those proposed in this chapter.

See: **www.theguardian.com/education/2015/jan/03/how-to-get-published-in-an-academic-journal-top-tips-from-editors** (accessed 7 January 2015).

In addition to taking into consideration the items in the checklist below and the other advice in this chapter, I would strongly recommend reading a few articles to become familiar with such conventions as how a literature review is presented; how it is linked to research questions; how an argument is constructed and maintained throughout; what needs to be included in the methods section; and what goes into (and indeed does not go into) the presentation of findings, the discussion, and the conclusions. The 'methods section' is often a source of problems. In addition to needing to ensure that you justify your choice of methods, as suggested in the previous paragraph, you need to ensure that your account of your methods is comprehensive. Remember the 'three Cs' (Zhang and Shaw 2012) outlined above.

It is important to recall the advice given in Chapter 5 concerning writing a literature review. The literature review can often be the point at which students fail to do justice to their research. As Reuber (2010) notes, because the literature review tends to appear early in a dissertation or article, it can create either a favourable impression or a negative one. The writer of a dissertation can improve their credibility at an early stage by providing a thoughtful literature review with a strong and clear argument.

Academic writing also tends to provide lots of signposts. As noted above, students often worry about giving away the plot if they do this, but it is actually a key element in academic writing. For example, in an article based on a cross-national study of religiosity in relation to volunteering, Ruiter and De Graaf (2006) conclude one section as follows:

> Parboteeah, Cullen, and Lim (2004) also find a strong positive effect of the national religious context, but unfortunately they do not control for church attendance at the individual level. We try to add to this research by providing new hypotheses on the influence of religious context and by testing them on a large-scale, international comparative dataset containing information on volunteering in 53 countries between 1981 and 2001.

> (Ruiter and De Graaf 2006: 192-3)

In this way, they establish that there is a problem with one of the most relevant studies *and* provide a clear signpost about what they are going to do in their article. They then move on to an outline of the relevant theory and their hypotheses. Having outlined their hypotheses concerning religiosity and volunteering, they have another section that presents hypotheses that begins:

> So far, we have formulated hypotheses on the impact of individual religiosity on volunteering. Next, we elaborate on the relation between the national religious context and volunteer work. This relation is somewhat neglected in the literature.

> (Ruiter and De Graaf 2006: 194)

Thus, the writing includes signposts about what is coming next along with a justification for the directions that the article will be taking. The authors also provide useful indications of where they have been so far in the journey ('So far, we have formulated hypotheses'), which gives additional meaning to the significance of the signposts of what is to come. When writing up your own research, try to provide some signposts along the way to give your reader a sense of where you are going and why, as well as some indications of where you have been.

Ensure that you are familiar with the writing conventions required by your department or institution. One of these is whether it is acceptable to use the word 'I' (the first person singular). Sometimes, you are required to write in the third person, such as:

> 'a questionnaire was administered' rather than 'I administered a questionnaire'

> 'it will be argued that' rather than 'I will argue'

> 'it has been shown that' rather than 'I have shown that'

> 'a thematic analysis was carried out' rather than 'I carried out a thematic analysis'

As Billig (2013) observes, third person writing is sometimes advocated because it conveys a sense of objectivity, but it does so at the cost of the disappearance of the researcher from the text. In the quotations from Ruiter and De Graaf in the previous paragraph, it is notable that they write in the first person plural and not in the third person ('*we* try to', '*we* have formulated', and '*we* elaborate'). I have an impression that third person writing is declining in popularity and that the researcher more frequently appears in the text. This is also a good thing from a stylistic point of view, as third person writing can sometimes lead to very tortuous sentences. I much prefer writing in the first person but I would advise you to find out what the conventions are in your department or institution.

Remember that writing is fundamentally about persuasion. You are trying to convince your readers of the quality of your work and of the contribution to understanding you are making. It is therefore important to write in a way that grabs the reader's attention and interest and not to provide your reader with ammunition with which to shoot you down (such as a methods section that is not comprehensive or poorly justified decisions). All too often, students rush writing up, and this was a recurring theme in many of the accounts that formed the basis for the Student experience boxes in this book. If writing is rushed, there is a risk that insufficient attention will be given to such things as writing style and constructing and maintaining an argument. Also, as I have suggested on several occasions, when presenting your research findings, many if not most conventions of

Tips and skills
How to write an article for *American Anthropologist*

It might appear perverse to have a boxed feature on how to write an article for *American Anthropologist* in a book that is principally aimed at the needs of students and early career researchers. *American Anthropologist* is a long-standing journal that has been in publication since 1888 and is a highly regarded outlet for the work of social anthropologists. Its editor, Tom Boellstorff, has written two articles advising readers how to get an article published in the journal and adds '(or anywhere)'. In other words, what Boellstorff (2008, 2010) aimed to provide was good advice about how to get an article published in most good peer-reviewed journals. What he offers is good advice that transcends both discipline and the style of research (for example, whether quantitative or qualitative or mixed methods). Moreover, it is sound advice to bear in mind for anyone who is writing for an academic audience. He recommends:

1. *Be professional.* Scrutinize your work for typos and grammatical errors. If you have used Word's Track Changes facility, make sure you have removed all evidence of it by confirming or rejecting all tracked changes.

2. *Link your data and your claims.* Boellstorff writes that one of the most common faults he encounters in his capacity as an editor is that the author's data and what they have inferred from the data are not aligned. Most notably, inferences are not sustainable from the data presented.

3. *Do not make sweeping generalizations.* Sweeping generalizations are far too easy to criticize so they are best avoided. Boellstorff says that articles often begin with such generalizations without any subsequent evidence to sustain them.

4. *Make effective use of citations.* Too often, Boellstorff suggests, authors fail to refer to significant work in the very area they are writing about. It is crucial to refer to the relevant areas of literature.

5. *Make sure that the typescript has an effective structure.* Boellstorff writes that it is crucial to ensure that there is a clear introduction and conclusion and that the intervening sections are well balanced in terms of length. Also, the thread of the article's core argument needs to be sustained throughout the article. Too often, he says, claims are made at the end of an article for which the prior evidence or reasoning is not apparent.

6. *Demonstrate your contribution.* Make clear what the contribution of your argument and findings is and why it is important to know it. Simply saying that something has not been studied before is not sufficient.

7. *Engage with the literature.* It is crucial not just to cite relevant references (see point 4 above) but also to engage with relevant literature. Boellstorff suggests that it is important to demonstrate a clear familiarity with the classic and more recent literature on a topic. He also recommends emphasizing literature that you found particularly influential in your own thinking and making clear why it is significant. Also, rather than what he calls a 'name-dropping' style of referencing, he advocates drawing out a sense that there is a community of scholars working on a certain topic and demonstrating how your own work will add significantly to that.

8. *Do not give data second hand.* Boellstorff argues that it is crucial to 'show' some of your data. I suspect that Boellstorff had in mind writing up qualitative investigations when he made this point. He suggests that it is important to show some of your interview transcript or field note evidence in the course of writing up, so that statements about what you found can be sustained. In other words, do not just summarize or generalize about what you found. Provide some of the evidence that lies behind what you say you found.

9. *Demonstrate the research methods used.* Be clear about how the data were collected in terms of sampling, measurement of concepts, techniques of data collection, analytic approaches, and so on. Information about when the research was done and over what period are also important to remember. I would add to this point that it is also crucial to justify your research methods. Why was a postal questionnaire or semi-structured interview used? Why are these documents appropriate to this research question?

10. *Keep revising.* Boellstorff suggests that revising should be a core element of writing. Your written output should be reread and revised on at least one occasion (and preferably more). Revising allows internal inconsistencies, poor phrasing, breaks in the argument, and key items of missing information to be addressed.

academic writing transcend the quantitative/qualitative/mixed methods distinctions. One of these, which has been mentioned several times in this article, is the need for a clear argument that runs through your work, so ensure that there is a clear flow from beginning to end and not a series of often unrelated points. Finally, do remember that research is a long haul and, if at all possible, try to find a topic that interests you, because you are much more likely to write about it in an engaged and engaging way.

Student experience *and* supervisor tips
Being interested

Alexandra Scherer was drawing on experience with her Master's dissertation on children's responses to representations of the child in award-winning picture books when she wrote:

> Make sure you have picked something you are fascinated in as your research question and topic, and that it is feasible to do in the time frame you have allocated, because if you are anything less than fascinated you will end up hating it by the end, and even if you are fascinated in it, there will still be times in the long process where you feel that there is no point in it and that what you have done is worthless! Everyone loses a sense of perspective about their research project at some point!

William Mason, when asked one bit of advice he would give to students beginning a research project, replied in similar terms:

> Choose something you enjoy and make it yours! This is your chance to be self-indulgent with your studies. Your dissertation is probably the longest piece of academic work you will have ever done and it's going to be a real slog if you choose the wrong topic. If you can choose a topic that suits you, you'll enjoy the process and this will almost definitely be reflected in your marks.

Similar views were expressed by several of the supervisors. They were asked what personal qualities and types of behaviour make for a successful dissertation student. Supervisor F replied:

> It would be fair to say, *pace* Blair, 'interest, interest, interest'—there is a strong correlation between how interested the student is in a topic, his or her engagement with the research process, and a quality outcome.

Similarly, Supervisor G wrote:

> A student has to want to write something like a dissertation or doctorate for more than a qualification. It has to be personal to be enjoyable.

Checklist
Issues to consider for writing up a piece of research

○ Have you clearly specified and justified your research questions?

○ Have you clearly indicated how the literature you have read relates to your research questions?

○ Is your discussion of the literature critical and organized so that it is not just a summary of what you have read?

○ Have you clearly outlined your research design and your research methods, including:

○ why you chose a particular research design?

○ why you chose a particular research method?

○ how you selected your research participants?

○ whether there were any issues to do with cooperation (for example, response rates)?

○ why you implemented your research in a particular way (for example, how the interview questions relate to your research questions, why you observed participants in particular situations, why your focus group guide asked the questions in a particular way and order)?

○ if your research required access to an organization, how and on what basis was agreement for access forthcoming?

○ steps you took to ensure that your research was ethically responsible?

○ how you analysed your data?

○ any difficulties you encountered in the implementation of your research approach?

○ Have you presented your findings in a manner that relates to your research questions?

○ Does your discussion of your findings show how they relate to your research questions?

○ Does your discussion of your findings show how they shed light on the literature that you presented?

○ Are the interpretations of the data that you offer fully supported with tables, figures, or segments from transcripts?

○ If you have presented tables and/or figures, are they properly labelled with a title and number?

○ If you have presented tables and/or figures, are they commented upon in your discussion?

○ Do your conclusions clearly allow the reader to establish what your research contributes to the literature?

○ Have you explained the limitations of your study?

○ Do your conclusions consist solely of a summary of your findings? If they do, rewrite them!

○ Do your conclusions make clear the answers to your research questions?

○ Does your presentation of the findings and the discussion allow a clear argument and narrative to be presented to the reader?

○ Have you broken up the text in each chapter with appropriate subheadings?

○ Does your writing avoid sexist, racist, and disablist language?

○ Have you included all appendices that you might need to provide (for example, interview schedule, letters requesting access, communications with research participants)?

○ Have you checked that your list of references includes *all* the items referred to in your text?

○ Have you checked that your list of references follows precisely the style that your institution requires?

○ Have you followed your supervisor's suggestions when he or she has commented on your draft chapters?

○ Have you got people other than your supervisor to read your draft chapters for you?

○ Have you checked to ensure that there is not excessive use of jargon?

○ Do you provide clear signposts in the course of writing, so that readers are clear about what to expect next and why it is there?

○ Have you ensured that your institution's requirements for submitting projects are fully met in terms of such issues as word length (so that it is neither too long nor too short) and whether an abstract and table of contents are required?

○ Have you ensured that you do not quote excessively when presenting the literature?

○ Have you fully acknowledged the work of others so that you cannot be accused of plagiarism?

○ Is there a good correspondence between the title of your project and its contents?

○ Have you proof read your writing?

○ Have you acknowledged the help of others where this is appropriate (for example, your supervisor, people who may have helped with interviews, people who read your drafts)?

» Key points

- Good writing is probably just as important as good research practice. Indeed, it is probably better thought of as a part of good research practice.
- Clear structure and a clear statement of your research questions are important components of writing up research.
- Be sensitive to the ways in which writers seek to persuade us of their points of view.
- The examination of writing strategies generally teaches us that social scientists do more than simply report findings.
- Writing is about persuasion. We all want to get our points across and to persuade our readers that we have got things right. We need to ask: Do we do it well? Do we make the best possible case? We all have to persuade others that we have got the right angle on things; the trick is to do it well. So, when you write an essay or dissertation, do bear in mind the significance of your writing strategy.
- It is crucial to have a clear argument running through your report of your work.
- Ensure that you are familiar with the conventions of academic writing.

? Questions for review

- Why is it important to consider the ways in which social research is written up?

Writing up your research

- Why is it important to be clear about your main argument when writing up your findings?

Writing up quantitative research

- Read an article based on quantitative research in a British sociology journal. How far does it exhibit the same characteristics as Kelley and De Graaf's (1997) article?
- What is meant by rhetorical strategy? Why might rhetorical strategies be important in relation to the writing-up of social research?

Writing up qualitative research

- Read an article based on qualitative research in a British sociology journal. How far does it exhibit the same characteristics as the article by Jones et al. (2010)?

- How far is the structure of the article by Jones et al. different from Kelley and De Graaf's?

- If you were writing up the results of a qualitative interview study you had undertaken, what would be your approach to using (or indeed not using) verbatim quotations from your transcripts?

Writing up mixed methods research

- Read an article based on mixed methods research in a British sociology journal.

- How far does it exhibit the same characteristics as the one by Poortinga et al. (2004)?

- How far does it succeed in integrating the quantitative and the qualitative findings?

Academic writing

- Outline some of the chief ways in which academic writing is distinctive.

Online Resource Centre
www.oxfordtextbooks.co.uk/orc/brymansrm5e/

Visit the Online Resource Centre to enrich your understanding of writing up social research. Follow up links to other resources, test yourself using multiple choice questions, and gain further guidance and inspiration from the Student Researcher's Toolkit.

Glossary

Terms with an entry elsewhere in the Glossary are in colour.

Abductive, abduction A form of reasoning with strong ties to *induction* that grounds social scientific accounts of social worlds in the perspectives and meanings of participants in those social worlds.

Action research An approach in which the action researcher and a client collaborate in the diagnosis of a problem and in the development of a solution based on the diagnosis.

Ad libitum sampling A sampling approach in *structured observation* whereby whatever is happening at the moment that observation is due to occur is recorded.

Adjacency pair The tendency for certain kinds of activity in talk to be characterized by linked phases.

Analytic induction An approach to the analysis of qualitative data in which the researcher seeks universal explanations of phenomena by pursuing the collection of data until no cases that are inconsistent with a hypothetical explanation (deviant or negative cases) of a phenomenon are found.

Arithmetic mean ($\bar{x}$) Also known simply as the 'mean', this is the everyday average-namely, the total of a *distribution of values* divided by the number of values.

Asynchronous online interview or focus group Online interviews may be asynchronous or *synchronous*. In the case of the former, the transactions between participants are not in real time, so that there may be long spaces of time between interviewers' questions and participants' replies, and, in the case of focus groups, between participants' contributions to the discussion.

Attached email questionnaire survey A survey in which respondents are sent a questionnaire, which is received as an attachment by email. Compare with *embedded email questionnaire survey*.

Audit trail. A term borrowed from accounting which, when transferred to social research, refers to ensuring that records are kept of key decisions in the research process and that an evidence base is maintained to ensure that the main findings and concepts are fully supported.

Behaviour sampling A sampling approach in *structured observation* whereby an entire group is watched and the observer records who was involved in a particular kind of behaviour.

Big Data Refers to extremely large sources of data that are not immediately amenable to conventional ways of analysing them.

Biographical method See *life history method*.

Bivariate analysis The examination of the relationship between two variables, as in *contingency tables* or *correlation*.

CAPI. An abbreviation of *computer-assisted personal interviewing*.

CAQDAS An abbreviation of *computer-assisted* (or *-aided*) *qualitative data analysis*.

Case study A *research design* that entails the detailed and intensive analysis of a single case. The term is sometimes extended to include the study of just two or three cases for comparative purposes. However, *multiple-case study* is the more common term for the examination of two or more cases.

Categorical variable See *nominal variable*.

Category In *grounded theory*, a category occupies a space between a researcher's initial theoretical reflections on and understanding of his or her data and a *concept*, which is viewed as a higher level of abstraction. Thus, a category has an intermediate position in terms of abstraction between *coding* and a theory.

CATI. An abbreviation of *computer-assisted telephone interviewing*.

Causality A concern with establishing causal connections between variables, rather than mere *relationships* between them.

Cell The point in a table, such as a *contingency table*, where the rows and columns intersect.

Census The enumeration of an entire *population*. Unlike a *sample*, which comprises a count of some units in a population, a census relates to all units in a population. Thus, if a *postal questionnaire* is mailed to every person in a town or to all members of a profession, the research should be characterized as a census.

Chi-square test Chi-square (χ^2) is a test of *statistical significance*, which is typically employed to establish how confident we can be that the findings displayed in a *contingency table* can be generalized from a *probability sample* to a *population*.

Closed-ended question A question employed in an *interview schedule* or *self-administered questionnaire* that presents the respondent with a set of possible answers to choose from. Also called 'fixed-choice question' and *pre-coded question*. Compare with *open-ended question*.

Cluster sample A sampling procedure in which at an initial stage the researcher samples areas (i.e. clusters) and then samples units from these clusters, usually using a *probability sampling* method.

Code, coding In quantitative research, codes are numbers that are assigned to data about people or other units of analysis when the data are not inherently numerical. In questionnaire-based research, the answer to a question (e.g. 'strongly agree') is assigned a number (e.g. 5) so that the information can be statistically processed. Thus, each person who answers 'strongly agree' will receive the same number (in this case 5). When answers are textual, respondents' answers must be grouped into categories and those categories are then coded. In qualitative research, coding is the process whereby data are broken down into component parts, which are given names.

Coding frame A listing of the codes used in relation to the analysis of data. In relation to answers to a structured interview schedule or questionnaire, the coding frame will delineate the categories used in connection with each question. It is particularly crucial in relation to the coding of *open-ended questions*. With *closed-ended questions*, the coding frame is essentially incorporated into the pre-given answers, hence the frequent use of the term *pre-coded question* to describe such questions.

Coding manual In *content analysis*, this is the statement of instructions to coders that outlines all the possible categories for each dimension being coded.

Coding schedule In *content analysis*, this is the form onto which all the data relating to an item being coded will be entered.

Comparative design A *research design* that entails the comparison of two or more cases in order to illuminate existing theory or generate theoretical insights as a result of contrasting findings uncovered through the comparison.

Computer-assisted personal interviewing (CAPI). A face-to-face survey interview in which the interviewer reads out questions as they appear on a computer and keys in respondents' answers. The software automates the skipping of questions that do not need to be asked due to the operation of *filter questions*.

Computer-assisted (or -aided) qualitative data analysis (CAQDAS). The use of computer software to provide an environment in which textual materials can be processed and analysed.

Computer-assisted telephone interviewing (CATI). A survey interview carried out over the telephone in which the interviewer reads out questions as they appear on a computer and keys in respondents' answers. The software automates the skipping of questions that do not need to be asked due to the operation of *filter questions*.

Concept A name given to a grouping of phenomena that organizes observations and ideas by virtue of their possessing common features. In *grounded theory*, a concept is a key building block in the construction of a theory.

Concurrent validity One of the main approaches to establishing *measurement validity*. It entails relating a measure to a criterion on which cases (e.g. people) are known to differ and that is relevant to the *concept* in question.

Confounding variable A variable that is related to each of two variables the result of which is to produce the appearance of a relationship between the two variables. Such a relationship is a *spurious relationship*.

Connotation, connotative A term used in *semiotics* to refer to the principal and most manifest meaning of a *sign*. Compare with *denotation*.

Constant An attribute in terms of which cases do not differ. Compare with *variable*.

Constant comparison A central tool of *grounded theory* that entails constantly comparing new data with existing data, concepts, and categories. It also entails comparing categories with each other and categories with concepts.

Construct validity. An assessment of the *measurement validity* of a measure that tests hypotheses deduced from a theory that is relevant to the underlying concept. If the findings are consistent with the theory, confidence in the validity of the measure is enhanced.

Constructionism, constructionist An *ontological* position (often also referred to as 'constructivism') that asserts that social phenomena and their meanings are continually being accomplished by social actors. It is antithetical to *objectivism*.

Constructivism See *constructionism*.

Content analysis An approach to the analysis of documents and texts that seeks to quantify content in terms of predetermined categories and in a systematic and replicable manner. The term is sometimes used in connection with qualitative research as well-see *qualitative content analysis*.

Contingency table A table, comprising rows and columns, that shows the *relationship* between two *variables*. Usually, at least one of the variables is a *nominal variable*. Each *cell* in the table shows the frequency of occurrence of the intersection of categories of each of the two variables and usually a percentage.

Continuous recording A procedure in *structured observation* whereby observation occurs for extended periods so that the frequency and duration of certain types of behaviour can be carefully recorded.

Control group See *experiment*.

Convenience sample, sampling A sample that is selected because of its availability to the researcher. It is a form of *non-probability sample*.

Convergent validity An assessment of the *measurement validity* of a measure that compares it to another measure of the same concept that has been generated from a different method.

Conversation analysis The fine-grained analysis of talk as it occurs in interaction in naturally occurring situations. The talk is recorded and *transcribed* so that the detailed analyses can be carried out. The analysis is concerned with uncovering the underlying structures of talk in interaction and as such with the achievement of order through interaction. Conversation analysis is grounded in *ethnomethodology*.

Core category In *grounded theory* this is a *category* that acts as an over-arching motif that brings together other categories.

Correlation An approach to the analysis of relationships between *interval/ratio variables* and/or *ordinal variables* that seeks to assess the strength and direction of the relationship between the variables concerned. *Pearson's r* and *Spearman's rho* are both methods for assessing the level of correlation between variables.

Covert research A term frequently used in connection with *ethnographic* research in which the researcher does not reveal his or her true identity. Such research violates the ethical principle of *informed consent*.

Cramér's V A method for assessing the strength of the relationship between two variables, at least one of which must have more than two categories.

Critical discourse analysis A form of *discourse analysis* that emphasizes the role of language as a power resource that is related to ideology and socio-cultural change. It draws in particular on the work of Foucault.

Critical realism A *realist* epistemology that asserts that the study of the social world should be concerned with the identification of the structures that generate that world. Critical realism is 'critical' because its practitioners aim to identify structures in order to change them, so that inequalities and injustices may be counteracted. Unlike a *positivist* epistemology, critical realism accepts that the structures that are identified may not be amenable to the senses. Thus, whereas *positivism* is *empiricist*, critical realism is not.

Cross-sectional design A *research design* that entails the collection of data on a *sample* of cases and at a single point in time in order to collect a body of quantitative or quantifiable data in connection with two or more variables (usually many more than two), which are then examined to detect patterns of association.

Data saturation The principle that the researcher should continue sampling cases until no new insights are apparent in the data. See also, *theoretical saturation*.

Deductive, deduction An approach to the relationship between theory and research in which the latter is conducted with reference to hypotheses and ideas inferred from the former. Compare with *inductive*.

Denotation, denotative A term used in *semiotics* to refer to the meanings of a *sign* associated with the social context within which it operates that are supplementary to and less immediately apparent than its *connotation*.

Dependent variable A *variable* that is causally influenced by another variable (i.e. an *independent variable*).

Diary A term that in the context of social research methods can mean different things. Three types of diary can be distinguished: diaries written or completed at the behest of a researcher; personal diaries that can be analysed as a *personal document*, but that were produced spontaneously; and diaries written by social researchers as a log of their activities and reflections.

Dichotomous variable A variable with just two categories.

Dimension Refers to an aspect of a *concept*.

Discourse analysis An approach to the analysis of talk and other forms of discourse that emphasizes the ways in which versions of reality are accomplished through language.

Distribution of values A term used to refer to the entire data relating to a *variable*. Thus, the ages of members of a *sample* represent the distribution of values for that variable for that sample.

Ecological fallacy The error of assuming that inferences about individuals can be made from aggregate data.

Ecological validity A concern with the question of whether social scientific findings are relevant and applicable to people's everyday, natural social settings.

Embedded email questionnaire survey A social survey in which respondents are sent an email that contains a *questionnaire*. Compare with *attached email questionnaire survey*.

Empiricism An approach to the study of reality that suggests that only knowledge gained through experience and the senses is acceptable.

Epistemology, epistemological A theory of knowledge. It is particularly employed in this book to refer to a stance on what should pass as acceptable knowledge. See *positivism*, *realism*, and *interpretivism*.

Eta(η) A test of the strength of the *relationship* between two variables. The *independent variable* must be a *nominal variable* and the *dependent variable* must be an *interval variable* or *ratio variable*. The resulting level of correlation will always be positive.

Ethnographic content analysis See *qualitative content analysis*.

Ethnography, ethnographer Like *participant observation*, a research method in which the researcher immerses him- or herself in a social setting for an extended period of time, observing behaviour, listening to what is said in conversations both between others and with the fieldworker, and asking questions. However, the term has a more inclusive sense than participant observation, which seems to emphasize the observational component. Also, the term 'an ethnography' is frequently used to refer to the written output of ethnographic research.

Ethnomethodology A sociological perspective concerned with the way in which social order is accomplished through talk and interaction. It provides the intellectual foundations of *conversation analysis*.

Evaluation research Research that is concerned with the evaluation of real-life interventions in the social world.

Event sampling. See *experience sampling*.

Experience sampling Also called 'event sampling', experience sampling refers to various methods that seek to capture affective states and/or behaviour at certain points in time. These 'points in time' are determined by the researcher and when they occur, research participants have to record such things as what they are doing or how they are feeling.

Experiment A *research design* that rules out alternative causal explanations of findings deriving from it (i.e. possesses *internal validity*) by having at least (a) an experimental group, which is exposed to a treatment, and a control group, which is not, and (b) *random assignment* to the two groups. Instead of a control group, an experiment may comprise a further group (or groups) that are exposed to other treatments.

Experimental group See *experiment*.

External validity A concern with the question of whether the results of a study can be generalized beyond the specific research context in which it was conducted.

Face validity A concern with whether an *indicator* appears to reflect the content of the *concept* in question.

Facilitator See *moderator*.

Factor analysis A statistical technique used for large numbers of *variables* to establish whether there is a tendency for groups of them to be inter-related. It is often used with *multiple-indicator measures* to see if the *indicators* tend to bunch to form one or more groups of indicators. These groups of indicators are called factors and must then be given names.

Field notes A detailed chronicle by an *ethnographer* of events, conversations, and behaviour, and the researcher's initial reflections on them.

Field stimulation A study in which the researcher directly intervenes in and/or manipulates a natural setting in order to observe what happens as a consequence of that intervention.

File drawer problem This occurs when research is conducted but it is found that the independent variable does not have the intended effect or the variables examined are unrelated, and as a result difficulty is experienced in publishing the findings. It is often suggested that the findings are then simply filed away in a drawer. The file drawer problem can produce bias when summarizing a field of research and especially when a *systematic review* (in particular a *meta-analysis*) is being conducted.

Filter question A question that is constructed so that on the basis of their replies, some respondents will answer another question to which the filter question is linked, whereas others will skip to a later question. For example, the filter question might ask respondents whether they have driven while intoxicated, but will only ask about the number of times that has happened to those respondents who reply 'Yes'; other respondents (those who have answered 'No') will skip to a later question.

Focal sampling A sampling approach in *structured observation* whereby a sampled individual is observed for a set period of time. The observer records all examples of whatever forms of behaviour are of interest.

Focus group A form of group interview in which there are several participants (in addition to the *moderator*); there is an emphasis in the questioning on a particular fairly tightly defined topic; and the emphasis is upon interaction within the group and the joint construction of meaning.

Frequency table A table that displays the number and/or percentage of units (e.g. people) in different categories of a variable.

Generalization, generalizability A concern with the *external validity* of research findings.

Grounded theory An iterative approach to the analysis of qualitative data that aims to generate theory out of research data by achieving a close fit between the two.

Hermeneutics A term drawn from theology, which, when imported into the social sciences, is concerned with the theory and method of the interpretation of human action. It emphasizes the need to understand from the perspective of the social actor.

Hypothesis An informed speculation, which is set up to be tested, about the possible relationship between two or more variables.

Independent variable A *variable* that has a causal impact on another variable (i.e. a *dependent variable*).

Index See *scale*.

Indicator A measure that is employed to refer to a *concept* when no direct measure is available.

Inductive, induction An approach to the relationship between theory and research in which the former is generated out of the latter. Compare with *deductive*.

Inferential statistics The domain of inferential statistics refers to tests of *statistical significance* that are used in inferring qualities of a *population* from data about a *sample* drawn randomly from that population. This process is referred to as *statistical inference*.

Informed consent A key principle in social research ethics. It implies that prospective research participants should be given as much information as might be needed to make an informed decision about whether or not they wish to participate in a study.

Inter-rater reliability The degree to which two or more individuals agree about the *coding* of an item.

Inter-rater reliability is likely to be an issue in *content analysis*, *structured observation*, and when *coding* answers to *open-ended questions* in research based on *questionnaires* or *structured interviews*.

Internal reliability The degree to which the indicators that make up a *scale* are consistent.

Internal validity A concern with the question of whether a finding that incorporates a causal relationship between two or more variables is sound.

Internet survey A very general term used to include any social survey conducted online. As such, it includes the *Web survey*, the *attached email questionnaire survey*, and the *embedded email questionnaire survey*.

Interpretative repertoire A collection of linguistic resources that are drawn upon in order to characterize and assess actions and events.

Interpretivism An *epistemological* position that requires the social scientist to grasp the subjective meaning of social action.

Interval variable A *variable* where the distances between the categories are identical across its range of categories.

Intervening variable A *variable* that is affected by another variable and that in turn has a causal impact on another variable. Taking an intervening variable into account often facilitates the understanding of the relationship between two variables. Also called a 'mediating variable'.

Interview guide A rather vague term that is used to refer to the brief list of memory prompts of areas to be covered that is often employed in *unstructured interviewing* or to the somewhat more structured list of issues to be addressed or questions to be asked in *semi-structured interviewing*.

Interview schedule A collection of questions designed to be asked by an interviewer. An interview schedule is always used in a *structured interview*.

Intra-rater reliability The degree to which an individual differs over time in the *coding* of an item. Intra-rater reliability is likely to be an issue in *content analysis*, *structured observation*, and when *coding* answers to *open-ended questions* in research based on *questionnaires* or *structured interviews*.

Item This term is used in *survey research* based on *questionnaires* and *structured interviews*. It refers to a statement to which the respondent is expected to respond in terms of a predetermined format (for example, by indicating his or her level of agreement or disagreement). A *Likert scale* is the kind of context in which items are encountered, as it is made up of several items. In effect, an item is a question on a questionnaire or interview schedule, but the term 'item' is preferred as it comprises a statement rather than a question in the sense that there is no question mark.

Item non-response The failure to respond to an *item* on the part of a survey respondent. See also *missing data*.

Key informant Someone who offers the researcher, usually in the context of conducting an *ethnography*, perceptive information about the social setting, important events, and individuals.

Life history interview Similar to the *oral history interview*, but the aim of this type of *unstructured interview* is to glean information on the entire biography of each respondent.

Life history method Also often referred to as the 'biographical method', this method emphasizes the inner experience of individuals and its connections with changing events and phases throughout the life course. The method usually entails *life history interviews* and the use of *personal documents* as data.

Likert scale A widely used format developed by Rensis Likert for asking attitude questions. Respondents are typically asked their degree of agreement with a series of statements that together form a *multiple-indicator* or *-item* measure. The scale is deemed then to measure the intensity with which respondents feel about an issue.

Longitudinal research A *research design* in which data are collected on a *sample* (of people, documents, etc.) on at least two occasions.

Mail questionnaire Traditionally, this term has been synonymous with the *postal questionnaire*, but with the arrival of email-based questionnaires (see *embedded email questionnaire survey* and *attached email questionnaire survey*), many writers prefer to refer to postal rather than mail questionnaires.

Maximum variation sampling A *purposive sampling* approach which is conducted to ensure as wide a variation as possible in terms of the dimension(s) of interest.

Mean See *arithmetic mean*.

Measure of central tendency A statistic, such as the *arithmetic mean*, *median*, or *mode*, that summarizes a *distribution of values*.

Measure of dispersion A statistic, such as the *range* or *standard deviation*, that summarizes the amount of variation in a *distribution of values*.

Measurement validity The degree to which a measure of a *concept* truly reflects that concept. See also *concurrent validity*, *construct validity*, *convergent validity*, *face validity*, and *predictive validity*.

Median The mid-point in a *distribution of values*.

Mediating variable Another term for intervening variable.

Member validation See *respondent validation*.

Meta-analysis A form of *systematic review* that involves summarizing the results of a large number of quantitative studies and conducting various analytical tests to show whether or not a particular variable has an effect across the studies.

Meta-ethnography A form of *systematic review* that is used to achieve interpretative synthesis of *qualitative research* studies and other secondary sources, thus providing a counterpart to *meta-analysis* in *quantitative research*.

Missing data Data relating to a case that are not available-for example, when a respondent in *survey research* does not answer a question. These are referred to as 'missing values' in *SPSS*. The term *item non-response* is often used to refer to unanswered questions.

Mixed methods research A term that is increasingly employed to describe research that combines both *quantitative research* and *qualitative research*. The term can be employed to describe research that combines just quantitative research methods or that combines just qualitative research methods. However, in recent times, it has taken on this more specific meaning of combining quantitative and qualitative research methods.

Mixed mode survey A *survey* that offers respondents more than one method of answering questionnaires, such as when *postal questionnaire* respondents are given the option of answering by *Web survey*.

Mode The value that occurs most frequently in a *distribution of values*.

Moderated relationship A *relationship* between two *variables* is said to be moderated when it holds for one category of a third variable but not for another category or other categories.

Moderator The person who guides the questioning of a *focus group*. Also called a 'facilitator'.

Multiple-case study A research design in which the researcher examines two or more cases in detail, usually but not necessarily to compare the findings deriving from the cases.

Multiple-indicator measure A measure that employs more than one *indicator* to measure a *concept*.

Multiple-item measure A measure that is made up of more than one *item*.

Multivariate analysis The examination of *relationships* between three or more *variables*.

Narrative analysis An approach to the elicitation and analysis of data that is sensitive to the sense of temporal sequence that people, as tellers of stories about their lives or events around them, detect in their lives and surrounding episodes and inject into their accounts. However, the approach is not exclusive to a focus on life histories.

Narrative review An approach to reviewing the literature that is often contrasted nowadays with a *systematic review*. It tends to be less focused than a systematic review and seeks to arrive at a critical interpretation of the literature that it covers.

Naturalism A confusing term that has at least three distinct meanings: a commitment to adopting the principles of natural scientific method; being true to the nature of the phenomenon being investigated; and a style of research that seeks to minimize the intrusion of artificial methods of data collection.

Negative relationship A *relationship* between two *variables* whereby as one increases the other decreases.

Netnography A form of *ethnography* which is applied to online or largely online communities. It has mainly been used in relation to topics in the fields of marketing and retailing.

Nominal variable Also known as a 'categorical variable', this is a variable that comprises categories that cannot be rank ordered.

Non-manipulable variable A *variable* that cannot readily be manipulated either for practical or for ethical reasons and that therefore cannot be employed as an *independent variable* in an *experiment*.

Non-probability sample A sample that has not been selected using a *random sampling* method. Essentially, this implies that some units in the population are more likely to be selected than others.

Non-response A source of *non-sampling error* that occurs whenever some members of a sample refuse to cooperate, cannot be contacted, or for some reason cannot supply the required data. This is more properly called 'unit non-response' to distinguish it from *item non-response*.

Non-sampling error Differences between the *population* and the *sample* that arise either from deficiencies in the sampling approach, such as an inadequate *sampling frame* or *non-response*, or from problems such as poor question wording, poor interviewing, or flawed processing of data.

Null hypothesis A *hypothesis* of no relationship between two variables.

NVivo A *CAQDAS* package that facilitates the management and analysis of qualitative data.

Objectivism An *ontological* position that asserts that social phenomena and their meanings have an existence that is independent of social actors. Compare with *constructionism*.

Observation schedule A device used in *structured observation* that specifies the categories of behaviour that are to be observed and how behaviour should be allocated to those categories.

Official statistics Statistics compiled by or on behalf of state agencies in the course of conducting their business.

Ontology, ontological A theory of the nature of social entities. See *objectivism* and *constructionism*.

Open-ended question A question employed in an *interview schedule* or *self-administered questionnaire* that does not present the respondent with a set of possible answers to choose from. Compare with *closed-ended question*.

Operational definition The definition of a *concept* in terms of the operations to be carried out when measuring it.

Operationism, operationalism A doctrine, mainly associated with an area of physics, that emphasizes the search for *operational definitions* of *concepts*.

Optimizing A cognitive process involved in answering survey questions that entails maximizing the amount of effort involved. The respondent expends a great deal of effort to arrive at the best possible answer. Compare with *satisficing*.

Oral history interview A largely *unstructured interview* in which the respondent is asked to recall events from his or her past and to reflect on them.

Ordinal variable A variable whose categories can be rank ordered (as in the case of *interval* and *ratio variables*), but the distances between the categories are not equal across the range.

Outlier An extreme value in a *distribution of values*. If a *variable* has an extreme value—either very high or very low—the *arithmetic mean* or the *range* will be distorted by it.

Paradigm A term deriving from the history of science, where it was used to describe a cluster of beliefs and dictates that for scientists in a particular discipline influence what should be studied, how research should be done, and how results should be interpreted.

Participant observation Research in which the researcher immerses him- or herself in a social setting for an extended period of time, observing behaviour, listening to what is said in conversations both between others and with the fieldworker, and asking questions. Participant observation usually includes interviewing *key informants* and studying documents and as such is difficult to distinguish from *ethnography*. In this book, 'participant observation' is employed to refer to the specifically observational aspect of ethnography.

Pearson's *r* A measure of the strength and direction of the *relationship* between two *interval/ratio variables*.

Personal documents Documents such as *diaries*, letters, and autobiographies that are not written for an official purpose. They provide first-person accounts of the writer's life and events within it.

Phenomenology A philosophy that is concerned with the question of how individuals make sense of the world around them and how in particular the philosopher should bracket out preconceptions concerning his or her grasp of that world.

Phi Phi (Φ) is a method for assessing the strength of the *relationship* between two *dichotomous variables*.

Photo-elicitation Typically, photo-elicitation is a visual research methods that entails getting interviewees to discuss one or more photographs in the course of an interview. The photograph(s) may be extant or may have been taken by the interviewee for the purpose of the research.

Population The universe of units from which a *sample* is to be selected.

Positive relationship A *relationship* between two *variables*, whereby as one increases the other increases as well.

Positivism An *epistemological* position that advocates the application of the methods of the natural sciences to the study of social reality and beyond.

Postal questionnaire A form of *self-administered questionnaire* that is sent to respondents and usually returned by them by postal mail.

Postmodernism A position that displays a distaste for master-narratives and for a *realist* orientation. In the context of research methodology, postmodernists display a preference for qualitative methods and a concern with the modes of representation of research findings.

Pre-coded question Another name for a *closed-ended question*. The term is often preferred, because such a question removes the need for the application of a *coding frame* to the question after it has been answered. This is because the range of answers has been predetermined and a numerical *code* will have been pre-assigned to each possible answer. The term is particularly appropriate when the codes appear on the *questionnaire* or *interview schedule*.

Predictive validity. An assessment of the *measurement validity* of a measure of a concept that uses a future benchmark as a criterion.

Probability sampling, sample A sample that has been selected using *random sampling* and in which each unit in the population has a known probability of being selected.

Purposive sampling, sample A form of *non-probability sample* in which the researcher aims to sample cases or participants in a strategic way, so that those sampled are relevant to the *research questions* that are being posed.

Qualitative content analysis An approach to documents that emphasizes the role of the investigator in the construction of the meaning of and in texts. There is an emphasis on allowing categories to emerge out of data and on recognizing the significance, for understanding the meaning of the context in which an item being analysed (and the categories derived from it) appeared. Also called 'ethnographic content analysis'.

Qualitative research Qualitative research usually emphasizes words rather than quantification in the collection and analysis of data. As a *research strategy* it is *inductivist*, *constructionist*, and *interpretivist*, but qualitative researchers do not always subscribe to all three of these features. Compare with *quantitative research*.

Quantitative research Quantitative research usually emphasizes quantification in the collection and analysis of data. As a *research strategy* it is *deductivist* and *objectivist* and incorporates a natural science model of the research process (in particular, one influenced by *positivism*), but quantitative researchers do not always subscribe to all three of these features. Compare with *qualitative research*.

Quasi-experiment A *research design* that is close to being an *experiment* but that does not meet the requirements fully and therefore does not exhibit complete *internal validity*.

Questionnaire A collection of questions administered to respondents. When used on its own, the term usually denotes a *self-administered questionnaire*.

Quota sample, quota sampling A *sample* in which participants are non-randomly sampled from a *population* in terms of the relative proportions of people in different categories. It is a type of *non-probability sample*.

Random assignment A term used in connection with *experiments* to refer to the random allocation of research participants to the experimental group and the control group.

Random digit dialling (RDD) A method of sampling, usually for a *computer-administered telephone interview (CATI)* survey, whereby telephone numbers are randomly generated.

Random sampling Sampling whereby the inclusion of a unit of a *population* occurs entirely by chance.

Randomized controlled trial A term used to describe a study that meets the criteria of a true *experiment*. The term is used in fields such as the health sciences in which the goal is to test the effectiveness of an intervention, such as a clinical intervention.

Range The difference between the maximum and the minimum value in a *distribution of values* associated with an *interval* or *ratio variable*.

Rapid review A literature review that conforms to the main principles of a *systematic review* but is deliberately limited in scope so that the review can be completed in a relatively short time.

Ratio variable An *interval variable* with a true zero point.

RDD An abbreviation of *random digit dialling*.

Reactivity, reactive effect A term used to describe the response of research participants to the fact that they know they are being studied. Reactivity is deemed to result in untypical behaviour.

Realism An epistemological position that acknowledges a reality independent of the senses that is accessible to the researcher's tools and theoretical speculations. It implies that the categories created by scientists refer to real objects in the natural or social worlds. See also *critical realism*.

Reflexivity A term used in research methodology to refer to a reflectiveness among social researchers about the implications, for the knowledge that they generate about the social world, of their methods, values, biases, decisions, and mere presence in the very situations they investigate.

Relationship An association between two variables whereby the variation in one variable coincides with variation in another variable. See also *negative relationship* and *positive relationship*.

Reliability The degree to which a measure of a concept is stable. See also *internal reliability*.

Replication, replicability The degree to which the results of a study can be reproduced.

Representative sample A *sample* that reflects the population accurately, so that it is a microcosm of the *population*.

Research design This term is employed in this book to refer to a framework or structure within which the collection and analysis of data takes place. A choice of research design reflects decisions about the priority being given to a range of dimensions of the research process (such as causality and generalization) and is influenced by the kind of *research question* that is posed.

Research question An explicit statement in the form of a question of what it is that a researcher intends to find out about. A research question not only influences the scope of an investigation but also how the research will be conducted.

Research strategy A term used in this book to refer to a general orientation to the conduct of social research (see *quantitative research* and *qualitative research*).

Respondent validation Sometimes called 'member validation', this is a process whereby a researcher provides the people on whom he or she has conducted research with an account of his or her findings and requests feedback on that account.

Response set The tendency among some respondents to *multiple-indicator measures* to reply in the same way to each constituent item.

Retroductive, retroduction A form of reasoning that entails making an inference about the causal mechanism that lies behind and is responsible for regularities that are observed in the social world. It is very much associated with *critical realism*.

Rhetoric, rhetorical A concern with the ways in which appeals to convince or persuade are devised.

Sample The segment of the population that is selected for research. It is a subset of the *population*. The method of selection may be based on *probability sampling* or *non-probability sampling* principles.

Sampling error Differences between a *random sample* and the *population* from which it is selected.

Sampling frame The listing of all units in the *population* from which a *sample* is selected.

Satisficing A cognitive process involved in answering survey questions that entails minimizing the amount of effort involved. The respondent does not expend enough effort to arrive at the best possible answer. Compare with *optimizing*.

Scale A term that is usually used interchangeably with 'index' to refer to a *multiple-indicator measure* in which the score a person gives for each component *indicator* is used to provide a composite score for that person.

Scan sampling A sampling approach in *structured observation* whereby an entire group of individuals is scanned at regular intervals and the behaviour of all of them is recorded at each occasion.

Secondary analysis The analysis of data by researchers who will probably not have been involved in the collection of those data, for purposes that may not have been envisaged by those responsible for the data collection. Secondary analysis may entail the analysis of either quantitative data or qualitative data.

Self-administered questionnaire A *questionnaire* that the respondent answers without the aid of an interviewer. Sometimes called a 'self-completion questionnaire'.

Self-completion questionnaire See *self-administered questionnaire*.

Semiotics The study/science of *signs*. An approach to the analysis of documents and other phenomena that emphasizes the importance of seeking out the deeper meaning of those phenomena. A semiotic approach is concerned to uncover the processes of meaning production and how signs are designed to have an effect upon actual and prospective consumers of those signs.

Semi-structured interview A term that covers a wide range of types of interview. It typically refers to a context in which the interviewer has a series of questions that are in the general form of an *interview guide* but is able to vary the sequence of questions. The questions are frequently somewhat more general in their frame of reference than those typically found in a *structured interview* schedule. Also, the interviewer usually has some latitude to ask further questions in response to what are seen as significant replies.

Sensitizing concept A term devised by Blumer to refer to a preference for treating a *concept* as a guide in an investigation, so that it points in a general way to what is relevant or important. This position contrasts with the idea of an *operational definition*, in which the meaning of a concept is fixed in advance of carrying out an investigation.

Sign A term employed in *semiotics*. A sign is made up of a signifier (the manifestation of a sign) and the signified (that idea or deeper meaning to which the signifier refers).

Simple observation The passive and unobtrusive observation of behaviour.

Simple random sample A *sample* in which each unit has been selected entirely by chance. Each unit of the *population* has a known and equal probability of inclusion in the sample.

Snowball sample A *non-probability sample* in which the researcher makes initial contact with a small group of people who are relevant to the research topic and then uses these to establish contacts with others.

Social desirability bias A distortion of data that is caused by participants responding to data collection exercises in terms of socially desirable traits so that their accounts conform to their perceptions of socially acceptable beliefs or behaviour.

Social survey See *survey research*.

Spearman's rho (ρ) A measure of the strength and direction of the *relationship* between two *ordinal variables*.

SPSS Short for **S**tatistical **P**ackage for the **S**ocial **S**ciences. SPSS is a widely used computer program that allows quantitative data to be managed and analysed.

Spurious relationship A *relationship* between two *variables* is said to be spurious if it is being produced by the impact of a third variable (often referred to as a *confounding variable*) on each of the two variables that form the spurious relationship. When the third variable is controlled, the relationship disappears.

Standard deviation A measure of dispersion around the *mean*.

Standard error of the mean An estimate of the amount that a sample *mean* is likely to differ from the population mean (μ).

Standardized interview See *structured interview*.

Statistical inference The process of inferring characteristics of a *population* from information about a *sample* drawn randomly from that population. See *statistical significance (test of)*.

Statistical significance (test of) Allows the analyst to estimate how confident he or she can be that the results deriving from a study based on a randomly selected *sample* are generalizable to the *population* from which the sample was drawn. Such a test does not allow the researcher to infer that the findings are of substantive importance. The *chi-square test* is an example of this kind of test. The process of using a test of statistical significance to generalize from a sample to a population is known as *statistical inference*.

Stratified random sample A *sample* in which units are *randomly sampled* from a *population* that has been divided into categories (strata).

Structured interview A research interview usually in the context of *survey research* in which all respondents are asked exactly the same questions in the same order with the aid of a formal *interview schedule*.

Structured observation Often also called 'systematic observation', structured observation is a technique in which the researcher employs explicitly formulated rules for the observation and recording of behaviour. The rules inform observers about what they should look for and how they should record behaviour.

Survey research A *cross-sectional design* in relation to which data are collected predominantly by *self-administered questionnaire* or by *structured interview* on a *sample* of cases drawn from a wider *population* and at a single point in time in order to collect a body of quantitative or quantifiable data in connection with a number of *variables*, which are then examined to detect patterns of *relationships* between variables.

Symbolic interactionism A theoretical perspective in sociology and social psychology that views social interaction as taking place in terms of the meanings actors attach to action and things.

Synchronous online interview or focus group Online interviews may be *asynchronous* or synchronous. In the case of the latter, the transactions between participants are in real time, so that there there will be only brief time lapses between interviewers' questions and participants' replies, and, in the case of focus groups, between participants' contributions to the discussion.

Systematic observation See *structured observation*.

Systematic review Systematic reviews are reviews of the literature in a domain that aim to provide an account of the literature that is comprehensive, capable of *replication*, and transparent in its approach. Systematic reviews pay close attention to assessing the quality of research in deciding whether a study should be included or not. *Meta-analysis* and *meta-ethnography* are both forms of systematic review.

Systematic sample A *probability sampling* method in which units are selected from a *sampling frame* according to fixed intervals, such as every fifth unit.

Test of statistical significance See *statistical significance (test of)*.

Text A term that is used either in the conventional sense of a written work or in more recent years to refer to a wide range of phenomena. For example, in arriving at a *thick description*, Geertz refers to treating culture as a text.

Thematic analysis A term used in connection with the analysis of qualitative data to refer to the extraction of key themes in one's data. It is a rather diffuse approach with few generally agreed principles for defining core themes in data.

Thematic synthesis Essentially, the application of *thematic analysis* to the synthesis of a set of qualitative studies in an area to arrive at an overall sense of what they show.

Theoretical sampling, sample A term used mainly in relation to *grounded theory* to refer to *purposive sampling* carried out so that emerging theoretical considerations guide the selection of cases and/or research participants. Theoretical sampling is supposed to continue until a point of *theoretical saturation* is reached.

Theoretical saturation In *grounded theory*, the point when emerging *concepts* have been fully explored and no new theoretical insights are being generated. See also *theoretical sampling*.

Thick description A term devised by Geertz to refer to detailed accounts of a social setting that can form the basis for the creation of general statements about a culture and its significance in people's social lives.

Time sampling In *structured observation*, a sampling method that entails using a criterion for deciding when observation will occur.

Transcription, transcript The text version of a recorded interview or *focus group* session.

Triangulation The use of more than one method or source of data in the study of a social phenomenon so that findings may be cross-checked.

Trustworthiness A set of criteria advocated by some writers for assessing the quality of *qualitative research*.

Turn-taking The notion from *conversation analysis* that order in everyday conversation is achieved through orderly taking of turns.

Unit non-response See *non-response*.

Univariate analysis The analysis of a single *variable* at a time.

Unobtrusive methods Methods that do not entail an awareness among research participants that they are being studied and that are therefore not subject to *reactivity*.

Unstructured interview An interview in which the interviewer typically has only a list of topics or issues, often called an *interview guide*, that are typically covered. The style of questioning is usually very informal. The phrasing and sequencing of questions will vary from interview to interview.

Validity A concern with the integrity of the conclusions that are generated from a piece of research. There are different aspects of validity. See, in particular, *measurement validity*, *internal validity*, *external validity*, and *ecological validity*. When used on its own, *validity* is usually taken to refer to *measurement validity*.

Variable An attribute in terms of which cases vary. See also *dependent variable* and *independent variable*. Compare with *constant*.

Web survey A survey conducted so that respondents complete a *questionnaire* via a website.

References

Abraham, J. (1994). 'Bias in Science and Medical Knowledge: The Opren Controversy', *Sociology*, 28: 717–36.

Abrams, K. M., Wang, Z., Song, Y. J., and Galindo-Gonzalez, S. (2015). 'Data Richness Trade-Offs Beteeen Face-to-Face, Online Audiovisual, and Online Text-Only Focus Groups', *Social Science Computer Review*, 33: 80–96.

Ackroyd, S. (2009) 'Research Designs for Realist Research', in D. Buchanan and A. Bryman (eds), *Handbook of Organizational Research Methods*. London: Sage.

Adler, P., and Adler, P. A. (1985). 'From Idealism to Pragmatic Detachment: The Academic Performance of College Athletes', *Sociology of Education*, 58: 241–50.

Adler, P. A. (1985). *Wheeling and Dealing: An Ethnography of an Upper-Level Drug Dealing and Smuggling Community*. New York: Columbia University Press.

Adler, P. A., and Adler, P. (1987). *Membership Roles in Field Research*. Sage University Paper Series on Qualitative Research Methods, 6. Newbury Park, CA: Sage.

Adler, P. A., and Adler, P. (2008). 'Of Rhetoric and Representation: The Four Faces of Ethnography', *Sociological Quarterly*, 49: 1–30.

Adler, P. A., and Adler, P. (2009). 'Using a Gestalt Perspective to Analyze Children's Worlds', in A. J. Puddephatt, W. Shaffir, and S. W. Kleinknecht (eds), *Ethnographies Revisited: Constructing Theory in the Field*. London: Routledge.

Adler, P. A., and Adler, P. (2012). Contribution to S. E. Baker and R. Edwards (eds), *How Many Qualitative Interviews is Enough? Expert Voices and Early Career Reflections on Sampling and Cases in Qualitative Research*. National Centre for Research Methods Review Paper. http://eprints.ncrm.ac.uk/2273/ (accessed 19 November 2014)

Adriaenssens, C., and Cadman, L. (1999). 'An Adaptation of Moderated E-mail Focus Groups to Assess the Potential of a New Online (Internet) Financial Services Offer in the UK', *Journal of the Market Research Society*, 41: 417–24.

Akerlof, K., Maibach, E. W., Fitzgerald, D., and Cedeno, A. Y. (2013). 'Do People "Personally Experience" Global Warming, and if so How, and Does it Matter?', *Global Environmental Change*, 23: 81–91.

Alderson, P. (1998). 'Confidentiality and Consent in Qualitative Research', *Network: Newsletter of the British Sociological Association*, 69: 6–7.

Allison, G. T. (1971). *Essence of Decision: Explaining the Cuban Missile Crisis*. Boston: Little, Brown.

Altheide, D. L. (1980). 'Leaving the Newsroom', in W. Shaffir, R. A. Stebbins, and A. Turowetz (eds), *Fieldwork Experience: Qualitative Approaches to Social Research*. New York: St Martin's Press.

Altheide, D. L., and Schneider, C. J. (2013). *Qualitative Media Analysis*, 2nd edn. Los Angeles: Sage.

Altschuld, J. W., and Lower, M. A. (1984). 'Improving Mailed Questionnaires: Analysis of a 96 Percent Return Rate', in D. C. Lockhart (ed.), *Making Effective Use of Mailed Questionnaires*. San Francisco: Jossey-Bass.

Alvesson, M., and Kärreman, D. (2000). 'Varieties of Discourse: On the Study of Organization through Discourse Analysis', *Human Relations*, 53 (9): 1125–49.

Alvesson, M., and Sandberg, J. (2013). *Constructing Research Questions: Doing Interesting Research*. London: Sage.

Andersen, M. (1981). 'Corporate Wives: Longing for Liberation or Satisfied with the Status Quo?', *Urban Life*, 10: 311–27.

Anderson, E. (1978). *A Place on the Corner*. Chicago: University of Chicago Press.

Anderson, E. (2006). 'Jelly's Place: An Ethnographic Memoir', in D. Hobbs and R. Wright (eds), *The SAGE Handbook of Fieldwork*. London: Sage.

Ang, I. (1985). *Watching Dallas: Soap Opera and the Melodramatic Imagination*. London: Methuen.

Angell, E., Bryman, A., Ashcroft, R., and Dixon-Woods, M. (2008). 'An Analysis of Decision Letters by Research Ethics Committees: The Ethics/Scientific Quality Boundary Examined', *Quality and Safety in Health Care*, 17: 131–6.

Arber, S., and Gilbert, G. N. (1989). 'Transitions in Caring: Gender, Life Course and the Care of the Elderly', in B. Bytheway, T. Keil, P. Allatt, and A. Bryman (eds), *Becoming and Being Old: Sociological Approaches to Later Life*. London: Sage.

Armstrong, D., Gosling, A., Weinman, J., and Marteau, T. (1997). 'The Place of Inter-Rater Reliability in Qualitative Research: An Empirical Study', *Sociology*, 31: 597–606.

Armstrong, G. (1993). 'Like that Desmond Morris?', in D. Hobbs and T. May (eds), *Interpreting the Field: Accounts of Ethnography*. Oxford: Clarendon Press.

Armstrong, G. (1998). *Football Hooligans: Knowing the Score*. Oxford: Berg.

Aronson, E., and Carlsmith, J. M. (1968). 'Experimentation in Social Psychology', in G. Lindzey and E. Aronson (eds), *The Handbook of Social Psychology*. Reading, MA: Addison-Wesley.

Asch, S. E. (1951). 'Effect of Group Pressure upon the Modification and Distortion of Judgments', in H. Guetzkow (ed.), *Groups, Leadership and Men*. Pittsburgh: Carnegie Press.

Atkinson, J. M., and Drew, P. (1979). *Order in Court: The Organization of Verbal Interaction in Judicial Settings*. London: Macmillan.

Atkinson, P. (1981). *The Clinical Experience*. Farnborough: Gower.

Atkinson, P. (1990). *The Ethnographic Imagination: Textual Constructions of Society*. London: Routledge.

Atkinson, P. (2006). *Everyday Arias: An Operatic Ethnography*. Oxford: AltaMira Press.

Atkinson, P., and Coffey, A. (2011). 'Analysing Documentary Realities', in D. Silverman (ed.), *Qualitative Research: Issues of Theory, Method and Practice*. 3rd edn. London: Sage.

Atkinson, R. (1998). *The Life Story Interview*. Beverly Hills, CA: Sage.

Atkinson, R. (2004). 'Life Story Interview', in M. S. Lewis-Beck, A. Bryman, and T. F. Liao (eds), *The Sage Encyclopedia of Social Science Research Methods*. 3 vols. Thousand Oaks, CA: Sage.

Atkinson, R., and Kintrea, K. (2001). 'Disentangling Area Effects: Evidence from Deprived and Non-Deprived Neighbourhoods', *Urban Studies*, 38: 2277–98.

Attar, A., and Genus, A. (2014). 'Framing Public Engagement: A Critical Discourse Analysis of GM Nation?', *Technological Forecasting and Social Change*, 88: 241–50.

Attride-Stirling, J. (2001). 'Thematic Networks: An Analytic Tool for Qualitative Research', *Qualitative Research*, 1: 385–404.

Bagguley, P., and Hussain, Y. (in press). 'Negotiating Mobility: South Asian Women and Higher Education', *Sociology*, doi: 10.1177/0038038514554329

Bahr, H. M., Caplow, T., and Chadwick, B. A. (1983). 'Middletown III: Problems of Replication, Longitudinal Measurement, and Triangulation', *Annual Review of Sociology*, 9: 243–64.

Bailey, A., Giangola, L., and Boykoff, M. T. (2014). 'How Grammatical Choice Shapes Media Representations of Climate (Un)certainty', *Environmental Communication*, 8: 197–215.

Ball, S. J. (1981). *Beachside Comprehensive: A Case Study of Secondary Schooling*. Cambridge: Cambridge University Press.

Ball, S. J. (1984). 'Beachside Reconsidered: Reflections on a Methodological Apprenticeship', in R. G. Burgess (ed.), *The Research Process in Educational Settings: Ten Case Studies*. London: Falmer Press.

Bampton, R., and Cowton, C. J. (2002). 'The E-Interview', *Forum Qualitative Social Research*, 3, **www.qualitative-research.net/fqs** (accessed 18 February 2015).

Banks, J. (2012). 'Edging Your Bets: Advantage Play, Gambling, Crime and Victimisation', *Crime Media Culture*, 9: 171–87.

Banks, J. (2014). 'Online Gambling, Advantage Play, Reflexivity and Virtual Ethnography', in K. Lumsden and A. Winter (eds), *Reflexivity in Criminological Research: Experiences with the Powerful and the Powerless*. Basingstoke: Palgrave Macmillan.

Banks, M. (2001). *Visual Methods in Social Research*. London: Sage.

Barbour, R. (2007). *Doing Focus Groups*. London: Sage.

Barker, E. (1984). *The Making of a Moonie: Choice or Brainwashing?* Oxford: Blackwell.

Barley, S. R., and Kunda, G. (2004). *Gurus, Hired Guns, and Warm Bodies*. Princeton: Princeton University Press.

Barnard, M., and Frischer, M. (1995). 'Combining Quantitative and Qualitative Approaches: Researching HIV-Related Risk Behaviours among Drug Injectors', *Addiction Research*, 2: 351–62.

Barter, C., and Renold, E. (1999). 'The Use of Vignettes in Qualitative Research', *Social Research Update*, 25.

Baruch, Y. (1999). 'Response Rate in Academic Studies—A Comparative Analysis', *Human Relations*, 52: 421–38.

Bauman, Z. (1978). *Hermeneutics and Social Science: Approaches to Understanding*. London: Hutchison.

Baumgartner, J. C., and Morris, J. S. (2010). 'MyFaceTube Politics: Social Networking Web Sites and Political Engagement of Young Adults', *Social Science Computer Review*, 28: 24–44.

Bazeley, P. (2013). *Qualitative Data Analysis: Practical Strategies*. London: Sage.

Beardsworth, A. (1980). 'Analysing Press Content: Some Technical and Methodological Issues', in H. Christian (ed.), *Sociology of Journalism and the Press*. Keele: Keele University Press.

Beardsworth, A., and Bryman, A. (2004). 'Meat Consumption and Meat Avoidance among Young People: An 11-Year Longitudinal Study', *British Food Journal*, 106: 313–27.

Beardsworth, A., Bryman, A., Ford, J., and Keil, T. (n.d.). '"The Dark Figure" in Statistics of Unemployment and Vacancies: Some Sociological Implications', discussion paper, Department of Social Sciences, Loughborough University.

Bechhofer, F., Elliott, B., and McCrone, D. (1984). 'Safety in Numbers: On the Use of Multiple Interviewers', *Sociology*, 18: 97–100.

Beck, U. (1992). *The Risk Society: Towards a New Modernity*. London: Sage.

Becker, H. S. (1958). 'Problems of Inference and Proof in Participant Observation', *American Sociological Review*, 23: 652–60.

Becker, H. S. (1963). *Outsiders: Studies in the Sociology of Deviance*. New York: Free Press.

Becker, H. S. (1967). 'Whose Side are We On?', *Social Problems*, 14: 239–47.

Becker, H. S. (1982). 'Culture: A Sociological View', *Yale Review*, 71: 513–27.

Becker, H. S. (1986). *Writing for Social Scientists: How to Start and Finish Your Thesis, Book, or Article*. Chicago: University of Chicago Press.

Becker, H. S., and Geer, B. (1957). 'Participant Observation and Interviewing: A Comparison', *Human Organization*, 16: 28–32.

Becker, S., Bryman, A., and Sempik, J. (2006). *Defining 'Quality' in Social Policy Research: Views, Perceptions and a Framework for Discussion*. Lavenham: Social Policy Association, **www.social-policy.org.uk/downloads/defining%20 quality%20in%20social%20policy%20research.pdf** (accessed 8 December 2014).

Becker, S., Sempik, J., and Bryman, A. (2010). 'Advocates, Agnostics and Adversaries: Researchers' Perceptions of Service User Involvement in Social Policy Research', *Social Policy and Society*, 9: 355–66.

Belk, R. W., Sherry, J. F., and Wallendorf, M. (1988). 'A Naturalistic Inquiry into Buyer and Seller Behavior at a Swap Meet', *Journal of Consumer Research*, 14: 449–70.

Bell, C. (1969). 'A Note on Participant Observation', *Sociology*, 3: 417–18.

Bell, C., and Newby, H. (1977). *Doing Sociological Research*. London: George Allen & Unwin.

Bell, E., and Bryman, A. (2007). 'The Ethics of Management Research: An Exploratory Content Analysis', *British Journal of Management*, 18: 63–77.

Belson, W. A. (1981). *The Design and Understanding of Survey Questions*. Aldershot: Gower.

Bengtsson, M., Berglund, T., and Oskarson, M. (2013). 'Class and Ideological Orientations Revisited: An Exploration of Class-Based Mechanisms', *British Journal of Sociology*, 64: 691–716.

Bennett, T., Savage, M., Silva, E., Warde, A., Gayo-Cal, M., and Wright, D. (2009). *Culture, Class, Distinction*. London: Routledge.

Benson, M. (2011). *The British in Rural France: Lifestyle Migration and the Ongoing Quest for a Better Way of Life*. Manchester: Manchester University Press.

Benson, M., and Jackson, E. (2013). 'Place-Making and Place Maintenance: Peformativity, Place and Belonging among the Middle Classes', *Sociology*, 47: 793–809.

Benson, M., Bridge, G., and Wilson, D. (2015). 'School Choice in London and Paris—A Comparison of Middle-Class Strategies', *Social Policy and Administration*, 49: 24–53.

Berelson, B. (1952). *Content Analysis in Communication Research*. New York: Free Press.

Berthoud, R. (2000a). 'Introduction: The Dynamics of Social Change', in R. Berthoud and J. Gershuny (eds), *Seven Years in the Lives of British Families: Evidence on the Dynamics of Social Change from the British Household Panel Survey*. Bristol: Policy Press.

Berthoud, R. (2000b). 'A Measure of Changing Health', in R. Berthoud and J. Gershuny (eds), *Seven Years in the Lives of British Families: Evidence on the Dynamics of Social Change from the British Household Panel Survey*. Bristol: Policy Press.

Beullens, K., and Schepers, A. (2013). 'Display of Alcohol Use on Facebook: A Content Analysis', *Cyberpsychology, Behavior, and Social Networking*, 16: 497–503.

Bhaskar, R. (1975). *A Realist Theory of Science*. Leeds: Leeds Books.

Bhaskar, R. (1989). *Reclaiming Reality: A Critical Introduction to Contemporary Philosophy*. London: Verso.

Bickerstaff, K., Lorenzoni, I., Pidgeon, N., Poortinga, W., and Simmons, P. (2008). 'Framing the Energy Debate in the UK: Nuclear Power, Radioactive Waste and Climate Change Mitigation', *Public Understanding of Science*, 17: 145–69.

Bilinski, H., Duggleby, W., and Rennie, D. (2013). 'Lessons Learned in Designing and Conducting a Mixed Methods Study to Explore the Health of Rural Children', *International Journal of Health Promotion and Education*, 51: 1–10.

Billig, M. (1991). *Ideology and Opinions: Studies in Rhetorical Psychology*. Cambridge: Cambridge University Press.

Billig, M. (1992). *Talking of the Royal Family*. London: Routledge.

Billig, M. (2013). *Learn to Write Badly: How to Succeed in the Social Sciences*. Cambridge: Cambridge University Press.

Billig, M., Condor, S., Edwards, D., Gane, M., Middleton, D., and Radley, A. (1988). *Ideological Dilemmas: A Social Psychology of Everyday Thinking*. London: Sage.

Bisdee, D., Daly, T., and Price, D. (2013). 'Behind Closed Doors: Older Couples and the Gendered Management of Household Money', *Social Policy and Society*, 12: 163–74.

Blaikie, A. (2001). 'Photographs in the Cultural Account: Contested Narratives and Collective Memory in the Scottish Islands', *Sociological Review*, 49: 345–67.

Blaikie, N. (2004a). 'Abduction', in M. S. Lewis-Beck, A. Bryman, and T. F. Liao (eds), *The Sage Encyclopedia of Social Science Research Methods*. 3 vols. Thousand Oaks, CA: Sage.

Blaikie, N. (2004b). 'Retroduction', in M. S. Lewis-Beck, A. Bryman, and T. F. Liao (eds), *The Sage Encyclopedia of Social Science Research Methods*. 3 vols. Thousand Oaks, CA: Sage.

Blatchford, P. (2005). 'A Multi-Method Approach to the Study of School Size Differences', *International Journal of Social Research Methodology*, 8: 195–205.

Blatchford, P., Edmonds, S., and Martin, C. (2003). 'Class Size, Pupil Attentiveness and Peer Relations', *British Journal of Educational Psychology*, 73: 15–36.

Blatchford, P., Bassett, P., Brown, P., and Webster, R. (2009). 'The Effect of Support Staff on Pupil Engagement and Individual Attention', *British Educational Research Journal*, 36: 661–86.

Blauner, R. (1964). *Alienation and Freedom*. Chicago: University of Chicago Press.

Bligh, M. C., and Kohles, J. C. (2014). 'Comparing Leaders Across Contexts, Culture, and Time: Computerized Content Analysis of Leader-Follower Communications', *Leadership*, 10: 142–59.

Bligh, M. C., Kohles, J. C., and Meindl, J. R. (2004). 'Charisma under Crisis: Presidential Leadership, Rhetoric, and Media Responses before and after the September 11th Terrorist Attacks', *Leadership Quarterly*, 15: 211–39.

Blom, A.G., Bosnjak, M., Cornilleau, A., Cousteaux, A.-S., Das, M., Douhou, S., and Krieger, U. (in press). 'A Comparison of Four Probability-Based Online and Mixed-Mode Panels in Europe', *Social Science Computer Review*, doi: 10.1177/0894439315574825

Blommaert, L., Coenders, M., and van Tubergen, F. (2014). 'Ethnic Discrimination in Recruitment and Decision Makers' Features: Evidence from Laboratory Experiment and Survey Data using a Student Sample', *Social Indicators Research*, 116: 731–54.

Bloor, M. (1978). 'On the Analysis of Observational Data: A Discussion of the Worth and Uses of Inductive Techniques and Respondent Validation', *Sociology*, 12: 545–52.

Bloor, M. (1997). 'Addressing Social Problems through Qualitative Research', in D. Silverman (ed.), *Qualitative Research: Theory, Method and Practice*. London: Sage.

Bloor, M. (2002). 'No Longer Dying for a Living: Collective Responses to Injury Risks in South Wales Mining Communities, 1900–47', *Sociology*, 36: 89–105.

Bloor, M., Frankland, S., Thomas, M., and Robson, K. (2001). *Focus Groups in Social Research*. London: Sage.

Blumer, H. (1954). 'What is Wrong with Social Theory?', *American Sociological Review*, 19: 3–10.

Blumer, H. (1956). 'Sociological Analysis and the "Variable"', *American Sociological Review*, 21: 683–90.

Blumer, H. (1962). 'Society as Symbolic Interaction', in A. M. Rose, (ed.), *Human Behavior and Social Processes*. London: Routledge & Kegan Paul.

Blyth, B. (2008). 'Mixed Mode: The Only "Fitness" Regime?', *International Journal of Market Research*, 50: 241–66.

Bobbitt-Zeher, D. (2011). 'Connecting Gender Stereotypes, Institutional Policies, and Gender Composition of Workplace', *Gender and Society*, 25: 764–86.

Boellstorff, T. (2008). 'How to Get an Article Accepted at *American Anthropologist* (or Anywhere)', *American Anthropologist*, 110: 281–3.

Boellstorff, T. (2010). 'How to Get an Article Accepted at *American Anthropologist* (or Anywhere), Part 2', *American Anthropologist*, 112: 353–6.

Boepple, L., and Thompson, J. K. (2014). 'A Content Analysis of Healthy Living Blogs: Evidence of Content Thematically Consistent with Dysfunctional Eating Attitudes and Behaviors', *International Journal of Eating Disorders*, 47: 362–7.

Bogdan, R., and Taylor, S. J. (1975). *Introduction to Qualitative Research Methods: A Phenomenological Approach to the Social Sciences*. New York: Wiley.

Bosley, S. L. C., Arnold, J., and Cohen, L. (2009). 'How Other People Shape our Careers: A Typology Drawn from Career Narratives', *Human Relations*, 62: 1487–520.

Bosnjak, M., Metzger, G., and Gräf, L. (2010). 'Understanding the Willingness to Participate in Mobile Surveys: Exploring the Role of Utilitarian, Affective, Hedonic, Social, Self-Expressive, and Trust-Related Factors', *Social Science Computer Review*, 25: 350–70.

Bosnjak, M., Neubarth, W., Couper, M. P., Bandilla, W., and Kaczmirek, L. (2008). 'Prenotification in Web-based Access Panel Surveys: The Influence of Mobile Text Messaging Versus E-mail on Response Rates and Sample Composition', *Social Science Computer Review*, 26: 213–23.

Bottomore, T. B., and Rubel, M. (1963). *Karl Marx: Selected Writings in Sociology and Social Philosophy*. Harmondsworth: Penguin.

Bourdieu, P. (1984). *Distinction: A Social Critique of the Judgement of Taste*. Cambridge, MA: Harvard University Press.

Bowen, G. A. (2008). 'Naturalistic Inquiry and the Saturation Concept: A Research Note', *Qualitative Research*, 8: 137–52.

Bradburn, N. A., and Sudman, S. (1979). *Improving Interview Method and Questionnaire Design*. San Francisco: Jossey-Bass.

Brannen, J. (2013). 'Life Story Talk: Some Reflections on Narrative in Qualitative Interviews', *Sociological Research Online*, 18, www.socresonline.org.uk/18/2/15.html (accessed 29 December 2014).

Brannen, J., and Nilsen, A. (2006). 'From Fatherhood to Fathering: Tradition and Change Among British Fathers in Four-Generation Families', *Sociology*, 40: 335–52.

Brannen, J., Lewis, S., Nilsen, A., and Smithson, J. (2002). *Young Europeans, Work and Family: Futures in Transition*. London: Routledge.

Brannen, J., O'Connell, R., and Mooney, A. (2013). 'Families, Meals, and Synchronicity: Eating Together in British Dual Earner Families', *Community, Work and Family*, 16: 417–34.

Braun, V., and Clarke, V. (2006). 'Using Thematic Analysis in Psychology', *Qualitative Research in Psychology*, 3: 77–101.

Braverman, H. (1974). *Labor and Monopoly Capital: The Degradation of Work in the Twentieth Century*. London: Monthly Review Press.

Brayfield, A., and Rothe, H. (1951). 'An Index of Job Satisfaction', *Journal of Applied Psychology*, 35: 307–11.

Bregoli, I. (2013). 'Effects of DMO Coordination on Destination Brand Identity: A Mixed-Method Study of the City of Edinburgh', *Journal of Travel Research*, 52: 212–24.

Brennan, M., and Charbonneau, J. (2009). 'Improving Mail Survey Response Rates Using Chocolate and Replacement Questionnaires', *Public Opinion Quarterly*, 73: 368–78.

Brewster, Z. W., and Lynn, M. (2014). 'Black-White Earnings Gap among Restaurant Servers: A Replication, Extension, and Exploration of Consumer Racial Discrimination in Tipping', *Sociological Inquiry*, 84: 545–69.

Bridgman, P. W. (1927). *The Logic of Modern Physics*. New York: Macmillan.

Briggs, C. L. (1986). *Learning How to Ask: A Sociolinguistic Appraisal of the Role of the Interview in Social Science Research*. Cambridge: Cambridge University Press.

Brooks, R., and Waters, J. (2015). 'The Hidden Internationalism of Elite English Schools', *Sociology*, 49: 212–28.

Brotsky, S. R., and Giles, D. (2007). 'Inside the "Pro-Ana" Community: A Covert Online Participant Observation', *Eating Disorders*, 15: 93–109.

Brown, A. D. (1998). 'Narrative, Politics and Legitimacy in an IT Implementation', *Journal of Management Studies*, 35: 35–58.

Brown, G. W., and Harris, T. W. (1978). *The Social Origins of Depression: A Study of Psychiatric Disorder in Women*. London: Tavistock.

Bruce, C. S. (1994). 'Research Students' Early Experiences of the Dissertation Literature Review', *Studies in Higher Education*, 19: 217–29.

Brüggen, E., and Willems, P. (2009). 'A Critical Comparison of Offline Focus Groups, Online Focus Groups and E-Delphi', *International Journal of Market Research*, 51: 363–81.

Bryman, A. (1974). 'Sociology of Religion and Sociology of Elites', *Archives de sciences sociales des religions*, 38: 109–21.

Bryman, A. (1988a). *Quantity and Quality in Social Research*. London: Routledge.

Bryman, A. (1988b). *Doing Research in Organizations*. London: Routledge.

Bryman, A. (1989). *Research Methods and Organization Studies*. London: Routledge.

Bryman, A. (1992). 'Quantitative and Qualitative Research: Further Reflections on their Integration', in J. Brannen (ed.), *Mixing Methods: Qualitative and Quantitative Research*. Aldershot: Avebury.

Bryman, A. (1994). 'The Mead/Freeman Controversy: Some Implications for Qualitative Researchers', in R. G. Burgess and C. Pole (eds), *Issues in Quantitative Research*, Studies in

Qualitative Methodology, volume 4. Greenwich, CT: JAI Press.

Bryman, A. (1995). *Disney and his Worlds*. London: Routledge.

Bryman, A. (1998). 'Quantitative and Qualitative Research Strategies in Knowing the Social World', in T. May and M. Williams (eds), *Knowing the Social World*. Buckingham: Open University Press.

Bryman, A. (1999). 'Global Disney', in P. Taylor and D. Slater (eds), *The American Century*. Oxford: Blackwell.

Bryman, A. (2003). 'McDonald's as a Disneyized Institution: Global Implications', *American Behavioral Scientist*, 47: 154–67.

Bryman, A. (2004). *The Disneyization of Society*. London: Sage.

Bryman, A. (2006a). 'Integrating Quantitative and Qualitative Research: How is it Done?', *Qualitative Research*, 6: 97–113.

Bryman, A. (2006b). 'Paradigm Peace and the Implications for Quality', *International Journal of Social Research Methodology*, 9: 111–26.

Bryman, A. (2007a). 'The Research Question in Social Research: What is its Role?', *International Journal of Social Research Methodology*, 10: 5–20.

Bryman, A. (2007b). 'Barriers to Integrating Quantitative and Qualitative Research', *Journal of Mixed Methods Research*, 1: 8–22.

Bryman, A. (2007c). 'Effective Leadership in Higher Education: A Literature Review', *Studies in Higher Education*, 32: 693–710.

Bryman, A. (2008a). 'The End of the Paradigm Wars?', in P. Alasuutari, J. Brannen, and L. Bickman (eds), *Handbook of Social Research*. London: Sage.

Bryman, A. (2008b). 'Why Do Researchers Integrate/Combine/Mesh/Blend/Mix/Merge/Fuse Quantitative and Qualitative Research?', in M. M. Bergman (ed.), *Advances in Mixed Methods Research*. London: Sage.

Bryman, A. (2012). Contribution to S. E. Baker and R. Edwards (eds), *How Many Qualitative Interviews is Enough? Expert Voices and Early Career Reflections on Sampling and Cases in Qualitative Research*. National Centre for Research Methods Review Paper, **http://eprints.ncrm.ac.uk/2273/** (accessed 19 November 2014).

Bryman, A. (2014). 'June 1989 and Beyond: Julia Brannen's Contribution to Mixed Methods Research', *International Journal of Social Research Methodology*, 17: 121–31.

Bryman, A., and Burgess, R. G. (1994a). 'Developments in Qualitative Data Analysis: An Introduction', in A. Bryman and R. G. Burgess (eds), *Analyzing Qualitative Data*. London: Routledge.

Bryman, A., and Burgess, R. G. (1994b). 'Reflections on Qualitative Data Analysis', in A. Bryman and R. G. Burgess (eds), *Analyzing Qualitative Data*. London: Routledge.

Bryman, A., and Burgess, R. G. (1999). 'Introduction: Qualitative Research Methodology—A Review', in A. Bryman and R. G. Burgess (eds), *Qualitative Research*. London: Sage.

Bryman, A., and Cramer, D. (2004). 'Constructing Variables', in M. Hardy and A. Bryman (eds), *Handbook of Data Analysis*. London: Sage.

Bryman, A., and Cramer, D. (2011). *Quantitative Data Analysis with IBM SPSS 17, 18 and 19: A Guide for Social Scientists*. London: Routledge.

Bryman, A., Becker, S., and Sempik, J. (2008). 'Quality Criteria for Quantitative, Qualitative and Mixed Methods Research: The View from Social Policy', *International Journal of Social Research Methodology*, 11: 261–76.

Bryman, A., Gillingwater, D., and McGuinness, I. (1996). 'Industry Culture and Strategic Response: The Case of the British Bus Industry', *Studies in Cultures, Organizations and Societies*, 2: 191–208.

Bryman, A., Haslam, C., and Webb, A. (1994). 'Performance Appraisal in UK Universities: A Case of Procedural Compliance?', *Assessment and Evaluation in Higher Education*, 19: 175–88.

Bryman, A., Stephens, M., and A Campo, C. (1996). 'The Importance of Context: Qualitative Research and the Study of Leadership', *Leadership Quarterly*, 7: 353–70.

Buckle, A., and Farrington, D. P. (1984). 'An Observational Study of Shoplifting', *British Journal of Criminology*, 24: 63–73.

Buckle, A., and Farrington, D. P. (1994). 'Measuring Shoplifting by Systematic Observation', *Psychology, Crime and Law*, 1: 133–41.

Bulmer, M. (1979). 'Concepts in the Analysis of Qualitative Data', *Sociological Review*, 27: 651–77.

Bulmer, M. (1980). 'Why Don't Sociologists Make More Use of Official Statistics?', *Sociology*, 14: 505–23.

Bulmer, M. (1982). 'The Merits and Demerits of Covert Participant Observation', in M. Bulmer (ed.), *Social Research Ethics*. London: Macmillan.

Bulmer, M. (1984). 'Facts, Concepts, Theories and Problems', in M. Bulmer, (ed.), *Social Research Methods*. London: Macmillan.

Burawoy, M. (1979). *Manufacturing Consent*. Chicago: University of Chicago Press.

Burawoy, M. (2003). 'Revisits: An Outline of a Theory of Reflexive Ethnography', *American Sociological Review*, 68: 645–79.

Burger, J. M. (2009). 'Replicating Milgram: Would People Still Obey Today?', *American Psychologist* 64: 1–11.

Burgess, R. G. (1983). *Inside Comprehensive Education: A Study of Bishop McGregor School*. London: Methuen.

Burgess, R. G. (1984). *In the Field*. London: Allen & Unwin.

Burgess, R. G. (1987). 'Studying and Restudying Bishop McGregor School', in G. Walford, (ed.), *Doing Sociology of Education*. Lewes: Falmer.

Búriková, Z., and Miller, D. (2010). *Au Pair*. Cambridge: Polity.

Burman, M. J., Batchelor, S. A., and Brown, J. A. (2001). 'Researching Girls and Violence: Facing the Dilemmas of Fieldwork', *British Journal of Criminology*, 41: 443–59.

Burrell, G., and Morgan, G. (1979). *Sociological Paradigms and Organisational Analysis*. Aldershot: Gower.

Burrell, I., and Leppard, D. (1994). 'Fall in Crime a Myth as Police Chiefs Massage the Figures', *Sunday Times*, 16 October: 1, 5.

Bury, M. (2001). 'Illness Narratives: Fact or Fiction?', *Sociology of Health and Illness*, 23: 263–85.

Business Week (1973). 'The Public Clams up on Survey Takers', 15 September: 216–20.

Buston, K. (1997). 'NUD*IST in Action: Its Use and its Usefulness in a Study of Chronic Illness in Young People', *Sociological Research Online*, 2, **www.socresonline.org.uk/2/3/6.html** (accessed 29 December 2014).

Butcher, B. (1994). 'Sampling Methods: An Overview and Review', *Survey Methods Centre Newsletter*, 15: 4–8.

Butler, T., and Robson, G. (2001). 'Social Capital, Gentrification and Neighbourhood Change in London: A Comparison of Three South London Neighbourhoods', *Urban Studies*, 38: 2145–62.

Calder, B. J. (1977). 'Focus Groups and the Nature of Qualitative Marketing Research', *Journal of Marketing Research*, 14: 353–64.

Callaghan, G., and Thompson, P. (2002). '"We Recruit Attitude": The Selection and Shaping of Routine Call Centre Labour', *Journal of Management Studies*, 39: 233–54.

Camerer, C. F. (1997). 'Taxi Drivers and Beauty Contests', *Engineering and Science*, 60: 11–19.

Campbell, D. T. (1957). 'Factors Relevant to the Validity of Experiments in Social Settings', *Psychological Bulletin*, 54: 297–312.

Campbell, R., Pound, P., Pope, C., Britten, N., Pill, R., Morgan, M., and Donovan, J. (2003). 'Evaluating Meta-Ethnography: A Synthesis of Qualitative Research on Lay Experiences of Diabetes and Diabetes Care', *Social Science and Medicine*, 56: 671–84.

Capstick, S. B., and Pidgeon, N. F. (2014). 'What *is* Climate Change Scepticism? Examination of the Concept using a Mixed Methods Study of the UK Public', *Global Environmental Change*, 24: 389–401.

Cassidy, R. (2014). '"A Place for Men to Come and Do Their Thing": Constructing Masculinities in Betting Shops in London', *British Journal of Sociology*, 65: 170–91.

Catterall, M., and Maclaran, P. (1997). 'Focus Group Data and Qualitative Analysis Programs: Coding the Moving Picture as well as Snapshots', *Sociological Research Online*, 2, **www.socresonline.org.uk/2/1/6** (accessed 7 January 2015).

Cavendish, R. (1982). *Women on the Line*. London: Routledge & Kegan Paul.

Cerulo, K. A. (2014). 'Reassessing the Problem: Response to Jerolmack and Khan', *Sociological Methods and Research*, 43: 219–26.

Chamberlayne, P., Bornat, J., and Wengraf, T. (2000). 'Introduction: The Biographical Turn', in P. Chamberlayne, J. Bornat, and T. Wengraf (eds), *The Turn to Biographical Methods in Social Science: Comparative Issues and Examples*. London: Routledge.

Charlton, T., Gunter, B., and Coles, D. (1998). 'Broadcast Television as a Cause of Aggression?: Recent Findings from a Naturalistic Study', *Emotional and Behavioural Difficulties*, 3: 5–13.

Charlton, T., Coles, D., Panting, C., and Hannan, A. (1999). 'Behaviour of Nursery Class Children before and after the Availability of Broadcast Television: A Naturalistic Study of Two Cohorts in a Remote Community', *Journal of Social Behavior and Personality*, 14: 315–24.

Charmaz, K. (1983). 'The Grounded Theory Method: An Explication and Interpretation', in R. M. Emerson (ed.), *Contemporary Field Research: A Collection of Readings*. Boston: Little, Brown.

Charmaz, K. (1997). 'Identity Dilemmas of Chronically Ill Men', in A. Strauss and J. M. Corbin (eds), *Grounded Theory in Practice*. Thousand Oaks, CA: Sage.

Charmaz, K. (2000). 'Grounded Theory: Objectivist and Constructivist Methods', in N. K. Denzin and Y. S. Lincoln (eds), *Handbook of Qualitative Research*. 2nd edn. Thousand Oaks, CA: Sage.

Charmaz, K. (2002). 'Qualitative Interviewing and Grounded Theory Analysis', in J. F. Gubrium and J. A. Holstein (eds), *Handbook of Interview Research: Context and Method*. Thousand Oaks, CA: Sage.

Charmaz, K. (2004). 'Grounded Theory', in M. S. Lewis-Beck, A. Bryman, and T. F. Liao (eds), *The Sage Encyclopedia of Social Science Research Methods*. 3 vols. Thousand Oaks, CA: Sage.

Charmaz, K. (2006). *Constructing Grounded Theory: A Practical Guide through Qualitative Analysis*. London: Sage.

Chase, S. E. (2011). 'Narrative Inquiry: Still a Field in the Making', in N. K. Denzin and Y. S. Lincoln (eds), *Handbook of Qualitative Research*. 4th edn. Los Angeles: Sage.

Chattoe, E., and Gilbert, N. (1999). 'Talking about Budgets: Time and Uncertainty in Household Decision Making', *Sociology*, 33: 85–103.

Chin, M. G., Fisak, B., Jr, and Sims, V. K. (2002). 'Development of the Attitudes toward Vegetarianism Scale', *Anthrozoös*, 15: 333–42.

Cicourel, A. V. (1964). *Method and Measurement in Sociology*. New York: Free Press.

Cicourel, A. V. (1968). *The Social Organization of Juvenile Justice*. New York: Wiley.

Cicourel, A. V. (1982). 'Interviews, Surveys, and the Problem of Ecological Validity', *American Sociologist*, 17: 11–20.

Clairborn, W. L. (1969). 'Expectancy Effects in the Classroom: A Failure to Replicate', *Journal of Educational Psychology*, 60: 377–83.

Clapper, D. L., and Massey, A. P. (1996). 'Electronic Focus Groups: A Framework for Exploration', *Information and Management*, 30: 43–50.

Clark, A. (2013). 'Haunted by Images? Ethical Moments and Anxieties in Visual Research', *Methodological Innovations Online*, 8: 68–81, **www.methodologicalinnovations.org.uk/** (accessed 21 January 2015).

Clark, A., and Emmel, N. (2010). 'Realities Toolkit #13: Using Walking Interviews', **http://eprints.ncrm.ac.uk/800/** (accessed 5 December 2014).

Clarke, V., and Braun, V. (2013). 'Teaching Thematic Analysis', *The Psychologist*, 26: 120–23.

Clayman, S., and Gill, V. T. (2004). 'Conversation Analysis', in M. Hardy and A. Bryman (eds), *Handbook of Data Analysis*. London: Sage.

Cloward, R. A., and Ohlin, L. E. (1960). *Delinquency and Opportunity: A Theory of Delinquent Gangs*. New York: Free Press.

Cobanoglu, C., Ward, B., and Moreo, P. J. (2001). 'A Comparison of Mail, Fax and Web-Based Survey Methods', *International Journal of Market Research*, 43: 441–52.

Coffey, A. (1999). *The Ethnographic Self: Fieldwork and the Representation of Reality*. London: Sage.

Coffey, A., and Atkinson, P. (1996). *Making Sense of Qualitative Data: Complementary Research Strategies*. Thousand Oaks, CA: Sage.

Coffey, A., Holbrook, B., and Atkinson, P. (1994). 'Qualitative Data Analysis: Technologies and Representations', *Sociological Research Online*, 2, **www.socresonline.org.uk/1/1/4.html** (accessed 5 December 2014).

Cohen, R. S. (2010). 'When It Pays to be Friendly: Employment Relationships and Emotional Labour in Hairstyling', *Sociological Review*, 58: 197–218.

Coleman, C., and Moynihan, J. (1996). *Understanding Crime Data: Haunted by the Dark Figure*. Buckingham: Open University Press.

Coleman, J. S. (1958). 'Relational Analysis: The Study of Social Organization with Survey Methods', *Human Organization*, 16: 28–36.

Collins, M. (1997). 'Interviewer Variability: A Review of the Problem', *Journal of the Market Research Society*, 39: 67–84.

Collins, R. (1994). *Four Sociological Traditions*. Rev. edn. New York: Oxford University Press.

Colman, I., Kingsbury, M., Weeks, M., Ataullahjan, A., Bélair, M-A., Dykxhoorn, J., Hynes, K., Loro, A., Martin, M. S., Naicker, K., Pollock, N., Rusu, C., and Kirbride, J. B. (2014). 'CARTOONS KILL: Casualties in Animated Recreational Theater in an Objective Observational New Study of Kids' Introduction to Loss of Life', *British Medical Journal*, doi: 10.1136/bmj.g7184 (accessed 17 December 2014)

Conger, J. A., and Kanungo, R. N. (1998). *Charismatic Leadership in Organizations*. Thousand Oaks, CA: Sage.

Converse, P. D., Wolfe, E. W., Huang, X., and Oswald, F. L. (2008). 'Response Rates for Mixed-Mode Surveys Using Mail and E-Mail/Web', *American Journal of Evaluation*, 29: 99–107.

Cook, T. D., and Campbell, D. T. (1979). *Quasi-Experimentation: Design and Analysis for Field Settings*. Boston: Houghton Mifflin.

Corbin, J., and Strauss, A. (2015). *Basics of Qualitative Research: Techniques and Procedures for Developing Grounded Theory*. 4th edn. Los Angeles: Sage.

Corden, A., and Sainsbury, R. (2006). *Using Verbatim Quotations in Reporting Qualitative Social Research: Researchers' Views*. Social Policy Research Unit Report, **www.york.ac.uk/inst/spru/pubs/pdf/verbquotresearch.pdf** (accessed 18 October 2014).

Corti, L. (1993). 'Using Diaries in Social Research', *Social Research Update*, 2, **http://sru.soc.surrey.ac.uk/SRU2.html** (accessed 7 January 2015).

Corti, L., Foster, J., and Thompson, P. (1995). 'Archiving Qualitative Research Data', *Social Research Update*, 10.

Couper, M. P. (2000). 'Web Surveys: A Review of Issues and Approaches', *Public Opinion Quarterly*, 64: 464–94.

Couper, M. P. (2008). *Designing Effective Web Surveys*. Cambridge: Cambridge University Press.

Couper, M. P., and Hansen, S. E. (2002). 'Computer-Assisted Interviewing', in J. F. Gubrium and J. A. Holstein (eds), *Handbook of Interview Research: Context and Method*. Thousand Oaks, CA: Sage.

Couper, M. P., Traugott, M. W., and Lamias, M. J. (2001). 'Web Survey Design and Administration', *Public Opinion Quarterly*, 65: 230–53.

Craig, G., Corden, A., and Thornton, P. (2000). 'Safety in Social Research', *Social Research Update*, 20, **http://sru.soc.surrey.ac.uk/SRU29.html** (accessed 5 December 2014).

Cramer, D. (1998). *Fundamental Statistics for Social Research*. London: Routledge.

Crawford, S. D., Couper, M. P., and Lamias, M. J. (2001). 'Web Surveys: Perceptions of Burden', *Social Science Computer Review*, 19: 146–62.

Creswell, J., and Plano Clark, V. L. (2011). *Designing and Conducting Mixed Methods Research*. 2nd edn. Thousand Oaks, CA: Sage.

Creswell, J., and Tashakkori, A. (2007). 'Developing Publishable Mixed Methods Manuscripts', *Journal of Mixed Methods Research*, 1: 107–11.

Croll, P. (1986). *Systematic Classroom Observation*. London: Falmer Press.

Croll, P., and Moses, D. (1985). *One in Five: The Assessment and Incidence of Special Educational Needs*. London: Routledge & Kegan Paul.

Crompton, R., and Birkelund, G. (2000). 'Employment and Caring in British and Norwegian Banking', *Work Employment and Society*, 14: 331–52.

Crook, C., and Light, P. (2002). 'Virtual Society and the Cultural Practice of Study', in S. Woolgar, (ed.), *Virtual Society? Technology, Cyperbole, Reality*. Oxford: Oxford University Press.

Crouch, M., and McKenzie, H. (2006). 'The Logic of Small Samples in Interview-Based Qualitative Research', *Social Science Information*, 45: 483–99.

Curasi, C. F. (2001). 'A Critical Exploration of Face-to-Face Interviewing vs Computer-Mediated Interviewing', *International Journal of Market Research*, 43: 361–75.

Curran, K., Mugo, N. R., Kurth, A., Ngure, K., Heffron, R., Donnell, D., Celum, C., and Baeten, J. M. (2013). 'Daily Short Message Service Surveys to Measure Sexual Behavior and Pre-exposure Prophylaxis Use among Kenyan Men and Women', *AIDS and Behavior*, 17: 2977–85.

Czarniawska, B. (2007). *Shadowing and Other Techniques for Doing Fieldwork in Modern Societies*. Malmö: Liber.

Dacin, M. T., Munir, K., and Tracey, P. (2010). 'Formal Dining at Cambridge Colleges: Linking Ritual Performance and Institutional Maintenance', *Academy of Management Journal*, 53: 1393–418.

Daigneault, P.-M., Jacob, S., and Ouimet, M. (2014). 'Using Systematic Review Methods within a Ph.D. Dissertation in Political Science: Challenges and Lessons Learned from Practice', *International Journal of Social Research Methodology*, 17: 267–83.

Dale, A. (1987). 'The Effect of Life Cycle on Three Dimensions of Stratification', in A. Bryman, B. Bytheway, P. Allatt, and T. Keil (eds), *Rethinking the Life Cycle*. London: Macmillan.

Dale, A., Arber, S., and Proctor, M. (1988). *Doing Secondary Analysis*. London: Unwin Hyman.

Daniel, W. W. (1968). *Racial Discrimination in Britain*. Harmondsworth: Penguin.

Davis, E. M. (2008). 'Risky Business: Medical Discourse, Breast Cancer, and Narrative', *Qualitative Health Research*, 18: 65–76.

Davis, J. A. (1964). '*Great Books and Small Groups*: An Informal History of a National Survey', in P. Hammond (ed.), *Sociologists at Work*. New York: Basic Books.

Davis, K., Randall, D. P., Ambrose, A., and Orand, M. (2015). '"I Was Bullied Too": Stories of Bullying and Coping in an Online Community', *Information, Communication and Society*, 18: 357–75.

Davis, S. N. (2003). 'Sex Stereotypes in Commercials Targeted toward Children: A Content Analysis', *Sociological Spectrum*, 23: 407–24.

Deacon, D. (2007). 'Yesterday's Papers and Today's Technology: Digital Newspaper Archives and "Push Button" Content Analysis', *European Journal of Communication*, 22: 5–25.

Deacon, D., Bryman, A., and Fenton, N. (1998). 'Collision or Collusion? A Discussion of the Unplanned Triangulation of Quantitative and Qualitative Research Methods', *International Journal of Social Research Methodology*, 1: 47–63.

Deacon, D., Fenton, N., and Bryman, A. (1999). 'From Inception to Reception: The Natural History of a News Item', *Media, Culture and Society*, 21: 5–31.

Deacon, D., Pickering, M., Golding, P., and Murdock, G. (1999). *Researching Communications: A Practical Guide to Methods in Media and Cultural Analysis*. London: Arnold.

Deakin, H., and Wakefield, K. (2014). 'SKYPE Interviewing: Reflections of Two PhD Researchers', *Qualitative Research*, 14: 603–16.

de Bruijne, M., and Wijnant, A. (2013). 'Comparing Survey Results Obtained via Mobile Devices and Computers: An Experiment with a Mobile Web Survey on a Heterogeneous Group of Mobile Devices Versus a Computer-Assisted Web Survey', *Social Science Computer Review*, 31: 484–504.

de Grosbois, D. (2012). 'Corporate Social Responsibility Reporting by the Global Hotel Industry: Commitment, Initiatives and Performance', *International Journal of Hospitality Management*, 31: 896–905.

Delamont, S. (1976). 'Beyond Flanders' Fields: The Relationship of Subject-Matter and Individuality in Classroom Style', in M. Stubbs and S. Delamont (eds), *Explorations in Classroom Observation*. Chichester: Wiley.

Delamont, S., and Atkinson, P. (2004). 'Qualitative Research and the Postmodern Turn', in C. Hardy and A. Bryman (eds), *Handbook of Data Analysis*. London: Sage.

Delamont, S., and Hamilton, D. (1984). 'Revisiting Classroom Research: A Continuing Cautionary Tale', in S. Delamont (ed.), *Readings on Interaction in the Classroom*. London: Methuen.

Delbridge, R. (1998). *Life on the Line: The Workplace Experience of Lean Production and the 'Japanese' Model*. Oxford: Oxford University Press.

Delbridge, R. (2004). 'Working in Teams: Ethnographic Evidence from Two "High-Performance" Workplaces', in S. Fleetwood and S. Ackroyd (eds), *Critical Realist Applications in Organisation and Management Studies*. London: Routledge.

De Leeuw, E. D., and Hox, J. P. (2011). 'Internet Surveys as Part of a Mixed-Mode Design', in M. Das, P. Ester, and L. Kaczmirek (eds), *Social and Behavioral Research and the Internet: Advances in Applied Methods and Research Strategies*. New York: Routledge.

De Leeuw, E. D., and Hox, J. P. (2015). 'Survey Mode and Mode Effects', in U. Engel, B. Jann, P. Lynch, A. Scherpenzeel, and P. Sturgis (eds), *Improving Survey Methods: Lessons from Recent Research*. New York: Routledge.

DeLorme, D. E., Zinkhan, G. M., and French, W. (2001). 'Ethics and the Internet: Issues Associated with Qualitative Research', *Journal of Business Ethics*, 33: 271–86.

Demetry, D. (2013). 'Regimes of Meaning: The Intersection of Space and Time in Kitchen Cultures', *Journal of Contemporary Ethnography*, 42: 576–607.

Denney, A. S., and Tewksbury, R. (2013). 'How to Write a Literature Review', *Journal of Criminal Justice Education*, 24: 218–34.

Denscombe, M. (2006). 'Web-Based Questionnaires and the Mode Effect: An Evaluation Based on Completion Rates and Data Contents of Near-Identical Questionnaires Delivered in Different Modes', *Social Science Computer Review*, 24: 246–54.

Denscombe, M. (2010). *Ground Rules for Good Research: Guidelines for Good Practice*. 2nd edn. Maidenhead: Open University Press.

Denyer, D., and Tranfield, D. (2009). 'Producing a Systematic Review', in D. Buchanan and A. Bryman (eds), *Handbook of Organizational Research Methods*. London: Sage.

Denzin, N. K. (1968). 'On the Ethics of Disguised Observation', *Social Problems*, 15: 502–4.

Denzin, N. K. (1970). *The Research Act in Sociology*. Chicago: Aldine.

Denzin, N. K. (1994). 'Evaluating Qualitative Research in the Poststructural Moment: The Lessons James Joyce Teaches us', *International Journal of Qualitative Studies in Education*, 7: 295–308.

Denzin, N. K., and Lincoln, Y. S. (1994). 'Introduction: Entering the Field of Qualitative Research', in N. K. Denzin and Y. S. Lincoln (eds), *Handbook of Qualitative Research*. Thousand Oaks, CA: Sage.

Denzin, N. K., and Lincoln, Y. S. (2000). *Handbook of Qualitative Research*. 2nd edn. Thousand Oaks, CA: Sage.

Denzin, N. K., and Lincoln, Y. S. (2005a). *Handbook of Qualitative Research*. 3rd edn. Thousand Oaks, CA: Sage.

Denzin, N. K., and Lincoln, Y. S. (2005b). 'Introduction: The Discipline and Practice of Qualitative Research', in N. K. Denzin and Y. S. Lincoln (eds), *Handbook of Qualitative Research*. 3rd edn. Thousand Oaks, CA: Sage.

Denzin, N. K., and Lincoln, Y. S. (2011). 'Preface', in N. K. Denzin and Y. S. Lincoln (eds), *Handbook of Qualitative Research*. 4th edn. Los Angeles: Sage.

Department of Health (2005). *Research Governance Framework for Health and Social Care*. London: Department of Health.

DeSoucey, M. (2010). 'Gastronationalism: Food Traditions and Authenticity Politics in the European Union', *American Sociological Review*, 75: 432–55.

Díaz de Rada, V. D., and Domínguez-Álvarez, J. A. (2014). 'Response Quality of Self-Administered Questionnaires: A Comparison Between Paper and Web Questionnaires', *Social Science Computer Review*, 32: 256–69.

Dickinson, H. (1993). 'Accounting for Augustus Lamb: Theoretical and Methodological Issues in Biography and Historical Sociology', *Sociology*, 27: 121–32.

Diener, E., and Crandall, R. (1978). *Ethics in Social and Behavioral Research*. Chicago: University of Chicago Press.

Diener, E., Inglehart, R., and Tay, L. (2013). 'Theory and Validity of Life Satisfaction Scales', *Social Indicators Research*, 112: 497–527.

Dillman, D. A., Smyth, J. D., and Christian, L. M. (2014). *Internet, Phone, Mail, and Mixed-Mode Surveys: The Tailored Design Method*. 4th edn. Hoboken, NJ: Wiley.

Dingwall, R. (1980). 'Ethics and Ethnography', *Sociological Review*, 28: 871–91.

Ditton, J. (1977). *Part-Time Crime: An Ethnography of Fiddling and Pilferage*. London: Macmillan.

Dixon-Woods, M., Angell, E., Ashcroft, R., and Bryman, A. (2007). 'Written Work: The Social Functions of Research Ethics Committee Letters', *Social Science and Medicine*, 65: 792–802.

Dommeyer, C. J., and Moriarty, E. (2000). 'Comparison of Two Forms of an E-Mail Survey: Embedded vs Attached', *International Journal of Market Research*, 42: 39–50.

Douglas, J. D. (1967). *The Social Meanings of Suicide*. Princeton: Princeton University Press.

Douglas, J. D. (1976). *Investigative Social Research: Individual and Team Field Research*. Beverly Hills, CA: Sage.

Dunne, C. (2011). 'The Place of the Literature Review in Grounded Theory Research', *International Journal of Social Research Methodology*, 14: 111–24.

Durkheim, E. (1938). *The Rules of Sociological Method*, trans. S. A. Solavay and J. H. Mueller. New York: Free Press.

Durkheim, E. (1952). *Suicide. A Study In Sociology*, trans. J. A. Spaulding and G. Simpson. London: Routledge & Kegan Paul.

Dyer, W. G., and Wilkins, A. L. (1991). 'Better Stories, Not Better Constructs, to Generate Better Theory: A Rejoinder to Eisenhardt', *Academy of Management Review*, 16: 613–19.

Edley, N., and Wetherell, M. (1997). 'Jockeying for Position: The Construction of Masculine Identities', *Discourse and Society*, 8: 203–17.

Edwards, R. (1979). *Contested Terrain*. New York: Basic Books.

Eisenhardt, K. M. (1989). 'Building Theories from Case Study Research', *Academy of Management Review*, 14: 532–50.

Elliott, C., and Ellingworth, D. (1997). 'Assessing the Representativeness of the 1992 British Crime Survey: The Impact of Sampling Error and Response Biases', *Sociological Research Online*, 2, **www.socresonline.org.uk/2/4/3.html** (accessed 11 December 2014).

Elliott, H. (1997). 'The Use of Diaries in Sociological Research on Health Experience', *Sociological Research Online*, 2, **www.socresonline.org.uk/2/2/7.html** (accessed 11 December 2014).

Emerson, R. M. (1987). 'Four Ways to Improve the Craft of Fieldwork', *Journal of Contemporary Ethnography*, 16: 69–89.

Erikson, K. T. (1967). 'A Comment on Disguised Observation in Sociology', *Social Problems*, 14: 366–73.

Erikson, M. G., and Erlandson, P. (2014). 'A Taxonomy of Motives to Cite', *Social Studies of Science*, 44: 625–37.

Eschleman, K. J., Bowling, N. A., Michel, J. S., and Burns, G. N. (2014). 'Perceived Intent of Supervisor as a Moderator Between Abusive Supervision and Counterproductive Work Behaviours', *Work and Stress*, 28: 362–75.

Evans, A., Elford, J., and Wiggins, R. D. (2008). 'Using the Internet in Qualitative Research', in C. Willig and W. Stainton Rogers (eds), *SAGE Handbook of Qualitative Methods in Psychology*. London: Sage.

Evans, J., and Benefield, P. (2001). 'Systematic Reviews of Educational Research: Does the Medical Model Fit?', *British Educational Research Journal*, 27: 527–41.

Ewick, P., and Silbey, S. (2003). 'Narrating Social Structure: Stories of Resistance to Legal Authority', *American Journal of Sociology*, 108: 1328–72.

Fairclough, N. (2003). *Analysing Discourse: Textual Analysis for Social Research*. London: Routledge.

Faraday, A., and Plummer, K. (1979). 'Doing Life Histories', *Sociological Review*, 27: 773–98.

Fenton, N., Bryman, A., and Deacon, D. (1998). *Mediating Social Science*. London: Sage.

Ferguson, H. (in press). 'Researching Social Work Practice Close Up: Using Ethnographic and Mobile Methods to Understand Encounters between Social Workers, Children and Families', *British Journal of Social Work*, doi: 10.1093/bjsw/bcu120

Ferrie, J., Shipley, M. J., Marmot, M. G., Stansfeld, S., and Smith, G. D. (1998). 'The Health Effects of Major Organizational Change and Job Insecurity', *Social Science and Medicine*, 46: 343–54.

Festinger, L., Riecken, H. W., and Schachter, S. (1956). *When Prophecy Fails*. New York: Harper & Row.

Fielding, J., Fielding, N., and Hughes, G. (2013). 'Opening Up Open-Ended Survey Data using Qualitative Software', *Quality and Quantity*, 47: 3261–76.

Fielding, N. (1982). 'Observational Research on the National Front', in M. Bulmer (ed.), *Social Research Ethics*. London: Macmillan.

Fielding, N., and Lee, R. M. (1998). *Computer Analysis and Qualitative Research*. London: Sage.

Filmer, P., Phillipson, M., Silverman, D., and Walsh, D. (1972). *New Directions in Sociological Theory*. London: Collier-Macmillan.

Finch, J. (1984). '"It's great to have someone to talk to": The Ethics and Politics of Interviewing Women', in C. Bell and H. Roberts (eds), *Social Researching: Politics, Problems, Practice*. London: Routledge & Kegan Paul.

Finch, J. (1987). 'The Vignette Technique in Survey Research', *Sociology*, 21: 105–14.

Finch, J., and Hayes, L. (1994). 'Inheritance, Death and the Concept of the Home', *Sociology*, 28: 417–33.

Finch, J., and Mason, J. (1990). 'Decision Taking in the Field-Work Process: Theoretical Sampling and Collaborative Working', in R. G. Burgess (ed.), *Reflecting on Field Experience*, Studies in Qualitative Methodology, volume 2. Bingley: Emerald Group, 25–50.

Fincham, B., Langer, S., Scourfield, J., and Shiner, M. (2011). *Understanding Suicide: A Sociological Autopsy*. Basingstoke: Palgrave.

Fine, G. A. (1996). 'Justifying Work: Occupational Rhetorics as Resources in Kitchen Restaurants', *Administrative Science Quarterly*, 41: 90–115.

Fisher, K., and Layte, R. (2004). 'Measuring Work-Life Balance using Time Diary Data', *Electronic International Journal of Time Use Research*, 1: 1–13, **http://ffb.uni-lueneburg.de/eijtur/pdf/volumes/eIJTUR-1-.pdf#pagemode** (accessed 11 December 2014).

Fjellman, S. M. (1992). *Vinyl Leaves: Walt Disney World and America*. Boulder, CO: Westview Press.

Flanders, N. (1970). *Analyzing Teacher Behavior*. Reading, MA: Addison-Wesley.

Fleming, C., and Bowden, M. (2009). 'Web-Based Surveys as an Alternative to Traditional Mail Methods', *Journal of Environmental Management*, 90: 284–92.

Fletcher, J. (1966). *Situation Ethics*. London: SCM Press.

Flint, A., Clegg, S., and Macdonald, R. (2006). 'Exploring Staff Perceptions of Student Plagiarism', *Journal of Further and Higher Education*, 30: 145–56.

Flyvbjerg, B. (2003). 'Five Misunderstandings about Case Study Research', in C. Seale, G. Gobo, J. F. Gubrium, and D. Silverman (eds), *Qualitative Research Practice*. London: Sage.

Foddy, W. (1993). *Constructing Questions for Interviews and Questionnaires: Theory and Practice in Social Research*. Cambridge: Cambridge University Press.

Forster, N. (1994). 'The Analysis of Company Documentation', in C. Cassell and G. Symon (eds), *Qualitative Methods in Organizational Research*. London: Sage.

Forth, J., Bewley, H., Bryson, A., Dix, G., and Oxenbridge, S. (2010). 'Survey Errors and Survey Costs: A Response to Timming's Critique of the Survey of Employees Questionnaire in WERS 2004', *Work, Employment and Society*, 24: 578–90.

Foster, J. (1995). 'Informal Social Control and Community Crime Prevention', *British Journal of Criminology*, 35: 563–83.

Foucault, M. (1977). *Discipline and Punish*. Harmondsworth: Penguin.

Fowler, B., and Bielsa, E. (2007). 'The Lives We Choose to Remember: A Quantitative Analysis of Newspaper Obituaries', *Sociological Review*, 55: 203–26.

Fowler, F. J. (1993). *Survey Research Methods*. 2nd edn. Newbury Park, CA: Sage.

Fowler, F. J., and Mangione, T. W. (1990). *Standardized Survey Interviewing: Minimizing Interviewer-Related Error*. Beverly Hills, CA: Sage.

Fox, B. H., and Jennings, W. G. (2014). 'How to Write a Methodology and Results Section for Empirical Research', *Journal of Criminal Justice Education*, 25: 137–56.

Fox, J., and Fogelman, K. (1990). 'New Possibilities for Longitudinal Studies of Intergenerational Factors in Child Health and Development', in D. Magnusson and L. R. Bergman (eds), *Data Quality in Longitudinal Research*. Cambridge: Cambridge University Press.

Frean, A. (1998). 'Children Read More after Arrival of TV', *The Times*, 29 April: 7.

Frey, J. H. (2004). 'Telephone Surveys', in M. S. Lewis-Beck, A. Bryman, and T. F. Liao (eds), *The Sage Encyclopedia of Social Science Research Methods*. 3 vols. Thousand Oaks, CA: Sage.

Frey, J. H., and Oishi, S. M. (1995). *How to Conduct Interviews by Telephone and in Person*. Thousand Oaks, CA: Sage.

Fricker, S., and Tourangeau, R. (2010). 'Examining the Relationship Between Nonresponse Propensity and Data Quality in Two National Household Surveys', *Public Opinion Quarterly*, 74: 934–55.

Fricker, S., Galesic, M., Tourangeau, R., and Yan, T. (2005). 'An Experimental Comparison of Web and Telephone Surveys', *Public Opinion Quarterly*, 69: 370–92.

Gabriel, Y. (1998). 'The Use of Stories', in G. Symon and C. Cassell (eds), *Qualitative Methods and Analysis in Organizational Research*. London: Sage.

Gallie, D. (1978). *In Search of the New Working Class: Automation and Social Integration within the Capitalist Enterprise*. Cambridge: Cambridge University Press.

Gallup, G. (1947). 'The Quintamensional Plan of Question Design', *Public Opinion Quarterly*, 11: 385–93.

Galton, M., Simon, B., and Croll, P. (1980). *Inside the Primary Classroom*. London: Routledge & Kegan Paul.

Gambetta, D., and Hamill, H. (2005). *Streetwise: How Taxi Drivers Establish their Customers' Trustworthiness*. New York: Russell Sage Foundation.

Ganann, R., Ciliska, D., and Thomas, H. (2010). 'Expediting Systematic Reviews: Methods and Implications of Rapid Reviews', *Implementation Science*, 5, **www.implementationscience.com/content/5/1/56** (accessed 19 December 2014).

Gans, H. J. (1962). *The Urban Villagers*. New York: Free Press.

Gans, H. J. (1968). 'The Participant-Observer as Human Being: Observations on the Personal Aspects of Field Work', in H. S. Becker (ed.), *Institutions and the Person: Papers Presented to Everett C. Hughes*. Chicago: Aldine.

Garcia, A. C., Standlee, A. I., Bechkoff, J., and Cui, Y. (2009). 'Ethnographic Approaches to the Internet and Computer-Mediated Communication', *Journal of Contemporary Ethnography*, 38 (1): 52–84.

Garfinkel, H. (1967). *Studies in Ethnomethodology*. Englewood Cliffs, NJ: Prentice-Hall.

Geertz, C. (1973a). 'Thick Description: Toward an Interpretive Theory of Culture', in C. Geertz, *The Interpretation of Cultures*. New York: Basic Books.

Geertz, C. (1973b). 'Deep Play: Notes on the Balinese Cockfight', in C. Geertz, *The Interpretation of Cultures*. New York: Basic Books.

Gephart, R. P. (1988). *Ethnostatistics: Qualitative Foundations for Quantitative Research*. Newbury Park, CA: Sage.

Gershuny, J., and Sullivan, O. (2014). 'Household Structure and Housework: Assessing the Contributions of All Household Members, with a Focus on Children and Youths', *Review of Economics of the Household*, 12: 7–27.

Gerson, K., and Horowitz, R. (2002). 'Observation and Interviewing: Options and Choices', in T. May (ed.), *Qualitative Research in Action*. London: Sage.

Gibson, L. (2010). 'Realities Toolkit #09: Using Email Interviews', **www.eprints.ncrm.ac.uk/1303/1/09-toolkit-email-interviews.pdf** (accessed 3 December 2014).

Gibson, N. (2004). 'Action Research', in M. S. Lewis-Beck, A. Bryman, and T. F. Liao (eds), *The Sage Encyclopedia of Social Science Research Methods*. 3 vols. Thousand Oaks, CA: Sage.

Gilbert, G. N. (1977). 'Referencing as Persuasion', *Social Studies of Science*, 7: 113–22.

Gilbert, G. N., and Mulkay, M. (1984). *Opening Pandora's Box: A Sociological Analysis of Scientists' Discourse*. Cambridge: Cambridge University Press.

Gill, R. (1996). 'Discourse Analysis: Practical Implementation', in J. T. E. Richardson (ed.), *Handbook of Qualitative Research Methods for Psychology and the Social Sciences*. Leicester: BPS Books.

Gill, R. (2000). 'Discourse Analysis', in M. W. Bauer and G. Gaskell (eds), *Qualitative Researching with Text, Image and Sound*. London: Sage.

Gioia, D. A., Corley, K. G., and Hamilton, A. L. (2012). 'Seeking Qualitative Rigor in Inductive Research: Notes on the Gioia Methodology', *Organizational Research Methods*, 16: 15–31.

Giulianotti, R. (1995). 'Participant Observation and Research into Football Hooliganism: Reflections on the Problems of Entrée and Everyday Risks', *Sociology of Sport Journal*, 12: 1–20.

Gladney, A. P., Ayars, C., Taylor, W. C., Liehr, P., and Meininger, J. C. (2003). 'Consistency of Findings Produced by Two Multidisciplinary Research Teams', *Sociology*, 37: 297–313.

Gladwell, M. (2008). *Outliers: The Story of Success*. London: Allen Lane.

Glaser, B. G. (1992). *Basics of Grounded Theory Analysis*. Mill Valley, CA: Sociology Press.

Glaser, B. G., and Strauss, A. L. (1967). *The Discovery of Grounded Theory: Strategies for Qualitative Research*. Chicago: Aldine.

Glock, C. Y. (1988). 'Reflections on Doing Survey Research', in H. J. O'Gorman (ed.), *Surveying Social Life*. Middletown, CT: Wesleyan University Press.

Glucksmann, M. (1994). 'The Work of Knowledge and the Knowledge of Women's Work', in M. Maynard and J. Purvis (eds), *Researching Women's Lives from a Feminist Perspective*. London: Taylor & Francis.

Goffman, A. (2009). 'On the Run: Wanted Men in a Philadelphia Ghetto', *American Sociological Review*, 74: 339–57.

Goffman, A. (2014). *On the Run: Fugitive Life in an American City*. Chicago: University of Chicago Press.

Goffman, E. (1956). *The Presentation of Self in Everyday Life*. New York: Doubleday.

Goffman, E. (1963). *Stigma: Notes on the Management of Spoiled Identity*. Harmondsworth: Penguin.

Gold, R. L. (1958). 'Roles in Sociological Fieldwork', *Social Forces*, 36: 217–23.

Golden-Biddle, K., and Locke, K. D. (1993). 'Appealing Work: An Investigation of How Ethnographic Texts Convince', *Organization Science*, 4: 595–616.

Golden-Biddle, K., and Locke, K. D. (1997). *Composing Qualitative Research*. Thousand Oaks, CA: Sage.

Goldthorpe, J. H., Lockwood, D., Bechhofer, F., and Platt, J. (1968). *The Affluent Worker: Industrial Attitudes and Behaviour*. Cambridge: Cambridge University Press.

Goode, E. (1996). 'The Ethics of Deception in Social Research: A Case Study', *Qualitative Sociology*, 19: 11–33.

Goode, W. J., and Hatt, P. K. (1952). *Methods of Social Research*. New York: McGraw Hill.

Goodings, L., Brown, S. D., and Parker, M. (2013). 'Organising Images of Futures-Past: Remembering the Apollo Moon Landings', *International Journal of Management Concepts and Philosophy*, 7: 263–83.

Gottdiener, M. (1982). 'Disneyland: A Utopian Urban Space', *Urban Life*, 11: 139–62.

Gottdiener, M. (1997). *The Theming of America: Dreams, Visions and Commercial Spaces*. Boulder, CO: Westview Press.

Goulding, C. (2009). 'Grounded Theory Perspectives in Organizational Research', in D. Buchanan and A. Bryman (eds), *Handbook of Organizational Research Methods*. London: Sage.

Gouldner, A. (1968). 'The Sociologist as Partisan', *American Sociologist*, 3: 103–16.

Graffigna, G., Bosio, A. C., and Olson, K. (2010). 'How do Ethics Assessments Frame Results of Comparative Qualitative Research? A Theory of Technique Approach', *International Journal of Social Research Methodology*, 13: 341–55.

Grant, A. M., and Wall, T. D. (2009). 'The Neglected Science and Art of Quasi-Experimentation: Why-to, When-to, and How-to Advice for Organizational Researchers', *Organizational Research Methods*, 12: 653–86.

Grant, D., Hardy, C., Oswick, C., and Putnam, L. L. (2004). 'Introduction: Organizational Discourse: Exploring the Field', in D. Grant, C. Hardy, C. Oswick, and L. Putnam (eds), *The SAGE Handbook of Organizational Discourse*. London: Sage.

Grazian, D. (2003). *Blue Chicago: The Search for Authenticity in Urban Blues Clubs*. Chicago: University of Chicago Press.

Greaves, F., Laverty, A. A., Cano, D. R., Moilanen, K., Pulman, S., Darzi, A., and Millett, C. (in press) 'Tweets about Hospital Quality: A Mixed Methods Study', *BMJ Quality and Safety*, doi:10.1136/bmjqs-2014-002875.

Green, J., Steinbach, R., and Datta, J. (2012). 'The Travelling Citizen: Emergent Discourses of Moral Mobility in a Study of Cycling in London', *Sociology*, 46: 272–89.

Greene, J. C. (1994). 'Qualitative Program Evaluation: Practice and Promise', in N. K. Denzin and Y. S. Lincoln (eds), *Handbook of Qualitative Research*. Thousand Oaks, CA: Sage.

Greene, J. C. (2000). 'Understanding Social Programs through Evaluation', in N. K. Denzin and Y. S. Lincoln (eds), *Handbook of Qualitative Research*. 2nd edn. Thousand Oaks, CA: Sage.

Grele, R. J. (1998). 'Movement without Aim: Methodological and Theoretical Problems in Oral History', in R. Perks and A. Thomson (eds), *The History Reader*. London: Routledge.

Grogan, S., Gill, S., Brownbridge, K., Kilgariff, S., and Whalley, A. (2013). 'Dress Fit and Body Image: A Thematic Analysis of Women's Accounts During and After Trying on Clothes', *Body Image*, 10: 380–8.

Groves, R. M. (2006). 'Nonresponse Rates and Nonresponse Bias in Household Surveys', *Public Opinion Quarterly*, 70: 646–75.

Groves, R. M., Fowler, F. J., Couper, M. P., Lepkowski, J. M., Singer, E., and Tourangeau, R. (2009). *Survey Methodology*, 2nd edn. Hoboken, NJ: Wiley.

Guba, E. G. (1985). 'The Context of Emergent Paradigm Research', in Y. S. Lincoln (ed.), *Organization Theory and Inquiry: The Paradigm Revolution*. Beverly Hills, CA: Sage.

Guba, E. G., and Lincoln, Y. S. (1994). 'Competing Paradigms in Qualitative Research', in N. K. Denzin and Y. S. Lincoln (eds), *Handbook of Qualitative Research*. Thousand Oaks, CA: Sage.

Guégen, N., and Jacob, C. (2012a). 'Lipstick and Tipping Behavior: When Red Lipstick Enhance Waitresses Tips', *International Journal of Hospitality Management*, 31: 1333–5.

Guégen, N., and Jacob, C. (2012b). 'Clothing Color and Tipping: Gentlemen Patrons Give More Tips to Waitresses with Red Clothes', *Journal of Hospitality & Tourism Research*, 38: 275–80.

Guest, G., Bunce, A., and Johnson, L. (2006). 'How Many Interviews are Enough? An Experiment with Data Saturation and Variability', *Field Methods*, 18: 59–82.

Guillemin, M., and Gillam, L. (2004). 'Ethics, Reflexivity, and "Ethically Important Moments" in Research', *Qualitative Inquiry*, 10: 261–80.

Gullifer, J. M., and Tyson, G. A. (2014). 'Who Has Read the Policy on Plagiarism? Unpacking Students' Understanding of Plagiarism', *Studies in Higher Education*, 39: 1202–18.

Gundersen, D. A., ZuWallack, R. S., Dayton, J., Echeverria, S. E., and DeInevo, C. D. (2013). 'Assessing the Feasibility and Sample Quality of a National Random-Digit Dialing Cellular Phone Survey of Young Adults', *American Journal of Epidemiology*, 179: 39–47.

Gusterson, H. (1996). *Nuclear Rites: A Weapons Laboratory at the End of the Cold War*. Berkeley, CA: University of California Press.

Halfpenny, P. (1979). 'The Analysis of Qualitative Data', *Sociological Review*, 27: 799–825.

Hall, W. S., and Guthrie, L. F. (1981). 'Cultural and Situational Variation in Language Function and Use—Methods and Procedures for Research', in J. L. Green and C. Wallatt (eds), *Ethnography and Language in Educational Settings*. Norwood, NJ: Ablex.

Hallett, R. E., and Barber, K. (2014). 'Ethnographic Research in a Cyber Era', *Journal of Contemporary Ethnography*, 43: 306–30.

Hammersley, M. (1989). *The Dilemma of Qualitative Method: Herbert Blumer and the Chicago Tradition*. London: Routledge.

Hammersley, M. (1992a). 'By what Criteria should Ethnographic Research be Judged?', in M. Hammersley, *What's Wrong with Ethnography?* London: Routledge.

Hammersley, M. (1992b). 'Deconstructing the Qualitative-Quantitative Divide', in M. Hammersley, *What's Wrong with Ethnography?* London: Routledge.

Hammersley, M. (1992c). 'The Paradigm Wars: Reports from the Front', *British Journal of Sociology of Education*, 13: 131–43.

Hammersley, M. (1997). 'Qualitative Data Archiving: Some Reflections on its Prospects and Problems', *Sociology*, 31: 131–42.

Hammersley, M. (2001). 'On "Systematic" Reviews of Research Literatures: A "Narrative" Response to Evans and Benefield', *British Educational Research Journal*, 27: 543–54.

Hammersley, M. (2009). 'Against the Ethicists: On the Evils of Ethical Regulation', *International Journal of Social Research Methodology*, 12: 211–25.

Hammersley, M. (2011). *Methodology: Who Needs It?* London: Sage.

Hammersley, M., and Atkinson, P. (1995). *Ethnography: Principles in Practice*. 2nd edn. London: Routledge.

Hammersley, M., and Gomm, R. (2000). 'Bias in Social Research', in M. Hammersley (ed.), *Taking Sides in Social Research: Essays in Partisanship and Bias*. London: Routledge.

Hammersley, M., Scarth, J., and Webb, S. (1985). 'Developing and Testing Theory: The Case of Research on Pupil Learning', in R. G. Burgess (ed.), *Issues in Educational Research: Qualitative Methods*. London: Falmer.

Hammond, C. (2005). 'The Wider Benefits of Adult Learning: An Illustration of the Advantages of Multi-Method Research', *International Journal of Social Research Methodology*, 8: 239–55.

Hammond, P. (1964). *Sociologists at Work*. New York: Basic Books.

Hanna, P. (2012). 'Using Internet Technologies (Such as Skype) as a Research Medium: a Research Note', *Qualitative Research*, 12: 239–42.

Hannah, D. R., and Lautsch, B. A. (2011). 'Counting in Qualitative Research: Why to Conduct It, When to Avoid It, and When to Closet It', *Journal of Management Inquiry*, 20: 14–22.

Hantrais, L. (1996). 'Comparative Research Methods', *Social Research Update*, 13, **http://sru.soc.surrey.ac.uk/SRU13.html** (accessed 5 December 2014).

Haraldsson, K., Lindgren, E.-C., Mattsson, B., Fridlund, B., and Marklund, B. (2011). 'Adolescent Girls' Experiences of Underlying Social Processes Triggering Stress in Their Everyday Life: A Grounded Theory Study', *Stress and Health*, 27: e61–e70.

Hardy, M., and Bryman, A. (2004). 'Introduction: Common Threads among Techniques of Data Analysis', in M. Hardy and A. Bryman (eds), *Handbook of Data Analysis*. London: Sage.

Harker, J., and Kleijnen, J. (2012). 'What is Rapid Review?: A Methodological Exploration of Rapid Reviews in Health Technology Assessments', *International Journal of Evidence-Based Medicine*, 10: 397–410.

Harkness, S., Moscardino, U., Bermúdez, M. R., Zylicks, P. O., Welles-Nyström, B., Blom, M., Parmar, P., Axia, G., Palacios, J., and Super, C. M. (2006). 'Mixed Methods in International Collaboration Research: The Experiences of the International Study of Parents, Children, and Schools', *Cross-Cultural Research*, 40: 65–82.

Harper, D. (2002). 'Talking about Pictures: A Case for Photo Elicitation', *Visual Studies*, 17: 13–26.

Harvey, S. A., Olórtegui, M. P., Leontsini, E., and Winch, P. J. (2009). '"They'll Change what they're Doing if they Know that you're Watching": Measuring Reactivity in Health Behavior Because of an Observer's Presence—A Case from the Peruvian Amazon', *Field Methods*, 21: 3–25.

Haslam, C., and Bryman, A. (1994). 'The Research Dissemination Minefield', in C. Haslam and A. Bryman (eds), *Social Scientists Meet the Media*. London: Routledge.

Hawkes, N. (2003). 'Close Shaves Beat Death by Whisker', *The Times*, 6 February: 1.

Hazelrigg, L. (2004). 'Inference', in M. Hardy and A. Bryman (eds), *Handbook of Data Analysis*. London: Sage.

Heap, J. L., and Roth, P. A. (1973). 'On Phenomenological Sociology', *American Sociological Review*, 38: 354–67.

Heath, C., Hindmarsh, J., and Luff, P. (2010). *Video in Qualitative Research*. London: Sage.

Heerwegh, D., and Loosveldt, G. (2008). 'Face-to-Face versus Web Surveying in a High Internet-Coverage Population: Differences in Response Quality', *Public Opinion Quarterly*, 72: 836–46.

Henwood, K., Shirani, F., and Finn, M. (2011). '"So you Think we've Moved, Changed, the Representation's got More What?" Methodological and Analytical Reflections on Visual (Photo-Elicitation) Methods Used in the Men-as-Fathers Study', in P. Reavey (ed.), *Visual Methods in Psychology: Using and Interpreting Images in Qualitative Research*. London: Psychology Press.

Heritage, J. (1984). *Garfinkel and Ethnomethodology*. Cambridge: Polity.

Heritage, J. (1987). 'Ethnomethodology', in A. Giddens and J. H. Turner (eds), *Social Theory Today*. Cambridge: Polity.

Hesse-Biber, S. (1995). 'Unleashing Frankenstein's Monster? The Use of Computers in Qualitative Research', in R. G. Burgess (ed.), *Computing and Qualitative Research*, Studies in Qualitative Methodology, volume 5. Greenwich, CT: JAI Press, 25–41.

Hewson, C. and Laurent, D. (2008). 'Research Design and Tools for Internet Research', in N. Fielding, R. M. Lee, and G. Blank (eds), *The SAGE Handbook of Online Research Methods*. London: Sage.

Hewson, C., Yule, P., Laurent, D., and Vogel, C. (2003). *Internet Research Methods: A Practical Guide for the Social and Behavioural Sciences*. London: Sage.

Hine, C. (2000). *Virtual Ethnography*. London: Sage.

Hine, C. (2008). 'Virtual Ethnography: Models, Varieties, Affordances', in N. Fielding, R. M. Lee, and G. Blank (eds), *The SAGE Handbook of Online Research Methods*. London: Sage.

Hine, C. (2014). 'Headlice Eradication as Everyday Engagement with Science: An Analysis of Online Parenting Discussions', *Public Understanding of Science*, 23: 574–91.

Hirsch, J. (1981). *Family Photographs*. New York: Oxford University Press.

Hobbs, D. (1988). *Doing the Business: Entrepreneurship, the Working Class and Detectives in the East End of London*. Oxford: Oxford University Press.

Hobbs, D. (1993). 'Peers, Careers, and Academic Fears: Writing as Field-Work', in D. Hobbs and T. May (eds), *Interpreting the Field: Accounts of Ethnography*. Oxford: Clarendon Press.

Hobbs, D., Hadfield, P., Lister, S., and Winlow, S. (2003). *Bouncers: Violence and Governance in the Night-Time Economy*. Oxford: Oxford University Press.

Hochschild, A. R. (1983). *The Managed Heart*. Berkeley and Los Angeles: University of California Press.

Hodges, L. (1998). 'The Making of a National Portrait', *The Times Higher*, 20 February: 22–3.

Hodkinson, P. (2002). *Goth: Identity, Style and Subculture*. Oxford: Berg.

Hodson, R. (1996). 'Dignity in the Workplace under Participative Management', *American Sociological Review*, 61: 719–38.

Hodson, R. (1999). *Analyzing Documentary Accounts*. Thousand Oaks, CA: Sage.

Hodson, R. (2004). 'Work Life and Social Fulfillment: Does Social Affiliation at Work Reflect a Carrot or a Stick?', *Social Science Quarterly*, 85: 221–39.

Hofmans, J., Gelens, J., and Theuns, P. (2014). 'Enjoyment as a Mediator in the Relationship Between Task Characteristics and Work Effort: An Experience Sampling Study', *European Journal of Work and Organizational Psychology*, 23: 693–705.

Holbrook, A., Bourke, S., Fairburn, H., and Lovat, T. (2007). 'Examiner Comment on the Literature Review in Ph.D. Theses', *Studies in Higher Education*, 32: 337–56.

Holbrook, A. L., Green, M. C., and Krosnick, J. A. (2003). 'Telephone versus Face-to-Face Interviewing of National Probability Samples with Long Questionnaires: Comparisons of Respondent Satisficing and Social Desirability Response Bias', *Public Opinion Quarterly*, 67: 79–125.

Holbrook, B., and Jackson, B. (1996). 'Shopping Around: Focus Group Research in North London', *Area*, 28: 136–42.

Holdaway, S. (1982). '"An Inside Job": A Case Study of Covert Research on the Police', in M. Bulmer (ed.), *Social Research Ethics*. London: Macmillan.

Holdaway, S. (1983). *Inside the British Police: A Force at Work*. Oxford: Blackwell.

Holdsworth, C. (2006). '"Don't you Think you're Missing Out, Living at Home?": Student Experiences and Residential Transitions', *Sociological Review*, 54: 495–519.

Holmes, L. (2012). 'Guidance for Ensuring Confidentiality and the Protection of Data', in S. Becker, A. Bryman, and H. Ferguson (eds), *Understanding Research for Social Policy and Social Work: Themes, Methods, and Approaches*. Bristol: Policy Press.

Holsti, O. R. (1969). *Content Analysis for the Social Sciences and Humanities*. Reading, MA: Addison-Wesley.

Homan, R. (1991). *The Ethics of Social Research*. London: Longman.

Homan, R., and Bulmer, M. (1982). 'On the Merits of Covert Methods: A Dialogue', in M. Bulmer (ed.), *Social Research Ethics*. London: Macmillan.

Hood, J. C. (2007). 'Orthodoxy vs. Power: The Defining Traits of Grounded Theory', in A. Bryant and K. Charmaz (eds), *The SAGE Handbook of Grounded Theory*. Los Angeles: Sage.

Huberman, A. M., and Miles, M. B. (1994). 'Data Management and Analysis Methods', in N. K. Denzin and Y. S. Lincoln (eds), *Handbook of Qualitative Research*. Thousand Oaks, CA: Sage.

Hughes, E. C. (1958). *Men and their Work*. Glencoe, IL: Free Press.

Hughes, G. (2000). 'Understanding the Politics of Criminological Research', in V. Jupp, P. Davies, and P. Francis (eds), *Doing Criminological Research*. London: Sage.

Hughes, J., Campbell, A., and Jenkins, R. (2011). 'Contact, Trust and Social Capital in Northern Ireland: A Qualitative Study of Three Mixed Communities', *Ethnic and Racial Studies*, 34: 967–85.

Hughes, J. A. (1990). *The Philosophy of Social Research*. 2nd edn. Harlow: Longman.

Hughes, K., MacKintosh, A. M., Hastings, G., Wheeler, C., Watson, J., and Inglis, J. (1997). 'Young People, Alcohol, and Designer Drinks: A Quantitative and Qualitative Study', *British Medical Journal*, 314: 414–18.

Hughes, R. (1998). 'Considering the Vignette Technique and its Application to a Study of Drug Injecting and HIV Risk and Safer Behaviour', *Sociology of Health and Illness*, 20: 381–400.

Humphreys, L. (1970). *Tearoom Trade: Impersonal Sex in Public Places*. Chicago: Aldine.

Humphreys, L., Gill, P., and Krishnamurthy, B. (2014). 'Twitter: A Content Analysis of Personal Information', *Information, Communication and Society*, 17: 843–57.

Humphreys, M., and Watson, T. (2009). 'Ethnographic Practices: From "Writing-up Ethnographic Research" to "Writing Ethnograpy"', in S. Ybema, D. Yanow, H. Wels, and F. Kamsteeg (eds), *Organizational Ethnography: Studying the Complexities of Everyday Life*. London: Sage.

Hutchby, I., and Wooffitt, R. (1998). *Conversation Analysis*. Cambridge: Polity.

Hycner, R. H. (1985). 'Some Guidelines for the Phenomenological Analysis of Interview Data', *Human Studies*, 8: 279–303.

Irvine, A., Drew, P., and Sainsbury, R. (2013). '"Am I not Answering Your Questions Properly?": Clarification, Adequacy and Responsiveness in Semi-Structured Telephone and Face-to-Face Interviews', *Qualitative Research*, 13: 87–106.

Israel, M., and Hay, I. (2004). *Research Ethics for Social Scientists*. London: Sage.

Jacobs, J. (1967). 'A Phenomenological Study of Suicide Notes', *Social Problems*, 15: 60–72.

Jamieson, J. (2000). 'Negotiating Danger in Fieldwork on Crime: A Researcher's Tale', in G. Lee-Treweek and S. Linkogle (eds), *Danger in the Field: Risk and Ethics in Social Research*. London: Routledge.

Janis, I. L. (1982). *Groupthink: Psychological Studies of Policy Decisions and Fiascos*. 2nd edn. Boston: Houghton-Mifflin.

Jayaratne, T. E., and Stewart, A. J. (1991). 'Quantitative and Qualitative Methods in the Social Sciences: Current Feminist Issues and Practical Strategies', in M. M. Fonow and J. A. Cook (eds), *Beyond Methodology: Feminist Scholarship as Lived Research*. Bloomington: Indiana University Press.

Jenkins, G. D., Nader, D. A., Lawler, E. E., and Cammann, C. (1975). 'Standardized Observations: An Approach to Measuring the Nature of Jobs', *Journal of Applied Psychology*, 60: 171–81.

Jenkins, N., Bloor, M., Fischer, J., Berney, L., and Neale, J. (2010). 'Putting it in Context: the Use of Vignettes in Qualitative Interviewing', *Qualitative Research*, 10: 175–98.

Jerolmack, C., and Khan, S. (2014). 'Talk is Cheap: Ethnography and the Attitudinal Fallacy', *Sociological Methods and Research*, 43: 178–209.

John, I. D. (1992). 'Statistics as Rhetoric in Psychology', *Australian Psychologist*, 27: 144–9.

John, P., and Jennings, W. (2010). 'Punctuations and Turning Points in British Politics: The Policy Agenda of the Queen's Speech, 1940-2005', *British Journal of Political Science*, 40: 561–86.

Johnson, P. (1998). 'Analytic Induction', in G. Symon and C. Cassell (eds), *Qualitative Methods and Analysis in Organizational Research*. London: Sage.

Jones, I. R., Leontowitsch, M., and Higgs, P. (2010). 'The Experience of Retirement in Secondary Modernity: Generational Habitus among Retired Senior Managers', *Sociology*, 44: 103–20.

Jose, A., and Lee, S.-M. (2007). 'Environmental Reporting of Global Corporations: A Content Analysis based on Website Disclosures', *Journal of Business Ethics*, 72: 307–21.

Kamberelis, G., and Dimitriadis, G. (2005). 'Focus Groups: Strategic Articulations of Pedagogy, Politics, and Inquiry', in N. K. Denzin and Y. S. Lincoln (eds), *Handbook of Qualitative Research*. 3rd edn. Thousand Oaks, CA: Sage.

Kamin, L. J. (1974). *The Science and Politics of IQ*. New York: Wiley.

Kanayama, T. (2003). 'Ethnographic Research on the Experience of Japanese Elderly People Online', *New Media and Society*, 5: 267–88.

Kandola, B. (2012). 'Focus Groups', in G. Symon and C. Cassell (eds), *Qualitative Organizational Research: Core Methods and Current Challenges*. Los Angeles: Sage.

Kapidzic, S., and Herring, S. C. (2015) 'Race, Gender, and Self-Presentation in Teen Profile Photographs', *New Media and Society*, 17: 958–76.

Kapsis, R. E. (1989). 'Reputation Building and the Film Art World: The Case of Alfred Hitchcock', *Sociological Quarterly*, 30: 15–35.

Katz, J. (1982). *Poor People's Lawyers in Transition*. New Brunswick: Rutgers University Press.

Kavanagh, J., Campbell, F., Harden, A., and Thomas, J. (2012). 'Mixed Methods Synthesis: A Worked Example', in K. Hannes and C. Lockwood (eds), *Synthesizing Qualitative Research: Choosing the Right Approach*. Chichester: Wiley.

Keat, R., and Urry, J. (1975). *Social Theory as Science*. London: Routledge & Kegan Paul.

Kelley, J., and De Graaf, N. D. (1997). 'National Context, Parental Socialization, and Religious Belief: Results from 15 Nations', *American Sociological Review*, 62: 639–59.

Kellogg, K. C. (2009). 'Operating Room: Relational Spaces and Microinstitutional Change in Surgery', *American Journal of Sociology*, 115: 657–711.

Kellogg, K. C. (2011). *Challenging Operations: Medical Reform and Resistance in Surgery*. Chicago: University of Chicago Press.

Kelly, L., Burton, S., and Regan, L. (1994). 'Researching Women's Lives or Studying Women's Oppression? Reflections on what Constitutes Feminist Research', in M. Maynard and J. Purvis (eds), *Researching Women's Lives from a Feminist Perspective*. London: Taylor & Francis.

Kendall, L. (1999). 'Recontextualizing "Cyberspace": Methodological Considerations for On-Line Research', in S. Jones (ed.), *Doing Internet Research: Critical Issues and Methods for Examining the Net*. Thousand Oaks, CA: Sage.

Kent, R., and Lee, M. (1999). 'Using the Internet for Market Research: A Study of Private Trading on the Internet', *Journal of the Market Research Society*, 41: 377–85.

Khan, S. (2011). *Privilege: The Making of an Adolescent Elite at St. Paul's School*. Princeton, NJ: Princeton Univesity Press.

Khan, S. (2014). 'The Science of Everyday Life', in S. Khan and D. R. Fisher (eds), *The Practice of Research: How Social Scientists Answer Their Questions*. New York: Oxford University Press.

Kimmel, A. J. (1988). *Ethics and Values in Applied Social Research*. Newbury Park, CA: Sage.

King, N. (1994). 'The Qualitative Research Interview', in C. Cassell and G. Symon (eds), *Qualitative Methods in Organizational Research*. London: Sage.

Kirk, J., and Miller, M. L. (1986). *Reliability and Validity in Qualitative Research*. Newbury Park, CA: Sage.

Kitsuse, J. I., and Cicourel, A. V. (1963). 'A Note on the Use of Official Statistics', *Social Problems*, 11: 131–9.

Kitzinger, J. (1993). 'Understanding AIDS: Researching Audience Perceptions of Acquired Immune Deficiency Syndrome', in J. Eldridge (ed.), *Getting the Message: News, Truth and Power*. London: Routledge.

Kitzinger, J. (1994). 'The Methodology of Focus Groups: The Importance of Interaction between Research Participants', *Sociology of Health and Illness*, 16: 103–21.

Kivits, J. (2005). 'Online Interviewing and the Research Relationship', in C. Hine, (ed.), *Virtual Methods: Issues in Social Research on the Internet*. Oxford: Berg.

Knights, D., and Willmott, H. (1990). *Labour Process Theory*. London: Macmillan.

Knights, D., Willmott, H., and Collinson, D. (1985). *Job Redesign: Critical Perspectives on the Labour Process*. Aldershot: Gower.

Koeber, C. (2005). 'Introducing Multimedia Presentations and a Course Website to an Introductory Sociology Course: How Technology Affects Student Perceptions of Teaching Effectiveness', *Teaching Sociology*, 33: 285–300.

Kozinets, R. V. (2001). 'Utopian Enterprise: Articulating the Meanings of *Star Trek*'s Culture of Consumption', *Journal of Consumer Research*, 28: 67–88.

Kozinets, R. V. (2002). 'The Field behind the Screen: Using Netnography for Marketing Research in Online Communities', *Journal of Marketing Research*, 39: 61–72.

Kozinets, R. V. (2010). *Netnography: Doing Ethnographic Research Online*. London: Sage.

Krahn, H. J., and Galambos, N. L. (2014). 'Work Values and Beliefs of "Generation X" and "Generation Y"', *Journal of Youth Studies*, 17: 92–112.

Kramer, A. D. I., Guillory, J. E., and Hancock, J. T. (2014). 'Experimental Evidence of Massive-scale Emotional Contagion through Social Networks', *Proceedings of the National Academy of Sciences of the United States of America*, 111: 8788–L 90, **www.pnas.org/content/111/24/8788** (accessed 13 May 2015).

Krause, M., and Kowalski, A. (2013). 'Reflexive Habits: Dating and Rationalized Conduct in New York and Berlin', *Sociological Review*, 61: 21–40.

Krosnick, J. A. (1999). 'Survey Research', *Annual Review of Psychology*, 50: 537–67.

Krosnick, J. A., Holbrook, A. L., Berent, M. K., Carson, R. T., Hanemann, W. M., Kopp, R. J., Mitchell, R. C., Presser, S., Ruud, P. A., Smith, V. K., Moody, W. R., Green, M. C., and Conaway, M. (2002). 'The Impact of "No Opinion" Response Options on Data Quality: Non-Attitude Reduction or an Invitation to Satisfice?', *Public Opinion Quarterly*, 66: 371–403.

Kross, E., Verduyn, P., Demiralp, E., Park, J., Lee, D. S., Lin, N., Shablack, H., Jonides, J., and Ybarra, O. (2013). 'Facebook Use Predicts Declines in Subjective Well-Being in Young Adults', *PLOS One*, 8, **www.plosone.org/article/info%3Adoi%2F10.1371%2Fjournal.pone.0069841** (accessed 16 February 2015).

Krueger, R. A. (1988). *Focus Groups: A Practical Guide for Applied Research*. Newbury Park, CA: Sage.

Krueger, R. A. (1998). *Moderating Focus Groups*. Thousand Oaks, CA: Sage.

Kuhn, T. S. (1970). *The Structure of Scientific Revolutions*. 2nd edn. Chicago: University of Chicago Press.

Kvale, S. (1996). *InterViews: An Introduction to Qualitative Research Interviewing*. Thousand Oaks, CA: Sage.

Labov, W. (1982). 'Speech Actions and Reactions in Personal Narrative', in D. Tannen (ed.), *Analysing Discourse: Text and Talk*. Washington, DC: Georgetown University Press.

Lacey, C. (1976). 'Problems of Sociological Fieldwork: A Review of the Methodology of "Hightown Grammar"', in M. Hammersley and P. Woods (eds), *The Process of Schooling*. London: Routledge & Kegan Paul.

Lamb, C. (2011). 'Model Student', *The Sunday Times Magazine*, 4 December: 40–7, **www.thesundaytimes.co.uk/sto/Magazine/Interviews/article829778.ece** (accessed 20 November 2014).

Lamont, M., and Swidler, A. (2014). 'Methodological Pluralism and the Possibilities and Limits of Interviewing', *Qualitative Sociology*, 37: 153–71.

Lankshear, G. (2000). 'Bacteria and Babies: A Personal Reflection on Researcher's Risk in a Hospital', in G. Lee-Treweek and S. Linkogle (eds), *Danger in the Field: Risk and Ethics in Social Research*. London: Routledge.

Lantz, P. M., and Booth, K. M. (1998). 'The Social Construction of the Breast Cancer Epidemic', *Social Science and Medicine*, 46: 907–18.

LaPiere, R. T. (1934). 'Attitudes vs. Actions', *Social Forces*, 13: 230–7.

Laub, J. H., and Sampson, R. J. (1998). 'Integrating Quantitative and Qualitative Data', in J. Z. Giele and G. H. Elder, Jr. (eds), *Methods of Life Course Research*. Thousand Oaks, CA: Sage.

Laub, J. H., and Sampson, R. J. (2003). *Shared Beginnings, Divergent Lives: Delinquent Boys to Age 70*. Cambridge, MA: Harvard University Press.

Laub, J. H., and Sampson, R. J. (2004). 'Strategies for Bridging the Quantitative and Qualitative Divide: Studying Crime over the Life Course', *Research in Human Development*, 1: 81–99.

Laurence, J. (2014). 'Reconciling the Contact and Threat Hypotheses: Does Ethnic Diversity Strengthen or Weaken Community Inter-Ethnic Relations?', *Ethnic and Racial Studies*, 37: 1328–49.

Laurie, H., and Gershuny, J. (2000). 'Couples, Work and Money', in R. Berthoud and J. Gershuny (eds), *Seven Years in the Lives of British Families: Evidence on the Dynamics of Social Change from the British Household Panel Survey*. Bristol: Policy Press.

Layder, D. (1993). *New Strategies in Social Research*. Cambridge: Polity.

Lazarsfeld, P. (1958). 'Evidence and Inference in Social Research', *Daedalus*, 87: 99–130.

Leake, J. (1998). 'Police Figures Hide Poor Clear-Up Rate', *The Times*, 21 June: 1, 5.

LeCompte, M. D., and Goetz, J. P. (1982). 'Problems of Reliability and Validity in Ethnographic Research', *Review of Educational Research*, 52: 31–60.

Ledford, C. J., and Anderson, L. N. (2013). 'Online Social Networking in Discussions of Risk: The CAUSE Model in a Content Analysis of Facebook', *Health, Risk and Society*, 15: 251–64.

Lee, R. M. (2000). *Unobtrusive Methods in Social Research*. Buckingham: Open University Press.

Lee, R. M. (2004). 'Danger in Research', in M. S. Lewis-Beck, A. Bryman, and T. F. Liao (eds), *The Sage Encyclopedia of Social Science Research Methods*. 3 vols. Thousand Oaks, CA: Sage.

Lee, R. M., and Fielding, N. G. (1991). 'Computing for Qualitative Research: Options, Problems and Potential', in N. G. Fielding and R. M. Lee (eds), *Using Computers in Qualitative Research*. London: Sage.

Lee, R. P., Hart, R. I., Watson, M. R., and Rapley, T. (in press) 'Qualitative Synthesis in Practice: Some Pragmatics of Meta-Ethnography', *Qualitative Research*, doi: 10.1177/1468794114524221

Lee-Treweek, G. (2000). 'The Insight of Emotional Danger: Research Experiences in a Home for the Elderly', in G. Lee-Treweek and S. Linkogle (eds), *Danger in the Field: Risk and Ethics in Social Research*. London: Routledge.

Leidner, R. (1993). *Fast Food, Fast Talk: Service Work and the Routinization of Everyday Life*. Berkeley and Los Angeles: University of California Press.

Lenzner, T. (2012). 'Effects of Survey Question Comprehensibility on Response Quality', *Field Methods*, 24: 409–28.

Leonard, M. (2004). 'Bonding and Bridging Social Capital: Reflections from Belfast', *Sociology*, 38: 927–44.

Letherby, G. (2003). *Feminist Research in Theory and Practice*. Buckingham: Open University Press.

Levitas, R., and Guy, W. (1996). 'Introduction', in R. Levitas and W. Guy (eds), *Interpreting Official Statistics*. London: Routledge.

Lewis, O. (1961). *The Children of Sánchez*. New York: Vintage.

Lieberman, J. D., Koetzle, D., and Sakiyama, M. (2013). 'Police Departments' Use of Facebook: Patterns and Policy Issues', *Policy Quarterly*, 16: 438–62.

Liebling, A. (2001). 'Whose Side Are We On? Theory, Practice and Allegiances in Prisons Research', *British Journal of Criminology*, 41: 472–84.

Liebow, E. (1967). *Tally's Corner*. Boston: Little, Brown.

Lincoln, Y. S., and Denzin, N. K. (2005). 'Epilogue: The Eighth and Ninth Moments—Qualitative Research in/and the Fractured Future', in N. K. Denzin and Y. S. Lincoln (eds), *Handbook of Qualitative Research*. 3rd edn. Thousand Oaks, CA: Sage.

Lincoln, Y. S., and Guba, E. (1985). *Naturalistic Inquiry*. Beverly Hills, CA: Sage.

Lincoln, Y. S., and Tierney, W. G. (2004). 'Qualitative Research and Institutional Review Boards', *Qualitative Inquiry*, 10: 219–34.

Lindesmith, A. R. (1947). *Opiate Addiction*. Bloomington: Principia Press.

Livingstone, S. (2006). 'Children's Privacy Online: Experimenting with Boundaries Within and Beyond the Family', in R. Kraut, M. Brynin, and S. Kiesler (eds), *Computers, Phones, and the Internet*. Oxford: Oxford University Press.

Livingstone, S., and Lunt, P. (1994). *Talk on Television: Audience Participation and Public Debate*. London: Routledge.

Livingstone, S., Kirwil, L., Ponte, C., and Staksrud, E. (2014). 'In Their Own Words: What Bothers Children Online', *European Journal of Communication*, 29: 271–88.

Lloyd, A. (2012). 'Working to Live, Not Living to Work: Work, Leisure and Youth Identity among Call Centre Workers in North East England', *Current Sociology*, 60: 619–35.

Locke, K. (1996). 'Rewriting *The Discovery of Grounded Theory* after 25 Years?', *Journal of Management Inquiry*, 5: 239–45.

Lockyer, S. (2006). 'Heard the One About . . . Applying Mixed Methods in Humour Research?', *International Journal of Social Research Methodology*, 9: 41–59.

Lofland, J. (1971). *Analyzing Social Settings: A Guide to Qualitative Observation and Analysis*. Belmont, CA: Wadsworth.

Lofland, J., and Lofland, L. (1995). *Analyzing Social Settings: A Guide to Qualitative Observation and Analysis*. 3rd edn. Belmont, CA: Wadsworth.

Lowe, D. (2011). 'The Lack of Discretion in High Policing', *Policing and Society*, 21: 233–47.

Lunt, P. K., and Livingstone, S. M. (1992). *Mass Consumption and Personal Identity*. Buckingham: Open University Press.

Lupton, D. (1996). *Food, the Body and the Self*. London: Sage.

Lynch, M. (2000). 'Against Reflexivity as an Academic Virtue and Source of Privileged Knowledge', *Theory, Culture and Society*, 17: 26–54.

Lynd, R. S., and Lynd, H. M. (1929). *Middletown: A Study in Contemporary American Culture*. New York: Harcourt, Brace.

Lynd, R. S., and Lynd, H. M. (1937). *Middletown in Transition: A Study in Cultural Conflicts*. New York: Harcourt, Brace.

Lynn, N., and Lea, S. (2003). '"A Phantom Menace and the New Apartheid": The Social Construction of Asylum Seekers in the United Kingdom', *Discourse and Society*, 14: 425–52.

Lynn, P., and Kaminska, O. (2012). 'The Impact of Mobile Phones on Survey Measurement Error', *Public Opinion Quarterly*, 77: 586–605.

MacLure, M. (2005). '"Clarity Bordering on Stupidity": Where's the Quality in Systematic Review? ', *Journal of Education Policy*, 20: 393–416.

Macnaghten, P., and Jacobs, M. (1997). 'Public Identification with Sustainable Development: Investigating Cultural Barriers to Participation', *Global Environmental Change*, 7: 5–24.

Madge, C., and O'Connor, H. (2002). 'On-Line with E-Mums: Exploring the Internet as a Medium of Research', *Area*, 34: 92–102.

Madriz, M. (2000). 'Focus Groups in Feminist Research', in N. K. Denzin and Y. S. Lincoln (eds), *Handbook of Qualitative Research*. 2nd edn. Thousand Oaks, CA: Sage.

Maitlis, S., and Lawrence, T. B. (2007). 'Triggers and Enablers of Sensegiving in Organizations', *Academy of Management Journal*, 50: 57–84.

Malinowski, B. (1967). *A Diary in the Strict Sense of the Term*. London: Routledge & Kegan Paul.

Malkin, A. R., Wornian, K., and Chrisler, J. C. (1999). 'Women and Weight: Gendered Messages on Magazine Covers', *Sex Roles*, 40: 647–55.

Manfreda, K. L., Bosnjak, M., Berzelak, J., Haas, I., and Vehovar, V. (2008). 'Web Surveys versus Other Survey Modes: A Meta-Analysis Comparing Response Rates', *International Journal of Market Research*, 50: 79–104.

Mangabeira, W. (1995). 'Qualitative Analysis and Micro-computer Software: Some Reflections on a New Trend in Sociological Research', in R. G. Burgess (ed.), *Computing and Qualitative Research*, Studies in Qualitative Methodology, volume 5. Greenwich, CT: JAI Press, 43–61.

Mangione, T. W. (1995). *Mail Surveys: Improving the Quality*. Thousand Oaks, CA: Sage.

Mann, C., and Stewart, F. (2000). *Internet Communication and Qualitative Research: A Handbook for Researching Online*. London: Sage.

Marcus, G. E. (1998). *Ethnography through Thick and Thin*. Princeton: Princeton University Press.

Markham, A. (1998). *Life Online: Researching the Real Experience in Virtual Space*. London and Walnut Creek, CA: AltaMira Press.

Marsh, C. (1982). *The Survey Method: The Contribution of Surveys to Sociological Explanation*. London: Allen & Unwin.

Marsh, C., and Scarbrough, E. (1990). 'Testing Nine Hypotheses about Quota Sampling', *Journal of the Market Research Society*, 32: 485–506.

Marshall, G., Newby, H., and Vogler, C. (1988). *Social Class in Modern Britain*. London: Unwin Hyman.

Martin, P., and Bateson, P. (2007). *Measuring Behaviour: An Introductory Guide*. 3rd edn. Cambridge: Cambridge University Press.

Marx, G. T. (1997). 'Of Methods and Manners for Aspiring Sociologists: 37 Moral Imperatives', *American Sociologist*, 28: 102–25.

Marzano, G., and Scott, N. (2009). 'Power in Destination Branding', *Annals of Tourism Research*, 36: 247–67.

Mason, J. (1996). *Qualitative Researching*. London: Sage.

Mason, J. (2002). 'Qualitative Interviewing: Asking, Listening, Interpreting', in T. May (ed.), *Qualitative Research in Action*. London: Sage.

Mason, M. (2010). 'Sample Size and Saturation in PhD Studies Using Qualitative Interviews' [63 paragraphs], *Forum Qualitative Sozialforschung/Forum: Qualitative Social Research*, 11 (3), article 8, **www.qualitative-research.net/index.php/fqs/article/view/1428** (accessed 18 October 2014).

Masterman, M. (1970). 'The Nature of a Paradigm', in I. Lakatos and A. Musgrave (eds), *Criticism and the Growth of Knowledge*. Cambridge: Cambridge University Press.

Mattley, C. (2006). 'Aural Sex: The Politics and Moral Dilemmas of Studying the Social Construction of Fantasy', in D. Hobbs and R. Wright (eds), *The SAGE Handbook of Fieldwork*. London: Sage.

Matza, D. (1969). *Becoming Deviant*. Englewood Cliffs, NJ: Prentice-Hall.

Mauthner, N. S., Parry, O., and Backett-Milburn, K. (1998). 'The Data are Out There, or Are They? Implications for Archiving and Revisiting Qualitative Data', *Sociology*, 32: 733–45.

Mavletova, A. (2013). 'Data Quality in PC and Mobile Web Surveys', *Social Science Computer Review*, 31: 725–43.

Mavletova, A., and Couper, M. P. (2014) 'Mobile Web Survey Design: Scrolling versus Paging, SMS versus E-mail Invitations', *Journal of Survey Statistics and Methodology*, 2: 498–518.

Mayhew, P. (2000). 'Researching the State of Crime: Local, National, and International Victim Surveys', in R. D. King and E. Wincup (eds), *Doing Research on Crime and Justice*. Oxford: Oxford University Press.

Maynard, M. (1994). 'Methods, Practice and Epistemology: The Debate about Feminism and Research', in M. Maynard and J. Purvis (eds), *Researching Women's Lives from a Feminist Perspective*. London: Taylor & Francis.

Maynard, M. (1998). 'Feminists' Knowledge and the Knowledge of Feminisms: Epistemology, Theory, Methodology and Method', in T. May and M. Williams (eds), *Knowing the Social World*. Buckingham: Open University Press.

Mays, N., Pope, C., and Popay, J. (2005). 'Systematically Reviewing Qualitative and Quantitative Evidence to Inform Management and Policy-Making in the Health Field', *Journal of Health Services Research and Policy*, 10 (Supplement 1): S6–S20.

Mazmanian, M., Orlikowski, W. J., and Yates, J. (2013). 'The Autonomy Paradox: The Implications of Mobile Email Devices for Knowledge Professional', *Organization Science*, 24: 1337–57.

McCabe, S. E. (2004). 'Comparison of Mail and Web Surveys in Collecting Illicit Drug Use Data: A Randomized Experiment', *Journal of Drug Education*, 34: 61–73.

McCall, M. J. (1984). 'Structured Field Observation', *Annual Review of Sociology*, 10: 263–82.

McCartney, J. L. (1970). 'On Being Scientific: Changing Styles of Presentation of Sociological Research', *American Sociologist*, 5: 30–5.

McDonald, P., Townsend, K., and Waterhouse, J. (2009). 'Wrong Way, Go Back! Negotiating Access in Industry-Based Research', in K. Townsend and J. Burgess (eds), *Method in the Madness: Research Stories you Won't Read in Textbooks*. Oxford: Chandos.

McGuigan, J. (1992). *Cultural Populism*. London: Routledge.

McKee, L., and Bell, C. (1985). 'Marital and Family Relations in Times of Male Unemployment', in B. Roberts, R. Finnegan, and D. Gallie (eds), *New Approaches to Economic Life*. Manchester: Manchester University Press.

McKeever, L. (2006). 'Online Plagiarism Detection Services: Saviour or Scourge?', *Assessment and Evaluation in Higher Education*, 31: 155–65.

McKeganey, N., and Barnard, M. (1996). *Sex Work on the Streets*. Buckingham: Open University Press.

Mead, M. (1928). *Coming of Age in Samoa*. New York: Morrow.

Mears, A. (2011). *Pricing Beauty: The Making of a Fashion Model*. Berkeley, CA: University of California Press.

Mears, A. (2013). 'Ethnography as Precarious Work', *Sociological Quarterly*, 54: 20–34.

Medway, R. L., and Fulton, J. (2012). 'When More Gets You Less: A Meta-analysis of the Effect of Concurrent Web Options on Mail Survey Response Rates', *Public Opinion Quarterly*, 76: 733–46.

Menard, S. (1991). *Longitudinal Research*. Newbury Park, CA: Sage.

Merton, R. K. (1967). *On Theoretical Sociology*. New York: Free Press.

Merton, R. K., Fiske, M., and Kendall, P. L. (1956). *The Focused Interview: A Manual of Problems and Procedures*. New York: Free Press.

Meterko, M., Restuccia, J. D., Stolzmann, K., Mohr, D., Brennan, C., Glasgow, J., and Kaboli, P. (2015). 'Response Rates, Nonresponse Bias, and Data Quality', *Public Opinion Quarterly*, 79: 130–44.

Michel, A. (2011). 'Transcending Socialization: A Nine-Year Ethnography of the Body's Role in Organizational Control and Knowledge Worker Transformation', *Administrative Science Quarterly*, 54: 1–44.

Michel, A. (2014). 'Participation and Self-Entrapment: A 12-Year Ethnography of Wall Street Participation Practices; Diffusion and Evolving Consequences', *Sociological Quarterly*, 55: 514–36.

Midgley, C. (1998). 'TV Violence has Little Impact on Children, Study Finds', *The Times*, 12 January: 5.

Mies, M. (1993). 'Towards a Methodology for Feminist Research', in M. Hammersley, (ed.), *Social Research: Philosophy, Politics and Practice*. London: Sage.

Miles, M. B. (1979). 'Qualitative Data as an Attractive Nuisance', *Administrative Science Quarterly*, 24: 590–601.

Milgram, S. (1963). 'A Behavioral Study of Obedience', *Journal of Abnormal and Social Psychology*, 67: 371–8.

Milkman, R. (1997). *Farewell to the Factory: Auto Workers in the Late Twentieth Century*. Berkeley and Los Angeles: University of California Press.

Millen, D. (1997). 'Some Methodological and Epistemological Issues Raised by Doing Feminist Research on Non-Feminist Women', *Sociological Research Online*, 2, **www.socresonline.org.uk/2/3/3.html** (accessed 6 November 2014).

Miller, A. G. (2009). 'Reflections on "Replicating Milgram" (Burger, 2009)', *American Psychologist*, 64: 20–7.

Miller, D., Jackson, P., Thrift, N., Holbrook, B., and Rowlands, M. (1998). *Shopping, Place and Identity*. London: Routledge.

Miller, D. D. (1956). *The Story of Walt Disney*. New York: Dell.

Miller, N., and Morgan, D. (1993). 'Called to Account: The CV as an Autobiographical Practice', *Sociology*, 27: 133–43.

Miller, R. L. (2000). *Researching Life Stories and Family Histories*. London: Sage.

Miner-Rubino, K., Jayaratne, T. E., and Konik, J. (2007). 'Using Survey Research as a Quantitative Method for Feminist Social Change', in S. N. Hesse-Biber (ed.), *Handbook of Feminist Research: Theory and Praxis*. Thousand Oaks, CA: Sage.

Mintzberg, H. (1973). *The Nature of Managerial Work*. New York: Harper & Row.

Mishler, E. G. (1986). *Research Interviewing: Context and Narrative*. Cambridge, MA: Harvard University Press.

Mitchell, J. C. (1983). 'Case and Situation Analysis', *Sociological Review*, 31: 186–211.

Mitchell, T. (1985). 'An Evaluation of the Validity of Correlational Research Conducted in Organizations', *Academy of Management Review*, 10: 192–205.

Mkono, M., and Markwell, K. (2014). 'The Application of Netnography in Tourism Studies', *Annals of Tourism Research*, 48: 289–91.

Molina-Azorín, J. F. (2012). 'Mixed Methods in Strategic Management: Impact and Applications', *Organizational Research Methods*, 15: 33–56.

Morgan, D. L. (1998a). *Planning Focus Groups*. Thousand Oaks, CA: Sage.

Morgan, D. L. (1998b). 'Practical Strategies for Combining Qualitative and Quantitative Methods: Applications for Health Research', *Qualitative Health Research*, 8: 362–76.

Morgan, D. L. (2002). 'Focus Group Interviewing', in J. F. Gubrium and J. A. Holstein (eds), *Handbook of Interview Research: Context and Method*. Thousand Oaks, CA: Sage.

Morgan, D. L. (2010). 'Reconsidering the Role of Interaction in Analyzing and Reporting Focus Groups', *Qualitative Health Research*, 20: 718–22.

Morgan, D. L., and Spanish, M. T. (1985). 'Social Interaction and the Cognitive Organization of Health-Relevant Behaviour', *Sociology of Health and Illness*, 7: 401–22.

Morgan, G. (1997). *Images of Organization*. Thousand Oaks, CA: Sage.

Morgan, G., and Smircich, L. (1980). 'The Case for Qualitative Research', *Academy of Management Review*, 5: 491–500.

Morgan, R. (2000). 'The Politics of Criminological Research', in R. D. King and E. Wincup (eds), *Doing Research on Crime and Justice*. Oxford: Oxford University Press.

Morley, D. (1980). *The 'Nationwide' Audience: Structure and Decoding*. London: British Film Institute.

Morse, J. M. (2004a). 'Purposive Sampling', in M. S. Lewis-Beck, A. Bryman, and T. F. Liao (eds), *The Sage Encyclopedia of Social Science Research Methods*. 3 vols. Thousand Oaks, CA: Sage.

Morse, J. M. (2004b). 'Sampling in Qualitative Research', in M. S. Lewis-Beck, A. Bryman, and T. F. Liao (eds), *The Sage*

Encyclopedia of Social Science Research Methods. 3 vols. Thousand Oaks, CA: Sage.

Moser, C. A., and Kalton, G. (1971). *Survey Methods in Social Investigation*. London: Heinemann.

Munday, J. (2006). 'Identity in Focus: The Use of Focus Groups to Study the Construction of Collective Identity', *Sociology*, 40: 89–105.

Nettleton, S., Pleace, N., Burrows, R., Muncer, S., and Loader, B. (2002). 'The Reality of Virtual Social Support', in S. Woolgar (ed.), *Virtual Society? Technology, Cyperbole, Reality*. Oxford: Oxford University Press.

Nichols, T., and Beynon, H. (1977). *Living with Capitalism: Class Relations and the Modern Factory*. London: Routledge.

Noblit, G. W., and Hare, R. D. (1988). *Meta-Ethnography: Synthesizing Qualitative Studies*. Newbury Park, CA: Sage.

Noy, C. (2008). 'Sampling Knowledge: The Hermeneutics of Snowball Sampling in Qualitative Research', *International Journal of Social Research Methodology*, 11: 327–44.

Nyberg, D. (2009). 'Computers, Customer Service Operatives, and Cyborgs: Intra-Actions in Call Centres', *Organization Studies*, 30: 1181–99.

Oakley, A. (1981). 'Interviewing Women: A Contradiction in Terms', in H. Roberts (ed.), *Doing Feminist Research*. London: Routledge & Kegan Paul.

Oakley, A. (1998). 'Gender, Methodology and People's Ways of Knowing: Some Problems with Feminism and the Paradigm Debate in Social Science', *Sociology*, 32: 707–31.

Oakley, A. (1999). 'Paradigm Wars: Some Thoughts on a Personal and Public Trajectory', *International Journal of Social Research Methodology*, 2: 247–54.

Oakley, A. (2000). *Experiments in Knowing: Gender and Method in the Social Sciences*. Cambridge: Polity.

O'Brien, K. (2010). 'Inside "Doorwork": Gendering the Security Gaze', in R. Ryan-Flood and R. Gill (eds), *Secrecy and Silence in the Research Process: Feminist Reflections*. London: Routledge.

O'Cathain, A. (2010). 'Assessing the Quality of Mixed Methods Research: Toward a Comprehensive Framework', in A. Tashakkori and C. Teddlie (eds), *SAGE Handbook of Mixed Methods in Social and Behavioral Research* (2nd edn). Los Angeles: Sage.

O'Cathain, A., Murphy, E., and Nicholl, J. (2007). 'Integration and Publication as Indicators of "Yield" from Mixed Methods Studies', *Journal of Mixed Methods Research*, 1: 147–63.

O'Cathain, A., Murphy, E., and Nicholl, J. (2008). 'The Quality of Mixed Methods Studies in Health Services Research', *Journal of Health Services Research* & Policy, 13: 92–8.

O'Connor, H., and Madge, C. (2001). 'Cyber-Mothers: Online Synchronous Interviewing using Conferencing Software', *Sociological Research Online*, 5, **www.socresonline.org.uk/9/2/hine.html** (accessed 9 December 2014).

O'Connor, H., and Madge, C. (2003). '"Focus Groups in Cyberspace": Using the Internet for Qualitative Research', *Qualitative Market Research*, 6: 133–43.

O'Connor, H., Madge, C., Shaw, R., and Wellens, J. (2008). 'Internet-Based Interviewing', in N. Fielding, R. M. Lee, and G. Blank (eds), *The SAGE Handbook of Online Research Methods*. London: Sage.

O'Grady, C., Dahm, M. R., Roger, P., and Yates, L. (2014). 'Trust, Talk and the Dictaphone: Tracing the Discursive Accomplishment of Trust in a Surgical Consultation', *Discourse and Society*, 25: 65–83.

Okely, J. (1994). 'Thinking through Fieldwork', in A. Bryman and R. G. Burgess (eds), *Analyzing Qualitative Data*. London: Routledge.

Olson, K., and Smyth, J. D. (2014). 'Accuracy of Within-Household Selection in Web and Mail Surveys of the General Population', *Field Methods*, 26: 56–69.

Onwuegbuzie, A. J., and Collins, K. M. T. (2007). 'A Typology of Mixed Methods Sampling Designs in Social Sciences Research', *The Qualitative Report*, 12: 281–L 316, **www.nova.edu/ssss/QR/QR12-2/onwuegbuzie2.pdf** (accessed 30 October 2014).

Onwuegbuzie, A. J., and Leech, N. L. (2010). 'Generalization Practices in Qualitative Research: A Mixed Methods Case Study', *Quality and Quantity*, 44: 881–92.

Oppenheim, A. N. (1966). *Questionnaire Design and Attitude Measurement*. London: Heinemann.

Oppenheim, A. N. (1992). *Questionnaire Design, Interviewing and Attitude Measurement*. London: Pinter.

O'Reilly, K. (2000). *The British on the Costa del Sol: Transnational Identities and Local Communities*. London: Routledge.

O'Reilly, K. A. (2010). 'Service Undone: A Grounded Theory of Strategically Constructed Silos and their Impact on Customer-Company Interactions from the Perspective of Retail Employees'. Doctoral dissertation, Utah State University, **http://digitalcommons.usu.edu/etd/669** (accessed 17 August 2014).

O'Reilly, K. A., Paper, D., and Marx, S. (2012). 'Demystifying Grounded Theory for Business Research', *Organizational Research Methods*, 15: 247–62.

O'Reilly, M., and Parker, N. (2013). '"Unsatisfactory Saturation": A Critical Exploration of the Notion of Saturated Sample Sizes in Qualitative Research', *Qualitative Research*, 13: 190–7.

O'Reilly, M., Dixon-Woods, M., Angell, E., Ashcroft, R., and Bryman, A. (2009). 'Doing Accountability: A Discourse Analysis of Research Ethics Committee Letters', *Sociology of Health and Illness*, 31: 246–61.

Orona, C. J. (1997). 'Temporality and Identity Loss due to Alzheimer's disease', in A. Strauss and J. M. Corbin (eds), *Grounded Theory in Practice*. Thousand Oaks, CA: Sage.

O'Shaughnessy, R., Dallos, R., and Gough, A. (2013). 'A Narrative Study of the Lives of Women who Experience Anorexia Nervosa', *Qualitative Research in Psychology*, 10: 42–62.

Owen, W. F. (1984). 'Interpretive Themes in Relational Communication', *Quarterly Journal of Speech*, 70: 274–87.

Pace, L. A., and Livingston, M. M. (2005). 'Protecting Human Subjects in Internet Research', *International Journal of Business Ethics and Organization Studies*, 10: 35–L 41, **http://ejbo.jyu.fi/pdf/ejbo_vol10_no1_pages_35–41.pdf** (accessed 17 August 2014).

Pahl, J. (1990). 'Household Spending, Personal Spending and the Control of Money in Marriage', *Sociology*, 24: 119–38.

Palys, T. (2008). 'Purposive Sampling', in L. M. Given (ed.), *The Sage Encyclopedia of Qualitative Research Methods*, Thousand Oaks, CA: Sage, vol. 2.

Park, C. (2003). 'In Other (People's) Words: Plagiarism by University Students: Literature and Lessons', *Assessment and Evaluation in Higher Education*, 28: 471–88.

Parker, M. (2000). *Organizational Culture and Identity*. London: Sage.

Parmelee, J. H., Perkins, S. C., and Sayre, J. J. (2007). '"What About People Our Age?": Applying Qualitative And Quantitative Methods to Uncover how Political Ads Alienate College Students', *Journal of Mixed Methods Research*, 1: 183–99.

Parreñas, R. S. (2011). *Illicit Flirtations: Labor, Migration, and Sex Trafficking in Tokyo*. Stanford, CA: Stanford University Press.

Pasquandrea, S. (2014). '"They Might Read a Fly Speck": Musical Literacy as a Discursive Resource in Louis Armstrong's Autobiographies', *Social Semiotics*, 24: 514–29.

Paterson, B. L. (2012). '"It Looks Great But How Do I Know if it Fits?": An Introduction to Meta-Synthesis Research', in K. Hannes and C. Lockwood (eds), *Synthesizing Qualitative Research: Choosing the Right Approach*. Chichester: Wiley.

Patrick, J. (1973). *A Glasgow Gang Observed*. London: Eyre-Methuen.

Patterson, M. G., West, M. A., Shackleton, V. J., Dawson, J. F., Lawthom, R., Maitlis, S., Robinson, D. L., and Wallace, A. M. (2005). 'Validating the Organizational Climate Measure: Links to Managerial Practices, Productivity and Innovation', *Journal of Organizational Behavior*, 26: 379–408.

Patton, M. (1990). *Qualitative Evaluation and Research Methods*. Beverly Hills, CA: Sage.

Paulus, T. M., Lester, J. N., and Britt, V. G. (2013). 'Constructing Hopes and Fears Around Technology: A Discourse Analysis of Introductory Research Methods Texts', *Qualitative Inquiry*, 19: 639–51.

Pawson, R., and Tilley, N. (1997). *Realistic Evaluation*. London: Sage.

Payne, G., and Grew, C. (2005). 'Unpacking "Class Ambivalence": Some Conceptual and Methodological Issues in Accessing Class Identities', *Sociology*, 39: 893–910.

Pearson, G. (2009). 'The Researcher as Hooligan: Where "Participant" Observation Means Breaking the Law', *International Journal of Social Research Methodology*, 12: 243–55.

Pearson, G. (2012). *An Ethnography of Football Fans: Cans, Cops and Carnivals*. Manchester: Manchester University Press.

Pearson, M., and Coomber, R. (2009). 'The Challenge of External Validity in Policy-Relevant Systematic Reviews: A Case Study from the Field of Substance Misuse', *Addiction*, 105: 136–45.

Peek, L., and Fothergill, A. (2009). 'Using Focus Groups: Lessons from Studying Daycare Centers, 9/11, and Hurricane Katrina', *Qualitative Research*, 9: 31–59.

Penn, R., Rose, M., and Rubery, J. (1994). *Skill and Occupational Change*. Oxford: Oxford University Press.

Peräkylä, A. (1997). 'Reliability and Validity in Research Based on Transcripts', in D. Silverman (ed.), *Qualitative Research: Theory, Method and Practice*. London: Sage.

Pernice, R. (1996). 'Methodological Issues in Unemployment Research: Quantitative and/or Qualitative Approaches?', *Journal of Occupational and Organizational Psychology*, 69: 339–49.

Pettigrew, A. (1985). *The Awakening Giant: Continuity and Change in Imperial Chemical Industries*. Oxford: Blackwell.

Pettigrew, A. (1997). 'What is a Processual Analysis?', *Scandinavian Journal of Management*, 13: 337–48.

Pettigrew, T. F., and Tropp, L. R. (2006). 'A Meta-Analytic Test of Intergroup Contact Theory', *Journal of Personality and Social Psychology*, 9: 751–83.

Peytchev, A., and Hill, C. A. (2010). 'Experiments in Mobile Web Survey Design: Similarities to Other Modes and Unique Considerations', *Social Science Computer Review*, 28: 319–35.

Phillips, N., and Hardy, C. (2002). *Discourse Analysis: Investigating Processes of Social Construction*. Thousand Oaks, CA: Sage.

Phillipson, C., Bernard, M., Phillips, J., and Ogg, J. (1999). 'Older People's Experiences of Community Life: Patterns of Neighbouring in Three Urban Areas', *Sociological Review*, 47: 715–43.

Phipps, A., and Young, I. (2015). 'Neoliberalisation and "Lad Cultures" in Higher Education', *Sociology*, 49: 305–22.

Phoenix, A. (1994). 'Practising Feminist Research: The Intersection of Gender and "Race" in the Research Process', in M. Maynard and J. Purvis (eds), *Researching Women's Lives from a Feminist Perspective*. London: Taylor & Francis.

Phoenix, C., Smith, P., and Sparkes, A. C. (2010). 'Narrative Analysis in Aging Studies: A Typology for Consideration', *Journal of Aging Studies*, 24: 1–11.

Pidgeon, N., and Henwood, K. (2004). 'Grounded Theory', in M. Hardy and A. Bryman (eds), *Handbook of Data Analysis*. London: Sage.

Pinch, T., and Clark, C. (1986). 'The Hard Sell: "Patter Merchanting" and the Strategic (Re)production and Local Management of Economic Reasoning in the Sales Routines of Market Pitchers', *Sociology*, 20: 169–91.

Pink, S. (2001). *Visual Ethnography*. London: Sage.

Pink, S. (2004). 'Visual Methods', in C. Seale, G. Gobo, J. F. Gubrium, and D. Silverman (eds), *Qualitative Research Practice*. London: Sage.

Platt, J. (1981). 'The Social Construction of "Positivism" and its Significance in British Sociology, 1950-80', in P. Abrams, R. Deem, J. Finch, and P. Rock (eds), *Practice and Progress: British Sociology 1950–1980*. London: George Allen & Unwin.

Platt, J. (1984). 'The *Affluent Worker* Revisited', in C. Bell and H. Roberts (eds), *Social Researching: Politics, Problems, Practice*. London: Routledge & Kegan Paul.

Platt, J. (1986). 'Functionalism and the Survey: The Relation of Theory and Method', *Sociological Review*, 34: 501–36.

Platt, J. (1996). *A History of Sociological Research Methods in America 1920–1960*. Cambridge: Cambridge University Press.

Plummer, K. (1983). *Documents of Life: An Introduction to the Problems and Literature of a Humanistic Method*. London: Allen & Unwin.

Plummer, K. (2001). 'The Call of Life Stories in Ethnographic Research', in P. Atkinson, A. Coffey, S. Delamont, J. Lofland, and L. Lofland (eds), *Handbook of Ethnography*. London: Sage.

Podsakoff, P. M., and Dalton, D. R. (1987). 'Research Methodology in Organizational Studies', *Journal of Management*, 13: 419–44.

Poland, B. D. (1995). 'Transcription Quality as an Aspect of Rigor in Qualitative Research', *Qualitative Inquiry*, 1: 290–310.

Pollert, A. (1981). *Girls, Wives, Factory Lives*. London: Macmillan.

Polsky, N. (1967). *Hustlers, Beats and Others*. Chicago: Aldine.

Poortinga, W., Bickerstaff, K., Langford, I., Niewöhner, J., and Pidgeon, N. (2004). 'The British 2001 Foot and Mouth Crisis: A Comparative Study of Public Risk Perceptions, Trust and Beliefs about Government Policy in Two Communities', *Journal of Risk Research*, 7: 73–90.

Pope, C., and Mays, N. (1995). 'Reaching the Parts Other Methods Cannot Reach: An Introduction to Qualitative Methods in Health and Health Services Research', *British Medical Journal*, 311: 42–5.

Porter, S. (1993). 'Critical Realist Ethnography: The Case of Racism and Professionalism in a Medical Setting', *Sociology*, 27: 591–609.

Porter, S. (2002). 'Critical Realist Ethnography', in T. May (ed.), *Qualitative Research in Action*. London: Sage.

Potter, J. (1996). *Representing Reality: Discourse, Rhetoric and Social Construction*. London: Sage.

Potter, J. (1997). 'Discourse Analysis as a Way of Analysing Naturally Occurring Talk', in D. Silverman (ed.), *Qualitative Research: Theory, Method and Practice*. London: Sage.

Potter, J. (2004). 'Discourse Analysis', in M. Hardy and A. Bryman (eds), *Handbook of Data Analysis*. London: Sage.

Potter, J., and Hepburn, A. (2012). 'Discourse Analysis', in S. Becker, A. Bryman, and H. Ferguson (eds), *Understanding Research: Methods and Approaches for Social Work and Social Policy*. Bristol: Policy Press.

Potter, J., and Wetherell, M. (1987). *Discourse and Social Psychology: Beyond Attitudes and Behaviour*. London: Sage.

Potter, J., and Wetherell, M. (1994). 'Analyzing Discourse', in A. Bryman and R. G. Burgess (eds), *Analyzing Qualitative Data*. London: Routledge.

Potter, J., Wetherell, M., and Chitty, A. (1991). 'Quantification Rhetoric: Cancer on Television', *Discourse and Society*, 2: 333–65.

Poulton, E. (2012). '"If You Had Balls, You'd Be One of Us!" Doing Gendered Research: Methodological Reflections on Being a Female Academic Researcher in the Hyper-Masculine Subculture of "Football Hooliganism"', *Sociological Research Online*, 17: 4, **www.socresonline.org. uk/17/4/4.html** (accessed 3 December 2014).

Pratt, M. G. (2008). 'Fitting Oval Pegs into Round Holes: Tensions in Evaluating and Publishing Qualitative Research in Top-Tier North American Journals', *Organizational Research Methods*, 11: 481–509.

Preisendörfer, P., and Wolter, F. (2014). 'Who Is Telling the Truth?: A Validation Study on Determinants of Response Behavior in Surveys', *Public Opinion Quarterly*, 78: 126–46.

Prichard, J., Turnbull, J., Halford, S., and Pope, C. (2014). 'Trusting Technical Change in Call Centres', *Work, Employment and Society*, 28: 808–24.

Prior, L. (2008). 'Repositioning Documents in Social Research', *Sociology*, 42: 821–36.

Procter, R., Vis, F., and Voss, A. (2013). 'Reading the Riots on Twitter: Methodological Innovation for the Analysis of Big Data', *International Journal of Social Research Methodology*, 16: 197–214.

Proksch, S.-O., and Slapin, J. B. (2010). 'Position Taking in European Parliament Speeches', *British Journal of Political Science*, 40: 587–611.

Psathas, G. (1995). *Conversation Analysis: The Study of Talk-in-Interaction*. Thousand Oaks, CA: Sage.

Punch, M. (1979). *Policing the Inner City: A Study of Amsterdam's Warmoesstraat*. London: Macmillan.

Punch, M. (1994). 'Politics and Ethics in Qualitative Research', in N. K. Denzin and Y. S. Lincoln (eds), *Handbook of Qualitative Research*. Thousand Oaks, CA: Sage.

Radley, A., and Chamberlain, K. (2001). 'Health Psychology and the Study of the Case: From Method to Analytic Concern', *Social Science and Medicine*, 53: 321–32.

Radley, A., Hodgetts, D., and Cullen, A. (2005). 'Visualizing Homelessness: A Study in Photography and Estrangement', *Journal of Community and Applied Social Psychology*, 15: 273–95.

Rafaeli, A., Dutton, J., Harquail, C. V., and Mackie-Lewis, S. (1997). 'Navigating by Attire: The Use of Dress by Female Administrative Employees', *Academy of Management Journal*, 40: 9–45.

Ragin, C. C., and Becker, H. S. (1989). 'How the Microcomputer is Changing our Analytic Habits', in G. Blank et al. (eds), *New Technology in Sociology: Practical Applications in Research and Work*. New Brunswick: Transaction Publishers.

Rayburn, R. L., and Guittar, N. A. (2013). '"This is Where You Are Supposed to Be": How Homeless Individuals Cope with Stigma', *Sociological Spectrum*, 33: 159–74.

Reed, M. (2000). 'The Limits of Discourse Analysis in Organizational Analysis', *Organization*, 7: 524–30.

Rees, R., Caird, J., Dickson, K., Vigurs, C., and Thomas, J. (2013). *The Views of Young People in the UK About Obesity, Body Size, Shape and Weight: A Systematic Review*. London: EPPI-Centre, Social Science Research Unit, Institute of Education, University of London.

Reiner, R. (2000a). 'Crime and Control in Britain', *Sociology*, 34: 71–94.

Reiner, R. (2000b). 'Police Research', in R. D. King and E. Wincup (eds), *Doing Research on Crime and Justice*. Oxford: Oxford University Press.

Reinharz, S. (1992). *Feminist Methods in Social Research*. New York: Oxford University Press.

Reiss, A. J. (1976). 'Systematic Observation of Natural Phenomena', in H. W. Sinaiko and L. A. Broedling (eds), *Perspectives on Attitude Assessment: Surveys and their Alternatives*. Champaign, IL: Pendleton.

Rettie, R. (2009). 'Mobile Phone Communication: Extending Goffman to Mediated Interaction', *Sociology*, 43: 421–38.

Reuber, A. R. (2010). 'Strengthening your Literature Review', *Family Business Review*, 23: 105–8.

Revilla, M. A., Saris, W. E., and Krosnick, J. A. (2014). 'Choosing the Number of Categories in Agree-Disagree Scales', *Sociological Methods and Research*, 43: 73–97.

Richards, L., and Richards, T. (1994). 'From Filing Cabinet to Computer', in A. Bryman and R. G. Burgess (eds), *Analyzing Qualitative Data*. London: Routledge.

Riches, G., and Dawson, P. (1998). 'Lost Children, Living Memories: The Role of Photographs in Processes of Grief and Adjustment among Bereaved Parents', *Death Studies*, 22: 121–40.

Riessman, C. K. (1993). *Narrative Analysis*. Newbury Park, CA: Sage.

Riessman, C. K. (2004). 'Narrative Interviewing', in M. S. Lewis-Beck, A. Bryman, and T. F. Liao (eds), *The Sage Encyclopedia of Social Science Research Methods*. 3 vols. Thousand Oaks, CA: Sage.

Riessman, C. K. (2008). *Narrative Methods for the Human Sciences*. Thousand Oaks, CA: Sage.

Rigby, M., and O'Brien-Smith, F. (2010). 'Trade Union Interventions in Work-Life Balance', *Work, Employment and Society*, 24: 203–20.

Ritchie, J., Spencer, L., and O'Connor, W. (2003). 'Carrying out Qualitative Analysis', in J. Ritchie and J. Lewis (eds), *Qualitative Research Practice: A Guide for Social Science Students and Researchers*. London: Sage.

Ritzer, G. (1975). 'Sociology: A Multiple Paradigm Science', *American Sociologist*, 10: 156–67.

Rocheleau, D. (1995). 'Maps, Numbers, Text, and Context: Mixing Methods in Feminist Political Ecology', *Professional Geographer*, 47: 458–66.

Röder, A., and Mühlau, P. (2014). 'Are They Acculturating? Europe's Immigrants and Gender Egalitarianism', *Social Forces*, 92: 899–928.

Rojek, C. (1995). *Decentring Leisure: Rethinking Leisure Theory*. London: Sage.

Rorty, R. (1979). *Philosophy and the Mirror of Nature*. Princeton: Princeton University Press.

Rose, G. (2001). *Visual Methodologies*. London, Sage.

Rosenfeld, M. J., and Thomas, R. J. (2012). 'Searching for a Mate: The Rise of the Internet as a Social Intermediary', *American Sociological Review*, 77: 523–47.

Rosenhan, D. L. (1973). 'On Being Sane in Insane Places', *Science*, 179: 350–8.

Rosenthal, R., and Jacobson, L. (1968). *Pygmalion in the Classroom: Teacher Expectation and Pupils' Intellectual Development*. New York: Holt, Rinehart & Winston.

Rosnow, R. L., and Rosenthal, R. (1997). *People Studying People: Artifacts and Ethics in Behavioral Research*. New York: W. H. Freeman.

Roulston, K., deMarrais, K., and Lewis, J. (2003). 'Learning to Interview in the Social Sciences', *Qualitative Inquiry*, 9: 643–68.

Rubin, G. J., Brewin, C. R., Greenberg, N., Simpson, J., and Wessely, S. (2005). 'Psychological and Behavioural Reactions to the Bombings in London on 7 July 2005: Cross Sectional Survey of a Representative Sample of Londoners', *British Medical Journal*, **www.bmj.com/content/early/2004/12/31/bmj.38583.728484.3A** (accessed 23 October 2014).

Rubin, G. J., Brewin, C. R., Greenberg, N., Hughes, J. H., Simpson, J., and Wessely, S. (2007). 'Enduring Consequences of Terrorism: 7-Month Follow-Up of Reactions to the Bombings in London on 7 July 2005 ', *British Journal of Psychiatry*, 190: 350–6.

Rubin, H. J., and Rubin, I. S. (1995). *Qualitative Interviewing: The Art of Hearing Data*. Thousand Oaks, CA: Sage.

Rubinstein, J. (1973). *City Police*. New York: Ballantine.

Ruiter, S., and De Graaf, N. D. (2006). 'National Context, Religiosity, and Volunteering: Results from 53 Countries', *American Sociological Review*, 71: 191–210.

Russell, R., and Tyler, M. (2002). 'Thank Heaven for Little Girls: "Girl Heaven" and the Commercial Context of Feminine Childhood', *Sociology*, 36: 619–37.

Ryan, G. W., and Bernard, H. R. (2003). 'Techniques to Identify Themes', *Field Methods*, 15: 85–109.

Ryan, S. (2009). 'On the "Mop-Floor": Researching Employment Relations in the Hidden World of Commercial Cleaning', in K. Townsend and J. Burgess (eds), *Method in the Madness: Research Stories you won't Read in Textbooks*. Oxford: Chandos.

Sacks, H., Schegloff, E. A., and Jefferson, G. (1974). 'A Simplest Systematics for the Organization of Turn-Taking in Conversation', *Language*, 50: 696–735.

Salancik, G. R. (1979). 'Field Stimulations for Organizational Behavior Research', *Administrative Science Quarterly*, 24: 638–49.

Sallaz, J. J. (2009). *The Labor of Luck: Casino Capitalism in the United States and South Africa*. Berkeley, CA: University of California Press.

Sampson, H. (2013). *International Seafarers and Transnationalism in the Twenty-first Century*. Manchester: Manchester University Press.

Sampson, H., and Thomas, M. (2003). 'Lone Researchers at Sea: Gender, Risk and Responsibility', *Qualitative Research*, 3: 165–89.

Sampson, R. J., and Raudenbush, S. W. (1999). 'Systematic Social Observation of Public Spaces: A New Look at Disorder in Urban Neighborhoods', *American Journal of Sociology*, 105: 603–51.

Samuel, R. (1976). 'Oral History and Local History', *History Workshop Journal*, 1: 191–208.

Sandberg, J., and Alvesson, M. (2011). 'Ways of Constructing Research Questions: Gap-Spotting or Problematization?', *Organization*, 18: 23–44.

Sandelowski, M. (2003). 'Tables or Tableaux? The Challenges of Writing and Reading Mixed Methods Studies', in A. Tashakkori and C. Teddlie (eds), *Handbook of Mixed Methods in Social and Behavioral Research*. Thousand Oaks, CA: Sage.

Sanders, C. R. (2009). 'Colorful Writing: Conducting and Living with a Tattoo Ethnography', in A. J. Puddephatt, W. Shaffir, and S. W. Kleinknecht (eds), *Ethnographies Revisited: Constructing Theory in the Field*. London: Routledge.

Sanders, T. (2005). 'Researching the Online Sex Work Community', in C. Hine (ed.), *Virtual Methods: Issues in Social Research on the Internet*. Oxford: Berg.

Sanjek, R. (1990). 'A Vocabulary for Fieldnotes', in R. Sanjek (ed.), *Fieldnotes: The Making of Anthropology*. Ithaca, NY: Cornell University Press.

Sarsby, J. (1984). 'The Fieldwork Experience', in R. F. Ellen (ed.), *Ethnographic Research: A Guide to General Conduct*. London: Academic Press.

Savage, M. (2005). 'Working-Class Identities in the 1960s: Revisiting the Affluent Worker Study', *Sociology*, 39: 929–46.

Savage, M. (2010). *Identities and Social Change in Britain since 1940: The Politics of Method*. Oxford: Oxford University Press.

Savage, M., and Burrows, R. (2007). 'The Coming Crisis of Empirical Sociology', *Sociology*, 41: 885–99.

Savage, M., Bagnall, G., and Longhurst, B. (2001). 'Ordinary, Ambivalent and Defensive: Class Identities in the Northwest of England', *Sociology*, 35: 875–92.

Savage, M., Bagnall, G., and Longhurst, B. (2005). *Globalization and Belonging*. London: Sage.

Schegloff, E. A. (1997). 'Whose Text? Whose Context?', *Discourse and Society*, 8: 165–87.

Scheper-Hughes, N. (2004). 'Parts Unknown: Undercover Ethnography of the Organs-Trafficking Underworld', *Ethnography*, 5: 29–73.

Schlesinger, P., Dobash, R. E., Dobash, R. P., and Weaver, C. K. (1992). *Women Viewing Violence*. London: British Film Institute.

Schneider, C. J. (in press) 'Police Presentational Strategies on Twitter in Canada', *Policing and Society*, doi: 10.1080/10439463.2014.922085

Schneider, C. J., and Trottier, D. (2012). 'The 2011 Vancouver Riot and the Role of Facebook in Crowd-Sourced Policing', *BC Studies*, 175: 57–72.

Schneider, S. M., and Foot, K. A. (2004). 'The Web as an Object of Study', *New Media and Society*, 6: 114–22.

Schuman, H., and Converse, J. (1971). 'The Effects of Black and White Interviewers on Black Responses in 1968', *Public Opinion Quarterly*, 35: 44–68.

Schuman, H., and Presser, S. (1981). *Questions and Answers in Attitude Surveys: Experiments on Question Form, Wording, and Context*. San Diego, CA: Academic Press.

Schutz, A. (1962). *Collected Papers I: The Problem of Social Reality*. The Hague: Martinus Nijhof.

Scott, J. (1990). *A Matter of Record*. Cambridge: Polity.

Scott, J. (2010). 'Quantitative Methods and Gender Inequality', *International Journal of Social Research Methodology*, 13: 223–36.

Seale, C. (1999). *The Quality of Qualitative Research*. London: Sage.

Seale, C., Ziebland, S., and Charteris-Black, J. (2006). 'Gender, Cancer Experience and Internet Use: A Comparative Keyword Analysis of Interviews and Online Cancer Support Groups', *Social Science and Medicine*, 62: 2577–90.

Seale, C., Charteris-Black, J., MacFarlane, A., and McPherson, A. (2010). 'Interviews and Internet Forums: A Comparison of Two Sources of Qualitative Data', *Qualitative Health Research*, 20: 595–606.

Seeman, M. (1959). 'On the Meaning of Alienation', *American Sociological Review*, 24: 783–91.

Sempik, J., Becker, S., and Bryman, A. (2007). 'The Quality of Research Evidence in Social Policy: Consensus and Dissension among Researchers', *Evidence and Policy*, 3: 407–23.

Shadish, W. R., Cook, T. D., and Campbell, D. T. (2002). *Experimental and Quasi-experimental Design for Generalized Causal Inference*. Boston: Houghton Mifflin.

Shapiro, S., and Humphreys, L. (2013). 'Exploring Old and New Media: Comparing Military Blogs to Civil War Letters', *New Media and Society*, 15: 1151–67.

Sharpe, K. (2000). 'Sad, Bad, and (Sometimes) Dangerous to Know: Street Corner Research with Prostitutes, Punters, and the Police', in R.D. King and E. Wincup (eds), *Doing Research on Crime and Justice*. Oxford: Oxford University Press.

Shaw, C. R. (1930). *The Jack-Roller*. Chicago: University of Chicago Press.

Sheehan, K., and Hoy, M. G. (1999). 'Using E-Mail to Survey Internet Users in the United States: Methodology and Assessment', *Journal of Computer-Mediated Communication*, 4, **http://onlinelibrary.wiley.com/doi/10.1111/j.1083–6101.1999.tb00101.x/full** (accessed 5 December 2014).

Sheller, M., and Urry, J. (2006). 'The New Mobilities Paradigm', *Environment and Planning A*, 38: 207–26.

Shepherd, J., Harden, A., Rees, R., Brunton, G., Garcia, J., Oliver, S., and Oakley, A. (2006). 'Young People and Healthy Eating: A Systematic Review of Research on Barriers and Facilitators', *Health Education Review*, 21: 239–57.

Shuy, R. W. (2002). 'In-Person versus Telephone Interviewing', in J. F. Gubrium and J. A. Holstein (eds), *Handbook of Interview Research: Context and Method*. Thousand Oaks, CA: Sage.

Siegel, M., Johnson, R. M., Tyagi, K., Power, K., Lohsen, M. C., Ayers, A. J., and Jernigan, D. H. (2013). 'Alcohol Brand References in U.S. Popular Music, 2009–2011', *Substance Use and Misuse*, 48: 1475–84.

Sillince, J. A. A., and Brown, A. D. (2009). 'Multiple Organizational Identities and Legitimacy: The Rhetoric of Police Websites', *Human Relations*, 62: 1829–56.

Silva, E. B., and Wright, D. (2005). 'The Judgment of Taste and Social Position in Focus Group Research', *Sociologia e ricerca sociale*, 76–7: 241–53.

Silva, E. B., and Wright, D. (2008). 'Researching Cultural Capital: Complexities in Mixing Methods', *Methodological Innovations Online*, 2, **www.pbs.plym.ac.uk/mi/pdf/Volume%202%20Issue%203/5.%20Silva%20and%20Wright%2050-62.pdf** (accessed 11 December 2014).

Silva, E. B., Warde, A., and Wright, D. (2009). 'Using Mixed Methods for Analysing Culture: The Cultural Capital and Social Exclusion Project', *Cultural Sociology*, 3: 299–316.

Silverman, D. (1984). 'Going Private: Ceremonial Forms in a Private Oncology Clinic', *Sociology*, 18: 191–204.

Silverman, D. (1985). *Qualitative Methodology and Sociology: Describing the Social World*. Aldershot: Gower.

Silverman, D. (1993). *Interpreting Qualitative Data: Methods for Analysing Qualitative Data*. London: Sage.

Silverman, D. (1994). 'Analysing Naturally-Occurring Data on AIDS Counselling: Some Methodological and Practical Issues', in M. Boulton (ed.), *Challenge and Innovation: Methodological Advances in Social Research on HIV/AIDS*. London: Taylor & Francis.

Silverman, D. (2010). *Doing Qualitative Research: A Practical Handbook*. 3rd edn. London: Sage.

Simon, H. (1960). *Administrative Behavior: A Study of Decision-Making Processes in Administrative Organization*, 2nd edn. New York: Macmillan.

Singer, E. (2003). 'Exploring the Meaning of Consent: Participation in Research and Beliefs about Risks and Benefits', *Journal of Official Statistics*, 19: 273–85.

Skeggs, B. (1994). 'Situating the Production of Feminist Ethnography', in M. Maynard and J. Purvis (eds), *Researching Women's Lives from a Feminist Perspective*. London: Taylor & Francis.

Skeggs, B. (1997). *Formations of Class and Gender*. London: Sage.

Skeggs, B. (2001). 'Feminist Ethnography', in P. Atkinson, A. Coffey, S. Delamont, J. Lofland, and L. Lofland (eds), *Handbook of Ethnography*. London: Sage.

Smith, D. J., and McVie, S. (2003). 'Theory and Method in the Edinburgh Study of Youth Transitions and Crime', *British Journal of Criminology*, 43: 169–95.

Smith, J. K. (1983). 'Quantitative versus Qualitative Research: An Attempt to Clarify the Issue', *Educational Researcher*, 12: 6–13.

Smith, J. K., and Heshusius, L. (1986). 'Closing down the Conversation: The End of the Quantitative-Qualitative Debate among Educational Enquirers', *Educational Researcher*, 15: 4–12.

Smithson, J., and Brannen, J. (2002). 'Qualitative Methodology in Cross-National Research', in J. Brannen, S. Lewis, A. Nilsen, and J. Smithson (eds), *Young Europeans, Work and Family: Futures in Transition*. London: Routledge.

Smyth, J. D., Dillman, D. A., Christian, L. M., and Stern, M. J. (2006). 'Comparing Check-All and Forced-Choice Question Formats in Web Surveys', *Public Opinion Quarterly*, 70: 66–77.

Smyth, J. D., Dillman, D. A., Christian, L. M., and McBride, N. (2009). 'Open-Ended Questions in Web Surveys: Can Increasing the Size of Answer Spaces and Providing Extra Verbal Instructions Improve Response Quality?', *Public Opinion Quarterly*, 73: 325–37.

Snee, H. (2013). 'Framing the Other: Cosmopolitanism and the Representation of Difference in Overseas Gap Year Narratives', *British Journal of Sociology*, 64: 142–62.

Snizek, W. E. (1976). 'An Empirical Assessment of "Sociology: A Multiple Paradigm Science" [Ritzer, 1975]', *American Sociologist*, 11: 217–19.

Snyder, N., and Glueck, W. F. (1980). 'How Managers Plan: The Analysis of Managers' Activities', *Long Range Planning*, 13: 70–6.

Spencer, L., Ritchie, J., Lewis, J., and Dillon, L. (2003). *Quality in Qualitative Evaluation: A Framework for Assessing Research Evidence*. London: Government Chief Social Researcher's Office, **www.civilservice.gov.uk/wp-content/uploads/2011/09/a_quality_framework_tcm6-38740.pdf** (accessed 4 December 2014).

Spradley, J. P. (1979). *The Ethnographic Interview*. New York: Holt, Rinehart & Winston.

Sprokkereef, A., Larkin, E., Pole, C. J., and Burgess, R. G. (1995). 'The Data, the Team, and the Ethnography', in R. G. Burgess (ed.), *Computing and Qualitative Research*, Studies in Qualitative Methodology, volume 5. Greenwich, CT: JAI Press, 81–103.

Squire, C. (2000). 'Situated Selves, the Coming-Out Genre and Equivalent Citizenship in Narratives of HIV', in P. Chamberlayne, J. Bornat, and T. Wengraf (eds), *The Turn to Biographical Methods in Social Science: Comparative Issues and Examples*. London: Routledge.

Stacey, J. (1988). 'Can there be a Feminist Ethnography?', *Women's International Studies Forum*, 11: 21–7.

Stacey, M. (1960). *Tradition and Change: A Study of Banbury*. London: Oxford University Press.

Stake, R. E. (1995). *The Art of Case Study Research*. Thousand Oaks, CA: Sage.

Stanley, L., and Temple, B. (1995). 'Doing the Business? Evaluating Software Packages to Aid the Analysis of Qualitative Data Sets', in R. G. Burgess (ed.), *Computing and Qualitative Research*, Studies in Qualitative Methodology, volume 5. Greenwich, CT: JAI Press, 169–97.

Stefani, L., and Carroll, J. (2001). 'A Briefing on Plagiarism' (Assessment Series No. 10), Learning and Teaching Support Network Generic Guidance.

Stewart, K., and Williams, M. (2005). 'Researching Online Populations: The Use of Online Focus Groups for Social Research', *Qualitative Research*, 5: 395–416.

Stewart, S., Prandy, K., and Blackburn, R. M. (1980). *Social Stratification and Occupations*. London: Macmillan.

Stige, B., Malterud, K., and Midtgarden, T. (2009). 'Toward an Agenda for Evaluation of Qualitative Research', *Qualitative Health Research*, 19: 1504–16.

Strauss, A. (1987). *Qualitative Analysis for Social Scientists*. New York: Cambridge University Press.

Strauss, A., and Corbin, J. M. (1990). *Basics of Qualitative Research: Grounded Theory Procedures and Techniques*. Newbury Park, CA: Sage.

Strauss, A., and Corbin, J. M. (1997). 'Commentary [on Orona, 1997]', in A. Strauss and J. M. Corbin (eds), *Grounded Theory in Practice*. Thousand Oaks, CA: Sage.

Strauss, A., and Corbin, J. M. (1998). *Basics of Qualitative Research: Techniques and Procedures for Developing Grounded Theory*. Thousand Oaks, CA: Sage.

Strauss, A., Schatzman, L., Ehrich, D., Bucher, R., and Sabshin, M. (1973). 'The Hospital and its Negotiated Order', in G. Salaman and K. Thompson (eds), *People and Organizations*. London: Longman.

Streiner, D. L., and Sidani, S. (2010). *When Research Goes Off the Rails: Why it Happens and What You Can Do About It*. New York: Guilford.

Sturges, J. E., and Hanrahan, K. J. (2004). 'Comparing Telephone and Face-to-Face Qualitative Interviewing: A Research Note', *Qualitative Research* 4: 107–18.

Sturgis, P., Allum, N., and Smith, P. (2008). 'An Experiment on the Measurement of Political Knowledge in Surveys', *Political Opinion Quarterly*, 85: 90–102.

Sturgis, P., Brunton-Smith, I., Read, S., and Allum, N. (2011). 'Does Ethnic Diversity Erode Trust? Putnam's "Hunkering Down" Thesis Reconsidered', *British Journal of Political Science*, 41: 57–82.

Sturgis, P., Brunton-Smith, I., Kuha, J., and Jackson, J. (2014a). 'Ethnic Diversity, Segregation and the Social Cohesion of Neighbourhoods in London', *Ethnic and Racial Studies*, 37: 1286–309.

Sturgis, P., Roberts, C., and Smith, P. (2014). 'Middle Alternatives Revisited: How the Neither/Nor Response Acts as a Way of Saying "I Don't Know?"', *Sociological Methods and Research*, 43: 15–38.

Sturridge, P. (2007). 'Class Belonging: A Quantitative Exploration of Identity and Consciousness', *British Journal of Sociology*, 58: 207–26.

Sudman, S., and Bradburn, N. M. (1982). *Asking Questions: A Practical Guide to Questionnaire Design*. San Francisco: Jossey-Bass.

Sullivan, C. F. (2003). 'Gendered Cybersupport: A Thematic Analysis of Two Online Cancer Support Groups', *Journal of Health Psychology*, 8: 83–103.

Sullivan, O. (1996). 'Time Co-Ordination, the Domestic Division of Labour and Affective Relations: Time Use and the Enjoyment of Activities within Couples', *Sociology*, 30: 79–100.

Sutton, R. I. (1992). 'Feelings about a Disneyland Visit: Photography and the Reconstruction of Bygone Emotions', *Journal of Management Inquiry*, 1: 278–87.

Sutton, R. I., and Rafaeli, A. (1988). 'Untangling the Relationship between Displayed Emotions and Organizational Sales: The Case of Convenience Stores', *Academy of Management Journal*, 31: 461–87.

Sutton, R. I., and Rafaeli, A. (1992). 'How we Untangled the Relationship between Displayed Emotion and Organizational Sales: A Tale of Bickering and Optimism', in P. J. Frost and R. Stablein (eds), *Doing Exemplary Research*. Newbury Park, CA: Sage.

Swain, J. (2004). 'The Resources and Strategies that 10-11-Year-Old Boys Use to Construct Masculinities in the School Setting', *British Educational Research Journal*, 30: 167–85.

Sweet, C. (2001). 'Designing and Conducting Virtual Focus Groups', *Qualitative Market Research*, 4: 130–5.

Swennen, M. H. J., van der Heijden, G. J. M. G., Boeije, H. R., van Rheenen, N., Verheul, F. J. M., van der Graaf, Y., and Kalkman, C. J. (2013). 'Doctors' Perceptions and Use of Evidence-Based Medicine: A Systematic Review and Thematic Synthesis of Qualitative Studies', *Academic Medicine*, 88: 1384–96.

Tashakkori, A., and Teddlie, C. (eds) (2003). *Handbook of Mixed Methods in Social and Behavioral Research*. Thousand Oaks, CA: Sage.

Tashakkori, A., and Teddlie, C. (eds) (2010). *Handbook of Mixed Methods in Social and Behavioral Research*. 2nd edn. Los Angeles: Sage.

Taylor, A. (1993). *Women Drug Users: An Ethnography of an Injecting Community*. Oxford: Clarendon Press.

Teddlie, C., and Yu, F. (2007). 'Mixed Methods Sampling: A Typology with Examples', *Journal of Mixed Methods Research*, 1: 77–100.

Teitler, J. O., Reichman, N. E., and Sprachman, S. (2003). 'Costs and Benefits of Improving Response Rates for a Hard-to-Reach Population', *Public Opinion Quarterly*, 67: 126–38.

Teo, P. (2000). 'Racism in the News: A Critical Discourse Analysis of News Reporting in Two Australian Newspapers', *Discourse and Society*, 11: 7–49.

Thøgersen-Ntoumani, C., and Fox, K. R. (2005). 'Physical Activity and Mental Well-Being Typologies in Corporate Employees: A Mixed Methods Approach', *Work and Stress*, 19: 50–67.

Thomas, D. R. (2006). 'A General Inductive Approach for Analyzing Qualitative Evaluation Data', *American Journal of Evaluation*, 27: 237–46.

Thomas, J., and Harden, A. (2008). 'Methods for the Thematic Synthesis of Qualitative Research in Systematic Reviews', *BMC Medical Research Methodology*, 8, **www.ncbi. nlm.nih.gov/pmc/articles/PMC2478656/pdf/1471- 2288-8-45.pdf** (accessed 17 November 2014).

Thomas, J., Harden, A., and Newman, M. (2012). 'Synthesis: Combining Results Systematically and Appropriately', in D. Gough, S. Oliver, and J. Thomas (eds), *An Introduction to Systematic Reviews*. London: Sage.

Thompson, C., Lewis, D., Greenhalgh, T., Taylor, S., and Cummins, S. (2013). 'A Health and Social Legacy for East London: Narratives of "Problem" and "Solution" Around London 2012', *Sociological Research Online*, 18: 1, **www.socresonline.org.uk/18/2/1.html** (accessed 18 March 2014).

Thompson, E. R., and Phua, F. T. T. (2012). 'A Brief Index of Affective Job Satisfaction', *Group and Organization Management*, 37: 275–307.

Thompson, P. (1989). *The Nature of Work*. 2nd edn. London: Macmillan.

Thomson, K. (2004). *Cultural Capital and Social Exclusion Survey*. London: National Centre for Social Research.

Thornberg, R., and Charmaz, K. (2014). 'Grounded Theory and Theoretical Coding', in U. Flick (ed.), *SAGE Handbook of Qualitative Data Analysis*. London: Sage.

Thornberg, R., Halldin, K., Bolmjső, N., and Petersson, A. (2013). 'Victimising of School Bullying: A Grounded Theory', *Research Papers in Education*, 28: 309–29.

Tilley, N. (2000). 'Doing Realistic Evaluation of Criminal Justice', in V. Jupp, P. Davies, and P. Francis (eds), *Doing Criminological Research*. London: Sage.

Timming, A. R. (2009). 'WERS the Validity? A Critique of the 2004 Workplace Employment Relations Survey', *Work, Employment and Society*, 23: 561–70.

Timulak, L. (2014). 'Qualitative Meta-Analysis', in U. Flick (ed.), *SAGE Handbook of Qualitative Data Analysis*. London: Sage.

Tinati, R., Halford, S., Carr, L., and Pope, C. (2014). 'Big Data: Methodological Challenges and Approaches for Sociological Analysis', *Sociology*, 48: 663–81.

Toepoel, V., and Lugtig, P. (2014). 'What Happens if You Offer a Mobile Option to Your Web Panel? Evidence from a

Probability-Based Panel of Internet Users', *Social Science Computer Review*, 32: 544–60.

Tourangeau, R., and Smith, T. W. (1996). 'Asking Sensitive Questions: The Impact of Data Collection Mode, Question Format, and Question Context', *Public Opinion Quarterly*, 60: 275–304.

Tourangeau, R., and Yan, T. (2007). 'Sensitive Questions in Surveys', *Psychological Bulletin*, 133: 859–83.

Tourangeau, R., Conrad, F. G., and Couper, M. P. (2013). *The Science of Web Surveys*. Oxford: Oxford University Press.

Townsend, K., and Burgess, J. (eds) (2009a). *Method in the Madness: Research Stories you won't Read in Textbooks*. Oxford: Chandos.

Townsend, K., and Burgess, J. (2009b). 'Serendipity and Flexibility in Social Science Research: Meeting the Unexpected', in K. Townsend and J. Burgess (eds), *Method in the Madness: Research Stories you won't Read in Textbooks*. Oxford: Chandos.

Tracy, S. J. (2010). 'Qualitative Quality: Eight "Big Tent" Criteria for Excellent Qualitative Research', *Qualitative Inquiry*, 16: 837–51.

Tranfield, D., Denyer, D., and Smart, P. (2003). 'Towards a Methodology for Developing Evidence-Informed Management Knowledge by Means of Systematic Review', *British Journal of Management*, 14: 207–22.

Tripp, T. M., Bies, R. J., and Aquino, K. (2002). 'Poetic Justice or Petty Jealousy? The Aesthetics of Revenge', *Organizational Behavior and Human Decision Processes*, 89: 966–84.

Trow, M. (1957). 'Comment on "Participant Observation and Interviewing: A Comparison"', *Human Organization*, 16: 33–5.

Tsang, E. W. K., and Kwan, K.-M. (1999). 'Replication and Theory Development in Organizational Science: A Critical Realist Perspective', *Academy of Management Review*, 24: 759–80.

Tse, A. C. B. (1998). 'Comparing the Response Rate, Response Speed and Response Quality of Two Methods of Sending Questionnaires: E-Mail vs Mail', *Journal of the Market Research Society*, 40: 353–61.

Tse, A. C. B. (1999). 'Conducting Electronic Focus Group Discussions among Chinese Respondents', *Journal of the Market Research Society*, 41: 407–15.

Turnbull, C. (1973). *The Mountain People*. London: Cape.

Turnbull, J., Prichard, J., Halford, S., Pope, C., and Salisbury, C. (2012). 'Reconfiguring the Emergency and Urgent Care Workforce: Mixed Methods Study of Skills and Everyday Work of Non-Clinical Call-Handlers in the NHS', *Journal of Health Services Research and Policy*, 17: 233–40.

Turner, B. A. (1994). 'Patterns of Crisis Behaviour: A Qualitative Inquiry', in A. Bryman and R. G. Burgess (eds), *Analyzing Qualitative Data*. London: Routledge.

Twine, F. W. (2006). 'Visual Ethnography and Racial Theory: Family Photographs as Archives of Interracial Intimacies', *Ethnic and Racial Studies*, 29: 487–511.

Underhill, C., and Olmsted, M. G. (2003). 'An Experimental Comparison of Computer-Mediated and Face-to-Face Focus Groups', *Social Science Computer Review*, 21: 506–12.

Upton, A. (2011). 'In Testing Times: Conducting an Ethnographic Study of Animal Rights Protestors', *Sociological Research Online*, 16, **www.socresonline.org. uk/16/4/1.html** (accessed 1 December 2014).

Van den Hoonaard, W. (2001). 'Is Research Ethics Review a Moral Panic?', *Canadian Review of Sociology and Anthropology*, 38: 19–36.

van Dijk, T. A. (1997). 'Discourse as Interaction in Society', in T. A. van Dijk (ed.), *Discourse as Social Interaction*, Discourse Studies: A Multidisciplinary Introduction, volume 2. Newbury Park, CA: Sage.

van Heerden, A. C., Norris, S. A., Tollman, S. M., Stein, A. D., and Richter, L. M. (2014). 'Field Lessons from the Delivery of Questionnaires to Young Adults Using Mobile Phones', *Social Science Computer Review*, 32: 105–12.

Van Maanen, J. (1978). 'On Watching the Watchers', in P. Manning and J. Van Maanen (eds), *Policing: The View from the Street*. Santa Monica, CA: Goodyear.

Van Maanen, J. (1988). *Tales of the Field: On Writing Ethnography*. Chicago: University of Chicago Press.

Van Maanen, J. (1991a). 'Playing back the Tape: Early Days in the Field', in W. B. Shaffir and R. A. Stebbins (eds), *Experiencing Fieldwork: An Inside View of Qualitative Research*. Newbury Park, CA: Sage.

Van Maanen, J. (1991b). 'The Smile Factory: Work at Disneyland', in P. J. Frost, L. F. Moore, M. R. Louis, C. C. Lundberg, and J. Martin (eds), *Reframing Organizational Culture*. Newbury Park, CA: Sage.

Van Maanen, J. (2010). 'A Song for my Supper: More Tales of the Field', *Organizational Research Methods*, 13: 240–55.

Van Maanen, J., and Kolb, D. (1985). 'The Professional Apprentice: Observations on Fieldwork Roles in Two Organizational Settings', *Research in the Sociology of Organizations*, 4: 1–33.

Van Selm, M., and Jankowski, N. W. (2006). 'Conducting Online Surveys', *Quality and Quantity*, 40 (3): 435–56.

Vasquez, J. M., and Wetzel, C. (2009). 'Tradition and the Invention of Racial Selves: Symbolic Boundaries, Collective Authenticity, and Contemporary Struggles for Racial Equality', *Ethnic and Racial Studies*, 32: 1557–75.

Vaughan, D. (1996). *The Challenger Launch Decision: Risky Technology, Culture, and Deviance at NASA*. Chicago: University of Chicago Press.

Vaughan, D. (2004). 'Theorizing Disaster: Analogy, Historical Ethnography, and the *Challenger* Accident', *Ethnography*, 5: 315–47.

Vaughan, D. (2006). 'The Social Shaping of Commission Reports', *Sociological Forum*, 21: 291–306.

Venkatesh, S. (2008). *Gang Leader for a Day: A Rogue Sociologist Crosses the Line*. London: Allen Lane.

Vidich, A. R., and Bensman, J. (1968). *Small Town in Mass Society*. Princeton: Princeton University Press.

Vincent, J., Kian, E. M., Pedersen, P. M., Kutz, A., and Hill, J. S. (2010). 'England Expects: English Newspapers' Narratives about the English Football Team in the 2006 World Cup', *International Review of the Sociology of Sport*, 45: 199–223.

Voas, D. (2014). 'Towards a Sociology of Attitudes', *Sociological Research Online*, 19, **www.socresonline.org. uk/19/1/12.html** (accessed 21 January 2015).

Voas, D., and Crockett, A. (2005). 'Religion in Britain: Neither Believing nor Belonging', *Sociology*, 39: 11–28.

Vogl, S. (2013). 'Telephone versus Face-to-Face Inteviews: Mode Effect in Semi-structured Interviews with Children', *Sociological Methodology*, 43: 133–77.

Von Wright, G. H. (1971). *Explanation and Understanding*. London: Routledge.

Wacquant, L. (2004). *Body and Soul: Notebooks of an Apprentice Boxer*. Oxford: Oxford University Press.

Wacquant, L. (2009). 'Habitus as Topic and Tool: Reflections on Becoming a Prize Fighter', in A. J. Puddephatt, W. Shaffir, and S. W. Kleinknecht (eds), *Ethnographies Revisited: Constructing Theory in the Field*. London: Routledge.

Wagg, S. (2010). 'Cristiano Meets Mr Spleen: Global Football Celebrity, Mythic Manchester and the Portuguese Diaspora', *Sport in Society*, 13: 919–34.

Wakeford, N., and Cohen, K. (2008). 'Fieldnotes in Public: Using Blogs for Research', in N. Fielding, R. M. Lee, and G. Blank (eds), *The SAGE Handbook of Online Research Methods*. London: Sage.

Walby, S., and Myhill, A. (2001). 'New Survey Methodologies in Researching Violence against Women', *British Journal of Criminology*, 41: 502–22.

Walker, J. (2010). 'Measuring Plagiarism: Researching What Students Do, Not What They Say', *Studies in Higher Education*, 35: 41–59.

Walklate, S. (2000). 'Researching Victims,' in R. King and E. Wincup (eds), *Doing Research on Crime and Justice*. Oxford: Oxford University Press.

Wall, R. (1989). 'The Living Arrangements of the Elderly in Europe in the 1980s', in B. Bytheway, T. Keil, P. Allatt, and A. Bryman (eds), *Becoming and Being Old: Sociological Approaches to Later Life*. London: Sage.

Walsh, I., Holton, J. A., Bailyn, L., Fernandez, W., Levian, N., and Glaser, B. (2015). 'What Grounded Theory is . . . A Criticially Reflective Conversation Among Scholars', *Organizational Research Methods*, doi: 10.1177/1094428114565028

Warde, A. (1997). *Consumption, Food and Taste*. London: Sage.

Warr, D. J. (2005). '"It Was Fun . . . But We Don't Usually Talk about These Things": Analyzing Sociable Interaction in Focus Groups', *Qualitative Inquiry*, 11: 200–25.

Warren, C. A. B. (2002). 'Qualitative Interviewing', in J. F. Gubrium and J. A. Holstein (eds), *Handbook of Interview Research: Context and Method*. Thousand Oaks, CA: Sage.

Warren, C. A. B., Barnes-Brus, T., Burgess, H., Wiebold-Lippisch, L., Hackney, J., Harkness, G., Kennedy, V., Dingwall, R., Rosenblatt, P. C., Ryen, A., and Shuy, R. (2003). 'After the Interview', *Qualitative Sociology*, 26: 93–110.

Watts, L. (2008). 'The Art and Craft of Train Travel', *Social and Cultural Geography*, 9: 711–26.

Weaver, A., and Atkinson, P. (1994). *Microcomputing and Qualitative Data Analysis*. Aldershot: Avebury.

Webb, E. J., Campbell, D. T., Schwartz, R. D., and Sechrest, L. (1966). *Unobtrusive Measures: Nonreactive Measures in the Social Sciences*. Chicago: Rand McNally.

Weber, M. (1947). *The Theory of Social and Economic Organization*, trans A. M. Henderson and T. Parsons. New York: Free Press.

Weinholtz, D., Kacer, B., and Rocklin, T. (1995). 'Salvaging Quantitative Research with Qualitative Data', *Qualitative Health Research*, 5: 388–97.

Weinmann, T., Thomas, S., Brilmayer, S., Heinrich, S., and Radon, K. (2012). 'Testing Skype as an Interview Method in Epidemiologic Research: Response and Feasibility', *International Journal of Public Health*, 57: 959–61.

Weitzman, E. A., and Miles, M. B. (1995). *Computer Programs for Qualitative Data Analysis*. Thousand Oaks, CA: Sage.

Wellings, K., Field, J., Johnson, A., and Wadsworth, J. (1994). *Sexual Behaviour in Britain: The National Survey of Sexual Attitudes and Lifestyles*. Harmondsworth: Penguin.

Wells, T., Bailey, J. T., and Link, M. W. (2013). 'Filling the Void: Gaining a Better Understanding of Tablet-based Surveys', *Survey Practice*, 6: **http://surveypractice.org/ index.php/SurveyPractice/article/view/25/html** (accessed 6 February 2015).

Westmarland, L. (2001). 'Blowing the Whistle on Police Violence: Ethics, Research and Ethnography', *British Journal of Criminology*, 41: 523–35.

Wetherell, M. (1998). 'Positioning and Interpretative Repertoires: Conversation Analysis and Post-Structuralism in Dialogue', *Discourse and Society*, 9: 387–412.

White, P. (2009). *Developing Research Questions: A Guide for Social Scientists*. Basingstoke: Palgrave Macmillan.

Whyte, W. F. (1955). *Street Corner Society*. 2nd edn. Chicago: University of Chicago Press.

Widdicombe, S. (1993). 'Autobiography and Change: Rhetoric and Authenticity of "Gothic" Style', in E. Burman and I. Parker (eds), *Discourse Analytic Research: Readings and Repertoires of Text*. London: Routledge.

Wiggins, S., and Potter, J. (2008). 'Discursive Psychology', in C. Willig and W. Stainton-Rogers (eds), *SAGE Handbook of Qualitative Research in Psychology*. London: Sage.

Wiles, R. (2014). 'Trust in GPs: Findings from Focus Groups', NCRM Working Paper, **http://eprints.ncrm.ac.uk/3270/** (accessed 8 December 2014).

Wilkinson, J. (2009). 'Staff and Student Perceptions of Plagiarism and Cheating', *International Journal of Teaching and Learning in Higher Education*, 20: 98–105.

Wilkinson, S. (1998). 'Focus Groups in Feminist Research: Power, Interaction, and the Co-Production of Meaning', *Women's Studies International Forum*, 21: 111–25.

Wilkinson, S. (1999a). 'Focus Group Methodology: A Review', *International Journal of Social Research Methodology*, 1: 181–203.

Wilkinson, S. (1999b). 'Focus Groups: A Feminist Method', *Psychology of Women Quarterly*, 23: 221–44.

Wilkinson, S., and Kitzinger, C. (2008). 'Conversation Analysis', in C. Willig and W. Stainton-Rogers (eds), *SAGE Handbook of Qualitative Research in Psychology*. London: Sage.

Williams, J. P. (2006). 'Authentic Identities: Straightedge Subculture, Music, and the Internet', *Journal of Contemporary Ethnography*, 35: 173–200.

Williams, M. (2000). 'Interpretivism and Generalisation', *Sociology*, 34: 209–24.

Williams, M. (2007). 'Cybercrime and Online Methodologies', in R. King and E. Wincup (eds), *Doing Research on Crime and Justice*. Oxford: Oxford University Press.

Williams, R. (1976). 'Symbolic Interactionism: Fusion of Theory and Research', in D. C. Thorns (ed.), *New Directions in Sociology*. London: David & Charles.

Willis, P. (1977). *Learning to Labour*. Farnborough: Saxon House.

Winch, P. (1958). *The Idea of a Social Science and its Relation to Philosophy*. London: Routledge & Kegan Paul.

Winlow, S., Hobbs, D., Lister, S., and Hadfield, P. (2001). 'Get Ready to Duck: Bouncers and the Realities of Ethnographic Research on Violent Groups', *British Journal of Criminology*, 41: 536–48.

Wolcott, H. F. (1990a). *Writing up Qualitative Research*. Newbury Park, CA: Sage.

Wolcott, H. F. (1990b). 'Making a Study "More Ethnographic"', *Journal of Contemporary Ethnography*, 19: 44–72.

Wolf, D. R. (1991). 'High Risk Methodology: Reflections on Leaving an Outlaw Society', in W. B. Shaffir and R. A. Stebbins (eds), *Experiencing Fieldwork: An Inside View of Qualitative Research*. Newbury Park, CA: Sage.

Wolfe, E. W., Converse, P. D., and Oswald, F. L. (2008). 'Item-Level Non-Response in an Attitudinal Survey of Teachers Delivered via Mail and Web', *Journal of Computer-Mediated Communication*, 14: 35–66.

Wolfinger, N. H. (2002). 'On Writing Field Notes: Collection Strategies and Background Expectancies', *Qualitative Research*, 2: 85–95.

Wolkowitz, C. (2012). '*Flesh and Stone* Revisited: The Body Work Landscape of South Florida', *Sociological Research Online*, 17, **www.socresonline.org.uk/17/2/26.html** (accessed 3 December 2014).

Wood, K., Patterson, C., Katikireddi, S. V., and Hilton, S. (2014). 'Harms to "Others" from Alcohol Consumption in the Minimum Unit Pricing Policy Debate: A Qualitative Content Analysis of UK Newspapers (2005–12)', *Addiction*, 109: 578–84.

Wood, R. T., and Williams, R. J. (2007). '"How Much Money Do You Spend on Gambling?" The Comparative Validity of Question Wordings to Assess Gambling Expenditure', *International Journal of Social Research Methodology*, 10: 63–77.

Wright, C., Nyberg, D., and Grant, D. (2012). '"Hippies on the Third Floor": Climate Change, Narrative Identity and the Micro-Politics of Corporate Environmentalism', *Organization Studies*, 33: 1451–75.

Wright, C. J., Darko, N., Standen, P. J., and Patel, T. G. (2010). 'Visual Research Methods: Using Cameras to Empower Socially Excluded Youth', *Sociology*, 44: 541–58.

Wright, R., Brookman, F., and Bennett, T. (2006). 'The Foreground Dynamics of Street Robbery in Britain', *British Journal of Criminology*, 46: 1–15.

Wu, M.-Y., and Pearce, P. L. (2014). 'Appraising Netnography: Towards Insights about new Markets in the Digital Tourist Era', *Current Issues in Tourism*, 17: 463–74.

Yager, Z., Diedrichs, P. C., Ricciardelli, L. A., and Halliwell, E. (2013). 'What Works in Secondary Schools? A Systematic Review of Classroom-Based Body Image Programs', *Body Image*, 10: 271–81.

Yang, K., and Banamah, A. (2013). 'Quota Sampling as an Alternative to Probability Sampling? An Experimental Study', *Sociological Research Online*, 19, **www.socresonline.org.uk/19/1/29.html** (accessed 3 December 2014).

Yardley, L. (2000). 'Dilemmas in Qualitative Health Research', *Psychology and Health*, 15: 215–28.

Yeager, D. S., Krosnick, J. A., Chang, L., Javitz, H. S., Levendusky, M. S., Simpser, A., and Wang, R. (2011). 'Comparing the Accuracy of RDD Telephone Surveys and Internet Surveys with Probability and Non-Probability Samples', *Public Opinion Quarterly*, 75: 709–47.

Yin, R. K. (2009). *Case Study Research: Design and Methods*. 4th edn. Los Angeles: Sage.

Young, N., and Dugas, E. (2011). 'Representations of Climate Change in Canadian National Print Media: The Banalization of Global Warming', *Canadian Review of Sociology*, 48: 1–22.

Zhang, Y., and Shaw, J. D. (2012). 'Publishing in *AMJ*—part 5: Crafting the Methods and Results', *Academy of Management Journal*, 55: 8–12.

Zickar, M. J., and Carter, N. T. (2010). 'Reconnecting with the Spirit of Workplace Ethnography: A Historical Review', *Organizational Research Methods*, 13: 304–19.

Zilber, T. B. (2002). 'Institutionalization as an Interplay between Actions, Meanings, and Actors: The Case of a Rape Crisis Center in Israel', *Academy of Management Journal*, 45: 234–54.

Zimdars, A. (2007). 'Challenges to Meritocracy? A Study of the Social Mechanisms in Social Selection and Attainment at the University of Oxford', D.Phil. thesis, Sociology, University of Oxford, **http://economics.ouls.ox.ac.uk/13935/** (accessed 20 February 2015).

Zimdars, A., Sullivan, A., and Heath, A. (2009). 'Elite Higher Education Admissions in the Arts and Sciences: Is Cultural Capital the Key?', *Sociology*, 43: 646–66.

Zimmerman, D. H., and Wieder, D. L. (1977). 'The Diary: Diary-Interview Method', *Urban Life*, 5: 479–98.

ZuWallack, R. (2009). 'Piloting Data Collection via Cell Phones: Results, Experiences, and Lessons Learned', *Field Methods*, 21: 388–406.

Name index

Subject index